KARUNAMIRTHA SAGARAM ON SRUTIS

A Treatise on Music
or
ISAI-TAMIL
Which is one of the main Divisions of Muttamil or Language, Music & Drama

Rao Sahib M. Abraham Pandither

GYAN

Published by

Gyan Publishing House
5, Ansari Road
Daryaganj, New Delhi-110002
Phone: 011-47034999, 9811692060
E-mail: books@gyanbooks.com

Distribution Network
gyanbooks.com
India, USA, Canada, UK, Australia, France

ISBN : 978-81-212-3375-0 (PB)
First Published, 1917

2nd Impression 2020

Printed at: Gyan Press, Delhi.

Karunamirtha Sagaram on Srutis
Author: Rao Sahib M. Abraham Pandither

KARUNAMIRTHA SAGARAM ON SRUTIS

KARUNAMIRTHA SAGARAM

FIRST BOOK
CONTENTS

FIRST PART

A Brief History of Indian Music

Page

FOURTH PART

The calculations for Srutis used in Isai-Tamil which is another name for Karnatic Music.

KARUNAMIRTHA SAGARAM.

FIRST BOOK.

ON SRUTIS.

KARUNAMIRTHA SAGARAM.

FIRST BOOK.

FIRST PART.

A BRIEF HISTORY OF INDIAN MUSIC.

THE DIGNITY AND ORIGIN OF MUSIC.

I BEGIN this work making obeisance to the beautiful feet of the Almighty, who created the whole universe with His word of command, who is Himself the universe, who is Himself incarnate and who rules the universe as the incarnation of virtue.

God, who is the Prime Being of the universe, rules the world first in the shape of Nadam, then life; He is the percept in the living beings. He is the Knowledge in the percept. He is the bliss in the Knowledge. He is the Nadam in the bliss. He is the Geetam in the Nadam. He is the Layam or concentration in the Geetam; thus He infuses His bliss into the created beings and rules the universe.

The Sages who felt in themselves the existence of the Being who is Sat, Chit and Anantham and who is reflected in all creation, fixed in Him their Sthoola and Sookshma faculties, partook in His reflected brightness as of myriads of Suns, loved the universe of creation, obtained their Mukti and thus gained the privilege of praising and worshipping Him eternally. Others who observed the exalted bliss of these Sages, aimed at the same bliss themselves, and obtained His grace by eternally worshipping this incarnation of bliss. All recipients of His grace have recourse to the higher Music which tells His praises, but never to the secular which has the tendency to demoralise. This Music has three sub-divisions, Abhinayam, Ragam and Talam corresponding to Thotam, Virdhi and Layam, analogous to the three separate functions of creation, destruction and preservation, of the deity. In the worship of the deity these three sub-divisions should be regarded as one. By so doing we may clearly understand that in all acts which are the results of His grace His presence is felt as the Perfect Being who manifests Himself through singing or dancing. The devotee who feels the presence of such a Being in him also joins in the act of worship with his own Music and dancing.

The devotees who worshipped the deity in such a manner found Him, according to their several conceptions either as a King, or as a parent or as a Guru, or as a timely helper, or as one who relieved them from all difficulties, or as a loving son, or as a loving bride-groom, and thus gave vent to their feelings in singing His praises; some worshipped by prostrating themselves before Him; some prayed to Him to deliver them from all their troubles; some prayed for the gift of obtaining whatever they desired; some bewailed their fate owing to separation from the deity; some, who realised His presence in themselves, danced for joy; many who desired His presence sent messengers for enquiry; others, filled with love, praised Him fervently. They described his several virtues and told the others about them by means of verse. They deplored their own unworthiness; conscious of their own faults, they implored pardon; some, owing to intense love, were so taken up with the contemplation of His image that they completely forgot this world and their food.

Their saintly life and the best parts of their works in praise of the deity were rolled into one and handed down by tradition for the benefit of future generations by our ancestors. Their successors wrote them down and called them the Vedas. All those who regulated their conduct according to the Vedas, converted some portions of it into verse and derived pleasure in singing them in the house of God, in public places and in their private worship. Those who had not the gift of singing, derived pleasure in hearing it sung by others. They made a number of musical instruments and thus produced a large volume of sound in the praise of the deity. Many forgot their own troubles and, knowing that universal and harmonious singing of His praises was the happiest state of man in this world and a foretaste of the musical service of the next, they were more and more encouraged. In order to develop their Music in different directions they invented one after another the harmonious Swarams, then Alapanam, and the time or Talam which enabled many voices to sing simultaneously. When they found such Music of use, they introduced singing during festivities, during the services of the church and even during their mealtime.

We must understand that Music is the development of ages through various stages. For, beginning with the percussion of sounding boards, boxes, doors, tin plates and the like, children proceed instinctively to the various sub-divisions of time or

Talam such as Jati, Ganam and Layam, and when they grow up they play little tomtoms made of the cocoanut shell and the Gengira. Those who have a special ear for Music proceed a step further at the next stage and play the percussion instruments such as Maddhalam, the Mrudangam. Beri, Oodukai. Nagara and the Thabila and become expert exponents of time or Thalam. The sense of time is instinctive in all. Infants when they are four or five months old keep time while swinging their body to and fro. Moreover the breathing and the heart beat of every human being is according to a definite time.

In the same manner, little children playing in the streets rolled the leaves of the Poovarasu tree, made a kind of reed out of the thinner end and produced Music by blowing through it. Finding that the sound was in proportion to the size and the mouthpiece, they played together three or four such reeds and felt elated when they found a certain kind of harmony existing between them. Then they made reeds out of the stems of the leaves of the Pumpkin and attached rolled up leaves to them and were delighted to find that the sound was either dull or bright in proportion to the length of the rolled up leaves. Of these, those who had a special ear for Music when they advanced in age made reeds of horns, conches and bamboos and later on of wood, gold, silver and brass of various shapes. In the same way they made progress in stringed instruments. They found that Music could be produced by tying the bent ends of a stick together either by a rope or a string. They proceeded to bend big bamboos in the form of a bow by means of leather thongs, tied bells to them to keep time and sang those particular songs used on the occasions of using bows. Finding by degrees that strings, either metallic or of catgut, sound better when passing through the medium of a vessel full of air or a box or a dried Sorakai with its contents scooped out, made instruments like Thoonthinama or the zither made of Sorakai, adjusted the strings to suit their voices and sang the praises of the deity.

Then they made instruments like the Kinnari made of the shell of the cocoanut and played them by means of bows instead of fingers. From this was developed the illustrious Veena which suited the compass of the human voice and which had its Swarams marked by means of frets. From these beginnings, Music, with its few fundamental rules, is making progress.

From all these we understand that from planks and other sounding objects used by children, instruments of percussion such as Tomtom, Berigai, Maddhalam Mridangam, Tapila, Oodukai, Kaithalam, Semakalam, Sellary, Bell, and Sathangai were developed; from playthings such as pipes made of twisted leaves were developed the wind instruments such as Tharai, Othu, Nagasuram. Mukhaveenai, Mahadi, the Flute the Horn and the Conch; from an accidental pleasant sound produced by a stretched string held between the teeth and the fingers were developed the stringed instruments such as Thunthinama (துந்தினம). Kinnari (கின்னரி). Thamburu (தம்புரு), Cocoanut shell Kinnari (குடுக்கைக்கின்னரி), Sundari Veenai (சுந்தரிவீணை), Rudhira Veena (ருத்திர வீணை). Periyal (பேரியாழ்), and Makarayal (மகரயாழ்). When we find this to be the case, we find how unworthy we are to understand the infinite wisdom of the Almighty!

The abovementioned instruments, however they may differ in shape and name according to the manufacturing skill or language of different nations, in reality are all instruments that contributed to the progress of Music. Seeing the beauty of the rules that guide Music and the instruments used therein, all nations are unanimous in declaring that their Music was derived from God. Just as a drop of dew reflects in itself even a big hill that stands opposite, the Music of every country reflects in itself not only the mind of the people, but also God who is himself a hidden hill full of all that is good.

"In the beginning was the Word (Nadam). The Word (Nadam) was with God. The Word (Nadam) was God. The same was in the beginning with God. All things were made by Him, and without Him was not anything made that was made. In Him was life; and the life was the light of men. That was the true light which lighteth every man that cometh into the world. He was in the world, and the world was made by Him and the world knew Him not. The Word (Nadam) was made flesh and dwelt among us full of grace and truth." (St. John. I. 1—14).

Through Nadam, which was the first principle, this world, in the course of time, obtained its Sookshama and Sthoola appearances. From the heart of living beings who had attained the three stages of Sthoola, Sookshma and Karanam, came many sweet sounds (Sookshamam) and gestures (Sthoolam) indicating their feelings. These sounds and gestures which were primarily intended for expressing the mind, became in course of time written language, from which were developed literature and the Shastras. They first wrote down the songs in praise of the deity which they considered very precious and which had been traditionally handed down for generations. It was for this reason known as Muthal Nool (முதல் நூல்) or the First Book. During the stage when it was known and practised by ear it was known as Sruti. When once the First Book had been written they made the Upangams, the Upanishads, the six Shastras and the sixty four Kalais to explain its hidden inner meaning, and to further elucidate them, they compiled the Itihasas and the Puranams. It is not easy to understand the real hidden meanings of those poems which come from the heart of servants devoted to the service of God. Just as we attach an importance to the Vedam which worships the Nada Brahmam in the form of Geetams, so an equal importance should be attached to the Gandharva Vedam or Music which also sings the virtues and praises of the deity. It is said, even at the present day, that Paramasivam taught Music at the Kailasa Malai, Niruthi Moolai, under the name of Niruththam (நிருத்தம்). [After this first Primary Book a number of Secondary Books have been written.]

My noble readers! what shall we say about the antiquity of Indian Music, if, in the Samaveda or the First Book, which is considered to be many thousand years old, not only mention is made of the Veena, which we consider the sweetest of all instruments, but also the rules to be observed in making it, and if it was given an importance as the only instrument by which the deity could be worshipped? If, again, it is said that sages like Sarasvati, Naradar, Thumburu and Hanuman are eternally singing the praises of the deity on their Veenas and that Paramasivam is for ever listening to the

Music of experts such as Kambalar and Asvatharar by wearing them as his ear ornaments (Kundalam) who can estimate the dignity of Veena Music and the antiquity of Music in general ?

When Grace Incarnate was born into this world, if the heavenly hosts appeared in the sky and sang to the hearing of the people of this earth, "Glory to God in the highest, on earth peace and goodwill towards men", we see the use of Music and the importance of the occasion in which it is used. However, if it is said that the saints and the angels in Heaven play their harps before the throne of God, singing new songs for ever, and thunder forth day and night saying "Holy, Holy, Holy, Lord God of hosts ; Heaven and earth are full of Thy glory," we have an idea of the importance of Music in this world and the world to come. Speaking of the glory and antiquity of Music we see its antiquity is as ancient as the eternity of God and creation ; its glory is as glorious as eternal bliss itself. We cannot find higher words of praise for Music.

We all know, the various poems in praise of the deity, composed by the sages of old, are able to influence the mind towards the deity only when they are sung to sweet Music. Just as the seeds which lie buried in the earth are brought out and made to yield fruit by the generative influence of rain, so also the poems of the ancients delight us by their inner and exalted meanings when they come under the ennobling influence of sweet Music. For example, the two lines

"கல்லேனும் ஐய ஒருகாலத்தில் உருகும் என் கன்னெஞ்சம் உருகவில்லையே"

(Even the hard stone may some time or other melt, but my heart which is hard as a stone refuses to melt.)

"நாடகத்தால் உன்னடியார்போல் நடித்து"

(Pretend to imitate your devotees without any real virtue.)

when subject to different expositions and variations of the same Ragam, affect the mind differently bringing out all the different ideas.

Moreover, Music gives peace in the midst of sorrow; it gives rest by alleviating physical pain ; it gives an exhilaration in the midst of hard work. For example, women who are working their hand looms at night forget their labour by singing the praises of their deity. In the same way the farmer who works at the picotah, the woman who grinds the flour, the boatman who plies his oar, the woman who plants the seedlings, the cooly who pounds the chunam — all forget the physical pain attendant on their work and spend their time merrily by singing songs in praise of God. Even the beggar with his cocoanut shell, the Thathan with his little gong and the Brahmachari who begs his oopathanam from door to door, spend their days in singing such inspiring songs like Ekkalakkanni (எக்காலக்கண்ணி) Paraparakkanni (பராபரக்கண்ணி) Oodarkooru (ஊடற்கூறு) and Nenjarivilakkam (நெஞ்சறிவிளக்கம்). The infant which is put to sleep by the gentle lullaby of the mother, desires for more when the lullaby stops. The cow which refuses the milk to its own calf, thinks better of it when under the influence of Music given forth by the cowherd. The cobra, which dwells in solitude hidden from the eye of man, forgets itself when it hears the weird strains of the Magadi, comes out of its hole and dances with its hood outspread. The cows follow the cowherd when he plays the flute for them. Martial Music rouses the spirit of the soldier. Even the horses keep time to the martial Music and are encouraged to advance.

We hear birds singing early in the morning while at the same time musical instruments and bells sound merrily in temples and palaces. In the same way we praise the deity by Music in the evening. There is nothing in the world that can make man happy as Music. Music wins in this world and the next.. God, our creator, desires worship with Music. Sages like Naradar, Thumbur, Hanuman, Ravana and King David obtained divine favor by their Music.

Music softens the mind and unites man with God. Music helps the growth of all virtues and finally leads man to God. Whatever nation practises it, it ennobles them and their country and makes them progress in all arts, wealth and godliness. If the king and his subjects will make much of this art and practise it. this king might justly be called a God and his subjects children of God; even the very land they live on might justly be called God-land. Those virtuous kings who worship the deity by Music will rule the country with such justice and equity, mercy, patience, love and peace, that the tiger and the cow will drink together in the same brook; such kings will consider the lives of their subjects as their own and will establish a heaven upon this earth. But those who abuse this ennobling Music, and make use of it in an unworthy manner, are sure to be cut off early.

Our ancestors, who held the worship of the deity as the chief end of Music, have written at length about the science and art of Music. But most of such works are now defunct; new theories have been advanced and many errors have also crept in. Hence the difficulty in understanding it. This is specially so as regards the period of the origin of Music, the place where it originated and its early patrons. However, we may derive some amount of pleasure if we could draw some legitimate conclusions from the traditionary as well as literary sources that are within our reach

II. PROOFS FROM THE HOLY BIBLE AS REGARDS THE ANTIQUITY OF MUSIC; MUSICAL INSTRUMENTS OF THE EARLY BIBLICAL PERIOD.

1. The existence of Musical instruments such as Kinnair (கின்னரி) and Nagasuram (நாகசுரம்) before the time of the Deluge.

BEFORE determining the age of South Indian Music, we shall do well to consider the age of Music in the neighbouring countries, from certain data from the Holy Bible which are accepted as historical by scholars. In the Book of Genesis, written by the sage Moses nearly 3,400 years ago, in the 4th chapter, in verses 20, 21 and 22 we read

"And Adah bare Jabal: he was the father of such as dwell in tents, and of such as have cattle; And his brother's name was Jubal: he was the father of all such as handle the harp and organ. And Zillah, she also bare Tubal-Cain, an instructor of every artificer in brass and iron."

Theologians have computed that Jubal, the father of those who played the harp and the organ, and Tubal-Cain, the father of those who worked in brass and iron, flourished about 4,000 years before the birth of Christ. If we add to this the 1914 years since the birth of Christ, their period is nearly 5,900 years from now. The Deluge came about 1,650 years after their period. From this we conclude, that the ancient inhabitants of Asia Minor were experts in Music and the lesser arts even before the period of the Deluge.

Moreover, it is said that Cain built a city and called it after his son Enoch. It is further said that there were giants on earth in those days and that people ordinarily lived for 700 to 1,000 years. These were all men of the ante-diluvian period. In the same way we shall see later on that in India also, long-lived men, giants, renowned cities, Kings, Musical instruments such as Kinnair, Nagasuram, Veena and the Flute, as well as the science and art of Music, flourished before the Deluge.

2. The Song of the sage Moses, the dance of Miriam and the song accompanied by the Tambourine.

We read in the 1st verse of XV Chapter of Exodus that (after the Deluge) Moses and the children of Israel sang the praises of God when they were delivered from their enemies who perished in the Red Sea. In the 20th verse of the same chapter we read

"And Miriam the prophetess, the sister of Aaron, took a timbrel in her hand; and all the women went out after her with timbrels and with dances."

When we note the verses they sang, we find that their songs in praise of God reflect a higher degree of civilisation than that of the present day. We see they were trained singers, that they had numerous high class instruments, and that even their women were experts in singing with instruments accompanied by proper dancing. This was nearly 3,400 years ago.

3. The song of Deborah.

Later on, in the 5th chapter of Judges we read that when Deborah the prophetess, the wife of Lapidoth, obtained victory over Sisera who came against her with his 900 chariots of iron, she sang in praise of God. The chapter is full of exquisite poetry. There, a realistic description, as of an eye-witness, is given of the battle, the glory of the Lord of hosts—the prowess of the princes—how the very stars fought against the enemy—the defeat of the enemy by the prowess of a woman—how God Himself fought on her side and gave her the victory. If a woman had the rare gift of making beautiful verses even at such an early period, we conclude that the ancients were experts in poetry and Music. This was nearly 3,200 years ago.

4. The dance of the daughter of Jephtha and the song accompanied by the timbrel.

Still further in the 34th verse of the 11th chapter of Judges we read that when Jephtha, the Judge, returned home victorious after defeating the children of Ammon, his daughter met him with timbrels and dances. This was nearly 3,070 years ago.

5. The Song of David, his piety, his dancing and the Musical instruments of his period.

In the 23rd verse of the 16th chapter of the first book of Samuel we read

"And it came to pass, when the evil spirit from God was upon Saul, that David took an harp, and played with his hand: so Saul was refreshed, and was well, and the evil spirit departed from him."

We learn from this that Music has the power to drive away evil spirits. The David mentioned here was a clever musician. He was an expert in making poems and in singing them to the accompaniment of the harp and the Veena. He was also skilful in making different kinds of musical instruments. He was devoted to the service of God. He not only delighted in singing and dancing before God but induced others to do the same. In the 5th, 14th and 15th verses of the 6th chapter of the Second Book of Samuel, it is written,

"And David and all the house of Israel played before the Lord on all manner of instruments made of firwood, even on harps, and on psalteries, and on timbrels, and on cornets, and on cymbals. And David danced before the Lord with all his might; and David was girded with a linen ephod. So David and all the house of Israel brought up the ark of the Lord with shouting, and with the sound of the trumpet."

We find from the above verses that songs accompanied by a number of Musical instruments and dancing were used in the service of God nearly 3,000 years ago. We must understand that David, the Musician mentioned above, was a mighty King of the Israelites, who might be called the very incarnation of Music. We may read his psalms, written in a profuse scale, in the Holy Bible. His psalms reflect in a remarkable degree the love of a devotee, the trust he has in God and his straightness of heart. It is difficult to come across such magnificent Musicians at the present day. The psalms written by him are of such a nature that a devotee will find in them a response to all his various moods — resignation, faith, joy and trust in God. A real devotee, if he is at a loss to find words to begin singing the praises of God, let him find them in the psalms of King David. For example, in the opening verses of the 92nd psalm, it is written

"It is a good thing to give thanks unto the Lord, and to sing praises unto thy name, O most high: To show forth thy loving kindness in the morning, and thy faithfulness every night, upon an instrument of ten strings, and upon the psaltery; upon the harp with a solemn sound."

And again in the 150th psalm

"Praise the Lord. Praise God in his sanctuary; praise him in the firmament of his power. Praise him for his mighty acts: praise him according to his excellent greatness. Praise him with the sound of the trumpet: Praise him with psaltery and harp, praise him with the timbrel and dance: Praise him with stringed instruments and organs: Praise him upon the loud cymbals: praise him upon the high-sounding cymbals. Let every thing that hath breath praise the Lord. Praise the Lord."

From this, we may have an idea of the dignity of Music, and the numerous instruments that have been in use which were solely employed in the service of God. This devoted servant of God was the first to organise a regular body of singers with their respective heads, and who in regular turns gave Music, both vocal and orchestral, in the service of the temple. His son Solomon also was a great patron of Music.

6. Music during the time of Solomon – the appointment of 288 singers for the service of the temple.

In the 32nd and 33rd verses of the 4th chapter of the first Book of Kings it is said

"He spake three thousand proverbs: and his songs were a thousand and five.

And he spake of trees, from the cedar tree that is in Lebanon even unto the hyssop that springeth out of the wall: he spake also of beasts, and of fowl, and of creeping things and of fishes."

This wise King followed in the footsteps of his father and introduced Music in the Service of God in the temple. We read in the 6th and 7th verses of the 25th chapter of the book of Chronicles that he had organised singing in regular turns in the magnificent temple that he had built. We read there

"All these were under the hands of their father for song in the house of the Lord, with cymbals, psalteries, and harps, for the service of the house of God, according to the King's order to Asaph, Jeduthun and Heman.

So the number of them, with their brethren that were instructed in the songs of the Lord, even all that were cunning, was two hundred four score and eight."

These 288 singers were sub-divided into twelve batches of 24 each, and sang in the temple morning, noon and night, in turns. We have never heard that such a large body of singers helped in regular turns in the services of any church in any of the kingdoms of this world. This is computed to be 2,930 years ago.

7. The Golden statue of Nebuchadnezzar in Babylon—the instruments that were used in the worship thereof.

We read in the opening verses of the 3rd Chapter of the Book of Daniel that Nebuchadnezzar, the King of Babylon (the Chief City of the Chaldeans), made an image of gold, whose height was three score cubits, and the breadth thereof six cubits; that he set it up in the plain of Dura, in the province of Babylon, and invited all people to be present at its dedication. In the 4th and 5th verses we read

"Then an herald cried aloud, to you it is commanded, O people, nations and languages,

That at what time ye hear the sound of the cornet, flute, harp, sack, sackbut, psaltery, dulcimer and all kinds of Music, ye fall down and worship the golden image that Nebuchadnezzar the King had set up."

From this we have an idea of the use of Musical instruments in ancient times.

8. How Music was used morning, noon and night in the palace at Babylon.

In the 18th verse of the 6th chapter of Daniel we read

"Then the King went to his palace, and passed the night fasting; neither were instruments of Music brought before him: and his sleep went from him."

From this we see that it was a custom for Kings to be treated to Music when they got up from bed in the morning, and when they were at rest after the day's work in the evening, and at night, after supper. The custom prevails even now. This custom is of great antiquity — one that was in use more than 2,450 years ago from calculations from the Bible.

To us who are inquirers after the antiquity of the Music of South India it will not be out of place to note a few points about the greatness and magnificence of the city of Babylon in whose palaces Music had played such a prominent part.

9. How Nimrod built Babylon, Nineveh and the cities thereof.

The Cities of Babylon and Nineveh were built on the Euphrates and the Tigris, respectively, in Asia Minor. We see accounts of these cities and the adjoining ones in the 10th chapter of the Book of Genesis.

"The Sons of Noah were Shem, Ham and Japheth. And the sons of Ham: Cush and Mizraim, and Phut and Canaan. And Cush begat Nimrod: he began to be a mighty one in the earth. He was a mighty hunter before the Lord: Wherefore it is said, even as Nimrod the mighty hunter before the Lord.

And the beginning of his Kingdom was Babel, and Erech, and Accad, and Calneh, in the land of Shinar.

Out of that land went forth Asshur, and builded Nineveh, and the city Rehoboth, and Calah, and Resen between Nineveh and Calah: the same is a great city."

From these verses we conclude that Babylon was the chief city of the kingdom of Nimrod. Besides this, he seems to have built Nineveh and other great cities. So the age of Babylon is 4,261 years according to the Bible. But the period of the reign of Nebuchadnezzar is 2,494 years ago *i.e.*, about B.C. 580. This Babylon was destroyed by Cyrus about 540 B.C.

10. The magnificence of the city of Babylon — its destruction.

This city was one of the most ancient and most extensive of the cities of antiquity. It was thrice in extent compared to London, the largest of modern cities. It was so magnificent that London is now called "Modern Babylon." Just as London is built on either side of the Thames, the great river Euphrates divided Babylon into two parts. On both sides of the river were splendid buildings, three and four storeys high, which reached very nearly its banks which were adorned by a breastwork of balustrades and broad ways. There was a strong and wonderful bridge across the river connecting the two banks. The city was a huge 15 miles square with 225 square miles. It was laid out in 625 squares formed by the intersection of 25 streets at right angles. The streets were so parallel that there were avenues to the river so that all the main streets might meet there. Each avenue opening into the riverside had a tremendous gate of brass. The framework as well as the doors thereof were of brass. In the same manner the 120 doors of the enormous wall were entirely of brass. This wall, which was entirely of brick and mortar, was 75 feet high and 32 feet broad. As the river was liable every year to overflow its banks, canals were made and the waters were turned temporarily into a reservoir about 40 miles square and 35 feet deep. The city was surrounded with a trench, very wide, deep and always full of water. On the summit of the city walls were watch towers, having space between them through which a chariot with four horses might easily pass and turn. Within the main wall there were two circular walls. Within these walls were the Royal palace and the park and the grand temple dedicated to Belus. This temple had huge gates of brass. Its frame work and steps were entirely of brass. There were many courts to this temple which were beautifully adorned, and the statues and utensils of the temple were of pure massive gold. The population and the commerce thereof were so immense that one was unable to distinguish night from day. The people were noted for their skill in costly manufactures such as rich carpets, delicate linen and cloth of velvet and gold. Among the spoils of Jericho which was destroyed by the Israelites about 3,365 years ago (Joshua VII 21) was a Babylonish garment. Achan says "*When I saw among the spoils a goodly Babylonish garment . . . I coveted them and took them.*" This clearly shows that at such an early age, very costly garments, highly valued by the neighbouring nations for their brilliancy of colour and fineness of texture, were manufactured by the Babylonians.

Moreover, in the centre of the great city was the lofty and extensive artificial hanging garden built by the great Cyrus. The ascent up to this garden was as to the top of a mountain, and it had buildings and apartments out of one into another, like unto a theatre. Under the steps to the ascent, were arches, one above another, rising gently by degrees, which supported the whole plantation. The highest of these arches was 50 cubits high. The garden itself was surrounded with battlements and bulwarks. Over several stories of this fabric were laid beams of huge massy stones. The roof was first covered with reeds daubed with brimstone; then upon them were laid double tiles, and over them was a covering with sheets of lead that the wet might not rot the foundation. Upon all these was laid earth of convenient depth for the growth of the largest trees. The arches, which stood one above another, had in them many stately rooms of all kinds and for all purposes. There were theatres, libraries, gymnasia, rest-houses and bazars in the lower stories, while the upper stories were reserved for Durbar halls and halls of justice. At times these were used for garden parties. There were engines to draw plenty of water from the river for watering this mighty garden, which were worked without any one being able to perceive the operation. So extensive and populous was the city that what was going on at one end of the city was utterly unsuspected by those at the other end. It was coveted by many merchants and princes on account of its wealth and extent.

Its inhabitants were noted for their skill in fine arts and manufactures. But at the same time they were notorious for their murders, robbery and adultery. The Kings of Babylon were in the habit of plundering and depopulating neighbouring countries and filling their own city with the spoils of war. In the same manner the neighbouring kingdoms, dazzled by its wealth and glory, had their eye on Babylon.

Many kings were burning to revenge themselves by burning and destroying this great city which had existed nearly 2,000 years. The city was invested by the victorious armies of Cyrus (B. C. 540) and, after a blockade of two years, was at last carried by stratagem. On the night of the great festival to Belus, the waters of the great river were turned off, and the channel through the city became a highway for the enemy. The approach of the enemy was not suspected till they attained the palace gate, and in the hour of godless profanity, intemperance and revelry, the sword of the conqueror was unsheathed upon them, and fire completed the destruction. The King was also put to death and the city passed into the hands of the victor. After the time of Cyrus it suffered a steady decline, and Babylon fell, never to rise again. Now, desolation alone meets the eye. The vast solitude, re-echoes only the savage shrieks of owls and jackals and other doleful creatures. Mass upon mass of shapeless ruin chills the heart of the appalled spectator. Modern visitors bring away with them many a memo of its ancient greatness and civilisation and inscriptions on stones.

11. The city of Nineveh — its grandeur — its destruction.

This City of Nineveh, built on the Tigris, by Nimrod, to rival the excellence of Babylon, was of such an extent that it took three days to travel from one end to the other. It was 19 miles in length and 11 in breadth, with a circumference of 60 miles and a population of over 6,00,000. It was surrounded by a wall one hundred feet high which was wide enough for three carriages to go abreast, and which was fortified by 1,500 towers of 200 feet in height. There were two inner walls and two deep moats which made this city unapproachable. It is this very city against which Jonah preached in B.C. 862. This great city was destroyed by King Ahasuerus in B.C. 753, so that its remains now are only a few walls and the moats.

12. The grandeur of the banquet of King Ahasuerus and his queen.

The book of Esther says that this King ruled over 127 provinces from India even unto Ethiopia. He made a grand feast to all the rulers of provinces, nobles and servants, which lasted 180 days. And when these days were expired, he made a feast unto all the people that were present in Sushan the palace, both unto great and small, for seven days, in the court of the garden of his palace. It is said that Vashti, the queen, also made a feast for the women in the Royal house. The beauty and magnificence of the palace is thus described in the 6th verse of the 1st chapter of Esther :—

> " Where were white, green and blue, hangings, fastened with cords of fine linen and purple to silver rings and pillars of marble : the beds were of gold and silver, upon a pavement of red and blue and white and black marble. And they gave them drink in vessels of gold."

The magnificence of a garden party given nearly 2,435 years ago is also described. Even this splendid kingdom of Ahasuerus, with its capital Shushan, was destroyed at a later period.

To sum up, we notice the following facts :—

That Nimrod built great cities after the deluge, which became the chief cities of his kingdom: that even in such ancient times there were many things which would fill the best of modern civilised nations with awe and wonder—the extent of Babylon,—the beauty of its structure,—the hanging gardens,—the monster engines—the numerous gates of brass—the huge reservoir,—the golden image 60 cubits high and 6 cubits broad, —the various musical instruments and their use,—the wall 70 cubits high and the surrounding ditch,—the magnificent banquet of 180 days—the grandeur of the palace of Shusan, and the garden party of the Royal pair. It is difficult to find parallels for all these in modern days in spite of advance of luxury, wealth and culture.

Before the great deluge, giants and mighty men lived for nearly a thousand years each; when these were destroyed by the deluge, the age of man became 120 years which gradually dwindled down to 70. If cities after the deluge were so illustrious what shall we say about the cities in ancient days built by long-lived giants and warriors of great prowess? If we fix the ante-diluvian period as the end of a Yugam, we may conclude that at that Yugam people were noted for their magnificent cities, long life, extensive skill in fine arts as well as the lesser arts of life.

13. The godliness of Enoch and Noah who lived before the Deluge.

We find that before the deluge men were as noted for their piety and godliness as for their longevity and courage. The instance of Enoch, who, after a life on earth with God, was taken bodily into the heavens, and that of Noah, the godly man of the Ark fame, who condemned the prevailing wickedness of the world and exhorted the people to repentance and became the ancestor of the post-diluvian generations, are in point.

III. THE TAMIL COUNTRIES AND ARTS DESTROYED BY THE DELUGE.

1. The difficulty of determining the period of historical events before the Deluge.

PEOPLE may not be interested in any minute description of events before the deluge. They may naturally look upon them as old wives' fables rather than as genuine history. But the conclusions of palaeontologists based upon the skeletons of monster animals and men buried deep into the earth, stone inscriptions, ancient records, ancient coins, buried cities, and natural fossils point to a still more remote period. This is also true. A number of great ports and ancient cities, which once had a brilliant history of their own, are now mere heaps of ruins. Their ancient glory, the prowess of their inhabitants, the magnificence of their arts and the renowned piety of the people are now merely credited as fables and nothing more. This is but natural.

In India also there have been, before the period of the great Deluge, brave giants, celebrated Rishis, Kings renowned for their justice and truth, warriors of prowess, merchants of repute, workmen skilful in arts, and professors and scientists advanced in the fine arts. But we are unable to determine them as the history of ancient India is not only buried in obscurity but is mixed up with a host of myths. In spite of it we may deduce some genuine conclusions from some of the ancient authentic literature. Even here, there are many contradictions. Being conscious of the above defects, we still make bold to arrive at truth regarding the antiquity of India from historical events and literature generally considered genuine by the world.

2. Satyavirata, the Dravidian King, and the deluge.

The following is a quotation from Bhagavatavachanam, Eighth Skandam, the 24th Athyayam :—

பாகவத வசனம், எட்டாவது ஸ்கந்தம், 24-ம் அத்தியாயம்.

"போன கல்பத்தினுடைய அந்தத்தில் பிரம்மாவினுடைய நித்திரையினால் உண்டான நைமித்திகமென்று சொல்லப்பட்ட பிரளயம் உண்டாச்சுது. அந்தப் பிரளயத்தில் பூமி முதலான லோகங்களெல்லாஞ் சமுத்திரத்தில் முழுகிப்போச்சுது. அப்போது காலவசத்தினால் நித்திரையடைந்து சயனிக்கவேணுமென்கிற இச்சையையுடையவனான பிரமதேவனுடைய முகத்தினின்றும் உண்டாகாநின்ற வேதங்களைச் சமீபத்திலிரா நின்ற அயக்கிரீவாசுரனானவன் அபகரித்தான். அப்போது ஸ்ரீ பகவானும் சர்வ நியந்தாவாயுமிருக்கிற ஸ்ரீ ஹரியானவர், தானவேந்திரனான அயக்கிரீவனுடைய சேஷ்டையை அறிந்து மச்சிய ரூபத்தைத் தரித்தார். அந்தக் காலத்தில் சத்திய விரதனென்று பெயரையுடையவனும் மகானும் பகவானிடத்தில் பக்தியுடையவனுமிருக்கிற ஒரு ராஜ ரிஷியானவன், ஜலத்தையே பானம் பண்ணிக்கொண்டு தபசு செய்துகொண்டிருந்தான். யாதொரு அந்த சத்திய விரதனென்கிற ராஜாவே இந்தக் கல்பத்தில் விவசுவானுடைய பிள்ளையாயும் சிரார்த்த தேவனென்று பிரசித்தனாயும் ஸ்ரீ ஹரியினால் மனுவாகக் கல்பிக்கப்பட்டிருக்கிறான். அந்த ராஜ ரிஷியானவன், ஒருக்கால் கிருதமாலா நதியில் ஜலதர்ப்பணஞ் செய்யும் போது, அவனுடைய கையில் இராநின்ற ஜலத்தில் ஒரு மச்சியமானது இருந்தது. திராவிட தேசாதிபதியான அந்தச் சத்திய விரதனென்கிற ராஜ ரிஷியானவன், தன்கையிலிராநின்ற அந்த மச்சிய ஜலத்தை நதிஜலத்திலே விட்டுவிட்டான். அப்போது அந்த மச்சியமானது மகா தயாளுவான அந்தச் சத்திய விரதனைக் குறித்து மிகவும் தைரியத்தோடு ஒரு வார்த்தை சொல்லிற்று.

* * * * * *

வாராய் ராஜரிஷியே! இன்றைக்கு ஏழாநாள் இந்தப் பூமி முதலான மூன்று லோகமும் பிரளய சமுத்திரத்தில் முழுகப்போகின்றது. அப்போது நம்மால் ஏவப்பட்டதாயும் விசாலமாயும் ஒரு ஓடமானது உன்னை அடையப்போகின்றது. நீயும் சமஸ்தமான ஔஷதிகளையும் நானாவிதங்களான வித்துக்களையும் அந்த ஓடத்தில் ஏற்றிக்கொண்டு, சப்தரிஷிகளோடும் சர்வ பலத்தோடுங் கூடினவனாய் அந்தப் பெரிதான ஓடத்தில் ஏறிக்கொண்டு, மகா அந்தகாரமான சமுத்திரத்தில் மகாரிஷிகளுடைய கடாட்சத்தினால் நிரனாய்ச் சஞ்சரிக்கப் போகிறாய். அப்போது மகா பலவானான வாயுவினால் அலைக்கப்பட்ட அந்த ஓடத்தைச் சமீபத்தில் வரா நின்ற என்னுடைய கொம்பிலே சேர்த்து, மகா சர்ப்பத்தினால் இழுத்துக் கட்டக்கடவாய். அப்போது நான், ரிஷிகளோடேகூட இராநின்ற உன்னையும் ஓடத்தையுமிழுத்துக்கொண்டு, பிரமாவினுடைய ராத்திரி காலமானது எவ்வளவோ, அவ்வளவு காலமும் சமுத்திரத்தில் சஞ்சரிக்கப்போகிறேன். அப்போது நீ பண்ணப்பட்ட பிரசினங்களினால் பரப்பிரம சொரூபமான என்னுடைய மகிமையை யதார்த்தமாக அறியப்போகிறாயென்று சொல்லிற்று. பின்பு சமுத்திரமானது வருஷிக்கப்பட்ட மேகங்களினால் விர்த்தியடைந்து, கரைபுரண்டு, பூமியெங்கும் வியாபித்தது. அந்த ராஜரிஷியும் பகவத் பாதாரவிந்தத்தைத் தியானம் பண்ணிக்கொண்டிருக்கும் போது தன்னண்டையே வராநின்ற ஓடத்தைப்பார்த்து, அந்த ஓடத்தில் ஔஷதிகளையெல்லா மேற்றிக் கொண்டு சப்தரிஷிகளோடேகூட தானுமேறிக்கொண்டான். அப்போது அந்த ரிஷிகளெல்லாம் சந்துஷ்டராய் அந்த ராஜரிஷியைப்பார்த்து, பகவானுடைய பாதாரவிந்தத்தைத் தியானம் பண்ணுவீராகில் நம்மை இந்தச் சங்கடத்தினின்றும் ரட்சிப்பாரென்று சொல்லாநின்ற அந்த ரிஷிகளுடைய வார்த்தையைக்கேட்டு, ராஜரிஷியும் பகவானையே தியானம் பண்ணிக்கொண்டிருந்தார்."

"The deluge, which is generally looked upon as the result of the sleep of Brahma, came at the close of the last Kalpam. The earth and the other worlds were submerged. The Vedas which proceeded from the face of Brahma, who was inclined to sleep on, became the coveted property of the giant Hayagreevan who stood close by the side of Brahma. The Omnipotent and omniscient Hari (Vishnu) who understood the thoughts of the giant took the shape of a Matsya (fish). At that time there was a devoted Rishi by name Satyaviratan, who was doing a very rigid penance, living solely on water. [It is this same Satyavirata who is represented by Sivan as the child of Vivasuvan (Manu) and as Srartha Deva.] When he was performing Tarpanam in the river

Kiruthamala, he found a small fish in the water he took with his hand from the river, and instantly dropped it again into the river. • • • • The fish was so thankful to him for the kindly act, that he spoke to Satyavirata as follows : O thou renowned sage ! This earth and the other two worlds will be submerged this day week. You will be then supplied by me with an extensive boat. By the grace of the rishis you are destined to live in all your glory in that boat, on the surface of the dark waters, with a stock of various drugs and seeds and in the company of the Saptarishis. You will then be careful to tie the boat, propelled by the might of the Vayu, on to my tusk using the great serpent as the rope. Then I shall take you and the Rishis on the surface of the waters so that you might live thereon as long as Brahma sleeps. From the deeds you will then perform you will understand my glory as the reflection of the very Brahmam.

Accordingly the gates of heaven opened, there was a heavy deluge and the oceans exceeded their shores. The Rishi, whose mind was solely on God, saw a boat approaching him, filled it with his stock of drugs and seeds, and got into it along with the Saptarishis. The Rishis were all delighted and told him that they all would be saved if he would worship and do service to God. He did accordingly."

ஷை. பாகவத வசனம் ஒன்பதாவது ஸ்கந்தம், முதலாம் அத்தியாயம்.

"திராவிடதேசாதிபதியான சத்தியவிரதனென்கிற யாதொரு ராஜரிஷியானவன் பூர்வ கல்பாந்தத்தில் மகாபுருஷனான ஸ்ரீ பகவானுடைய சேவையினால் உத்தமமான ஞானத்தையடைந்தானோ, அந்த ராஜரிஷியே இப்போது வைவஸ்வதமனுவாக இருக்கிறானென்று என்னால் கேட்கப்பட்டது. இக்ஷ்வாகு முதலான ராஜாக்கள் அந்த மனுவினுடைய புத்திரரென்று உம்மாலே சொல்லப்பட்டார்கள்."

Again, in the same book, ninth Skandam and first Adhyayam, it is written

"I heard you declare that Satyavirata, the ruler of the Dravidam, the great Rishi, who obtained the favour of God by devoted service to him, was the same who is now Vyvaswatamanu, and that Ikshvaku and others were the descendants of Manu."

From this we gather that Satyaviratan, the Dravidian King, was performing a rigid Tapas, that the earth was then destroyed by the deluge, that he, along with the seven Rishis and his stock of drugs and seeds, was saved by a boat which brought him to the foot of a hill and that Vishnu became a fish incarnate (his last incarnation) to help his devotee. This account very nearly resembles the account of the great deluge in the time of Noah which is mentioned in the Holy Bible. Only the scene of the deluge is different, the Biblical account locating it in Asiatic Turkey and the other, in South India.

3. Sri Krishna, the ruler of Dwaraka, and the Deluge.

பாகவதம், பதினோராவது ஸ்கந்தம், 30-அத்தியாயம். ஸ்ரீ பகவான் வாக்கியம்.

"வாராய்சாரதி! நீ துவாரகாபட்டணத்துக்குப்போய், பந்துக்களுக்கு யாதவர்கள் ஒருத்தருக்கொருத்தர் யுத்தம்பண்ணி அடிபட்டுப்போனதையும், யோகமார்க்கத்தினால் பலராமர் பரமபதத்தையடைந்ததையும், நான் இச்சரீரத்தை விட்டுவிட்டதையுஞ் சொல்லக்கடவாய். பந்துக்களோடே கூடிக்கொண்டிருக்கிற நீங்கள் துவாரகையிலிருக்கவேண்டாம். என்னால் விடப்பட்டிருக்கிற இந்தத் துவாரகாபட்டணத்தைச் சமுத்திரமானது முழுகிப்போனதாகப் பண்ணப்போகிறது. ஆகையினால் நீங்கள் சமஸ்தமானபேர்களும் அவரவர் பந்துஜனங்களையும் நம்முடைய மாதா பிதாக்களையும் அழைத்துக்கொண்டு அர்ச்சுனனாலே ரக்ஷிக்கப்பட்டவர்களாய் இந்திரப்பிரஸ்தத்தைப் போயடையுங்களென்று பந்துக்கள்பொருட்டுச் சொல்லக்கடவாய்."

In Bhagavatam, 11th Skandam and 30th Adhyayam it is said

"O thou charioteer! I instruct you herewith to proceed at once to Dwaraka and inform our relations how the Yathavas destroyed each other in the war, how Balarama has obtained Mukti by his rigid yoga, and how I have relinquished this body. Tell them to leave Dwaraka at once as it is going to be destroyed by a deluge. Tell them that they, along with the inhabitants of Dwaraka, their parents and relations, should proceed forthwith to Indraprasta to be under the protection of Arjuna".

ஸ்ரீ பாகவத வசனம், ஸ்ரீ ஸ்கந்தம், 31-ம் அத்தியாயம். ஸ்ரீ சுகர் வாக்கியம்.

"வாராய்மகானுபாவனே! அந்தக்ஷணத்தில் சமுத்திரமானது ஸ்ரீ கிருஷ்ணனுடைய கிரகத்தை விட்டுவிட்டு அவரால் விடப்பட்டிருக்கிற துவாரகாபட்டணம் சமஸ்தத்தையு முழுகப் பண்ணியது.

* * * * * * * * *

"பிற்பாடு அர்ச்சுனனானவன் அசேஷர்களாயிருக்கிற பாலவிருத்தர்களை யழைத்துக்கொண்டு இந்திரப்பிரஸ்தத்தை வந்தடைந்து, அவ்விடத்தில் வச்சிரனுக்குப் பட்டாபிஷேகம் பண்ணிவைத்தான்."

Again, in the 31st Adhyayam of the same Skandam, Sri Sukar says

"O thou man of excellence! at that very moment the ocean left Sri Krishna's strong hold and submerged the whole of Dwaraka."

"Then Arjunah took with him children and the aged who were helpless, brought them to Indraprastha, and there had Vajran crowned King."

ஸ்ரீ பாகவத வசனம் பன்னிரண்டாவது ஸ்கந்தம், 2-ம் அத்தியாயம்.

"எப்போது பகவானுன ஸ்ரீ விஷ்ணுவினுடைய அம்சமாயும் சத்துவசொரூபமாயுள்ள தேகமானது ஸ்ரீ வைகுண்டத்தையடைந்ததோ, அப்போதே கலியானதுண்டானது ஸ்ரீ லட்சுமிபதியான ஸ்ரீ கிருஷ்ண ராஜாவர் தம்முடைய பாதபத்மங்களால் ஸ்பரிசித்துக்கொண்டு பூமியிலிருந்தவரையில் அந்தக் கலியானது பூமியை ஆக்கிரமிக்கைக்குச் சமர்த்துள்ளதல்லாமற்போயிற்று."

Further, in Sri Bhagavata Vachanam, the 12th Skandam and the 2nd Adhyayam, he says

"When the body of Sri Krishna, the hamsam of Sri Vishnu, entered Vykuntam, the Kaliyugam came into existence. So long as Sri Krishna, the Lakshmipati, had this earth under his beautiful feet, Kali was powerless to command this earth."

From the above extract we conclude that Sri Krishna was on this earth at the close of the Dvaparayugam, that, foreknowing the destruction of Dwaraka by the deluge, he sent instructions to Arjuna to remove all his people to Indraprastha (the modern Delhi), that Arjuna did so and crowned Vajran King and that Kaliyugam commenced when Sri Krishna relinquished his incarnate body. It is generally understood that Kaliyugam commenced about 5,014 years ago. The city of Dwaraka is at the western corner of Kathiawar near Kutch which is at the mouth of the Indus. The very appearance of Kutch and Kathiawar indicate that they must have been once submerged. There is evidence to suppose that the Gulf of Kutch, the Persian Gulf, the Gulf of Aden and the Red Sea destroyed, to some extent, parts of the low lands opposite to them. It is an approved geological fact that the latent fire in the centre of the earth, at times appears on the surface and affects the appearatnce of it by converting land into water and *vice versa*. Applying this natural geological law to Arabia, India and Burma, we may conclude that large parts of land which once existed opposite to them must have been submerged at a later period. There is also reason to suppose that the period of the submersion of

Dwaraka is the same as deluge of the time of Noah. It may not be wrong to conclude that the two deluges, dated 4,263 years and 5,000 years from now, are identical. (A difference of seven or eight hundred years is nothing where thousands of years are concerned.) We understand from ancient Tamil literature that the 40 provinces of South India and their capital city Madura were destroyed by sea.

4. The ancient temple of Avudayarkoil, and the 300 Sholya Brahmins who were saved from the deluge.

Visitors interested in South Indian Archaeology will remember the incidents mentioned in connection with the temple of Avudayarkoil noted for its sculptural excellence.

South Indian Railway Illustrated Guide for 1913.

"In the village of Avudayarkoil is an ancient temple which, though small, is considered one of the most perfect specimens of its class in Southern India. . . . . . According to legends the temple occupies the site where, after the deluge, Siva, established a colony of three-hundred disciples called Solias, for the purpose of propagating the Brahman religion."

This leads us to conclude that the Southern part of India must once have been submerged and that people from the south must have proceeded to the neighbouring highlands to save themselves just as the inhabitants of Dwaraka removed to Indraprastha.

5. The Provinces destroyed by the deluge; the Period of the deluge.

[It may be supposed that in some cases, the sea receded and so provided an inhabitable area.] The fact that sea sand is plentiful in some inland parts of Africa adjoining the Red Sea, in Arabia, Asiatic Turkey, Persia, Beluchistan and the eastern part of India, the existence of the ruins of villages and cities amidst piles of sea sand, and the fact that we see the original layer of earth in many places when all the sand is scraped off, makes us conclude that once many cities must have been destroyed by the deluge.

There is difference of opinion among scholars as regards the actual period of the deluge. The Jews place it at 2105 B.C. i.e. 4,019 years ago; Clement Alexandrinaus says that it took place 5,389 years from now, i.e., in B.C. 3475; Euribius thinks that in B.C. 2459, i.e., 4,373 years ago the deluge came; the Venerable Bede places it still earlier in B.C. 3544 or 5,458 years ago; Ursher says that B.C. 2349 is the year of the deluge i.e. that it happened 4,263 years from now, while Hales declares that the year of the deluge is B.C. 3153 or that it took place 5,067 years ago.

It is but natural that these opinions should be conflicting, for those who computed the age of the deluge were not scholars who lived at the time, but who lived thousands of years later. There are no authentic records to throw any light upon the age of the deluge. Historical authenticity should be determined by records or inscriptions found in large cities. But as such cities were destroyed the records perished with them and we have to be satisfied with the external evidence of historians. The fate of the renowned cities of Dwaraka and Indraprastha, which were destroyed thousands of years ago, must also have been the fate of many an illustrious city.

6. The Greater part of South India destroyed by the deluge.

There is evidence to show that, irrespective of the small parts of earth destroyed by the deluge, great parts of Southern India were submerged.

Illustrious readers! The Holy Bible declares that in the antediluvian period there were musicians of repute who not only made musical instruments such as the Kinnair (கின்னரம்) and the Nagaswaram (நாகசுரம்) but played on them; in the same way the literature of South India says that in South Madura which was submerged by the sea there existed musical instruments such as the Narada periyal (நாரதப்பேரியாழ்) with thousand strings and other Veenas, and literary gems such as Naradeeyam, Ahathiyam, Perunarai, Perunkurugu and the like. So, we think, it will not be out of place to say a few words about that province as it may throw light upon the antiquity of South Indian Music. To save time and place, we shall merely quote what others have to say on the subject, without troubling you with any remarks of our own.

7. South India and the deluge.

The following extracts show that in ancient times the Southern part of India was destroyed by the deluge, that it was a huge piece of land and that it was the primary habitation of the ancient man.

Vol. I of the Manual of the Administration of the Madras Presidency P. 33 Foot-note (2).

"*Hypothesis of the genealogy and general migrations of the races of man*: "There are a number of circumstances (especially chronological facts), which suggest that the primæval home of man was a continent now sunk below the surface of the Indian Ocean, which extended along the south of Asia, as it is at present (and probably in direct connection at some points with it); to wards the east as far as Further India and the Sunda Islands, towards the west as far as Madagascar and the south-eastern shores of Africa. Many facts in animal and vegetable geography render the former existence of such a South Indian continent very probable. To this continent has been given the name of Lemuria, from the primitive mammals of that name which were characteristic of it. By assuming Lemuria to have been man's primæval home, the explanation of the geographical distribution of the human species by migration is much facilitated."

Vol. I of the Manual of the Administration of the Madras Presidency, P. 110, 111.

"Investigation in relation to race show it to be by no means impossible that Southern India was once the passage-ground by which the ancient progenitors of Northern and Mediterranean races proceeded to the parts of the globe which they now inhabit. Human remains and traces have been found on the East coast of an age which is indeterminate but quite beyond the ordinary calculations of History."

"Antiquarian research is only now beginning to find means of supplementing the deficiency caused by the absence of material constructed or collected by usual historic methods. These results are specially to be regretted, as without doubt the population who have for many ages occupied this portion of the peninsula are a great people, influencing the world not much perhaps by moral and intellectual attributes, but to a great extent by superior physical qualities."

From these extracts it appears that the ancient inhabitants of South India were a powerful race and resembled in physical build those giants (mentioned in the Bible) who lived for nearly thousand years in the antediluvian period.

Vol. I of the Manual of the Administration of the Madras Presidency, Chapter 1, Page (4).

"The Sanskrit authors of the Pooranas, writing in the north described Ceylon as much more extensive than it now is, and as stretching specially towards the west and south; thereby not representing, no doubt, the fact in Pooranic times, but embodying nevertheless traditions current among Indian Nations. * * * * * *

The Sanskrit astronomers placed their chief Meridian in Lunka, but it was a line to the west of the present Ceylon. These remarks bear on the theory, that in the most ancient times there was a connection between Southern India and Madagascar. * * * *

It also accords with the local tradition recorded by the Buddhists which state that Ceylon was gradually contracted by submergence. * * * *

The date assigned to the Noachian deluge of Scripture is 2,348 B. C. That of the severance of Ceylon from the mainland according to the Booddhists is 2387 B.C. The Rajauvaly, one of the Ceylon Sacred books, records in detail a great submergence on the west, and a tradition exists that the great and little Basses rocks on the east are left by an eastern submergence."

This enables us to conclude that a deluge similar to that of the time of Noah took place in South India and destroyed the greater part of the island of Ceylon which had far extended into the Sea. The time of the deluge has been reckoned by scientists of the east and the west, and we shall not be far wrong in considering the two deluges as identical.

8. The time of the deluge as reckoned by Buddhists.

Vol. I of the Manual of the Administration of the Madras Presidency P. 110, 111.

"The most ancient facts regarding Southern India are remarkable. Geology and Natural history alike make it certain that at a time within the bounds of human knowledge, this country did not form part of Asia. A large southern continent, of which this country once formed part has even been assumed as necessary to account for the different circumstances. The Sanskrit Pooranic writers, the Ceylon Booddhists, and the local traditions of the west coast, all indicate in different manners a great disturbance of the point of the Peninsula and Ceylon within recent times. The date given by English theologians to the Noachian deluge is 2,348 B. C.; and that given by the Ceylon Booddhists to the latest submergence in the region of Ceylon is 2387 B. C. The two dates cannot have been arrived at with mutual knowledge. Investigations in relation to race show it to be by no means impossible that Southern India was once the passage ground by which the ancient progenitors of Northern and Mediterranian races proceeded to the parts of the globe which they now inhabit."

From this we may infer that the greater part of Ceylon was destroyed about 4,300 years ago *i.e.* in B.C. 2387 which is the period of the deluge according to Buddhist priests. Again it is clear that. when the south part of Southern India was destroyed by the sea, the inhabitants migrated through Southern India to other places.

9. The ship in which Satyavirata was saved and the Malaya mountains

The Tamilian Antiquary by Pandit D. Savariroyan, M.R.A.S.

"Before this diluvial catastrophe, the western Ghats were known as the Northern mountains, in relation to the southern Land which was submerged by the ocean. The Satapatha Brahmana relates that the ark of Manu rested in the Northern mountains and the Puranas mention that he, the 'Lord of the Dravida', underwent austere penance in the Malaya. The Mahabharata and the Puranas give an account of seven other Rishis who accompanied Manu and settled in the new colony. This indicates the advent of other clans led by other Rishis who followed the footsteps of the "Lord of the Dravida". Thus it appears that the Tamilian race that settled in the Pandya land belonged to these eight Rishis or Prajapatis, one of whom was the famous Rishi Pulastya of the extreme south, from whom were descended Agastya, the Tamil Muni and Ravana, the king of South.

The Satapatha Brahmana, in which the story of Manu first occurs, does not mention the name of the Northern Mountains. However, there is ample evidence in the Puranic accounts to identify the 'Northern Mountain' with the Western Ghats, and the particular spot on which the ark rested with Malaya."

Here we read that the ship in which Satyavirata, the Dravidian King, was saved found a haven in the Malaya hill along with the Rishis. Malayam is another name for the Pethigai hill. The river Kritamala is not found in modern geography. It will be absurd to suppose that Satyavirata performed his Tapas on the banks of the Vaigai near Madura. Further, Malaya hill must have been to the south of North Madura and not to the north of it. But there is reason to suppose that just as the Kumari river, (which took its rise in the western ghats) the northern boundary of the South Pandya Kingdom, disappeared from the face of the earth, the river Kirutamala, which had its origin in the Pothangai hill might have once been the scene of the penance of Satyavirata near South Madura, and might have disappeared later on. Our inference, therefore, is that when South Madura, which was very far south of Southern India, was destroyed by the Sea, King Satyavirata, who was there, reached the Malaya hill, which is to the north of South Madura, with the help of his ship.

10. The ancient temples in Cape Comorin.

Essays by S. V. Thomas, M.A. Page 84.

"The earliest mention of Cape Comorin by European writers is contemporaneous with the time of Alexander the Great. We have reason to believe that so early as the time of the *Periplus* the Cape was already famous as a sacred shrine of the Hindus. The temple was dedicated to Siva's wife, called Kumari, or young woman, as emblematic of eternal youth and beauty. It is impossible to decide the precise site of the ancient temple seen by the Greek sailors. There are at present three temples at Cape Comorin. One is in complete ruins, and the sea is every day swallowing it up. This probably is the ancient of the three. Another is situated on an elevated rock the foot of which is constantly washed by the waves. The temple is antique in appearence and structure, but is dedicated evidently to Siva's son, not wife, as it contains a rude stone image of Ganesa. The third is the temple which pilgrims now go to visit. This has a comparatively modern look about it. * * * * * * * * *

"It is very probable that the most ancient temple has been buried under the sea, and that when the encroachments of the sea were arrested by the solid rocks that now stand out to check its progress, another temple was built and dedicated to the same goddess. This view is supported by the report that is current among the fishermen living in the neighbourhood. They say that in 1883, when the green Sun perplexed the scientific world, the sea receded all of a sudden some furlongs that there were then seen the ruins of old buildings with brazen gates and other accompaniments, that some of the fishermen ventured out to drag them ashore, but that before they could succeed the sea came back to assert her ancient dominion, and the enterprise was given over. If this be true, we have strong reasons for supposing that the temple which astonished the Greeks is imbedded in sea, and that the present temple afterwards rose to the honour of the tutelary goddess of the Cape."

We find from the above extracts that the temple dedicated to Parvati—the emblem of eternal youth and beauty-which is in Cape Comorin, the southernmost point of India, has been submerged, and that temples which were built later on, including a temple to Ganesha, are being washed by the sea. It is said that these temples which had been submerged, appeared above the surface in 1883 when the sea receded a little, that some fishermen tried to bring ashore the gates of brass belonging to them, but had to give it up when they saw the waters of the sea rising once more. We gather again that gates of gold and brass were used in the building of palaces and temples by those ancient people. The destruction by sea of the ancient temples of Cape Comorin is also inferred.

11. The location of Lemuria.

Castes and Tribes of Southern India Vol. I, Intro. P. 20, 21 by E. Thurston.

"In the chapter devoted to 'Migration and distribution of organisms,' Haeckel, in referring to the continual changing of the distribution of land and water on the surface of the earth, says: "The Indian ocean formed a continent, which extended from the Sunda Islands along the Southern Coast of Asia to the east coast of Africa. This large continent of former times Sclater has called Lemuria, from the monkey-like animals which inhabited it, and it is at the same time of great importance from being the probable cradle of the human race. The important proof which Wallace has furnished by the help of chronological facts, that the present Malayan Archipelago consists in reality of two completely different divisions, is particularly interesting. The western division, the Indo-Malayan Archipelago, comprising the large islands of Borneo, Java, and Sumatra, was formerly connected by Malacca with the Asiatic continent, and probably also with the Lemurian continent just mentioned. The eastern division, on the other hand, the Austro-Malayan Archipelago, comprising Celebes, the Moluccas, New Guinea, Solomon's Islands, etc., was formerly directly connected with Australia."

The above extracts enable us to infer that the ancient continent of India, which was to the South of India in the Indian Ocean, was the original habitation of man, that it was the cradle of all nations, and that after the destruction of the continent the various races occupied the shores which were against them. Natural historians who have made a comparative study of the nations, the fauna and the flora of the neighbouring countries, conclude that all races should have originated from this continent of Lemuria. Moreover, the ancient history of almost all nations is unanimous in acknowledging a deluge, and in saying that particular nations are the descendants of a saint who was miraculously saved from the deluge.

12. Some noteworthy points in connection with the deluge.

The New Popular Encyclopedia Vol. IV, Page 325.

"Many other nations mention, in the mythological part of their history, inundations which in their essential particulars, agree with the scriptural account of Noah's preservation. Hence many persons have inferred the universality of this inundation. To this, it has been replied that each nation localizes the chief events and actors as connected with itself, necessitating an Ararat, an ark and a Noah in each instance. Fohi in the Chinese mythology, Sottivrata or Satyavrata in the Indian, Xisuthrus in the Chaldæn, Ogyges and Deucalion in the Greek, have each been recognized by many as the Noah of the sacred scriptures under a different name. Even

Tolgauppyam complete should consist of three parts; on letters, words and prosody, or rather versification as an art. Of these the last part cannot be found complete. Tolgauppyam has had three commentaries written upon it by Natchinarkiny, Yilampooran, and Shenauvareiyan [Nunnool.]

The Sootrams of Tholkappiam are looked upon by the Tamilians of even the present day as precious as gold. Yet there are few who have understood the author and practised his sayings. Doctor McLean speaks of 8,000 Sutras whereas only as few as 1,612 are in use at present. This makes us think that the others must have been destroyed by moth. There is reason to think that the 12,000 Sutrams referred to by Dr. Winslow might be Chittahathiyam. The Tholkappiam treats about the ancient manners and customs of the Tamils, law and politics, division of the country and Music. Its grammar is so elegant and chaste that it beats any style of Tamil even in its advanced stage. There is no further proof necessary for the glory and dignity of Tamil.

14. Some evidence for proving antiquity.

When we speak of the First Sangam and its Presidents who lived 4,400 years before the author of Tholkappiam, our readers may doubt our statements as these lead one to the belief that nine and ten thousand years have passed since creation, whereas the recognised period of the creation is but 6,000 years from now. It is the opinion of historians that the 'days' mentioned in the opening chapter of the book of Genesis written by the sage Moses about 3,400 years ago, are each of them an Ooli (a certain number of years). This is supported by the fact that the skeletons of animals buried deep into the earth now discovered are much bigger than those of animals which went into the ark with Noah. The skeletons of giant men are also being unearthed from time to time. The age of some trees which grow on hilly places is reckoned to be over 20,000 years. Age of trees based upon their separate layers is always reliable. The following extract will throw some light on it.

Doubts of Infidels, Page 26.

"The bones of man, of the type of the North American Indian, have been exhumed from the delta of the Mississippi at New Orleans, which were found lying below the fourth forest level, and making large allowance, must have lain there for more than fifty-thousand years. The exhumed relics of ancient civilisation in the valley of the Nile antedate the History of the Jewish theocracy and the foot prints of the Creator are found in the granite pages of the primary and fossiliferous rocks, long anterior to the fabulous era of this Genesaical history of creation. Humboldt describes a tree now growing in the famous gardens of Montezuma, as more than six-thousand years old, and another in Central America as but little less than twenty-thousand years old."

Here the author says that bones of men, resembling those of the North American Indians, have been exhumed near New Orleans, and that they must be at least 50,000 years old. The deluge seems to have converted large forests into areas of sand, on which other forests rose. And these forests, after thousands of years, in their turn again became seas of sand, and so this process was going on for ages as the result of four different deluges. Judging from the flora and fauna of these separate layers of earth, Paleontologists ascribe thousands of years to the formation of each layer. When they found the bones of the type of North American Indians in the last of these four layers they reckoned that they must have been under the earth for over 50,000 years. On the banks of the Nile were also unearthed many relics which throw light upon her ancient civilisation. Among long-lived trees is mentioned the Paparapuli (Adansonia digitata) whose age is computed to be 20,000 years. This species is found in Southern India. This is a trèe indigenous to South India and not an importation. Yogis who understand the virtue of its juice make a small incision in the trunk, apply the lime ot the sulphate of copper to the place and receive the milk that exudes from it in a small vessel. The drinking of this juice makes them go off into a trance and they remain in a state of unconciousness for nearly four days. It is considered that this juice is of great help to them in the performance of yoga and other rigid functions. The fact that the properties of a tree are well known in a particular country proves beyond doubt that the tree is indigenous to that country. In some parts of Southern India it is known as the Bhuta tree; and it is considered so sacred that no one destroys its branches or leaves. Its trunk is very broad and the top tapers gradually into a conical shape. This tree is found in great abundance in the Tanjore District, and it is also seen in some places of Madura and Tinnevelly Districts. In the city of Tanjore, one of them may be seen in the Sivaganga garden and another near the banks of the Vennar. Many may be found in the delta of the Cauvery. When a section is made of the trunk of this tree, different layers seen there help in reckoning the age of it which may be placed at the first Ooli. The existence of this tree in many other places is made out by the following extract.

Dravidian comparative Grammar by Bishop Caldwell, Page 66, Foot-note.

"Huge old specimens of the Baobab, or Adansonia Digitata, an African tree of which the Hindus do not know even the name, may still be seen in or near various sites of foreign commerce in the extreme south of the Indian peninsula: *e. g.* in Kottar, near Cape Comorin, and near Tuticorin in Tinnevelly --possibly on the site of the ancient Kolkhi."

The author says that the Baobab is an African tree which may be seen in or near sea coast towns in India engaged in foreign commerce and that the Hindus are ignorant even of its very name. But to those South Indian people, who are cognisant of its virtues, it is not unknown. There is reason to think that this tree must have once been found in abundance in the land between Africa and South India before it was submerged and it is now found in the adjoining countries. Particulars of this tree are given in the following extracts:—

Winslow's Dictionary P. 728.

பப்பரபுளி—(also பெருக்கமரம்) A species of large tree, Adonsonia degitata."

and again in

Vasudeva Naidu's Ayurveda Paravaram P. 676.

யானைப்புளியமரம், பப்பரப்புளி, புரிமரம், Adonsonia digitata, Baobob, Monkey bread tree. This tree has spread to a large extent in Africa and our own country. The fruit of the tree has the virtues of relaxing the nerves and the pulse and of stopping the flow of blood and puss. It also causes the relaxation of pulse by curing the burning sensations. It might also be administered with effect for diarrohea and fever arising from phlegmatic cold."

The above extract shows the various names by which this tree is known. There is reason to think that Yogis largely used it on account of the peculiarly good properties it possessed. This long-lived tree must have been found in earliest times in

Lemuria whose sages did rigid penance to obtain long life. It is but natural that after the destruction of the continent it should have survived in those parts of land which were adjoining, namely in Africa and South India. The fact that these trees are found near Pothigai hills and on the banks of the Cauvery shows that these were not importations from other countries.

Castes and Tribes of Southern India by E. Thurston Vol. I, Introduction P. XXIV.

"On the evidence of the very close affinities between the plants and animals in Africa and India at a very remote period, Mr. R. D. Oldham concludes that there was once a continuous stretch of dry land connecting South Africa and India."

This extract also proves our point. It is based upon the peculiar resemblance between the flora of Africa and South India.

Another proof for the antiquity of nations is furnished by the Egyptians who, according to calculations, seem to have been in existence 10,000 years ago, and who were skilful in manufacturing earthen vessels entirely by their hand without the usual aid of the rod and the wheel. The following extract proves our statement:—

Hutchinson's History of the Nations, Page 5.

Early Egyptians making pottery 10,000 years ago.

"The most abundant handwork of the early Egyptians was the finely made pottery entirely formed by hand. It was built up from the base and in form so true that no error is perceptible. The facing was finished with a coat of red haematite, which turned to a brilliant black in the furnance. It is interesting to note that the same materials are used in the same kind of patterns by the hill tribes at the back of Algeria at the present time."

The extract enables us to infer the existence of men not only 10,000 years ago, but long before that period also. For judging the age of man by the progress mankind has made since creation, we may divide the ages into three :—the first stage is that in which man lived on fruits, seeds and honey; the second is the age when the properties of fire were known which enabled man to broil raw roots, raw fruit and seeds in the fire, and the third stage is that in which earthen vessels were used for cooking grains and greens and herbs. Historians prove antiquity by various other means also, such as the implements, clothing, and the dwelling place used in the various stages of existence. If an Egyptian had made earthen vessels 10,000 years ago in the third stage of man's existence, it is not improbable that skeletons of men 50,000 years old should have been exhumed. The existence of things in America and Egypt in ancient times proves the existence of man in the continent of Lemuria also from the earliest times.

From the above statements we find it is not beyond the chances of probability to say that the author of Tholgaupiam lived 8,000 years ago and that the First Sangam was instituted 12,000 years ago. The statement that Agastyar flourished in the time of the First Sangam over 8,000 years ago and that he was the author of the grammar which treated about the three divisions of Tamil, Iyal, Isai and Natakam, is rather surprising to us, short-lived men. Why should we not believe Nakkeeranar who wrote the commentary on Irayanar Ahapporul 1,800 years ago? Could we imagine him capable of an untruth who fought with Paramasivam by saying " Even if one had an eye in the forehead (as Sivan has) one must acknowledge one's mistake"? Even if he stated an untruth, would it not have been refuted by the learned vidwans of the Tamil Sangam which then existed? Those days were not the same as the modern times when people hesitate to refute others out of sheer regard for the preservation of peace. This period is also made mention of by Adyarkunallar. Hence the undoubtedness of its antiquity. It is enough for our purpose that the boundaries of countries which existed at the end of the first Ooli, and the magnificent grammar of the Tamil literature, are made mention of by reliable authorities such as Tholkappiam even 8,000 years ago.

15. The religion of South India.

Glancing into the antiquity of South India, we see that it abounds with Kings who were famous for their equity and justice, devotees whose sole business was the worship of the deity, and Rishis well known for their devotion and culture. We may conclude by the following extracts that the inhabitants of the continent of Lemuria were chiefly responsible for the Hindu religion, the worship of the deity and the arts of civilised life and were also instrumental in disseminating their religion in the North.

District Manual of Madura, Pt. III, Page 48.

"Mr. Pope in his edition of the Abbe Dubois' work says that in South India numberless legends relating to devout worshippers of the Linga are current: that some of them are curious, and they are exclusively of southern origin. And Wilson states in his introduction to the catalogue that tradition uniformly points to an extension of Hinduism and civilization from the extreme south of the Peninsula."

We may conclude from the above extracts and from the facts that Sri Krishna instructed Arjuna to remove his people from Dwaraka to Indraprastha in the North-East to be safe from the deluge and that Paramasivan protected the 300 Solia Brahmins, the remnants of those saved from the deluge, at Avudayarkoil for the purpose of disseminating the Brahmin religion, that there was an exodus of the people from the South to the North.

Again, we see in all the chief centres of South India enormous temples, magnificent sculptural work, huge cars and a number of temples dedicated to Siva and many lingams, while such sights are rare in North India.

Again, we see the people of South Madura were specially devoted to the service of Siva, both Siva and his two sons Ganesha and Subramania being held in the highest esteem by them. It is to be noted that in all the provinces of the destroyed Lemuria the worship of Siva predominated. It is believed that Siva and his son were the chief guides of the Kingdom of South Madura for many years, that they patronised Tamil literature by being Presidents of the first Sangam which had a long life of nearly 4,400 years. It is for that reason, and also being struck by the Godhood that was manifest in them, that the people of South Madura built splendid temples for them, set up the lingam in the most holy places, and made enormous cars to be of use in the temple processions. Vast maniyam lands and other offerings have been given so that the festivals and the daily poojahs might go on for ever. By means of daily and monthly gifts they have perpetuated the daily service of the temple. Arrangements have been made so that one might definitely know what poojah should be performed, at what hour of the day or night, with what particular libations and offerings and by what particular priest. Those who are appointed to sing and dance during the services of the temple do their work most regularly. The arrangements for poojahs are so perfect that people, religiously inclined, may go at any part of the day or night with their gifts and offer them to god. The small ministrations such as watering the temple garden which supplies flowers for worship, gathering the flowers early in the morning for the poojah, sweeping the precincts of the temple and lighting it are performed with the greatest enthusiasm. They sing soul-inspiring songs such as Thevaram and Thiruvachagam in the worship of the deity. They commune with the deity by being in the same posture for hours having their five senses under the most perfect control. They perform viratams to keep the body, which is the birth place of all that is evil, in strict subjection. In short the temple is always filled with the music and dancing and offering and other requisites of divine service. Those who have attended the services of Parvatiamman in the temple of Alavai in Ootaramadura will testify to the beauty of temple poojahs. The services of the temples are so arranged that a man in any one of the four stages of existence—sarithai, kiriai, yogam, and gnanam—may find in them all that is requisite to satisfy his spiritual needs.

It is also seen that those who escaped from the deluge came and occupied South India and there built temples similar to their ancient ones and introduced there the worship of their old deities.

We now proceed to prove that just as the Hindu religion was found in the vast provinces of South of India in the remotest times, so also the Tamil language was a pure unmixed language which existed there from the ancient times.

IV. THE ANTIQUITY OF TAMIL.

1. The Antiquity and beauty of the Tamil language used by the inhabitants of Southern India.

NOBLE readers! if we want to understand clearly the sublety and antiquity of Indian music we would do well to make a few observations on the Tamil language which includes within itself the poetry of the Music and the Drama. The period of the origin of Indian Music is as ancient as the period of the Tamil language, and the sweetness of Indian Music is the sweetness of the language itself. Just as the language stands unmixed and unaffected by other languages, so also the Music of South India is perfect in itself having special rules of its own without seeking the aid of other music. So, before we speak about the music of South India which is held in the highest esteem by musicians of repute, we would do well to say a few words about the antiquity and dignity of the Tamil language. As the remarks that we are about to make are but the good or evil to the Tamil language derived from the comparison of different languages and different countries by different scholars, we earnestly implore our readers not to imagine that we have any special motive for decrying any language or any nation.

Historians say that the inhabitants of the destroyed continent of Lemuria were highly civilised long before the historic period and quite prior to the period of the dawn of civilisation in other countries. In support of this we find that South Madura, which was a part of it, had an ancient brilliant history of its own, that the Pandyan Kings who ruled over it as well as the presidents of the Tamil Sangam, yea, even the Tamil language itself—had an antiquity and excellence of their own which were indisputable.

The first two letters of the word (தமிழ்) Tamil namely (தமி) Tami mean "peer-less" "standing by itself", and the word Tamil means "sweetness". We shall presently see that in conformity with its derivative meaning, the Tamil language, according to eminent scholars, was perfect in itself without, in the least, being dependent on other languages.

Vol. I, of the Manual of the Administration of the Madras Presidency, Page (42.)

"There is little doubt that the Dravidian languages are incomparably older in point of time than the Sanskrit. It is not an unreasonable supposition that they once occupied the whole of Hindustan and have been driven to their present position to the south and along the coast by the encroachment of other languages coming from the North-west."

We see from the above extract, that the language spoken in India before the advent of the Aryans, was Tamil.

Further, we shall see, that although the language has undergone some change owing to the exigencies of time, its grammar is intact and perfect. That it was in this perfect and unchangeable state thousands of years ago, is proved by the following.

Vol. I, of the Manual of the Administration of the Madras Presidency Page (112.)

"As far as present evidence goes, however, they are indigenous to India, and perhaps specially indigenous to Southern India.........As to their language, no other is known to which it can be affiliated. It stands alone, without any immediate predecessor. In origin, it must be long anterior to the Sanskrit, which has subsequently played so important a political part with regard to it. Its original strength is shown by the great persistence of its grammatical formations through all the vicissitudes of history."

Here the author says, that some of the Greek characters were derived from Hebrew, some Pali characters from Greek, some Sanskrit characters from Pali, and most of the Prakrit characters from Sanskrit; but he is at a loss to derive the Tamil characters from any other language. The Tamil language stands by itself. He further says that its strength is shown by the great persistence of its grammatical rules through all the vicissitudes of history.

The same fact is established by the following extract.

Vol. I, of the Manual of the Administration of the Madras Presidency, Page (49.)

"North Indian Civilization, when it came as far south as the Tamul country, found the people already in possession of the art of writing and of cultivated language. In consequence of this, Sanskrit did not regulate the Tamul phonetic system, and merely held the place of a foreign learned language."

The above extracts show that the Tamilians were equally civilised and cultured like the Aryans who came from the North. The Aryans were not able to influence the Tamil language to any appreciable extent as they did with the other languages which they came in contact with. It is the Aryans who gave the name, 'Dravidam' to the oldest Tamil words, the name "Dravida Desam" to the place where the language was used, and the name "Dravidians" to the people who spoke the language. We shall see from the following extract that being unable to write in their own exalted language the simple name 'Tamil' they called it by some other name which had not the slightest connection with it!

சிங்காரவேலு முதலியார் எழுதிய அபிதான சிந்தாமணி பக்கம். 489.

"தமிழ்நாட்டரசர் மூவரும் சூரிய சந்திர வம்சத்திலிருந்து பிரிந்தவர்கள்; இவர்கள் துவாபரயுகத்திற்கு முன்பும் அரசாண்டதாகத் தெரிகிறது. ஒரு பாண்டியன் பாரத யுத்தத்தில் பாண்டவர்களின் சேனைக்கு அன்னமிட்டதாகத் தெரிகிறது. இவன் தமிழ்ப்புலவரை ஆதரித்தவன். * * * * * * பின்னும் இவ்வரிய பாஷை மற்றைப் பாஷைகள்போல் வேறு பாஷைகளின் துணைவலி பெறாது தானே விளங்கும் வற்றமுற்றது; இதனை அறிவுள்ளோர் பலர் பழைய நூல்களிற் கண்டறியலாம். ஆயின் தமிழ் என்பது திராவிடம் என்பதின் திரிபென்றேவெனின் திரிபாகாது. தமிழ், தெலுங்கு, கன்னடம், மகாராஷ்டிரம், கூர்ச்சரம் இவைகளையும் திராவிடமென்பவாகலின் இதற்கேயுரியதாகாது. ஆயினும் அப்பெயர் கூறவந்த வடநூலார் அக்காலத்திற்கு முன்னரே தோன்றிய பாஷைக்குத் தாங்கள் பெயரிடாது அந்நாட்டில் தாங்கள் வந்தகாலத்து இட்ட பெயராகவுமிருத்தலின் இது வடமொழிக்குப் பிந்தியதாகாது. வடமொழி வடநாட்டிலிருந்ததுபோல் தென்மொழி தென்னாட்டிலிருந்தது. இதனால் தமிழ்ப் பாஷை தனித்த பூர்வபாஷையென்பது கொள்ளக்கிடக்கிறது."

Abithana Chintamani by Singaravelu Mudaliar, Page 489.

"All the three Kings of the Tamil Country were descendants of either the Soorya or the Chandra kulams. They seem to have ruled even before the Dvaparayuga. One of the Pandya Kings evidently fed the whole army of the Pandavas in the great war. He was also a patron of Tamil scholars. * * * * * * Moreover, this unique language has the peculiarity of standing by itself without being influenced at all by other languages. Scholars will be able to find this out by reference to ancient literature. It is absurd to say that the word "Tamil" is derived from "Dravidam", as the term is equally applied to other languages such as, Telugu, Malayalam Canarese, Maharashtra and Guzrati. In any case the Sanskrit language is by no means prior to the Tamil language, as the Aryans found this language in the South when they imigrated southwards, and were ignorant of its name. Just as the Sanskrit was the language of the north, Tamil was the language of the South. This clearly shows that Tamil was an ancient independent language."

The Aryans, who hated to pronounce the name Tamil, called it the Dravidian language. They tried to establish a derivative connection between the words "Tamil" and "Dravidam" thus trying to establish that 'Tamil' was derived from Sanskrit. They said "Dravidam" became "Thiramilam" as 'l' might in some cases be used for 'd'; the long 'ra' became short thus giving 'Thiramilam'; then it became "Thamilam" by dropping the second letter 'ra', which in its turn became 'Tamil' by dropping the end syllable 'am'. But what about the letter 'vi'? What is the connection between 'vi', and 'mi,'? As they are capable of interpreting things in a round-about way like the man who tries to reach his nose by taking his hand round the head instead of going straight in front, they interpreted an easy slokam in the Sangeetharatnakaram of Sarangadevar in 20 different ways without in the least arriving at the truth! When we notice that they interpret the meaning by taking letter after letter, they must only hold their peace and keep their mouths shut, as the man who realised that every thing was Brahmam kept his mouth shut in proof thereof! Though we realise that Sanskrit is a superior language and that its literature contains many precious gems, yet we cannot be blind to the fact that it is a dead language.

They changed the forms of many words from time to time that people might think that they were derived from Sanskrit, and supported the transformation by writing books, puranams and fables. If they barefacedly declare that the Tamil word 'Neer' (நீர் = water) was derived from Sanskrit 'Neeram', and that 90 p. c. of the Tamil words are derived from Sanskrit there is no limit to which they may go! Do they mean to say that the Tamil Scholars, who conducted the Sangam for nearly 4,400 years before the first Ooli, and the innumerable people who lived long before that time, never drank water? Or were they at a loss to find a suitable name for water? Was it after the advent of the Aryans that they were able to distinguish hot water (வெந்நீர்) from cold water (தண்ணீர்), and differentiate (ஆற்றுநீர்) river water from ஊற்றுநீர் (spring water), சேற்றுநீர் (Mud water), செந்நீர் (red water), வெடிநீர் (Philosopher's acid), கடனீர் (sea water) குடிநீர் (drinking water) இளநீர் (water of the tender cocoanut), கண்ணீர் (tears from the eye), and உமிழ்நீர் (spittle) and such waters? They did the same with many other words. To prove that these Tamil words were derived from Sanskrit they mutilated many a word by lengthening or shortening the sounds or by bringing in alien sounds. They gave Sanskrit names to many an important hill, river, city and people in the Tamil country and perpetuated the fraud by composing Puranams and history to suit the same. These puranams and poems were preached broadcast before kings and subjects, and they were made to believe them as true. People who believed their derivation of 'Naratham' and 'Narayanan' from 'Neera' "Neeram" and 'naram' believed also their philology which derived 'Neer' from "Naram" and "Neeram" and their other trumped up tales! When once the Sanskrit language obtained adherents in the Tamil country many a Sanskrit word was boldly introduced. We need not say more. All right minded people understand it.

We had to say all these on account of the undisputed fact that Poetry which is the chief adjunct of Music, and which is one of the three angams of the language itself, flourished from the earliest times in the South and that it was carried north by the Aryans who came from there. We shall speak about the subject later on.

We may see from the following extracts how Sanskrit was largely introduced into the Tamil language.

2. The process of the introduction of Sanskrit words into Tamil.

Manual of the administration of the Madras Presidency, Vol. I, Page 4.

"It is to be observed that though the long list of names mentioned in the Pooranas are all Sanskrit, these are only book names. The names of the country reported or ascertained by Aryan travellers and settlers were invariably translated into Sanskrit by the literary caste of the Aryans. It is a very common error to suppose that because none but Sanskrit names are found in the ancient literature of the country, it was therefore a country occupied by an Aryan people, and that all the places mentioned were founded by the Aryans. But in fact as the Aryan visitors to India had the monopoly of literature, the indigenous names could only appear in a Sanskrit form; and no argument is to be thence deduced in one direction or another as to the extent of the Aryan colonizations. In later times Aryan influence has undoubtedly given current names to geographical places even in Southern India. * * * It will be seen from the next note that Greek literature is analogous to Sanskrit in presenting indigenous Indian names in such a Greek dress that they are not easily recognisable; but the Greeks did not at all to the same extent actually translate Indian names."

The above extract shows that the Tamil words were changed into Sanskrit and introduced into the puranas by the Aryans and that they were adepts in building castles in the air and in giving Sanskrit names to cities and houses which they had never built! The Aryans were naturally clever in representing as genuine truth anything which they heard or anything which they imagined to be true. Some of them are so clever that even if a new phenomenon appeared in the world they would trace the existence of it in their puranas from the ancient times! The Indians have become habituated to believe such stories. The Aryans who entered India more or less in modern times, ignored, or kept in the back ground, its ancient people, its language and literature, and the history of its ancient Kings and great men, and made much of their own language, their own literature and their own great men. It is said that when the Greeks who invaded India changed some of the Indian names into their own language, the names could hardly be recognised as Indian, but the sin of the Aryans in this respect was much greater. Doctor McLean says that it is a common error to suppose that India was a country inhabited by the Aryans and that all the chief cities there were established by them. We must, on the same lines, assert that it is equally an error to suppose that Tamil is derived from Sanskrit, and that Tamil language has no charms but for the introduction of a number of Sanskrit words. It appears that when the first Tamil Sangam, its literature and the country were destroyed in the first Ooli, Tholkappiam was the only work that survived. Later works of the time of the Middle Sangam were destroyed in the second Ooli. We shall see that even the few which survived this are found mutilated by the introduction of Sanskrit words and by Sanskrit works which support the mutilation.

தமிழ்ப் பண்டிதர், சூரிய நாராயண சாஸ்திரியார், B.A., எழுதிய தமிழ் மொழியின் வரலாறு பக்கம் 14. 15.

"வடமொழியாளர் தமிழர்களது ஒழுக்கவழக்கங்களை யுணர்ந்து அவற்றிற்கேற்ப வடமொழியில் நூல்கள் வகுப்பான் புகுந்தனர். அவர்களெல்லாம் ஆன்ம நூற்பயிற்சி மிக்குடையாராயும், கலை யுணர்ச்சி சான்றவராயு மிருந்தமைபற்றித் தமிழரது திவ்விய ஸ்தலங்களுக்குப் புராணங்கள் வகுத்தனர்; தமிழர்களிடத் தில்லாதிருந்த 'அந்தணர், அரசர், வணிகர், வேளாளர்' என்ற நால்வகைச்சாதி முறையை மெல்ல மெல்ல நாட்டிவிட்டனர்.

'முற்படைப்பதனில் வேறுஇய முறைமைபோல்
நால்வகைச் சாதியிந் நாட்டினீர் நாட்டினீர்.'

என்று ஆரியரை நோக்கி முழங்குங் கபிலரகவலையுங் காண்க. இன்னும் அவர் தம் புத்திநலங்காட்டித் தமிழரசர்களிடம் அமைச்சர்களெனவும் மேலதிகாரப் பிரபுக்களெனவும் அமைந்துகொண்டனர்; தமிழரிடத் திருந்த பல அரிய விஷயங்களையும் மொழிபெயர்த்துத் தமிழர் அறியு முன்னரே அவற்றைத் தாமறிந்தன போலவும் வடமொழியினின்றுமே தமிழிற்கு அவை வந்தனபோலவும் காட்டினர். * * * *
தாங்கள் செல்லுமிடங்களுக்குத் தக்கபடி புதிய புதிய இலிபிகள் ஏற்படுத்திக்கொள்ளு மியல்புடைய ஆரியர் தமிழ்நாட்டிற்கேற்றபடி, தமிழிலிபியை யொட்டிக் 'கிரந்தம்' என்னும் பெயரிற் புதியதோர் இலிபி வகுத்தனர்; தமிழரை வசீகரிக்குமாறு அவ்விலிபியிற் பல நூல்கள் வரைந்தனர். தமிழ்ப்புலவராவார் எதற்கும் அசையாது தங்கள் தமிழ்மொழியின் போக்கையே தழுவிச் செல்வாராயினர்."

" சித்தெலா நிறைந்து சித்தா யமர்ந்த
தேசிகர் மரபில் சிறந்து விளங்கும்
மடாதி பதிகளா மாண்பமை ஞானியர்
அளவிற் படுவதவ் வதீன காலம்."

The Tamil language by Pandit Sooryanarayana Sastriar B.A., p. 14. 15.

The upholders of Sanskrit learnt the manners and customs of the Tamilians and wrote works in Sanskrit to be in conformity with them. They were also responsible for devising puranams in connection with their sacred shrines as they were well-versed in religion and arts. They gradually introduced the division of castes into Brahmins, Kings, Vaisyas and Agriculturists which were unknown among the Tamilians. Compare with this what Kapilar says in his ahaval where he denounces the Aryans, for having established the four castes as having existed from the time of creation. Further by the display of their intelligence they got round the Tamil Kings and obtained the coveted posts of prime-ministers and nobles. They copied into Sanskrit many precious things found amongst the Tamilians, and boasted that they had knowledge of them before the Tamilians and made out that they were copied from their own literature into the Tamil language. The Aryans who were clever in devising characters and letters to suit the different places they emigrated to, introduced the 'grantham' to suit the Tamil Country and the Tamil literature. They wrote many works in the new 'characters' in praise of the Tamilians. But the scholars and admirers of the indigenous language were never affected by these fulsome praises but went on cultivating their own language without being influenced by the Aryan novelties.

We have to accept the above statement as it comes from a learned Sanskrit scholar who is himself an Aryan. There is every reason to suppose, judging from what the Pandit says, that many of the Tamil works were written out in Sanskrit, and that alterations were made here and there to make them appear that they were prior in time to the Tamil works. To give a few instances, we find that some of the chootrams in Perahathiyam and in Tholkappiam, and some treatises in connection with medicine, alchemy, yogam, gnanam and astronomy betray many interpolations which lead us to conclude they must have been tampered with by Sanskrit writers. This is glaringly evident from the work called " Perisai Choothiram" generally ascribed to Kalarambar, a disciple of Ahastya The book speaks about ten different Kalams (periods) through which the language has passed. The first kalam was in the shape of sound; the second, of letters; the third, of grammar; the fourth, of Sangams; the fifth, of the rule of Matathipathis; the sixth, of the Jains; the seventh, of the Puranas; the eighth, of unrighteousness; the ninth, of the play of the deity; and the tenth, of the modern times This arrangement is found in the works of S. V. Damodaram Pillai, the commentator of Veerasholyam 34 years ago. So we conclude that this " Perisai Chootram" ascribed to Kalarambar must have been written in the year " Vishu" a few decades ago. Even here a change has been made converting the fifth Anatharakalam of Damodaram Pillai into the " time of the predominance of the Rulers of Mutts" or Matathipathis. All this clearly shows that the work could not have been by the disciple of Ahasthiyar. The language also tells the same tale. Again, it is absurd to suppose that Kalarambar who flourished during the time of Ahasthiyar could have known anything about the " modern times." Even supposing he prophesied anything about the " modern times" how came he to omit the " future times" altogether? This is surely the later work of some one who was interested in upholding the antiquity of Sanskrit.

The ancient Tamil musical works also shared the same fate. They have been so cleverly manipulated as to make people think Indian musical treatises were derived from Sanskrit literature. But experts would clearly see the difference between Indian Music as expounded by Sanskrit writers and the Music of the Carnatic country. Though the rules of music given by Sanskrit writers are not used in the South, yet the different musical terms of the North are found here. Of this more anon.

The following extract shows that the large introduction of Sanskrit words into the language is to be attributed to the influence of the Jains and Aryans of the period of the last Sangam. During the same period there was also a large introduction of Tamil words into other languages.

Vol. I, of the Manual of the Administration of the Madras Presidency Page 41, 42.

"The greater number of the Sanskrit and Pracrita words in the Dravidian languages were introduced by the Jaina writers. Some tatsamas, however, were introduced by the three comparatively modern philosophic schools: the Sheiva Siddhaunta, the school of Sankaracharya and the school of Ramanujacharya. Sanskrit words are said to have been introduced even before the time of the Jains, but it is doubtful whether these are not ancient words common to both Aryan and Dravidian languages."

The author here seems to doubt whether some of these words were not common to the Aryan and the Dravidian languages. It is a known fact that the Aryans, who were interested in the Sanskrit language, wrote many works having the Tamil words and ideas for a basis but clothing them with the Sanskrit garb. So, many Tamil words must have also found their way into Sanskrit. It is but natural, that when once the mingling has been perpetuated, for scholars to doubt whether they were originally Aryan or Dravidian. It is also the way of the world that when one determines never to return an article borrowed, to shape and transform it beyond recognition. There is a Tamil proverb which says "Though the article is a borrowed one, it so much suits my fancy that, by my father, I swear I will not return it."

We shall see from the following extract that the Aryans made bold to derive all Tamil from Sanskrit only after a thorough fusion of the two languages, both in words and literature, had been made.

Dravidian Comparative Grammar by Bishop Caldwell, P. 34.

"Professor Wilson observes that the spoken languages of the South were cultivated in imitation and rivalry of the Sanskrit, and but partially aspired to an independent literature; that that the principal compositions in Tamil, Telugu, Canarese, and Malayalam are translations or paraphrases from Sanskrit works; and that they largely borrow the phraseology of their originals. This representation is not perfectly correct, in so far as the Tamil is concerned; for the compositions that are universally admitted to be the ablest and finest in the language, viz., the Kural and the Chintamani, are perfectly independent of the Sanskrit, and original in design as well as in execution."

Here Prof. Wilson doubts the facts that Sanskrit was prior to Tamil, that the spoken languages of the South were cultivated as rival languages, that the Dravidian literature are but paraphrases or translations of Sanskrit and that their style betrays the original. This is exactly what every Sanskrit scholar believes undoubtedly at the present day. The fusion between the two languages was so complete that they made bold in saying it.

It is no doubt true that within the last 800 years a few Puranams and books on Vedanta philosophy have been translated into Tamil. But from this one cannot jump to the conclusion that ancient literature which was prior to Sanskrit was derived from the later language. "Thirukural" and "Chintamani" are examples of works which are purely Tamil without any admixture of Sanskrit. But there are also ignorant people who imagine that some of the Tamil words here are Sanskrit.

It is a recognised fact that 'Thirukural' was composed at the period of the decadence of the Tamil Country and its rulers. And the superior books treating on grammar, Music and dancing (the three angams of Tamil) and on morality were destroyed by the two deluges. Works like 'Thirukural' came into existence after the advent of the Aryans and the Jains and at the close of the Third Sangam. By glancing at 'Tholkapiam' we may see the grandeur and independence of Tamil words and the complete and perfect rules of grammar of that period. Persons convinced of the antiquity of Tamil will never dream of deriving it from Sanskrit.

3. How Tamil was the mother of languages.

The following extracts will go to prove how the Tamil language had an excellence of its own from the earliest times and how its grammatical rules were perfect.

Dravidian Comparative Grammar by Bishop Caldwell, P. 29.

"No person who has any acquaintance with the principles of comparative philology and who has carefully studied the grammars and vocabularies of the Dravidian languages, and compared them with those of the Sanskrit, can suppose that the grammatical structure and inflexional forms of those languages and the greater number of their more important roots are capable of being derived from the Sanskrit by any process of corruption whatsoever."

Dravidian Comparative Grammar by Bishop Caldwell, P. 4.

"This language (Tamil) being the earliest cultivated of all the Dravidian idioms, the most copious, and that which contains the largest portion and the richest variety of indubitably ancient forms, it is deservedly placed at the head of the list."

The above quotations show how Tamil was the mother language to all languages whom the Aryans named Dravidian, that its grammar is perfect, that it is of great antiquity and that it is quite different from Sanskrit.

The following extract shows the antiquity of Tholkappiam, its minutest rules of grammar and the existence of Tamil Vidwans prior to the time of Tholkappiam, by certain references made in it.

Manual of the Administration of the Madras Presidency, Vol I, P. (56.)

"Tamul literature is the oldest among the Dravidian languages. To the sage Agastiya (of unknown date) are attributed not only the formation of the alphabet and first treatise upon grammar, but also a number of treatises on various sciences. But nothing authentic survives from such an ancient time. The oldest extant Tamul grammar is called the 'Tolgauppiam' that is to say 'The ancient book': Such a work must have been preceded by centuries of literary culture as it lays down rules for different kinds of poetical compositions, deduced from examples furnished by the best authors whose works were then in existence. Its date cannot, however, be fixed."

The above extract shows that the formation of the Tamil Alphabet, its grammar and its early prose treatises are attributed to the sage Ahastyar. But his date is not clear. But he is sure that there must have been Tamil authors long before this time for Ahastya himself says that not only the language but also excellent treatises in the language existed before him. It may be seen from the following stanzas :—

பேரகத்தியம்.

"இலக்கண மென்பதிலக்கிய முறையுற
வைத்ததென் றுரை வழங்கப்படுமே."

"இலக்கிய மின்றி யிலக்கண மின்றே
எள்ளின் றாகி லெண்ணெயு மின்றே
எள்ளினின் றெண்ணெ யெடுப்பதுபோல
இலக்கியத் தினின் றெடுபடு மிலக்கணம்"

Perahathiyam.

1. Grammar was devised according to the strict rules of poetry or prose writing.

2. No grammar could exist without prose or poetry. There can be no gingelly-oil without the sesamum seed. Just as the oil is derived from the seed, grammar is derived from written works."

This shows the excellence of the Tamil language even before the time of Ahastya. Thiruvilayadal Puranam also bears this out. The following extract shows that his grammar was composed in accordance with the culture of the times to suit the three angams of Tamil—Iyal, Isai, and Natakam (Grammar Music and Dancing.)

"வடவேங் கடந் தென்குமரியாயிடைத்
தமிழ்கூறு நல்லுலகத்து
வழக்குஞ் செய்யுளுமாயிருமுதலின்
எழுத்துஞ் சொல்லும் பொருளுநாடிச்
செந்தமிழியற்கை சிவணியநிலத்தொடு
முந்துநூல்கண்டு முறைப்படவெண்ணிப்
புலந்தொகுத்தோனே. - - - - "

Ahastya, who after a deep study of the Tamil literature in existence in the good Tamil country extending from Venkatagiri in the north to Cape Comorin in the South, devised the regular grammar explaining the characters, words and ideas found both in the colloquial prose works and the poems previous to his time.

This extract shows the antiquity and perfection of the language.

4. How the Tamil words were used by traders from foreign countries.

The extract quoted below shows that the Greeks and the Phoenicians who traded with South India called the articles of trade, which they carried from India, after their Tamil names, transliterating them into their respective languages.

Preface to Winslow's Dictionary.

"It is said that the Language of the Mountaineers of Rajah Mahal abounds in terms identified with Tamil and Telugu. What is more singular, the names by which the ivory, apes, and peacocks, conveyed by Solomon's ships of Tarshish were known, are the same with those still used in Tamil; seeming to imply that the traders visited Ceylon, or India, and obtained with these novelties their Tamil names, *Danta*, *Kapi*, and *Togai*, as found in the Hebrew Bible."

This shows that the period of the trade with India was about 1,000 B.C. These traders, then, must have used the Tamil names for articles exported from the Tamil country even 3000 years ago. But the imports into India are not mentioned which probably might have been marbles, porcelain, or toys then considered a novelty in India. So it is not likely that foreign Greek or Hebrew words could have been largely introduced into Tamil.

Manual of the Administration of the Madras Presidency, Vol. I, P (48.)

"The Phœnicians were the first to adopt a purely alphabetic system. The general voice of antiquity gives them this credit and the facts agree with the rumour. The Indo-Arabian alphabet is held to represent the Himyarite of South Arabia and the alphabets of India as shown in the Asoka's inscriptions. It will be seen later that this scheme does not provide for the original alphabet of the Dravidian nations, which remains thus unaffiliated in the same way as are the Dravidian languages themselves."

The above extract declares that written Alphabet was first used in Phoenicia, in Asiatic Turkey, in the Mediterranean. He says that the inscriptions of Asoka were derived from the picture writing of South Arabia and the Indian Alphabet. But it is noteworthy that the Dravidian Alphabet stands unique without being affected by other alphabets.

5. How the Dravidian characters are independent of the Phoenician and Sanskrit Alphabets.

The following extracts say that the Indian Alphabet could not have been derived from the Phoenician.

Sanskrit-English Dictionary by Monier Williams, M. A., Preface, P. XVI.

"According to Mr. Edward Thomas (Prinsep's Indian Antiquities, Vol. II, Page 42,) the theory by which Professor Weber has sought to establish a Phœnician origin for the indian alphabets is untenable. There are, however, two sets of Buddhist inscriptions, and that of Kapurdigiri is decidedly traceable to a Phœnician source. Those on the rock of Girnar (Giri-nagara) in Kathywar, Gujarat, which are said to be most important in their relation to the present Indian alphabets, are not so clearly traceable. Mr. Thomas appears to have good ground for thinking that many of the Nagari letters were derived from the Dravidians of the south."

The above shows that, judging from stone inscriptions, it is clearly seen that the Indian language has hardly any resemblance to the Phoenician. So the Tamil language cannot be said to have been derived from the Phoenician language; nor does it warrant us to derive it from Sanskrit.

The following quotation shows the striking differences between the grammars of the Tamil and the Sanskrit languages.

Preface to Winslow's Dictionary. (Tamil English).

"Unlike several of the vernaculars of India, it is not, as some have supposed, a daughter of the Sanskrit. Its Alphabet differs not only in character, but in sound; and is more limited. Its grammar, though conformed to the Sanskrit, as far as the genius of the Language would allow, is still very different. It has no article, no relative pronoun, no dual number, no optative mood. It differs in its numerals, in many nouns, verbs, and adverbs, and in technical terms in grammar. In the declension of its nouns, the conjugation of its verbs, and the arrangement of its sentences, it more resembles the Latin."

The author says here, after comparing the grammars of the Tamil and Sanskrit languages, that Tamil resembles Latin, that its letters and words are more limited than those of Sanskrit in sound, and that in shape and sound it is very different from Sanskrit. It is the Tamil language which has small words to suit children who lisp their mother-tongue, classical words to suit the requirements of the learned, and easy words to serve the purpose of the common people. The Tamil language has such a remarkable distinction of letter sounds, that a letter has the same sound wherever it might be used and the pronunciation is so easy that what is written can be interpreted easily by any one.

The following shows that the Tamil language can be spoken perfectly without the mixture of Sanskrit words.

Preface to Winslow's Dictionary.

"It is evident that there was an early literature in Tamil independent of Sanskrit; it is certain that Tamil could do without Sanskrit much better than English without Latin.

* * * * * * * * *

The reason why Tamil is more independent of Sanskrit than the Northern Languages, and even than the other Dravidian tongues, is, that it has not been left, like those, principally to the cultivation of the Brahmans."

In spite of the harm done to the Tamil language and literature by the Aryan scholars, the Tamilians are under a deep debt of gratitude to them for having been the chief instruments in mastering the music of South India and of disseminating and preserving it from destruction at a period when decadence had set in owing to the disappearance of works on music and dancing.

6. The Excellent literature in the Tamil language.

The following extract says that Tamil is a language of beautiful words, of ancient literature and literary men.

Preface to Winslow's Dictionary.

"A native author of repute, well versed in English, as well as his own vernacular, has said, adopting the words of Mr. Taylor before mentioned 'it is one of the most copious, refined, and polished languages spoken by man.' This author has added, what may admit of doubt, 'few nations on earth can perhaps boast of so many poets as the Tamils'. As, however, all their earlier literature was in poetry, even Dictionaries and Grammars, and works on Medicine, Law, Architecture and Theology, the number of poets, so called, must have been great.'

The above warrants us to conclude that all the arts and sciences of a great country were in one language, and that language Tamil. It was in the Tamil country that Paramasivam demonstrated each of the sixty four kalais (sciences) in the form of Thiruvilayadal (drama). This enables us, then, to infer that all possible arts and sciences were found in ancient times in the Tamil Country and were destroyed later on.

Preface to Winslow's Tamil—English Dictionary.

"It is not perhaps extravagant to say, that, in its poetic form, the Tamil is more polished and exact than the Greek, and in both dialects, with its borrowed treasures, more copious than the Latin. In its fulness and power it more resembles English and German than any other living language. Its prose style is yet in a forming state, and will well repay the labor of accurate scholars in moulding it properly. Many natives who write poetry readily, cannot write a page of correct prose."

The Tamil language, then, is as polished and perfect as any of the languages of the Indo-European group and is a living language, capable of being spoken.

Preface to Winslow's Dictionary.

"The Tamil is not a vulgar dialect. Before the principal basis of the English had a written character, it was a highly polished language. Its name signifies sweetness, and though not so musical as the Telugu, in its poetic form especially, it is not without its claim to euphonic charms and 'linked sweetness'."

The Tamil language, then, was a highly polished language long before the characters of the English language came into use.

7. Some points about the origin of Sanskrit.

Preface to Winslow's Dictionary.

"In the opinion of the Rev. William Taylor, the able Editor of Dr. Rottler's Dictionary, 'there was originally one simple homogeneous dialect, spoken by rude, simple aborigines from the Himalaya to cape Comorin.' Mr. Taylor, thinks that, 'the earliest probable refinement of it was the Pali of the North, and the Tamil of the extreme South,' and that, 'the Sanscrit assumed its own form by engrafting numerous Chaldaic terms of science and others of common use in the old Pali.' It is evident from their names, that the Pali must have been anterior to the Sanscrit, the former signifying root or original, and the latter finished or polished. It is stated by Colonel Sykes that very ancient inscriptions on rocks and coins, are found in Pali and Pracrit four hundred years earlier than in Sanscrit."

The author here says that the ancient inhabitants of India occupied the country between the Himalayas and Cape Comorin, that they spoke one simple homogeneous language which was known as Pali in the North and Tamil in the South, and that Sanskrit was the outcome of the adaptation of many words from the Pali language and the Chaldean. Inscriptions on stones and coins are in the Pali language. The Pali as well as the Pracrit were 400 years anterior to Sanscrit. The Pali is the original rude language and the Sanskrit is its refined daughter. The word 'Sanskrit' itself means 'finished' or 'polished,' while 'Pali' means 'root'. This warrants us to conclude that the Aryans borrowed the words from the languages of the provinces they emigrated to, and compiled a fresh language (Sanskrit) and also devised rules of grammar for its guidance. Hence we find a large introduction into Sanskrit of words from Greek, Latin, Hebrew, Scythian, Pali, Pracrit, Tamil and other languages.

Again, names given to things for a special purpose were of a later introduction, the earlier names being natural. The fact that the musical treatises in Sanskrit are full of derivative terms in preference to the ancient natural names used in Tamil, is a proof that such Sanskrit treatises are a later introduction.

8. How the Hebrew, Scythian, European and the Sanskrit languages have borrowed from Tamil.

The following shows that even the classical Sanskrit language has borrowed some words from Tamil.

Preface to Winslow's Dictionary.

"While nearly all the vernaculars of India have been greatly enriched from the Sanskrit, that wonderful language has condescended to borrow even from the Dravidian group, of which the Tamil is the oldest, and the principal. Dr. Caldwell in his learned Dravidian Comparative Grammar, instances 31 words in Sanscrit taken from Dravidian tongues, and 25 borrowed by both from some common source. He is of opinion that the Sanscrit derived its cerebral consonants from the Dravidian."

Here we see that Sanskrit has many Tamil words. that words common to Tamil and Sanskrit are found there, and that the letters ட, ண, ள, and ற (da, na, lla and ra) are borrowed from Tamil.

There is also reason to suppose that originally there must have been a common home from which all the races branched out, and that the language which they spoke in their ancient common home was Tamil. This migration must have taken place in prehistoric times. The races so migrating must have spoken their language very imperfectly. For it is natural that at the time of a deluge the cultured and the literary should succumb while the peasant and the common man should escape. Such common people would only know about two or three hundred words of their old language. In course of time, owing to contact with others, even the little they know of their language might be forgotten. While gradually getting initiated into a new language, the words of their own original language might get shortened or lengthened or get corrupted by the introduction of new sounds. The prefixes and suffixes might change, in course of time, and the words might be considered altogether new.

From a comparative study of the words in different languages we may derive the following conclusions.

(i) That Tamil, which was under the patronage of the First Sangam for 4,400 years i.e., 8,000 years ago, in the time of the author of Tholgaupiam, was the ancient language of the continent of Lemuria (ii) That the Tamilians after the destruction of their original abode migrated to the opposite shores (iii) That they were classified as different races speaking different languages according to the changes formed in them by climatic differences, by difference of food, difference of manufacturing skill and culture.

The fact that many Tamil words are found in these languages is a sufficient proof for the above conclusions. There are many letters and words in use in Sanskrit which have been borrowed from Tamil.

Preface to Winslow's Dictionary.

"But from affinities traced out by him, in addition to those hereafter given, it would be seen that we may go farther back for many roots and forms in these tongues, to some common fountain both for them and for the languages of the Indo-European family, including Sanscrit, nearer to the time when 'the whole earth was of one language.' He specifies 85 words in the Dravidian, as having Scythian affinities, 31 as Semitic, and 106 connected with the west Indo-European family, distinct from those in Sanscrit."

Comparative Grammar By Bishop Caldwell P. 453.

" Some of the words which are contained in the following list, have Sanskrit as well as classical or West Aryan analogies; but they have been placed in this, rather than in the preceding list, because the West Aryan affinities are clearer, more direct, and more certain than the Sanskrit ones. The greater number, however, of the words that follow, though indubitably connected with the western tongues, and especially with the Greek and Latin, exhibit no analogy whatever to any words contained in the Sanskrit. If the existence of this class of analogie can be clearly established, it must be concluded either that the Dravidians were at an early period near neighbours of the West Aryan tribes, subsequently to the separation of their tribes from the Sanskrit speaking people, or that both races were descended from a common source The majority of the Dravidian words which exibit West Aryan analogies, do not belong to that primary, rudimental class to which the words that the Dravidian languages have in common with the Scythian are to be referred. Neverthless, they are so numerous, many of them are so remarkable, and when all are viewed together, the analogy which they bring to light is so distinct, that an ultimate relation of some kind between the Dravidian and the Indo-European families, may be regarded as conclusively established."

The above extracts warrant us to infer from the analogy of many languages and their close relation to Tamil, that all nations must have originally sprung from a common stock, and that they must have spoken one language in their common home, namely, Tamil.

The following quotations are also in point.

List of Sanskrit words borrowed from Tamil.

I

1. அக்கா (Sister)
2. அத்தா (Mother)
3. அடவி (Jungle)
4. ஆணி (Nail)
5. அம்பா (Mother)
6. அம்மா (Mother)
7. அடே (Interjection)
8. ஆளி (A Female friend)
9. கடு (Sharp)
10. கலை (Learning)
11. காவேரி (Cauvery)
12. குசம் (Female breast)
13. கூச்சல் (Din)
14. குடி (House)
15. கூன் (Hunchback)
16. குளம் (Tank)
17. கோட்டை (Fortification)
18. கட்டில் (Cot)
19. சவம் (Corpse)
20. சா (Die)
21. சாய் (Lean)
22. [illegible] (Several)
23. நீர் (Water)
24. பட்டணம் (City)
25. பொன் (Gold)
26. பள்ளி (Village)
27. பாகம் (Part)
28. மீன் (Fish)
29. வெள் (Silver)
30. வளை (Bend)
31. மோதிரம் (Ring)

II

Words Common to Sanskrit and Tamil.

1. அடி (Beat)
2. உதை (Kick)
3. அடை (Obtain)
4. என (To speak)
5. ஊர (To creep)
6. கட (Cross)
7. கழுதை (Ass)
8. சின்ன (Little)
9. குதிரை (Horse)
10. கீற (To cut)
11. கிழி (Tear)
12. கெடு (Spoil)
13. சிரை (Shave)
14. சிலிர் (Shiver)
15. செ (To be red)
16. தடி (Rod)
17. தூவு (Sprinkle)
18. தூற (Shower)
19. நட (Walk)
20. பாடு (Sing)
21. பாகு (Division)
22. பிற (Other)
23. பால் (Milk)
24. பேசு (Speak)
25. பூ (Flower)

III

Tamil words found in the Indo-European languages.

1. அசை (Shake)
2. அருவி (Brook)
3. அலை (Wave)
4. அவா (Desire)
5. ஐயை (Mother)
6. ஆவி (Vapour)
7. இழு (Pull)
8. இரும்பு (Iron)
9. ஈனு (Bring forth)
10. உயர் (High)
11. எரி (Burn)
12. உழு (Plough)
13. உளை (Mire)
14. ஊளை (Howl)
15. எய் (Shoot)
16. எழு (Rise)
17. எல்லாம் (All)
18. ஓரம் (Edge)
19. கடிதல் (Reproving)
20. கண் (Eye)
21. கரடி (The bear)
22. கழுகு (Eagle)
23. களவு (Theft)
24. கெவி (Cave)
25. காய் (To burn)
26. செய் (Do)
27. கிண்டு (Stir up)
28. கிழம் (Old)
29. கிழமை (Day of week)
30. கிளை (Branch)
31. குப்பை (Dust)
32. குறு (Short)
33. குருடு (Blind)
34. குளிர் (Cold)
35. கேள் (Hear)
36. கொல் (Kill)
37. சாக்கு (Sack)
38. சாத்து (Shut)
39. சாடி (Jar)
40. சால் (Water pot)
41. சீறு (Hiss)
42. சுடு (Burn)
43. செப்பு (Speak)
44. செல் (Proceed)
45. தகு (Fit)
46. தயிர் (Curd)
47. தின் (Eat)
48. திற (Open)
49. தீண்டு (Touch)
50. தெள் (Clear)
51. தொலை (Distance)
52. திருப்பு (Turn)
53. நசுக்கு (Squash)
54. நரம்பு (Vein)
55. நினை (Think)
56. நீந்து (Swim)
57. நெய்ய (To weave)
58. படு (Suffer)
59. படி (Lie down)
60. பண்ண (To make)
61. அனுப்பு (Send)
62. பழ (Old)
63. பழு (Get ripe)
64. பல (Many)
65. பள்ளி (Town)
66. பிய்க்க (To tear)
67. பிரி (Divide)
68. பிள்ளை (Child)
69. புகழ் (Praise)
70. புறம் (Side)
71 பூனை (The cat)
72. பெரு (Big)
73. பெறு (Bring forth)
74. பேய் (Devil)
75. பையன் (Boy)
76. பொறு (Bear)
77. பொழுது (Time)
78. பொங்கு (To be puffed up)
79. போ (Go)
80. போடு (Put)
81. விழு (Fall)
82. மகன் (Son)
83 மயிர் (Hair)
84. மற (Forget)
85. மா (A Male)
86. மாழ்கு (To die)
87. மிகு (Much)
88. முழுகு (Immerse)
89. முகில் (Cloud)
90. முயலு (Endeavour)
91. முறுமுறு (Murmur)
92. மூக்கு (Nose)
93. மெத்தை (Cushion)
94. மெல் (Fine)
95. வலி (Strength)
96. வளர் (Progress)
97. விண் (Heaven)
98. விறை (To be numb)
99. வீண் (Vain)
100. வேண்டு (Want)
101. வேறு (Other)

IV

Tamil words found in Hebrew and other languages.

1. அப்பா (Father)
2. அம்மா (Mother)
3. ஆறு (River)
4. அல் (Not)
5. அவா (Desire)
6. இரு (Sit)
7. இறங்கு (Descend)
8. எரி (Burn)
9. ஊர் (Village)
10. எறி (Throw)
11. எரு (Manure)
12. கூர் (Point)
13. சாக்கு (Sack)
14. சால் (Bucket)
15. சாய் (Recline)
16. சினம் (Anger)
17. சீறு (Hiss)
18. சுமை (Load)
19. கவர் (Seize)
20. செம்மை (Straightness)
21. நாட்டு (Plant)
22. ஈட்டு (Produce)
23. நோக்கு (Notice)
24. பழு (Ripen)
25. பால் (Milk)
26. பெறு (Receive)
27. வா (Come)
28. மாய் (Die)
29. மாறு (Change)
30. மிலேச்சன் (A vile person)
31. மெத்தை (Cushion)

V

Scythian words borrowed from Tamil.

1. அக்கா (Sister)
2. அத்தன் (God or Father)
3. ஆத்தாள் (Mother)
4. அன்னை (Mother)
5. அப்பன் (Father)
6. அம்மாள், அம்மை, அம்மன் (Mother)
7. அரு (Formless)
8. அல், எல் (Negative Suffixes)
9. ஔவை (Mother)
10. அலை (Wave)
11. ஆறு (River)
12. ஆம் (Yes)
13. இரும்பு (Iron)
14. நீஞ்சு (Swim)
15. உயர (To rise up)
16. உள் (In)
17. எழுது (Write)
18. எலும்பு (Bone)
19. ஒக்க (Together with)
20. கத்தி (Knife)
21. கடி, கறி (Bite)
22. கட்டு (Bind)
23. கண்ணீர் (Tear)
24. கப்பல் (Ship)
25. கரு (Black)
26. கரடி (The bear)
27. கழுகு (The eagle)
28. கழுத்து (The neck)
29. கல் (Stone)
30. கள்ளம் (Guile)
31. காற்று (Air)
32. காய்ச்சு (Boil)
33. கால் (Leg)
34. கிழ (Old)
35. கீழ் (Under)
36. குதிரை (Horse)
37. குடில் (Hut)
38. குளிர் (Cold)
39. கை (Hand)
40. கெபி (Cave)
41. செவி (Ear)
42. கேள் (Hear)
43. கொல் (Kill)
44. கோ, கோன் (King)
45. கோழி (Fowl)
46. சாரல் (Spray)
47. சா (Die)
48. சேறு (Mud)
49. தலை (Head)
50. தீ (Fire)
51. தூசி (Dust)
52. தோல் (Skin)
53. நக்கு (Lick)
54. நகை (Laughter)
55. நாய் (Dog)
56. நெற்றி (Brow)
57. நெய் (Ghee)
58. நோக்கு (Notice)
59. ஞாயிறு (The Sun)
60. பசுமை (Greenness)
61. பையன் (Boy)
62. பழமை (Antiquity)
63. பல் (Tooth)
64. பால் (Milk)
65. பிடி (Catch)
66. பிறகு (After)
67. பிள்ளை (Child)
68. புகை (Smoke)
69. பெண் (Girl)
70. வயிறு (Belly)
71. வாழ் (Prosper)
72. மனை (House)
73. மரம் (Tree)
74. மதி (Cheek)
75. மலை (Hill)
76. முறுமுறு (Murmur)
77. முட்டை (Egg)
78. வானம் (Sky)
79. வாய் (Mouth)
80. விழி (Wake)
81. வெளிச்சம் (Light)

The words in the above five tables are words very commonly used in the Tamil country by the illiterate masses, and not classical words. There is reason to believe that these words must have been carried to other countries and there became changed by various processes. Tamilians know very well that a number of new words have been formed, with these words as the root, by the processes of prefixes, suffixes and other changes. There is no doubt that the above words are all Tamil. It is said that the words common to Tamil and Sanskrit, derived from a third language, are 25 in number. So it goes without saying that these words must have been in the Tamil language from time immemorial and that the same were found in Tholgaupiam. Scholars must admit that the above 25 words are Tamil words.

On further investigating into the existence of many Tamil words in a changed form in other languages also, we shall be able to conclude that the common Tamil words must have been the root from which they have been derived.

A few instances of Tamil words which exist in other languages in various shapes.

The natural cries of some of the animals resemble the sound of Tamil letters and words. Hindus are familiar with the cry of the calf 'amma'. The cuckoo or the Akka bird makes the sound 'Akka' or 'Akki'. We are also familiar with the cries of animals beginning with the letters ka, ki, ku, koo, chu, ee, oo, ma, ma, and nga.

Judging from the words that are used in accordance with these cries, we conclude that these sounds, as well as words, were in use from the first appearance of man. In all languages, from the earliest infant stage, the sound of 'Ma' and 'Mma', are in use. This first word is very easily pronounced with the help of the tongue and the lips, and the words Abba, Akka, Athai, Mama, Thatha, Pāppa are acquired gradually later on. On close enquiry we find that first letter 'ah', the cry of the calf 'Amma' and the cry of the bird 'Akka' were the earliest letter and sounds in use.

1. *Amma.*—This Tamil word is 'Amba' and 'Amma' in Sanskrit; in old High German and Oscan 'Amma'; in Icelandic 'Amma'=grand-mother; in German 'Ammi nurse; in Samoiede 'Amma'; in Jenesei, 'Aur' or 'Amma'; in Estrian, 'Emma'; in Finish 'Ema'; in Sindan 'Ama'; in Malaya, 'ama'; in Tulu, 'amme'—father, and appi —mother; in Mongolian 'Ama'—father; in Tibetan, Ma or Mo=woman; in Hebrew 'Em', and 'im', in Syriac 'Amo'.

2. '*Appa*'—In Telugu and Canarese 'Appa'; in Bhotiya, 'Aba'; in Hebrew 'ab'; in Chaldee, 'abba'; in Syriac, abo'; in Aramaic 'abba', and in Sinhalese 'Appa.'

3. *Akkal.*—In Sanscrit Akka—mother; in Telugu and Canarese 'Akka'—an elder sister; in Mahratta, aka; in Tungusian 'aki'; in Mongolian 'Akkan' in Tibetan, 'achche'; in Turkish, 'ege'; in Mordwin 'aky'; in Ugrian 'iggen'; in Lappish "ake" = wife or grand-mother; in Mongol. 'aka'—an elder brother; in Uigur, 'acha'—an elder brother; in Tungusian, aki'—an elder brother; in Ostiak, 'iki'—an old man; in Finish, 'ukko'—an elder and in Hungarian, 'agg'—an old man.

The changes formed in the roots of Tamil words is something analogous to the following:—

There was a pot full of 10 seers of pure unadulterated milk. The first man took away a seer and substituted water, and the same process was repeated by many other. At the end there was nothing left of the milk but water. The same has been the fate of Tamil words. The Tamil root 'amma' became in turn 'amme', 'ammei', 'ama', 'ama' 'am', 'ema' 'emma' 'em', 'im' 'amba', 'appe', 'amo', 'Ma', and 'mo'. The Tamil word 'akkal' became 'akka'. akkam', 'akin', 'ake' 'aha', ahi', 'akki', 'aha', 'ikki', 'ehai' 'ikiam' 'ooko' and 'ak'. The Tamil word 'Appa' became 'abba', 'aba', 'abo' and 'ab'.

4. The Tamil word '*Ko*' or *Kou*' is found in the Dravidian languages. The same is found in the Turkish and Mongolian as 'Khan' and 'Khagan'; in Ostiak, 'khon' and in Scythian 'ko'.

5. *Kol* (கொல்); in Russian Kolya; in English 'kill' and 'quell', in Finnish 'kuol'; in Theremiss, 'kolem'; in Syrjanian, 'kula'; in Hungarian, 'hal'; in Norwegian, 'Killa'; in Dutch, 'kollam' and in Icelandic 'kollah'.

6. *Kud* (குடி—வீடு); in Sanscrit 'kuti', S. Patakutiram—a hut of leaves; also 'Kudumba' in Sans; 'kuti! or kutisai'=temple or small habitation in Telugu and Canarese; in Finnish, 'kota'; in Tscheremiss, 'kuda'; in Mordwin, 'kudo'; in Ostiak and Saxon "chot".

7. *Neer* (நீர்=water); in Sanskrit 'Neera' and "Neeran" in Telugu, 'Neeramu', 'Neeru' and 'Neellu'; in Gond 'ir'; in Brahin, it is 'dir' and in Modern Greek, 'Neero'.

8. '*Meen*' (மீன்=fish); in Sanskrit it is 'Meenam' and 'Meen'.

9. *Pattanam or Patti* (பட்டணம், பட்டி=city or village). In Canarese it is 'hatti'; in Telugu, it is 'patti', and in Sanskrit it is 'pettah', 'pattam', 'pattanam" and 'pattanam'.

10. *Kadu, kadimei or kadi* (கடு, கடுமை, கடி=sharp) is 'kati', 'katukah' and 'kadugu' in Sanscrit.

So the Tamil words are found mixed up with the other languages of the world having undergone different changes. The softness of the words, the fewness of the letters and the comparative ease with which the words are pronounced warrant us to infer that the Tamil language must have been the language of early mankind. Our list of words is by no means exhaustive The fact that Tamil words are well mixed up with other languages after undergoing various changes of form, and that the mixture has been justified by new rules of grammar, is to be noted. For it is significant that Tamil stands by itself without being affected by other languages, in spite of other languages borrowing from it. This is a clear proof for the independence of the language.

When we go into the root of Sanskrit and other members of the Indo-European group and find that a number of words have been borrowed by the Scythian, Hebrew, and Sanskrit tongues, we have reason to believe that Tamil might have been the root of all these languages. This is further supported by ancient Tamil literature which speak about the antiquity of the language and the high efficiency of music of the period of the first Tamil Sangam. The following is an extract from Dr. Caldwell who speaks about the necessity of encouraging a language with such antiquity and glory :—

Dravidian Comparative Grammar by Bishop Caldwell, P. 31.

"The Tamil, however, the most highly cultivated *ab-intra* of all Dravidian idioms, can dispense with its Sanskrit altogether, if need be, and not only stand alone but flourish without its aid."

The Tamil language was preserved in a pure and unmixed state by the savants of the first and second Tamil Sangams, while during the time of the Third Sangam it became corrupt by the admixture of foreign words. During this period many Buddhist and Aryan scholars, who had a great admiration for the language, began to produce a number of works on grammar, poetry and prose, while a few others were engaged in writing commentaries on the ancient Tamil works. It was this that caused the introduction of many Sanskrit words and ideas into Tamil which made people think that Tamil was a dialect of Sanskrit. Yet we have to thank these Sanskrit scholars for substituting other works for those destroyed during the close of the first two Sangams and for writing commentaries on them. The Aryan scholars of those days considered the Music of South India as a precious buried treasure, just as we do at the present day, and introduced into it a number of names from the Sanskrit. If the Tamilians of this country will be as much interested and be as enthusiastic over their language as the late Bishop Caldwell, who was an eminent philologist and Scholar in Tamil, the language, we are sure, will recover its former glory.

9. The chief incontrovertible argument to prove that Tamil must have been the Mother tongue is the Pranavamantra.

It is a well known fact that the Pranava letter 'Om' indicates Paramasivam, that he who devotedly prays to it obtains the Paramasivam and becomes God himself. It is also well known that the Tamilians considered this letter as the Prime Manthiram and used it in their daily devotions, as they were sure that any work commenced with it ensured success. Their Yogis used this Manthiram while practising their breathing, and obtained not only length of life but also felt the presence of God in them. Compare what the Tamil Poet says.

" வாசி வாவென்று வாசியில் ஊடாடி
வாசியை உள்ளே வைத்து நீ பூஜித்தால்
வாசியும் ஈசனும் மருவி ஒன்றாகும்
வாசியைப்போல் சித்தி மற்றொன்றும் இல்லையே."

"If you invite breath, make it a part of yourself, without letting it out and pray to God, breath and God will become one and inseparable. There is nothing like breath to gain success."

These Yogis held that out of the Sivam, represented by this letter, proceeded the five Saktis of Siva—Eesanam, Tharpurusham, Aboram, Vamadevam and Satiyosatham; that in order to obtain the fruition of these saktis one should pronounce the Panchakshara manthiram with the letters ந, ம, சி, வ, ய (Na, ma, si, va, ya). They further multiplied these panchaksharams into 125 by permutation, and repeated each of these 125 mantrams with the addition of the letter "Om". They not only practised it themselves but preached the same to others and obtained the eight Karma Sithis namely, the magical arts of Thambanam, Mohanam, Vasyam, Maranam, Ootchadanam, Aharudanam, Vitthuvadanam, and Pathanam. They have also discoursed at great length on the rules and regulations for the use of the Chidambarachakaram in the various temples, which is based on these five letters. They felt within themselves that these five letters were the five Saktis of Pranavam, that these five Saktis were contained in the Pranavam, that Pranavam was the Brahmam, that Brahmam was the great and small Andam (world), that Pranavam was the Pranam or life, that the Pranavam was the combination of Aharam, Ooharam and Maharam or 'Om', that Pranavam was the Satthu, Chitthu and Anandam or Sirushti, Sthithi and Layam by which the world was being governed, that it represents the figure ten formed by the combination of eight and two, that Pranavam resolved itself into the three kalais and was the life of the living beings, that this Pranan was the life, that this life which was free from the three faults Anadam, Kamam and Maya was the Sivam, that Tapas or Penance or Yogam or Mukti was the practising of the deeds of Siva to the exclusion of the deeds of living beings.

So we find that these Panchaksharams formed the basis of all their works written to suit different minds. The importance and virtue of these five aksharams may be seen in their works on Yogam and Gnanam.

If we note the six letters om, na, ma, si, va, ya we shall find that they correspond to the six Atharams into which the human body is divided, namely, Moolatharam, Sivathishtanam, Manipooragam, Anagatham, Visutthi and Aginai. If we note the

The figure showing how the five letters Om, Na, Ma, Si, Va and Ya distribute themselves in the human body.

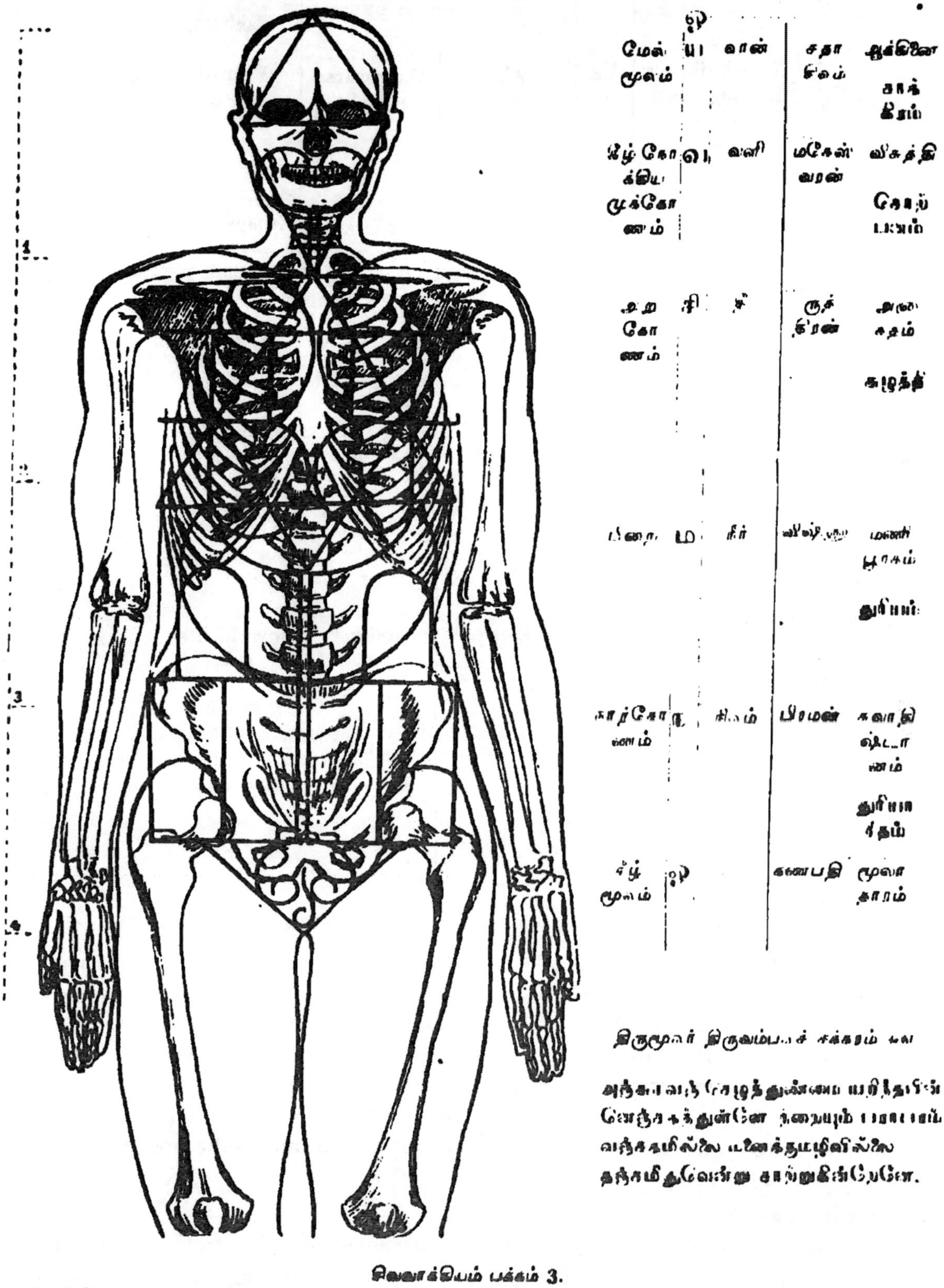

திருமூலர் திருவம்பலச் சக்கரம்

அஞ்சுவமைந் தெழுத்துள்ளமை யறிந்தபின்
செஞ்சுடருள்ளே நிறையும் பராபரம்
வஞ்சகமில்லை மனைக்குமிழிவில்லை
தஞ்சமிதுவென்று சாற்றுகின்றேனே.

சிவவாக்கியம் பக்கம் 3.

நவ்விரண்டு காலதாய் நவின்றமர் வயிறதாகி
சிவ்விரண்டு தோளதாய்ச் சிறந்த வவ்வுவாயதாய்
யவ்விரண்டு கண்ணதாய் யமர்ந்துநின்ற நேர்மையிற்
செவ்வியொத்து நின்றதே சிவாயமஞ் செழுத்துமே.

The top Moolam	**Oh Ya**	Ahasa	Sathasivam	Aginai
				Sakiram
The Thirikonam looking downwards	**Va**	Air	Mahesvaran	Visuthi
				Swarpanam
The six Konams	**Si**	Fire	Rudran	Anagatham
				Suluthi
Pirai	**Ma**	Water	Vishnu	Moni-pooragam
				Thuryam
The four Konams	**Na**	Earth	Brahma	Suvathishtanam
				Thuryatheetham
The bottom Moolam	**Oh**		Ganapati	Moolatharam

திருமூலர் திருவம்பலச் சக்கரம் ௯௭.

அஞ்சுகவஞ் செழுத்துண்மை யறிந்தபின்
னெஞ்சகத்துள்ளே நிறையும் பராபரம்
வஞ்சகமில்லை மனைக்குமழிவில்லை
தஞ்சமிதுவென்று சாற்றுகின்றேனே.

சிவவாக்கியம் பக்கம் ௩.

நவ்விரண்டு காலதாய் நவின்றமவ் வயிறதாய்ச்
சிவ்விரண்டு தோளதாய்ச் சிறந்த வவ்வுவாயதாய
யவ்விரண்டு கண்ணதாய மர்ந்திருந்த நாதனைச்
செவ்விபோர்த்து நின்றதே சிவாயமஞ்செழுத்துமே.

Thirumoolar Thiruvambala Chakaram 97.

Com.—When you have understood the truth of the five letters, beware; God fills himself into your heart; there is no cheating here nor is the house perishable; I say that this is the refuge for man.

Sivavakiyam page 3.

Com:—Na becomes the two legs; Ma becomes the belly; Si the two shoulders; the excellent Va becomes the mouth; the Ya becomes the two eyes. This combination of the five letters was excellent.

order in which these six letters stand, we shall find that from the Mooladharam (which looks down) to the Aginasthanam (which looks up) it is a progress upwards. The Omkaram in the ய 'ya' at the top indicates the head, and the Omkaram at the bottom indicates the Marmasthanam. If we note the structure of the organs at these two ends we find that they resemble the letter 'Om', or the head of an elephant or the shape of a half frog. Only sages can understand the meaning of the circular formation of the right eye, and the circular formation of the left, with a line drawn downwards for partition between the two eyes and with a circle at the end (which is exactly the shape of the letter 'om' 'ஓம்' in Tamil.)

Inasmuch as the sages alone could understand the mystery by which Akaram and Ukaram became Makaram, it is given to others in the form of a manthram. This character which has been given as a manthram, just as it developed itself into the two circles (or the two eyes), the two lobes of the brain, and the line indicating the breath which rises from the brain, it also stood for the same character which is the shape of the generative organs. Sages will tell us that this body, in its first shape, had a circular head and a short tail like that of a half frog. So this Omkaram, which represents the shape of the body at the top and at the bottom, was made the Moolamanthra Aksharam. A knowledge of the inner meaning of this character was considered the knowledge of self, and the knowledge of the self was looked upon as the first step towards the knowledge of God. They have written at length on the five Tatvams of the Sthoola and the Sookshma sareerams which lead to a knowledge of the self.

This character which conveys the inner meaning of the Vedanta Shastra belongs exclusively to Tamil. The shape of the Sthoola aksharam is seen in this Tamil character. This 'Om' or Pranava manthram shows how a+u+m became 'Om' and reflects its sound and Sthoola shape as it is. This mystic letter with its peculiar shape and inner meaning is a stranger to other languages. How could the Aryans who attach an importance to this letter, and consider it essential to the life of this world and the next, write it in any other character but the Tamil? If a differently shaped letter be used, will it convey the inner meaning equally well? Will praying to the deity with a strange letter be of any efficacy.?

10. How the Sthoola Sareeram manifests itself by the combination of the Panchaksharams.

The sages have declared definitely, and at great length, how the five places marked by these five aksharams represent the five Bhutas (—Prithvi, Appu, Thajus, Vayu and Akasam), the five Karthas—(Brahma, Vishnu, Rudran, Mahesvaran and Sadasivan), the five Saktis, the five Colours, the 51 Aksharams [formed by the gradual development of four into six, six into ten, ten into twelve, twelve into sixteen and sixteen into three], the Gods, Goddesses and Saktis represented by these 51 Aksharams, the one body, the one life, the spouse of the deity, the Vahanam of the deity and the temple of the deity. In accordance with the Manthram of Tirumoolar, which says

" ஐம்ப தெழுத்தே அமர்ந்தவே தங்கள்
ஐம்ப தெழுத்தே ஆகமம் ஆகின்
ஐம்ப தெழுத்தின் அதிலை அறிந்தபின்
ஐம்ப தெழுத்தே ஐஞ்செழுத் தாமே."

"All the Vedas are contained in the fifty letters, all literature is contained within the fifty letters. If one has fully the knowledge of the fifty letters one will understand that the fifty are reducible to the five." These sages obtained all the Divine saktis with the help of these five letters in the five Sthanams as five Karthas or Saktis. Great men who understood the importance of these letters wrote for the benefit of the world the various means and ceremonial rules in the shape of Vedams for teaching the people to obtain Mukti by eschewing evil and doing good, and by attaining that state of self-abnegation in which one loves one's neighbour as one self. Those who realise in themselves the significance of the silent Aksharam (Mounaksharam) which is the key to all the Vedas, will clearly understand this.

When we note the shape of the Pranava aksharam or the Panchaksharams we find that when the first letter ந (nakaram) is written on both sides of the human trunk (with the turnings left and right) in the Swadhishthana Chakram, the two legs are formed; the second letter ம (makaram) when written in the same manner in the Manipooraga Chakram gives us the belly; the third letter சி (sikaram) if written in the same manner on both sides of the trunk results in the two hands and the heart; the fourth letter வ (vakaram) when written in the fifth stharam gives the lungs and the neck, and the fifth letter ய (yakaram) in the Aginasthanam results in the 'head' which is the shape of Omkaram. Thus we see that the Panchaksharams represent the various organs of the body and their shape, the shape of the Omkaram at the top representing the head and the shape of it in a triangular form at the bottom representing Prajapati.

Thus the letter 'Om' represents the Sthoola, Sookshma and Karanams of this body, and the connection between this Primary Aksharam, the five Aksharams and this Sareeram has been clearly set forth. The figure which represents this is found in all Tamil Shastras. These five letters with their particular shapes are not found in any other language. This primary Manthram and the letter which contains its inner meaning are peculiarly the heritage of the Tamil language. Others might have repeated the Manthram but they lacked the particular letters. This is a strong argument for proving the antiquity of Tamil.

11. How the various modulations of the letters க, ச, ட, த and ப (ka, cha, da, tha and pa) were a later introduction, just as the one became the many.

It is a law of nature that from the primary 'one' all the rest were developed. From God, the Prime Being, everything else was created. It is natural, in languages, to multiply the one into many and not combine the many into one. So it is but natural that from the primary sounds க, ச, ட, த, and ப, (ka, cha, da, tha and pa) were derived the three other sounds of affinity which are at present used in the Sanskrit language. We are to be glad of this, because by the introduction of these new sounds we are able to express all our thoughts. We have not touched upon other Sanskrit letters as it is not necessary. This proves that the Tamil language is very ancient, that it is independent and that other languages must have sprung after it.

The important letter 'ழ' (lla) is not found in other languages and the very sound of it is unknown. This is also a fact to be remembered.

This ancient and independent language was, for long, patronised by the Pandya kings who ruled in South Madura. They were presidents of the great Tamil Sangam, which brought together scholars from the 49 Tamil provinces (which were later on destroyed by the deluge), which discussed great and glorious things and which gave its stamp of authority to all newly produced Tamil works.

12. How South Madura, and after its destruction, South India was noted for ancient Music.

From all that has gone before we infer that there was an extensive continent named Lemuria in the South Indian Ocean, that it was the cradle of the nations of the earth and that the inhabitants of it migrated to the adjacent islands and provinces after its destruction. Judging from the fauna and flora of those regions, the skeletons of men and animals and the words found mixed in their languages, we may safely assert that they had attained a very high degree of civilisation even in the earliest times, that they all spoke the Tamil language in their ancient home and that they were long lived and mighty.

When the Tamil country, famous for its language whose greatness was seen in grammar, music and dancing, was destroyed, the remnants of those who were saved took refuge in the opposite shores, and as the new land was also a portion of the Tamil country, we may safely assert that the three amsams or departments of the Tamil language—grammar, music and dancing, were already known there. This is the very reason that the Music of South India has ever been held in the highest esteem as being very scientific. The same music has been handed down from generation to generation and has been maintained and preserved chiefly through dancing girls, their instructors, players of different instruments as the Nagaswaram, the Flute, and the Veena and through drummers who have all been supported by gifts from temples. Indian Music has been learnt by others from these and is being learnt of them even at the present day. Even to-day we have some players on the Nagaswaram who have the ability to instruct even the best of singers and players on the Veena. So we have reason to conclude that Bharatam, Singing, playing on the Veena, Flute or Nagaswaram and playing the Melam have been preserved from falling into disuse, and have been taught to others by a body of professional musicians attached to the service of temples. The fact that the North which has so many renowned musicians cannot boast of such eminent music as that of South India is conclusive evidence to prove that Music first existed in the Tamil language in South India and that the Aryans cultivated it only after their advent into South India. This eminent music of South India has been from ancient times under the patronage of kings, princes and scholars who flourished 4,440 years ago at the time of the first sangam and music made enormous advances at the time helped by the number of musical works written at the period. We shall, therefore, do well to make a few remarks on the three sangams which existed in South Madura, Kapatapuram and North Madura respectively.

13 A few remarks on the three Sangams which existed in South Madura, Kapatapuram and North Madura.

Of the three Sangams which patronised the language, the first is said to have existed at the close of the first Ooli. It is very necessary we should know the period and literature of this Sangam which existed 8,000 years ago, and especially the literature showing the greatness of South Indian Music. We shall, therefore, consider the remarks of eminent scholars on these three Sangams.

Ilankovadigal, the brother of king Senguttuvan who ruled over the Chera country 1,800 years ago, has written a work named 'Silappadhikaram.' We learn from it the grandeur of kingdoms which then flourished, the nature of kings and their government. In the place where he makes a reference to the hero, Kovalan, and his lover, the dancer Mathavi, he says, how clever both were in playing the Veena, how the heroine was an expert exponent of the art of dancing: and he concludes by making mention of a few special amsams of that special art. Further light is thrown upon it by works on music and commentaries on them written during the time of Adiyarkunallar, the commentator on Silappadhikaram. We give below the remarks made by Mahamahopadhyaya V. Saminatha Iyer, the publisher of the above work.

சிலப்பதிகாரம் இளங்கோவடிகள் வரலாறு, பக்கம் 10, 11.

"இளங்கோவடிகள் காலம் கடைச்சங்கப் புலவர் காலமென்று நிச்சயிக்கப்படுகிறது. அக்கடைச்சங்கப்புலவருட் சிறந்தவரும் மதுரைக் கணக்காயனார் மகனாருமாகிய நக்கீரனார் இறையனாரகப் பொருளுக்குத் தாம் இயற்றியவுரையில் இந்நூலிற் கானல் வரியிலுள்ள "நிணங்கொள்," "துறைமேய் வலம்புரி" "சேர்ந்தகன்காதலர்" ' புணர்துணை " என்னும் பாடல்களை யெடுத்து உதாரணமாகக் காட்டியிருப்பதுங் காண்க. இளங்கோவடிகளுக்குத் தமையனாகிய செங்குட்டுவன் பத்தினிக் கடவுளாகிய கண்ணகியார்க்குக் கோயில் சமைத்து விழாக்கொண்டாடிய காலத்து இலங்கை யரசனாகிய கயவாகுவென்பவன் உடனிருந்தானென்ற வரலாற்றையாலும், அக்கயவாகுவும் இலங்கையிற் கண்ணகியார்க்குக் கோயில் கட்டுவித்து விழாக்கொண்டாடினனென்று இந்நூற்பதிகத்தைச் சார்ந்த உரைபெறு கட்டுரையாலும் தெரிகின்றன. இற்றைக்குச் சற்றேறக்குறைய 1,760 வருடங்களுக்கு முன்பு கயவாகுவென்னு மரசனொருவன் இருந்தானென்று இலங்கைச் சரித்திரத்தால் (மகாவம்சம்) புலப்படுகின்றது. பின்னும் சற்றேறக்குறைய 760 வருடங்களுக்கு முன்பு கயவாகு வென்னும் மற்றோரரசனிருந்ததாகவும் அச்சரித்திரத்தால் தெரிகின்றது. ஆயினும், இந்நூலிற் கூறிய வேறு சில அரசர்களுடைய காலத்தை ஆராயும்போது இந்நூலாசிரியர் காலம் இரண்டாங் கயவாகுவின் காலத்திற்கு முந்தியதாகத் தெரிகின்றமையின், இவர்காலம் முதற்கயவாகுவின் காலமென்றே துணியப்படுகின்றது."

Silappadhikaram of Ilankovadigal P. 10, 11.

The age of Ilankovadigal is reckoned to be contemporaneous with that of the scholars of the last Sangam. This is supported by the fact that Nakkeerar, son of Kanakayanar of Madura and one of the most distinguished among the scholars of the last Sangam, in his commentary on 'Irayanarahapporul' quotes a few stanzas beginning "நிணங்கொள்", "துறைமேய் வலம்புரி" "சேர்ந்தகன்காதலர்" and "புணர்துணை" all from Silappadhikaram. Again, in the "Varandarukathai of the above work we read that Gayavahu, the King of Lanka, was present at the dedication festival of the temple built in honour of Kannahi by the wife of Shenkuttuvan, the brother of Ilankovadigal, and in the preface to the above work we read that the same Gayavahu built a temple to Kannahi in Lanka and had its dedication festival celebrated. It appears from 'Mahavamsam'—the history of the Kings of Lanka—that Gayavahu ruled about 1,760 years ago. From the same history we understand that there was another King Gayavahu 760 years ago. However, we have reason to conclude that the age of the author of Silappadhikaram must have been contemporaneous with that of Gayavahu I, and not with that of Gayavahu II, judging from the history of other kings.

We gather from the above extract and from the geneology of the kings of Lanka named 'Mahavamsam' that Gayavahu, Ilangovadigal and Nakkeeranar, one of the literary savants of the last Sangam, were all contemporaries. The time of Gayavahu was about 1,800 years ago. Again when we notice that Natchinarkiniyar speaks highly of 'Manimekhalai' the work of Koolavanikan Sattanar we are led to infer that Ilangovadigal and Sattanar were also contemporaries. There is also reason to infer that the commentary on Silappadhikaram of Ilangovadigal written by Adiyarkkunallar must have been after the time of Nakkeeranar, one of the scholars of the last Sangam. In the above work written nearly 1,800 years ago, distinct mention is made of the first Sangam which was in South Madura destroyed by the deluge, and of Kapatapuram, the seat of the second Sangam.

14. The destruction by deluge of the first Sangam and the 49 provinces of South Madura.

சிலப்பதிகாரம், வேனிற்காதையுரை, பக்கம் 197.

"நெடியோன் குன்றம்—வேங்கடமலை. தொடியோள்—பெண்பாற் பெயராற் குமரியென்பதாயிற்று. ஆகவே தென்பாற் கன்னியென்னும் ஆற்றிற்குப் பெயராம். ஆனால், நெடியோன் குன்றமும் தொடியோள் நதியுமென்னாது பௌவமுமென்றது என்னையெனின், முதலூழியிறுதிக்கண் தென்மதுரையகத்துத் தலைச்சங்கத்து அகத்தியனாரும் இறையனாரும் குமரவேளும் முரஞ்சியூர் முடிநாகராயரும் நிதியின் கிழவனும் என்றிவருள்ளிட்ட நாலாயிரத்து நானூற்று நாற்பத்தொன்பதின்மர் எண்ணிறந்த பரிபாடலும் முதுநாரையும் முதுகுருகும் களரியாவிரையு முள்ளிட்டவற்றைப் புனைந்து தெரிந்து நாலாயிரத்து நானூற்று நாற்பதிற்றியாண்டு இரீஇயினார் காய்சின வழுதிமுதற் கடுங்கோனீறாயுள்ளார் எண்பத்தொன்பதின்மர்; அவருட் கவியரங்கேறினார் எழுவர் பாண்டியருள் ஒருவன் சயமாகீர்த்தியனாகிய நிலந்தரு திருவிற்பாண்டியன் தொல்காப்பியம் புலப்படுத்து இரீஇயினான். அக்காலத்து அவர் நாட்டுத் தென்பால் முகத்திற்கு வடவெல்லையாகிய பஃறுளியென்னும் ஆற்றிற்கும் குமரியென்னும் ஆற்றிற்கு மிடையே எழுநூற்றுக் காவதவாறும் இவற்றின் நீர்மலிவானென மலிந்த ஏழ்தெங்கநாடும் ஏழ்மதுரைநாடும் ஏழ்முன்பாலைநாடும் ஏழ்பின்பாலைநாடும் ஏழ்குன்றநாடும் ஏழ்குணகாரை ஏழ்குறும்பனைநாடுமென்னும் இந்த நாற்பத்தொன்பது நாடும் குமரிகொல்ல முதலிய பன்மலைநாடும் காடும் நதியும் பதியும் தடநீர்க்குமரி வடபெருங்கோட்டின் காறும் கடல்கொண்டொழிதலாற் குமரியாகிய பௌவமென்றாரென் றுணர்க. அஃது என்னை பெறுமாறெனின், 'வடிவேலெறிந்த வான்பகை பொறாது, பஃறுளி யாற்றுடன் பன்மலையடுக்கத்துக் குமரிக்கோடுங் கொடுங்கடல் கொள்ள' என்பதனாலும் கணக்காயனார் மகனார் நக்கீரனாருரைத்த இறையனார் பொருளுரையானும் உரையாசிரியராகிய இளம்பூரண வடிகள் முகவுரையானும் பிறவாற்றானும்பெறுதும். அஃதேல் அற்றாக, வடக்கின்கண் வேங்கடமலை தெற்கின்கட் குமரிக்கடலெனக் குறியாற் கூறினவர் கீழ்பால் மேல்பாற்கு எல்லை கூறாதது என்னையோவெனில், நெடுந்திசையாகிய வடபாற்கெல்லை குன்றமென்றும் தென்பாற்கெல்லை குமரிப்பௌவமென்றும் கூறினமையான் ஒழிந்த திசைகட்கு ஒழிந்த பௌவம் எல்லை என்பதாயிற்று; என்னை? வேங்கடக்குமரி

தீம்புனற் பௌவமென் றிந்நான்கெல்லை தமிழது வழக்கே. என்றார் சிகண்டியாருமாகலின். அன்றியும் வடதிசைக்கண் வடுகொழிந்த திரிபுடை மொழி பலவுளவாகலான் மலையெல்லை கூறி நீங்கிய திசை மூன்றிற்கும் திரிபின்மையாற் கடலெல்லை கூறினரெனினுமமையும்."

Silappadhikaram. Venirkathayurai. P. 197.

The term Nediyon Kundram corresponds to Venkatamalei. The expression தொடியோள் must refer to 'Kumari' as the termination is feminine. So it is the name of a river in the South. But he says "நெடியோன் குன்றமுந் தொடியோள் பௌவமும்" instead of "நெடியோன் குன்றமுந் தொடியோள் கரியும்." He uses the term "பௌவம்" (sea) because at the end of the first Ooli, 4,449 presidents of the first Sangam at South Madura lived, such as Agasthyanar, Irayanar, Kumaravel (Subramanya) Muranjiyur Mudi Naga Rayar (Siva) who had composed such eminent works as "Paripadal," "Muthugurugu" and "Kalariayavirai" for a period of 4,440 years, of whom there were 89 kings beginning from "Kaisina Valuthi" and ending with "Kadunkoan", seven of whom made original compositions which were approved by the Sangam, and Nilandaruthiruvil Pandyan wrote annotation on Tolgauppiam. There was the distance of 700 leagues between the river Pahtruli which was the northern boundary of its southern end, and the 49 fertile provinces made up of the seven Thenga Nadu, the seven Madura Nadu, the seven Menpalai Nadu, the seven Pinpalai Nadu, the seven Kundra Nadu, the seven Kunakarai Nadu and the seven Kurumpani Nadu, along with the mountainous regions of Kumari and Kollam, rivers and forests were destroyed by sea. Hence the use of the term "பௌவம்." This is further supported by the quotation "வடிவேலெறிந்த வான்பகை பொறாது, பஃறுளியாற்றுடன் பன்மலையடுக்கத்துக் குமரிக்கோடுங் கொடுங்கடல் கொள்ள", and by what we read in the Irayanar Porul of Nakkeeranar, the son of Kanakayanar, and in the preface of Ilangovadigal. When he has specified the Northern limit to be Venkatamalai and the Southern to be Kumari-kadal why has he omitted the Eastern and Western boundaries.? The reason is that the Eastern and Western limits were destroyed by sea. The Sage Sil andi also supports this statement that the two boundaries above mentioned were the limits of the Tamil country.

We infer from the above that the River Kumari was the northern boundary to the province of Kumari in the south of South India, and that the 49 provinces as far as Kumari were destroyed by the deluge We may see particulars about the 49 provinces in the following extract.

15. A few remarks on the 49 Tamil provinces which existed during the first Ooli.

தமிழ்மொழியின் வரலாறு, பக்கம் 60-63.

"புறநானூற்றிற் பாண்டியன் பல்யாகசாலை முதுகுடுமிப்பெருவழுதியை நெட்டிமையார் பாடிய பாட்டில் 'பஃறுளியாற்று மணலினும் பலவே' என்றதனால் பஃறுளியாறு வடிம்பலம்ப நின்ற பாண்டியனும் உண்டாக்கப்பட்டதென்பது குறிக்கப்பட்டுளது; இன்னும் முன்னர் வெளிப்பட்ட 'செங்கோன்றரைச் செலவு' என்றதோர் சிறு நூலினுற் சிலவிஷயங்கள் விளங்குகின்றன. மேல் அடியார்க்கு நல்லாருரையான் விளங்கிய ஏழ் தெங்கநாடு முதலிய நாடுகளில் சார்ந்து 'பெருவளநாடு' முதலிய பிறநாடுகளும், 'மணிமலை' முதலிய சில மலைகளும், 'மூத்தூர்' முதலிய சிலவூர் களும், சக்கரக்கோ, பேராற்று நெடுந்துறையன், இடைக்கழிச் செங்கோடன் முதலிய புலவர் சிலரதுபெயர் களும், 'பெருநூல்', 'இயனூல்' எனச் சில நூற்பெயர்களும் அந்நூலானும் அதனுரையானும் வெளியாகின்றன அந்நூல் முதலூழியில் தலைச்சங்கத்தார் காலத்திற் குமரியாற்றிற்கும் பஃறுளியாற்றிற்கும் இடையேயுள்ள பெருவளநாட்டரசனுகிய செங்கோனை முதலூழித் தனியூர்ச் சேந்தன் பாடியதென்பது.

"செங்கோன் றரைச்செலவைச் சேந்தன் றனியூரான்
றுங்கன் றமிழ்த்தாப் புலித்தோடரா—லங்கிசைத்தான்
சக்கரக்கோ முன்னின்று சாற்றும் பெருவூழி
யக்கரக்கோ நாமஞ்சு வாம்."

என்ற பஃறுளியாற்றுத் தலைப்பாச்சல் ஏழ்தெங்கநாட்டு முத்தூர் அகத்தியன் கூறிய பாட்டினுற் புலனுகின்றது. இவையனைத்தையும் உற்றுநோக்குமிடத்து, எழுநூற்றுக்காவதம் அகன்று கிடந்த நாற்பத்தொன்பது தமிழ்நாடுகள் கடல் கொள்ளப்பட்டன வென்பது புலனும். இக்காலத்து அளவின்படி ஒரு காவதமென்பது பத்து மைலாக, எழுநூறு காவதமும் ஏழாயிர மைலெல்லையனவாம். 'இந்துமகா சமுத்திரம் இருநூற்றைம்பது லக்ஷம் சதுரமைலுள்ளது. இதனல் அது சிறிது குறையப் பதினறு லக்ஷம் மையில் நீளமும் பதினறு லக்ஷம் மையில் அகலமுடையதென்பது பெறப்படும். பெறவே இப்பதினறு லக்ஷம் மையில் நீளத்தில் ஏழாயிர மைலளவு நிலனுயிருந்து கடல் கொள்ளப்பட்டிருத்தல் வேண்டும். இனி மோரீசுத்தீவுக்கும், பம்பாய் நகரத்துக்கும் இடையிலுள்ள நீர்ப்பரவை இரண்டாயிரத்தைந் நூறுமையில் நீளமுள்ளதாம். மோரீசுத்தீவிற்கும் அதற்குத் தெற்கிலுள்ள கெர்கியூலன்' என்னுந் தீவிற்கும் இடையிலுள்ள நீளமும் அவ்வளவினதேயாம். ஆகவே நீளத்தில் இக்காலத்திலுள்ள 'குமரிமுனை' யிலிருந்து கெர்கியூலன் தீவின் தெற்கு வரையிலும், அகலத்தில் 'மடகாசிகர்தீவு' முதற் 'சுமாத்திரா,' 'ஜாவா' முதலியவற்றை யுள்ளடக்கிய 'சந்தாத் தீவுகள்' அளவும் விரிந்து கிடந்த குமரிநாடு கடல் கொள்ளப்பட்ட தென்பது போதரும்.

இக்குமரிநாடுதான், கிழக்கே சந்தாத்தீவுகள் வரையிலும் மேற்கே மடகாசிகர் தீவு வரையிலும் அகன்று கிடந்ததாகக் கூறப்படும் 'லெமூரியா' என்ற நிலப்பரப்பாம். இந்நிலப்பரப்பு ஒருகாலத்தெழுந்த பெருவெள்ளத்தில் ஆழ்ந்துபோயிற்றென்றும் அவ்வாறு ஆழ்ந்துபோன பெருநிலம் இவ்வுலக முழுவதற்கும் நடுவிற்கிடந்த பெரும்பரப்பாகலான் மக்கள் முதன் முதல் இந்நிலத்திலிருந்து பின் நாற்றிசையினும் பிரிந்து சென்று வேறுபட்டனரென்றும், அங்ஙனம் இதிலிருந்த தொல்லோர் வழங்கியது தமிழ்ப்பாஷையா மென்றும், பலகாரணங்கள் காட்டி விளக்கி நிறுவினர் மேற்புல விஞ்ஞானிகளுளொருவர்.

The history of the Tamil language Page, 60 -63.

In Purananooru, in the stanza ascribed to Nettimayar it is said that the river Pahtruli was dug by Vadimbalamba Nindra Pandyan. Some other things are also brought to light by the little book "Senkonetarai chilavu" which was published recently. In connection with the 49 provinces mentioned by Adiyarkkunallar, other provinces such as 'Peruvalanadu', other hills such as 'Manimalai' other towns such as 'Muttoor', the names of a few other scholars as well as books such as 'Perunool' are brought to light. It is presumed that the book was written by "Thaniyoor Chendan", King of Peruvalanadu between the rivers Kumari and Pahtruli, during the period of the first Sangam in the first Ooli.' Again a stanza sung by Muthoor Agathyan of the seven Thenga Nadu proves our point. All these distinctly show that the 49 provinces which extended 700 leagues were destroyed by sea. According to modern computation a league equals 10, (3) * miles. So the 700 leagues amount to 7,000, (2,100) * miles. The extent of the Indian Ocean is 25,000,000 square miles; in other words its length and breadth are about 16,00,000, (5,000) * miles each way. So 7,000, (2,100)* miles out of this 16,00,000, (5,000)* miles should have been land submerged. The distance between the island of Mauritius and Bombay is 2,500 miles. The distance between Mauritius and the island of Kerguelen is about the same. So we may see that the province of Kumari, submerged, must have extended from Cape Comorin to the island of Kerguelen in length, and from the island of Madagascar to the Sunda Islands.

This province of Kumari whose limit is mentioned above was the continent of Lemuria. So by various reasonings a western scholar establishes the facts that this continent was once destroyed by sea, that the submerged portion was the centre of the world from which races became scattered in different regions, and that the language used by the ancient inhabitants of the destroyed continent was Tamil.

* The figures within brackets are preferable.

We see, there, that for this ancient province South Madura was the chief city, that its inhabitants spoke only Tamil, that there were 549 scholars in the Tamil Sangam and that the Sangam was carried on for 4,440 years with 4,449 eminent men as its presidents.

We may see from the following extract that the Second and the Third Sangams were carried on without any break on the same lines.

16. The Period of the three Sangams, the literary men—the Kings that flourished at the time—and the literary works that were produced.

The history of the Tamil language, P. 95–100.

1. முதற்சங்கம்.

"இம்முச்சங்கங்களையும் பற்றி 'இறையனாரகப்பொருளுரை' யின்கட் கூறப்பட்டிருப்பதே மிகப் பழமையான சரிதம். அதன் கண்ணே, தலைச்சங்கமிருந்தார் அகத்தியனாரும் திரிபுரமெரித்த விரிசடைக் கடவுளும் குன்றெறிந்த முருகவேளும் முரஞ்சியூர் முடிநாகராயரும் நிதியின்கிழவனுமென இத்தொடக்கத்தார் ஐஞ்ஞூற்று நாற்பத்தொன்பதின்மர் என்ப. அவருள்ளிட்டு நாலாயிரத்து நானூற்று நாற்பத்தொன்பதின்மர் பாடினாரென்பது. அவர்களாற் பாடப்பட்டன எத்துணையோ 'பரிபாட'லும் 'முதுநாரை'யும் 'முதுகுருகு'ங் 'களரியாவிரை'யும் என இத்தொடக்கத்தன. அவர் நாலாயிரத்து நானூற்று நாற்பதிற்றியாண்டு சங்கமிருந்தாரென்ப. அவர்களைச் சங்கம் இரீஇயினார் காய்சினவழுதி முதலாகக் கடுங்கோனீறாக எண்பத்தொன்பதின்மரென்ப. அவருட் கவியரங்கேறினார் எழுவர் பாண்டியரென்ப. அவர் சங்கமிருந்து தமிழாராய்ந்து கடல் கொள்ளப்பட்ட மதுரையென்ப. அவர்க்கு நூல் 'அகத்தியம்' என்ப எனத் தலைச்சங்கத்தைப் பற்றியும்.

I. The First Sangam.

What Irayanarahapporul says about the three Sangams is the most ancient of records concerning them. There the names of the 549 presidents of the first Sangam are given; among them we find the names of Agasthyanar, Siva, Subramanya and others. The names of 4,449 scholars who composed works like 'Paripadal', 'Muthunarei' 'Muthukurugu', 'Kalariyavirai' are also mentioned. These carried on the work of the Sangam for a period of 4,440 years. Those who organised the Sangam were 89 sovereigns from Kaisina Valuthi to Kadunkoan. Seven of those Pandyan kings placed their original compositions before the Sangam and obtained their stamp of authority. The seat of their sangam was the destroyed province of Madura. "Agasthyam" is the literary work that gives the history of the first Sangam.

தமிழ்மொழியின் வரலாறு, பக்கம் 95—100.

2. இடைச்சங்கம்.

இனி யிடைச் சங்கமிருந்தார் அகத்தியனாருந் தொல்காப்பியனாரும் இருந்தையூர்க் கருங்கோழி மோசியும் வெள்ளூர்க் காப்பியனும் சிறுபாண்டரங்கனும் திரையன் மாறனும் துவரைக் கோமானும் கீரந்தையுமென இத்தொடக்கத்தார் ஐம்பத்தொன்பதின்மரென்ப. அவருள்ளிட்டு மூவாயிரத்தெழுநூற்றுவர் பாடினாரென்ப. அவர்களாற் பாடப்பட்டன 'கலி'யும் 'குருகு'ம் 'வெண்டாளி'யும் 'வியாழமாலையகவ'லுமென இத்தொடக்கத்தனவென்ப. அவர்க்கு நூல் 'அகத்திய'மும் 'தொல்காப்பிய'மும் 'மாபுராண'மும் 'இசைநுணுக்க'மும் 'பூதபுராண'முமென இவை. அவர் மூவாயிரத்தெழுநூற்றியாண்டு சங்கமிருந்தாரென்ப. அவரைச்சங்கம் இரீஇயினார் வெண்டேர்ச்செழியன் முதலாக முடத்திருமாறனீறாக ஐம்பத்தொன்பதின்மரென்ப. அவருட் கவியரங்கேறினார் ஐவர் பாண்டியரென்ப. அவர் சங்கமிருந்து தமிழாராய்ந்தது கபாடபுரத்தென்ப. அக்காலத்துப்போலும் பாண்டியநாட்டைக் கடல்கொண்டது என இடைச்சங்கத்தைப்பற்றியும் பல கூறப்பட்டுள.

" இக்கூற்றுகளை நாம் ஆராய்ந்து பார்க்குமிடத்து, தலைச்சங்கத்தை ஒவ்வொரு பாண்டியனும் ஏறக்குறைய ஐம்பதைம்ப தாண்டுகளாக நடாத்த அது நடந்து வந்திருத்தல் வேண்டுமென்பதும், இடைச் சங்கத்தை ஒவ்வொரு பாண்டியனும் ஏறக்குறைய அறுபத்துமூன் றறுபத்துமூன் றாண்டுகளாக நடாத்த அது நடந்து வந்திருத்தல் வேண்டுமென்பதும் போதருகின்றன. இச் சங்கங்களிரண்டும் நீடித்த காலம் நடந்து வந்திருக்கவேண்டுமென்பதிலும் பலநூல்களியற்றப் பட்டனவென்பதிலும் பாவலர் பலர் சங்கத்தை யொட்டி வாழ்ந்தனரென்பதிலும், சங்கமிரண்டும் முறையேயிருந்த மதுரையும் கபாடபுரமும் கடல் கொள்ளப்பட்டன வென்பதிலும், அது காரணமாகப் பல அரிய தமிழ் நூல்கள் அழிந்துபட்டன வென்பதிலும் ஐயப்பாடில்லை யென்னலாம். மற்றுப் பாண்டிய ராசர்கள் முறையே ஐம்பதாண்டும் அறுபத்துமூன்றாண்டுமாக ஆண்டு வந்தன ரென்றுரைத்தல் ஐயுறற்பாலதே. ஆயினும், பாண்டியர் எண்பத்தொன்பதின்மரும் பாண்டியர் ஐம்பத்தொன்பதின்மரும் ஒரே தொடர்ச்சியாக ஆண்டுவந்தனரென்று கருதாது, நடுவில் இடையிடையிட்டு அரசின்றிக் கழிந்த ஆண்டுகளும் இவ்வாண்டுகளுடன் கூட்டிக்கொள்ளப் பட்டிருத்தல் வேண்டுமென்று கருதுக. இவ்வாறு தலைச்சங்கமிருந்த நாலாயிரத்து நானூற்று நாற்பதிற்றியாண்டில் இடையிடு பட்டுக் கழிந்தன எத்துணை யாண்டுகளோ? இடைச்சங்கமிருந்த மூவாயிரத்தெழுநூற்றியாண்டில் இடையிடுபட்டுக் கழிந்தன எத்துணையோ? இவற்றிற்கும் ஒருவாறு உத்தேச வகையால் தக்க கணக்கிட்டுக்கொள்ளின் மேற்கூறிய பாண்டியர் எண்பத்தொன்பதின்மரும் பாண்டியர் ஐம்பத் தொன்பதின்மரும் ஆண்ட காலத்தின் அளவு குறைந்து நம்புதற் பாலதாகு மென்க. இத்துணை யுய்த்துணரமாட்டாத சிலர் வேறுபடக் கூறுவர்."

The history of the Tamil language, P. 95-98.

2. The Middle Sangam.

The scholars that lived during this period Agasthyanar, Tolgauppyan, and others, were 59 in all. 3,700 Vidwans have made original compositions under them. Their minor works were 'Kair', 'Kurugu', 'Vendali' and such others. The chief literary works of the period were 'Tolgauppyam', 'Agattyam', 'Mapuranam', 'Isainunukkam' and 'Bhutapuranam'. The Sangam existed for 3,700 years. The kings who patronised this Sangam were 59 in number, beginning from Vender Chelian up to Mudathirumaran. Five of the Pandyan kings were authors of compositions which were approved by the Sangam. The seat of the Sangam was Kapatapuram. It is said that the kingdom of the Pandyas was destroyed by the sea just as the seat of the first Sangam was submerged.

From all these data we may infer that the first Sangam was conducted, on an average, for 50 years each, by each of the Pandya kings and that the second one, for 63 years each, by each of the sovereigns of the same dynasty; that these Sangams must have been carried on for a number of years, that many literary works were published then, that a number of Vidwans were under the patronage of the Sangams and that the seats of the two Sangams were destroyed by the sea which resulted in the destruction of many eminent literary productions in the Tamil language. But the statement that the Pandyan kings organised them for a definite period of 50 years and 63 years is rather open to doubt. It is improbable that they continually reigned for such periods, so we must infer that the years in which there were no kings reigning must also have been added on. We do not know for how many years there were no sovereigns in the first period of 4,440 years and in the second period of 3,700 years. So speaking approximately, the Pandyas must have reigned only for a less number of years. Different theories are given by others who cannot understand this.

தமிழ்மொழியின் வரலாறு, பக்கம் 98-99.

3. கடைச்சங்கம்.

" களவியற் பொருள்கண்ட கணக்காயனார் மகனார் நக்கீரனாரினின்றும் பத்தாம் தலைமுறையாளராகிய நீலகண்டனார் "கடைச்சங்கமிருந்து தமிழாராய்ந்தார் சிறுமேதாவியாரும் சேந்தம்பூதனாரும் அறிவுடையரனாரும் பெருங் குன்றூர் கிழாரும் இளந்திருமாறனும் மதுரையாசிரியர் நல்லந்துவனாரும் மருதனிள நாகனாரும் கணக்

காயனார் மகனார் நக்கீரனாருமென இத்தொடக்கத்தார் நாற்பத்தொன்பதின்மரென்ப. அவருள்ளிட்டு நானூற்று நாற்பத்தொன்பதின்மர் பாடினாரென்ப. அவர்களாற் பாடப்பட்டன 'நெடுந்தொகைநானூறும் 'குறுந்தொகை நானூறும்' 'நற்றிணைநானூறும்' 'ஐங்குறுநூறும்' 'பதிற்றுப்பத்தும்' நூற்றைம்பதுகலியும்' 'எழுபதுபரிபாடலும்' 'கூத்தும்' 'வரியும்' 'பேரிசை'யும் 'சிற்றிசை'யுமென்று இத்தொடக்கத்தன. அவர்க்கு நூல் 'அகத்திய'மும் 'தொல்காப்பிய'முமென்ப. அவர் சங்கமிருந்து தமிழாராய்ந்தது ஆயிரத்தெண்ணூற்றைம்பதிற்றியாண்டென்ப. அவர்களைச் சங்கம் இரீஇயினார் கடல் கொள்ளப்பட்டுப் போந்திருந்த முடத்திருமாறன் முதலாக உக்கிரப் பெருவழுதி யீறாக நாற்பத்தொன்பதின்மரென்ப. அவர் சங்கமிருந்து தமிழாராய்ந்தது 'உத்தரமதுரை' யென்ப. அவருட்கவியரங்கேறினார் மூவர் பாண்டியரென்ப" என்று கடைச்சங்கத்தைப் பற்றிக் கூறுகின்றனர்."

The History of the Tamil language, P. 98-99.

3. The Last Sangam.

The scholars of this period were about 49 in number, such as Nakkeeranar, Neelakantanar (tenth in descent from Nakkeeranar), Sirumedhaviar, Sendampootanar, Arivudayaranar and others. 449 poets made compositions under the above distinguished scholars. The works composed by them were 'Neduntarai Nanooru', "Kuruntarai Nanooru', 'Nattinai Nanooru', 'Ainguru Nanooru' and such like. Their literary authorities were the great standard works 'Agattyam' and 'Tolgauppyam'. The Sangam continued its literary researches into the language for a period of 1,850 years. The Pandya kings who patronised it were 49 in number, beginning from Mudatirumaran up to Oograperuvaludi. The seat of the Sangam was Oottara Madura. Three of the Pandya sovereigns composed original works which were approved by the Sangam.

The scholars of the last Sangam, who lived when Tiruvalluvar submitted his Tirukkural for their acceptance, have made certain references to certain authors. From those references we gather the names of the following scholars who lived at the close of the third Sangam, and they are:—

1.	இறையனார்	1.	Irayanar.
2.	உக்கிரப்பெருவழுதியார்	2.	Oograperuvaluthiar.
3.	கபிலர்	3.	Kapilar
4.	பரணர்	4.	Paranar
5.	நக்கீரர்	5.	Nakkeerar
6.	மாமூலனார்	6.	Mamoolanar
7.	கல்லாடர்	7.	Kalladar
8.	சீத்தலைச் சாத்தனார்	8.	Seettalai Sattanar
9.	மருத்துவன் தாமோதரனார்	9.	Maruttuwan Damodaranar
10.	நாகன்தேவனார்	10.	Nagan Devanar
11.	அரிசிற்கிழார்.	11.	Arisirkilar
12.	பொன்முடியார்	12.	Ponmudiyar
13.	கோதமனார்	13.	Gothamanar
14.	நத்தத்தனார்	14.	Nattattanar
15.	முகையலூர்ச் சிறுகருந்தும்பியார்	15.	Mugayalur Sirukarunthumbiar
16.	ஆசிரியர் நல்லந்துவனார்	16.	Asyriar Nallanduvanar
17.	கீரந்தையார்	17.	Keerandaiyar
18.	சிறுமேதாவியார்	18.	Siru Medhaviar

19.	நல்கூர் வேள்வியார்	19.	Nalkoor Velviar
20.	தொடித்தலை விழுத்தண்டினர்	20.	Thodittalai Villuttandinar
21.	வெள்ளிவீதியார்	21.	Velli Veethiar
22.	மாங்குடி மருதனர்	22.	Mangudi Marudanar
23.	எரிச்சலூர் மலாடனர்	23.	Erichchalore Maladanar
24.	போக்கியார்	24.	Pokyar
25.	மோசிகீரனர்	25.	Mosikeeranar
26.	காவிரிப்பூம்பட்டினத்துக்காரிக்கண்ணனர்	26.	Karikkannanar of Cauveripoompattinam
27.	மதுரைத் தமிழ்நாயகனர்	27.	Madura Tamil Nayakanar
28.	பாரதம்பாடிய பெருந்தேவனர்	28.	Perundevanar, author of Bharatham
29.	உருத்திர சன்மகண்ணர்	29.	Rudhira Sanmakannar
30.	பெருஞ்சித்தனர்	30.	Peruncheettanar
31.	நரிவெரூஉத்தலையார்	31.	Nariveruttalayar
32.	மதுரைத் தமிழாசிரியர் செங்குன்றூர்கிழார்	32.	Senkuntroorkilar, Tamil Author
33.	மதுரையறுவைவாணிகர் இளவேட்டனர்	33.	Ilavettanar, Vanigar of Madura
34.	கவிசாகரப் பெருந்தேவனர்	34.	Perundevanar Kavi Sagara
35.	மதுரைப்பெருமருதனர்	35.	Perumarudanar of Madura
36.	கோவூர்கிழார்	36.	Kovoorkilar
37.	உறையூர் முதுகூற்றனர்	37.	Mudukootranar of Woriyur
38.	இழிகட் பெருங்கண்ணனர்	38.	Ilikat Perunkannanar
39.	செயிர்க்காவிரியார்மகனர் சாத்தனர்	39.	Sattanar, son of Seyirkaviriar
40.	செயலூர்க் கொடுஞ்செங்கண்ணனர்	40.	Kodunchenkannanar of Seyalore
41.	வண்ணக்கஞ் சாத்தனர்	41.	Vannakkam Sattanar
42.	களத்தூர்கிழார்	42.	Kalattoor Kilar
43.	நச்சுமனர்	43.	Natchumanar
44.	அக்காரக்கனி நச்சுமனர்	44.	Akkarakkini Natchumanar
45.	நப்பாலத்தனர்	45.	Nappalattanar
46.	குலபதிநாயனர்	46	Kulapati Nayanar
47.	தேனிக்குடிக்கீரனர்	47.	Thenikkudi Keeranar
48.	கொடிஞாழன் மாணிபூதனர்.	48.	Kodignalan Manipoodanar
49.	கவுணியனர்	49.	Kavunianar
50.	மதுரைப்பாலாசிரியனர்	50.	Madurai Palasirianar
51.	ஆலங்குடி வங்கனர்	51.	Alangudi Vanganar

The interest which the above scholars had in the Tamil literature may be gathered from their compositions.

தமிழ் மொழியின் வரலாறு, பக்கம் 99

"அக்கூற்றை யாராயுமிடத்துப் பாண்டியர் நாற்பத்தொன்பதின்மரும் ஆண்டகாலம் இடையீ டெட்டுக் கழிந்த காலத்தோடுங்கூடி ஆயிரத் தெண்ணூற் றைம்பதிற்றி யாண்டாகின்றது. பாண்டியரொவ்வொருவரும் (இடையீட்டுக் காலத்தொடுங்கூடி) முப்பத்தெட்டாண்டுகள் அரசாட்சி செய்தவராகின்றனர். இது நம் புதற்பாற்றே. இனித்தலைச்சங்கமிருந்த நாலாயிரத்து நானூற்று நாற்பது வருஷங்களும் இடைச்சங்கமிருந்த மூவாயிரத்தெழுநூறு வருஷங்களும் கடைச்சங்கமிருந்த ஆயிரத் தெண்ணூற்றைம்பது வருஷங்களுமாகக் கூடி ஒன்பதினாயிரத்துத் தொள்ளாயிரத்துத் தொண்ணூறு வருஷங்களாகின்றன' இதனைக் கி. பி. நூற்றிலிருந்து

பிற்கணக்கிட்டுச் சென்றால் தலைச்சங்கம் கி. மு. ஒன்பதினாயிரத் தொள்ளாயிரத் தொண்ணூறு வருஷங்கட்கு முன்னர்ஸ்தாபிக்கப்பட்டிருத்தல் வேண்டும். தமிழ் மொழியின் தொன்மை மாட்சி கூறிவந்த விடத்து, கி. மு. 8,000 ஆண்டுகட்கு முற்பட்ட எழுத்துச் சாதனங்கள் கண்டுபிடிக்கப்பட்டுளவென்றமையால் அதனினும் ஏறக்குறையப் பத்தொன்பது நூற்றாண்டுகள் முன்னரே தலைச்சங்கமேற்பட்டு விட்டதென்றல் சாலாதென வாதித்தற்கும் இடமுண்டு.

இவ்வாதி காலத்து நூல்களுட் கடல்கொண்டழிந்தனவும் இன்னும் கண்டு பிடிக்கப்படாதனவும் போக, இப்போழ்தத்துக் கிடைப்பன தலைச்சங்கத்தார் காலத்துச் செய்யப்பட்ட 'அகத்தியம்' என்ற நூலின் கட்சில சூத்திரங்களும், இடைச்சங்கத்தார் காலத்துச் செய்யப்பட்ட 'தொல்காப்பியம்' என்ற இலக்கண நூலும், கடைச்சங்கத்தார் காலத்துச் செய்யப்பட்ட 'எட்டுத்தொகை' என்ற நூற்றொகையுள்ளடங்கிய எட்டு நூல்களும் 'பத்துப்பாட்டு'ம், 'பதினெண்கீழ்க்கணக்கு' மாம். எட்டுத்தொகை நூல்களைப்பின்வரும் பாட்டாலுணர்க.

"நற்றிணை நல்ல குறுந்தொகை யைங்குறுநூ
றொத்த பதிற்றுப்பத் தோங்கு பரிபாடல்
கற்றறிந்தார் ஏத்துங் கலியோ டகம்புறமென்
றித்திறத்த வெட்டுத் தொகை."

இவ்வெட்டுத் தொகையுட் 'கலித்தொகை' ஐங்குறுநூறு, புறநானூறு' என்ற மூன்று நூல்களும் அச்சாகி வெளிப்போந்தன. இம்மூன்றனுள் முன்னைய இரண்டும் அகப்பொருளும் பின்னையதொன்றும் புறப்பொருளும் கூறுவனவாம்."

The History of Tamil language, P. 99.

Judging from the above, we find that the total number of years during which the 49 Pandyas reigned (including the period in which there were no Kings) comes to 1,850, *i. e.* on an average of 38 years each. This is quite probable. Now adding together the period of the existence of the three Sangams we get 9,990 years. Going backwards, then, from the year of the birth of Christ, we calculate that the first Sangam should have been established in 9,990 B. C. But speaking about the antiquity of the Tamil language it is said that inscriptions as old as 8,000 B. C. only have come to light; so some may object that the First Sangam could not possibly have been instituted 19 centuries before that time.

Among the literary productions of this ancient period we find the following remnants, the others having been destroyed by the sea or still being searched for. These are a few of the Sootrams from Ahattyam produced during the first Sangam, the grammar 'Tolgauppyam' of the Middle Sangam, and 'Ettutogai', 'Pattupattu' and 'Padinenkeelkanakku' of the third Sangam. Some of the works comprised under 'Ettutogai' are 'Kalitogai', 'Aingurunooru, and 'Purananooru'. These have been printed and published. Of these the first two treat about matters indigenous while the latter speaks of extraneous matters.

We gather from the above that Ilankovadigal, the author of 'Silappadhikaram', flourished at the period of the last Sangam and that he was a contemporary of Gayavahu, the king of Lanka, who lived 1,800 years ago. The facts that Nakkeeranar, commentator on Irayanarahapporul' quotes from 'Silappadhikaram' and that he was one of the members of the last Sangam show that he flourished about the same time. We gather from Nakkeeranar's commentary, that the first Sangam at South Madura lasted for 4,440 years about the close of the first Ooli, that the Sangam had 4,449 presidents successively at the rate of one per year, that 89 Pandyan kings beginning from 'Kaisina

Valuthi' to 'Kadunkone' ruled at the time and that seven of these Pandyan kings presided over the deliberations of the Sangam owing to their excellence of literary composition. During the reign of one of these ruling sovereigns, namely Nilandarutiruvil Pandyan, the eminent literary work 'Tolgauppyam' seems to have been written. It was during the reign of this monarch that South Madura and its 49 provinces were destroyed by the sea. We learn from 'Purananooru' that the river 'Pahtruli' in the South was dug by Vadimbalambanindra Pandyan. We also learn from the small book Senkontrarichchelavu' the names of a few provinces, hills, and cities, and the names of a few scholars and their works. This small book is attributed to the king 'Senkovei Taniyoor Seyndan' the ruler of the fertile province between the Kumari and the Pahtruli. The period then was the first Ooli.

The highly efficient state of the language during the first Ooli.

Those who realise the importance of the Tamil language know how it was pure and easy and unmixed and had attained a high state of excellence at the period of the first Ooli as seen from the works of Narada, Agastya and other sages who flourished then. But after the deluge, as the Tamilians spread over different regions and as people with different languages of the period of the second and the third sangams mixed freely with them, the original grandeur of the language was lost. The same remark applies also to the Music of South India. In addition to this, some portions of ancient works, such as Agattyam, were destroyed along with Korkei or Kapatapuram during the time of the Middle Sangam. It is said, at the present day, that the ruins of a city with magnificent temples, palaces and forts may be seen submerged to the east of the modern Korkei which is situated at about 10 miles from the temple walls of Tiruchendoor, in south-west Tinnevelly, washed by the waves of the sea. There is reason to believe that there may be many a temple and fort in the eastern shores of South India submerged in the same manner.

Those who have seen the submerged temple of Subramanya near Vizagapatam and that dedicated to Siva near Mahabalipuram will easily realise this.

We may understand, then, that the Tamil Sangams were carried on for nearly 9,000 years in South Madura, Kapatapuram and Madura which were later on destroyed. We also understand that there were 657 members of the Sangam and 8,598 presidents, that they were under the patronage of 197 Pandya kings of whom 15 were great scholars who composed works of their own.

'Silappadhikaram' of Ilankovadigal, brother of Shenguttuvan,' 'Tolgauppyam' of Tranadhoomagni, 'Manimekhalai' of Koolavanigan Sattanar, 'Ettutogai', 'Pattupattu', 'Padinenkeel kanakku' and other literary works in Tamil have become the ancient heritage of the Tamilians, patronised as they were by eminent scholars of the Sangam as well as by rulers of the Tamil Country. Inasmuch as they preeminently possess beautiful words and ideas and are free from grammatical flaws, they are held in the highest esteem even by the Tamil scholars of the present day. The fact that the style of these ancient Tamil works is considered so very eminent is a proof for the antiquity and excellence of the language.

Who is there who does not appreciate the rare excellence and beautiful ideas contained in the 'Tirukkural of Tiruvalluvanayanar held in the highest esteem by all the world? Are there any children in the Tamil country who do not first learn by rote the 'Attichoudi' (mainly of two words) and 'Kondraivendan' (of four words) composed by his sister 'Avvaiyar'? The excellence and antiquity of works like the 'Kural' and the 'Attichoudi' which contain in themselves in an easy explanatory style all that is indispensably necessary for the well being of mankind, will be clearly manifest to scholars who have made a comparative study of works of a similar nature in other languages. Who can express the beauty and excellence of religious works like Devaram, Tiruvachakam and Tiruvoimoli?

17. The efficient state of Music at the period of the First Sangam.

This Sangam existed for 4,440 years during the first Ooli. The works Mudunarai, Mudukurugu, Panchabharateeyam and Kalariavirai which were the works of this Sangam along with their Muthal Nool, the Agattyam, were destroyed by the sea. The portion relating to Music in Agattyam, and the works Perunarai, Perunkurugu and Panchabharateeyam which mainly related to Music—all these must have been in extensive use during the first Ooli. 'Perungalam' or the Yal with 1,000 strings and other Veenas with 21, 17 and 14 strings, which are referred to in the above works, were all destroyed. 'Perungalam' was the Narada Veena. The fact that the works of the period refer to Narada as 'Yalasrian' (Master of the Yal) enables us to infer that he was an expert on the Veena, that he taught the instrument to others and that he was the author of the musical work 'Panchabharateeyam.'

But the musical works of this period are more or less extinct, and remnants of them, in the shape of quotations, are found in the few Sootrams of Agastya and Narada at the present day. Those Sootrams are referred to in Silappadhikaram written 1,800 years ago and in its commentary written by Adiyarkunallar. If a prince who flourished 1,800 years ago, and a scholar who lived 1,000 years ago, make mention of Sangams which existed for 4,440 years under the presidentship of 4,449 Tamil scholars, and of great literary works and musical instruments like the Perungalam, who could disbelieve them? The age of Karikal Cholan and Gayavahu is about the same period *i. e.*, about 1,800 years ago.

18. How Music, which was in an efficient state in the first Ooli, declined in the next.

Judging from ancient history, we find that music was very much in use in the service of God. From Kings downwards, every one had practised music for its own sake. Just as the Bible says that King David sang and danced before the ark of God along with his subjects, it is also said that Karikal Cholan (1,800 years ago) in Kauveripoompattinam, Rajasekhara Pándyan in Madura, and Natarajan in Chidambaram were experts in Bharata Shastram and danced before God. It is said that it was Paramasivam who sang the Ragam 'Sadhari' to the accompaniment of the Veena for the sake of his devotee Banaputtiran, and who came as a witness to testify to the excellence of the Veena music of the wife of the same Banaputtira. It is a matter for regret that such eminent music and dancing deteriorated in course of time by the apathy of the Jains, the Buddhists and kings who did not appreciate its excellence, and that it is now found in the possession of the poor and the despised.

When the ancient literature on music as well as the renowned musicians who used such music in the services of the temple perished by the deluge, only a few musicians survived, just as the few saved by Noah's ark. There is reason to infer that when South Madura, the capital of the 49 Tamil provinces in the extreme south of India, was submerged, only a few people in the north of it escaped. Many scholars and musicians perished as they were ignorant of the approach of the deluge. Some of the presidents of the first Sangam who survived this destruction, like the sage Agastya, established a second Sangam in Kapatapuram, similar to the first. We find from records that the Pandyan kings who ruled in South Madura, were different from those who ruled at Korkei, though they might have been of the same dynasty. We infer from the ruins of forts and walls of the present day that Pandyan kings similarly ruled over Ugramannankottai, Sundarapandyapuram, Tenkasi, Karuvainallur, Kottaru, Valliyur, Pandrikulam, Srivilliputtoor, Adittyapuram, Manarpadei, Shencottai and other smaller provinces. So this second Sangam was instituted by a few of the minor kings who were ruling provinces to the north of South Madura and by the few scholars who survived the deluge. Most of these must have been ignorant of Isai and Natakam (Music and Dancing). The remnants of those who remained after the deluge were not much interested in the advancement of Music. Perhaps they did not care to instruct those short-lived men in those rare arts which they had cultivated for many hundreds of years, for we read in the Puranas that the men of the first Ooli lived for thousands of years. Even if we suppose that these Puranas are given to exaggeration, there must be some truth in their statements as we read in the Holy Bible that men, (6,000 years ago) had a long life of 960 years, and that Noah begat Shem in his 500th year (4,500 years ago). On the strength of this we may say that it is not beyond the range of probability to believe in the 4,400 presidents of the South Madura Tamil Sangam and the 4,400 years of its existence. The members of the Sangam must have then cultivated for many years the three divisions of the language, Iyal, Isai and Natakam; but men who came after the deluge, being short-lived, gradually gave up cultivating the use of instruments like the Periyal with 1,000 strings. Being ignorant of the science of Music according to Narada, they took a dislike for it. Being unable to understand the excellence of the Bharata Shastra, where the gestures of each one of the organs of the five senses had a special significance, they got confounded. When such was the state of affairs, Kapatapuram, the seat of the Middle Sangam, was destroyed by the sea. Then, Mudattirumaran, the Pandyan king who was there, proceeded northwards, found the forest of Kadamba a suitable place for a new capital, built North Madura there (the modern Koodal Alawai) and established the third Sangam. This third Sangam was, to a certain extent, affected by Buddhism and Jainism and by some of the ruling chiefs who adopted one or other of these religions. The Aryans also gradually established themselves in the south.

19. The influence of the Aryans on the Music of South India.

We have already noticed that the renowned grammar 'Tolgauppyam', which dates from the close of the first Ooli, was the standard work during the second and third Sangams. The author says there that during the first Ooli, justice and truth had their sway, while in later days many corruptions had crept in. In proof of this he refers to some new introductions made by the Rishis in connection with marriages.

தொல்காப்பியம், பொருளதிகாரம், 4 வது கற்பியல், 144-வது சூத்திரம்.

" மேலோர் மூவர்க்கும் புணர்த்த கரணங்
கீழோர்க் காகிய காலமு முண்டே "

Natchinarkiniyar, who commented on the above, says that the law of marriage was the same for the four castes in ancient times, but that the Vellalars (Sudras) were excluded from it from the time of the second Ooli. He further says that the members of the first Sangam also speak in their poems about the uniformity of marriage laws for the four castes according to the rules laid down by Agastiya.

தொல்காப்பியம், பொருளதிகாரம், 4-வது கற்பியல், 145-வது சூத்திரம்.

" பொய்யும் வழுவுந் தோன்றிய பின்ன
ரையர் யாத்தனர் கரண மென்ப "

The Commentator on the above says that inasmuch as in-justice and un-truth prevailed from the beginning of the second Ooli, the great sages fixed different laws of marriage for the high and the low castes. The term 'ஐயர்', he says, does not refer to the first author but to the northern or Aryan writers. Moreover, as the author composed this work at the end of the first Ooli, he mentions how un-chastity and un-truth naturally followed after once the border line of honesty was passed, and how sages accordingly made different laws for the different castes. So from the above literary works we gather that at the time of Tolgauppyam the Aryans instituted different marriage laws for the higher and the lower castes, but that at the time of the first Sangam they were the same for all. It was only after the advent of the Aryans we find that the Vedas were divided and the special duties for the four castes prescribed. This enables us to conclude that the Vedas were one and un-divided in the first Ooli, the ceremonial duties of the four classes were the same and that the period was one in which truth and equity reigned supreme. From that time forward Sanskrit words were gradually introduced into the Tamil language.

We learn from the Second Chapter of " தமிழ் மொழியின் வரலாறு " (the History of the Tamil language) of Mr. Sooryanarayana Shastrial, B.A., that the Aryans rendered some help to the language from the time of their coming to South India, but that others who could not appreciate the excellence of the language did their best to strangle the language and its ancient literature. This is but the way of the world. When a thing of antiquity lacks supporters it is sure to become defunct. The same fate attended the Tamil language. Again, some of the Brahmins of South India who were born there and who had Tamil as their mother-tongue did not care to write down in Tamil what they had learnt from their own language but wrote them down in Sanskrit. For example, about 360 years ago, there was one Venkatamakhi, the son of Govinda Dikshitar, who was a prime minister of the Tamil Chola country. He arranged together in Sanskrit the modes of the Ragas used in South Indian Music, composed Mela-kartas and Lakshana-geetams to indicate the position of the swarams in the various Ragas and called his work 'Chaturdandi prakasika.' Though it is a work on the Music of South India, it does not help one to understand the srutis thereof, but rather confuses one, as it is written in Sanskrit. Some of the Musicians of South India who have studied the theory of the 22 Srutis from purely Sanskrit works approve of the theory but they criticise this work. There are others again who do not subscribe to the 72 Mela-kartas. We cannot understand the secret intention of Maha Vydyanatha Iyer, who composed the 'Ragamalika' for the 72 Mela-kartas, in writing his poetry in Sanskrit although he was a good Tamil scholar responsible for many excellent Kirtanams whose substance was from the Peria Puranam. Such constant changes, therefore, from one language to another naturally lead to a number of errors and admixtures, so much so, that the original form of a thing is completely lost and a new form springs up like the creation of Visvamitra. If one who knows the language is incapable of understanding the idea of the author how could people of alien tongues understand it? Some of the Sanskrit slokas on the 22 Srutis written by Sarangadevar have been interpreted in twenty different ways. In course of time Buddhist and Jain musicians gradually established their own theories (which clashed with each other) with the help of kings who were persuaded to support them and Tamil scholars who became their interested partisans. They not only abhorred music and dancing as they were mainly instrumental in appealing to our gross nature but did their best to stifle them altogether.

20. The efforts of Buddhists and Jains to strangle Music and dancing and the works which were destroyed by them.

தமிழ் மொழியின் வரலாறு, பக்கம் 34, 35.

"இத்துணைப்பெருமை வாய்ந்த நாடகத் தமிழின் தோற்றமென்னை? தமிழ்நாடகம் முதலி லுண்டானது மதவிடயமாகவே யென்பது துணியப்படும். அது கடவுளர் திருவிழாக்காலங்களில் ஆடல் பாடலிரண்டையுஞ் சேர நிகழ்த்துவதினின்றும் உண்டாயிற்று. சிலகாலத்தின் பின்னர்க் கதை நடையான மனப்பாடங்களும் உடன்கூடின; அதன்மேல் முதலிற் பாடலாயுள்ள சம்பாஷணை களும் பின்னர் வசனமாயுள்ள சம்பாஷணைகளும் அவற்றுடன் சேர்க்கப்பட்டன. பிற்பாடு நாடகத்தமிழ் 'வேத்தியல், பொதுவியல்' என்ற இருபிரிவினதாகி அரசர்களாலும் ஏனையோராலும் ஆதரித்து வளர்க்கப் பட்டது. கி. மு. மூன்றுநூற்றாண்டினுதல் அல்லாக்கால் அதனினுஞ் சற்று முற்காலத்தினுதல் நாடகத் தமிழ் உயர்நிலையுற்றிருந்திருத்தல் வேண்டும். நாமுணர்ந்த பழமையான நாடகத்தமிழ் நூல்கள் அனைத்தும் அக்காலத்தே நின்று நிலவினவாதலினென்க. ஆகவே அது குற்றங்குறைவு இல்லாது உண்டானதொரு தொழிலென்றே ஆதியில் மதிக்கப்பட்டது என்று 'நாடகவிய' லின் முகவுரைக்கட் கூறிய கூற்றையுங் காண்க.

இவ்வாறு தோன்றிவளர்ந்த நாடகத்தமிழ் வீழ்நிலையடையப் புகுந்தது. அதற்குற்ற காரணம் யாது? ஒழுக்க நிலை வகுக்கப்புகுந்த ஆரியருஞ் சைனரும் நாடகக் காட்சியாற் காமமே அறிவினும் மிகப்பெருகு கின்றதென்ற போலிக்கொள்கையுடையராய்த் தமது நூல்களிற் கடியப்படுவனவற்றுள் நாடகத்தையுஞ் சேர்த்துக் கூறினர். அக்காலத்திருந்த அரசர்களுக்குந் துர்ப்போதனைசெய்து நாடகத் தமிழைத் தலையெழ வொட்டாது

அடக்கிவந்தனர். ஔவையாருந் திருவள்ளுவரும் ஒருங்கே புகழ்ந்த இல்லற வாழ்க்கையையே தீவினை யச்சத் தின்பாற் படுத்துக் கூறுஞ் சைனர்கள் நாடகத்தமிழைக் கடிந்தது ஓராச்சரியமன்று. இவ்வளவு கட்டுப்பாட்டுக் கிடையில் நாடகத்தமிழ் எவ்வாறு தலையெடுத்து ஓங்கப்போகின்றது ?"

The History of the Tamil language, P. 34, 35.

What was the origin of this grand Nataka Tamil? The drama had its origin in matters religious. It arose from the Singing and Dancing which were the necessary accompaniments of religious festivities. Later on, a little bit of history, in the form of Kathas, was added. And again dialogues in the form of verse and prose were introduced. Then the drama became divided into 'Vethyal' and 'Pothuvyal' and was under the patronage of Kings and others. Drama must have attained a recognised place in Tamil literature about the third century B.C. or a little earlier. All dramatic literature known at present is dated from that period only. So we read in the preface to 'Natakavyal' that it was looked upon as pure and flawless in ancient times.

The Drama, which began under such auspicious circumstances, began to decline. What was the cause of it? The Aryans and the Jains who drew up the moral code for the Tamil country, being under the false impression that the drama appealed more to our gross nature than the spiritual, condemned it in their works. They tried to strangle the drama as much as possible by influencing the ruling sovereigns of the period also in condemning it. It is not a matter for surprise that while the Jains condemned married life which was held in such high esteem by Avvayar and Tiruvalluvar they should speak disparagingly of the drama. How could the drama lift up its head under such discouraging circumstances?

தமிழ் மொழியின் வரலாறு, பக்கம் 32, 33, 35, 36.

" இவ்வுலக வாழ்க்கைக்கு அறம் பொருளின்பமென்ற மூன்றுஞ் சிறந்தனவாமென்னு முண்மையை நன்குணராது, 'அறமே யாவரும் பின்பற்றுதற்குரியது, மற்று இன்பம் கைவிடுதற்குரியது" என்று எண்ணி, இசையினால் இன்பம் மிகுதலின் அதனையுங் கடியவேண்டுமென்று புகுந்து, ஆரியருஞ் சைனரும் ஒருங்கு சேர்ந்து, இசைத்தமிழைப் பெரிதும் அலைத்துத் தொலைக்க முயன்றனர். [இசை நாடகங் காமத்தை விளைக்குமென்றுரைத்தார் உரையாசிரியர்களுள் தலைநின்ற நச்சினார்க்கினியரும்.] அம் முயற்சிகளில் அநேக நூல்கள், அந்தோ! அழிந்துபோயின. இப்போழ்தத்து எஞ்சியிருப்பன மிகச் சிலவே இவற்றை இறைவன் பாதுகாத்தருள்க.

பண்டிதராயினர் கடிந்து நாடகத் தமிழைக் கைவிடவே, அது பாமரர் கையகப்பட்டு இழி வடைந்து தெருக்கூத்தளவிலே நிற்கின்றது. அக்காலத்துச் சங்கப் புலவர்கள் செய்த 'பரதம்', 'அகத்தியம்', 'முறுவல்', 'சயந்தம்', 'குணநூல்', 'செயிற்றியம்', 'மதிவாணர் நாடகத் தமிழ்நூல்', 'கூத்தநூல்', 'நூல்', என்ற நாடகத் தமிழ்நூல்களெல்லாம் யாண்டுப்போ யொளித்தன ?"

The History of the Tamil language, P. 32, 33, 35, 36.

Being unable to understand that Dharmam, riches and pleasure are the three indispensable necessaries for the well-being of man in this world, the Aryans and the Jains held that Dharmam was necessary but pleasure was not a necessity for human beings; hence they condemned music also as it was a source of pleasure and tried their best to put down Isai Tamil. [The chief of commentators, Natchinarkinyar, also held that drama and music only produced low desires.] Under the above circumstances many works on drama and music disappeared altogether. May God preserve the remnants.

When the learned scholars treated the drama and the music with such contempt, it gradually lost its prestige and is now found under the patronage of low class people and has come down to the streets! We do not know the fate of such excellent works on drama such as 'Bharatam', 'Agathyam', 'Muruval', 'Sayantam', 'Gunanool', 'Seyitiam', 'Muthivanar Nataka Tamil Nool', 'Koottanool' and 'Nool' which were composed by the scholars of those days.

The above extracts show that the Tamil language was affected by other languages only after the advent of the Aryans, Buddhists and Jains. It appears that inasmuch as the 'Peragattyam' of the sage Agastya was very elaborate, the author made an abridged edition of it and called it 'Chittagattyam'. This shows the extensiveness of prose literature at the time. As rules of grammar are framed for the sake of poetic or prose literature, such an elaborate grammar presupposes the existence of elaborate poetry and prose literature As the work of Agastya was very comprehensive, the author of Tolgauppyam confined himself to the rules of Iyal Tamil (orthography and etymology). To Pavanandi Munivar is ascribed 'Nannul' and to Veeramamunivar, 'Thonnul'. Further abridged grammars were also written, like 'Veerasoliyam', 'Ilakkana Vilakkam', 'Ilakkanam' by Rev. G. U. Pope. 'Ilakkana Churukkam', 'Ilakkana Vilakka Chooravali', 'Ilakkana Choodamani' and 'Muttu Veeriam'. All these speak invariably of Iyal Tamil. When we note that rules of grammar have been made only for a few varieties of poems out of 700 mentioned in Peragattyam we have reason to suppose that the ancient works on music, on musical instruments and dancing had a similar fate and gradually declined. To add to this, those inhabitants of Southern India who were not indigenous to the soil, in trying to do it good, became, in reality, its enemies. Thus at the time of the last Sangam most of the works on music became defunct owing to these adventitious foreigners.

We noted above that the author of Tolgauppyam concerned himself only with the first of the three parts of the language. Those that came after him abridged it still further. At the time of Agasthya (as we read from his Sootrams), Music, Dancing and the attendant gaieties were largely cultivated in the Tamil country. The following is the Sootram of the author of Tolgauppyam where he speaks about the four kinds of soil, (Mullai, Kurinji, Marudam and Neydal) and their respective productions :—

"தெய்வ முணவே மாமரம் புட்பறை
செய்தி யாழின் பகுதியொடு தொகைஇ
யவ்வகை பிறவுங் கருவென மொழிப."

Here the author enumerates the particular deity, the grains, animals, trees, birds, drums, the different kinds of labour and the various kinds of musical instruments pertaining to different soils. We read about this more clearly in the commentary of Natchinarkiniar. Where the author of Tolgauppyam annotates upon his work he distinctly mentions that poets should bear in mind the respective headman and woman of the soil in describing the deity, the grains and productions of it.

நால்வகை நிலத்தின் கருப்பொருள் விபரம்.

"முல்லைக்கு உணா, வரகுஞ்சாமையும் முதிரையும்; மா, உழையும் புல்வாயும் முயலும்; மரம், கொன்றையுங்குருந்தும்; புள், கானக்கோழியுஞ் சேவலும்; பறை, ஏறுகோட்பறை; செய்தி, நிரைமேய்த்தலும்

வரகு முதலியன களை கட்டலுங் கடாவிடுதலும்; யாழ், முல்லையாழ், பிறவு மென்றதனுற், பூ, முல்லையும் பிடவுந் தளவுந் தோன்றியும் ; நீர், கான்யாறு ; ஊர், பாடியுஞ் சேரியும் பள்ளியும்.

குறிஞ்சிக்கு உணு, ஐவன நெல்லுந் தினையும் மூங்கிலரிசியும் ; மா, புலியும் யானையுங் கரடியும் பன்றியும் ; மரம், அகிலும் ஆரமுந் தேக்குந் திமிசும் வேங்கையும் ; புள், கிளியும் மயிலும் ; பறை, முருகியமுந் தொண்டகப் பறையும் ; செய்தி, தேன் அழித்தலுங் கிழங்கு அகழ்தலுந் தினை முதலியன விளைத்தலுங் கிளி கடிதலும் ; யாழ், குறிஞ்சியாழ் ; பிறவுமென்றதனுற், பூ, காந்தளும் வேங்கையுஞ் சுனைக்குவளையும் ; நீர், அருவியுஞ் சுனையும் ; ஊர், சிறுகுடியுங் குறிச்சியும்.

மருதத்திற்கு உணு, செந்நெல்லும் வெண்ணெல்லும் ; மா, எருமையும் நீர்நாயும் ; மரம், வஞ்சியுங் காஞ்சியும் மருதமும் ; புள், தாராவும் நீர்க்கோழியும் ; பறை, மணமுழவும், நெல்லரிகிணையும் ; செய்தி, நடுதலுங் களை கட்டலும் அரிதலுங் கடாவிடுதலும் ; யாழ், மருத யாழ். பிறவுமென்றதனுற், பூ, தாமரையுங் கழுநீரும் ; நீர், யாற்றுநீரும் மனைக்கிணறும் பொய்கையும் ; ஊர், ஊர்களென்பனவேயாம்.

நெய்தற்கு உணு, மீன் விலையும் உப்பு விலையும் ; மா, உமண்பகடுபோல்வன ; முதலையுஞ் சுறவும் மீனுதலின் மாவென்றல் மரபன்று. மரம், புன்னையும் ஞாழலுங் கண்டலும் ; புள், அன்னமும் அன்றிலும் முதலியன ; பறை, மீன் கோட்பறை ; செய்தி, மீன்படுத்தலும் உப்புவிளைத்தலும் அவை விற்றலும் ; யாழ், நெய்தல் யாழ். பிறவு மென்றதனுற், பூ, கைதையும் நெய்தலும் ; நீர், மனைக்கிணறும் உவர்க்குழியும் ; ஊர், பட்டினமும் பாக்கமும்.

பாலைக்கு உணு, ஆறலைத்தனவுஞ் சூறைகொண்டனவும் ; மா, வலியழிந்த யானையும் புலியுஞ் செந்நாயும் ; மரம், வற்றின இருப்பையும் ஓமையும் உழிஞையும் ஞெமையும் ; புள் கழுகும் பருந்தும் புறவும் ; பறை, சூறை கோட்பறையும் நிரைகோட்பறையும் ; செய்தி, ஆறலைத்தலுஞ் சூறைகோடலும் ; யாழ், பாலையாழ் ; பிறவுமென்றதனுற், பூ, மராவுங் குராவும் பாதிரியும் ; நீர் அறுநீர்க்கூவலுஞ் சுனையும் ; ஊர், பறந்தலை."

The particular adjuncts for the four different soils.

For Mullai. The *grains* are, ragi, millet and pulses ; the *animals* are the deer, the hart and the bear ; the *trees*, the trichilia and Cassia; the *birds*, wild fowl and partridge; the *drum*, Erukoteparai ; the *work*, the grazing of cattle, storing up grains and breeding sheep ; the *yal*, Mullayal ; the *flower*, the different species of the Jasmine and the lily ; the *water*, wild stream ; and the *village*, Padi, chari and Palli.

For Kurinji. The *grains* are, the five kinds of cereal grains, the millet and the rice of the bamboo ; the *animals*, the tiger, the elephant, the bear and the boar ; the *trees*, the eaglewood, the sandalwood, the teak and the kino tree ; the *birds*, the parrot and the peacock ; the *drum*, the mountain drums ; the *work*, procuring honey and roots, cultivating millet and other grains, and scaring away parrots ; the *yal*, the mountain yal ; the *flowers*, the November flower, the flower of the Kino tree and the water-lily ; the *water*, from the hill ; the *village*, Sirukudi and Kuritchi.

For Marutham. The *grains* are, paddy of the red and the white kind ; the *animals*, the buffalo and the beaver ; the *trees*, the winding plant, Kanji and the Vanji ; the *birds*, the duck and the water-fowl ; the *drum*, the kettle drum and the drum played while binding the sheaves of corn ; the *work*, planting, removing the tares and sheep-breeding ; the *yal*, peculiar to the Marutha nilam ; the *flowers*, the lotus and the red water-lily ; the *water*, river, well, and tank water ; the *villages* all oors.

For Neydal. The *eatables* are fish and salt ; the *animals*, like the bullock of burden (the crocodile and the shark cannot be classified under animals as they are fish) ; *trees*, punnai, the Kongu and the Kandal ; the *birds*, the swan and the nightingale of India ; the *drum*, the drum of maritime districts ; the *work*, fishing and manufacturing and selling salt ; the *yal*, Neythal yal ; the *flowers*, the flower of the wild pine and the Neydal (*water flower*) ; the *water*, from wells sunk in sand in salt pans ; the *villages*, pattinam and paukam.

For Palai. The *means of livelihood* are highway robbery and pillaging ; the *animals*, the powerless elephant, the tiger and the red dog ; the *trees*, the *Ilupai* with hardly any sap in it, the mango and the cotton shrub; the *birds*, the vulture, the kite and the dove; the *drums*, those used in plundering ; the *work*, highway robbery and plunder ; the *yal*, Palaiyal ; the *flowers*, that of the Kadambu tree, the kuravu and the trumpet flower ; the *water* from the wells which contain excellent water, and from mountain rills.

We learn from the above that even during the time of the author of Tolgaup-pyam, *i. e.*, 8,000 years ago, mention has been made of different kinds of Yal and the rules for the playing of such instruments. How swarams were marked in these instruments will be noted later on.

21. The ancient works on Music.

Where Adiyarkunallar speaks about Isai Tamil in the preface to Silappadhika-ram, he deplores the extinction of works on Music and Musical instruments, and quotes a few works that helped him in his annotation. He says :—

"இனி இசைத்தமிழ்நூலாகிய பெருநாரை பெருங்குருகும் பிறவும் தேவவிருடி நாரதன் செய்த பஞ்சபாரதீய முதலாயுள்ள தொன்னூல்களுமிறந்தன. நாடகத் தமிழ்நூலாகிய பரதம் அகத்தியமுதலாயுள்ள தொன்னூல்களுமிறந்தன. பின்னும் முறுவல், சயந்தம், குணநூல், செயிற்றிய மென்பனவற்றுள்ளும் ஒருசாரார் சூத்திரங்கள் நடக்கின்ற அத்துணையல்லது முதல்கடைநிகழ்ச்சி காணாமையின் அவையும் இறந்தனபோலும். இறந்தவேவரும் பெருங்கலமுதலிய பிறவுமாம். இவற்றுட் பெருங்கலமாவது பேரியாழ்; அது கோட்டினளவு பன்னிருசாணும் வணரளவு சாணும், பத்தரளவு பன்னிருசாணும், இப்பெற்றிக்கேற்ற ஆணிகளும், திவவும், உந்தியும்பெற்று ஆயிரங்கோல் தொடுத்தியல்வது; என்னை? ஆயிர நரம்பிற் றாகியாழாகு, மேனை யுறுப்பொப்பன கொளலே, பத்தர தளவுங் கோட்டின தளவு, மொத்த வென்ப விருமூன் றிரட்டி, வணர்சா ணொழித்தென வைத்தனர் புலவர்" என்றாருள்ளும் "தலமுத லூழியிற் றானவர் தருக்கறப், புலமக ளாளர் புரிநரப் பாயிரம், வலிபெறத் தொடுத்த வாக்கமை பேரியாழ்ச், செலவுமுறை யெல்லாஞ் செல்லையித் தெரிந்து, மற்றை யாழுங் கற்றுமுறை பிழையான்" எனக் கதையினுள்ளுங் கூறினாராகலாற் பேரியாழ் முதலியனவும் இறந்தனவெனக்கொள்க.

இனித் தேவவிருடியாகிய குறுமுனிபாற்கேட்ட மாணாக்கர் பன்னிருவருட் சிகண்டியென்னும் அருந்தவமுனி, இடைச்சங்கத்து அநாகுலனென்னுந் தெய்வப்பாண்டியன் தேரொடு விசும்புசெல்வோன் திலோத்தமையென்னுந் தெய்வமகளைக்கண்டு தேரிற்கூடினவிடத்துச் சனித்தானைத்தேவரும் முனிவரும் சபித்தலிற் றோன்றினமையிற் சாரகுமாரனென அப்பெயர்பெற்ற குமரன் இசையறிதற்குச்செய்த இசை நுணுக்கமும், பாரசைவமுனிவரில் யாமளேந்திரர் செய்த இந்திரகாளியமும், அறிவனார்செய்த பஞ்சமரபும், ஆதிவாயிலார்செய்த பரதசேனாபதீயமும் கடைச்சங்கமிரீஇய பாண்டியருட் கவியரங்கேறிய பாண்டியன்மதி வாணனார்செய்த முதநூல்களினுள்ள வசைக்கூத்திற்கு மறுதலையாகிய புகழ்க்கூத்தியன்ற மதிவாணர் நாடகத் தமிழ்நூலு மெனவைந்தும் இந்நாடகக் காப்பியக்கருத்தறிந்த நூல்களன்றேனும் ஒருபுடை யொப்புமைகொண்டு முடித்தலைக்கருதிற்று இவ்வுரையெனக் கொள்க."

The preface to Silappadhikaram.

The Perunarei, the Perungurugu and other works treating on Isai Tamil, as well as Panchabharateeam written by the sage Narada and other ancient productions, have become extinct. Again, it is presumed, that works like 'Muruval', 'Sayantham', 'Gunanool' and 'Seyttyam' are also dead inasmuch as only a few sootrams from them are in use and the beginning, middle and end of these works are not easily discernible. Some of the famous instruments of the ancient days are also extinct such as the Perunkalam. The Perunkalam is the Periyal. Its length was 12 spans and it was constructed with nails, frets and belly proportionately large and big and it had 1,000 strings. This fact is supported by literature as well as history. But such instruments have all perished.

The five works mentioned below, namely *Isai Nunukkam*, composed by the sage Sikhandi (one of the twelve disciples of the great Muni) for the benefit of Sarakumara born to the Pandyan King Anakulam and the celestial beauty Tilottamai, the *Indrakalyam* ascribed to Yamalendirar, the *Panchamarabu* of Ariwanar, the *Bharatasenapateeyam* of Audi vayilar, and the *Mathivanar Nataka Tamil Nool* written by the Pandya King Mathivanar of the last Sangam as a set off to his vasakoottu—these five works, although they have scarcely grasped the meaning of the drama, we have included them here along with the others.

We see from the above that 'Panchabharatheeyam', 'Bharatam' and 'Agattyam as well as the instrument 'Periyal' (in the first Ooli) ascribed to the sage Narada, became defunct; the works 'Muruval', 'Sayantham', 'Gunanool', 'Seyttyam' and others of the period of the middle Sangam were nearly dead; but that works like 'Isai nunukkam' written during the period of the middle Sangam were helpful to Adiyarkunallar in writing his annotation. Even the latest works he mentions are in an incomplete state now.

We shall do well, therefore, to examine a few of the works on music that existed at the time of Adiyarkunallar, as they may throw some light on the antiquity of South Indian Music.

"அகத்தியம்—இஃது இயல் இசை நாடகமென்னும் முத்தமிழிலக்கணத்தையும் தெரிவிப்பதாகிய ஒரு பெரிய இலக்கண நூல்; தென்மதுரைக்கணிருந்த தலைச்சங்கப் புலவர்களுள் முதல்வராகிய அகத்திய முனிவரா லருளிச் செய்யப்பட்டது. இது நச்சினார்க்கினியர் காலத்திலேயே இறந்து போயிற்றென்று தெரிகிறது. ஆயினும் இதிலுள்ள சில சூத்திரங்கள்மட்டும் பழையவுரைகளில் ஆங்காங்கு காணப்படுகின்றன.

இசை நுணுக்கம்—இதுசாரகுமாரன் அல்லது சயந்தகுமாரனென்பவன் இசையறிதற்பொருட்டு, அகத்தியமுனிவர் மாணாக்கர் பன்னிருவருள் ஒருவராகிய சிகண்டியென்னும் அருந்தவமுனிவரால் வெண்பாவாலி யற்றப்பட்ட இசைத் தமிழ் நூல்; இஃது இடைச்சங்கமிருந்த காலத்துச் செய்யப்பட்டதென்று அடியார்க்கு நல்லாருரையாலும், அச்சங்கப்புலவர்க்கு நூலாகவிருந்ததென்று இறையனாரகப்பொருளுரையாலும் தெரிகிறது.

இந்திரகாளியம்—இது யாமளேந்திரரென்னும் ஆசிரியரால் செய்யப்பட்ட இசைத்தமிழ்நூல்; அடியார்க்கு நல்லார் உரையெழுதுவதற்கு மேற்கோளாகக்கொண்ட நூல்களுளொன்று.

குணநூல்—இது நாடகத்தமிழ் நூல்களுளொன்று. இதிலுள்ள சில சூத்திரங்கள்மட்டுமே நடைபெறுகின்றனவென்றும் நூல் இறந்துபோயிற்றென்றும் அடியார்க்கு நல்லார் எழுதியிருக்கின்றனர்.

கூத்தநூல்—இது நாடகத்தமிழ்நூல். இதன் வரலாறு வேறொன்றுந் தெரியவில்லை.

சயந்தம்—இது நாடகத்தமிழ் நூல்களுளொன்று. இதிலுள்ள சூத்திரங்களிற் சில நடைபெறுகின்றனவன்றி நூலின் முதனடுவிறுதி காணாமையின் இந்நூல் இறந்ததுபோலுமென்று அடியார்க்கு நல்லார் எழுதியிருக்கின்றனர்.

செயிற்றியம்—இது செயிற்றியனாரென்னும் ஆசிரியரால் சூத்திரரூபமாக இயற்றப்பட்ட நாடகத் தமிழ்நூல். இதின் சூத்திரங்களிற் சில நடைபெறுகின்றனவன்றி நூலின் முதனடுவிறுதி காணாமையின் இறந்தது போலுமென்று அடியார்க்கு நல்லார் எழுதியிருக்கின்றனர்.

தாளவகையோத்து—இது தாளவிலக்கணத்தைக் கூறு நூல்களுள் ஒன்று ; இதன் வரலாறு வேறொன்றுந் தெரியவில்லை.

நூல்—இது நாடகத்தமிழ் நூலுளொன்றன் பெயரென்று மட்டுந்தெரிகிறது. இதன் வரலாறு வேறு யாதொன்றுந் தெரியவில்லை.

பஞ்சபாரதீயம்—இது தேவவிருடி நாரதன் செய்த இசைத்தமிழ்நூல்; தம்முடைய காலத்திலேயே இந்நூலிறந்துபோயிற்றென்று அடியார்க்கு நல்லார் எழுதியிருக்கின்றனர்.

பஞ்சமரபு—இஃது அறிவனாரென்னும் ஆசிரியராற் செய்யப்பட்ட இசைத்தமிழ் நூல். சிலப்பதிகாரவுரை எழுதுவதற்கு அடியார்க்கு நல்லார் மேற்கோளாகக்கொண்ட நூல்களுளொன்று.

பரதசேனாபதீயம்—இஃது ஆதிவாயிலாரென்னும் ஆசிரியரால் வெண்பாவாற் செய்யப்பட்ட நாடகத்தமிழ்நூல்; சிலப்பதிகாரவுரை எழுதுவதற்கு அடியார்க்கு நல்லார் மேற்கோளாகக்கொண்ட நூல்களுளொன்று.

பரதம்—இது நாடகத்தமிழ் நூலுளொன்று ; இதனை இறந்துபோன நூல்களுள் ஒன்றாக அடியார்க்கு நல்லார் எழுதியிருக்கின்றனர்.

பெருங்குருகு—இது தலைச்சங்கப்புலவரியற்றிய இசைத்தமிழ் நூல்களுளொன்று; இந்நூல் தமது காலத்தேதானே இறந்து போயிற்றென்று அடியார்க்கு நல்லார் எழுதியிருக்கின்றனர். இது முதுகுருகென்றும் சொல்லப்படும்.

பெருநாரை—இது தலைச்சங்கப்புலவரியற்றிய இசைத்தமிழ் நூல்களுளொன்று; அடியார்க்கு நல்லார் காலத்தேதானே இஃது இறந்துபோயிற்றென்று தெரிகிறது.

மதிவாணர் நாடகத் தமிழ்நூல்—இது சூத்திரப்பாவாலும் வெண்பாவாலும் மதிவாணனாரென்னும் பாண்டியரொருவராற் செய்யப்பட்ட நாடகத்தமிழ்நூல்; அடியார்க்கு நல்லார் உரை எழுதுவதற்கு மேற்கோளாகக்கொண்ட நூல்களுளொன்று.

முறுவல்—இது பழைய நாடகத்தமிழ் நூல்களுளொன்று ; இந்நூல் அக்காலத்தே இறந்துபோயிற்றென்று அடியார்க்கு நல்லார் எழுதியிருக்கின்றனர்."

Agattyam.—This is an elaborate work on grammar which treats of Iyal, Isai and Natakam, whose author is Agattya Muni, the leading scholar of the Tamil Sangam in South Madura. This seems to have become defunct even during the time of Natchinarkiniar. But some of the Sootrams appear in old commentaries.

Isainunukkam.—This is a work on Isai Tamil composed in the form of Venbas by Sikandi muni, one of the twelve disciples of Agattya, for teaching music to Sarakumara or Sayantakumara. From what we gather from the annotation of Adyarkunallar and Irayanarahapporul it seems to have been a standard work of the Second Sangam.

Indirakalyani.—This is a work on Isai Tamil written by Yamalendr which helped Adyarkunallar in his annotation.

Gunanool.—A work on Nataka Tamil. Adyarkunallar says that only a sootrams of it are in use whereas the work is extinct.

Kootanool.—This is a work on Nataka Tamil of which no particulars are known.

Sayantam.—This is also a work on Natakam. Adyarkunallar says that the work must be considered to have become extinct as only a few sootrams are now in use while the major portion of the beginning, the middle and the end are unknown.

Seyttyam.—This is a work on Natakam written in the shape of Sootrams by Seyttyanar. This is also considered defunct by Adyarkunallar as only a few Sootrams remain.

Talavahaiyottu.—One of the works which speak about the gram r of Thalam. Particulars are not known.

Nool.—Another work on Natakam of which no particulars are forthcoming.

Panchabharateeam.--Isai Tamil Nool of Narada the divine sage. It was dead even during the time of Adyarkunallar.

Panchamarabu.—Isai Tamil Nool by Ariwanar, which served as an authority for the annotation on Silappadhikaram.

Bharatasenapateeam.—A work on Natakam in the form of venbas writtien by Audivayilar, which helped Adiyarkunallar in his annotation on Silappadhikaram.

Bharatam.—A work or Natakam which is now defunct according to Adyarkunallar.

Perungurugu.—One of the Isai Tamil works of the first Sangam, now extinct according to Adyarkunallar. It is also known as Mudugurugu.

Perunarei.—An Isai Tamil work of the First Sangam. It was extinct even during the time of Adyarkunallar.

Mathivanar Nataka Tamil Nool.—A Nataka work written by Mathivanar in the form of Sootrams and Venbas, one of the works which helped Adyarkunallar in his commentary.

Muruval.—An extinct work on Natakam as Adyarkunallar says.

We may not be wrong in inferring from the above that during the period of the first Sangam (i.e. before the deluge) literature on music, as well as highly efficient musical instruments, were known; that during the period of the middle Sangam some of them were destroyed and a few remained; that during the last Sangam even the few that remained became defunct and only a few Sootrams remained which had been learnt by rote and handed down by tradition. Even the works which Adiyarkunallar quoted from, have perished. Only a few Sootrams have been preserved owing to the disinterested efforts of Mahamahopadhyaya V. Saminatha Iyer, who collected and printed 'Silappadhikaram.' It is a matter for regret that works on South Indian Music have thus perished for want of supporters. In spite of this, a few Ragas, Bharatam and Talam which had been learnt by rote have been happily preserved for us. These have been kept up and preserved as precious mainly by the gifts from various temples to the instrumental musicians, singers and dancers attached to them. But the absence of books for obtaining first hand knowledge of the rules of music has resulted in the destruction of the ancient purity of Indian Music and the very Srutis are doubted. Yet the Hindus and the foreigners who have made a deep study of it testify to the advanced state of its efficiency, its scientific merit and its purity and independence. The ancient civilisation of India, the godliness of its inhabitants, the music of their religious worship and their language are highly worthy of praise.

22. The wealth and civilisation of the Tamil country.

Hitherto we concerned ourselves about the antiquity of the Tamil country, its culture, the numerical abundancy of the scholars of the Sangams and the excellence of its literature. We next proceed to note its wealth and civilisation.

We may infer that the Pandyans were a cultured race who ruled over a fertile country from the Ramayana of ancient date where Sugreeva describes to the Vánaras in glowing terms the residence of Seeta. The sage Valmiki says that Sugreevan describes to the Vanaras going southward how they will recognise at sight the city gate of the Pandyas which is imbedded with gold, pearls and precious stones and which is built in continuation with the walls of the fort. Here he describes at length the magnificent city gates of the Pandya kings. It is to be noted that while speaking about the beauty and wealth of a city he is in raptures with its gates. So he leaves us to draw our own inference as to the wealth and grandeur of the city. The very fact, that the first thing that might catch their eye, he says, will be a gate, enables us to have an idea about the height and breadth of the ponderous gate. We know that the age was famous for animals and living beings of an abnormal size. It was also the custom to have high and broad gates so that there might be room enough for huge elephants to pass under, carrying the sovereign seated in a howdah inlaid with precious stones with the attendants to hold the umbrella over him. As the gates were of gold, the reflection of its brightness enabled people to see them from afar. Again, when Ravana's fort was seized by Sri Rama, he was struck with surprise when he saw the priceless and magnificent emeralds that had been used for flooring the bathroom of Ravana. We infer from this that the wealth and grandeur of the city of Ravana was equal to that of the cities of the South Pandya Kingdom. Lankah should be considered not the only province over which Ravana ruled, but one of the many, and the seat of his government must have been somewhere far south in the Indian Ocean.

It is again said that Oodiyan Cheralatham, the Chera King, helped the armies of the Pancha Pandavas with victuals as long as the war lasted.

We read again that Ravana, the ten-headed giant, ruled long over an extensive kingdom which had the Vindhya range as its northern boundary, and that his lieutenants Kharan and Dushanan fought against Rama with their 14,000 chariots of bronze, as Sisera came against the Israelites with his 900 chariots of iron. Ravana also possessed high literary merit and was specially an expert in Music. It is said that when he attempted to uproot the Kailasa hill, Paramasivam very nearly crushed him under the hill with the might of his toe; that he then played on the Veena and sang the praises of Sivan by chanting the Sama Vedam and thus obtained divine favour. It appears that the Rig Vedam of his time was chanted with the four Oodatta and Anudatta Swarams, Ri and Dha and Ga and Ni and that later on Sama Vedam was chanted with the additional three Swarita swarams, Sa, Ma and Pa. Sama Vedam possesses in full the Sampoorana sapta swarams with which Ravana, for the first time, praised the deity. The fact that he was the first to introduce the three new swarams melted the heart of the deity in his favour. His ganam resembles that of South India with its perfect modes.

It is manifest from some of the Sootrams of Agastya that music, dancing and such rare arts flourished in this country long anterior to the time of 'Agattiyam' which treated about Iyal, Isai and Natakam. Again, the fact that the Holy Bible speaks about musicians skilful in playing the Kinnair and the Nagaswaram during the ante-diluvian period, authorises us to say that music was extensively in use in South Madura and its 49 provinces. It is difficult to come across such tremendous gates of brass as were found in Babylon and Nineveh. Such gates were in hundreds in those cities, but now not even one is to be seen like them. There must have been many such gates inlaid with gold and precious stones, in South Madura. There is reason also to think that the fortress of Ravana, and its grandeur must have been equally great.

We read in the Puranas that (when the Pandavas were living a retired life in the forest,) Arjuna, who had married Subhadra, the sister of Sri Krishna, the ruler of Dwaraka, came to Madura (known as Manavur), and that he married Chitrangada, the daughter of Chitravahana Pandiyan and remained at his court for three years. Further, we read that Arjuna taught the art of Bharatam to the women in the palace of Viratapuram in the Matchya Desa, and that the Kings of the Chera, Chola and Pandya countries were present at the marriage of his son Abhimanyu. The strong ties of friendship that existed among the kings of that period, their culture, and there enthusiasm for music and the art of dancing were so great that they are incomprehensible to us. We do not need a better instance for this than that of Kusan and Lavan, sons of Sri Rama, who distinguished themselves in the art of making Kathas from Ramayana, in the presence of royalty, being trained by the sage Valmiki. Again, we read in the Holy Bible that when Daniel, the devoted servant of God, (during the reign of Darius in Babylon) was cast into the den of lions, the King being filled with grief for his act, could not eat but kept awake the whole night and would not allow any musical instruments to be played before him. This, along with the custom of having music in royal palaces morning and evening at the present day, warrants us to suppose that the same custom, which was in vogue 2,500 years ago must have prevailed in ancient South Madura also. Apart from their excellence in culture and music, the ancients, (as we read in the chapters describing the city and village in 'Silappadhikaram' of Ilankovadigal) were noted for their enormous wealth as reflected by their large emporiums, grain stores, different kinds of cloth of cotton, silk, wool and lace, different kinds of spices like eaglewood, sandalwood, camphor and the like, and different kinds of precious stones like diamonds, rubies, pearls and coral.

23. The excellence of South Indian architecture.

We shall be surprised at the architectural skill of our ancestors. We may find at the present day in the temples at Madura, Avudayarkoil, Tenkasi, Mahabalipuram, Tiruchendoor, Srirangam, Chidambaram, Vellore, Conjeevaram, Tanjore and other places remarkable specimens of architecture which reflect great skill on the workmen, such as verandahs built with rafters and joists of granite stone, capitals of pillars worked like folded rolls, huge images carved out of a single granite stone, highly polished images cut out of black granite, life-like petals of flowers made of chunam, bows and bow-strings carved out of granite and chains of granite. Again, Emperor Krishnadevarayalu, who ruled over Vijayanagaram (Bellary) 500 years ago began building on a tremendous scale the entrance gopurams to the big temples at Madura and Srirangam. Many might have seen the exquisite beauty of the work which is wholly on granite and the huge granite door-frames. The proverb, "like the foundation of Rayalu's gopuram", is in use even at the present day. The work which he commenced has been so elaborate that it is left incomplete because no one could continue it and it excites the wonder of the beholder.

24. The deities of the Tamil Country—their scholarship in Tamil.

Nakkeeranar, the annotator on 'Irayanarahapporul' says that the first Sangam existed long before the deluge, and that Agastya as well as Siva, (the deity with matted locks of hair, who burnt Tripurams) and Skanda (Subramanya, who cleft the mountain with his lance) were presidents thereof. This warrants us to say that Paramasivam himself ruled over South Madura and that he and his son Subramanya patronised the Tamil language and were presidents of the Sangam.

The following facts show that the Tamil language was one best loved by Paramasivam :—

It is said that during the period of the last Sangam, when Champaka Pandyan Vangisha Choodamani was ruling over North Madura, Paramasivan composed a poem on the subject that was uppermost in the mind of the ruler and gave it to one Dharmi who was thus enabled to carry away the prize of the 1,000 pieces of gold promised by the sovereign. Again, many scholars praise Paramasivam in their poems in the following terms.

"தமிழ் அறியும் பெருமானே
தன்னைச் சேர்ந்தார் நன்னிதியே
திருவாலவாய் என்னும் மதுரைக்கரசனே"

Again,—"பாட்டுக்குருகுந்தமிழ்ச்சொக்க நாதர்"

again—"தெய்வத்தமிழ்க் கூடல்"

and again.—"சங்கம் பொரக்கும் பண் முத்தமிழ்க்கோர்
பயனே சவுந்தர பாண்டியனே."

It is said, again, that Sundara Pandya (who married Thatathaka), and his son Oogra Pandya, who ruled over North Madura, were considered incarnations of Siva and Subramanya respectively.

Again, the Pandya Kings are all known by the names of Tamil nadan, Thennavan, Tamilar koman, Koodar koman, Kadamba vana nadhan, Madhu rasan, Pandivalanadhan, and scholars have used these flattering epithets for Siva and Subramanya and the Pandyan Kings descended from them. We see then that Siva and Subramanya and the Pandyan Kings, who descended from them, were rulers over South Madura, Korkaei and North Madura and were great patrons of the three divisions of Tamil—Iyal, Isai and Natakam. People built temples for the more celebrated of these Kings and deified them. All those who descended from these Kings were traditional worshippers of Siva and his son Subramanya, who were the first Presidents of the first Sangam. We might see a number of temples dedicated to Siva and Vigneswara in South India and the islands of Sumatra and Java. Such temples are rare in Northern India and other parts.

We read in the Sthalapurana of North Madura, named "Tiruvalavoy" and in "Tiruvilayadal Purana" that the Kings who ruled at North Madura for 130 generations were the descendants of Somasundara Pandya, (another name for Siva.) We read also about Music, Bharatam and Talam in the Viragu-vitra Padalam, or Yal vasitta Padalam, Isaivathuventra Padalam and Kal-mari-yadiya Padalam of the same Purana.

25. How we may determine the ancient history of India from the period of the three Tamil Sangams.

My noble readers, the age of ancient India is not reckoned merely by numbers as 2 years or 3 years, but more minutely, as in the period of such and such Manu, in a particular Yuga, in a particular 'Parivrutti' (120 years), in a certain year (as Bhava or Yuva) and in such and such a Rasi-month. It is customary to say that a man was born, say in the year Bahudhanya, in the Kataka-ravi. But as the particular Bahudhanya year is not mentioned (there are so many of them, one for every sixty years), or the particular Parivrutti or Ayilya Tiruvila or the Yuga it is very difficult to say what the age of the man is. Again, in some of the Indian Royal families, the names of ancestors are constantly repeated in the succeeding generations just to show how the names of the progenitors are revered. But it throws considerable difficulty in the way of reckoning the age of any particular king.

Again the authors of Puranas and Itihasas of old, being ignorant of the worth of historical age, have given the number of years according to their own fancy. Presuming that a human year was 365 days, and a divine year 360 of those 365 days, they say that a king ruled for 10,000 or 40,000 or 60,000 of the divine years! They say again that many rishis lived for a number of Oolis and many chathur-yugas. Hence the hopelessness of the ancient history of India as regards age. Histories abound in such improbabilities. To add to this, the scholars, who wrote on principles of morality and equity, never cared to enlighten the reader, from beginning to end, on their country, name or age. Readers of Kural, Attichoudi, Kondreiventhan, Moothurai, Nanneri, Nalvali and other similar works will testify to this. There was, again, no registry of new books in those early days. Even if they did register them, such a fact was mentioned either in the first or the last page which were surely destined to be destroyed by moth within a short time! Such destruction would naturally cause difficulty in computing the age. Again, a wrong idea has entered into the minds of people that it was a glorious thing to pass off works of recent date as works of great antiquity, and to assign the names of ancient authors for works written by them. But this is mostly confined to works made up of trumped up stories like the Puranas and does not apply to works on justice and morality and the accurate sciences. For example, we are aware how Sthalapuranas spring up every day. The author borrows the services of a Vyasa to relate the story, a Soothapuranika to relate it to Janamajaya, and a Narada to inspire the author, another Vyasa. In course of time all their works will become converted into Vedas and Puranas written by Vyasa. The names Soothapuranika, Narada and Vyasa, though they appear different, the author of the Puranas is one and the same. Though we are cognisant of the real authors of these Sthalapuranas and their historical worth, we believe them to be genuine because the names of the above mentioned sages, and those of a few of the deities, occur there. This blind belief is peculiar to India. It is unsafe to determine the age of the history of India by these Puranas alone.

It is impossible to gauge the authenticity of the history of thousands of years except through ancient records that are available. The age of the three Sangams appears to be genuine, and so, later histories might well be calculated from that period. As south Madura was destroyed along with its 49 provinces, we have no other authentic records to fall back upon.

What the historians say about Lemuria, the natural features of the countries that adjoined it, the antiquity of the Tamil language and the admixture of Tamil words in many foreign languages, appears to be true. Time may yet reveal facts of greater authenticity. We concur with the scholars who declare that Tamil was the language of ancient Lemuria, and that it was prior to every other language. The great land portion in the South of Indian Ocean which extended as far as the Kerkulan Isles must have been the original habitation of the Tamilians before the first Ooli, and the seat of the first Tamil Sangam for 4,400 years It is said that there was the peak Kumari, surrounded by hills, in the south of this continent, and that the river Pahtruli which takes its rise from these hills, was artificially dug by Vadimbalambaninda Pandya. This may be analogous to the case of the river Vygai whose course was diverted to the east, though it would naturally empty itself into the Arabian Sea taking its rise from the Western Ghats. This river Pahtruli must have been a great and broad river. This river, as well as the Kumari must have taken their rise from the Kumari hills which could be compared to the Himalayas in height and grandeur. When this hill and the river were destroyed, the Kumari river, the northern boundary of the continent, must also have disappeared. Although we have no records to understand the antiquity of this period, yet we may be sure that Mudathirumaran, the last of the Pandyas, who came to Kapatapuram after the deluge, as well as the Presidents of the first Sangam, like Agasttya and the author of Tolgauppyam, must have given the members of the Second Sangam an idea of the glory and grandeur of the first. For the 4,440 years of the Sangams, presided over by 4,449 eminent literary men, would not have been so definitely stated. As there was another deluge 3,700 years after, the incidents of the first deluge are but casually stated. However, there is no reason to doubt the truth of the incidents as they were traditionally handed down and considered to be real facts. It is a known fact that the third Sangam came to an end nearly 1,800 years ago, yet no mention is made of the existence of a Sangam. After the demise of the last Sangam in the 2nd century A. D. the Tamil country has been ruled by the Pandya Kings for nearly 1,000 years i.e., till 1200 A. D. After the Pandya kings, a Muhammadan ruler named Athi Sultan reigned for 50 years, and after him kings of the Naik dynasy such as Visvanatha Naik and Tirumalai Naik; and these were followed by Murari Rao, Appaji Rao, Chanda Saheb, Khan Saheb and a few minor kings, who fought with each other often and ruled for very short periods. There was no peace in the country till Madura and its nighbouring provinces came under the benign British government in 1801 A. D. The demise of the Sangam is due to the times when everybody's life and property were so insecure. The language also suffered at the same time owing to the predominance of works written in alien tongues and the introduction of foreign words.

26. How the fourth Tamil Sangam at Madura came into existence during the reign of Her Gracious Majesty Queen-Empress Victoria.

The benign British government brought India into a state of tranquillity and security by putting down internecine war, preventing foreign invasion, removing turbulent rulers, and introducing such facilities as Telegraphs, Postal service, good roads and railways, water works, Hospitals, Schools, Colleges and Universities, Courts of Justice and the like. Her Gracious Majesty Queen-Empress Victoria who has graciously ruled over India, and looked upon her subjects as her own children became Empress in 1858 and ruled the British Empire peacefully for 64 years. The disappearance of civil wars, the subjugation of many cruel acts, and the formation of many an association for bringing people together as brethren of the same community, all these were the results of the benign government. So an association was formed of members who had an exalted idea of the antiquity of Tamil and its eminent literature, for the purpose of making researches into, and collecting and printing, ancient Tamil works. So in the year 1901—the 64th year of the reign of Her Majesty who was the first Empress—the fourth Tamil Sangam was organised.

How can we disbelieve the first three Sangams and their grandeur when we know for certain that the fourth Tamil Sangam sprang up in the 5,002nd year of the Kaliyuga, *i. e.* 1,800 years after the demise of the third, and has been going for the last 13 years with 251 members on its rolls where researches into the language are being made! This Sangam was organised chiefly by the efforts of the Zemindar of Palaivanattam and Sriman Pandidorai Thevar. It might well have been named Palaivanattam Tamil Sangam or Pandidorai Tamil Sangam. But the fact that it has been named Madura Tamil Sangam shows the continuity of it with the first three Sangams.

We shall do well to notice here the origin of the Sangam, the first presidents, the patrons, the active workers and members of the same so that it may convince those who are ignorant of the particulars of the first three Sangams.

THE FOURTH MADURA TAMIL SANGAM

INSTITUTED BY

SRIMAN P. PANDI THORAI THEVAR.

On May 24th, 1901.

The following were its Presidents for the last 13 years.

1. Sriman Pandi Thorai Thevar, Avl.
2. „ S. Saminatha Vijaya Thevar, Avl.
3. „ P. S. Subramania Iyer, Avl.
4. Rajarajesvara Mutturamalinga Setupati, Avl.
5. Sriman Rao Bahadur M. Arumugam Pillai, Avl.
6. „ Honourable K. Rama Iyengar, Avl.

7. Honourable P. Ramanathan, Avl.
8. M.R.Ry. Maha mahopadhyaya V. O. Saminatha Iyer, Avl.

The following gentlemen are the patrons of the Sangam :—

1. Palavanattam Zemindar Śriman P. Pandi Thorai Thevar Avl., (Founder).
2. His Highness Bhaskara Sethupati Avl.
3. „ Rajarajeswara Mutturamalinga Setupati Avl.
4. „ The Maharajah of Pudukota, Avl.
5. „ The Maharajah of Travancore, Avl.
6. „ The Maharajah Gaikwar of Baroda, Avl.
7. „ The Maharajah of Mysore, Avl.
8. „ The Maharajah of Darbhanga, Avl.
9. „ The Maharajah of Cochin, Avl.
10. „ The Rajah of Ettiyapuram, Avl.
11. Sriman Pettatchi Chettiar Avl., Andipatti Zemindar.
12. Sriman V. T. S. Savuha Pandya Thevar Avl., Setur Zemindar.
13. Sriman A. L. A. R. Arunachallam Chettiar.
14. Sriman Ramachandra Thevar, Avl.
15. Sriman Subramania Teerthapati, Zemindar of Singampatti.
16. „ Raja M. Dinakara Bahadur, Avl.
17. „ R. M. C. Vyravan Chettiyar, Avl., Devikottah.
18. „ M. L. M. Ramanathan Chettiar, Avl., „
19. „ M. R. N. Ramanathan Chettiar, Avl., „
20. „ R. A. A. R. Arunachalam Chettiar, Avl., „
21. „ A. A. S. Somasundram Chettiar, Avl., „
22. „ M. A. A. Arunachalam Chettiar, Avl., „
23. „ M. V. Alagappa Chettiar, Avl., „
24. „ V. L. R. L. Petthaperumal Chettiar, Avl., Devikottah.

The following are active Members of the Sangam who are responsible for its efficient working —

1. His Highness Sriman Rajarajesvara Setupati, (President.)
2. M.R.Ry. S. R. M. M. T. T. Pettatchi Chettiar, Avl., (Vice-President).
3. „ Maha mahopadhyaya V. O. Saminatha Iyer, Avl.
4. „ V. Gopalasami Raghunatha Rajaliar Avl.
5. „ Dakshanamoorti Durai Raja, Avl., B.A., B.L.
6. „ Nallasami Pillai, Avl., B.A., B.L.
7. „ Ct. A. V. Somasundram Pillai Avl., B.A., B.L.
8. „ T. A. Ramalingam Chettiar Avl., B.A., B.L.
9. „ R. Raghava Iyengar, Avl.
10. „ Rao Sahib M. Abraham Pandithar, Avl.
11. „ V. S. Ramasami Shastrial, Avl.
12. „ Khan Bahadur H. Abdul Subhan Sahib, Avl.
13. „ S. Gopalasami Iyengar, Avl., B.A.
14. „ T. N. Sundararaja Iyengar, Avl., B.A., B.L. } Secretaries.
15. „ T. C. Srinivasa Iyengar, Avl., B.A., B.L., } Secretaries.

The following is a list of members who have made original compositions and researches in the Tamil literature and have obtained the sanction of the Sangam from time to time.—

1. M.R.Ry. V. O. Saminatha Iyer, Avl., Maha Mahopadhyaya, Presidency College, Madras.
2. „ R. Raghava Iyengar, Avl., Samasthana Vidwan, Ramnad.
3. „ T. Narayana Iyengar, Editor of Sen-Tamil, Madura.
4. „ Sri Arangasami Iyengar, Avl., Head Master, Tamil Sangam College, Madura.
5. „ Setur R. Subramania Kavirayar, Vidwan, Tiruvaduthurai Mutt.
6. „ A. Shanmugam Pillai, Avl., Tamil Vidwan, Sholavandan.
7. „ Ambalavana Navalar, Avl., Tamil Vidwan, Tinnevelly.
8. „ Poovai Ashta-avadhanam Kalyanasundara Mudaliyar, Avl., Tamil Vidwan, Madras.
9. „ A. Narayanasami Iyer Avl., Head Tamil Pandit, Town High School, Kumbakonam.
10. „ T. P. Sivarama Pillai Avl., Head Tamil Pandit, Hindu College, Tinnevelly.
11. „ A. Muttuthambi Pillai, Avl., Tamil Vidwan, Navalaikotam, Jaffna.
12. „ A. Kumarasami Pillai, Avl., Tamil Vidwan, Sunnagam, Jaffna.
13. „ Kaviraj Nallayappa Pillai, Avl., Tamil Vidwan, Tinnevelly.
14. „ R. Appu Iyengar, Avl, Tamil Pandit, Hindu High School, Srivilliputtur.
15. „ P. A. Muttu tandavaraya Pillai, Avl., Tamil Vidwan, Tranquebar.
16. „ P. S. Devasikhamani Iyer, Avl., Tamil Pandit, Raja's High School, Sivaganga.
17. „ M. R Kandasami Kavirayar, Avl., Editor, Vidyabhanu, Madura.
18. „ M. R. Arunachala Kavirayar, Avl., Tamil Vidwan, Vivekabhanu Office, Madura.
19. „ Kanji Nagalinga Mudaliar Avl., Tamil Vidwan, Madras.
20. „ M. S. Subramania Kavirayar, Avl., Tamil Pandit, Hindu College, Tinnevelly.
21. „ K. Sreenivasachariar, Avl., Head Tamil Pandit, Hindu College, Mysore.
22. „ T. Kylasam Pillai, Avl., Head-master, Saivaprakasa Vidyasala, Jaffna.
23. „ V. SadasivaChettiar, Avl., Tamil Pandit, S. P. G. College, Trichinopoly.
24. „ V. Kuppusami Raju, Avl., Vidwan, Govindan & Brothers, Tanjore.
25. „ N. Swami Vedachalam, Avl., Madras.
26. „ K. Gopalachariar, Avl., Head Tamil Pandit, Christian College, Madras.
27. „ T. S. Subramania Pillai, Avl., Tirugnanasambandha Matalaya Sabha, Tuticorin.
28. „ P. M. Muttaiya Pillai, Avl., Tuticorin.
29. „ Swami Rudra Koteesvarar, Dharma Lodge, Poottan Sandai, Travancore.
30. „ C. Rangasami Naicker, Avl., George Town, Madras.
31. „ V. Gopalasami Regunatha Rajaliar, Avl., Haridwara Mangalam, Tanjore District.
32. „ M. Sambasiva Nayanar, Avl., Tamil Vidwan, Saliyamangalam, Tanjore Dt.
33. „ G. Sathasivam Pillai, Avl., Editor, "Neelalochini", Negapatam.
34. „ Nalla Kuttalam Pillai, Avl., Tamil Pandit, Setupati High School, Madura.
35. „ C. S. Chokkalingam Pillai, Avl., Tamil Pandit, Coimbatore.
36. „ R. M. Palanivelu Pillai, Avl., Iron Merchant, East Gate, Tanjore.
37. „ M. V. Ramanujachariar, Avl, Tamil Pandit, College, Kumbakonam.
38. „ M. Palanisami Goundar, Avl., Kumaralingam, Palni Taluq.
39. „ S. M. Syed Mahamed Alim Pulavar, Avl., Keelakarai.
40. „ S. Radhakrishna Iyer, Avl., B.A., F.M.U., Pudukotah.
41. „ G. Subramania Iyer, Avl., Editor, "Swadesha Mitran", Madras.
42. „ T. Ramakrishna Pillai, Avl., B.A., High Court, Madras.
43. „ K. Sundararamier, Avl., M.A., Lecturer, Kumbakonam.

44. M.R.Ry. J. M. Nallasami Pillai, Avl., B.A., B.L., Member, Tamil Sangam Committee, Madura.
45. „ K. G. Sesha Iyer, Avl., B.A., B.L., High Court, Vakil, Trivandrum.
46. „ B. S. Subramania Iyer, Avl., B.A., Revenue Board Office, Madras.
47. „ S. V. Kallapiran Pillai, Avl., B.A., Special Deputy Collector, Trichinopoly.
48. „ Pagadal S. P. Narasimhalu Naidu, Avl., Editor, "The Crescent", Coimbatore.
49. „ S. Saminatha Iyer, Avl., Sannadhi Street, Ramnad.
50. „ S. Paulvanna Mudaliar, Avl., Secretary, S. V. Sabha, Tinnevelly.
51. „ M. S. Pooranalingam Pillay, Avl., B.A., Bridge, Tinnevelly.
52. „ T. C. Sreenivasa Iyengar, Avl., B.A., B.L., Honorary Secretary, Tamil Sangam.
53. „ I. Saminatha Mudaliar, Avl., Supervisor of Primary Schools, Tanjore.
54. „ V. P. Subramania Mudaliar, Avl., G. B. V. C., Dy.-Supt., Civil Veterinary, Madras.
55. „ V. Muttukumarasami Mudaliar Avl., B.A., Inspector, Rangoon.
56. „ Chit-Kylasam Pillai, Avl., Secretariat, Colombo.
57. „ Karkulam Kuppusami Mudaliar, Avl., B.A., Government Secretariat, Madras.
58. „ S. Krishnasami Iyengar, Avl., M. A., M. R. A. S., Bangalore City.
59. „ T. Kanakasundram Pillai, Avl., B.A., 315, Mint Street, Madras.
60. „ P. Vencatasami Mudaliar, Huzur Sheristadar, Tinnevelly.
61. „ V. J. Thambi Pillai, Avl., M. R. A. S., Wellavetti, Colombo.
62. „ T. A. Ramalinga Chettiar, Avl., B.A., B.L., Coimbatore.
63. „ N. V. Sundara Raja Iyer, Avl., B.A., First Grade Pleader, Ramnad.
64. „ K. Devanadhachariar, Avl., Tamil Pandit, Maharaja's College, Mysore.
65. „ T. Lakshmana Pillai, Avl., B.A., Huzur Office, Trivandrum.
66. „ K. V. Subba Iyer Avl., Head-Master, T. H. School, Madras.
67. „ M. R. Sreenivasa Iyengar, Avl., Tamil Vidvan, Pudukotah.
68. „ M. K. M. Andul Kadir Rowther, Avl., Hakhdhar, Sothukudi.
69. M. Julien Vinsen Esq., Professor al ' Ecolede Langues Orientals, 58, rue' del Universite, Paris.
70. „ M. N. Sesha Iyer, Avl., Teacher, Sethupati High School, Madura.
71. „ Peruhavaluthan Rangachariar, Avl., Maha Mahopadhyaya, Kumbakonam.
72. „ T. E. Srinivasachariar, Avl., Sanskrit Pandit, College, Kumbakonam.
73. „ V. Srinivasachariar, Avl., Sanskrit Vidwan, Ramnad.
74. „ Veerasami Iyengar, Avl., Samasthana Viyakarana Vidwan, Ettiyapuram.
75. „ Chandrasekhara Sastrial, Avl., Maha Mahopadhyaya, Sanskrit Pandit, Madras.
76. „ R. Krishnamachariar, Avl., M.A., Inspector of Sanskrit Schools.
77. „ L. K. Thulasi Ram, Avl., B.A., B.L., Vakil, Madura.
78. „ Dakshanamurti Dorai Rajah, Avl., B.A., B.L., High Court Vakil, Madura.
79. „ Sundaralingaswami Kamaya Naicker, Avl., Madura.
80. Khan Bahadur H. Abdul Subhan Sahib, Avl., Retired Asst. Police Supt., Madura.
81. „ K. Annamalai Pillai, Avl., Tamil Pandit, Ammanur, Tiruturaipoondi.
82. „ K. P. Seygutambi Palar, Avl., Sandi Street, Kotar.
83. „ S. Kalyana Goundar, Avl., Servampatti Zemindar, Trichengode.
84. „ M. Kadiresa Chettiar, Avl., Mahipalanpatti, Ramnad.
85. „ N. Somasundaram Pillai, Avl., Police S. H. O. Tirumakotai, Tanjore Dt.
86. „ J. V. Subramania Iyer, Avl., B.A., Manager, P.W.D., Bellary.
87. „ T. A. Muttusami Konar, Avl., Secretary, Saiva Samaj, Trichengode.
88. „ M. P. Mascarenhas, Esq., Coral Mills Co., (Ltd.), Tuticorin.
89. „ T. A. Gopinatha Row, Avl., M. A., Archeological Supdt. Trivandrum.
90. „ Nellaiappa Pillai, Avl., B.A., Sub-Magistrate, Oodumalpet.

91. M.R.Ry. Mutturathna Mudaliar, Avl., Tiruvarur.
92. „ M. V. Minakshisundra Mudaliar, Avl., First-Grade Pleader, Coimbatore.
93. „ P Ramanatha Mudaliar, Avl., Chintadripet, Madras.
94. „ Y.,S. Taylor Bodhakar, East Gate, Madura.
95. „ T. N. Tangavelu Mudaliar, Avl., Assistant Auditor, Madras.
96. „ Bava Vydilinga Mudaliar, Avl., Mirasidar, Tiruvarur.
97. „ Rao Bahadur K. S. Sreenivasa Pillai, Avl., Pleader, Tanjore.
98. „ Ramasubba Mudaliar, Avl., Mirasidar, Alttambadi, Tiruturaipoondi.
99. „ Sri la Sri Anantha Shanmuga Saranalaya Swamigal, Tillaivilagam, Tanjore Dt.
100. „ S. V. M. Swaminatha Pillai, Avl., Merchant, Velipalayam, Negapatam.
101. „ P. Samson Esq., Advocate, Mynchien, Burma.
102. „ A. Sundaranatha Pillai, Avl., Tamil Pandit, S.P.G. College, Trichinopoly.
103. „ Kumarasami Mudaliar, Avl., Big House, Kunnur, Srivilliputtoor.
104. „ M. Mariappa Pillai Avl., Mirasidar, Karuvappanaickanpettah, Trichinopoly.
105. O. S. P. S. E. Pakeer Mytheen Rowther, Madura.
106. „ S. Krishnasami Senaiya Nadar, Avl., Mirasidar, Palliyur.
107. „ A. Chithambara Mudaliar, Avl., Police Inspector, Oottaranmerur, Chingleput.
108. „ S. Krishnasami Iyer, Avl., Tamil Pandit, College, Trivandrum.
109. „ V. M. Thangayya Naicker, Avl., Mirasidar, Valatamangalam, Tanjore Dt.
110. „ S. Govindasami Pillai Avl., Manager, S. S. School Avalivanallur, Tanjore Dt.
111. „ S. Krishnasami Thevar Avl., Mirasidar, Avalivanallur, Haridwaramangalam, Tanjore Dt.
112. „ A. M. Satagoparamanujachariar, Avl., Tamil Pandit, N. H. School, Trichy.
113. „ Ramasami Vannyar Avl., Mirasidar, Pulavarnattam, Tanjore Dt.
114. „ Pampya Sethurayar, Avl., President, Nattamil Sangam, Ilankadu.
115. „ S. Gnanasikhamani Mudaliar, Avl., B.A., Srivaikuntam.
116. „ K. R. Venkatarama Iyer, Avl., B.A., B.L., High Court Vakil, Madura.
117. „ M. Panchanatham Pillai, Avl., East Main Street, Trivadi.
118. „ M. Vencatasami Nattar, Avl., Head Tamil Pandit, S. P. G. College, Trichinopoly.
119. „ V. R. Pakkirisami Pillai Avl., Negapatam.
120. „ Ramasami Pillai, Avl., Teacher, Pudukotah.
121. „ T. N. Sundara Raja Iyengar, Avl., B.A., B.L., Honry Secretary, Tamil Sangam, Madura.
122. „ Rao Saheb M. Abraham Pandither, Avl., Karunanithi Medical Hall, Tanjore.
123. „ Muttu Vijaya Ragunadha Muttukumara Vanangamudi Valuvadi Devar, Avl., Zemindar, Tanjore.
124. „ R. Saminatha Vijaya Thevar, Avl., Zemindar of Papanad, Tanjore.
125. „ T. Bhaktavatchalam, Avl., B.A., Vepery, Madras.
126. „ C. V. Krishnasami Iyer, Avl., District Munsiff, Tiruvarur, Tanjore Dt.
127. „ P. S. Ramalinga Vijaya Thevar, Avl., Younger Zemindar of Papanad, Tanjore.
128. „ P. Kumarasami Pillai Avl., B.A., Head Clerk, Munsiff Court, Madura.
129. „ L. Gopalasami Iyengar Avl., B.A., Vakil and Auditor, Tamil Sangam.
130. „ Hon. S. Rm. M. Ramasami Chettiar, Avl., Municipal Chairman, Chidambaram.
131. „ N. A. V. Somasundaram Pillai, Avl., B.A., B.L., Bridge, Tinnevelly.
132. „ Oobhayavedagama Pandither of Yalpanattunallur, Singapore.
133. „ S. Somasundaram Pillai Avl., High Court Vakil, Madras.
134. „ Rajamannarsami Nadalvar Avl., Seeralur, Tanjore Dt.
135. „ Venkatachala Regunatha Rajaliar Avl., Mirasidar, Tanjore.

136. M.R.Ry. V. Appasami Vandayar Avl, Landlord, Poondi, Tanjore.
137. „ K. Sadasiva Chettiar Avl., Mint Street, Madras.
138. „ Mosur Munisami Mudaliar Avl., 175, Mint Street, George Town, Madras.
139. „ K. P. Arunachala Mudaliar Avl., Mirasidar, Kotivinayakanallur, Tiruturaipoondi.
140. „ Valmeekalingam Pillai Avl., Mirasidar, Menali, Tiruturaipoondi.
141. „ M. Gopalakrishna Iyer Avl., Tamil Pandit, College, Madura.
142. „ S. D. Krishna Iyengar Avl., B.A., B.L., High Court Vakil, Madura.
143. „ M. S. Sesha Iyengar Avl., B.A., First Grade Pleader, Madura.
144. „ A. Gopalamuttusami Naidu Avl., Teacher, Govt. School, Pahoor.
145. „ V. Sundaram Iyer Avl., B.A., B.L., High Court Vakil, Madura.
146. „ V. S. Lakshminarayana Iyer, Avl., B.A., B.L., High Court Vakil, Madura.
147. „ K. Venkoba Row Avl., Thanappa Mudaliar Agraharam, Madura.
148. „ C. Natesa Iyer Avl., B.A., B.L., High Court Vakil, Madura.
149. „ C. Srinivasa Rao Saheb Avl., B.A., B.L., High Court Vakil, Madura.
150. „ C. S. Venkatachariar Avl., High Court Vakil, Madras.
151. „ T. Ramasami Iyengar, Avl., B.A., B.L., Vakil, Madura.
152. „ P. N. Naganatha Iyer Avl., B.A., Vakil, Madura.
153. „ M. Mathuvier Avl., B.A., B.L., High Court Vakil, Madura.
154. „ C. Srinivasa Iyer Avl., B.A., B.L., High Court Vakil, Madura.
155. „ A. Rangasami Iyer Avl., Government Pleader, Ramnad.
156. „ V. R. Satagopa Iyengar Avl., B.A., B.L., Vakil, Madura.
157. „ G. Somayaji Iyer Avl., B.A., B.L., High Court Vakil, Madura.
158. „ V. Ramachandra Iyer, Avl., B.A., B.L., Govt. Pleader, Madura.
159. „ S. Ramasami Iyengar Avl., B.A., B.L., Vakil, Madura.
160. „ G. A. Sundaram Iyer Avl., B.A., B.L., Vakil, Madura.
161. „ S. Harihara Iyer Avl., Vakil, Madura.
162. „ Honourable K. Rama Iyengar Avl., B.A., B.L., High Court Vakil, Madura.
163. „ M. R. N. Ramanathan Chettiar Avl., Devakotah.
164. „ N. Natesa Iyer Avl., B.A., B.L., Vakil, Madura.
165. „ Janakaraja Thevar Avl., Madura.
166. „ S. Bhupalam Pillai Avl., Chief Clerk, P. W. D. Batticaloa, Ceylon.
167. „ A. Oograpandiam Pillai Avl., Vakil, Ramnad.
168. „ Namperumal Iyengar Avl., Muhavoor, Tiruparchethi Post, Ramnad Dt.
169. „ Karai M. Sabharatna Iyer Avl., Tamil Pandit, Jaffna.
170. „ V. S. Ramasami Sastrigal, B.A., B.L., Vakil, Madura.
171. „ S. A. Subramania Iyer, Avl., Headmaster, Madura College.
172. „ S. Rm. M. Ct. Pettatchi Chettiar, Avl., M. R. A. S., (Vice-President, Tamil Sangam, Madura) Kanadukathan.
173. „ G. Ramasami Iyengar, Avl., Landlord, Madura.
174. „ M. Raghava Iyengar, Avl., Tamil Pandit, Tamil Lexicon Office, Madura.
175. „ Subramania Pillai, Avl., Peishkar, Tirupparchethi Post.
176. „ P. Subbaraya Iyer, Avl., Vakil, Madura.
177. „ A. Sundaram Iyer, Avl., Vakil, Madura.
178. „ K. Gopala Iyengar, Avl., Pleader, Paramakudi.
179. „ M. Nagalingam Pillai, Avl., Pleader, Ramnad.
180. „ M. C. Anaiappa Mudaliar, Avl., Tamil Pandit, Namakal.
181. „ C. M. Raju Chettiar, Avl., M. B. P. G. Madras.

182. M.R.Ry. Muthu K. M. Natesan Chettiar, Avl., Devakota.
183. „ P. K. Ramasami Iyengar, Avl., High Court Vakil, Madura.
184. „ S. Vedantam Iyengar, Avl., Pleader, Paramakudi.
185. „ T. V. Kothandarama Iyer, Avl., Pleader, Paramakudi.
186. „ A. S. Subbiar, Avl., Pleader, Paramakudi.
187. „ A. L. V. R. Rm. Chithambaram Chettiar, Avl., Devakota.
188. „ S. Nagalingan Pillai, Avl., Pleader, Paramakudi.
189. „ T. V. Ramasami Iyengar, Avl., Pleader, Paramakudi.
190. „ S. Gangadharam Iyer, Avl., Ramnad.
191. „ B. B. Subbarama Iyer, Avl., Tamil Pandit, Madura.
192. „ N. R. Subramania Sarma, Avl., Tamil Pandit, A. M. P. High School, Pasumalai.
193. „ M. Govindasami Iyer, Avl., Tamil Pandit, Madura.
194. „ T. R. Sreenivasa Iyengar, Avl., Vakil, Madura.
195. „ A. R. Narayana Iyer, Avl., Pleader, Srivilliputoor.
196. „ S. R. Venkatachariar, Avl., Pleader, Srivilliputoor.
197. „ R. K. Nallakuttalam Pillai, Avl., Pleader, Srivilliputoor.
198. „ S. Subbiar, Avl., Pleader, Srivilliputoor.
199. „ D. Sundararaja Iyengar, Avl., Pleader, Madura.
200. „ M. S. Vengusami Iyer, Avl., Pleader, Madura.
201. „ N. S. R. Natchiappa Mudaliar, Avl., Negapatam.
202. „ Rao Bahadur G. Sreenivasa Rao, Avl., First Grade Pleader, Madura.
203. „ T. Ramanuja Iyengar, Avl., Vakil, Ramnad.
204. „ K. V. Ramachariar, Avl., South Masi Street, Madura.
205. „ A. A. A. R. Arunachalam Chettiar, Avl., Karaikudi.
206. „ C. M. Venkatachalapati Iyer, Avl., Municipal Councillor, Madura.
207. „ S. V. A. Nagasami Chettiar, Avl., Ilayangudi.
208. „ S. M. Muthaya Rodrigo, Avl., Shop-keeper, Chilaw, Ceylon.
209. „ R. Satagopachariar, Avl., Manager, Setur.
210. „ T. V. Chithambara Iyer, Avl., Tamil Pandit, Trivandrum.
211. „ R. Krisnamachariar, Avl., Madura.
212. „ K. A. Venketasubramania Iyer, Avl., Pleader, Madura.
213. „ D. S. Rengachariar, Avl., B.A., B.L., High Court Vakil, Sivaganga.
214. „ V. Manikkam Pillai, Avl., Pleader, Madura.
215. „ C. Padmanabha Iyengar, Avl., Pleader, Mylapore.
216. „ M. V. Subramania Iyer, Avl., Pleader, Madura.
217. „ R. S. Narayanasami Iyer, Avl., Vakil, Madura.
218. „ R. R. Krishnamachariar, Avl., Tamil Vidvan, Madura.
219. „ P. K. Subramania Pillai, Avl., Sub-Assistant Surgeon, Madura.
220. „ K. Vadivelu Chettiar, Avl., Editor, "Lokopakari" Madras.
221. „ V. T. Srinivasa Iyengar, Avl., Tamil Pandit, College, Pudukotah.
222. „ A. Kandasami Pillai, Avl., Tamil Pandit, Katuputtur, Trichy.
223. „ C. A. C. Kasinathan Chettiar, Avl., Kothamangalam, Ramnad District.
224. „ A. A. A Annamalai Chettiar, Avl., Money lender, Keelaseevalpatti.
225. „ P. Eswaramoorthia Pillai, Avl., Merchant, Tuticorin.
226. „ A. Varadhananjaya Pillai, Avl., Suramangalam, Salem.
227. „ B. J. M. Kulasekhara Raj, Avl., Prakasapuram, Nazareth (Tinnevelly District.)
228. „ V. Srineevasa Desikachariar, Avl., First Grade Pleader, Madura.

229. M.R.Ry. V. R. Venketarama Iyer, Avl., Thambipatti, Watrap.
230. „ V. Rengachariar, Avl., 40, Tank Square, Triplicane.
231. „ Pandit S. Sivanandam Pillai, Avl., Native Doctor, Madras.
232. „ V. Muthusami Iyer, Avl., M. A., L. T., Inspector of Schools, Arpukkota.
233. „ P. Chithambarapunnai Vananathan, Avl., Tamil Pandit, Hindu College, Tinnevelly.
234. „ K. M. Muthukrishna Pillai Avl., Landholder, Kalakadu, Tinnevelly District.
235. „ Rao Bahadur S. Bhavanandam Pillai, Avl., F. R. H. S., M. R. A. S., Assistant Commissioner of Police, Madras.
236. „ T. S. Subramania Iyer, Avl., B. A., B. L., First Grade Pleader, Madura.
237. „ R. Rengachariar, Avl., B. A., B. L., First Assisant, Madanapalle.
238. „ R. Ganapathi Iyer, Avl., B. A., B. L., High Court Vakil, Madura.
239. „ Nagesvara Iyer, Avl. Journalist, Madura.
240. „ M. Rangasami Iyer, Avl., B.A.,B.L., Vakil, Ramnad.
241. „ S. P. Nagasami Iyer, Avl., Pleader, Ramnad.
242. „ S. Sreenimuragam Pillai Avl., Vakil, Tripatur, Ramnad.
243. „ Dewan Bahadur L. D. Swami Kannu Pillai, Avl., M. A., B. L., L.L.B., Registrar of Co-operative Societies, Madras.
244. „ M. V. Visvanatha Pillai, Avl., Tamil Pandit, G. T., Madras.
245. „ W. Narayana Iyer, Avl., Sheristadar, District Court, Chittoor.
246. „ D. Gopalacharlu, Avl., Vaidyaratna Pandit, Principal, Ayurvedic College, Madras.
247. „ The Honourable Rao Bahadur P. Kesava Pillai, Avl., Pleader, Gooty.
248. „ V. M. Ratnesvara Iyer, Avl., Tamil Pandit, S. M. S. Karakudi.
249. „ T. V. Oomamahesvaram Pillai, Avl., B. A., B. L., Vakil, Tanjore.
250. „ P. Sambanda Mudaliar, Avl., B.A., B.L., High Court Vakil, Madras.
251. „ A. G. Pichamuttu Pillai, Avl., B.A., L.T., Hd. Master, St. Peter's High School, Tanjore.

27. Some probable conclusions as regards the age of the three Sangams.

It is now 1914 years since Christ was born and 5,014 years since kaliyugam began. It is said that the third sangam was in existence till 100 A. D. But inasmuch as it existed in North Madura for 1,850 years, we may put down the commencement of the sangam to 3,664 years from now. We have noted already that the kaliyugam began, after the destruction of Dwaraka and that about the same time there was a deluge in the provinces adjoining the Indian Ocean. It appears that Kapatapuram, the seat of the Second Sangam, was then submerged. So the third Sangam must have come into existence about the year 1,350 of the kaliyugam. If one asks where the Pandya Kings of Korkei were, during these 1,350 years, we may say that they came to Manavur, five or six miles east of North Madura, built their palaces there and settled down. While there, they built the city of modern Madura and a small temple there, and transferred the seat of Government also to the new city. Their old capital of Manavur is called old Madura, where ruins of palaces and temples may still be seen. We read in the Puranas that Arjuna was at Manavur where he married the daughter of the Pandya King Chitravahanan. From all these we are enabled to infer that, after the destruction of Kapatapuram by deluge, the Pandya Kings made Manavur the seat of their Government, that Madura was built by them while they were at Manavur and that the Sangam was established by them about the same time. We have also noted that there was a previous deluge before the kaliyuga. This is the deluge where Satyavrata figures. From the fact that there was the Pandya rule as well as a Sangam in Kapatapuram 3,700 years before the commencement of the kaliyugam, we are not wrong in concluding that there was a deluge 8,700 years ago. Again, when it is said that the author of Tolgauppiam, contemporary with Nilandarutiruvil Pandyan ruling at South Madura before this deluge, existed during the period of the Middle Sangam, we may infer that Tolgauppiam must have been written over 8,700 years ago when South Madura was destroyed. Again when it is said that the Sangam existed in South Madura for 4,440 years we may fix the probable date of the First Sangam to be 13,000 years ago. Moreover, a survey of the geneology for a number of generations, the number of Patron-Sovereigns whose literary works were approved and stamped by the authority of the Sangams, the style of the Tamil literature of the period — all these undoubtedly support the accuracy of our conclusions as regards the age of the Sangams. We cannot rely upon the Puranas for determining the age of the Sangams as they are partly mixed with fables, and as their age, according to eminent scholars, is only about 1,000, or 1,500 years. In Madura Tiruvilayadal Puranam, Pandya Kings are credited with 5,000, 8,000, 10,000 and even 15,000 years of rule each! But judging from the life of generations of sovereigns we find on an average they are either 50, 63 or 38 years, in which the interregnum period must also be included.

We are not far wrong in concluding, then, that the Tamil language with its three angams of Iyal, Isai, and Natakam, and consequently Music, flourished even 13,000 years ago.

Noble readers! it may surprise you or perhaps you may even think it absurd to be told that there was a Tamil Sangam 13,000 years ago, and that the Tamil language, with its three angams, was patronised and cultivated by ruling sovereigns, sages and scholars. But as the ancients have left no records, our task of reckoning the age of anything is so very hopeless. Age, even at the modern day, is calculated by the aid of extraneous literature and a few other means. At the present time books are registered, which is a permanent record of age. The ancients on the other hand, merely noted the name of the year as Vahudhanya or Virodhikritu without mentioning to which particular cycle the year belonged. This undoubtedly resulted in last being first and first last.

The dotting of some Tamil letters such as ஏ and ஒ mentioned by the author of Tolgauppiam (which letters are considered to belong to a rude stage) is a testimony to the antiquity of the language.

Again, our readers are not unaware of the opinion of Professor Haeckel as regards the natural evolutionary growth of the earth. He determines from the shape of the conches and cover plates of snails that this earth must have had living beings in it even five millions of years ago. We come across such fossilised plates even now. He establishes the evolution of man from the lower animals by means of skeletons of animals, the structure and primary shape of the embryo and the peculiar development of the teeth and the head.

We shall do well to give his theory as regards the age and primary residence of the first man and the language of the first inhabitants.

28. How man was descended from the monkey.

"The Evolution of Man." by Professor Haeckel. P. 352.

"Hence in the genealogy of the mammals we must derive man immediately from the Catarrhive group, and locate the origin of the human race in the Old World. Only the early root form from which both descended was common to them"

The above extract shows that man was descended from the monkey and that the generative organs of the two species are alike. He says that the first men inhabited the Old World. This Old World is the continent of Lemuria which was submerged in the Indian Ocean. The author determines the limits of this continent and mentions the islands and lands that surrounded it by deriving them from some of the plants and trees that grew there.

We may see from the following extract that man must have descended from the eastern apes.

"The Evolution of Man." by Professor Haeckel. P. 259.

"The other group, to which man belongs, are the Eopitheca or eastern apes; they are found in Asia and Africa, and were formerly in Europe. All the eastern apes agree with man on the features that are chiefly used in Zoological classification to distinguish between the two Simian groups, especially in the dentition."

By Eastern countries he means Asia and Africa. A particular species of ape found in the shores of Asia and Africa must have been the ancestor of man.

"The Evolution of Man." by Professor Haeckel. P. 261.

"The apes of the Old World or all the living or fossil apes of Asia, Africa and Europe, have the same dentition as man."

Here he says that, judging from the dentition of fossilised apes of the Old World man must have belonged to the same species as there is a similarity in the dentition. The survivors of the species are now found in the following places :—

"The Evolution of Man." by Professor Haeckel. P. 257.

"These living survivors are scattered far over the southern part of the Old World. Most of the species live in Madagascar, some in Sunda Islands, others on the mainland of Asia and Africa. Some of these were almost as big as men, such as the diluvial lemurogonon Megaladapis of Madagascar."

We see from the above that the remnants of the species which escaped from the deluge are found in Madagascar and Sunda Islands and in the land portions of Asia and Africa.

29. The period of the first appearance of man.

The following extract throws some light on the period of the origin of the species Man, and the period when he was endowed with speech.

"The Evolution of Man." by Professor Haeckel. P. 203.

"The first appearance of man, or, to be more precise, the development of man from some closely related group of Apes, probably falls in either the Miocene or the Pliocene period, the middle or the last section of the Tertiary period. Others believe that man properly so-called, man endowed with speech was not evolved from the non-speaking ape-man (Pithecan thropus) until the following, the Anthropozoic age. In this fifth and last section of the organic history of the earth we have the full development and dispersion of the various races of men, and so it is called the Anthropozoic as well as the Quarternary period. In the imperfect condition of Palæontological and Ethnographical science we cannot as yet give a confident answer to the question whether the evolution of the human race from some extinct ape or lemur took place at the beginning of this or towards the middle or the end of the Tertiary period. However this much is certain—the development of civilisation falls in the Anthropozoic age, and this is merely an insignificant fraction of the vast period of the whole history of life. When we remember this, it seems ridiculous to restrict the word "history" to the civilised period. If we divide into a hundred equal parts the whole period of history of life, from the spontaneous generation of the first monera to the present day, and if we then represent the relative duration of the five chief sections or ages, as calculated from the average thickness of the strata they contain, as percentages of this, we get something like the following relation :—

(i)	Archeolithic or Archeozoic (Primordial) age		...	53 6
(ii)	Paleolithic or Paleozoic (Primary)	„	...	32 1
(iii)	Mesolithic or Mesozoic (Secondary)	„	...	11 5
(iv)	Cenolithic or Cenozoic (Tertiary)	„	...	2 3
(v)	Anthropolithic or Anthropozoic (Quarternary)		...	0 5
				100 0

In any case, the "Historical period" is an insignificant quantity compared with the vast length of the preceding ages, in which there was no question of human existence on our planet. Even the important Cenozoic or Tertiary period in which the first placentals or higher mammals appear, probably amounts to little over two per cent of the whole organic age."

The author here computes the age of living beings to be 50 millions of years from now. He divides the whole of this period into 100 equal divisions, and takes five of those chief sections. He makes out that the monkey species came into existence in the middle of the fourth period and man later on, and that in the fifth period man was endowed with speech and with the privilege of going about as he liked. This fifth period is reckoned by him to have comprised 2,50,000 years. If man was endowed with speech 2,50,000 years ago, he must have attained some degree of civilisation and culture at least 50,000 years ago, and must have learned writing and civilised arts at least 20,000 years ago.

30. That Lemuria was the cradle of the human race.

We shall be enabled to conclude from the following extract that the first civilised man must have occupied the Old World or the continent of Lemuria and after the destruction of the continent must have become scattered in different countries.

"The Evolution of Man." by Professor Haeckel. P. 264.

"The third, and last, stage of our animal ancestry is the true or speaking man (Homo) who was gradually evolved from the preceding stage by the advance of animal language into articulate human speech. As to the time and place of this real "creation of man" we can only express tentative opinions. It was probably during the Diluvial period in the hotter zone of the Old World either on the mainland in tropical Africa or Asia, or on an earliar continent (Lemuria—now sunk below the waves of the Indian Ocean), which stretched from East Africa (Madagascar, Abyssinia) to East Asia (Sunda Islands, further India). I have given fully in my "History of Creation" the weighty reasons for claiming this descent of man from the anthropoid eastern apes and shown how we may conceive the spread of the various races from this "Paradise" over the whole earth. I have also dealt fully with the relations of the various races and species of men to each other.

The above extract warrants us to say that the man endowed with speech was a development from the ape which has no power of speech, that the language of nan was a development from that of the lower animals, that the man with the power of speech first lived in the tropics, that the land inhabited by him was once submerged, that the submerged continent was Lemuria adjoining the land portions of Africa, Madagascar, Abyssinia, Sunda and India, and that was the "Paradise" of the first man from which the various races spread over the whole earth. We have already noted that South Madura was in the Old World Lemuria, that the Tamil Sangam established there was destroyed by the sea after an existence of 4,400 years, and that the Tamil language spoken there was carried to different countries and was found in many languages. We have also noted that the Tamil language possesses some natural sounds of animals not found in other languages and is a unique and independent language. Perhaps we may doubt whether one language could have possibly been the ancestor of all languages. We shall note below the view of Professor Haeckel on the subject.

"The Evolution of Man." by Professor Haeckel. P. 203.

"All philologists of any competence in their science now agree that all human languages have been gradually evolved from very rudimentary beginnings."

The above extracts prove that the earliest language spoken was in Lemuria inhabited by man who spoke the articulate human language which was a development from animal language, and that the primitive language of the world was the one that was in use in the seven great provinces of that continent.

31. Lemuria, the habitation of the first Man and the place where the first language was spoken.

"The Evolution of Man." By Professor Haeckel. P. 204.

"As we have been convinced from Comparative anatomy and ontogeny, and from paleontology, that all past and living vertebrates descend from a common ancestor, so the comparative study of dead and living Indo-Germanic tongues proves beyond question that they are all modifications of one primitive language. This view of their origin is now accepted by all the chief philologists who have worked in this branch and are unprejudiced."

Just as we derive all living animals from a common ancestor by a comparative study of their physical structure and the vertebral column, so also scholars who have studied the philology of different languages agree that all languages were modifications of one primordial language.

We have already mentioned that when the first inhabitants became scattered in different places their ancient language also gradually got corrupted and was known by different names. Professor Haeckel says we have more definite proofs to show that all languages were derived from one primitive tongue than to establish the evolution of animals from one common ancestor from zoological data.

"The Evolution of Man." by Professor Haeckel. P. 205.

"We find just the same thing in comparing the various dead and living languages that have developed from a common primitive tongue. If we examine our geneological tree of the Indo-Germanic languages in this light, we see at once that all the older or parent tongues, of which we regard the living varieties of the stem as divergent daughter and grand-daughter languages, have been extinct for some time. The Aryo-Romanic and the Slavo-Germanic tongues have completely disappeared; so also the Aryan, the Greco-Roman, the Slavo-Lettic, and the ancient Germanic. Even their daughters and grand-daughters have been lost; all the living Indo-Germanic languages are only related in the sense that they are divergent descendants of common stem forms. Some forms have diverged more, and some less, from the original stem-form.

This easily demonstrable fact illustrates very well the analogous case of the origin of the vertebrate species. Phylogenetic comparative philology here yields a strong support to phylogenetic comparative zoology. But the one can adduce more direct evidence than the other, as the paleontological material of philology the old monuments of the extinct tongue have been preserved much better than the paleontological material of zoology the fossilised bones and imprints of vertebrates."

The above quotation clearly shows that all modern languages were derived from one primitive language, and that language was first spoken in the Old World, *i. e.* Lemuria. Inasmuch as the words of this first language are found mixed in many languages of the present day, it will not be difficult to determine the origin of the animal world and the evolution of man from lower animals. Some of the words of the first language now found in modern languages are more startling proofs to establish our theory than the fossils of animals.

32. The language of Lemuria was Tamil.

We have established by incontestible proofs that the habitation of the first man was Lemuria. Judging from the species of men, apes and other animals and the plant-life found in the regions about South India, it may be clearly seen that Lemuria was the same as the province of Kumari which was once to the south of South India but which was later on destroyed by the sea. The first habitation of man seems to be the South Pandya Kingdom, made up of the 49 fertile provinces between the rivers Pahtruli and Kumari, namely the Seven Tenga, the Seven Madura, the Seven Munpalai, the Seven Pinpalai, the Seven Kundra, the Seven Gunakarai, and the Seven Kurumpanei. This speaking of the 49 provinces warrants us to suppose that the seven great land portions—the land of the Naawel tree, the land of the Peepul tree, the land of the Reed, the land of the Andil bird (the nightingale of India), the land of the Elephant, the land of the cocoanut and the land of the Arecanut palm—correspond to the seven great islands such as Australia, Sumatra and Java, and that each of these was divided into seven provinces. The trees and animals commonly found in South India, such as the naawel, the peepul, the reed, the andil bird, the elephant, the cocoanut and the areca-nut palm, were found in abundance in these seven islands. We do not find them in other places. Ancient literary works declare that the Sapta swarams originated from these seven islands. We have noted already, that, before these 49 provinces were submerged, they were very fertile, possessing all the natural advantages of the soil, and were ruled by Pandya Kings. South Madura was the capital of these provinces. Tamil was the sole language spoken there, now found mixed with many other languages. When most of the eminent literary works in Tamil were destroyed, only a few books remained. Some of the words used in ancient works cannot be understood even now. Many pregnant words went out of use altogether. When all the pregnant ideas and words disappeared, only a few common colloquial words remained, just as remnants of leaves only fall to the share of children in the process of preparing ghee. Judging from the facts that this language was spoken in Lemuria from ancient times, that it became mixed with other languages in course of time, that the sounds of the language had a close resemblance to natural sounds, that the shape of its characters was easy and each letter had the same sound wherever it occurred, we may definitely conclude that Tamil was the first language. But inasmuch as the Tamilians and their eminent literary productions were destroyed when Lemuria and its 49 provinces were submerged, the language was treated with contempt and was looked down upon by others. Only a few productions obtained some prominence during the period of the second Sangam, just like the smell that still sticks to the asafœtida pot after the article is removed. Tolgauppiam and other literary works testify to the fact that medicine, alchemy, yogam, gnanam, astrology, painting, music and the 64 kalais had attained a high state of efficiency in the Tamil country. Eighty-nine Pandya sovereigns, beginning from Kaisina Valuthi up to Kadunkoan, ruled over South Madura, the seat of the First Sangam. Seven of these Pandya Kings obtained the stamp of the Sangam as literary savants. During the time of one of these sovereigns, namely, Sayamakeerthian or Nilandarutiruvil Pandyan the 49 Pandya provinces, whose extent was seven-hundred leagues, were destroyed by the sea.

33.—A Comparison of the views of different writers on the Southern Country, its Language and Government.

It has been already noted that Bishop Caldwell who had spent the greater part of his life in the Tamil Country and who had made thorough researches into the philology of the Tamil language gave instances of Tamil words which had been introduced into the Sanskrit, Hebrew, Anglo-Saxon, Scythian and other tongues. We have also shown how Tamil might well have been the primitive tongue from which all other languages sprang up. The fact that Tamil words are found in many languages proves that either the Tamilians must have spread in other countries or other people must have come into some contact with them. But Professor Haeckel says how Lemuria, the continent to the south of South India was the ancient Old World, and that it was the "Paradise" of the first man. He further says, that in spite of the constant changes which languages are undergoing day by day, the words found in it are the chief means to prove that they have been derived from one primitive language, indicating at the same time the origin of man, the land of his origin and first language spoken by him.

Bishop Caldwell who concludes that Tamil must have been an independent tongue from the fact that its words are found in other languages, and professor Haeckel who concludes that the destroyed continent of Lemuria to the south of South India must have been the " Paradise" of the first man, were scholars who lived within the last 50 years. But Nakkeerar, the commentator on " Irayanarahapporul", and Ilankovadigal, the author of " Silappadhigaram " (which throws light upon the kings, countries and arts of the age,) declare that the 49 provinces between the river Kumari (in the south of South India) and Pahtruli (which was 700 leagues off from the Kumari) were destroyed by the sea. And these authors lived 1,800 years ago. They further say that South Madura was the capital of these provinces, that they were ruled for 4,440 years by 89 hereditary Pandya Kings who patronised the Tamil Sangam. If Bishop Caldwell and Professor Haeckel had been cognisant of the writings of the above two literary men they would have been deeper in their researches about the Tamil country, the language and the Pandya Kingdom.

Considering what these authors say, we find that one speaks about the antiquity and eminence of the Tamil language, and another, about the natural features of the land of Lemuria where this language was in use, while a third speaks about the 49 provinces (having all the features of the Lemurian continent), some villages, mountains, rivers, kings, presidents of Sangams, and the extant literature which were all destroyed by the sea during the reign of the victorious Nilandarutiruvil Pandyan. This author lived 1,800 years ago. But it is said in the preface to the Tolgauppiam that the great work was first presented for approval before Athankotasan in the durbar of Nilandarutiruvil Pandyan, who ruled in South Madura 8,700 years ago. Putting the theories of the various scholars who have made independent researches together we may unhesitatingly conclude that the continent of Lemuria and the ancient Tamil country, namely, the South Pandya Kingdom, were identical. To add to this, we understand by means of ancient literary works and later Puranams that for 13,000 years and as recent as 700 years ago—Pandya Kings had been ruling in South Madura, Kapatapuram and North Madura. These Kings of the Sandor caste have been off and on praised by Tamil Scholars under the appellations of Nadân, Nadan, Pandyan, Tennavan and Tamil nadan. One might enquire what has become of this kingly caste who have been rulers for many thousands of years. Have they disappeared? No. At the close of the third Sangam, owing to some misunderstanding between the ruling Pandya monarch and the presidents of the Sangam, the Sangam became disorganised, researches into the language became rare and the kings themselves lost prestige. Though the Pandya Kings ruled for nearly another thousand years their rule gradually came to an end owing to internal troubles. The Mahammadans, the Naiks and others who succeeded them became the enemies of the Sandors. So in course of time these lost their landed property and became poor. Scholars of the present day, who have had occasion to understand their sterling qualities, such as godliness, loyalty, courage, truthfulness, industry, thrift and forbearance, and who have noticed their tribal and family appellations will not hesitate in concluding that the Tamilians of the Sandor caste who are found in such large numbers in South India are the descendants of the ancient Pandya royal family.

Readers of history know the present despised condition of the Jews who were sovereigns of Judæa ruled by the godly king David and his wise son Solomon receiving tribute from the neighbouring monarchs. Who does not know the American Red Indians, now poor and despised but who were once celebrated kings? The case of the Zulus and Kaffirs of South Africa, who have likewise come to a low condition, is also a parallel. In the same way the descendants of the once mighty Pandya Kings are now found in large numbers in an impoverished state in one corner of their extensive kingdom, namely in the south part of the Deccan, but are now gradually improving their condition.

Just like the Sun, which is at its highest in the Aries, comes to its lowest in the Libra, and once more regains its height in the Aries, and just like the double-headed serpent, whose head becomes its tail, and *vice versa,* this also has happened. It is but the course of nature. Man conforms himself to his condition whether it be high or low. We have heard of kings, who, when driven from their kingdoms by their own subjects, have made the jungle their place of abode and have earned their livelihood by cutting wood, and living upon the fruits of the forest.

Just as the swarams in a ragam by their sancharam in the three octaves according to the rules of Arohanam and Avarohanam (going up and coming down) and Vadi and Samvadi, produce the keenest pleasure to the hearer, God, the creator of the whole universe, seems to enjoy the fun of making people having their "ups and downs" in this world.

With the destruction of the Pandya Kingdom works on music were also destroyed. The remnants of the Pandyas were scattered in different countries. Their Tamil language, though it became an altered one in course of years, yet has not lost its common colloquial words. In the same manner, the music of South India, though it has become corrupt, losing some of its features by local peculiarities, yet the main swarams in use are still found there. Though people hold different opinions as regards the number of Srutis, they are unable to demonstrate what they say by means of an instrument nor are they able to prove how the Srutis ought to be used. But South Indian Music is based upon the 12 main swarams and the minute srutis that come between them. They are ignorant that the rules of this superior Music are found in their own ancient Tamil works. They forget that the harmonious succession of these swarams is the all important consideration in Music. What has been traditionally handed down for generations has been the means of preserving all that is correct in Music.

We shall prove later on, that those who wrote the secrets of Indian Music in the Sanskrit tongue have all erred. They have changed altogether the Tamil Musical terms and the names of ragams and wrote works in Sanskrit so that the Tamil names might be forgotten and ignored. In the meanwhile we shall do well to give the opinions of scholars on Indian Music in general, and on Northern, Hindustani and South Indian Music in particular.

V.—DIFFERENT OPINIONS ON INDIAN MUSIC IN GENERAL.

I.—The generally accepted opinion on Indian Music.

AFTER the destruction of the 49 ancient Pandya provinces now known as Lemuria, all the culture they had attained perished. There was no means of arriving at definite conclusions about this culture by any documentary or oral evidence either by means of writings on palm leaves or inscriptions on brass plates or stones. However, some little light is thrown upon it by remnants of scattered literary Tamil works and by the sayings of some of the scholars of the second and the third Sangams. More trustworthy evidence is obtained by means of music traditionally handed down and by other arts of civilised life, which go to prove that there was a time when South India had attained a high degree of civilisation. But even here there are differences of opinion, yet what is commonly held to be true is enough for our purpose.

It is wonderful how, by means of the Astrological science, it was reckoned that a bright celestial body would appear at the time of the incarnation of Christ, the Paramatma, when Saturn would be in the house of the Pisces (மீனம்) with the auspicious conjunction of Jupiter (குரு) and Moon (சந்திரன்) as well as Moon and Mars (மங்களன்); that a great Avatara Purusha would be born in that part of the earth which corresponded to the belt of this celestial body. Further it was wonderfully reckoned that he would be born at 48¾ naligais, on the 18th of the month of Arpasi in the year Rakshasa, because the chief planet Sun (இலக்கினாதிபதி) was in an ascendant lucky state having lost its malign influence, and Mercury (புதன்) was in the ascendancy as well as Rahu in the Putrasthana. Again the minuteness with which this was reckoned by the eastern sages who travelled from afar to worship Him with their offerings, the accurateness of the astronomical science and their religious devotion reflected in their desire to worship the Avatara Purusha, are all matters of great wonder. [It is presumed that these three sages were the three kings of the Tamil Country]. It is also a matter for surprise that these ancients had distinct names for the minutest fraction as well as for integers up to 36 places. They had an equally high repution in sculpture and music. Who can adequately express their cleverness in manufacture if they could make shawls so delicate that one of 10 feet square could be compressed in the palm of your hand? There were many renowned artists who could divide the husk of a grain of paddy into two equal parts, inscribe in the grain of rice inside the complete figures of Vighnesvarar and Subramania and close it up again as before, and who could make strong destructive traps and images which could annihilate the enemy even at the contact. It is acknowledged by all that many arts and sciences such as manufacture, painting, music, yogam and medicine flourished in India from the ancient times. But inasmuch as the artists were unwilling to disclose the secrets of their art even to their own children, even at their dying moments, they gradually dwindled away. To those who make researches into ancient arts even though they understand some of them, it is, at best, only guess work and not the genuine art. However, we shall note below the opinions of some of the scholars which are the results of their researches into ancient India.

Hindu Music and the Gayan Samaj. Part II, P. 8.

"But upon the testimony of works of great antiquity lying around us (some 4,000 to 8,000 years old), we can safely affirm that Hindu music was developed into a system in very ancient times, in times of which we have no genuine records, in times when all other nations of the world were struggling with the elements for existence, in times when Hindu Rishis were enjoying the fruits of civilization and occupying themselves with the contemplation of the mighty powers of the eternal Brahma."

Here the author says that ancient literature testifies to the existence of Music in India even 8,000 years ago.

We may gather from the following extract that Indians were experts not only in Music but in weaving, dyeing with fast colours and in manufacturing different kinds of musical instruments.

Mill's History of Br. India. Vol. I, P. II.

"Of the exquisite degree of perfection to which the Hindus have carried the productions of the loom, it would be idle to offer any description.

Among the acts of the Hindus, that of printing and dyeing their cloths has been celebrated and the beauty and brilliancy as well as durability of the colours they produce are worthy of particular praise.

Dr. Tennant says, "If we are to judge merely from the number of instruments and the frequency with which they apply them, the Hindus might be regarded as considerable proficients in music."

The following extracts show that the inhabitants of ancient India were civilised long before the advent of the Aryans into India.

Steele's India through the ages. P. I.

"Even if we go so far back as B.C. 2000, the voices of men who have lived and died are still to be heard in the earlier hymns of the Rig-Veda.

"These same hymns incidentally tell us that the Aryan invaders found a people in India civilised enough to have towns and disciplined troops, to have weapons and banners, women whose ornaments were of gold, poisoned arrows whose heads were of some metal that was probably iron."

The above extract tells us that when the Aryans invaded India they found the people of South India civilised enough to have fortified cities, well-disciplined armies, beautiful jewels and cloths and poisoned arrows. We also learn from the Vedas that the Aryans, who emigrated to India in search of new and fertile lands for themselves as well as their cattle, were in the habit of performing yagams and drinking the juice of the Soma plant. And we learn from ancient Tamil literature that many of the ancient Tamilians were not in the habit of killing animal life but were pure vegetarians according to the strict rules of saivism before the advent of the Aryans.

We must not forget also that they are gradually giving up the rules of chanting the hymns in their Vedas and are practising South Indian Music to a large extent.

We may gather from what follows that Music was one of the fine arts that was responsible for the culture of the Indians, that it had become a science even in the time of Panini nearly 2,300 years ago, and that it was introduced into Egypt, Persia, Arabia and Greece from here.

W. W. Hunter's, The Indian Empire. P. 110-112.

INDIAN MUSIC.

"The Indian art of Music (Gandharva veda) was destined to exercise a wider influence. A regular system of notation had been worked out before the age of Panini (350 B. C.), and the seven notes were designated by their initial letters. This notation passed from the Brahmans through the Persians to Arabia and was thence introduced into European music by Guido L' Arezzo at the beginning of the 11th century. Some indeed, suppose that our modern word gamut comes not from the Greek letter gamma, but from the Indian gama (in Prakrit; in Sanskrit, Grama) literally a musical scale."

We might infer from the following that as early as between 2500 and 1400 B.C. (i e., 4,400 years ago), during the so-called Brahman period, the Indian Musical scale was in existence, that more minute researches might point to a still earlier period and that the greater part of the science of Music orginated from India.

Hindu Musical scale and the 22 Srutis by K. B. Deval. P. 1.

"It might be stated here at the outset that the Hindu musical scale dates as far back as the Brahman Period which is calculated, according to modern researches, to extend from 2,500 B.C. to 1,400 B. C. It is possible that further researches might modify this date or might, perhaps carry it still farther back. But we may be certain that our scale dates farther back than the Greek scale which is acknowledged to be the parent of modern European scales. Capt. Day in his 'Music of Southern India'—observes:—The Historian Strabo shows that the Greek influence extended to India, and also that Greek musicians of a certain school attributed the great part of the science of music to India."

We gather from the above that Indian Music originated during the Brahman period, *i.e.*, between 3,000 and 4,000 years ago, that it was in a flourishing state at the age of Panini (B.C. 350) and that it spread in other countries through the Brahmans. He says that further researches, perhaps, might carry the date still farther back. In the Tolgauppiam, where he refers to the products peculiar to the four different kinds of soil, he makes mention of four different kinds of Yal. If we notice the Srutis of the four Yals—Marutham, Kurinji, Neythal and Palai—we find that Music is produced out of them by having the Shadjamam, Madhyamam, Panchamam and Nishadam as the basis notes. The author of Tolgauppiam only made mention of the rules of Music in use before his time. The sages Agastya and Narada have also written at length on the subject. This period is contemporaneous with the existence of the Sangam in South Madura. [We might presume the existence of Music anterior to the Sangam.] Men of understanding will admit that after the destruction of South Madura, the survivors might have developed a few of the swarams in their own country, and that they might have improved their own music with the help of the Music of South India. We shall see later on how Pythagoras, the Greek philosopher copied the swarams used in South

Indian Music by the ratios of $\frac{4}{3}$ and $\frac{3}{2}$. Being ignorant of the minute increase or decrease possible in the case of swarams, a number of doubts have arisen.

It was a custom in India that, while performing a sacrificial rite, two Brahmans played on the Veena while a third chanted the Vedas. Unless this was done, it was considered that the Yagam had no efficacy. This is seen in the following extract.

Hindu Music and the Gayan Samaj. Part I, P. 21.

"The system of instrumental music was in practice in the earliest times of the history of our land and it was held that sacrificial rites (yagams) had no efficacy unless two Brahmans played upon the Vina in concert with a third Brahman singing."

The following shows how Indian Music has the virtue of softening the mind and concentrating it on devotion to God.

Hindu Music and the Gayan Samaj. Part II, P. 30.

"Music is one of the most innocent and elevating indoor amusements. It affords pleasure to all and delights specially those who cultivate and develop a taste for it. It softens and refines the mind and elevates its devotion to the Creator of the Universe. Relying upon the testimony only of works of great antiquity lying around us some 4,000 to 8,000 years old, we can safely affirm that Hindu Music is of very ancient origin, and was developed into a system and science when Hindu Rishis resided and meditated in the primeval forests, and inagurated civilization."

The above extract warrants us to say that music was one of the oldest of sciences in India, that it was practised by sages, that by writing down its rules they developed it into a science, and that it was the root of all civilisation.

Just as Nadam is the first cause of all creation, the nadam or music which proceeds from the heart of man is the cause of his culture and devotion. The omnipresent Being is reflected in the hearts of all living beings. If the heart of a man has in it the image of God (Truth) he is considered as possessing every bliss; on the other hand, one who has no God (Truth) in himself gradually loses all that he has. He who does not possess a good heart has no good words to say, and he has no truth in himself. The courteous words and agreeable sounds of a man redound upon himself (bring courteous words in return.) When a man's life is one round of such agreeable and pleasant sounds he is lifted to the region of the highest bliss. True Nadam is the cause of true bliss. Men of understanding call the first cause, which leads to truth, 'Atmam' and 'Param'. The Anandam or bliss which proceeds from truth, and the geetam which is the result of this Anandam only go to adorn the place from which they spring. In other words it helps to concentrate the mind on the deity who is present in them as truth. The sages who felt in themselves the presence of God performed their penance with the help of music. They lived as bright lights in this world as children of God, being blessed with the virtues of kindliness, self-restraint, patience, obedience and love. But all music which individuals make apart from truth, brings such individuals into endless trouble and makes them liars.

We infer from the following extract that the Vedas were chanted from the time of their first appearance, that they were chanted with the help of only one, two or three swarams at the beginning, and that five, six and seven swarams as well as harmonic swarams were later introductions under the names of Udatta, Anudatta and Swarita swarams.

Hindu Music and the Gayan Samaj. P. 4.

"As has been already observed, our Rishi ancestors, in very early times had been chanting vedic hymns and setting them to music, and mention of this fact in the vedas is frequently made in the Rigveda, as for instance, in such assertions as Archino Gayanti, Ganthino Gayanti and Samino Gayanti. Again, in later times Panini and other acharyas or teachers describe the science, and all this goes to show distinctly that music was cultivated among our ancestors to a large extent, and with great assiduity and taste. The Arka system of music, it is said, was based upon only one note, the Gathika system upon two, and the Samika upon three, and to these was subsequently added another system termed the swarantara (another note) based upon four notes. There was thus vital difference between the system adopted by the Rishis and those adopted by the Acharyas; and Panini, to make up the difference, while regarding in his vyakarana Sutras, the three swaras (Udatta, Anudatta and Swarita), as the main notes, points out in his (Siksha), the connection between the system by three and those by seven notes thus :--

(Udatta) includes (ni and ga)
(Anudatta) includes (ri and dha) and
(Swarita) includes (sa, ma, pa)."

We find here that the Sapta swarams, as well as a few important characteristics, in music were known at the time of Panini, the author of the Sanskrit grammar, and that the Aryans who came from the north used at the beginning only one, two and three swarams as Udatta and Anudatta. But there is evidence to establish that king Ravanesvara of South India chanted the Sama Veda with the Sapta swarams, and that the use of these Sapta swarams as well as their Vikruti swarams in Sama Veda was posterior to the time of Ravanesvara. We have already noted that music was in a highly efficient state even during the time of the author of Tolgauppiam, who flourished during the Second Sangam. This was many thousand years before Panini. The age of Panini was long posterior to the period of Ravana as well as the author of Tolgauppiam, he (Panini) being more or less a contemporary of Ilankovadigal. We must understand that the method of chanting the Sama Veda was given by Ravanesvara long before the time of Panini and that works on Music (Isai) were written by Agastya and Narada long before him.

The following extract proves how musical instruments were made by Ravanesvaran.

History of Music by Hunt. P. 141.

"The family of stringed instruments played with a bow has been a very numerous one. The most ancient *Viol* on record appears to be the ravenstrom (or ravanstron), still played in India by the mendicant monks of Buddha. Tradition says that this primitive instrument was invented by one of the kings of Ceylon, but the date assigned to this monarch is somewhat about five thousand years before Christ. It is said, that the ravenstrom was the precursor of the gondok, or Russian Fiddle, and the Welsh crwth, which has six strings strung across a flat bridge, and was played partly with the bow, and partly by plucking with the fingers."

Reading the above extract one is inclined to think that the Ravanesvaram was more or less like the fiddle made of the cocoanut shell sold in the streets for six pies. But it is absurd to suppose that Ravanan made this instrument, or one slightly bigger than this, which could be played by the bow. He should certainly have made a superior instrument commensurate with his high efficiency in music which was helpful to him in securing the favour of Paramasivam by chanting the Sama Veda with the Sapta swarams which were unknown even to the best Aryan musicians. It is quite absurd to think that he could have been the inventor of the trumpery toy fiddle which Kuravas make out of cocoanut shell and sell for six pies to earn their daily bread ! It is true that small toy-fiddles were made of the shell of the cocoanut which was found in abundance in the islands over which Ravana ruled, and sold to little children and destitute religious mendicants. Perhaps this toy-fiddle might have been known as the Ravanesvaram.

The Rig Veda which contains 10,417 slokas is the most ancient of the Vedas. It comprises within itself the other three Vedas, namely, Yajur, Sama and Atharvana. It is clear that inasmuch as Ravanan was well-versed in the Rig Veda that he selected out of it the particular slokas in praise of Paramasivam and chanted them in the Sapta Swarams according to the rules of the music of South India then in use. As Paramasivam pardoned Ravana having been delighted with his music, he (Paramasivam) is known even at this day as "Sama gana priar" or one who delights in Samaganam.

Ravana, who was conversant with the four Tantras—Sama, Dana, Bheda and Danda, chanted certain portions of the Rig Veda with the help of the Veena and asked pardon of Paramasivam. Samam + Vedam = Sama Vedam. Samam = pacifying. As Ravanan chanted this to pacify the deity, this chanting might have been called Sama Ganam or Sama Vedam.

The chants sung in praise of the deity while Somayagam is performed are called Sama ganam. The word "Somam" means a tree or a plant. Forests full of Soma trees as well as branches of the Soma creeper (plant) are spoken of. It appears that the juice of the plant produces a kind of exhilaration as well as giddiness when taken in.

The following extract shows that people were in the habit of drinking the Soma juice as much as they required after they had cooked and partaken of the food prescribed for a yagam. Then followed the chanting to the moon on behalf of their ancestors who were supposed to be in the land of the moon.

Music of Hindustan by Fox Strangways. P. 249, 250.

"Samaveda. The symbol round which the elaborate ritual of the Samaveda gathers is that sacrifice of which the drinking of the juice of the Soma plant was the central point. The virtues of this juice are recapitulated in the ninth book of the Rig Veda, from which mainly the words for the Saman chants are taken. Soma is translated 'moon-plant'; and the Samaveda is specially connected with the worship of ancestors, whose abode was the moon. Great care was taken not to deviate from the original melody-types and rhythms and the religious efficacy of the hymns was held to depend largely on the right application of directions contained in the Brahmanic explanations (Brahmana not later than the sixth century B. C.) of the Vedic text 'Samhita.' The expense of the full ceremonial was not small; the Soma sacrifice involved days in performance and months in preparation. A full description of its elaborate and gorgeous ritual is to be found in the Aitareyabrahmana of the Rig Veda translated into English by Martin Haug, 1863, and its close connection with the fire-worship of the Zorastrians is there detailed."

It is very likely that the chant addressed to Soman or the moon might have been known as 'Somaganam' or 'Samaganam' or the chanting that followed the drinking of the Soma juice might have been so called. But we must think that the name 'Samaganam' was introduced only after Ravanesvaran praised Paramasivam with his sweet chanting. It is the general belief of the world that the Slokas from Rig Veda after they had been chanted by Ravanesvara became the Sama Veda.

The historical fact contained in the above extracts is not unknown to us. We have also seen the image in the temple at Madura which perpetuates this historical fact. We see there that Ravana is represented as playing a Veena with his twenty hands. Again in the temple at Avadayarkoil near Madura and other Sivite temples, and in the Ravana Vahanam made of silver, the same representation is found. Judging from the pictures of the same found in temples more than two and three thousand years old there is no reason to think that the Ravanesvaram was an instrument played with the bow. It will be more in accordance with the laws of proportion to suppose that Ravanan invented the Periyal, the most ancient of Indian Musical instruments with 1,000 strings (unknown at the present day), and played it with all his twenty hands! We may surely say that even before this time Music was in an efficient state. We read that there were a number of yals, such as Periyal, Sakotayal, Makarayal, Sengotiyal in those days but never a Kinnari made of the cocoanut shell.

We read in the following extract that the habit of singing a melody to the accompaniment of an instrument was a very ancient practice in Indian Music.

H. M. Scale and the 22 Srutis by K. B. Deval. P. 46.

"The essential basis of music is melody and this is contained admittedly in the Hindu scale to its full extent. This has been the main charm of the Hindu system of music for thousands of years in the past and will continue to remain so for a number of years in the future."

Here he says that the singing of melodies is very charming and that in future also it will be considered the main charm of Indian music. The real reason for the excellence of Indian melody is given below..

The Indian Empire by W. W. Hunter. P. 111.

"It is, indeed, impossible to adequately represent the Indian system by the European notation; and the full range of its effects can only be rendered by Indian instruments a vast collection of sound-producers, slowly elaborated during 2,000 years to suit the special requirements of Hindu music. The complicated structure of its musical modes (Rags) rests upon three separate systems, one of which consists of five, another of six, and the other of seven notes. It preserves in a living state some of the early forms which puzzle the student of Greek music, side by side with the most complicated developments."

Judging from the above it is seen that the author is one who has understood the science of Indian music in detail. He says that the minute swarams of Indian music cannot be adequately represented by the staff notation of the European system. He further says that they can only be reproduced by the Indian musical instruments and that such minute swarams constitute the main charm of the Indian system of music. But in spite of this, the Indians are unable to reproduce these swarams either vocally or by means of written symbols. Again he says that Indian musical instruments are more than 2,000 years old, and that the ragams sung in the Oudava, Shadava and Sampoorna scales are so complicated and advanced that it puzzles the best exponents of music.

Captain Day gives below the difference between Eastern and Western music, the excellence of the Indian melody and the reason for its want of further development.

Hindustan Sangita Paddhati. P. 329, 330.

"'The wide divergence of taste in the matter of music between European and Asiatic nations has doubtless arisen from the fact that while the western nations gradually discarded the employment of mode, and clothed the melody with harmony, the Eastern nations in this respect made little or no progress; and now, in India, the employment of authentic modes and melody types (or ragas) is still jealously adhered to.

Speaking of this, Capt. Willard remarks "To expect an endless variety in the melody of Hindustan would be an injudicious hope as their authentic melody is limited to a certain number, said to have been composed by professors universally acknowledged to have possessed not only real merit but also the original genius of composition, beyond the precincts of whose authority it would be criminal to trespass. What the more reputed of the moderns have done is that they have adopted them to their own purposes, and found others by the combination of two or more of them. Thus far they are licensed, but they dare not proceed a step further. Whatever merit an entire modern composition might possess, should it have no resemblance to the established melody of the country, it would be looked upon as spurious. It is implicitly believed that it is impossible to add to the number of these one single melody of equal merit. So tenacious are the natives of Hindustan of the ancient practices."

The continued employment of mode combined with the almost entire absence of harmony, has prevented Indian music from reaching any higher pitch of development such as has been attained elsewhere. It stands to reason also that this is the chief cause of the monotony which causes Indian music to be little appreciated by, if not repellent to, European ears.

Since the early periods of Indian history, music would seem to have been cultivated more as a science than as an art. More attention seems to have been paid to elaborate and tedious artistic skill than to simple and natural melody. Hence arose technical rules that marred the pristine sweetness of melody, the very life of all real music. To a great extent this must be attributed to the art falling into the hands of illiterate "Virtuosi." Their influence which caused music to suffer both in purity of style and simplicity is being felt less and less. The great aim of music—"Rakti" or the power of affecting the heart—now asserts itself more and more, and is slowly but surely bringing about a return to the early type of sweet, simple melody.'"

He says here that the Western nations discarded the melody sung to fixed modes, but clothed the melody with four parts made of the harmonious swarams, Shadjamam, Gandharam, Panchamam and the Octave Shadjamam, while the eastern nations jealously adhered to the melody. This is true. It was a custom in ancient days when the Vedas were chanted in two, three or four swarams to chant them in harmonious swarams, one singing it in Shadjamam and the other in its octave. [This custom is found even at the present day among those who chant the Vedas where a number of voices blend together in harmony. It is a matter for pride that this system of harmony was copied from India where it existed from ancient times, and then developed by other nations. The truth of this may be appreciated if we observe the chanting that takes place by the crowd of worshippers that follow the deity in procession.] But after the introduction of the seven swarams when they found that many Ragas could be generated by the variation and combination of these swarams they found that the beauty of melody was far superior to that of harmony. Shankarabharanam which commences in Shadjamam becomes Hanumatodi when begun in Gandharam and Harikambodhi when commenced in Panchamam. So the simultaneous singing of the three Ragas will not have a pleasing effect either to the ear or the mind. Perhaps at the commencement or at the end where the harmonious swarams blend together it might be tolerable. Harmony is not helpful in the exalted state of mind where it is thoroughly unconscious of its surroundings. It is for this reason that melody and not harmony has been highly cultivated in India by the sages who found it very helpful in their solitary state while performing penance. People living in tropics like India have long life if their faculties are concentrated and subdued and short life when they let them roam about at will. But those living in cold climes like Europe will be short-lived and die of numbness if they do not give a free play to their physical and mental faculties. Hence, the latter require the necessary food, clothing and activity to keep themselves warm. Nature also, it should be noted, provides for this purpose cool springs in the tropics and hot springs in the cold climes. Conforming to nature we find that the music of the cold regions is such as to make every one sing and dance. On the other hand the music of India is so beautifully constituted with so many varieties of exposition that the wandering mind may be concentrated so as to hold communion with the diety, so that a sage may sit in the same posture in silent meditation for any length of time. He who has a tendency to dance and to sing will appreciate Western music, but he who desires silent, contemplative worship will sing or hear an Indian ragam sung continually even for six months. This is but natural. We notice that winter fruit are comparatively less sweet and stand in the tree for a long time without getting ripe, and flowers in winter have less fragrance and last in the plants for days. On the other hand fruits in summer are very sweet and ripen fast, and flowers in this season are also very fragrant but they drop their petals very soon. So the sages who performed their penance in cool places, such as the shady banks of rivers and mountain caves, played and practised the same melody for a number of days on the celebrated Veena and found it very helpful to them in their devotion. The beauty of melody which inspires in one the sentiments of the morning, though it is evening time, and *vice versa*, is altogether alien to harmony. So those who have appreciated the beauty of Indian music, which is sung in the proper season according to a given mode with the variations of Oudava, Shadava and Sampoorna and according to the rules of Vakram and Varjyam, will never care forh armony.

He further says that, in conformity with their rigid conservatism, the Vidwans sincerely believe that the creation of a new Ragam is impossible. We subscribe fully to this view of the author. The ancient sages of India wrote down the exposition of each ragam in the form of *Geetams*. Modern musicians base their expositions of a Raga on these Geetams only. But the rules for composing such Geetams have all been destroyed. So at the present day, only those Ragas are in use for which Geetams have been written. fI one attempts a new Ragam in a new mode, one gets so hopelessly mixed that one gives it up in despair. Indian music is like a lock which has been locked but has no key to open it or relock it.

He says further that music has been cultivated more as a science than as an art. He makes this statement as he came across some musical works where the practice entirely contradicted the theory. If he had understood the secret of the science of music he would not have done so. We quite agree with him where he says that Indian music lost its dignity as it came into the hands of inferior and ignorant men. When men of knowledge found that music which was originally used in ennobling and elevating the soul is now being made a marketable commodity they are right in despising Indian music.

The chief reason for the decline of music is that the science which was once practised and made much of by crowned heads, Avataramurtis and Rishis is now imperfectly practised by acrobats and dancers and is mainly in the hands of those who pretend to be clever vidwans. Want of interest and patronage on the part of Indian nobles resulted in Indian music losing its established rules (Margam) and becoming, to a large extent, corrupted (Desikam).

We see from the following extract that music was held in the highest esteem in India and that our chief resource lies in those Geetas which had been traditionally handed down by oral transmission.

Doctor Coomarasawmy's Foreword to "The Study of Indian Music by E. Clements."

"Long anterior to this, however, music was a most highly cultivated—perhaps the most highly cultivated—of Indian arts, and to the present day it has remained the most continuously vital and most universally appreciated art of India."

"It is far better that the method of oral transmission should be maintained."

The statement that the method of oral transmission should be maintained is noteworthy because it throws some light upon the chief customs in India. We know that the secret of many precious cults and manufactures are whispered by a dying father to his son secretly in his last moments. The mystery or the key of some mantras, the mystery of the Vedanta philosophy, the secret of alchemy and of the three salts were all contained in a single word or two. Any number of books written on the above subjects, which do not contain the 'Key', are absolutely useless. Again, some of these precious sciences require practical demonstration, without which they are difficult to be understood. The extant literature on many of the occult sciences, such as medicine, alchemy, astronomy, yogam and vedantam, do not supply the 'Key' which is necessary for their right interpretation and understanding. For example, the middle ingredient and the five elements in medicine and alchemy, the mathematical calculations in astronomy and yogam, the operation of the five elements and the three tatwas in the human body in connection with the Vedanta Philosophy — all these absolutely necessary things have been omitted. (" எல்லார் கண் முன்னிற்கும் எடுத்துரைக்கும் குரு அருளில்லாமற் போனால் சொல்லாலும் வாராது.") "It will be so plain as to be seen by all eyes, but without the favour of the Guru (without the key) any amount of explanation will be of no effect" is a truism, for even the most elaborate of works have some secrets in them which could be explained only by the great sages. Just as a man who does not possess the key of a locked house is helpless, so the shastras without the 'Key' to them, which could be supplied only by the guru, are hopeless without being in a position to be rightly interpreted. Just as the light of a single match is able to expel the darkness around and show things as they are, so the light thrown upon a science by a single word of the Guru enables us to understand it right. We shall prove later on how there is such a secret in connection with the science of Indian music also.

If we but understand this secret we shall be able to find that South Indian music alone is scientific while other music is less so. We must understand that the Ragas of South India and their respective combination of swarams have been preserved intact up to the present day by the servants of temples, by oral transmission, and that is the chief reason for the purity of Carnatic music. The ignorance of the Carnatic Music has resulted in different books with different theories on the subject and in many controversies.

Just as birds and dried leaves are carried east or west according to the direction of the wind, the music of other countries has undergone many changes according to the vicissitudes of time, but the music of the Tamil country alone has remained intact, unaffected by the ravages of time. We can assure our readers that through the ancient literary works on the music of the Tamil Country are all destroyed, those Ragas which have been preserved by oral transmission are quite sufficient to make us understand the secrets of the science, their help is sufficient not only to determine the chief characteristics of the science but to enable one to make further discoveries on the same lines. This will be fully dealt with in the Second Book on Ragas. Just as the expansion of the one into many sometimes enable us to understand the one hidden idea, the expansion of ideas in music reflects the secret of the Srutis which has not been explicitly stated. The very beauty of the Ragas handed down by oral transmission reflects, as we shall presently see, the secret of those Ragas. We earnestly request those gentlemen who practise Carnatic Music not to spoil it and spoil themselves also (like the insect which is attracted by a light stifles the light as well as its own life) by following its corrupt forms of Desikam but to preserve it pure and unalloyed.

In the following extract he gives the reason why the sweetness of Indian music is not appreciated by others.

The Indian Empire by W. W. Hunter. P. 111.

"Melodies which the Indian composer pronounces to be the perfection of harmony, and which have for ages touched the hearts and fired the imagination of Indian audiences, are condemned as discord by the European critic. The Hindu ear has been trained to recognise modfications of sound which the European ear refuses to take pleasure in. Our ears on the other hand, have been taught to expect harmonic combinations of its own. The Indian musician declines altogether to be judged by the few simple Hindu airs which the English ear can appreciate."

We may gather from the following extract that the Indian Music is of very ancient origin, that each swaram was divisible into three and it was well suited for the chanting of the Vedas.

Hindu Music and the Gayan Samaj. Pt. ii, P 36. (Kunte.)

" It is now positively established by documentary evidence that at least 7,000 years before Christ, India had developed a system of musical notation, that the seven notes were scientifically arranged, each note being divided into three—the sharp, flat, and the proper note itself. All the inscriptions as yet discovered, and the Sanskrit literature that has been brought to light, place this statement beyond doubt. This fact has a scientific side. Though all the world over, notes, the elements of music, are seven only, yet the great variety of modes and melodies differ in European and Indian music which is either ancient or modern, Southern or Northern. The Southern or the Dravidian system is more Vedic than the Northern or Hindustani Dhanga. There is what is called a constant mode in Maharashtra. This is the remnant of the system of singing vedic psalms. It consists of opening modulation, soft, steady and slow in its progress. This is followed by notes the pitch of which is high, the modulation is strong, varied and rapid in its flow. This is followed by a combination of both leading to agreeable cadences. In a treatise on music, which is at any rate as ancient as the third century before Christ, a connection between physiological condition of human blood in the course of a day, and the changes of temper which these conditions necessitate are explained."

We have to note here that each swaram had three divisions, namely, the swaram itself, its sharp and its flat. But when we ask by how much was a swaram sharpened or flattened it lands us in the region of doubt as to the number of srutis and their intervals. At the rate of three for each swaram the total is 21, which contradicts the theory of the 22 srutis. Making such casual statements about the srutis is the cause of the springing up of different theories as to their number.

Again, he says that the music of South India is very useful for the purpose of chanting the Vedas. We must observe that this statement is made by a northern vidwan. We know that Ravanesvaran was the originator of the practice of chanting the Sama Veda with the help of the seven swarams and that he was the king of Lanka adjacent to South India. The different srutis that were used along with the seven swarams have been mentioned in the ancient Tamil literature. From this we may reasonably conclude that South India was primarily responsible for Vedic chanting as well as other music.

2. How South Indian Music became corrupt by mixture or Desikam.

We may infer from the following that South Indian Music was carried to the north by many and it became diversified in practice according to the peculiarities of the countries through which it passed and their various dialects.

Oriental Music by Chinnasawmi Moodr, M. A. P. 12, Art. 30.

"Considering the prodigious number of nationalities and the diversity of provincial dialects in existence throughout the length and breadth of the Indian Empire, it should be no matter for astonishment if there be found any number of heterogeneous systems, as well as incongruous classifications in standard works forming the músical literature of the land. The primary distinction is into two classes, Marga (celestial) and Desi (terrestrial); the latter is now broadly divided into Hindustani and Karnata, the former representing the school established by Hanuma, and the latter the much more ancient and authentic system introduced by Narada, the inventor of all arts and sciences. It is clear however that local tastes and methods of training have considerably upset the theories originally propounded.

In the extreme North, there is a system of six Ragas and thirty-six Raginis which are grouped together differently by different authors; in the west of India the divergences are still wider, though the origin is traceable to the same source; in the extreme south only thirty-two are recognised as principal Ragas, of which 8 are classed as Purusha and 24 as Stri, while a few more are designated by other fanciful names. Another classification is into 32 ancient and 42 recent Ragas. All these are manifestly incomplete. Of late the Hindustani element (which has itself much deteriorated owing to foreign admixture) has been ingrafted on the Dravidian modes to an alarming extent, so that it is a matter of no small difficulty to distinguish the purely classical from the adulterated systems. The tendency is at present to demolish all system and to sail clear of all trammels rules and regulations imposed by the ancient framers of the science; but it is evident that this is not the proper method of effecting reform or insuring progress. Each system should be taken up separately by itself, and while its true original and individual character is jealously maintained, it should be divested of all useless encumbrances and incrustations which obstruct or retard improvement.

Here he says that music had two divisions, Margam and Desikam, (that Margam was divine music, Desikam comprised Hindustani and Karnatic music,) that Hanuma was the author of the prior one viz., Hindustani and that the latter was attributed to Narada. He further says that the system established by Narada, the inventor of all arts and sciences, was the right one, and most ancient, but that it became corrupt by local exigencies. But we must understand that Margam was the system invented by the Rishis, that it was the music practised by Hanuma, Narada, Ravanesvara and others, that that was the genuine system, and that the Carnatic music of South India possessess all the characteristics of a pure system. It is absurd to attribute Hindustani music to Hanuma, for the Margam of Narada was carried to the north where it became corrupt by local influences and was known as Desikam. It is said that Desikam is for the benefit of children with no musical ear, and may be practised by women and foreigners. We must remember that Desikam has infringed the rules of music and is a corrupt system.

The old commentator on Silappadhikaram says that there were 11,991 indigenous ragas in the Tamil Country from ancient times. The Kalyani raga, which has a Prati Madhyamam, according to the Southern system, was taken to the north where two other Madhyamams, as well as two other swarams in Gandharam and Nishadam were introduced in it quite against established rules. It was brought back in its altered form once again to the South and the vidwans here have perpetuated the corruption as they found it very good! Such has been the fate of the other ragas such as Ananda-bhairavi, Kambodhi and Todi. Such admixture of swarams will result in all the Carnatic ragas sounding as one. The stricture we pass on Hindustani Music will also apply to Carnatic music.

We may gather from the following extract that Carnatic music was an eminently regular system while Buddhist and Hindustani music were looked upon as Desikam.

Hindu Music and the Gayan Samaj. Part I, P. 8.

"The Margi system, although preserved still in Sanskrit works on Music, owing to want of cultivation, political influence, and other adventitious circumstances has almost become extinct. Desi with its numerous ramifications is the system now obtaining in India. Music is divided into Nibadha and Anibadha, that set in words and that not, the former being Margi and the latter Desi. The Desi system first acquired importance from the Buddhist musicians, and received fuller development from Mussulmans who introduced Khyal from the Hindu Dhruvapada system and from that the Tappa. Besides these, there is the Southern Indian system, distinct in itself, and constituting an important section of the Indian musical system, termed the Carnataka system"

It appears from this that Margam existed only in theory without being put into practice but that Desikam improved in many directions. The Buddhists and, after them, the Mahammadans, who did not know the music of South India to perfection, patronised Desikam. It is noteworthy that an author who belongs to the north where the mixed and corrupt Desikam is largely in use should speak about a pure unmixed system in the south. Further, we know that their system of singing Thurbath, Kayal, Tappa, Tomari, and other Geetams is a very easy one. But the Geetam, Tanavarnam, Choukavarnam, Keertanam, Pallavi, and Ragamalika in Karnatic music are quite in accordance with scientific principles and are elaborately developed both in time and other scientific requisites.

We shall observe in the following extract how the Hindustani Desikam developed by the Mahammadans was an offshoot of the music of South India which was carried north from here when some of the vidwans of South India were taken captives by Allauddin, and that Nayak Gopal was one of those southern musicians so carried as captives. We have the authority of Subbarama Dikshatar who quotes Kallinadhar, the commentator on Sarangadeva, to say that the above Nayak Gopal was the author of Thalarnavam, Ragakadambam, Prabandham and other works 400 years ago. Venkatamakhi, the author of Chaturdandi-prakasika testifies that he (Naik Gopal) had a profound knowledge of the Srutis. It is said of him that he made a light miraculously ignite and burn of itself by singing the Ragam "Deepacam".

Universal History of Music. P. 84.

"The Mahomedans as a ruling nation came in contact with the people of India for the first time in the 11th century, and since then a change has been worked into the music system of the country. The Mahomedans did not encourage the theory of the art, but they patronized practical musicians and were themselves instrumental in composing and introducing several styles of songs or devising new forms of musical instruments. It is related by Mahomedan historians of the period that when Dacca was invaded by Allaudin in 1294 and the conquest of the south of India was completed (1310) by his Mogul general Malik Kafer, music was in such a flourishing condition, that all the musicians and their Hindu preceptors were taken with the armies, and settled in the North. It is said that the celebrated Persian poet and musician Amir Khosru came to India during the rule of Allaudin and defeated in a contest the musician of the South, Nayak Copal who had come to Delhi with a view to challenge the musicians of the court. Amir Khosru is reported to have given the name of *Satar* to the *Tri-tantri* Vina of the classic days and to have divided the *Rags* into twelve *Mokams* which were subsequently subdivided by other Mahamedan musicians into 24 *Sobhas* and 48 *Guswas*."

We have reason here to suppose that as the system of music in North India was found inferior to that in the south, South Indian musicians were taken to the north for the cultivation of superior music. It is also traditionally said that Alexander the Great took with him a number of musicians and other artists.

We read in the following extract that the Indian Music in the North became degenerate under Mahammadan rulers and came to be known as Hindustan Music.

The Music and the Musical Instruments of Southern India by C. R. Day. P. 5.

" In later years music became a distinct trade, especially under Musalman rulers and passed into the hands of the lower orders and the unlearned; and to this cause operating through a long succession of years, the differences between the Hindustani and Karnatic systems must be in a great measure attributed."

The following extract speaks about the musical experts in the time of Akbar, and the minuteness of the Srutis used by them.

The Indian Empire by W. W. Hunter. P. 110-111.

"Hindu music, after a period of excessive elaboration sank under the Mahomedans into a state of arrested development. Of the 36 chief musicians in the time of Akbar, only 5 were Hindus. Not content with tones and semitones, the Indian musicians employ a more minute subdivision, together with a number of tonal modifications, which the Western ear neither recognises nor enjoys. Thus they divide the octave into 22 subtones instead of the 12 tones and semitones of the European scale. This is one of several fundamental differences, but it alone suffices to render Indian music barbaric to us; giving it the effect of a Scotch ballad in a minor key, sung intentionally a little out of tune."

Here we read that during of time of Akbar the Great (1556-1605), who ruled India so eminently for nearly 50 years, there were 36 chief musicians at his court, of whom only 5 were Hindus. Compare with this the fact that in Aryaloor, belonging to the Tanjore Samasthanam, there was a Jagirdar, by name Katchiyuvaranga bhoopati, who supported during his time 365 renowned Karnatic musicians, that there are a number of Varnams and Keertanams composed by them with the name Katchiyuvaranga bhoopati. This shows the dearth of musicians in North India. Moreover he says that they used very minute swarams such as the quarter and the one-eighth tones. In the same breath he says that they divided the octave into 22 Srutis. There is a contradiction here. How could 7 swarams be proportionately or equally divided into 22 with the ratio of one-fourth or one-eighth ? We shall see that this ratio will not hold good in dividing the octave into 22 srutis.

3. The South Indian Music and the Music of North India are entirely different from each other.

To sum up what we have said before, the music of South India introduced by Narada and Agastya was taken to the north and became Desikam by the addition of a few swarams.

The following quotation also shows that Margam or Deva-ganam was in use in South India while Desika-ganam was peculiar to the north.

The Music and the Musical Instruments of Southern India by C. R. Day. P. 12.

" Of the two systems practised in Southern India at the present time, the *Hindustani* is somewhat akin to that of Northern India and Bengal. It is practised mostly by Mussalman musicians while the *Karnatic* is confined more to those of the Southern races. The latter which may be called the national music of the South, is far more scientific and refined than the Hindustani and its professors are as a rule, men of much better education, a fact that is not without influence upon their music and seems apparent in all their melodies but particularly in the renderings they give of them."

Here he says how Carnatic music which is the national music of South India is far more scientific and refined than Hindustani music, how it is cultivated by men of education and how it is capable of beautiful renderings.

We have noted before the period of the existence of South Madura in the destroyed continent which existed to the South of India, the members who presided at the meetings of the Sangam and the highly efficient state of music at the time. When we specially note who the musical experts were who excelled in singing, playing on the Veena and dancing before the deity in the act of worship, we are proud to find they were ruling kings, Avataramurtis, princes and nobles of the country. When the subjects found that their rulers were interested in music and Bharatam they also came down south, followed the footsteps of their leaders, and became famous for their music and dancing. Further, the royal rishis, who had relinquished their kingdoms for the sake of practising tapas, their disciples and the Brahmans of the south, practised it to a large extent as they found it very helpful to their penance. Thus, music came into the hands of sages, highly intellectual men and the Aryans who were all considered leaders of society and held in great esteem, so much so that it was considered a necessary adjunct of services in the temple and of secular rites and ceremonies such as marriage.

When the Pandya kingdom declined, music also declined for want of patronage, but was upheld to a small measure by the Chola Rajas of the Tamil country. But after the fall of the Chola kingdom, the Tamil country was ruled till recently by Nayak Rajas and after them by the Mahrattas. These sovereigns patronised music and dancing to a certain extent.

The following extract says music has flourished in South India without interruption from very ancient times.

The Music and the Musical Instruments of Southern India by C. R. Day. P. 5.

" Music has almost without interruption flourished there (in Southern India) from very remote ages.

The higher branches of musical profession were formerly confined to the Brahmins (Bhagavatars) or to men of very high caste. Music being of divine origin was regarded as sacred and it was considered impious for any but men of the caste to wish to acquire any knowledge of its principles. It was and still is called the fifth Veda. Hence the ancient Brahmins of the country would have excommunicated any of their number who would have so far presumed as to betray the sacred writings to any but the elect, whose mouths only were esteemed sufficiently holy to utter words so sacred. Indeed it was the knowledge of which they were possessed that was the chief cause of the reverence and adoration paid to the Brahmins of old and which gave them power and influence they prized so much. It was thus that the ancient musicians sang their own composition."

It was held, as we see, that music was of divine origin and, as such was regarded as sacred, and that its secret was preserved religiously so that others might not know it.

Our readers will remember how we said before that music and its various parts such as Bharatam and Talam had attained high excellence and were practised with the help of instruments such as the Veena, the piccolo, and Mridangam long before the advent of the Aryans into South India, and how music was in great demand in temples and royal palaces. These Aryans became experts in South Indian music after they came to the south. Just as they are determined to keep the slokas of the Vedas as a sealed book to others they are also unwilling to teach others the South Indian music which they had learnt from others. Again, they discarded all the existing Tamil fragments in music, and composed new ones in Sanskrit and Telugu and used them exclusively and handed them down to their generations also. But in spite of it they unconsciously follow the ancient Tamil style only. So in course of time the music which originated in South India came to be considered to have been derived from the Sanskrit literature of the north.

We may see in the following extract that Karnatic and Hindustani music are two distinct systems, that Karnatic music which looks more as if it were of divine origin than the other is surrounded by a halo of sanctity, and that almost all the religious literature of the South is redolent of music.

The Music and the Musical Instruments of Southern India, by C. R. Day. P. 2, 3 and 4.

" Since the *Sangita Parijata* which is believed to be one of the latest of these Sanskrit works, had been written by *Ahobila*, two separate *schools* or *systems* of music have arisen and are now known by the names of Hindustani and Karnatic. The Karnatic appears to have been elaborated as a distinct system subsequent to the advent of the Aryans to the south of India. The two systems although sprung from the same origin have since undergone independantly considerable changes and are now totally distinct from each other.

Of Hindu music in Southern India, since the fall of the Hindu Empire of Vijayanagar, Tanjore has been the only *school* and from it those of Travancore and other places have doubtless been founded.

Mahomedan music taken as a whole, has little to recommended itself even at the present day. The ideas professed by Hindus offer a curious contrast for music from a Hindu standpoint. It is associated with all that is bright and sweet in life; its origin ascribed directly to divine providence causes it to be regarded as surrounded by a halo of sanctity. Almost all the religious literature of the Hindus breathes music."

We see here that the author of ' Parijatam ', who lived 300 years ago, evidently held that the Srutis of the South Indian system of music did not correspond with the

Sruti system of 'Sangeeta Ratnakaram' (which was 400 years anterior) and so gave the intervals for the 12 main swarams of the Veena only giving up as hopeless the remaining 10 minute srutis. He says he would give the Raga-lakshanam for the 12 swarams, excluding the ten. From this it appears that even during his time the controversy, that the Srutis of the two systems were entirely different, had existed. [We shall later on enquire how the name 'Dwavimsati Srutis' came into use.] Evidently Captain Day has been mislead by those who told him that Karnatic music was posterior to 'Parijatam.' If he had been told by those who understood the real truth about South Indian Music, he would have declared to the world the most minute and incontestible arguments in support of it. It is a matter for regret that many European gentlemen who come to India to gather information about the antiquity of India, its ancient arts and culture, are very often misled by those who have a very imperfect knowledge of it. Their case is analogous to that of the bull which is led by the nose-string in the direction in which the driver intends that it should go. This is but the nature of the times. This is why we find even men of understanding erring at times. But if we remember that a controversy as regards Indian Music has been going on for the past 2,500 years mainly owing to the ignorance of the secrets of it, we shall not be surprised at what Captain Day says.

He further says that the Karnatic music was organised as a system subsequent to the advent of the Aryans. This is true. We have already pointed out how the Aryans might have entered South India during the period of the last Sangam, how they might have subsequently learnt the Tamil language writing commentaries and fresh works in the same, how that might account for the presence of Sanskrit words here and there which made people doubt the antiquity of the language and how they might have clothed the ideas borrowed from destroyed Tamil literature with a Sanskrit garb. In the same way it appears that the exclusive Karnatic system of music has been mistaken at the present day for the Hindustani music. But Captain Day distinctly says that, although both systems might have been derived from a common origin, each has undergone a number of modifications independently of each other. Again he mentions how, in complete ignorance of the Sruti System of South India, two different systems have sprung up, one the Sanskrit system of the 22 srutis, and the other system advocated in Sanskrit works like 'Parijatam' by South Indian musical experts in accordance with the rules of South Indian music. He mentions how the South Indian system was chiefly found in Tanjore, from which it seems to have been copied in other places. We have already said how 'Chaturdandi-prakasika' which was written by Tanjore Venkatamakhi nearly 300 years ago in Sanskrit and other smaller works after his time have all declared the truths of this South Indian system. We have to be thankful that after the destruction of the Tamil works which described the 103 modes (பண்கள்) and 12,000 ragas derived from the four Palis (பாலைகள்) (original airs) they were at least good enough to systematise on behalf of the Karnatic music the 12 swarams of the Ayappalai and the 72 Melams derived from them. But they have completely changed the names of some of the ancient ragams and techincal terms, giving Sanskrit names with Sanskrit letters as mnemonics for determining them thus giving them derivative names. They further classified the ragams on some principle introducing some of the chief Sanskrit ideas into it. They gave new Sanskrit names to some of the ancient places, cities and kings in South India and wrote Sanskrit works to perpetuate the names as they did in music.

We have heard the chanting of Thevaram, Thiruvachakam, Thiruvoimoli and other songs in praise of the deity in temples by Brahmans and other devotees. The different ragas to which they should be sung are given in those books which is strictly followed. But the ancient names of these ragas such as Pan Indalam, Pan Gandharam, Pan Kolli, Pan Seekamaram, Pan Takkasi, Pan Kurunji, Pan Nattapadai, Pan Kuruntogai, Pan Tiruttandagam are not found in Sanskrit works on music. So we must understand that the ancient Thevarams are now found as Ragas in a new Sanskrit garb. We have heard so much already about the tendency for changing existing names.

From all this we conclude that the original South Indian system of music was represented under different names—by the Greek Philosopher Pythagoras as $\frac{2}{3}$ and $\frac{3}{4}$, by Sanskrit musicians like the authors of Bharatam and Sangeeta Ratnakaram as 22 srutis, by Venkatamakhi, by the author of Sangeeta Parijatam and by Bosanquet as 12 swarams. Each wanted to establish his theory as the right one like the man who obstinately held some other animal to be the elephant.

It is a great proof for the profound scholarship of Captain Day that he should have made such minute researches about Indian music when it was in such a chaotic state.

We have already noted that after the fall of Oottara Madura and the Pandya kingdom the Cholas and, after them, the Nayak Rajas, who were Telugus, ruled over it. At that time they took with them the music which they considered precious, as well as musicians of repute, and fostered them in their own kingdom. It is for this reason that Vizayanagaram and Tanjore are considered great centres of music even at the present day. But men of understanding will know how the music of the Tamil country centres round Tamil kings and Tamil deities up to the present day.

Captain Day, who had clearly understood the importance of Karnatic music and the way in which it was handled, says that it is surrounded by a halo of sanctity. We cannot adequately express our deep admiration for this gentleman. If a nobleman from the West has such an exalted idea about Indian music, what should be the idea of men in South India who are practising it as a profession ? If they really had such a consideration for Indian music will they delight in music which is contrary to established rules ?

We must understand that Karnatic music is long prior to the author of Sangeeta-parijatam (A. D. 1600), to Saranga-deva, the author of Sangeeta-ratnakaram (A. D. 1200) and to Bharatar (A. D. 500), as it was in existence many thousand years before these authors in the first Ooli. Again, after the fall of the Pandya kingdom, it was fostered and patronised by some of the kings in South India, such as those of Vizayanagaram, Tanjore, Travancore and Mysore.

We may see from the following extract that when North India was in a chaotic condition owing to internal wars, South India was comparatively in a peaceful condition and the science of music was cultivated and developed here more than in the north.

The Music and the Musical Instruments of Southern India by C. R. Day. P. 13.

"The theory, modes and notation in present use throughout the whole of India are derived from that taught originally by the earlier Sanskrit musicians; but owing to the south of India having been less disturbed by internal commotions and having been more subject to Hindu rule than either Deccan or Northern Province, the science of music would seem to have been maintained and cultivated long after the original art had been lost in the north.

Hence Southern India music or as it is more usually called Karnatic, bears as far as we can judge, a very close resemblance to what the Sanskrit must have been, and in many cases we can clearly trace the development and refinements introduced from time to time upon the original Ragas."

We have noted already that works on Tamil prosody, such as Ahattyam, Panchabharateeyam, Perunarei, Perunkurugu, were destroyed by the deluge, and the remnants were lost during the destruction of Kapatapuram. Even the few minor works that survived gradually disappeared for want of patronage. Since then, Sanskrit works alone are in use. But scholars know there is a vast difference between music as found in those Sanskrit writings and the music of Southern India. We have already noted the opinion of experts as to the fact that the music of North India and that of the South are based on two entirely different systems.

The vast difference between the two systems is found in the following extract.

The Music and the Musical Instruments of Southern India by C. R. Day. P. 15.

"The exact definition of what constituted a *sruti* is difficult to determine; but it is thus vaguely given by the Sangita Ratnakara 'A *sruti* is formed by the smallest intervals of sound and and is perceivable by the ear; it is of 22 kinds; also every distinct audible sound is a *sruti*; it is a *sruti* because it is to be heard by the ear.'

"Doubts however exist as to whether the intervals of the strutis were equal or not."

"In the arrangement of the srutis, modern usage is diametrically opposite to the classical one; the latter placing them before the note to which they respectively belong, while the former gives position after the notes. It is difficult to determine when or by whom the alteration was effected. The arrangement of the frets of the Vina and other stringed instruments accord with the modern acceptation of the principle. According to the rule laid down in the classical treatises, the disposition of the notes is reversed in the case of the *Darve* instruments and out of this reversed arrangement perhaps the modern theory about the arrangement of the position of all sruties has been worked. (Tagore)"

Here he says that the author of Sangeeta-ratnakaram speaks of 22 srutis formed by the smallest intervals of sound but doubts whether the intervals of the srutis were equal. This doubt is caused by the fact that there is a difference between the ancient and the modern systems. But he says that the distribution of the frets on the Veena agrees with the modern principle, namely the South Indian system. But it appears that this particular arrangement of the frets was reversed in the case of the

Darve instruments. It is but natural that when once Desikam (Hindustani) was practised, the position of srutis in stringed instruments should also have altered in accordance with it. Many are of opinion that Sangeeta-ratnakaram is a work that brings out in full the details of the South Indian system, while it contradicts a few of the principles of the Hindustani system. We shall establish later on that the determination of srutis by Mr. Clements, Mr. Deval and others who wrote solely on Hindustani is not based on work of Sarngadeva; for, according to this author the srutis should be of equal interval whereas their srutis are not so.

The following extract proves that there is a world of difference between the intervals of the srutis according to the Northern system and those of the South.

Oriental Music by Chinnasawmi Moodr, M. A. P. 14 Art. 37.

"The mathematical ratios of the Indian Gamut likewise vary in the north and south of India. But this extremely complicated question may be left open for the present, because for all practical purposes the system of Equal Temperament which coincides almost exactly with the adjustment of frets on the Vina is found to meet all existing requirements more or less satisfactorily. It is admitted on all hands that this curious coincidence has been arrived at by the two nations through distinct processes, quite independently of each other; and historical research so far as it has been made, has established the fact that the Indian system has remained *in statu quo* for ages before the *Lux ab oriente* dawned upon the *West*."

We find here that as the system of the modern arrangement of frets on the Veena exactly resembles the system of Equal Temperament for all practical purposes the Veena is found to meet all requirements of music. The concensus of opinion of the Eastern and Western musicians in this respect is surprising, he says, and history proves that this system had existed in India from the remotest times.

We have noted before that the four different kinds of Yal and the rules for their practice were in existence in South Madura even 8,000 years ago. The rules for their tuning and other particulars will be given later on.

We must enquire whether the system of 22 srutis propounded by Sarngadeva will be of any help to Karnatic music. But it will be out of place to give a comparison of the srutis of Karnatic music and the 22 srutis as the former have not yet been definitely formulated. When the comparison is made, the merit or demerit of the two systems will be made manifest. But it is very necessary to examine the theories of those who profess to follow Sangeeta-ratnakaram and compare their mathematical calculations with those of Sarangadeva.

Sarngadeva says that the srutis in an octave should have equal intervals and should rise gradually without allowing space for any other srutis in the middle. But the music of North India seems to have srutis with unequal intervals. We shall see later on how it is caused by measuring the strings in the proportions of $\frac{2}{3}$ and $\frac{3}{4}$. The music of South India, on the other hand, seems to be entirely different from these. Moreover, Pythagoras, the Greek philosopher, who was well conversant with the srutis used in the South Indian system as well as in Sangeeta-ratnakaram, being unaccustomed to tuning an instrument by sounding

Madhyamam and Panchamam, as is the South Indian system, took with him the measurements $\frac{3}{2}$ and $\frac{4}{3}$ and developed Western music out of it. From that time forward the intervals of the Swarams in the South Indian system varied. As time went on there arose a school which argued that this system was wrong, that the system of Pythagoras, namely, the Diatonic scale, was the correct one because some musical experts, who had seen the same method advocated in works like Sangeeta-parijatam, found it conforming to a few Ragas which they were using, and that the system of Equal Temperament introduced later on in Europe for purposes of modulation was incorrect. To add to the confusion, the 22 srutis according to the systems of the author of Sangeeta-ratnakaram were also said to conform to the above system. Those who are determined to establish as truth whatever was said in Sanskrit slokas, knowing that no weight would be attached to their words unless they cried down the system of srutis of South Indian music and the instrument Veena which reproduces things as they are, begin to propound new theories. If they only realise what a stumbling block this theory of 22 srutis is they would never commit themselves as they have done. Ignorance of this fact has resulted in doubt, contention and chaos as regards the theory of the srutis. There is also a little room to say that this theory of the 22 srutis may be correct because a few Ragas, with minute Swarams in South Indian music, are capable of being interpreted by this system. But can we sacrifice thousands of Ragas for the sake of ten or fifteen?

The following extract shows how there are 12 Swarams in an octave and how they exactly correspond to the Swarams of South Indian music and the Swarams of a Veena.

The Music and the Musical Instruments of Southern India by C. R. Day. P. 20.

"The Hindu Octave, like the European, is divided into twelve semitones. (This view is supported by both Sir W. Jones and Mr. Fowke 'Asiatic researches.') Sir W. Jones remarks "I tried in vain to discover in practice any difference between the Indian scale and that of our own but knowing my ear to be very insufficiently exercised, I requested a German professor of music to accompany on his violin a Hindu lutenist who sang by note some popular airs on the loves of Krishna and Radha and he assured me that the scales were the same; and Mr. Shore afterwards informed me that when the voice of a native singer was in tune with his Harpsichord he found the Hindu series of seven notes to ascend like ours by a sharp Third. From many experiments I am led to believe that a wrong idea as to the temperament of the Indian scale as practically employed has hitherto been held. I played over all the various scales shown later upon a pianoforte tuned to Equal Temperament in the presence of several well known Hindustani and Karnatic musicians, all of whom assured me that they corresponded exactly to those of the Vina. Upon comparing the two instruments this was found to be the case as far as could be judged by the ear alone, in every instance. Maula Bux, a man of considerable attainments, took pains to explain to me that the tempering of the modern Indian scales differed in no whit from the European."

Here Captain Day, whose work on South Indian music is so very helpful in making us understand many things about Karnatic music, says, after elaborate researches, that the 12 swarams of European as well as South Indian music are identical. He further says that there is a misapprehension in the minds of many as regards these Swarams which are the result of Equal Temperament. Those who know the detail about the four different kinds of Yal understand that this system of Swarams according to Equal Temperament but also far minuter srutis were known in very ancient times in the Tamil country and in South Madura. This ancient system lost its subtlety and became corrupt owing to later mathematical calculations and also by the fact that it was carried to the West. In the same way, being ignorant of the 22 numbers, the Rasis and the relation between these 12 Swarams, it was wrongly established in later works that there were 22 srutis in an octave. This wrong system combined with the haphazard system carried by Pythagoras resulted in many books being written on the subject with contradictory theories. These two wrong systems, mutilated as they are, try to mutilate South Indian music also, just like the man who not only spoiled himself but spoiled the sacred tank Chandra Pushkarani by immersing in it.

South Indian music after losing the patronage of the Pandya kings was fostered chiefly by the Cholas. This music which was so much in use in the Chola country is now being knocked about in various places like the birds in a tank which has run dry.

However, it is a certainty that so long as there are sacred places of pilgrimage and Vaishnavite temples in South India, South Indian music will surely live. For the instruments such as the Veena and the Flute which are the chief exponents of music are in use at present as of old. These instruments are so constituted as to bring out clearly tones, half-tones and minuter Swarams also.

The following extract tells us that Karnatic music possessed such a dignified and permanent system from the earliest times.

The Music and the Musical Instruments of Southern India by C. R. Day. P. 29.

"The following table kindly sent me by Mr. Ellis shows the results obtained from a most minute and careful examination made by him and by Mr. A. J. Hipkins of a beautiful old Vina, in perfect condition now in my possession. This instrument is between two or three hundred years old and is from the collection in the Tanjore palace. The results as will be seen tend to prove that the frets were purposely arranged for something like Equal Temperament. We see therefore that in India much the same results have been independently arrived at by the native musicians as have been attained by subsequent science in Europe."

In the above he gives a few important particulars about the Veena that was taken to England from Tanjore. This instrument appears to have been from the collections at the Tanjore palace museum and the frets in it seem to have been arranged so as to produce srutis in accordance with Equal Temperament. He says that on examination of it by Mr. Ellis and Mr. A. J. Hipkins it was found that the frets were arranged not in conformity with the Diatonic scale used in Europe for 2,000 years but in accordance with Equal Temperament used for purposes of modulation for the past century or two, and that the Indian Musicians had arrived at this system independently before it was ever discovered by the Europeans.

We have already referred to the eminence of this Captain Day, who, after laborious researches, discovered the fact that the Swarams of the Veena were in accordance with Equal Temperament and mentioned the truth that this system was known in

India from remotest times. A little deeper research in the field would certainly convince such a great man that we could conclude from what we find from Silappadhikaram of Ilankovadigal, written 1,800 years ago, and from Tolgauppyam, written many thousand years ago, that this system is referred to in the ancient music of the Tamil country and that the Tamilians have been practising the same to the present day.

In addition to the 12 Swarams with equal intervals, there is also an important system in use in South India to the present day where more minute srutis are used. But as singers as well as hearers are unable to find out what these srutis are they are at a loss to understand the secret of South Indian music. Those who are ignorant of the construction, secret and the antiquity of this splendid instrument declare that the frets of the Veena were arranged in accordance with the European system of Equal Temperament quite recently for the benefit of Sèvappa Naik who ruled in Tanjore. If they had known the truth, they would never have erred by making such a statement. We shall clearly prove later on in the Sruti system of South India that the chief Swarams of our Ragas are the Swarams found in the Veena according to its arrangement of frets, that the system by which one or two of its Swarams are either a little flat or sharp is found in ancient Tamil works and that the very same had been in use in the Tamil country from very early times.

We have already noted briefly how the Tamil country noted for its different cults was the cradle of the human race, how the language spoken by the early inhabitants got mixed with other languages, how three Sangams in the Tamil country existed where researches were made in the branches of the language—Iyal, Isai and Natakam, how a number of works had been written on (Isai music), how these works were twice destroyed by the sea and how music declined in later days. We also noted the opinions of writers bearing on the declining state in which music was found at present. We also noted the clearly stated opinions of others how South Indian music which was the one that closely followed prescribed rules, was also more scientific when compared with Northern and Hindustani music and was capable of a large variety of Ragas. The permanency of the rules of South Indian Music and the never-changing beauty of its Ragas are to be attributed to the fact that it has been traditionally taught for generations how the Swarams of a particular Ragam should be of particular srutis while used in Arohanam and Avarohanam, how the Swarams omitted in Ragas of the Shadava and Oudava type should be carefully avoided altogether, how the Vikruti swarams should be in close harmony with their allied ones in the Sanchara of the whole Ragam where such Swarams are used, and how the Swarams not found in the Arohanam or Avarohanam of a Ragam should never be made use of contrary to established order; they have been taught what the Jeevaswarams of a Ragam are, how different Ragams should be sung to suit different occasions and how particular Puns (பண்) should be sung to particular Ragas. Such a system has been maintained from the earliest times and perpetuated chiefly by the patronage of kings who gave maniyam lands and gifts to temples for the fostering of the particular system of music. Moreover, music was largely in demand in the durbars of kings, during marriage festivities and triumphant entries into cities. Orders were given for the daily use of music, morning, noon and night in palaces and temples and a body of singers were appointed for the purpose. It was a custom with the kings of the early days to build temples in different parts of their kingdom, endow them with lands so that the ringing of bells, the sounding of the conch and the playing of various instruments such as the drum, Mattalam, Nagaswaram, Flute and the Veena might take place regularly during the services, to appoint suitable musicians and dancers for chanting the religious poems in praise of the deity such as Thevaram, Thiruvachagam and Thiruvamoli and encourage them by giving them houses to dwell in and gifts for their daily maintenance. We know of many a Sivavite and Vaishnavite temple where such arrangements have been made. The musicians so appointed for the service of the temple have made music their profession and have been practising and cultivating it up to the present time. This system was not started yesterday but has been going on for many thousand years. This is the chief reason why Karnatic music is so pure without the admixture of any Desikam. Musical experts could appreciate the difference between the vocal music of Northerners and the pure music of an expert in Nagaswaram. Many nobles and other musicians who were charmed with the music of instruments such as the Veena, the Flute, the Mridangam, the Nagaswaram used in temples not only delighted in learning the music themselves but also imparted their ecstasy to others. Some of them who became eminent musicians were highly esteemed and respected. Others spent their time in praise of the deity without the expectation of any reward. A few others wrote about some of the parts of the science of music.

We shall no doubt desire to learn some particulars about the chief of those eminent musicians referred to above.

VI. A FEW PARTICULARS ABOUT SOUTH INDIAN MUSICIANS.

1. General Points.

WE have noted briefly that the celebrated South Indian continent or the province of Kumari was Lemuria, that Tamil was its language, that the rulers thereof were Pandya kings, that they organised the first Sangam by bringing together kings, sages and scholars who were noted for their learning, and made researches into various sciences and wrote them down. We also mentioned how music which was practised as one of the divisions of the language became degenerate in course of time by the loss of all its existant literature. that the remnants of works that remained during the next two sangams complety disappeared at a later stage. There is reason to think that South Indian music was practised by many who imigrated to South India during the period of the last sangam and in the subsequent period and that the science of music was written in many languages even then. For we find that the 22 numbers (அலகுகள்) that occur in the music of the ancient Tamil country were misinterpreted by them to be the 22 srutis in an octave and written in other languages so as to cause doubt in the minds of people. But the music in vogue at present in the Tamil country is quite systematic and antagonistic to the principle of the 22 srutis. Some of the Sootrams written in a foreign language which are said to be 400, 500 and even 1,000 years old, although they do not possess any scientific authenticity and firmness of their own have unfortunately brought South Indian music, which was on a firm basis, to a tottering condition of doubt. Even this doubt chiefly exists among those who study works on music in other languages and not among those professional musicians patronised for generations by temples who have practised Karnatic music as handed down by tradition. We have already noted the opinion of musicians who say that if there were 22 srutis in the octave it would neither suit the system of South India nor would it suit the Swarams used in chanting the Vedas and that the system of 22 srutis is highly impracticable. There are many musicians at the present day who are ignorant of the 22 srutis, nay, who have never heard the very name. There are others who are incapable of testing the South Indian music they have been practising on the light of the 22 srutis.

But in spite of the scarcity of literature as regards srutis, South Indian music has been preserved and taught to others by those professional musicians, supported for generations by ancient temples who learnt music by oral transmission and who became experts in playing instruments such as the Veena, the Flute, the Nagaswaram, the drum, and the Mridangam, and in dancing and singing.

When we read that God, who found all things He had created to be good, is enthroned on high listening to the singing of the *Ter sanctus* by all the saints, with their respective musical instruments, and their dancing before the throne, it distinctly appears that God is the primary cause for music and its progress. Again, we see the highest use of music from the fact that it is God alone who accepts the praise of all devotees and living beings. All beings created by God seem to praise them with their natural sweet sounds.

A certain kind of music is produced by the rapid rotation of the planets and other celestial bodies round their own axes. As the bodies are of different magnitudes, different kinds of sounds are produced. We know that the sound produced by the wings of a small gnat when it flies is higher in pitch than that produced by the wings of a large musquito. A slow rotation of a body produces a low sound while a rapid rotation of the same produces a sound of a higher pitch. The celestial bodies praise God by the sound produced by their rotation. In the same way all living beings praise Him by their good lives, devotion and music. The Vegetable Kingdom praise Him and induce others to do the same by the fragrance of their flowers, the sweetness of their fruits and the usefulness of their produce. We know how the birds in a grove sing His praises. In the same way the nine kinds of precious gems by their brilliancy, rills by the noise of their fall, streams by their gentle murmur, and oceans by their eternal roar keep praising the deity. Thus, the commendable habit of eternally praising the deity is natural to all creation. Yet only a few are endowed with the special gift of practising music and of singing it to the delight of others. History has not recorded definitely the period in which they lived. Yet a few words about their history might remind us of the efficiency of their music and their eminence.

History has recorded how, after the dismemberment of the last Sangam, the Pandya kingdom declined in many ways retaining its independence for some time while being conquered by the Cholas at other periods, that this decadence was going on for 2,000 years and how it has been in the hands of foreigners for the last seven or eight hundred years.

2. Music under the Cholas.

We read in the history of Ceylon how the son and daughter of Asoka, the Buddhist king who ruled in the north between 272 and 231 B.C., came to the South, how they concluded treaties with the Chera, Chola and Pandya kings, and how the Cholas invaded Lanka in B.C. 247 and later on in B.C. 150 also.

After them, Karikal Cholan I who was king of the Chola kingdom from A.D. 50—95, ruled with great fame making Cauviripoompatnam his capital. He built great anicuts and banks for the rivers having the fertility of his kingdom at heart. He constructed canals. He had extensive trade with China, Burma, Greece and Java by means of boats and ships which he possessed in large numbers. He encouraged land and sea industry by helping specialists who excelled in them. He organised a cabinet of specialists in the departments of law, religion, medicine, astronomy and war and governed the country having these as an advisory body. Tamil and its eminent arts flourished during his reign. He patronised scholars of both sexes who were eminent in the three angams of the language—Iyal, Isai and Natakam.

Cheran Chenguttuvan, the ruler over the Chera kingdom, was his contemporary. Ilankovadigal, the brother of Chenguttuvan, was an ascetic at the time, doing penance. The Pandya king Nedunchelian who ruled at Madura and the Pandya king Peruvaluthy (who is known as one who held his durbar from a silver swing) seem to have been also his contemporaries. The death of this Pandya king Nedunchelian was under the most tragic circumstances. There was one Kovalan, son of a tradesman by name Masathuvan, who lived in Cauveripoompatnam at the mouth of the Cauvery. He fell in love with a dancing girl, by name Madhavi, in the same city, attracted by her singing and dancing. He lost all his property through this unfortunate love and had only an anklet (சிலம்பு) left. He took this jewel to the great city of Madura for the purpose of selling it. The jewel was identified by a goldsmith as that which was lost from the palace, and accordingly when King Nedunchelian was informed of it, he condemned Kovalan to death. The wife of Kovalan, by name Kannahi, when she heard of this, proceeded to the king and proved to him satisfactorily that the jewel was hers. The king, when he heard this, was so struck with remorse for having rashly condemned a man to death without going into his case thoroughly, suddenly fell down dead from his throne. The crowd that assembled accompanied Kannahi who proceeded weeping to the street where the goldsmith, who wrongly accused her husband, lived. The whole street was reduced to ashes as the result of divine wrath. This incident appears to have taken place during the time of Karikal Cholan.

The Veena seems to have been efficiently played in the Chola kingdom, one of the three Tamil provinces. Particulars about Veena music are given by Ilankovadigal who belonged to the Chera kingdom. We have already seen how music was extensively used in the Pandya kingdom, how extensive researches were made in the realm of music and how a number of works were written on the subject. After the fall of the Pandya kingdom, which was the foremost among the three, music and other arts flourished under the Cholas who were the conquerors of the Pandyas. We have read off and on how ancient kings when they conquered a country never cared to seize the treasure or property of the conquered but took musicians and other artists as captives of war, transplanted them in their own country for the purpose of disseminating those sciences and arts in which they were found experts. In the same way Karikal Cholan also improved the sciences and arts of his kingdom. Details of his reign may be found in the " Pattinappalai" written by Rudhirankannar who lived during his time and in the " Silappadhikaram" of Ilankovadigal.

After him his son Nalankilli, the Cholan, reigned from A. D. 95 to 105.

His son Killivalan and his brother Perunarkilli ruled from 105 to 150 A. D. It was during the time of the latter that Worayur was made the capital. It also appears that during his reign he performed a royal sacrifice to which were invited the kings of Chola, Pandya and Lanka kingdoms. The kingdom lasted for two generations after him. From 130 to 246 A. D. Worayur was the seat of the Chola kingdom. No particulars are available about the Chola kings from this time.

We learn from the Tanjore Gazetteer that about 600 A. D. there was a Chola king by name 'Wochengannan' who was a great devotee and who built more than 70 Sivite and Vishnavite temples.

We gather from stone inscriptions in various places that Vijialayan, the Cholan, conquered Tanjore while he was at Conjeevaram and ruled over Ookal, Conjeevaram, Tirukoilur, Sucheendram and other places from 846 to 880 A. D. with the title of Parakesarivarman.

After a time came his son Muthal Aditya Rajakesarivarman who reigned from 880-907. He conquered the Pandya king Varagunapandyan and Pallava Aparajith and added the Kongu country to his dominions.

He was succeeded by Parantaka I. who ruled from 907 to 947 with the titles of Parakesarivarman and Veeranarayanan. He overcame the Pandya king Rajasimha in 910 A. D. He adorned the big hall in the temple at Chidambaram with tiles made of gold. For 37 years out of the 40 of his reign he was engaged in incessant warfare with Lanka and finally subdued it. He had five sons.

His first son Rajadityan succeeded him under the name of Rajakesarivarman.

After him came his brother Kandaradityan. After his death his wife built a temple in his memory at Konarirajapuram and placed his statue also in it. His brother was Arunjayan or Arjuna, whose son was Parantaka II or Sundara Cholan.

His successor was Aditya II or Karikalan II.

He was succeeded by Parakesarivarman or Oottama Cholan who reigned from 970 to 985. He promised his kingdom to Rajaraja Cholan after him and ruled the country when the latter was a minor. Rajaraja Cholan was one of the most celebrated of Chola sovereigns. He was as famous as Karikal Cholan I who ruled over the ancient Chola kingdom when Cauveripoompatnam was its capital. He was known by the name of Arumolidevan when he was the yuvaraj. He styled himself Mummudi Cholan during the third year of his reign. He captured a number of sea-coast towns such as Kandalur about the tenth year of his rule. He conquered Gangapadi, Nulambapadi, Thadigaipadi, Vengainadu about the beginning of the fourteenth year. He conquered the Pandya kingdom during the latter part of the fourteenth year, Quilon and Kalinga at the twentieth year and Lanka during the twentieth year of his reign. It is said that he subdued the 12,000 islands belonging to the Laccadives group in the twenty-ninth year. In his latter days he was known as Jayankondan and Rajasrayan. He seems to have built the Brahadeeswara Swami's temple at Tanjore. From the inscriptions in this temple we understand that he, his wife and his relations were the donors of many gifts. We may notice that music and other noble arts progressed during his reign. He has appointed musicians for the service of many of the famous temples in the Chola kingdom, and has given them dwellings and maniyams and daily gifts. Before his death he had conquered the whole of the Madras Presidency with the exception of Madura and Tinnevelly. It appears that "he wept that he had no more worlds to conquer". This valiant king died in 1013.

His son Rajendra or Gangaikonda Cholan ruled from 1010 to 1042 assuming the titles of Mudikonda Cholan and Oottama Cholan. He conquered the Kalinga country, the plains of the Ganganad and Burma during his time.

He was followed by his son Rajadhirajan in 1042. There was incessant warfare between him and Someswara Chalukyan. He died in the battle of Koppam near the Tungabhadra in 1052.

At his death, his brother was victorious over Someswara Chalukyan, and ruled from 1052-1061.

After him ruled Veera Ragendran or Sakala-Bhuvanasrayar from 1062 to 1070. He was the brother of Rajendran mentioned above. During his time, Vikramaditya invaded the country from Gangaivadi but was defeated by him. He was victorious over Vaikalan in Venginadu. He defeated the Chalukyans at Bezwada and at the mouth of the Tungabhadra. He conquered the provinces of Kollam, Pandyam and Kalingam during the fifth year of his reign and ruled under the title of Rajadhiraja.

His son Adhirajarajan ruled only for a year.

After him Rajendra Cholan, the grandson of Rajaraja by his daughter, was appointed king regent in his twelfth year in Conjeevaram, under the title of Kulottunga Cholan. He became king of Kuntalam on the banks of the Cauvery. He conquered the Pandya king and overran the Gulf of Mannar. In 1085 he conquered Tinnevelly Pothiamalai, Cape Comorin, Kotaru, Syamalai, Kudamalainadu, Vilingam and Salai. During his time the whole of the Madras Presidency with the exception of Madura was under the Cholas. A land survey was made during his time. The measurement-rod was known as the Sripadam. Jayankondan, the prince of poets, flourished during his reign. He conquered Venginadu and Kalingam in 1084 and was considered famous among Chola sovereigns. Sakilar was a contemporary of his. He was styled "Sungantavirta Cholan" as he abolished some of the taxes (Sungam) during his reign.

He was succeeded by Vikrama Cholam (1118-1135). He was the fourth son of Kulottungan.

After him came Kulottungan II who ruled from 1135 to 1150 styling himself Tribhuvana Chakravarti. Ottakoottan belongs to this period.

Rajadhiraja Cholan reigned from 1164 to 1178. Sakilar, Kamban, Ottakoottan Pugalendi, Adiyarkku-nallar and other eminent literary men flourished at this time.

Kulottungan III reigned from 1178 to 1216. He was a pious king who built many new Sivite temples and had a number of old temples renovated.

Thri Vikrama Chakravarti or Rajadhiraja Cholan III ruled after him from 1216 to 1244.

He was succeeded by Rajendra Chola Devar (1245 to 1267).

The history of these early Chola kings might be seen in detail in "Ancient India" by S. Krishnaswami Aiyangar, M. A., and in the District Gazetteer of Tanjore.

Owing to the absence of competent sovereigns, the Chola kingdom gradually declined after 1267 and passed through troublous times for 300 years after. In 1310 Malik Kafir, the Mahammadan ruler, overran Madura and Trichinopoly and ruled over them for 50 years. Then the Kingdom of the Cholas passed into the hands of the sovereigns of Imperial Vizianagar.

Bukkaraylu from 1335 to 1343 and after him Virupakshan seized the Chola kingdom.

From 1374-1375 Kempanna Oodayar ruled over Trichinopoly.

Harihararayalu was in possession of Trichinopoly from 1379 to 1391. But it appears from the stone inscriptions recording royal grants of land in Tanjore of the years 1443 that Devarayalu was in possession. The inscriptions recording grants of land presented by Tirumalarayalu in 1455 are also in Tanjore.

From 1475 to 1500 the Chola kingdom appears to have been under the Chalukyan dynasty, the prime ministers of the Emperors of Vizianagaram. We understand from inscriptions that Krishnadevarayalu ruled from 1517 to 1518. In 1532 Atchutadevarayalu conquered the Pandya king and built an obelisk in commemoration of it on the banks of the Tambraparni. In 1537 he conquered Tanjore, Negapatam and the Karnatic coast and brought them under Vizianagar. In 1539 he has given royal grants of land as seen from inscriptions. Savappa Naicker, the vizier of this Atchyuta Devarayalu ruled the Chola country from 1549 to 1572.

Atchyutappa Naicker reigned from 1572 to 1614. It is said that Venkatamakhi, the son of his prime minister Govinda Deekshatar, wrote about the 12 swarams occurring in the Ayappalai and the 72 Melakartas formed by permuting and combining those swarams. Of this more later on.

It is believed that Raghunadha Naicker ruled from 1614, and was succeeded by Vijayaraghava Naicker who died in 1673.

Shaji, who ruled over the Mahratta country, had two sons, Sivaji and Venkaji. The elder became the ruler of his father's kingdom after him, while the younger brother Venkaji invaded Tanjore with a small army and easily conquered it. He was also known as Ekoji. From this time, the Chola kingdom came under the Mahrattas. Venkaji ruled from 1674 to 1687.

His son Shaji ruled from 1687 to 1711, and Shaji's brother Sarabhoji I from 1711 to 1727.

After him his brother Tukoji reigned from 1728 to 1735. After the death of Tukoji, Bava Saheb, the eldest of his three sons ruled for a year, and his wife for two years.

She was succeeded by the Second son Sayaji who ruled till 1740 for two years.

The third son Pratap Singh reigned from 1740 to 1763.

After him came Thulajaji Maharaja (1763—1787). There was a revival of music during his reign. He seems to have invited vidwans from various places and organised musical parties. He and his queen were not only experts in music but also in other arts and sciences. Hearing of the musical fame of Sendil-velannavi of Tinnevelly in dancing, singing and playing the Veena, he sent a palanquin to bring him to Tanjore with all honours, but the old veteran musician was unable to accept the invitation owing to his infirmity but sent his son Mahadevan instead. It is said up to the present day that music made great progress in Tanjore under him.

After him, as his son Sarabhoji was too young to undertake the duties of government, Amarasingh, the brother of Thulajaji, succeeded him and ruled from 1787 to 1798.

He was succeeded by Maharaja Sarabhoji II (1798—1824). His son Sivaji sat on throne between 1824 and 1865. The Chola kingdom after his death, for want of an heir, came under the benign British Government who take a deep interest in the progress of education, manufactures and sanitation.

It must be understood that from the time of Maharaja Thulajaji the number of musicians in the Chola country increased. For the Maharaja has been encouraging musicians by gifts of free lands and dwellings in the most fertile parts of the country and by treating them with great consideration. His gifts are even at the present day enjoyed by the descendants of those musicians. It appears that, through Mahadevan Annavi, music and some of its beautiful and rare characteristics made progress. His descendants are found in many places in the Chola and other Tamil countries.

We noted how the Chola kingdom was first conquered by Vizianagar and later on by the Nayak and Mahratta kings in succession.

We find that the Chera, Chola and Pandya kings lived even as early as the third and fourth century B. C. and that the son and the daughter of Asoka made treaties with them. But tradition, puranas and literature ascribe to them even a still earlier date. Of these the Pandya kingdom seems to have the most ancient history, and there is reason to believe that the Pandyas were called 'the oldest' (பழையர்) on account of their antiquity. We have already spoken in brief about South Madura, the first capital of the Pandya kingdom, the Tamil Sangam that was organised there, the kings that ruled there and the Tamil language. We noted also how the words of Tamil, famous as a spoken as well as a written language, got mixed up with the many languages of the world. We also noted how a number of excellent words of the Tamil language which were in use under the Pandya kings gradually went out of use when the power of the sovereigns declined, how after the last Sangam they got mixed with foreign languages owing to the advent of alien sovereigns and how this admixture was the cause of great many doubts.

The Pandya kingdom seems to have been in an exalted condition many thousands of years before the dawn of the Christian era. We find that Chola kings then became powerful and scored victories over the Pandyas as well as other kings. Though the capital of the Pandyas was changed from time to time owing to circumstances of the deluge yet these Pandyas have ruled over Madura till the last. But the Cholas, though they were not affected by the deluge, never kept to a particular city as their capital, but had different capitals at different times in Oorayur, Kauveripoompatnam, Conjeevaram and Tanjore. Moreover, they seem to have ruled over the whole of the Madras Presidency with the exception of Madura. Unlike the Pandya kingdom, different dynasties ruled over the Chola kingdom at different periods. The descendants of the Chola sovereigns may be found at the present day in the Chola country either as Zemindars under the titles of Cholar, Choladevar, Cholangadevar, Vijayar, Vijayadevar and Mudikondan or as big Mirasdars, while the majority are in a very poor condition. When the ancient Chola kings conquered the Pandya kingdom once and again they captured a few small forts and cities and gradually spread themselves over the Pandya country. These Cholas afterwards declined owing to internal jealousies and quarrels. The Chera kingdom alone escaped from the vicissitudes of fortune and is continuing up to the present day. Karikal Cholan I must be mentioned as the foremost among the Chola kings in whose reign the kingdom was in a most flourishing condition. Madhavi, the expert in playing the Veena. and Kovalan the Veena expert, both of Kauveripoompatnam, lived during his reign. Ilankovadigal, this brother of the Chera king Chenguttuvan, makes mention of the proficiency of the above two in music, in Silappadhikaram. From this we may conclude that music and dancing had attained a high degree of efficiency in the Tamil country even as early as the time of Karikal Cholan. Even during this time we find that the 12 swarams which are formed by the Shadjama Panchama series are according to the system of Ayappalai. As the modern musicians are ignorant of that system they declare that ancients did not know the art of having permanent frets for the Veena but had them adjusted from time to time to suit different ragas, and that the modern system of having permanent frets originated from the time of Savappa Naicker of very recent date, having the English notes of a scale for a model. But we shall prove later on that a system of more minute srutis was also in use during his time.

This Karikalan lived from 50 to 95 A.D. We have already noted how he invited many Vidwans and artists from different places and made them live in Kauveripoompatnam. We find that Kochengannan, who was a sovereign of distinction after Karikal Cholan, built as many as 70 Sivite and Vishnuvite temples. His time may be about 600 A. D.

We understand that Vijayalayar conquered Tanjore when he was at Conjeevaram in 846, and that Parakesarivarma or Parantaka I who came to the throne in 907 presented tiles made of gold to the temple at Chidambaram.

Rajarajan, the Chola king, came to the throne in 985. While he was young, he was known as Arumolidevar and later on he was called Mummudi Cholan. The Chola kingdom was in a powerful state during his time. The big temple at Tanjore seems to have been built at this time. We may find in the walls surrounding the temple many stone inscriptions recording gifts to the temple by himself and his relations. Again, we may find among the inscriptions a regular system by which temple-music had been organised during his time. We find that he invited musicians from different parts of the country and patronised them by giving them houses to dwell in along with lands and gifts for their maintenance. It appears that music was in a progressive state from his time forward. Long after him Kulottunga Cholan I, his grandson by his daughter, ruled over the country. A survey of lands was made during his time. The measuring rod was called Sripadam. His survey was so perfect and minute that in a Vali of land there was not even the mistake of a square inch. Jayamkondan, the prince of poets, lived about this time. Ottakoottan lived during the time of Kulottungan II (1135—1150) and Sakilar, Kamban, Puhalandi and Adiyarkku-nallar belong to the time of Rajadhi Rajan (1164).

In 1572, during the reign of Atchyutappa Naicker, the second of the Nayak kings who ruled over the Chola country, Venkatamakhi the son of the king's prime minister Govinda Deekshatar lived. Having the 12 Swarams of South Indian music as the basis, he derived 72 Melakartas from them and also composed Geetams and Lakshana Sahityam for the same. He also noted the different Janya Ragas (Secondary Ragas) that might be derived from each mother Ragam. Though be had definitely noted the mother Ragas which contain the Janya Ragas with minute srutis yet he failed to note the minute srutis themselves. So modern musicians have a tendency to spoil these also and bring them down to the position of Hindustani music.

So we conclude that music was made much of during the reign of Atchyutappa Naicker. There is reason to think that music had made enormous strides during the reign of the Mahratta king Tulajoji Maharaja who ruled over the Chola country in 1763. He seems to have patronised the excellent Veena, singing, dancing, gestures, flute and other ancient systems of instrumental and vocal music. We have declared that music did make great progress under the Cholas. In proof thereof if we see a stone inscription dated 1,000 years ago found on the walls of the big Temple at Tanjore we shall certainly come to the conclusion that music was in an excellent condition even as early as that period. Though a few extracts from those inscriptions will be quite enough for our purpose, yet we find that it will be expedient to quote the inscriptions as they are, seeing that they are so ancient and speak entirely about the musicians of that period. The following are from " South Indian Inscriptions, Vol. II, Pt. III.

3. The Stone inscriptions in the Temple of Brahadeeswara at Tanjore.

These inscriptions are found on the walls of the outer courts of the temple in the North-Western corner.

Hail! Prosperity! Until the twenty-ninth year (*of the reign*) of Ko-Rajakesarivarman, *alias* Sri Rajarajadeva who in his life of growing strength, during which (*in*) the belief that, as well as the Goddess of fortune, the Goddess of the great earth had become his wife, - he was pleased to destroy the ships (*at*) Kandalur-Salai, and conquered by his army, which was victorious in great battles, Vengai-nadu, Ganga-padi, Tadigai-padi, Nulamba-padi Kudamalai-nadu, Kollam, Kalingam, Iramandalam, (*which was the country*) of the Singalas who possessed rough strength, the seven and a half lakhs of Irattapadi, and twelve thousand ancient islands of the sea, deprived the Seriyas of (*their*) splendour at the very moment when (*they were*) resplendent (*to such a degree*) that *they were* worthy to be worshipped everywhere - the lord Sri Rajarajadeva had given for reciting the *Tiruppadiyam* before the lord of the Sri Rajarajesvara (*temple* forty eight musicians (*Pidarar*), one person who should constantly beat the small drum in their company, and one person who should constantly beat the big drum (*Kottai-mattalam*) in their company. These fifty persons were to receive from the city treasury of the lord a daily allowance (nibandha of three *Kuruni* of paddy each (*measured*) by the *Marakkal* called (*after*) Adavallan, which is equal to a *rajakesari*. Instead of those among these persons, who would die or emigrate the nearest relation of such persons were to receive that paddy and to recite the *Tiruppadiyam*. If the nearest relations of such persons were not qualified themselves, they were to select (*other*) qualified persons, to let (*these*) recite the *Tiruppadiyam*, and to receive that paddy. If there were no near relations to such persons, the (*other*) incumbents of such appointments were to select qualified persons for reciting the *Tiruppadiyam*, and the person selected was to receive the paddy in the same way, as that person (*whom he represented*) had received it. Accordingly (*the names of these fifty persons*) were engraved on stone as the lord Sri Rajarajadeva had been pleased to order :—

1. To Palan (*i.e.*, Bala) Tiruvanjiyattadigal, *alias* Rajaraja Pichchan, *alias* Sadasivan, three Kuruni of paddy per day.
2. To Tiruvenaval Semborchodi *alias* Dakshina-Meru Vitanka Pichchan, *alias* Nana-Sivan, three Kuruni of paddy per day.
3. To Pattalagan Ambalattadi *alias*, Manotma Sivan three Kuruni of paddy per day.
4. To Pattalagan Sirudaikkaral *alias*, Purva Sivan three Kuruni of paddy per day.
5. To Porchuvaran Tirunavukkaraiyan, *alias* Purva Sivan, three Kuruni of paddy per day.
6. To Madevan (i.e., Mahadeva) Tirunanasambadan *alias* Nana-Sivan, three Kuruni of paddy per day.
7. To Kayilayan (*i.e.*, Kailasa) Arur, *alias* Dharma Sivan three Kuruni of paddy per day.
8. To Setti Eduttapadam *alias* Kavacha-Sivan three Kuruni of paddy per day.
9. To Iraman (*i.e.*, Rama) Sambandan *alias* Satya Sivan three Kuruni of paddy per day.
10. To Ambalavan Pattargal *alias* Vama Sivan three Kuruni of paddy per day.
11. To Kamban Tirunavukkaraiyan (*alias*) Sadasivan, three Kuruni of paddy per day.
12. To Nakkan (*i.e.*, Nagna) Siralan, *alias* Vama-Sivan three Kuruni of paddy per day.
13. To Appi Tirunavukkaraiyan, *alias* Netra Sivan, three Kuruni of paddy per day.
14. To Sivakkorundu Siralan, *alias* Dharma-Sivan, three Kuruni of paddy per day.
15. To Ainnurruvan Venkadan, *alias* Satya-Sivan, three Kuruni of paddy per day.
16. To Araiyan Anukkan, *alias* Tirumaraikka *alias* Dharma-Sivan, three Kuruni of paddy per day.
17. To Araiyan Ambalakkuttan, *alias* Omkara Sivan, three Kuruni of paddy per day.
18. To Aruran Tirunavukkaraiyan, *alias* Nana Sivan, three Kuruni of paddy per day.
19. To Kuttan Maralaichchilambu, *alias* Purva-Sivan, three Kuruni of paddy per day.
20. To Ainnurruvan Siyarur, *alias* Tatpurusha-Sivan, three Kuruni of paddy per day.
21. To Sambandan Aruran, *alias* Vama-Sivan, three Kuruni of paddy per day.
22. To Araiyan Pichchan, *alias* Dharma-Sivan, three Kuruni of paddy per day.
23. To Kasyapan Eduttapada-Pichchan *alias* Rudra Sivan, three Kuruni of paddy per day.
24. To Subrahmanyan Achchan, *alias* Dharma Sivan, three Kuruni of paddy per day.
25. To Kuttan Amarabhujamgan *alias* Satya-Sivan, three Kuruni of paddy per day.
26. To............Venkadan, *alias* Aghora-Sivan, three Kuruni of paddy per day.
27. To Madevan Tirunavukkaraiyan, *alias* Vijnana Sivan, three Kuruni of paddy per day.
28. To Kuttan Venkadan, *alias* Rudra Sivan, three Kuruni of paddy per day.
29. To Ainnurruvan Tiruvaymur, *alias* Aghora-Sivan, three Kuruni of paddy per day.
30. To Tirumalai Kuttan, *alias* Vama-Sivan, three Kuruni of paddy per day.
31. To Ainnurruvan Eduttapadam, *alias* Dharma-Sivan, three Kuruni of paddy per day.
32. To Araiyan Tillaikkaraisu, *alias* Purva-Sivan, three Kuruni of paddy per day.
33. To Kalisambandan, *alias* Dharma-Sivan, three Kuruni of paddy per day.
34. To Kapalika-Vali, *alias* Nana-Sivan, three Kuruni of paddy per day.
35. To Venkadan Namassivayam, *alias* Rudra-Sivan, three Kuruni of paddy per day.
36. To Sivan Anantan *alias* Yoga Sivan, three Kuruni of paddy per day.
37. To Sivakkorundu Sambandan, *alias* Aghora-Sivan three Kuruni of paddy per day.
38. To Iraman Kanavadi (*i.e.*, Ganapati) *alias* Nana-Sivan three Kuruni of paddy per day.
39. To Pichchan Venkadan *alias* Aghora Sivan, three Kuruni of paddy per day.
40. To Maraikkadan Nambi-Aruran *alias* Nana-Si an three Kuruni of paddy per day.
41. To Soman (*i.e.* Soma) Sambandan *alias* Nana-Sivan three Kuruni of paddy per day.

42. To Satti (*i.e.*, Sakti) Tirunavukkaraiyan, *alias* Isana Sivan, three Kuruni of paddy per day.
43. To Porchuvaran Nambi-Aruran *alias* Dharma Sivan. three Kuruni of paddy per day.
44. To Achchan Tirunavukkaraiyan, *alias* Netra Sivan three Kuruni of paddy per day.
45. To Aiyaran Pennorbagan, *alias* Hridaya-Sivan three Kuruni of paddy per day.
46. To Rajadittan Ambalattadi, *alias* Sikha Sivan three Kuruni of paddy per day.
47. To Selvan Kanavadi Temban *alias*, Dharma Sivan three Kuruni of paddy per day.
48. To Kuttan Tillaikkuttan *alias* Nana-Sivan three Kuruni of paddy per day.
49. For beating the small drum, to Suryadeva Kramavittan, *alias*.........Vidanga-Udukkai Vijjadiran, *alias* Soma-Sivan, the son of Tattaya-Kramavittan of Dvedaigomapuram three Kuruni of paddy per day.
50. For beating the big drum to Gunappugar Marudan, *alias* Sikha-Sivan three Kuruni of paddy per day.

Inscription in the Tanjavur Brahadiswarar Temple recording Sri Rajarajadeva's grant to 614 persons including 400 dancing girls for temple service.

Hail! Prosperity! Until the twenty-ninth year (of the reign) of Ko-Rajakesarivarman, *alias* Sri Rajarajadeva, who etc.,—the lord Sri-Rajarajadeva had (1) given (a number of) Nivandakkarar as Nivandakkarar of the lord of the Sri-Rajarajesvara (temple), and (2) transferred (a number of) temple women from (other) temple establishments of the Chola country (Soramandalam) as temple women of the lord of the Sri-Rajarajesvara (temple). To (these persons) shares (pangu) were allotted as allowance (Nibandha). (The value) of each share (which consisted of the produce) of (one) veli of land was to be one hundred Kalam of paddy, (measured by the marrakkal called (after) Adavallan, which is equal to a rajakesari. Instead of those among these share holders, who would die or emigrate, the nearest relations of such persons were to receive that allowance (Kani) and to do the work. If the nearest relations were not qualified themselves, (they) were to select (other) qualified persons, to let (these) do the work, and to receive (the allowance). If there were no near relations, the (other) incumbents of such appointments were to select qualified persons from those fit for such appointments, and the person selected was to receive the allowance. Accordingly (the names of those persons) were engraved on stone as the lord Sri-Rajarajatheva had been pleased to order.

1. The temple women (were the following):—
2. To Seramangai, a girl (who has been transferred from the establishment of the temple) of Lokamahadevi-Isvara at Tiruvaiyaru, (and who resides in) the first house of the southern row (Siragu) of the temple street on the south (of the temple), one share.
3. „ Iranamugarami, a girl of the same temple, (who resides in) the second house, one share.
4. „ Udaram, a girl of the same temple, (who resides in) the third house, one share.
5. „ Pattali, a girl of the same temple, (who resides in) the fourth house, one share.
6. „ Eduttapadam, a girl of the same temple, (who resides in) the fifth house, one share.
7. „ Sorakulasundari, a girl of the same temple, (who resides in) the sixth house, one share.
8. „ Ekaviri, a girl of the same temple, (who resides in) the seventh house, one share.
9. „ Rajakesari, a girl of the Tirukkaronam (temple) at Nagapattanam, (who resides in) the eighth house, one share.
10. „ Tesichchi, a girl of the Koyiltali (temple) in the same village, (who resides in) the ninth house, one share.

11. To Periya Tesichchi, a girl of the same temple, (who resides in) the tenth house, one share.
12. „ Vichchadiri *i.e.*, Vidyadhari), a girl of the Tirukkaronam (temple) in the same village, (who resides in) the eleventh house, one share.
13. „ Maraikkadu, a girl of the same temple, (who resides in) the twelfth house, one share.
14. „ Ammari, a girl of the Naduviltali (temple) in the same village, (who resides in) the thirteenth house, one share.
15. „ Tiruvaiyaru, a girl of Rajakesarinallur, (who resides in) the fourteenth house, one share.
16. „ Tillai Aragi, a girl of the Vikramavijaya-Isvara (temple) at Jananathapuram, (who resides in) the fifteenth house, one share.
17. „ Echchumandai, a girl of the same temple, (who resides in) the sixteenth house, one share.
18. „ Parami, a girl of Pagavadiseri (i.e., Bhagavati-seri) (a quarter of the same village), (who resides in) the seventeenth house, one share.
19. „ Tillaikkaraisu, a girl of Tiruvidaimarudil, (who resides in) the eighteenth house, one share.
20. „ Aragi, a girl of the same village, (who resides in) the nineteenth house, one share.
21. „ Saduri, a girl of the same village, (who resides in) the twentieth house, one share.
22. „ Maduravasagi, a girl of the same village, (who resides in) the twenty-first house, one share.
23. „ Madevadigal, a girl of the same village, (who resides in) the twenty-second house, one share.
24. „ ...., a girl of the same village, (who resides in) the twenty-third house, one share.
25. „ Iravikulamanikkam, a girl of the Komakkambhisvara (temple), (who resides in) the twenty-fourth house, one share.
26. „ Arur, a girl of the Mullurnakkantali (temple) at Paraiyaru, (who resides in) the twenty-fifth house, one share.
27. „ Virani, a girl of the Vadatali (temple) in the same village, (who resides in) the twenty-sixth house, one share.
28. „ Tennavanmadevi, a girl of the same temple, (who resides in) the twenty-seventh house, one share.
29. „ Tiruvaiyaru, a girl of Avaninarayanapuram, (a quarter) of the same village, (who resides in) the twenty-eighth house, one share.
30. „ Madevadigal, a girl of the Tentali (temple) at Paraiyaru, (who resides in) twenty-ninth house, one share.
31. „ Pugari, a girl of the Sritari-Vinnagar (temple) at Arapuram, (who resides in) the thirtieth house, one share.
32. „ Panjadi, a girl of the Tigaippiratti-Isvara temple in the same village, (who resides in) the thirty-first house, one share.
33. „ Karanavichchadiri, a girl of the same temple, (who resides in) the thirty-second house, one share.
34. „ Sangi, a girl of the Eriyurnattuttali (temple) at Tanjavur, (who resides in) the thirty-third house, one share.
35. „ Tarani a girl of the same temple, (who resides in) the thirty-fourth house, one share.
36. „ Setti, a girl of the same temple, (who resides in) the thirty-fifth house, one share.
37. „ Aravam, a girl of the same temple, (who resides in) the thirty-sixth house, one share.
38. „ Nakkam, a girl of the same temple, (who resides in) the thirty-seventh house, one share.

39. To Sirudaiyal, a girl of Periyatalichcheri, (a quarter) of Tiruvarur, (who resides in) the thirty-eighth house, one share.

40. „ Paravai, a girl of the Brahmisvara (temple) in the same village, (who resides in) the thirty-ninth house, one share.

41. „ Maralaichchilambu, a girl of Periyatalichcheri, (a quarter) of the same village, (who resides in) the fortieth house, one share.

42. „ Aramudu, a girl of the Tiruvaraneri (temple) in the same village, (who resides in) the forty-first house, one share.

43. „ Sikandi, a girl of the Arumori Isvara (temple) in the same village, (who resides in) the forty-second house, one share.

44. „ Paranderuman, a girl of the Ulagisvara (temple) in the same village, (who resides in) the forty-third house, one share.

45. „ Narayani, a girl of the Tiruvaraneri (temple) in the same village, (who resides in) the forty-fourth house, one share.

46. „ Aravam, a girl of the same temple, (who resides in) the forty-fifth house, one share.

47. „ Sodivilakku, a girl of the Brahmisvara (temple) at Tiruvarur, (who resides in) the forty-sixth house, one share.

48. „ Tigaichchudar, a girl of the Ulagisvara (temple) in the same village, (who resides in) the forty-seventh house, one share.

49. „ Ali, a girl of the Brahmisvara (temple) in the same village, (who resides in) the forty-eighth house, one share.

50. „ Sikandi, a girl of the Tentali (temple) at Mattai, (who resides in) the forty-ninth house, one share.

51. „ Perratiru, a girl of the same village, (who resides in) the fiftieth house, one share.

52. „ Vira-Sori, a girl of the Tanjaimamanikkoyil (temple) at Tanjavur, (who resides in) the fifty-first house, one share.

53. „ Tiruvalangadi, a girl of Sikandapuram, (who resides in) the fifty-second, house, one share.

54. „ ...., a girl of Parantakapuram, (who resides in) the fifty-third house, one share.

55. „ Uttamadani, a girl of the same village, (who resides in) the fifty-fourth house, one share.

56. „ ...., a girl of the Arikulakesari Isvara (temple) at Niyamam, (who resides in) the fifty-fifth house, one share.

57. „ Venkadu, a girl of the same temple, (who resides in) the fifty-sixth house, one share.

58. „ Kuttadi, a girl of the same temple, (who resides in) the fifty-seventh house, one share.

59. „ Sorasulamani, a girl of the same temple, (who resides in) the fifty-eighth house, one share.

60. „ Pungavi, a girl of Ariyattali, (a quarter) of the same village, (who resides in) the fifty-ninth house, one share.

61. „ Nanjuri, a girl of the Arikulakesari-Isvara (temple), in the same village, (who resides in) the sixtieth house, one share.

62. „ Devi, a girl of the Ayirattali (a quarter) of Niyamam (who resides in) the sixty-first house, one share.

63. „ Nanguri, a girl of the Tirumagalam (temple) at Ambar, (who resides in) the sixty-second house, one share.

64. „ Rajaraji, a girl of the same temple, (who resides in) the sixty-third house, one share.

65. „ Atimasi, a girl of the same temple, (who resides in) the sixty-fourth house, one share.

66. To Udaiyam, a girl of the Avaninarayana-Vinnagar, (temple) in the same village, (who resides in) the sixty-fifth house, one share.
67. „ Kamakkodi, a girl of the Tirumagalam (temple) in the same village, (who resides in) the sixty-sixth house, one share.
68. „ Nichchal, a girl of the Mudubagavartali (temple) in the same village, (who resides in) the sixty-seventh house, one share.
69. „ Kuppai, a girl of the Tiruvilangoyil (temple) at Kadambur, (who resides in) the sixty-eighth house, one share.
70. „ Vidividangi, a girl of the same (temple), (who resides in) the sixty-ninth house, one share.
71. „ the younger Nakkam, a girl of the same (temple), (who resides in) the seventieth house, one share.
72. „ the elder Nakkam, a girl of the same (temple), (who resides in) the seventy-first house, one share.
73. „ Dharanivarahi, a girl of the Ittachchi-Isvara (temple) in the same village, (who resides in) the seventy-second house, one share.
74. „ Madevi, a girl of Tirumaraikkadu, (who resides in) the seventy-third house, one share.
75. „ Ammari, a girl of Vidaiyapuram, (who resides in) the seventy-fourth house, one share.
76. „ ....tappagai, a girl of Velur, (who resides in) the seventy-fifth house, one share.
77. „ Tirunilagandi, a girl of Nayadirapuram, (who resides in) the seventy-sixth house, one share.
78. „ Manabarani, a girl of Virapuram, (who resides in) the seventy-seventh house, one share.
79. „ Perratiru, a girl of the Tirumerrali (temple) at Pachchil, (who resides in) the seventy-eighth house, one share.
80. „ Soram, a girl of the Tiruvachchiramam (temple) in the same village, (who resides in) the seventy-ninth house, one share.
81. „ Sengulam, a girl of the Tirumerrali (temple) in the same village, (who resides in) the eightieth house, one share.
82. „ ....a girl of Virapuram, (who resides in) the eighty-first house, one share.
83. „ Porkesi, a girl of Tirukkolambudur, (who resides in) the eighty-second house, one share.
84. „ Arayiram, a girl of the same village, (who resides in) the eighty-third house one share.
85. „ Tillaikkutti, a girl of the Karpagadanipuram, (who resides in) the eighty-fourth house, one share.
86. „ Arur, a girl of the same village, (who resides in) the eighty-fifth house, one share.
87. „ Samundi, a girl of the same village, (who resides in) the eighty-sixth house, one share.
88. „ Abaiyam, a girl of the same village, (who resides in) the eighty-seventh house, one share.
89. „ Tirumangalam, a girl of the Brahmakuttam (temple) at Tanjavur, (who resides in) the eighty-eigth house, one share.
90. „ Pichchi, a girl of the same temple, (who resides in) the eighty-ninth house, one share.
91. „ Tiruvadigal, a girl of Pallavanaranapuram, (who resides in) the ninetieth house, one share.
92. „ Sattam, a girl of Tirumaraikkadu, (who resides in) the ninety-first house, one share.
93. „ Tirumalai, a girl of the same village, (who resides in) the ninety-second house, one share.
94. „ Vikkiramatongi, a girl of the Lokamahadevi-Isvara (temple) at Tiruvaiyaru, (who resides in) the first house, of the northern row of the same temple street, one share.

95. To Pugari, a girl of the same (temple), (who resides in) the second house, one share.
96. „ Manikkam, a girl of Miraiyil, (who resides in) the third house, one share.
97. „ Madevi, a girl of Periyatalichcheri, (a quarter) of Tiruvarur, (who resides in) the fourth house, one share.
98. „ Tirumulattanam, a girl of the same temple, (who resides in) the fifth house, one share.
99. „ Arur, a girl of the Brahmisvara (temple) in the same village, (who resides in) the sixth house, one share.
100. „ Kandiyur, a girl of Periyatalichcheri, (a quarter) of the same village, (who resides in) the seventh house, one share.
101. „ Achcham, a girl of the Ulagiswara (temple) in the same village, (who resides in) the eighth house, one share.
102. „ Aravam, a girl of the Tiruvaraneri (temple) in the same village, (who resides in) the ninth house, one share.
103. „ Karambiyam, a girl of the same (temple), (who resides in) the tenth house, one share.
104. „ Kandiyur, a girl of Periyatalichcheri (a quarter) of the same village, (who resides in) eleventh house, one share.
105. „ Vidividangi, a girl of the same (temple), (who resides in) the twelfth house, one share.
106. „ Innilavanji, a girl of the Avaninarayana-Vinnagar (temple) at Ambar, (who resides in) the thirteenth house, one share.
107. „ Maralaichchilambu, a girl of the same temple, (who resides in) the fourteenth house, one share.
108. „ Sembon, a girl of the Tirumagalam (temple) in the same village, (who resides in) the fifteenth house, one share.
109. „ ....a girl of Tiruvaiyuru, (who resides in) the sixteenth house, one share.
110. „ Aiyaru, a girl of the same village, (who resides in) the seventeenth house, one share.
111. „ Tiruvennaval, a girl of the same village, (who resides in) the eighteenth house, one share.
112. „ Umai, a girl of the Tiruvachchiramam (temple) at Pachchil, (who resides in) the nineteenth house, one share.
113. „ Perratiru, a girl of the Tentali (temple) at Paraiyaru, (who resides in) the twentieth house, one share.
114. „ the younger Sirudaiyal, a girl of Killigudi, (who resides in) the twenty-first house, one share.
115. „ the elder Sirudaiyal, a girl of the same village, (who resides in) the twenty-second house, one share.
116. „ Olokamata, a girl of Talichchattangudi, (who resides in) the twenty-third house, one share.
117. „ Tiru, a girl of Pagandiseri (a quarter) of Jananathapuram, (who resides in) the twenty-fourth, house, one share.
118. „ Madevi, a girl of the Tanjaimamanikkoyil (temple) at Tanjavur, (who resides in) the twenty-fifth house, one share.
119. „ Kali, a girl of Talaiyalangadu, (who resides in) the twenty-sixth house, one share.
120. „ Tiruppuvanam, a girl of the Sritari-Vinnagar (temple) at Arapuram, (who resides in) the twenty-seventh house, one share.
121. „ Marudamanikkam, a girl of Kaipagadanipuram, (who resides in) the twenty-eighth house, one share.

122. To Karpagamanikkam, a girl of the same village, (who resides in) the twenty-ninth house, one share.

123. „ Kayilam (i.e., Kailasa), a girl of the Tiru-Amalisvara (temple) at Nannilam, (who resides in) the thirtieth house, one share.

124. „ Achcham, a girl of Ayirattali, (a quarter) of Niyamam, (who resides in) the thirty-first house, one share.

125. „ Paranderuman, a girl of the Tirumerrali (temple) at Pachchil, (who resides in) the thirty-second house, one share.

126. „ Sorakulasundari, a girl of the Vadatali (temple) at Paraiyaru, (who resides in) the thirty-third house, one share.

127. „ Adavallal, a girl of the Pagaividai Isvara (temple) at Paravur, (who resides in) the thirty-fourth house, one share.

128. „ Ilangoyil, a girl of the Nandi-Isvara (temple) at Kadambur, (who resides in) the thirty-fifth house, one share.

129. „ Arivatti, girl of the Mahadevi-Iswara (temple) (who resides in) the thirty-sixth house, one share.

130. „ Madevadigal, a girl of the Eriyurnattuttali (temple) at Tanjavur, (who resides in) the thirty-seventh house, one share.

131. „ Ponnalamandal, a girl of the Vikrama-Vijaya-Iswara (temple) at Jananathapuram, (who resides in) the thirty-eighth house, one share.

132. „ Karayil, a girl of the Sripudi-Vinnagar (temple) at Pambuni, (who resides in) the thirty-ninth house, one share.

133. „ Tiruvaiyaru, a girl of . . . . (who resides in) the fortieth house, one share.

134. „ Aiyaru, a girl of Ayirattali, (who resides in) the forty-first house, one share.

135. „ Perramai, a girl of the Niraimadi-Isvara (temple), (who resides in) the forty-second house, one share.

136. „ Mari, a girl of Tirumaraikkadu, (who resides in) the forty-third house, one share.

137. „ Tiru, a girl of the Vikramavijaya-Isvara (temple) at Jananathapuram, (who resides in) the forty-fourth house, one share.

138. „ Nandi Eruman, a girl of the same temple, (who resides in) the forty-fifth house, one share.

139. „ Tillaikkaraisu, a girl of the Tiruvamalisvara (temple) Pachchil, (who resides in) the forty-sixth house, one share.

140. „ Umai, a girl of the Tiruvachchiramam (temple) in the same village, (who resides in) the forty-seventh house, one share.

141. „ Siriyal, a girl of the Mahadevi-Isvara (temple), (who resides in) the forty-eigth house, one share.

142. „ Achcham, a girl of Tiruvidaimarudil, (who resides in) the forty-ninth house, one share.

143. „ Kadugal, a girl of the same village, (who resides in) the fiftieth house, one share.

144. „ Panchavanmadevi, a girl of the same village, (who resides in) the fifty-first house, one share.

145. „ Sikandi, a girl of the same village, (who resides in) the fifty-second house, one share.

146. „ Kallarai, a girl of the same village, (who resides in) the fifty-third house, one share.

147. „ Sittiravalli, a girl of the Sritari-Vinnagar (temple) at Arapuram, (who resides in) the fifty-fourth house, one share.

148. „ Nallur, a girl of the Nigalangi-Isvara (temple) in the same village, (who resides in) the fifty-fifth house, one share.

149. To Peruvari, a girl of the same temple, (who resides in) the fifty-sixth house, one share.
150. „ Semani, a girl of the Tiruvilangoyil (temple) at Kadambur, (who resides in) the fifty-seventh house, one share.
151. „ Konadi, a girl of the same (temple), (who resides in) the fifty-eighth house, one share.
152. „ Nambugari, a girl of the Tiruvaraneri-Isvara, (temple) at Tiruvarur, (who resides in) the fifty-ninth house, one share.
153. „ Tirumulattanam, a girl of the Periyatalichcheri (a quarter) of same village, (who resides in) the sixtieth house, one share.
154. „ Somanadi, a girl of the Brahmisvara (temple) in the same village, (who resides in) the sixty-first house, one share.
155. „ Irami, a girl of Periyatalichcheri, (a quarter) of the same village, (who resides in) the sixty-second house, one share.
156. „ Echchumandai, a girl of the Brahmisvara (temple) in the same village, (who resides in) the sixty-third house, one share.
157. „ Sundara Sori, a girl of the Tirumandali (temple) in the same village, (who resides in) the sixty-fourth house, one share.
158. „ Pandal, a girl of the Ulagisvara (temple), (who resides in) the sixty-fifth house, one share.
159. „ Kami, a girl of the Avani Narayana-Vinnagar (temple) at Ambar, (who resides in) sixty-sixth house, one share.
160. „ Asarapanjari, a girl of the same temple, (who resides in) the sixty-seventh house, one share.
161. „ Ekaviri, a girl of the Mudupagavartali (temple) in the same village, (who resides in) the sixty-eighth house, one share.
162. „ , a girl of the same (temple), (who resides in) the sixty-ninth house, one share.
163. „ Sangam, a girl of the same temple, (who resides in) the seventieth house, one share.
164. „ Kandam, a girl of Tiruvaiyaru, (who resides in) the seventy-first house, one share.
165. „ Pavai, a girl of the same village. (who resides in) the seventy-second house, one share.
166. „ Tutti, a girl of the Avaniyamadarpapuram, (a quarter) of Paruvur, (who resides in) the seventy-third house, one share.
167. „ Arikulakesari, a girl of the Pagavidai-Isvara (temple) in the same village, (who resides in) the seventy-fourth house, one share.
168. „ Kulaman, a girl of the Pugarmadil-Isvara (temple) at.........ndali, (who resides in) the seventy-fifth house, one share.
169. „ Karumanikkam, a girl of the same temple, (who resides in) the seventy-sixth house, one share.
170. „ Nagarattal, a girl of Puraiyachcheri, (who resides in) the seventy-seventh house one share.
171. „ Sandiram, a girl of Ayirattali, (a quarter) of Niyamam, (who resides in) the seventy-eighth house, one share.
172. „ Vadavagil, a girl of the Arikulakesari-Isvara (temple) in the same village, (who resides in) the seventy-ninth house, one share.
173. „ Paranderuman, a girl of the Niripakesari-Isvara (temple) in the same village, (who resides in) the eightieth house, one share.
174. „ Tiruvengadam, a girl of the Sandiramallisvara (temple) in the same village, (who resides in) the eighty-first house, one share.

175. To Sarpadevi, a girl of the Arikulakesari-Isvara (temple) in the same village, (who resides in) the eighty-second house, one share.
176. „ Amattur, a girl of the Tirumerrali (temple) at Nannilam, (who resides in) the eighty-third house, one share.
177. „ Udari, a girl of Kavirippumbattanam, (who resides in) the eighty-fourth house, one share.
178. „ Silasulamani, a girl of the Araiyerumantali (temple) at Paraiyaru, (who resides in) the eighty-fifth house, one share.
179. „ Vikkiramaditti, a girl of Avani-Narayanapuram, (a quarter) of the same village, (who resides in) the eighty-sixth house, one share.
180. „ Tillainiraindal, a girl of the same village, (who resides in) the eighty-seventh house, one share.
181. „ Nayanavalli, a girl of the Vadatali (temple) in the same village (who resides in) the eighty-eighth house, one share.
182. „ Perratiru, a girl of the same temple, (who resides in) the eighty-ninth house, one share.
183. „ Madanavalli, a girl of the Mallisvara (temple) at Ayiratalli, (who resides in) the ninetieth house, one share.
184. „ Eduttapadam, a girl of Karuppur, (who resides in) the ninety-first house, one share.
185. „ Minavanmadevi, a girl of Virapuram (who resides in) the ninety-second house, one share.
186. „ Muvargandi, a girl of the Brahmisvara (temple) at Tiruvarur, (who resides in) the first house of the southern row of the temple street on the north (of the temple), one share.
187. „ Sirudaiyal, a girl of the Tirukkaronam (temple) at Nagapattanam, (who resides in) the second house, one share.
188. „ Tiru, a girl of the Nigalangi-Isvara (temple) at Arapuram, (who resides in) the third house, one share.
189. „ Perratiru, a girl of the Gunavati-Isvara (temple) at Kottur (who resides in) the fourth house, one share.
190. „ Pal, a girl of Sripudi-Vinnagar (temple) at Pambuni, (who resides in) the fifth house, one share.
191. „ Karpagadani, a girl of Karpagadanipuram, (who resides in) the sixth house, one share.
192. „ Pandal, a girl of Periyatalichcheri, (a quarter) of Tiruvarur, (who resides in) the seventh house, one share.
193. „ , a girl of the same village, (who resides in) the eighth house, one share.
194. „ Ambalam, a girl of Talichattangudi, (who resides in) the ninth house, one share.
195. „ Viraiyachchilai, a girl of Periyatalichcheri, (a quarter) of Tiruvarur, (who resides in) the tenth house, one share.
196. „ Anavarata Sundari, a girl of Ayirattali, (who resides in) the eleventh house, one share.
197. „ Rajasulamani, a girl of the same village, (who resides in) the twelfth house, one share.
198. „ Araneri, a girl of Nayadirapuram, (who resides in) the thirteenth house, one share.
199. „ Pattam, a girl of Ayirattali, (who resides in) the fourteenth house, one share.
200. „ Ilanga, a girl of the same village, (who resides in) the fifteenth house, one share.
201. „ Modi, a girl of the Arumori-Isvara (temple) at Tiruvarur, (who resides in) the sixteenth house, one share.
202. „ Karuvur, a girl of the same village, (who resides in) the seventeenth house, one share.

203. To Tiruvanaikkavi, a girl of the Parantaka-Isvara (temple), (who resides in) the eighteenth house, one share.
204. „ Aravam, a girl of Tiruvaiyaru, (who resides in) the nineteenth house, one share.
205. „ Sundari, a girl of the Panchavan-Mahadevi-Isvara (temple) at Kottur, (who resides in) the twentieth house, one share.
206. „ Nambandi a girl of the same temple, (who resides in) the twenty-first house, one share.
207. „ Umai, a girl of the same temple, (who resides in) the twenty-second house, one share.
208. „ Tittaichcheri, a girl of the same temple, (who resides in) the twenty-third house, one share.
209. „ Umai, a girl of the same temple, (who resides in) the twenty-fourth house, one share.
210. „ Sittiravalli, a girl of the Tiruvaraneri-Isvara (temple) at Tiruvarur, (who resides in) the twenty-fifth house, one share.
211. „ Pichchi, a girl of Ayirattali, (who resides in) the twenty-sixth house, one share.
212. „ Perratiru, a girl of the Pugarisvara (temple) at Vidaiyapuram, (who resides in) the twenty-seventh house, one share.
213. „ Sikandi, a girl of the Tirumandali (temple) at Tiruvarur, (who resides in) the twenty-eighth house, one share.
214. „ Kundavai, a girl of the same temple, (who resides in) the twenty-ninth house, one share.
215. „ Pakkari, a girl of the Mallisvara temple at Ayirattali, (who resides in) the thirtieth house, one share.
216. „ Pon, a girl of the Brahmisvara (temple) at Tiruvarur, (who resides in) the thirty-first house, one share.
217. „ Porkumaran, a girl of the Vikramavijaya-Isvara (temple) at Jananathapuram, (who resides in) the thirty-second house, one share.
218. „ Somakon, a girl of the Parantaka-Isvara (temple), (who resides in) the thirty-third house, one share.
219. „ Ekaviri, a girl of the Arumori-Isvara (temple) at Tiruvarur, (who resides in) the thirty-fourth house, one share.
220. „ Devi, a girl of Ayirattali, (who resides in) the thirty-fifth house, one share.
221. „ Tiruvadigal, a girl of the same village, (who resides in) the thirty-sixth house, one share.
222. „ the dark Tiruvadi, a girl of the same village, (who resides in) the thirty-seventh house, one share.
223. „ Kandarachchi, a girl of the Tiruvedigudi, (who resides in) the thirty-eighth house, one share.
224. „ Kulamanikkam, a girl of the same village, (who resides in) the thirty-ninth house, one share.
225. „ …………, a girl of Arruttali, (who resides in) the fortieth house, one share.
226. „ Vembi, a girl of the same village, (who resides in) the forty-first house, one share.
227. „ Porkesi, a girl of the Niraimadi-Isvara (temple), (who resides in) the forty-second house, one share.
228. „ Orriyur, a girl of Tiruchchorrutturai, (who resides in) the forty-third house, one share.
229. „ …………, a girl of Tirumaraikkadu, (who resides in) the forty-fourth house, one share.
230. „ Sangani, a girl of the Tirumerrali (temple) at Nannilam, (who resides in) the forty-fifth house, one share.

231. To Eri, a girl of the Tiru-Amalisvara (temple) in the same village, (who resides in) the forty-sixth house, one share.

232. „ Puvanam, a girl of Uttamadanipuram, (who resides in) the forty-seventh house, one share.

233. „ Adigal, a girl of Ayirattali, (a quarter) of Niyamam, (who resides in) the forty-eighth house, one share.

234. „ Nirani-Pavarakkunru, a girl of the Araiyerumantali (temple) at Paraiyaru, (who resides in) the forty-ninth house, one share.

235. „ Arumori, a girl of the same temple, (who resides in) the fiftieth house, one share.

236. „ Achcham, a girl of the Tentali (temple) in the same viilage, (who resides in) the fifty-first house, one share.

237. „ To the younger Achcham of the same temple (who resides in) the fifty-second house, one share.

238. „ Amudam, a girl of the Vadatali (temple) in the same village, (who resides in) the fifty-third house, one share.

239. „ Sulamani, a girl of the same temple, (who resides in) the fifty-fourth house, one share.

240. „ Ekaviri, a girl of the same temple, (who resides in) the fifty-fifth house, one share.

241. „ Virani, a girl of the Mullurnakkantali (temple) in the same village, (who resides in) the fifty-sixth house, one share.

242. „ Oruppanai, a girl of the same temple, (who resides in) the fifty-seventh house, one share.

243. „ Kannaradevi, a girl of Korramangalam, (who resides in) the fifty-eight house, one share.

244. „ Kanavadi, a girl of Tiruttengur, (who resides in) the fifty-ninth house, one share.

245. „ Etti, a girl of Sellur, (who resides in) the sixtieth house, one share.

246. „ Ambalakkutti, a girl of Tiruvaiyaru, (who resides in) the sixty-first hourse, one share.

247. „ Anantam, a girl of Senamugam, (a quarter) of Nagapattanam, (who resides in) the sixty-second house, one share.

248. „ Varuvanilai, a girl of the Tanjai Mamanikkoyil (temple) at Tanjavur, (who resides in) the sixty-third house, one share.

249. „ To Sidevi, a girl of the Lokamahadevi-Isvara (temple), (who resides in) the sixty-fourth house, one share.

250. „ To Eruvanai, a girl of Parantakapuram, (who resides in) the sixty-fifth house, one share.

251. „ Pon, a girl of Tiruvaiyaru, (who resides in) the sixty-sixth house, one share.

252. „ Paruvur, a girl of the Pagaividai-Isvara (temple) at Paruvur, (who resides in) the sixty-seventh house, one share.

253. „ Sivadevi, a girl of the Ittachchi-Isvara (temple) at Kadambur, (who resides in) the sixty-eighth house, one share.

254. „ Sikurugur, a girl of Periyatalichcheri, (a quarter) of Tiruvarur (who resides in) the the sixty-ninth house, one share.

255. „ Sangani, a girl of the Tirumerrali (temple) at Nannilam, (who resides in) the seventieth house, one share.

256. „ Sembiyanmadevi, a girl of Tiruvidaimarudil (who resides in) the seventy-first house, one share.

257. „ Kamamogi, a girl of the Jaya-bhimatali (temple) at Tanjavur, (who resides in) the seventy-second house, one share.

258. „ Ponnali, a girl of Periyatalichcheri, (a quarter) of Tiruvarur, (who resides in) the seventy-third house, one share.

259. To Virasikhamani, a girl of the Nripakesari-Isvara (temple) at Niyamam, (who resides in) the seventy-fourth house, one share.

260. „ Arur, a girl of the Sripudi-Vinnagar (temple) at Pambuni, (who resides in) the seventy-fifth house, one share.

261. „ Virabogi, a girl of Talaiyalamgadu, (who resides in) the seventy-sixth house, one share.

262. „ Ponnambalam, a girl of the same village, (who resides in) the seventy-seventh house, one share.

263. „ Oruppanai, a girl of Vadatali (temple) at Paraiyaru, (who resides in) the seventy-eighth house, one share.

264. „ Umai, a girl of the Tiruvilangoyil (temple) at Kadambur, (who resides in) the seventy-ninth house, one share.

265. „ Arangam, girl of Kavirippumbattanam, (who resides in) the eightieth house, one share.

266. „ Perratiru, a girl of the Mudubagavartali (temple) at Ambar, (who resides in) the eighty-first house, one share.

267. „ Rajaraji, a girl of Tiruvidaimarudil, (who resides in) the eighty-second house, one share.

268. „ Munji, a girl of the Tiruvamalisvara (temple) at Pachchil (who resides in) the eighty-third house, one share.

269. „ Porkali, a girl of Periyatalichcheri, (a quarter) of Tiruvarur, (who resides in) the eighty-fourth house, one share.

270. „ Tigaimanikkam, a girl of the Ulagisvara (temple) in the same village, (who resides in) the eighty-fifth house, one share.

271. „ Seyyapadam, a girl of the Mudubagavartali (temple) at Ambar, (who resides in) the eighty-sixth house, one share.

272. „ Aiyal, a girl of Viralur, (who resides in) the eighty-seventh house, one share.

273. „ Nambugamari, a girl of Naduvittalichcheri, (a quarter) of Nagapattanam, (who resides in) the eighty-eighth house, one share.

274. „ Araiyam, a girl of the Komakkambhisvara (temple), (who resides in) the eighty-ninth house, one share.

275. „ Nittangai, a girl of the Tirumandali (temple) at Tiruvarur, (who resides in) the ninetieth house, one share.

276. „ Siriya Umai, a girl of the Parantaka-Isvara (temple), (who resides in) the ninety-first house one share.

277. „ To Kamamogi, a girl of the Jayabhimatali (temple) at Tanjavur, (who resides in) the ninety-second house, one share.

278. „ Tiruvaragu, a girl of the Tanjaimamanikkoyil (temple) in the same city, (who resides in) the ninety-third house, one share.

279. „ Seyya Soram, a girl of Tirukkollambudur, (who resides in) the ninety-fourth house, one share.

280. „ Tirukkuravi, a girl of Kadambur, (who resides in) the ninety-fifth house, one share.

281. „ Irami, a girl of the Tirukkaronam (temple) at Nagapattanam, (who resides in) the first house of the northern row of the temple street on the north (of the temple), one share.

282. „ Karrali, a girl of the same temple, (who resides in) the second house, one share.

283. „ Kannam, a girl of the same temple, (who resides in) the third house, one share.

284. „ Uttamasundari, a girl of the Panchavan-Mahadevi Isvara (temple) at Kottur (who resides in) the fourth house, one share.

285. To Kunjaramalli, a girl of the Avanikesari-Isvara (temple) at Annali, (who resides in) the fifth house, one share.
286. „ Seyyapadam, a girl of Karpagadanipuram, (who resides in) the sixth house, one share.
287. „ Siriya-Aravam, a girl of Periyatalichcheri (a quarter) of Tiruvarur, (who resides in) the seventh house, one share.
288. „ Silasulamani, a girl of the Vadatali (temple) at Paraiyaru, (who resides in) the eighth house, one share.
289. „ Ananti, a girl of Velur, (who resides in) the ninth house, one share.
290. „ Porkali, a girl of the Tiruppadali-Isvara (temple) at Pambuni, (who resides in) the tenth house, one share.
291. „ Araamudu, a girl of Uttamadanipuram (who resides in) the eleventh house, one share.
292. „ Venkadu, a girl of Ayirattali (who resides in) the twelfth house, one share.
293. „ Porkoyil-Tillai-Aragi, a girl of the same village, (who resides in) the thirteenth house, one share.
294. „ Okkuri, a girl of Uttamadanipuram, (who resides in) the fourteenth house, one share.
295. „ Asangi, a girl of Ayirattali, (who resides in) the fifteenth house, one share.
296. „ Pugalogamanikkam, a girl of the Arumori-Isvara (temple) at Tiruvarur, (who resides in) the sixteenth house, one share.
297. „ Devadi, a girl of Periyatalichcheri, (a quarter) of the same village, (who resides in) the seventeenth house, one share.
298. „ Kuttadi, a girl of the Gunavati-Isvara (temple) at Kottur, (who resides in) the eighteenth house, one share.
299. „ ....a girl of the Mahadevi-Isvara (temple), (who resides in) the nineteenth house, one share.
300. „ Pakkari, a girl of Talichchattangudi, (who resides in) the twentieth house, one share.
301. „ Eranadevi, a girl of the Panchavanmahadevi-Isvara (temple) at Kottur, (who resides in) the twenty-first house, one share.
302. „ Nambinangai, a girl of the Tiruppugari-Isvara (temple) at Vidaiyapuram, (who resides in) the twenty-second house, one share.
303. „ Sipattali, a girl of the Panchavanmahadevi-Isvara (temple) at Kottur, (who resides in) the twenty-third house, one share.
304. „ Kunjaramalli, a girl of the same (temple) (who resides in) the twenty-fourth house, one share.
305. „ Karayil, a girl of the Pugarisvara (temple) at Vidaiyapuram, (who resides in) the twenty-fifth house, one share,
306. „ Kamuttiri, a girl of Periyatalichcheri, (a quarter) of Tiruvarur, (who resides in) the twenty-sixth house, one share.
307. „ Kariya-Aravam, a girl of Nayadirapuram, (who resides in) the twenty-seventh house, one share.
308. „ Nambiyamai, a girl of the Avaninarayana-Vinnagar (temple) at Ambar, (who resides in) the twenty-eighth house, one share.
309. „ Karuvur, a girl of the Tirumandali-Isvara (temple) at Tiruvarur, (who resides in) the twenty-ninth house, one share.
310. „ Sembou, a girl of the Tirumangalam (temple) at Ambar, (who resides in) the thirtieth house, one share.
311. „ Porcheyyal, a girl of the Mallisvara (temple) at Ayirattali, (who resides in) the thirty-first house, one share.

312. To Pattatiru, a girl of the Vikramavijaya-Isvara (temple) at Jananathapuram, (who resides in) the thirty-second house, one share.
313. „ Venkadu, a girl of Tiruvidaimarudil, (who resides in) thirty-third house, one share.
314. „ Murungai, a girl of the Nigalangi-Isvara (temple) at Arapuram, (who resides in) the thirty-fourth house, one share.
315. „ Orriyur, a girl of Ayirattali, (who resides in) the thirty-fifth house, one share.
316. „ Adal-Aragi, a girl of the same village, (who resides in) the thirty-sixth house, one share.
317. „ Kumaradi, a girl of the same village, (who resides in) the thirty-seventh house, one share.
318. „ Nangali, a girl of Tiruvedigudi, (who resides in) the thirty-eighth house, one share.
319. „ Tiribuvanamadevi, a girl of the Parantakar-Isvara (temple), (who resides in) the thirty-ninth house, one share.
320. „ Irami, a girl of Arruttali, (who resides in) the fortieth house, one share.
321. „ Sirudaikkaral, a girl of the Niraimadi-Isvara (temple), (who resides in) the forty-first house, one share.
322. „ Maraikkadu, a girl of Tiruchchorrutturai, (who resides in) the forty-second house, one share.
323. „ Umai, a girl of Tirukkollambudur, (who resides in) the forty-third house, one share.
324. „ Ilavam, a girl of the Tiruvamalisvara (temple) at Nannilam, (who resides in) the forty-fourth house, one share.
325. „ Orriyur, a girl of Tirumerrali (temple) in the same village, (who resides in) the forty-fifth house, one share.
326. „ Soramadevi, a girl of the Tiruvamalisvara (temple), (who resides in) the forty-sixth house, one share.
327. „ Adavallal, a girl of Ayirattali, (a quarter) of Niyamam, (who resides in) the forty-seventh house, one share.
328. „ Nambiyamai, a girl of the Sandiramalli-Iswara (temple) in the same village, (who resides in) the forty-eighth house, one share.
329. „ Amudam, a girl of the Araiyerumantali (temple) at Paraiyaru, (who resides in) the forty-ninth house, one share.
330. „ Sidevi, a girl of the Mudubagavartali (temple) at Ambar, (who resides in) the fiftieth house, one share.
331. „ Pitti, a girl of the Tentali (temple) at Paraiyaru, (who resides in) the fifty-first house, one share.
332. „ Irami, a girl of the Vadatali (temple) in the same village, (who resides in) the fifty-second house, one share.
333. „ Singadi, a girl of the same temple, (who resides in) the fifty-third house, one share.
334. „ Silasulamani, a girl of the same temple, (who resides in) the fifty-fourth house, one share.
335. „ Koyil, a girl of the Sangisvara (temple) in the same village, (who resides in) the fifty-fifth house, one share.
336. „ Malaiyaman, a girl of the Mullurnakkantali (temple) in the same village, (who resides in) the fifty-sixth house, one share.
337. „ Aiyaru, a girl of Avaninarayanapuram, (who resides in) the fifty-seventh house, one share.
338. „ Nakkam, a girl of Tirunettanam, (who resides in) the fifty-eighth house, one share.
339. „ Perramai, a girl of Tiruttengur, (who resides in) the fifty-ninth house, one share.

340. To Parippili, a girl of the Tiruvamalisvara (temple) at Nannilam, (who resides in) the sixtieth house, one share.

341. „ Pattali, a girl of the Ulagisvara (temple) at Tiruvarur, (who resides in) the sixty-first house, one share.

342. „ Manra mudaiyal, a girl of the Eriyurnattuttali (temple) at Tanjavur, (who resides in) the sixty-second house, one share.

343. „ Kuppai, a girl of Velur, (who resides in) the sixty-third house, one share.

344. „ Aditti, a girl of the Pagaividai-Isvara (temple) at Paruvur, (who resides in) the sixty-fourth house, one share.

345. „ Nakkam, a girl of the Arikulakesari-Isvara (temple) at Niyamam, (who resides in) the sixty-fifth house, one share.

346. „ To Villavanmadevi, a girl of Periyatalichcheri, (a quarter) of Tiruvarur, (who resides in) the sixty-sixth house, one share.

347. „ Eduttapadam, a girl of the Mudubagavartali (temple) at Ambar, (who resides in) the sixty-seventh house, one share.

348. „ Pumi (i.e., Bhumi), a girl of the Nandisvara (temple) at Kadambur, (who resides in) the sixty-eighth house, one share.

349. „ Tiruvadigal, a girl of Tiruvaiyaru, (who resides in) the sixty-ninth house, one share.

350. „ Tuduvi, a girl of the Brahmakuttam (temple) at Tanjavur, (who resides in) the seventieth house, one share.

351. „ Maralaichchilambu, a girl of Kanjaranagaram, (who resides in) the seventy-first house, one share.

352. „ Perratiru, a girl of Avaniyamadarpapuram, (a quarter) of Paruvur, (who resides in) the seventy-second house, one share.

353. „ Pugalogamanikkam, a girl of the Lokamahadevi-Isvara (temple), (who resides in) the seventy-third house, one share.

354. „ Sundari, a girl of the Sripudi-Vinnagar (temple) at Pambuni, (who resides in) the seventy-fourth house, one share.

355. „ Madevi, a girl of the Tirukkaronam (temple) at Nagapattanam, (who resides in) the seventy-fifth house, one share.

356. „ Ponnambalam, a girl of Killigudi, (who resides in) the seventy-sixth house, one share.

357. „ …………, a girl of Tiruvidaimarudil, (who resides in) the seventy-seventh house, one share.

358. „ Vembi, a girl of Periyatalichcheri, (a quarter) of Tiruvarur, (who resides in) the seventy-eighth house, one share.

359. „ Pugalogamanikkam, a girl of Tiruvidaimarudil, (who resides in) the seventy-ninth house, one share.

360. „ Karaikkal, a girl of the same village, (who resides in) the eightieth house, one share.

361. „ Vira-Sori, a girl of the Arikulakesari-Isvara (temple) at Niyamam, (who resides in) the eighty-first house, one share.

362. „ Muttal, a girl of Kavirippumbattanam, (who resides in) the eighty-second house, one share.

363. „ Sandarasegari, a girl of the Arikulakesari-Isvara (temple) at Niyamam, (who resides in) the eighty-third house, one share.

364. „ Pumi, a girl of Ayirattali, (a quarter) of the same village, (who resides in) the eighty-fourth house, one share.

365. „ Sundari, a girl of Killigudi, (who resides in) the eighty-fifth house, one share.

366. To Aiyaru, a girl of Miraiyil, (who resides in) the eighty-sixth house, one share.
367. „ Aiyaru, a girl of the Nandisvara (temple) at Kadambur, (who resides in) the eighty-seventh house, one share.
368. „ Arumori, a girl of Tiruvaiyaru, (who resides in) the eighty-eighth house, one share.
369. „ Sandai, a girl of the Komakkambhisvara (temple), (who resides in) the eighty-ninth house, one share.
370. „ Nallur, a girl of the Brahmakuttam (temple) at Tanjavur, (who resides in) the ninetieth house, one share.
371. „ Paranderuman, a girl of the Parantaka-Isvara (temple), (who resides in) the ninety-first house, one share.
372. „ Kanavadi, a girl of Tirupparanam, (who resides in) the ninety-second house, one share
373. „ Kuditangi, a girl of the Tiruppadali-Isvara (temple) at Pambuni, (who resides in) the ninety-third house, one share.
374. „ Soradevi, a girl of Tirukkollambudur, (who resides in) the ninety-fourth house, one share.
375. „ Tunganai, a girl of the Ittachchi-Isvara (temple) at Kadambur, (who resides in) the ninety-fifth house, one share.
376. „ Perramai, a girl of the Brahmakuttam (temple) at Tanjavur, (who resides in) the ninety-sixth house, one share.
377. „ a girl of , (who resides in) the first house, of , one share.
378. „ Nittasundari, a girl of the same village, (who resides in) the second house, one share.
379. „ Pattali, a girl of Tirunettanam, (who resides in) the third house, one share.
380. „ Karonam, a girl of Arapuram, (who resides in) the fourth house, one share.
381. „ Attanappon, a girl of Ayirattali, (who resides in) the fifth house, one share.
382. „ Maralaichchilambu, a girl of the Avanikesari-Isvara (temple) at Andali, (who resides in) the sixth house, one share.
383. „ Tigaimanikkam, a girl of the same temple in the same village, (who resides in) the seventh house, one share.
384. „ Kulamanikkam, a girl of the same temple, (who resides in) the eighth house, one share.
385. „ Tayam, a girl of Miraiyil, (who resides in) the ninth house, one share.
386. „ Arangam, a girl of the same village, (who resides in) the tenth house, one share.
387. „ Seyyavaymani, a girl of Puraiyachcheri, (who resides in) the eleventh house, one share.
388. „ Ponmalai, a girl of the Mahadevi-Isvara (temple) (who resides in) the twelfth house one share.
389. „ Ponnambalam, a girl of Tiruvedigudi, (who resides in) the thirteenth house, one share.
390. „ Nambandi, a girl of Talaiyalangadu, (who resides in) the fourteenth house, one share.
391. „ Mandai, a girl of Tangattartali, (who resides in) the fifteenth house, one share.
392. „ Nilam, a girl of Manninagaram, (who resides in) the sixteenth house, one share.
393. „ Pattali, a girl of Vayalur, (who resides in) the seventeenth house, one share.
394. „ Sunangai, a girl of the same village, (who resides in) the eighteenth house, one share.
395. „ Umai, a girl of the same village, (who resides in) the nineteenth house, one share.
396. „ Porkesi, a girl of the Avanikesari Isvara (temple) at Paruvur, (who resides in) the twentieth house, one share.
397. „ Vanavanmadevi, a girl of the Pagaividai-Isvara (temple) in the same village (who resides in) the twenty-first house, one share.

398. To Ariyal, a girl of the same village, (who resides in) the twenty-second house, one share.
399. „ Arinjai, a girl of Pandananallur, (who resides in) the twenty-third house, one share.
400. „ Puvanam, a girl of Thiruvaiyaru, (who resides in) the twenty-fourth house, one share.
401. „ Panchavanmadevi, a girl of the Gunavati-Isvara (temple) at Kottur, (who resides in) the twenty-fifth house, one share.
402. For one dancing-master who directs the dancing, to Araiyan Sundara-Soran, *alias* Mummadi Sora-Nirttamarayan, two shares.
403. „ another, to Kumaran Vadavayil, *alias* Mummadi-Sora Nirttapperayan, two shares.
404. „ another, to Vikki Pattalagan, two shares.
405. „ another, to Araiyar Abhimanatongan, *alias* Arumori-Nirttapperayan, two shares.
406. „ another, to Mallan Irattaiyan and to Sittiran Kesuvan, two shares.
407. „ another, to Araiyan Mananjeri, *alias* Vagaiyili—Nirttapperaiyan.
408. „ one........, to Kuravan Vira Soran, *alias* Panchavanmadevi-Nadagamayyan, one and a half share.
409. „ another, to Maraikkattu-Kanavadi, *alias*, Tiruvellarai-Sakkai, one and a half share.
410. „ another, to Orriyuran Singan *i. e.*, Simha one and a half share.
411. „ another, to Orriyuran Ilangavan, one and a half share.
412. „ one..........., to Araiyan Rajasrayan, *alias* Nittavinodavadyamarayan, two shares.
413. „ another, to Araiyan Ninra-Narayanan, two shares.
414. „ three singers, to Mundadari Anukkan, four and a half shares.
415. „ two others, to Achchan Kirttibhushanan, *alias* Arinjigai Kamarapperaiyan, three shares.
416. „ one pipe (Vangiyam), to Tanjai Kanavadi, who has joined (his new appointment) from the Nigarili Sora-Terinda Udanilai Kudiraichchevagar, one and a half-share.
417. „ another, to Seru-Vattaviraiyan, (who belongs) to the Sirudanattu Vaduga Kalavar, one and a half share.
418. „ another, Rajendradasaraiyan, one and a half-share.
419. „ one..........., to Kuttan Bahu......Vidangan, two shares.
420. „ another, to Araiyan Vadyamarayan, two shares.
421. „ another, to Brahmakuttan Kanavadi *alias* Irumadi-Sora-Vadya Marayan, two shares.
422. „ another, to Pogayan-Poriyilan, *alias* Mummadi-Sora-Vadyamarayan, two shares.
423. „ one person who beats the small drum (udukkai) to Virasoran Vidangan, *alias* Raja-raja—Srihastan, one and a half share.
424. „ another, to Kuttan Adittan, *alias* Rajaraja-Sahasrabahu, one and a half-share.
425. „ two persons why play the lute (vinai), to Subrahmanyan Kuttan, *alias* Sembiyan Vinai-Adittan, three and a half-shares.
426. „ If he should die, Araiyan Sadasivan, the son of his paternal uncle, who has married his daughter, shall receive the allowance.
427. „ three persons who sing in Sanskrit (Ariyam) to Araiyan Ambalanadan, *alias* Sembi-yan-Vadyamarayan, four and a half-shares.
428. „ one person who sings in Tamir, to Pattalagan Kamarapperaiyan, one and a half share.
429. „ another to Amudan Kali, one and a half share.
430. „ another, to Vanaraai Kuttan, one and a half share.
431. „ another, to Araiyan Surri, one and a half share.
432. For one big drum (kotti-mattalam), to Gandharvadasan, one share.

433. For another, to Gandharvaturai-Kavali, one share.
434. „ blowing one conch (muttirai sangu), to Tayilan (*i.e.*, Taila) Vikkiyannan, one share.
435. „ another, to Surri-Nadan, (who belongs) to the Mummadi-Sora-Terinda-Anaippagar, one share.
436. „ another, to Porkali Tondayan, a drummer of the Eriyurnattuttali (temple) at Tanjavur, one share.
437. To Aiyaran Andari (one of) the Pakkavadyar (?) (who belongs to) the Aragiya-Sora-Terinda-Valangai-Velailkkarar, three quarters of a share.
438. „ Satti Arur, (one of) the same, (who belongs) to the Kshatriyasikhamani-Terinda-Valangai-Velaikkarar, three quarters of a share.
439. „ Pada-Sivan Achchan Pichchan, (one of) the same of Karugavur in Avur-kurram, (a subdivision) of Nittavinoda-valanadu, three quarters of a share.
440. „ Satti Ponnan, (one of) the same, (who belongs) to the Satrubhujamga-Terinda-Valangai-Velaikkarar, three quarters of a share.
441. „ Kaman, Aiyaran, (one of) the same (who belongs) to the Vira-Sora Anukkar, three quarters of a share.
442. „ Erubattaivan, (one) of the musicians (Gandharvar), shall receive three quarters of a share.
443. „ Pattalagan Ambalam, (who belongs) to the Rajakanthirava-Terinda-Valangai-Velaikkarar, three quarters of a share.
444. „ Kuppai Tirumananjeri (one) of the musicians, three quarters of a share.
445. „ Aiyaran Kandarachchan, a drummer of the Brahmakuttam (temple) at Tanjavur, three quarters of a share.
446. „ Varagunan Siralan, (who belongs) to the Rajaraja-Terinda-Valangai-Velaikkarar three quarters of a share.
447. „ Kirtti Nadan, (who belongs) to the Parantaka Kongaval, three quarters of a share.
448. If he should die his younger brother Kirtti Kilaitangi shall receive the allowance.
449. To Nurrenman Surri, (who belongs) to the Aridurgalanghana-Terinda-Valangai-Velaikkarar, three quarters of a share.
450. If he should die, his younger brother Nurrenman............shall receive the allowance.
451. To Mangalavan Mani, (who belongs) to the Murttavikramabharana-Terinda-Valangal Velaikkarar, three quarters of share.
452. „ Tandan-Kamban, (who belongs) to the same troop (padai), three quarters of a share.
453. „ Arur Devan (who belongs) to the same troop, three quarters of a share.
454. „ Kandi-Kali, (who belongs) to the Mummadi-Sora-Terinda-Parikkarar, three quarters of a share.
455. „ Adigal Setti, (who belongs) to the Ranamukhabhima-Terinda-Valangai-Velaikkarar, three quarters of a share.
456. „ Kalari Achchan, a drummer of Kunargal-Munniyur in Avur-kurram, (a subdivision) of Nittavinoda-valanadu, three quarters of a share.
457. „ Parantakan Viman, (*i.e.*, Bhima) a Vira-Sora-Anukkan of the Tanjai-mamanikkovil (temple) at Tanjavur, three quarters of a share.
458. „ Sundaran Kalakalan, a Vira-Sora Anukkan of the Jayabhimatali (temple) in the same city, three quarters of a share.
459. „ Pisangan Siralan, a Vira-Sora-Anukkan of the same temple, three quarters of a share.
460. „ Devan Sengulavan, a Vira-Sora-Anukkan of the same temple, three quarters of a share.
461. „ Iraman Kamban, (who belongs) to the Vikramabharana-Terinda-Valangai-Velaikkarar, three quarters of a share.

462. To Achchan-Adavallan, (who belongs) to the Ilaiya-Rajaraja-Terinda-Velangai-Velaikkarar, three quarters of a share.

463. „ Uttaman-Kuttan, (who belongs) to the Rajakanthirava-Terinda-Valangai-Velaikkarar, three quarters of a share.

464. For one person who proclaims the sacred commands (of the god) to Kumaran Jayamanan, *alias* Mummadi-Sora-Kadigaimarayan, one share.

465. „ another to Kumaran Arumori, *alias* Rajaraja Kadigaimarayan, one share.

466. „ another, to Rajakesari Kodandaraman, *alias* Jayankonda Sora Kadigaimarayan, one share.

467. „ another, to Achchan Madigiravan, *alias* Aragiya-Sora Kadigaimarayan, one share.

468. „ another, to Mogiliyan-Soman-Paranderuman of Vangaram, *alias* Tirunarayana-chaturvedimangalam, in Mi-Sengili-nadu, (a subdivision) of Pandyakulasani-valanadu, one share.

469. „ superintending the temple women and the female musicians, (Gandharvi) to Savur Paranjodi, two shares.

470. „ the same, to Govindan-Somanadan, two shares.

471. To the accountant (Kanakku) Tannichchai-Saduravidangan, a native of Sembangudai in Vira-Sora valanadu, (a subdivision) of Nittavinoda-valanadu, two shares.

472. „ two persons who write the accounts under him, one and a half share, *viz*, three quarters of a share each.

473. To Madevan Sivalokasundaran, a native of Kadaikkudai in Mi-Sengili-nadu, (a subdivision) of Pandyakulasani-valanadu, two shares.

474. „ two persons who write the accounts under him, one and a half share, *viz.*, three quarters of a share each.

475. „ Nakkan Peruman, a native of Kirkkudai in Tiruvarur-kurram, a subdivision of Kshatriyasikhamani-valanadu, two shares.

476. „ two persons who write the accounts under him, one and a half share, *viz.*, three quarters of a share each.

477. „ Aiyaran Porchuvaran, a native of Mangudai, in Nallur-nadu, (a subdivision) of Nittavinoda-valanadu, two shares.

478. „ two persons who write the accounts under him, one and a half share, three quarters of a share each.

479. „ eleven men engaged in drumming, who are headed by Aiyan Poyyili of Nallur *alias* Panchavanmahadevi-chaturvedimangalam, in Nallur nadu, (a subdivision) of Nittavinoda-valanadu, five and a half shares *viz.*, half a share each.

480. „ eleven men (engaged in) the same, (who belong) to the Sagadaikottigal, and who are headed by Tamodiran (i.e., Damodara) Setti, five and a half shares *viz.*, half a share each.

481. „ eleven men engaged in the same, (who belong) to the Sagadaikottigal, and who are headed by.........Arangam, five and a half shares, *viz.*, half a share each.

482. „ eleven men engaged in the same, (who belong) to Sagadaikottigal, and who are headed by Sattan Ambalam, five and a half shares, *viz.*, half-a-share each.

483. „ eleven men engaged in the same, (who belong) to the Sagadaikottigal, and who are headed by Satti Iranakolan, five and a half shares, *viz.*, half a share each.

484. „ eleven men engaged in the same, who shall (eventually) take the place (of the former) and who are headed by Araiyan Udaiyamattandan (*i.e.*, Udayamartanda), five and a half shares, *viz.*, half a share each. These men shall receive the allowance........ Having thus received the allowance, they shall do the work.

485. For one man belonging to the persons who hold the sacred parasol (tiruppallittongal), one share, and for ten (other) men, eight twentieths of a share each, altogether, to

Udaiyan Tiruvisalur, *alias* Mummadi-Sora-Tongarperaiyan, and to Kuppadi Vanni *alias* Kshatriyasikhamani-Tongarperaiyan, five shares.

486. For one man belonging to the lamp-ligters, one share, and for seven other men, three and a half shares, *viz*., half a share each; altogether, to Puvanisegaran (*i.e.*, Bhuvanasekhara) Karpagam, *alias* Panchavan-Peraiyan, four and a half shares.

487. ,, four men who sprinkle water, half a share each; altogether, to the above-mentioned person, two shares.

488. ,, two Sannaliyal (?), three quarters of a share each; altogether, to the above-mentioned person, one and a half share.

489. ,, one man belonging to the potters (Kusavar) of the sacred kitchen (tiru-madaippalli) one share, and for ten (other) men, half a share each; altogether, to the potters of the high street of Surasikhamani, six shares.

490. ,, two washermen, one share each; altogether, to the washermen of the same street, two shares.

491. ,, one person who performs the duty of accountant (Kavidi), to Araiyan Manalilingan, *alias* Sembiyan Perungavadi, half a share.

492. ,, another, to Achchan Tiruvengadam, *alias* Rajaraja-Perungavidi, half a share.

493. ,, two persons who perform the duty of barbers, to Seyadaran (*i.e.*, Jayadhara) Nettanan *alias* Rajaraja-Perunavisan, one share.

494. ,, one astrologer and two subordinates, to Tunaiyan Adittan, *alias* Sembiyan-Korrapperungani, two shares.

495. ,, another and two subordinates, to Parantakan Pandyakulasani, *alias* Rajaraja-Ganitadhirajan, two shares.

496. ,, two persons who perform the duty of.........to Araiyan Pavaruttiran (*i.e.*, Bhavarudra) *alias* Panchavan-Mangalapperaiyan, three shares.

497. To the barber (Ambattan) Kon Sadangavi (*i.e.*, Shadangavid), *alias* Rajaraja-Prayogadaraiyan, one share.

498. For one tailor (Tayyan), to Devan Kavali, *alias* Vira-Sora-Perundayyan, one share.

499. ,, another, to Sippan Marapadi, *alias* Keralantaka-Perun dayyan, one share.

500. To the jewel-stitcher Achchan Karundittai, one and a half share.

501. For one brazier (Kannan), to Idaikkaraigari, *alias* Kshatriyasikhamani-Perungannan, one share.

502. ,, one master carpenter (Tachch-acharya) one and a half share, and for two (other) men, one and a half share; altogether, to Vira-Soran Kunjaramallan, *alias* Rajaraja-Perundachchan three shares.

503. ,, one carpenter, to Gunavan Madurantakan, *alias* Nittavinoda-Perundachchan, three quarters of a share.

504. ,, another, to Ilatti Sadaiyan, *alias* Kandaraditta-Perundachchan, three quarters of a share.

505. To the tailor Panan Uttaman Surri, *alias*, Arikulakesari-Sakkai, one and a half share.

506. ,, another, Aiyaran Arinji, one and a half share.

507. ,, another, Abarayidan (i.e., Aparajita) Vadavayil, *alias* Pallavan Sakkai, one and a half share.

508. ,, another, Vaduvur Arinji, one and a half share.

509. For a person who performs the duty of superintending goldsmith (Kankani tattan) by selecting one man and letting him do the work—to Kuttan Kanavadi *alias* Kshatriyasikhamani-Perundattan, the superintending goldsmith of the minor treasure of the lord Sri-Rajarajadeva, one share.

4. Some important points to be noted in the above Inscriptions.

We see from the inscription of Rajaraja Cholan known as "Nam Edupiththa Thirukatrali." (The sacred gift built by us), that he himself built the Big Temple at Tanjore. We gather from other inscriptions that his queens and other members of his family have done many a service as well as given many gifts to the temples at Tanjore and Tiruvadi. It is said that he ruled for 29 years between 985 and 1013. He had his son Rajendran crowned as his successor even during his life time in 1010 and was managing the affairs of the state for him. The Big Temple must have been built about the close of his reign. Judging from the fact that he came to the throne while quite young and that "he wept because he had no more provinces to conquer" we may conclude that he died in the prime of life. He must have handed over the reins of government to his son three years before his death and must have spent his whole time in superintending the building of the Temple. Or else, he could not have succeeded in obtaining the huge granite stone out of which the gigantic Nandi in the temple was hewn, nor could he have obtained the single block of granite 25½ft. square, weighing 80 tons, to be placed at the top of the temple gopuram, in a place like Tanjore where no granite is available, and at a time when the country was full of wars and invasions. It appears that he encouraged the sculptors and masons who worked in stones and in chunam by his own presence and by supplying them with eatables and betel-leaf. It is traditionally said even at the present day, that once a sculptor who was executing some very fine work held out his hand to a servant that was standing behind for some betel-leaf; the king observing this, supplied him with the folded betel-leaf. The sculptor noticing the difference between that and the previous folds turned back to see who it was that gave him the betel-leaf. Finding that it was the king himself, he made a deep obeisance to him. We hear of many other such incidents also.

Further, from these inscriptions we learn something about the prowess of Kings, their victories, and their royal titles which are given at the head of these inscriptions. After this, we find the names of the servants of the temple who sing and dance before the deity, the daily or annual gifts to them and their dwelling places. The name of a particular servant and his heirs of generations who should receive the gifts in turn are mentioned. All these might be clearly seen in the inscriptions. In the first of these inscriptions we find the names of 50 persons, 48 of whom are players on the Nagaswaram, and the other two, players on the drum (கொட்டி மத்தளம்) and the Oodukkai. When we note the names of these individuals we find that they are named after Siva, Thirugnana Sambandan, Thirunavukkarayan and Ganapati as was the custom in those days. Even in the modern day the names of players on the Nagaswaram are Sivakolundu, Mahadevan, Ganapati, Thirumarul Natesan, Koranattu Natesan, Swaminadhan, Kulandai Velan, Jagathratkshakan, Subramanian, Sabhapati, Rangan, Gurumoorti, Balaguru, Dakshanamoorti, Sambamurti or Kandan. These players on the Nagaswaram, as we see from the inscriptions, received three Kurunis (6 Marcals) daily for their service.

At the beginning of the second inscription, we find names of the dancers, who were 400 in number. It is stated where they originally came from and in what temples they served before. We find in the inscriptions, "to the girls from Thalichchery brought from the Chola kingdom". This enables us to conclude that dancers from Thirukaronam (Negapatam), Thiruvidamarudur, Tiruvarur, Tanjai Mamanikoil near the banks of the Vennar in Tanjore, Thirumagalam, Kadambur, Thirumaraikadu, Vidayapuram, Velur, Tiruvayar, Thalayalankadu, Nannilam, Kauveripoompatnam, Palayaru, Kotur, Thiruchotruthurai, Ootthamadanapuram, Nemam, Paychil, Thiruvethakudi, Thiruneythanam, Thiruchendoor, Paluvoor, Pandanallur and other places were brought to Tanjore and employed there long before the Brahadeeswara temple was built by Rajaraja Cholan at Tanjore. This implies that even before the time of this sovereign *i.e.*, even a thousand years ago there were Sivite and Vishnavite temples and dancers and musicians attached to them in the above places. But we have already noted how there was singing and dancing in temples and royal palaces even before this time during the period of the three sangams. The constant repetition of the inscriptions (இவ்வூர் நக்கன்) "nakkan of this place", (இத்தளி நக்கன்) "nakkan of this temple," (தஞ்சாவூர் நக்கன்) "nakkan of Tanjore" indicates that even before this temple was built, and before the time of Rajaraja Cholan, there were many dancers and musicians in Tanjore. The expression 'Thalichcheri' (தளிச்சேரி) means 'colony round the temple'. The expression 'நாம் எடுப்பித்த கற்றளி' means 'the temple built by us of granite stones'. So 'இத்தளி' means 'this temple'. 'Thalichcheri' means 'a street round the temple.'

From the numbers 402 to 407 we find the names of those who taught the art of dancing. These teachers are known as 'Nattuvan' and 'Annavi'.

We see the names of five singers, three in number 414 and two in the next. From 416 to 418 are the names of those who played the Mukhaveena. Numbers 423 and 424 give the names of those who played the Oodukkai. The names of Veena players are found in 425 and 426, while 427 contains the names of three musicians who chanted the Aryam. The numbers 428 to 431 give the names of Tamil chanters; 432 and 433, the names of those who played the Kotimaddalam; 434 to 436, the names of those who sounded the Mutthirai Changu; 437 to 463, the list of those who played the secondary instruments; 464 to 468, the names of heralds; while 469 and 470 give the names of two Gandharvas. The gifts for 66 drummers and their names are mentioned from 479 to 484.

Besides these the names of other temple-servants such as lamp lighters, sprinklers of water, those who carry minor things in procession, potters, dhobies, barbers, astrologers, blacksmiths, tailors, coppersmiths, carpenters, goldsmiths, lute players and accountants, the rules for their guidance and their share of gifts are mentioned.

One share implies 100 kalams of the modern day as is evident from the second inscription where he says "பங்கு வழிப்பங்கு ஒன்றினுக்கு நிலம் வேலியினுக்கு ராஜகேஸரியோடொக்கும் ஆடவல்லான் என்னும் மரக்காலால் நெல்லு நூற்றுக் கலனாகவும்" "The value of each share which consisted of the produce of one Veli of land, was to be 100 kalams of paddy, measured by the Maracal called Adavallan which is equal to a Rajakesari." This was one year's produce from a vali of land in those days. This implies that it excludes what must be paid to the government for kudivaram. We see that these 100 kalams obtained by Melvaram are given as gifts to Vidwans and others even at the present day. It appears that those who had two shares obtained 200 kalams. while others who had 1½ or ½ share received in proportion for their service in the temple. The shares for two Veena players are also given here. We hear that the same kind of gifts were granted to musicians attached to temples in ancient times. We have seen the Ravana Vahanam made of silver where Ravana is represented as playing the Veena. We know how Paramasivam under the guise of a wood cutter appeared on behalf of his devoted servant Banaputtiran and conquered Hemanadhan by singing the Ragam called 'Sathari'. It is but proper that Veena music should be played in temples dedicated to the worship of Ṣiva who delights in Veena music. Again we all hold the Veena in high esteem as a sweet and living instrument. Paramasivam is called 'Veena-Gana-Priar' one who delights in Veena music. We shall speak later on about the Veena and its construction.

We read of three persons who sang the Aryam. We must conclude that 'Aryam' means 'Sanskrit' and 'singers of Aryam' means singers of Sanskrit songs. There is no reason to suppose they chanted the Vedas. For the name "Sembiam Vathian Arayan" cannot be that of a Brahman. The term 'Arayan' is applied to Nattuvans in 419 to 422 and to heralds in 464. 465, 466 and 467. We know very well to which caste heralds and Nattuvans belong and that Brahmans will never undertake these duties. So "singers of Aryam" means "singers of Sanskrit songs."

There were four Tamil singers. They were in the habit of singing heart-melting Tamil keertanams in praise of the diety such as Thevaram, Thiruvachakam, and Thiruvoimoli. Worshippers who go to temples are even at the present day, in the habit of singing the praises along with these professional musicians or by themselves.

In number 432 we find "To a Gandharva who plays the Kottimattalam"; in 432, "to Duraikavali, the Gandharva" and in 469 "to superintend the Thalichchery dancers and Gandharvis". Gandharvas are, there, singers, "song" is known as "Gandharvam". But this term is now gone out of use. Just as some terms found in these inscriptions such as 'Perayan'. 'Sembian', 'Arayan', 'Oovaichan', 'Nattuvan', 'Nakkan' have become either corrupted into 'Ochan' and 'Nattuvan' or have become extinct altogether, the term 'Gandharva' also has disappeared. Both the Gandharvas and the Gandharvis must have been expert singers and of an attractive appearance. Hence the Puranas proudly speak of them as having come from the celestial regions and as having sung in the Sabha of the gods. We do not hear that any one else sang before gods or danced before them except Gandharvas and the dancing girls. So the Gandharvas appear to be a professional class of singers who made music their means of livelihood. We find them as servants in the Tanjore temple also. These do not belong to the celestial regions; they are of this earth, and some of them do exist even at the present day.

From all this we may conclude that music and Bharatam were extensively known in South India and were in a highly efficient state not only 1000, years ago but many thousands of years ago. We have already noted how music was cultivated as one of the main Angams of the Tamil language in the Pandya Kingdom during the period of the three Sangams. We must understand how music was known in the Tamil country for the last 12,000 years; how it was one of the Angams of the language; how it spread in various places after the destruction of South Madura or Lemuria; how the people of South Madura, after the destruction of their musical literature, orally handed down the few gems in music which they knew to the future generations and how that is the very reason why South Indian music is held in the highest esteem up to the present day. Just as we find in the temples of the Chola Kingdom, professional musicians are attached to the temples of Madura, Thiruchendoor, Tinnevelly, Alvartirunagari, Sankaranayanarkoil, Srivilliputtoor, Tenkasi and other places. It is immaterial and unnecessary to speak about the musicians of those temples.

5. The names of Experts in South Indian Music with a few remarks on each.

We have established how the Pandya kings patronised, up to the end of the Third Sangam, i.e. up to the first century A. D., the three Angams of the Tamil language held more precious than gold by the ancients, namely Iyal, Isai and Natakam and how the interest in the language waned after this period. We find now from 50 A.D. Karikal Cholan, the Chola sovereign, patronised Tamil Vidwans of both the sexes by giving them many gifts and by encouraging associations for such literary experts. He seems to have attracted during his time many such Vidwans from various parts of India. We also noted how the Chola sovereigns conquered the Chera and Pandya kingdoms, Lanka and the adjoining islands and the Telugu country also from time to time. This might have been one of the reasons for the presence of so many literary men in the Chola country. We find that Parakesari Varma Rajaraja Cholan, otherwise known as Mummudi Cholan, finished the building of the big temple at Tanjore in the year 1013 A.D. From the time of Rajaraja Cholan, Tanjore seems to have been the capital of the Chola kingdom, though it is mentioned that Vijayalayan the Chola king conquered Tanjore while Conjeevaram was his capital and ruled in Tanjore from 846 to 880 A.D. So from the time of Rajaraja Cholan, Tanjore became the centre of literary men who excelled in the three Angams of the Tamil language. We find that there were many literary men in Tanjore during the reign of Rajendra Cholan (Kulottunga Cholan) in 1084 A.D., and in the reign of Kulottunga II in 1135 A.D. Jayamkondan, the Kavichakravarti, lived during the reign of Kulottunga I, and Ottakoottan, during the time of Kulottunga II.

At the time of Rajadhi Raja Chola (1164-1178) there lived Kamban, Ottakoottan, Pugalendi and Adiyarkunallar. From that time forward the extent of the Chola kingdom as well as its influence was in the decline. A number of rulers succeeded each for a few years. So the association of literary men gradually became extinct. Moreover, the later sovereigns of the Chola country were either Telugu or Mahratta.

During the time of Atchyutappa Naick (1572-1614), Venkatamakhi seems to have paid attention only to one of the Angams of the language, namely Isai or Music.

Thulajaji Maharaja (1763-1787) seems to have invited many literary men, well versed in music, and encouraged the art by patronising them. It was during his reign that Mahadeva Annavi, the son of Senthilvel Annavi, was brought from Tinnevelly, and other musicians also from different parts of the country and encouraged by extensive maniyam lands such as 10 velis, 5 velis, 2 velis and 1 veli and dwelling places. Many excellent musicians flourished in the Chola kingdom during his reign and in that of his son Sarabhoji maharaja. The art of music has declined at the present day for want of patronage by sovereigns. Moreover many subtle points and excellent rules in vocal music are looked upon as mere fables at the present day for want of those interested in such things. We do not know the future of those excellent rules which are now treated as fables. However, we shall do well to note a few points about those musical experts. The time of some of these Vidwans is unknown, a thing very common in connection with anything Indian. Just as the year of the publication of any important book is purposely omitted so that it might be considered a recent work, some Vidwans do not state the time in which they lived so as to clothe themselves with an odour of antiquity. However, we have determined, as far as we can, the time in which these vidwans lived, by the history of the kings and leading Vidwans of the period. The term "lives at the present day" means that the musician was alive in 1914.

The history of many of the Vidwans of modern and ancient times is not fully known. We are still trying to find out the history of many players on the Nagaswaram who have been traditionally musicians in the various districts of the Presidency. Their mames and history will be published in the second volume. Any particulars as regards time or remarks about the Vidwans whose names are found in the following list will be thankfully received and added on.

அ

அகிலாண்ட ஐயர்—(Akilanda Iyer) a native of Tanjore. He was practising as a Barrister-at-Law at Hyderabad. He was good in playing the Veena. He has been teaching Indian Music to the westerners.

அஹோபிலர்—(Ahobilar). He lived near Ahobila Matam in Cuddapah District about 300 years ago. He wrote the 'Sangeeta Lakshanam' in accordance with the system found in Sangeeta Ratnakaram and Anjaneyam.

அக்கில்ஸ்வாமி—(Akkil Swami). He was living in a village near Chidambaram. He has composed Keertanams in Sanskrit. It is said that he was cured of a dire disease which he was subject to by singing the keertanam "[illegible]" in praise of God in Kalyani Raga. He lived about 70 years ago.

அங்கண்ணா—(Ankanna) of Tanjore. He was clever in the art of playing the Mridangam according to the rules of Karnatic music. He was perfect in Layagnanam. He is living at the present day.

அங்கண்ணா—(Ankanna). He belonged to Venkatagiri Samasthanam. He could play the Veena well.

அண்ணசாமி சாஸ்திரி—Annasami Sastri 1827-1900. He was the eldest grandson of Samasastrial. He was clever in singing and playing the violin. He has composed many Kirtanams and Tanams.

அண்ணாச்சி ஐயர்—Annatchi Iyer. He was Samasthana Vidwan under Sarabhoji maharaja in Tanjore between 1798 and 1824. He was celebrated for his Veena playing and singing.

அண்ணு, சோழமுத்து, இராமஸ்வாமி—Annu, Cholamuttu, and Ramaswami. Three brothers. Annu and Ramaswami were experts in playing the Mridangam, while Cholamuttu was famous for teaching the art of dancing and for playing the Violin.

அத்துகான்—Attukhan. Samasthana Vidwan of Gwalior. He distinguished himself by singing in the durbar of Sarabhoji maharaja and received distinction.

அப்பன்—Appan. He was a charming and skilful player on the Violin. He had five sons, of whom the eldest, Appukutti, was a neat player on the Violin, while the others were good in singing and playing the Veena.

அப்பாக்கண்ணு—Appakanna a disciple of Ponnusami. He was good in playing the Violin. Manickyam and Narayanasami, his sons-in-law, were also good on the Violin.

அப்பாக்கண்ணுபிள்ளை—Appakannu Pillai known as Veenai Appakannu Pillai. He is at Chidambaram now. He is clever on the Veena and in teaching the art of dancing. Many have learnt the art from him.

அப்பாசாமி ஐயர்—Appasami Iyer, younger brother of Maha-Vydyanatha Iyer. He spent his days with his brother. Has a good ear for music. He lives now.

அப்பாஜி ஐயர், வெங்கட ஐயர்—Appaji Iyer and Venkata Iyer of Coimbatore. Very neat players on the Mridangam.

அப்பாத்துரை ஐயங்கார்—Appadurai Iyengar a disciple of Sreenivasa Iyengar of Ramnad. He is clever in playing the Jalatarangam.

அப்பாத்துரை ஐயர்—Appadurai Iyer of Tirupanthuruthi. He was a student of Veenai Thirumalai Iyer. He was Samasthana Vidwan under Sivaji maharaja (1824-1865). He was clever in music and the art of dancing. His son Panchapakesa Bhagavatar, and his disciple Krishna Bhagavatar, are famous musicians.

அபோய்—Abboy, son of Sabhapati. He could play the Violin well. His son Kanni was clever in playing the Mridangam.

அப்பாவு—Appavu. Brother of Nagalingam. He could play the Violin well.

அப்புக்குட்டி, சாமுக்குட்டி—Appukutti and Samukutti. Two brothers clever in vocal music.

அப்பு பாகவதர்—Appu Bhagavatar. A disciple of Paramesvara Bhagavatar. A cunning singer. His brother was good on the Violin.

அப்பையர்—Appaier. The grandson of Veenai Vijayavarahappier. He was good at playing many instruments and has obtained many presents from different Samasthanams for his Hindustani singing. His son is Dasavadyam Krishna Iyer.

அமியப்பா, முனிசாமி, முத்து—Amiappa, Munisami and Mutthu were clever in playing the Mridangam very skilfully.

அம்பயிரம்—Ambayiram. He was skilful on the Violin. Paidala Gurumoorti Sastri who heard him play the violin at the bungalow of Rama Naidu in Tanjore gave him the name of "the young lion." His son Appan was a cunning player on the violin. He had five sons. The eldest of whom, Appukutti, could play the violin very neatly, while the others were good in singing and playing instruments such as the Veena.

அகிலாண்டம்—Akhilandam. She belonged to Srirangam, and learnt the Veena and dancing under Gurumoorti Nattuvan. Her daughters also were good on the Veena, in singing Ragas and Pallavi, and in singing Kshetrayya Padams and dancing with appropriate gestures. Ranganayaki, Kuntalam and Sokku were clever in singing and on the Veena.

அரிகர பாகவதர்—Harihara Bhagavatar. He lives at Veeravanallur. He is good on the Violin and in performing Harikathas and Sivakathas. He is the brother of Muttya Bhagavatar.

அரிதீர்த்த ஐயர்—Hariteertha Iyer. He is a disciple of Rama Bhagavatar. He is good in vocal music. He is now at Pudukotah.

அரிராவ்—Hari Row. He is clever in playing the Mridangam.

அருணாசல ஐயர்—Arunachala Iyer of Conjeevaram. He is a student of Ayyavier of Thiruvalankadu. He is skilful in playing the Mridangam and the Ghatam.

அருணாசல ஐயர்—Arunachala Iyer of Madras; clever in vocal music.

அருணாசலக் கவிராயர்—Arunachala kavirayar. Originally belonged to Shiyali. He was well versed in the Ilakkanam of the Tamil language. He lived during the time of Tulajaji Maharajah (1763—1787). He composed Tamil Kirtanams for all the six kandams of the Ramayana with appropriate *rasam* to suit the stories and in proper *Ragas* in order to bring out the Varnakramams, sang them for the first time in the Sabha of Manali Muddukrishna Mudaliar of Madras, and was literally anointed with gold in appreciation of his excellent work.

அருணாசலஞ் செட்டியார்—Arunachalam Chettiar. The Zemindar of Devakottah. Well versed in vocal music and in instruments like the Surabat. He knew the science of music well.

அருணாசலம், குருசாமி—Arunachalam and Gurusami. Both of Conjeevaram; clever in playing the Mridangam and the Ghatam.

அருணாசலம்—Arunachalam a descendant of Mahadevan. Brother of Nallappa. He was good in music.

அருணாசலம்—Arunachalam of Karvetinagaram; clever in vocal music and in playing the Kinjira.

அழக சிங்கையா—Alagasingayya son of Veenai Jeeyar. Clever on the Veena and in teaching music.

அழக நம்பி—Alaga Nambi a very cunning player on the Mridangam. He is at Kumbakonam.

அனந்தராம பாகவதர்—Anantarama Bhagavatar. He is known as Palghat Anantarama Bhagavatar. He lives at Kumbakonam now. He is clever in vocal music, in making kathas and in playing instruments like the violin.

அனந்தராமையர்—Anantarama Iyer a disciple of Mahadeva Iyer. He is clever in singing with great beauty and elaborateness. He could also perform Harikathas. He is alive now.

அனந்தராமையர்—Anantarama Iyer known as Sathanoor fiddle Anantarama Iyer. Skilful on the Violin and in singing. He lives at Kumbakonam.

அனந்தாச்சாரியர்—Anantachariar of Coimbatore famous for his playing the Ghatam.

அஷ்டராக கங்காராம்—Ashtaraga Gangaram. He is a disciple of Balavanta Row of Gwalior. Very clever in music.

ஹரிநாயக்—Harinayak 1500. He is the author of "Sangeeta Saram".

ஆ

ஆதப்ப பச்சிமிரியம்—Adappa *Pachimiriam*, a great musician of the Pudukotah Samasthanam. He has composed many Varnams and Keertanams. His grandson is Veenai Subbukutti Iyer. He could play the Veena neatly and skilfully. His son Subbanna could play the Veena scientifically.

ஆதப்பையர்—Audappier. He was the Court Vidwan of Tanjore under Pratapsingh and Thulajaji maharajahs (1740—1787). He is not only the author of many Varnams and Geetas in the Rakti as well as Desika Ragas for the instruction of the young, but also has composed many Keertanams in the chief gamaka jatis with the stamp of Sri Venkatarama. He has systematically arranged Raga Alapanas, Pallavi of the Madhyama Kala and Pans. He has composed the Tana Varnam called 'Viriboni' in the Bhairavi Ragam which is so very sweet when sung or played on the Veena. Veenai Krishna Iyer was his son.

ஆதி மூர்த்தி ஐயர்—Audimurti Iyer son of Pallavi Gopala Iyer. He was the Samasthana Vidwan under Sivaji maharajah (1824—1865). He is a near relation of Challagali Krishna Iyer. He could play the Veena beautifully. Veenai Venkatachalam Iyer was his son.

ஆயில்ய மஹாராஜா--Ayilya Maharajah. Maharajah of Travancore. He excelled in vocal music and in playing the Veena. He lived about 40 years ago.

ஆறுமுகம்—Arumugam of Royapuram. A good player on the violin.

ஆனந்த குமாரஸ்வாமி—Ananda Coomaraswamy. A son of the Honourable P. Kumarasami. Both he and his wife are clever in composing Sahityam as well as in playing the Veena. He has written the Preface to Clement's "Introduction to Indian music." He is the author of "Essays in National Idealism" 1909, the first twenty pages of which speak about Indian Music. Though a native of Colombo he lives in London mainly.

ஆனை ஐயர்—Anei Iyer. Brother of Iyyavier. He is generally known as 'Anai yya'. He was the samasthana Vidwan under Sarabhoji maharajah (1798—1824). He Iwas skilled in Sanskrit, Tamil and Telugu languages as well as in Music. He has composed many Keertanams in Tamil.

இ

இரகுபதிராவ்—Raghupati Row, son of Khamasdar Madhava Row. He could sing well and play the Surabath and the Mridangam skilfully.

இரங்கசாமி—Rangaswami of Srirangam. A disciple of Andanoor Subbier. He has composed many Varnams and Kritis. He is a graceful singer. He could play the Surabath and the violin well. His son-in-law Subbayya is equally a good singer.

இரங்கசாமி ஐயங்கார்—Rangasami Iyengar. He has established a school of Indian music in Vepery for the benefit of the young and is also editing a monthly musical magazine. He is good on the Veena and the violin.

இரங்கசாமி முதலியார்—Rangasami Moodaliar Kulitalai. He is a Sangeetha Vidwan at Chidambaram now.

இரங்காச்சாரியார்—Rangachariar. He is known as Rangachariar of Sriperumbuttoor. He is a disciple of Alasoor Krishna Iyer. He has a good ear for Talam (time). He could sing Pallavi in many Jatis.

இரங்காச்சாரியார்—Rangachariar a disciple of Tanjore Subbaraya Sastri. He could play the violin very gracefully and neatly. Chinna Singalachariar and Periya Singalachariar of Madras are his disciples.

இரங்காச்சாரியார்—Rangachariar of Chandragiri. A disciple of Subbaraya Sastri the son of Alasoor Krishna Iyer. He could play the Gamakams on the violin very gracefully.

இரத்தின தேவி—Rathina Devi noted for her Sangeeta Sahithyam and vocal music. She published 30 Nepaul and Punjab Keertanams in 1913.

இரவீந்திரநாத் தாகோர்—Rabindranath Tajore. He belongs to the famous Tagore family of Bengal, he is a well known Vidwan in Sangeetam and Sahithyam of Bengal; author of the famous Gitanjali.

இராகவாச்சாரியார்—Raghavachariar. of Bangalore. A good singer.

இராகவையங்கார்—Raghava Iyengar. The munsiff of Mannargudi at present. He could sing the Gana Ragas well and could play the Veena also.

இராகவையர்—Raghavier. He is known as Ragavier of Coimbatore. He could sing beautifully appreciating and understanding the difference between Ghana, Naya and Desika Ragas. He is a disciple of Paramesvara Bhagavatar of Travancore State.

இராகவையர், இராமாநுஜ ஐயர், எம்பெருமானார்—Raghava Iyer, Ramanuja Iyer and Yemberumanar. These are three brothers, of whom Raghava Iyer and Yemberumanar are very skilful on the violin. Ramanuja Iyer could sing Karnataka Ragas neatly. Namberumalaya, the son of Raghava Iyer, could play the Violin well.

இராகவையர்—Raghava Iyer. He and his son are noted for their skill on the Veena.

இராஜா ஜெகத் ஜோதிர் மல்லா—Raja Jagath Jothir Mulla. 1650. The author of "Sangeeta Sara Sangraham" and "Sangeetha Bhaskaram."

ராஜா ஜெகதீஸ்வர ராம வெங்கடேஸ்வர எட்டப்ப ராஜா—Raja Jagadeesvara Rama Venkatesvara Ettappa Raja. 1899. The Raja of Ettiyapuram. One who appreciated music. He was clever in composing Sahityams. He has composed the Keertanam 'குருநாதநடுவே' in the Khamas Ragam and "ஏனோ நீ என்னை மறந்தாய்" in Bhairavi. Subbarama Deekshatar was his court Vidwan. He helped the Deekshatar in publishing his book "Sangeeta Sampradaya Pradarsani."

ராஜா சுரேந்திர மோகன் தாகோர்—Raja Surendra Mohan Tagore. He belongs to the well-known Tagore family who were considered unrivalled in Fine Arts and Painting. He was celebrated for his Sangeetha Sahityam in Bengal. He has written many books on music. He is a cousin of Rabindranath Tagore.

ராஜா மான்—Raja Mon King of Gwalior. He systematized the Thurubath.

ராஜு ஐயர்—Raju Iyer of Lalgudi. He could play the Violin.

ராணா கும்பகர்ண மகிமேந்திரா—Rana Kumbhakarna Mahimendra. (1450). Author of "Rasikapriya", "Sangeetha Meemamsa" and Sangeetha Raja."

ராதாகிருஷ்ணையர்—Radhakrishna Iyer of Chitoor. He was a disciple of Thyagaraja Iyer of Trivadi. He could sing religious Keertanams with great taste.

ராதாகிருஷ்ண பாகவதர்—Radhakrishna Bhagavatar. He is at Kumbakonam at present. He could play the Violin and the Harmonium.

ராதாகிருஷ்ண பாகவதர்—Radhakrishna Bhagavatar. Son of Pallavi Soma Iyer of Talainayar. He is skilful on the Violin. He is alive now.

ராதாகிருஷ்ணையர்—Radhakrishna Iyer, son of Rama Iyer of Lalgudi. Clever in singing and playing the Violin. He is alive now.

ராதாகிருஷ்ணையர்—Radhakrishna Iyer, son Gopala Bhagavatar. He attained proficiency in music under Krishna Iyer of Kunnangudi.

ராதாகிருஷ்ணையர்—Radhakrishna Iyer. He could play the Kinjira. His son Thyagaraja Iyer is a graceful singer.

ராம காளாஸ்திரி ஐயர்—Ramakalastri Iyer. He is known as Veena Ramakalastri Iyer. He was a well known Vidwan in music and playing the Veena. Veena Perumal Iyer was his disciple. Kasturi Ranga Iyer of Deepambalpuram, Sonthi Venkata Subbier, his son Sonthi Venkatarama Iyer, Sunkam Veerabhadra Iyer, Sunkam Seenu Iyer—all these six were great Vidwans.

ராமகிருஷ்ண ஐயர்—Ramakrishna Iyer of Salyamangalam. He could play the Veena.

ராமகிருஷ்ண பாகவதர்—Ramakrishna Bhagavatar of Tinnevelly. He plays the Veena.

ராமகிருஷ்ணையர்—Ramakrishna Iyer. He is the Samasthana Vidwan of Trevandrum. Son of Paramesvara Bhagavator. He is well-skilled in singing and playing the Violin. He lives now.

ராமகிருஷ்ணையர்—Ramakrishna Iyer of Velur. He sings well.

ராமகிருஷ்ணையர் B.A., B.L.--Ramakrishna Iyer, B.A., B.L. Retired Sub-Judge, Palghat. He is very proficient in Music. He plays the veena well. He is the author of many Essays on 'South Indian Music' and on 'Srutis.'

இராமஸ்வாமி—Ramaswami of Karur. A good singer.

இராமஸ்வாமி அண்ணாவி—Ramaswami Annavi. He was well known for his veena playing and for his knowledge of the science of Bharatam in Tinnnevelly during the life time of Dalava Mudaliar. He taught singing and the veena to Vellai of Tinnevelly, Marimuttu, Sornam, Madura Kalimuttu and her daughter.

இராமஸ்வாமி ஐயர்—Ramaswami Iyer, son of Venkatarama Iyer of Mysore. He and his brother Lakshmana Iyer are skilful players on the Veena.

இராமஸ்வாமி—Ramaswami. Generally known as Ramaswami of Koranadu. A disciple of Muttusami Deekshatar ; skilful in Sangeetha Lakshanam.

இராமஸ்வாமி—Ramaswami of Tiruvidamarudur. He could play the Mridangam with strict adherence to Thalam.

இராமஸ்வாமி—Ramasami of Mayavaram. A player of Nagaswaram.

இராமஸ்வாமி ஐயங்கார்—Ramaswami Iyenger of Srirangam. He plays the Veena.

இராமஸ்வாமி ஐயர்—Ramaswami Iyer. He is a Vidwan in the Court of Trevandrum. His sons also are proficient in playing the Violin, Mridangam and other instruments.

இராமஸ்வாமி ஐயர்—Ramaswami of Conjeevaram. A Vidwan in music.

இராமஸ்வாமி ஐயர்—Ramaswami Iyer. Elder brother of Maha Vydianatha Iyer. He was a well known vidwan in Tamil, Telugu and Music. He has written Periya Puranam, and the biographies of Manickyavachakar, Markandeyar, Prahladan and others and Seetakalyanam in the shape of keertanams. He has composed "Thiruvaiyattrandadi" and "Thiruchendoor Santha Viruttam". He obtained the title of "Monaisingam" when he was Tamil vidwan in the Sethu Samasthanam. His son Vyai R. Subramania Iyer is a Tamil Pandit in St. Peter's High School, Tanjore and he has a good taste for music.

இராமஸ்வாமி ஐயர்—Ramasami Iyer son of Kittu Bhagavatar of Trevandrum. A splendid player on the violin. He is now living.

இராமஸ்வாமி ஐயர்—Ramasami Iyer. A disciple of Thirukodikaval Krishna Iyer. He could play the violin well.

இராமஸ்வாமி ஐயர்—Ramaswami Iyer. He belongs to the family of Varahappa Iyer. He is a veena vidwan.

இராமஸ்வாமி தீக்ஷிதர்—Ramaswami Deekshatar. 1735. Son of Venkatesvara Dikshatar. He learnt the Veena and Chathurdandiprakasika under Vythianatha Dikshatar, the grandson of Venkatamahki's uncle in Madhyarjunam. He was Court Vidvan under Amara Singh Maharaja of Tanjore and received many honours. He had three sons,—Muttusami Dikshatar, Chinnasami Dikshatar, and Balasami Dikshatar. This family was patronised by Manali Mutthukrishna Mudaliar and his son Chinnya Mudaliar. He was anointed with gold in appreciation of the 108 Ragatala Malika he composed in the name of Chinnaya Mudaliar. It is said that when his second son, Chinnasami Dikshatar, lost his eyesight, he spent 45 days in the presence of the god Venkatachala Swami at Tirupati, praising him by singing the Ragam 'Vehavahini' as Pallavi and composing Raga Malika in 48 other ragas, and returned with his son's eye sight restored. He has composed a Raga Malika on Meenatchi Amman in 44 ragas Chouka Varnams in Reethigoula, Inthola, Manohari and Poornachandrika Ragas, Thana Varnams in the Sankarabharana Raga and many keertanams with the stamp of Venkata Krishna. He was a specialist in the Hamsadhwani Ragam and has composed padams in it.

இராமஸ்வாமி பாகவதர்—Ramasami Bhagavatar. Of Lalgudi. A Sangeetha Vidwan.

இராமஸ்வாமி பாகவதர்—Ramasami Bhagavatar. A Sangeetha Vidwan.

இராமஸ்வாமி பாகவதர்—Ramasami Bhagavatar. A yogi and a disciple of Kittu Bhagavatar. He could play beautifully.

இராமஸ்வாமி பாகவதர்—Ramasami Bhagavatar of Thiruvisanallur. A Sangeetha Vidwan.

இராமசேது பாலஸ்வாமி—Ramasetu Balaswami. He could not only play the Veena and the Mridangam but could sing very sweetly. He learnt Kshetraya Padams under Kuppiyer.

இராமச்சந்திர தொண்டமான் மகாராஜா—Ramachandra Thondaman Maharajah. Of Pudukotai. He learnt music and the Veenai under Veenai Subbukutti Iyer. He could sing well.

இராமச்சந்திர பாகவதர்—Ramachandra Bhagavatar. He is the younger brother of Veenai Kalyanakrishna Iyer of Trivandrum. He could also play the Veena with great skill and charm. He is now living.

இராமச்சந்திர பாகவதர்—Ramachandra Bhagavatar. He was the Samasthana Vidwan of Ettiyapuram. He could sing with great skill and with strict adherence to Talam.

இராமச்சந்திர பாகவதர்—Ramachandra Bhagavatar Samasthana Vidwan of Trivandrum.

இராமச்சந்திர ஐயர்—Ramachandra Iyer of Tiruvattoor. He plays the violin well.

இராமச்சந்திரையர்—Ramachandra Iyer of Keevalur near Negapatam. He sings with great charm. He is now living.

இராமண்ணா ஸ்வாமி—Ramanna. He belongs to the line of Matadhipatis. He plays the Veena and the Mridangam.

இராமதாசர்—Rama Dasar, son of Gopannamathyar. He lived about 300 years ago. It is said that when he was Tahsildar in the Bhadrachalam Taluq, he was imprisoned by the Nawab for spending the Government funds in improving the temple of Ramabhadrar and in making jewels for the deity. He then prayed and sang many keertanams on Sri Rama. These kirtanams are in use even at the present day. He was very clever in Sangeeta Sahityam.

இராமதாஸுலு—Rama Dasulu. The younger brother of Seshachalla Bhagavatar the Samasthana Sangeeta Vidwan of Pudukotah. He is skilled in composing Sahityam. He has composed many a keertanam with the stamp of Rama.

இராமதாஸ்—Ramadoss of Bangalore. He could sing well.

இராமதாஸ்சுவாமி—Ramadoss Swami of Tanjore. He belongs to the line of Mahratta Matadhipatis. He plays the Mridangam well.

இராமநாதன்—Ramanadhan Honourable P. He wrote the history of Harischandra in the form of a play in English, staged it in London and other great cities of Europe and made a name. He is a member of the Ceylon Legislative Council.

இராம பாரதி, கலியாண பாரதி—Rama Bharathi and Kalyana Bharathi. They belong to the village of Vettanoor in the Tanjore District. Both are clever in music and in singing. They were Samasthana Vidwans at Sivaganga and Pudukota respectively. Gopala Bhagavatar, the son of Rama Bharathi, is a good singer.

இராம ராவ்—Rama Row. Plays the Mridangam well.

இராமாஞ்சுலு—Ramanjulu. A disciple of Singalachariar. He sings Karnatic and Hindustan Keertanams well.

இராமாஞ்சுலு நாயுடு—Padala Ramanjulu Naidu. He could sing the padams of Kshetragnar, Sarangapani and Shetti Pattanam Seenu Iyer.

இராமாஞ்சுலு நாயுடு—Ramanjulu Naidu. He plays the Mridangam neatly.

இராம மாத்தியர்—Ramamatyar 1550 A. D. son of Thimma Mathya. He was Samasthana Pandithar in the court of Venkatadri, the Emperor of Vizianagar. He was a magnificent exponent of the art of Bharatam. In appriciation of his skill he was called "அபிநவ பரதாசாரியர்" in the Samasthanam. He is the author of 'Ela', 'Kathambam', 'Svaraangam', 'Vadya Prabandham', 'Panchathalesvariam', 'Sriranga vilasam' and other works. He also composed the important work "Sangeetha-swara-mela-Kalanithi, which contains all the lakshanams of music, at the request of the Emperor.

இராமாமிர்தம்—Ramamritham grandson of Krishna Iyer of Umayalpuram. He is clever in vocal music and in playing the Violin.

இராமானந்த யதீந்திரலு—Ramananda Eteendrulu. He is the author of "Gouriraga Prabandham" in Sanskrit. He seems to have lived after Ahobilar.

இராமானுஜ ஐயர்—Ramanuja Iyer of Thirunagari. He is skilled in playing the Veena and composing Sahithyams.

இராமானுஜாசாரியர்—Ramanujachariar. Brother of Doraisami Iyengar of Tirupati. An excellent Vidwan in Veena and Violin.

இராமானுஜாசாரியர்—Ramanujachariar. Generally known as Ramanujachariar of Padakapet. A disciple of Veena Kuppier. He could play the Veena in strict accordance to rules. He has composed many Varnams.

இராமுடு பாகவதர்—Ramudu Bhagavatar. Of Thirumalairajan Patnam. He is clever in elaborating Pallavi with Swarams and sounds.

இராமையங்கார்—Rama Iyengar. Of Srivilliputoor. He plays the violin well. His student Kanthadai Thirumalai Iyengar could sing well.

இராமையங்கார்—Rama Iyengar. A Sangeetha Vidwan.

இராமையர்—Rama Iyer. He and his son Krishnasami are clever on the violin.

இராமையர்—Rama Iyer. Generally known as Thirukunnam Rama Iyer. A student of Anantasayanam Govinda Perumal. He could sing the Shatkalam well. His son Sami Sastriar is also well-known for his singing.

இராமையர்—Rama Iyer of Lalgudi. A great musician. His son is Gurusami Iyer. He could sing well in strict adherence to rules. He is an excellent player on the Ghatam. His second son Radhakrishnier is also good in singing and in playing on the violin.

இராம்சாகேப்—Ram Saheb. Also known as "Nimlakar Saheb". He is a charming and beautiful singer. He plays the Veena and the violin also with great taste. He has established his reputation as a great Vidwan by exhibiting his talents in places like Baroda.

இராயாச்சாரியர்—Rayachariar. Samasthana Vidwan of Vizianagaram. Learnt music under Gururayachariar. He could sing many Jatis in Kathamargam in strict accordance to Talam.

இருதய நாராயணர்—Hridaya Narayanar. The author of "Hridayaprakasika", a treatise on music.

இலட்சுமணாச்சாரியர்—Lakshmanachariar. He is a Vidwan with wonderful Satavadhanam powers. He is very skilful in performing Harikathas and Bhagavat Katha prasangam.

இலட்சுமிகாந்த மகாராஜா—Laksmi Kanta maharajah. Proficient in Sanskrit and Music. He has composed Keertanams, Varnams and Sahityams. They are held in high esteem even at the present day.

இலட்சுமி நாராயண பாபு—Lakshmi Narayana Babu of Vizianagaram Samasthanam is well known for his skill in playing the Rudra Veena.

இலட்சுமையர்—Lakshmier. A disciple of Venkatarama Bhagavatar who learnt music under Sadasiva Row. He could sing the Keertanams of Sadasiva Row and Tyaga Iyer very neatly. Iyah Iyah, his brother-in-law could also sing Sadasiva Row's Keertanams with great taste.

உ

உபேந்திர கிசோரே—Upandra Kiso Ray. A great Calcutta musician.

எ

எம்பெருமானார்—Yemberumanar. He could play the violin wonderfully well. His son Desikulu is a charming player of Veena and the violin.

ஏ

ஏனாதி—Yenadi. Renowned for his cleverness in teaching the art of Bharatam.

ஐ

ஐயசாமி—Iyasami of Negapatam. A neat player on the Violin.

ஐயசாமி—Iyasami of Tiruvarur. Disciple of Muttusami Deekshatar. He has composed many Tanams, Varnams and Keertanams.

ஐய பாகவதர்—Iya Bhagavatar. One of the best students of Tyaga Iyer ; known for his excellence on the Veena and the violin and in singing Ragam and Pallavi. His student was Sivaramakrishna Iyer.

ஐயவையர்—Iyavaier of Tiruvalam in N. Arcot. Famous for singing Pallavi and Ragam. He was Samasthana Vidwan of Mysore under Maharajah Krishna Raja Oodayar. His disciple was Sadasivarayar of Mysore.

ஐயவையர்—Iyavaier. Son of Venkatasubbier of Tanjore and brother of Anai Iyer. He was Samasthana Vidwan during the reign of Sarabhoji maharajah (1787—1798). A great scholar in Sanskrit, Tamil and Telugu. Vyacheri Dorasami Iyer *alias* Panchanada Iyer was his student.

ஓ

ஓதப்பையர்—Odappier generally known as Chikka Odappier. He was an excellent Vidwan on the Veena in the Tanjore Samasthanam. Veenai Vijayavarahappa Iyer and Challagali Veeraraghaviah were two brothers who belonged to the same family.

க

கச்சி—Katchi. A skilful player of Mridangam.

கச்சி சாஸ்திரி—Katchi Sastri. The nephew of Syamasastri. He could sing well and play the violin also. He has a good ear for Talam.

கஸ்தூரிரங்கையர்—Kasturirangier of Deepambalpuram. A student of Veena Chinna Kalastri Iyer. He was noted for his music.

கடுவா பாகவதர்—Kaduva Bhagavatar ; otherwise known as Muttya Bhagavatar also. He belonged to the village of Samboor Vadagari of Trevandrum. He has earned a good name for his vocal music and for his particular skill in Talam.

கணபதி ஐயர்—Ganapati Iyer. Generally known as Mukkay Ganapati Iyer. He is the Samasthana Vidwan of Travancore A student of Paramesvara Bhagavatar. He could sing exceedingly well.

கணபதி ஐயர்—Ganapati Iyer of Tanjore. He was a Sub-judge ; very clever in playing the Veena and in singing.

கணபதி சாஸ்திரிகள்—Ganapati Sastrigal of Melatoor. Uncle of Subramania Iyer. He could sing very charmingly without shaking his head and with knives tied round. He knew the science of Talam well. He has obtained special honours in all the chief samasthanams. Those who have learnt Nrityam under him in the art of dancing are specially clever in Talam.

கணேச கிர்கி-பாவகிர்கி—Ganesa girki and Bava girki—Residents of Poona. They were specialists in singing Thurbath, Kyal, Tillana, Thomreel, Kajal, Lavani, Tharanal and other ragas and also Tappa Ragam which would try the patience of other singers.

கன்னுசாமி பிள்ளை—Kannusami Pillai. A Vidwan in Bharata Sangeetam and Sahityam. He has received numerous presents in Samasthanams like Malayalam and Ramnad. He was employed in the court of Baroda on a monthly salary of Rs 75 and a batta of Rs. 15 and taught music there to many for 10 years.

கன்னுசாமி ராவ்—Kannusami Row. Brother of Chittu Swami Row. The brothers were at Pudukota Samasthanam. Kannusami Row is noted for his excellent playing on the flute, violin, harmonium and Sarabat. He is now living.

கந்தசாமி—Kandasami of Tanjore. A charming singer, skilled in the science of Talam. He is clever in teaching the art of dancing.

கந்தசாமி பிள்ளை—Kandasami Pillai. He is the son of Meenakshisundara Annavi, a descendant of the Nattuva family who were hereditary servants attached to the temple of Meenakshisundarar at Madura. He is clever for his Bharata Sangeetam and Sahityam.

கலியாண கிருஷ்ணையர்—Kalyanakrishnier. He belonged to the court of Travancore. He is a wonderfully charming player on the Veena. His brother Ramachandra Bhagavatar could play the Veena in strict accordance with established rules and with neatness.

கலியாணசுந்தரம் பிள்ளை—Kalyanasundaram Pillai. A proficient in Bharata Sangeeta Sahityam. Son of Meenakshisundaram Annavi, a descendant of the Nattuva family who were hereditary servants attached to the temple at Madura.

கலியாண பாரதி—Kalyana Bharati of Vetanoor in the Pattukkota Taluq. He was at the Samasthanam of Pudukotah. A good singer.

கல்லிநாதர்—Kallinathar 1553 A. D. Son of Lakshmanachariar who belonged to the family of Ramamatya. He was the Samasthana Vidwan at Imperial Vizianagar during the reign of Immidi Devaraya Chakravarti. His commentary on the "Sangeeta Ratnakaram" is held in the highest esteem by all. On account of his profound scholarship he received the appellations of "Chatura Kallinadha" "Abhinava Bharatachariar" and "Kalkinatha."

கர்ப்புரி, தர்மபுரி வாரு—Garbhapuri. Darmapuri Varu. These have composed many Javalies with the stamp of Garbhapuri and Darmapuri.

கன்னி—Kanni, son of Fiddle Abboyee of Kumbakonam. He could play the Mridangam well.

கன்னி—Kanni. Goldsmith Kanni. He is skilful on the violin, Mridangam and Ghatam.

கன்னையா—Kannaya. Kannaya garu of Tanjore. A great Lakshana Vidwan. His students are Mukundayya, Chintamani, and Vaddi Subbayya. He is now living.

கா

காந்தீஸ்வர அண்ணாவி—Kanteesvara Annavi. A descendant of the Nattuva family which was hereditarily attached to the temple of Meenakshisundaresar at Madura. He is clever in Bharata Sangeeta Sahityam.

காபிரியேல் உபதேசியார்—Gabrial .Catechist of Nallur in the Tinnevelly District. He has composd many Keertanams pregnant with beautiful ideas.

காமராஜு—Kamaraju. He was at the Samasthanam of Vizianagaram. He was a noted Vidwan on the violin and Abhinayam (gestures) and he possessed Talagnanam.

காளாஸ்திரி ஐயர்—Kalastri Iyer-*Veenai.* Brother of Veenai Samba Iyer. He was the Samasthana Vidwan in Tanjore under Sarabhoji maharajah (1798—1824). His wife also had a good knowledge of the Veena which she exhibited before the Ranees. It is traditionally said that he was professionally jealous of his own son because he (the son) was a skilful player on the Veena.

கி

கிட்டு பாகவதர்—Kittu Bhagavatar. Samasthana Vidwan of Travancore. A student of Paramesvara Bhagavatar. He could play the Surabat charmingly. Yogi Ramaswami Bhagavatar was his disciple.

கிரி ராஜ கவி—Giri Raja Kavi of Thiruvarur. He was the Court Vidwan at Tanjore during the time of Shaji maharajah (1687-1711), the second of the Mahratta sovereigns who ruled over Tanjore. He considered music as his great treasure. He has composed many Keertanams which reflect devotion to God and which contain the essence of Vedantam.

கிரிவாசப்பா—Girivasappa. He was clever in teaching Bharatam (dancing).

கிருஷ்ணசாமி ஐயர்—Krishnasami Iyer. Son of Veenai Kuppier of Tiruvattoor. A very skilful player on the Veena and the violin. His voice was as sweet as the sounds produced on the strings.

கிருஷ்ணசாமி யாதவராவ் சாஹேப்—Krishnasami Yadava Row Saheb. Brother-in-law of Sivaji maharajah of Tanjore. A good singer and player on instruments like the Veena. He learnt music under Maha Vydyanatha Iyer.

கிருஷ்ண பாகவதர்—Krishna Bhagavatar of Tanjore. He had a good knowledge of Karnatic and Hindustani music. He could skilfully play the Surabat, the Violin, the Mridangam and the Kinjira. He could delight an audience by the performance of Harikathas. He originated the new method of performing Harikatha in which the northern method of interspersing the Katha with the Kannis, and the southern method of performing it with a mixture of Keertanams, prose, Pattu and dancing were happily combined. So his Kathas consisted of Keertanams, Dindi, Jakies and Pattu. It was only after him the Katha performers were recognised as a separate school. He had the special gift of charming an audience by his performance. His well known disciple is Panchapakesa Bhagavatar.

கிருஷ்ணப்பா—Krishnappa. He is known as Bidaram Krishnappa. He is a Vidwan in the Samasthanam of Mysore. He plays the Veena well and is able to sing in all the three Sthayis.

கிருஷ்ணப்பா—Krishnappa. Known as Nartaka Krishnappa, a resident of Tanjore. He could play the Melam beautifully.

கிருஷ்ணமாச்சாரியார்—Krishnamachariar. Generally known as Krishnamachariar of Kolattur. A disciple of Subramania Iyer of Madras. He could play the Violin with great charm and is well-known as a proficient in the art of teaching music.

கிருஷ்ணமாச்சாரியார்—Krishnamachariar. Noted for his Veena playing and singing.

கிருஷ்ணமாச்சாரியார்—Krishnamachariar of Kalattipeta. A student of Singalachariar of Madras. He could play the Violin.

கிருஷ்ணமூர்த்தி—Krishnamoorti. Generally known as Vasu Krishnamoorti. He could play the Veena neatly and charmingly in strict accordance with the rules of Gamakam.

கிருஷ்ணாஜி—Krishnaji. A well-known skilful player of Nagaswaram in Tanjore.

கிருஷ்ணாஜி பல்லால் தேவால்—Krishnaji Ballal Deval. Retired Deputy Collector. He has made many researches into the theory of the 22 srutis with the help of Abdul Kareem, a celebrated Hindustani Musician, and has produced a book on the same as a result of his labours.

கிருஷ்ணையங்கார்—Krishna Iyengar. He was the District Munsiff of Trichinopoly. He was clever on the Veena and in singing.

கிருஷ்ணையங்கார்—Krishna Iyengar of Madura. He was a skilful musician and could sing Ragam and Pallavi well.

கிருஷ்ணையர்—Krishnayyar. Generally known as Krishna Iyer of Palghaut. A good player on the Mridangam.

கிருஷ்ணையர்—Krishnayyar of Umayalpuram. A student of Venkatasubbier of Manombuchavadi, Tanjore. He is proficient in music, and is a good teacher of music. Panchapakesa Sastriar of Mayavaram learnt under him.

கிருஷ்ணையர்—Krishna Iyer. Generally known as Veenai Krishnayya. Son of Adaippayyar. He is skilful in playing the Veena and music in general. He was a great adept in the science of Talam. He has composed songs in praise of the Maharajas of Mysore, Vizianagaram and Pudukotah. He was such a master of Seven Talams that while he sang in Dhruva Talam and six others in six different Talams he could begin again in the Dhruva Talam when be finished with his Pallavi. Veenai Subbukutti Iyer was his son.

கிருஷ்ணையர்—Krishnayyar. A Sangeeta Vidwan.

கிருஷ்ணையர்—Krishnayyar. Known as Challagali Krishnayyar. Son of Pallavi Gopalayyar. He was the Samasthana Vidwan during the reign of Sivaji maharajah of Tanjore (1824-1865). An adept in singing and playing the Veena. He could play the Veena in strict accordance to rules and with great charm without touching the side strings at all. His singing and playing were so sweet and gentle as the southerly breeze that he received the surname of Challagali Krishnayyar. His disciples were

Tyagaraja Deekshatar of Tiruvalangadu, Sadasiva Iyer of Venukkurutchi, Neelakanta Sastri of Conjeevaram, Dharma Deekshatar of Akhilandapuram and Veena Vydyanatha Iyer of Mayavaram.

கிருஷ்ணையர்—Krishnayyar. Known as Ghanam Krishnayyar of Udayarpalayam. A Vidwan in Tamil and music. Clever in singing Pallavi. His padams were noted for their Sringara Rasam and difficult Varnakramams. He has composed many padams on the Zemindar of Udayarpalayam. He is said to be a contemporary of the great Tyagayyar.

கிருஷ்ணையர்—Krishnayyar of Tirukkalukkundram. He could sing 'Ghanams' tying knives round his head. He has composed many keertanams.

கிருஷ்ணையர்—Krishnayyar known as Dasavadyam Krishnayyar. Son of Appayyar. He has been honored in many Samasthanams for his playing on many instruments and for his special singing of Hindustani songs.

கிருஷ்ணையர்—Krishnayyar. Son of Amancham Kuppayar of Tanjore. A good singer.

கிருஷ்ணையர்—Krishnayyar of Chidambaram. A disciple of Pallavi Sivarama Iyer. Very proficient in music. He could sing strictly in accordance with the rules of Karnatic music.

கிருஷ்ணையர்—Krishnayyar of Tirukodikaval. He has practised violin playing to a very large extent. He could play with great charm.

கிருஷ்ணையர்—Krishnayyar of Umayalpuram. Very clever in music. Rajaram Row, who is his relative and who learnt under him, is a clever exponent of Tyagayyar's keertanams.

கிருஷ்ணையர்—Krishnayyar of Kumbakonam. He could sing even very difficult Swarams with skill, and charm.

கிருஷ்ணையர்—Krishnayyar of Kunnangudi. Very clever in music. His desciples were Radhakrishnayyar and Dasarathi Iyer, son of Gopala Bhagavatar.

கிருஷ்ணையர்—Krishnayyar. Generally known as Surabat Krishnayyar. He was Samasthana Vidwan at Pudukotah. Specially gifted in playing on the Surabat. He had practised the instrument so well that he could play it in strict accordance to Talam and make it sound like the Veena to hearers from outside.

கிருஷ்ணையர்—Krishnayyar of Palani. He had great skill in playing the Ghatam.

கிருஷ்ணையர்—Krishnayyar of Kunnargudi. He was Samasthana Vidwan of Ramnad. He has composed many Varnams and Tillanahs.

கிருஷ்ணையர்—Alasoor Krishnayyar a student of Pallavi Sivaramayyar. He was Vidwan at the Mysore Samasthanam and made himself famous for singing Pallavi and in keeping to strict Talam. He taught music to Nakhas Rudrappa, his grandson Subbanna and to Rangachariar of Sriperumboothoor. His son is Subbaraya Sastriar.

கிருஷ்ணையர்—Krishnayyar. Generally known as Tirupalli Krishnayyar. He could play the violin well.

கிருஷ்ணையர்—Krishnayyar known as Mylapore Krishnayyar. He had a gift for music. He has composed many Varnams.

கிருஷ்ணையர்—Krishnayyar a native of Talainayar. He was the court jester under Sarabhoji maharajah of Tanjore (1798-1824). He knew music. Pallavi Somu Iyer was his son.

கிருஷ்ணையர்—Krishnayyar known as Pondicherry Krishnayyar. He was in Tinnevelly. He could play the Violin well.

கிருஷ்ணையர்—Krishnayyar. Known as Niraghautam Krishnayyar. He was attached to Vijayanagaram Samasthanam. He could sing well.

கிருஷ்ணையர்—Krishnayyar known as Kote Vadyam Krishnayyar, for his efficiency in that particular art.

கிரோஸ்ஸே—J. Grosset of Lyons (France). A French gentleman greatly interested in Indian music. He has mastered Sanskrit and has translated the Bharata Natya Sastram of Bharata into French and has published it.

கிளெமெண்ட்ஸ்—E. Clements I.C.S. He is a Judge at Satara in Bombay. He has written the preface to "Deval's twenty-two Srutis" and has published a book of his own called "Introduction to the study of Indian music."

கு

குஞ்சு மேனன்—Kuuju Menon. Sub-judge of Calicut. He was skilled in playing the Veena and in singing.

குட்டைய செட்டியார்—Kuttaya Chettiar. A student of Pallavi Somu Iyer. He has practised all kinds of instruments. He sings well and is a patron of musicians.

குப்புசாமி—Kuppuswami. Two brothers elder and younger Kuppusami of Hyderabad. The senior can play the Violin very neatly in strict accordance to rules. He has composed many Varnams. The younger brother is equally good on the violin.

குப்புசாமி ஐயர்—Kuppuswami Iyer. He was at the Tanjore Samasthanam during the reigns of Amar Singh maharaja and Sarabhoji maharajah. His Keertanams are noted for their devotional element and his padams for their 'Sringara rasam. He has composed many Keertanams and Padams with the stamp of Varada Venkata.

குப்புசாமி ஐயர்—Kuppuswami Iyer. A native of Conjeevaram. He learnt music under Veena Kuppayyar of Madras. He could play the violin in strict accordance to rules.

குப்பையர்—Kuppayyar. Known as Veenai Kuppayyar and Tiruvattoor Kuppayyar. 1850. He could play the Veena wonderfully well. He was also a beautiful singer. He was a great patron of Vidwans. He could also play the violin. He is the author of many Varnams, Keertanams and Tillanahs. Hundreds of students learnt music of him. He not only taught them but kept them and fed them in his own house. He specially celebrated the festivals of Sri Rama Navami and Siva Ratri. He obtained the title of "Gana Chakravarti" as he was proficient in all music. Venkataramana Iyer of Kurattavasi, Seetaramayyar and Ponnusami were the chief students of his. Krishnaswami Iyer, Ramaswami Iyer and Tyagaraja Iyer, his sons, were also clever in music. His son Tyagaraja Iyer has published the Varnams, Keertanams and Tillanahs of the father.

குப்பையர்—Kuppayyar. Known as Amancham Kuppayyar. He was Vidwan in the Tanjore Samasthanam. He could sing padams very charmingly. His son Krishna Iyer could sing well.

குமாரசாமி முதலியார்—Kumaraswami Mudaliar of Alvarkuritchi. A relation of Dalava Mudaliar. He was at Tinnevelly. He was skilful in music and in playing the Veena.

குருசாமி—Guruswami of Conjeevaram. He and his brother Arunachalam are noted for their skill in playing the Mridangam and the Ghatam.

குருசாமிஐயர்—Gurusami Iyer. Son of Rama Iyer, the Sangeeta Vidwan of Lalgudi. He could sing Karnatic music neatly and could also play the Ghatam.

குருசாமி ஐயர்—Guruswami Iyer. A relation of Subramania Iyer of Madras and the student of Subbayyar of Andanoor. He plays the violin well.

குருமூர்த்தி சாஸ்திரியார்—Gurumoorti Sastriar. He lived in the village of Kayatraru (Tinnevelly District) during the closing years of Ramaswami Deekshatar. He possessed extraordinary skill in music. He is the author of many Geeta Prabandhams and Keertanams. He was very much honored by Manali Chinnayya Mudaliar of Madras.

குருமூர்த்தி சாஸ்திரியார்—Gurumoorti Sastriar. Known as Paidala Gurumoorti Sastri. He lived in Madras. He could sing the Ghana, Naya and Desikams very neatly and skilfully. He has composed many Geeta Prabandhams and Keertanams. His brother Paidala Subbaraya Sastriar also sings well.

குருமூர்த்தி நட்டுவர்—Gurumoorti Nattuvar. Son of Mahadeva Annavi who came from Tinnevelly. He was a famous Vidwan in playing the Veena, in teaching the art of Bharatam and in composing Sahityam. He was invited to Madras by Cunniah Chettiar for teaching to his relations and was treated by him with great kindness. He taught music to Muttusami and Thambusami, his sons, and to Ponnusami and Appakannu, and many other students.

குருராயாச்சாரியார்—Gururayachariar. He was Samasthana Vidwan at Vizianagaram. He was famous for singing the Ghana, Naya and Desikams with great discrimination. He is the author of many Tanams, Swarajatis, Ragachittas, Swarapallavis, Pallavimurais and Geetas. He could elaborately play the Shatkalams on the Veena. He was presented with an umbrella, white fans etc., by the maharajah as a mark of honour. Many learnt music of him.

குலசேகரப் பெருமாள்—Kulasekharaperumal. The Maharajah of Travancore. He was gifted with the knowledge of Malayalam, Telugu, Hindustani, Sanskrit and the English language. He was very learned in music and took a special interest in it. He has composed many Chouka Varnams and Keertanams in Rakti and Desika Ragas with the name of 'Padmanabha' at the end. He patronised many Sangeeta Vidwans. He invited Vadivel Nattuvanar from the Tanjore Samasthanam and kept him at his Court for teaching music and dancing and presented him with a Veena, violin and Tambur, all made of ivory.

குலாபு மான்டில்—Gulab Mantil. He was a descendant of Meean Tansen (Tatachari) who was Vidwan at the Court of Akbar. He became Samasthana Vidwan of Sivaganga. He was skilful in playing the instruments.

குலாபு மொயிதீன்—Gulab Moideen of Hyderabad. A charming singer of Hindustani. His nephew could also sing and play well on the Sittara and Tapela.

கூ

கூவனசாமி ஐயர்—Koovanaswami Iyer. His Tala Varnam in the Nataikurinchi Ragam has earned a very good name. He was the brother of Govindasami Iyer who was Samasthana Vidwan at Karvadi.

கெ

கெங்கைமுத்து பிள்ளை—Gangaimuthu Pillai of Tinnevelly. He is Vidwan attached to the temple of Anavarata dana nather at Madura. He has taught the art of dancing to many in Madura. He has written a treatise called "Natanadi Vadya Ranjanam" at the request and permission of Kaviraj Nellayappa Pillai who is the brother of Mutthirappa Pillai, the son of Kuppaiandi Pillai, Mirasdar of Kallumadai in Ramnad District.

கெங்கைமுத்து நட்டுவனார்—Gangaimuttu Nattuvanar of Tanjore. Famous for his Bharata Sangeeta Sahityam. Subbaraya Nattuvanar and Chidambara Nattuvanar are his sons.

கே

கேசவையா—Kesavayya known as Bobbili Kesavayya. He was Samasthana Vidwan at Bobbili. He visited diffierent Samasthanams and received honours. He visited Tanjore during the reign of Sarabhoji maharajah (1798-1824). He has successfully solved many knotty points in music which were considered impossible by others.

கொ

கோண்டையர்—Kondayyar. Brother of Veena Perumal Iyer. Had a special gift in music.

கொண்டையர்—Kondayyar of Masulipatam. He could sing the Sapta Swarams, Pallavis, and Grahaswarams strictly in accordance with established rules. He was, therefore, known as "Swaram Kondayyar."

கோ

கோட்டைசாமித் தேவர்—Kottaiswami Tevar. Zemindar of Palavanattam. He made himself skilful in music and playing the Veena by having Radhakrishna Iyer, the Sangeeta Vidwan of Lalgudi, always with him. It is only twelve years since he died.

கோட்டையா—Kottayyah of Masulipatam. He could play the violin and accompany it with singing at the same time.

கோதண்டராமையர்—Kodandaramayyar of Srirangam. He could play Karnatic Ragas on the violin tuned on English Musical principles but in strict accordance with rules. His brother was equally clever in doing so.

கோபாலகிருஷ்ண பாரதி—Gopalakrishna Bharati. He was at Anaitandavapuram. He was extensively imaginative. He is the author of Nandanar Charitram, Ragamalikas and many Keertanams.

கோபாலசாமி ஐயர்—Gopalaswami Iyer. Samasthana Vidwan of Pudukottah. Son of Matru-bhootayyah. He was one who understood Sangeeta Lakshanams well. He could sing Pallavi with great skill, with due appreciation of old Ragas and the amsams of Ragas.

கோபாலசாமி ஐயர்—Gopalaswami Iyer. A descendant of Veenai Varahappayar; specially skilled in playing the Veena and in Sangeeta Lakshanam. He has received honours in many places. He is now Vidwan at the court of the Zemindar of Ilaiyarasanendal.

கோபால நாயக்கர்—Gopala Naicker, a Sangeeta Vidwan in Tanjore.

கோபால பாகவதர்—Gopala Bhagavatar of Varahoor. He was extensively known for his skill in performing Harikathas.

கோபால பாகவதர்—Gopala Bhagavatar. Son of Rama Bharati. He learnt music under his father and Tyagaraja Iyer. He could sing well.

கோபால பாகவதர்—Gopala Bhagavatar, a disciple of Paramesvara Bhagavatar of the Travancore Samasthanam. He could sing well.

கோபாலையர்—Gopalayyar, a student of Venkataramayyar of Karur. He plays the violin.

கோபாலையர்—Gopalayyar, known as Pallavi Gopalayyar. A disciple of Patchimiriam Audappayyar. He was Samasthana Vidwan during the reigns of Amarasing maharajah and Sarabhoji maharajah of Tanjore. He has composed many Varnams and Keertanams. The Tana Varnam called '*Vanajakchi*' shows his extreme skill in adapting Swarams to suit his Sahityam. He has composed Tana Varnams in Autitalam in Kambodi and Todi Ragas with the name of 'Venkata' at the end. As he was very clever in singing Pallavi, he was called 'Pallavi' Gopalayyar.

கோபாலையர்—Gopalayyar, known as Nerur Gopalayyar. He is a charming singer. He is living now.

கோபால் நாயக்—Gopala Naik 1313. He was the most famous of the Vidwans taken by Malik kafar, the general of Alauddin, Emperor of Delhi, from South India.

கோவிந்த ஐயர்—Govinda Iyer. Son of Doraswami Iyer. Famous for his Veena playing and music.

கோவிந்தசாமி—Govindasami of Coimbatore. A good violinist.

கோவிந்தசாமி ஐயர்—Govindasami Iyer. Samasthana Vidwan of Karvadi. A very learned musician. He has composed very charming Sahityams making a collection of Telugu Padams. He is also the author of many Varnams in Navaroja and Kedara gowla Ragas. He seems to have lived before the time of Audappayyar.

கோவிந்தசாமி ஐயர்—Govindasami Iyer. A very learned professor of music and Sahityam. He has composed five excellent Varnamettus. He is also a good singer.

கோவிந்தசாமி பிள்ளை—Govindasami Pillai of Trichinopoly. A good violinist. He is now living.

கோவிந்தசிவம்—Govinda Sivam. Son of Madhyarjunam Doraswami Iyer. He and his brother Sabhapati Iyer learnt music under Tyagaraja and were well-known for their skill in Sangeetam and Sahityam. He has composed many Keertanams in Tamil in praise of Siva.

கோவிந்த தீக்ஷிதர்—Govinda Deekshatar. He was prime minister to Atchutappa Naicker, the second of the Nayak sovereigns who ruled over Tanjore (1572-1614). He was well-versed in music, and has composed many Lakshana Geetams. It is traditionally believed that he was the first to introduce the 24 frets in the Veena, and that before his time they were adjusted with reference to Prakriti and Vikriti swarams according as occasion arose.

கோவிந்தமாரார்—Govinda Maran. He was in the Travancore Samasthanam. He was known as Shatkala Govinda Doss. He was a famous Vidwan in music and Veena playing. He once visited Tyagaraja Iyer at Tiruvadi and played on his Veena so wonderfully that the latter sang the Keertanam beginning with the words "எந்தரோ மகானுபாவுலு அந்தரிகி வந்தனமு." There are many gifted persons; thanks to them all.

ச

சகஸ்ர புத்தி—Sahastra Buddhi. Secretary of the Poona Gayan Samaj and author of "Sangeeta Bodhini."

சங்கம சாஸ்திரி—Sangama Sastri. Brother-in-law of Nandigama Venkayya of Bobbili Samasthanam. He could play the Veena and violin with charm.

சங்கரராவ் விஸ்வநாதராவ்—Sankara Row and Visvanatha Row. Two brothers. Besides being the Court physicians at Tanjore, they possessed the gift of music. The former was a skilful player on the Surabath and a clever singer.

சங்கரையர்—Sankarayyar of Cannanore. He was clever in Sangeetam and Sahityam.

சங்கரையர்—Sankarayyar. A student of Tyagaraja Iyer of Tiruvattur, and a very successful teacher of music.

சஞ்சீவிஐயர்—Sanjeevi Iyer. A disciple of Patchimiriam Audappayyar and brother of Pallavi Gopalayyar. He is a proficient musician. Pallavi Sitaramayyar is his son.

சஞ்சீவி ராவ்—Sanjeevi Row. A disciple of Sarabha Sastri. He plays the flute well. He is a living musician.

சடகோபநாயுடு—Sathagopa Naidu. A very skilful player on the Veena.

சட்டம்பிள்ளை—Chattam Pillai of Prakasapuram in Tinnevelly District. He has composed many Keertnams full of beautiful ideas.

சதாசிவ ஐயர்—Sadasiva Iyer, known as Velukuritchi Sadasiva Iyer. A disciple of Challagali Krishna Iyer. He is very clever in music.

சதாசிவபிரம்மம்—Sadasiva Brahmam. He lived in Karur, Nerur and other places. His Sanskrit Keertanams are still in use. He lived about 175 years ago.

சதாசிவம்—Sadasivam. He was good on the violin and Harmonium.

சதாசிவராயர்—Sadasivarayar. He was Sangeeta Vidwan in the Mysore Samasthanam. He was well-versed in Sanskrit and Telugu. He has composed many Varnams and Tillanahs. His compositions are in use even at the present day under the title of "the Kritis of Mr. Rayar." He was rich and patronised vidwans in a very generous manner, knowing the merits of different individuals.

சத்தியநாதன் உபதேசியார்—Sattyanathan. Catechist of Tanjore. He is the author of many Keertanams full of excellent ideas.

சத்ரசிங்—Chatrasingh. A good Hindustani singer. His nephew Sundarasingh was a good violinist.

சந்திர சேகரசாஸ்திரியார்—Chandrasekhara Sastriar of Bangalore. He was a learned scholar in Sangeetam and Sahityam. He has composed many Javalis which finish with the name of Balachandra.

சந்திர பிரபு—Chandra Prabhu. A famous Vidvan of Bhownagar.

சபாபதி—Sabhapati of Chidambaram. A student of Krishna Iyer of Chidambaram. A charming singer.

சபாபதி—Sabhapati. He was very clever in playing the Melam and in teaching the art of dancing.

சபாபதி—Sabhapati. Brother of Amboiyiram. He is famous for his singing and playing the violin. His son Abboy is a good violinist while his other son Kanni plays the Mridangam well.

சபாபதி ஐயர்—Sabhapati Iyer of Mannargudi. A famous Vidwan in the science of dancing. He has written many Padams in praise of Rajagopal.

சபாபதி ஐயர்—Sabhapati Iyer. Son of Duraisami Iyer of Madhyarjunam. He learned music under Tyagaraja Iyer and was good in Sangeetam and Sahityam.

சபாபதி நட்டுவனார்—Sabhapati Nattuvanar of Tanjore. He was famous for his Bharata Sangeeta Sahityam. He has received many honours in the shape of Toda and Kanthi from many kings and nobles.

சபேசையர்—Sabhesa Iyer. Son of Sambasiva Iyer and a student of Maha Vydyanatha Iyer. He is clever in Sangeetam and Sahityam. He is also good on the violin. He lives in Madras. Mutthya Bhagavatar of Harikesavanallur is his student.

சப்தரிஷி பாகவதர்—Saptarishi Bhagavatar of Tanjore. A learned Pandit in Sanskrit and the Vedas. Has a special gift for music. He performs Harikathas also.

சரப சாஸ்திரியார்—Sarabha Sastri of Kumbakonam. Was specially good at Sangeetam and Sahityam. He had the gift of elaborating Ragas with great charm on the flute.

சர்வ சாஸ்திரியார்—Sarva Sastriar (Sishtu). A great Veena Vidwan in the court of Bobbili. His brother was Sishtu Chalamayya.

சலமய்யா—Chalamayya, known as Sishtu Chalamayya. He could play the Veena in strict accordance with rules. His brother Sishtu Bhagavanlu has practised the Veena to a remarkable degree.

சவ்யஸாசி ஐயங்கார்—Savyasachi Iyengar. He was Vidwan at the Mysore Samasthanam. He could play the Veena so skilfully with either hand that he received the surnams of "Savyasachi". He has practised the Veena to such a large extent that when he combines different Mettu Jatis on the Veena it is exquisite.

சற்குணம் வின்ப்ரெட்—Satgunam Winfred. A preacher. He has composed many Keertanams noted for their extreme devotion.

சா

சாமண்ணு—Samannah, known as Veenai Samannah· Samasthana Vidwan at Mysore. He could play the gamakamargams on the Veena very charmingly and in accordance with rules. His son is also good on the Veena. His son-in-law Subbarayar is a good singer. He has the gift of teaching music.

சாமராஜ உடையார்—Chamaraja Udaiyar. The Maharajah of Mysore. Famous for his music and Veena playing.

சாமளையர்—Syamalayyar of Tinnevelly. A good violinist.

சாமா சாஸ்திரியார்—Syama Sastriar 1763. He was born at Tiruvarur. A famous Vidwan in Sangeetam and Sahityam. He is the author of many Keertanams. His Sahityams, Swarajatis, Tanavarnams with the name of Syama Krishna specially display his imaginative skill and minuteness of Talam. Subbaraya Sastriar, the son of Alasoor Krishnayyar, was his student.

சாமிநாத ஐயர்—Swaminatha Iyer, known as Palamaneri Swaminatha Iyer. A disciple of Maha Vydyanatha Iyer. He is a famous Vidwan in Sangeeta Lakshyam and Lakshanam. He could sing in the three Sthayis with great charm playing the violin for his accompaniment. He is the author of "Ragavibodhini". He is one of the present day musicians who could play the Karnatic Ragas neatly.

சாமிநாத சாஸ்திரி—Swaminatha Sastri, son of Ramayyar of Tirukunram. A good singer.

சாமிநாதன்—Swaminathan of Tanjore. He knows music and Bharata Shastram. He is good at teaching the art of dancing. His son Govindasami has the same reputation in music like the father.

சாமிநாதன்—Swaminathan of Tanjore. Clever in teaching the art of Bharata Shastram.

சாமிநாதன்—Swaminathan of Chidambaram. He and his brother Vengu are well known for their skill in playing the Mridangam.

சாமிய பிள்ளை—Samia Pillai, son of Thyagaraja Pillai of Tanjore. He is clever in teaching singing and the violin.

சாமிராவ்—Sami Row, a skilful player of Mridangam.

சாமுகுட்டி—Syamukutti. He and his brother Appukutti are specially famous for their music and singing.

சாமய்யர்—Samayyar, son of Mahadeva Iyer who is the disciple of Paramesvara Bhagavatar. He is clever in playing the Veena and in singing.

சாமய்யர்—Samayyar. He and his son Balakrishna Iyer are good violinists.

சாமய்யர்—Samayyar of Karur. He and his brothers Periya Devayya and Chinna Devayya are good singers and violinists.

சாம்ப ஐயர்—Samba Iyer, known as Veenai Samba Iyer of Tanjore. He was Samasthana Vidwan at Mysore. He could sing the Vedas and Upanishads well with Veena accompaniment. He was specially gifted for Ghanamargam. He would bring on each separate aksharam in a Thillanah with such clearness and elaborateness that his playing would sound so grand as if produced by hundreds of Veenas. Bangaruswami Iyer was his son.

சாம்பசிவ ஐயர்—Sambasiva Iyer, son of Sabhapati Iyer. A good violinist. His son Sabhesa Iyer is the teacher of Muttya Bhagavatar.

சாம்பமூர்த்தி ராவ்—Sambamurti Row, B. A., B. L. of Tanjore. He plays the Veena well and has a gift for music.

சாரங்க தேவர்—Sarngadevar of Kashmere. Son of Soddaladevar. He was Samasthana Vidwan at the court of Simgana Raja who ruled at Doulatabad or Deogiri or Devagiri between 1210 and 1247 A.D. He was very learned in Sanskrit and music. He wrote a book on Vedanta philosophy, called 'Adhyatma Vivekam' and also the well known standard work 'Sangeeta Ratnakaram' based on the opinions of musical experts such as Bharata, Matanga, Keertidhara, Kohala, Kambala, Aswatara, Anjaneya, Abhinavagupta and Somesvara. He received the surname of "Nis-sanka which means" free from any doubt."

சாரங்கபாணி—Sarangapani. He was at the Samasthanam of Karveti Nagar. He was very clever in Sangeetam and Sahityam. He has composed many Padams full of great charm.

சாரங்கபாணி நாயுடு—Sarangapani Naidu. He and his grand-father Sathagopa Naidu were clever on the Veena and in teaching Music.

சி

சிங்களாசாரியர்—Singalachariar, two brothers. Known as Periya Singalachariar and Chinna Singalachariar of Tatchoor. They lived in Madras. They learnt music under Subbaraya Sastriar, son of Samasastriar, and his disciple Rangachariar, the violinist. Periya Singalachariar plays the violin in strict accordance with rules. He has composed Sahityams in Sanskrit and Telugu. He is very learned in music and is the author of a number of keertanams and Javalis. His brother Chinna Singalachariar is widely known for his singing and his playing on the Surabath and the Violin. They have published the following works for the advancement of music 'Swara-manjari,' 'Gayaka-parijatam,' 'Sangeeta-kalanithi,' 'Gayaka-lochanam,' and 'Gayaka-sidhanjanam.' Among his students the following are well known; Venkataramayya, Jalayya, Doraiswami Iyengar, Ramanujachariar, Narasimhachariar of Tenmatham, Varadachariar, and his brother and Baubiah Sastri.

சிட்டுசாமிராவ்—Chittu Swami Row. Brother of Kannuswami Row of Pudukottah Samasthanam. He has practised the Surabath to a large extent, which he could play with great charm.

சிதம்பர ஐயர்—Chidambara Iyer, known as Polakam Chidambara Iyer. He is specially skilled in singing and in playing the Ghatam.

சிதம்பர நட்டுவனர்—Chidambara Nattuvanar of Tanjore, known for his skill in Bharata Sangeeta Sahithyam.

சிந்தாமணி—Chintamani. A Sangeeta Vidwan.

சிந்தாமணி—Chintamani. A disciple of Kanniah Garu of Tanjore. He could play the Sarandah with great skill.

சிவகாசி அப்பாவு அண்ணாவி—Sivakasi Appavu Annavi. He is a descendant of the family which hereditarily rendered musical service in the temple at Sivakasi. He is very clever in Bharata Sangeetam.

சிவசாமி உடையார்—Sivasami Oodayar of Tanneerkunnam. He is a great Vidwan in singing and in playing the Veena and other instruments.

சிவசாம்பையர்—Sivasambayyar of Negapatam. A good singer.

சிவராம பாகவதர்—Sivarama Bhagavatar known as Andami Sivarama Bhagavatar. He is clever in performing Harikathas.

சிவராம பாகவதர்—Sivarama Bhagavatar of Tanjore. He is well-known for his Sangeeta Sahityam and skill in performing Harikathas. He is known as "Chitrakavi" Sivarama Bhagavatar.

சிவராமாச்ரமுலு—Sivaramasramulu 1827. He lived at Tiruvarur. He is the author of "Nijabhajana Sukhapaddhati". Many of his Keertanams noted for devotion are in existence.

சிவராமையர்—Sivaramayyar, known as Pallavi Sivaramayyar. Son of Sanjeevi Iyer, brother of Pallavi Gopalayyar. He has a great reputation for singing Pallavi. His son is Fiddle Subbarow.

சிவராமகிருஷ்ணையர்—Sivaramakrishna Iyer. A good player on the Violin.

சிவராமகிருஷ்ணையர்—Sivaramakrishnayyar, son of Subbarama Bhagavatar, the disciple of Venkatasubbayyar of Manombuchavadi. He could play the Keertanams of Tyagaraja Iyer on the violin with charm.

சிவானந்தம்—Sivanandam. Son of Mahadeva Annavi of Tinnevelly. He was clever in Sangeetam and Bharatam. He had two sons, Mahadevan and Swaminathan. He has taught the art of dancing to Sadaimudi, Sundaram, Desur Subbalakshmi and Pudukotah Ammalu.

சிவானந்தம் நட்டுவனர்—Sivanandam Nattuvanar. Brother of Vadivalu Nattuvanar of Tanjore. He was well-skilled in the science of Bharata Sangeetam, and in teaching gestures. He was made much of by Sivaji maharajah. He has taught the art of gesticulation to many.

சின்னசாமி—Chinnaswami of Tirukkalukkundram; clever in playing the harmonium.

சின்னசாமி தீக்ஷிதர்—Chinnaswami Deekshatar, brother of Muttuswami Deekshatar. He was a proficient Vidwan in music, playing the Veena and in singing. He has composed many Keertanams in the Kalyani Ragam.

சின்னசாமி தேவர்—Chinnasami Tevar of Chokkampatti, brother of the Zemindar of Chokkampatti. He is a great Vidwan in Sangeeta Sahityam, in playing the Veena and in the Tamil literature.

சின்னசாமி பாகவதர்—Chinnasami Bhagavatar of Tiruvalur. He has written many essays in Tamil, Telugu and Sanskrit.

சின்னசாமி முதலியார்—Chinnasami Mudaliar, M.A. He was in a high position in Madras Chief Secretariat Office. He took a very deep interest in music, spending all his energy and wealth for organising and systematising Indian music. He set to music a number of Indian Keertanams by writing them in European staff notation, and printed some of them. He did not live long enough to complete the work he had undertaken.

சின்னசாமையா—Chinnasamayyah. Nephew of Nakkaya, the goldsmith. He could sing with great charm and skill.

சின்னத்தம்பி அண்ணாவி—Chinnatambi Annavi. A descendant of the hereditary Nattuva family attached to the service of the temple of Meenakshisundaresa of Madura. Skilled in dancing.

சின்னதேவையா—Chinnadeviah of Karur. He could sing well and also play the violin neatly to the rules of Karnatic music.

சின்னபாரதி—Chinna Bharati of Mayavaram. A good scholar in Tamil literature and music.

சின்ன வைத்தி, பெரிய வைத்தி—Peria Vythi and Chinna Vythi, two brothers. Natives of Radhamangalam near Sivaganga. They are well-known Vidwans in Sivaganga Samasthanam. The combined singing of the two brothers will be exquisite.

சின்னையா, பொன்னையா, வடிவேலு—Chinnayya, Ponnayya and Vadivelu. These three have composed Swarams, Talam, Jati, Varnams, Tillanahs and Ragamalikas in connection with the art of dancing. They could hold the audience spell-bound with their singing. They were at Travancore Samasthanam.

சின்னையா—Chinnayya 1500 A.D., known as Talapakkam Chinnayya. He lived at Tirupati spending his time in devotedly worshipping Venkatachalapati. He was the first who composed Todayam, Mangalam, Charanam, Keertanams for awakening and Keertanams to be used in the ceremonial worship of the deity. He appears to have lived before the time of Ramamatya.

சின்னையா நட்டுவனார்—Chinnayya Nattuvanar. It is said that he stood unrivalled in the art of teaching dancing. He lived during the time of Sivaji maharajah. Those who read his science of Bharatam all learnt the Art. The Maharajah introduced male dancing (specially in processions with the cows) for the first time and encouraged it. He was well-skilled in Bharata Sangeeta Sahityam.

சின்னையா பாகவதர்—Chinnayya Bhagavatar. He lived in Tinnevelly. A great Vidwan in Veena playing. He had many students. He was rich and generous enough to maintain Vidwans from other places.

சீ

சீதாராம பாகவதர்—Sitarama Bhagavatar. A student of Paramesvara Bhagavatar of Travancore. A very good singer.

சீதாராமையர்—Sitaramayyar. Tahsildar of Madura. He learnt music under Subbayya of Audavanallur and was very clever in playing instruments like the Veena and in singing.

சீதாராமையர்—Sitaramayyar known as Soldier Sitaramayyar. A student of Thygaraja Iyer of Tiruvadi. He could sing Ragam and Pallavi with skill.

சீதாராமையர்—Sitaramayyar. Samasthana Vidwan of Vizianagaram. Son of Gururayachariar. He succeeded his father as Samasthana Vidwan. He could play the shatkalams on the Veena with great skill. As he had well practised the art of playing the Veena he was able to elaborate Pallavis and Ragas well.

சீதாராம ஐயர்—Sitaramayyar known as *Todi* Sitaramayyar. He was in Tanjore at the beginning of the reign of Sarabhoji maharajah. He specially cultivated the Todi Ragam and completely mastered it. He could elaborate the ragam with special skill and a number of variations.

சீதாராமையர்—Sitaramayyar. Son of *Veenai* Kuppayyar of Tiruvattoor. He could sing Ragam and Pallavi with neatness.

சீதாராமு—Sitaramu of Hyderabad. Brother of Peria and Chinna Kuppusamies. A very good violinist.

சீனிவாச ஐயர்—Sreenivasa Iyer of Tinnevelly. A Vidwan who knew many of the knotty points in the science of Music. A good violinist.

சீனிவாச ஐயங்கார்—Sreenivasa Iyengar. A student of Subbayyar of Madras. A good exponent of Ragam and Pallavi. He is a proficient scholar who knows Sangeta Laksyam and Lakshanam. He has visited many places and has been specially honored wherever he went. He is now Samasthana Vidwan in the Ramnad Samasthanam and is teaching music to many.

சீனிவாசராவ்—Sreenivasa Row of Srirangam. Son of Bheemachariar. The father and son are clever singers. Bheemachariar plays the Veena.

சீனிவாசராவ்—Sreenivasa Row of Kumbakonam. A student of Oomayalpuram Swaminatha Iyer who learnt music under Maha Vydyanatha Iyer. He is a sweet player on the flute.

சீனிவாசராவ்—Sreenivasa Row known as *Kotu Vadyam* Sreenivasa Row. He could play the *Kotu Vadyam* and the violin very sweetly with gamakams. He is also a magnificent singer.

சீனிவாச ஐயர்—Sreenivasayyar. He has composed many Padams and Keertanams pregnent with ideas in Tamil, finishing them with the name of Vijayagopala. He was prime minister at Madura in the reign of Vijayaranga Chokkanatha Naicker.

சீனுவையர் சௌக்கம்—Seenu Iyer, *Choukam.* He was Samasthana Vidwan in the Tanjore Samasthanam under Sarabhoji and Sivaji maharajahs. He obtained the surname because of his imaginative and elaborative skill in singing Raga Alapanams.

சீனுவய்யங்கார்—Seenu Iyengar of Shettipattanam. A great vidwan in music who has composed many Padams.

சீனய்யா—Seenayya known as *Ghanam* Seenayya, son of Seshayyar and a student of Vatoola-desikar. He was proficient in Sanskrit and Telugu and music. He was minister in the reign of Vijayaranga Chokkanatha Naicker. He is the author of many Keertanams and Padams which end with the name of Mannar Ranga. He is held to be a contemporary of Kshetragnar.

சு

சுதாகலச—Sudhakalasa 1324 A.D. Author of "Sangeeta Upanishad" and "Sangeeta Upanishad Saram".

சுந்தர ஐயர்—Sundara Iyer. He could sing and play the violin at the same time and make the singing and playing blend together sweetly.

சுந்தர ஐயா—Sundara Iyah. Son of Paidala Subbaraya Sastrulu. A very charming singer.

சுந்தர சிங்—Sundara Singh .He and his brother Chatra Singh are good singers of Hindustani Music. Sundara Singh plays the violin with great charm.

சுந்தர நாயக்கர்—Sundara Naickar of Negapatam. He was a Sub-judge. He was a good player of the Veena and the violin and also a singer.

சுந்தரப்பையர், சுப்பராமையர், சேஷையர்—Sundarappayyar, Subbaramayyar and Seshayyar. Three brothers who were vidwans in music. They have composed Padams and Keertanams in Tamil.

சுந்தரம் ஐயர்—Sundaram Iyer of Umayalpuram. A student of Venkatasubbayya of Manambuchavadi. He was clever in singing Ragas, Pallavis and Keertanams. He taught music to Panchapakesa Iyer, Koratavasi Venkataramana Iyer and Fiddle Natesa Iyer. Natesa Iyer is a skilful player on the violin.

சுந்தர ஐயர்—Sundara Iyer of Chittoor. A pleader. He is good in playing the Veena and in singing.

சுந்தரராவ்—Sundara Row of Tanjore. He had a beautiful voice. He was known as *Todi* Sundara Row. He belonged to the Tanjore Mahrattas. His son was also a specialist in singing Todi Ragam.

சுபங்கர்—Subhankar 1700 A.D. Author of "Sangeeta Damodaram."

சுப்பண்ணா—Subbannah. Son of *Veenai* Subbukutti Iyer. He could play the Veena neatly and in strict accordance with the rules of Karnatic music.

சுப்பண்ணா—Subbannah known as Bhakshi Subbannah. He is Veena Vidwan at the Mysore court. A student of *Veena* Sambayyar. His singing to his own accompaniment on the Veena will be something wonderful. He could also play many other instruments.

சுப்பராம ஐயர்—Subbarama Iyer. Son of Seshachala Iyer. He is a good violinist and his brother, a good singer.

சுப்பராம தீக்ஷிதர்—Subbarama Deekshatar. Grandson of Balaswami Deekshatar (through his daughter) and his adopted son. He was a proficient scholar in Sanskrit, Telugu and music. He learnt Kavya, Veena, Nataka, Alankara and Sangeeta Lakshya and Lakshana from Balaswami Deekshatar and Krishnamatyar of Vilattikulam. He was Samasthana Vidwan at Ettiyapuram during the time of Jagadeesvara Rama Venkatesvara Rajah. He is the author of many Choukavarnams, Tanavarnams, Keertanams, Ragamalikas and Ragasamcharas. These may be seen in the "Sangeeta Sampradaya Pradarsani" published by him and Chinnasami Mudaliar with the help of the Rajah of Ettiyapuram. Tyagarajayyar of Ettiyapuram is his student.

சுப்பராமையர்—Subbaramayyar of Vydeesvarankovil. A Vidwan in Tamil and music. He has composed many Padams which end with the name of Muttukumara. He lived about 50 years ago.

சுப்பராய அண்ணாவி—Subbaraya Annavi. A descendant of the Nattuva family hereditarily attached to the temple of Subramania at Tiruchendoor. His service was to chant Thevaram and Thiruvasakam. He was good in music and in Bharata Sangeeta Sahityam.

சுப்பராய சாஸ்திரியார்—Subbaraya Sastriar 1803. Son of Syama Sastriar. He was a scholar in Tamil, Telugu, Sanskrit and music. He has composed many Keertanams and Swarajatis. Ponnusami was his student.

சுப்பராய சாஸ்திரியார்—Subbaraya Sastriar. Brother of Padala Gurumoorti Sastriar of Madras. A good singer. He has composed many Varnams. His son Sundara Iyer is a charming singer.

சுப்பராய சாஸ்திரியார்—Subbaraya Sastriar. Son of Krishna Iyer of Alasoor. He was a great Vidwan and a student of Syama Sastriar. He is the author of many Keertanams which end with the name of Kumara. His son Annasami Sastriar, and his son-in-law Katchi Sastriar, were skilful Vidwans held in great esteem. Krishna Iyer of Perambore, Rangachariar of Chandragiri, Tirugnana Mudaliar, Chimata Raghavulu Chetty and *fiddle* Balu were his students.

சுப்பராய நட்டுவனார்—Subbaraya Nattuvanar. Proficient in Bharata Sangeeta Sahityam. His Varnams and Keertanams are in praise of Tulajaji maharajah and the deity. He was presented by the Maharajah with a palanquin and other paraphernalia, with land, jewels and with the residence known as Nattuvan Chavadi. He has taught music to many. His three sons, Ponnayya, Chinnayya and Sivanandam were also efficient musicians.

சுப்பராயர்—Subbarayar, known as Subbarayar of Pichandar Kovil. A student of Neelakanta Iyer. A splendid musician. His singing was so exquisite like the liquid sounds of a stringed instrument that the audience would be quite charmed.

சுப்பராயலு—Subbarayalu of Pichandarkoil. An exquisite singer. Sivasamba-Iyar was his student.

சுப்பராயலு—Subbarayalu of Tiruvallur. Son of Chengalrayudu of Tiruvallur. A good player of Nagaswaram.

சுப்பராயலு—Subbarayalu of Tirupapuliyur. He and Vyapuri and Muttu are expert players of Mridangam.

சுப்பராவ்—Subba Row known as *fiddle* Subba Row. Son of *Pallavi* Sivaramayyar. He could play the violin neatly keeping excellent time.

சுப்பராவ்—Subba Row. Samasthana Vidwan at Pittapuram. An expert Veena player.

சுப்பிரமணிய ஐயர்—Subramania Iyer known as Pattanam Subramania Iyer. Originally he was a resident of Tiruvadi but removed to Madras later on. He could sing Ghana, Naya and Desikams, Ragas and Pallavi with great skill in strict accordance to rules. He has composed a number of Keertanams, Varnams, Javalis, Tillanas, with excellent Varnamettu. He could reproduce the Keertanams of the great Vidwans exactly as they were originally sung. Those who have heard him and his brother Panchanada Sastri sing Keertanams will hardly be inclined to listen to the Pallavi of others. Sreenivasa Iyengar of Ramnad, *fiddle* Krishnamachariar, Kanchi Seshayyar and Seshagiri Row are his disciples who could exactly imitate their master in singing Keertanams and Pallavis. He died about 15 years ago.

சுப்பிரமணிய ஐயர்—Subramania Iyer of Kangundi. He could sing in strict accordance with established rules.

சுப்பிரமணிய ஐயர்—Subramania Iyer known as Tiruvadi Subramania Iyer. Samasthana Vidwan at Mysore. He is specially gifted in the science of Talam. He could sing Pallavi with great discrimination of different Jatis.

சுப்பிரமணிய ஐயர்—Subramania Iyer of Nemam. A student of Tyagaraja Iyer. He could sing Ragam and Pallavi and also the Keertanams of his master neatly and with great effect.

சுப்பிரமணிய ஐயர்—Subramania Iyer of Vettanur. A good singer. He lives at Pudukotah.

ஸ்ரீ ல ஸ்ரீ சுப்பிரமணிய தேசிகர்—Sri La Sri Subramania Desikar. The Tambiran Swami of Tiruvaduturai Mutt. He learnt music under Maha Vydyanatha Iyer and was efficient in singing and in playing the Veena.

சுப்புக்குட்டி ஐயர்—Subbukutti Iyer known as *Veenai* Subbukutti Iyer. Grandson of *Patchimiriam* Audappayya, Samasthana Vidwan at Pudukotah. He is an exquisite player on the Veena in which he could play Raga Alapanam, Pallavi of Madhyamakalam so as to bring out his imaginative and discriminating skill in arranging Swarams and his command of the ten kinds of Gamakams, so that the Ateeta, Anagata, Sama and Vishama grahams may boldly stand out. He was playing the Veena even in his seventieth year and died about 1870. *Veena* Subbannah is his son.

சுப்புக்குட்டி ஐயர்—Subbukutti Iyer of Mylapore. A student of *Veenai* Venu who was the disciple of Tiruvattur Tyagayyar. A good musician.

சுப்புச்சவையர்—Subbuchavayyar of Kumbakonam. A pleader. He could sing the Keertanams of Tyagayyar with a charming voice. A disciple of Umayalpuram Krishna Sundara Bhagavatar.

சுப்பையர்—Subbayyar known as Andanoor Subbayyar. A student of Nangapuram Neelakanta Iyer who learnt music from Tyagayyar. He could play with the utmost ease the Gamakamargams and Ateeta-Anagatams which would defy the skill of ordinary musicians. He could sing with and without accompaniment the Padams of Kshetragnar. His student Gurusami Iyer (a relation of Pattanam Subramania Iyer) is a good violinist. Rangasami of Srirangam is also his student.

சுப்பையர்—Subbayyar known as *Janjhamarutam* Subbayyar. Student of Kannayyar of Tanjore. He could sing gracefully in the three sthayis. He obtained his surname in the durbar of the Maharajah of Mysore.

சுப்பையர்—Subbayyar known as Vaddy Subbayyar. He is also a disciple of Kannayyar of Tanjore. A good singer.

சுப்பையர்—Subbayyar of Srivaikuntham. A very charming singer.

சுப்பையர்—Subbayyar of Srirangam. Son-in-law of Rangasami, the student of Andanoor Subbayyar. A good singer.

சுப்பைய பாகவதர்—Subbayya Bhagavatar of Tinnevelly District. A good violinist and a performer of Harikathas.

சுயம்பிரகாச யதீந்திரலு—Swayamprakasa Yeteendrulu. He lived in Mayavaram about 60 years ago. He has composed Keertanams in Sanskrit.

சுவாமி பாகவதர்—Swami Bhagavatar known as Swami Bhagavatar of Umayalpuram. Nephew of Krishna Bhagavatar and Sundara Bhagavatar. He has mastered many of the Keertanams of Tyagayyar. He is a living musician.

சுவேதாரண்ய ஐயர்—Swetaranya Iyer. Son of Vettanur Venkatarama Iyer, the disciple of Deekshatar. A good violinist.

சூ

சூரியநாராயண சாஸ்திரிகள்—Sooryanarayana Shastriar. "Doorvasa" was his house name. He was at the Samasthanam of Vizianagaram. He was specially gifted in playing the Shatkalams on the Veena and in making each aksharam ring with effect. He has practised the Veena to a very large extent. He has also composed many Sahityams.

செ

செந்தில்வேலண்ணாவி—Sendilvelannavi of Tinnevelly of the Otchar caste. He was playing the Veena in the temple of Nelliappa and teaching dancing as well as the right method of chanting to those who were specially engaged in it. He was under the patronage of a great nobleman, by name Pulayan. Tulaja maharaja who heard the chanting of those who learnt under him was so struck with their charm that he sent for his son Mahadeva Annavi and kept him at his court thus helping the progress of Carnatic music in his Samasthanam.

செந்து மேனன்—Chendu Menon of Palghat. A Munsiff. A good player on the Veena and a singer. He learnt music under Paramesvara Bhagavatar.

செல்வகணபதி தீக்ஷிதர்—Selva Ganapati Deekshatar of Chidambaram. A student of Singalachariar of Madras. A gifted musician.

சென்ன மல்லப்ப—Chenna Mallappa of Bangalore. He plays the Veena in accordance with established rules.

சே

சேதுராமராவ்—Seturama Row. A good player on the Mridangam.

சேது ராமராவ்—Seturama Row of Tanjore. A student of Mridangam Tukkaram Row. He plays the instrument with great skill.

சேத்தூர் ஜமீந்தார்—Zemindar of Setur. He is proficient in Sangeeta Sahityam in Tamil and in playing the Veena. These Zemindars were all good in Tamil literature and music. He practised music under the guidance of Muttya Bhagavatar of Srivilliputtur who always lived with him.

சேஷ ஐயங்கார்—Sesha Iyengar. He came to Srirangam from Oudh and sang many Keertanams in praise of Sri Ranganadha, many of which are in use at present. He was surnamed "*Margadarsi*" because his Keertanams follow the scientific method.

சேஷகிரி சாஸ்திரியார்—Seshagiri Sastriar, M.A. Sanskrit Professor in the Madras Presidency College. He was specially famous for his proficiency in Sangeetam and Sahityam. A good player on the Veena. His brother Venkatesa Sastri was good on the Veena and the Violin. He was well known for his gift of teaching.

சேஷண்ணு—Seshanna. Surnamed *Veenai* Seshanna. A student of *Veenai* Subbanna. He was Samasthana Vidwan at Mysore during the time of Maharajah Chama Raja Oodayar and Krishna Raja Oodayar. He could play the Ravai Jatis on the Veena with wonderful skill. He also plays the violin and the Jalatarangam. He has made a name in many Samasthanams.

சேஷாசல ஐயர்—Seshachala Iyer. He was a musician at the Pudukotah Samasthanam. He could sing according to established rules.

சேஷாசல பாகவதர்—Seshachala Bhagavatar, a student of Syama Shastrial. Samasthana Vidwan at Pudukotah. Clever in Sangeeta Sahityam and singing. He has composed many Keertanams in Telugu. His son Matrubhootayya and his brother Ramadoss are also musicians.

சேஷையர்—Seshayyar known as Gootala Seshayyar of Conjeevaram. A student of Gurumoorti Sastriar and a famous Vidwan. He has composed many Keertanams. His son Subbayyar and his student Nagoji Row are good in singing.

சேஷையர்—Seshayyar. Brother of Sundarappayyar and Subbaramayyar. Clever in Sangeetam and Sahityam. He has composed many Keertanams and Padams in Tamil.

சேஷையர்—Seshayyar. He lived in Neykarpatti a village near Salem. He has composed many Keertanams and Varnams.

சோ

சோட்டுமியான்—Chottu mian. A good singer of Hindustani music.

சோமநாதர்—Somanatha 1609 A.D. Author of "Ragavibotha". This has been translated and published in the "Indian Music Journal" by Mr. H. P. Krishna Row, B. A., of Mysore.

சோமாஜி பாகவதர்—Somaji Bhagavatar. A great vidwan at the Samasthanam of Travancore.

சோமு ஐயர்—Somu Iyer. Surnamed *Pallavi* Somu Iyer of Talainayar (Tanjore District). Son of Krishna Iyer, the court jester at Tanjore. He could sing Ragam and Pallavi with great skill and in accordance with known rules. His son Radhakrishna Iyer, is good in singing and playing the violin. Kuttayyan Chettiar of Devakottah learnt music under him.

சோழமுத்து—Cholamuttu. Brother of Annu and Ramasami. Clever in teaching the art of dancing and in playing the Violin.

ஜ

ஜகதீஸ்வர ராமகுமார எட்டப்ப ராஜா—Jagadeesvara Ramakumara Ettappa Rajah, Raja of Ettayapuram. He was a proficient scholar in Tamil, Telugu, Sanskrit and music. He played the Veena. He has composed many Choornikas and Slokas on Ganapati addressing him as Kartikeya, and many Keertanams in Rakti and Desika ragas. He was a patron of many musicians. The chief musicians of his court were, Balaswami Deekshatar, Appukutti Iyer, Meenakshisundaram Iyer, Veenai Subbayya Annavi, Vengu Bhagavatar, Ramayya of Madura and Subramania Iyer of Thevoor.

ஜகதீஸ்வர ராமவெங்கடேஸ்வர எட்டப்பராஜா—Jagadisvara Rama Venkatesvara Ettappa Rajah Raja of Ettayapuram. He was keen on music and had practised many instruments such as the Veena, Surabath, Sither, Jalatarangam, Ghatam and Mridangam. He has composed the Swarajati commencing "முருகா உன்னை நம்பினேனையா" (Muruga Unnai Nambinen Iyah).

ஜயதேவர்—Jayadevar 1100 A.D. Son of Bojjala Devar who lived in a village in Bengal, known as "Kundavilva" or "Kundubilvam". A student of Govardhanachariar. He was musician at the court of Lakshmana Sena Maharajah, the son of Vallala Sena Maharajah. His contemporaries were Oomapati Das, Saranar, Govardhanachariar and Thopi Kaviraja. He has not only set to music the Ashtapadi Grantham known as "Geetagovindam" but has also composed a drama known as "Prasanna Raghavam".

ஜா

ஜாலய்யா—Jalayya, a disciple of Singalachariar. A very good singer. He was employed for 18 years at the Devastanam of Kanyaka Paramesvari at Madras. He has taught music to many.

ஜானகிராமய்யர்—Janakiramayyar. A student of *Veena* Kuppayar of Tiruvattoor A charming singer.

ஜான் பாமர்—John Palmer. Writer of Nagercoil. He has composed many Keertanams full of fine ideas.

ஜீ

ஜீயர்— Jeeyar. A good player on the Veena. His son Alagasingayyar is also good on the Veena. He has taught music to many.

ஸ்

ஸ்ட்ராங்வேஸ்—Fox Strangways A. H.—A European musician who travelled through India to make researches on Indian music; he has published the result of his consultation with many Indian musicians in the form of a book, "the Music of Hindustan."

ஷா

ஷாஜி மகாராஜா—Shaji maharajah. Son of Ekoji maharajah of Tanjore, and second sovereign of the Mahratta line. He ruled the Chola Kingdom from 1687-1711. He was specially proficient in Maharashtram, Telugu, Hindustani and other languages. He has not only composed many Keertanams, but has set to music the drama called "Pallaki" in Telugu, in praise of Tyagaraja Swami of Tiruvarur.

க்ஷே

க்ஷேத்ரக்ஞர்—Kshetragnar—He was in the habit of singing the praises of, and praying to, the deity at the Gopalaswami Temple at Muvvapuri, in the Chandragiri Taluq of the Chittoor District. He composed many Padams well known for their beautiful words and ragas, representing man and God in the relation of two lovers, bringing out the characteristics of God with appropriate beauty and sense. His Padams stand unrivalled so far as their meaning and beauty are concerned. He visited the courts of Madura, Tanjore and Golconda and was specially honored for his Padams. His Padams on Kanchi Varadarajar and Sevantilingesar and with the name of "Muvva Gopala." We gather from old works that he lived during the reign of Vijayaraghava Naicker of Tanjore and was the author of as many as 1,000 Padams.

க்ஷேமகர்ணர்—Kshemakarna 1570 A.D. The author of "Ragamala".

த

தம்பியப்பன்—Tambiappan. Son of Gurumoorti Nattuvanar. He did duty as Nattuvan in the Temple of Tyagaraja at Tiruvarur during the time of Sarabhoji and Sivaji maharajahs. He taught music and dancing to Gnanam and Kamalam of Tiruvarur. He was so clever in music and playing the Mridangam specially in Lakshyam and Lakshanam that he was surnamed "*Suddha Mridangam* Tambiappa." He received a monthly salary from the Maharajah besides being given a residence and manyam lands. He helped Ramasami Deekshatar and Muttuswami Deekshatar.

தர்மதீக்ஷதர்—Dharma Deekshatar of Akhilandapuram. A disciple of Challagali Krishna Iyer, very clever in playing the Veena.

தக்ஷிணாமூர்த்தி—Dakshinamoorti of Pudukottah. A student of Mamundiapillai of Kinjira fame. He is an expert in playing the Ghatam, Mridangam and Kinjira.

தக்ஷிணாமூர்த்தி—Dakshinamoorti of Tanjore. A good player on the Mridangam.

தக்ஷிணாமூர்த்தி சாஸ்திரி—Dakshinamoorti Shastri of Masulipatam. A good singer.

தா

தசரதி ஐயர்—Dasarathi Iyer, son of Kola Bhagavatar. He became proficient in music which he learnt from Krishnayyar of Kunnankudi.

தாசரி—Dasari. A skilful player on the Surabatt.

தாண்டவராயத் தம்பிரான்—Tandavaraya Tambiran. He was Kharbar Tambiran in the Mutt at Kalladakurchi. He was very skilful in Tamil, in Sangeetam and Sahityam and in playing the Veena. He is the author of many Keertanams.

தாதாச்சாரியார்—Tatacharriar. One of the Karnatic musicians taken to Delhi from South India by Emperor Akbar. He became a Mahamadan and was known as " Mian Tansen, the proficient musician."

தாமோதர மிச்ரா—Damodara Misra 1560-1647. He is the author of "Sangeeta Darpana" 1625.

தாவூத் சாயபு—Dawood Saheb of Tanjore. A skilful Vidwan in playing the Saranda. He could also sing with great charm.

தி

திம்ம மத்தியர்—Timma Matyar 1550-1600. He and his son Rama Matya are the joint-authors of "Swara mela kala nidhi."

தியாகராஜ ஐயர்—Tyagaraja Iyah. Grandson of Girirajakavi who was Samasthana Vidwan in the reign of Shaji maharajah of Tanjore. Son of Rama Brahmam. He left Tiruvarur, his native place, came to Tiruvadi on the river Kaveri and learnt Sanskrit, the Vedas, Kavyam, Natakam and descriptive composition. He then learnt Sangeeta Lakshanam, Talam, elaboration of Ragas, Pallavi and other subtle points in music under Sunthi Venkataramanayya, and became so extraordinarily proficient that he rose to the pinnacle in Sangeetam and Sahityam. He was in the habit of spending his whole time in the presence of Sri Rama, composing new Keertanams daily and in singing them to the accompaniment of the Veena. He had the rare gift of composing Keertanams without any premeditation. His Varnams and Keertanams number over 2,000. There will not be a Vidwan in South India who would not have heard his Keertanams. His many disciples are Iyah Bhagavatar, Subbarama Bhagavatar, Ganesa Iyer, Venkatarama Bhagavatar of Walajapet, Soldier Sitaramayya, *Veenai* Kuppayyar of Tiruvattur, Amritalingam Pillai, Rama Iyengar of Tillaisthanam, Venkatasubbayya of Manambuchavadi, Krishna Iyer of Oomayalpuram and his brother Sundaram Iyer. Of these *Veena* Kuppayyar and Venkatasubbayya were men of great fame.

தியாகராஜ ஐயர்—Tyagaraja Iyer, surnamed: Tiruvattur Tyagaraja Iyer and Tyagaraja Iyer of Peddunaickanpet. Son of *Veenai* Kuppayyar who learnt music under Tyagaraja Iyer of Tiruvadi. He learnt music and playing the Veena under his own father also. He distinguished himself as a Vidwan in singing Ragam and Pallavi and in Veena playing. He not only composed many Varnams and Keertanams but published them along with his father's compositions.

தியாகராஜ ஐயர்—Tyagaraja Iyer of Mysore. Son of Radhakrishna Iyer of Kinjira fame. A good singer.

தியாகராஜ ஐயர்—Tyagaraja Iyer. Student of Subbarama Deekshitulu of Ettiyapuram. A good singer.

தியாகராஜ சாஸ்திரிகள்—Tyagaraja Sastrial of Tiruvalankadu. He was the Guru of Veena Vydyanatha Iyer. He was a great Vidwan in musical composition, singing and in playing the Veena.

தியாகராஜ தீக்ஷிதர்—Tyagaraja Deekshatar of Tiruvalankadu. Student of *Challagali* Krishna Iyer. He was clever in music and in composition, and a talented player on the Veena.

தியாகராஜ பிள்ளை—Tyagaraja Pillai, a student of Doraswami Iyer of Vyaicheri. He was specially good in Sangeetam, Talam, Pallavi and in giving instruction in music. He has mastered a number of Keertanams of Tyagaraja Iyer. He taught music to his son Samia Pillai (Pattu), to Madhava Row, Ameen at Orthanad and to Sivasamba Iyer of Negapatam.

திரிகூடராசப்ப கவிராயர்—Tirikooda Rasappa Kavirayar. A native of Mela Agaram near Tirukuttalam. Specially proficient in Tamil and in musical composition. He is the author of "Kuttalakuravanchi" and other works. He has been given a Manyam named " Kuravanchi Medu."

திருக்கடவூர் பாரதி—Tirukadavur Bharati of Mayavaram, specially proficient in Tamil and music.

திருமலை ஐயங்கார்—Tirumalai Iyengar, house-name Kanthadei. Disciple of Rama Iyengar of Srivilliputoor. A good singer.

திருமலை ஐயங்கார்—Tirumalai Iyengar, known as Tirumalai Iyengar of Aunmarainadu. He lived at Srivilliputoor. A scientific singer.

திருமலை ஐயர்—Tirumalai Iyer, son of *Veenai* Audappayar. He was Samasthana Vidwan at Tanjore during the time of Tulaja Maharajah. Very clever in Sangeetam and in playing the Veena. Appadurai Iyer of Tirupoonduruti was his student.

திருமலைராவ் சாஹெப், ஜாகீர்தார், ஆரணி—Tirumalai Rao Sahib, Jagirdar of Arni. He practised music and playing the Veena under the guidance of *Veenai* Sadasiva Row of Mysore and *Kinjirah* Radhakrishna Iyer who always lived with him.

திருவேங்கடப்பய்யர்—Tiruvenkatappayyar specially gifted in playing the Veena. He has composed many Tanams.

திருவேங்கடாச்சாரியார்—Tiruvenkatachariar of Needamangalam. Known as Sarasvati Tiruvenkatachariar. A pundit in Sanskrit and Bharata Shastra.

து

துக்காராம்—Tukaram, a famous Mahratta musician. He holds the same eminent position as regards Mahratta music as Tyagaraja Iyer holds for Karnatic music.

துக்காராம் ராவ்—Tukaram Row. A skilful player on the Mridangam.

துரைசாமி ஐயங்கார்—Doraswami Iyengar. A disciple of Singalachariar of Madras. Clever in music and in playing the Veena. He is teaching the Veena to the Mahunt of Tirupati.

துரைசாமி ஐயர்—Doraswami Iyer. He lived at Tiruvadi during the time of Sarabhoji maharajah. A clever Vidwan in music and composition. He has composed many Keertanams with the name of Subramania.

துரைசாமி ஐயர்—Doraswami Iyer of Madhyarjunam. Famous for his Sangeetam and Sahityam. A very charming singer. He has two sons, Sabhapati Iyer and Govinda Sivan.

துரைசாமி ஐயர்—Doraswami Iyer. Son of Appu Bhagavatar of Travancore Samasthanam. He is a lawyer at the court of Cochin. He is a beautiful singer. His brother is very good on the violin.

துரைசாமி ஐயர்—Doraswami Iyer. Son of Vytti Iyer of Manitattu. An exquisite singer.

துரைசாமி ஐயர்—Doraswami Iyer. Native of Vyaicheri near Tanjore. He was Samasthanam Vidwan during the time of Sarabhoji maharajah. A disciple of Anai Iyah, who was the son of his (Duraisami Iyer's) grand uncle. His sons were Sambamoorti Iyer, Ramaswami Iyer, Maha Vydyanatha Iyer and Appaswami Iyer. Thyagaraja Pillai was his disciple. The Rajah gave him a residence at Tiruvadi and Manyam lands at Tirupoonduruti.

துரைசாமி ஐயர்—Doraswami Iyer of Tiruvadi. He could sing the Keertanams of Tyagaraja Iyer, Tillanas and Javalis so as to charm an audience.

துளஜ மகாராஜா—Thulaja maharajah 1716-1787. The fifth Mahratta king who ruled over the Chola country from Tanjore. He was specially keen and interested in music. He and his queen Ammani Boi Saheba were good players on the Veena. He patronised musicians by encouraging them with gifts and Manyam lands. He sent for Mahadeva Nattuvan from Tinnevelly in order to arrange and systematise Karnatic music with special reference to Bhavam, Ragam and Talam and kept him at his court to disseminate music. The special Vidwans of his court were Audappayyar, Sunthi Venkatasubbayyar, *Veenai* Subbukutti Iyer, Venkatasubbayyar, Mahipalei *Veenai* Perumal Iyer and Mahadevan. He wrote the musical work called "Sangeeta Saramritam" in 1770.

தே

தேவநாயக ஐயங்கார்—Devanayaka Iyengar of Travancore. Specially proficient in Sangeetam and Sahityam. He has composed many good Keertanams. His sons could also sing well.

தேவராஜுலு நாயுடு—Devarajulu Naidu. Son of Govindaswami of Tanjore. He could play the Moresing and Ghatam well.

தேவய்யா—Devayyah of Karur. One of three brothers, Devayya Senior and Junior and Samayyah. All are good singers and scientific players on the violin.

ந

நக்கய்ய—Nakkayya, known as Nakkayyar the goldsmith. Has made a special study of music. A magnificent singer. He has composed many beautiful Keertanams.

நஞ்சுண்டப்பா—Nanjundappah of Bangalore, a charming player on the violin.

நடராஜ பாகவதர்—Nataraja Bhagavatar of Tirukattupalli. Clever in music and in the performance of Harikathas.

நடேச ஐயர்—Natesa Iyer. A student as well as a relation of Sundara Iyer of Umayalpuram. Very clever in singing and playing the Violin and in giving music lesson.

நடேச ஐயர்—Natesa Iyer. Son of Subramania Iyer of Nemam, a disciple of Thyagaraja Iyer. A charming singer.

நடேச கிர்கி—Natesa Girki of Poona. He is a skilful player of Thurabath, Kyal, Thillanah, Thomereelu, Katchal, Ilavani, Tharanal and other compositions.

நடேச தீக்ஷதர்—Natesa Deekshatar of Kumbakonam. Skilful in performing Harikathas.

நடேச பாகவதர்—Natesa Bhagavatar of Melatur. He is skilful in music and in the performance of Harikathas.

நடேசன்—Natesan of Koranadu near Mayavaram. A very skilful player of Nagaswaram.

நம்பெருமாளய்யர்—Namberumalayyar. Son of Raghavayyar. A charming player on the Violin.

ஸ்ரீ-ல-ஸ்ரீ நரசிம்ம அபிநய ஸ்வாமி, சிருங்கேரி, சாரதா பீடாதிபதி—Sri La Sri Narasimha Abhinaya Swami, Sringeri, Sarada Peethadhipati. He was specially gifted in, and famous for Veena playing, singing and powers of composition.

நரசிம்ம ஐயங்கார்—Narasimha Iyengar of Namakal. He is a scientific singer of ragam and pallavi.

நரசிம்ம பாகவதர்—Narasimha Bhagavatar. Though a resident of Namakal, he stays at Srirangam performing Harikathas. He has a sound knowledge of music.

நரசிம்ம பாகவதர்—Narasimha Bhagavatar. He could perform Harikathas with special reference to the devotional element.

நரசய்யர்—Narasayyar. Surnamed "Shatkala." He was a native of Salem, though he spent a great part of his time in Bangalore. Besides composing many Varnams and Keertanams, he has been giving lessons in music to many a Vidwan.

நரசய்யர்—Narasayyar. Surnamed *Padala*. He could sing beautifully. He has composed Pathantaram to many Padams.

நரசையா—Narasiah. Surnamed *Shankarabaranam* Narasiah. He was Sangeetha Vidwan at the Tanjore Samasthanam under Sarabhoji maharajah. He has composed many Padams in Tamil which are highly imaginative. He is specially famous for elaborating the Shankarabharana Ragam.

நல்லப்பா—Nallappa. A descendant of Mahadevan of Nagaswaram fame. He could play the Nagaswaram in strict accordance to time. His brother Arunachalam is also a gifted musician.

நன்னுமியா, மீரலி—Nannumeah, Meerali. Two brothers noted for their skill in playing the Dolak.

நன்னேகான்—Nannekhan. A well-known musician in Bhownaggar.

நா

நாகபூஷணம்—Nagabhushanam. A Samasthana Vidwan of Vizianagaram and a disciple of Gururayachariar. A skilful player on the Veena.

நாகலிங்கம் அப்பாவு—Nagalingam Appavu. A good violinist.

நாகராஜ பாகவதர்—Nagaraja Bhagavatar. A student of Govindaswami Bhagavatar of Tanjore. He performs Harikathas well and is a good violinist.

நாகராஜ ராவ்—Nagaraja Row. Of Kumbakonam. A good flutist.

நாகராஜராவ்—Nagaraja Row of Tanjore. Father-in-law of Seturama Row, the famous player on Mridangam. He is clever in playing the Veena, Violin, Mridangam and in singing. Venkasami Row is his student.

நாகசாமி மாடிகாராவ் சாயப்—Nagasami Madigarow Saheb. Son-in-law of Maharajah Sarabhoji. He could play the Veena and other instruments. Vidwans were in the habit of singing their compositions before him for approval.

நாகோஜிராவ்—Nagoji Row, disciple of Gootala Seshayyar of Conjeevaram. A good singer.

நாகோஜி ராவ்—Rao Bahadur C. Nagoji Row, B.A., F.M.U. Retired Inspector of Schools. One who is very keen cn, and much interested in music. He is the author of Raga Swarakramam written for the benefit of school children. His essay on the 22 Srutis was translated into Tamil and read before the second conference of the Tanjore Sangeeta Vidya Mahajana Sabha. He has manufactured Veenas for the 22 Srutis out of deal wood, and has given them to many. He also prepared a harmonium with 22 srutis while he was at Kumbakonam with the help of Radhakrishna Bhagavatar.

நாராயண ஐயங்கார்—Narayana Iyengar. Known as Narayana Iyengar of Setlur. Author "Abhinaya Sara Samputam."

நாராயண ஐயர்—Narayana Iyer of Umayalpuram. He plays the Ghatam well.

நாராயணசாமி—Narayanaswami of Shiyali. Good on the violin and harmonium.

நாராயணசாமி—Narayanasami of Needamangalam. He and his son are good singers.

நாராயணஸ்வாமி—Narayanaswami of Tirupati. Plays the Veena.

நாராயணஸ்வாமி அப்பா—Narayanaswami Appa. Member of a Mahratta family in Tanjore. He was an exquisite player on the Mridangam. He could so clearly and neatly play the instrument as an accompaniment to singing or to an instrument or as a sola, that the Ravai Jaties will be clearly and distinctly heard.

நாராயணஸ்வாமி ஐயர்—Narayanaswami Iyer. Samasthana Vidwan of Pudukotah. Grand-son of Appukutti Iyer. He was also known as *Fiddle* Narayanaswami Iyer. He lives at Tirugokarnam near Pudukotah. He is a world-known Vidwan in Sangeetam and in playing the violin.

நாராயணஸ்வாமி ஐயர்—Narayanaswami Iyer of Umayalpuram. He is surnamed *Bharatam* Narayanaswami Iyer. He is skilful in music and Bharatam.

நாராயணஸ்வாமி ஐயர்—Narayanaswami Iyer. Brother of Veenai Perumal Iyer. A very good player on the Veena.

நாராயணஸ்வாமி ஐயர்—Narayanaswami Iyer of Thiruvisanallur. He could sing Ragam and Pallavi and could play the Veena and the violin with great charm. He is a disciple of *Pallavi* Somu Iyer.

நாராயணஸ்வாமி முதலியார்—Narayanaswami Mudaliar. He was Tahsildar at Satur. He is a great Vidwan in playing the Veena and singing.

நாராயண தாஸ்—Narayana Doss of Vizianagaram, skilful on the Veena and in the performance of Harikathas.

நாராயண தீர்த்தர்—Narayana Teerthar. He lived about 300 years ago. He is the author of the Sanskrit work "Krishnatarangam". His Pans are very beautiful.

நாராயண தேவர்—Narayana Thevar 1765. Author of "Sangeeta Narayana."

நீ

நீலகண்ட ஐயர்—Neelakanta Iyer, known as Nangavaram Neelakanta Iyer. A student of Tyagaraja Iyer. A good Vidwan in music. He is a very earnest and successful teacher of music. His students are, Subbayyar of Andanoor, his brother Sundaram Iyer, Manitattu Vydi and others.

ப

பகவான்தாஸ்—Bhagavan Doss. A good player on the harmonium.

பகவான்லு—Bhagavanlu known as Sishtu. Brother of Veenai Sishtu Sarva Shastriar. He has practised the Veena to a very large extent.

பக்கிரி—Packiri of Kumbakonam. He could play the Mridangam well.

பங்காருஸ்வாமி ஐயர்—Bangaruswami Iyer. Sangeeta Vidwan at Mysore. Son of Veenai Samba Iyer. A good player on the Veena.

பஞ்சநத ஐயர்—Panchanada Iyer. He could sing with great charm according to established rules and could melt an audience. He has composed a few Varnams.

பஞ்சநத சாஸ்திரியார்—Panchanada Sastriar. A student of Syama Sastrial of Tranqebar. He, like his master, has composed many Keertanams. A good singer.

பஞ்சநத சாஸ்திரியார்—Panchanada Shastriar. Brother of Pattanam Subramania Iyer. He spent his time with his brother and had a gift for music. A very charming singer.

பஞ்சாபகேச ஐயர்—Panchapakesa Iyer. He learnt music under Venkataramana Iyer of Kuratavasi and Sundaram Iyer of Umayalpuram. He could sing Ragam, Pallavi and Keertanams strictly in accordance with rules.

பஞ்சாபகேச ஐயர்—Panchapakesa Iyah. Grandson of Tyagaraja Iyah, and student of Venkatasubbayya of Manambuchavadi. A very sweet singer.

பஞ்சாபகேச சாஸ்திரி—Panchapakesa Sastri of Kumbakonam. Generally known as Panchapakesa Bhagavatar of Tirupayanam. He is specially proficient in Sanskrit Sangeeta Sahityam and in performing Harikathas.

பஞ்சாபகேச சாஸ்திரி—Panchapakesa Sastri of Tiruvarur. He could sing Ragam and Pallavi in the style of old masters. He could sing the Keertanams of Deekshatar scientifically.

பஞ்சாபகேச சாஸ்திரி—Panchapakesa Sastriar. A student of Krishna Iyer of Umayalpuram. A gifted musician and a good teacher.

பஞ்சாபகேச பாகவதர்—Panchapakesa Bhagavatar. Son of Appadurai Iyer who taught Bharatam to Krishna Bhagavatar. A student of Krishna Bhagavatar of Tanjore. A gifted musician in Lakshya Lakshanam and in singing Pallavi. He is such an exquisite and neat player on the violin that even the minutest Gamaka Swarams can be distinctly heard. He is widely known for his skill in the performance of Harikathas. He is also an earnest and successful teacher. Sesha Bhagavatar is his student.

பஞ்சாபகேசன்—Panchapakesan of Tanjore, good in Talam and in teaching dancing.

பஞ்சு ஐயர்—Panchu Iyer. Famous for his singing and playing the Surabath.

பஞ்சுசாமி சாகிப்—Panchu Sami Saheb. A wonderful player of Surabath and Mridangam.

பஞ்சுசாமி ராவ்—Panchuswami Row. A relation of the Rajah of Tanjore. He could play the Veena, violin, Surabath and Mridangam.

பட்கோஸ்வாமி—Bhatgoswami known as Jagannātha Bhatgoswami of Tanjore. A renowned player of Balasarasvati. When King Edward VII visited India as Prince of Wales, he honored him for his wonderful playing on the instrument. His son Moni Bhatgoswami plays the Veena, Mridangam and the harmoniam.

பட்டாபிராம ஐயர்—Pattabhirama Iyer. He was attached to the Mysore Samasthanam. He has composed many Sahityams, and also many Javalies in the shape of Natakas.

பத்மநாப நாயுடு—Padmanabha Naidu of Tanjore. Clever in playing the fiddle and in giving music lessons.

பத்மநாபாசாரியார்—Padmanabhachariar attached to the Samasthanam at Vijianagaram, well known for his Sangeeta Sahityam and skill in playing the Veena.

பரமேஸ்வர ஐயர்—Paramesvara Iyer of Ariyalur. A student of Narayanasami Appa, the famous Mridangam player of Tanjore. He plays the Mridangam well.

பரமேஸ்வர பாகவதர்—Paramesvara Bhagavatar. Samasthana Vidwan at Travancore. A famous Vidwan in playing the Veena and the Surabath and in performing Harikathas. His voice will be as sweet as the music produced by the instrument itself. He is the author of many Varnams. Kittu Bhagavatar, Appu Bhagavatar, Gopala Bhagavatar, Seetarama Bhagavatar, Mukkay Ganapati Iyer, and Coimbatore Raghava Iyer are his students. His sons are Mahadeva Iyer and Ramakrishna Iyer.

பரிமள ரங்கன்—Parimala Rangan. He lived in the Northern parts of India about 200 years ago. He is the composer of many Padams with Yethi-prasams in Telugu, ending with the name of Parimala Ranga.

பலவந்தராவ்—Balavanta Row. House-name Dharvada. He was in the Bellary District. He was gifted in Hindustani and Karnatic music. He could sing Hindustani Music in the three Sthayis bringing out the Gamakams distinctly. His two sons also could sing Hindustani Music so as to delight an audience.

பலவந்தராவ், பையா சாகேப்—Balavanta Row and Bayya Saheb, younger brothers of Maharajah Madhava of Gwalior. He was very skilful in Sangeeta Sahityam and on the Veena. He has composed many Keertanams in praise of Sri Krishna.

பாவ்பட்டர்—Bhava Bhatta 1640. Author of "Sangeetanupankusa".

பாவ்பட்டர்—Bhava Bhatta 1680. Author of "Anoopa Sangeeta Vilas," "Muraliprakasa," and "Nashta-uddishta Prabodhaka Darpana Teeka"

பேனேகான்—Baney Khan. A native of Nepaul skilled in singing Hindustani music as Pathantarams and in elaborating the Ragam 'Tappa'. He could elaborate Hindustani Pallavis on a large scale just as in Karnatic music.

பா

பாக்கியநாதன்—Bhagyanathan P. of Sivakasi, author of many Christian Keertanams.

பாண்டித் துரைசாமித்தேவர்—Pondi Dorasami Tevar, Zemindar of Palavanattam. He is widely known for his scholarship in Tamil, Sangeeta Sahityam, singing and instrumental playing. President-founder of the Fourth Madura Tamil Sangam.

பாப்பையா—Bappiah of Bangalore. He could sing so sweetly that it will be difficult to differentiate between an instrument and his voice.

பாரதி—Bharati of Mayavaram. Tirukadavur Bharati and Chinna Bharati are brothers, specially proficient in Tamil and music.

பார்த்தசாரதி நாயுடு—Parthasarathi Naidu of Madras. A student of Venu, the famous Veena player. A distinguished Vidwan in music and in playing the Veena.

பாலகிருஷ்ண செட்டியார்—Balakrishna Chettiyar. He could play the Veena and accompany it by his own sweet singing. He could play many instruments with skill with the exception of the Violin.

பாலகிருஷ்ணய்யர்—Balakrishnayyar, student of Krishna Bhagavatar. He and his father Samayyar are good violinists.

பாலஸ்வாமி தீக்ஷிதர்—Balaswami Deekshatar (1786-1859). Son of Ramasami Deekshatar. He was well acquainted with Sangeeta Lakshyam and Lakshanam. He learnt to play the Violin also under an English gentleman in Madras through the influence of Manali Chinnayya Mudaliar. He could play the Veena, Surabath and the Sithar. He was Samasthana Vidwan at Ettiyapuram. He has composed in the Saranga, Durbar, Kannada and Rudrapria Ragas. He also composed Darus in praise of Venkatesvara Ettappa Rajah in Rudrapria, Durbar and Vasanta Ragas with the Muttayee Swarams, and received many gifts by the Rajah. Subbaraya Dikshatar is his grandson as well as adopted son.

பாலபுவனநாதபட்—Bala Bhuvananatha Bhut. Grandson of Bava of Gwalior. Could perform Harikathas in Hindustani.

பாலு ஐயர்—Balu Iyer of Madras. A clever violinist.

Dr. பாலு முதலியார்—Dr. Balu Mudaliar of Trichinopoly. Famous for singing and Veena playing. He learnt music under Subbarayar of Pichandar Kovil.

பாவவிநாச முதலியார்—Pavavinasa Mudaliar; clever in Tamil and music. He has composed many Mock-heroic Padams with the name of Pavavinasa. He lived during the time of Tulaja maharajah.

பாவா--Bava. He came from Gwaliar. He could perform Harikathas in Hindustani with special skill.

பாஸ்கர சேதுபதி—Bhaskara Setupati. Raja of Ramnad. Skilful in Tamil and Sangeeta Sahityam. He could sing with great charm.

பி

பிங்களர்—Pingal, B.A. He wrote a book in 1898, on Hindustani Music in English and Marati known as "Indian Music".

பிச்சைமுத்து, B.A.,L.T.—Pichaimuthu A.G., B.A.,L.T.—Organist of S. Peter's Church, S.P.G. Tanjore. He is very keen on, and much interested in music. He has passed very high examinations in European Music. He plays the organ and the Piano with great skill. Many of his students are organists in different places of this Presidency.

பிரதாபசிம்ம மகாராஜா—Maharaja Pratap Singh of Madhyarjunam. Son of Amar Singh Maharajah of Tanjore. He knew music well, and could play the Mridangam with skill. He has published the notation for a Raga Tala Malika known as "Navaratna Malika" in the Mahratta language so that the Varnakramams might be easily understood. He died a few years before Sivaji Maharajah.

பிரதாப ராமஸ்வாமி பாகவதர்—Pratapa Ramaswami Bhagavatar of Puvanur near Nidamangalam. He is specially clever in music and in Sanskrit compositions.

பு

புண்டரீக விட்டலர்—Pundareeka Vitthala. He lived about the end of the XVI Century. He is the author of "Nartana Nirnaya", "Ragamanjari", "Seegrabodhini", "Namamala," "Shadraga Chandrodaya", "Ragamala", and "Sangeeta Vritta Ratnakara".

புரந்தர விட்டலதாஸ்—Purandara Vithaldoss. He was a millionaire of Poona, who was so devoted to the God Sri Panduranga Perumal that he was in the habit of singing his praises daily by a new Keertanam. He has composed many Alankarams, Pillayar Geetams, Keertanams, Suladis, Prabandhams, Tanams and Bhagavan Nama Kritis. All the above treat about Vedantam and are in use at the present day in the Mathams in the North.

புருஷோத்தம மிஸ்ர—Purushottama Misra 1730. The author of "Sangeeta Narayana."

பெ

பெரியகுப்புசாமி—Periya Kuppuswami of Hyderabad. He could play on the violin very charmingly and in strict accordance with rules. He has composed many varnams.

பெரியதம்பி அண்ணாவி—Periatambi Annavi. Surnamed "Sooryamoorti." A decendant of the Nattuva family hereditarily attached to the service of the temple of Meenakshi Sundaresa at Madura. Skilled in Bharatam.

பெரிய தேவையா—Periya Deviah of Karur. A good singer. He could play the violin strictly adhearing to the rules of Karnatic music.

பெரிய பக்கிரி—Periya Packiri. Surnamed Mannargudi Packiri. A wonderful player on the Nagaswaram.

பெரிய வைத்தி—Periya Vyddi. He was Samasthana Vidwan at Sivaganga. He and his brother Chinna Vyddi were widely known for their skill in Sangeeta Sahityam and singing.

பெருமாளையர்—Perumalayyar. Surnamed Mahipalai *Veenai* Perumalaiyar. He was Sangeeta Vidwan at Tanjore during the reign of Maharajah Sarabhoji (1798-1824). Student of Veenai Kalahasti Iyer. The members of his family have been distinguished for Veenai playing for generations. He was well known for his handling of Ghana Raga Talams. He could play the Rakti Ragas like the Bhairavi for ten days together never once repeating what he had first played. He has been honored in the Samasthanams of the North receiving palanquins and other paraphernalia and Veenais inlaid with precious stones as presents. He played a single ragam with elaborations for 20 days together in the Pudukotah Samasthanam and was honored. He was widely known for his skill in playing the Veena with strict adherence to Talam. The village of Mahipala was presented to him by the Maharajah of Tanjore. His brother *Veenai* Narayanasami is also good on the Veena.

பெருமாளையர்—Perumalaiyar of Madura. He and his father are clever in playing the Mridangam.

பை

பையா—Byah of Tanjore. A good singer of Hindustani music and a skilful player on the Surabath.

பொ

பொன்னம்பலம்—Ponnambalam. Son of Nagalingam Appa. He could play the violin and the harmonium well.

பொன்னுசாமி—Ponnuswami of Irupoor. A good violinist.

பொன்னுசாமி—Ponnuswami of Tiruvattoor. He was known as a good musician owing to his constant association with Kuppayar. He was a good violinist. He has composed many Varnams. He was living in Madras.

பொன்னுசாமி—Ponnuswami. A disciple of Subbaraya Shastrial of Tanjore. He could sing well the Keertanams of his guru as well as the Keertanams and Padams of Syama Shastrial.

பொன்னுசாமி—Ponnuswami of Madura. A very good player of Nagaswaram.

பொன்னுசாமி அண்ணாவி—Ponnuswami Annavi of Madura, who belonged to the hereditary Nattuva family of the temple of Sundaresar. He was well-known for teaching dancing and for playing on instruments.

பொன்னையா—Ponnayya. He was well-known for his skill in teaching dancing in the Samasthanam at Travancore. He has composed Tana Sahityam necessary for the art of dancing in collaboration with Vadivelu.

பொன்னையா நட்டுவனார்—Ponnayya Nattuvanar. He has composed many Keertanams and Varnams being a profound scholar in Tamil and Telugu. He was made much of in the court of Maharajah Sivaji at Tanjore and in the court of Krishna Raja Woodayar, Rajah at Mysore. He has composed many Keertams and Sahityams on the Maharajahs of Mysore, Malayalam and Tanjore. He is held in the highest esteem by the Vidwans of the present day as one who was the author of Varnams, Sahityams and Padams necessary for the art of dancing and which are in use now from the Himalayas to Cape Comorin. A well-known master in Bharata Sangeeta Sahityam.

பொன்னையா பிள்ளை—Ponnayya Pillai of Tanjore. A Vidwan in Bharata Sangeetam. A very clever Vidwan in singing Ragam and Pallavi and in teaching dancing. He has been teaching the art to many.

ம

மகமது ஷர்க்கீவி—Mahamed Sharkvi of Janpore. The originator of Kyal Paddhati.

மகம்மேரு—Mahammeru. A native of Tanjore who was Samasthana Vidwan at Travancore. He could sing to the compass of three Sthayis and a half. He belonged to the family of Mathadhipatis.

மகாதேவ அண்ணாவி—Mahadeva Annavi. Son of Chendilvel Annavi of Tinnevelly. He was brought to Tanjore by Maharajah Tulaja and was appointed Samasthana Vidwan. He has composed many Varnams, Keertanams and Swarajatis in Tamil and Telugu, which are in use even at present. He made the dancers Vanajatshi and Muttumannar, brought by him from Tinnevelly, dance in the Durbar hall of Maharajah Tulajaji to the Varnam called "Bosaley Thulajendra Rajah" in the Todi

Ragam. Those who were Samasthana Vidwans at the time, such as Audappayyar, *Veenai* Subbukutti Iyer, Thirumalai Iyer, Venkatasubbayyar learnt the Veenai under him and improved their Bhava, Raga, Talams. Syama Sastrial of Conjeevaram and Muttusami Deekshatar of Tiruvarur practised their Veenai and dancing under him. The Maharajah was so delighted with his musical genius that be built a residence for him in the Western Main Street of Tanjore, gave him 10 velis of land as Sarvamanyam and appointed him Samasthana Vidwan. Sivanandam, Vadivelu and Gurumoorti are his sons. These were also well-known vidwans in Sangeeta Sahityam, the art of dancing and in playing the Veena.

மகாதேவ ஐயர்—Mahadeva Iyer. Son of Paramesvara Iyer who was Samasthana Vidwan at Travancore. He had a magnificent voice and was capable of singing in the three Sthayis. He could play the violin so skilfully that each aksharam could be distinctly heard. *Veenai* Swami Iyer is his son, and Anantaramayyar, his student.

மகாதேவ நட்டுவனார்—Mahadeva Nattuvanar of Tanjore. He was very much learned in Bharata Sangeeta Sahityam. He has been honored by many kings and nobles with Toda, Kanthi and other presents.

மகாதேவன்—Mahadevan. A genuis. He could play the Nagaswaram so effectively as to melt the hearts of his hearers. Nallappa, a descendant of his, could play the Nagaswaram with strict adherence to Talam.

மதனபாலதேவ—Madanapaladeva 1528. Author of the musical treatise "Ananda Sanjeevana".

மதிராஜம் பாகவதர்—Matirajam Bhagavatar. He could sing in the Madhyamakalam very sweetly. He was at Ettiyapuram in Tinnevelly.

மரியான் உபதேசியார்—Marian, Catechist of Elayirampannai in Tinnevelly. He has composed many Keertanams.

மா

மாசிலாமணி முதலியார்—Masilamani Mudaliar. He was a well-known photographer in Madras. He learnt music and became an efficient violinist. His student is Johannas Sundararajam.

மாணிக்கம்—Manickyam. A good violinist.

மாதவ மகாராஜா—Madhava Maharajah of Gwalior. He is good in music and in playing instruments like the Veena and violin.

மாதவராவ்—Madava Row (Khamasdar). He could sing according to established rules. His son Raghupati Row is well-known for his singing and playing the Surabath and the Mridangam.

மாதவராவ்—Madhava Row. Surnamed "Dharwar." A native of Bellary. He could sing Karnatic as well as Hindústani music. He had a voice which sounded like music played on the strings.

மாத்ரு பூதய்யா—Matrubhootayya of Pudukotah. Son of Seshachala Bhagavatar. A very proficient musician.

மாத்ருபூதையர்—Matrubhootayya of Trichinopoly, surnamed *Kavi* Matrubhootayya. He is the author of many Keertanams in praise of Sri Sugandhi Kuntalambal where he sets forth her sense of justice and the people's devotion to her. He has composed many Padams also full of Sringara rasam. He has written the work ' Parijatapaharanam" in the form of Keertanams. His Keertanams invariably end with the name of "Tri Sira Giri".

மாமுண்டியா பிள்ளை—Mamundiah Pillai of Pudukotah. A wonderful player of the Kinjira. He was specially a genius in Talam. His student is Dakshinamoorti.

மீ

மீனாக்ஷிசுந்தரம் அண்ணாவி—Meenakshisundaram Annavi. A lineal descendant of the Nattuva family of the temple of Meenakshisundara at Madura. He was famous for his Bharata Sangeeta Sahityam. He made a collection of Arya, Dravida, Andhra Bharata Shastras.

மு

முத்து இராமலிங்க சேதுபதி ராஜா—Muttu Ramalinga Setupati Rajah of Ramnad. He was clever in Tamil and in Sangeeta Sahityam. Many of his compositions have been printed and are in use. He lived about 45 years ago.

முத்து இராமலிங்க சேதுபதி ராஜா—Muttu Ramalinga Setupati Rajah of Ramnad. He was well-practised in Tamil, Sangeeta Sahityam and in playing instruments like the Veena and violin.

முத்துக்கிருஷ்ண நாயுடு—Muttukrishna Naidu. He and his son are skilful players of Mridangam.

முத்துக்கிருஷ்ண முதலியார்—Muttukrishna Mudaliar of Madras. Surnamed "Manali." He and his son Manali Chinnaya Mudaliar, *alias* Venkatakrishna Mudaliar, were much interested in music. They patronised a number of Tamil scholars as well as Sangeeta Vidwans. Sonthi Venkatasubbayyar, Ramaswami Deekshatar, Govinda Deekshatar, Gurumoorti Sastri, Muttu Tandava Kavirayar, Arunachala Kavirayar, Muttusami Deekshatar are the most distinguished Vidwans of his Sabha.

முத்துசாமி—Muttuswami. Son of Mariappan. He was specially proficient in Bharatam, Talam and singing. He has been honored with gifts in many Samasthanams.

முத்துசாமி தீக்ஷிதர்—Muttuswami Deekshatar *1775*. Son of Ramasami Deekhsatar. He was Samasthana Vidwan at Ettiyapuram. He has composed Keertanams in Mayamalavagoula, Ragatalas with Varnakramams for Ashtapadis in praise of Rama, Navagraha Keertanams in Sooladi Sapta Talas, nine Keertanams in praise of Kamalambal and Keertanams in Megharanjita and Amrita Varshini Ragas in praise of Venkatesvara Ettappa Bhoopati. He has also composed Keertanams which end with the name of "Guruguha" on Tyagaraja Swami and many other swamis in Ragas specially recommended by Venkatamakhi so as to bring out the Gamakajatis, the Jeevaswarams of the different Ragas and the Raga names. Tirukadavur Bharati,

Veena Venkataramaniah of Avudayarkovil, Tevur Subramania Iyah, *Suddha* Mridangam Tambiappan of Tiruvarur, Ponnayya of Tanjore. Vadivelu, Vettanoor Subbarayalu, Koranadu Ramaswami, Tiruvalundoor Vilvavanam, Iyaswami of Tiruvarur, Kamalam of Tiruvarur and Ammanni of Vallalarkoil are his students.

முத்துசாமித் தேவர்—Muttusami Thevar of Ramnad. A good violinist.

முத்துசாமி நட்டுவர்—Muttusami Nattuvar. Son of Gurumoorti Nattuvar. Native of Madras. A very famous Vidwan in Veena and in the art of Bharatam. He was Samasthana Vidwan at Venkatagiri and Arni and taught music to the Rajahs. He was such a genuis as to sing Pallavis in the 108 talas. Periya Vydyanatha Iyer, Chinna Vydyanatha Iyer, Pattanam Subramania Iyer, *Maha* Vydyanatha Iyer, Coimbatore Raghava Iyer, *Veenai* Venu, Chidambaram Appakannu, Panchanadam of Tirumulaivoil, Pudukota Mamundia Pillai, Talai Nayar Radhakrishna Iyer, *Veenai* Dhanam, and Dancing girl Krishna of Triplicane were among his students. Of these the last named Krishna was a famous Veena player in the court of Venkatagiri. Singaram *alias Veenai* Venu is his son.

முத்துசாமி முதலியார்—Muttuswami Mudaliar. Tahsildar of Tiruturaipoondi. He learnt music under Krishnayyar of Umayalpuram and was skilled in playing the violin and in singing.

முத்துசாமி நட்டுவர்—Muttuswami Nattuvar. Surnamed "*Oochita Bhava Alankara.*" He was Samasthana Vidwan at Sivaganga and was honored with a necklace for his success in a trial of skill in music.

முத்துசாமி முதலியார்—Muttuswami Mudaliar of Palamcottah. A descendant of Vengu Mudaliar. He was clever in singing and in playing the Veena. He is the composer of many Keertanams.

முத்துத்தாண்டவர்—Muttuttandavar. He lived before Arunachala Kavirayar. A Vidwan in Tamil and music. He has composed many Padams and Keertanams on Nataraja of Chidambaram which are noted for their devotional and love elements.

முத்து முனுசாமி—Muttu Munuswami. These could play Mridangam so exquisitely that it will resemble the kiss of lovers.

முத்தையர்—Muttayya of Bodinaickanur. Clever in playing the Mridangam.

முத்தையர்—Muttayyar. Surnamed "Kehara". He could sing Ragas, Pallavis and Keertanams purely in accordance with the rules of Karnatic music.

முத்தைய பாகவதர்—Muttya Bhagavatar of Srivilliputtoor. He could sing Ragam and Pallavi with skill.

முத்தைய பாகவதர்—Muttya Bhagavatar of Harikesavanallur in the Tinnevelly District. A disciple of Sabhesayyar of Madras. A learned Vidwan in Sangeetam and Sahityam. He could play the Kote Vadyam with exquisite taste. He is widely known for his skill in performing Harikathas. He has visited many places and has been honoured every where.

முனுசாமி—Munuswami. He could play the harmonium and the violin.

மே

மேருஸ்வாமி—Meruswami. A descendant of the Tanjore Matadhipati ; he was in the Samasthanam of Malayalam. He could sing well in the three Sthayis.

யு

யுவரங்க பூபதி—Yuvaranga Bhoopati. Surnamed " Katchi." He was Zemindar of Udayarpalayam during the reign of Maharajah Tulajaji. He was cognisant of the nobleness and the dignity of music and was a keen musician. He was so very charitable and generous that he established a Sangeeta Sabha at his court and was maintaining a number of Vidwans. It is said that when once the Maharajah Tulajaji went in disguise along with his minister, in order to find out how things were being carried on in his kingdom, he found that a number of Vidwans were assembled at the court of Udayarpalayam and were having a musical party. He watched them for a long time and was so struck with wonder and shame, that on his return he sent for many famous Vidwans at the recommendation of the Zemindar to come to his court and from that time forward patronised the art and its savants. He has composed many Padams which end with the name of " Yuvaranga".

ஜோ

ஜோசேப்பு கவிட்டர்—Joseph of Neyoor in Trevandrum. Author of many Keertanams full of beautiful ides.

வ

வடிவேல் நட்டுவனர்—Vadivelu Nattuvanar. A learned Vidwan in Bharata Sangeeta Sahityam ; he was unrivalled in singing and in playing instruments like the Veena and the violin. It is traditionally said that when once at a musical party in the house of Tanjore Sama Naicker at Madras where he played the violin, the Veena player *Veenai* Kuppayar of Tiruvattiyoor who was lounging in a comfortable cushion, known as " Kathilodu" was so struck with his wonderful skill on the violin that he honored him by giving up the seat of honor to him and made a vow never to lounge in a Kathilodu again. He sang his Keertanams in the presence of Tyagaraja Iyer who was his contemporary and was very much esteemed by him. Vidwans were in the habit of singing their Keertanams before Tyagaraja Iyer in order to obtain his approval. But seldom would they receive even a nod of appreciation from him. But it is traditionally said that when the Nattuvanar sang a Telugu Padam in the presence of Iyer (named " Na Samiga Namida Daya Chooda Rada"). *நா ஸாமிக நாமித தயசூட ராத* in the Bhoorikalyani Ragam in a most melting manner, the Iyer was so much moved that he appreciated his singing by nodding as well as by clapping his hands. Again, he was appointed by Kulasekhara Maharajah of Travancore as his court Vidwan on a monthly salary of Rs. 105. Under his tutelage, the Maharajah has composed many Keertanams, Swarajatis and Varnams. He stayed at this court for 11 years and obtained a name which stands unrivalled and was presented also in 1834 with a violin and a box made of ivory with the stamp of the Maharajah. He seems to have received many other presents also.

வடிவேல் நட்டுவனார்—Vadivelu Nattuvanar of Tanjore. He has received many an honor in different Samasthanams and has been held in the highest esteem by distinguished vidwans. He received a new honor called "Naradar Tamboolam" during the Dusserah festivities by Bhaskara Setupathi Avergal at the court of Ramnad. He was clever in Bharata Sangeeta Sahityam and has taught the same to many.

வரதப்பா—Varadappa. Professional name Nartaka. A good teacher of Bharatam. His son was also clever in the art.

வரதாச்சாரியார்—Varadachariar. Brother of Narasimhachariar of Tenmatam. Both the brothers were clever Vidwans in Veena and the violin.

வரதாச்சாரியார்--Varadachariar K., B.A. A charming singer.

வராகப்பையர்—Varahappayyar. He was Asthana Bakshi and Samasthanam Vidwan under Maharajah Sarabhoji. A profound scholar and player of English as well as Karnatic instruments. He has obtained a medal from the Governor of Madras for his skill as a violinist. The Maharajah has given him a residence in Tanjore and a gift of Manyam lands at Pasupatikoil. Lakshmana Gosayi, Paramesvara Bhagavatar, and Vadivelu are his students. His decendants are skilful Veena Vidwans even now.

வராகம் ஐயர்—Varaham Iyer. A distinguished Vidwan in Veena playing. His son is *Veenai* Gopalaswami Iyer.

வா

வாஞ்சிய சாஸ்திரியார்—Vanchia Sastriar. A very charming singer.

வி

விசாக மகாராஜா—Visakha Maharajah. Maharajah of Travancore. A distinguished vidwan in Sangeeta Sahityam, singing and playing the Veena. He is the author of many compositions. He lived about 25 yearg ago.

விசுவநாத ஐயர்—Visvanatha Iyer. Son of Maha Vydyanatha Iyer. He could sing as well as his father.

விசுவநாத கவிராயர்— Visvanatha Kavirayar. A great Vidwan in music who flourished in the XIV century in the Vanga Desam. Author of "Sahitya Darpanam."

விசுவநாதராவ்—Visvanatha Row. He could play the violin and the Surabath with skill.

விஜயகோபால்—Vijayagopal. He has composed Sahitya keertanams which end with the name of Vijayagopal.

விஜயவராகப்பையர்—Vijaya Varahappayar. He was Veena Vidwan at the Tanjore Samasthanam. He is the grandson of Veena Chikka Odappayyar.

வீ

வீரபத்திர ஐயர்—Veerabhadra Iyer. He composed many imaginative Keertanams, Padams and Tillanahs in the Rasika and Desika ragas during the reign of Maharajah Pratapsingh (1740—1763). He tried his best to bring the South Indian Music to an organised system.

வீரபத்திரப் பிள்ளை—Veerabhadra Pillai of Tinnevelly. A good singer and a player on the Veena. He has composed many Keertanams.

வீரமாமுனிவர்—Veeramamunivar *alias* Beschi 1680. A European Roman priest. After his coming to India, he learnt the Tamil language and became a distinguished scholar. He is well known as the author of "Tembavani", "Vediarolukkam", "Sathuragaradi" and "Tonnool" and the works on medicine such as "Pancharatnam", "Navamanimalei," and "Nasalkandam." He is also composer of many keertanams distinguished for their language as well as their beautiful ideas and devotional character. He was placed in Samadhi in the village of Manapadu (Tinnevelly Dt.)

வீரசாமி—Veeraswami of Irupoor. A good violinist.

வீரசாமி—Veeraswami. House-name Attaikandi. He is the author of a few Ragamalikas, Tillanahs and Swarajatis. He is a successful teacher in music.

வீரசாமி சாஸ்திரி—Veeraswami Sastri of Nayudupettah. A good singer.

வீரசாமி நாயக்கர்—Veeraswami Naicker of Tanjore. A Tahsildar. He was clever in playing the Veena and in singing. He has composed many keertanams.

வீரசாமி நாயுடு—Veeraswami Naidu of Tanjore. He was Samasthana Vidwan at Ramnad. He was such a charming player on the Saranda that he was known as "*Saranda* Naicker".

வீரராகவாச்சாரியார்—Veeraraghavachariar of Bandanapalli. A good player on the Veena.

வீரராகவையர்—Veeraraghavayyar. He was Samasthana Vidwan at Tanjore. His charming voice got him the appellation of "*Challagali*".

வெ

வெங்கடகிருஷ்ண நாயுடு—Venkatakrishna Naidu. Generally known as "Modiram" Venkatakrishna Naidu. He could sing Hindustani Ragas beautifully and distinctly.

வெங்கடசுப்பையர்—Venkatasubbayar T. B.A., B.L., of Madras. A student of Tyagaraja Iyer of Tiruvattoor. He could play the Veena well and could perform Harikathas which will be noted for their devotional element.

வெங்கடசுப்பையர்—Venkatasubbayyar of Manombuchavadi. He was a relation of Thyagaraja Iyer of Tiruvadi and became a distinguished musician learning the art under him. He has composed many Keertanams in praise of Venkatasami. He was a good violinist also. Panchapakesa Iyer and Sivarama Iyer are his students.

வெங்கடசுப்பையர்—Venkatasubbayyar. He was Samasthana Vidwan under Maharajah Tulajaji. He is the author of many Varnams and Keertanams. It is said that he was able to sing 4,000 ragas. The Maharajah gave him 5 velis of wet land as Manyam at Tiruvadi.

வெங்கடசுப்பய்யர்—Venkatasubbayyar. House name "Sonthi". Student of Veena Kalahasti Iyer. He was Samasthana Vidwan in the court of Maharajah Tulajaji. He composed a Varnam in praise of the Maharajah in the Bilahari Ragam with special Kalpana. There are many compositions of his which were composed in the Sabha of Manali Chinnayya Mudaliar. Sonthi Venkataramanayya is his son.

வெங்கடபதி ராஜா—Venkatapati Rajah. Rajah of Karvetinagar. Clever in music and in playing the Veena. He played the Veena to entertain Emperor Edward VII when he visited India in 1875 as Prince of Wales.

வெங்கடாசலமய்யர்—Vencatachalam Iyer. Son of *Veenai* Audimoorti Iyer of Tanjore. A distinguished Vidwan in music and the Veena. He is also Veena Vidwan in the Tanjore palace like his ancestors.

வெங்கடேச சாஸ்திரி—Venkatesa Sastri. He belongs to Pallavur near Palghat. A good Mridangam player.

வெங்கடேச சாஸ்திரி—Venkatesa Sastri. A beautiful player of Veena and violin. Good at giving music lessons.

வெங்கடேச சாஸ்திரியார்—Venkatesa Shastriar. A distinguished vidwan in music and in playing the Veena. He wrote the treatise called "Sangeeta Swaya Bodhini" in 1892.

வெங்கட ஐயர்—Venkata Iyer of Coimbatore. A charming player of Mridangam.

வெங்கடசாமி ராஜு—Venkataswami Raj of Kalahasti. He plays the Veena well and is a good teacher of music.

வெங்கடரமண ஐயர்—Venkataramana Iyah of Kooratavasi. Disciple of Veena Kuppayyar of Tiruvattoor. A great scholar in Sangeeta Sahityam, and a good singer. He has composed many Varnams.

வெங்கடரமணய்யா—Sonthi Venkataramanayya. Son of Sonthi Venkatasubbayyar. He was Sangeeta Vidwan in the court of Maharajah Sarabhoji (1798-1824). He was as clever as his father in Sangeeta Sahityam and singing. He is the author of many Varnams and can sing Pallavis wonderfully well.

வெங்கடராம ஐயர்—Venkatarama Iyer of Karur. A Sangeeta Vidwan.

வெங்கடராம சாஸ்திரியார்—Venkatarama Sastriar. A native of Melatoor, near Tanjore. He was Sangeeta Vidwan under Maharajahs Sarabhoji and Sivaji (1798-1865). His compositions excel in combining a number of good Kysiki Padams with many Padams noted for their lighter vein.

வெங்கடராம பாகவதர்—Venkatarama Bhagavatar of Kumbakonam. He could perform Harikathas.

வெங்கடராம பாகவதர்—Venkatarama Bhagavatar. Noted for his music and skill in performing Harikathas.

வெங்கடராமய்யர்—Venkataramayyar. He was surnamed "*Irumbukadalai*" because his musical compositions were so difficult to be sung by others. He has composed a Keertanam in Todi, named "Satamani", in praise of Bodhendra Swami and a few Keertanams on Maruthanallur swami which all end with the name of Gopalakrishna. He seems to have lived during the closing years of Audappayyar.

வெங்கடராமையர்—Venkataramayyar. A native of Ammapet near Tanjore. A good violinist.

வெங்கடராமையர்—Venkataramayyar of Velipalayam. A Sangeeta Vidwan.

வெங்கடராமையர்—Venkataramayyar of Tinnevelly. A good musical instructor. His student Gopalayyar is a good violinist.

வெங்கடராமையர்—Venkataramayyar. Brother of Samba Iyer of Mysore. A proficient scholar in music. He and his sons Ramaswami Iyer and Lakshmana Iyer play the Veena well.

வெங்கடராமையர்—Venkataramayyar. A student of Singalachariar. A good singer.

வெங்கடராமையர்—Venkataramayyar of Varahoor. A charming singer.

வெங்கடராமையர்—Venkataramayyar. Surnamed "*Konugolu*". A good singer on the higher octaves.

வெங்கடராமையர்—Venkataramayyar of Vettanur. Student of Dikshatar. He plays the Veena well and his son Swetaranya Iyer is a good violinist.

வெங்கடராவ்—Venkatarow of Kumbakonam. Clever in singing and in playing the violin and the Mridangam.

வெங்கடராவ்—Venkatarow. A violinist. He is Sangeeta Vidwan at the court of Pittapuram. He is a wonderful player on the violin.

வெங்கட வைத்தியநாதர்—Venkata Vydyanathar. He and Muddu Venkatamakhi were Vidwans who belonged to the Venkatamakhi school.

வெங்கடேசுவர எட்டப்பராஜா—Venkatesvara Ettappa Rajah 1816-1839. Rajah of Ettyapuram. Much interested in music. He patronised and supported many musicians. He learnt music as well as the Veena. He has composed a Keertanam in Tamil in the Mukhari Ragam, named "Sivagurunadanei".

வெங்கசாமி ராவ்—Venkasami Row of Madras. Sheristadar in the Revenue Board office. He was clever in music, in singing and in playing the Veena.

வெங்கு—Venku of Chidambaram. He and his brother Swaminathan were skilful in playing the Mridangam and in Talam.

வெங்கு பாகவதர்—Venku Bhagavatar of Tinnevelly. A student of Vadivelu Nattuvanar. He knew a good number of old Keertanams. He was good in singing Raga Alapanas and Pallavi Swarams. He is the author of many Darus, Keertanams, Tanams and Varnams. He lived about 60 years ago. Brahmananda Paradesi is his son.

வெங்கு பிள்ளை—Venku Pillai of Tinnevelly. He was very clever in playing Ragas and Pallavi on the violin very neatly and with elaborative skill.

வெங்கோபராவ்—Venkoba Row. A student of Krishna Sundara Iyer of Umayalpuram. He was a distinguished vidwan in playing the violin, Jalatarangam and Mridangam and in vocal music. He belonged to Tanjore. His brother Rama Row was equally distinguished.

வே

வேங்கடகிரியப்பா—Venkatagiriappa of Hyderabad. Many Javalis have been composed by him.

வேங்கடசாமி—Poosala Venkataswami. A good player of Nagaswaram.

வேங்கடமகி—Venkatamakhi 1660. Son of Govinda Deekshatar. He learnt music, instrumental playing, singing and Lakshya Lakshanams from his brother Yegna Narayana Deekshatar and from Sangeeta Vidwan Tanappa Acharyar. He is the author of the musical work "Chaturdandiprakasika" which treats in an extensive manner about Veena, Sruti, Swaram, Melam, Ragam, Tayam, Geetam, Prabandham and Talam. He has also composed 24 Ashtapadis on Tyagarajayya of Tiruvarur.

வேங்கடரமணதாஸ்—Venkataramanadoss. He is now Veena Vidwan at the court of Vijayanagaram. Grandson of *Veena* Gururayachar. A distinguished vidwan in Sangeeta Sahityam and in singing ragam and pallavi. He has so mastered the Veena by his tremendous practice that he could play even the most intricate music with the greatest ease and rapidity.

வேணு—Venu. Son of Muttuswami Nattuvar of Madras. He is a well known musician who learnt the art under his father and under *Veena* Tyagayyar of Tiruvattiyur, and is very proficient on the Veena. Subbukutti Iyer of Mylapore and Parthasaradhi Iyer are his students.

வேணுகோபாலதாஸ் நாயுடு—Venugopala Doss Naidu. Surnamed "Veera Soora Veerakanthamani." He is a vidwan who obtained the Kantamani for coming out successfully in a musical trial at Sivaganga.

வேணுகோபாலன்—Venugopalan of Negapatam. A very good player of Nagaswaram.

வேதநாயகசாஸ்திரியார்—Vedanayaga Shastriar. 1774-1864. A distinguished vidwan in Tamil and musical composition. He was Sangeeta vidwan in the court of Sarabhoji maharajah when Bava Pandithar was prime minister. He wrote the history of the Bhonsle Royal family in the shape of poems and received special honors. He is the author of 120 works, great and small, such as "Gnanapada Keertanams," "Bethlehem Kuravanji," "Gnanakummi," "Paraparakanni," "Aranathintham," "Gnanavulah," "Jepamalai" and "Perinbakadal". His descendants still live in the house built for him by the Rajah and are singers. Gnanadeepammal, Gnanasikhamani Shastriar, Noah Gnanadhickyam Shastriar and Elias Devasikhamani Shastriar are his descendants who were gifted in Tamil and musical composition.

வேதநாயகம் பிள்ளை—Vedanayagam Pillai of Mayavaram. A munsif. Student of Meenakshi Sundaram Pillai. A celebrated vidwan in Tamil and Sangeeta Sahityam and a good player on the Veena. More than a thousand of his Keertanams have been printed and are in use. His wife and children were also proficient in Veena and singing. He is also the author of other works treating on justice and morality.

வேதபுரிகுப்புசாமி தீக்ஷிதர்—Vedapuri Kuppuswami Deekshatar of Kumbakonam. Proficient in playing all kinds of instruments.

வேதர்—Veda. Author of " Sangeeta Makaranda ".

வேதாந்த பாகவதர்—Vedanta Bhagavatar of Kalladakuritchi. Son of Muttu Sastriar. Clever in vocal music.

வை

வைகுண்டசாஸ்திரி—Vaikunta Shastri. He is the author of many Keertanams in Sanskrit, especially in the Desika Ragas. which are well known for their charm and beautiful ideas. They end with the name of " Vaikunta ".

வைத்தி—Vyddi known as Manatattu Vydyanatha Iyer. He could sing Karnatic music purely without any admixture. His brother Ramaswami Iyer and his son Dorasami Iyer are charming singers.

வைத்யநாத ஐயர்—Vydyanatha Iyer of Mayavaram. A distinguished player on the Veena. He possesses good laya gnanam. He is a great vidwan in singing Pallavi. His son Sabhesa Iyer could play the Veena very well.

வைத்யநாத ஐயர்—Vydyanatha Iyer of Kaverirajapuram. A clever singer.

வைத்யநாத ஐயர்—Vydyanatha Iyer of Arantangi. A good whistler and a good singer.

வைத்யநாத பாகவதர்—Vydyanatha Bhagavatar of Soolamangalam. He could perform Harikathas bringing out specially the devotional element.

வைத்யநாத பாகவதர்—Vydyanatha Bhagavatar of Nemali. Rajamannarkoil. He could perform Harikathas.

வைத்யநாதபாகவதர்—Vydyanatha Bhagavatar of Melatur. He could perform Harikathas beautifully.

வைத்யநாதையர் மகா—*Maha* Vydyanatha Iyer. Son of Duraiswami Iyer of Vyacheri, a village near Tanjore. Even when very young he learnt the art under his father, and pratised it so well that he could sing with the greatest charm in public Katcheris. He was a man of principles. He was a distinguished and profound scholar in Sangeeta Sahityam and singing. He could sing Keertanams magnificently well with a due discrimination of Ghana, Naya and Desika Ragas. He has been honored in good many Samasthanams. He was Sangeeta Vidwan in the court of Sakaram Saheb. He sang the Ragamalika on the 72 Melakartas in the Sangeeta Mahal at Tanjore in the presence of Sakaram Sahib and received special honors in appreciation thereof. He received the title of " Maha Vydyanatha Iyer " in his 12th year when he was singing in the midst of many Vidwans assembled at the Mutt of Tiruvaduturai near Kallidakuritchi. His students are *Fiddle* Swaminatha Iyer of Palamaneri, Saminatha Iyer of Umayalpuram, Sabhesa Iyer of Madras, and *Veena* Vydyanada Iyer.

வையாபுரி முத்து—Vyapuri Muttu of Tirupapuliyur. A good player of Mridangam.

For Additional Names See Appendix.

6. Some points to be noted in the above list.

We have not had complete information about the history of the Vidwans mentioned in the above list and their musical talents. Moreover, as the particulars about many of the Vidwans were obtained after a long delay, we were not able to mention them here. There is also some doubt about the musical works of these vidwans. However, we must say that great men like Purandara Vithal Das, Kshetragnar, Tyagaraja Iyer and Arunachala Kavigal whose names are found in the list are among those who made many compositions in Karnatic music and helped to preserve the Karnatic ragas from being altogether forgotten. The element of devotion which their works reflect and the Sancharam of those Ragas which are specially suited to such devotion are something marvellous. They are held in the highest esteem like the nectar of gods which never satiates. After them many Vidwans have composed Padams, Keertanams, Varnams, Ragamalikas and Chittaswarams quite commensurate with the dignity of Karnatic music which are in use at the present day. Among these, the following prominent Vidwans have been regarded as worthy of the highest esteem :—Purandara vital Dos, Kshetragnar, Tyagaraja Iyer, Arunachala Kavigal, Venkatamakhi, Gururayacharlu, *Veena* Kuppayyar, Sadasiva Rayar, *Veena* Venkataramana Doss, Singalachariar, Mahadeva Annavi, Vadivelu Annavi, Subramania Iyer, Syamasastrial, Muttuswami Deekshatar, Venkatasubbayyar, Subbarama Iyer, Talapakkam Chinnaya, Venkatasubbayyar of Manombuchavadi, *Maha* Vydyanatha Iyer, Kaduva Bhagavatar and Somu Iyer of Talaignayar. Being gifted with the powers of original musical composition, they have composed many works in Tamil, Sanskrit and Telugu and have sung them also with the greatest charm. The following eminent vidwans have been singing them and are singing them so as to bring out their chief rasams so that their singing itself might be considered celestial :—Maha Vydyanatha Iyer, Subbarayar of Pitchandarkoil, Raghavayyar, Madras Subramania Iyer, Singaram *alias* Venu, Chinna Vyddi, Peria Vyddi, Sarabha Shastrial, Madras Sabhesa Iyer, Seenu Iyengar of Ramnad, Paramesvara Bhagavatar, Packiri of Mannargudi, Ponnusami of Madura, Gururayacharlu of Vizianagaram, Soorya Narayana Somayaji, Venkataramana Doss, Samannah of Mysore, Subbannah of Mysore, Seshannah of Mysore, *Challagali* Krishna Iyer, Veena Perumalayyar, Veena Subbukutti Iyer, Veena Kalyanakrishna Iyer, Fiddle Thirukodikaval Krishnayyar, Palamaneri Swaminatha Iyer, Bidaram Krishnappa, Tirupayanam Panchapakesa Sastrial, Anantarama Bhagavatar, Konerirajapuram Vydyanatha Iyer, Tiruvadi Subramania Iyer, Mayavaram Veena Vydyanatha Iyer, Mridangam Narayanasami Appah, Mridangam Alaganambi, Mridangam Dakshinamoorti, Mridangam Krishnayyar, Flute Sanjeevi Row, Fiddle Panchapakesa Bhagavatar, Kotevadyam Muttya Bhagavatar, Fiddle Masilamoni Pillai, Fiddle Govindasami Pillai and others. Besides these, the following distinguished musicians have composed many Keertanams and printed and published them so that the Tamilians might use them for years :—Thevur Anantabharati, Gopalakrishna Bharati, Arunachala Kavigal, Kavikunjaram Iyer, Ramasami Iyer, Muttu Ramalinga S.tupati, Vedanayaga Shastriar, Vedanayagam Pillai and others. Their musical genius, the beautiful ideas in their compositions and the beautiful language in which they are clothed have taken the hearts of the Tamilians by storm and they are used by them with great reverence even now. But it is a matter for regret that many other Keertanams are in use at the present time the ideas of which are not clear even to the singers or the hearers, to the exclusion of the old Keertanams full of pregnant ideas which appeal most tellingly to the hearts of the people. If the singing of the devotional Keertanams like those of Tyagaraja Iyer were preceded by an explanation of the meanings thereof they could be better appreciated. Mere sounds without the ideas are entirely fruitless, and they serve but to kill time. We desire very much that the Tamilians of South India should hear more than they now do the singing of Tamil Keertanams and devotional compositions like Thevaram, Thiruvachagam, Thiruvoimoli, and Thayumanavar Padal so that they might easily understand the ideas in them and be benefited. All Keertanams in alien languages should first be interpreted before being sung. One who understands the meaning of a song in praise of God and appreciates it derives more benefit than one who hears it merely in a foreign tongue. Just as a hart gives up its life when it hears the sweet sound of bells, the life of men who strive after sweet sounds only ends fatal. A geetam which possesses no good ideas is lifeless and devoid of any use. When a man who delights in singing the excellence of the deity expresses it by means of songs, his heart is entranced and gets concentrated in the deity and he obtains the high privilege of seeing him face to face. Those who hear such devotional songs obtain the same privilege. But those who hear the mere sweet sounds do not derive any benefit but forget the sounds soon. Man whose nature is wicked certainly requires devotional music which has the tendency of eradicating his evil nature. One to whom Iyal Tamil does not appeal will at least be affected by Isai Tamil or music. Great sages have declared that a Brahmin who sings mere sounds without any meaning in them should not be allowed to remain in the company of Brahmins while having their dinner. We are sure that if Vidwans are requested to give a short interpretation of the Keertanams they intend to sing they will only be too glad to understand them themselves and give the meaning to others.

7. The Maharajahs and Nobles who patronised Karnatic music on a large scale.

It will not be out of place here to make honourable mention of those Maharajahs and nobles who maintained and patronised Sangeeta Vidwans by giving residences to them, gifts of lands and endowments and also encouraged them from time to time by giving them clothes, jewels and other presents and helped the continued progress of music :—

Tanjore Samasthanom—Maharajahs Tulajaji and Pratap Singh.
Malayalam—Maharajahs Kulasekhara Perumal and Ayilya.
Ramnad—Muttu Ramalinga Setupati Avergal.
Venkatagiri—Maharajah Rajagopalakrishna.
Visianagaram—Maharajah Pasupati Ananda Gajapati.
Pittapuram—Rajah Venkata Kumara Soorya Row Bahadur.
Pudukotah—Maharajah Ramachandra.
Mysore—Maharajahs Krishna Raja Oodayar and Chama Raja Oodayar.

Karvetnagar—Rajah Venkatapathi.

Ettiyapuram—Maharajahs Jagadeesvara Ettappa and Jagadeesvara Rama Kumara Ettappa.

Arni—Jageerdar Thirumalai Row.

Ariyalur—Jageerdar Uvaranga Bhoopati.

Tiruvaduthurai—Mathadhipatis Ambalavana Desikar, Subramania Desikar and Ambalavana Desikar.

Manali—Muttukrishna Mudaliar alias Chinnaya Mudaliar and Venkatakrishna Mudaliar.

The above mentioned have not only patronised musicians by giving them everything they required but were themselves capable of correcting the mistakes of these vidwans and to sing and make original compositions themselves and leave them in use for the future generations with their stamp of authority. Although Indian music cannot boast apparently of so many eminent patrons who have left an everlasting name in the field of music yet we have at the present day the Maharajahs of Mysore. Travancore, Cochin, Pudukotah. Vizianagaram, Pithapuram, Ramnad, Ettiyapuram and other provinces who are keen patrons of musicians.

8. The Many whose names are left out in the list of traditional musicians.

Besides the musicians whose names occur in the above list, there are legions of musicians who have been distinguished for their Sangeeta Sahityam and for their efficiency in the three important elements of music, viz., Bhava, Raga and Talam who are found among the class of Ochars, Annavis, Players of Nagaswaram, Davul, Mridangam, Veena and Mukhaveena, Gandharvas, Devadasis and Dancing girls. We know that these who had attained special efficiency in the three chief elements of music, Bhava, Raga and Talam had learnt the art from the very beginning and had made it their means of livelihood. Among these, the Gandharvis (female singers) were and are excellent singers. Of these we find that there were many excellent players on the Veena at a very early period as we see from the case of Madhavi who lived 2,000 years ago during the reign of Karikal Cholan and from the Veena music of Gandharvadattayar. Such musicians are found at present also. As we have been unable to obtain their names and other particulars regarding them in time we have not mentioned them here. That they were the original storehouse from which all music was disseminated later on is a well established fact. It is a world-known truth that Brahmins and others learnt the art of playing the Mridangam about 30 years later on and appeared before the public. But the time when music was learnt because it was a means of livelihood is very modern, viz., within the last 1,000 years. For even in the Puranas and Kathas which we consider ancient we find Gandharvas, Yakshas, Kinnarer, Kimpurushar, Nagar and persons like Tumburu, Naradar, Rambha, Tillottama, Oorvasi and Menaka who appeared before the durbar of Rajahs and performed their music before them in public. It is said that in the same period the Brahmins prepared the Homam, chanted the Vedas, blessed others, obtained Tapam and were fed. But it is nowhere said that a Brahmin sang or danced at the time or played the Nagaswaram or the Veena. Further as the Upanishads declare that those who perform dancing, singing and gesticulating should be excluded from dining with the Brahmins it is clearly seen that the Brahmins had nothing to do with those arts. Yet they are included in the category of those who pronounced the name of the deity and extolled him before others.

The above mentioned Sangeeta Vidwans sang only the Karnatic music though they did not have any decided opinion on the Srutis that were in use there.

9. Some points as regards the 72 Melakartas.

The twelve Swarams of the Karnatic music and the Ragas that are formed by the various combinations of them have been held from ancient times as the Mother-Ragas by the Tamilians as well as others who made the Tamil Country their abode and such has been the use even at the modern time. Some of these without troubling themselves to understand what the Srutis are, quote a few Sootrams to contend that the 22 Srutis mentioned by the author of Sangeeta Ratnakaram are the one in use in the music of South India. Distinguished musicians like Kshetragnar and Tyagaraja Iyer have not definitely stated which Srutis are used in particular ragas. But musicians like Venkatamakhi and Maha Vydyanatha Iyer have composed Geetams and Ragamalikas in the 72 Melakartas. Chinnasami Mudaliar, M.A., has stated that Venkatamakhi says in his "Chaturdandiprakasika" that he is the originator of these 72 Melams and that it is impossible to prove the existence of either more or less than the number. Mr. Mudaliar says as follows :—

Ottaramelam 36.

(*a*) The division of Ragas mentioned in the chapter on Raga Vivekam in the "Sangeeta Ratnakaram" of Sarngadevar is not in use.

(*b*) The number of melams in use mentioned in "Swara Mela Kalanidhi" of Ramamatya is evidently not correct as there were only 19 in use at the time.

(*c*) Venkatamakhi, in his "Chaturdandiprakasika" has distinctly held that if the Melaprastaram were made in regular order without changing the beginning and ending Swarams in Poorvangam and Oottarangam and without omitting any of the Vikriti Swarams, there could only result 72 Melams, 36 with the Suddha Madhyamam and 36 with the Prati Madhyamam.

2. If anybody objects and says that there are only a few of them in use, while the others are useless and are put down just for the sake of adding importance, Venkatamakhi has the following answer ready :-

(*a*) There are diversities in men.

(*b*) There are diversities in countries.

(*c*) Many Desika ragas which have been taught in the past are being taught in the present and will be taught in the future by singers and musicians who have mastered different kinds of systems, have crept in, which have either become familiar to us by constant use or are found only in treatises, in course of time these have also melams common to many of the ragas.

(*d*) The existence of some important Desika ragas such as Pantu Varali and Kalyani and the Melas common to them.

(*e*) These 72 Melakartas have been made by us to comprehend all these ragas. So any opinion that some of these are useless cannot stand.

(*f*) To say that an important Vrittam is useless which is found in the midst of an ocean of Vrittams proved to be absolutely true by "Vrittaratnakaram"; and which is obtained by virtue of the extensive process of Prastaram, will never hold.

(*g*) To say that a Talam is absolutely useless which is arrived at by the tedious process of Talaprastaram, and which is found among a vast collection of such Talams will, not hold either.

(*h*) No one will dare to add or take away a Melam from the 72 Melams which have been very carefully derived from the well known 12 Swarams. If any one does so, all my efforts have been in vain. Even Sivan who has an eye in the forehead will find it impossible to do so. So just as the letters known as "Matrukaighal" are fixed at 51, the 72 Melams are fixed. There could be neither more nor less. Thus I have established the theory of 72 Melams, &c., &c."

Although these 72 Melakartas and the Ragas derived from them refer to Karnatic music, they have been arrived at so as to create some doubt in the process of formation. The Geetams and Sahityas of Purandhara Vithal Das who lived in 1500 A.D. before Venkatamakhi are in use even now. In the treatise known as "Vyasaghatakam" which is even prior to the time of Purandhara Vithal Das we see the Ragas Kanakangi, Ratnangi, and Ganamoorti with the marks of Graha, Nyasa and Amsa Swarams. It seems that Purandhara Vithal Das lived before Venkatamakhi and that the treatise "Vysaghatakam" was anterior to his time. The fact that the names "Kanakangi", "Ratnangi" and "Ganamoorti" which occur in the 72 Melakartas have been mutilated into "Kanakambari", "Penadyuti" and "Ganassamavarali" warrants us to say that a new treatise has been written with the help of the old, thus expunging the prior one completely. Compare the fact how treatises in alien tongues, which only copied the ideas in the old Tamil works, have been written so as to hide completely the original.

10. The New garb in which the old 103 modes (பண்கள்) appear.

There are those who would not accept the theory of the 72 Melakartas but would persistently declare that there are only 19 Ragas in accordance with the views of the author of Sangeeta Ratnakaram and Ramamatya. We might wonder how the 103 modes which were in use 2,000 years ago went out of use. But the truth is they have not disappeared. The old ragas are still in use at present. But only their names are found changed in alien languages and different Sahityams are found in them but the old Varna Mettus still remain. But in course of time when the ragas, the swarams and the Srutis became open to doubt, different theories were put forward, many mixtures resulted and the original ragas were marred. No one cared to find out the errors nor to ascertain the Srutis which occurred in the ragas in use. So there is no chance of learning any of these by means of books but one has to serve 10 or 12 years before one is able to master them. As we were making researches into Swarams, Srutis and Ragas, we found it expedient to organise a Sabha of Vidwans so that they may be systematised, and the result was the establishment of the Tanjore Sangeeta Vidya Mahajana Sangam.

VII. THE TANJORE SANGEETA VIDYA MAHAJANA SANGAM.

1. Why the Sangam was started.

WE tried for a long time to have a knowledge of music, which is held superior even to nectar, and to find out its secrets. Many essays on music appeared from time to time in the journals for the past few years, which were more or less of a conflicting character. But in the midst of them we found many doubts as regards Srutis and Ragas, a few doubts which resulted from the confusion of the Dwavimsati Srutis with the Srutis of the Karnatic music. Knowing that there was no reason why such doubts should arise and being assured that there must be many distinguished Vidwans in South India who would be able to clear those doubts, and whose words would be of much benefit to the public, we sent the following article to "Sentamil" the organ of the Madura Tamil Sangam, to "Swadesa Mitran" and to the "Hindu"

INDIAN MUSIC.

"O thou journal which is illustrious and famous as fine gold! we were very much pleased and encouraged to see an article in your columns with the heading "Indian Music", specially as we have been making researches into the secrets of Indian Music for the past 10 years. We write the following article to be published in your valuable journal as we find that under the patronage of many distinguished Vidwans and Maharajahs you publish many new and interesting articles day by day.

INDIAN MUSIC.

"Sir,

I was highly delighted to read in the brilliant columns of your paper the article under the title of "Indian music".

For the last ten years I have been an earnest student of that subject, and my enquiries in respect of it have been chiefly directed towards finding out the secret scientific principle which underlies and pervades Indian Music. I venture to send you these lines, as your organ is patronized by many excellent men of culture, and the columns thereof are everyday luminous in the discussion of many a new and valuable topic.

Every body knows that in creation, man. bird, beast and reptile, each is endowed with a strong love of music and an inherent sound sufficient for the expression of pain or pleasure on the part of the individual.

From the level of herbs onwards, throughout the whole range of the Vegetable Kingdom endowed with a single sense, the influence of music could be traced. The Mango, the Jack, the Date, the Tamarind, the Gooseberry, the Margosa, the Champaca, and other trees that flower with the advent of the south wind, Mallika, Kundumallika, and other plants and hill trees that blossom by the sway of the west wind, the Naval, the Tazhai and others of same species, the Parijata, the Pichy, Mullai, Samanti, the Rose, the Lotus, and other plants, Sampangi, Jimiki and other trees, the many species of herbs—all these put forth their blossom in response to the placid vibration that pervades the wind. If that be so, it goes without saying, that human beings endowed with a six sense also are moved by concord of sounds. When we reflect that God in the shape of a still small voice (1 Kings 19-13) spoke to a devotee, we may realise that He alone exists as Universal Harmony, flooding and penetrating the heavens and the Universe and all things animate as well as inanimate, in varying degrees of vibration. From infancy to old age, it is melody that makes life sweet and cheerful. From the finite harmony on the material plane, the consciousness is uplifted and becomes fit for the perception of spiritual joy which opens the door to Divine ecstacy which is the mould or channel through which harmony flows. The universe is the expression of the Divine Sound Aum, and the Divine Life that pervades it and constitutes its origin is Vibration which is fundamentally Sound-Word which was God (John I—1). If this is Divine, what better analogy could be given for the potentiality of melody ? He, the embodiment of vibration, is the Life of all existence, the energy of the Life, the emotion of the energy, the perception, the sound and expression of the joy.

The saints introduced the seven essential tones of scale out of the Divine sound, that is, out of the tonal relationship of God to matter, made Srutis of all its modulations, its rhythmical flexibilities and ramifications; praising Him who is the limit of all vibrations and the embodiment of all harmony, they (the saints) wedded themselves with the spirit of Eternal Good. And people who could not perceive the real value of music, employed it to serve their ends on the material plane which appeared to them all in all.

Music is thus valuable on the material plane as well as on the spiritual. There is a natural tendency on the part of people to learn it, to practise it, to teach it to others and enjoy it while alone and in the company of others as well ; and even students who are unable to carry on their practice to the full measure of their desire, always cherish to be lifted into at-one-ment with the highest altitudes of music. Of such I am one. I request that accomplished musicians who read this will clear my doubts and thus pave the way for the growth and better understanding of Indian music.

1. What is the origin of the 'Sapta Swaras'. What was the order of their development ? Is there at present any rule which would enable any one to sound the various 'Swarams' in order ?

2. Is it true there are 22 Srutis in the Octave ? If so, what are they ? What are the views of the celebrated Sarnga Devar and Matanga Rishi on the subject ? Are the different names used by them for the Srutis such as 'Teevra', 'Kumudvati,' 'Manda', 'Chandovati' etc., and the names for the 'Jatis' such as 'Deepta', 'Ayata', 'Mridu', 'Madhya' and 'Karuna' still in use ? According to the two authors mentioned above, there are the 4 'Sas', 4 'Mas', 4 'Pas', 3 'Ris', 3 'Dhas', 2 'Gas' and 2 'Nis' in the Octave. Could any one state the names and their places in the Octave ? Are such 'Swarams' in practical use ?

3. Are there only 1,008 varieties of 'Ragams' which could be derived by the permutation and combination of all the 'Swarams' except the permanent 'Shatjamam' and 'Panchamam' ? Or, is there room for the birth of more Ragas ?

4. Are there any fixed principles satisfying all the Sruti rules allowing for 'Vakram' and 'Varjyam', by which one could easily understand the 'Sancharam' (ramification) of any Ragam and detect mistakes in them while being sung?

5. Some say that the 'Sancharam' of a ragam is determined by its 'Geetam'. Are there any who have a knowledge of those 'Geetams' and can they prepare a 'Geetam' for the Ragam specified below in any time they choose and give the rules which guided them in such a composition?

Sa, Ga4, Ma2, Dha6, Pa, Dha6, Ni6, Sa; Sa, Ni6, Pa, Ma2, Ri4, Sa. The name of the Ragam is Navanita Panchamam; Sub-Ragam of Varuna Priya; 24th Tayi-Ragam (mother tone).

6. The KIRTANAMS of many renowned musicians such as Mudduswami Dikshatar of Tiruvalur, Syamasastrial of Tanjore, Subramania Iyer of Trivady, Sadasiva Rao of Mysore, and Tyagaraja Iyer of Trivady are held in the highest estimation in South India. What was the basis of these KIRTANAMS? Have they handed down to any one the mysteries of their science? It is traditionally known that the sage Narada furnished Tyagaraja Iyer with a Chuvadi (book) containing rules which enabled him to compose a fresh KIRTANAM every day for the worship of the Deity. This tradition, coupled with the peculiar excellence of his Kirtanas, makes me bold to think that such a work exists. If so, who has it now?

7. Does the primary Melakarta which is the basis of all possible Ragams exist anywhere at the present day?

8. From the Eighth Tayi Ragam, Hanumat-todi, which has SUDDHA RE and SADHARANA GA in the Scale, is it scientifically correct to derive the following as JANYA-RAGAM?

TODI with the 2nd Sruti RE and 3rd Sruti GA etc., BHOOPALAM with the third Sruti RE, and the 5th Sruti GA etc., ASAVERI with the first Sruti RE and the third Sruti GA etc? Perhaps, for the sake of effect, they used the 3rd Sruti instead of the 2nd and the 5th instead of the 4th Sruti in the BHOOPALA Ragam, and they constructed the ASAVERI by substituting the 1st in the place of the 2nd and the third in the place of the 4th. What is the reason for this violation of principles? If two different kinds of Srutis (one of them decidedly unscientific) are used in many Ragams, will it not confound those who strive to learn the science of music? My humble opinion is there must exist somewhere a definite set of rules by learned musicians which will certainly not lead any one astray. I suggest this for the main reason that if such rules exist, it will be a decided boon that will open a royal road to the study of scientific Indian music.

9. At the present day there is no unanimity of opinion as regards the interval between the 12 semitones of the octave. Some hold that with the exception of the never varying SA and PA, the other notes are arranged on the principle of Equal Temperament. Along with this, there is the idea that Indian music cannot be literally played on the Piano or the Harmonium. My firm belief is that all possible Ragams that could be brought under the 72 Melakartas which have the 12 Semitones as their basis can correctly be played on these instruments. But it will be impossible to play

those Ragams which are derived from the 22 Srutis which are made up of quarter tones. The insufficiency of the harmonium, for Indian music, is partly derived from the inability to discriminate between the Ragams that could be played on it and the Ragams that could not be played. To give an instance, it is possible to play the DHEERA SANKARABHARANA Ragam which has in its scale the 4th Sruti RE and DHA etc., but not the brilliant and effective SANKARABHARANAM which has the 5th Sruti RE and DHA etc. If these two notes. the 5th Sruti RE and DHA are given up, the brilliant Ragam will have lost its life, though it might resemble the Ragam in other respects.

N. B. Though my view as regards the 22 Srutis and the quarter tones is slightly different from the ordinary view. I make this statement assuming the truth of the latter.

If my readers could give any other opinion and point out the difference between the Swarams on a Veena and the half-Swarams on a Harmonium, I shall be thankful.

10. It is popularly said that many of the musicians of old were able to spin out a Ragam for 10 or 20 nights without repetition, whereas, it is very rare to find a modern musician who could sing a Ragam for two hours. It makes one conclude that the former had learnt by heart many PRASTARAS which helped them in spinning out a Ragam. If so, how many kinds of PRASTARAS are there ? Where can one obtain them now ?

Many learned men who take a special interest in the science of Indian Music when they make enquiries about Swarams other than the Semitones. invariably get the following answer. "The quarter Swarams are Gamakams of which there are 10 varieties. These are a sealed book and have been handed down to us by our Gurus; they cannot be written down, but can be acquired only by intelligent study for years."

In this age of the benign British rule, Englishmen unfold without reserve their valuable discoveries in the field of science and their invention in machinery and instruments; and as standing evidence of their power of original research and, what is more, far-reaching sympathy with mankind, they immortalize every bit of scientific discovery in books and establish institutions for the benefit of students who are in quest of knowledge. If Indians will only publish, for the benefit of all, their achievements in the art of music, its secret principles, fundamental laws and regulations, the reputation of Indian music will advance beyond their wildest reckoning. It is with this object that I have ventured to set forth my doubts on the subject, and I beg the favor of accomplished musicians to be pleased to clear them."

No reply of any kind has been yet received in answer to the above article.

2. The Essay that was sent to Europe about Indian Music.

A few days after, the following article was sent to the "Royal Society of Arts," John Street, Adelphi, London, to "The Music News" 3, Wine Office Court, Fleet Street, London, to the "Musical Standard" 83, Charing Cross Road, London and to the "Musical Times", 160, Wardour Street, London, for the benefit of those English musicians interested in Indian Music.

INDIAN MUSIC.

"Indian Music has been, for some time, an attractive and interesting study to Englishmen. Some of them have also been touring in this country in order to make their own researches and obtain first-hand information in the field of Indian Music. One of these tourists, Mr. A. H. Fox Strangways, was recently in our midst here at Tanjore, holding interviews with the eminent musicians of the place with a view to know the inherent quality and worth of Indian Music. Writing on this subject in the "Madras Mail," a few months ago, he observed that Indian musicians who are disposed to wrap up their musical practice in mystery and who deliberately withhold the knowledge which their pupils had paid for. have no need of an acoustic theory. He regretted that not even one in a hundred cared to inquire into the theory of the SRUTI. He further said that there was room for good work in recording the excellent Indian songs, but that no Indian would think of it; that the work, however, would be published in Germany and sold in America.

With regard to these remarks of his, I wish to say a few words. Students of Indian Music who wish to have a knowledge of the Srutis ransack all their books in vain to find out (a) the principle which underlies and pervades them all, (b) the method of constructing melodies out of the Srutis, and, (c) the MELAKARTHA which contains all the melodies. No problem relating to Indian Music could be solved without a definite knowledge of these three things. Professors of Indian Music have devoted a whole life-time to a single RAGAM and have composed GEETAMS. VARNAMS, KIRTANAMS and PALLAVIS out of it, leaving the fundamental theory thereof to remain an enigma. Only the old Ragams are sung at the present day and nobody thinks of attempting the various new Ragams, although they are furnished with the basis-scales of all the Ragams. New discoveries and unusual phenomena relating to earth and sky are coming to light every day, but, in the realms of Indian Music, time honoured methods prevail. and so the music remains where it was. While allowing that there are a few things that are, of course, excellent in what is ancient, my humble opinion is, that in respect of Indian Music, time-honoured methods have been the *bete noir* of progress.

Before proceeding to explain what I have to say regarding SRUTI, RAGASPHUTAM and KARTHA, I wish to say a few words as to the MOTHER-RAGAM in Indian Music and the JANYAMS or melodies that are born of them.

1. In the Piano or the Harmonium, the scale played from the middle C to its octave and back is the basis scale for the 29th Mother-Ragam in Indian Music, known as Dheerasankarabharanam. In English notation the scale and Ragachurukkam (a simple specimen of the Ragam) of this will be as I on page 216 A.

2. With D as keynote, if 8 successive white notes be sounded, we get the basis-scale for the 22nd Mother-Ragam known as Karaharapriya. The scale and Ragachurukkam is as 2 on page 216 A.

3. With E as the keynote, if 8 successive white notes be played we get the basis-scale for the 8th Mother-Ragam known as Hanumattodi. The scale and Ragachurukkam is as 3 on page 216 A.

4. With F as the keynote if 8 successive white notes be played we obtain Meshakalyani, the 65th Mother-Ragam. The scale and Ragachurukkam will be as 4 on page 216 A.

5. With G as the keynote, if 8 successive white notes be played we obtain Harikambhodi the 28th Mother-Ragam, The basis-scale and Ragachurukkam will be as 5 on page 216 B.

6. With A as the keynote, if 8 successive white notes be sounded we get the 20th Mother-Ragam or Natabhairavi. The basis-scale and Ragachurukkam will be as 6 on page 216 B.

7. With B as keynote if 8 successive white notes be sounded, we get a Ragam named Sudda Todi without G. This is regarded as a Janyam from Hanumat-todi, the 8th Mother-Ragam. The basis-scale and Ragachurukkam will be as 7 on page 216 B.

N.B.—In all Indian Music, each Ragam commences with C which is the first note of the basis-scale: therefore when we speak of scale commencing with G we really mean it commences with C, but the intervals are arranged as if the scale were played on the white notes only, from G to G. For example, if the Harikambhoji scale be G A B C D E F G, the semi tones fall between 3 and 4, and 6 and 7. So the real Harikambhoji scale will be C D E F G A B flat and C. The 12 white and black notes of an octave in the Harmonium and the 12 notes of the octave on the Indian Veena are just the same. Only the intervals between these 12 Swaras, say, tones less than a semitone, cannot be sounded on the Harmonium. So, at the outset, it is easy to understand what are popularly known as the 72 Mother-Ragams, derived from these twelve notes and their tonal relationship. The peculiar excellence of Indian Music consists in singing according to given Sruti the thousands of melodies derived from the 72 Melams or Mother-Ragams based on the 12 notes of the octave, without allowing any admixture of other notes, and strictly according to given laws. But this unique system of singing is undergoing a gradual change in the hands of Indian musicians from time to time, either by the Sruti of a melody getting a little changed or by the admixture of strange sounds or by the absence of a definite system of laws to which all the various melodies may conform. As a result of this, some melodies, Keertanams and Varnams have become individualised and handed down to posterity, nay, they have become family treasures. In course of time, some characteristic errors have also crept in. Some Ragams have become invested with certain errors which embarrass even the best Indian musician. These errors are now justified either on the score of antiquity or heredity, or considered too sacred to be rectified as they originated from Rishis or sages of old. Recently, an Indian musician who noticed a Sruti difference in the Anandabhairavi, derived from the Natabhairavi, (the 20th Mother-Ragam) was afraid that he had to regard it as generating from 8 different Mother-Ragams. Another musician held that the very error had its beauty. And others said that when it was sung rightly, according to the Sruti pertaining to the Mother-Ragam, the result was simply charming. As there is such a variety of opinion among musicians

No. 1. Sankarabaranam Scale and its simple ramifications.

No. 2. Karaharapiria Ragachurukam Scale and its simple ramifications.

No. 3. Hanumathodi Ragachurukam Scale and its simple ramifications.

No. 4. Meshakalyani Scale and its simple ramifications.

No. 5. Harikambothi Scale and its simple ramifications.

No. 6. Natabairavi Ragachurukam Scale and its simple ramifications.

No. 7. Hanumathodi Ragachurukam Scale and its simple ramifications.

of repute, they do not care to rectify themselves but go on singing it as they have received it from their predecessors and do not care to inquire into the fundamental theory of Music. It has scarcely occurred to them that there must be in existence one theory and one law of constructing melody for all people from the Himalayas to Cape Comorin and from the Indus to the Bay of Bengal. If there be one such law acceptable to all, Indian Music is sure to reach a position of eminence.

Though at the outset it may appear an Herculean task, yet it is possible to sing all the 171,396 melodies, every one of which has a charm of its own. A precise knowledge of the law of melody is all that is required to get over the existing doubts and errors. The practice will be found comparatively easy by those who had a real ear for Music.

Talking of Western Music, it may be said that, of the 6 melodies based on the 8 white notes from C to C, the first, namely the Dheerasankarabharanam is sung in English Music with the admixture of Srutis belonging to the other 5 melodies and some times clean without them. The resultant melody resembles Sankarabharanam in several places, but it is not entirely that, nor is it Todi or Kalyani.

The Indian musician has "Moods" to express the thoughts of his mind and Alapanams to bring out the choicest parts of a Ragam, while the subtlety of time and his own ingenuity are shown by means of the Pallavis. It is impossible to harmonise such intricate portion of the Indian Music. But I know, however, from my own experience, that simple Keerthanams and Swarajatis (plain singing without Alapanams and Gamakams) can be beautifully harmonised. Musicians who have heard Indian Music sung to four parts admit that it is exquisite. I am of opinion that, as the Indian musician cultivated melody alone, he advanced beyond the middle stage of simple and popular Music into realms of intricate and subtle Music to show off his ingenuity in exposition and variation.

My idea is to give a specimen Keerthanam or Swarajati for each of the above mentioned 6 Ragams in the course of my next article. I have given however, the following.

What I have already said and what I intend to say in the succeeding articles many not be altogether new to my readers and may not be any real value to them, or, it may be considered impracticable. Again in some respects I may be overrating the importance of my subject or may fail to do it justice. Yet it is my earnest desire to try to meet all objection as far as I can, either by private correspondence or through the medium of any Journal. If I find that at least I have roused an interest in a few of my readers, I have had my reward."

ROYAL SOCIETY OF ARTS,
JOHN STREET, ADELPHI,
LONDON, W. C.
25th August 11.

DEAR SIR,

I beg to acknowledge with many thanks your letter of 2nd instant.

Articles on Music scarcely come within the scope of the journal, which deals, as you know rather with the applied arts than fine arts.

If however, you would care to send me your Mss. I should be glad to look at it.

The principal papers that deal with the subject of Music are, the "Musical News" 3, Wine Office Court, Fleet Street, "The Musical Standard," 83, Charing Cross Road, and "The Musical Times" 160, Wardour Street, the addresses given all being in London.

Yours faithfully,
G. K. MENZIES,
Asst. Secretary.

Rao Sahib M. Abraham Pandither,
Karunanithi Medical Hall,
Tanjore.

Replies to my above articles.

ROYAL SOCIETY OF ARTS,
JOHN STREET, ADELPHI,
LONDON, W. C.
17th Nov. 1911.

DEAR SIR,

Since receiving your letter of September 13th I have been making inquiries in different directions, but I am sorry to say without any satisfactory results. It is difficult to find any people in this Country with interest in or knowledge of Indian Music. I am therefore returning the Mss. which you were kind enough to send me, with much regret that I have not been able to assist you.

Yours faithfully,
G. K. MENZIES,
Editor of the Journal.

M. Abraham Pandither,
Karunanithi Medical Hall,
Tanjore.

3. The origin of the Tanjore Sangeeta Vidya Mahajana Sangam.

Though subsequent personal enquiries were made of many Vidwans we did not receive any satisfactory answer for the above queries. When doubt existed as regards the fundamental ideas of Indian music, namely as regards Swarams and Srutis how could we establish other theories which are based on them? The Ragakramam could only result from the realisations of the position of the Swarams. Music can stand only after the mathematical calculation of the Srutis has been established. Just like the Tamil saying that the life of men who are ignorant of "numbering their days" is one series of trouble, music without mathematical precision is open to endless doubt. How could a science without precision in its fundamental ideas and a house without a foundation ever hope to stand? So, having our fears that the music of South India might get mixed with Desikam in course of time and become corrupt like other music we had to establish the above Sangam.

When His Excellency Lord Carmichael, the Governor of Madras, visited Tanjore in February 1912, a number of Musical Vidwans were present here for the purpose of paying their respects. Among them were the following musicians.—

Veena Vydyanatha Iyer of Mayaveram, Muttya Bhagavatar of Harikesavanallur, Panchapakesa Bhagavatar of Tanjore, A. G. Pichaimuttu, B.A., L.T., of Tanjore, Harihara Bhagavatar, R. Subramania Iyer, Subramania Shastrial, N. P. Subramania Iyer, Veena Vencatachalam Iyer, Ramalinga Gurukkal, Vydyanatha Iyer of Konerirajapuram and Krishna Iyer of Tirukodikaval. At a meeting of the above musicians I placed my views before them and it was unanimously resolved that a musical Sangam was very necessary and that it should be organised. Later on, the idea of such a Sangam was placed before the following gentleman who gladly promised to become patrons of the Sangam:—Maharajah Setupati of Ramnad, M.R.Ry. Rai Bahadur Saminatha Vijaya Thevar Avargal, Zemindar of Papanad, M.R.Ry. V. A. Vandayar Avergal of Poondi, M.R.Ry. Rao Bahadur Annasami Tevar Avergal of Ukkadai, M.R.Ry. Avidayappa Pillai Avergal, M.R.Ry. P. V. Krishnasami Naik Avergal, M.R.Ry. T. Sambamoorti Row Avergal, M.R.Ry. Venkatasubbayyar Avergal, M.R.Ry. Rao Bahadur C. Nagoji Row Avergal and others. Others have since become members and have promised their help. The Sangam has been conducted at my own expense till now because I first wanted to prove to the world the usefulness and expediency of such a Sangam before asking for help from outside. I hear that many who have heard about the work of the Sangam either through others or through the published reports are willing to render all possible assistance. I hope that this Sangam will make its progress and be of genuine usefulness in developing the music of South India in many ways. Other particulars as regards the working of the Sabha may be gathered from the following remarks :—

It will be of use if we notice here some particulars about the object of the Sangham, the members thereof and the work done by them.

4. The objects of the Sangam.

1. To make a study of such data as would tend to the development of South Indian music and to publish them.

2. To establish an academy for the systematic teaching of South Indian music and its fundamental rules.

3. To arrange for examining its pupils and others desirous of being examined and give certificates of merit to those who are proficient.

4. To search for and publish works on music which would be of help to Karnatic Music as well as Keertanams which have not hitherto been published.

5. To make arrangements about developing the art of performing Kathas and singing.

6. To deliberate upon, and remove the doubts about, some of the important items of Karnatic music.

7. To purify the Karnatic Ragas by weeding out a few of its errors.

8. To reward distinguished Vidwans by means of medals and honorific titles.

9. To place before the Sangam for its approval new treatises, essays, opinions, or, new Keertanams in connection with Karnatic music and have Karnatic Ragas and modes sung by distinguished musicians.

Many noblemen, gentlemen, richmen and Vidwans have become members of this Sangam and are working in it sacrificing their substance and their energy.

5. The Members of the Mahajana Sangam.

Founder and President.

M. R. Ry. Rao Sahib M. Abraham Pandither.

Chairmen of the Reception Committee.

„ Panchapakesa Bhagavatar Avl.
„ Muttya Bhagavatar Avl.

Secretaries.

„ A. G. Pichaimuthu Avl., B.A., L.T.
„ N. P. Subramania Iyer Avl.

Chairmen of the First Meeting.

„ *Veena* Vydyanatha Iyer Avl.
„ Swaminatha Iyer Avl. of Palamaneri.

Chairmen of the Second Meeting.

„ T. Sambamurti Row Avl., B.A., B.L.
„ A. G. Pichaimuthu Avl., B.A., L.T., Tanjore.
„ P. V. Naganatha Sastrial Avl., B.A., B.L., Tanjore.

Chairmen of the Third Meeting.

„ *Veena* Venkataramanadoss Avl., Vijayanagaram.
„ H. P. Krishna Row Avl., B.A., Mysore.
„ Sabhesa Iyer Avl. Madras.

Chairmen of the Fourth Meeting.

„ V. P. Madhava Row Avl., C.I.E., Dewan, Baroda.
„ Doraisami Iyengar Avl., Madras.

Chairman of the Fifth Meeting.

„ T. A. Ramakrishna Iyer Avl., (Retired) Sub-Judge, Palghat.

Chairman of the Sixth Meeting.

„ A. S. Balasubramania Iyer Avl, B. A., B. L., Sub-Judge, Kumbakonam.

Patrons.

1. H. H. Maharajah Holkar, Indore.
2. H. H. Setupati Maharajah, Ramnad.
3. The Right Honourable Viscountess Churchill, V. A., London.
4. M. R. Ry. Sivaji Rajah Saheb Avl., Tanjore.
5. „ Pratapsingh Rajah Saheb Avl., Tanjore.
6. „ Rai Bahadur Swaminatha Vijaya Tevar Avl, the Zemindar of Papanad.
7. „ V. P. Madhava Row Avl, C. I. E., Dewan, Baroda.
8. „ Rao Bahadur Annasami Tevar Avl, Ukkadai.
9. „ V. Appasami Vandayar Avl, Poondi.
10. „ V. Gopalasami Raghunatha Rajaliar Avl, Haridwaramangalam.
11. „ Sivashanmuga Meygnana Sivacharya Swamigal, Tirupapuliyur.
12. „ Rao Bahadur C. Nagoji Row Avl, B. A., Coimbatore.
13. „ Rao Saheb J. Sunam Bhut, Hadakalli, Bellary.
14. „ S. R. M. C. T. Pettatchi Chettiar Avl, Zemindar of Andipatti.
15. „ Rai Bahadur J. S. Gnanayyar Nadar Avl, B.A., B.L., Sub-Judge, Negapatam.
16. „ T. A. Ramakrishna Iyer Avl, Retired Sub-Judge, Palghat.

17. M. R. Ry. A. S. Balasubramania Iyer Avl, B. A., B. L., Sub-Judge, Kumbakonam.
18. ,, Rao Bahadur N. Krishnasami Iyengar Avl, B. A., B. L., Kumbakonam.
19. ,, T. Sambamurti Row Avl, B. A., B. L., Tanjore.
20. ,, Audinarayana Iyer Avl, Pannayar, Pavoor.
21. ,, S. Venkatasubbayyar Avl, B. A., B. L., Tanjore.
22. ,, Dr. T. N. Govinda Iyer Avl, M. B. and C. M. Tinnevelly.
23. ,, Radhakrishna Iyer Avl, B. A., Pudukotah.
24. ,, T. D. Swaminatha Iyer Avl, Tanjore.

The Musical Vidvans present at the Meetings.

1. M. R. Ry. *Veena* Venkatramanadoss Pantulu, Vizianagaram.
2. ,, *Fiddle* Sabhesa Iyer Avl, Madras.
3. ,, *Fiddle* Swaminatha Iyer Avl, Palamaneri.
4. ,, Krishna Iyer Avl, Ernakulam.
5. ,, *Veena* Vydyanatha Iyer Avl, Mayavaram.
6. ,, *Fiddle* Panchapakesa Bhagavatar Avl, Tanjore
7. ,, Muttya Bhagavatar Avl, Harikesavanallur.
8. ,, Pratapa Ramaswami Bhagavatar Avl, Poovanur.
9. ,, *Veena* Venkatachalam Iyer Avl, Tanjore.
10. ,, Nagaraja Bhagavatar Avl, Tanjore.
11. ,, Doraiappah Iyer Avl, Tanjore.
12 ,, Saptarishi Bhagavatar Avl, Tanjore.
13. ,, Radhakrishna Bhagavatar Avl, Kumbakonam.
14. ,, *Veena* Ramasami Iyer Avl, Tanjore.
15. ,, *Veena* Appakannu Pillai Avl, Chidambaram.
26. ,, *Fiddle* Narayanasami Iyer Avl, Tanjore.
17. ,, *Fiddle* Johannes Sundararajam Avl, Madras.
18. ,, Govinda Bhagavatar Avl, Karuntattangudi, Tanjore.
19. ,, Syamasastri Avl, Tanjore.
20. ,, Jagannatha Bhutgosami Avl, Tanjore.
21. ,, Visvanatha Sastriar Avl, Tanjore.
22. ,, Appasami Iyer Avl, Vyaicheri.
23. ,, R. Subramania Iyer Avl, Tamil Pandit, Tanjore.
24. ,, *Sangeeta* Ramachandra Iyer Avl, Ukkadai.
25. ,, Saminatha Pillai Avl, Tanjore.
26. ,, *Fiddle* Padmanabha Naidu Avl, Tanjore.
27. ,, *Mridangam* Swami Iyer Avl, Tanjore.
28. ,, *Mridangam* Mani Bhutgosami Avl, Tanjore.
29. ,, *Ghata Vadyam* Sundara Ramayyar Avl, Kumbakonam.
30. ,, S. V. Rangasami Iyengar Avl, Madras.
31. ,, M. K. Sreenivasa Iyengar Avl, Madras.
32. ,, K. V. Sreenivasa Iyengar Avl, Trichinopoly.
33. ,, Sadhu Ganapati Subramania Sastrial, Tiruvadi.
34. ,, K. Ramachandra Iyer Avl, Keevalur,
35. ,, Seshayya Avl, Mayavaram.
36. ,, Chokkalinga Nadar Avl, Nadukaveri.
37. ,, Swamidoss Hastings Avl, Vijayapuram.
38. ,, A. G. Pichaimuthu Avl, B. A., L. T., Tanjore.

39. Sri Mathi *Veena* Bhagyam Ammal (Mrs. Abraham Pandither)
40. „ *Veena* Annapoornam Ammal (Mrs. Gnanasikhamani)
41. „ *Fiddle* Marakatavalli Ammal (Miss Pandither)
42. „ *Fiddle* Kanakavalli Ammal (Miss Pandither)

The Names of those who read Essays at the Meetings and the subjects thereof.

1. M. R. Ry. A. G. Pichaimuthu Avl, B. A., L. T., Tanjore, on the dignity and usefulness of music, the history of European music and a few important points thereon.
2. „ R. Subramania Iyer Avl, Tanjore, on the dignity and utility of music.
3. „ Saptarishi Bhagavatar Avl, of Tanjore, on Sangitam and Sahityam, the determination of the 22 Srutis and their usefulness.
4. „ A. P. Ganesa Iyer Avl, of Mylapore, on Karnatic Music, its present condition, the secrets of Indian music and the method of singing.
5. „ Muttya Bhagavatar Avl, of Harikesavanallur, on the system of practising music.
6. „ Panchapakesa Bhagavatar Avl, of Tanjore, on the art of singing, and the 22 Srutis.
7. „ Radakrisnna Bhagavatar Avl, of Kumbakonam, on the dignity of music, and researches into the Bhairavi Ragam on the principle of the 22 Srutis.
8. „ S. Subramania Sastrial, Sanskrit Pundit, Tanjore, on the system of teaching music, some side issues on the enquiry into the Srutis, the enquiry into the principle of Talam.
9. „ S. V. Nataraja Iyer Avl, Sengalipuram, on the progress of Indian Music.
10. „ *Veena* Venkatachalam Iyer, Tanjore, on the Nattai Ragam.
11. „ P. V. Krishnasami Iyer Avl, B.A., Vakil, Tanjore on Nada Brahmam, Nadopasanai, Nada Mahimai, History of Tyagaraja Swami and Nadam and Navarasam.
12. „ P. S. Sundaram Iyer Avl, B. A., L. T., Tanjore, on the 22 Srutis.
13. „ C. Tirumalayya Naidu Avl, M. R. A. S., Madras, on Mayamalava Ragam.
14. „ Appasami Iyer Avl, of Vyaicheri, on the 22 Srutis.
15. „ Syama Sastrial Avl, on the 22 Srutis.
16. „ *Veena* Venkataramanadoss of Vijayanagaram, on the method of practising the Veena.
17. „ T. A. Venkatarama Sastrial of Tanjore, on NadaBrahmam.
18. „ *Veena* Appakannu Pillai Avl, of Chidambaram, on the Veena.
19. „ Ranganatha Swamigal of Chidambaram, on Nadam.
20. „ Johannes Sundararajam Avl of Madras, on some important points helpful to the progress of Indian Music.
21. „ Seturama Bharatiar Avl, Tamil Pandit, Tanjore, on the indigenous 'Modes' in use in the Tamil Country.
22. „ Nagaraja Bhagavatar Avl, Tanjore on the life of Tyagaraja Swamigal.
23. „ Sabhesa Iyer Avl, of Madras, on the 22 Srutis.
24. „ Rao Saheb M. Abraham Pandither Avl, on some general remarks about the 22 Srutis, and the dignity and antiquity of music.
25. „ Pratapa Ramasami Bhagavatar Avl of Poovanur, on the 22 Srutis.

The list of those promoters of the Sangam who were present at its meetings.

1. M. R. Ry. K. V. Sreenivasa Iyengar Avl., B. A., L. T., Deputy Collector, Tanjore.
2. „ G. Kodandaramanujulu Naidu Avl., B. A., B. L., Sub-Judge, Tanjore.
3. „ P. C. Thiruvenkatachariar Avl., B. A., B. L., Sub-Judge, Tanjore.
4. „ T. Seshayyar Avl., B. A., Deputy Collector, Tanjore.
5. „ Rao Sahib D. Dravia Nadar Avl., B. A., Deputy Collector, Tanjore.
6. „ D. K. Kunhunni Menon Avl, B. A., Deputy Collector, Tanjore.
7. „ Y. V. Sreenivasa Iyer Avl, B. A., Deputy Collector, Tanjore.
8. „ S. Sundaram Iyer Avl., Receiver, Tanjore.
9. „ Abdul Karim Khan Sahib Bahadur, Inspector of Police, Tanjore.
10. „ Mulhari Rao Avl, Retired District Munsif, Tanjore.
11. „ Vijayaraghavachariar Avl, M. A., Post Master, Tanjore.
12. „ Rao Bahadur K. Sreenivasam Pillai Avl., Tanjore.
13. „ Purushottama Mudaliar Avl, B. A., M. B., C. M., Tanjore
14. „ T. D. Govindayyar Avl, B. A., M. B., C. M., Tanjore.
15. „ P. V. Naganatha Sastrial Avl., B. A., B. L., Tanjore.
16. „ N. K. Ramasami Iyer Avl, B. A., B. L., Tanjore.
17. „ T. K. Anantapadmanabha Iyer Avl., B. A., Madura.
18. „ K. Natarajan Avl, B. A., B. L., Tanjore.
19. „ P. V. Mahalinga Iyer Avl, B. A., B. L., Tanjore.
20. „ E. Sooryanarayana Iyer Avl, B. A., B. L., Tanjore.
21. „ P. V. Ramaseshayyar Avl, B. A., B. L., Tanjore.
22. „ T. V. Panchapakesa Iyer Avl, B. A., B. L., Tanjore.
23. „ Bhavani Row Saheb Avl, Tanjore.
24. „ T. S. Sundaram Iyer Avl, Tanjore.
25. „ V. Mangala Vedakar, Editor, "Modern world," Mylapore.
26. „ T. V. Sreenivasa Iyengar Avl, B. A., L. T., M. R. A. S., Tanjore.
27. „ Rev. J. B. Gnanavoluvu Avl, B. A., L. T., Negapatam.
28. „ S. A. Israel Pillai Avl, B. A., L. T.
29. „ S. Daniel Pillai Avl, B. A., L. T.
30. „ R. Sundaram Iyer Avl, B. A., L. T.
31. „ A. B. Paul Avl, B. A.
32. „ V. Vamana Row Avl, B. A.
33. „ K. Brahadeesan Avl, B. A.
34. „ V. Ramayya Garu B. A., Madras.
35. „ Ramachandra Iyer Avl.
36. „ M. P. Durasami Iyer Avl.
37. „ S. V. Nataraja Iyer Avl, Sengalipuram.
38. „ Vidwan Arasan Shanmugam Pillai Avl.
39. „ D. Savariraya Pillai Avl, M. R. A. S. Trichy.
40. „ S. Olaganatha Pillai Avl, Tamil Pandit, Tanjore.
41. „ Devaprasadam Pillai Avl, Madras.
42. „ O. N. Appasami Iyer Avl, Tanjore.
43. „ V. Krishnamachariar Avl.
44. „ Natesa Sastrial.
45. „ T. Subramaniam Avl, Madras.
46. „ A. Venkatasubramania Iyer Avl.

47. M. R. Ry. V. S. Seshayya Avl, Tanjore.
48. „ T. S. Subramania Iyer Avl., Tanjore.
49. „ T. A. Ganapati Iyer Avl, Tanjore.
50. „ Rajagopala Iyer Avl, Tanjore.
51. „ Sambaparamesvara Iyer Avl.
52. „ Ramasami Iyer Avl.
53. „ Pakirisami Pillai Avl, Tanjore.
54. „ Ramachandra Row Avl.
55. „ Ranganatha Bhut Avl.

Other promoters and wellwishers of the Sangam.

1. M. R. Ry. His Highness Maharajah Sri, Sir Krishnaraja Oodayar Bahadur, G. C. S. I., Maharajah of Mysore.
2. „ Sri Padmanabhadasa Vanchi, Sir Balaramavarma Kulasekhara Kireetadhipati. Mannai Sultan, G. C. I. E., G. C. S. I., Maharajah of Travancore.
3. „ His Highness Maharajah Holkar Sivaji Row Holkar Bahadur, Indore.
4. „ H. H. Martanda Bhairava Tondaman, Maharajah of Pudukotah.
5. „ Rama Gajapati Avl, Maharajah of Vijayanagaram.
6. „ Row Venkataswetachalapati Ranga Row, Maharajah of Bobbili.
7. „ Row Venkatakumara Mahipati Soorya Row, Maharajah of Pittapuram.
8. „ Jagaveerarama Venkatesa Ettappa Maharajah of Ettyapuram.
9. „ Mutturamalinga Setupati Avl, Rajah of Ramnad.
10. „ Tirumalai Row Saheb Avl, Jagirdar of Arni.
11. „ Vyricharla Veerabhadra Raju Avl, Rajah of Kuruppam.
12. „ Honourable Dewan Bahadur V. Ramabhadra Naidu Avl, Zemindar of Vadakarai.
13. „ Lakshmipati Naicken Avl. Zemindar of Idyakotai, Dindigul.
14. „ Subramania Teerthapati Avl, Zemindar of Singampatti, Tinnevelly.
15. „ Vadamalai Tiruvanatha Sevuba Pandya Thevar Avl, Zemindar of Setur.
16. „ Gowri Vallabha Thevar Avl, Zemindar of Sivaganga.
17. „ Muttu Ramasami Kalingarayan Avl, Zemindar, Oothukuli.
18. „ Varadappa Naidu Avl, Zemindar of Nekondi, Dharmapuri, Salem.
19. „ A. L. A. R. Arunachalam Chettiar Avl, Zemindar, Devakotah.
20. „ Nagayasami Thumitchi Naicker Avl, Zemindar, Poraiyar.
21. „ Ramasami Naicker Avl, Zemindar, Ammayanaickanur, Madura.
22. „ Katchi Yuvarangappa Kolakkakola Oodyar Avl, Zemindar, Udayarpalayam
23. „ Krishnavijaya Boochayanaicker Avl, Zemindar. Marungapuri, Trichy.
24. „ Parthasaradhi Chettiar Avl, Zemindar, Anumammatti.
25. „ Samba Iyer Avl, Zemindar, Sandapalli, Salem.
26. „ Venkatasubbayyar Avl, Zemindar, Soolamalei, Salem.
27. „ Balasubramania Chettiar Avl, Zemindar, Mandalanainagunta, Salem.
28. „ Moorti Chettiar Avl, Zemindar, Vanipatti, Salem,
29. „ Prasannah Venkatachala Reddiar Avl, Zemindar, Turaiyur.
30. „ Somasundra Chettiar Avl, Zemindar, Kalattoor.
31. „ Krishnasami Iyengar Avl, Zemindar, Kadatur, Salem.
32. „ Subramania Koundan Avl, Zemindar, Palamedu, Salem.
33. „ Raja Koundar Avl, Zemindar Manatti, Salem.
34. „ A. L. A. R. Vyravan Chettiar Avl. Mittadar, Rajampalayam.

35. M. R. Ry. Venkata Subbayyar Avl, B.A., B.L., Zemindar, Tuttikulam, Namakkal, Salem.
36. ,, Doraisami Reddiar Avl, Zemindar, Pudukottai, Namakkal.
37. ,, Gopalasami Chettiar Avl. Zemindar, Pavithram, Namakkal.
38. ,, Kanakasabhapati Mudaliar Avl, Zemindar, Konankurichi. Salem.
39. ,, Muttukumaraswami Mudaliar Avl, Zemindar, Ponneri.
40. ,, Honourable Rao Bahadur Subba Row Avl, Mangalore.
41. ,, Rao Bahadur S. T. Shanmukham Pillai Avl, Dewan, Ettiyapuram.
42. ,, Rao Bahadur C. Hanumanta Goud Garu Hospet. Bellary.
43. ,, Jagarlamoodi Lakshmayya Naidu Garu Avl, Karamchedu, Bapatla.
44. ,, Parthasarathi Iyengar Avl, Karnool.
45. ,, G. Adinarayana Reddiar Avl, Kondapuram, Anantapur.
46. ,, K. Adinarayana Reddiar Avl, Alur, Nellore.
47. ,, Sri Ankitam Venkata Jaggarow Garu Shermuhammada puram, Vizagapatam.
48. ,, P. T. Rangaswami Iyengar Avl, Kulitalai.
49. ,, Marella Gangaraju Pantulu garu Potuloor, Ganjam.
50. ,, B. C. Avidayappa Pillai Avl, Pichandarkoyil, Trichinopoly.
51. ,, Dr. Govindayyar Avl. Tinnevelly.
52. ,, *Veena* Ramakrishna Bhagavatar Avl, Tinnevelly.
53. ,, Narayanaswami Iyengar Avl, Vakil, Veeraraghavapuram, Tinnevelly.
54. ,, Gurusami Iyer Avl, Vakil, Tinnevelly.
55. ,, Dr. Appavu Pillai Avl, Veeraraghavapuram, Tinnevelly.
56. ,, Subbayya Bhagavatar Avl, Kodayanallur, Tinnevelly.
57. ,, Vedanta Bhagavatar Avl, Kallidaikurichi.
58. ,, N. Subramania Iyer Avl. Vakil, Kakatop, Madura.
59. ,, M. V. Meyappa Chettiar Avl, Devakotta.
60. ,, Ramalinga Gurukkal Avl, Virudupatti.
61. ,, T. S. Subramania Iyer, Avl, Vakil, Tiruturaipoondi.
62. ,, *Kote Vadyam* Sakaram Row Avl, Tiruvidamarudur.
63. ,, *Fiddle* Govindasami Pillai Avl, Trichinopoly.
64. ,, Anantarama Bhagavatar Avl, Kumbakonam.
65. ,, Panchapakesa Bhagavatar Avl, Kumbakonam.
66. ,, Dewan Bahdur P. Parankusa Naidu Garu, Madras.
67. ,, Dewan Bahadur P. Rajaratna Mudaliar Avl, C. I. E., Madras.
68. ,, Honourable Mr. Nawab Syed Mahamed Bahadur, Madras.
69. ,, P. Lakshminarasu Naidu Garu, B.A., Professor, Pachaiyappa's College, Madras.
70. ,, Honourable Dewan Bahadur L. A. Govindaraghava Iyer Avl, B. A., B. L., Madras.
71. ,, V. Ryru Nambiar Avl, B. A., B. L., Madras.
72. ,, Honourable Dewan Bahadur M. Audinarayana Iyer Avl, Madras.
73. ,, Honourable Rao Bahadur P. Tyagaraja Chettiar Avl, B. A., Madras.
74. ,, V. Arunagiri Nayudu Avl, B. A., Madras.
75. ,, Honourable T. V. Seshagiri Iyer Avl, B. A., B. L., Puisne Judge, High Court, Madras.
76. ,, Pandit D. Gopalacharlu Garu, Madras.
77. ,, A. V. B. A. C. Parthasarathi Naidu Avl, Madras.
78. ,, T. Rangachariar Avl, Retired Judge, Madras.
79. ,, K. B. Ramanatha Iyer Avl, M. A., B. L., L. T., Madras.

80. M. R. Ry. S. Gopalasami Iyengar Avl, B. A., B. L., Madras.
81. " T. Gopalasami Mudaliar Avl, Madras.
82. " C. Gopalamenon Avl, B. A., Madras.
83. " G. A. Vydyarama Iyer Avl, B. A., Madras.
84. " *Fiddle* Gopalakrishna Iyer Avl, Marungapuri.
85. " Anantarama Iyer Avl, Vidvan, Kumbakonam.
86. " Radhakrishna Bhagavatar Avl, Talainayar.
87. " *Flute* Vydyarama Iyer Avl, Tillaivilagam.
88. " *Veena* Ramasami Iyer Avl, Travancore.
89. " Ramasami Bhagavatar Avl, Lalgudi.
90. " Nimmari Paramesvara Bhagavatar Avl, Palghat.
91. " A. Rangaswami Iyengar Avl. Madras.
92. " *Flute* Nagaraja Row Avl, Kumbakonam.
93. " *Flute* Sanjivi Row Avl, Palladam.
94. " Iyan Sambasiva Iyer, Avl. Karaikudi, Madura.
95. " P. R. Natesa Iyer Avl, B. A., B. L., Tanjore.
96. " K. Natarajan Avl, B. A., B. L., Tanjore.
97. " Kannusami Nattuvanar Avl, Tanjore.
98. " Ramanna Avl, Musician, Tanjore.
99. " *Fiddle* Venkoba Row Avl, Tanjore.
100. " Rama Row Avl, Musician, Tanjore.
101. " *Fiddle* Ganapati Iyer Avl, Mylapore, Madras.
102. " *Veena* Iyavayyar Avl, Pudukotah.
103. " *Kinjira* Mamundia Pillai Avl, Pudukotah.
104. " Srikantha Iyer Avl, Triplicane, Madras.
105. " *Fiddle* Subbayyah Avl, Tiruvadamarudur.
106. " Panchu Bhagavatar Avl. Tillaisthanam, Tanjore.
107. " *Veena* Ramakrishna Iyer Avl, Salyamangalam, Tanjore.
108. " R. Sreenivasa Iyengar Avl, Ettyapuram.
109. " Vedaranya Bhagavatar Avl, Tiruvadi.
110. " Tyagayyar Avl, Musical Vidvan, Madras.
111. " Row Bahadur N. Krishnasami Iyengar Avl, B. A., B. L., Kumbakonam.
112. " L. C. R. Lakshmivaraha Iyengar Avl, B. A., B. L., Kumbakonam.
113. " Rao Bahadur Appu Sastriar Avl, B. A., Kumbakonam.
114. " A. R. Chakrapani Chettiar Avl, Kumbakonam.
115. " S. Rajaram Iyer Avl, Kumbakonam.
116. " Er. M. C. Bhagavansingh Avl, Kumbakonam.
117. " Honourable Rao Bahadur V. K. Ramanujachariar Avl, B. A, Kumbakonam
118. " S. Sivagurunatha Chettiar Avl, B. A., B. L., Kumbakonam.
119. " K. Anantarama Iyer Avl, M. A., B. L., Tanjore.
120. " Sitarama Bhagavatar Avl, Soolamangalam, Tanjore.
121. " Vydyanatha Bhagavatar Avl, Soolamangalam, Tanjore.
122. " Ramasami Bhagavatar Avl, Mayavaram.
123. " Govinda Bhagavatar Avl, Tanjore.
124. " Ramasami Iyer Avl, Vidwan, Conjeevaram.
125. " Gavinda Bhagavatar, Avl, Karantattangudi, Tanjore.
126. " S. Santappa Avl, B. A., Tanjore.

127. M. R. Ry. Subramania Iyer Avl, Tiruvenkatanatharkovil.
128. " Koteesvara Iyer Avl, Madras.
129. " Tiruvenkatachariar Avl, Ariyalur.
130. " G. D. Dawson Avl, Shiyali.
131. " N. G. Kalidasan Avl, Calcutta.
132. " Narasingarow Pantulu Garu, Kadayam, Godaveri.
133. " Jesudasan Avl, Kulittalai.
134. " S. E. Ranganadham Avl, M. A., Madras.
135. " J. V. Thomas Avl, M. A., Madura.
136. " M. Koil Pillai Avl, M. A., Trichinopoly.
137. " G. S. Abraham Avl, B. A., Madura.
138. " Peter Isaac Avl., B. A., Madura.
139. " A. Periyanayakam Avl, B. A., Ramnad.
140. " Rev. J. X. Miller Avl, M. A., Pasumalai.
141. " Dewan Bahadur L. D. Swamikannu Pillai Avl, M. A., L. L. B., Madras.
142. " Honourable Chidambaranatha Mudaliar Avl, B. A., Shiyali.
143. " Rao Bahadur G. Arogiaswami Pillai Avl, B. A., Coimbatore.
144. " Rao Bahadur M. Arumugam Pillai Avl, Retd. Dy. Collector, Madura.
145. " Khan Bahadur H. Abdul Sultan Saheb Avl, Madura.
146. " Rao Bahadur Dharmaranga Raju Avl, Madras.
147. " Rao Bahadur Ramakrishna Iyer Avl, Tinnevelly.
148. " Rao Bahadur A. V. Ramalingam Iyer Avl, Supdg. Engineer, D. P. W., Madras.
149. " Rao Bahadur G. Sreenivasa Row Avl, Madura.
150. " Rao Saheb Dr. Bhandarkar, B. A., L. M. S., Indore.
151. " Rao Saheb T. Ramakrishna Pillay Avl, B. A., F. M. U., M. R. A. S., F. R. N. S., President, Tamil Acadamy, Madras.
152. " Mahamahopadhyaya V. Saminatha Iyer Avl, Presidency College, Madras.
153. " V. Gopalayya Pantulu Garu, B. A., B. E. Executive Engineer, Tanjore.
154. " M. Neelakanta Iyer Avl, B. E. Executive Engineer, Tanjore.
155. " J. Muttaya Avl, Sub-Engineer, Trichinopoly.
156. " Dr. T. M. Nair Avl, Madras.
157. " Dr. James Harris Avl, Madras.
158. " Chockalinga Pillai Avl, Dewan. Ramnad.
159. " T. Dorasami Avl, Sub-Asst. Surgeon, Kondanur Madura.
160. " T. M. Thamba Pillai Avl, Sub-Asst. Surgeon, Rayachuti, Cuddapah.
161. " Dr. J. Mathuranayagam Avl, Negapatam.
162. " Dr. Maduram Avl, Trichinopoly.
163. " T. D. Madurainayagam Avl, Gnanasundara Vydyasala, Colombo.
164. " Dr. Lamech, L. R. C. P. and S. Rangoon.
165. " S. Balasingam Satya Avl, M. A., Madras.
166. " G. Devasahayam Avl, B. A., B. L.,
167. " K. R. Ramachandra Iyer Avl., B. A., B. L., Tanjore.
168. " A. Rangasami Iyer Avl., Vakil, Nagore.
169. " Ranga Row Avl., Vakil, Tanjore.
170. " Vakil Natesa Iyer Avl, Sarada Sangeeta Sabha, Triplicane.
171. " M. Subbanna Iyer Avl, Vakil, Ponmanjanallur. Papanasam.
172. " K. Subramania Iyer, Avl., B, A., B. L., Trichinopoly.

173. M. R. Ry. D. V. Ramaswami Iyer Avl, Vakil, Tiruvannamalai.
174. „ A. K. Sundaram Iyer Avl, B. A., B. L., Tinnevelly.
175. „ M. Narayanasami Iyer Avl., B. A., B. L., Tanjore.
176. „ T. Kodandarama Iyengar Avl, B. A., M. L.. Tanjore
177. „ G. P. Subramania Iyer Avl, B. A., B. L., Tanjore.
178. „ R. Ramaseshayyar Avl., B. A.. B. L.. Tanjore.
179. „ E. Varada Iyengar Avl. B. A., B. L., Tanjore.
180. „ D. Panchanada Iyer Avl. B. A.. B. L., Tanjore.
181. „ K. Anantarama Iyer, Avl, M. A., B. L.
182. „ S. Krishna Iyer Avl. B. A., B. L., Tanjore.
183. „ N. A. V. Somasundram Pillai Avl, B. A., B. L., Tinnevelly Bridge.
184. „ T. A. Ramlingam Chettiar Avl, B. A., B. L., Coimbatore.
185. „ V. S. Ramasami Sastriar Avl, B. A., B. L., Madura.
186. „ Subramania Iyer Avl, B. A., Pleader, Madura.
187. „ T. C. Sreenivasa Iyengar Avl, B. A., B. L., H. C. Vakil, Madura.
188. „ T. N. Sundararaja Iyengar Avl, B. A., B., L., H. C. Vakil, Madura.
189. „ Mangudi Natesa Iyer Avl, B. A., B. L., Vakil, Madura.
190. „ N. Kuppuswami Iyer Avl, B. A., Vakil, Tirupati.
191. „ R. Yegnyaramayyar Avl, B. A., Vakil, Guntur.
192. „ N. K. Chandrasekhara Iyer Avl, B. A., B. L., H. C. Vakil, Mylapore.
193. „ B. C. Raghavayyar Avl, B. A., B., L., Public Prosecutor, Chittoor.
194. „ S. Hanumanta Row Pantulu garu, B. A., B. L., Public Prosecutor, Masulipatam.
195. „ K. Venkatappayya Pantulu garu, B. A., B. L., Vakil, Guntur.
196. „ Subramania Iyer Avl, Music Vidvan, Tinnevelly.
197. „ Veerasami Iyer Avl. Vakil, Tiruvarur.
198. „ I. Kumarasami Pillai Avl, B. A., B L.. Tanjore.
199. „ Umamahesvaram Pillai Avl, B. A., B. L., Tanjore.
200. „ Dorairaja Pillai Avl, B. A., B. L., Pudukotah.
201. „ Gnanadurai Avl, B. A., B. L., Trichinopoly.
202. „ Desikachariar Avl, B. A., B. L., Trichinopoly.
203. „ N. S. Venkatarama Iyer Avl, B. A., B. L., Tanjore.
204. „ Navamani David Nadar Avl, B. A., B. L, Trichinopoly.
205. „ Nellayappa Pillai Avl, B. A., B. L., Tinnevelly.
206. „ Kumarasami Reddiar Avl, B. A., B. L., Palamcottah.
207. „ A. K. Sundara Iyer Avl, B. A., B. L., Tinnevelly.
208. „ Thomas Nadar Avl, B. A., B. L., Palamcottah.
209. „ Rev. N. G. Ponniah Avl, B. A., L. T., Mannargudi.
210. „ Rev. L. P. Larsen Avl, M. A., Bangalore.
211. „ Rev. G. E. Phillip Avl, M. A., Bangalore.
212. „ Rev. Frances Avl, Tamil Pulavar, Bangalore.
213. „ Dr. A. C. Asirvada Nadar Avl, Madras.
214. „ Rev. D. Samuel Avl, B. A., L. T., Mannargudi.
215. „ S. K. Devasikhamani Avl, B. A., L. T., Trichinopoly.
216. „ T. D. Manikyavachakam Avl, B. A., L. T., Mannargudi.
217. „ J. R. Isaac Avl, B. A., Madras.
218. „ G. Devadasan Avl, B. A., L T., Palamcottah.
219. „ N. G. Devasahayam Avl, B. A., Coimbatore.

220. M. R. Ry.—S. Chinnaya Avl, B. A., Shiyali.
221. „ J. S. Devasahayam Avl, B. A., Palamcottah.
222. „ T. Abhyudayan Avl, B. A., L. T., Tinnevelly.
223. „ Isaac Gnanam Avl, B. A., L. T., Trichinopoly.
224. „ Samuel Joseph Avl, B. A. Trichinopoly.
225. „ J. Gnanamuttu Avl, B. A. L. T., Trichinopoly.
226. „ T. Gnanamuttu Avl, B. A., L. T., Tinnevelly.
227. „ S. Arulnayakan Avl, B. A., L. T., Madura.
228. „ S. Nallamuttu Avl, B. A., Madras.
229. „ P. E. Devadasan Avl, B. A., L. T., Madras.
230. „ S. P. Arumanayagam Avl, B. A., L. T., Madras.
231. „ C. N. Subramania Iyer Avl, Retd. Asst. Inspector of Schools, Travancore.
232. „ T. M. Kuppusami Pillai Avl, Teacher, Anaikuppam, Cuddalore.
233. „ P. S. Subramania Iyer Avl, B. A., S. Joseph's College, Trichy.
234. „ Chelvakesava Mudaliar Avl, M. A., Pachaiyappa's College, Madras.
235. „ Rangachariar Avl, M. A., L. T.. Botanist, Coimbatore.
236. „ Pakianada Pillai Avl, G. L. M. School, Tanjore.
237. „ W. S. Haddaway Esq., Supdt. School of Arts, Madras.
238. „ Y. Devavaram Avl, Normal School, Rangoon.
239. „ Rajanayakam Avl, B. A., L. T., Sub-Assistant Inspector of Schools, Dharapuram.
240. „ S. G. Daniel Avl, B. A., Sub-Assistant Inspector of Schools, Saidapet.
241. „ James Sargunam Avl, B. A., Sub-Assistant Inspector of Schools, Vellore.
242. „ Paul Appasami Avl, M. A., L. L. B., Madras.
243. „ T. Jesudasan Avl, B. A., Madras.
244. „ S. D. Sundaram Avl, B. A., Madras.
245. „ Sankara Iyer Avl, B. A., Tanjore.
246. „ J. M. Nallasami Pillai Avl, B. A., B. L., Madura.
247. „ Manickyavasaka Nadar Avl, B. A., Head Master, Virudupatti.
248. „ Chellaia Avl, B. A., Tuticorin.
249. „ Y. D. Charles Avl, B. A., Customs Office, Rangoon.
250. „ Samuel Avl, B. A., Rangoon.
251. „ V. P. Ramanuja Chettiar Avl, of Messrs Perumal Chettiar & Sons, Madras.
252. „ V. P. Alwar Chettiar Avl, Do. do.
253. „ V. Krishnayya garu Avl, Vakil, Chittoor.
254. Mr. D. S. Duff of Messrs Duff, Osler & Co., Madras.
255. „ D. Bose of Messrs John Dickinson & Co., Madras.
256. M. R. Ry. Mitra Avl, Messrs John Dickinson & Co., Madras.
257. „ Kalahasti Venkataramaraju Avl, Veena Vidwan, Madras.
258. „ Gireesa Bhagavatar Avl, Kotayur, Madura.
259. „ Hariteertha Iyer Avl, Music Vidwan, Tirugokarnam, Pudukotah.
260. „ *Fiddle* Balu Iyer Avl, Madras.
261. „ Ramachandra Iyer Avl, Sangeeta Vidwan, Kewalur.
262. „ Krishnamachariar Avl, Sangeeta Vidwan, Madras.
263. „ Rajaguru Meru Swamiar Avl, Tanjore.
264. „ Muddukrishna Iyer Avl, Sangeeta Vidwan, Melatore.
265. „ *Fiddle* Raju Iyer Avl, Lalgudi.

266. M. R. Ry. D. Ponnaia Avl, Music Master, Pasumalai.
267. „ *Nagaswaram* Ramasami Avl, Semmanarkoil, Tanjore.
268. „ *Nagaswaram* Periya Packiri Avl, Mannargudi.
269. „ *Nagaswaram* Ramasami Avl, Mayavaram.
270. „ *Nagaswaram* Natesan Avl, Koranadu, Mayavaram.
271. „ *Nagaswaram* Ponnusami Avl, Madura.
272. „ *Nagaswaram* Kannayyan Avl, Tanjore.
273. „ Tavul Saminathan Avl, Tanjore.
274. „ Tavul Darmalingam Avl, Negapatam.
275. „ K. V. Sreenivasa Iyengar Avl, Music Vidwan, Trichinopoly.
276. „ Vydyanatha Bhagavatar Avl, Melatur.
277. „ Natesa Bhagavatar Avl, Melatur.
278. „ Krishnamachariar Avl, Music Vidwan, Trichinopoly.
279. „ Radhakrishna Bhagavatar Avl, Karantattangudi, Tanjore.
280. „ Chidambara Bhagavatar Avl, Mangudi, Tanjore.
281. „ Namakal Narasimha Bhagavatar Avl, Srirangam.
282. „ Samavedam Lakshmana Srowtigal, Varahur.
283. „ Samavedam Nagu Srowtigal, Varahur.
284. „ Nemam Natesa Iyer Avl, Music Vidwan, Palamaneri.
285. „ Sesha Bhagavatar Avl, Tanjore.
286 „ R. Ramasami Bhagavatar Avl, Tiruvisanallur.
287. „ K. Krishnasami & Bros., Govindappa Naickan Street, Madra
288. „ Nataraja Bhagavatar Avl, Palamaneri.
289. „ *Nagaswaram* Krishnamurti, Tanjore.
290. „ S. Subramania Iyer Avl, Music Vidwan, Mysore.
291. „ *Vidwan* Venkatarama Iyer Avl, Velipalayam, Negapatam.
292. „ *Veena* Gopalasami Iyer Avl, Tiruvisanallur.
293. „ *Veena* Ramasami Iyengar Avl, Srirangam.
294. „ R. Raghava Iyengar Avl, Setu Samasthana Vidwan.
295. „ Palni Subramania Bhagavatar Avl.
296. „ *Veena* A. Subba Row Avl, Samasthana Vidwan, Pittapuram.
297. „ *Fiddle* H. Venkata Row Avl, Samasthana Vidwan, Pittapuram.
298. „ M. K. Ramasami Iyer Avl, Salt Office, Tanjore.
299. „ Srinivasa Iyer Avl, Music Vidwan, Triplicane, Madras.
300. „ *Chittrakavi* Sivarama Bhagavatar Avl, Tanjore.
301. „ *Bharatam* Narayanasami Iyer Avl, Umayalpuram, Tanjore.
302. „ *Veena* R. Kuppusami Iyer Avl, H. C. Vakil, Madras.
303. „ Vedanta Bhagavatar Avl, Kallidakurichi.
304. „ M. D. Subramania Iyer Avl, Sub Registrar, Tirumangalam.
305. „ Subramania Iyer Avl, Sub Registrar, Tiruvidamarudur.
306. „ M. Veeraraghava Chettiar Avl, Retd. Sub-Registar, Cuddalore N. T.
307. „ P. R. Krishnamachariar Avl, Tamil Pandit.
308. „ Ramasami Sastrigal, Sanskrit Pandit, Tanjore.
309. „ M. V. Ramanujachariar Avl, Tamil Pandit, Kumbakonam.
310. „ M. V. Gopalachariar Avl, Tamil Pandit, Triplicane, Madras.
311. „ M. Venkatasami Nattar Avl, Tamil Pandit, Trichinopoly.
312. „ Tirumalai Velu Kavirayar Avl, Madura.

313. M. R. Ry. Kandasami Kavirayar Avl, Madura.
314. „ N. S. Venkatarama Iyer Avl, M. A., L. T., Guntur.
315. „ Durai Raya Vanangamudi Veluvatti Thevar Avl, Zemindar, Nagaram.
316. „ Mannaba Saheb Avl, Tanjore.
317. „ Chota Saheb Avl, Tanjore.
318. „ S. Balasubramania Nadar Avl, Madras.
319. „ Panchapakesa Oodayar Avl, Nidamangalam.
320. „ A. Natesa Iyer Avl, Mirasdar, Kumbakonam.
321. „ Singaravelu Oodayar Avl, Thannerkunnam.
322. „ Srila Sri Pandara Sannidhi Thambiran of Tiruvaduturai.
323. „ Srila Sri Pandara Sannidhi Thambiran of Tirupanandal.
324. „ S. V. Nataraja Iyer Avl, Mirasdar, Sengalipuram, Tanjore.
325. „ Chinnatambia Pillai Avl, Reddipalayam, Tanjore.
326. „ V. Arumanayaka Nadar Avl, Photographer, Tuticorin.
327. „ Kaliaperumal Pillai Avl, Tanjore.
328. „ Velayudha Mudaliar Avl, Negapatam.
329. „ T. S. Akhilandam Avl. Ilanchi, Tinnevelly.
330. „ H. V. V. Chettiar Avl, Vani Villa, Mylapore.
331. „ M. R. R. M. Ramasami Chettiar Avl, Pudukotah.
332. „ V. Govindarajulu Naidu Avl, Pondicherry.
333. „ Munisami Naidu Avl, Mint Street, Madras.
334. „ Parthasaradhi Iyengar Avl, Tambu Chetti St. Madras.
335. „ Neerala Vencatesaperumal Chettiar, Govindappa Naicker St. Madras.
336. „ Ramanujacharriar Avl, Veeraraghava Mudali Street, Teriplicane.
337. „ C. Gopalachettiar Avl, Pycroft's Road, Triplicane.
338. „ V. R. L. S. T. Ramanathan Chettiar Avl, Devacottah.
339. „ M. C. T. Vyravan Chettiar Avl, do.
340. „ P. G. Sundaresa Sastrial, B.A., Trichinopoly.
341. „ A. Jesudasan Appasami Avl, Manorama, Palamcottah.
342. „ Rathna Sastrial Avl, Palamaneri.
343. „ A. K. Raghavachariar Avl. Srirangam.
344. „ R. Krishna Row Avl, Nungumbaukam, Madras.
345. „ P. S. Natesa Sastrial, Ellore.
346. „ M. M. P. L. Palaniappa Chettiar Avl, Nemathanpatti, Pudukotah.
347. „ M. M. P. L. Narayanam Chettiar Avl, do. do.
348. „ Annamalai Chettiar Avl. Kumbakonam.
349. „ M. L. M. Saminatha Chettiar Avl, Devakottah.
350. „ M. C. T. Somasundaram Chettiar Avl, do
351. „ P. K. Subramania Sastrial Avl, Palamaneri.
352. „ Kalyanaramayyar Avl, Survery office, Chepauk, Madras.
353. „ Kesavaram Naidu Avl, B.A., Revenue Survey office, Chepauk, Madras.
354. „ S. Rajaram Avl, Trichinopoly.
355. „ C. Bhaktavatsalu Avl, Madras.
356. „ Sri Swami Vedachalam Avl, Pallavaram.
357. „ C. Veeraraghava Mudaliar Avl, Pursewalkam, Madras.
358. „ K. Natanasabhapati Avl, Zemindar, Pudupalayam, Salem.
359. „ V. T. Subramania Mudaliar Avl, Vellal, Tenkasi.

360. M. R. Ry. K. Thyagaraja Iyer Avl, Collector's Office, Nellore.
361. " K. Rajaram Iyer Avl, B.A., B.L., Kumbakonam.
362. " Palvanna Mudaliar Avl, Tinnevelly.
363. " A. Mahalinga Iyer Avl, Sanyasigramam, Tinnevelly.
364. " C. N. Ganesa Iyer Avl, Chief Secretary office, Rangoon.
365. " J. R. Sivasubramaniam Avl, Svarnavilas, Egmore, Madras.
366. " J. T. Iyapillai Avl, Madras.
367. " V. Ramakrishnayya Garu, Dubash, Messrs. Oakes & Co., Madras.
368. " K. Chandrasekharam Pantulu garu, Dy. Superintendent of Police, Rajahmandry.
369. " Ramasami Sivam Avl, Coimbatore.
370. " Ranga Raju Avergal, Saidapet.
371. " Selvaranga Raju Avl, Coimbatore.
372. " Kumarasami Merkondar Avl, Mirasdar, Koonampatti, Tanjore.
373. " S. Isaac Avl, B.A. M.B. & C.M., Madras.
374. " V. Arumanayagam Nadar Avl, Tuticorin.
375. " Shanmugam Pillai Avl, Palamcottah.
376. " Sivakolandu Mudaliar Avl, Negapatam.
377. " Sreenivasa Mudaliar Avl, Mannargudi.
378. " Sathagopa Mudaliar Avl, do.
379. " Asirvadam Pillai Avl, Palamcottah.
380. " Mannarsami Pillai Avl, Trichinopoly.
381. " Cornelius Nadar Avl, Salem.
382. " Koilpillai Nadar Avl, Trichinopoly.
383. " Nargunam Nadar Avl, Deputy Collector, South Arcot District.
384. " Aaron Devadasan Avl, B.A., Negapatam.
385. " F. B. Selvanayagam Avl, B.A. Deputy Superintendent, Calicut.
386. " Vellaye Tevar Avl, Surandai, Tinnevelly.
387. " Arunachala Mooppanar Avl. do.
388. " Venkatarama Iyengar Avl, Village Munsiff, Surandai, Tinnevelly.
389. " Dorasami Nadar, Anamalaipatti.
390. " Ponnambala Pulavanar Avl, do.
391. " Devabhakti Kavundar Avl, Vehambur, Dindigul.
392. " A. Nallatambi Conductor Avl, Octumbe est Demodera, Ceylon.
393. " Periakaruppam Servai Avl, Kandi, Ceylon.
394. " William Lamech Avl, B.A., Tahsildar, Tanjore District.
395. " A. V. Velupillai Avl, Rangoon.
396. " Narayanasami Mudaliar Avl, Retired Post Master, Tiruvarur.
397. " Subramania Iyer Avl, Rao Bahadur, Superintendent District Jail, Tanjore.
398. " Nyina Pillai Maraycayar Avl, Muttupet.
399. " Satagopa Ramanujachettiar Avl, Messrs. Wenlock & Co., Madras.
400. " G. Alwar Chettiar Avl, G. R. C. Press, Madras.
401. " Dorasami Iyer Avergal, Madras.
402. " Mahmed Khan Saheb Avl, Deputy Superintendent of Police, Tanjore.
403. " Satyanesa Nadar Avl, B.A., Tahsildar, Nagercoil.
404. " Arumanayagam Avl, B.A., B.L., District Munsiff, Trevandrum.
405. " R. Asirvadam Avl, Govt. Telegraph Master, Bellary.

406. ,, A. Samuel Avl, Asst. Supdt. of Police, Nagercoil.
407. ,, Abel Arulanandam Avl, M.A., Professor, Kumbakonam.
408. ,, Manonmani Nadar Avl, B.A., Inspector of Salt, Tanjore.
409. ,, Kumarasami Nadar Avl, Inspector of Salt, Porayar.
410. ,, B. Abraham Avl, British Customs Collector, Pondicherry.
411. ,, Siluvaimuttu Avl, B A., B.L., Madura.
412. ,, Athicha Nadar Avl, B.A., B.L., Srivaikuntam.
413. ,, Visuva Nadar Avl, Vakil, Satur.
414. ,, A. V. Joseph Avl, Timber Merchant, Rangoon.
415. ,, Daniel G. Moses Avl, B.A.,L.T., Chingleput.
416. ,, Paul C. Joseph Avl, Nagercoil.
417. ,, Sundararaj Gnanaolivu Avl, B. A., L. T., Madras.
418. ,, S. K. I. Abdul Rahiman Saheb Avl, Salem.
419. ,, Dorasami Nadar Avl, Police Inspector, Guntakal.
420. ,, Rao Bahadur J. Manickyavasaka Nadar Avl, Supdt. of Police, Tinnevelly.
421. ,, Moses Tangayya Avl, M. A., Christian College, Madras.
422. ,, Moses Andrew Avl, M. A., Madras.
423. ,, Devanesam Avl, M. A, Christian College, Madras.
424. ,, Chinnasami Nadar Avl, B. A., Sub-Registrar, Walajapet.
425. ,, Gnanasikhamani Nadar Avl, B. A., B. L., District Munsiff, Salem.
426. ,, Joseph Nadar Avl, Vakil, Srivaikuntam.
427. ,, S. Swamidas Avl, Vepery, Madras.
428. ,, M. S. Santanam Iyengar Avl, Sanskrit College, Tiruvadi.

---

1. The first Inaugural Sub-Committee assembled on 14th February, 1912.
2. ,, first Conference met on 27th May 1912.
3. ,, second ,, ,, 21st August 1912.
4. ,, third ,, ,, 19th April 1913.
5. ,, fourth ,, ,, 9th August 1913.
6. ,, fifth ,, ,, 18th April 1914.
7. ,, sixth ,, ,, 24th October 1914.

6. Opinion of Dewan V. P. Madhava Row, C. I. E., on the Sangam.

He felt it a great honour to preside over this assembly of learned Musicians and he was indebted to Mr. Pandither for that kindness. While listening to various papers, he had formed certain impressions. His first observation was that Mr. Pandither had laid the public under great indebtedness to him by organising that Sangam and bringing together the Pandits to lecture to them on the various aspects of Indian Music. He had thereby helped the revival of that fine-art, which had, for several causes, been dwindling in that city—once the home of Music, as of many other Arts and many an Industry,—and offered substantial encouragement to those who were still devoted to it. He had, practically, created the opportunity and the means for the study and practice of the Indian system of music in this country, which was once the duty of kings to patronise. Such indeed was the work which Mr. A. Pandither had imposed upon himself to do, and it was extremely creditable to him that the work had also been financed solely by him. It was equally complimentary to the members and other well-wishers of the Sangam that they had all thought of relieving him, to some extent, by undertaking, gradually, to contribute their "mite" to the Sangam. Such co-operation was as necessary as it was praiseworthy, in great efforts like that. The day had come when the people themselves should come forward of their own accord, to support such movements as the Sangam, instead of expecting kings to do it for them. What Mr. A. Pandither had done is quite in line with the modern spirit of democracy, which has transferred the patronage of fine-arts from the hands of kings to those of the people. A spirit of democracy is clear in all the thoughts and deeds of the people, everywhere, and no wonder, what Mr. Pandither has well begun is enthusiastically taken up by his friends, interested in the famous Art. Mr. Pandither has revived the democratic spirit, and the spirit of co-operation as well. Another noticeable feature was that all the papers read at the meeting were in the Vernacular of the District. He would however, suggest that the papers be translated into English and widely published in all parts of this country. That would be in keeping with the recent awakening of their National consciousness due, in a measure, to the influence of English education. The effort to instruct the people in their own vernaculars was, indeed, praiseworthy. Almost every one of the papers read at the meeting deserved to be published, while, particularly, Mr. Pichamutthu Pillai's excellent discourse on some aspects of Indian and English Music is, perhaps, a revelation to those who have formed a poor, or, no idea, of Western Music. Mr. Abraham Pandither's happy idea of organising the Sangam had thus brought together such good thinkers and rendered exchange of thoughts easy and profitable. For all such services, the public are bound to be grateful to our host, Mr. Pandither, whose yeoman services are well known, and who has been helping the progress of his country in many ways. He would only pray that the Institution might continue for ever to grow in strength and usefulness and be an honour to the city, with which good music had always been associated. thanked them all for inviting him to take part in the proceedings of the Sangam.

7. Opinion of Mr. Ramakrishnaiyar Retired Sub-Judge of Palghat on the Sangam.

The Chairman then concluded the morning session by a short speech in the course of which he expressed his high appreciation of the two papers that had been just then read. He felt extremely grateful to Mr. Pandither for the task he had imposed upon himself in the cause of Indian Music. It was also appropriate that such a work should proceed from Tanjore as that town was once the home of that fine art and has been the birth place of many leading musicians of Southern India. Mr. Pandither has won the gratitude of all the Vidwans in this part of the country and elsewhere by the organisation of this Conference and though, at the outset, it may seem up-hill work, the periodical Conferences of the renowned musicians from different parts of the country might be productive of much good to the science itself. Nothing should discourage him. Music is given the foremost place among fine arts. No nation is without it. It is divine in its nature and inspires the spiritual in man. Indian music had reached a very high stage of perfection like other Indian arts as also the literature and philosophy of India. There is no department of life in India but has the inspiring influence of Music. At home, in social life, in temples, and in all functions of life Music is employed to enrich and to elevate. It was once the duty of kings in India to patronise the art and it is now the duty of people to work steadily for the revival, growth and development of that art.

8. Opinion of Mr. T. S. Balasubramania Iyer, Sub-Judge of Kumbakonam on the Sangam.

" Music in India is an ancient science. It is said that Indian Music was first revealed to the sages of India by the Gods. The ecstatic dancing of the God Nataraja, narrated in Hindu Mythology, is the first instance of the practice of music by the Gods. Music was a source of infinite delight to the Gods and lyrical songs were sung by them to the accompaniment of "Talam". Music is the essence of the Vedas. The recitation of the Veda is based on musical principles. The Rig Veda has evolved out of one sound and in the other Vedas we find a multiplicity of sounds evolving out of this one sound. In this manner "Gadhai" has two sounds and "Samam" exhibits three. How out of these three, seven sounds came into existence has been discussed by writers like Panini. Thus, music which had its origin in the Vedas and which was practised in the Deva Loka gave rise to other arts such as the art of dancing and Sahityam. Music is otherwise called the Gandharva Vedam, because of the many arts that are allied to it. The glory of music is only known to those that practise it with devotion. In the dance of the God, Sabhesa, Maha Vishnu, Brahma, Ganesa and all the Devas round the seat of the

Lord took part. Vishnu kept time and the audience were delighted with the music of His flute. Narada came to know the significance of this Great Dancer whereby Sabhesa danced away the mutability of human affairs and the transient nature of the things of this world. Saint Narada spread a knowledge of this music and unfolded its secrets to the three worlds. In the court of Indra music was abundantly popular. Sage Narada, sage Valmiki and his well known Sishyas, Sri-krishna and his trusted devotee Arjuna and many other illustrious people are known to have enjoyed and encouraged the practice of Music. In ancient India, musicians were generously rewarded and music had considerable influence on the formation of character. To elevate the mind, to help divine contemplation, music had a power which is peculiarly its own. In America and other places music is taught in schools and experts in this art received titles, degrees and diplomas. A distinguished lady, accomplished in English Music, was once in Madras. An ordinary Vydika Brahmin entertained her at a music party where he sang the Gopika Gitai. The lady was extremely pleased and exclaimed that it was only then that she really understood what true melody was—melody which is held so valuable in English music. The lady had never known what true melody was until she heard the Brahmin sing the Gopika Gita. Such singers are unfortunately becoming fewer in India. Abul Fazal has said that in the days of Emperor Akbar music was taught in all schools and a study of the science was made compulsory. Expert musicians from Arabia, from Europe and other countries joined hands with the Indian musicians in the court of the Emperor and a comparative study of the music of these three countries opened the way to much interesting musical research. In these days, alas! music is considered an impediment to a student's education. In the reign of Aurangazeb a knowledge of music was considered a crime. Musicians were punished. The benefits of the rule of Akbar were in course of time altered or modified. Manusi, the historian, has given a heart-rending account of Aurangazeb's hatred of music. The Emperor found a grave for music. One result of the researches in the field of music in the days of Akbar, we find in the songs of Kabhir Das, Vitthal Das, Purandhar Das and other illustrious musicians. Their songs are a medium between the ancient and the modern systems of music. Extremely delightful, these songs elevate the consciousness of man from the normal into the divine. There is much difference between the music of Das and modern music. Music is practised in various ways. Every country has its own method. We should acquire a knowledge of these methods in a way and enrich Indian music by importing into it all that is best in those methods. Indian musicians have not realised their duty in this respect. In South India we are told music attained considerable progress and became popular only recently. In the Telugu country the songs of Kshethria are original and full of ingenuity. The composition is plain, simple and figurative; the mind of the hearer is purified, redeemed and purged of all sins so as to become fixed in God. The songs of Kshethriya are rarely heard now-a-days. Nobody sings them. They are in vogue in dancing. Where is the glory of Indian music when songs of Kshethria are so neglected? Tanjore is described as the seat of Indian Music. Here, however, no two musicians agree. Each has his own mode of singing. Who could forget the songs of Dhikshatar, Tyagayya, Sama Sastri and other Mahatmas. Their soul-stirring lyrics embody the wisdom of Upanishads. Indeed, each lyric is an Upanishad by itself coming out of the author's heart in which the wisdom of the Upanishads is enshrined. All music is an expression of the divine and its power consists in purifying the mind and lifting it to a contemplation of the Eternal. That is the purpose of Musical Science. Brahmam, manifested as sound, is the cause of all creation, preservation and dissolution. Other manifestations of life are helping forces. That sound has the power to create, to preserve and to destroy is proved by science. The human soul that has evolved out of sound finds its expression in the seven sounds and penetrating through them becomes absorbed into the one. This aspect of the power of music has been revealed in the works of Alfred Tennyson, the poet-laureate. He describes his vision when contemplating upon the word which is the symbol of his name. The power of sound, of Manthra, has been understood by people of other religions belonging to other countries. Jesus and Muhammed are known to have realised the potentiality of sound.

In India the value of music depends upon the nature of those who practise it. Its value is judged by the purpose for which it is employed. Those who do not understand the glory of music bring discredit upon the science by its indiscriminate use. Music, as now-a-days practised in India, has this draw-back. On account of incompetent singers, the science itself suffers. The practice and employment of music must be on the lines of spiritual devotion. Music, bereft of the spiritual element in it and employed exclusively for bread-winning, is of no use. That generation of musicians who understood the right use of music seems to have become extinct. There is no one who now practises the science on the lines adopted by them. Modern singers sing under cover of what they call Manobhavam. One could scarcely identify the songs of Tyagayya when sung by these people. The mode of singing adopted by these musicians is altogether new and does not conform to any science or rule or definite purpose; there is no consistency. This, they call the play of their Manobhavam. What wonder then, if, in these circumstances, the sicence of music should deteriorate? No science will thrive if practised in the manner adopted by these musicians. Astrology, music, medicine and other sciences will be no-where if understood and practised in this way. Students of music live upon the reputation of their ancestors and neglect the rules of the science itself. Where practice does not conform to the rules of the science no true knowledge can be gained. No science will flourish where the students make a departure from the accepted rules. India needs accomplished musicians endowed with a sense of responsibility and competent students who could learn the science and carry their knowledge with dignity. Students of music should realise the harm they may do to the science itself by indiscrete use of their gifts. In view of these defects it has long been my desire to establish a Sabha. That desire is fulfilled and I owe that good fortune to Mr. Pandither. It is beyond my power to complement him adequately for the trouble he has taken. My joy is unbounded when I think of the object of the Sabha and the excellent manner in which everything is conducted. We all now heard the children Mr. Abraham Pandither sing. All the characteristics of a good song, such as Talam, Layam, Swaram, Varnam, Mettu &c. are there. To these are added a distinct voice, a deep seated devotion and invention all their own. When I contemplate on the music I have just heard from them, I feel that the ancient reputation of Indian music has come back and all the corruptions that have crept into it have disappeared. We in Madras were working hard for several years to found a Sabha to encourage the practice of music and to reward competent musicians. It had long been my desire to organise a Library of Musical works, to have a collection of all musical instruments, to gather together all the Vidwans and encourage music in all possible ways. There are in Madras the Saraswati Sabha, the Parthasarathi Sabha and the Krishna Gana Sabha. To earn money by singing, or, to reward musicians for their skill, is no good to the science itself. To use Music for mercenary ends is not the right use of music. We cannot understand the real power of music when one sings for money. The effect of music is to stimulate the divine in us. When this object is realised and when music is practised in the light of that principle then alone could we talk of doing something for the up-keep of the science itself. If the practice of music is allowed to go on as hitherto, very soon Indian Music would dwindle like the art of dancing and would be on the same level with it. Nobody has investigated minutely the art of dancing. There is no one to explain to us its significance. Indian music is threatened with a similar fate. Like other sciences this science of music also should be studied according to the rules laid down by the Great Ones. A firm devotion to God, purity of body, purity of word, thought and deed, a realisation of the glory of music and the methods of its use—these are the necessary qualifications for a student of Indian music. No true idea of the science of music can be gained without deep seated piety to God. The musicians from Bengal are well known. They earn thousands of rupees every day, yet it can by no means be said that our Vidwans are in any respect behind them. The Guvais of Bengal are much respected for the knowledge of science and their scientific training they show. The Vidwans in this part of the country have no taste for research. They are content to exhibit their own skill in order to earn money. They forget their duty to the science itself and do nothing to show its glory. The end of Music is the attainment of spiritual bliss and I have nothing but pity for those who sing for money. I appeal in the name of the almighty to the Vidwans, present here to do all that lies in their power to promote the object of this Sangam. The scientific methods of the savants of India should be carefully investigated, and modern music should be purged of all its defects. Let Music be studied and practised for the Divine. All music is but an expression of His glory and those that hear a musician should feel the presence of the Divine sound and be absorbed into it. Such is the state to which Indian music should be restored by the united efforts of the Vidwans that belong to this Sabha and I appeal to them to pray to God for help to gain this object of the Sabha. If every Vidwan will bear this view in mind he will not only earn the blessings of the Supreme, but will become a source of inspiration to the other nations abroad who will learn to see in the musical system of India a science that is no less marvellous than any of the other sciences for which it has become justly famous. May this credit become ours.

9. A few important remarks about the Sangam.

When we look back upon the circumstances that led to the establishment of the Sangam we notice that M.R.Ry. Muttya Bhagavatar Avergal of Harikesavanallur was of great help to us. M.R.Ry. *Veena* Venkataramanadoss, Samasthana Vidwan of Vijayanagaram was also very helpful in spite of many difficulties. Again, M.R.Ry. Panchapakesa Bhagavatar Avergal who has taken great pains in teaching the violin and Karnatic music to my children, M.R.Ry. A. G. Pichaimutthu Avergal, B.A.,L.T., of Tanjore, the English Music instructor to them, and M.R.Ry. *Veena* Vencatachalam Iyer, the Veena tutor, helped in singing along with my children at the commencement and end of every conference. Many Vidwans read essays on subjects approved and selected by the conference, and many others demonstrated the Sancharams of Ragas by singing them, and by minutely enquiring into the subtle points which came for discussion. M.R.Ry. V. Ramayya Garu, B.A. is also rendering all possible help by looking to the comforts of the guests assembled at the conferences.

As a result of the enquiry made as regards Srutis, many new theories which have not the slightest connection with those of the Karnatic music have come to light, such as the Dwavimsati Srutis, the Enharmonic Scale, the 53 Srutis of Bosanquet, the 27 of Clements and other theories. The cropping up of these theories although it has robbed us of precious time, yet, seeing the advantage of considering these theories before the Srutis of the Karnatic music are firmly established, we have entered into their merits fully. Some are trying their best to fix the Srutis occurring in the Geetams in use by various means. Others are quite anxious that enquiries should be made into Karnatic music in all possible directions and to join the Sangam and render every help. M.R.Ry. Madhava Row Avergal, C.I.E., the Dewan of Baroda, M.R.Ry. Ramakrishna Iyer Avergal, B.A.,B.L., Retired Sub-Judge of Palghat, and M.R.Ry. Balasubramania Iyer Avergal, B.A.,B.L., Sub-Judge of Kumbakonam, presided at the meetings of the conference and encouraged the members and advised them on many rare subjects. Leading gentlemen like M.R.Ry. Rai Bahadur Swaminatha Vijaya Thevar Avergal, Zemindar of Papanad, M.R.Ry. Appasami Vandayar Avergal of Poondi, M.R.Ry. Rao Bahadur Annasami Tevar Avergal of Ukkadai, M.R.Ry. K. V. Sreenivasa Iyengar Avergal, B.A.,L.T., Deputy Collector, M.R.Ry. Tiruvenkatachariar, Avergal, B.A.,B.L., Sub-Judge, M.R.Ry. Kodandaramanjulu Naidu Avergal, B.A.,B L., Sub-Judge, M.R.Ry. T. Seshayya Avergal, B.A., Deputy Collector, M.R.Ry. Rao Sahib D. Dravya Nadar Avergal, B.A., Deputy Collector, M.R.Ry. Y. V. Sreenivasa Iyer Avergal, Deputy Collector, M.R.Ry. Vijayaraghavachariar Avergal, M.A., Postmaster, M.R.Ry. Rao Bahadur K. S. Sreenivasam Pillai Avergal, M.R.Ry. Gopalasami Ragunatha Rajaliar of Haridwaramangalam and others, and distinguished Tamil Vidwans like Arasan Shanmukham Pillai Avergal, M.R.Ry. Savariroya Pillai Avergal, M.R.A.S., M.R.Ry. Seturama Bharatiar Avergal, M.R.Ry. Olaganatha Pillai Avergal and M.R Ry. Devaprasadam Pillai Avergal, and others were present at the meetings to the encouragement of the members.

Seeing that all the distinguished musicians and others who attend the meetings take a deep interest, show mutual love and look upon the meeting day as a great festival, we have cause to say that good days are in store for the Tanjore Sangeeta Vidya Mahajana Sangam.

10. Conclusion.

The doubt about the Srutis in use in South Indian music, which arose from the discussions in the Sangeeta Vidya Mahajana Sangam, led us to write the above few lines. Before fixing the Srutis in use in South Indian music, it was found expedient to discuss fully the established theories of others in the same field. So it was found necessary to enquire fully into the different opinions of the authors of the Sanskrit works, such as Sangeeta Ratnakaram, Sangeeta Parijatam, Raga vibodham, and Swara mela kala nidhi, the theory of the Enharmonic Scale of the west and the system of Pythagoras, the theories of Mercator, Poole, Thompson, White and Bosanquet with their 53 Srutis, the 22 Srutis of Nagoji Row and Deval, the 27 Srutis of Clements and the opinion of Helmholtz, the author of "Sensations of Tone", on the subject.

On entering into the merits of the above theories, we had to enquire into the opinion of the ancient Tamil literature on the subject. This led us on to conclude that the music of South India and the fundamental rules thereof were of great antiquity, that music had attained a high state of efficiency even during the period of the first Sangam which existed in Madura which was in the destroyed continent of Lemuria, and that the three Angams-Iyal Isai and Natakam, were first found in the Tamil language only and were afterwards practised and cultivated in other countries and languages. Moreover, it was seen that the system of Srutis as well as Ganams found in ancient literature were so varied as to render it impossible to be mastered. So we were led on to jot down a few historical records as regards South Indian Music which was in use in the Tamil Country. But these are only very few. However, we hope that these will serve at least as land marks which might lead earnest enquirers into the way of truth.

Space did not allow us to commit to writing all the results of our researches. But we have noted the following points:—After offering a few remarks about the existence of music for four and five thousand years only in places other than India, we went on briefly to say how music was in India prior to and posterior to the Deluge, 5,000 years ago, how South India was noted for its very ancient music, how South Madura which existed long before and the Tamil Sangam were in an exalted state, how the Tamil language was an ancient one and how music was largely used by those who spoke the Tamil language alone, how music degenerated and passed into other hands after the destruction of South Madura and Kapatapuram and the decline of the Pandya kingdom and how Desikam was introduced into South Indian Music from that time forward.

In addition to this we have also recorded the opinions of many gentlemen on South Indian Music, and Hindustani and Indian Music.

We have also given to a certain extent the history of the three Sangams patronised by the Pandya sovereigns, and of the fourth Sangam which exists at the present day; we have also quoted the two inscriptions which go to prove how music was under the patronage of the Chola sovereigns after the extinction of the Pandya kingdom and how it was maintained by gifts to the temple musicians; we have also pointed how the Nayak and the Mahratta Rajas as well as many nobles in the Chola kingdom helped to maintain the progress of music and we have appended also a list of the renowned musicians past and present.

We have next attempted to give the objects with which the Tanjore Sangeeta Mahajana Sangam was organised, *viz*, for enquiring into the primary system which would throw light upon the fundamental Srutis and Ragas of the Karnatic Music which are so difficult to be understood and to disseminate the system broadcast for the benefit of all. The names of those gentlemen who presided at the deliberations of the conference, the names of those who read essays on various subjects, and the names of the patrons, members and well wishers of the Sangam have also been appended.

What we have mentioned above are but a drop in the vast ocean of the history and progress of music. We shall mention from time to time, whenever space permits, other matters connected with music. Any suggestions by learned gentlemen, either in the way of corrections or additions, will be very thankfully received and given a place in the next edition.

It is a matter for universal acceptance that the chief elements of the science of music are the Swarams and the minuter Srutis. Yet there is a vast difference of opinion on this fundamental subject. To come to a definite conclusion regarding them is a matter of the highest importance. As our primary duty is to examine the merits of the various theories as regards Srutis we have reserved our enquiry into the 22 Srutis for the Second part.

END OF PART I.

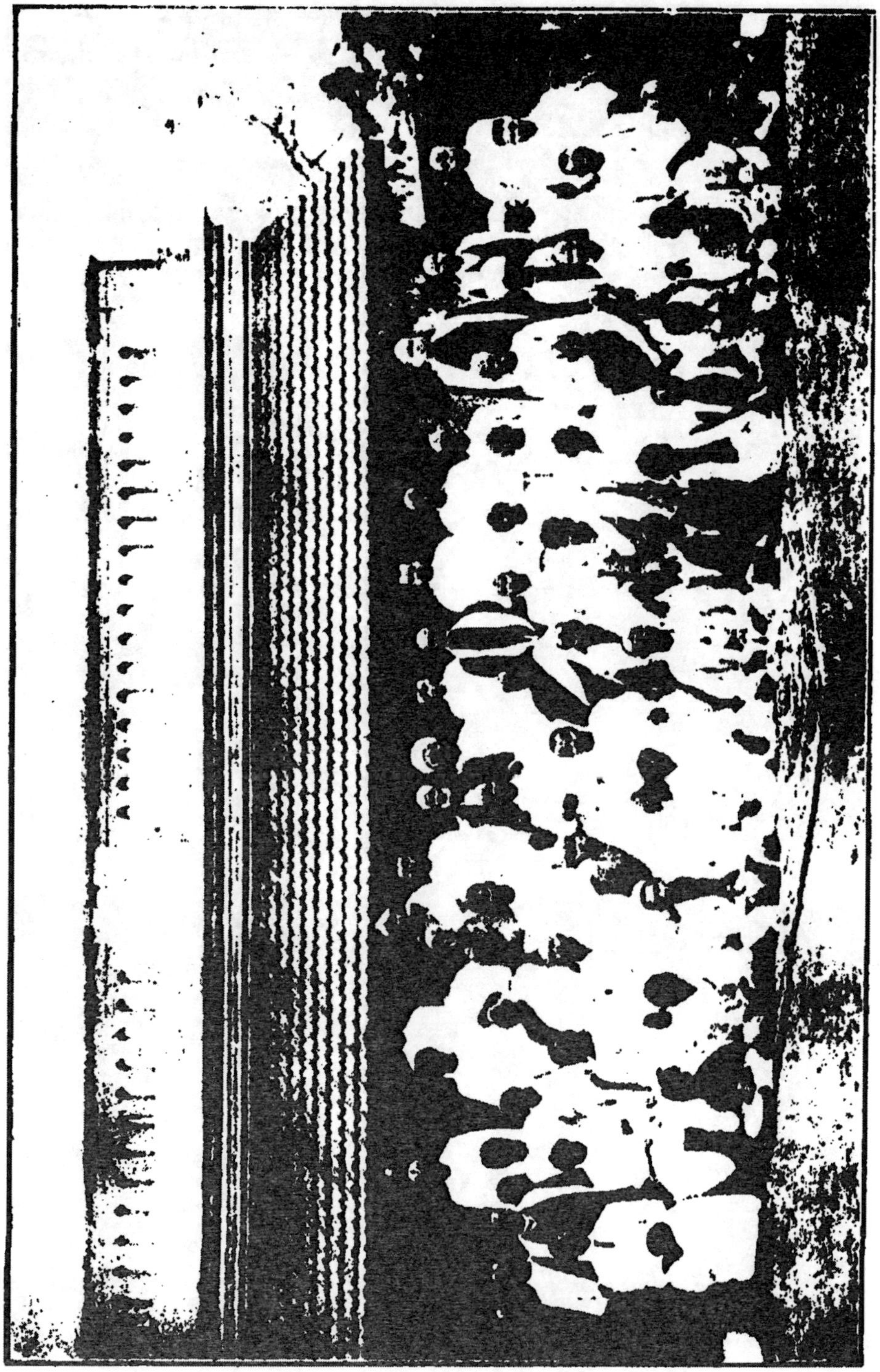

A Group Photo of the Musicians and Members of the Sabha who were Present at the 1st Conference, 27th May, 1912.

A Group Photo of the Musicians and Members of the Sabha who were present at the 2nd Conference, 31st August, 1912.

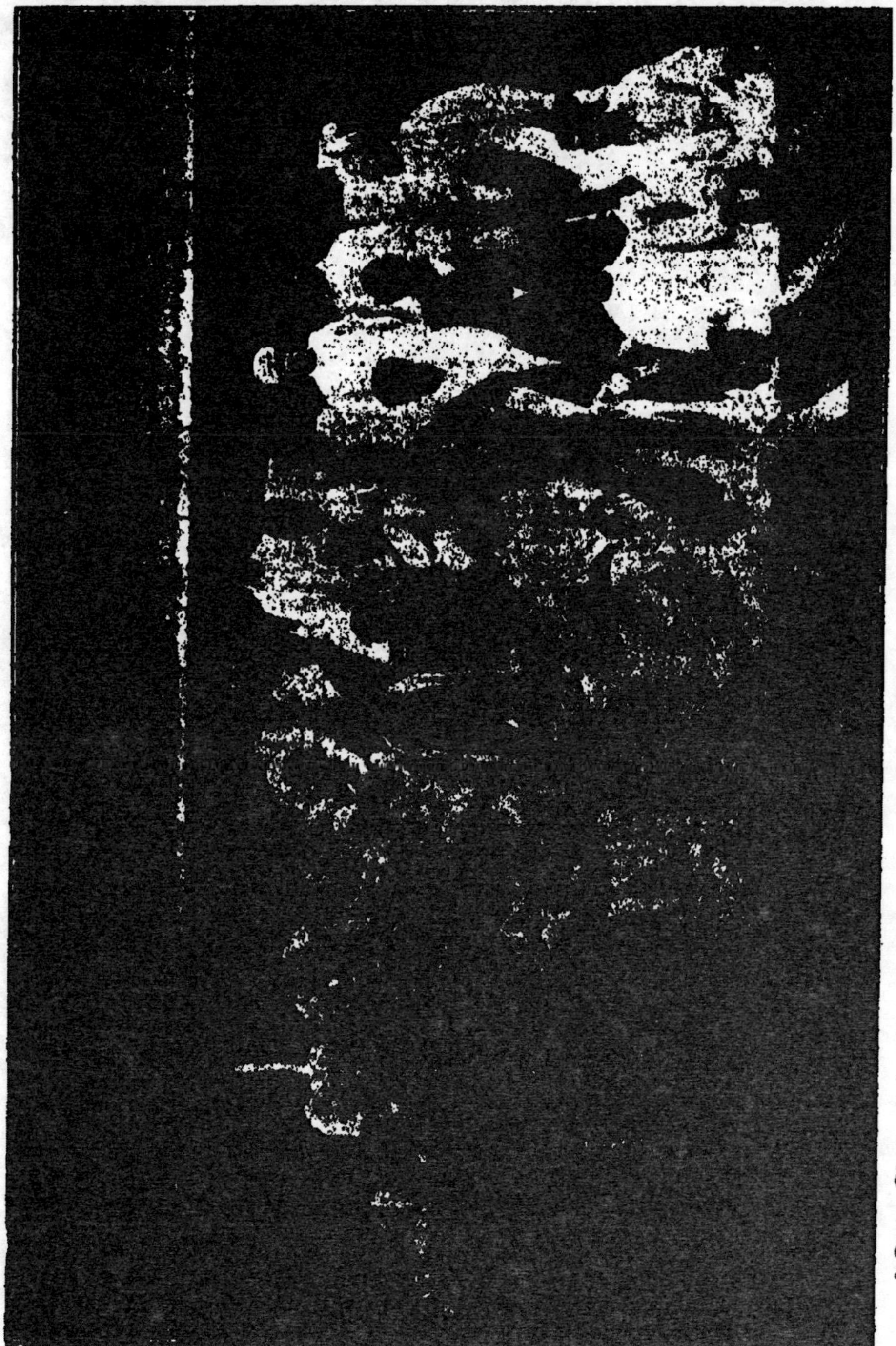

A Group Photo of the Musicians and Members of the Sabha who were present at the 3rd Conference, 19th April, 1913.

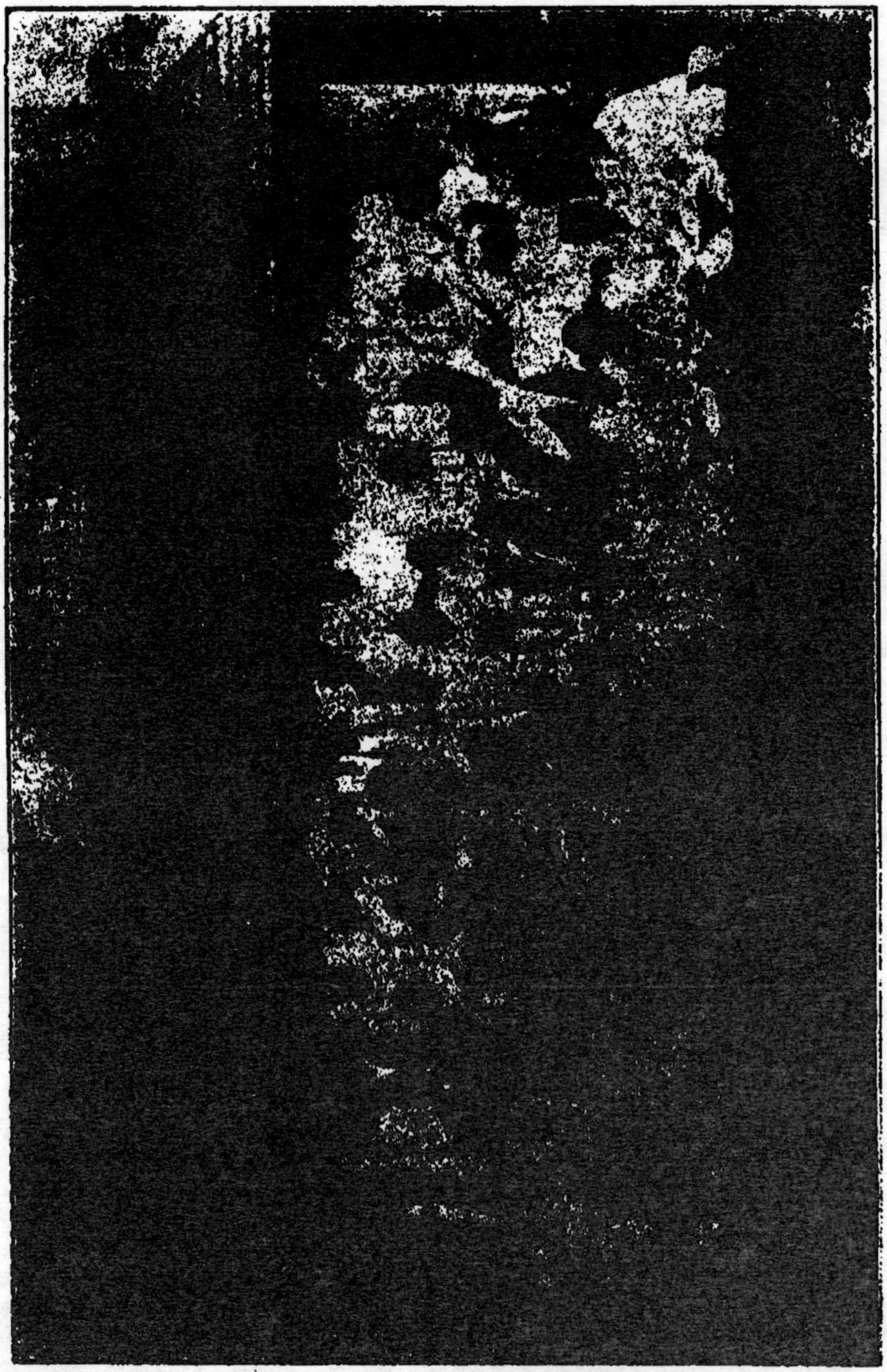

A Group Photo of the Musicians and Members of the Sabha who were present at the 4th Conference, 9th August, 1913.

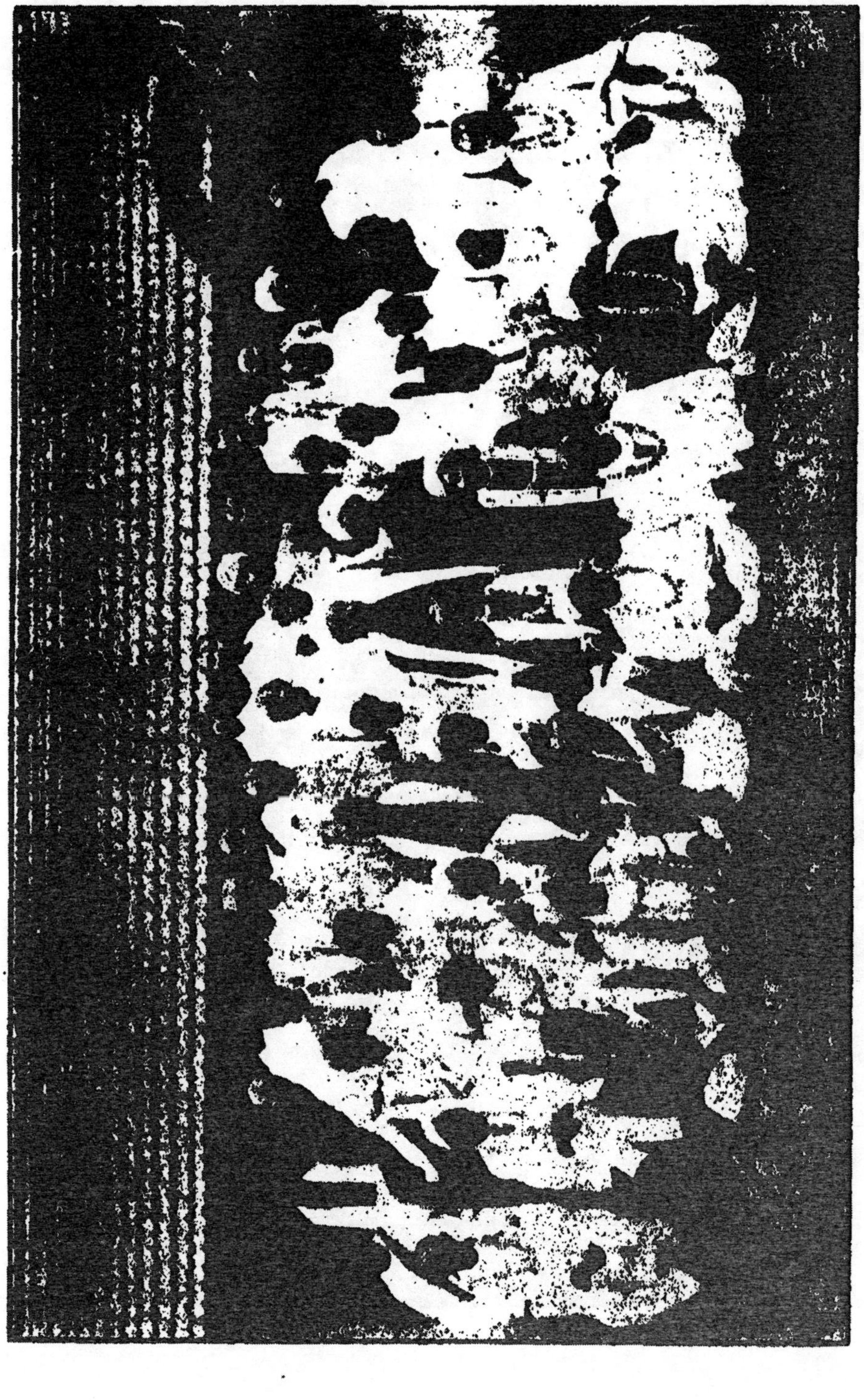

A Group Photo of the Musicians and Members of the Sabha who were present at the 9th Conference, 19th April, 1914.

A Group Photo of the Musicians and Members of the Sabha who were present at the 6th Conference, 24th October, 1914.

KARUNAMIRTHA SAGARAM.

FIRST BOOK.

SECOND PART.

ON SRUTIS.

KARUNAMIRTHA SAGARAM.

FIRST BOOK.

SECOND PART.

THE 22 SRUTIS.

WE shall do well first to enquire into the theory of the 22 Srutis as popularly held and as propounded by Sarnga Devar and then proceed to examine the Srutis of the Karnatic music, inasmuch as many in this famous country hold pronounced opinions on the 22 Srutis that they are the conclusions of Sarnga Devar and many of the Vidwans of South Indian music are also of opinion that the Srutis in use in South Indian music are the same.

A few points about Sarnga Devar and the Sootrams he quotes in favour of his theory of Srutis.

The author of Sangeeta Ratnakaram is Sarnga Devar who was a native of Kashmir. He belonged to the Varunaganarishi Kulam. He was the contemporary of Singana Raja (Somaraja Maharaja) who ruled in Deogiri (near Aurangabad in Hyderabad) from 1210-1247 A. D. This work seems to have been written at the request of this Raja. He has brought out beautifully in his work all the important elements of the music in use during his time. It is the first duty of every musician to know his views on Srutis, inasmuch as he discusses the subject fully and his work has the additional sanction of antiquity. We quote *verbatim* a few Sootrams from the chapter on "Swarams" in his work "Sangeeta Ratnakaram".

Prepare two Veenas with 22 wires each. Tune the string of one of the Veenas so that it might sound the lowest possible note. Tune the next wire so that it might give a little higher note but see that no other sound is possible between the 2 notes given by the 2 wires. Go on tuning all the wires on this principle. Then the 22 wires will give 22 ascending series of notes. Tune the other Veena also on the same principle. Of these the SA will be a Swaram of 4 Srutis and will sound on the 4th wire. The 3 Srutis of RI will be on the 5th, 6th and 7th wires. The 2 Srutis of GA will be on the 8th and 9th wires. The 4 Srutis of MA will sound on the 10th, 11th, 12th and the 13th wires. The 4 Srutis of PA will be on the 14th, 15th, 16th and the 17th wires. The 3 Srutis of DHA will sound on the 18th, 19th and 20th wires. The 2 NIS will sound on the 21st and 22nd wires. Grant that one of these Veenas is the Dhruva Veena and the other Chala Veena. Change the notes of the Chala Veena according to my direction. If Sapta Swarams were arranged from the 3rd Sruti of the Shadjamam which comes after the 4th Shadjamam you will have one Sruti less. Again if 2 Srutis were lessened, the GA and the NI will obtain one of the srutis of RI and DHA. If 3 srutis were lessened, the RI and the DHA will obtain 4 of the Srutis of SA and PA. If 4 Srutis were lessened, the NI, GA, MA of the Dhruva Veena will correspond to the SA, MA, PA of the Chala Veena. In other words the SA, MA, PA will commence on the 22nd, 9th and the 13th wires respectively. The alteration of 4 Srutis in this manner, makes the swarams of the Dhruva Veena correspond with those of the Chala Veena. This is how Swarams are mathematically calculated. From these Srutis the 7 Swarams SA, RI, GA, MA, PA, DHA and NI are created.

We shall do well to quote here a few lines from Clements who has literally translated some of the Sootrams from Sangeeta Ratnakaram.

We give below the translation of Clements of some of the Sootrams from Sangeeta Ratnakaram treating on the 22 Srutis :—

Introduction to the Study of Indian Music by E. Clements, P. 53.

THE SANGIT RATNAKAR.

"Take two Vinas with 22 wires each and tune as follows. Let the first wire give the lowest possible note. The next a note a little higher and so on, so that between the notes given by any two adjacent wires a third note is impossible.

These successive notes are the Srutis. *Sa* will stand on the fourth wire, being a Svara of four Srutis ; *Ri* will be on the third wire counting from the fifth ; *Ga* which has only two Srutis will fall on the second counting from the eighth ; *Ma* being of four Srutis on the fourth counting from the tenth ; *Pa* on the fourth, counting from the fourteenth ; *Dha* on the third after *Pa* ; *Ni* on the second after *Dha* ; so *Ni* will fall on the twenty-second Sruti."

The two translations given above are identical in our opinion. But the interpretation of the two in different ways has given rise to conflicting opinions as regards Srutis. To add to this, a number of books are being published which have mixed together the theory of Srutis according to the author of Parijatam, that according to Western Science and that according to Karnatic Music and which at the same time retain the name of Dwavimsati Srutis so as to bring about a kind of compromise between ancient and modern theories and which in addition enforce their own mixed theories upon others and fix the mode of singing also on the same lines. Those who realise these variety of opinions will surely sympathise with the miserable state of Indian music. Just as people in India do not realise the importance of pure drinking water, so also they do not care for the purity of Indian music, which is one of the chief causes of its decline. However, a few amsams have been happily preserved, more owing to the system of oral transmission and the practice of learning by rote than by any other cause, and are as bright gems which serve to reflect the glory of the ancient music. So it is not an easy matter to establish the right theory about the Srutis with the help of these varied opinions.

However, we also desire to say a few words about the Srutis in use in Indian music. We also make bold to say that our opinions on the Srutis are the correct ones and we hope to put an end for ever to the controversy on the Srutis in Indian Music, just as the other gentlemen who have handled the subject have declared before. We beg to be excused for our boldness. We were led on to study this subject mainly by reading the works of many authors who have spent their time, energy and substance on this question. We dare say that enquirers on Srutis would have deeply studied tbe Adhyaya on Swarams in the ancient and elaborate work Sangeeta Ratnakaram. But we arrive from the mathematical calculations of those who have written on Srutis, that the Srutis mentioned in the Adhyaya are all gone out of use. We find, for example, that with the exception of the Sa and its octave above, no Sruti agrees in calculation with the 22 Srutis mentioned in Sangeeta Ratnakaram. It is not fair that, in an attempt to remove a few errors that had crept into an ancient system, the whole system itself should be radically changed. Moreover, we do not find many reasons for the existence of diversity of opinion as regards Srutis, nor do we find any definite arrangements in the few reasons given.

It is clearly seen that the Sootrams of Sangeeta Ratnakaram have not been properly interpreted. When we notice the conflicting opinions on Srutis of writers in the North, we come to the conclusion that either the system of modern music or the opinion of Sarnga Dev must be wrong. Sarnga Dev has explained a difficult system in very easy language. Just as the eye which sees everything and which can be seen by every one is not seen by the possessor himself, so also is this system of Sarnga Dev, which can be easily grasped by all. We shall do well to consider *first* the theories of Sahasra Buddhi, Raja Surendra Mohan Tagore and others whose theories are to a certain extent based upon the system of Sarnga Devar, *secondly*, the theories of writers like Deval and Clements whose system is based upon Hindustani music, and *thirdly*, the theories of those who confuse together the Srutis of Western and other alien music and declare it to be the Karnatic system. After dealing with these we shall give the right interpretation of the system of Sarnga Devar and close with the Srutis as found in Karnatic music.

FIRST.

I. The first class of writers whose theory of Srutis resembles that of Sarnga Dev in measurement.

THE 22 SRUTIS OF SAHASRA BUDDHI.

The following is the opinion of Srutis of Sahasra Buddhi, the Honorary Secretary of the Poona Gayan Samaj, who has taken great pains in working for the progress of Indian music.

Hindu Music and the Gayan Samaj. Pt. ii. P. 13.

"If a monochord with moveable bridge be taken, and a space equal to 44 units be measured and the bridge shifted to this point, the string when struck will yield a note; if we start with this note as the tonic or key-note and run through the Gamut by shifting the bridge (the Sanskrit writers affirm) the following facts will be observed. Sa will be produced at the distance 44; *Ri* at 40; *Ga* at 37; *Ma* at 35; *Pa* at 31; *Dha* at 27; *Ni* at 24; and *Sa* again at 22; but latter *Sa* will be twice as intense as the former."

In order to make the statement of the author clear to our readers we have appended a table where we first state his own measurement of the 22 Srutis and then their measurement if 32 inches be taken, adding also the fractions to show the respective places of the srutis in the octave and the number of vibrations of the other srutis if Sa were five hundred and forty.

N. B. As the opinions and measurements and vibrations of the Srutis are different in different writers we have taken 32 inches as the standard length of the wire and 540 as the number of vibrations of the Tonic Sa and have converted the calculations of others to this uniform standard, so that every one can understand them easily at sight.

Though this does not at all agree with the system of 22 Srutis of Sarnga Dev, we have given the cents for each Sruti as well as the difference between Srutis. Our readers can easily compare them.

N. B. He takes the length of the wire to be 44, and places the Sa of the Tara Sthayi in the exact middle. This is easily understood. Then the length of the Madhya Sthayi below the Tara Sthayi becomes 22 and thus the 22 Srutis are located in each of the 22 places. For example, if we take the whole length to be 44 inches, then we get a sruti for each of the inches and the Madhya Sthayi Sa comes on the 22nd Sruti. He takes the 1st of the four Srutis of Sa as the Tonic or the ground Sa. So the 4 Srutis of Sa come between the 44th and the 41st inches, the 3 of Ri between 40 and 38, the 2 of Ga on the 37th and 36th, the 4 Srutis of Ma between the 35th and 32nd, the 4 of Pa between 31st and 28th, the 3 of Dha between 27th and 25th and the 2 Srutis of Ni on the 24th and 23rd inches. Thus he accounts for the 22 Srutis, 4 Sas, 3 Ris, 2 Gas, 4 Mas, 4 Pas, 3 Dhas and 2 Nis.

TABLE 1

Showing the 22 Srutis of the Indian Music according to Mr. Sahasra Buddhi's

Interpretation of Sangeeta Ratnakaram.

The No. of the Swaram or Sruti.	The Name of the Swaram or Sruti.	Fraction showing the position of other Swarams or Srutis granting that Tonic SA is 1.	Decimal Fractions.	The position of the Swarams or Srutis in a wire of 32 inches length.	Cents.	Cents for the intervals of the Srutis.	The Number of vibrations of each Sruti granting Tonic SA=540.
1	2	3	4	5	6	7	8
			⊕	⊕	⊕	⊕	⊕
1	S_1	1	1·0000	32	0		540
2	S_2	43/44	·9773	31·27	40	40	552·6
3	S_3	42/44	·9545	30·55	81	41	565·7
4	S_4	41/44	·9318	29·82	122	41	579·5
5	Ri_1	40/44	·9091	29·09	165	43	594
6	Ri_2	39/44	·8864	28·36	209	44	609·2
7	Ri_3	38/44	·8636	27·64	254	45	625·3
8	G_1	37/44	·8409	26·91	300	46	642·2
9	G_2	36/44	·8182	26·18	347	47	660
10	M_1	35/44	·7955	25·45	396	49	678·9
11	M_2	34/44	·7727	24·73	446	50	698·8
12	M_3	33/44	·7500	24	498	52	720
13	M_4	32/44	·7273	23·27	551	53	742·5
14	P_1	31/44	·7045	22·55	606	55	766·5
15	P_2	30/44	·6818	21·82	663	57	792
16	P_3	29/44	·6591	21·09	722	59	819·3
17	P_4	28/44	·6364	20·36	783	61	848·6
18	D_1	27/44	·6136	19·64	845	62	880
19	D_2	26/44	·5909	18·91	911	66	913·8
20	D_3	25/44	·5682	18·18	979	68	950·4
21	Ni_1	24/44	·5455	17·45	1049	70	990
22	Ni_2	23/44	·5227	16·73	1123	74	1033
1	S'_1	22/44	·5000	16	1200	77	1080

The Calculations in Columns marked ⊕ are our own.

There is one point to be noted here. In his Sangeeta Ratnakaram, Sarnga Devar says, " Tune the first wire so that it may give the lowest possible note, and the second that it might give the next higher note. See that no other sound is possible between the two wires. Tuning on this principle will give you an ascending series of notes." Here he only speaks about an ascending series of sounds, but does not imply that the length of the wires should also be equal and graduated. Sahasra Buddhi who has interpreted Saranga Dev will also remember the fact that if the sound of the Mandara Sthayi is one, that of Madhya Sthayi is double of it, while that of Tara Sthayi is four times of it and so on. If so, granting that the Madhya Sthayi ends with 22 inches, the Tara Sthayi must end with 11 inches, for as we ascend, the sound and the length of the wire vary in inverse ratio. In the same way the Swarams in a Sthayi gradually ascend and the octave ends with 2, if the Tonic Sa is 1. We all know that the Madhya Sthayi's range is the first half of a wire, that of the Tara Sthayi is a fourth from the centre, and that of Atitara Sthayi, an eighth from that of the Tara Sthayi, thus ascending in Geometrical Progression. In the same way as each Swaram in an octave progresses upwards, the length of the wire is diminished in Geometrical Progression. The Ri above the Tara Shadjam has half the length of the wire pertaining to Ri in the Madhya Sthayi while the Ri of the Madhya Sthayi has its length of wire double that of the Ri of the Tara Sthayi. But the Ni below the Shadjam of the Tara Sthayi is $\frac{1}{8}$ more than the measurement of the Ri above. Though there is a diminution of $\frac{1}{8}$ in the length of wire yet in sound it is $\frac{1}{8}$ more. Thus we see that the Sapta Swarams as they proceed to the next higher Sthayi gain in the vibrations of sounds but lessen in the length of wire. Instead, if the measurement of the wire be made exactly equal they differ in Swaram. In other words they will not agree with the Swarams mentioned by the author of Sangeeta Ratnakaram. Thus we see that the opinion of Sarnga Dev which says that the Swarams proceed in a gradual ascending series without any difference in the vibrations of sounds or in the measurement thereof contradicts the opinion of Sahasra Buddhi who emphasises the fact that the measurement of the Swarams as regards the length of wire should be equal and uniform. But we must notice that he says that Nadam should be of equal measurement. We may see in the Table on P. 247 his measurement of wire and that of Sarnga Dev, and also his calculation of the vibrations of each Swaram and that of Sarnga Dev.

He divides a Sthayi into 22 parts and says that the first 4 Srutis belong to Shadjam, but we all know that the 4th Sruti of the Shadjam is sounded near the Meru.

SECOND.

THE 22 SRUTIS OF RAJA SURENDRA MOHAN TAGORE.

Tagore was a resident of Calcutta. He made a collection of Indian musical instruments and sent them to the Paris Exhibition and wrote many treatises so that the Western nations might know Indian music also. In 1875 he wrote the work "Victoria Geetika" in the name of our Queen Empress and her ancestors. He has divided the Srutis of the Indian music as follows :—

Although we were unable to get at his original work we quote his system from Deval.

Hindu Musical Scale and 22 Srutis by K. B. Deval, P. 34.

Mr. Deval says that he (Raja Surendra Mohan Tagore) divided the whole speaking length of the wire into two halves, the whole giving the *Sa* or fundamental note and the half giving the *Sa*, the octave; both these notes are correct. Again he divided the first half into two equal parts, each being ¼ of the whole length. The first quarter of the wire he sub-divided into 9 equal parts calling each part a Sruti. And at the end of the 9th part is sounded a note Ma (at ¾ of the wire) which is correct. In the next quarter of the wire he made 13 equal subdivisions, each being also called a Sruti. Thus in all he got the 22 Srutis.

Deval mentions in the 34th and 35th pages of his book that Mᴀ comes exactly in the middle of the Sthayi. It seems, therefore, that he wants to divide the Sthayi into 22 Srutis.

TABLE 2

Showing the 22 Srutis of the Indian Music according to Mr. Rajah Surendr Mohana Tagore's Interpretation of Sangeeta Ratnakaram.

No. of Swaram or Sruti.	Name of Swaram or Sruti.	Fraction showing the Sthanam of other Srutis, granting that the Tonic SA is 1.	Decimal Fractions.	The position of Srutis in a wire of 32 inches length.	Cents.	Cents for the Sruti intervals.	No. of vibrations of each Sruti when SA=540.
1	2	3	4 ●	5 ●	6 ●	7 ●	8 ●
1	S_1	1		32·0			540·
2	S_2	35/36	·9722	31·1	49	49	555·4
3	S_3	34/36	·9444	30·2	99	50	571·8
4	S_4	33/36	·9167	29·3	151	52	589·1
5	Ri_1	32/36	·8889	28·4	204	53	607·5
6	Ri_2	31/36	·8611	27·5	259	55	627·1
7	Ri_3	30/36	·8333	26·6	316	57	648
8	G_1	29/36	·8056	25·7	374	58	670·3
9	G_2	28/36	·7778	24·8	435	61	694·3
10	M_1	27/36	·7500	24·0	498	63	720·
11	M_2	19/26	·7307	23·38	543	45	738·9
12	M_3	37/52	·7115	22·77	589	46	758·9
13	M_4	18/26	·6923	22·15	637	48	780·
14	P_1	35/52	·6731	21·54	685	48	802·3
15	P_2	17/26	·6538	20·92	736	51	825·9
16	P_3	33/52	·6346	20·31	787	51	850·9
17	P_4	16/26	·6154	19·69	841	54	877·5
18	D_1	31/52	·5962	19·08	895	54	905·8
19	D_2	15/26	·5769	18·46	952	57	936
20	D_3	29/52	·5577	17·85	1011	59	968·3
21	Ni_1	14/26	·5385	17·23	1072	61	1002·9
22	Ni_2	27/52	·5193	16·62	1135	63	1040
	S_1	13/26	·5000	16·00	1200	65	1080·

The Calculations in Columns marked ● are our own.

We notice a difference in the opinions of this writer and Sahasra Buddhi; Tagore divides the first quarter length of the wire into 9 exactly equal parts and the second quarter length above it into 13 equal parts. Though the parts might have been equally divided on the whole, we shall see there is a slight difference in the Swara Sthanams. When an octave is divided into 22 equal parts, according to Sahasra Buddhi, the 12th Sruti Sthanam becomes the exact centre. That means there are 2 Srutis above the MA which is the tenth. In other words the 3rd Sruti of the MA, which has 4 Srutis, becomes the middle. But in the opinion of Tagore, the middle Sruti is the MA with 9 Srutis. When the Madhya Sthayi is divided into equal parts by Sahasra Buddhi the 12th place becomes the ordinary MA in popular use. In other words it is $\frac{3}{4}$, and according to Tagore's calculation, the third MA. But his first MA or the 10th Sruti sounds exactly in the middle of the wire. So there is the difference of 2 Srutis between the two writers. According to Tagore the first of the 4 Srutis of MA sounds in the centre of the wire, whereas the third of the 4 Srutis of MA sounds in the middle according to Sahasra Buddhi. This difference of opinion should be noted.

Though MA sounds in the first quarter length of the wire (it may be a little above or below) Sarnga Dev does not say that the length below should be divided into 9 equal parts and the length above into 13 equal parts. Moreover as the length of the wire of the three Sthayis gradually becomes proportionately less as the sounds increase in pitch, the Swarams that occur in an octave need not necessarily have an equal length of wire. It is to be noted that instead of saying that the sounds should be equally divided, Tagore says that Srutis should occur in wires of equal length.

He divides the first quarter length of a wire into 9 equal parts and the next quarter length into 13 equal parts. Appended is the table which indicates where the Srutis occur in a wire of 32 inches length and the progression of the number of vibrations of the Srutis granting the SA to be 540 vibrations per second.

When we compare the Tables of Sahasra Buddhi and Tagore we find that with the exception of the Tonic SA and its octave no other Srutis agree. When we find that when even PA and MA do not agree we need not point out any further absurdity. We know the importance of these 2 Swarams in an octave. If we neglect these two there will be no other Swaram to harmonize with SA. Other Swarams might disagree but these two must agree. This is not what the author of Sangeeta Ratnakaram says. His theory is quite plain. But writers have interpreted it in many different ways. Their opinions will be noted one by one later on.

Tagore divides the octave into 22 parts and ascribes the first 4 srutis to SA. But we know that the fourth SA sounds near the Meru.

It is unnecessary to say further on this subject here. The author of Sangeeta Ratnakaram does not advocate this kind of division of the Octave.

THIRD.

II. The second class of writers who say that the Hindustani music is an adaptation of the system of Sarnga Dev.

THE 22 SRUTIS OF K. B. DEVAL.

Deval is a retired Deputy Collector of Sangli in the Southern Mahratta Country. He has written a treatise on Indian Music where he says that there are 22 Srutis in an octave. The following are the thirteen rules by which he derives his 22 Srutis :—

Sa$_1$ (C$_1$) ; Sa$_2$ (C$_2$).

1. "The whole length of the wire between the two fixed bridges gives the Fundamental Note *Sa*$_1$ (*C*$_1$). Let the length of the wire be 36 inches, let the note produced be called *Sa*$_1$ (*C*$_1$) and let its vibrations be 240 per second.

2. The note produced on half the length is in value equal to *Sa*$_1$ (*C*$_1$) and in pitch or vibrations it is double the Fundamental Note (*F. N.*)

The note produced on the length 18" is therefore *Sa*$_1$ (*C*$_1$) itself, but one octave higher. Let this note be called *Sa*$_2$ (*C*$_2$) to distinguish it from *Sa*$_1$ (*C*$_1$) the F. N. ; then the vibrations of *Sa*$_2$ (*C*$_2$) are double *i.e.* $2 \times 240 = 480$ per second.

3. The pitch of a note or its vibrations are inversely proportional to the length of the wire.

This rule is a legitimate inference from the above two rules. Rule (1) permits us to take any length for the Fundamental Note (F. N.) and according to rule (2) if the length is halved the pitch is doubled, and if the length is doubled the pitch or the number of vibrations is halved. If therefore $\frac{1}{3}$ length is taken the pitch or the number of vibrations produced will be trebled. Or, by generalization

4. The pitch varies inversely as the length and *vice versa*.

The above four rules may therefore be put in the form of a simple Formula for convenience of working and ready reference.

Let V_n = vibrations or pitch of the note on wire l_n inches long. U_n = The vibrations or pitch of *Sa*$_1$ (*Ca*$_1$) the F. N., here = 240.

l = the length of the wire of the F. N. here = 36 inches = 36".

Then

$$V_n \times l_n = U \times l \quad \ldots \ldots \ldots \ldots \text{(A)}$$

$$V_n = U \times \frac{l}{l_n} \quad \ldots \ldots \ldots \text{(B)}$$

$$l_n = U \times \frac{l}{V_n} \quad \ldots \ldots \ldots \text{(C)}$$

therefore if $V_n = 2\,U$

$$l_n = l/2 \quad \ldots \ldots \text{(D)}$$

Ma (F).

5. The note *Ma* (*F*) or the fourth note is produced at the middle of the Fundamental Note and its octave.

The note *Ma* is therefore produced at half the length of Sa_1 (C_1) and Sa_2 (C_2) or at $\frac{1}{2}$ (36"+18")=$\frac{1}{2}$ (54")=27". In other words the note of the wire 27" or 27 inches of the executive part of the wire will give out the 4th note or *Ma* (*F*) and by rule (4) formula (B) the pitch or vibrations of *Ma* (*F*) are equal to 320.

The formula (B) is

$$V_n = U \times \frac{l}{l_n}. \text{ Here } U = 240, l = 36 \text{ and } l_n = 27.$$

$$V_n = 240 \times \tfrac{36}{27} = 320 = \text{Vibrations of } Ma.$$

And Formula (C) is

$$l_n = U \times \frac{l}{V_n}; \therefore l_n = 240 \times \frac{l}{320} = \tfrac{3}{4}\, l = \tfrac{3}{4} \times 36$$

or the length of *Ma* is $\frac{3}{4}$ of the length of the F. N. and the vibrations of *Ma* are $\frac{4}{3}$ of the F. N. and it may be laid down

6. That the length of the wire of *Ma* (*F*) or the 4th note is $\frac{3}{4}$ of that of the Fundamental Note and the vibrations of *Ma* (*F*) are $\frac{4}{3}$ of the vibrations of the Fundamental Note Sa_1 (C_1).

Pa (G).

7. The fifth or *Pa* (*G*) note is produced on $\frac{1}{3}$ or $\frac{2}{3}$ of whole length of the wire. The former note is one octave higher than the latter.

The length of the wire is 36". Therefore a length of 12" or 24" will give the fifth note *Pa* (*G*). But we want the length between 18" and 36" — the two limits of the octave. Therefore the length 24" is that which we require and it will give out the note *Pa* (*G*).

Let us apply the formulæ (B) and (C) to the case of *Pa* (*G*).

$$V_n = U \times \frac{l}{l_n} \quad \ldots \quad \ldots \quad \ldots \quad \text{(B)}$$

Substitute the values $U = 240$, $l = 36$ and $l_n = 24$.

$V_n = 240 \times \frac{36}{24} = 360 =$ Vibrations of *Pa* (*G*) $= U \times \frac{36}{24} = \frac{3}{2}\, U$.

or the vibrations of *Pa* (*G*) are $\frac{3}{2}$ of its Sa_1 or F. N.

and

$$l_n = U \frac{l}{V_n} \quad \ldots \quad \ldots \quad \ldots \quad \ldots \quad \text{(C)}$$

$\therefore l_n = \frac{240}{360} \times l = \frac{2}{3}\, l = 24.$

or the length of *Pa* is $\frac{2}{3}$ of its Sa_1 (C_1) or F. N.

These facts may be noted down under rule (8) below

8. The length of the wire of *Pa* (*G*) or the fifth note is $\frac{2}{3}$ of that of Sa_1's (C_1) wire and its vibrations or pitch is $\frac{3}{2}$ of that of Sa_1 (C_1).

Ri (D).

9. In the interval of a given octave Sa_1 (C_1) with *Pa* (*G*) and *Ma* (*F*) with Sa_2 (C_2) form perfect concords; it may be noted that Sa_1 (C_1) with *Ma* (*F*) and *Pa* (*G*) with Sa_2 (C_2), the inverted interval, form imperfect concords.

This rule is very important and is made use of in finding out the lengths and vibrations of the other notes *Ri* (*D*), *Ga* (*E*), etc, etc.

According to Rule (1) any length may be said to give the fundamental note and its *Pa* will be the 5th note from it. This *Pa* will form a perfect concord with it. This gives us the following consonant notes.

F. N. Sa_1 (C_1)		consonant note Pa or Ma (F)	
Sa_1	C_1	,, ,, Pa	G
Ri	D	,, ,, Dha	A
Ga	E	,, ,, Ni	B
Ma	F	,, ,, Sa_2	C_2
Pa	G	,, ,, Ri_2	D_2
Sa_2	C_2	,, ,, Pa_2	G_2 or Pa G.

Let us take *Pa* (*G*) itself as the starting or fundamental note; then its *Pa* or fifth will be *D* in the higher octave which may be called Ri_2 (D_2.) Apply the formula (B)

$$V_n = U\frac{l}{l_n};\ \text{here } U = 360,\ l = 24,\ \text{and } l_n = \tfrac{2}{3} \times 24.\ \therefore l_n = 16.$$

Rule 7. Substituting the values of U, l and l_n

$$V_n = 360 \times \tfrac{24}{16} = 540.$$

540 are the vibrations of Ri_2 or *Ri* (*D*) in the 2nd octave. Therefore the vibrations of *Ri* in the first octave are $= \frac{1}{2} \times 540 = 270$; Vide Rule (2)

Formula C is $l_n = U \times \frac{l}{V_n}$; substituting $U = 240$, $l = 36$ and $V_n = 270$

we have $l_n = 240 \times \frac{36}{270} = 32$. Hence—

10. The length of *Ri* (*D*) is 32 inches and its vibrations are 270; or, the length is $\frac{4}{3}\,l$, and vibrations $\frac{3}{4}\,U$.

Dha (A).

11. The length of *Ri* is 32" If we take this as the starting note then its *Pa* is *Dha*. Therefore the length of *Dha* is $\frac{2}{3}$ of $32 = 21\frac{1}{3}$ by Rule 8 and its vibrations are $\frac{3}{2}$ of $270 = 405$.

Ga (E).

The length of *Dha* (*A*) is $21\frac{1}{3}$ and its vibrations are 405. Let us take *Dha* as the fundamental note (Rule I); then Ga_2 (*E*) or *Ga* in 2nd octave becomes its *Pa* or the 5th note (Rule 9) Therefore its length is $\frac{2}{3} \times 21\frac{1}{3}$ and vibrations $\frac{3}{2} \times 405$; but these are for Ga_2. Therefore according to Rule (2) the length of *Ga* is $= 2 \times \frac{2}{3} \times 21\frac{1}{3} = 2 \times \frac{2}{3} \times \frac{64}{3} = \frac{256}{9} = 28\frac{4}{9}$,

and the vibrations of $Ga = \frac{1}{2} \times \frac{3}{2} \times 405 = \frac{1215}{4} = 303\frac{3}{4}$.

Ni (B).

The length of *Ga* is $28\frac{4}{9}$ and its vibrations $303\frac{3}{4}$ (Rule 12). If we take *Ga* as the Fundamental note, then *Ni* becomes its *Pa* or the fifth note. Therefore

the length of $Ni = \frac{2}{3} \times 28\frac{4}{9} = \frac{2}{3} \times \frac{256}{9} = \frac{512}{27} = 18\frac{26}{27}$,

and the vibrations of $Ni = \frac{3}{2} \times 303\frac{3}{4} = \frac{3}{2} \times \frac{1215}{4} = \frac{3645}{8} = 455\frac{5}{8}$.

TABLE 3

Showing the 22 Srutis of the Indian Music in accordance with Mr. Deval's Interpretation of Sangita Ratnakaram, Ragavibodham and Parijatam.

The No. of the Swaram or Sruti.	The Name of the Swaram or Sruti.	Fraction showing the position of other Swarams or Srutis granting that Tonic SA is 1.	Fractions for the intervals of the Sruti.	Decimal Fractions.	The position of the Swarams or Srutis in a wire of 32 inches length.	The position of the Srutis in a wire of 36 inches length.	Cents.	Cents for the intervals of the Srutis	The Number of vibrations of each Sruti granting Tonic SA=540.	The Number of Vibrations of each Sruti granting Tonic SA=240.
1	2	3	4	5 @	6 @	7	8	9	10 @	11
	S	1		1·0000	32	36	0		540	240
1	Ri1	20/21	20/21	·9524	30·48	34– 5·71	84	84	567	252
2	Ri2	15/16	63/64	·9375	30	33–15	112	27	576	256
3	Ri3	9/10	24/25	·9000	28·8	32– 8	182	71	600	266·67
4	Ri4	8/9	80/81	·8889	28·44	32	204	22	607·5	270
5	G1	27/32	243/256	·8438	27	30– 7·5	294	90	640	284·44
6	G2	5/6	80/81	·8333	26·67	30	316	22	648	288
7	G3	4/5	24/25	·8000	25·6	28–10	386	71	675	300
8	G4	64/81	80/81	·7901	25·28	28– 8·89	408	22	683·4375	303·75
9	M1	16/21	27/28	·7619	24·38	27– 8·57	471	63	708·75	315
10	M2	3/4	63/64	·7500	24	27	498	27	720	320
11	M3	32/45	128/135	·7111	22·76	25–12	590	92	759·375	337·50
12	M4	45/64	2025/2048	·7031	22·5	25– 6·25	610	20	768	341·33
13	P	2/3	128/135	·6667	21·33	24	702	92	810	360
14	D1	40/63	20/21	·6349	20·32	22–17·14	786	84	850·5	378
15	D2	5/8	63/64	·6250	20	22–10	814	27	864	384
16	D3	3/5	24/25	·6000	19·2	21–12	884	71	900	400
17	D4	16/27	80/81	·5926	18·96	21– 6·67	906	22	911·25	405
18	Ni1	9/16	243/256	·5625	18	20– 5	996	90	960	426·67
19	Ni2	5/9	80/81	·5556	17·78	20	1018	22	972	432
20	Ni3	8/15	24/25	·5333	17·07	19– 4	1088	71	1012·5	450
21	Ni4	128/243	80/81	·5267	16·86	18–19·26	1110	22	1025·15625	455·625
22	S	1/2	243/256	·5000	16	18	1200	90	1080	480

The Calculations in Columns marked @ are our own.

Again

Ga (E).

12. If the vibrations of *Ga* (*E*) be taken as 300 (and there is a reason for doing so) in place of $303\frac{3}{4}$ as obtained in Rule (2) above, then

$$l_n = \frac{Ul}{V_n} \ldots\ldots\ldots\ldots(C);\ U=240,\ l=36 \text{ and } V_n=300.$$

$$\therefore l_n = \frac{240 \times 36}{300} = \frac{144}{5} = 28\tfrac{4}{5}.$$

Hence the length of *Ga*$=28\frac{4}{5}$" and its pitch $=300$.

The *Ga* (*E*) obtained by the foregoing process has $303\frac{3}{4}$ vibrations and bears with the F. N. a complicated ratio *vis* 81 : 64. The *Ga* (*E*) obtained as the fifth harmonic when reduced by two octaves has 300 vibrations and bears with the F.N. the simple ratio of 5 : 4 ; and it sounds more consonant with it. It is clearly heard on the bass string (the fourth, giving *Sa* or F. N.) of the Vina. Sanskrit writers have adopted this in preference to the other. They tested their notes by harmonics ; the author of Ragavibodha clearly lays down this.

Ni (B).

13. If *Ga* (*E*) is taken as the Fundamental Note, then *Ni* (*B*) become its *Pa* the fifth in the same octave.

$\therefore 300 \times \frac{3}{2} = 450 =$ the vibrations of *Ni* by Rule (8) ;
and the length is $\frac{2}{3} \times 28\frac{4}{5} = \frac{2}{3} \times \frac{144}{5} = \frac{288}{15} = 19\frac{3}{15} = 19\frac{1}{5}$;

i.e. The vibrations of *Ni*$=450$
and the length of *Ni*$=19\frac{1}{5}$ inches. Etc. Etc.

N.B.—It is manifest that Deval has spent years to arrive at a conclusion regarding the 22 Srutis. We are glad that he has made researches and published a book on Srutis while those professional musicians of India have been indifferent about it. Among musical works held in esteem at the present day "*Ragavibodham*" and after that "*Sangeeta Parijatam*" are considered ancient. This writer draws his conclusions as regards Srutis from "*Ragavibodham*", while he derives the swarams step by step after the system of *Parijatam*. In the fifth step where he determines Ni from Ga, he recommends 300 vibrations for Ga instead of $303\frac{3}{4}$. He says there is reason for such a step. But the only reason he gives for the alteration is that it is pleasant to the ear.

When we proceed by the Sa-Pa series, if at the fourth step (*i.e.*, from Dha to Ga) we get a difference of $3\frac{3}{4}$ vibrations, it is but just to suppose that at each step there must be a lessening of the number of vibrations. Moreover, he lessens $3\frac{3}{4}$ vibrations to suit $\frac{5}{4}$ or *Major third* of Western writers so that the two Swarams may be in the ratio of 240 : 300 or 4 : 5. Further he takes the Sruti with $303\frac{3}{4}$ vibrations as one above Ga, and says that 240 is to $303\frac{3}{4}$ as 64 to 81. We cannot say why he lessened the number of vibrations, but probably he found the ratio of 64 to 81 difficult to proceed with or he wanted to suit his Ga to the $\frac{5}{4}$ of Western musicians. But he gives the reason that Sanskrit Vidwans found this more pleasant to the ear. In the same way in the fifth step he alters the $455\frac{5}{8}$ vibrations of Ni into 450, and says that $455\frac{5}{8}$ must be another Sruti after 450. We doubt very much whether such a calculation where there is a difference in the number of vibrations even at the fourth or fifth step, could be accurate. More minute calculations might be seen in the table appended. In the 8th line of the 11th column of the 3rd table we read of 300 vibrations and in the next line of 303¾ vibrations. The Ga we obtain at the fourth step of the Sa-Pa series has 303¾ vibrations. He makes it 300 by reducing the 3¾. When he says that this is in accordance with Western music he is not far wrong. But it is not at all in accordance with the system of 22 Srutis of Sarnga Dev. In the same manner when we proceed in the same series from 303¾ we get another Sruti with 455⅝ vibrations Here again he cuts off 5⅝ vibrations and calls it 450 in the 20th line. This is the Ni of the Western musicians or $\frac{15}{8}$. This western view is also allied to the system of the author of Parijatam which proceeds by the Sa-Pa series. But it is absurd to say that 22 Srutis result from either system and that it is also the system of Sarnga Dev. Sarnga Dev never makes mention of such calculation, nor does it agree with the system of Indian music. By looking at his table we find that he accounts for the 22 Srutis thus :—1 Sruti with 20 Cents, Six with 22, 3 with 27, 1 with 63, 4 with 71, 2 with 84, 3 with 90 and two Srutis with 92 cents. On the other hand, according to the system of Sarnga Dev the series must ascend gradually with equal intervals, so that no other Sruti might possibly come between.

Again, under this system it is not possible to sing Grahasvaram in the Shadja Gramam, Gandhara Gramam and Madhyama Gramam as the Srutis are not of equal intervals. In the eighth column we see that if the Tonic Sa is 0, the four Ris have 84, 112, 182 and 204 cents respectively. These are not of equal intervals and hence cannot suit the purpose of singing Grahasvaram. Again, he gives the total number of Srutis as 22—4 Sas, 3 Ris, 2 Gas, 4 Mas, 4 Pas, 3 Dhas and 2 Nis, but does not say that Ri, Ga, Dha and Ni have 4 Srutis each. So it conflicts with the theory of Sarnga Dev. We need not dwell upon each of the Srutis here as the Table given is clear enough.

Making the Srutis sound at ½, ⅓, ¼, ⅕ and ⅙ lengths of the wire from Meru will not give the exact Sruti. This was given as an approximate measurement for those who have no ear for music. To call this Just Temperament will not be accurate. If there is a difference of 3¾ vibrations at the fourth step it follows that there must be differences in each step. If a more accurate and certain system had been framed out by him it would have been more useful. The system by which he locates the Swarams and Srutis does not accord with 'Sangeeta Ratnakaram'. We need not dwell on this subject any further. In short, he does not account for the 22 Srutis as given in 'Sangeeta Ratnakaram', but fixes the Seven Swarams according to the system given in Parijatam and accounts for the other Swarams and Srutis according to his own fancy. He is not supported by any authority. Moreover, many other minute intervals such as between Gas and Nis *i.e.*, (300—303¾, 450—450⅝) might possibly occur.

Again, the method he adopts for making half-Swarams and Srutis in the intervals of the Sapta Swarams is nowhere mentioned in the Sanskrit works. It seems to have been his own. He divides the interval between Sa and Ri *i.e.*, between 36 inches and 32 inches into four Sruti Sthanams. Of these the first is 1, the second $\frac{35}{36}$, the third $\frac{15}{16}$, the fourth $\frac{9}{10}$, and the fifth $\frac{8}{9}$. Thus 4 Srutis occur in 36 inches, $34\frac{2}{7}$ inches, $33\frac{3}{4}$ inches, $32\frac{2}{5}$ inches and 32 inches respectively. These intervals are not of equal measurement. Their vibrations are 240, 252, 256, $266\frac{2}{3}$ and 270 respectively. Thus we see an unequal difference in the number of vibrations, 12, 4, $10\frac{2}{3}$ and $3\frac{1}{3}$ being the respective difference in the four srutis. He also uses many fractions which do not agree together. Evidently these are his own views. In criticising his theory of 22 Srutis, if he had erred in one or two places, it might be of use to correct him, but when his view teems with errors the task is hopeless. However, we give him credit for the trouble he has taken in finding out the Srutis.

The following is the opinion of Clements on his Sruti Sthanams :—

In his Introduction to Hindu Musical scale and the 22 Srutis of Deval E. Clements says

"Secondly, it will be found that although Mr. Deval did not test his Shrutees throughout by the harmonic intervals 5:4, 6:5 and 7:6 which may be called the Major Third, Minor Third and Septimal Third, they are clearly built up from those intervals.

"Indeed the importance attached to the Septimal intervals, *that is* those derived from the seventh harmonic, places the Music of India in the first rank of intellectual developments of the musical art. Some writers on Harmony have elaborated theories based upon the supposition that the subdominant (corresponding with Komal Madhyam) and dominant seventh (that is Atikomal Madhyam) are for all practical purposes the same note. No one who has attentively listened to Indian Ragas could entertain such an idea for a moment, as the Septimal Seventh, is very much flatter than the ordinary Seventh, the interval 7:6 being easily distinguishable even by the untrained ear from the interval 6:5.

"The 22 shrutees are as Mr. Deval points out a selection from the total number of shrutees used in Indian Raginis. Mr. Deval had not only to ascertain what Shrutees were made use of by different singers but also to pick out the 22 which might justly be considered essential."

* * * * * * * * *

"Mr. Krishnaji Mahadev Gokhale of Miraj who makes use of considerably more than 22 Shrutees has kindly sung over to me 83 Ragas and Raginis and given me the names of the notes used in them. It appeared to me that the extra Shrutees used were chiefly those necessary to give the exact Septimal intervals in some of those cases which I have marked 'nearly' in the footnote. An additional 'Atikomal Gandhar' of 280 relative number of vibrations was also used but in one Raga only. Mr. Deval tells me that some singers use a similar septimal 'Atikomal Nishad'. The 'Atikomal Nishad' chosen by him is however a vital necessity as the fourth above Madhyam, and if the Shrutees are to be restricted to 22, I am afraid one must give up these two septimal notes, pleasing though their effect must be acknowledged to be.

"The intervals between each Shrutee and the next, as given in Mr. Deval's table D., are of no great significance."

Regarding Mr. Deval's Shrutees Dr. Coomarasamy says :—

"It is true that Mr. Deval did not succeed in his endeavour to improve his case by importing aid and corroboration from scientific acoustics and Sanskrit philology ; but I think that certain of his critics fall into more serious error when they judge the results of his patient and invaluable experimental work by weakness or inaccuracies in his mode of presentation."

Deval quotes a few slokas from Sanskrit writers in support of his theory of the 22 Srutis, copies the 13 out of the 18 Swarams of the Enharmonic scale of the

Western musicians and accounts for the other 9 by placing them above and below these 13. He quotes 'Parijatam' in support of the above 13 Srutis, but does not quote any reliable authority for the remaining 9. He does not establish his theory by practically finding out what Srutis are in use in the Ragas of India at the modern day, though he was born and brought up in India, nor does he follow the system of 'Sangeeta Ratnakaram', nor does he dogmatise suiting his method to that given in 'Sangeeta Parijatam.' The minute Srutis in use in Indian music are only capable of being sung or reproduced in the Veena. To think that by the adjustment of frets they could be sounded in the Veena, or, sounded on instruments like the Harmonium, is altogether a false idea. To attempt such things is to sin against the elaborateness of Indian music and destroy its eminent beauty. Again, it appears that the Westerners have adopted the system of locating the Swarams by measurement as is done by the author of Parijatam. Yet they use these Swarams approximately correct for the purpose of harmony. Even while Deval copies the Enharmonic scale he does not do it wholesale. But it is to be noted that he emphatically declares " this is the opinion of the author of ' Sangeeta Ratnakaram' and these are the Srutis in use in Indian music." However, his attempt to publish his theory for the benefit of the Indians who have long neglected their music is very praiseworthy.

FOURTH.

The theory of Srutis by E. CLEMENTS (District Judge).

Clements gives a two-fold opinion as regards the Srutis in use in Indian music. The *one* is the theory of 22 Srutis adapted from Bharata and Sarnga Dev and the *other* is his own with a few modifications taken from Deval. We shall first give the two theories and their mathematical calculations and then offer a few remarks of our own on the same.

Introduction to the study of Indian Music, By E. Clements, I.C.S., P. 2.

"The present work deals with Hindustani music only; the author hopes to be able to show that a great part of it is directly traceable to the systems set forth in Bharata's Natya-Shastra of about the fifth century A. D., and the Sangit Ratnakar of the thirteeth century. These are the most closely reasoned and critically worded of the early text books. It is reputed that Sarnga Dev the author of the Sangit Ratnakar was an inhabitant of Kashmir. From internal evidence one would conclude that the music he describes is that of Hindustan. However, the pandits of Southern India endeavour to appropriate him to themselves. The present writer hopes to show that it is only by doing violence to his theory that it can be applied to Karnatic music. Roughly speaking, Hindustani music may be said to prevail in the north and west of India and Deccan, while Karnatic music is confined to the south and east. Many scales are common to both but the general spirit of the two systems is apparent from the scales which are first taught to beginners; in the west, the scale is the same as the just major scale of Europe, in the south, it is a chromatic scale (known in Hindustani music as the scale of the Raga Bhairava) with semi-tones between the first and second, third and fourth, fifth and sixth and seventh and eighth degrees."

We gather from the above that he derives his theory of 22 Srutis from the system of Bharata and Sarnga Devar and that the system applies only to Hindustani music. Clements is justified in thinking that he has written about Hindustani music only as Sarnga Dev lived in Devagiri or Daulatabad, near the great city of Aurangabad in Hyderabad which is a Hindustani province. But if we enter deep into the book, we shall find that in many *amsams* his statements are wrong.

First, let us take the theory of 22 Srutis. The opinions of Deval and Clements are entirely different from that of Sarnga Dev. But we may concede a little and say that the Srutis which he obtained from researches with the help of Abdul Karim, the distinguished Hindustani Vidwan, may belong entirely to Hindustani music. But we shall see clearly from the Table of 22 Srutis of Sarnga Dev that the Srutis of Clements and Deval are entirely different.

Secondly, it appears that Sarnga Dev was the Asthana Vidwan of the Court of Simgana Raja, one of the native Kings of India and that he wrote his Sangeeta Ratnakaram at the King's request.

Thirdly, when we notice in Sangeeta Ratnakaram the names of the three Deities—Brahma, Vishnu and Rudran, the Beejaksharams—Akara, Ookara, Makaram and Onkaram, the four Vedas, the four Jatis, the seven Devatas—Agni, Brahma, Sarasvati, Aran, Ari, Vinayaka and Sooryan corresponding to the Seven Swarams, the names of Indra, Brahma, Chandran, Vishnu, Narada and Thumburu who invented the Swarams and the nomenclature of the Ragas, we are led to think that there is not the slightest connection between Hindustani music and Sangeeta Ratnakaram.

Fourthly, when we compare the period of the invasion of Mamood of Gazni (1024), the period of Mahammed Ghori who established for the first time a Kingdom at Delhi (1206) and the time of Simgaņarajah Maharajan at Devagiri, we may conclude that Sarnga Dev could not possibly have written this work on behalf of Hindustani music. It does not appear from history that the Mahamedans came to the South of the Vindhya range prior to 1294. We do not take objection to the statement of Clements when he says he writes about the Srutis in Hindustani music. But we do take objection, and that strongly, when he says that he adopts the system of Sarnga Dev. This is what Clements says in the 6th and the 7th pages of his work :—

Introduction to the Study of Indian Music, By E. Clements, P. 6, 7.

" He persevered for years at this investigation deriving assistance from many of the best singers that India could produce. As regards most of the notes in use, his conclusions, when referred back to ancient theory, may be summed up in the statement that two Srutis make a just semitone, three Srutis a Minor-tone and four Srutis a Major-tone. In respect of these notes the accuracy of his conclusions can fairly be said to be beyond controversy.

" The author has through Mr. Deval's courtesy, and with the help of Abdul Karim and other singers, been able to verify all the various scales mentioned in the following pages upon this instrument (Deval's Sruti Harmonium).

" The following table describes the twenty-four notes in most frequent use, showing which of them are adopted in the Indian Harmonium and their relationship with the ancient Srutis."

Here he says that he arrived at the following Table about Srutis from the results of his labours with the help of Abdul Karim and from those of Deval.

TABLE 4

Showing the Srutis of the Hindustani music in India in accordance with **Clements' Views.**

The number of the Sruti.	The Name of the Sruti.	Fraction showing the position of other Swarams or Srutis granting Tonic Sa is 1.	Fractions for the intervals of the Srutis.	Decimal Fractions.	The position of the Srutis in a wire of 32 inches length.	Cents.	Cents for the intervals of the Srutis.	The Number of vibrations of each Sruti granting Tonic Sa=540.	The Number of vibrations of each Sruti granting Tonic Sa=240.
1	2	3	4	5	6	7	8	9	10
			⊛	⊛	⊛	⊛	⊛	⊛	
	S	1		1·0000	32	0		540	240
1	Ri₁	20/21	20/21	·9524	30·48	84	84	567	252
2	Ri₂	15/16	63/64	·9375	30	112	27	576	256
3	Ri₃	9/10	24/25	·9000	28·80	182	71	600	266·67
4	Ri₄	8/9	80/81	·8889	28·44	204	22	607·50	270
5	G₁	27/32	243/256	·8438	27	294	90	640	284·44
6	G₂	5/6	80/81	·8333	26·67	316	22	648	288
7	G₃	4/5	24/25	·8000	25·6	386	71	675	300
8	G₄	64/81	80/81	·7901	25·28	408	22	683·44	303·75
9	M₁	16/21	27/28	·7619	24·38	471	63	708·75	315
10	M₂	3/4	63/64	·7500	24	498	27	720	320
11	M₃	20/27	80/81	·7407	23·70	520	22	729	324
12	M₄	32/45	24/25	·7111	22·76	590	71	759·375	337·50
13	M₅	45/64	2025/2048	·7031	22·50	610	20	768	341·33
14	P	2/3	128/135	·6667	21·33	702	92	810	360
15	D₁	40/63	20/21	·6349	20·32	786	84	850·5	378
16	D₂	5/8	63/64	·6250	20	814	27	864	384
17	D₃	3/5	24/25	·6000	19·20	884	71	900	400
18	D₄	16/27	80/81	·5926	18·96	906	22	911·25	405
19	Ni₁	4/7	27/28	·5714	18·29	969	63	945	420
20	Ni₂	9/16	63/64	·5625	18	996	27	960	426·67
21	Ni₃	5/9	80/81	·5556	17·78	1018	22	972	432
22	Ni₄	8/15	24/25	·5333	17·07	1088	71	1012·5	450
23	Ni₅	135/256	2025/2048	·5273	16·88	1108	20	1024	455·11
24	S	1/2	128/135	·5000	16	1200	92	1080	480

The Calculations in Columns marked ⊛ are our own.

N.B.—This Table is mearly a copy of the Table D on the 29th page of Deval's book. But it is to be noted that he introduces two new Srutis after the 10th and the 17th of Deval. Deval gives 320 vibrations for the 10th Sruti and 337½ for the 11th. Clements admits this but says there must be another Sruti with 324 vibrations after the 10th. Again, admitting the 17th and 18th Srutis of Deval with 405 and 426⅔ vibrations respectively, he introduces one between them with 420 vibrations. He says that these Srutis were used by Abdul Karim in his music and are very charming to the ear. It is very commendable that he observed from practical experience the existence of these two swarams and told it to the public without the slightest doubt on the poin. It is not easy for Western musicians to find out the Srutis in use in Indian music and to come to a definite conclusion about them. These two Srutis occur above MA and DHA. But there are such Srutis and even more minute ones between other Swarams also. But this fact cannot be mathematically proved by Indian musicians but they can only sing them. This is the reason why there is no unanimity among Indian musicians as regards Srutis. Just as the Srutis between 320 and 337½ vibrations and between 405 and 426⅔ vibrations, many other minute Srutis may occur between 455⅝ and 480, between 432 and 450, between 384 and 400, between 360 and 378, between 341⅓ and 360, between 288 and 300, between 270 and 284 4/9 and between 240 and 252 vibrations. If after 320 a Sruti sounds at 324, why could not there be two Srutis at 328 and 332. In the same way if there are two Srutis 420 and 426⅔ why should not there be Srutis at 408 and 414? If we grant these, we shall have many harmonious and charming Srutis with equal measurements. We shall notice them later on in the Table of Srutis of South Indian music.

The same critisism we offered to Deval pointing out errors in his mathematical calculations when he attempted to give the same number of vibrations to Indian Srutis like the Western, applies also to this writer.

Deval gives 455⅝ vibrations to the 21st Sruti. But according to Clements it is 455 1/9. This slight difference is owing to fractional calculations. In other respects, there is no difference between the theories of the two writers.

FIFTH.

The three new Srutis of Clements which result from the change of Grahams according to Sarnga Dev

Adapted from Sootrams 24 to 38 of the third Prakaranam in Sangeeta Ratnakaram.

In the following table 3 Srutis are added on to the 22. He claims that these 3 Srutis result from the change of Srutis in the Shadjama, Madhyma and Gandhara Gramams according to Sarnga Dev who is an advocate of 22 Srutis only. These three are accounted for as follows :—A Sruti with $296\frac{8}{27}$ vibrations before Antaragandharam with 300 vibrations, another with $355\frac{5}{9}$ vibrations before PA with 360, and a third with $444\frac{4}{9}$ vibrations before KAKALI NI with 450 vibrations. There is not much difference between his and Deval's except in the following places :—The first Sruti has 250 vibrations in place of 252, the ninth Sruti has $316\frac{4}{81}$ instead of 315, the twelfth has $345\frac{3}{5}$ in place of $341\frac{1}{3}$ and the fourteenth has 375 for 378. When the Srutis are changed according to the three Gramas of Sarnga Dev no other Srutis but the 22 can possibly result. When the Swarams are arranged in equal semitones in an octave, the change of a Swaram would not result in any new Swaram. The same applies to the scale with 22 Srutis also. No new swaram can possibly occur in the middle in spite of the change of Gramam To sing a Gramam means to sing an ascending and descending scale where the Srutis for each Swaram are definite and fixed. The general opinion is that, however the Srutis might be changed for a Gramam, the total number of Srutis cannot possibly be more than 22. In the Shadjama Gramam there are 4 SAS, 3 RIS, 2 GAS, 4 MAS, 4 PAS, 3 DHAS and 2 NIS, in all 22 Srutis. These will respectively commence in the 4th, 3rd, 2nd and the first SAS and end accordingly. For the Madhyama Gramam there are 4 SAS, 3 RIS, 2 GAS, 4 MAS, 3 PAS, 4 DHAS and 2 NIS. These also commence in the 4th, 3rd, 2nd and the first SAS. For the Gandhara Gramam there are 4 SAS, 2 RIS, 4 GAS, 3 MAS, 3 PAS, 3 DHAS and 3 NIS. In all 22. These also commence respectively in the 4th, 3rd, 2nd and the first SAS.

Here we see that in Shadja Gramam, when we shift the four Srutis of SA one by one to the left, if we commence the 4 Srutis of SA in the second Sruti of the SA in the top row, the GA and the NI with two Srutis each reach their layam in RI and DHA. In other words, the third Sruti of RI and DHA respectively become GA and NI. In the same way when we commence the fourth Sruti of SA in the first Sruti, the RI and the DHA with three Srutis each reach their layam in SA and PA. In other words SA and PA become RI and DHA respectively. When the fourth SA commences in NI which is the twenty-second Sruti, SA speaks in NI, MA in GA and PA in MA. Then the first SA commences in the second of the Srutis of DHA, namely in the nineteenth. In the same manner each Gramam proceeds regularly with the number and measurements of its respective Swarams. Clement's table of Srutis has been appended. If the measurements be noted in four different pieces of paper each half an inch broad and the Grahams changed we may see what a number of Srutis and intervals result therefrom.

TABLE 5

Showing the Srutis in use in Hindustani Music in India in accordance with **Clements' Views**

With the three Srutis which result from change of Gramam according to the system of Sarnga Dev.

The Number of 22 Srutis or Swarams.	The Number of 25 Srutis or Swarams	Name of Sruti or Swaram.	The fractional value of Swarams if the Tonic SA be 1.	Fraction of Sruti Intervals.	Decimal fractions.	Location of Srutis in a wire of 32 in length.	Cents.	Cents for the Sruti Intervals.	Number of vibrations if SA=540.	Number of vibrations if SA=240.
1	2	3	4	5	6	7	8	9	10	11
	⊛			⊛	⊛	⊛	⊛	⊛	⊛	
4	1	S_2	1		1·0000	32			540	240
5	2	S_3	24/25	24/25	·9600	30·72	71	71	562·50	250
6	3	R_1	15/16	[illegible]	·9375	30	112	41	570	256
7	4	R_2	9/10	24/25	·9000	28·80	182	71	600	266·67
8	5	R_3	8/9	80/81	·8889	28·44	204	22	607·50	270
9 {	6	G_1	27/32	[illegible]	·8438	27	294	90	640	284·44
10	7	G_2	5/6	80/81	·8333	26·67	316	22	648 }	288
		G_3	81/100	[illegible]	·8100	25·92	365	49	666·67 }	296 8/27
11	8	G_4	4/5	80/81	·8000	25·6	386	22	675	300
12	9	M_1	243/320	[illegible]	·7594	24·3	477	90	711·11	316 4/81
13	10	M_2	3/4	80/81	·7500	24	498	22	720	320
14	11	M_3	18/25	24/25	·7200	23·04	569	71	750	333·33
15 {	12	M_4	32/45	80/81	·7111	22·76	590	22	759·38	337·50
16	13	P_1	25/36	[illegible]	·6944	22·22	631	41	777·6 }	345·6
	14	P_2	27/40	[illegible]	·6750	21·60	680	49	800 }	355 5/9
17	15	P_3	2/3	80/81	·6667	21·33	702	22	810	360
18	16	P_4	16/25	24/25	·6400	20·48	773	71	843·75	375
19	17	D_1	5/8	[illegible]	·6250	20	814	41	864	384
20	18	D_2	3/5	24/25	·6000	19·20	884	71	900	400
21	19	D_3	16/27	80/81	·5926	18·96	906	22	911·25	405
22 {	20	N_1	9/16	[illegible]	·5625	18	996	90	960 }	426·67
1	21	N_2	5/9	80/81	·5556	17·78	1018	22	972 }	432
	22	N_3	27/50	[illegible]	·5400	17·28	1067	49	1000	444 4/9
2	23	N_4	8/15	80/81	·5333	17·07	1088	22	1012·5	450
3	24	S_1	81/160	[illegible]	·5063	16·20	1178	90	1066·67	474·07
4	25	S_2	1/2	80/81	·5000	16	1200	22	1080	480

The Calculations in Columns marked ⊛ are our own.

The following plan will show clearly the change of Gramam according to Sarnga Dev.

• Shadja Gramam.

In accordance with the views of the author of Sangeeta Ratnakaram.

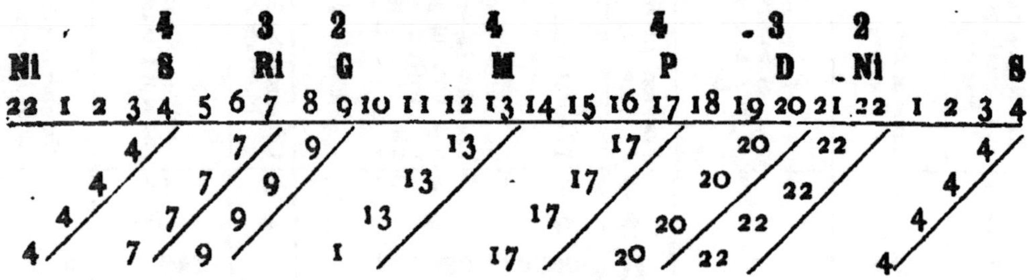

• Madhyama Gramam.

In accordance with the views of the author of Sangeeta Ratnakaram.

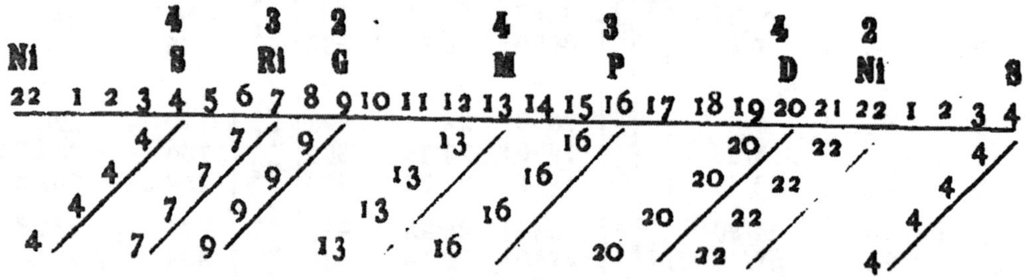

• Gandhara Gramam.

In accordance with the views of the author of Sangeeta Ratnakaram.

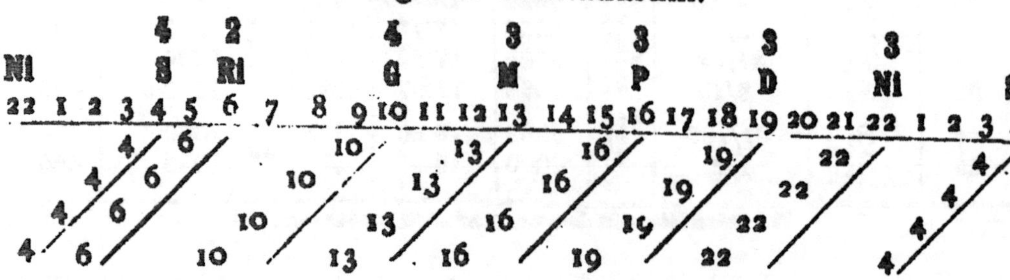

Further, when we refer to the cents' table in the ninth column of Table V, we see that he speaks of five different kinds of unequal Srutis with 22, 41, 49, 71 and 90 cents. But in Table IV he gives eight different kinds of unequal Srutis with 20, 22, 27, 63, 71, 84, 90 and 92 cents. When Srutis change according to Graham, these different kinds of measurements will surely land us in a number of unequal Srutis. Though it cannot be held that 3 new Swarams result from the system of changing of Grahams yet it is praiseworthy that he took pains to arrive at these extra Swarams over the 22 with the help of singers who knew music.

Besides the three Gramams mentioned by Sarnga Dev, there is another mentioned in the old literary work in Tamil, known as Silappadhikaram. There we read of 4 Gramams, known as Ayappalai, Trikonappalai, Sadurappalai and Vattappalai. In Vattappalai Gramam the 22 Srutis are spoken of as 22 Alagus. These are KURAL (SA) 4, Tuttam (RI) 4, KYKKILAI (GA) 3, OOLAI (MA) 2, ILI (PA) 4, VILARI (DHA) 3 and THARAM (NI) 2. It appears that this system of Vattappalai Gramam is different from that of Sarnga Dev. Moreover, no Alagus are given for the other three Gramams mentioned in Silappadhikaram. When we go deeply into this, we find that the 22 Srutis in the octave were equally adjusted to the Seven Swarams and the Seven Swarams were thus located. Again, it appears there were only two systems, the first being the system where by changing the Graham the four Srutis of SA were taken from right to left and the other where they were taken from left to right. The latter system is not found in Sangeeta Ratnakaram, but in some of the old Tamil literature. Other particulars will be found in the Table. Out of the 22 Srutis of Sarnga Dev which Clements says are in use in Indian music, 15 are taken from the English Enharmonic scale. He accounts for 3 out of the remaining 10 by saying they are resultant from the change of Graham and the other 7 to the 25 Srutis in general.

On the whole, we regret that Clements was mislead by adopting the conclusions of Deval while we are glad of his patient researches into the subject. We quite agree with him where he says that these Srutis which he heard sung by Abdul Karim and others belong to Hindustani music. Like many other Hindustani systems which are entirely opposed to Hindu systems in actual practice, this system of Hindustani music is also opposed to indigenous Indian music. But it goes without saying there must be a regular system which must produce definite Ragas, no matter where a Sruti is commenced within the octave. It is a matter for deep gratification that Clements, an European has made researches into the Srutis and has published his views for the benefit of the public while there are thousands of Vidwans in Indian music who have never read the Sanskrit work of Sarnga Dev, or who have never understood the meaning of it even if they were able to read it, or who never knew the inner meaning of it even if they understood the meanings of individual words or who have never practised it even if they knew the hidden meaning of it.

Though it is impossible to construct a Harmonium to suit the Srutis in Indian music, the fact that Clements attempts the construction of one with a few Srutis foreshadows the possibility of further development in this line and is a matter for congratulation.

Other points in connection with his theory of Srutis which have been left out without any comment might be found clearly in the appended Table V.

SIXTH.

III—The third class of writers who declare that South Indian Music is after the system of Srutis of Sarnga Dev.

The theory of 22 Srutis by Rao Bahadur C. Nagoji Row, Retired Inspector of Schools.

The theory of 22 Srutis in Indian music by Mr. Nagoji Row written in English was translated into Tamil by M.R.Ry. P. R. Sundaram Iyer, B.A., L.T., and read in the Second Conference of the Tanjore Sangeeta Vidya Mahajana Sangam.

The following are some of the chief points of Mr. Nagoji Row :—

Learned musicians speak about 12 Srutis in the scale. These are Sa, Suddha Ri, Chatur Sruti Ri, or, Suddha Ga, Sadharana Ga, or, Shat Sruti Ri, Antara Ga, Suddha Ma, Prati Ma, Pa, Suddha Dha, Chatur Sruti Dha, or, Suddha Ni, Kaishiki Ni, or, Shat Sruti Dha and Kakali Ni. Western musicians speak of these same Srutis as 7 full tones and 5 semitones. Others say there are more minute Srutis in Indian music besides the 12, such as quarter tones and still more minute tones. And if one asks for an explanation why Ragams based on the same scale have different effects upon the hearers, they explain it away by saying that the difference is caused by Gamakams. But our science distinctly says there are but 22 Srutis. So the conclusion we arrive at is that there must be more than 12 Swarams.

So, we have first to determine how many distinct Swarams there could be in an octave and what they are.

So far as we have made researches we find, in accordance with what is said in the literature of music, that there are 22 Srutis in an octave, neither more nor less.

Western musicians say that a Swaram is caused by the vibration of a string. If, in a fixed time a string vibrates more, it produces a note of a higher pitch and less number of vibrations indicate a note of lower pitch. They also say that the Tara Sa or Sa' has double the number of vibrations of Madhya Sa. According to them the following is the table showing the relative pitch of the ascending notes in an octave:

Sa	... 1					Pa	... $\frac{3}{2}$		
Ri_1	... $\frac{25}{24}$	Ga_1	... $\frac{32}{27}$	Ma_1	... $\frac{4}{3}$	Dha_1	... $\frac{25}{16}$	Ni_1	... $\frac{16}{9}$
Ri_2	... $\frac{16}{15}$	Ga_2	... $\frac{6}{5}$	Ma_2	... $\frac{27}{20}$	Dha_2	... $\frac{8}{5}$	Ni_2	... $\frac{9}{5}$
Ri_3	... $\frac{10}{9}$	Ga_3	... $\frac{5}{4}$	Ma_3	... $\frac{45}{32}$	Dha_3	... $\frac{5}{3}$	Ni_3	... $\frac{15}{8}$
Ri_4	... $\frac{9}{8}$	Ga_4	... $\frac{81}{64}$	Ma_4	... $\frac{25}{18}$	Dha_4	... $\frac{27}{16}$	Ni_4	... $\frac{48}{25}$
								Sa'	2

If Sa has 240 vibrations, Ri_1 has $\frac{25}{24}$ or 250 vibrations and Ri_2 $\frac{16}{15}$ or 256 vibrations and so on.

In the Tanjore Sangeeta Mahajana Sangam and Quarterly Report it is said :—

I shall now proceed to give reasons why there could possibly be *no more* Srutis than 22 in the Octave.

In European music the notes Sa, Ga, Pa and Sa' form a concord. These four are consonant notes. The chord is the basis of all harmony, and European Music is nothing *if it were not harmony*. One reason why this is called a consonant chord is this: If a string is struck, it not only sounds the Tonic, but also the Mediant and the Dominant at the same time, and, moreover, as soon as the Tonic is sounded, our mind is prepared to hear the other consonant notes; hence the combination of Sa, Ga, Pa and Sa' is called the "Chord of Nature." In the same way if these notes are sounded in succession, the series of these consonant notes will form a Melody or a Ragam.

If we take the series Sa, Ga, Pa and Sa', the interval between the two Sas is 2; in other words Sa' has double the number of vibrations of Sa. It is so hard to distinguish between the two Sas when sounded together; they are therefore called '*Unison*'. So the interval 2 is a consonant one.

The interval between Pa and Sa is 3/2; in other words Pa has one-and-a-half times the number of vibrations of Sa. These are also consonant notes, but in a lesser degree.

In the same way the interval between Pa and Sa' is 4/3, for Pa × 4/3 = Sa'; and 3/2 × 4/3 = 2.

Again, the interval between Ga_3 and Sa is 5/4 and that between Pa and Ga_3 is 6/5 for Ga_3 × 6/5 = Pa, and 5/4 × 6/5 = 3/2.

From the above we conclude that 2, 3/2, 4/3, 5/4 and 6/5 are consonant intervals. A well-ordered succession of these intervals will produce a pleasing Ragam.

Western Musicians are of opinion that there are also other consonant intervals besides these; and they are:

(1) The Major Tone which has 9/8 or 1 and 1/8th the number of vibrations of Sa,

(2) The Minor Tone which has 10/9 or 1 and 1/9th the number of vibrations of Sa,

(3) The Major Semi-tone having 16/15 or 1 and 1/15th the number of vibrations of Sa, and

(4) The Minor Semi-tone having 25/24 or 1 and 1/24 the number of vibrations of Sa.

From these we may conclude that notes with consonant intervals which produce harmony when sounded together may also produce a sweet melody when sounded in succession.

From this we understand that the Swarams with the following intervals are consonant: 25/24. 16/15, 10/9, 9/8, 6/5 and 5/4.

As everybody is agreed that the combination of the Swarams Sa, Pa and Sa' is harmonious, their intervals, *viz*, 4/3, 3/2 and 2 are also consonant.

I. We must next find out what consonant intervals there might possibly be between Sa and Ga_3, Ga_3 and Pa and between Pa and Sa'.

We can easily recognise the Swaram Ri_1 between Sa and Ga_3 for the interval between Sa and Ri_1 is 25/24 and that between Ri_1 and Ga_3 is 6/5; for 25/24 × 6/5 = 5/4 and Ri_1 × 6/5 = Ga_3; which means that if we make Ri_1 the standard Sruti, Ga_3 will be its Sadharana Gandharam, and Ri_2 which comes in between Sa and Ga_3 agrees well with both of them; for, the interval between Ri_2 and Sa is 10/9, and that between Ga_3 and Ri_2 is 9/8. This may be easily demonstrated—

$$10/9 \times 9/8 = 5/4$$
$$Ri_2 \times 9/8 = Ga_3$$

that is, if we have Ri_2 as the standard Sruti, then Ga_3 will be its Ri_4.

Again, Ri_4, if it comes between Sa and Ga_4 will be very pleasing to the ear ; for, the interval between Ri_4 and Sa is 9/8, and that between Ga_4 and Ri_4 is 10/9. This may be proved as follows :—

$$9/8 \times 10/9 = 5/4$$
$$Ri_4 \times 10/9 = Ga_4$$

that is, if we have Ri_4 as the standard Sruti, then Ga_4 will really be Ri_3.

N. B.—The intervals 6/5, 9/8 and 10/9 are among the list of consonants occurring between Sa and Ga_4. The interval between Ga_4 and Sa is 6/5 and that between Ga_3 and Ga_2 is 25/24.

This may be proved as follows:—

$$6/5 \times 25/24 = 5/4$$
$$Ga_2 \times 25/24 = Ga_3$$

that is, if Ga_2 were made the standard Sruti, then Ga_3 will become Ri_1.

To sum up, then, the following are consonant intervals :—

Sa, Ri_1, Ga_3
Sa, Ri_3, Ga_3
Sa, Ri_4, Ga_3
Sa, (Ga_2 = Re_6) Ga_3.

In the same manner let us determine the consonant Swarams between Ga_3 and Pa.

In the first place, Ma_1 will be consonant, for—

$$5/4 \times 16/15 = 4/3$$
$$Ga_3 \times 16/15 = Ma_1$$

that is, if Ga_3 were the standard Sruti, Ma_1 will be Suddha Rishabham.

The interval between Pa and Ga_3 is 9/8—

$$4/3 \times 9/8 = 3/2$$
$$Ma_1 \times 9/8 = Pa$$

that is, if Ma_1 were the standard Sruti, then Pa will be Ri_4.

Again Ma_2 is another consonant interval between Ga_3 and Pa. The interval between Ma_2 and Ga_3 is 9/8—

$$5/4 \times 9/8 = 45/32.$$
$$Ga_3 \times 9/8 = Ma_2.$$

The interval between Pa and Ma_2 is 16/15. This can be thus proved :—

$$45/32 \times 16/15 = 3/2.$$
$$Ma_2 \times 16/15 = Pa.$$

[These intervals are also among the list of consonant intervals given above.]

To sum up, therefore

Ga_3, Ma_1, Pa
Ga_3, Ma_2, Pa are consonant sets of Swarams.

II. Just as Sa, Ga_3, Pa and Sa' when sounded together, produce harmony, so also Sa, Ga_2, Pa and Sa' produce harmony. The combination of the latter four Swarams is called the Minor Chord in European Music.

We will apply the same principle as we did before to determine the consonant Swarams that can possibly occur between Sa and Ga_2 and between Ga_2 and Pa.

We may find Ri_2 between Sa and Ga_2. The interval between Ri_2 and Sa is 16/15, and that between Ga_2 and Re_2 is 9/8 ; for—

$$16/15 \times 9/8 = 6/5$$
$$Ri_2 \times 9/8 = Ga_2$$

Re_4 might also occur between these two, for the interval between Re_4 and Sa is 9/8, and that between Ga_2 and Re_4 is 16/15; for –

$$9/8 \times 16/15 = 6/5$$
$$Ri_4 \times 16/15 = Ga_2$$

To sum up, therefore,

$$Sa, Ri_3, Ga_3$$
$$Sa, Ri_4 \text{ and } Ga_2 \text{ are harmonious.}$$

Next, we shall enquire what consonant intervals there are between Ga_2 and Pa: Ma_1 may be one of them; for, the interval between Ma_1 and Ga_2 is 10/9; for—

$$6/5 \times 10/9 = 4/3.$$
$$Ga_2 \times 10/9 = Ma_1$$

The interval between Pa and Ma_1 is 9/8; for—

$$4/3 \times 9/8 = 3/2$$
$$Ma_1 \times 9/8 = Pa.$$

Again Ma_2 is another consonant interval, for the interval between Ga_2 and Ma_2 is 9/8. This may be proved as follows:—

$$6/5 \times 9/8 = 27/20$$
$$Ga_2 \times 9/8 = Ma_2$$

The interval between Pa and Ma_2 is 10/9; for—

$$27/20 \times 10/9 = 3/2$$
$$Ma_2 \times 10/9 = Pa.$$

Again Ma_4 is another consonant. The interval between Ma_4 and Ga_2 is 6/5; for —

$$6/5 \times 6/5 = 36/25$$
$$Ga_2 \times 6/5 = Ma_4.$$

The interval between Pa and Ma_4 is 25/24; for—

$$36/25 \times 25/24 = 3/2$$
$$Ma_4 \times 25/24 = Pa.$$

So the following are also consonants:—

$$Ga_2, Ma_1, Pa.$$
$$Ga_2, Ma_2, Pa.$$
$$Ga_2, Ma_4, Pa.$$

From all these we conclude that between Sa and Pa there are the following Swarams: — Ri_1, Ri_2, Ri_3, Ri_4; Ga_2, Ga_3; Ma_1, Ma_2, Ma_3, Ma_4. Some of these when played together will sound harmoniously.

III. We must next turn our attention to see how many Swarams might occur between Pa and Sa′. The interval between Pa and Sa′ is the same as the interval between Sa and Ma_1. In other words, if Pa were made the standard Sruti, Sa′ will be the Madhyamam. So, the same number of Swarams must occur between Pa and Sa′ as between Sa and Ma_1. The following is a list of the Swarams that might occur between Sa and Ma_1 and the corresponding ones between Pa and Sa′.

List of Swarams.	Corresponding Swarams.	List of Swarams.	Corresponding Swarams.
Sa ... 1	Pa ... 3/2	Ri_4 ... 9/8	Dha_4 ... 27/16
Ri_1 ... 25/24	Dha_1 ... 25/16	Ga_2 ... 6/5	Ni_2 ... 9/5
Ri_2 ... 16/15	Dha_2 ... 8/5	Ga_3 ... 5/4	Ni_3 ... 15/8
Ri_3 ... 10/9	Dha_3 ... 5/3	Ma_1 ... 4/3	Sa′ ... 2

In other words, if Pa were made the standard Sruti, it has its Ri_1, Ri_2, Ri_3, Ri_4, Ga_2, Ga_3 in the same way as Sa has.

IV. We proceeded upwards from Pa and determined the possible Srutis; now we shall proceed downwards from Sa', and see how many Srutis might occur.

The interval between Pa and Dha_1 is the same as that between Ni_4 and Sa'.

$$48/25 \times 25/24 = 2$$
$$Ni_4 \times 25/24 = Sa'.$$

In other words, if Ni_4 were made the standard Sruti, Sa' will be in the position of Suddha Rishabham Ri_1.

In the same manner, the interval between Dha_3 and Pa is the same as that between Sa' and Ni_3

$$15/8 \times 16/15 = 2$$
$$Ni_3 \times 16/15 = Sa'.$$

If we proceed upwards in the same way and make Ni_1 the standard Sruti, then Sa' will be in the position of Re_4

$$16/9 \times 9/8 = 2$$
$$Ni_1 \times 9/8 = Sa'.$$

So we find two new Srutis Ni_1 and Ni_4 between Pa and Sa'.

If we carry the analogy further and suppose the Srutis with the same intervals might occur between Sa and Ma_1, we obtain two new Srutis Ga_1 and Ga_4. The interval between Ga_1 and Ma_1 is 9/8; for

$$32/27 \times 9/8 = 4/3$$
$$Ga_1 \times 9/8 = Ma_1.$$

The interval between Ga_4 and Ma_1 is 25/24; for —

$$32/25 \times 25/24 = 4/3$$
$$Ga_4 \times 25/24 = Ma_1.$$

So we found that there were 22 Srutis in the Scale, namely :—Sa, Ri_1, Ri_2, Ri_3, Ri_4, Ga_1, Ga_2, Ga_3, Ga_4, Ma_1, Ma_2, Ma_3, Ma_4, Pa, Dha_1, Dha_2, Dha_3, Dha_4, Ni_1, Ni_2, Ni_3 and Ni_4.

If there be other Srutis they cannot be consonant. I have reason to believe that these *are the 22 Srutis* mentioned in our Shastras.

Though we find these 22 Srutis in one Sthayi, yet all these 22 are not used in a Ragam. Melody is made up of a few selected Srutis only. Moreover, there can be only one Swaram between Sa and Ga_3 as between Ga_3 and Pa. And two Swarams occur between Sa and Ma as between Pa and Sa'. To sum up there are seven Swarams made up as follows :—Sa one, another between Sa and Ga_1, Ga a third, the fourth between Ga and Pa_1, Pa a fifth, and the sixth and the seventh between Pa and Sa'. The succession of these seven Swarams in a scale forms the basis of a Ragam. As they are seven, they are called **Sapthaswarams**. The middle of these seven swarams forms the Madhyamam and the fifth one Panchamam.

Some Ragams commence with Sa and others with different Swarams. In the latter case the succeeding Swarams will change correspondingly. But no other Swarams are in use except the 22 mentioned above.

Now we shall take note of some peculiar expressions used in connection with Indian Music, and we shall interpret them in the light of the theory of the 22 Srutis.

We shall note the meaning of Vadi and Samvadi Swarams. The interval between Sa and Pa is 3/2 and there are 12 Srutis between them. So Vadi and Samvadi Swarams are those which have 12 Srutis between them according to Shastras.

The interval between Pa and Sa' is 4/3 and there are 8 Srutis between Pa and Sa'. According to the Shastras these are also called Vadhi and Samvâdhi Swarams, though they have only 8 Srutis between them.

We cannot distinctly make out the compass of Shadjagramam, Madhyamagramam and Gandharagramam. But my opinion is ...

(1) **Shadjagramam** commences with a Sa and has the following Swarams :— 4 Sas, 3 Ris, 2 Gas, 4 Mas, 4 Pas, 3 Dhas and 2 Nis. We see here that the Saptha Swarams—Sa, Ri_2, Ga_1, Ma_1, Pa, Dha_2, Ni_1 and Sa' are the basis of the Sadjagramam. The Mela Ragam having the above Sapta Swarams in its scale very nearly resembles the **Mukhari**. But the Dha_2 sometimes used in the Ragam must be put down to an embellishment not belonging to the scale proper.

(2) **Madhyamagramam** :—This commences with Madhyamam as Sa and proceeds onwards. In the Madhyamam compass it is said that there are 3 Srutis for Pa and four for Dha. So the Scale would go thus :—

Ma_2, Pa, Dha_2, Ni_2, Sa', Re'_4, Ga'_2 and Ma'_2.

Among these Sapta Swarams Dha_2 is not consonant with Ma_2 ; so, Dha_2 should be given up. The rest of the Swarams occur in Ragams like Madhyamavati and Sriragam.

(3) **Gandharagramam** :—It is said that in this compass Sa alone has 4 Srutis, and the rest three each. So the scale would be as follows :—, Ga_2, Ma_1, Ma_4, Dha_2, Ni_1, Ni_4, Sa', Re'_2, and Ga'_2. Ga becomes the Sa of this scale, and hence the name.

Among these Ma_1 and Ma_4 are Vivadi Swarams ; so also Ni_1 and Ni_4 ; so, in each of these couples one should be given up. I think that these Srutis occur in Hindustani and Todi Ragams.

* * * * * * * * *

As I said before, Musicians of the present day all accept the existence of the 22 Srutis in the Scale. But either owing to the ignorance of what the Srutis really are, or owing to singing them unconciously, they think they have only 12 Swarams—(5 full and 7 half Swarams) in the Scale. And again in instruments like the Veena they have only 12 bridges (*mettus*). If one places the fingers exactly on those bridges, one could never produce any Ragam. Again all musicians say that the beauty of a ragam could be brought out only if the strings of the Veena are pulled a little to the left. So the real Sruti is not in the locus indicated by the bridge, but in pulling the string. Hence the absurdity of having the 12 bridges.

From all these we see there is a difference between what musicians preach and what they practise. Hence the division of Melakarthas into 72 is not quite accurate as it may sometimes land us in difficulties. Both Ri_1 and Ri_2 are called by them as Suddha Rishabham, Ri_3 and Ri_4 are called Chatursruti Rishabham, Ga_1 and Ga_2 are called Sadharana Gandharam, Ga_3 and Ga_4 Antara Gandharam, Ma_1 and Ma_2 Suddha Madhyamam, Ma_3 and Ma_4 Prati Madhyamam, Dha_1 and Dha_2 Suddha Dhaivatam, Dha_3 and Dha_4, Chatursruti Dhaivatam, Ni_1 and Ni_2 Kaisiki Nishadam and Na_3 and Ni_4 Kakali Nishadam.

Anyhow the division into 72 Melams is very ingenious, and its usefulness may be seen later on.

TABLE 6

Showing the 22 Srutis in use in Indian Music in accordance with Nagoji Row's

Interpretation of Sangeeta Ratnakaram and other Sanskrit works.

The number of the Sruti.	The Name of the Sruti.	Fraction showing the position of other Swarams or Srutis granting Tonic S_A is 1.	Fractions for the intervals of the Srutis.	Decimal Fractions.	The position of the Srutis in a wire of 32 inches length.	Cents.	Cents for the intervals of the Srutis.	The Number of vibrations of each Sruti granting Tonic S_A=540.	The Number of vibrations of each Sruti granting Tonic S_A=240.
1	2	3	4	5	6	7	8	9	10
			⊛	⊛	⊛	⊛	⊛	⊛	⊛
	S	1		1·0000	32	0		540	240
			24/25				71		
1	Ri1	24/25		·9600	30·72	71		562·50	250
			125/128				41		
2	Ri2	15/16		·9375	30	112		576	256
			24/25				71		
3	Ri3	9/10		·9000	28·8	182		600	266·67
			80/81				22		
4	Ri4	8/9		·8889	28·44	204		607·50	270
			243/256				90		
5	G1	27/32		·8438	27	294		640	284·44
			80/81				22		
6	G2	5/6		·8333	26·67	316		648	288
			24/25				71		
7	G3	4/5		·8000	25·60	386		675	300
			125/128				41		
8	G4	25/32		·7813	25	427		691·20	307·2
			24/25				71		
9	M1	3/4		·7500	24	498		720	320
			80/81				22		
10	M2	20/27		·7407	23·70	520		729	324
			24/25				71		
11	M3	32/45		·7111	22·76	590		759·375	337·5
			125/128				41		
12	M4	25/36		·6944	22·22	631		777·60	345·6
			24/25				71		
13	P	2/3		·6667	21·33	702		810	360
			24/25				71		
14	D1	16/25		·6400	20·48	773		843·75	375
			125/128				41		
15	D2	5/8		·6250	20	814		864	384
			24/25				71		
16	D3	3/5		·6000	19·20	884		900	400
			80/81				22		
17	D4	16/27		·5926	18·96	906		911·25	405
			243/256				90		
18	Ni1	9/16		·5625	18	996		960	426·67
			80/81				22		
19	Ni2	5/9		·5556	17·78	1018		972	432
			24/25				71		
20	Ni3	8/15		·5333	17·07	1088		1012·50	450
			125/128				41		
21	Ni4	25/48		·5208	16·67	1129		1036·80	460·8
			24/25				71		
22	S	1/2		·5000	16	1200		1080	480

The Calculations in Columns marked ⊛ are our own.

N.B.—Though the scale of Srutis of Nagoji Row resembles more or less the English Enharmonic scale and the scales of Deval and Clements, it is an improvement upon all these. 17 out of the 22 Swarams of Nagoji Row can be accounted for thus :—16 notes of the Enharmonic scale and one Sruti with $\frac{32}{25}$ or 307·20 vibrations from that of Chinnasawmy Mudaliar. There is also an unanimity between Nagoji Row and Deval in 17 Srutis. The second Sruti with 250 vibrations, the 12th Sruti $\frac{36}{25}$ with 345·6 vibrations and the 14th $\frac{25}{16}$ with 375 vibrations are found among the 25 Srutis of Clements which he adopts from Sangeeta Ratnakaram. These are nothing but the notes of the Enharmonic scale. The 10th Sruti of Nagoji Row with 324 vibrations is the new 11th Sruti with 324 vibrations found in the list of 24 Srutis of Clements and Deval. But there is a new Sruti in Nagoji Row's list, namely, the 21st $\frac{48}{25}$ with 460·8 vibrations.

The Table showing the list of Srutis is appended on P. 274.

The writer *thinks* that these are the 22 Srutis found in our Sangeeta Shastras. He does not definitely quote either from Sangeeta Ratnakaram or Parijatam. Again it is one of the fundamental laws of music that swarams must occur in the same intervals both while ascending and descending. In this respect it is remarkable to note that according to the principle by which the multiplication of the first Sruti $\frac{25}{24}$ with the 21st Sruti $\frac{48}{25}$ gives $\frac{2}{1}$. Nagoji Row has fixed the 21st Sruti with 460·8 vibrations as $\frac{48}{25}$. But according to Deval the multiplication of his first $\frac{25}{24}$ with his 21st $\frac{243}{128}$ does not give the result $\frac{2}{1}$. In some other places also Deval has fixed some Srutis which do not satisfy the above general rule. So it is praiseworthy that Nagoji Row's theory satisfies this principle in many cases. But the 10th Sruti before Prati Ma, and the 12th Sruti after Prati Ma and Prati Ma itself do not satisfy this. If these also follow the general principle then the 22 Srutis might be found satisfactory in one respect at least. But it will be perfect if all the Srutis are of equal intervals.

It is noteworthy that Nagoji Row locates 3 Srutis between Ma and Pa and one between Ga and Ma. This is as it ought to be. But Deval locates two Srutis with very close intervals between Ma and Pa and two more very close Srutis between Ga and Ma. He fixes two Srutis where there ought to be three, and two where there should be one. We may remember that Deval took away $3\frac{3}{4}$ from a Sruti with $303\frac{3}{4}$ vibrations when he proceeded by the Sa-Pa Series and fixed it at 300. What shall we say about his calculation if he makes this $303\frac{3}{4}$ a separate Sruti ? Nagoji Row gives three Srutis with $\frac{25}{18}$, $\frac{36}{25}$, and $\frac{64}{45}$ between Ma and Pa or $\frac{4}{3}$ and $\frac{3}{2}$. On the other hand, Deval gives only two Srutis, $\frac{45}{32}$ and $\frac{64}{45}$. Again, between Ga and Ma or $\frac{5}{4}$ and $\frac{4}{3}$, Deval gives two Srutis $\frac{81}{64}$ and $\frac{32}{25}$ instead of a single Sruti. All these may be clearly seen in Table VI. Other advocates of the 22 Srutis have 6 and 8 different kinds of Sruti intervals with different cents but Nagoji Row's Sruti intervals are of 4 different kinds only having 22, 41, 71 and 90 cents. It is also to be noted that $\frac{2}{1}$ is the product of the multiplication of the intervals taken from the two ends *Seriatim*. On the whole this is not the system of Sarnga Dev; nor, does it suit Karnatic music. As he says in the beginning of his essay his scale is "according to Western Musicians"

We know personally the years spent by Nagoji Row in his researches on Srutis and also the time of the construction of a Veena to suit his srutis and the time when it became public property. As a result of his labours many were induced to work in the same field. Finding that their own attempts were in vain they were compelled to accept the theory of Nagoji Row as no other course was open to them.

Nagoji Row says that these are probably the Srutis that are used in the music of India but he does not particularly say in what music. So we need not dwell at length on this question. Nagoji Row, who had observed the very minute Srutis used, tried his best to bring about a kind of uniformity between what was practised by Vidwans of Karnatic music and what was said in literature about the 22 Srutis. But the Vidwans who found that according to Nagoji Row the Srutis not only differed in ascending and descending scales but also that the Ragams became altered gave it up in despair. The mathematical calculations were also new to them. On the other hand, if they had stood by him firmly and found its merits and demerits by practice they would have benefited the world. It is the bane of Karnatic musicians that they would neither correct themselves nor correct others but leave everything in a state of doubt. Many of the sciences of India have been made known to the public in the shape of dialogues between a Guru and his disciple. If they had done the same here it would have been of much use ; on the other hand, no attempt was made to assist Nagoji Row and he was left severely alone.

The chief defect in Nagoji Row's theory is that the Srutis instead of having the same pitch while ascending and descending (which is a necessary condition in Karnatic music) are different in pitch. The rule of Vadi and Samvadi here are not quite satisfactory. About the above conditions which are a neeessary adjunct of all music our readers may clearly see them in the Chapter on Karnatic system of music. We have already dwelt on the change of Grahams on page 266.

Nagoji Row has also given his opinion on Melakartas and the 12 semitones. Our readers will hear more about them in the chapter on Sruti system of South Indian music.

SEVENTH.

The theory of Srutis of Subramania Sastrial who says that the 22 Srutis of Sarnga Dev are the Srutis of South Indian Music.

Subramania Shastrial read two essays on the above subject in two conferences of the Tanjore Sangeeta Vidya Mahajana Sangam. Finding the two essays to be of no use, he gave a third view which he says was the result of his researches. His third resembles that of Nagoji Row. But he changes the three Sthanams between Ma and Pa. We find the same chief defects here as are found in the theory of Deval. It will be well if we take no notice of his essays or his calculations of Srutis. However, as he is one of those who say that the Karnatic music should be sung according to the 22 srutis and as he has a few followers, we deem it necessary to point out some of the chief errors in his systems.

In the Second Conference Report of the Sangeeta Vidya Mahajana Sangam, Sastrial says as follows :—

1. "In ancient times we had only a few instruments like the Veena and a practical ear for Ragams but no up-to-date instruments by which the subtlest differences in tone can be recognised as the Westerner had. So, having the conclusions of Western musical science for a basis, I shall try, as far as lies in my poor knowledge, to make a comparison between them and our own, and find out how far they are at one."

Here he says that we did not possess subtle instruments in ancient days for noting the minutest differences but only posessed a few musical instruments like the Veena and a practical hear-say knowledge of Ragams. He finds fault with our ancestors, because, he is incapable of understanding the beautiful order of their minute Swarams and the inner meaning of the Sootrams which they handed down. It is a well known fact that the ancients, without any of the help of the modern up-to-date instruments, have calculated the minutest divisions in the science of Astronomy, have computed the periods of the eclipses of the Sun and the Moon and have laid down the rules for finding out the five necessary informations of Natchatram, Tidhi, Varam, Yogam and Karanam. Without the use of modern instruments have they not perfected the science of Anatomy? Have they not, by virtue of their rigid penance, written about the spiritual science of Ashtanga Yoga Sastram? Why do such sages need these modern instruments? An instrument is a necessity for one who has lost the keenness of perception. Only a man ignorant of Arithmetic needs a mathematical table in his pockets! If he had actually followed Sarnga Dev in his calculations of the 22 srutis, as he professes to do, he will not have made such a statement. In his essays he pretends to understand the meaning of Sarnga Dev and says "*In the literature bearing on Indian music it is said that Sruti is a factor, 22 of which go to compose an octave.*" After having made such a statement he is at a loss to find out the real truth in it and tries to establish another method which may conform to Western Science and modern Indian methods.

He has not understood the principle that the Tara Sthayi should be double that of Madhya Sthayi and the Atitara Sthayi double that of Tara Sthayi, nor the calculations of the 22 Srutis of Sarnga Dev by which the Swarams should gradually ascend in pitch without admitting any other Sruti in the middle, nor the Srutis of Karnatic music. So, instead of appreciating the musical genius of the ancients whose system was to learn the Srutis by rote, like the crocodile which let go the leg of the fox and caught hold of the root of the Nowal tree instead, he enunciates a number of wrong theories and deplores the absence of advanced scientific instruments among the ancients! If he would only understand the Veena, the glory and the subtle structure thereof and the genius of our ancestors, he would certainly acknowledge that it is the Indian music which lent its lustre to the music of the world. If he would only observe the flute with seven holes, and the numerous Srutis that could be produced out of a single one of these holes, he will have some idea of the genius of the ancients.

In the Second Conference Report he further says as follows :—

" 2. Prathamasravanach chhabdah sruyate hrasvamatrakah.
Sa srutih saumparijñeya svaravayavalakshana.

Sruti is the minimum of audible sound, which is capable of continued vibration. Sruti when it vibrates continually, becomes a Swaram. The most ancient authority on Srutis is the book called **Sangeeta Ratnakaram.** It speaks about the method to be adopted in discriminating Srutis and recommends two Veenas with 22 different strings each. To construct such an instrument at the present day is impracticable; so we may adopt a different method. First, let us take a porcelain cup which, when filled with water and struck, gives a particular Sruti. We will take this as the standard Sa; then take another cup with a Sruti slightly higher in pitch and so on. If we have 26 such cups arranged in ascending order, and if we strike them in succession, we shall find that the sound of the 23rd, 24th, 25th and the 26th is but the repetition, in a higher Sthayi of the Srutis produced by 1, 2, 3 and 4.

Suppose we take a similar series of cups and sound them also. We shall find that the cups numbering 4, 7, 9, 13, 17, 20, 22 and 26 in both the sets will sound the fundamental Swarams Sa, Ri, Ga, Ma, Pa, Dha, Ni and Sa'. Now, if we fix this series as the standard and sound the cups numbering 3, 6, 8, 12, 16, 19, 21 and 25 as an ascending scale, this series of sounds will be quite distinct from the standard series. Then, if we begin the scale at 2 and go on with 5, 7, 11, 15, 18, 20 and 24, we shall find that the Ga and Ni of this series (7 and 20) is the same as the Ri and Dha (7 and 20) of the standard series, thus proving beyond doubt that Suddha Ga and Suddha Ni are capable of two varieties. In the same way, by sounding the series 1, 4, 6, 10, 14, 17, 19 and 23, and the series 3, 5, 9, 13, 16, 18, and 22 for Ri, Ga, Ma, Pa, Dha, Ni, and Sa we may establish beyond doubt that Suddha Ri and Suddha Dha are capable of three varieties each, and that Sa, Ma and Pa have four varieties each—thus giving the sum total of the possible Srutis within the Scale as 22 ".

The writer has translated the Sootrams in Sangeeta Ratnakaram which speak about the Srutis very accurately. He has also grasped fully the Srutis of the Sapta Swarams and the system by which they commence respectively from the four Srutis of Sa. He is as clear as the author of *Sangeeta Ratnakaram* and equally so in interpreting it. But he has not understood the mystery of it. It is no wonder that he has erred where others before him have erred also in not understanding the hidden meaning. If he had really understood it he would not have given several separate tables showing the 22 Srutis.

He declares that he has not the slightest doubt about the identity of the Suddha Swarams mentioned in Sangeeta Ratnakaram, but then he proceeds to give entirely different mathematical calculations to prove the truth of the same. We cannot understand this procedure of his.

It is a matter for wonder that he recommends porcelain cups to a beginner for determining Srutis without mentioning any other percussion instrument. To regulate sounds by means, of adding to, or, lessening the water in a cup is only possible in the case of people with very good ear for music; and it is not possible either to get cups regulated for the 22 Srutis. People of understanding will easily know that this is not the best means of making the Srutis known to beginners.

Again he says in the second conference report as follows :—

"3. If we examine the ascending scale of the first series of fundamental swarams, we may recognise it as the scale of the modern *Bhairavi*. That is why, in some treatises *Bhairavi* is considered the Audiragam. So I have no hesitation in saying that the Suddha Swarams mentioned in Sangeeta Ratnakaram are the ascending scale of Bhairavi. The following slokam is on the same presumption :—

Chatus chatus chatus chaiva shadjamadhyamapañchamāh
Dve dve nishādagāmdhārau tris trī rishabhadhaivatau.

This means that SA, MA and PA have each of them 4 Srutis, NI and GA have 2 each and RI and DHA have 3 Srutis each.

In *Ragavibodham* it is said

Teshām srutayaḥ kramato vedā (4), rāmā (3), drisau (2), tathāmbudhayaḥ (4),
Nigamā (4), dahanāḥ (3), pakshav (2), evaṃ dvavimsatihsarvaḥ
Turyāyāṃ saptamyāṃ tāsu navamyaṃ srutau trayodasyam
Saptadasīvimsīdvavimsīshu cha te sphutaḥ kramataḥ.

All other writers, with the exception of the author of Sangeeta Ratnakaram, only repeated like a parrot the mathematical calculations of the Srutis, without caring to demonstrate them in actual practice. For example, it is a known fact that the Suddha Swarams of the scale occur in 4, 6, 8, 13, 17, 19, 21 and 26th places, whereas the above quotation contradicts it. So we must not be led away by the special names used at the modern times for the different Srutis in the scale.

The author of *Sangeeta Parijatam*, who first establishes the calculations for the Suddha Swarams and then determines the Swara Sthanams in the Veena, makes mention of 12 Sthanams for both the Suddha and the Vikruti Swarams.

The following are the slokas he quotes :—

Dhvanyavachchhinnavīnayām madhye tārakasaḥ sthitaḥ.

The Tara Sthayi is just in the centre of the sounding Veena.

Ubhayoḥ shadjayor madhye madhyamaṃ svaramācharet.

The Sthanam for Madhyamam should be fixed between the Shadja Sthanam of the Meru and the Shadja Sthanam of the Tara Sthayi.

Tribhāgatmakavīnāyam pañchamaḥ syāt tadagrime.

Panchamam is located at the end of the first part when the whole Veena is divided into three equal parts.

Shadjapañchamayor madhye gâmdhârasya sthitir bhavet.

Ga will be in the exact middle between Sa and Pa.

Sapayoh pûrvabhâge cha sthâpanîyo'tha risvaraḥ.

Ri will be placed at the end of the first part in the three equal divisions between the Meru and Pa.

Sapayor madhyadese tu dhaivatam svaramâcharet.

Dha will be between Tara Shadjam and Pa.

Tatrâmsadvayasamtyâgân nishâdasya sthitir bhavet.

Ni should be located in the very same place after two Sthanams.

Bhâgatrayânvite madhye mero rishabhasamjñitât.

Bhâgadvayottaram meroḥ kuryât komalarisvaram.

Komala Ri should be placed between the Meru and the Ri after two Sthanams

Merudhaivatayor madhye tîvragamdhâramâcharet.

The Teevra Gandharam should be between the Meru and the Dha.

Bhâgatrayavisishte'smims tîvragâmdhârashadjayoḥ.

Pûrvabhâgottaram madhye mam tîvratamamâcharet.

The Teevra Ma should be located between Teevra Ga and Sa after one Sthanam.

Bhâgatrayânvite madhye pañchamottarashadjayoh

Komalo dhaivataḥ sthpâyah pûrvabhâge manîshibhih.

The Komala Dha must be between Pa and Tara Sa after one Sthanam.

Tâthaiva dhasayor madhye bhâgatrayasamanvite

Pûrvabhâgadvayâdûrdhvam nishâdam tivramâcharet.

The Teevra Ni should be between Dha and Tara Sa after two Sthanams.

Thus, if we should produce on the Veena the 13 successive swarams beginning from Madhya Sa to Tara Sa, the following lengths of wires are necessary :- (a) If the length of wire of Madhya Sa be 1, then Komala Ri should have $\frac{17}{18}$ of the length, Ri $\frac{8}{9}$, Ga $\frac{5}{6}$, Teevra Ga $\frac{19}{24}$, Ma $\frac{3}{4}$, Teevra Ma $\frac{32}{45}$, Pa $\frac{2}{3}$, Komala Dha $\frac{11}{18}$, Dha $\frac{7}{12}$, Ni $\frac{5}{9}$, Teevra Ni $\frac{18}{35}$ and Tara Sa $\frac{1}{2}$.

Thus the relative length of wire determines the pitch of the sound. It is a known fact that the Madhya Sa and Tara Sa are in perfect Unison, because the Tara Sa has double the number of vibrations of Madhya Sa. This gives us the rule that if we want the octave of a note, the length of wire should be exactly half of that of the original. So the vibrations of swarams from Madhya Sa to Tara Sa range from 1 to 2. The fractions representing the length of wire when inverted give the following:— (b) Madhya Sa 1, Komala Ri $\frac{18}{17}$, Ri $\frac{9}{8}$, Ga $\frac{6}{5}$, Teevra Ga $\frac{24}{19}$, Ma $\frac{4}{3}$, Teevra Ma $\frac{45}{32}$, Pa $\frac{3}{2}$, Komala Dha $\frac{18}{11}$, Dha $\frac{12}{7}$, Ni $\frac{9}{5}$, Teevra Ni $\frac{35}{18}$, Tara Sa 2.

The same principle is spoken of in the Sanskrit work Sesha Lilavati as follows:—

Tantrītantusvaro jñeyas taddairghyavyastamānataḥ.

So, if we take a wire 32 inches long for the Madhya Sadjam, then, according to the above calculation, Komala Ri will require 29 17/27, in., Ri 28 4/9 in., Ga 26 2/3 in., Theevra Ga 25 1/3 in., Ma 24 in., Theevra Ma 22 2/9 in., Pa 21 1/3 in., Komala Dha 19 5/9 in., Dha 18 2/3 in., Ni 17 7/9 in., Theevira Ni 16 8/9 in., and Tara Sadjam 16 inches of wire.

The relation between sounds is determined by their respective vibrations per second. If we suppose that a wire 32 inches long produces 240 vibrations per second when struck, we may easily conclude that Madhya Sa (wire, 32 in. long) has 240, Komala Ri 259 1/5, Ri 270, Ga 288, Theevra Ga 303 3/19, Ma 320, Teevra Ma 345 3/5, Pa 360, Komala Dha 392 8/11, Dha 411 3/7, Ni 432, Theevra Ni 454 14/19 and Tara Sadjam 480 vibrations per second.

It is a recognised fact that relative proportion of vibrations per second for the Srutis from Sa to Ma and Pa to Sa' in the Scale is the same. This is also the theory of **Pythagoras**, the Greek Philosopher. According to him the seven fundamental notes of the scale have the following vibrations per second :—Madhya Sa 240, Ri 270, Ga 303 3/4, Ma 320, Pa 360, Dha 405, Ni 455 5/8, Tara Sa 480. Here also we see that the vibrations for notes between Sa and Ma are in the ratio of 8 : 9, 8 : 9, and 243 : 256. The same is the ratio for the notes between Pa and Tara Sa.

If we notice the relation between the same Swarams as given in Sangeeta Parijatam, we see that the following is the ratio for the respective vibrations of notes between Madhya Sa and Ma, namely—25 : 27, 24 : 25, 15 : 16, 19 : 20 and 18 : 19, and between Pa and Tara Sa 11 : 12, 21 : 22, 20 : 21, 19 : 20 and 18 : 19. Here we see a difference in the Komala Dha and Dha. But we cannot alter Komala Ri and Ri to suit these, as they are also recognised Swarams both in Science and practice.

So the surmise is that the author has unconsciously erred in reckoning their vibrations. If we also notice the system of Sarnga Dev for Suddha Swarams we must conclude that the author of Parijatam has erred. So in trying to correct the latter part so that it may conform to the former, I was compelled to alter his slokas here and there, and the following altered slokas were the result."

Our readers are requested to pay particular attention to this.

We see in the above extract that the author, with a view to change Dha in conformity with Ri, multiplies some of the Srutis of Ri by 3/2, and distributes them accordingly after the Sa-Pa system of the author of *Parijatam*. He multiplies the 12/11 Komala Ri and 8/7 Ri by 3/2 and determines Komala Dha as 18/11 and Dha as 12/7 respectively. Not satisfied with altering these swarams according to his own fancy, he blames the author of *Parijatam* by saying that he has unconciously erred, and in order to set it right he alters the slokas of a Sanskrit work which, according to his own statement, is 300 years old. He has not understood that the system given by the author of *Parijatam* is for the benefit of those who have no musical ear and not for geniuses in music. The very statement "Sa-Pa system" is the key note for determining all the Srutis. But to those who have no musical ear this is nothing but a stumbling block. This has confounded a number of musical Vidwans and even philosophers like Pythagoras. So it is no wonder that Sastrial has been taken in. This is the Corner Stone of all musical edifice, and the key for determining all ancient music.

Again in the Second Conference of the Sangam he has quoted the following slokas :—

Dhvanyavachchhinnavînayam madhye tarakasaḥ sthitaḥ.
Ubhayoḥ shadjayor madhye madhyamaṃ svaramâcharet.
Tribhâgâtmakavinâyam pañchamaḥ syât tadagrime.
Shadjapañchamayor madhye gâṃdharasya sthitir bhavet.
Sapayoḥ pûrvabhâge cha sthâpanîyo'tha risvaraḥ.

This is plain.

* Pasayor dvyamasamtyâgâ nishâdasya sthitir bhavet.

1. Ni must be located between Pa and Tara Sa after two sthanams.

Dhaivatasya sthitir madhye nipayor dvyamsataḥ param

2. Dha stands between Pa and Ni after two places.

Bhâgatrayânvite madhye mero rishabhasamjñitât.
Bhagadvayottaraṃ meroḥ kuryat komalarisvaram.

3. This is also plain.

Madhyamaḥ syât tîvratamo madhye rishabhashadjayoḥ.

4. Teevra Ma is placed between Ri and Tara Sa

* Tîvramarshabhayor madhye tîvragâmdhâramâcharet.

5. Teevra Ga must be located between Ri and Teevra Ma.

* Bhagatrayânvite sthâpyaḥ komalo dhaivataḥ svaraḥ.
* Bhâgadvayât paraṃ madhye padhayos tu manîshibhiḥ.

6. Komala-Dha must come after the second Sthanam when the interval between Pa and Dha is divided into three Sthanams.

* Tathaiva nisayor madhye nishâdaṃ tîvramâcharet.

7. Teevra Ni must come between Ni and Tara Sa.

We are afraid Mr. Sastrial is in the habit of altering slokas. Perhaps this custom has been in existence from ancient times. We cannot but be reminded here of the words of Rameschandra Dutt and Sooryanarayana Sastrial. Great men like Sastrial, who appeared from time to time, have put their sacrilegious hands on ancient Sastras and have destroyed the first place of India among countries of the world and have confounded others also. We very much doubt whether another Sastrial might not have given his mutilated view as regards the 22 Srutis.

With a view to display his knowledge of Sanskrit the author has mutilated 10 out of the 17 padams, and he makes bold to say that he was compelled to alter the slokas in some places to suit his own view of Srutis.

The following are the results of his alterations as given in his essay read at the second conference of the Sangam :—

Fractions.

" (a) Madhya Sa 1, Koma Ri $\frac{15}{16}$, Ri $\frac{8}{9}$, Ga $\frac{5}{6}$, Teevra Ga $\frac{64}{81}$, Ma $\frac{3}{4}$, Teevra Ma $\frac{32}{45}$, Pa $\frac{2}{3}$, Komala Dha [illegible], Dha $\frac{16}{27}$, Ni $\frac{5}{9}$, Teevra Ni $\frac{8}{15}$, and Tara Sa $\frac{1}{2}$.

Pitch.

(*b*) Madhya SA 1, Komala RI $\frac{27}{25}$, RI $\frac{9}{8}$, GA $\frac{6}{5}$, Teevra GA $\frac{24}{19}$, MA $\frac{4}{3}$, Teevra MA $\frac{36}{25}$, PA $\frac{3}{2}$, Komala DHA $\frac{81}{50}$, DHA $\frac{27}{16}$, NI $\frac{9}{5}$, Teevra NI $\frac{36}{19}$, and Tara SA 2.

Length of the wire.

(*c*) Madhya SA 32, Komala RI 29 $\frac{17}{27}$, RI 28$\frac{4}{9}$, GA 26$\frac{2}{3}$, Teevra GA 25$\frac{1}{3}$, MA 24, Teevra MA 22$\frac{2}{9}$, PA 21$\frac{1}{3}$, Komala DHA 19$\frac{61}{81}$, DHA 18$\frac{26}{27}$, NI 17$\frac{7}{9}$, Teevra NI 16$\frac{8}{9}$, Tara SA 16.

Vibrations.

(*d*) Madhya SA 240, Komala RI 259$\frac{1}{5}$, RI 270, GA 288, Teevra GA 303 $\frac{3}{19}$, MA 320, Teevra MA 345$\frac{3}{5}$, PA 360, Komala DHA 388 $\frac{4}{5}$, DHA 405, NI 432, Teevra NI 454$\frac{14}{19}$, and Tara SA 480.

Intervals between Fractions.

(*e*) From Madhya SA to MA, 25:27, 24:25, 15:16, 19:20 and 18:19. From PA to Tara SA, 25:27, 24:25, 15:16, 19:20 and 18:19.

This is, I presume, what the author of *Parijatam* must have had in mind. But of his Suddha Swarams and Vikruti Swarams the former are not mathematically accurate. For his RI, GA, DHA and NI are located above the Sthanams given for them in *Sangeeta Ratnakaram*. There can, therefore, be only 3 Madhya SAS, 4 RIS, 2 GAS, 3 MAS, 4 PAS, 4 DHAS, and 2 NIS (3 Tara SAS,) in all 22."

Here we see that he gives the length of wire, the vibrations and fractional measurements for the Suddha Swarams and says that he believes that this must have been in the mind of the author of *Parijatam*. Why has he not interpreted the mind of the author of *Sangeeta Ratnakaram* when he has been able to know the mind of the author of *Parijatam* who flourished only 300 years ago? Again he says that we may make bold to say that the Suddha Swarams of *Parijatam* do not conform to those of *Sangeeta Ratnakaram*. Perhaps Mr. Sastrial has not realised the fact that the system of determining the 22 Srutis of *Sangeeta Ratnakaram* is entirely different from the system of determining the Suddha Swarams of *Parijatam*. The appended tables will clear his doubts. We do not think he is right in confounding the two, before understanding the tables.

Again he says in the Second Conference essay as follows :—

"Now we shall determine which of these Suddha Swarams obtained from *Parijatam* are in conformity with the opinion of the ancients and with science. According to the opinion of Western Scientists who have made special researches into harmony the following are common to both. SA 240, RI 270, MA 320, PA 360, Tara SA 480. Watson, the Scientist, accepts Komala RI 259$\frac{1}{5}$, GA 288, and Teevra MA 345$\frac{3}{5}$. Though Western scientists do not accept Teevra GA 303$\frac{3}{19}$, yet Pythagoras accepts a note with 303$\frac{3}{4}$ vibrations which very nearly approaches it. We have also to accept other Srutis according to the principle that the intervals between SA and MA should be identical with the intervals between PA and Tara SA. We might also accept 455$\frac{5}{8}$ for NI which is recognised by Pythagoras."

He says that the Swaram with 303$\frac{3}{19}$ vibrations given in *Parijatam* is recognised by Pythagoras with a slight alteration 303$\frac{3}{4}$, and in the same manner the Ni with 455$\frac{5}{8}$ vibrations. We have found fault with this in our criticism of Deval.

In Table 7 Shastrial selects Srutis with vibrations (303¾ and 307½), (320 and 324), (360 and 364½), (384 and 388·8), (405 and 410$\frac{1}{16}$) and (455⅝ and 461¼) *i.e.*, with differences of 3¾, 4, 4½, 4·8, 5$\frac{1}{16}$, 5⅝ vibrations. Again in Table 12 he selects Srutis with vibrations (300, 303$\frac{1}{27}$ and 307⅕), (333⅓, 337½ and 341⅔), (355⅝ and 360), (375, 379$\frac{13}{18}$ and 384), (400 and 405), (426⅔ and 432) and (450, 455⅛ and 460$\frac{4}{9}$) *i.e.*, with differences of 3$\frac{25}{27}$, 3$\frac{101}{135}$, 4⅙, 3⅚, 4$\frac{4}{9}$, 4$\frac{13}{18}$, 4$\frac{5}{18}$, 5, 5⅓, 5⅛, 5$\frac{1}{9}$.

If there are Srutis with 300, 303¾, 307½ vibrations with 3¾ vibrations as difference why not there be Srutis with vibrations of 311¼ and 315 with the same 3¾ vibrations as difference; 307½ + 3¾=311¼; 311¼ + 3¾=315.

Again, if there are Srutis with 320, 324, 333⅓, 337½ and 341⅔ *i.e.*, with 4 vibrations as difference why not there be one with 328$\frac{8}{9}$ vibrations 4$\frac{8}{9}$ vibrations more than 324 and 4$\frac{4}{9}$ vibrations less than 333$\frac{1}{3}$.

Similarly, if there are Srutis with 355$\frac{5}{9}$, 360, 364½, 375, 379$\frac{13}{18}$ and 384 vibrations *i.e.*, with 4$\frac{4}{9}$, 4½, 4$\frac{13}{18}$ and 4$\frac{5}{18}$ vibrations as differences, why not there be one with 370 vibration,—5½ vibrations more than 364½ and 5 vibrations less than 375.

Following the same argument between 410$\frac{1}{16}$ and 426⅔ we can have 415 and 420 and between 432 and 450 we can have 438 and 444 and so on.

The *Fractions* and *Cents* for most of these vibrations are to be found in Table 20. For others 311¼v=450c. 315v=$\frac{21}{16}$=471c; *vide* Deval. 328$\frac{8}{9}$v=$\frac{37}{27}$=545c; 370v =$\frac{37}{24}$=749c, 444v=$\frac{37}{20}$=1065c, the 25th, 34th and 48th of Shastrial's 53. 444$\frac{4}{9}$v=$\frac{50}{27}$ =1067c. and 420v=$\frac{7}{4}$=969c. of Clements. 415v=948c. 438v=1041c.

The privilege which Ga enjoys might be extended to other swarams! Sastrial will clearly see from this that there may be more srutis than 22 in an octave. When he is confounded with the 22 Srutis mentioned in *Ratnakaram*, he says that "these Srutis, in my humble opinion, are in conformity with modern science". If he had clearly stated what modern science says on the subject it would have been more useful. He has only quoted what Pythagoras said 2,400 years ago, but has not stated anything new. He makes this statement because he is ignorant of the beautiful system in vogue amongst the Tamilians many thousand years before the time of Pythagoras.

Again he says in the same essay as follows:—" We have now determined 12 out of the 22 Srutis mentioned in *Ratnakaram*. We shall now proceed to find the others. Any amount of discussion of the theory of the author of *Parijatam* will be fruitless without bringing his opinion to light. So in my attempt to bring his theory to light I accidentally stumbled against a system which has been a hidden mystery till now. This has enabled me to determine the whole series.

Let us take, according to *Parijatam*, Ma as the Standard. (This will be the *10th* Sthanam as we shall presently see). If we imagine this to be Sa we may locate Tara Sa which will be its Panchama Sthanam. As Tara Sa is right in the centre of the string, the Madhya Sa will naturally be at the Meru Sthanam. This is the *first* Sthanam. From this we may determine its Pa which will be the *14th* Sthanam. The Pa from this becomes the fifth Sthanam of Tara Sa. If the length of the string for the above be doubled, we arrive at the *5th* Sthanam of the Madhya Sthayi. The Pa from this becomes the Sthanam for our *18th* Sruti. From this we derive the *8th* Sthanam of the Tara Sthayi. Doubling the length of string of the above Sruti we arrive at the 8th Sthanam of the Madhya Sthayi. If we proceed in the manner till we arrive at the 17th

TABLE 7

The first table of 22 Srutis of South Indian Music given by Subramanya Sastrial at the first two Conferences of the Sangam.

Adapted from Pythogoras and Watson and from the altered Slokas from Parijatam.

Number of Swaram.	Name of Swaram.	Fraction showing the Srutis if Tonic SA is 1.	The measurement of Srutis in a wire 32 inches long.	Cents.	Vibrations of Srutis if SA=540.	Vibrations of Srutis if SA=240.	After Parijatam (1st Conference). Fractions.	Measurement of Srutis in a wire 32 inches long.	Cents.	Vibration.
1	2	3	4	5 ⊛	6 ⊛	7	8	9 ⊛	10 ⊛	11 ⊛
	S	1	32		540	240	1	32	0	240
1	R_1	80/81 §	31·60	22	546·75	243	—			
2	R_2	15/16 §	30	112	576	256	—			
3	R_3	25/27 *	29·63	133	583·20	259·2*	25/27	29·63	133	259·2
4	G_1	8/9	28·44	204	607·5	270	8/9	28·44	204	270
5	G_2	640/729 §	28·09	225	615·094	273·375	—			
6	M_1	5/6 *	26·67	316	648	288*	5/6	26·67	316	288
							19/24	25·33	404	303 3/19
7	M_2	64/81 ‡	25·28	408	683·438	303·75				
8	M_3	32/41 §	24·98	429	691·875	307·5	—			
9	M_4	3/4	24	498	720	320	3/4	24	498	320
10	P_1	20/27 §	23·70	520	729	324	—			
11	P_2	45/64 §	22·50	610	768	341·33	—			
12	P_3	25/36 *	22·22	631	777·6	345·6*	25/36	22·22	631	345·6
13	P_4	2/3	21·33	702	810	360	2/3	21·33	702	360
14	D_1	160/243 §	21·07	723	820·125	364·5	—			
15	D_2	5/8 §	20	814	864	384	—			
16	D_3	50/81 †	19·75	835	874.8	388·8				
							11/18	19·56	853	392 8/11
17	N_1	16/27 †	18·96	906	911·25	405				
18	N_2	1280/2187 §	18·73	927	922·641	410·063				
							7/12	18·67	933	411 3/7
19	S_1	5/9	17·78	1018	972	432	5/9	17·78	1018	432
							19/36	16·89	1106	454 14/19
20	S_2	128/243 ‡	16·86	1110	1025·156	455·625				
21	S_3	64/123 §	16·65	1131	1037·813	461·25	—			
22	S_4	1/2	16	1200	1080	480	1/2	16·	1200	480

§ Sastrials own Srutis † Srutis resulting from alteration of Slokas.
‡ Srutis after Pythogoras. * Srutis after Watson.

The Calculations in Columns marked ⊛ are our own.

Sthanam, the following series will be the result, viz. 21, 12, 3, 16, 7, 20, 11, 2, 15, 6, 19, 9, 22, 13, 4, 17. Do we not now see as clear as day light the 12 Sthanams and the other hidden Sthanams also? There is another secret in connection with this which will be given out by me on another occasion."

In the above extract he says "I accidentally stumbled against a system which has been a hidden mystery till now," but only gives the method of determining swarams by the SA-PA series. Following this method he proceeds by 14 Sthanams if the first Sruti is included, or, 13 Sthanams if the given Sruti is left out of consideration. This proceedure of 13 by 13 is not a new method discovered by Mr. Sastrial but is only the method of the authors of *Sangeeta Ratnakaram* and *Parijatam* and Pythagoras. Again, his procedure by thirteens is open to criticism, as will be seen from the tables he gives.

TABLE 8

Table showing the formation of 22 Srutis by the SA-PA system.

1 Proceeding by thirteens or SA-PA system **The system of Sarnga Dev.**				2 Proceeding by thirteens or SA-PA system **Where Subramania Sastrial has erred.**			
		10	M_1			10	M_1
1	M_1	10+13−22= 1	S_1	1	M_1	10+13−22= 1	S_1
2	S_1	1+13 =14	P_1	2	S_1	1+13 =14	P_1
3	P_1	14+13−22= 5	Ri_1	3	P_1	14+13−22= 5	Ri_1
4	Ri_1	5+13 =18	D_1	4	Ri_1	5+13 =18	D_1
5	D_1	18+13−22= 9	G_2	5	D_1	**18+13−22= 8**	G_1
6	G_2	9+13 =22	Ni_2	6	G_1	8+13 =21	Ni_1
7	Ni_2	22+13−22=13	M_4	7	Ni_1	21+13−22=12	M_3
8	M_4	13+13−22= 4	S_4	8	M_3	12+13−22= 3	S_3
9	S_4	4+13 =17	P_4	9	S_3	3+13 =16	P_2
10	P_4	17+13−22= 8	G_1	10	P_3	16+13−22= 7	Ri_2
11	G_1	8+13 =21	Ni_1	11	Ri_3	7+13 =20	D_3
12	Ni_1	21+13−22=12	M_3	12	D_3	20+13−22=11	M_2
13	M_3	12+13−22= 3	S_3	13	M_2	11+13−22= 2	S_2
14	S_3	3+13 =16	P_3	14	S_2	2+13 =15	P_2
15	P_3	16+13−22= 7	Ri_3	15	P_2	15+13−22= 6	Ri_2
16	Ri_3	7+13 =20	D_3	16	Ri_2	6+13 =19	D_2
17	D_3	20+13−22=11	M_2	17	D_2	**19+13−22= 9**	G_2
18	M_2	11+13−22= 2	S_2	18	G_2	9+13 =22	Ni_2
19	S_2	2+13 =15	P_2	19	Ni_2	22+13−22=13	M_4
20	P_2	15+13−22= 6	Ri_2	20	M_4	13+13−22= 4	S_4
21	Ri_2	6+13 =19	D_2	21	S_4	4+13 =17	P_4
22	D_2	19+13−22=10	M_1	22	P_4	17+13−22= 8	G_1
					G_1	8+13 =21	Ni_1
					Ni_1	21+13−22=12	M_3
					M_3	12+13−22= 3	S_3
					S_3	3+13 =16	P_3
					P_3	16+13−22= 7	Ri_3

For example the 18th Sruti DHA is obtained from the 5th Sruti RI. He says from this we may obtain the 8th Sthanam of the Tara Sthayi. This is wrong, because we should obtain the Second GA or 9th Sruti of the Tara Sthayi (13th Sruti) and not the 8th Sruti. In other words $18+13-22=9$. He gives 8 instead. As he has erred in one sthanam, his series is 8, 21, 12, 3, 16, 7, 20, 11, 2, 15, 6 and 19 instead of 9, 22, 13, 4, 17, 8, 21, 12, 3, 16, 7 and 20.

Again instead of $19+13=32$; and $32-22=10$, he gives 9. Again, owing to this initial error, he locates Srutis at 9, 22, 13, 4 and 17. But, 11, 2, 15, 6, 19 and 10 must be the series. He has changed GA_2 into GA_1 in the 5th line and MA_1 into MA_2 in the 17th line. But as we see from Table 8 with the exception of GA_1 and GA_2 in the 5th and the 17th lines respectively all that follows conform to the SA-PA series. If the 13th Sruti from the 18th Sthanam be an error all that follows must also be considered wrong. In the same manner if there is an error in the Second GA in the 18th line all that follows must also be wrong. Instead of that we find only 2 Swarams changed. This forces us to say that the above 2 have been specially altered by the author to suit his own convenience.

As is seen from the first half of the above Table when we proceed by thirteens from the 10th Sruti we should obtain all the 22 Srutis in the octave step by step. In other words, whether we commence at the 1st, the 10th or the 14th Sruti or any other we must return again in a cycle to the place we started from. But in the second half of the above Table such a procedure is impossible. If we start from the GA, which is obtained at the fifth step, and proceed onwards, only the 17 steps from the GA to PA_4 which is the 21st step will come in a cycle while the others will not at all recur. In the same manner, in the second half if we get 10 ($19+13=32$; and $32-22=10$) at the 17th step, only the first 17 places will come in a cycle and not the remaining five. Mr. Shastrial who found that five places above and below do not satisfy the general rule has made a little alteration both at the end of the first five and the last five. He has reduced two Srutis, therefore, at the fifth and the seventeenth steps. This has necessitated him to say that we should proceed by SA-PA series from the 10th step. For, this procedure of going up by thirteens gives us MA_1, SA_1, PA_1, RI_1 and DHA_1. Finding that he does not arrive at GA_1 and NI_1 by this method, in the fifth line, instead of getting GA_2 he accounts for GA_1 and gives 8 instead of $(31-22=)9$ as the number of the Sruti. With the object of obtaining all the Second Srutis of the main swarams in a serial order as M_2, SA_2, PA, RI_2, DHA_2, GA_2, NI_2, just as he obtained the first Srutis of the Sapta swarams, he reduces one Sruti and makes it 9 instead of $(32-22=)$ 10. But in due course MA_1 must follow DHA_2. So he tries in vain to regulate a wrong system, forgetting that there is the right method. He has altered the fractions also to reduce these two Srutis. For he knows very well that unless he gives up these two Srutis, his theory of 22 Srutis in the octave will not stand. Men of brains will understand that he unconciously and unwittingly suspected the truth like the young lad who, with a view to save his father that was hidden in the paddy store-house declared "My father is not inside the paddy store-house." Why should be commit an error to establish his Srutis as 22? He has deliberately done this. It would be a great boon

TABLE 9

The table showing there are more Srutis than 22 in an octave when we proceed by the Sa-Pa and Sa-Ma series or by 701·955 and 498·045 cents.

1. Sa-Pa system.				2. Sa-Ma system.		
Number of Sruti.	The system of determining Srutis by the Sa-Pa system.	The Sruti Sthanam.	Name and place of Sruti.	Number of Srutis.	The system of determining Srutis by the Sa-Ma system.	Name and place of Sruti.
1	2	3	4	5	6	7
1	0 + 701·955	= 701·955	13 P	1	498·045	9 M_1
2	701·955 + 701·955 − 1200	= 203·910	4 R_4	2	996·090	18 N_1
3	203·910 + 701·955	= 905·865	17 D_4	3	294·135	5 G_1
4	905·865 + 701·955 − 1200	= 407·820	8 G_4	4	792·180	14 D_1
5	407·820 + 701·955	= 1109·775	21 N_4	5	90·225	1 R_1
6	1109·775 + 701·955 − 1200	= 611·730	12 M_4	6	588·270	10 M_2
7	611·730 + 701·955 − 1200	= 113·685	3 R_3	7	1086·315	19 N_2
8	113·685 + 701·955	= 815·640	16 D_3	8	384·360	6 G_2
9	815·640 + 701·955 − 1200	= 317·595	7 G_3	9	882·405	15 D_2
10	317·595 + 701·955	= 1019·550	20 N_3	10	180·450	2 R_2
11	1019·550 + 701·955 − 1200	= 521·505	11 M_3	11	678·495	11 M_3
12	521·505 + 701·955 − 1200	= 23·460	2 R_2	12	1176·540	20 N_3
13	23·460 + 701·955	= 725·415	15 D_2	13	474·585	7 G_3
14	725·415 + 701·955 − 1200	= 227·370	6 G_2	14	972·630	16 D_3
15	227·370 + 701·955	= 929·325	19 N_2	15	270·675	3 R_3
16	929·325 + 701·955 − 1200	= 431·280	10 M_2	16	768·720	12 M_4
17	431·280 + 701·955	= 1133·235	1 R_1	17	66·765	21 N_4
18	1133·235 + 701·955 − 1200	= 635·190	14 D_1	18	564·810	8 G_4
19	635·190 + 701·955 − 1200	= 137·145	5 G_1	19	1062·855	17 D_4
20	137·145 + 701·955	= 839·100	18 N_1	20	360·900	4 R_4
21	839·100 + 701·955 − 1200	= 341·055	9 M_1	21	858·945	13 P
22	341·055 + 701·955	= 1043·010	22 S	22	156·990	22 S
23	1043·010 + 701·955 − 1200	= 544·965	13 P	23	655·035	9 M.
24	544·965 + 701·955	= 1246·920	4 R.	24	1153·080	18 N_1

to the world if such errors be corrected instead of being perpetuated. It is not right that he who came to establish the truth of what was written in Sanskrit should commit an error. However we see by the first column of Table 8 that the 22 Srutis in an octave are obtained if we proceed by the SA-PA series. But we shall see from Table 9 that his theory will not be in conformity with that of Sarngadev as his (Sastrial's) SA-PA system and the 2/3 system or SA-PA of others are entirely different.

If we fix 1200 cents for the Madhya Sthayi, the PA of the SA-PA series will have 701·955 cents. If we measure from PA this SA-PA we arrive at RI. So RI will have 701·955+701·955=1403·910 or, 203·910 cents above the 1200 cents of the Madhya Sthayi. If we add to this the 701·955 cents of SA-PA we arrive at DHA_4 with 905·865 cents. If we proceed in this manner for the 22 Srutisthanams Mr. Sastrial says we find we come to the end of a Sthayi at 1043·010 cents. But this is wrong, for this is less than 1200 cents by 156·990 cents. If we proceed, then, by the above system a Sthayi finishes at the 24th step with about 47 cents in excess. This excess can be easily accounted for. In the same way, it is apparent that in SA-MA series also we must proceed 24 steps; only here it is 47 cents less; whether proceeding by SA-PA or by SA-MA series we get in a Sthayi 24 steps. Understanding that the ancient Dwavimsati Sruti scale will not suit this exact scale of SA-PA he tries to supress the two srutis.

Just as a Sthayi is complete in 22 srutis, the sum of 9 Srutis and 13 Srutis, this must be complete according to cents also exactly. But according to this procedure there is an excess of 47 cents in the SA-PA series and a deficiency of 47 cents in the SA-MA series. I do not think that Sarngadev who theorises that the pitch of the upper Sthayi should be twice that of the lower Sthayi would have ever allowed so much difference as this. All that he says is that SA-MA is of 9 Srutis and SA-PA of 13 srutis. In no portion of his book do we find the theory of 3/4 and 2/3; and intelligent people will understand that an excess of 47 cents in the SA-PA system and a deficiency of 47 cents in the SA-MA system is an impossiblity; such being the case, who would accept a scale of 22 srutis in which the 22nd of the SA-MA series ends with an excess of 157 and SA-PA with a deficiency of 157 cents? Again the calculation must be entirely wrong where he leaves out 2 srutis in the octave and fixes the srutis at 22 proceeding by the principle of 2/3. It is palpable that he purposely omits two steps so as to leave out these two Srutis.

It is clear that there is not the slightest connection between his Srutis, their vibrations and fractions and between those resulting from the SA-PA series. Mr. Sastrial and others think that the position of PA is at 2/3 of the length of the wire. If we proceed with the series on this principle of 2/3 as 2/3, 2/3×2/3, 2/3×2/3×2/3 each of the 22 Srutis must result. The calculation may be seen in the following Table.

We see clearly the system of determining Srutis by the SA-PA system. He takes MA or 3/4 as the standard and asks us to proceed by the fifths. So we should get 1/2 if we mutiply 2/3 by 3/4. This 1/2 multiplied by 2/3 gives us 1/3. Doubling it we get 2/3 or PA of Madhya Sthayi. Multiplying this by 2/3 we get $4/9=2^2/3^2$ or RI. As this RI belongs to the upper Sthayi, when we double it we get $2^3/3^2$ or RI. Proceeding in this manner by multiplying by 2/3 he doubles the Swaram of the Tara Sthayi and locates them in the Madhya Sthayi. We may see clearly from column 6 of Table 10 how the order of

TABLE 10.

The table of 22 Srutis of the South Indian Music taken from **Subramanya Shastrial's** essay at the Second Conference.

Adapted from Parijatam on the Sa-Pa=⅔ System.

Number of Srutis according to Mr. Sastrial.	Number of Srutis according to correct method.	The order of Srutis.	Name of Swaram or Sruti.	Fraction of Srutis if Tonic SA be 1.	Decimal Fractions for Same.	The position of Srutis in a wire 32 inches long.	Cents.	How Srutis generate.	The Number of vibrations SA=540.	The Number of Swarams or Srutis.
1	2	3	4	5	6	7	8	9	10	11
	⊛	⊛			⊛	⊛	⊛	⊛	⊛	
1	1	2	S_1	1	1·000000				540	1
2	3	14	S_3	$2^{19}/3^{12}$	·986540	31·569	23	12s	547	2
3	4	9	S_4	$2^{11}/3^{7}$	·936443	29·966	114	1c+ 7s	577	3
5	5	4	Ri_1	$2^{3}/3^{2}$	·888889	28·444	204	2c+ 2s	608	5
4	6	21	Ri_2	$2^{30}/3^{19}$	✱·923837	29·562	137	1c+19s	585	4
6	7	16	Ri_3	$2^{22}/3^{14}$	·876925	28·062	227	2c+14s	616	6
7	8	11	G_1	$2^{14}/3^{9}$	·832393	26·637	318	3c+ 9s	649	7
8	9	6	G_2	$2^{6}/3^{4}$	·790123	25·284	408	4c+ 4s	683⅓	8
	10	23		$2^{33}/3^{21}$	★·821188	26·278	341	3c+21s	658)	
10	10	1	M_1	3/4	·750000	24·000	498	5c− s	720	10
9	11	18	M_2	$2^{25}/3^{16}$	✱·779489	24·944	431	4c+16s	693	9
11	12	13	M_3	$2^{17}/3^{11}$	·739905	23·677	522	5c+11s	730	11
12	13	8	M_4	$2^{9}/3^{6}$	·702332	22·475	612	6c+ 6s	769	12
(—	14	25	—	$2^{36}/3^{23}$	★·729945	23·350	545	5c+23s	740	)
14	14	3	P_1	2/3	·666667	21·333	702	7c+ s	810	14
13	15	20	P_2	$2^{28}/3^{18}$	✱·692879	22·172	635	6c+18s	779⅓	13
15	16	15	P_3	$2^{20}/3^{13}$	·657694	21·046	725	7c+13s	821	15
16	17	10	P_4	$2^{12}/3^{8}$	·624295	19·977	816	8c+ 8s	865	16
18	18	5	D_1	$2^{4}/3^{3}$	·592593	18·963	906	9c+ 3s	911	18
17	19	22	D_2	$2^{31}/3^{20}$	✱·615891	19·709	839	8c+20s	877	17
19	20	17	D_3	$2^{23}/3^{15}$	·584617	18·708	929	9c+15s	924	19
20	21	12	Ni_1	$2^{15}/3^{10}$	·554929	17·758	1020	10c+10s	973	20
21	22	7	Ni_2	$2^{7}/3^{5}$	·526749	16·856	1110	11c+ 5s	1025	21
22	2	19	S_2	$2^{26}/3^{17}$	✱.519658	16·629	1133	11c+17s	1039	22
(—	23	24	—	$2^{34}/3^{22}$	★·547459	17·519	1043	10c+22s	987	)
	1	2	S'	½	·5	16	1200	12c	1080	

The Calculations in Columns marked ⊛ are our own.

the Srutis, and that of decimal fractions, cents and vibrations of the Srutis come backwards and forwards, when we proceed this way.

The PA sounds at $\frac{2}{3}$= ·666667 of the wire ; PA_3 at ·692879 which is wrong, as ·692879 must come between the limit of the MA_4 and PA. If it comes out of order the calculation is certainly wrong. In the same manner, DHA_1 sounds at ·592593 of the wire and DHA_2 at ·615891. Instead of getting a smaller fraction for DHA_2 we get one larger in the limit of PA_4. Likewise, the MA_2 and RI_2 come out of order. His system itself creates a good deal of disorder among many of the Swarams. He locates SA_2 below SA_1 whereas it should come above it.

Again, in the number of the Srutis in the first column, we see 5 before 4, 10 before 9, 14 before 13 and 18 before 17. In the same way, their fractions, places, cents and vibrations are not in regular order.

Again when we proceed by $\frac{3}{4}$ at the 23rd step we come to an end at the 10th Sthānam just below $\frac{3}{4}$. But it ought to end at $\frac{3}{4}$ itself. If it does end there, it ends at 24th inch of a wire with 32 inches length, with ·75 as its decimal fraction and with its cents as 498. On the other hand it ends with 26·278 as length of wire at ·821188 having 341 cents. So this has 498—341 or 157 cents less as we pointed out in a previous Table. Only if we go two more steps further (23 and 24) an octave will very nearly come to an end. These may be seen with an asterisk* in the Table against the numbers 23, 24 a. d 25. The difference between the 545 cents against number 25 in the third column and the 498 cents against $\frac{3}{4}$ in the same column is 47 cents. So it is clear that when we proceed by fifths or $\frac{2}{3}$ unless there are more Srutis than 22 we do not come to an end. Whether we proceed by fifths ($\frac{2}{3}$) or fourths ($\frac{3}{4}$). *i.e.* whether the series be SA-PA or SA-MA, both must come to an end at one and the same place without the slightest difference in calculation. But as we get either 47 cents more or 47 cents less SA-PA and SA-MA do not exactly correspond to the $\frac{2}{3}$ and $\frac{3}{4}$. This may be clearly seen in the system treating about Karnatic music later on. Also 702 – 545 = 157 cents and 1200 – 1043 = 157 cents.

Again, the system of $\frac{2}{3}$ and $\frac{3}{4}$ will never correspond to the system of Sarnga Dev which proceeds by thirteens and nines. This may be clearly seen from the above Table. The same has been shown in Table 9 also. Again, it is a matter to be noted that he proceeds by the SA-PA system from MA and not from SA. He ought, on the other hand, to have commenced from the Tonic SA. Knowing that the MA could not be located in the right place, (or $\frac{3}{4}$) if he commenced from Tonic SA, he proceeds from MA so that he might get the MA, PA, and SA' right. If he commenced from Tonic SA and proceeded by Panchamams or $\frac{2}{3}$ he would get $1 \times \frac{2}{3} = \frac{2}{3}$ or PA. From this of RI_4 or $\frac{2}{3} \times \frac{2}{3} \times 2 = \frac{8}{9}$ is obtained. From this he gets DHA_1 or $\frac{8}{9} \times \frac{2}{3} = 2^4/3^3$. If this is multiplied by $\frac{2}{3}$ he gets GA_2 or $2^4/3^3 \times \frac{2}{3} = 2^5/3^4$ of the Tara Sthayi. If this is doubled $2^6/3^4$ or GA_2 of the Madhya Sthayi results. As we proceed in this manner at the 22nd step we obtain $2^{33}/3^{21}$ with 341 cents but not $\frac{3}{4}$ with 498 cents, or MA. Unless two more steps are taken MA cannot be obtained So, knowing that MA cannot be obtained at the 22nd step if he started from Tonic SA, he starts purposely from MA. There is not the slightest reason for such a process.

Again he says in his essay read at the 3rd Conference as follows :—

" 'Although in (the strings of) the harp as well as in the human vocal chord there could be produced various srutis with very slight shades of difference according to the theory of professors of Indian Music, yet they say that there are only twenty-two Srutis in the relationship of Shadja-Panchama both in the harp and the human voice.' From what I have said in my paper read before the last Conference, it will be apparent, that the author of the *Sangitaparijata* has after determining the positions of the twenty-two Srutis according to this theory, for convenience sake selected twelve out of the twenty-two for the harp. Adopting his theory of Shadjapanchamabhava if we proceed beyond the twenty-two stages we shall find that there are 53 distinct stages. Proceeding any further we shall only find that the same stages recur again.

Besides, even if we adopt the method of *Shadjamadhyamabhava*, we get the same fifty three stages which go to form a perfect scale. We can also show that the notes of the European scale are all comprised within these fifty three; so that if with the help of this Sonometer we could establish these facts, it should be conceded that such an instrument is in entire accord with, and satisfies the requirements of the science of music—Eastern and Western. If we should attempt to select any notes not based on this scale we must find that they are anything but concordant.

In the European system of music only certain intervals between notes are recognised as leading to harmony. Of these (i). *minor semi-tone* is one. This represents an interval between one note and another 2 stages apart, either above or below it. This may be designated as Ekasruti in our nomenclature. (ii). The *major semi-tone* of the European system may be represented by the interval between a note and another 4 stages apart, either above or below. This corresponds to the Dvisruti of our books. (iii). *The minor tone* of European music which is the Trisruti of our system has an interval of 7 stages above or below. (iv). The *major tone* which corresponds to our Chatusruti has an interval of 8 stages. (v). The *minor third* which may be designated Sadharanagamdharasruti has an interval 13 stages. (vi). The *major third* or Antaragamdharasruti as it may be called has 16 intervals above or below. (vii). The *fourth* which we call Madhyamasruti has an interval of 21 stages. (viii) The *fifth* which may appropriately be called Panchamasruti represents an interval of 30 stages above or below. (ix). The *Octave* which we shall name Sthayisruti represents an interval of 52 stages. Some writers recognise in certain places the *septimal third* and *septimal seventh* as suitable intervals. These respectively represent intervals of 11 and 42 stages according to our calculation. Of these—

Ekasruti is the interval between a note and another producing [illegible] times its vibration.
Dwisruti " " " [illegible] " "
Trisruti " " " [illegible] " "
Chatusruti " " " [illegible] " "
Sadharanagandharasruti " " [illegible] " "
Antaragandharasruti " " [illegible] " "
Madhyamasruti " " [illegible] " "
Panchamasruti " " [illegible] " "
Sthayisruti " " [illegible] " "

From the above it will be apparent that in our books the term Sruti is used in certain places to denote the intervals between specific notes.

We shall now see if our Sonometer could be profitably used in determining the several musical notes referred to as Suddhasvaras in the Samgitaratnakara. For this purpose let us take the Meru, *i.e.,* the first stage, to indicate *Adharashadja* or fundamental note. The 8th stage from this gives us the *Trisrutirishaba*. The 5th thence gives the *Dwisrutigandhara*. The 9th thence gives the *Chatusrutimadhyama*. The 9th after this the *Chatusrutipanchama*. Similarly the 8th from the *Panchama* gives the *Trisrutidhaivata*. The 5th thereafter the *Dwisrutinishada* and the 9th therefrom the *Chatusrutishadja*.

If we further examine the gradation of these stages we will note that the stages from *Adharashadja* to *Suddhamadhyama* correspond to stages from *Panchama* to *Shadja* of the higher *sthayi* inasmuch as each of the former groups bears the same ratio in interval to each of the latter. Also it may be noted that the interval between the 1st, 2nd, 3rd, and 4th of the former group, and the 1st, 2nd, 3rd, and 4th of the latter respectively will be what has been already referred to as *Panchamasruti*. Hence we may naturally expect that with *Panchamasruti* as our basis all other stages that are possible between *Adharashadja* and *Suddhamadhyama* will have as many corresponding stages between *Panchama* and *Shadja* of the higher *Sthayi* as their counterparts. Proceeding on the method detailed *supra* we will find that the 23rd stage from the *Adharashadja* of our sonometer gives us the Sruti assigned to *Suddhamadhyama*. We should now determine all possible stages above *Adharashadja* and those below *Suddhamadhyama* which will produce musical concord. We know that there are 4 intervals, *viz*., minor semitone, major semi-tone, minor-tone, and major-tone between one note and another either immediately above or below it. By proceeding above *Adharashadja* and below *Suddhamadhyama* and finding out the four intervals referred to above, we get the following ten stages, *viz*, 1, 4, 6, 9, 10, 14, 15, 18, 20 and 23. The counterparts corresponding to these will be 32, 35, 37, 40, 41, 45, 46, 49, 51 and 54 respectively. Of these as the 54th stage belongs strictly speaking to the next higher *Sthayi* we have thus so far got 19 *Srutis* within one *Sthayi* barring the interval between Suddhamadhyama and Panchama which has not been taken into account. As the interval between *Suddhamadhyama* and *Panchama* is a *Chatuhsruti* one there should be three Srutis between the two. In this matter the doubt may naturally arise whether these 3 Srutis are to be got by ascending from *Suddhamadhyama* or by descending from *Panchama*. This difficulty may, in a way, be tided over if we, for a moment, observe the effect of striking the string of a harp or any other stringed instrument. Let us see what happens. If we strike that string of a harp which produces the Shadja note, any one who has an ear for music cannot but note that along with that its third (Antaragamdhara) and perfect fifth (*Panchama*) notes are also produced. This is what is known as the harmonic triad in European music. Similarly if we strike the Panchama string, *Kakalinishada* and *Chatuhsrutirishabha* of the higher *Sthayi* are also produced which three merging together form a harmonic triad. From this it will be evident that just as Panchama and *Kakalinishada* correspond to *Shadja* and *Antaragamdhar* respectively, similarly *Chatuhsrutirishabha* of the higher *Sthayi* is the note which corresponds to *Panchama*. Similarly we may presume that the notes between the *Shadja* and the *Chatuhsrutirishabha* of the higher *Sthayi* on the same principle correspond to the notes between *Suddhamadhyama* each to each. The notes of the higher Octave between *Shadja* and *Chatuhsrutirishabha* are, as we know, 4th, 6th and 9th of the same *Sthayi*. Thus it will be seen that the three notes required are got by ascending from *madhyama* and not otherwise, and these three are 26th and 31st. Hence from the Sonometer we may find that out of the 53 stages we need take into account only the following twenty-two :—1, 4, 6, 9, 10, 14, 15, 18, 20, 23, 26, 28, 31, 32, 35, 37, 40, 41, 45, 46, 49 and 51.

From a detailed study of certain portions of our literature on Indian Music we find that in the place of the minor semi-tone we have considered here a certain interval which may be designated sub-minor second and which has been recognised by our professors. This can be determined by our Sonometer and is denoted by the interval between a stage and its 4th either above or below. According to this process the follows stages, *viz*. :—1, 5, 6, 9, 10, 14, 15, 18, 19, 23, 27, 28, 31, 32, 36, 37, 40, 41, 45, 46, 49 and 50 of our Sonometer can be easily identified as the required Srutis. This is in entire accord with the theory promulgated by the philosopher PYTHAGORAS. But as our method of investigation closely follows the European system and as the interval known as minor semi-tone has been employed in determining several pairs of corresponding notes by the author of the *Sangitaparijata* we have based our theory on this method."

TABLE 11.

The Table showing the 53 Srutis of
Subramania Sastrial
obtained by the SA-PA = $\frac{3}{2}$ = 701·955c and the SA-MA = $\frac{4}{3}$ = 498·045c Series.

1				2				3			
Number of 53 Srutis	How they are obtained.	Cents by the SA-PA System.	Names Selected for the 22 Srutis.	Number of 53 Srutis.	How they are obtained.	Cents by the SA-MA System.	Selected Srutis.	Number of 53 Srutis.	Order of Srutis by the SA-MA System.	Order of Srutis by the SA-MA System.	Name of the 22 Srutis.
1	2	3	4	5	6	7	8	9	10	11	12
	1	0			1	0		1	0	0	Chandowati
1	32	701·955	Rykika	1	23	498·045	Kenavi	2	23·460	19·845	
2	10	203·910	Kurali	2	45	996·090	Yownika	3	46·920	43·305	
3	41	905·865	Kowravi	3	14	294·135	Rudnika	4	70·380	66·765	Dayavati
‡4	19	407·820		4	36	‡792·180		5	‡93·840	90·225	
‡5	50	1109·775		5	5	‡90·225		6	113·685	110·070	Ranjani
6	28	611·730	Nykari	6	27	‡588·270		7	137·145	133·530	
7	6	113·685	Neerada	7	49	1086·315	Ganavati	8	160·605	156·990	
8	37	815·640	Dhokati	8	18	384·360	Venila	9	184·065	180·450	Raktika
9	15	317·595	Depika	9	40	882·405	Bhonati	10	203·910	200·295	Rowdri
10	46	1019·550	Jayanti	10	9	180·450	Meenaja	11	227·370	223·755	
11	24	521·505		11	31	678·495	Mynaki	12	250·830	247·215	
12	2	23·460		12	53	1176·540		13	274·290	270·675	
13	33	725·415		13	22	474·585		14	297·750	294·135	Krodha
14	11	227·370		14	44	972·630		15	317·595	313·980	Vajrika
15	42	929·325		15	13	270·675		16	341·055	337·440	
16	20	431·280	Chetika	16	35	768·720	Sona	17	364·515	360·900	
17	51	1133·235	Mayika	17	4	66.765	Heena	18	387·975	384·360	Prasarini
18	29	635·190		18	26	564·810	Hynuka	19	‡407·820	404·205	
19	7	137·145		19	48	1062·855		20	431·280	427·665	Precti
20	38	839·100		20	17	360·900		21	454·740	451·125	
21	16	841·055		21	39	858·245		22	478·200	474·585	
22	47	1048·010		22	8	156·990		23	501·660	498·045	Marjani
23	25	544·965		23	30	655·035		24	521·505	517·890	
24	3	46·920		24	52	1153·080		25	544·965	541·350	
25	34	748·875		25	21	451·125		26	568·425	564·810	Kshiti
26	12	250·830		26	43	949·170		27	‡591·885	588·270	
27	43	952·785		27	12	247·215		28	611·730	608·115	Rakta
28	21	454·740		28	34	745·260		29	635·190	631·575	
29	52	1156·695		29	3	43·305		30	658·650	655·035	
30	30	658·650		30	25	541·350		31	682·110	678·495	Sandipini
31	8	160·605		31	47	1039·395		32	701·955	698·340	Alapini

1				2				3			
1	2	3	4	5	6	7	8	9	10	11	12
32	39	862·560		32	16	337·440		33	725·415	721·800	
33	17	364·515		33	38	835·485		34	748·875	745·260	
34	48	1066·470		34	7	133·530		35	772·335	768·720	Madanti
35	26	568·425	Hynuka	35	29	631·575		36	‡795·795	792·180	
36	4	70·380	Heena	36	51	1129·620	Mayika	37	815·640	812·025	Rohini
37	35	772·335	Sona	37	20	427·665	Chetika	38	839·100	835·485	
38	13	274·290		38	42	925·710		39	862·560	858·945	
39	44	976·245		39	11	223·755		40	886·020	882·405	Ramya
40	22	478·200		40	33	*721·800		41	905·865	902·250	Ugra
41	53	1180·155		41	2	19·845		42	929·325	925·710	
42	31	682·110	Mynaki	42	24	517·890		43	952·785	949·170	
43	9	184·065	Meenaja	43	46	1015·935	Jayanti	44	976·245	972·630	
44	40	886·020	Bhonati	44	15	313·980	Depika	45	999·705	996·090	Kshobhini
45	18	387·975	Venila	45	37	812·025	Dhokati	46	1019·550	1015·935	Teevra
46	49	1089·930	Ganavati	46	6	110·070	Neerada	47	1043·010	1039·395	
‡47	27	591·885		47	28	608·115	Nykari	48	1066·470	1062·855	
‡48	5	93·840		48	50	‡1106·160		49	1089·931	1086·315	Kurrudvati
‡49	36	795·795		49	19	‡ 404·205		50	‡1109·775	1106·160	
50	14	297·750	Rudnika	50	41	902·250	Kowravi	51	1133·235	1129·620	Manda
51	45	999·705	Yownika	51	10	200·295	Kurali	52	1156·695	1153·080	
52	23	501·660	Kenavi	52	32	698·340	Rykika	53	1180·155	1176·540	
53	1	1203·615	Panasa	53	54	1196·385	Panasa	54	1203·615	1196·385	Chandowati

‡ Indicates the Srutis of Pythagoras.

If we notice the 22 Srutis obtained while proceeding by fourths or powers of $\frac{4}{3}$, $[\frac{4}{3}, (\frac{4}{3})^2, (\frac{4}{3})^3]$ and so on we will find a difference between the swarams 1, 4, 6 and 9 of Table 11 and the same number of swarams in the Table 12.

From the above extract we see that apart from the 22 Srutis which he establishes in an octave by the Sa-Pa series, he also makes mention of 53 Sthanams in an octave obtainable by the same process in which the 22 are included. He says the same 53 result from the Sa-Ma series. His words are :—" Adopting his theory of Shadja-Panchama-bhava if we proceed beyond the 22 stages we shall find that there are 53 distinct stages. The process of Shadja-Madhyamam also gives us the same 53 stages in an octave."

We have clearly stated before that when we proceed by Sa-Pa or $\frac{3}{2}$, the octave is not perfect unless there are the additional Sthanams 23rd and 24th. We have also given the reason why Mr. Sastrial has left out the two Sthanams. In the 8th column of the same Table we have marked the respective cents for the 22 Srutis. We shall now note there is not the slightest uniformity between these calculations and the cents for the 22 Srutis marked in the 53 Sthanams. In Table 11 which is appended we have shown how he proceeds by thirty ones in the Sa-Pa series, the order of their procedure and the particular Srutis he selects to make up his 22. These have been specially underlined. In the same way in the next side of the same Table we have shown his system of arriving at the 53 steps proceeding by twenty twos in the Sa-Ma series, and have underlined the 22 Srutis he selects out of them in the third column. These have been calculated on the principle of 1200 cents for an octave with 701·955 for $\frac{3}{2}$ or Pa and 498·045 for $\frac{4}{3}$ or Ma. We may notice in the first part where he proceeds by the Sa-Pa series he leaves 17 swarams severely alone from the 18th to the 34th, rejects 5 Sthanams after the 10th step and 4 after the 37th step. Likewise in the Sa-Ma series the 17 Srutis between 19 and 35, four Srutis after the 11th step and five after the 37th are given up. Why have these (5+17+4 continuous=) 26 Sthanams been left out without choosing any of the 22 out of them?

In the third column we have arranged side by side his Srutis by the Sa-Pa and the Sa-Ma series respectively. He has said before that the same Srutis result from the two series. We have put them side by side just to show that the Srutis in the two series are different. Again, out of the 27 Sthanams he has selected, leaving out the 22 Sthanams of Sarnga Dev, we have marked the Sthanams of Pythagoras. Those are the 5th, the 19th, the 27th, the 36th and the 50th. When he has said there could be no more Srutis than 22 in the octave, why does he waver and mark 27? Moreover, men of understanding know that the same Sthanams will not result in the two series $\frac{3}{2}$ and $\frac{4}{3}$ as there is some slight difference in calculation between the two. But he declares that their calculation is uniform. But he is wrong, for example, the 4th Sruti Dayavati obtained by the Sa-Pa series has a difference of 3·6 cents when compared with the same obtained by the Sa-Ma series. When one is 70 and the other 66 how can we say that the same Sthanam results from the two series? Again, Ranjani the 6th Sthanam has a difference of 3·6 cents. Again, the 10th Sthanam by the Sa-Pa series has 204 cents while the same by the Sa-Ma series has 200. The 23rd Sthanam by the Sa-Pa series has 502 cents and the same in Sa-Ma series has 498. For, the 32nd Sthanam 701·9 and 698·3 are the cents. If there is no unanimity in the 23rd and 32nd places—Ma and Pa—how could other Sthanams agree? Again, for the 54th place or the end of the Sthayi he gets 1203·615 cents instead of 1200 i.e., 3.615 cents in excess. This imperfection proves that the division of the octave into parts is wrong. In the same way, he gets 1196·385 cents for the 54th place by the Sa-Ma series or 3·615 cents less. A system which results in 3½ cents, more or less, must be wrong. So, by these we conclude that the statement that 22 Srutis are exactly obtained in an octave by the Sa-Pa or Sa-Ma series is incorrect. Again if we compare the cents for the 22 Srutis with those ascribed to them by him in Table 10 we may notice a vast difference between them. We need not point them out here as they may be clearly seen from the Tables. Again we think it unnecessary to dwell upon the names of the 22 Srutis of Sarnga Dev and the names of the 53 Srutis of Mr. Sastrial, as the calculations for them is primarily wrong.

Mr. Sastrial, besides accepting the 22 Srutis of Sarnga Dev as being in use in South Indian music, introduces a new system by accepting the five new Srutis of Pythagoras as also in use and says they satisfy the requirements of modern science. The measurement of these Srutis in the wire, their cents and the difference between them may clearly be seen from Table 12 which is appended. In the sixth column of this table we have indicated by a bracket ~ those Srutis of Pythagoras which correspond to any particular Sruti among his 22 Srutis while the Sruti Sthanams of Pythagoras himself are indicated by a double dagger ‡. In the same column, the Srutis 10, 11 and 12 which do not come under the 22 Srutis of Nagoji Row are marked by an asterisk*.

Again, he says in his essay read at the Third conference as follows :—

"Calculating this way we find that we obtain 22 Srutis in an octave which are useful for singing the Ragas in Karnatic music, that these are the 22 referred to in ancient treatises like *Ratnakaram* and that these, in my humble opinion, satisfy all the requirements of modern science."

Here Mr. Sastrial says that only 22 Swara Sthanams there are in an octave which are utilised for singing the Karnatic Ragas. But in the same breath he says there may be 27 Srutis in an octave, nay even 53 by the SA-PA, SA-MA series!! He makes a selection of 22 out of these 53. We ask why cannot the other 31 be also in use?

Helmholtz, the German Scientist, one of the professors who have made researches into Srutis, seems to say that an octave can be divided into 12, 19, 22, 29, 31, 43, 50, 53, 55, 301 equal parts, and that the 53 equal divisions will give us fractions which are more or less those of the Srutis in use at the modern day. But he does not give any reason why these particular equal divisions should result in an octave. Just as no reason is assigned for the number 22, the other numbers are also left equally unaccounted for. But Mr. Shastrial declares that the 53 Sthanams are obtained by the SA-MA series. The SA-MA system proceeds by powers of $\frac{4}{3}$. But proceeding by this principle he must understand that we do not finish at the Madhya Sthayi. The Madhya SA should have half the length of the wire. We have shown in the previous Tables that unless two more Srutis are added the length of wire will not be approximately half nor would the octave come to an end there. Again, if the 53 Sthanams are obtained by the SA-MA system why not have them all in use? Why should the particular Sthanams 1, 4, 6, 9, 10, 14, 15, 18, 20, 23, 26, 28, 31, 32, 35, 37, 40, 41, 45, 46, 49, 51 and 54 be chosen out of the whole lot? What is the principle of this selection? When he has accepted the Sruti intervals of the author of *Ratnakaram*, such as 4, 3, 2, 4, 4, 3, 2, why should he not subscribe to his 22 Srutis but create a new theory of 53? It will be a great boon if he could repeat here his feat of altering the 10 Sootrams of the author of *Parijatam*! He would have created a few more doubts here also. We get the intervals 3, 2, 3, 1, 4, 1, 3, 2 respectively from the numbers 1, 4, 6, 9, 10, 14, 15, 18 and 20. So the intervals between the Srutis vary from 1 to 4. Sarnga Dev never meant such intervals to exist nor have they ever been found in our Karnatic music. Mr. Shastrial will clearly see that his theory stands in the way of the singing of Moorchanas and Grahaswarams so much in use amongst the ancients.

Mr. Shastrial while attempting to establish the 22 Srutis of Sarnga Dev, instead of dividing the octave into 22 parts divides into 53, and picks out 22 out of them. He would have done well to hold fast the other words just as he had done with the number 22. If we would only be guided by the experience of others in locating the Sapta Swarams and experiment it himself he will find that all his fantastic mathematical calculations are completely inaccurate. Instead of being guided by what has been in practice among distinguished musicians from time immemorial, he is guided by what is said in Sanskrit. The result is he has altogether deviated from truth.

Again, he says that he obtains a few Swarasthanams by taking the 4th, 6th, 9th and the 10th out of the 53 and proceeding upwards from Sa and downwards from the fourth Ma.

Such a system was never mentioned by Sarnga Dev. These approximate swarams are not useful either for Moorchanas or Grahaswaram. He says, these irregular swarams result from the Sa-Ma series. He proceeds by twenty twos in the Sa-Ma series and by thirty ones in the Sa-Pa series.

No doubt it is possible to confuse together a number of systems and arrive at irregular Srutis by the change of Sthanams here and there. But Karnatic musicians of high repute will never accept these.

When we notice the Table 12 we find the names of the 22 Srutis of Sarnga Dev in the fourth column. Chandovati, the fourth Sruti of Sa, is the first name. The three other Srutis of Sa, namely, Teevra, Kumudvati and Mandah, are marked under Tara Sa as the 19th, 20th and the 21st Srutis. Besides these, in the fifth column we see some names for the 22 Srutis. While we have not definitely decided about Sruti Sthanams and their calculations, it is not advisable to enter into controversy about the names of the Srutis. Moreover, we give this up for the present, because the names of the 22 Srutis, the names of the 53 Srutis of Mr. Sastrial and the names of Srutis now in use in Karnatic music are all conflicting. The measurements of 19 Sthanams in a string for the Srutis found in the sixth column are a copy from Nagoji Row's and not anything new. The five Sthanams marked with a double dagger ‡ are the ones found among the 53 Srutis obtained by the Sa-Pa or Sa-Ma series. He says that these five are obtained from the system of Pythagoras. But we find a slight difference between these swarams and those of Pythagoras. The three Srutis of Ma, namely 10, 11 and 12 are entirely different from those of Nagoji Row. These may be clearly seen in numbers 10, 11, 12 of Table 6. They may be still more clearly noted in the 11th column of Table 12 where the cents for the intervals between srutis are given as 71, 41, 71 and 22. But in the 8th column of Table 6 we see that between the 9th, 10th, 11th, 12th and the 13th Srutis we have the cents 22, 71, 41 and 71. Again, he says that the four Srutis of Ri should have the intervals 71, 41, 71 and 22. Although this may be said to be true as regards the four Srutis of Ma, how does he declare these four Srutis for Ri and that these are the identical ones? What has become of Sarnga Dev who declared that Ri could have no more than 3 Srutis? If he thus mercilessly alters the system of the ancients wherever he lays his hands, how will he obtain any one to support his views? Perhaps the learned have the privilege of altering ancient theories to suit modern ones. But we may be sure that unless a system is capable of being put into practice it will not be accepted by the Public. It is not fair to try to establish the truth of an ancient usage by introducing and mixing in it a number of modern usages.

We might see by Table 11 how he arrives at the 53 srutis by the Sa-Pa and Sa-Ma series and how he picks out 22 out of the lot. In Table 12 we might see the fractional calculations of 27 Sruti Sthanams found in the 6th column and how Sthanams 2, 10, 13, 18 and 26 are those of Pythagoras. The following Table 13 will clearly show the disagreement between the calculations of the Srutis obtained by the Sa-Ma series in Table 11 and those of the Srutis found in column 6 of Table 12.

TABLE 12

Showing the 27 Srutis in use in South Indian Music as read by **Subramanya Shastrial** in the III conference in accordance with the theories of science and Pythagoras as written in Sangita Ratnakaram.

Number of the 22 Srutis.	Number of the 27 Srutis.	No. of Srutis.	Names of 22 Swarams or Srutis.	Names of 22 Swarams or Srutis.	Fractions showing the positions of other Srutis when Tonic SA is 1.	Fractions showing the intervals between Srutis.	Positions in a String of 32 inches.	Positions of Srutis in a String of 36 inches.	Cents.	Cents for intervals.	Vibrations for each Sruti if Tonic SA=540.	Vibrations for each Sruti if Tonic SA=240.
1	2	3	4	5	6	7	8 @	9	10 @	11	12 @	13
		4	Chandowati	Shadjam	1		32	36-0			540	240
										71		
1	1	5	Dayavati	Ekasruti Rishabham	24:25 }	24:25	30·72	34-11⅕	71		562½	250
	2				128:135‡ }		30·34	34-2⅜	92	41	569½	253⅛
2	3	6	Ranjani	Dvisruti Rishabham	15:16	125:128	30·	33-15	112	71	576	256
3	4	7	Raktika	Suddha Rishabham	9:10	24:25	28·80	32-8	182	22	600	266⅔
4	5	8	Rowdri	Chatursruti Rishabham	8:9	80:81	28·44	32-0	204	90	607½	270
5	6	9	Krodha	Suddha Gandharam	27:32	243:256	27·	30-7⅛	294	22	640	284⁴⁄₉
6	7	10	Vajrika	Sadharana Gandharam	5:6	80:81	26·67	30-0	316	71	648	288
7	8	11	Prasarini	Antara Gandharam	4:5	24:25	25·60	28-16	386	41	675	300
8	9	12	Preeti	Chyu. Madh. Gandharam	25:32 }	125:128	25·	28-2⅛	427		691⅕	307⅕
	10				405:512‡ }		25·31	28-9⅛	406	71	682⅔	303⅓⅐
9	11	13	Marjani	Suddha Madhyamam	3:4	24:25	24·	27-0	498	71	720	320
10	12	14	Kshiti	Teevra Madhyamam	18:25* }	24:25	23·04	25-18⅞	569		750	333⅓
	13				32:45‡ }		22·76	25-12	590	41	759⅜	337½
11	14	15	Rakta	Teevratara Madyamam	45:64*	125:128	22·50	25-6¼	610	71	768	341⅓
12	15	16	Sandipini	Teevratama Madyamam	27:40*	24:25	21·60	24-6	680	22	800	355⅝
13	16	17	Alapini	Panchamam	2:3	80:81	21·33	24-0	702	71	810	360
14	17	18	Madanti	Ekasruti Dhaivatam	16:25 }	24:25	20·48	23-0⅛	773		843¾	375
	18				256:405‡ }		20·23	22-15	794	41	854⅛	379⅛⅛
15	19	19	Rohini	Dvisruti Dhaivatam	5:8	125:128	20·	22-10	814	71	864	384
16	20	20	Ramya	Suddha Dhaivatam	3:5	24:25	19·20	21-12	884	22	900	400
17	21	21	Ugra	Chatursruti Dhaivatam	16:27	80:81	18·96	21-6⅜	906	90	911¼	405
18	22	22	Kshobhini	Suddha Nishadam	9:16	243:256	18·	20-5	996	22	960	426⅔
19	23	1	Teevra	Kaisika Nishadam	5:9	80:81	17·78	20-0	1018	71	972	432
20	24	2	Kumudvati	Kakali Nishadam	8:15	24:25	17·07	19-4	1088	41	1012½	450
21	25	3	Manda	Chyu. Shadja Nishadam	25:48 }	125:128	16·67	18-15	1129		1036⅛	460⅘
	26				135:256‡ }		16·88	19-0	1108	71	1024	455⅑
22	27	4	Chandowati	Shadjam	1:2	24:25	16·	18-0	1200		1080	480

The Calculations in Columns marked @ are our own. ‡ Srutis after Western Music. * New Srutis substituted for Nagoji Row's.

In the first column of Table 13 we have indicated the system of arriving at 22 Srutis by the SA-MA series commencing from MA. The Srutis obtained after the system of Pythagoras proceeding by $\frac{4}{3}$ are found in column 2. Sarnga Dev's Srutis are mentioned in column 3. The cents calculation of Srutis which result from the SA-MA series is found in column 8. In column 12 are found the fractions for his own Srutis. In the 11th column are found the cents corresponding to the fractions mentioned in column 12. In the 10th column the difference between the cents of the Srutis of the SA-MA series and those corresponding to the fractions found in column 11. We shall find here the same difference which we found between the Srutis of the SA-PA and the SA-MA series. Should there be no unanimity between the Srutis of the SA-MA series and the cents obtained for the corresponding fractions? As he commences with MA in the SA-MA series the cents corresponding to it are 498.045. This is $\frac{4}{3}$ we know. But $\frac{3}{2}$ or PA obtains 698.340c instead of 701.955c. So also in the SA-PA series MA has 501·660c instead of 498·045. We have already pointed out that this is the difference that occurs in the middle between the SA-PA and the SA-MA series. This is a slight difference come to by dividing the length of the wire into exactly $\frac{3}{2}$ or $\frac{4}{3}$. This slight difference which results in either series confounds the best of musicians and goes on lengthening without coming to an end in the octave like the tail of Anjaneya which lengthened at every touch! But for this slight difference either series would completely end in an octave. The details of these will be found later on in the chapter on Karnatic music. Just as there is a difference at the step $\frac{3}{2}$ so there is a difference of 3.615 cents where the TARA SA should end in 1200 cents. In the same manner, there is something less in RI, GA, MA, PA, DHA, NI and SA. In other cases also there is the slight deficiency of 2 or 1½ cents. We need not dilate upon these differences any further. The necessary detailed information may be found in the tables.

Mr. Shastrial also makes mention of another system which he gave out at the fifth conference.

In an essay on "Srutinirnayam" read by Mr. Shastrial in the fifth conference, he says as follows:—

"One and all of the ancient books on Indian Music written in the Sanskrit language such as the Natyasastra of Bharata, with one accord say that within the same Octave, Shadja has the 4 srutis—Tivra, Kumudvati, Manda and Chandovati; Rishabha has the 3 Srutis—Dayavati, Ranjani and Raktika; Gandhara the 2 Srutis—Raudri and Krodha; Madhyama the 4 Srutis—Vajrika, Prasarini, Priti and Marjani; Panchama the 4 Srutis—Kshiti, Rakta, Samdipini and Alapini; Dhaivata the 3 Srutis—Madanti, Rohini and Ramya; and Nishada the 2 srutis—Urga and Kshobhini. The following extract from some ancient Tamil work '[illegible],' will show that Tamil works on Indian Music also recognise only 22 Srutis.

Before we fix the positions of these 22 stages in our instrument let us for a while proceed to find out the nature of the Ekasruti interval which is slightly shorter than the Dvisruti one. What is referred to as Major-tone in works on European Music is but the Chatussruti of ours and similarly their Minor-tone and Major-semi-tone are respectively our Trisruti and Dvisruti intervals. The shorter interval Minor semi-tone of theirs is taken by some as corresponding to the Ekasruti interval of our system. The minor semi-tone is in our instrument the interval between

TABLE 13.

The Table which will be useful for making a comparison of the 22 Srutis suitable to South Indian Music picked out by Subramanya Sastrial out of his 53, and the 22 Srutis of Pythagoras and Western Science in conjunction with Tables XI and XII.

No. of Srutis out of the 53.	The 22 Srutis after Pythagoras.	The 22 Srutis picked out from the scientific treatises by Mr. Shastrial.	Decimal fractions.	Position of Srutis in a wire 32 inches long.	How Srutis result.	Number of vibrations of Srutis.	Cents after the SA-MA series.	Cents for intervals.	Difference between cents resulting from SA-MA series and the cents of Sastrial's fractions.	Cents corresponding to Sastrial's fractions.	The Swara Sthanams of Sastrial if Tonic SA be 1.
1	2	3	4	5	6	7	8	9	10	11	12
⊕	⊕	⊕	⊕	⊕	⊕	⊕	⊕	⊕	⊕	⊕	
	S	S	1·0000	32·00		540	0			0	1
17		1 R_1	·9622	30·79	1c — 17k	561	*66·765	67	+3·908	*70·673	24/25
(5)	(1) R_1		·9492	30·38	1c — 5k	569	‡90·225		+1·954	‡92·179	128/135
46	2 R_2	2 R_2	·9384	30·03	2c — 46k	575½	110·070	43	+1·661	111·731	15/16
10	3 R_3	3 R_3	·9010	28·83	2c — 10k	599⅓	180·450	70	+1·954	182·404	9/10
51	4 R_4	4 G_1	·8907	28·50	3c — 51k	606	200·295	20	+3·615	203·910	8/9
3	5 G_1	5 G_2	·8438	27·00	3c — 3k	640	294·135	94	—	294·135	27/32
44	6 G_2	6 M_1	·8341	26·69	4c — 44k	647	313·980	20	+1·661	315·641	5/6
8	7 G_3	7 M_2	·8009	25·63	4c — 8k	674½	384·360	70	+1·954	386·314	4/5
(49)	(8) G_4		·7917	25·34	5c — 49k	682	‡404·205		+1·661	‡405·866	405/512
37		8 M_3	·7811	24·99	5c — 37k	691⅓	*427·665	43	−0·292	*427·373	25/32
1	9 M_1	9 M_4	·7500	24·00	5c — 1k	720	498·045	70	—	498·045	3/4
18		10 P_1	·7216	23·09	6c — 18k	748	*564·810	67	+3·908	*568·718	18/25
(6)	(10) M_2		·7119	22·78	6c — 6k	758½	‡588·270		+1·954	‡590·224	32/45
47	11 M_3	11 P_2	·7038	22·52	7c — 47k	767	608·115	43	+1·661	609·776	45/64
11	12 M_4	12 P_3	·6758	21·62	7c — 11k	799	678·495	70	+1·954	680·449	27/40
52	13 P	13 P_4	·6681	21·38	8c — 52k	808½	698·340	20	+3·615	701·955	2/3
16		14 D_1	·6414	20·53	8c — 16k	841½	*768·720	70	+3·908	*772·629	16/25
(4)	(14) D_1		·6328	20·25	8c — 4k	853⅓	‡792·180		+1·954	‡794·134	256/405
45	15 D_2	15 D_2	·6256	20·02	9c — 45k	863	812·025	43	+1·661	813·686	5/8
9	16 D_3	16 D_3	·6007	19·22	9c — 9k	899	882·405	70	+1·954	884·359	3/5
50	17 D_4	17 N_1	·5938	19·00	10c — 50k	909⅓	903·250	20	+3·616	905·866	16/27
2	18 N_1	18 N_2	·5625	18·00	10c — 2k	960	996·090	94	—	996·090	9/16
43	19 N_2	19 S_1	·5561	17·79	11c — 43k	971	1015·935	20	+1·661	1017·597	5/9
(7)	20 N_3	20 S_2	·5339	17·09	11c — 7k	1011⅓	1086·315	70	+1·954	1088·260	8/15
(48)	(21) N_4		·5278	16·89	12c — 48k	1023	‡1106·160		+1·661	‡1107·821	135/256
36		21 S_3	·5207	16·66	12c — 36k	1037	*1129·620	43	−0·293	*1129·327	25/48
53	22 S	22 S_4	·5010	16·03	13c — 53k	1078	1196·385	67	+3·615	1200·000	1/2

The Calculations in Columns marked ⊕ are our own. * Srutis after science. ‡ Srutis after Pythagoras.

any stage and the 3rd after that. If we closely subject the 22 Srutis recognised by our system to scrutiny we shall find that 11 of them are got from the Suddha Madhyama stage known as Marjani by employing the Shadja-panchama standard of measurement one after another, and 10 others from the Marjani by employing the Shadja-madhyama standard one after another. The same result will be got by starting from the last note obtained by the above method and measuring backward with the Shadja-panchama standard. Having fixed the 22 stages thus, when we try to find out which of the intervals recognised in European Music would give us this result, we shall see that the interval Minor semi-tone has no place in this series. But if we employ the interval known as larger Limma in European Music in its place we get at the correct result. Thus we find that it is larger Limma and not Minor semi-tone that corresponds to the Ekasruti of our system and that it is the 4th stage after the starting point.

The stage right in the middle of the interval between the basic stage and its counterpart of the next higher Octave is Suddha Madhyama which forms as it were the very heart or centre of life of the scale. This is the 23rd stage obtained as above and is known as Marjani in the works on Music handed down to us from our ancestors. By proceeding from this according to the Shadja-panchama standard we arrive successively at the following stages the 54th or the 1st known as Chhandovati, the 32nd Alapini, the 10th Raudri, the 41st Urga, the 19th Priti, the 50th Manda, the 28th Rakta, the 6th Ranjani, the 37th Rohini, the 15th Vajrika, and the 46th Tivra. Then again proceeding from the same Marjani according to Shadja-madhyama standard we get in order the 45th Kshobhini, the 14th Krodha, the 36th Madanti, the 5th Dayavati, the 27th Kshiti, the 49th Kumudvati, the 18th Prasarini, the 40th Ramya, the 9th Raktika and the 31st Samdeepani. As will be seen from above we have thus got at the 22 Srutis referred to in our works as belonging to Shadja and other notes of the Octave."

From the above extract we see the names of the Dwavimsati Srutis and those of the seven fundamental swarams. The number of vibrations for the seven swarams is also given according to Tamil scientific treatises. These are well-known to all. After this he says how the 12 swarams, Marjani, Chhandovati, Alapini, Rowdri, Urga, Preeti, Manda, Rakta, Ranjani, Rohini, Vajrika, and Tivra result from the SA-PA series and how the 11 Srutis Marjani, Krodha, Madanti, Dayavati, Kshiti, Kumudvati, Prasarini, Ramya, Raktika and Sandeepini are arrived at by the SA-MA series. All particulars about these are clearly stated in Table 11. All treatises speak about the deriving of the 22 Srutis either by the SA-PA or the SA-MA series. The modern opinion of Vidwans is, whether we derive 9 srutis by the SA-MA system or 13 srutis by the SA-PA system that in either case the octave must completly finish with them. Finding that MA and PA while thus proceeding by 9 and 13 according to Sarnga Dev do not result in the usual pitch, he takes the principle of $\frac{4}{3}$ and $\frac{3}{2}$. But finding that this principle threatens to give him more than 22 srutis in the octave, he adopts another. Again, knowing that he gets an excess of 157 cents at the 22nd step in the SA-MA or $\frac{4}{3}$ series and 157 cents less in the SA-PA or $\frac{3}{2}$ series he uses a stratagem so that there may not be much difference in the number of cents. In other words he chooses the first 11 Srutis while proceeding by thirty ones in the SA-PA series, and the first 11 Srutis in the SA-MA series while proceeding by twenty twos. Even this does not save his position. The inconsistencies and errors in this principle will be seen in the appended Table 14.

TABLE 14

Showing the Dwawimsati Srutis in use in South Indian Music as read by Subramania Sastrial in the V Conference in accordance with the theory of Shadja-Panchama and Shadja-Madhyama.

Number of Srutis.	Name of Sruti.	Fractions showing the positions of other Srutis when Tonic SA is 1.	Number according to SA-MA series.	Fractions showing the positions of the other Srutis when Tonic SA is 1.	Number according to SA-PA Series.	Decimal Fractions showing the position of other Srutis when Tonic SA is 1.	Decimal fractions showing the Positions of Srutis in a string of 32 inches.	Cents.	The order in which Srutis arise.	Vibrations for each Sruti if Tonic SA=540.	When properly arranged. Name of Sruti.	Cents.	Cents for Intervals.
1	2	3		4		5	6	7	8	9	10	11	12
		●	●	●	●	●	●	●	●	●	●	●	●
	S	$3^0/2^0$		1	2	1·0000	32	0		540	S	0	90
1	R_1	$3^5/2^8$	5	243/256		·9492	30·38	90·225	c − 5s	569	R_1	90	24
2	R_2	$3^{10}/2^{16}$	10	59049/65536		·9010	28·83	180·450	2c − 10s	599⅓	R_3	114	66
3	R_3	$2^{11}/3^7$		2048/2187	9	·9364	29·97	113·685	c + 7s	576⅔	Ri_2	180	24
4	R_4	$2^3/3^2$		8/9	4	·8889	28·44	203·910	2c + 2s	607½	Ri_4	204	90
5	G_1	$3^3/2^5$	3	27/32		·8438	27	294·135	3c − 3s	640	G_1	294	24
6	G_2	$3^8/2^{13}$	8	6561/8192		8009	25·63	384·360	4c − 8s	674¼	G_3	318	66
7	G_3	$2^{14}/3^9$		16384/19683	11	·8324	26·64	317·595	3c + 9s	648⅔	G_2	384	24
8	G_4	$2^6/3^4$		64/81	6	·7901	25·28	407·820	4c + 4s	683	G_4	408	90
9	M_1	$3^1/2^2$	1	3/4	1	·7500	24	498·045	5c − s	720	M_1	498	90
10	M_2	$3^6/2^{10}$	6	729/1024		·7119	22·78	588·270	6c − 6s	758½	M_3	588	24
11	M_3	$3^{11}/2^{18}$	11	177147/262144		·6758	21·62	678·495	7c − 11s	799	M^2	612	66
11	G_3	$2^{17}/3^{11}$		131072/177147		7399	23·68	521·505	5c + 11s	729⅘	M_4	678	
12	G_4	$2^9/3^6$		512/729	3	7023	22·48	611·730	6c + 6s	769			24
13	P	$2^1/3^1$		2/3	3	·6667	21·33	701·955	7c + s	810	P	702	
14	D_1	$3^4/2^7$	4	81/128		·6328	20·25	792·180	8c − 4s	853⅓	D_1	792	90
15	D_2	$3^9/2^{15}$	9	19683/32768		·6007	19·22	882·405	9c − 9s	899	D_3	816	24
16	D_3	$2^{12}/3^8$		4096/6561	10	·6243	19·98	815·640	8c + 8s	865	D_2	882	66
17	D_4	$2^4/3^3$		16/27	5	·5926	18·96	905·865	9c + 3s	911¼	D_4	906	24
18	N_1	$3^2/2^4$	2	9/16		·5625	18	996·090	10c − 2s	960	Ni_1	996	90
19	N_2	$3^7/2^{12}$	7	2187/4096		·5339	17·09	1086·315	11c − 7s	1011⅓	Ni_3	1020	24
20	N_3	$2^{15}/3^{10}$		32768/59049	12	·5549	17·76	1019·550	10c + 10s	973	Ni_2	1086	66
21	N_4	$2^7/3^5$		128/243	7	·5267	16·86	1109·775	11c + 5s	1025	Ni_4	1110	24
22	S	$3^0/2^1$		1/2		·5000	16	1200·000	12c	1080		1200	90

The Calculations in Columns marked ● are our own.

From the above Table we see that he arrives at 12 Sthanams commencing from Madhyamam, the 9th Sruti. Next, he arrives at 10 places by the SA-MA system. These are clearly indicated in the fourth column.

When we proceed by $\frac{3}{2}$ we obtain the following srutis :—

The first step gives us MA, the 9th Sruti.
The second step gives us Tonic SA.
The third gives us PA, the 14th Sruti.
The fourth gives us RI, the 4th Sruti.
The fifth gives us DHA, the 17th Sruti.
The sixth gives us GA, the 8th Sruti.
The seventh gives us NI, the 21st Sruti.
The eighth gives us MA, the 12th Sruti.
The ninth gives us RI, the 3rd Sruti.
The tenth gives us DHA, the 16th Sruti.
The eleventh gives us GA, the 7th Sruti.
The twelfth gives us NI, the 20th Sruti.

The above are indicated in Antique numbers in the Table. In the same way, when we proceed by the SA-MA series or $\frac{4}{3}$, we obtain at the second step $\frac{16}{9}$ or the 18th sruti. The third step gives us the fifth Sruti and the fourth step the 14th Sruti. Proceeding in this manner at the 11th step we obtain [illegible] or the 11th Sruti. Here if we proceed by the SA-PA series to the 13th step it must give us MA$_2$ or the 11th Sruti. But the 11th Sruti by the SA-MA series is MA$_2$. But the MA$_2$ which results from the 11th step of the SA-PA series, and the MA$_2$ which results from the 11th of the SA-MA series are entirely different. If we observe the number of cents for the two Srutis in column 3, we find that the MA$_2$ of the SA-MA series has 678·495 cents while the MA$_2$ of the SA-PA series has 521·505 cents. Thus a difference of 156·990 *i.e.* 157 cents between the two is noticeable. We have already seen from previous Tables that these 157 cents are wanting to complete an octave. If Mr. Sastrial had minutely calculated his fractions he would not have been led into this error. The same difference occurs in the $\frac{3}{2}$ or SA-PA series. The MA$_2$, or the 11th Sruti by either series must be the same. Whereas we find one 78½ cents above and the other 78½ cents below 600 cents which is therefore admittedly the M$_2$ or Prati Madhyamam. This may be clearly seen from Table 14. From the Table we may see that he gives in the third column 11 Srutis by the SA-PA series, and in the fourth column 11 Srutis by the SA-MA series.

Again, we have pointed in Table 10 how he obtains Srutis in irregular order while proceeding by $\frac{3}{2}$. The same irregularity occurs here also. In column seven we notice that the cents pertaining to the second Sruti are given for the third and *vice versa*. In the same manner the 6th and the 7th Srutis interchange. The same is to be said of the Srutis 10 and 11, 15 and 16 and 19 and 20. If we regulate them as we see in column 10 and 11, we find the kinds of Sruti intervals with 90, 24 and 66 cents alone (which we see in column 12) are complete in an octave. These three intervals come in the order of 15, 4, 11. These intervals are possible only when an octave is divided into 200 equal parts. This may be found in column 12. So the attempt of Mr. Shastrial in deriving 11 Srutis by the SA-PA series and 11 Srutis by the SA-MA series has resulted in his catching a Tartar !!, and has proved the possibility of dividing an octave into 200 Srutis !!.

If we concede that the Dwavimsati Srutis are the ones in use in Karnatic music we must also concede that Sarnga Dev and Bharata before him are authorities on Karnatic music as they have written at length about the 22 Srutis. Sarnga Dev who advocates the 22 Srutis says that there is the relation of Vadi and Samvadi between SA and PA and SA and MA. He fixes 8 Srutis between SA and MA and 12 between SA and PA. In other words, he fixes 10 and 14 in an octave including the starting Sruti, and 9 and 13 excluding it. So, in the ascending series of an octave we get 22 Srutis namely 9 and 13. In other words, from SA to MA 9 and from MA to SA 13, 9+13=22, or, from SA to PA 13 and from PA to SA 9, 13+9=22. He also states clearly whether proceeding from SA to PA *i. e.* MA to SA, or, SA to MA *i. e.* PA to SA the Srutis should stand in the relation of Vadi and Samvadi. He emphasises this in many places in his treatise. We understand clearly from this that there are 22 Srutis in the octave and that these should be used in Ganams by the SA-PA and SA-MA systems. Again, in the process of determining Srutis, if we proceed by thirteens or SA-PA system in the 22nd step the 22 Srutis should fill 13 Sthayis completely leaving neither blank Sthanams nor going beyond the 13th Sthayi. In other words, the Srutis in an octave go on in an ascending series and come back in a cycle to the first Sruti without creating any other possible intervals between. There is no confusion of any kind here. This may be seen from the appended Table 15. The same result is obtained if we proceed by nines or the SA-MA system where in the 22nd step the 22 Srutis should fill in the 9 Sthayis completely. These two views of the author of Sangeeta Ratnakaram are perfectly right. When such is the case, why should Vidwans depart from this time-honored view of 22 Srutis which are in use in our Ganams? Why should 53 Srutis occur in an octave in which there were only 22 before? Does their octave end with these 53 Srutis at least? Men of understanding will notice how while proceeding 22 Sthayis by the SA-MA series there are seven Sthanams less and how while proceeding 31 Sthayis by the SA-PA series there are seven Sthanams more. These have been clearly shown in the Tables. A reference to the Tables will clearly show that the theory of 53 Srutis in an octave obtained by the SA-PA or by the SA-MA series is incorrect. Modern music does not conform to the view of Sarnga Dev who says that the 22 Srutis in the octave should be of equal intervals. All that Mercator, Poole, Cheve, White, Thompson and Bosanquet say is that if an octave were divided into 53 equal Srutis, some of them (P. 313) will be harmonious, but they do not say they will obtain 53 Srutis by the SA-PA or SA-MA series. We have already pointed that some slight differences arise as we proceed upwards by $\frac{3}{2}$ or $\frac{4}{3}$. There is not the slightest connection between this and the 53 Srutis of Bosanquet &c., Mr. Shastrial has been trying his best to bring together two most irregular systems with the same disastrous result as that of the shepherd who, mistaking the bear and its young ones which were being carried by the flood to be sheep jumped into the river, and was caught in their embrace! If he divided

TABLE 15

Showing that according to Sa-Pa System when we take 13 steps each time, 22 Srutis will fill 13 Sthayis according to Ratnakaram.

	1	2	3	4	5	6	7	8	9	10	11	12	13	14	15	16	17	18	19	20	21	22
1													P_{1}									
2				P_{2}													P_{3}					
3								P_{4}													P_{5}	
4												P_{6}										
5			P_{7}													P_{8}						
6							P_{9}													P_{10}		
7											P_{11}											
8		P_{12}													P_{13}							
9						P_{14}													P_{15}			
10										P_{16}												
11	P_{17}													P_{18}								
12					P_{19}													P_{20}				
13									P_{21}													P_{22}
14													P_{23}									
15				P_{24}													P_{25}					
16								P_{26}													P_{27}	
17												P_{28}										
18			P_{29}													P_{30}						
19							P_{31}													P_{32}		
20											P_{33}											
21		P_{34}													P_{35}							
22						P_{36}													P_{37}			
23										P_{38}												
24	P_{39}													P_{40}								
25					P_{41}													P_{42}				
26									P_{43}													P_{44}
27													P_{45}									
28				P_{46}													P_{47}					
29								P_{48}													P_{49}	
30												P_{50}										
31			P_{51}													P_{52}						
32							P_{53}															
	1	2	3	4	5	6	7															

TABLE 16

Showing that according to Sa-Ma System when we take 9 steps each time, 22 Srutis will fill 9 Sthayis according to Ratnakaram.

	1	2	3	4	5	6	7	8	9	10	11	12	13	14	15	16	17	18	19	20	21	22
1									M1									M2				
2					M3									M4								
3	M5									M6									M7			
4						M8									M9							
5		M10									M11									M12		
6							M13									M14						
7			M15									M16									M17	
8								M18									M19					
9				M20									M21									M22
10									M23									M24				
11					M25									M26								
12	M27									M28									M29			
13						M30									M31							
14		M32									M33									M34		
15							M35									M36						
16			M37									M38									M39	
17								M40									M41					
18				M42									M43									M44
19									M45									M46				
20					M47									M48								
21	M49									M50									M51			
22						M52									M53							
	1	2	3	4	5	6	7	8	9	10	11	12	13	14	15							

the octave into 77, 118, 200 or 301 equal parts he would get Swarams which are still more harmonious! Yea, if he makes still larger divisions of the octave he is sure to obtain 22 Srutis, by a still more minute process.

Finding that the theories he put forward hitherto were open to criticism, he gives another theory in his essay on "Arya Sangeeta Dwavimsati Sruti Nirnaya" read at the Sixth Conference.

It became the first duty of the Sangam to determine the Srutis in use in South Indian Music. But some of the distinguished musicians who had only a traditional knowledge of singing without knowing anything of the science of it stopped away for fear of committing themselves, while others, though present, were unable to give reasons for their views. Some of them read essays, armed with the authority of Sanskrit works, saying that the Dwavimsati Srutis were the ones in use in South Indian music. But finding that their opinions and the Dwavimsati Srutis conflicted with Carnatic music, they said their theories referred to Aryan music. We shall not dwell here on Aryan music as we are ignorant of it. Yet, we shall do well to note a few points in connection with it at least for the benefit of those who practice that music. We have noticed before that though the three different kinds of music—South Indian, Hindustani and Bengali—are made mention of by a few, yet a great number of them subscribe to the pre-eminence of South Indian music. But nowhere we see any mention made of Aryan music. We have also read the opinions of many historians that the people of South India had attained a very high degree of civilisation long before the advent of the Aryans into India. We know well that there is hardly a race of men which is completely ignorant of singing, that the very sound produced by the human being in its infant stage, the primary sound of all living beings and the sound produced by the elements as well as by the rotation of the planets—all this is music. We do not say that the Aryans never sang and that they never wrote treatises on music. Far from it. But as our business is to enquire into the Srutis of South Indian music, we need not bother our heads with the Srutis of Aryan music. However, we think it necessary to note a few points in connection with his essay on " Arya Sangeeta Dwavimsati Sruti Nirnaya" as the Dwavimsati Sruti of the author of Ratnakaram is in complete conflict with Mr. Sastrial's theory owing to an error of interpretation.

The following is an extract from his essay on Arya Sangeeta Dwavimsati Sruti Nirnaya read at the sixth conference :—

Though we have to discuss a number of subjects in connection with the science of music, as the subject before us is "Sruti" I venture to make a few observations on it. I have read many essays on this subject before this conference. In one of those I have placed the views of the author of Parijatam before you and have arrived at definite conclusions on the subject. On another occasion I have established our 22 srutis on the light of Western science and have pointed out the difference between these srutis and the 22 srutis in use in Karnatic music. In another essay I have pointed out the good and bad points in the theories of others. I have also criticised the view of those writers, ignorant of the Vedas who claim 24 srutis in the octave. In the same essay it has been shown that 53 srutis result from the Sa-Pa or Sa-Ma series and how the 22 are picked out of them. My opinion has been held to be correct by my friends as well as those vidwans who entered into the merits of it. But I have a few friends who have not the patience enough to know how I arrived at these conclusions. There are yet others who think they will lose their prestige if they interfere in this matter by giving their opinion. There are others who stand entirely aloof as they do not understand this difficult matter."

The above extract shows that here he attempts to sum up what he has said in the previous conferences. These points are :—

(1) "I have come to definite conclusions as regards the theory of srutis of the author of Sangeeta Parijatam."

(2) "The 22 srutis of our sciences have been examined in the light of European science and firmly established."

(3) "In some places I have pointed out the 22 srutis in use in Karnatic music which are entirely different."

(4) "I have criticised the views of others pointing out their merits and demerits."

(5) "I have criticised the view of those writers ignorant of the Vedas who claim 24 srutis in the octave."

(6) "I have shown that 53 sthanams are obtained in an octave by the SA-PA or the SA-MA series and how the 22 can be selected out of them."

The SA-PA and the SA-MA systems of determining Srutis have been in use among our ancient writers on music. Ahobilar seems to have written the work Parijatam having been dissatisfied with the theory of the author of Sangeeta Ratnakaram. There he gives the 22 Srutis as an introduction and then proceeds to mention the system of arriving at Srutis by the SA-PA series after Narada. There the SA-PA series proceed by $\frac{2}{3}$. But according to the author of Ratnakaram the SA-MA and the SA-PA series, proceed by nines and thirteens respectively. Men of understanding know that PA, which is the 13th Sruti in an octave, does not sound exactly on $\frac{2}{3}$. Seeing that there is such a difference between the Dwavimsati Srutis and the Ganams in actual use Ahobilar must have written his Parijatam. When we hear that this system of proceeding by $\frac{2}{3}$ is that of Narada, we are reminded of his appellation of "Narada, the Yalasrier found in ancient Tamil treatises on music. We see from this that he was the master of Yal, and that the instrument itself was one that was peculiar to the Tamil Country. To add to this, the author of Tolgauppiam makes mention of the four kinds of Yal—Marudai, Kurinji, Neydal and Palai Yal—and the four big Puns (பண்கள்) that are derived from the SA-PA series. This shows that the SA-PA system was in use in the Tamil country from ancient times. But Narada never made mention of the fraction $\frac{2}{3}$. The Yalasrian of those days was well-versed with the harmonious tuning of SA with PA, as is seen from the extract, "[illegible]" (possessing the musical ear necessary to tune the [illegible] or SA in harmony with [illegible] or PA). According to this inasmuch as the Panchamam speaks at about $\frac{2}{3}$ the length of a wire, Ahobilar suggested that PA should be placed at $\frac{2}{3}$. This is common with those musicians who adjust the frets of Veena. But a more minute measurement and calculation may be seen in the part treating on the Srutis in use in South Indian music.

We have already pointed out how Mr. Shastrial has tried his best to mutilate and change the opinions of the author of Parijatam. In some places he says that the opinion of the Ratnakaram is the correct one, and that others are like parrots which repeat what they had heard without understanding it, while in another place he says that the author of Parijatam has fallen into an error so much so his Slokas had to be altered, that he had to reject some of the Swarams of that author, that he had to accept some of the Swarams of Pythagoras, the philosopher, and of one Watson ; he further uses the doubtful expressions "we may conclude", "we may determine", "we might take it to be the opinion of the ancients" etc. Knowing that all his essays are being minutely studied and criticised, he goes on giving opinions at every conference. Not satisfied with this he advocated the theory of 53 Srutis hoping thereby to satisfy all parties and to choose the 22 Srutis out of them. He found that the SA-PA system or proceeding by $\frac{2}{3}$

gave him more than 22 Srutis in an octave. Realising the sad fate of the 22 Srutis advocated by Sarnga Dev in his Sanskrit work, he is anxious to establish the 22 in an octave which lands him in a number of errors as regards mathematical calculations. We only pity him. The Sanskrit treatise is not responsible for this error. The fact that he is obstinate in establishing what is wrong and excluding what is right shows that he is a blind admirer of the Sanskrit language and nothing less. This may be seen in different places.

He says "I have criticised the views of those writers ignorant of the Vedas who claim 24 Srutis in the octave". The view by which he condemns speakers of truth as "Avaideeks" and exalts liars as Vaideeks", is indeed praiseworthy! He is only guided by the Puranas and Ithihasas in which he firmly believes!

Again, in the essay read at the Sixth Conference he says as follows :—

"I try once more to state my theory clearly by means of this essay. European musicians have conventionally granted 12 sthanams in an octave with equal intervals in instruments like the Harmonium for the sake of a particular principle according to their theory, the Tonic SA has 0 cents, the Dwi Sruti RI 100 cents, Chatursruti RI 200 cents, Sadharana GA 300 cents, Antara Ga 400 cents, Suddha MA 500 cents, Teevra MA 600 cents, Pa 700 cents, Dwi Sruti DHA 800 cents, Chatur Sruti DHA 900 cents, Kyshiki NI 1000 cents, Kakali NI 1100 cents and the octave SA 1200 cents. The cents calculation thus became the primary subject for discussion in the controversy on srutis. Even proceeding by the SA-PA series the 13th sthanam will never finish with the octave. If five or seven clever musicians will give me two hours of their time any morning in a quiet place I could demonstrate to them the truth of my statements. For this very purpose a friend of mine and myself have prepared an instrument with 14 strings. If I could be given an opportunity they may clear their doubts by this means. Another instrument to show the 53 sthanams has already been constructed. But those who have deeply studied it with a view to arrive at the truth are not more than three or four."

We have already spoken about the 53 Sthanams in the octave. He also speaks about an octave being divided into twelve equal Swarams in European instruments like the Harmonium for a particular reason. Being anxious to establish the truth of his 22 Srutis and 53 Srutis he says that the octave does not end in the 13th step of the SA-PA series If he is obstinate in saying that the hare he caught has only three legs who is there prepared to accept it?

Again in his essay read at the Sixth Conference he says as follows :—

"Some musicians, while accepting the fact that an octave cannot come to an end within 12 sthanams, hold that there are 22 sthanams in an octave with equal intervals and that the 22 sthanams are reckoned to be the 22 srutis by the Aryan treatises on music. Yea, they are bold enough to declare that the ancients were unable to time the SA with the PA harmoniously for PA which should have 702 cents is given 7 cents more or 709 cents in their calculation. In as much as the ancients had a special knowledge of the relation between SA and PA and SA and MA, the above opinion is certainly wrong. If we hold that there are 24 Sruti Sthanams with equal intervals in an octave, though PA with 702 cents has but 709 (not much of a difference), still Antara GA which should have only 386 cents has 14 cents more or 400 cents. So this kind of division also lands us in error. But if we take 53 sthanams in an octave with equal intervals, though Antara GA an un-important sruti, has only a cent less, the important PA and MA occur exactly at 702 cents and 498 cents respectively. Therefore, it is clear that the sthanams we require are either connected with the SA-PA or the SA-MA series. When we proceed to choose the 22 sthanams, handed down by science and tradition, out of these 53, we shall start from Suddha MA and arrive at the other sthanams. In the SA-PA series SA results from MA.

MA.
SA results from MA.
PA results from SA.
Chathur Sruti RI from PA.
Chathur Sruti DHA from Chatur Sruti RI.
Chyutha Madhyama GA from Chatur Sruti DHA.
Chyuta Shadja NI from Chyuta Madhyama GA.
Theevrathara MA from Chyuta Shadja NI.
Dwisruti RI from Theevrathara MA.
Dwisruti DHA from Dwisruti RI.
Sadharana GA from Dwisruti DHA.
Kaisika NI from Sadharana GA.

Inasmuch as a certain sthanam very near to the important Suddha MA results from Kaisiki NI they have not taken it into account.

In the same way

Suddha MA results from Suddha NI.
Suddha NI results from Suddha GA.
Suddha GA results from Ekasruti DHA.
Ekasruti DHA results from Ekasruti RI.
Ekasruti RI results from Teevra MA
Teevra MA results from Kakali NI.
Kakali NI results from Antara GA.
Antara GA results from Suddha DHA.
Suddha DHA results from Suddha RI.
Suddha RI results from Teevratara MA.

As Teevratara MA results from a sthanam very nearly equal to that of the important SA they have not taken that into account either.

Thus, we see that the 11 swarasthanams from the central sruti Suddha MA and the 10 swarasthanams which generate from it, including the original sruti form the 22 sruti sthanams advocated by the ancients. These are the srutis in use in our country. A friend of mine has read an essay pointing out how these sruti sthanams occur in the various Ragas. If we want more srutis than the above 22 we have to look for them in the octave with 53 sthanams."

He says that the ancients were very clever in discriminating the harmony of the SA-PA sounds. According to the author of Ratnakaram, PA which is the 13th Sruti should have 709 cents, but according to the author of Parijatam it should be 702. Of these the author of Ratnakaram distinctly states that SA to MA form 9 and SA to PA 13 Srutis. Then an octave ends with 22 Srutis. But in the systems of Pythagoras which say that PA speaks at ⅔ the length of the wire PA has 702 cents. This system exactly indicates that there must be nearly 24 Srutis in the octave. He alters the calculation of these Srutis which are obtained in the usual course, and tries his utmost to prove that the system of Parijatam as well as the modern system of Karnatic music have erred and that the Dwavimsati Srutis are the ones in use in Karnatic music. The result is that he is landed in various conflicting opinions. He says that it is but right that PA should have 702 cents and MA 498 cents proceeding by the SA-PA series and arrives at 12 Sthanams by the SA-PA series and another 12 Sthanams by the SA-MA series. But he leaves out of calculation MA which results from NI, as well as another Sthanam below Tara SA from which Teevra MA is obtained. We have indicated in various Tables how 2 Sthanams have been omitted in the two systems. He gives up these two places of his own accord and says that this is the opinion of the ancients and that the Srutis may be determined in this wise. We may quote the testimony of the ancients in support of a just cause, but it is absurd to quote them in support of one's own miscalculations. Did the ancients support the theory of 53 Sthanams in the octave? Picking out 22 of them at random, at irregular intervals, was it the opinion of the ancients? Is it the *Tantrum* of Mr. Shastrial to leave out a Sthanam above Suddha MA and one below Tara SA? The truth of this must come out.

He says we are sure that the ancients determined it in this manner. When he is quite sure, why does he worry himself with so many conflicting opinions. If we proceed by the SA-PA and SA-MA series we may arrive at many more Srutis. Why has he not made sure of them also?

Again, this is what he says in his essay read at the sixth conference.

"According to the theory of *Just Intonation* of the Europeans, an Ekasruti has 92 cents, a Dwisruti 112 cents and a Trisruti 182 cents and a Chatursruti 204 cents. According to this we get the following results :—

	cents.		
Tonic SA	0	Teevratara MA	610
Ekasruti RI	92	Teevratama MA	680
Dwisruti RI	112	Pa	702
Suddha RI	182	Ekasruti DHA	794
Chatursruti RI	204	Dwisruti DHA	814
Suddha GA	294	Suddha DHA	884
Sadharana GA	316	Chatursruti DHA	906
Antara GA	386	Suddha NI	996
Chyuta Madhyama GA	406	Kaisiki NI	1088
Suddha Madhyamam	498	Kakali NI	1018
Teevra MA	590	Chyuta Shadja NI	1108
		Octave SA	1200

Having these 22 Srutis as the basis, our ancient treatises speak of 4 Srutis each for SA, MA and PA, 3 Srutis each for RI and DHA and 2 Srutis each for GA and NI. These are the Suddha Swarams of Sama Veda. I have spoken at length about these in my previous essays."

We may find from the Dwavimsati Sruti system of Sarnga Dev that he never mentioned 22 Srutis with the intervals as calculated by Mr. Shastrial. Though the number of his 22 Srutis is accounted for as 4, 3, 2, 4, 4, 3, 2=22, they are never mentioned as the Suddha Swarams of the Sama Veda. If such an use had been in existence in his time, he would doubtless have made mention of it. Again, he makes mention of 92, 112, 182 and 204 cents above the Tonic SA for the four RIS, and gives 264 cents for Suddha GA. Here we see there are 4 RIS, the fourth of them being known as Chathur Sruti RI and that the DHA above PA has also 4 Srutis. GA and NI have also 4 Srutis each. So in his essays we see that RI, GA, DHA and

Ni have 4 Srutis each. But Sarnga Dev never said so. All that he said was that the Srutis which he ascribed for the Swarams while the Grahams were changed might occur in the other Srutis, but that the numbers would never get mixed but always stand 4, 3, 2 etc. The four Sthanams below Pa should only be called by the name of Pa, just as the places below Suddha Ma should be called by the name of Ma. Because this principle is not adhered to, instead of having Eka Sruti, Dwi Sruti, Suddha and Chatur Sruti Ris we get names mixed up. Unless we give the names Ga and Ni to the Sthanams below Suddha Ga and Suddha Ni we cannot get 3 Ris and 3 Dhas and 2 Gas and 2 Nis.

He gives the cents calculation for the 22 Srutis mentioned above. As he calls it the Sruti Nirnaya of Aryan music let us see whether there is any truth in those calculations.

We have already pointed out the absurdity of his theory which, while granting there are 53 Srutis in the octave, declares that they are obtained in the 31st Sthayi by the Sa-Pa series and in the 22nd Sthayi by the Sa-Ma series. For, all that Bosanquet Mercator, Poole, White, Cheve, Thompson and others say is this:—that if an octave were divided into 53 equal intervals, the 12 swarams obtained by proceeding from any one of them by 31 intervals will be harmonious and will be the 12 notes of an octave. *i.e.*, any successive 12 of 1, 32, 10, 41, 19, 50, 28, 6, 37, 15, 46, 24, 2, 33, 11, 42, 20, 51, 29, 7, 38, 16, 47, 25, 3, 34, 12, 43, 21, 52, 30, 8, 39, 17, 48, 26, 4, 35, 13, 44, 22, 53, 31, 9, 40, 18, 49, 27, 5, 36, 14, 45, 23. They never said that these were obtained in the Sa-Pa or Sa-Ma series. In other words they never said that these 53 were obtained by the process of $\frac{3}{2}$ or $\frac{4}{3}$. They first divided the octave into 53 equal parts. We may see from Tables 15 and 16 (P. 306-7) that the Sa-Pa and the Sa-Ma series do not come to an end in the 31st or the 22nd Sthayis. The system of 53 Srutis was never in use in the music of India. We have clearly shown in Table 11 that there is not the slightest relation between these and the 22 Srutis. We have also stated there, therefore, that the first 11 Srutis out of the 53 obtained in the 31 Sthayis of the Sa-Pa series and the first 11 of the 53 Srutis obtained in the 22 Sthayis of the Sa-Ma series can never be the correct Srutis. If he had followed the Western scientists he would not have been far wrong. But we would never use them. Having rejected the theory of Westerners which advocates equal divisions of the Octave, and the theory of Sarnga Dev which derives 22 Srutis by the Sa-Pa, Sa-Ma series, he proceeded to determine the Srutis of Karnatic music by the system of Pythagoras $\frac{3}{2}$ and by $\frac{4}{3}$; finding that this also landed him in difficulties he tries to establish his own theory of picking out 22 Srutis from 53 and says they belong to Sama Veda and that he has successfully determined the Srutis of Aryan music! We look for these 53 Srutis in vain in any of the treatises on Sama Veda or Aryan Music. We may see clearly from the following Table 17 how he rejects two Srutis near Ma and Sa out of the first 12 Srutis of the Sa-Pa and the Sa-Ma series respectively.

We find in the following Table 17 that the Sa-Pa and Sa-Ma series commence with Ma as the Tonic Sruti. The ancients have declared that the ground Sa is the fundamental note of all progressive Swarams, just as Pa is derived from Sa and Ri from Pa. We have shown in Table 14 (P. 303) that he is driven to this necessity or else he would not obtain the important Swarams SA and PA correctly. In the same Table we have shown that his system of proceeding from Suddha MA is equally wrong. His MA and PA obtain 498 and 702 cents respectively. This corresponds to the $\frac{3}{4}$ and $\frac{2}{3}$ measurements of a string. We obtain the first 12 Swarams if we go on adding 702 cents from 498 or Suddha MA. He says he obtains 406 cents in the fifth step instead of 408. In other words he adds 700 cents instead of 702. Why should he do this ? If by an oversight he has given 406 instead of 408 cents he might have corrected himself at least at the sixth step. But he does not do this. The lessening of these two cents in the fifth line makes him continue the same mistake in the seven Sthanams (See column 6). We have specially indicated the fifth line with Antique letters where he lessens the cents

TABLE 17.

Calculations as regards the 22 Srutis of Aryan Music. How the first 11 Srutis out of 53 of each of the SA-PA and the SA-MA series form the Dwavimsati Srutis.

Number of Srutis.	The 11 Srutis obtained in the SA-PA series or proceeding by 702 cents.				The wrong calculation of Mr. Shastrial.	The Sruti Sthanams by the SA-PA series	Number of Srutis.	The 11 Srutis obtained in the SA-MA series or proceeding by 498 cents.				The wrong calculation of Mr. Shastrial.	The Sruti Sthanams by the SA-MA series.
1	2	3	4	5	6	7	8	9	10	11	12	13	14
1	498+	702	=	1200	1200	22	1	0+	498	=	498	498	9
2	1200+	702−	1200=	702	702	13	2	498+	498	=	996	996	18
3	702+	702−	1200=	204	204	4	3	996+	498−	1200=	294	294	5
4	204+	702	=	906	906	17	4	294+	498	=	<u>792</u>	<u>794</u>	14
5	906+	702−	1200=	<u>408</u>	<u>406</u>	8	5	792+	498−	1200=	90	92	1
6	408+	702	=	1110	1108	21	6	90+	498	=	588	590	10
7	1110+	702−	1200=	612	610	11	7	588+	498	=	1086	1088	20
8	612+	702−	1200=	114	112	2	8	1086+	498−	1200=	384	386	7
9	114+	702	=	816	814	15	9	384+	498	=	882	884	16
10	816+	702−	1200=	318	316	6	10	882+	498−	1200=	180	182	3
11	318+	702	=	1020	1018	19	11	180+	498	=	678.	680	12
12	1020+	702−	1200=	− 522*			12	678+	498	=	1176*		

The Calculations in Columns marked ● are our own.

* The two Sthanams left out by Mr. Shastrial for making 24 Srutis appear as 22.

by 2. We have shown in the 5th column the right calculation of cents if we proceed by 702c. As Tara Sthayi SA is obtained in the SA-PA series if we start from Suddha MA we may note in the first line, that it is given 1200 cents at the 22nd Sruti. In the 12th line might be seen the Sruti which he had rejected.

In the second part of the Table, the 12 Srutis obtained by adding 498 cents in the SA-MA series are mentioned. Here we see that in the 4th line he gives 500 cents instead of 498. In other words instead of getting 294+498=792, he has 294+500=794. Perhaps he has erred in adding figures as may be seen from Table 8 of page 286. But the eight succeeding Sthanams have also each 2 cents in excess. This may be seen in column 13 of the Table. But the correct cents are given in column 12. In the SA-PA series he has reduced 2 cents from line 5, but in the SA-MA series he has added 2 cents from line 4. This addition and subtraction seem to have been done with a purpose, namely, that of establishing the Dwavimsati srutis. Again, this seems to have been done to get the fractions for Srutis in column 12 of Table 13 (P. 301) right. In the 10th column of the above Table 13 we find 92, 112, 182, 204, 294, 316 &c. He gets into trouble wherever he sets his foot. Trying to strike out a uniformity between the theories of Mr. Nagoji Rao, Pythagoras and the author of Parijatam, he flounders into many a pitfall which excites our pity.

Again, when we arrange in order the Srutis obtained by the SA-PA and the SA-MA series and compare them with the 22 Srutis of Aryan music, we may see the difference between them. It may be seen from the appended Table 18.

In Table 18, (columns 2 and 3), we have shown how the various Srutis are obtained in the SA-MA, SA-PA series starting from Suddha MA. We have also shown the cents valuation of the Srutis in the 4th column. In the 5th column may be found the cents for the intervals between Srutis. We may notice here that there are three kinds of Sruti intervals with 90, 66 and 24 cents as found in Table 14 (P. 303) also. But in column 6, according to Mr. Shastrial there are 5 different kinds of Sruti intervals, 92, 90, 71, 22 and 20 which are also found in Tables 12 and 13. If Sruti-intervals are so every different we can imagine how Ragas would sound when Grahams are changed and sung!

Again, he rejects a Sruti Sthanam which is closely akin to the important Suddha MA which is obtained from Kaishiki Ni in the SA-PA series. The above Sthanam is obtained in the 12th step of the SA-PA series with 522 cents. It has 24 cents in excess of the previous Sruti Suddha MA, which has 498 cents. In the same manner, he rejects another Sruti which gives rise to Teevra MA; for this is very closely akin to the important SA in the SA-MA series.

When we examine one of these rejected Srutis, we find that it is a NI with 1176 cents obtained at the 12th step of the SA-MA series. This is 24 cents less than the Tara SA which has 1200 cents. The other is a MA, (next to Suddha MA), which is obtained at the 12th step of the SA-PA series. He says the ancient writers have rejected these two Srutis. It may be clearly seen from the Table. Their names are found in column 8, and their number among the 22 Srutis in column 9. There it is clearly seen that the 10th and the 23rd Srutis have been left out. Can Mr. Shastrial

TABLE 18
Showing the absurdity of the 22 Srutis of Aryan Music.

The true SA-PA and SA-MA Series.						The false SA-PA and SA-MA series of Mr. Sastrial.			
Number of Srutis.	How Srutis are obtained by SA-PA or SA-MA series.	The different steps in which the Srutis are obtained in the series. SA-PA	SA-MA	Arrangement of Srutis according to the order in which they are obtained.	The intervals between Srutis.	The wrong intervals between Srutis.	The wrong calculation of cents for Srutis.	Mr. Shastrial's nomenclature for the 22 Srutis.	Number of Srutis.
⊕ 1	⊕ 2	3	⊕ 3	⊕ 4	⊕ 5	⊕ 6	7	8	⊕ 9
1	S-M		5	90	90	92	92	Ekasruti Rishabham	1
2	S-P	8		114	24	* 20	112	Dwisruti Rishabham	2
3	S-M		10	180	66	70	182	Suddha Rishabham	3
4	S-P	3		204	24	22*	204	Chatursruti Rishabham	4
5	S-M		3	294	90	90	294	Suddha Gandharam	5
6	S-P	10		318	24	22*	316	Sadharana Gandharam	6
7	S-M		8	384	66	70	386	Antara Gandharam	7
8	S-P	5		408	24	* 20	406	Chyu. Madh. Gandharam	8
9	M		1	498	90	92	498	Suddha Madhyamam	9
10	S-P	12		<u>522</u>	24	92			
11	S-M		6	588	66	* 20	590	Teevra Madhyamam	10
12	S-P	7		612	24	70	610	Teevratara Madhyamam	11
13	S-M		11	678	66	22*	680	Teevratama Madhyamam	12
14	S-P	2		702	24	92	702	Panchamam	13
15	S-M		4	792	90	* 20	794	Ekasruti Dhaivatam	14
16	S-P	9		816	24	70	814	Dwisruti Dhaivatam	15
17	S-M		9	882	66	22*	884	Suddha Dhaivatam	16
18	S-P	4		906	24	90	906	Chatursruti Dhaivatam	17
19	S-M		2	996	90	22*	996	Suddha Nishadam	18
20	S-P	11		1020	24	70	1018	Kaisiki Nishadam	19
21	S-M		7	1086	66	* 20	1088	Kakali Nishadam	20
22	S-P	6		1110	24		1108	Chyu. Shadja Nishadam	21
23	S-M		12	<u>1176</u>	66				
24	S-P	1		1200	24	92	1200	Shadjam	22

The Calculations in Columns marked ⊕ are our own.

quote the authority of ancient writers for rejecting these two Srutis? He cannot establish his theory of 22 Srutis by any reasonable calculation or process.

Again, the reason for rejection is the fact that they are Sthanams which occur very closely to important Srutis. In other words, they are rejected because their interval is very short. It is said in ancient treatises that the Sa-Pa has 13 Sruti-intervals and Sa-Ma 9 Sruti-intervals. But their Sa-Pa and Sa-Ma will never correspond to $\frac{3}{2}$ and $\frac{4}{3}$. But Mr. Shastrial gives up the above two Sthanams to establish his 22 Srutis on the principle of $\frac{3}{2}$ and $\frac{4}{3}$. We have already pointed out in page 305 that there is no connection whatever between the 22 Srutis obtained by the Sa-Pa series and the same obtained by the systems of $\frac{3}{2}$ and $\frac{4}{3}$. That he confuses himself by identifying the two for arriving at the 22 Srutis may be easily understood by men of knowledge.

We saw that there was a difference of 24 cents between the Sruti above Suddha Ma with 522 cents and Suddha Ma. And again there was a difference of 24 cents between Ni below Sa with 1176 cents (see opposite 23rd number) and Tara Sa. In the 6th column which gives the intervals of his Srutis may be seen the 5 Srutis with 20 cents marked * and the 5 Srutis with 22 cents marked °. For one who rejected two Srutis with 24 cents each on the plea of their having only a few cents as intervals, it is surprising he accepts intervals with 20 and 22 cents! It will be just if he had rejected the 10 Srutis with 20 and 22 cents while he has rejected Srutis with 24 cents. In the same manner, the different systems which he advocates when tested by the touchstone of mathematical calculation are found to be wanting. To say that this system is the one in use in Aryan music is thoroughly absurd.

He again says that the Sapta Swarams of the 22 Srutis occur in the order of 4, 3, 2, 4, 4, 3, 2 in the Sama Veda, and that they are given in detail in his previous essays. We shall do well here to say a few words on this point which will go to prove that this was not at all the object of Sama Veda. The terms 53 and 22 occur nowhere in the Sama Veda. But Mr. Shastrial has given fancy names for his 53 Srutis such as Chetika, Chotika, Dhenuka, Kurali and the like, has reserved some of them for Vydeeka Sampradayam, others for Loukeeka Sampradayam and has left the remaining ones adrift in the streets! This will be seen from the appended Table.

In Table 19 we may see that when we proceed by thirty ones by the Sa-Pa series, how the 12 Swarams of Vydeeka Sampradayam (Column 1), the 12 Swarams of Swaya Sampradayam (Column 2) and the 12 Swarams of Loukeeka Sampradayam (Column 3) are arrived at along with their respective Sruti Sthanams. Here also he says that the Sa-Pa series has 31 Srutis and the Sa-Ma series, 22. We need not take any particular notice of his theory, but if he errs in his calculations we cannot but point them out. We may see from the Table that in all the three systems, the Sa-Pa, Sa-Ma series do not give the same measurements for Srutis. Just as he tried a dodge before to hide two Srutis in each of the Sthayis before, he gives here also a wrong interval for one Sruti in the Sa-Pa series and for another in the Sa-Ma series. For example, in the first column he accounts for the 53 Srutis as follows:—4+4+5+4+5+4+5+4+4+4+5+4+5 =53. This system of having a Sruti more or less for each of the Swarams is entirely

TABLE 19

Showing the division into 12s and 7s according to Vydeeka, Swaya and Loukeeka Sampradayams of Mr. Shastrial, and those of Pythagoras and the authors of Parijatam and Ratnakaram of the 53 Swarams obtained by the SA-PA and SA-MA series.

Vydeeka Sampradayam.	Swaya Sampradayam.	Loukeeka Sampradayam.	22 Srutis according to Pythagoras.	22 Srutis according to Parijatam.	Dwavimsati Suddha Swarams.	The wrong calculation of Dwavimsati Srutis.	The right calculation of the Srutis.
1	2	3	4	5	6	7	8
S 1	S 1	S 1	S4 1	S4 1	S 1		
2	2	2	2				
4 3	3	3	5 3				
4	4 4	5 4	4	R1 4			
R 5	R 5	5	R1 5				
6	6	R 6	R2 6	R2 6		9	$9\frac{14}{22}$
7	7	7	7				
4 8	5 8	4 8	4 8				
R 9	9	9	R3 9	R3 9			
10	R 10	R 10	G1 10	G1 10	R 10		
11	11	11	11				
5 12	12	5 12	5 12				
13	4 13	13	13				
G 14	G 14	14	G2 14	G2 14		8	$7\frac{5}{22}$
15	15	G 15	M1 15	M1 15			
16	16	16	16				
4 17	4 17	4 17	4 17				
G 18	G 18	18	M2 18	M2 18	G 18		
19	19	G 19	M3 19				
20	20	20	20	M3 20		5	$4\frac{18}{22}$
5 21	5 21	21	4 21				
22	22	4 22	22				
M 23	M 23	M 23	M4 23	M4 23	M 23		
24	24	24	24				
4 25	4 25	25	5 25				
26	26	5 26	26	P1 26			
M 27	M 27	27	P1 27				
28	28	M 28	P2 28	P2 28		9	$9\frac{14}{22}$
29	29	29	29				
5 30	5 30	30	4 30				
31	31	4 31	P3 31	P3 31			
P 32	P 32	P 32	P4 32	P4 32	P 32		
33	33	33	33				
4 34	4 34	34	5 34				
35	35	5 35	35	D1 35			
D 36	D 36	36	D1 36				
37	37	D 37	D2 37	D2 37		9	$9\frac{14}{22}$
38	38	38	38				
4 39	5 39	39	4 39				
D 40	40	4 40	D3 40	D3 40			
41	D 41	D 41	N1 41	N1 41	D 41		
42	42	42	42				
5 43	43	43	5 43				
44	4 44	5 44	44				
N 45	N 45	45	N2 45	N2 45		8	$7\frac{5}{22}$
46	46	N 46	S1 46	S1 46			
4 47	47	47	47				
48	4 48	48	4 48				
N 49	N 49	4 49	S2 49	S2 49	N 49		
50	50	N 50	S3 50				
51	51	51	51	S3 51			
5 52	5 52	52	4 52			5	$4\frac{18}{22}$
53	53	4 53	53				
S 54	S 54	S 54	S4 54	S4 54	S 54		

contrary to the ancient usage of singing Grahaswaram and to modern usage and to the view of the author of Sangeeta Ratnakaram.

Vydeeka Sampradayam.

When we proceed from the Ri_2 or the 9th Sruti to PA, the 32nd Sruti, by the SA-MA series, we obtain 5+4+5+4+5=23 Srutis. This ought to be 22 Srutis. Again when we proceed by SA-PA series from PA, the 32nd Sthanam, we should properly obtain the Ri_2. But it comes as the 30th Sruti or 4+4+5+4+4+5+4=30. We must notice here that in the SA-PA series we get one Sruti less, 30 for 31, and in the SA-MA series one Sruti more, 23 for 22. This has been clearly shown before in the different tables. In an Octave we find 2 Srutis different. At this rate the octave will never come to an end even if we proceed 31 Sthayis.

Swaya Sampradayam.

In the *Swaya Sampradayam* he says there are 12 swarams on the same principle of 4+5+4+4+5+4+5+4+5+4+4+5=53. Here also we find that some of the Swarams of the SA-PA and the SA-MA series are inaccurate. When we proceed by the SA-MA series, from the Ga_2, 18th Sthanam to Dha_2, 41st Sthanam he gets 5+4+5+4+5 or 23, whereas he ought to get 22. In the same way when he proceeds by the SA-PA series from the Dha_2, 41st Sruti he obtains Ga_2, 18th Sruti whereas he ought to get 41+31=72; 72—53=19, but he gets 18; or 4+4+5+4+5+4+4=30. This ought to be 31. In the other Sampradayam also we noticed such differences.

Loukeeka Sampradayam.

He accounts for the 12 swarams here also by the same principle of 5+4+5+4+4+5+4+5+4+5+4+4=53. Here when he proceeds by the SA-MA series from Ma_1, 23rd Sruti to Ni_1, 46th Sruti he gets 5+4+5+4+5 or 23 Srutis. But it ought to be 22. Ni_1 should result at the 45th step. In the same way, while proceeding by the SA-PA series, Ma_1 should result from Ni_1, 46th Sruti. In other words 46+31=77; 77−53=24. This comes as the 23rd Sthanam, or 4+4+5+4+5+4+4=30. But he ought to get 31. He locates the Ma_1 at the 23rd place instead of the 24th.

The Three Sampradayas.

To sum up our criticism on the three Sampradayas we see,

(1) In the *Vydeeka Sampradayam*, while proceeding by the SA-MA series from Ri_2 to PA, and by the SA-PA series from PA to Ri'_2 he gets a Sruti more and a Sruti less.

(2) In the *Swaya Sampradayam* also while proceeding from Ga_2 to Dha_2 (SA-MA series) and from Dha_2 to Ga_2 (SA-PA series) he is landed in the same error.

(3) In the *Loukeeka Sampradayam* also he fares no better. The same error is repeated while proceeding from Ma_1 to Ni_1 and Ni_1 to Ma_1 in the two series.

We have never come across a system which errs in all its three directions, in any treatise. Have the wise men ever declared that to behave in three different ways is the virtue of the noble and good?

While comparing these Sampradaya Srutis with those which he gave out at the Sixth conference we find the following :—

(1) *Vydeeka Sampradayam.*			(2) *Sama Veda Sampradayam.*		
Ri_1	90·225	cents.	Ri_1	92	cents.
Ri_2	180·450	„	Ri_2	182	„
Ga_1	294·135	„	Ga_1	294	„
Ga_2	384·360	„	Ga_2	386	„
Ma_1	498·045	„	Ma_1	498	„
Ma_2	588·270	„	Ma_2	590	„
Pa	698·340	„	Pa	702	„
Dha_1	792·180	„	Dha_1	794	„
Dha_2	882·405	„	Dha_2	884	„
Ni_1	996·090	„	Ni_1	996	„
Ni_2	1086·315	„	Ni_2	1088	„
Sa	1196·385	„	Sa	1200	„

While we notice the Vydeeka Sampradayam, the twelve out of the 53 places, namely, 5, 9, 14, 18, 23, 27, 32, 36, 40, 45, 49 and 54, mentioned in Part 3 Column 11 of Table 11 (P. 294-5) (by the Sa-Ma series) are the same Swarams of this Sampradayam. But this does not exactly correspond to the 12 Swarams of the Sa-Ma series. The cents of the Swarams also do not end in 1200. In Table 18 (P. 316) may be seen the various steps by which the swarams are obtained in the two series, to which are also appended the right method showing the difference in the two series along with Mr. Shastrial's wrong method. The series that proceeds by 90,180 etc., pertaining to Vydeeka Sampradayam, is entirely different from the Sama Veda series proceeding by 92,182 etc. It is clearly seen that there is not the slightest connection between the two. So either of the two Sampradayas must be wrong. We see that he establishes the Vydeeka Sampradayam by proceeding by $\frac{3}{2}$ (the method of Pythagoras) and the same Sama Veda Sampradayam by taking the Just Intonation of the Western Scientists.

This has been shown in page 312. We do not say that the Vydeeka Sampradayam should differ from that of Sama Vedam. On the other hand, it should be based on Sama Vedam. Is the Sama Vedam prior to or later than the period of the 53 Srutis of Bosanquet or that of the $\frac{3}{2}$ and $\frac{4}{3}$ system of Pythagoras or that of the system of Intonation? If the Dwavimsati Sruti system of Sarnga Dev be considered ancient, what about Bharata and Upanishads which flourished before his time? Mr. Shastrial who finds that 22 Srutis in an octave would conflict with the system of $\frac{3}{2}$ and $\frac{4}{3}$ and that modern music on the other hand is based entirely on the system of $\frac{3}{2}$ and $\frac{4}{3}$ tries his utmost to establish his 22 Srutis, thus committing himself to many an error in calculation. This only creates our laughter, and the emphatic way in which he tries to saddle his wrong theories on others excites our commiseration.

According to Bosanquet the series will be: 5, 10, 14, 19, 23, 28, 32, 36, 41, 45, 50, 54.

The System of Pythagoras in Table 19.

In the above Table his Srutis are compared with those of Pythagoras, those of the author of Parijatam and the Dwavimsati Srutis. Here also we find the same contradictions. In the SA-MA series of Pythagoras we should get SA'$_1$ from PA$_1$. The 27th Sruti is PA$_1$. So SA$_1$ ought to be 27+22=49. But it comes as the 46th or 3 Srutis less. In the same way, proceeding by the SA-PA series from SA$_1$ to PA$_1$ we get 46+31=77; 77−53=24. But in Mr. Shastrial's system PA$_1$ occurs as the 27th Sruti. Again SA$_2$ must result from PA$_2$ by the SA-MA series. He gets 49 instead of 28+22=50. In the same way, PA$_2$ obtained from SA$_2$ will also differ. SA$_3$ should be obtained from PA$_3$ by the SA-MA series. But he gets it as 50 or 3 Srutis less whereas it outhg to be 31+22 or 53.

The System of Parijatam.

In this system also the same mistakes, as we pointed before, occur. Proceeding by the two series from PA$_1$ to SA$_1$, PA$_2$ to SA$_2$, PA$_3$ to SA$_3$, MA to DHA and from GA$_2$ to NI$_2$ the same differences in Srutis result.

The Suddha Swarams of the Dwavimsati series.

Mr. Sastrial tries to inculpate Sarnga Dev also by making him subscribe to his theory of 53 Srutis. But each Swara Sthanam should be at a distance of 22 in one way and 31 in the other way. But columns 6, 7 and 8 will show that this is not the case. The two series do not produce the right Srutis proceeding by twenty twos and thirty ones.

For example, the GA$_2$ or the 18th Sruti of the SA-MA series should be DHA$_2$. He fixes it at the 41st place instead of at the 40th (18+22=40). In the same way GA$_2$ obtained from DHA$_2$ by the SA-PA series is fixed at the 18th instead of the 19th Sthanam, for 41+31=72; 72−53=19. Again he derives Suddha NI from MA at the 49th step instead of at the 45th; for, MA$_1$ or 23+22=45. Again, proceeding by the SA-PA series from NI$_2$ or 49th Sruti to MA$_1$, he fixes it at 23 instead of 27, for 49+31=80; 80−53=27. This is all inaccurate. This also conflicts with the opinion of Sarnga Dev that the Swarams of the SA-PA and SA-MA series stand in the relation of Vadi and Samvadi. He tries to prove that SA-PA or $\frac{3}{2}$ is the same as the SA-PA of Sarnga Dev. Hence all this trouble. We are prepared to accept him if he proves it. But he cannot. Sarnga Dev merely mentions that (SA to MA, or 9)+(SA to PA, or 13)=22 Srutis and nothing more.

Mr. Sastrial first declared that the Swarams in use in South Indian Music were not the correct ones, that our ancient musicians used only the Dwavimsati Srutis of Sarnga Dev and they were the Vydeeka Ganam. Now he relinquishes that position and says that Sarnga Dev's SA-MA and SA-PA series are the same as SA-MA or $\frac{4}{3}$ or proceeding by 22nd and SA-PA or $\frac{3}{2}$ or proceeding by 31st. But we may clearly see that Mr. Sastrial's Srutis do not agree well with these 2 fundamental Swarams of Sarnga Dev.

Again, there is a vast difference between the system of Sarnga Dev 4+3+2+4+4+3+2=22, and the system of 53 Srutis of Mr. Sastrial 9+8+5+9+9+8+5=53 found in col 7 of the Table. However long or short an octave might be all the Srutis should stand at intervals of 4, 3, 2, 4, 4, 3, 2. But his measurements are quite different. For example,

(1) $\frac{53}{22}\times 4=9\frac{14}{22}$. But he gives 9

(2) $\frac{53}{22}\times 3=7\frac{5}{22}$. But his is 8

(3) $\frac{53}{22}\times 2=4\frac{18}{22}$. But his number is 5

Sarnga Dev never allowed Mr. Sastrial the privilege of adding in one or subtracting in another according to his own fancy. The object of Sarnga Dev in having Srutis numbered as 4, 3, 2 was to indicate the three castes Brahma, Kshatriya and Vaisya. But Mr. Sastrial, in contradiction to that has indicated a new system of 9, 8 and 5. While advocating ancient works he goes against them in the same breath. He condemns all ancient writers, with the exception of Sarnga Dev, that they learnt music like parrots. The case of Mr. Sastrial is like that of the following silly parrots:—A hunter finding that the parrots would not be deceived by his snares but bit them into pieces, had recourse to a stratagem. He had a number of Korukai reeds which were hung on an iron wire, and he tied these to the branches of a tree. A parrot mistaking the wire for the branch settled down on it. As the wire was light, it could not sit on it, but rolled down along with the reeds head downwards and began to scream flapping its wings at the same time. The parrot completely ignorant of the cause was holding on to the reeds with grim determination. Other parrots who heard the scream, seeing their comrade in danger, also came and settled by the side of him and began screeching with their heads down each holding on to a reed. The hunter came at this juncture and seized them all. The poor parrots being ignorant of the fact that if they let go their hold they would be out of danger, were all caught. Ignorant men are also caught in this wise. Those who made researches into the theory of Srutis in Indian Music and those others, like Mr. Sastrial, who have written on the Srutis of South Indian Music have caught grim hold of the 22 Srutis and are entangled like the parrots who got hold of the Korukai reeds!

The chief of these is Mr. Sastrial. This is clear from the calculations he gives. If we compare his calculations with those of the 53 Srutis of Bosanquet we could see his errors as clear as in a glass. It may be seen from Table 20.

We have criticised at length the various theories put forward by Mr. Sastrial from time to time. We shall do well to sum them up here for our remembrance:—

Table 7, Page 285.

(1) It is clearly seen here that the Dwavimsati Srutis are not derived after the Sruti system of Sarnga Dev.

(2) Swarams are obtained according to the length of wire for Srutis suggested by the author of Parijatam. Their respective length of wire, fractions and cents are found in the 8th, 9th, 10th and 11th columns of the Table. He accepts Parijatam's

Tara Sa $\frac{2}{1}$ with 1200 cents, the Pa $\frac{3}{2}$ with 702 cents, the Ma $\frac{4}{3}$ with 498 cents, the Ga_1 $\frac{9}{8}$ with 204 cents, and the Sa'_1 $\frac{9}{5}$ with 1018 cents on their own merits.

(3) He says that inasmuch as Watson approves of [illegible] (line 3), [illegible] (line 6) and [illegible] (line 12) obtained after the system of Parijatam we might also accept them.

(4) With the exception of these 8 Swarams he changes the Srutis of Parijatam by correcting [illegible] into [illegible] in line 16, and [illegible] into [illegible] in line 17, and alters the Sootrams of the author to suit his own convenience. Again, in line 7 he changes [illegible] of Parijatam into [illegible], and in line 20, [illegible] into [illegible], and calls these the system of Pythagoras.

(5) He accepts the [illegible], [illegible], [illegible], [illegible] and [illegible] of Parijatam. In the other 7 Swarams he accepts [illegible], [illegible] and [illegible] as Watson approves of them. But he changes the [illegible] and [illegible] of Parijatam into [illegible] and [illegible] after the system of Pythagoras. Again, he changes the 16th and the 18th Srutis, namely [illegible] and [illegible] of Parijatam into [illegible] and [illegible] to suit his own theory and alters the Sootrams accordingly.

(6) Among the Swarams obtained after the method of Parijatam, the 1st, 2nd, 3rd, 5th, 6th, 7th, 10th and 12th are intact. Of the other four, two are altered after the system of Pythagoras and the other two are his own to suit which the Sootrams of Parijatam have been altered. These four changes are unwarranted.

(7) Apart from the 12 Swarams obtained after the measurement of Ahobilar, the author of Parijatam, he locates 10 other Srutis in different places. Regarding the 10 Srutis occurring opposite to the numbers 1, 2, 5, 8, 10, 11, 14, 15, 18 and 21, the 10th [illegible], the 1st [illegible], the 14th [illegible], the 5th [illegible] and the 18th [illegible] are obtained successively from the 10th Ni_1 [illegible] of Parijatam by Sa-Pa [illegible] system; the 2nd [illegible] and the 15th [illegible] are obtained by the same process from the 11th [illegible] which must have been taken from Deval's and Clement's scales; so also the 21st [illegible] from the 8th [illegible]. But wherefrom does he get this 41st harmonic?

Table 8, Page 286.

When we notice all this we are reminded of the bag of the beggar which was filled with a quantity of different grains! This is entirely conflicting with the Srutis of Karnatic music and the theory of Srutis of Parijatam.

We have shown here that we can never obtain 22 Srutis in a Sthayi when we proceed by 13s in the Sa-Pa series. In the first half of the Table we have given the right series of the Sa-Pa system and in the other half the wrong series of Mr. Shastrial.

If we proceed by the 13s by the Sa-Pa series according to Sarnga Dev we will obtain only 22 Srutis. But if Sa-Pa is taken as [illegible] we will get more Srutis than 22 in the octave. Where Mr. Shastrial has erred in lines 5 and 17 have already been clearly set forth.

Table 9, Page 288.

Here we have shown by means of cents calculation how more than 22 Srutis are obtained in the octave if we take Sa-Pa = [illegible] and Sa-Ma = [illegible]. The measurements of the extra Srutis are also indicated.

Table 10, Page 290.

Here we have shown how the system of Sa-Pa or proceeding by $\frac{3}{2}$ is not after the method of Parijatam or Pythagoras. We have also shown here how the 22 Srutis occur in a very irregular order when we proceed by $\frac{3}{2}$ from the 10th Sthanam. It is shown how we get 157 cents less when proceeding by $\frac{3}{2}$ we arrive at the 23rd Sruti, thus showing the possibility of more Srutis. We shall also observe from this Table that there is not the least resemblance between the Srutis of Parijatam arrived by the Sa-Pa series in Table 7 and the Srutis derived while taking Sa-Pa to be $=\frac{3}{2}$.

Table 11, Page 294.

In the second part of this Table may be found the 22 Srutis which result from the Sa-Ma series taking successive multiples of 498·045 cents after the system of 53 Srutis of Mr. Shastrial. In the first part, how the 22 Srutis result from the Sa-Pa series is given. In the third part, we may see how the Srutis contradict and differ from each other while proceeding by the two series. In the same part, we may see that the difference which exists between Pa opposite the 32nd number and the Pa of the Sa-Ma series is repeated as regards the other Srutis such as Ma, Ga, and Ri etc.

Table 12, Page 299.

Here he says that his 22 Srutis after the system of Ratnakaram were obtained from his 53 Srutis. The names of the respective Srutis are also given. If we compare the cents found in Columns 10 and 11 of this Table and those of Nagoji Row in Columns 7 and 8 of Table 6 we shall find that they are just the same. The only change is that the order for Sruti intervals from Ma, 22, 71, 41 and 71 cents of Mr. Rowji is changed into 71, 41, 71, and 22 cents.

Table 13, Page 301.

Here we see the vast difference in cents calculation between the Srutis of the Sa-Ma series in column 7 and those of Mr. Shastrial in Table 12. We may see here that his words and actions do not tally. In the 9th column may be seen the difference in calculations more or less.

Table 14, Page 303.

Here we may see how Mr. Shastrial obtains 12 Srutis by the Sa-Pa series and 10 by the Sa-Ma series starting from Ma, knowing that the octave does not come to an end even at the 53rd Sruti, assuming 53 to be the number of possible Srutis in the octave. Here again we might see the irregularities in Srutis and their measurement. It is also shown how there is a difference of 678½ − 521½ or 157 cents between the Ma_2 of the Sa-Pa series (13th Sruti) and Ma_2 of the Sa-Ma series (11th Sruti) showing how they are exactly 78½ cents more and 78½ cents less than 600 cents (the 12th Sruti.)

Table 15, Page 306.

This Table shows how the 22 Srutis are obtained within 13 Sthayis when we assume Sa-Pa=13 according to the system of Sarnga Dev. It also shows how the octave does not end even with 31 Sthayis but requires 7 more places to complete.

Table 16, Page 307.

This shows how 22 Srutis are obtained within 9 Sthayis when we assume Sa-Ma=9 according to Sarnga Dev. It also shows how 53 Srutis result even 7 places earlier before 22 Sthayis are finished.

Table 17, Page 314.

This table shows how the successive twelve Srutis are not selected by Mr. Shastrial when he proceeds by 702s in the Sa-Pa series and 498s in the Sa-Ma series while speaking about the Srutis of Arya Sangeetam. It also shows how in the 5th and the 4th places he gets 2 cents more sometimes and 2 cents less sometimes.

Table 18, Page 316.

This table indicates the order of the Srutis of the Sa-Pa and the Sa-Ma series and the special Swarams of the 10th and 23rd places. In the second part, it is shown how he rejects the 10th and the 23rd places with 24 cents each while he has accepted 5 places with 20 cents each and another 5 with 22 cents each.

Table 19, Page 318.

In this Table his selection from the 53 Srutis for the three Sampradayas—Vydeeka, Loukeeka, and Swaya—is given along with the Suddha Swarams of the Dwavimsati Srutis and those of the author of Parijatam and of Pythagoras. It is also shown how the Srutis from the Sa-Pa and the Sa-Ma series are unsatisfactory even as regards the seven fundamental Swarams.

TABLE 20 Pages 326, 327, 328 and 329.

This table shows the difference between the 53 Srutis of Bosanquet and the 53 Srutis of Mr. Shastrial obtained (1) by the Sa-Pa and (2) by the Sa-Ma series, and the difference in Srutis resulting from the collection of opinions of Mr. Shastrial from various sources. The different conferences and the Tables in which they have been previously given are also indicated.

TABLE 20.

For comparing the 53 Srutis of Bosanquet with the 53 of the SA-PA and SA-MA series.

Number of 53 Srutis.	The 53 Sthanams of Mercator, Poole, White, Thompson, Cheve, Bosanquet and Bhandarkar.	The 53 Srutis of SA-PA series.				The 53 Srutis of SA-MA series.				Names of Srutis.	
		Fraction of Srutis if SA = 1.	Location of Swarams in a wire 32 in long.	Cents.	How the 53 Srutis are produced.	Fraction of Srutis if SA = 1.	Location of Swarams in a wire 32 in long.	Cents.	How the 53 Srutis are produced.	53 Srutis.	22 Srutis.
1	2	3	4	5	6	7	8	9	10	11	12
1	0	1	32·000	0		1	32·000	0		Panasa	Chandovat
											...
2	22·641	·98654	31·569	23·460	12s	·98859	31·635	19·845	c − 41s	Deepani	...
3	45·283	·97326	31·144	46·920	24s	·97530	31·209	43·305	c − 29s	Likucha	...
4	67·924	·96016	30·725	70·380	36s	·96217	30·790	66·765	c − 17s	Heena	...
										,,	*Dayavati*
5	90·566	·94724	30·312	93·840	48s	·94922	30·375	90·225	c − 5s	Leena	Dayavati
											...
						·93838	30·029	110·070	2c − 46s	Heerada	Ranjani
6	113·207										*Ranjani*
		·93644	29·966	113·685	c + 7s					,,	...
											...
7	135·849	·92384	29·563	137·145	c + 19s	·92577	29·625	133·530	2c − 34s	Mithya	....
9	181·132	·89914	28·772	184·065	c + 43s	·90102	28·833	180·450	2c − 10s	Meenaja	Raktica
											Raktica
						·89073	28·504	200·295	3c − 51s	Khurali	Rowdri
10	203·773	·88889	28·444	203·910	2c + 2s					,,	*Rowdri*
											...
11	226·415	·87693	28·062	227·370	2c + 14s	·87874	28·120	223·755	3c − 39s	Sooryaka	...
14	294·339	·84200	26·944	297·750	2c + 50s	·84375	27·000	294·135	3c − 3s	Rudnika	Krodha
						·83412	26·692	313·980	4c − 44s	Dhepika	Vajrica
15	316·981										*Vajrica*
		·83239	26·637	317·595	3c + 9s					,,	...
16	339·623	.82119	26·278	341.055	3c + 21s	·82293	26·333	337·440	4c − 32s	Vepani	...
18	384·906	·79923	25·575	387·975	3c + 45s	·80090	25·629	384·360	4c − 8s	Venila	Prasarini
											Prasarini
						·79176	25·337	404·205	5c − 49s	Kerali	Preethi
19	407·547										...
											...
		·79012	25·284	407·820	4c + 4s					,,	...
											Preethi
						·78112	24·996	427·665	5c − 37s	Chetika	...
20	430·188										...
		·77949	24·944	431·280	4c + 16s					,,	...
23	498·114	·74845	23·950	501·660	4c + 52s	·75000	24·000	498·045	5c − s	Kenavi	Marjani
											...
24	520·755	·73991	23·677	521·505	5c + 11s	·74144	23·726	517·890	6c − 42s	Jypila	...
25	543·396	·72995	23·358	544·965	5c + 23s	·73147	23·407	541·350	6c − 30s	Gykuti	...

TABLE 20.
For comparing the conflicting opinions of Subramania Sastrial.

Number of 53 Srutis.	Pa or Ma.	What Srutis are obtained by Sa-Pa and Sa-Ma.	Cents for the 22 or 78 Srutis of Mr. Shastrial.	Fractions.	Vibrations for Swarams.		27 Srutis of Pythagoras.	Sud. Swrms. of Pythagoras.	12 of Parijatam.	The altered 12 of Parijatam.	22 of Parijatam.	22 by Sa-Pa Series.	Mr. Rowji's altered.	27 from 53 by Sa-Ma series.	22 by Sa-Pa and Sa-Ma series.	Just Intonation.	Prata Ramaswami Bhagavatar.	Conference Reports.			Table.
					If Sa = 240.	If Sa = 540.												Number.	Page.	Line.	
13	14	15	16	17	18	19	20	21	22	23	24	25	26	27	28	29	30	31	32	33	34
1				1	240	540												3	41	15	
		R_1	21·506	$\frac{80}{81}$	243	$546\frac{3}{4}$	...	...	...	...	1	...	...	...	...	...	...	2	52	30	7
2	P		23·460	...	...	547·4	1	...	...	...	...	1	...	...	...	...	...	2	51	16	9, 10, 11
3	P		* 46·920	...	...	554·9	...	...	...	...	...	...	...	...	...	...	...	...	...	...	9, 11
4	M	R_1	66·765	...	...	561·2	...	...	...	...	...	...	...	1	...	...	...	3	41	15	11
		R_1	70·673	$\frac{24}{25}$	250	562·5	...	...	...	...	...	...	1	...	...	...	...	3	40	12	12
5	M		90·225	$\frac{243}{256}$	$252\frac{5}{8}$	$568\frac{8}{9}$	2	...	...	...	...	...	...	$\frac{1}{2}$	1	...	1	3	42	7	11, 14
			92·179	$\frac{128}{135}$	$253\frac{1}{8}$	569·5	...	...	...	...	...	...	$\frac{1}{2}$	...	...	1	...	6	...	...	12, 18
	M	R_2	110·070	...	...	575·4	...	...	...	...	...	...	...	2	...	...	...	3	41	15	11
6		R_2	111·731	$\frac{15}{16}$	256	576·	...	...	...	...	2	...	2	...	...	2	2	3	40	14	7, 12, 18
	P		113·685	$\frac{2048}{2187}$	$256\frac{37}{128}$	576·6	3	...	...	...	...	2	...	...	2	...	...	2	51	16	9, 10, 14
		R_3	133·237	$\frac{25}{27}$	$259\frac{1}{5}$	583·2	...	...	1	1	3	...	...	...	...	...	...	2	49	29	7
7	P		137·145	...	...	584·6	...	...	...	...	...	3	...	...	...	...	...	2	51	16	9, 10
9	M	R_3	180·450	...	...	599·3	4	...	...	...	...	...	...	3	3	...	...	3	41	15	11, 14
		Su. R	182·404	$\frac{9}{10}$	$266\frac{2}{3}$	600·	...	...	...	...	...	...	3	...	...	3	3	3	40	15	12, 18
10	M	R_4	200·295	...	...	606·3	...	...	...	...	...	...	...	4	...	...	...	3	41	15	11
	P	G_1 or R_4	203·910	$\frac{8}{9}$	270	$607\frac{1}{2}$	5	1	2	2	4	4	4	...	4	4	4	3	40	16	7, 9, 10, 12,
		G_2	225·416	$\frac{225}{256}$	$273\frac{1}{15}$	615	...	...	...	...	5	...	...	...	...	...	...	2	52	34	7 [14, 18
11	P		227·370	...	...	615·8	6	...	...	...	...	5	...	...	...	...	...	2	51	16	9, 10
14	M	Su. G_1	294·135	$\frac{27}{32}$	$284\frac{4}{9}$	640	7	...	...	...	...	...	5	5	5	5	5	3	41	15	11, 12, 14, 18
	M	G_2	313·980	...	...	647·4	...	...	...	...	...	...	...	6	...	...	...	3	41	15	11
15		Sa. Su. G. M_1	315·641	$\frac{5}{6}$	288	648	...	...	3	3	6	...	6	...	...	6	6	3	40	18	7, 12, 18
	P		317·595	...	...	648·7	8	...	...	...	...	6	...	...	6	...	...	2	51	16	9, 10, 14
16	P		§ 341·055	...	...	657·5	...	...	...	...	...	?	...	...	...	...	...	...	...	...	9, 10
18	M	G_3	384·360	...	...	$674\frac{1}{4}$	9	...	...	...	...	...	...	7	7	...	...	3	41	15	11, 14
		Anta. G.	386·314	$\frac{4}{5}$	300	675·	...	...	...	...	...	...	7	...	...	7	7	3	40	19	12, 18
	M		404·205	...	...	682	...	...	...	...	...	...	...	$\frac{7}{8}$	...	...	...	3	42	7	11
19			*404·442	$\frac{19}{24}$	$303\frac{3}{19}$	682·1	...	...	4	...	...	...	...	...	...	...	...	2	49	29	7
			405·864	[illegible]	303[illegible]	$682\frac{2}{3}$	...	...	...	...	...	...	$\frac{7}{8}$	...	...	8	...	3	42	7	12, 18
	P	M_2	407·820	$\frac{64}{81}$	$303\frac{3}{4}$	$683\frac{7}{16}$	10	2	...	4	7	7	...	...	8	...	8	2	50	27	7, 9, 10, 14
		Su. M. G_4	427·373	$\frac{25}{32}$	$307\frac{1}{5}$	691·2	...	...	...	...	...	...	8	...	...	...	...	3	41	16	11, 12
	M		427·665	...	...	$691\frac{1}{3}$	...	...	...	...	...	...	...	8	...	...	...	3	41	41	
20		M_3	429·062	$\frac{32}{41}$	$307\frac{1}{2}$	$691\frac{7}{8}$	...	...	...	...	8	...	...	...	...	...	...	2	52	37	7
	P		431·280	...	...	$692\frac{3}{4}$	...	...	...	...	...	8	...	...	...	...	...	2	51	16	9, 10
23	M	Su. M_1. M_4	498·045	$\frac{3}{4}$	320	720	11	3	5	5	9	9	9	9	9	9	9	3	40	20	7, 10, 11, 12,
		P_1	519·552	$\frac{20}{27}$	324	729	...	...	...	...	10	...	...	...	...	...	...	2	52	39	7 [14, 18
24	P		521·505	...	...	729·8	12	...	...	...	...	10	...	...	?	...	...	2	51	16	9, 10, 14
25	P		§ 544·965	...	...	739·8	...	...	...	...	...	?	...	...	...	...	...	...	...	...	9, 10,

1	2	3	4	5	6	7	8	9	10	11	12
26	566·038	·72012	23.044	568·425	5c + 35s	·72163	23·092	564·810	6c − 18s	Hynuka	...
27	588.679	·71043	22·734	591·885	5c + 47s	·71191	22·781	588·270	6c − 6s	Kynavi	*Kshiti* Kshiti
28 {	611.321					·70379	22·522	608·115	7c − 47s	Nykhari	... Rakta *Rakta*
		·70233	22·475	611·730	6c + 6s					„	...
29	633·962	·69288	22·172	635·190	6c + 18s	·69433	22·218	631·575	7c − 35s	Mica	... ...
31	679·245	·67435	21·579	682.110	6c + 42s	·67576	21.624	678·495	7c − 11s	Mynaki	Sandipini
32 {	701·886					·66805	21·378	698·340	8c − 52s	Rykhika	*Sandipini* Alapini
		·66667	21·333	701·955	7c + s					„	*Alapini*
33	724·528	·65769	21·046	725·415	7c + 13s	·65906	21·090	721·800	8c − 40s	Chotika	... ...
35	769·811	·64011	20·483	772.335	7c + 37s	·64145	20·526	768·720	8c − 16s	Sona	...
36	792·452	.63150	20·208	795·795	7c + 49s	·63281	20·250	792·180	8c − 4s	Khonika	*Madanti* Madanti
37 {	815·094					·62559	20·019	812·025	9c − 45s	Dhokati	... Rohini *Rohini*
		·62430	19.977	815·640	8c + 8s					„	...
38	837·735	·61589	19·708	839·100	8c + 20s	·61718	19·750	835·485	9c − 33s	Ghotika	... ...
40	883·018	·59942	19·182	886·826	8c + 44s	·60068	19·222	882·405	9c − 9s	Bhonati	... Ramya
41 {	905·660					·59382	19·003	902·250	10c − 50s	Kyravi	*Ramya* Ugra
		·59259	18·963	905·865	9c + 3s					„	*Ugra*
42	928·301	·58462	18·708	929·325	9c + 15s	·58583	18·747	925·710	10c − 38s	Towkali	... ...
45	996·226	·56134	17·962	999·705	9c + 51s	·56250	18·000	996·090	10c − 2s	Younika	... Kshobhini
46 {	1018·867					·55608	17·795	1015·935	11c − 43s	Jayanti	Teevra *Teevra*
		·55493	17·758	1019·550	10c + 10s					„	...
47	1041·509	·54746	17·519	1043·010	10c + 22s	·54860	17·555	1039·395	11c − 31s	Gayani	... [ti
49	1086·792	·53282	17·050	1089·930	10c + 46s	.53394	17·086	1086·315	11c − 7s	Ganavati	Kumudva
50 {	1109·433					·52784	16·891	1106·160	12c − 48s	Nakhara	*Kumudva* Manda
		·52675	16·856	1109·775	11c + 5s					„	... ...
51 {	1132·075					·52075	16·664	1129·620	12c − 36s	Mayika	*Manda* ...
		·51966	16·629	1133·235	11c + 17s					„	... ...
53	1177·358	·50376	16·184	1180·155		·50682	16·218	1176·540		Maninee	... ... [ti
54 {	1200·000					·50104	16·038	1196·385	13c − 53s	Panasa	Chandova *Chandova*
		·49897	15·967	1203·615	11c + 53s					„	...

13	14	15	16	17	18	19	20	21	22	23	24	25	26	27	28	29	30	31	32	33	34
26	M	M_2	564·810	...	...	748·4	...	...	...	...	...	...	...	10	...	...	...	3	41	41	11
		T.M.	568·718	[illegible]	333⅓	750	...	...	...	...	...	...	10	...	...	...	...	3	41	41	12
27	M		588·270	[illegible]	337[illegible]	758·5	13	...	...	...	...	...	...	[illegible]	10	...	10	3	42	7	11, 14
			590·224	[illegible]	337½	759·4	...	...	...	...	...	...	[illegible]	...	...	10	...	3	42	7	12, 18
	M	M_3	608·115	...	...	767·3	...	...	...	...	...	...	...	11	...	...	...	3	41	41	11
28		T.Tr.M.P_2	609·776	[illegible]	341⅓	768	...	...	...	...	11	...	11	...	...	11	11	3	42	7	7, 12, 18
	P		611·731	[illegible]	341[illegible]	768·9	14	...	...	...	...	11	...	...	11	...	...	2	51	16	9, 10, 14
		P_3	631·283	[illegible]	345[illegible]	777·6	...	...	6	6	12	...	...	...	...	...	...	2	49	49	7
29	P		635·190	...	...	779⅓	...	...	...	...	...	12	...	...	...	...	...	2	51	16	9, 10
31	M	M_4	678·495	...	...	799	15	...	...	...	...	...	...	12	12	...	...	3	41	41	11, 14
		T.Tam. M.	680·449	[illegible]	355[illegible]	800	...	...	...	...	...	...	12	...	...	12	12	3	42	7	12, 18
32	M	P	698·340	...	...	808¼	...	...	...	...	...	...	...	13	...	...	...	3	41	17	11
	P	P., P_4	701·955	2/3	360	810	16	4	7	7	13	13	13	...	13	13	13	3	40	22	7, 9, 10, 12,
		D	723·461	[illegible]	364½	820[illegible]	...	...	...	...	14	...	...	...	...	...	...	2	52	31	7 [14, 18
33	P		725·415	...	...	821	17	...	...	...	...	14	...	...	...	...	...	2	51	16	9, 10
35	M	D_1	768·720	...	...	841·6	...	...	...	...	...	...	...	14	...	...	...	3	41	17	11
		D_1	772·628	[illegible]	375	843¾	...	...	...	...	...	...	14	...	...	...	...	3	41	41	12
36	M		792·180	[illegible]	379[illegible]	853⅓	18	...	...	...	...	...	...	[illegible]	14	...	14	3	42	...	11, 14
			794·134	[illegible]	379[illegible]	854·3	...	...	...	...	...	...	[illegible]	...	...	14	...	6	...	...	12, 18
	M	D_2	812·025	...	...	863·1	...	...	...	...	...	...	...	15	...	...	...	3	41	17	11
37		D_2	813·686	[illegible]	384	864	...	...	...	...	15	...	15	...	...	15	15	2	52	30	7, 12, 18
	P		815·640	...	...	865	19	...	...	...	...	15	...	...	15	...	...	2	51	16	7, 9, 10, 14
		D_3	835·192	[illegible]	388[illegible]	874·8	...	...	...	8	16	...	...	...	...	...	...	2	49	31	7
38	P		839·100	...	...	876¾	...	...	...	...	...	16	...	...	...	...	...	2	51	16	9, 10
			*852·592	[illegible]	392[illegible]	883[illegible]	...	...	8	...	...	...	...	...	...	...	...	2	49	29	7
40	M	D_3	882·405	...	...	899	20	...	...	...	...	...	...	16	16	...	...	3	41	17	11, 14
		Su. D	884·359	[illegible]	400	900	...	...	...	...	...	...	16	...	...	16	16	6	...	...	12, 18,
41	M	D_4	902·250	...	...	909·5	...	...	...	...	...	...	...	17	...	...	...	3	41	18	11
	P	D_4, N_1	905·866	[illegible]	405	911⅓	21	5	...	9	17	17	17	...	17	17	17	2	48	20	7, 9, 10, 12,
42	P	N_2	927·371	[illegible]	410[illegible]	922·6	...	...	...	...	18	...	...	...	...	...	...	2	52	35	7 [14, 18
			929·325	...	...	923·7	22	...	...	...	...	18	...	...	...	...	...	2	51	16	9, 10
			*933·129	[illegible]	411[illegible]	925·7	...	...	9	...	...	...	...	...	...	...	...	2	47	12	7
45	M	Su. N_1	996·090	[illegible]	426[illegible]	960·	23	...	...	...	...	...	18	18	18	18	18	3	41	18	11, 12, 14, 18
	M	N_2	1015·935	...	...	971·	...	...	...	...	...	...	...	19	...	...	...	3	41	18	11
46		Ki. N., S_1	1017·597	4/5	432	972·	...	...	10	10	19	...	19	...	...	19	19	6	...	...	7, 12, 18
	P		1019·550	...	...	973·1	24	...	...	...	...	19	...	...	19	...	...	2	51	16	9, 10, 14
47	P	§	1043·010	...	...	987·3	...	...	...	...	...	?	...	...	...	...	...	...	...	...	9, 10
49	M	N_3	1086·315	...	...	1011·4	25	...	...	...	...	...	...	20	20	...	...	3	41	18	11, 14
		Ka. N	1088·269	[illegible]	450	1012⅓	...	...	...	...	...	...	20	...	...	20	20	6	...	...	12, 18
	M		1106·160	...	...	1023	...	...	...	...	...	...	...	[illegible]	...	...	...	3	42	8	11
50		*	1106·397	[illegible]	454[illegible]	1023⅓	...	...	11	...	...	...	...	...	...	...	...	2	49	20	7
			1107·821	[illegible]	455⅓	1024	...	...	...	...	...	...	[illegible]	...	...	...	...	6	...	...	12, 18
	P	S_2	1109·775	[illegible]	455[illegible]	1025½	26	6	...	11	20	20	...	...	21	21	21	2	50	32	7, 9, 10, 14
		S. Sha., N	1129·327	[illegible]	460[illegible]	1036·8	...	...	...	...	...	...	21	...	...	...	...	...	...	...	12
	M	N_4	1129·620	...	...	1037·	...	...	...	...	...	...	...	21	...	...	...	3	41	18	11
51		S_3	1131·017	[illegible]	461½	1037·8	...	...	...	...	21	...	...	...	...	...	...	2	52	38	7
	P		1133·235	...	...	1039½	...	...	...	...	...	21	...	...	...	...	...	2	51	16	9, 10
	P	*	1176·540	...	...	1065·4	...	...	...	...	...	...	...	...	...	...	...	6	...	...	9, 11, 17, 18
	M	Sha.	1196·385	...	...	1077·8	...	...	...	...	...	...	...	22	...	...	...	3	41	48	11, 13
54		Sha., S_4	1200·	1/2	480	1080·	27	7	12	12	22	22	22	...	22	22	22	...	...	...	7, 10, 12, 14,
	P	*	1203·615	...	...		...	...	...	...	...	...	...	...	...	...	...	...	...	...	11 [18

We find 4 pages of statement in Table 20. In the 326 and 327 pages only 25 out of the 53 Srutis and those below 545 cents are dealt with, and the rest will be found in pages 328 and 329. Our readers will do well to consider the 4 pages as one and compare the Srutis.

We see that in this Table 20, in the first and second columns are given the calculations of Mercator, Poole, White, Thompson, Cheve, Bosanquet, Bhandarkar and others, dividing the octave into 53 equal parts. The 3rd, 4th, 5th and 6th columns contain the calculations to show that the opinion of Mr. Shastrial that 53 Srutis are obtained by the SA-PA series is wrong. The 7th, 8th, 9th and 10th columns prove the same mistake of Mr. Sastrial as regards the SA-MA series. The 11th and the 12th columns give the names of the Srutis. We shall see clearly here that there is not the remotest connection between the calculations of the Western scientists who divide the octave into 53 equal parts and the 53 Srutis obtained by Mr. Shastrial while proceeding by $\frac{3}{2}$ and $\frac{4}{3}$. We might also notice that the 53 Srutis obtained by the SA-PA series and the same obtained by the SA-MA series are different from each other, and that Mr. Shastrial's calculations as regards the same are wrong.

We might see in column 5 that the PA or 701·955 obtained at the 32nd Sruti Sthanam is of the SA-PA series. But the PA obtained by the SA-MA series is 698·340 as given in column 9. So, when we see a difference of about 4 cents for main Swarams in the two series, how can we conclude that the same Srutis result from them? Again, the 23rd Sruti MA has 501·660 cents in the SA-PA series (see column 5) while the same MA has 498·045 cents (see column 9). Here again we see a difference of nearly 4 cents. So Mr. Shastrial's conclusions are wrong. He makes such bold statements knowing that the Karnatic musicians will blindly believe anything he says. We have shown on various occasions that every one of his statements is completely wrong. We are compelled to have recourse to so many Tables so that every one might be fully convinced that the various calculations he gave to prove his 22 Srutis are entirely wrong.

Again we noted already that there was a difference of 3·546 cents between the PA of the Western scientists (701·886c) and the PA=698·340c of the SA-MA series of Sastrial. He may say that the PA of his SA-PA series has only the very slight difference of ·069 cents. But if we disregard this slight difference it gathers moment as it proceeds and results in the difference of 3·615 in an octave! So, even in the main Swarams MA and PA we see a difference between him and the Westerners. The Table will show that there is the difference of 2, 3 and 4 cents in the other Srutis also. Again in the 23rd Sthanam we see 498·114 cents in the calculations of Western scientists, but in his we see 501·660 in the SA-PA series. When there is the difference of 3·546 cents, how can he say that his system resembles that of Bosanquet? So, it is absurd on Mr. Shastrial's part to say that the SA-PA series end in 31 Sthayis and the SA-MA in 22 Sthayis having irregular calculations as his basis. We have shown in the 15th and the 16th Tables how the SA-PA series has 7 places more and the SA-MA series 7 places less.

In pages 327 and 329, we have shown how he has borrowed all his Srutis either from Pythagoras, the author of Parijatam, Nagoji Row and Pratapa Ramasami Bhagavatar and from the series of Just Intonation. Here, in columns 15 and 16 the

Swarams of the SA-PA and SA-MA series, their respective cents, and in column 17 the fractions he borrows from other writers and in columns 18 and 19 the vibrations for the fractions, are given. The calculations for the Swarams of the two series and for the Swarams of the fractions are given in the 19th column, assuming that the Madhya Sthayi SA has 540 vibrations. In the Second Conference Report p. 48, he gives his calculations assuming that the Tonic SA has 240 vibrations. This we have converted into 540. We shall compare the following according to the above calculation. He says that the RI_1 (22 cents) in column 24 is obtained after the 22 Srutis of Parijatam (see Second Conference Report p. 52, line 30). Again he says that the RI_1 (23 cents) in col. 20 is obtained after the 27 Srutis of Pythagoras and by the SA-PA series in col. 25 (see Second Conference Report p. 51, line 16). He says again that the RI (67 cents) found in col. 27 is obtained by the SA-MA series (see Third Conference Report p. 41, line 15). The RI_1 (71 cents) in col. 26 is borrowed from Nagoji Row. He gives it as his own in the Third Conference Report p. 40, line 12. The RI_1 (90 cents) in col. 28 of the SA-MA series is claimed as his own in the Third Conference Report page 42. This same is claimed by Pratapa Ramaswami Bhagavatar as his own. The RI_1 (92 cents) obtained from the series of the Just Intonation is said to be derived from the Sama Veda system as given in his essay at the Sixth Conference. (We cannot quote page and line as the report is not printed yet).

Thus we see that his RI_1 varies from 540 to 546$\frac{3}{4}$, 547·4, 561, 562$\frac{1}{2}$, 568$\frac{4}{5}$ and 569·5 in the number of vibrations, and from 22 to 23, 67, 71, 90 and 92 as regards cents. We may notice the same irregularity as regards other Srutis also. He first came to establish 22 Srutis, then moved on to 53. He was not stable there either but tried to establish 78 Srutis, being led by the opinions of others.

Besides these 78 Srutis there are three marked *; of these 47 cents is the 24th in SA-PA series and is nearer to the octave than the 22nd; 1177c is rejected because it is too close to 1200c; and 1204c is not mentioned as it is beyond Madhya Sthayi though it is the 53 in SA-PA series. Two marked §; in the SA-PA series beginning from SA, the 9th Sruti, or, Suddha Madhyamam must be 498 cents; but it comes out as 341 with 157 cents less; so also, the 22nd as 1043 instead of as 1200. Lastly the four marked ★ are from Parijata's scale for which Mr. Shastrial substitutes others.

Overleaf is a comparative statement Table 20 A. of some of the scales of Srutis given by Mr. Shastrial. It is divided into three parts. Taking parts I and II together and comparing the values of any given Sruti, we find there is a difference of either 157, 159, or 161 cents between the highest and the lowest values.

Even if we take the most charitable view and rearrange the 9th and 10th tables according to their values and give them as in part III and compare again the values of each Sruti in parts II and III, we find a difference of 24 cents between the lowest and the highest occuring 7 times, 47 cents thrice, 51 cents twice, 67 cents twice, 71 cents 4 times, 73 cents twice, and 92 and 94 cents once each.

As in table 20, so also here, we find from his essays read at the 6 conferences, from the scales he gives explicitly and the scales which are implied in his words, leaving out of consideration those Srutis which he rejects he really arrives at 94 Srutis in a Sthayi and not 22.

TABLE 20-A.

A Comparative Statement of the highest and lowest values assigned to each Sruti by Mr. Sastriar.

Comparison of Tables in I and II.				I		II				III			Comparison of Tables in II and III.		
Highest cents.	Lowest cents.	Difference in cents.	No. of Sruti.	Cents in Table 9-2	Cents in Table 9-1.	Cents in Table 13.	Cents in Table 11—1.	Cents in Table 12.	Cents in Table 7.	Cents in Table 9-2 re-arranged.	Cents in Table 9-1 re-arranged.	No. of Sruti.	Highest cents.	Lowest cents.	Difference in cents.
1	2	3	4	5	6	7	8	9	10	11	12	13	14	15	16
1292—	1133=	159	1	90	1133	90	70	92	22	67	23	1	92—	22=	70
180—	23=	157	2	180	23	110	114	112	112	90	114	2	114—	90=	24
271—	114=	157	3	271	114	180	184	182	133	157	137	3	184—	133=	51
361—	200=	161	4	361	204	200	204	204	204	180	204	4	204—	180=	24
298—	137=	161	5	294	137	294	298	294	225	271	227	5	298—	225=	73
384—	227=	157	6	384	227	314	318	316	316	294	318	6	318—	294=	24
475—	318=	157	7	475	318	384	388	386	408	361	341	7	408—	341=	67
565—	404=	161	8	565	408	404	431	406	429	384	408	8	431—	384=	47
502—	341=	161	9	498	341	498	502	498	498	475	431	9	502—	431=	71
588—	431=	159	10	588	431	588	568	590	520	498	522	10	590—	498=	92
678—	522=	156	11	678	522	608	612	610	610	565	612	11	612—	565=	47
769—	612=	157	12	769	612	678	682	680	631	588	635	12	682—	588=	94
859—	698=	161	13	859	702	698	702	702	702	678	702	13	702—	678=	24
794—	635=	159	14	792	635	792	772	794	723	769	725	14	794—	723=	71
882—	725=	157	15	882	725	812	816	814	814	792	816	15	816—	792=	24
973—	816=	157	16	973	816	882	886	884	835	859	839	16	886—	835=	51
1063—	906=	157	17	1063	906	902	906	906	906	882	906	17	906—	882=	24
1000—	839=	161	18	996	839	996	1000	996	927	973	929	18	1000—	927=	73
1086—	929=	157	19	1086	929	1016	1020	1018	1018	996	1020	19	1020—	996=	24
1177—	1020=	157	20	1177	1020	1086	1090	1088	1110	1063	1043	20	1110—	1043=	67
1267—	1106=	161	21	1267	1110	1106	1133	1108	1131	1086	1110	21	1133—	1086=	47
1357—	1043=	314	22	1357	1043	1196	1204	1200	1200	1176	1133	22	1204—	1133=	71

As regards his 53 Srutis we fear Mr. Shastrial has copied some portions from 461st and 462nd. sections of Barton's Text Book on Sound (p. 503 and given them in the Fifth Conference Report page 35. But Shastrial has not observed what the author says in Section 463, page 504. "*But is it a practical temperament? We fear not.*"

In a division of the Octave into 53 equal parts, the Swara Sthanams are placed by Barton at intervals of 9, 8, 5, 9, 8, 9, 5 and by Bosanquet at 9, 9, 4, 9, 9, 9, 4, whereas Mr. Shastriar has the intervals 8, 9, 5, 9, 8, 9, 5 for *Vydika*, 9, 8, 5, 9, 9, 8, 5 for *Swaya* and 9, 9, 4, 9, 9, 9, 4 for *Loukika* Sampradayams. As these are not in the ratios of 4, 3, 2, 4, 4, 3, 2 of Sarnga Dev's Sruti scale we have already stated in Page 322 that they are not suitable. On the whole, we see that by his conflicting systems we can never arrive at the Srutis in use in South Indian Music.

To sum up our criticism on Mr. Shastrial's theory of Srutis, it is clearly seen that he has tried his best

(1) *To prove the truth of the term "Dwavimsati Srutis" of the author of Ratnakaram.*

(2) *To hide the additional Srutis obtainable by the Sa-Pa and the Sa-Ma series.*

(3) *To confound the eminent Karnatic musicians and to impose upon them a theory of his own.*

(4) *On the whole, his Srutis are not after the system of the author of Ratnakaram, nor, are they in use in Karnatic music.*

(5) *The Sa-Pa and the Sa-Ma series for which he claims originality are nothing new. In neither of the series will 53 Srutis result in an octave.*

(6) *Bosanquet divided the Sthayi into 53 equal parts. But the idea of Mr. Shastrial in thinking he would obtain 53 Srutis by the Sa-Ma series which proceeds by the ratios of 498 cents, is entirely wrong.*

(7) *To say that we derive the identical Swarams while proceeding by 702 and 498 cents in the two series is also wrong.*

(8) *His wrong system has nothing to do with the system of Sama Vedam.*

(9) *We do not see whether sound has, at any time, been divided into Loukeekam and Vydeekam. But Geetams have been so divided with reference to their subject.*

We may notice in different places in his essays some remarks of his which are given in disparagement of others.

In this essay read at the Fifth Conference he says as follows :—

"From this it will be seen that the beginnings of Indian music have to be traced to the chanting of the hymns of Sama Veda by our ancestors in ancient times. While this fact is as clear as noonday light, it really passes strange, why professors of South Indian Music of the present day want to avoid the light and seek shelter in the darkness of lethargy. What is worse is, if any one among them picks up courage enough to find out the truth, he is branded by the others as a mad man, not because of any fault of his, but because the others can see nought with their jaundiced eyes. It is not till we have several such mad men in this country that there will be any scope for the dispelling of the darkness that envelopes us."

Here he says that the 22 Srutis out of his 53 are obtained from the Sama Veda, that they ought to be in use in the music of South India, that they are sure and bright as day light, but the professors of South Indian music avoid it and seek shelter in darkness. We have seen in the Tables how he hides the real Srutis obtainable by the Sa-Pa and Sa-Ma series and tries to establish the Srutis as 22. It is but just that to such a bright (?) intellect the professors of South Indian music appear to be blind! This reminds us of the bats which are in the habit of dwelling in dark places with their heads always hanging downwards belittling the rays of the brilliant Sun! Though he has had the privilege of hearing the beautiful master pieces of Kshetrignar, Tyagarajar, Venkatamakhi, Maha Vydyanatha Iyer and other great musicians, and precious Geetas like those Puns (பண்கள்) selected from Thevaram and Thiruvachakam, it passes strange that he should make such statements. We hope that the musicians of South India will make a note of it.

He says again in the same essay, "The Science of Music, as is the case with every other Science, is developing day by day, and, as such, new combinations of notes, sweet to the ear, cannot but spring into existence from time to time. It will be beyond the power of any one of us to make such combinations conform to cannons of Music divised by us, after all, with our imperfections. Those that try to do so will but reduce themselves to the predicament of one who tries to make the head fit the cap ! The truth underlying the harmony of sounds as designed by Providence is the same everywhere, and the professors of European music have, with much zeal and patient research, arrived at it. I have elsewhere dealt with the harmonic intervals they have fixed. The method we have adopted in finding out the Sruti-stages mentioned above is more or less a royal road."

It is but natural that one who tries to hide the Swarams which stand out boldly as land marks in South Indian music with a view to suit the Sootrams of Sarnga Dev which try to establish 22 Srutis in the octave, should make such remarks. We who have studied for the past 12 years some of the systems of South Indian Music, noticed its downward tendency with regret, and the probability of its being completely destroyed owing to the admixture of Desikam. We have also been writing books from time to time on Srutis, the method of generating Ragas, the system of elaborating Prastharas and on Grahaswarams. We have submitted our views on the above subjects to eminent musicians of Karnatic music from time to time and have obtained their approval. Mr. Shastrial, who is perfectly cognisant of the above fact, introduces his criticisms of our views here and there in his essays. We do not mean reproducing all of them here. We are glad he has been the means of bringing truth to light though he has been scorched in the act, just like the little stick, which is used for trimming a light, gradually gets itself burnt in the act.

He says "that the truth underlying the harmony of sounds as designed by Providence is the same everywhere, and the professors of European music have, with much real patient research arrived at it"

We have seen that this 22 Srutis are not the result of the systems of $\frac{3}{2}$ and $\frac{5}{4}$ of the Europeans ; nor, do they conform to the natural series of Sarnga Dev. The system of arriving at such an irregular series is called by him *" a royal road "*. We draw the attention of South Indian musicians to this fact also.

Again, in his essay read at the Fifth Conference he says,

" Venkatamakhin, an eminent professor of Indian music, who flourished about 250 years ago, seems to have been brought up in the atmosphere of the above school. It was he who fixed for the first time, 12 frets employed in the Vina of the present day."

We have already dealt with (see Page 209) Venkatamakhin, his work "Chathurdandiprakasika" and the 72 Melakarthas mentioned there. Although there were conflicting opinions in his time as regards the Srutis of South Indian music and the Dwavimsati Srutis, they seem to have been disregarded and the Melakarthas made entirely with the help of the Swarams in use in South Indian music. We must understand that the Vina which was then in use was his chief help in making the Melams. It would be absurd to say that he arranged the Swarams of the Vina to suit those Swarams used at present by European musicians. From the Silappadhikaram of Ilankovadigal written about 1800 years ago and from the Sootrams of Tolgauppyam dated many thousand years before that, we find that the Senkoti Yal which we see now with 7 strings and the other kinds of Yal and the Swarasthanams of the present day were in use even then. In his attempt to establish the Dwavimsati Srutis of Saranga Dev who flourished 700 years ago, Mr. Shastrial says that the Vina and its Swarams (dated 8000 years ago) were made by Venkatamakhin who lived 250 years ago. Nothing can be more absurd than this. Of course, it is not expected that one should have a knowledge of everything. Yet, to be ignorant about the very ancient Vina and its Swara Sthanams, is inexcusable. We shall deal with the subject in detail in the Musical system of South India.

He also gives a few criticisms in his essay at the Fifth Conference (Vide Pages 51, 52 and 53) on our remarks about the Vina and the Melams, which were made by us as regards Brahma, Vishnu, Rudra and Mahesa Melams in the First Conference. (Vide Pages 57, 58 and 59). They are quoted below :—

"GENTLEMEN,

I am sure the warm discussion that has been going on for the past hour and a half on the Ragam "*Nattai*" will be of great benefit to us. I am really glad that you have all entered heartily into the discussion and have frankly given your opinions conflicting though they were in some points.

I am sure such a sangam will be productive of some benefit at least. We heard with thankfulness the opinion of Rao Bahadur C. Nagoji Row Avergal, and those of M. R. Ry. P. S. Sundaram Iyer Avergal, B.A., L.T., that granting the existence of the 22 Srutis, in this Ragam the GA and the NI in Arohanam should be Kakaly NI as in NI SA RI SA and in Avarohanam Pancha Sruti as in NI PA DHA NI PA. We also listened to the opinions of M. R. Ry. K. V. Sreenivasa Iyengar Avergal, on the subject slightly differing from them. I rise to say a few words just to emphasise the fact that there is no use of raising any objection to what they said so long as we have not discussed the existence of the 22 Srutis. Though I was not prepared to say anything on the subject at this meeting, my main object being to listen to what others have to say, yet the thoughtful words of some of the speakers urged me on to give my views.

It gives me great pleasure to acknowledge that Indian Music had attained great progress under the great sages of old. Four Melams have been mentioned by ancient writers *viz.*, Mahesvara Melam, Rudra Melam, Vishnu Melam and Brahma Melam.

We understand from the Bharatam of Aravath Navalar of Tiruperundurai that Agastyar mentions in his Bharatam that the ancient Rishis Vasishtar, Veda-Vyasar, Bharadawajar and Satthiar received the 32 Ragams direct from Brahma to be used for the purpose of reciting the four Sacred Vedas (at the rate of 8 Ragams each for the 4 Vedas). We might also see from Tamil Dictionaries at the present time, that they generally speak of 32 Tamil Ragams, their respective characteristic features and their relations with each other. These 32 Ragams are derived from the 12 Prakriti Swarams only. They are accounted for as follows :—

16 Ragams generate when Suddha-Madhyamam goes along with the four varieties of RI and GA, DHA and NI, and the other 16 generate when Prati Madhyamam goes with those varieties. This fact is generally recognised by all.

Besides the 32 Melams mentioned above, 16 different varieties of Ragams generate from the combination of Vikrithi Swarams in RI., GA., DHA., and NI., thus creating 36 Ragams from the 6 varieties in each of RI, GA, DHA, and NI with Suddha-Madhyamam, and another 36 Ragams with Prati Madhyamam —in all 72 Ragams. The 12 Srutis are used in the 12 Sthanams. But owing to the difference caused by the Vikriti Swarams they are generally calculated as 16. The Melam based upon the 16 Srutis is known as Rudra Melam and the Veenai marked with those 16 Srutis Rudra Veenai. Many of the Ragams in use at the present day are derived from this Mela Karta. The Ragam we are discussing at present generates from Jala Nattai which is the 36th Mela Karta in the Rudra Melam. So we must first determine its Arohanam and Avarohanam in relation to this Mela Karta. Though the works of ancient writers consider the Arohanam to be Sampoornam and look upon Ga and Dha as Varjyams in Avarohanam, yet from Geetams in use we see that the practice is different, some considering Ri. Dha as Varjyams both in Arohanam and Avarohanam while others in Avarohanam only. It is our duty to reconcile these conflicting ideas and to arive at some definite conclusion at least as regards Arohanam and Avarohanam. Even this will be of great use to students of Music.

Moreover, there are many consonant Srutis which add beauty to a Geetam and which occur from time to time in the course of a Ragam. Brahma Melam gives us the rules for determining those consonant Srutis so that we might sing them and also recognise them while being sung. They are over 4,600 in number. The Ragam Nattai generates from the 1050th Mother Ragam known in the Brahma Melam. It is my idea to publish in a book-form all the particulars about this Ragam as well as the 200 Vishnu Mela Karthas. All the possible consonant Srutis which could be sung in three Kalams will be found there. At our next meeting after discussing the existence of the 22 Srutis we may enter into the question of the using of the *Ga* and the *Dha* in Arohanam and Avarohanam in the Ragam, along with other particulars concerning it."

Mr. Shastrial who thinks that the above remarks of ours are open to criticism will be convinced of his false position if he would only note clearly what he has said in his essay and the remarks that are to follow.

In his essay read at the Second Conference (Vide Report Page 52, 2nd Para) he says "though the Tamil spoken language has many hard and soft vowel and consonant sounds yet we are wanting in many letters to represent the sounds fully. Although this is a matter which we all admit from experience, yet the general idea has prevailed that the Tamil language is perfect in its characters."

It is a fixed rule that the words of a language should be pronounced according to the sound indicated by individual letters. The letters which are silent in a word is a privilege reserved for the highly proficient scholars ! But in the Tamil language no such irregularity is found ; when words are introduced into the Tamil language from alien tongues they could not possibly conform to the grammatical rules of the language. We find no such mixtures in the classical works of ancient Tamil literature.

Moreover the hard sounds க, ச, ட, த, ப, and ற which come after the soft letters ங, ஞ, ண, ந, ம and ன appear to have lost their original hardness and to have acquired a third sound like Sanskrit characters. But we must remember that these sounds were not introduced into the Tamil language yesterday or the day before, but have existed from ancient times. We may see that in the following words the hard sound resembles that of Sanskrit characters :—தங்கம், திங்கள், மங்கை, பஞ்சு, நெஞ்சு, தஞ்சம், பஞ்சை, நெஞ்சை, தொண்டு, பண்டம், பெண்டாட்டி, உண்டி, தந்தம், சந்தை, தந்தை, முந்தா. பிந்து. இந்தளம், தொந்தி, கொம்பு, வம்பு, நம்பு, தும்பு, பம்பை, தும்பை, உம்பர். அம்பலம், செம்பு, இன்பம். துன்பம், நன்று, தென்றல், நன்றி, வென்றி, நின்றும் and the like. When we notice this, we see that he finds fault with the Tamil language being ignorant of the greatness and dignity of the language with the existing characters is able to represent all sounds. He thinks highly of the use of fresh letters instead of making use of the existing letters in their proper places to represent proper sounds. In the same way, the hard sounds which come after the Tamil letter ஃ lose their hardness, obtain the sound of ha, the Sanskrit letter, and become more or less consonants in their sound. When we notice the Tamil words அஃகம், எஃகு, பஃறுளியாறு, இருபஃது, கஃச, பஃறி, அஃறிணை, and அஃகான் we are led to believe that there were six different letter sounds in use in Tamil from ancient times. The second and the fourth varieties of the Sanskrit letters, Ka, Cha, Ta, Tha and Pa are but the emphatic forms of the first and the third sounds. In the Tamil language we find inanimate consonants used in their place. Moreover, we find that many words in Tamil have very charming sounds and they have been so pronounced from time immemorial. After we got ourselves accustomed to write and talk Tamil style (Tamil and Sanskrit the red coral and beads) we have begun to doubt whether words are Tamil or alien words.

Just as a promissory note becomes time-barred after 3 years, a mortgage bond after 12 years, an hypothecation with enjoyment (othi), after 60 years and a permanent lease, after 99 years, so the words that were borrowed into Tamil from alien tongues have become naturalised Tamil words in course of time. From this one must not suppose that there have not been enough words in the language for the Tamilians to make known their thoughts.

In his essay on the 22 Srutis of Aryan music read at the Sixth Conference he says,

"Those who observe how words like கண் the (eye), செவி (the ear), வாய் (the mouth) have been introduced into the Tamil language from Prakrit are enabled to judge how Sanskrit has been a feeder to the Tamil language for years" and again, "for one to attempt to bring into use something which has been destroyed, is like trying to establish one's right to a property by a copy of a document which had once been made null and void."

We have already noticed in Part I, the opinion of many scholars how Tamil is an independent language, how the Tamilians had attained a high degree of culture from the earliest times, how they had been rulers and know the art of government among other arts even in prehistoric times, and how the grammar of the language had attained such a perfect state so as to admit of no change even when kingdoms underwent many changes. We had also established the fact that at one time the whole of India had one language and one race of people, the Tamils, that the language was known as Pali in the North and Tamil in the South, that the admixture of many languages from people who came from the North-West gave rise to Prakrit, that because Sanskrit became a dead language owing to the rise of many Prakrit dialects a number of scholars arose who made it their life-work to establish the Sanskrit language on a firm basis by collecting many words from different dialects, by devising a grammar for it and writing a number of Puranas, Itihasas and Shastras to support it. They preached a crusade in favour of the language and made so many commentaries and expositions that other languages were stifled in the competition. The word Sanskrit itself means "well made". This shows that it was "made up" of words from other languages and therefore was later in time.

Again, it is a custom to call a country or a ruled province after the particular language spoken there. So, we have Tamil Nadu, Sentamil Nadu, Koduntamil Nadu, the Tamil kings, the three kings speaking the three different Tamils, the Maharashtra king, the Mahratta country, the Telugu country, the Canarese province, the Hindu country, Bangalam, the Hindustani kingdom and the Malayalam country. But we have to search in vain for the expressions "Sanskrit province" or "king of Sanskrit country." If such countries existed they would surely have been found in the so called ancient Puranas. We all know well that even Sanskrit scholars when they were children spoke the mother-tongue or the Vernacular of the country in which they were born, but never lisped in Sanskrit! We know very well that the birth place of Mr. Shastrial is Tanjore, a Tamil city ruled over by the Cholas who were one of the three kings of the countries where the three Angams of the Tamil language were fostered. We should like to ask him whether his mother while he was an infant taught him the sweet Tamil words like feeding a babe with milk and sugar or Sanskrit words. When he grew up a child was he delighted to hear sweet Tamil words or Sanskrit words? Was not the Tamil language comprehensive enough for him to express his thoughts and obtain all his wants when he became a man? This case is analogus to that of those excellent (?) men who forget their mothers after the advent of the wife! We are at a loss to know from which scholar his mother learnt the words கண் மூக்கு, வாய், காது and the like. We do not blame him for extolling the Sanskrit language for which he seems to have an admiration. But will the world have any high opinion of a man who despises the mother that gave him birth? In Sanskrit we have no roots for கண், மூக்கு, வாய், காது.

When the Sanskrit language was first intended to be introduced they got hold of what are called 'Nagari' letters and had some rules framed for the use of the same. The characters of this newly formed language were known as 'Devanagari' letters. The same eyes and ears which heard the words of Sir M. E. Grant Duff, Ex-Governor of Madras in his address to the Graduates of the University that "when comparing the antiquity of the Dravidians with that of the Aryans, the latter may be compared to a Reuter's telegram received a few minutes ago."! are still in existence. We wonder whether Mr. Shastrial was ignorant of this. We have dealt in Part I about the words that have been borrowed in different languages from Tamil. If he had accounted for these words also in the light of his own theory he would have been more consistent. We have given many instances to prove how words that are borrowed into a language from a primary one are found there with their original prefixes or suffixes or the body of the word itself lengthened, shortened or changed in some other way. There are many evidences to show that Tamil words like கண், கை, கால், காது, மூக்கு, வாய், மெய், நீர், தீ, வான், நிலம், are found in other languages with a few changes consequent on their peculiar sounds, that the first language of Man is Tamil, that the first land occupied by Man was Lemuria, that the earliest countries were Tamil countries, that people became scattered in different countries from the Tamil country, that a number of years after the Tamils spread themselves in different countries speaking different languages and returned to India, Sanskrit language and literature came into use.

One sufficient proof for the above statement is that during the period of Asoka, i.e., 2000 years ago, there were no Sanskrit inscriptions in stones of any kind. We were compelled to say a few words in Part I about the antiquity of the term "முத்தமிழ்" in general and of "இசைத்தமிழ்" in particular, to establish the fact that the Science of Music must have been originally in the Tamil language. So, we spoke at length on the Tamil language, the Tamil provinces, the Tamil kingdoms, the three Sangams and the literature thereof. When we examine the very ancient Tamil literature we are led to conclude that the theory of Dwavimsati Srutis written in Sanskrit by Sarnga Dev and other writers has been written in recent times as a result of misunderstanding. Mr. Shastrial who knows that we hold this view compares our attempt to that of the man "who tried to establish his claims to a property by means of a document which had been made null and void." Leaving alone the periods and kingdoms which are thought of beneath notice, modern research is bringing to light many things of antiquity which excites our wonder.

We cannot easily estimate the zeal and patriotism of those scholars who are engaged in such reseaches. Only such scholars can appreciate excellence of those Tamil works and not Mr. Sastrial whose knowledge is confined to literature which is as extensive as a little toy box! Hence, he made such statements. This stigma on Tamil literature can soon be removed if the Tamilians would talk and write and preach purely in their own sweet language without allowing any admixture of foreign words which only mar its inherent beauty.

Again, in his essay read at the Second Conference Mr. Shastrial says,

> "We who support a system do not rely mainly on reason and experience alone but are also guided by the literature on the subject."

As usual, Mr. Shastrial uses the terms Sruti, Yukti and Anubhavam without knowing their meaning. The three results of actions, namely, Thottram, Vriddhi and Layam correspond to the three sources Manam, Vakku and Kayam. The same are otherwise known as the Sthoolam, Sookshmam and Karanam. Sruti, Yukti and Anubhavam must correspond to the above three. Yukti is connected with the Karana Sareera. Sruti is that which is spoken and heard. The Manam thinks, the Vakku gives expression to it in words and the accomplishment according to the expression forms the Anubhavam. That which is spoken by mouth is heard by the ears and is acted upon; this when committed to writing becomes the Sruti. So it is clear that, of these steps, Yukti comes first and then Sruti and lastly Anubhavam. One who has no advanced Yukti of his own stands in need of a Sruti which embodies the Yukti of others. To one who examines the Srutis which contain the Yuktis of others, may strike a new Yukti which is not found in the Srutis. So, when the new Yukti is put into practice the previous Sruti becomes useless. Such new Yuktis and experiences are being formed from time to time, their author being God himself.

Does not Mr. Shastrial understand that the result of such new Yuktis and Anubhavam are being published as new Srutis day by day? What is the earthly use of Srutis to one who has no Yukti? A light is useful to one who walks about at night and who has no Anubhavam. When urgency requires many people walk about without a light. In the same way, many have accomplished great things entirely by their own Yukti and without any guidance from Sruti. That which first originated from Yukti was then brought to experience and then written down as Sruti. Just as in nature we find different flowers with different fragrance and sweetness, so also Srutis have different kinds of usefulness to the world. How many Srutis have been which appeared in support of the Srutis and then dwindled away because they were not put into practice! We do not know what the state of Indian music will be if we rest upon the old Srutis without creating new ones to suit our new Anubhavam. How can we trust those Srutis which only confound without enlightening us. It is not fair that we should confound others. It is best that we should conform ourselves to the traditional views of eminent scholars of various countries who had attained a high state of efficiency in music. Though Mr. Shastrial lives in the midst of eminent Vidwans who have been born and brought up in the atmosphere of Karnatic music, yet like the man who could not quench his thirst though he is in the midst of water, he takes the 22 Srutis first but finds no way out of it; then he takes the system of Parijatam but finds it also unsatisfactory; then he borrows two Srutis from Pythagoras and still keeps on to the number 22; then he flies off at a tangent to the 19 and 53 Srutis of the Westerners and mixes them all together and picks out 22 which he considers to be the Srutis of Karnatic music! This only excites our laughter! But we shall find that our ancestors have not placed us in such a desperate plight. This may be understood by what follows.

Eighth.

The view of M.R.Ry. Panchapakesa Bhagavatar that the Dwavimsati Srutis of the author of Sangeeta Ratnakaram are the Srutis in use in South Indian Music.

When we carefully analyse the view of the above Vidwan we find that it is entirely based upon the view of the previous writers, M.R.Ry. Subramania Sastrial. Moreover he looks upon the view of Mr. Shastrial as that of his Guru and heartily supports him. Though his view does not in any way correspond either to the Dwavimsati Srutis of Sarnga Dev or to the system of Parijatam which proceeds by the SA-PA series, he emphatically declares that his view is the correct one, and that the Srutis of South Indian music ought to be as he declares. In spite of his great proficiency in Karnatic music he has been led away and deceived by the calculations of Mr. Shastrial. Though it is unnecessary to speak about the calculations of his Srutis, yet we have to say a few words regarding it in order to dispel his confusion as well as that of some of his admirers. We note below a few important points from his essay read at the Fourth Conference.

In the above essay read at the Fourth Conference he says as follows :—

"That there are 12 main Swarams in the octave is a fact accepted by all musicians including the Carnatic musicians. When we enquire whether there are only 12 Srutis or more in an octave we find that writers on Indian music speak about 22 of them in an octave. Although these 22 Srutis are not each of them so clearly discernible as the 12 main Swarams, yet the fact of their existence is conclusive from the fact that they occur severally in many Ragas. Our ancestors were sure about this and they ascribed to the seven Swarams SA, RI, GA, MA, PA, DHA, NI 4 Srutis, 3 Srutis, 2 Srutis, 4 Srutis, 4 Srutis, 3 Srutis and 2 Srutis respectively. It is only the different combinations of these 22 Srutis we hear in Kirtanams as well as instrumental music.

I may prove this by taking the Veena as the standard. When the Veena is tuned for the purpose of playing, the note that is primarily sounded we may take as the Shadjam. By placing our fingers over the frets in succession we obtain in order Komala RE, Tivra RE, Komala GA, Tivra GA, Komala MA, Tivra MA, PA, Komala DHA, Tivra DHA, Komala NI and Tivra NI. Thus we obtain the 12 main Swarams. Thus we see that SA and PA do not admit of variety, whereas the other five Swarams are capable of 2 varieties each thus giving the total 12. But as each of the five varieties is further capable of 2 varieties according to the principle of Chala and Dhruva the total 22 Srutis may be easily accounted for, the Sapta Swarams being 4, 3, 2, 4, 4, 3, 2 respectively. These 22 Srutis are named in ancient books as follows:—(1) Tivra (2) Kumudvati (3) Manda (4) Chendovati (5) Dayavati (6) Ranjani (7) Raktika (8) Rowdri (9) Krodha (10) Vajrika (11) Prasarini (12) Preethi (13) Marjani (14) Kshithi (15) Raktika (16) Sandeepani (17) Alapini (18) Madanthi (19) Rohini (20) Ramya (21) Oogra and (22) Kshobhini. According to this if each of the Srutis RE, GA, MA, DHA, NI admit of 4 varieties with the inclusion of SA and PA they make 22.

If we are to calculate how many Sruti Sthanams are found in an octave we may never come to the end of it, if a Sruti may admit of many minute varities. But if we proceed by the SA-PA series we will have to stop with the 12 Srutis (SA, PA, RE, DHA, GA, NI, MA, RE (Komala), DHA (Komala), GA (Komala), NI (Komala), MA (Komala) and SA and thus get disappointed. But the mystery of it could only be understood by an instrument I have made called Nadamani. Before I discovered this instrument I myself was wallowing in a pool of doubt. But I am very thankful to say that my doubts have all been entirely cleared by Brahmasri Subramania Sastrial. I must here mention how Sastrial spent a good deal of his time and energy in solving this mystery, all with disinterested motive of the welfare of the Sabha. He was not only satisfied in acquiring the knowledge himself by his minute researches but also explained the whole thing to me and cleared my doubts. If any one in this Sabha is deserving of any recognition of merits, it is he. He is worthy of such a distinction.

Now to proceed to the way of obtaining the 22 Srutis, Devadattan proceeded upwards by fifths or by SA-PA series and another man Danavadattan proceeded downwards by the same series and they met at the 54th place (Sa) having set their foot on 53 different places. So, we see there are 53 minute Srutis in an octave. Of these on some principle 22 have been selected. The principle is to proceed by 12, as 1, 13, 25, 37, and 49 and select a Sruti at that place. The next number being 61, they deducted 53 from 61 (obtaining 8), and then proceeded from 8 on the same principle 8, 20, 39, 44, fixing a Sruti there and so on obtaing the 22 important Srutis.

I am placing before you a plan arranged in the form of a lotus flower, where the Srutis can be distinctly seen. Those who practise these 53 Srutis daily will become musical experts."

Mr. Bhagavatar starts with giving the names of the 12 Swarams. In which Sastram do we find these names of the Swarams for the 12 Sthanams? Can Mr. Shastrial quote chapter and verse in support of the names? The names that have been given to these Srutis in works like "Sangeeta Ratnakaram", "Shadraga Chandrodayam", "Ragavibodham", "Swaramelakalanidhi," "Chathurdandiprakasika", "Sangeeta Saramritam" and "Sangeeta Parijatam" are given in the form of a Table by M.R.Ry. Pratapa Ramaswami Bhagavatar in his essay read at the Fourth Conference (Pp. 57 to 61). Our readers are referred to Table 26. There we shall find that no names are given for the 5th, 6th, 18th and the 19th Srutis. The names of some of the other Sthanams also are conflicting. Leaving out of consideration the names Laghu, Mridu, Poorva and Suddha which convey the same meaning, if we notice the Sruti Sthanams, we find that there is no unanimity in some places. On the whole, four Sthanams are nameless. But he has taken the 12 Veena Swarams of the author of Parijatam as the chief ones. We do not there find the names which Mr. Bhagavatar ascribes to them. The names of other 10 Swarams do not correspond with the names given to them by others. Again, he commits this mistake being ignorant of the fact that there is not the slightest connection between the Swarams arising from the 22 Srutis and those given in Parijatam. How can we expect unanimity in other names when the names of PA and MA are different in different writers? As the terms Tivram and Komalam mean a slight increase or decrease to a fixed Swaram, it is clear that there must be other Swarams. If the 2nd Sruti is Komala RI and the third Suddha RI, the fourth should be Tivra RI. The same principle should apply to other Srutis also. Such mistakes occur because one is not sure which are the fundamental Srutis and which the minute derived ones.

The numbers 4, 3, 2, 4, 4, 3, 2 when added give us 22. The author of Sangeeta Ratnakaram says that these are the Srutis in an octave or rather the Sapta Swarams of the octave. From that, it is clear that the Sapta Swarams should have the intervals shown in 4, 3, 2, 4, 4, 3, 2. Moreover, Sarnga Dev distinctly says that in an octave the

22 Sthanams should gradually rise and should obtain their fixed intervals without allowing the possibility of any other Swaram in the middle. But Mr. Bhagavatar completely changes the interval system of Saranga Dev, namely, 4, 3, 2, 4, 4, 3, 2 and gives a new one, 1, 4, 4, 4, 1, 4, 4. Here he converts the SA and PA with 4 Srutis each into single Srutis, and the RI, GA, DHA and NI with 2 or 3 Srutis each into 4 Srutis each. This is a case of humbling the exalted and exhalting others instead. We have reason to doubt whether Mr. Shastrial has perverted the Sootrams of Sarnga Dev also just as he did with those of Parijätam ! Again, there is not the slightest resemblance between intervals like, 1, 10, 18, 23, 32, 41, 49 and 54, and 4, 3, 2, 4, 4, 3 and 2.

Mr. Shastrial who declared that we should not be led away by our reasoning and experience but should be guided by written works, completely changes the view of Sarnga Dev and makes his admirers to follow his intervals 1, 4, 4, 4, 1, 4, 4. Besides this, Mr. Bhagavatar declares that the 12 Swarams of the Veena obtained by the SA-PA system, namely, SA, PA, RI, DHA, GA, NI, MA, RI, DHA, GA, NI, MA and SA have completely confounded him. He makes bold to say this in spite of his own conviction that the 12 Swarams obtained by the SA-PA system are the very life of Karnatic music, that from time immemorial they have been fixed in the Veena, the celestial instrument and are a testimony to every one. It has become a custom amongst the people of the Karnatic country that one who is a proficient musician may say anything he likes which will be swallowed by others. If each one gives a different opinion according to one's own fancy what will be the fate of the remnant of the Karnatic music that is still left to us ? He says that all that is subtle in music could be understood by means of the Nadamani, an instrument which he has himself constructed. When we examined this instrument in person we found it to be one where the frets were arranged as in a Tambura according to his own measurement but which sounded only false notes! There were 22 frets in it arranged in disorder. Karnatic Ragas could neither be played in it nor sung to it. We are obliged to pass the same judgment on this instrument just as we said that the calculations about 22 Srutis given by Mr. Shastrial were neither those of Sarnga Dev nor were they in accordance with the experience of Karnatic musicians. On the other hand it is like the Kurali which came to spoil the eminent view of Sarnga Dev and the dignity of Karnatic Ragas. These gentlemen gave the calculation for the 22 Srutis in accordance with the theory of Nagoji Row to start with, then proceeded to pick out the 1st, 5th, 6th, 9th, 10th Sthanams out of the 53 Srutis which they declared were found in the octave. But at the third opportunity they used dots instead of frets to fix the Swarasthanams knowing that they would be compromised if they used frets ! Supposing they commit themselves to another theory, we wonder what name they will give it ! Mr. Bhagavatar has spared no pains to explain the process of obtaining the 53 subtle Srutis in the octave with a view to glorify his Guru, Mr. Shastrial. We give him credit for generosity of mind which seems to have been very much pleased not only at his own success in establishing his theory but was anxious that others should also enjoy the same happiness. But it would have been of real use, if he had propounded a right theory and taught it to others.

We criticise below his 22 Srutis pointing out the errors in his calculations.

He says "Beginning from SA Devadattan proceeded upwards by fifths. In the same way, another person Danavadattan proceeds downwards from the top SA by fifths. Each proceeded 53 steps and stopped at the SA which was the 54th Sthanam."

This is something to be specially noted here. He first states that a Sthayi comes to an end after 12 Swarams if we proceed by the SA-PA series. He declares in the same breath that it is very misleading. But again he has recourse to the same system. Men of understanding know that the SA-PA system will give only 12 Swarams in the octave. But as there is a minute difference between the sounding of fifths and their proportionate length of wire, slight difference gathers momentum at every step and becomes such an appreciable quantity as to create difference in the 12 Swarams. Only men endowed with musical ear can appreciate this. However, we have not yet come across any system where the sounding of a fifth and its mathematical calculations are exactly alike. If there had been such a system, he would not have said that the SA-PA system ever confounded him. It is certain that the relation between SA and PA is as important, and as consonant as the relation between a husband and the wife, the king and the subjects, the sour taste and the sweet, lamp and the oil, the flowing canal and its draining channel, and the body and the life. They are the fundamental swarams from which every other swaram originates. Though Brahmam is the first cause of all external appearance, nothing is possible without Maya the Sakti. In the same manner, though SA be the fundamental Swaram, yet no consonance can result unless PA, which is nearly half as much again in sound as the SA, sounds in perfect concord with it. In the same manner SA and MA are next in consonance as one is nearly half of the other in length of wire and in sound they stand in the relation of 1 to $1\frac{1}{3}$ nearly. The intervals SA-PA and SA-MA in an ascending scale become SA-MA and SA-PA respectively and MA-SA and SA-MA in the descending scale. Just as these Swarams stand out prominent in the ascending and descending scales they stand out marked in Ragams also. Any Ragam without the Swarams MA and PA will be insipid. We determine the other Swarams having these two as the standard. All the ancient treatises on music declare that there are four Srutis between MA and PA. All the trouble arose owing to our inability to determine these four Srutis. The intervals SA to RI have the same relation as MA to PA as regards sound. For example, let us substitute PA-RI for SA-PA. Then PA stands for SA, then the top SA stands in the relation of SA to MA. The Tara SA becomes MA. If we take its fifth or SA-PA in the ascending scale it is PA-RI; and in the descending scale it is SA-MA. The RI that occurs between these two fifths must stand in the relation of MA to PA. So there must be 4 Srutis between SA and RI just as there are 4 Srutis between MA and PA. This is the fundamental rule by which all Swarams are derived. Being ignorant of this fundamental rule, one gives 3 Srutis between MA and PA and another two Srutis; they not only give conflicting opinions in measurement and calculation, but try to prove on paper what they should practically demonstrate. As they were unable to get at the right way of determining these Swarams, one gave 22 Srutis, another 25, a third 27, and others 53 Srutis in the octave. Just as there is a whirlpool at the top surface when water goes under a bridge, there was a great whirlpool of doubt between the ascending and the descending scales. Just as the dried leaves that are caught in the whirlpool are tossed about here and there, so was the fate of these writers. We pity Mr. Bhagavatar who is also caught in this whirlpool in spite of his eminence in South Indian music. We do not know how many more there are in the same pitiable plight.

Only those who are confounded will acknowledge that there are 53 Sthanams in the octave when we proceed by the Sa-Pa system. As there is a slight difference between the calculation for Sa-Pa and its length of wire $\frac{2}{3}$, learned men advocate that in tuning the fifths we should make it slightly flatter than a perfect fifth. In other words, they say, that tuning should be done by ear and not by arithmetical minuteness.

When we procced by fifths in an octave, that is by $\frac{2}{3}$, $(\frac{2}{3})^2$, $(\frac{2}{3})^3$ and so on, we have to double the measurements of the Swarams occurring in the higher octave; then we shall find that there will be more than 22 Srutis in the octave. These measurements, again, will never come in a regular order, but backwards and forwards. This may be seen from Tables 8, 9 and 10.

We shall give below a suggestion to find out how many Swarams will result in an octave when we proceed by the Sa-Pa series, but that the number could never be 53. Let us divide an octave into 1200 cents. Everybody thinks that Sa to Pa is 13 Srutis, and that its length of wire is $\frac{2}{3}$ of the whole. Proceeding by fifths the 13th Sruti should be obtained at the 13th step. If our friend Devadattan proceeds by fifths he ought to put his first step on the 13th Sruti, and then at the 4th which is 13th from the 1st and after that on the following steps:—13, 4, 17, 8, 21, 12, 3, 16, 7, 20, 11, 2, 15, 6, 19, 10, 1, 14, 5, 18, 9, 22. He will then come back to the place he started from. Now, if according to their theory, we add Sa and Pa to the 20 Srutis belonging to Ri Ga, Ma, Dha and Ni we get the 22 Srutis. These Swarams appear also to satisfy the rules of Vadi and Samvadi. In the same way, when Sa to Ma is 9 Srutis if Sa and Pa are added to the 20 Srutis of Ri, Ga, Ma, Dha and Ni we get the 22 Srutis.

Now, when we proceed by $\frac{2}{3}$ from Sa, we get 701·955 cents out of 1200 for Pa. If we proceed over the octave deducting 1200 at each step, the 13th Sruti gives us 701·955 cents, the 4th Sruti 203·910 cents, the 17th Sruti 905·865 cents, the 8th Sruti 407·820 cents, and Ma, the 9th Sruti gives us 341·055 instead of 498·045, in other words 157 cents less. What is the use of saying we obtain the 22 Srutis in such an irregular way? The criticism of this system, the cents calculation and Srutisthanams are given in Table 11 page 294.

In Table 9 page 288, we may find that the 22nd Sruti has 1043·010 cents. This ought to be 1200 cents. But it is 157 cents less or in other words some Srutis have been left out. Again, in the Sa-Ma series, the 22nd Sruti has 157 cents more than 1200. Here we get a few Srutisthanams more. Seeing we get some Srutis less in the Sa-Pa series and some more in the Sa-Ma series when we proceed by $\frac{2}{3}$ and $\frac{3}{4}$ respectively, we clearly understand that there must be some other measurement for the two series and not $\frac{2}{3}$ and $\frac{3}{4}$. Everybody will acknowledge that Sa-Pa is $\frac{2}{3}$ and Sa-Ma is $\frac{3}{4}$. These two Swarams are known to everybody. So, if we want to arrive at 22 Srutis in an octave according to the system of Sarnga Dev we must have a different measurement for SA and PA. So, we must first determine the measurement of SA-PA and SA-MA if we want to derive 22 Srutis in the octave.

If 1200 cents are distributed equally among 22 Srutis we get 54$\frac{6}{11}$ for each Sruti. Then MA which has nine Srutis should have 54$\frac{6}{11}$ × 9 or 490·9 cents, and PA with 13 Srutis should have 709·1 cents. Then the 22nd Sthanam in both the series will end with 1200 cents. Their cents, measurement, and Srutisthanams with the names of Srutis will be found in the Table of Sarnga Dev given later on.

It is only when we proceed by $\frac{3}{2}$ and $\frac{4}{3}$ that in the 11th Sthanam of the SA-PA series we get 521½ cents, and in the same Sthanam of the SA-MA series 678½ cents, with a difference of 157 cents. But if we look at the Table of Sarnga Dev we shall find that the 11 Sthanams of the two series get 600 cents each and that 521½ cents come before 600 and 678½ after 600. When there is such an easy royal road why should Mr. Bhagavatar confound himself with his 53 Sthanams? Perhaps this is an example of the Dharma of this Kali Yugam!

We can never arrive at the Dwavimsati Srutis if PA and MA are taken as $\frac{3}{2}$ and $\frac{4}{3}$. Mr. Shastrial who found that this did not give him his 22 Srutis makes 18+13=31; 31−22=8 instead of 9: and 19+13=32; 32−22=9 instead of 10! (*Vide* Table 8 page 286); will 22 taken from 31 give us 8, and 22 taken from 32 give us 9? If he errs in one place it would not matter much. He left out two of the Srutis of the SA-PA series and made them 22. His admirers not knowing that this was a dodge to get at the number 22 got confounded. We have dwelt very clearly on this subject in our remarks on Mr. Shastrial's theory of Srutis. If we take a measurement which will never give us the 22 places we may go on until Doomsday without coming to an end! When such is the case, if he says that there are 53 subtle Srutis in the octave, that our ancestors have known and marked these to be the results of the SA-PA and the SA-MA series and that they have picked out 22 of them here and there, how could other people swallow such a pill! Only silly people will be taken in. Do we read in any of the ancient works on music that our ancestors believed in it? Does it stand to reason? Can it be practically demonstrated and proved by any one in the world? Will men of understanding accept a theory which is contrary to Sruti, Yukti and Anubhavam?

The 53 Srutis and their names are something like the following myth which might easily deceive silly people:—There were three royal princes who were well known for their courage and good disposition. They lived in the city of nowhere (Soonyam). Two of the three were never born while the third was never even conceived in the womb!!

However, we give below a circle showing the 53 Srutis and other details. He picks out 22 Srutis out of these 53, calls them by fancy names such as Dhenuka, Chetika, Chotika, Kodika, Nadika and Mayika! If all the 53 names were written out this will also become a huge Shastram just as 53 is an improvement on 22! We will not then require anything else to destroy Karnatic music! We have already shown in Table 11 (p. 294) the method of arriving at the 53 Srutis by the SA-PA and SA-MA series and the system of selecting 22 out of them. We might see there clearly that the resultant Swarams of the two series do not agree with each other.

We may see below the circle of Mr. Bhagavatar which is divided into 53 compartments to show how the Srutis are obtained by the Sa-Pa series. Therein we might also see how the 22 Srutis are obtained by the ascending and descending series of the Sa-Pa system.

TABLE 21.

The Chakaram showing how the Dwavimsati Srutis are obtained while Devadattan comes round by the right from the 1st or the 54th place by the Sa-Pa series and Danavadattan comes round by the left in the same way. (Chakram).

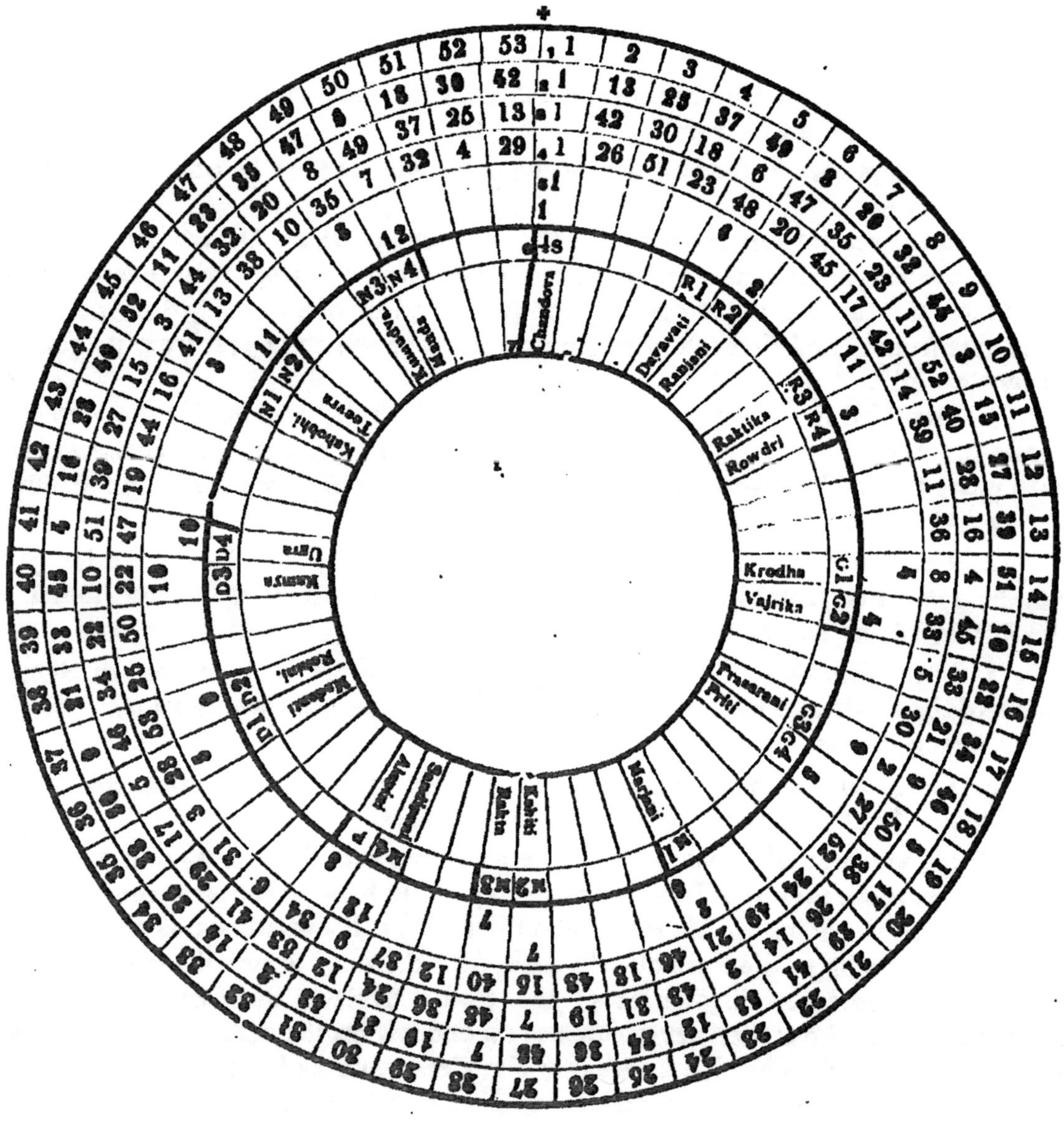

When we notice this Chakram we find that there is not the slightest connection between the system of Mercator, Poole, White, Bosanquet &c., which divides an octave into 53 equal parts giving 31 to Sa-Pa and 22 to Sa-Ma, and the system of Mr. Bhagavatar which says that 53 Sthanams are obtained in an octave where Sa-Ga is $\frac{4}{5}$, Sa-Pa $\frac{3}{2}$ and Sa-Ma $\frac{4}{3}$. The Sa-Pa and Sa-Ma series come to perfection after 53 Sthanams while in this system we get sometimes more and sometimes less than 53 Sthanams which have either 4 cents more or 4 cents less. (*Vide* Table 11 p. 294). While working towards the object of establishing the Dwavimsati Srutis of Sarnga Dev they commit themselves to the 53 Srutis which is completely antagonistic to his system and say that the Sa-Pa and the Sa-Ma system was the one in use among the ancients. We shall note below how this entirely conflicts with the system of Sarnga Dev. They attach so much importance to written Sruti but are entirely unconscious of the fact that their view is against Sruti and that they spoil the existing Srutis. This may be seen from their essays.

We must particularly observe the following so that we might clearly understand the 21st figure, the Chakram.

1. The numbers in the first line of the outer edge of the Chakram point out the 53 Srutis.

2. In the second line may be seen the Sruti-steps which Devadattan takes by the Sa-Pa system in the ascending series proceeding by 31s. For example, he proceeds from the 1st step to the 2nd or 32nd place, and thence to the 3rd or 10th place which is 31st from it, and thence to the 4th or 41st place which is 31st from it, coming round by the right.

3. The third line gives the Srutisthanams which he obtains by the descending series proceeding round the left by 31s. For example, proceeding backwards from the 54th place by 31s, he places his second step at 23, the third step at 45 and the fourth step at 14 and so on.

4. The fourth line gives the Sthanams we obtain by the Sa-Ga series proceeding by 17s. For example, the second step is at 18, the third at 35, the fourth at 52, the fifth at 16 and so on.

5. In the fifth line of the Chakram, the top figures indicate the 12 Swarasthanams of the Sa-Ma series, and the bottom figures the 12 Swarasthanams of the Loukika Sampradayam.

6. The sixth line gives the Srutis of the Swarams which correspond to the names of the 22 Srutis found in the seventh compartment.

When we minutely observe these we shall find that there is no difference between these and those found in Table 11 page 294. He has picked out the 11 Srutisthanams of the ascending Sa-Pa series and the first 11 Swarasthanams of the same series while descending. We have clearly dealt with these 22 Swarasthanams obtained in the ascending and descending series of the Sa-Pa system, their cents calculation and have pointed out how they never come to an end within the octave. We have also stated how there is no connection between the modern system of proceeding by $\frac{3}{2}$ and $\frac{4}{3}$ and the system of Sarnga Dev proceeding by Sa-Pa and Sa-Ma. It is clearly seen that they vainly attempted to get the calculations right by multiplying the fractions and fell back upon the method of setting it right by adding and subtracting the Sruti-sthanams! The 22 Swarams must end in the octave by both the SA-PA and the SA-MA systems. Instead of showing the right calculation by which these series end within the octave, they pick out the first 11 in the SA-PA series and another 11 in the SA-MA series and reject the rest! What is the earthly use of such a system? To say that this is the view of the ancients, and that they did the same, is absurd.

While Devadattan proceeded by the SA-PA series or by 31s, he came to grief at the 12th step and fell into a pit which was not found in the Dwavimsati system! In the same manner, Danavadattan proceeding backwards slipped at the 13th step which was against the Dwavimsati system and his fate is still unknown! So we find they will never reach the surface again if they try to come up by the Dwavimsati steps or 53 steps! With the exception of the first 11 steps of either of them, we are afraid whether the other Sthana Sancharas are like the Athichara Sancharam of the nine planets! The steps which they take and their mathematical calculations may be seen from the following table.

TABLE 22

Showing how the first Eleven Sthanams of the steps of Devadattan and Danavadattan while proceeding by the SA-PA series right and left have no connection whatever with the Dwavimsati Srutis.

1. The progress of Devadattan by the right.				2. The progress of Danavadattan by the left.			
Number.	How Srutis are arrived at by the SA-PA System.	Sruti Sthanam.	Names of the Srutis.	Number.	How Srutis are arrived at by the SA-PA System.	Sruti Sthanam.	Names of Srutis.
						1	Chandovati
1		1	Chandovati	1	1+53−31=	23	Marjani
2	1+31 =	32	Alapini	2	23+53−31=	45	Kshobhini
3	32+31−53=	10	Rowdri	3	45 −31=	14	Krodha
4	10+31 =	41	Ugra	4	14+53−31=	36	Madanti
5	41+31−53=	19	Priti	5	36 −31=	5	Dayavati
6	19+31 =	50	Manda	6	5+53−31=	27	Kshiti
7	50+31−53=	28	Rakta	7	27+53−31=	49	Kumudvati
8	28+31−53=	6	Ranjani	8	49 −31=	18	Prasarani
9	6+31 =	37	Rohini	9	18+53−31=	40	Ramya
10	37+31−53=	15	Vajrika	10	40 −31=	9	Raktika
11	15+31 =	46	Teevra	11	9+53−31=	31	Sandipani
	46+31−53=	24	Govinda		31 −31=	0	Govinda
	24+31−53=	2	,,		53 −31=	22	,,
	2+31 =	33	,,		22+53−31=	44	,,

In the first part of the Table is shown how the 11 Sthanams are obtained while Devadattan proceeds by 3rs and how he gets no further Sthanams to rest his tired feet. In the second part we show how Danavadattan comes to grief in the same way after the 11th step proceeding backwards. The ancients never contemplated a system like this nor did they pick out the 22 from the 53. It is clearly seen that this system is alien to South Indian music.

Again, if we notice the intervals of the Srutis given in the Chakram we find they are very irregular, and this is contrary to the use of Srutis in South Indian music. We have already dwelt at length on these points in our criticism of the previous essay.

Again, having first impressed the fact that if Devadattan proceeded by the Sa-Pa system and Danavadattan by the Sa-Ma series right and left they would go through 53 steps and end the octave. Mr. Shastrial found later on that this system could not stand ; and therefore he now suggests to his admirers that even if they proceeded by the Sa-Ga system they would end the octave in the same number of steps. Just as $\frac{3}{2}$ or Sa-Pa and $\frac{4}{3}$ or Sa-Ma series do not support the Srutis of Sarnga Dev, the system of $\frac{5}{4}$ or Sa-Ga also does not help him in any way.

We have from the very beginning criticised the number of vibrations of the Ga (4th Sruti) obtained while proceeding by $\frac{5}{4}$. He gave 300 as the vibrations while it ought to be 303¾. We have to repeat the same criticism here as regards calculation of cents. The Ga with 300 vibrations gets 386·314 cents. He says he obtains all the Srutis while proceeding thiswise by the Sa-Pa and the Sa-Ma series. We may see from the appended table that the Sa-Ga series will never be satisfactory, just as the Sa-Pa and the Sa-Ma series are, in giving 22 Srutis.

We shall have to specially note the Sa-Ga system in the fourth compartment of the Chakram as it is a novel one. But this is nothing new as it has already been stated in line 19 of page 40 of the Third Conference report where it is known as 1¼ or Gandhara Sruti.

Here, knowing that the Ma-Pa, Tara Sa and other Sthanams are not obtained with the right measurement, he tries to prove their correctness by the Chakram.

Sa-Ga or $\frac{5}{4}$ should proceed by 386·315 cents at each step. In Table 23 we give the cents for all the 53 Srutis proceeding by the Sa-Ga series.

Here, while we go on multiplying 386·315 by numbers 1, 2, 3, 4, 5 all excess over 1200 are noted. The 54th Sruti or Tara Sa should end in 1200 cents whereas we get 74·695 cents in excess. In the second part of Table 23 the Srutis are arranged in the order of their cents. In other words, the respective measurement of each of the 53 Srutis is noted. Of these, the Sa-Ma or the 22nd Sruti gets 502 for 498·450 or 4 cents more. Again, the 32nd Sruti or Pa ($\frac{3}{2}$) gets only 690·520 cents for 702 or 11 cents less. The 54th Sruti or Tara Sa has 1175·765 for 1200 or nearly 24 cents less. The Sa-Ga or the 18th has 362·800 cents. But if Sa-Ga or $\frac{5}{4}$ occurs as the 19th Sruti what shall we say of such an irregular system ? Or else, it would be absurd to say that Sa-Ga proceeds

TABLE 23

Showing that 53 Srutis are obtained in the SA-GA series = $\frac{5}{4}$ or 386·315 cents according to **Mr. Shastrial and Mr. Bhagavatar**

Swarams that are obtained when SA-GA = $\frac{5}{4}$ and the interval between Srutis is 386·315 cents.						The Swarams of the SA-GA series arranged in a regular order.					
1	0	19	953·670	37	707·340	1	0	19	386·315	37	789·450
2	386·315	20	139·985	38	1093·655	2	16·820	20	403·135	38	830·505
3	772·630	21	526·300	39	279·970	3	57·875	21	444·190	39	871·560
4	1158·945	22	912·615	40	666·285	4	74·695	22	485·245	40	888·380
5	345·260	23	98·930	41	1052·600	5	98·930	23	502·065	41	912·615
6	731·575	24	485·245	42	238·915	6	115·750	24	526·300	42	929·435
7	1117·890	25	871·560	43	625·230	7	139·985	25	543·120	43	953·670
8	304·205	26	57·875	44	1011·545	8	156·805	26	567·355	44	970·490
9	690·520	27	444·190	45	197·860	9	181·040	27	584·175	45	994·725
10	1076·835	28	830·505	46	584·175	10	197·860	28	608·410	46	1011·545
11	263·150	29	16·820	47	970·490	11	222·095	29	625·230	47	1035·780
12	649·465	30	403·135	48	156·805	12	238·915	30	649·465	48	1052·600
13	1035·780	31	789·450	49	543·120	13	263·150	31	666·285	49	1076·835
14	222·095	32	1175·765	50	929·435	14	279·970	32	690·520	50	1093·655
15	608·410	33	362·080	51	115·750	15	304·205	33	707·340	51	1117·890
16	994·725	34	748·395	52	502·065	16	321·025	34	731·575	52	1134·710
17	181·040	35	1134·710	53	888·380	17	345·260	35	748·395	53	1158·945
18	567·355	36	321·025	54	74·695	18	362·080	36	772·630	54	1175·765

by 17 steps. A system which gives 24 cents less in one place and 75 cents more in another to Tara SA must certainly be completely wrong. Men of understanding, of course, will never be misled.

Again, there is not the slightest connection whatever between these 53 Srutisthanams and the Sama Veda, Vydeeka and Loukeeka Sampradayas. The Srutis agree less in the SA-GA system than they do in the SA-PA and the SA-MA series.

In the SA-GA series the Tara SA gets 74·695 cents more than 1200. When we arrange the Srutis of the above series in a regular order we get the cents for the fourth Sruti. But in their 53 Srutis this occurs as the 3rd of the 9 Srutis of RI. While there is such a difference in calculation how would one believe that there are the same Sruti Sthanams in the SA-GA series as are obtained in the other two series ?

TABLE 24.

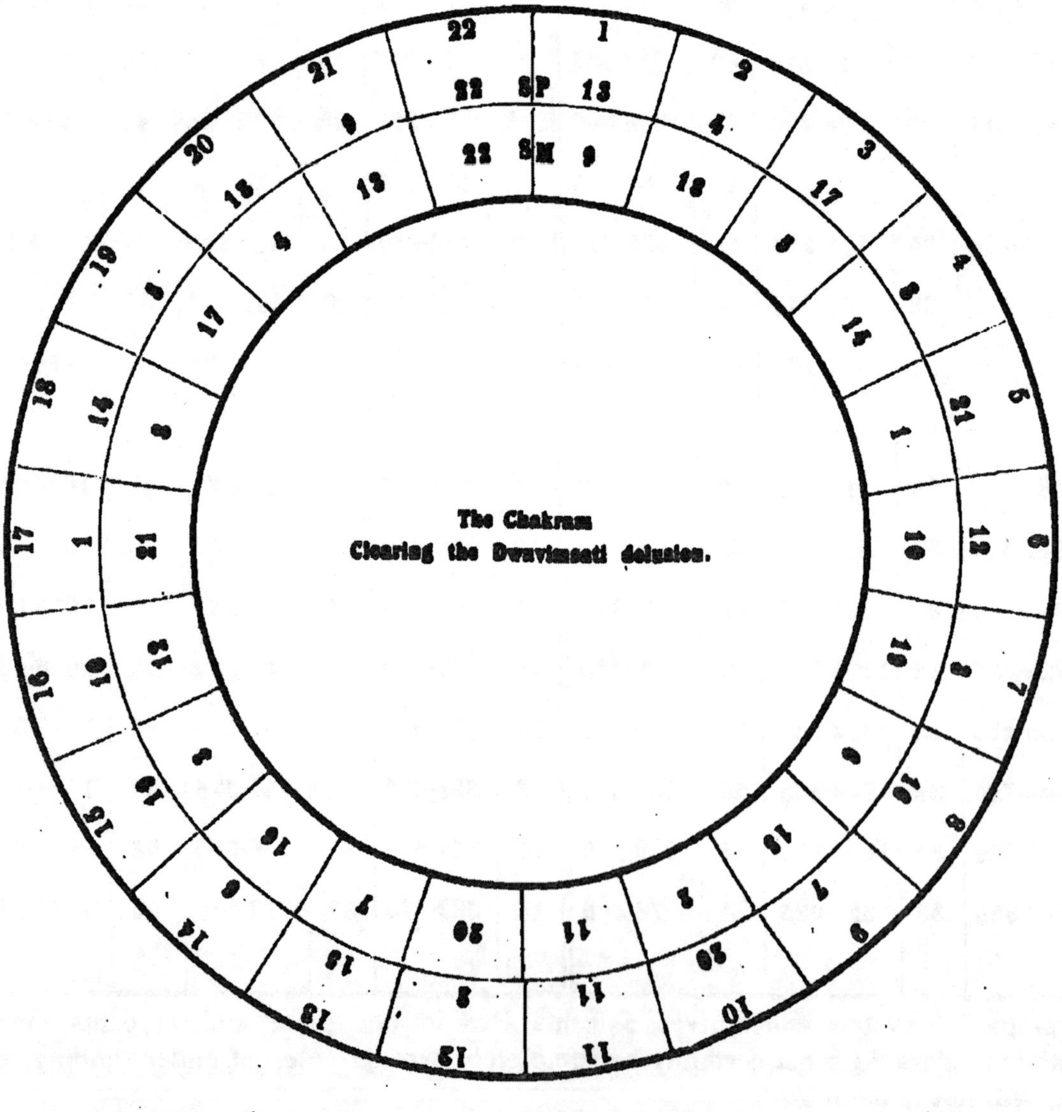

We have seen that the above theory of the 22 Srutis will never hold good. According to Sarnga Dev there will be 22 Srutis in the octave, Sa to Pa being 13, and Sa to Ma 9. The following table shows his system very clearly.

1. The first line from outside shows the numbers of the 22 Srutis.

2. The second line of the first compartment gives the number of the Srutis obtained by the Sa-Pa series. It shows the Srutisthanams obtained by adding 13 and subtracting 22 wherever the number exceeds 22; for example, we have 13 as the first Sthanam, $13+13=26$; $26-22=4$ as the 2nd, $4+13=17$ as the 3rd step and so on.

3. The third line shows the Srutisthanams of the Sa-Ma series. That is 9 has been added to each, and wherever the total exceeded 22, 22 has been subtracted.

These two series correspond to the Sruti system of Sarnga Dev. The calculation of cents for these Srutis and their measurements may be clearly seen in the system of Sarnga Dev which is given below. When we definitely obtain 22 Srutis by the two series there is no necessity for a new system which takes 11 from the Sa-Pa series and 11 from the Sa-Ma series. As there is a difference between the systems of $\frac{4}{?}$ and $\frac{?}{?}$ and the Dwavimsati system of Sarnga Dev an attempt was made to mix together the Srutis of modern Karnatic music and the result was a curious admixture.

The 22 Srutis are obtained at the 13th Sthayi in the Sa-Pa series. The same result at the 9th Sthayi in the Sa-Ma series. If Mr. Bhagavatar, who says that Pa is the 13th Sruti and Ma the 9th would only use his observation, all his doubts will clear in an instant like the dew before the rising Sun. Leaving this he says we proceed 31 Sthayis by the Sa-Pa series and 22 by the Sa-Ma series. Even proceeding by such a method, does his octave come to an end by the 22 Srutis? No. Why then should he advocate this measurement? That the 53 steps are Srutisthanams is not advocated in any of the musical works of our ancestors. Perhaps he was led away by the Western scientists like Thompson, Mercator, Poole, etc., who say that all the minute Srutis used in music may be easily derived if we take Sa-Pa to be 9, Pa-Ri to be 8, Ri-Dha to be 9, and Ni-Ga to be 5. Was he consistent even there? He changed it into a new system 9, 8, 5, 9, 9, 8, 5. What is to become of the system of Sangeeta Ratnakaram? If people like Mr. Shastrial and Bhagavatar who swear by existing Srutis do this, what shall we say about others? We give due credit to Mr. Bhagavatar and his Guru Mr. Shastrial who were anxious to do good to the world by establishing the 22 Srutis by hiding a few of the Srutis actually in use in South Indian music.

Ninth.

The theory of M. R. Ry. Pratapa Ramaswami Bhagavatar Avl. that the Dwavimsati Srutis of Sarnga Dev and the Srutis of South Indian music are identical.

When we note the essence of the essay of Mr. Bhagavatar read at the third Conference, we find that out of the 22 Srutis which he says he obtained by a new method, 17 are those of Deval and 15 are those of Nagoji Row. It is best not to take any notice of his theory because he has followed the Sa-Pa and the Sa-Ma system of the above two writers and has said nothing new. However, some of the other members of the Tanjore Sangeeta Sabha may be mislead as regards the Srutis in use in South Indian music believing some of his Sootrams to be Shastraic. If such a thing happened, even the remnent of what is pure in Karnatic music may be completely destroyed. So we think it necessary to prove from his essay that the Dwavimsati Srutis are not the ones in use in South Indian music. Hence the necessity of criticising him. It is more for the sake of his admirers than for anything else.

He says in his essay read at the 3rd Conference

2. " All the following works on music unanimously declare that the Srutis are but 22. These works are Sangeetha Ratnakaram, Ragavibodham, Swaramelakalanidhi, Sangeeta Parijatam, Shadraga Chandrodayam, Chaturdandiprakasika and Sangeeta Saramritam. In some parts of the above works it is distinctly stated that there could be neither more nor less than 22 Srutis.

3. I shall let you know of an easy method which I found out, so that any one might easily understand the 22 Srutis.

4. Take a Tambur with a metallic string. Tighten the string by the Merus at each end. Having the centre of this string as the standard all the Srutis may be derived, whatever the length of the string might be. The sound of this string when struck gives us the standard Swaram Adhara Shadjam.

5. If the string be divided into two parts and a pen-knife be placed in the centre, the octave to the first Sa will sound on either side of the penknife.

6. If the string be divided into 3 equal parts and the knife be placed at the end of the first part, the Pa will sound on the right side and Tara Pa on the left.

7. If the wire were divided into 4 equal parts then Suddha Ma will sound at the end of the first part on the right side, and Atitara Shadjam on the left.

8. In the same way the division of it into 5 equal parts will give us Antara Gandharam and Atitarantara Gandharam.

9. Likewise Sadharana Ga and Atitara Pa will result from a division of the wire into 6 equal parts.

10. We have now arrived at 5 out of the 22 Sthanams, namely (1) Sa, (2) Pa, (3) Suddha Ma, (4) Antara Ga and (5) Sadharana Ga. I shall show below how the other 17 Sthanams can be derived from these 4 Sthanams omitting the Sa.

The figure given below will help in understanding what we stated above :—

Scale of the Thambur.

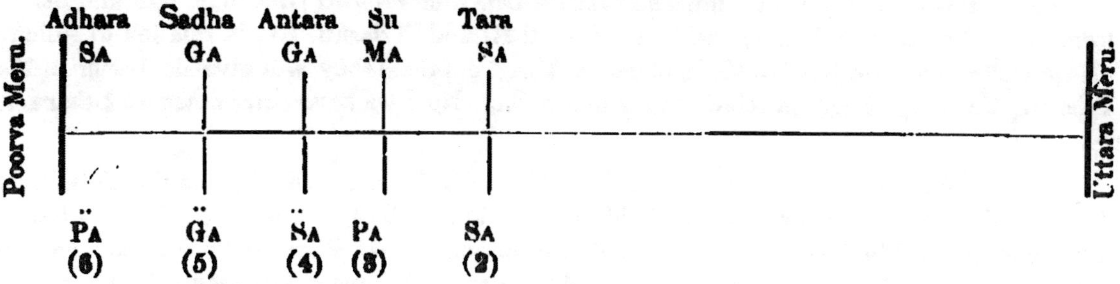

The numbers refer to those in para 10 above.

11. If the Sadharana GA be made into SA, and the measurement of the wire after it be left out, and if the other portion before it be made into 3 equal parts, on the right side of the first part will sound PA. (Taken from Adhara SA it will be Kysiki NI). On the left side will sound Tara Sruti RI. In the same way the division of the wire into 4 equal parts will give us Suddha MA on the right and Tara Suddha MA on the left. (From Adhara SA it will give us Dwisruti DHA).

12. In the same manner, make Antara Gandhara the SA, divide the length of the wire before it into 3 and 4 equal parts, on the right side you will get PA and MA, but on the left side Tara Dwisruti RI and Tarantara Gandharam in Trisruti DHA. (From Adhara SA they will be Kakali NI and Trisruti DHA.

13. Again, from Suddha MA as SA, by the like division of the wire into 3 and 4 parts you will get PA and MA. (Taken from Adhara SA they will be Tara SA and Suddha NI). So we have obtained another 5 Srutis or 10 in all. See the figure below.

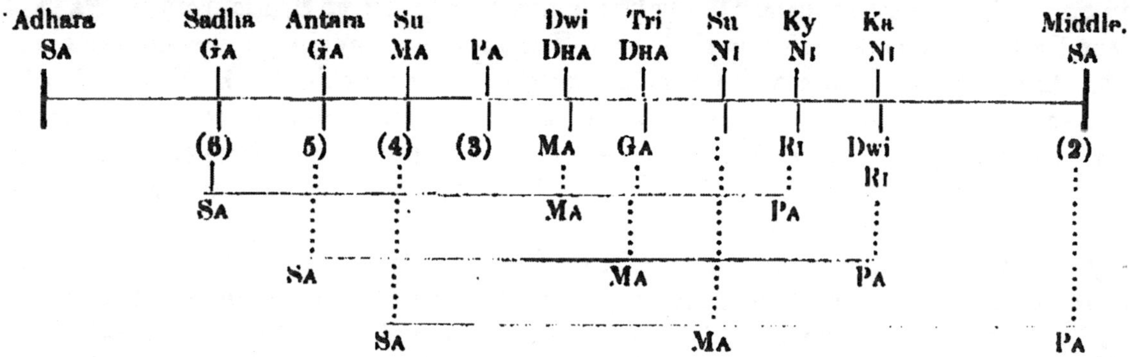

14. We shall now try to determine the remaining 12 Srutis. Let us assume the Suddha NI given in the figure to be PA. This is how we derive Adhara SA from it. We know that PA sounds at the end of the first part when the wire is divided into three. So, if Suddha NI be taken for PA and if the measurement for the above Sthanam be 2 parts in front, the remaining will be one part. So add on this latter after the NI Sthanam and place the knife there. That which sounds here will be the Adhara SA for the Suddha NI PA. (But from Adhara SA it will be Suddha GA).

15. If we make this Suddha GA into SA, and divide the space over it into four equal parts, that which sounds in the $\frac{3}{4}$ of the wire will be MA to it (from Adhara SA it will be Ekasruti Dha).

Now we have determined 12 Srutisthanams.

16. Let us proceed to find out the other 10. Convert Ekasruti DHA into PA, do as before, it will be Ekasruti RI in relation to Adhara SA. If RI be made SA and the MA sounded, then it will be Ekasruti MA in relation to Adhara SA.

17. In the same way if we suppose Dwisruti DHA and Trisruti DHA to be PAs and derive SAs from them, then those Sthanams will be Dwisruti RI and Trisruti RI in relation to Adhara SA. If we make these two RIs into SA and derive MAs from them they will give us Dwisruti MA and Trisruti MA respectively in relation to Adhara SA. Now we have determined 18 Sthanams clearly.

18. There are four more to be found out. If we divide into 3 equal parts the distance of wire between the Poorva Meru and PA or divide the whole length of wire between the two Merus into nine equal parts, Chathusruti RI will sound in either case if we place the knife at the end of the first part. Or again, if we suppose PA to be MA the same Sthanam will result in relation to Adhara Sa. On the left side will sound the Chathusruti RI of the 5th Sthayi. If this were made SA, the fifth from it will be Chathusruti DHA in relation to Adhara SA.

19. If the above Chathusruti DHA were made into MA and if we proceed to the fifth place we derive Tivra GA in relation to SA.

20. If the above Tivra GA were made SA and if we proceed 5 Sthanams we get Tivra Kakali Ni in relation to Adhara SA.

Now we know the 22 Srutis.

21 We see how these 22 Srutis are related to each other. This is the view of ancient writers like the author of Sangeeta Ratnakaram. We might also notice the Vadi-Samvadi relations here which are spoken of in those Granthams.

It appears that Mr. Bhagavatar is a Sanskrit scholar. He seems to have read many Sanskrit works on music. Though it is possible to derive Srutis from SA-PA, SA-MA and SA-GA which are perfect in their Vadi-Samvadi relationship, yet we must remember that the author of Sangeeta Ratnakaram nowhere says that SA-PA, SA-MA and SA-GA are the same as $\frac{2}{3}$, $\frac{3}{4}$, $\frac{4}{5}$ and $\frac{5}{6}$. Again, the author of Parijatam who rejected 10 out of the 22 Srutis, though he gives the measurements $\frac{2}{3}$, $\frac{3}{4}$, $\frac{5}{6}$ never mentions $\frac{4}{5}$. However, Mr. Bhagavatar must certainly know that he gave these measurements after his experience of the Veena. We have already pointed out in connection with Deval's theory of Srutis, that even while proceeding by $\frac{2}{3}$ or SA-PA series according to Parijatam, we get, in the 5th step, a difference of $3\frac{3}{4}$ and $5\frac{5}{8}$ vibrations for GA and NI, that he has given up these slight differences and made the Srutis 300 and 450 vibrations exactly, and that this is contrary to the system of Parijatam. We see similar mistakes here also. When we take the mere measurement of the SA-PA series without troubling ourselves about the sound we see that PA gets an increase of 1 in 350 cents, comparing the sound of it from experience with that of the measurement. This slight increase gathers force when we proceed by *fifths* as SA-PA, PA-RI, RI-DHA, DHA-GA and GA-NI whereas it loses (cents) while proceeding by *fourths* into SA-MA. So there is a good deal of difference between the two series. These differences might be clearly seen in our table of Karnatic Srutis. It is for this very reason that Western scientists say from experience that in tuning by *fifths*, we must have them slightly flat.

1. According to him $\frac{2}{3}$ is the 13th Sruti by the SA-PA series, $\frac{8}{9}$, the 4th Sruti, $\frac{16}{27}$ is the 17th Sruti, $\frac{64}{81}$ is the 8th Sruti and $\frac{128}{243}$ is the 21st Sruti. After this by the SA-MA series he derives $\frac{3}{4}$ as the 9th Sruti, $\frac{9}{16}$ as the 18th, $\frac{27}{32}$ as the 5th, $\frac{81}{128}$ as the 14th, $\frac{243}{256}$ as the 1st and $\frac{729}{1024}$ as the 10th.

2. Again from Antara GA or $\frac{5}{4}$, by the SA-MA series he derives $\frac{5}{3}$ as the 16th Sruti, $\frac{10}{9}$ as the 3rd and $\frac{40}{27}$ as the 12th Sruti and by SA-PA series $\frac{15}{8}$ as the 20th.

3. Again he makes $\frac{6}{5}$ the 6th Sruti and from it by the SA-MA series he obtains $\frac{8}{5}$ as the 15th Sruti, $\frac{16}{15}$ as the 2nd, $\frac{64}{45}$ as the 11th and by SA-PA series $\frac{9}{5}$ as the 19th Sruti.

We notice here that most of his Srutis resemble those of Deval with the exception of the 1st, the 10th, the 12th and the 14th which differ only very slightly from those of Deval. We have already said that Deval has not proceeded by the system of Sangeeta Ratnakaram. We have to repeat the same remark here also. Clements and Bhandarkar who have given the same calculations have distinctly declared that those Srutis belonged to Hindustani and not Karnatic music. Karnatic musicians will never accept these Srutis when they know clearly that they belong to Hindustani music. If Mr. Bhagavatar had clearly grasped the meaning of the author of Sangeeta Ratnakaram he would never have committed himself like this. The opinion of Sarnga Dev is that there should be 22 Srutis in the octave; they must rise gradually with equal number of cents, without admitting other Srutis in the middle. While such is the case how did Mr. Bhagavatar dare to give a system of Srutis irregular in order, quite contrary to that of Sarnga Dev and palm it on others as the theory of Sarnga Dev?

For example, if we suppose a Sthayi to be 1200 cents, we must get 22 Srutis with 54½ cents each. On the other hand he has Srutis with irregular cents like 90, 22, 71, 22, 90, 22, 71, 22, 90 and 90 and says they are the Srutis of Sarnga Dev. It is quite clear from the Sootrams of Sarnga Dev that a Sthayi with 22 Srutis should have 54½ cents for each Sruti if we suppose the whole octave to be 1200 cents. Just as he is strong in affirming that the octave has 22 Srutis, he must also strongly affirm that the octave has 22 Srutis, and that these Srutis should have regular and equal intervals. On the other hand if he affirms one Sruti to have 22 cents which is less than half of 54½, another to have 71 cents which is 1⅓, a third to have 90 cents which is 1⅔ of the standard taken, is he not going altogether against the system of Sarnga Dev? Will not men of common sense laugh at his theory which gives 22 for one Sruti, 90 which is four times as large for another, and 71 which is three times as large for a third?

If we assume 22 as the number of Srutis in an octave, $\frac{4}{3}$ and $\frac{3}{2}$ will never be MA and PA respectively. If there is no unanimity as regards the calculations of MA and PA which are perfectly consonant with SA, how could other Swarams agree? For example, MA which is $\frac{4}{3}$ of the whole should have 498 cents and PA which is $\frac{3}{2}$ should have 702 cents. Instead of that, MA the 9th Sruti, gets 491 cents (*i.e.* 7 cents less) while PA, the 13th Sruti gets 709 (*i.e.* 7 more). We who find fault even with great Vidwans when they err even to the slightest extent in tuning the Tambura, and make fun of singers when they sing out of tune even to the extent of a hair breadth, if we give out such conflicting theories what shall we say about them? We need not dilate more on this.

Other details may be found in Table 25.

TABLE 25.

The theory of **Pratapa Ramaswami Bhagavatar** as regards the Srutis in use in South Indian music.

(According to the System of Parijatam).

Number of Swaram or Sruti.	Name of Swaram or Sruti.	Location of Swarams in a wire 32 inches long.	Fractions showing the places of Swarams assuming Adhara SA to be 1.	Cents.	Cents for intervals between Srutis.	No. of Vibrations of Swarams if SA=540.	No. of Vibrations of Swarams if SA=240.	TABLES OF SRUTIS.								
1	2*	3*	4	5*	6*	7*	8*	9	10	11	12	13	14	15	16	17
	S	32	1			540	240	...	...	...	...	...	...	...	...	...
					90											
1	R_1	30·375	243/256	90		568·89	252·84	...	...	...	...	...	11	...	14	...
					22											
2	R_2	30	15/16	112		576	256	3	6	7	...	...	...	12	...	18
					71											
3	R_3	28·80	9/10	182		600	266·67	3	6	...	...	...	...	12	...	18
					22											
4	R_4	28·44	8/9	204		607·50	270	3	6	7	9	10	...	12	14	18
					90											
5	Su. GA.	27	27/32	294		640	284·44	3	6	...	...	...	11	12	14	18
					22											
6	Sa. GA.	26·67	5/6	316		648	288	3	6	7	...	...	...	12	...	18
					71											
7	An. GA.	25·60	4/5	386		675	300	3	6	...	...	...	...	12	...	18
					22											
8	Tiv. GA.	25·28	64/81	408		683·4375	303·75	...	...	7	9	10	...	...	14	...
					90											
9	M_1	24	3/4	498		720	320	3	6	7	...	10	11	12	14	18
					90											
10	M_2	22·78	729/1024	588		758·52	337·12	...	...	...	...	...	11	...	14	...
					22											
11	M_3	22·50	45/64	610		768	341·33	3	...	7	...	...	...	12	...	18
					71											
12	M_4	21·60	27/40	680		800	355·56	...	...	...	...	...	...	12	...	18
					22											
13	P	21·33	2/3	702		810	360	3	6	7	9	10	...	12	14	18
					90											
14	D_1	20·25	81/128	792		853·33	379·26	...	...	...	...	...	11	...	14	18
					22											
15	D_2	20	5/8	814		864	384	3	6	7	...	...	...	12	...	...
					71											
16	D_3	19·20	3/5	884		900	400	3	6	...	...	...	...	12	...	18
					22											
17	D_4	18·96	16/27	906		911·25	405	3	6	7	9	10	...	12	14	18
					90											
18	Su. N.	18	9/16	996		960	426·67	3	6	...	...	10	11	12	14	18
					22											
19	N_2	17·78	5/9	1018		972	432	3	6	7	...	...	...	12	...	18
					71											
20	N_3	17·07	8/15	1088		1012·50	450	3	6	...	...	...	...	12	...	18
					22											
21	N_4	16·86	128/243	1110		1025·15625	4555·62	3	...	7	9	10	...	...	14	...
					90											
22	S	16	1/2	1200		1080	480	3	6	7	...	10	11	12	...	18

The Calculations in Columns marked * are our own.

In the 2nd col. of the above table we find that the 5 Swarams Ri, Ga, Ma, Dha and Ni have four Srutis each, while Sa and Pa have one Sruti each. This is quite contrary to the view of Sarnga Dev. The names of the Srutis also, it must be noticed, are not those of Sarnga Dev but which are found in the modern work of Venkatamakhi namely "Chaturdandiprakasika". If we notice again the fractions of the Srutisthanams in col. 4, we find that the 17 Srutis, 2, 3, 4, 5, 6. 7, 9, 11, 13, 15, 16, 17, 18, 19, 20, 21 and 22 have the same fractions as the Srutis of Deval (Vide 3rd col. of Table 3, P. 255). We have pointed them out in col. 9. We have already remarked that they are based on the system that Sa-Pa $= \frac{3}{2}$, but which will never give us the right Srutis. The fractions $1, \frac{1}{2}, \frac{1}{3}, \frac{1}{4}, \frac{1}{8}$ and $\frac{1}{4}$ are used conveniently for the purpose of demonstrating to those who have no ear for music. That they will never suit Karnatic music may be seen from the system of Karnatic music to be given later on.

Again, his calculations for Srutis 1. 8, 10, 12 and 14 differ from those of Deval. The same calculations are found in Tables 10, 11 and 12 of Subramania Sastrial of 53 Srutis fame (Vide cols. 13, 14 and 15 of the above Table 25). If we notice the intervals between Srutis in col. 6, we shall find that while Ri, Ga, Dha and Ni are regular with 90, 22, 71, and 22 cents, we see that Ma has 90, 90, 22 and 71. In the same manner Pa has 22 and Sa 90. If we sing Grahaswaram with intervals so varied, the result will be glorious! Only gods and Mr. Bhagavatar must appreciate the celestial music!! Sarnga Dev never gave such measurement.

Besides the above, Mr. Bhagavatar read an essay at the Sixth Conference under the heading "The 22 Srutis in use in Aryan music". Here he gives the same views given above but confirms them in the following words :—

(4) "Just as Gnostics in the world believe in the existence of one God and four Vedas, so they also believe that there are only 22 Srutis in Aryan music. Again just as the Vedas are the chief means by which God could be understood, so are the musical Shastras of writers beginning from Bharata, Matanga, Dattila, Kohala and Narada and ending with Sarnga Dev. But after Sarnga Dev, the writers Somanath, Ahobila, Ramamatya, Pundareekavittala, Venkatamakhi and Thulaja Maharajah and their works Ragavibodham, Sangeetha Parijatam, Swaramelakalanidhi Shadraga Chandrodayam, Chaturdandiprakasika and Sangeeta Saramritham treat only about Sruti, Swaram, Gramam and Moorchana, more or less adopting the views of the writers of the earlier period. Those who have read these works will clearly see that as regards Ragam, Talam and other parts their theories are conflicting.

Of these ancient works only "Bharata Natya Shastram" written by Bharata is in print; I have read this book. It is difficult to obtain the other works."

(5) "Therefore it is a well-known fact that from time immemorial there are only 22 Srutis in Aryan music. In the Bharata Natya Shastram also, which I have quoted above, the Srutis are given as 22. In the 28th Chapter of the book it is said

"From the above Slokas it is clear there are only 22 Srutis. I have only quoted the Slokas necessary for the Srutis from Prakrit. I have not quoted the others.

"The Grandham known as "Sangeeta Ratnakaram" written by Sarnga Dev who is also known as "Nissanka" adopts the view of Bharata in many respects. Therefore all Vidwans will agree that Sangeeta Ratnakaram is an excellent guide to go by."

(6) "Among Smritis there is one known as "Yajnyavalkya Smriti". It is held in as great esteem by the ancients as the Smriti of Manu. It has a commentary known as "Mitaksharee". The period of the author of this commentary seems to be far anterior to that of Sarnga Dev. There it is said, that in a particular sloka the term "Sruti" means one of 22 Srutis and the term "Jati" means one of 18 Jatis, namely seven Suddha Jatis in Shadjagramam and 11 Vikriti Jatis in Madhyamagramam. Therefore there is not the slightest doubt that Srutis are but 22."

(7) In the "Mahavakya Vivarana Bhashyam" of Sri Sankaracharyar our Jagat Guru, where he speaks about the differences in Nadam he says that there are 22 different kinds of Nadam. As we all have the greatest respect for our Guru, it is clear that the time of Sri Sankaracharyar is prior to that of the commentator on "Yajnyavalkya Smriti". So even the great saints say there are only 22 Srutis. No body could possibly controvert this."

(8) "So when it is clearly stated in the ancient works that Srutis are but 22, the position of men who add two to them and say they are 24 or subtract two from them and say there are only 20, is altogether untenable. Those who say so only display their ignorance. Again in the chapter on Srutis in Sangeeta Ratnakaram where he speaks about the difference between Srutis, he says there is only one Sruti. He further says there, that there may be 2 kinds of Srutis, three kinds, four kinds, nine kinds, 22 kinds, 66 kinds, or multitude of Srutis. But later on criticises the other kinds but establishes 22 Srutis on a firm basis after quoting a number of arguments in favour of it. There he never says the number 24 as regards Srutis. If there had been an ancient work which spoke about 24 Srutis, he would certainly have made mention of it. So it is clear that such a work was never in existence. Even if such an one was in existence and I brought it before the public, I will be pooh-poohed by musicians as it will be contrary to ancient recognised works."

(9) "Again, our Tamil Pandits know very well that in the Tamil works "Silappadhikaram" and "Chathurakaradi" the seven Swarams, Sa, Ri, Ga, Ma, Pa, Dha and Ni are known respectively as Kural, Thuttham, Kaikkilai, Oolai, Ili, Vilari and Tharam, and the Srutis belonging to each Swaram are known as "Mathras" etc.

So even Tamil works say there are only 22 Srutis, so we must confess our utter inability to controvert it."

(10) "My Aryan friends! it is a matter well known to you all that only 22 Srutis have been in use from ancient times up to the present day in Aryan music. This I have definitely proved having for my support the ancient recognised writings on music such as Bharata Natya Shastram ; you will also accept the fact that those who read those works have not only made use of them themselves but also taught the same to their disciples, and that even those who were not learned enough to understand the Sanskrit works have followed the practice of the learned up to this day. I have only reminded you of the facts already known to you, just acting the part of a stick which brightens up a lamp dimly burning. If we find fault with an ancient theory, not knowing the real meaning of ancient works and propagate a new theory just because those works do not subscribe to our own views, even ordinary people will be afraid to accept it as they are not supported by Shastras. Even if they do accept it they will not only derive no credit from it but will bring down upon them the dishonour of the world. They will hang between the two roads and lose all happiness in this world and the next."

(11) At the present day, many richmen, Sanskrit Pandits and musicians of the North in Bombay, Calcutta and Poona have formed themselves into Sabhas for the purpose of improving the music of their country. They make researches into ancient musical works for the purpose of dispelling their doubts. The result of all their researches is that they find the ancient methods most satisfactory and so do not attempt anything new, like the man Choku who was quite satisfied with the old Choku! They print journals like "Lakshya Sangeetam" and Hindustani Sangeetam and teach their own countrymen by distributing them broadcast and send them to us also. Moreover they consider our Karnatic music far superior to their own. This may be seen in many of their Grandhams. These are facts well known to you."

(12) "I request the all knowing, all noble, all religious and all generous members of this Sabha to try their best through the means of this Sabha to develop the Aryan music on ancient Shastraic lines, so that it may spread everywhere as in ancient times."

In section (4) given above, he says that Bharata, Matanga Rishi, Dattila, Kohala, Narada, Sarnga Dev and others were the pioneers of the science of music, while Somanatha, Ahobila Pandit, Ramamatya, Pundareeka Vittala, Venkata Makhi, Tulaja Maharaja and others came after them. If we examine them we find, that among them, there are advocates of 22 Srutis, besides others who speak about the Srutis of Karnatic music. When we notice the system of the author of Parijatam, who says he takes after Narada, we find that Pa has $\frac{3}{2}$, while Chaturdandiprakasika of Venkatamakhi, who proceeds also by $\frac{3}{2}$, speaks about the Srutis in use in Karnatic music. But Mr. Bhagavatar says in the 5th section that all the above writers subscribe to the 22 Srutis. He says that the Bharata Natya Shastram, the most ancient of Granthams, speaks about 22 Srutis only and that Sangeeta Ratnakaram, which came after it, is also an excellent guide and that also speaks about 22 Srutis only. We are not concerned here with the Srutis of Aryan music. It is to be noted that Mr. Bhagavatar whose object was to speak about the Srutis in Karnatic music goes off to speak about those of Aryan music. He further says that the later treatises adopt the view of the former ones as regards Sruti, Swaram, Gramam and Moorchana but as regards Ragam and Thalam they give conflicting opinions. We daily come across many a rule and mantram which are found in books but are never put into practice. In the same way it is a habit with a few writers to pretend to know things said in the books of their ancestors of which they are really ignorant and to display their scholarship by giving strange names to things which they know!

He says again in section (6) that inasmuch as Mitakshara, the commentator on Yajnyavalkya Smriti, who lived before Sarnga Dev, speaks of 22 Srutis, there is not the slightest doubt about the truth of the 22 Srutis.

Again in section (7) he says that as "Maha Vakya Vivarana Bhashyam" of Sri Sankaracharya refers to 22 Nadams, no body could controvert the theory of 22 Srutis.

In section (8) it is said that those who say there are either more or less than 22 Srutis in the octave only display their ignorance, and that Sarnga Dev speaking about different kinds of Srutis says there is only one kind, there are 2 kinds, 4 kinds, 9 kinds, 22 kinds, 66 kinds of Srutis, yea, there are multitudes of Srutis, and that he has picked out 22 out of them.

The 9th Section says that there could be only 22 Srutis, as the fact is supported by the Tamil works Silappadhikaram and Chathurakaradi.

In the 10th Section he emphasises the fact that only 22 Srutis are in use even at the present day in Aryan music and that no body should gainsay it.

In the 11th Section he speaks how many Vidwans in Bombay, Calcutta and Poona have organised Sabhas for making researches into music and how they are satisfied with the old ways and how they are singing according to tradition saying that the old Choku was quite enough for them ! Again he says how they hold the Karnatic music of the South in higher esteem than their own, which fact is supported by their writings.

We all know very well that many Vidwans in the North have organised Sabhas for making researches into the Srutis of Indian music and are trying their best to establish their theories. We have discussed the theories of some of them in the Second Part such as (1) Sahasrabuddhi, (2) Raja Surendra Mohan Tagore, (3) K. B. Deval, (4) E. Clements and (5) Dr. Bhandarkar. We find very conflicting opinions among them. Besides these, Chinnasami Mudaliar, M.A., who had taken so much pains as regards Indian music, is quite satisfied with 12 Swarams and says, in his remarks about Srutis, that we should not interfere in this matter which is so full of difficulties. So we find that the conclusion of Mr. Bhagavatar is that as we are unable to come to any definite conclusions as regards Srutis, let us be singing in the old way without worrying ourselves about Srutis and let us be saying there are only 22 Srutis as Sarnga Dev has said so !

Further, we have never heard about the term Aryan music nor read about it in any book hitherto. We do not think it right that we should call it Arya Sangeetam because the Aryans alone were singing it or that everything written in Sanskrit is the monopoly of the Aryans.

We may deduce from the above that the Northerners who are proficient in Aryan Music and in the Aryan language have their music after the Hindustani system and that they think highly of Karnatic music. We have dwelt at length on this in Part I.

We have adduced many arguments criticising the views of the advocates of 22 Srutis that they are not after Sarnga Dev nor suited to Karnatic music. There is no connection whatever between the Srutis of the Sa-Pa series and the Dwavimsati Srutis of Sarnga Dev.

We are of opinion that the theory of 22 Srutis in the octave will never hold. We shall find later on that this system was put forth in later days by writers who were completely ignorant of the Srutis of the Tamil country where the three Angams of Tamil, Iyal, Isai, and Natakam were in use. It is not wise to blindly affirm like the man who said that the hare he had caught had only three legs, that because such works were only found in Sanskrit, all that is written in Sanskrit is infallible. While speaking about the Srutis in use in the Karnatic country which is full of Tamil Vidwans who were bold enough to speak the truth even before Paramasivam saying," a fault is a fault even though committed by Paramasiwam who has an eye in his forehead", is it relevant to say that there are 22 Srutis in use in Aryan music? If Mr. Bhagavatar would only deeply consider the matter he would find that his 22 Srutis and the Srutis of the Karnatic music will never agree and it will be impossible to make any kind of Ganam with the help of the former.

In short, Mr. Bhagavatar does not follow either Sangeeta Ratnakaram or Parijatam. Without examining what Swarams are used in the Karnatic Ragas which he himself sings traditionally he only blindly affirms the existence of 22 Srutis. Did he examine whether the Swarams occurring in Ragams like Kalyani, Todi and Shankarabharanam, which he is in the habit of singing at the present day, will come right in an instrument with 22 Srutis?

Like those eminent (?) men who fly off into a rage when all argument fails, he also does when he finishes his argument on the Dwavimsati Srutis! We do not know what the fate of the 22 Srutis will be! In short, his adopting the view of Parijatam and discarding that of Ratnakaram by saying there are 22 Srutis is completely wrong and will never suit Karnatic music.

Besides this, it is also necessary to look into the Table which Mr. Bhagavatar gives as regards the names of Srutis. We see there that there are different names given in the different books for Srutis. The names of Srutis and their Srutisthanams are different in different writers. Again, as there were varied views as regards Srutis many have attempted to remedy it by putting down in the form of books the views that were prevalent during their time. Mr. Bhagavatar declares that these books do not agree with each other in matters of Ragam and Thalam, but we shall see from the Tables that they do not agree in Srutis and their names either.

There is a great difference in the number and names of Ragas in use at the time of the author of Sangeeta Ratnakaram and the later period.

By Table 26 we find that there were 19 Swarams in all, 7 Suddha and 12 Vikriti Swarams. There is reason to believe that inasmuch as there were only 19 Karta Ragas, he might have created 19 Melams to suit the 19 Swarams.

According to Parijatam we shall find 29 Swarams in Table 27, 7 Suddha, 5 Vikriti, and 17 further Vikriti Swarams.

Shadraga Chandrodayam gives 17 Swarams in all, of which 7 are Suddha Swarams, 7 Vikriti and 3 more Swarams in ordinary use.

Seventeen Swarams are mentioned in Ragavibodham, of which 7 are Suddha Swarams and 10 Vikriti.

Swaramelakalanithi, on the other hand, gives 7 Suddha Swarams, 7 Vikriti Swarams in all 14 and 4 Swarams allied to the Suddha and Vikriti Swarams.

Chathurdhandiprakasika has 16 Swarams, 7 Suddha and 9 Vikriti; of which the 9th and 22nd are common; while Sangeeta Saramritam gives 17, 7 Suddha and 10 Vikriti Swarams of which the 9th, the 13th and the 22nd are common.

The different views may be clearly seen from the Table. The various authors speak of 14, 16, 17, 18, 19, 20, 22 and 29 Srutis. If so many different Srutis and different names could be found in Madhya Sthayi which has half the length of wire, we must

TABLE 26

Suddha and Vikriti Swarams according to Sangita Ratnakaram.

Page 57 of the Fourth Conference Report of the Sangeeta Vidya Mahajana Sangham.

Sruti No.	Suddha Swarams.	Vikriti Swarams.	Srutis in each.	Fractions in a wire where the Swarams sound.
1	2	3	4	5
1		1. Kysika Nishadam ...	3	
2		2. Kakali Nishadam ...	4	
3		3. Chyutha Shadjam ...	2	
4	1. Suddha Shadjam ...	4. Achyutha Shadjam ...	2	1
7	2. „ Rishabham ...	5. { Chatursruti Rishabham or, Vikriti Rishabham ...	4	10/9
9	3. „ Gandharam ...			
10		6. Sadharana Gandharam ...	3	32/27
11		7. Antara Gandharam ...	4	
12		8. Chyuta Madhyamam ...	2	
13	4. „ Madhyamam ...	9. Achyuta Madhyamam ...	2	4/3
16		10. Trisruti Panchamam ...	3	
		11. Kysika Panchamam ...	4	3/2
17	5. „ Panchamam ...			
20	6. „ Dhaivatam ...	12. { Chatusruti Dhaivatam or, Vikriti Dhaivatam ...	4	5/3
22	7. „ Nishadham ...			16/9

Suddha Swarams 7. Vikriti Swarams 12.

Suddha and Vikriti Swarams 19.

conclude that the works are entirely conflicting. We clearly see further that though each of them makes mention of 22 Srutis, in ordinary use they seem to have used a variety of Swarams. But they all agree in saying there are 7 Suddha Swarams. Even there we find that the author of Parijatam differs in respect to 4 Swarams, while he agrees with others as regards Ma, the 9th Sruti, Pa, the 13th Sruti and Ni, the 22nd Sruti.

Besides this, we find that with the exception of the author of Parijatam, others have followed the system of Sarnga Dev in having the Srutis as 4, 3, 2, 4, 4, 3 and 2. On the whole, we find that as regards the number of Srutis in a Sthayi there is difference of opinion (1) as regards the number (2) as regards the names of Srutis and (3) that even as regards the Sapta Swarams the author of Parijatam gives different Sthanams.

TABLE 27

Suddha and Vikriti Swarams of the Sangita Parijatam.

Page 58 of the Report of the Fourth Conference of the Sangita Vidya Mahajana Sangham.

Sruti No.	Suddha Swarams.	Vikriti Swarams.	Vikriti Swarams.
1	2	3	4
1			1. Poorva Rishabham.
2		1. Komala Rishabham.	
3	1. Suddha Rishabham...		2. „ Gandharam.
4			3. Tivra Rishabham.
5	2. „ Gandharam...		4. Tivratara Rishabham
6		2. Tivra Gandharam ...	
7			5. „ Gandharam.
8			6. Tivratama „
9	3. „ Madhyamam.		7. Ati Tivratama „
10			8. Tivra Madhyamam.
11		3. Tivra Madhyamam.	
12			9. Tivratama Madhyamam.
13	4. „ Panchamam.		10. Ati Tivratama „
14			11. Poorva Dhaivatam.
15		4. Komala Dhaivatam.	
16	5. „ Dhaivatam ...		12. Poorva Nishadam.
17			13. Tivra Dhaivatam.
18	6. „ Nishadam ...		14. Tivratara Dhaivatam.
19		5. Tivra Nishadam ...	
20			15. „ Nishadam.
21			16. Tivratama „
22	7. Tara Shadjam ...		17. Atitivratama „
	Suddha Swarams 7.	Vikriti Swarams 5.	Vikriti Swarams 17.

Suddha and Vikriti Swarams 29.

However, every one of them has mentioned the term 22 Srutis. Putting together the views of these authors which say there are 14, 16, 17, 18, 19, 20, 22 and even 29 Srutis and that of Sarnga Dev who says the Srutis are 1, 2, 3, 4, 9, 22, 66 yea there are multitudes of Srutis, we may come to the definite conclusion that according to these authors the number of Srutis is in a glorious state of uncertainty! We are driven to the necessity, therefore, of supposing that these authors erred in interpreting the music that has been in use from ancient times among the inhabitants of South Madura and the scholars of the three Tamil Sangams. Mr. Bhagavatar who said that the

TABLE 28.

Suddha and Vikriti Swarams mentioned in Shadraga Chendrodaya.	Suddha and Vikriti Swarams mentioned in Ragavibodham.

Page 59 of the Report of the Fourth Conference of the Sangita Vidya Mahajana Sangam.

Sruti No.	Suddha Swarams.	Vikriti Swarams.	Suddha Swarams.	Vikriti Swarams.
1	2	3	4	5
1		1. Kysika Nishadam ...		1. Kysika Nishadam.
2		2. Kakali " ...		2. Kakali Nishadam.
3		3. Laghu Sadjam ...		3. Mridu Shadjam.
4	1. S. Shadjam ...		1. S. Shadjam ...	
7	2. S. Rishabham.		2. S. Rishabham.	
8		4. Chatusruti Rishabham*		4. Tivra Rishabham
9	3. S. Gandharam.		3. S. Gandharam.	
10		5. Sadharana Gandharam		5. Sad. Gandharam.
11		6. Antara Gandharam ...		6. Antara "
12		7. Laghu Madhyamam...		7. Mri. Madhyamam
13	4. S. Madhyamam		4. S. Madhyamam	
14		8. Pan. Sruti Madhyam*		8. Tivrtara "
15				
16		9. Laghu Panchamam ...		9. Mrid Panchamam.
17	5. S. Panchamam.		5. S. Panchamam.	
20	6. S. Dhaivatam...		6. S. Dhaivatam...	
21				
22	7. S. Nishadam ...	10. Chat. Dhaivatam* ...	7. S. Nishadam ...	10. Tivra Dhaivatam.

Suddha Swarams 7.	Vikriti Swarams 10.	Suddha Swarams 7.	Vikriti Swarams 10.
Suddha and Vikriti Swarams 17.		Suddha and Vikriti Swarams 17.	

* Swarams marked thus are in practice.

later authors are at one with the ancient writers in Sruti, Swaram, Gramam and Moorchana, never cared to look into the table of Srutis given by himself. In the same manner there is no unanimity in Ragam and Thalam, he says. Just because there is a difference as regards the names of Ragas as well as the Swarams and Srutis used in Arohanam and Avarohanam, we have taken so much trouble in enquiring into them When we notice the views of modern authors also we find there is anything but unanimity in their opinions. We hope Mr. Bhagavatar will take cognisance of this at least in the future. No sane man builds a house whose foundations are made up of heaps of

TABLE 29.

Prakriti and Vikriti Swarams as mentioned in Swaramela Kalanidhi.

Page 60 of the Report of the Fourth Conference of the Sangita Vidya Mahajana Sangam.

Sruti No.	Suddha Swarams.	Vikriti Swarams.	Vikriti Swarams.
1	2	3	4
1		1. Kysika Nishadam ...	1. Shatsruti Dhaivatam
2		2. Kakali Nishadam ...	
3		3. Chyuta Shadja Nishadam	
4	1. Suddha Shadjam.		
7	2. ,, Rishabham.		
9	3. ,, Gandharam.		2. Panchasruti Rishabham.
10		4. Sadharana Gandharam ...	3. Shatsruti Rishabham
11		5. Antara Gandharam ...	
12		6. Chyu. Pan. Gandharam...	
13	4. ,, Madhyamam		
16		7. Chyu. Pan. Madhyamam.	4. Panchasruti Dhaivatam.
17	5. ,, Panchamam.		
20	6. ,, Dhaivatam.		
22	7. ,, Nishadam ...		
	Suddha Swarams 7.	Vikriti Swarams 7.	These four are allied to the Prakriti and Vikriti Swarams
	Prakriti and Vikriti Swarams 14.		

irregular stones. The term 22 becomes the real cause why Indian music is pooh-poohed as music which does not agree even in Srutis and as a science without foundation.

If we notice the two pages of Table 31 we shall find a vast difference between the number of the Srutis and the names of Srutis given. It is clear that Swaramela-kalanidhi, Chathurdandiprakasika and Sangeeta Saramritam were written after Sangeeta Parijatam. When we notice the numbers 1, 2, 3, 4, 5 and 6 in connection with the Srutis of Ri and Dha they appear to conform to Karnatic music. However, we must suppose that the author of Parijatam lived prior to the period of the other writers, and that he has to a very large extent made sure of the Srutis in Karnatic music though he errs in a few points owing to miscalculation. The details may be seen by a comparative study of the Tables.

TABLE 20.

Chaturdandiprakasika | **Sangita Saramritam**

Page 61 of the Fourth Conference Report of the Sangita Vidya Mahajana Sangam.

Sruti No.	Sruti Swarams.	Vikriti Swarams.	Suddha Swarams.	Vikriti Swarams.
1	2	3	4	5
1		1. Kysika Nishadam ... 2. Shatsruti Dhaivatam..		1. Kysika Nishadam. 2. Sh. Sr. Dhaivatam.
3		3. Kakali Nishadam ...		3. Kakali Nishadam.
4	1. S. Shadjam ...		1. S. Shadjam ...	
7	2. S. Rishabham..		2. S. Rishabham.	
9	3. S. Gandharam	4. Pan. Sruti Rishabham	3. S. Gandharam.	4. P. Sr. Rishabham.
10		5. Shatsruti Rishabham.. 6. SadharanaGandharam		5. Sh. Sr. Rishabham. 6. Sad. Gandharam.
12		7. Antara Gandharam ...		7. Antara Gandharam.
13	4. S. Madhyamam		4. S. Madhyamam	8. S. M. Gandharam.
16		8. Varali Madhyamam ...		9. V.Pan. Madhyamam.
17	5. S. Panchamam.		5. S. Panchamam	
20	6. S. Dhaivatam...		6. S. Dhaivatam	
22	7. S. Nishadam ...	9. Pan. Sruti Dhaivatam.	7. S. Nishadam	10. P. Sr. Dhaivatam.

Suddha Swarams 7 } Vikriti Swarams 9. | Suddha Swarams 7. } Vikriti Swarams 10.

Suddha and Vikriti Swarams 16. | Suddha and Vikriti Swarams 17.

He who first affirmed that there could be only 22 Srutis in the Octave and that the others should not attempt to make either more or less than the 22, gives himself away by trying to prove from his own Tables that there may be 16, 17, 18, 19, 20, 22 and even 29 Srutis in the octave. Men of understanding will know by what sort of people such contradictory statements will be freely indulged.

Moreover, he goes on further to say that the Northerners were quite content to be satisfied with the old Choku, or the old modes of singing, seeing there was such a wide controversy as regards the Dwavimsati Srutis, and declares that there is not much use in discussing the Srutis of Karnatic music but that every one may use what Ragams or what Srutis he likes and may help to introduce Desikam and admixture into the pure Karnatic music! We shall prove later on that Karnatic music is not after the 22 Srutis. We have already refuted clearly, and pointed out the errors committed by the advocates of the 22 Srutis.

TABLE 31.

Names of Sruti Sthanams for the 22 Srutis as given in Sangita Ratnakaram, Shadraga Chandrodayam, Ragavibodham, Swaramelakalanidhi, Chaturdandi Prakasika, Sangita Saramritam and Sangita Parijatam.

	Sangita Ratnakaram		Sruti.		Shadraga Chandrodayam.	Ragavibodam	Swara Mela Kalanidhi.	Chaturdandi Prakasikai.	Sangita Saramritam.	Sangita Parijatam.			
1	2	3	4	5	6	7	8	9	10	11	12	13	15
1	...	Ky. Nisadam.	3	...	Ky.Nishadam	Ky.Nishadam	6 S. Daivatam ... Ky. Nisadam.	6 S.Dhaivatam Ky. Nishadam	6 Sr. Dhaivatam Ky.Nishadam	19	...	Ti. Nishadam	...
2	...	Ka. „	4	...	Ka. „	Ka. „	Ka. „	Ka. „	...	20	...	...	Ttr. Nisadam.
3	...	Ch. Shadjam.	3	...	La. Shadjamam	Mri. Shadjamam	Ch. Shadjam.	...	Ka. „	21	...	...	Ttm. „
4	Su.Sa.	Ac. Shadjam.	2	...	...	...	...	...	...	22	Su.Sa.	...	A. Ttm. „
5	...	...	...	...	...	...	...	...	...	1	...	...	Pu. Rishabam
6	...	...	...	...	...	...	...	...	...	2	...	Ko. Rishabham	...
7	„ Ri.	4 S.Rishabam or, Vi. Rishabam	4	[illegible]	...	...	...	...	...	3	„ Ri.	...	„ Gandaram
8	...	...	...	...	4 S.Rishabam	Ti. Rishabam	...	5 Sr.Rishabam	...	4	...	...	T. Rishabam.
9	„ Ga.	...	...	...	...	...	5 S.Rishabam	6 „ „	5 S.Rishabam	5	„ Ga.	...	Ttr. „
10	...	Sa. Gandaram	3	[illegible]	Sa. Gandaram	Sa. Gandaram	6 „ „ ... Sa. Gandaram	Sa. Gandaram	6 „ „ ... Sa. Gandaram	6	...	Ti. Gandaram	...
11	...	An. „	4	...	An. „	An.Gandaram	An. „	An. „	...	7	...	...	„ Gandaram
12	...	Ch. Madhyam	2	...	La. Madhyamam	Mr. Madhyam	Ch. Ma. „	...	An. „	8	...	...	Ttm. „
13	„ Ma.	Ac. „	2	[illegible]	...	...	...	...	Su. Ma. „	9	„ Ma.	...	A. Ttm. „
14	...	...	...	...	5 S. Madyam.	...	...	...	...	10	...	Ti. Madhyamam	...
15	...	...	...	...	...	Ttr. Madyam.	...	...	...	11	...	...	Ttr. Madyamam
16	...	3 S. Panchamam Ky. „	3 4	...	La. Panchamam	Mri. Panchamam	„ P. Madyam.	V.Madyam.	V.P.Madyam.	12	...	...	Ttm. „
17	„ Pa	...	...	[illegible]	...	...	...	...	...	13	„ Pa.	...	A. Ttm. „
18	...	...	...	...	...	...	...	...	...	14	...	...	Pu. Daivatam
19	...	...	...	...	...	...	...	...	...	15	...	Ko. Dhaivatam	...
20	„ Dh.	4 S.Daivatam Vi. „	4	[illegible]	...	...	...	...	...	16	„ Dh.	...	Pu. Nishadam
21	...	...	...	[illegible]	4 S. Dhaivatam	Ti.Dhaivatam	...	...	...	17	...	...	Ti. Dhaivatam
22	„ Ni.	...	...	...	...	...	5 S. Daivatam	5 Sr.Daivatam	5 Sr. Dhaivatam	18	„ Ni.	...	Ttr. „

A. Ati; Ac. Achyuta; An. Antara; Ch. Chyuta; Ka. Kakali; Ko. Komala; Ky. Kysiki; La. Laghu; Mr. Mri. Mridu; P. Panchma; Pu. Purva; S. Sr. Sruti; Sa. Sadharana; Su. Suddha; Ti. Tivra; Ttr. Tivratara; Ttm. Tivratama; V. Varali; Vi. Vikriti.

Tenth.

The opinion of M. R. Ry., S. Manickya Mudaliar of Sankhagiri Drug as regards arriving at the Srutis in use in South Indian Music.

The above author published a book in 1902 known as Sangeeta Chandrika. He does not say with the help of what treatise he wrote it. It is well to give here his calculations as regards Srutis.

HOW FRETS ARE FIXED IN A VEENA TO SUIT THE SRUTIS.

First, How Srutis are fixed by sound (by the ear).

"We have already dealt with the names of the seven wires of the Veena in the 15th head under the Srutis. Tune the seven wires, namely, Anumandaram, Panchamam, Saranai, Talamandaram, Tala Panchamam, and Talasaranai according to the usual rule; sound the wire Sarana and fix the fret called ✱ exactly at the place in the wire where Talasaranai or the higher Sa speaks.

The Melam or fixing of frets should be done carefully, observing the figure of the Veena and the Sarana wire given below.

The fret for Pa should be fixed in the place in the same wire where Tala (Hecchu= high) Panchamam or the sound equivalent to its octave speaks.

The *fifth* or the Panchamam from the above fret will give you the place of Ri_2.

The *fifth* from Ri_2 will give you the place of Dha_2.

The *fifth* from Dha_2 gives you Ga_2.

The *fifth* from Ga_2 gives Ni_2, the *fifth* or Panchamam from Ni_2 gives Ma_2, the Panchamam from Ma_2 gives Ri_1, the Panchamam from Ri_1 gives Dha_1, the *fifth* from Dha_1 gives Ga_2, the Panchamam from Ga_2 gives Ni_2, and the *fifth* from Ni_2 gives Ma_1.

So, the 12 frets thus fixed give us the Madhya Sthayi in the wire Saranai. If the above 12 frets were fixed according to the rule given above they will give us the following Swarams:—

The Saranai wire is Taggu Shadjam. The Ri denotes Suddha Ri, the Ri_2 Suddha Ga or Chathusruti Ri, the Ga_2 Sadharana Ga or Shatsruti Ri, the Ga_2 Antara Ga, the Ma_1 Suddha Ma, the Ma_2 Prati Ma, the Pa denotes Panchamam, the Dha_1 Suddha Dha, the Dha_2 Suddha Ni or Chathusruti Dha, the Ni_2 Kaisika Ni or Shatsruti Dha, and the Ni_2 denotes Kakali Ni or Octave Sa. The places denoted by dots in the above figure of the Veena and wires are the ones used in playing Prathama Sarali Varisai. If the octaves for the above 12 places could be found out and frets fixed there, then we have the 24 frets of the Veena. The fret marked (*b*) on the right end of the Veena in the shape of a horse where the wires stand over the pot and the fret on the left end marked (*a*) or the piece of wood where the last fret stands, and the 24 frets should be shaped and fixed regularly according to rules. Then the 24 frets representing the 24 Swarasthanams of the wire Saranai will also clearly represent the Swarasthanams of the other three wires Panchamam, Mandaram and Anumandaram. In other words, the 24 Swarasthanams of the Anumandara wire, commencing from the Suddha Ma of Taggumandara Sthayi up to Panchamam of Madhya Sthayi, the 24 Swarasthanams of the Mandara wire commencing from Suddha Dha of Mandara Sthayi up to the Panchamam of Tara Sthayi and the 24 Swarasthanams of Saranai wire, commencing from Suddha Ri of the Madhya Sthayi up to the Octave Sa of the Tara Sthayi will be respectively denoted by the 24 frets. This is how the frets are fixed in a Veena by ear.

Fixing of frets by measurement.

The first mode of fixing frets is only for those who have a good ear for music. The second method is given for the benefit of those who have no ear for music. The frets should be fixed by closely observing the figure of the Veena and wires given below.

Divide the whole length of the Saranai wire *that is*, the length of the wire from (*a*) to (*b*) and fix the fret ச̇ in the middle. Next, divide the right half of the wire from ச̇ to (*b*) into equal parts and fix the fret ச̈ there. The fret for ம$_1$ MA$_1$ will be exactly in the middle of (*a*) to ச̇. Divide the distance between ச̇ and ச̈ into two equal parts and fix ம̇$_1$ ma$_1$ there. The exact middle between ம$_1$ and ம̇$_1$ will be நி$_2$ NI$_2$. Take half the length between NI$_2$ and sa and measure that distance from ச̈ towards (a) and place நி̇$_2$ ni$_2$ there. The exact middle between நி$_2$ and நி̇$_2$ will give க̇$_2$. Take double the length of ச̇ sa and க̇$_2$ ga$_2$ and measure that length from (*a*) and place the fret க$_2$ GA$_2$. The exact middle between க$_2$ and க̇$_2$ will give the fret த$_1$ DHA$_1$. Take half the length of த$_1$ DHA$_1$ and ச̇ sa and measure that distance from ச̈ towards (*a*) and place த̇$_1$. The exact middle between த$_1$ and த̇$_1$ will give ரி̇$_1$ ri$_1$. Take double the length of ச̇ sa and ச̈ ரி$_1$ ri$_1$ and measure that distance from (*a*) and place ரி$_1$ RI$_1$. ம$_2$ MA$_2$ will come between ரி̇$_1$ ri$_1$ and ரி$_1$ RI$_1$. Take half the length between ம$_1$ MA$_1$ and ம$_2$ MA$_2$ and measure that distance from ம̇$_1$ ma$_1$ towards (*b*) and place ம̇$_2$ ma$_2$ there. Place நி$_3$ NI$_3$ between ம$_2$ MA$_2$ and ம̇$_2$ ma$_2$. Take half the length between நி$_3$ NI$_3$ and ச̇ sa and measure that distance from ச̈ towards (*a*) and place நி̇$_3$ ni$_3$ there. Place க̇$_3$ between நி$_3$ NI$_3$ and நி̇$_3$ ni$_3$. Take double the distance between க̇$_2$ ga$_2$ and க̇$_3$ ga$_3$ and measure that distance from க$_2$ GA$_2$ towards ச̇ sa and it will be க$_3$ GA$_3$. Place த$_2$ DHA$_2$ between க$_3$ and க̇$_3$. Take half the length between த$_1$ DHA$_1$ and த$_2$ DHA$_2$ and measure that distance from த̇$_1$ dha$_1$ towards (*b*) and place த̇$_2$ dha$_2$ there. Place ரி̇$_2$ ri$_2$ between த$_2$ and த̇$_2$. Take double the length between ரி̇$_1$ ri$_1$ and ரி̇$_2$ ri$_2$ and measure that distance from ரி$_1$ RI$_1$ towards (*b*) and place ரி$_2$ RI$_2$ there. Place ப between ரி̇$_2$ ri$_2$ and ரி$_2$ RI$_2$. Take half the length between ம$_2$ MA$_2$ and ப PA and measure that distance from ம̇$_2$ ma$_2$ towards (*b*) and call it ப̇ pa.

So, if the 24 frets given above, namely ரி$_1$, ரி$_2$, க$_2$, க$_3$, ம$_1$, ம$_2$, ப, த$_1$, த$_2$, நி$_2$, நி$_3$, ச̇, ரி̇$_1$, ரி̇$_2$, க̇$_2$, க̇$_3$, ம̇$_1$, ம̇$_2$, ப̇, த̇$_1$, த̇$_2$, நி̇$_2$, நி̇$_3$, and ச̈ were fixed according to the exact measurement given above, they represent as they stand the 24 Swarasthanams of the Madhya and Tara Sthayis."

He gives two methods of tuning the Veena, the one for those who have a good ear for music, and the other, by measurement, for those who possess no such gift. Though we accept his first method of tuning to be the correct one, yet as the second method goes by certain measurements which are tangible and which could be understood by others we have to pass a few remarks on the same.

We see that he divides the length of the wire into two equal parts, and makes the lower half into Madhya Sthayi and the half of the upper half into Tara Sthayi. He locates Madhya Sthayi MA in the exact centre of Madhya Sthayi, and Tara Sthayi MA in the exact centre of the Tara Sthayi. He locates NI$_2$ in the exact centre of the wire between Madhya Sthayi MA and Tara Sthayi MA. He divides the distance between Tara SA and Madhya NI$_2$ into two equal parts and locates NI below Atitara SA at a distance of one of the equal parts. From this, he proceeds to locate GA and the 12 Swarams. When we look into this deeply, we find that he advocates the SA-MA system or dividing the lengths of the wire into 2 equal parts. He gives at the close that PA comes between RI$_2$ and Tara Sthayi ri$_2$. We know well that Swarams which result from such measurement will be only approximately correct. Taking SA to be 540 vibrations, we get 720 for $\frac{4}{3}$, and 810 for $\frac{3}{2}$. He commences from MA or 720, proceeds 12 Swarams and finishes at PA. Even though he commences from 720, when he proceeds 12 steps by $\frac{4}{3}$ he gets 799 for PA. To say that

TABLE 32.

The Table showing the Swarams in use in Indian music according to the author of **Sangeeta Chandrika.**

No. of Swaram.	How it is obtained.	Name of Swaram.	The location of the Swaram in a wire 32 inches long.	Fractions for Swarams if Adhara Sa be 1.	Cents.	Difference in the Cents.	The Vibration of each Swaram if SA=540.	The Vibrations by the right system of tuning the Saranai.	The difference between the two.
1	⊕ 2	⊕ 3	⊕ 4	⊕ 5	⊕ 6	⊕ 7	⊕ 8	⊕* 9	⊕ 10
	1	S ஸ	32.000	1	0		540	540	
1	6	R_1 ரி$_1$	30·375	243/256	90	90	568·89	572·11	3
2	11	R_2 ரி$_2$	28·833	59049/65536	180	90	599·319	606·13	7
3	4	G_2 க$_2$	27·000	27/32	294	114	640	642·17	2
4	9	G_3 க$_3$	25·628	6561/8192	384	90	674·239	680·35	6
5	2	M_1 ம$_1$	24.000	3/4	498	114	720	720·81	1
6	7	M_2 ம$_2$	22·781	729/1024	588	90	758·519	763·68	5
7	12	P ப	21·624	177147/262144	678	90	799·092	809·09	10
8	5	D_1 த$_1$	20·250	81/128	792	114	853·333	857·20	4
9	10	D_2 த$_2$	19·222	19683/32768	882	90	898·985	908·17	9
10	3	N_2 நி$_2$	18·000	9/16	996	114	960	962·17	2
11	8	N_3 நி$_3$	17·086	2187/4096	1086	90	1011·358	1019·38	8
12	1	s ஸ்	16·000	1/2	1200	114	1080	1080	

The Calculations in Columns marked ⊕ are our own.

*** Details about the 9th Column will be found in Part IV.**

PA must be $\frac{3}{2}$ is approximately correct. But he gets [illegible] for PA. When we take the length of wire as $\frac{3}{4}$ and $\frac{2}{3}$, $\frac{4}{3}$ becomes a little less and $\frac{3}{2}$ a little more than the natural measurement. Taking this alone into consideration the slight difference does not show much. But when he proceeds 12 steps by $\frac{4}{3}$, as $\frac{4}{3}$, $\frac{4}{3}\times\frac{4}{3}$ and so on, this slight difference gathers momentum and lessens 10 vibrations (809—799). In the same way, the other Swarams also, beginning from RI, have the difference of 3, 7, 2, 6, 5, 1, 10, 4, 9, 2 and 8 vibrations respectively. Table 32 gives the fractions, length of wire and vibrations of the Swarams according to his measurement.

We must note here that his measurements are all for the Swarasthanams of the Veena and that he proceeds by the SA-MA system. His calculations for the 12 Swarams of the Veena are very different from those of Parijatam. But we are of opinion, that but for the slight natural difference of a *fourth* or MA, the 12 Swarasthanams will be quite correct in accordance with the SA-MA system. His system of proceeding by $\frac{4}{3}$ is certainly superior to the system of Parijatam. The SA-PA system of Parijatam and the SA-MA system are, as it were, the keys for opening out and determining the Swarams used in music.

Looking into the above Table, we see that he determines the Swarams by the SA-MA system. But we should not forget that he recommends this method for those who have no ear for music. The first method is distinctly for the benefit of those who have a good ear for music, inasmuch as he recommends that the three wires used for keeping time should be tuned by *fifths*. There could be no mistake if we proceed by this method. But, as it is argued that the system of tuning by ear is inaccurate and that the system of doing it by measurements and calculations is correct, we are compelled to examine and see whether such a system gives the results correctly.

In the first column of the above Table the numbers of the 12 Swarams are found. The second column gives their order in the SA-MA series. For example, if SA-MA be the first and the second, MA-NI becomes the third, NI-GA the fourth, GA-DHA the fifth, DHA-RI the sixth, RI-MA the seventh, MA-NI the eighth, NI-GA the ninth, GA-DHA the tenth, DHA-RI the eleventh and RI-PA the twelfth. Each step proceeds by the addition of 498 cents and if any goes over 1200, 1200 is deducted from it. This is found in col. 6. The cents for each is given in col. 7. These calculations may be also found in the second part of Table 17, in columns 9, 10, 11 and 12, page 314.

He says that there is a difference in the calculation of cents of SA-MA as obtained by tuning it by ear and proceeding by $\frac{4}{3}$. So we must conclude that SA-MA is $\frac{4}{3}$ in the 498 cents for those who have no ear for music. As he distinctly says that this method is for those who have no ear for music, there must be another more correct method for those gifted with a musical ear. The correct length of the wire, cents calculation, and number of vibrations for the benefit of those with a musical ear may be found in the Karnatic system of music which will be given later.

On the whole, we conclude, that his 12 Swarams are those in Karnatic music. Evidently he is of opinion that the Dwavimsati Srutis will not suit Karnatic music.

Eleventh.

How the author of Sangeeta Parijatam determines the Srutis after the System of Narada.

Ahobila Panditer was the author of Sangeeta Parijatam. He was born in Ahobilam, a village near the Tungabhadra in the district of Kurnool. There is a small hill in the village, and a cave on the top of the hill, and a temple of Narasimhamoorti within that cave. There is reason to believe he was called Ahobila after the village where he was born. He seems to have written Parijatam with a view to explain clearly the theory of Srutis given in Sangeeta Ratnakaram. He gives his measurements just to suit the Swarasthanams found in the Veena of his time, *i.e.* nearly 400 years ago. However it is distinctly seen that he first quotes the views of Sarnga Dev and then proceeds to give his own. We will do well to know what he says about Srutis. He says, " There are 22 Nadis (breath) which run right across the three Nadis of the heart namely, Idaikalai, Pingalai and Sushumnai. These are the birthplaces of sound. With the help of the stomach, the heart, the Kantam, the head and the mouth the sound gradually increases and is brought out. Just as the snake is known by the names of Ahi and Kundali, the sound is known as Sruti and Swaram. Wise men are of opinion that there are a number of Srutis, with the difference of the top of a blade of grass, in our body just as in the Veena."

" In a Veena with the Meru and the Mettu, there are 22 Srutis by the system of SA-PA. I give below the explanation of the Srutis after the system of Narada, etc., etc. A Swaram can never result from a Sruti. There are 29 Srutis, of which 7 are Suddha Swarams and 22 are Vikriti Swarams. SA, MA and PA have four Srutis each. GA and NI have two Srutis, and RI and DHA, three Srutis each. (He then proceeds to give how each Swaram is arrived at).

The Tara SA is exactly at the middle of the whole wire in a Veena. MA comes between Tara SA and Meru SA. If the whole length of the wire is divided into three equal parts PA will sound in the first part. GA will occur in the middle between Meru SA and PA. Divide the length of the wire between Meru SA and PA into three equal parts and locate RI in the first part. DHA occurs between Tara SA and PA. Divide the length between Tara SA and PA into three equal parts and locate NI after the second part."

Sangita Parijata's scale for the determination of 12 Swarams.

N.B. —The measurements have been converted to fractions for comparison with those of others.

The measurement of each Swaram in a wire in accordance with Sangita Parijatam.	Names of Swarams.	Fractions
In the full length of the wire...	Adhara Shadjam	1
In half the „ „ „	Tara Shadjam	$\frac{1}{2}$
In ⅔ of the „ „ „	Panchamam	$\frac{2}{3}$
In the middle of the Adhara Shadjam and Tara Shadjam	Madhyamam	$\frac{3}{4}$
In the middle of the Adhara Shadjam and Panchamam	Gandharam	$\frac{5}{6}$
In the middle of the Panchamam and Tara Shadjam	Dhaivatam	$\frac{7}{12}$
In ⅓ of the length of the wire between Adhara Shadjam and Panchamam (nearer the former) ...	Rishabham	$\frac{8}{9}$
In ⅓ of the length of the wire between Tara Shadjam and Panchamam (nearer the former) ...	Nishadham	[illegible]

The above seven are Suddha Swaras.

The measurement of each Swaram in a wire in accordance with Sangita Parijatam.	Names of Swarams.	Fractions.
In a wire		
Make three equal divisions between Adhara Shadjam and Rishabham and in the second division place	Komala Rishabham	25/27
Between Adhara Shadjam and Dhaivatam	Tivra Gandharam	19/24
Make three equal divisions between Tivra Gandharam and Tara Shadjam and in the first division place	Tivra Madhyamam	25/36
Make three equal divisions between Panchamam and Tara Shadjam and in the first division place	Komala Dhaivatam	11/18
Make three equal divisions between Dhaivatam and Tara Shadjam and in the second division place	Tivra Nishadam	19/36
These are Vikriti Swarams.		

Number.	Names of Swaram.	General Interpretation. Positions of Swarams.	Cents.	Location of Swarams if wire is 216 units.	Intervals in units.	Location of Swarams if wire is 32 inches.	Intervals in inches.	According to G. G. Barve. Positions of Swarams.	Cents.	Location of Swarams if wire is 216 units.	Intervals in units.	Location of Swarams if wire is 32 inches.	Intervals in inches.
	Adhara Shadjam ...	1	0	216		32·00		1	0	216		32·00	
					16		2·37				12		1·78
1	*Komala Rishabham**	25/27	133	200		29·63		17/18	99	204		30·22	
					8		1·19				6		0·89
2	*Rishabham* ...	8/9	204	192		28·44		11/12	151	198		29·33	
					12		1·78				18		2·67
3	Gandharam ...	5/6	316	180		26·67		5/6	316	180		26·67	
					9		1·33				9		1·33
4	Tivra Gandharam *	19/24	404	171		25·33		19/24	404	171		25·33	
					9		1·33				9		1·33
5	Madhyamam ...	3/4	498	162		24·00		3/4	498	162		24·00	
					12		1·78				12		1·78
6	Tivra Madhyamam *	25/36	631	150		22·22		25/36	631	150		22·22	
					6		0·89				6		0·89
7	Panchamam ...	2/3	702	144		21·33		2/3	702	144		21·33	
					12		1·78				12		1·78
8	Komala Dhaivatam*	11/18	853	132		19·56		11/18	853	132		19·56	
					6		0·89				6		0·89
9	Dhaivatam ...	7/12	933	126		18·67		7/12	933	126		18·67	
					6		0·89				6		0·89
10	Nishadam ...	5/9	1018	120		17·78		5/9	1018	120		17·78	
					6		0·89				6		0·89
11	Tivra Nishadam *	19/36	1106	114		16·89		19/36	1106	114		16·89	
					6		0·89				6		0·89
12	Tara Shadjam ...	1/2	1200	108		16.00		1/2	1200	108		16·00	

* These five are Vikriti Swarams.

Now he proceeds to give the method of arriving at Vikriti Swarams.

"Komala Ri occurs in the second of the three equal parts into which the length between Meru Sa and Ri is divided.

"Teevra Ga comes between Meru Sa and Dha. Divide the length between Teevra Ga and Tara Sa into three equal parts and locate Teevra Ma in the first part. Komala Dha occurs in the first of the three equal lengths of the wire between Pa and Tara Sa. Divide the length between Suddha Dha and Tara Sa into three equal parts and locate Teevra Ni in the second part."

Next, he gives the different names by which Vikriti Swarams are known.

Suddha Ga is otherwise known as Teevratara Ri, Suddha Ma as Atiteevratama Ga, Suddha Dha as Poorva Ni and Suddha Ni as Teevratara Dha.

A Suddha Swaram, when it becomes sharper in the first stage, is called Teevram, and in the next step Teevrataram, and in the third step Teevratamam and in the fourth step Atiteevratamam. In the same way, when it becomes flat by one Sruti it is called Komalam, and Poorvam when it is flatter by two Srutis. He further says that he has given the Raga Lakshanam for all the Srutis with the exception of the following ten :—

"(1) Poorva Ri, (2) Teevra Ri, (3) Teevratara Ga, (4) Teevratama Ga, (5) Teevra Ma, (6) Teevratara Ma, (7) Poorva Dha, (8) Teevra Dha, (9) Teevratara Ni and (10) Teevratama Ni."

The above Table shows (first column) where the seven Suddha Swarams and the five Vikriti are located in the different lengths of the wire in order. The second column shows what the different Srutis will be in integers if Adhara Sa be assumed to be 216. The third column gives the only two differences in the calculation for the Srutis, namely 204, 198 units of the Ri Sthanam, according to Ganapati Row Gopala Row Barve of Ahmedabad who had followed the system of Parijatam. We feel glad that he has minutely followed Parijatam as far as possible. Besides this, there is also something noteworthy in his Swarasthanams as regards Ri. The Sootram of Parijatam which says that Komala Ri should be located in the length between Adhara Sa and Ri is capable of two interpretations, some saying that there should be three Srutis for Ri according to Sarnga Dev and others giving only two. Here, although we have given Komala Ri to be $\frac{25}{27}$ to suit the opinion of Pratapa Ramaswami Bhagavatar who follows the division into three according to Sarnga Dev, yet we believe that the system of Barve which divides it into two giving 204 units or $\frac{17}{18}$ instead of 200 units to Komala Ri is far more preferable. Again, Barve gives Ri 198 units or $\frac{11}{12}$. This foreshadows the possibility of another Ri between $\frac{8}{9}$ and $\frac{17}{18}$.

Of the four units 216, 204, 198 and 192, if we omit 216 or Adhara Sa, we get three Srutis. But according to the common idea that Ri should have four Srutis we get the following four with a difference of 6 between, namely, 192, 198, 204 and 210. If $\frac{8}{9}$ were made $\frac{32}{36}$, the above four become $\frac{32}{36}$, $\frac{33}{36}$, $\frac{34}{36}$ and $\frac{35}{36}$ respectively. If we thus get the four Srutis of the Ri then the method of Parijatam is something good. Of the other Swarams, Ga, Teevra Ga, Ma, Pa, Ni and Teevra Ni more or less resemble the

Swarams of the Veena. We have never come across a method which is so very accurate while proceeding by measurements alone. The other Swarams also are more or less accurate and not so glaringly different as those of others. If we substitute the $\frac{15}{16}$ of Barve in place of $\frac{25}{27}$, the 12 Swarams of Parijatam will exactly correspond to the 12 Swarams of the Veena. The author of Parijatam says there are 22 Srutis which are derived by the SA-PA system. In the same breath he says he follows the system of Narada and gives the above method. This should be noted. This makes us suppose there must have been an instrument which had its Swarams marked according to his measurement. He must have made that instrument the basis of his calculations. We conclude, therefore, that there must have been a system named after Narada which is the correct system of the present day, from the following facts:—The author of Parijatam says that he follows the method of Narada. Narada is called Yalasrian, in Silappadhikaram the ancient Tamil treatise. There was at one time a Veena called Narada Veena. There was a musical treatise called Naradeeyam or Panchabharateeyam. He was called the son of Brahma. In spite of all this, the method for those with a good musical ear will never agree with this method which is only meant for others. These methods were given for the benefit of the latter which will be only approximately correct. This method was only an approximate one so that those who began with it might in course of time learn to tune their instruments by the ear. But there is not much difference between the two methods. The slight differences in the Swarasthanams of this method and other details may be seen in the following Tables.

The third column of the above Table gives the 12 Swarams and their measurements in the wire, the fourth column gives their fractions while the sixth, their respective cents. In the 6th column

the second Swaram or RI_2 gets 204 cents,
the fourth Swaram or GA_2 gets 404 „
the fifth Swaram or MA_1 gets 498 „
the seventh Swaram or PA gets 702 „
the tenth Swaram or NI_1 gets 1018 „
the eleventh Swaram or NI_2 gets 1106 „
and the twelfth or Tara SA gets 1200 „

Here we find there is approximately a difference of 100 cents between each of the Swarams. The 1st, the 3rd, the 6th, the 8th and the 9th Swarams get a little over 100 cents each. Their difference is due to the fractional division of the wire. Though the fractions $\frac{8}{9}$ and $\frac{3}{4}$ are the only ones that agree with the previous calculations, the other Swarams more or less agree with those of the Karnatic music which cannot be said of the Srutis of others.

Looking a little more deeply we find the interval of the two Swarams between the second and the fourth Srutis (*i.e.*, 204 to 404) is 200 cents. Secondly, the interval between the first and the ninth Swarams (*i.e.*, between 133 and 933) is 800 cents *i.e.*, 100 cents for each Sruti. Thirdly, the interval between the sixth and the ninth Srutis is (933-631) 302 cents, for the three Srutis. All these distinctly show that each Sruti should have 100 cents.

TABLE 33.

The view of Parijatam as regards Srutis occurring in Indian Music.

No. of Swaram or Sruti.	Name of Swaram or Sruti.	Location of Swarams in a wire 32 inches long.	Fraction of Swarams if Adhara SA be 1.	Decimal fractions of Swarams if Adhara SA be 1.	Cents.	Cents for the intervals between Srutis.	The Number of vibrations of each Swaram if SA=540.	The Number of vibrations of each Swaram if SA=240.	Measurements of Srutis in wire if the whole wire is 216.	The difference.
● 1	● 2	● 3	● 4	● 5	● 6	● 7	● 8	● 9	● 10	● 11
	S ஸ	32·00	1	1·0000			540·00	240·00	216	
						133				16
1	R_1 ரி$_1$	29·63	25/27	·9259	133		583·20	259·20	200	
						71				8
2	R_2 ரி$_2$	28·44	8/9	·8889	204		607·50	270·00	192	
						112				12
3	G_1 க$_1$	26·67	5/6	·8333	316		648·00	288·00	180	
						88				9
4	G_2 க$_2$	25·33	19/24	·7917	404		682·10	303·16	171	
						94				9
5	M_1 ம$_1$	24·00	3/4	·7500	498		720.00	320·00	162	
						133				12
6	M_2 ம$_2$	22·22	25/36	·6944	631		777·60	345·60	150	
						71				6
7	P ப	21·33	2/3	·6667	702		810·00	360·00	144	
						151				12
8	D_1 த$_1$	19·56	11/18	·6111	853		883·64	392·73	132	
						80				6
9	D_2 த$_2$	18·67	7/12	·5833	933		925·71	411·43	126	
						85				6
10	N_1 நி$_1$	17·78	5/9	·5556	1018		972·00	432·00	120	
						88				6
11	N_2 நி$_2$	16·89	19/36	·5278	1106		1023·16	454·74	114	
						94				6
12	s ஸ்	16·00	1/2	·5000	1200		1080	480	108	

The Calculations in Columns marked ● are our own.

He determines the Swarasthanams being cognisant of the difference, even during his time, between the Dwavimsati Srutis and the Srutis in use in the Ragas. He gives the method for generating Ragas with the help of the 12 Swarams only saying that he omits the other 10 as they are open to doubt and not in practical use. We should not think lightly of the fact that he has taken these 12 Swarams only.

If, in an age when Dwavimsati Srutis were in practice, he established only the 12 and rejected the ten, musicians of the time would have taken him to task. Evidently they were silent because only these 12 Swarams were in actual use. From that time up to the present day, it is clearly seen that musicians who sing Ragas as well as writers on Srutis only use these 12 Swarams as the fundamental ones. Seeing there was the same doubt as regards the other Swarams even then, as it is now, to clear the doubt once for all, he rejected the doubtful ten and established only the 12, and thus saved music from a great danger. Thenceforward, the objections raised against the 22 Srutis were not so virulent. To those who consider deeply, his system would certainly appear an ancient one as clear as daylight. For, the SA-PA system implies that each Swaram used in a Ganam should have the right measurement common to the series, should agree in sound with its *fifth*, and should have a difference which should be common to the progressive series. A comparison as to how far the Swarams obtained by the SA-PA series and the Swarams according to Parijatam which discusses the Srutis in an octave agree with one another may be seen from the Table which gives the Srutis of South Indian music.

After having learnt some of the Sanskrit Slokas of Parijatam with the help of those who are eminent in Sanskrit literature and music we have interpreted them in the correct manner and have given the measurements. We presume they are correct, as the same measurements are given by Bhandarkar and Barve. Though there is a slight difference as regards the two RIs with 99 and 151 cents respectively, given by Barve, we conclude he is not wrong in interpreting them in such a manner.

Twelfth.

The opinion of Rao Sahib R. Bhandarkar, B.A., L.M.S., of Edward Hospital, Indore, as regards the Swarams in Indian Music.

We think it right to give the opinion of the above gentleman as he is in many respects the best of the writers on Srutis of Indian music we came across his essay on Srutis in Indian Music in the "Indian Musical journal" edited by Veena Krishna Rao, the Samasthana Vidwan of Mysore. We requested the gentleman to send us further contributions if any, seeing that he was so interested in music. Accordingly we obtained a few more essays which he had written to "the Indian Antiquary." Out of which we quote below what he says on Srutis in the Indian Music journal.

"The Indian Music Journal, 1912 May and June Issue, Volume II. No. 2 Page 42--43 edited by Mr. H. P. Krishna Row, B.A., Mysore.

" For instance, the following experiment may be tried. Ahobila, author of the S. P. gives the tuning of the four wires of the vina as anumandra SA, anumandra PA, mandra Sa and mandra PA. This is also one of the recognised modes of tuning with the Carnatic school. This tuning does not necessitate a recourse to the scale of equal temperament. But for practical purposes of playing we must not have more than twelve notes to the octave and we shall have therefore to make a selection in the case of chromatically altered notes. [Of course there is no such restriction in the case of the human voice or stringed instruments without frets.] I would suggest the following values for the twelve notes, using the nomenclature of the modern Hindustani school :—

WIRE I.		WIRE II.	
SA =	1	PA =	$\frac{3}{2}$
Komala RI =	$\frac{16}{15}$	Komala DHA =	$\frac{8}{5}$
RI =	$\frac{10}{9}$	DHA =	$\frac{5}{3}$
Komala GA =	$\frac{6}{5}$	Komala NI =	$\frac{9}{5}$
GA =	$\frac{5}{4}$	NI =	$\frac{15}{8}$
MA =	$\frac{4}{3}$	Mandra SA =	2
Tivra MA =	$\frac{45}{32}$	Mandra Ko RI =	$\frac{32}{15}$

WIRE III.		WIRE IV.	
SA =	2	PA =	3
Komala RI =	$\frac{32}{15}$	Komala DHA =	$\frac{16}{5}$
RI =	$\frac{20}{9}$	DHA =	$\frac{10}{3}$
Komala GA =	$\frac{12}{5}$	Komala NI =	$\frac{18}{5}$
GA =	$\frac{5}{2}$	NI =	$\frac{15}{4}$
MA =	$\frac{8}{3}$	Madhya SA =	4

This is the arrangement for the first six frets. The remaining frets should be so adjusted as to produce on wire IV notes with accepted intervals. As in the case of the other tuning, the first three wires are to be used only for the production of notes lower than the note of the fourth wire open. Unfortunately with this tuning it is not at all easy to find the correct positions for the frets as in the other case, and it would be necessary to do the work with the help of proper tuning-forks if tolerable accuracy is to be secured. Having built such an instrument, it would be interesting to compare the performance with that of one tuned to equal temperament. I need hardly add that the performance will have to be judged by competent persons."

TABLE 34.

The Table showing the opinion of Bhandarkar as regards the Swarams in use in Indian Music.

No. of Swaram or Sruti.	Name of Swaram or Sruti.	Location of Swarams in a wire 32 inches long.	Fraction of Swarams if Adhara Sa be 1.	Intervals between Srutis.	Decimal fractions of Swarams if Adhara Sa be 1.	Cents.	Cents for the intervals between Sruti	The Number of vibrations of each Swaram if Sa-540.	Number of vibrations of Swarams if Sa-240.
1	2	3	4	5	6	7	8	9	10
	S ஸ	32·00	1		1·0000	0		540	240
				16/15			112		
1	R_1 ரி$_1$	30·00	15/16		·9375	112		576	256
				25/24			70		
2	R_2 ரி$_2$	28·80	9/10		·9000	182		600	266⅔
				27/25			134		
3	G_1 க$_1$	26·67	5/6		·8333	316		648	288
				25/24			70		
4	G_2 க$_2$	25·60	4/5		·8000	386		675	300
				16/15			112		
5	M_1 ம$_1$	24·00	3/4		·7500	498		720	320
				16/15			112		
6	M_2 ம$_2$	22·50	45/64		·7031	610		768	341⅓
				135/128			92		
7	P ப	21·33	2/3		·6667	702		810	360
				16/15			112		
8	D_1 த$_1$	20·00	5/8		·6250	814		864	384
				25/24			70		
9	D_2 த$_2$	19·20	3/5		·6000	884		900	400
				27/25			134		
10	N_1 நி$_1$	17·78	5/9		·5556	1018		972	432
				25/24			70		
11	N_2 நி$_2$	17·07	8/15		·5333	1088		1012·50	450
				16/15			112		
12	s ஸ	16·00	½		·5000	1200		1080	480

The Calculation in Columns marked ● are our own.

When we look into the above Table and notice some of his statements we find that he mentions 12 Swarams in an octave which should be of equal measurement. He distinctly says that our ancient music never admitted of Srutis with unequal intervals. But his measurements show four different kinds of intervals, $\frac{17}{18}$, $\frac{33}{34}$, $\frac{35}{36}$ and $\frac{143}{144}$; and the order of the 12 Swarams is according to that of Clements, Deval and Nagoji Row. He also says clearly that the 12 Swarams belong to Hindustani music. We could not say further on his theories as we do not know what his views are. But when we find that he rejects the 10 Srutis on which there is a difference of opinion and chooses only the 12, we are led to believe that he does not view the 10 Srutis to be correct.

Further, he says that the Karnatic system is superior and that the determination of Swarams by the Veena is highly reliable. Further, he gives the following calculations of Parijatam as regards the Srutis.

The Indian Music Journal, 1912 May and June Issue, Vol. II No. 2.

Making these corrections this scale stands thus: --

OPEN STRING = 1

Sa =	1	Pa =	$\frac{2}{3}$
Ko-Ri =	$\frac{17}{18}$	Ko-Dha =	$\frac{17}{27}$
Su-Ri =	$\frac{11}{12}$	Su-Dha =	$\frac{11}{18}$
Su-Ga =	$\frac{5}{6}$	Su-Ni =	$\frac{5}{9}$
Ti-Ga =	$\frac{19}{24}$	Ti-Ni =	$\frac{19}{36}$
Su-Ma =	$\frac{3}{4}$	Tara-Sa =	$\frac{1}{2}$
Ti-Ma =	$\frac{13}{18}$		

In the 36th and 37th pages he critisises the view of G. G. Barve as his does not resemble that of Parijatam in the Rishabha Sthanams though it agrees in other respects.

From the above table, we see that he gives the same fractions for Srutis as are found in Table 33 in p. 380 which gives the system of Parijatam. Evidently he has interpreted the system given in Parijatam distinctly as given in the book. He gives things as they are and not like other writers who attempt to improve upon Parijatam and give different calculations. His measurements are clearly stated in Table 35, where we see that with the exception of the 3rd Swaram or $\frac{5}{6}$, the 5th Swaram or $\frac{3}{4}$, the 7th Swaram or $\frac{2}{3}$, the 10th Swaram or $\frac{5}{9}$, the other seven resemble those of the other writers.

To conclude, we must say that though he was well aware of the opinions of Parijatam, he has changed his views to suit Western music, contrary to his own conviction.

TABLE 35.

Bhandarkar's interpretation of Parijata's slokas regarding the Srutis practised in Indian Music.

No. of Swaram or Sruti.	Name of Swaram or Sruti.	Location of Swarams in a wire 32 inches long.	Fraction for Swarams if Adhara Sa be 1.	Decimal fractions of Swarams if Adhara Sa be 1.	Cents.	Cents for the intervals between Srutis.	The Number of vibrations of each Swaram if Sa=540.	The Number of vibrations of each Swaram if Sa=240.	Measurements of Srutis in wire if the whole wire is 216.	The difference.
❀ 1	❀ 2	❀ 3	❀ 4	❀ 5	❀ 6	❀ 7	❀ 8	❀ 9	❀ 10	❀ 11
	S ஸ	32.00	1	1·0000			540·00	240·00	216	
						133				16
1	R_1 ரி$_1$	29·63	25/27	·9259	133		583·20	259·20	200	
						71				8
2	R_2 ரி$_2$	28·44	8/9	·8889	204		607·50	270·00	192	
						112				12
3	G_1 க$_1$	26·67	5/6	·8333	316		648·00	288·00	180	
						88				9
4	G_2 க$_2$	25·33	19/24	·7917	404		682·10	303·16	171	
						94				9
5	M_1 ம$_1$	24.00	3/4	·7500	498		720·00	320·00	162	
						133				12
6	M_2 ம$_2$	22·22	25/36	·6944	631		777·60	345·60	150	
						71				6
7	P ப	21·33	2/3	·6667	702		810·00	360·00	144	
						151				12
8	D_1 த$_1$	19·56	11/18	·6111	853		883·64	392·73	132	
						80				6
9	D_2 த$_2$	18·67	7/12	·5833	933		925·71	411·43	126	
						85				6
10	N_1 நி$_1$	17·78	5/9	·5556	1018		972·00	432·00	120	
						88				6
11	N_2 நி$_2$	16·89	19/36	·5278	1106		1023·16	454·74	114	
						94				6
12	s ஸ்	16·00	1/2	·5000	1200		1080·00	480·00	108	

The Calculations in Columns marked ❀ are our own.

Thirteenth.

The opinion of Mr. G. G. Barve as regards the Swarams in use in Indian Music.

The Indian Musical Journal May and June 1912 Vol. II No. 2 edited by Mr. H. P. Krishna Rao, B. A., Page 36 and 37.

" In very recent years the verses in the Samgita Parijata which give the Scale by describing the necessary division of a stretched string, have attracted considerable attention. The first writer to my knowledge, to bring them to the public notice in print was Mr. Ganapatrao Gopal Rao Barve of Ahmedabad. According to his interpretation of the verses the division of the stretched string is as follows.

Samgita-Parijata's scale according to Mr. Barve's interpretation.

Open String = 1

Sa =	1	Pa =	$\frac{2}{3}$
Ko—Ri =	$\frac{17}{18}$	Ko—Dha =	$\frac{11}{18}$
Su—Ri =	$\frac{8}{9}$	Su—Dha =	$\frac{7}{12}$
Su—Ga =	$\frac{5}{6}$	Su—Ni =	$\frac{5}{9}$
Ti—Ga =	$\frac{19}{24}$	Ti—Ni =	$\frac{19}{36}$
Su—Ma =	$\frac{3}{4}$	Tara—Sa =	$\frac{1}{2}$
Ti—Ma =	$\frac{25}{36}$		

This interpretation is quite correct except for the note Su. Ri. and consequently, except for Ko. Ri. also. *Sapavoh purvabhage cha, sthapaniyo tha ri swarah.* It must be admitted that these lines are loosely worded."

The following table gives the calculations of Barve for the theory of Parijatam.

We find from the above Table that all Swarams are correct with the exception of the first two Sthanams *i. e.* Komala Ri and Suddha Ri. This too seems to have resulted from the particular interpretation of the Sootram " Sapayoh purvabhage cha, sthapaniyo tha Ri swarah." He locates Ga dividing the $\frac{1}{3}$ of the length of the wire between Sa and Pa into two. That is $\frac{1}{3} \times \frac{1}{2} = \frac{1}{6}$; $1 - \frac{1}{6} = \frac{5}{6}$. The fraction $\frac{11}{12}$ between Sa and Ga or $\frac{5}{6}$, he calls Ri. That is $1 - \frac{5}{6} = \frac{1}{6}$; $\frac{1}{6} \times \frac{1}{2} = \frac{1}{12}$; and $1 - \frac{1}{12} = \frac{11}{12}$. This is 151 cents. Further, he divides the half length below it into three equal parts and locates Komala Ri there. In other words, Komala Ri is $1 - \frac{11}{12} = \frac{1}{12}$; $\frac{1}{12} \times \frac{1}{3} = \frac{1}{36}$; $\frac{11}{12} + \frac{1}{36} = \frac{17}{18}$. This is 99 cents. We may find that there is another Swaram by the side of it which has nearly 50 cents. For $\frac{5}{6} = \frac{30}{36}$. Then the 7 Swarams of the series are $\frac{30}{36}$, $\frac{31}{36}$, $\frac{32}{36}$, $\frac{33}{36}$, $\frac{34}{36}$, $\frac{35}{36}$ and $\frac{36}{36}$ which is Sa. $\frac{30}{36}$ or $\frac{5}{6}$ is Ga. So $\frac{31}{36}$ may become another Ga. We have said already that $\frac{33}{36}$ occurs as a half Sruti in the interval below Ga with 151 cents. He divides the interval by the side of this into three equal parts and locates another Swaram which is $\frac{34}{36}$ or $\frac{17}{18}$, with 99 cents. But Bhandarkar gives here another Swaram $\frac{32}{36}$ or $\frac{8}{9}$ with 204 cents. For, the interval between Sa and Pa is divided into 3 equal parts and the Swaram located in the first. $1 - \frac{2}{3} = \frac{1}{3}$; $\frac{1}{3} \times \frac{1}{3} = \frac{1}{9}$; $1 - \frac{1}{9} = \frac{8}{9}$. This is Suddha Ri, and the interval below it is divided into 3 parts and the first part or $\frac{25}{27}$ is called Komala Ri with 133 cents. We conclude, then, that the Komala Ri must also have an interval of 100, just as we have shown the 2nd, the 4th, the 5th, the 7th, the 10th, the 11th and the 12th Swarams have. So, the Komala Ri of Barve $\frac{17}{18}$ with 99 cents must be the real first Swaram.

TABLE 36

The opinion of Barve as regards the Swarams in use in Indian Music, according to the system of Parijatam.

No. of Swaram or Sruti.	Name of Swaram or Sruti.	Location of Swarams in a wire 32 inches long.	Fraction for Swarams if Adhara Sa be 1.	Cents.	Cents for the intervals between Srutis	The Number of vibrations of each Swaram if Sa-540.	Measurements of Srutis in wire if the whole wire is 216.	The difference.
		@		@	@	@	@	@
1	2	3	4	5	6	7	8	9
	Sa ஸ	32·00	1	0	0	540	216	
1	Ko - Ri கோ - ரி	30·22	17/18	99	99	571·77	204	12
2	Su - Ri ச - ரி	29·33	11/12	151	52	589·09	198	6
3	Su - Ga ச - க	26·67	5/6	316	165	648·00	180	18
4	Ti - Ga தீ - க	25·33	19/24	404	88	682·10	171	9
5	Su - Ma ச - ம	24·00	3/4	498	94	720·00	162	9
6	Tiv - Ma தீ - ம	22·22	25/36	631	133	777·60	150	12
7	Pa ப	21·33	2/3	702	71	810·00	144	6
8	Ko - Dha கோ - த	19·56	11/18	853	151	883·64	132	12
9	Su - Dha ச - த	18·67	7/12	933	80	925·71	126	6
10	Su - Ni ச - நி	17·78	5/9	1018	85	972·00	120	6
11	Ti - Ni தீ - நி	16·89	19/36	1106	88	1023·16	114	6
12	Sa ஸ	16·00	1/2	1200	94	1080	108	6

The Calculations in Columns marked @ are our own.

It will be more or less consistent with the regular order of Swarams if we accept the Ri of Bhandarkar ($\frac{9}{8}$ or 204 cents), and the Komala Ri of Barve ($\frac{18}{17}$ or 99 cents). The Sootram we have quoted above is capable of being interpreted either way. " Sapayoh Poorvabhage Cha" means, divide the interval between Sa and Pa into three parts and locate Ri in the Poorva bhaga or the first part. We get by this means Ri which is $\frac{9}{8}$. This is how it is commonly interpreted. The other interpretation is, Ga comes between Adhara Sa and Pa, Dha between Pa and Tara Sa, so Ri and Dha may come in the middle of the Purva Bhaga between Adhara Sa and Ga, and Pa and Dha. We may also assume Sa-Ga as Poorvabhagam and Ga to Pa as Oottarabhagam and take the middle of Sa to Ga or Poorvabhagam. As he does not say that three divisions should be made and as he divides Sa to Pa and Pa to Sa into two equal parts he might mean that this interval should also be divided into two parts, the former of which will be Poorvabhagam. It appears that Barve has also interpreted this in the same manner.

It appears that if we accept the Ri between Sa and Ga which is $\frac{12}{11}$ with 151 cents we also accept the other two Ris, $\frac{18}{17}$ with 99 cents, and $\frac{9}{8}$ with 204 cents. By this method we may obtain all the Srutis in the octave.

We find from the remarks of Dr. Bhandarkar about Barve, that the latter printed and circulated the system of Parijatam as regards determining Srutis. So he deserves all praise as being the first who attempted the system of determining the Srutis in Indian music.

On the whole, we conclude that his 12 Swarams more or less resemble the 12 Srutis of Karnatic music.

Fourteenth.

The opinion of Fox Strangways for determining the Srutis in use in Indian Music.

We know that this gentleman travelled a good deal and took great pains to gather information about the customary and traditional use of Indian music. When he came to South India in the course of his travels in 1912, we were given to understand that he was anxious to get information about Indian music and wanted our help. So when we met, we asked him whether he wanted any information about the Srutis or Ragas in use. He said that he was not particularly anxious to get information about those points. However, we shall do well to say a few words about his tables of Srutis published in 1914 in his "Music of Hindustan."

Music of Hindostan by Fox Strangways P. 115, 116.

"In the following diagram, column I gives the constituent elements of each note in terms of the Major Tone ($a=\frac{9}{8}$), the minor Tone ($b=\frac{10}{9}$), and the Semitone ($c=\frac{16}{15}$). Columns IV and V give the representative fractions, distributed into 'quintal' (those derived from the fifth ($\frac{3}{2}$) alone) and 'tertian' (those derived jointly from the fifth and the third $\frac{5}{4}$). Column II gives the equivalent of these in cents and column III their differences (or, speaking in ratios, their quotients) Columns VI and VII are adjustments proposed by Mr. Clements on the strength of observations taken by Mr. Deval of Poona on a dichord; his two tertian intervals are a Fourth apart, and his two septimal, a Fifth. [Septimal intervals are derived from the septimal seventh $\frac{7}{4}$=969 cents.]

Music of Hindostan by Fox Strangways P. 118.

"First, the Carnatic system 'merges'; it recognizes not twenty two, but only sixteen nominal and twelve real sub-divisions of the scale."

In the first col. of the above Table the 26 Srutisthanams, and in the second col. he gives the 22 Srutis he has chosen out of them. The third column gives the names of the Srutis and the following Swarams are given their alternate ones. RI_1, MA_3, DHA_1, and NI_4, which are specially marked. In the fifth col. we see the fractions for the Srutisthanams and in the sixth, their cents calculations.

Of these Sthanams, we find that, with the exception of $\frac{81}{80}$, the first Sthanam, [illegible] the 17th and [illegible] the 25th, the rest are found in the Table of Srutis of Clements and [illegible] in that of Deval. We have noticed already how Clements and Deval say that their Srutis belong to Hindustani music only. In the same way, Strangways seems to give the Srutis for Hindustani Music and recognises only 12 Swarams definitely for Karnatic Music. But it is to be noted that their Dwavimsati Srutis do not agree with those of Saranga Dev and their Sruti intervals are not in uniform order but varied as 84, 28, 70, 22 and 90. This enables us to say that there is no agreement between the Srutis of Sarnga Dev, the Dwavimsati Srutis and the Srutis of these writers. This may be clearly understood from the table of Srutis of Sarnga Dev.

TABLE 37.

The table of Fox Strangways which gives the Srutis in use in Indian Music.

Names and No.		Constituents.	Cents.	Differences.	Fractional Ratios. Quintal.	Fractional Ratios. Tertian.	Adjustments. Cents.	Adjustments. Ratios.	
		I.	II.	III.	IV.	V.	VI.	VII.	VIII.
Ni.	22.	3a+2b+2c	1200		2	2	...	...	C
				(90					
	21.	[Samvadi to No. 8]	[1110]		...	(243 : 128)			♯ B
			1108				1108	256 : 135 (tertian)	
				22)					
Dha.	20.	3a+2b+ c	1088		...	15 : 8	...		B
				70					
	19.	3a+ b+2c	1018		...	9 : 5	...	...	B♭
				22					
	18.	2a+2b+2c	996		16 : 9	...	...	...	♭ B♭
				90					
Pa.	17.	3a+ b+ c	906		27 : 16	...	...	...	A
				22					
	16.	2a+2b+ c	884		...	5 : 3	...	...	A
				70					
	15.	2a+ b+2c	814		...	8 : 5	...	...	A♭
				22					
	14.	a+2b+2c	792		128 : 81	...			♭ A♭
			787				787	63 : 40 (septimal)	
				90					
Ma.	13.	2a+ b+ c	702		3 : 2	...			G
				22					
	12.	a+2b+ c	680			40 : 27			♯ F♯
				70					
		a+ b+2c	610			64 : 45	} 610	64 : 45 (tertian)	
				20					
	11.	2a+ b	590			45 : 32			F♯
				70					♯
	10.	(2a+ c)	(520)		...	(27 : 20)	...	...	F
				22					
Ga.	9.	a+ b+ c	498		4 : 3	...	...	...	F
				90					
	8.	(2a)	(408)		(81 : 64)	...	...	...	♯ E
				22					
Ri.	7.	a+ b	386		...	5 : 4	...	...	E
				70					
	6.	a+ c	316		...	6 : 5	...	...	E♭
				22					
	5.	b+ c	294		32 : 27	...	...	...	♭ E♭
				90					
Sa.	4.	a	204		9 : 8	...	...	...	D
				22					
	3.	b	182		...	10 : 9	...	...	♭ D
				70					
	2.	c	112		...	16 : 15	...	...	D♭
				(90					
			84				85	21 : 20 (septimal)	
	1.	[Samvadi to No. 10]	[22]		...	[81 : 80]			♭ D♭
				22)					
Ni.	0.		0		1	1	...	...	C

The table on the opposite page wile help in understanding this easily.

TABLE 38.

The Table of Srutis of Fox Strangways

(Adapted from Sangeeta Ratnakaram).

No. of Swaram or Sruti.		Name of Swaram or Sruti.	Location of Swarams in a wire 32 inches long.	Fraction of Swarams if Adhara SA be 1.	Cents.	Cents for the intervals between Srutis	The Number of vibrations of each Swaram if SA=540.
●		●	●				●
1	2	3	4	5	6	7	8
		S ச	32·00	1	0	0	540
						22	
1	1 {	R_1 ரி$_1$	31·60	80/81	22		546¾
						63 } 90	
2		R_1 ரி$_1$	30.48	20/21	84		567
						28	
3	2	R_2 ரி$_2$	30·00	15/16	112		576
						70	
4	3	R_3 ரி$_3$	28.80	9/10	182		600
						22	
5	4	R_4 ரி$_4$	28·44	8/9	204		607½
						90	
6	5	G_1 க$_1$	27.00	27/32	294		640
						22	
7	6	G_2 க$_2$	26·67	5/6	316		648
						70	
8	7	G_3 க$_3$	25·60	4/5	386		675
						22	
9	8	G_4 க$_4$	25·28	64/81	408		683⅓
						90	
10	9	M_1 ம$_1$	24·00	3/4	498		720
						22	
11	10	M_2 ம$_2$	23·70	20/27	520		729
						70	
12	11 {	M_3 ம$_3$	22.76	32/45	590		759⅜
						20 } 90	
13		M_3 ம$_3$	22·50	45/64	610		768
						70	
14	12	M_4 ம$_4$	21·60	27/40	680		800
						22	
15	13	P ப	21·33	2/3	702		810
						84 } 90	
16	14 {	D_1 த$_1$	20·32	40/63	786		850½
						6	
17		D_1 த$_1$	20·25	81/128	792		853⅓
						22	
18	15	D_2 த$_2$	20·00	5/8	814		864
						70	
19	16	D_3 த$_3$	19·20	3/5	884		900
						22	
20	17	D_4 த$_4$	18·96	16/27	906		911¼
						90	
21	18	N_1 நி$_1$	18·00	9/16	996		960
						22	
22	19	N_2 நி$_2$	17·78	5/9	1018		972
						70	
23	20	N_3 நி$_3$	17·07	8/15	1088		1012½
						20 } 22	
24	21 {	N_4 நி$_4$	16·88	135/256	1108		1024
						2	
25		N_4 நி$_4$	16·86	128/243	1110		1025¼
						90	
26	22	S ச	16	1/2	1200		1080

The Calculations in Columns marked ● are our own.

Fifteenth.

The opinion of Chinnasami Mudaliar, M. A., as regards the Srutis of South Indian Music.

The above author has published a book on music where the Ragas and Ragamalikas of South Indian music are represented in English *Staff notation*. Here he seems to approve of the 72 Melakartas based on the 12 fundamental Swarams. However, we shall sift his opinion also as regards Srutis. In the first place, he gives a Table showing the names of Srutis as used among the Italians, the French, the German and the English musicians and their calculations. And side by side, he gives the names and the calculations as used by South Indian musicians. He points out how there is a slight difference of opinion among the various nations. So we need not dwell very much on this question.

He says, " The Chief Musical nations of Europe have also adopted different names for distinguishing the Vikriti Bedhas of the several notes ; the following comparative table exhibits in one view their nomenclature as well as their mathematical values from a strictly scientific point of view (N.B. The last column is inserted merely to show the corresponding Indian names ; the notes are not identical with the European varieties printed in the same parallel columns, nor are their mathematical values exactly the same."

The following Table 39 must be compared with Table 40, and the calculations given in cols. 5 and 6 of Table 39 may be easily understood by a look at the subsequent table.

We notice 20 Srutisthanams in the above Table. Though the number appears to be 21, yet when we notice $\frac{33}{32}$ above Sa, and ·92 above Adhara Sa this appears to be a Swaram below Madhya Sthayi. So we say there are 20 Swarasthanams. But if we accept 17·39 (½ of 34·78) above the 19th Sthanam we shall have 21 Srutis. Besides this, the Swarams against 3, 5, 6, 7, 8, 11, 13, 14, 15, 16, 17, 19 and 20 in col. 1 are the notes of the Enharmonic scale. Their cents calculations and their difference and their vibrations are found in other columns.

We have already seen how Pa taken as equivalent to $\frac{3}{2}$ and Ma to $\frac{4}{3}$ will never help the music of South India.

Besides this Table he gives another showing the names of Srutis and Vikriti Bedhas. We shall consider that Table also.

In the above Table, the names of the 22 Srutis are found in col. 11, and their corresponding English names in col. 10. The Sapta Swarams to which new names are given by Govinda Dikshitar are to be seen in col. 8. Apart from this, the measurements and fractions for the 22 Srutis are not indicated. So we are unable to make any remarks on them. Moreover, as the opinions of writers differ as regards Prakriti and Vikriti Swarams, we are not able to say anything as regards them also. The difference in Srutisthanams of different writers of ancient times has been already clearly dealt with in Tables 26, 27, 28, 29, 30 and 31.

All his music has been based upon the 16 fundamental Swarams formed by the combination of Prakriti and Vikriti Swarams. Though these are in a way the Swarams used in South Indian music, he does not give their mathematical calculations.

He further says, that we should not trouble ourselves with the determination of Srutis which is an intricate affair but that the 12 frets of the Veena are quite enough for all practical purposes. So we conclude that his view is not to support the cause of the 22 Srutis.

TABLE 39.

The chief *Musical* nations of Europe have also adopted different names for distinguishing the *Vikriti Bedhas* of the several notes ; the following Comparative table exhibits in one view their nomenclature as well as their *Mathematical* values from a strictly scientific point of view. (N. B. The last column is inserted merely to show the corresponding Indian NAMES ; the notes are not identical with the European varieties printed in the same parallel columns, nor are their mathematical values exactly the same—vide remarks infra on *Melakartas*.)

No.	Nomenclature used in Harmony.	Signature.	Intervals.	Relative vibration No.	Ratio.	Italian Names.	French Names.	German Names.	English. Names.	Tonic sol-fa Names.	Indian Names.	
1	2	3	4	5	6	7	8	9	10	11	12	
1	Tonic or Keynote.	♭	Diminished first ...	·9200	25:23	Do bemolle	Ut bémol	Ces	C flat	...	...	
		♮	First or unison ...	1·0000	1:1	Do	Ut	C	C	D	Sa	Shadjama.
		♯	Augmented first ...	1·0417	24:25	Do diesis	Ut dièse	Cis	C sharp	De	...	
2	Super tonic ...	♭	Minor second ...	1·0800	25:27	Re bemolle	Re bémol	Des	D flat	Ra	Ra	
		♮	Major second ...	1·1250	8:9	Re	Re	D	D	R	Ri	Rishaba.
		♯	Augmented second.	1·1719	64:75	Re diesis	Re dièse	Dis	D sharp	Re	Ru	
3	Mediant ...	♭	Minor third ...	1·2000	5:6	Mi bemolle	Mi bémol	Es	E flat	Ma	Ga	
		♮	Major third ...	1·2500	4:5	Mi	Mi	E	E	M	Gi	Gándhàra.
		♯	Augmented third...	1·3021	96:125	Mi diesis	Mi dièse	Eis	E sharp	Me	Gu	
4	Subdominant	♭	Diminished fourth	1·2800	25:32	Fa bemolle	Fa bémol	Fes	F flat	...	...	
		♮	Perfect fourth ...	1·3333	3:4	Fa	Fa	F	F	F	Ma	Madhyama.
		♯	Augmented fourth	1·3889	18:25	Fa diesis	Fa dièse	Fis	F sharp	Fe	Mi	
5	Dominant ...	♭	Diminished fifth ...	1·4400	25:36	Sol bemolle	Sol bémol	Ges	G flat	Sa	...	
		♮	Perfect fifth ...	1·5000	2:3	Sol	Sol	G	G	S	Pa	Panchama.
		♯	Augmented fifth ...	1·5625	16:25	Sol diesis	Sol dièse	Gis	G sharp	Se	...	
6	Submediant or Superdominant.	♭	Minor sixth ...	1·6000	5:8	La bemolle	La bémol	As	A flat	La	Dha	
		♮	Major sixth ...	1·6667	3:5	La	La	A	A	L	Dhi	Daivata.
		♯	Augmented sixth	1·7361	72:125	La diesis	La dièse	Ais	A sharp	Le	Dhu	
7	Leading note or Subtonic.	♭	Minor seventh ...	1·8000	5:9	Si bemolle	Si bémol	Bes	B flat	Ta	Na	
		♮	Major seventh ...	1·8750	8:15	Si	Si	B	B	T	Ni	Nishàda.
		♯	Augmented seventh	1·9531	64:125	Si diesis	Si dièse	Bis	B sharp	Te	Nu	
8	Octave ...	♮	Perfect eighth ...	2·0000	1:2	Do	Do	c	C	D	Sa	Shadjama.

TABLE 40.
The Sruti Scale of Chinnasawmy Mudaliar.

No. of Swaram or Sruti.	Name of Swaram or Sruti.	Location of Swarams in a wire 32 inches long.	Fraction of Swarams if Adhara SA be 1.	Decimal fractions of Swarams if Adhara SA be 1.	Cents.	Cents for the intervals between Srutis	The Number of vibrations of each Swaram if SA=540.	Number of vibrations of Swarams if SA=240.
1	2 ⊛	3 ⊛	4	5	6 ⊛	⊛ 7	8 ⊛	9 ⊛
1		34·78	25/23	·9200			496·80	220·80
2	S_1	32·00	1	1·0000	0		540·00	240·00
3	S_2	30·72	24/25	1·0417	71	71	562·50	250·00
4	R_1	29·63	25/27	1·0800	133	62	583·20	259·20
5	R_2	28·44	8/9	1·1250	204	71	607·50	270·00
6	R_3	27·31	64/75	1·1719	275	71	632·81	281·25
7	G_1	26·67	5/6	1·2000	316	41	648·00	288·00
8	G_2	25·60	4/5	1·2500	386	70	675·00	300·00
9	G_3	25·00	25/32	1·2800	427	41	691·20	307·20
10	M_1	24·58	96/125	1·3021	457	30	703·13	312·50
11	M_2	24·00	3/4	1·3333	498	41	720·00	320·00
12	M_3	23·04	18/25	1·3889	569	71	750·00	333·33
13	P_1	22·22	25/36	1·4400	631	62	777·60	345·60
14	P_2	21·33	2/3	1·5000	702	71	810·00	360·00
15	P_3	20·48	16/25	1·5625	773	71	843·75	375·00
16	D_1	20·00	5/8	1·6000	814	41	864·00	384·00
17	D_2	19·20	3/5	1·6667	884	70	900·00	400·00
18	D_3	18·43	72/125	1·7361	955	71	937·50	416·67
19	N_1	17·78	5/9	1·8000	1018	63	972·00	432·00
20	N_2	17·07	8/15	1·8750	1088	70	1012·50	450·00
21	N_3	16.38	64/125	1·9531	1158	70	1054·69	468·75
	S_1	16·00	1/2	2·0000	1200	42	1080·00	480·00

The Calculations in Columns marked ⊛ are our own.

TABLE

Oriental Music by

"The number of variable sounds within an octave which could be clearly distinguished by could not produce pleasing melodic effects when taken together in succession, some had to be with others for purposes of determining the position of frets on the *Vina*. (In the subjoined state- they are not identical with the other names in common use, and that even their redistribution under the Prakriti and Vikriti Bhedas.)

SAPTA SVARAS.	PRAKRITI.		VIKRITI.			Total number of varieties.
			Notes Retained.		Notes Rejected.	
	Distinct notes.	Identical with others.	Distinct notes.	Identical with others.		
1	2	3	4	5	6	7
1. Shadjam ... Sa	...	...	...	...	Achyuta...	1
	Suddha ...	...	...	...	...	2
	...	...	...	...	Chyuta ...	3
2. Rishabham ... Ri	...	...	...	...	Sadharana	4
	Suddha ...	...	...	...	...	5
	...	...	Chatusruti	...	...	6
	...	...	...	Shatsruti	...	7
3. Gandharam ... Ga	...	Suddha ...	...	...	...	8
	...	...	Sadharana	...	...	9
	...	...	Antara	...	...	10
4. Madhyamam ... Ma	...	...	...	...	Achyuta...	11
	Suddha ...	...	...	...	...	12
	...	...	Prati ...	...	Chyuta ...	13
5. Panchamam ... Pa	...	...	...	...	Trisruti ...	14
	Suddha ...	...	...	...	...	15
	...	...	...	...	Kaisiki ...	16
6. Dhaivatam ... Dha	Suddha ...	...	...	...	...	17
	...	...	Chatusruti	...	...	18
	...	...	...	Shatsruti	...	19
7. Nishadam ... Ni	...	Suddha ...	...	...	...	20
	...	...	Kaisiki ...	...	...	21
	...	...	Kakali ...	...	...	22
Total number of audible notes. ...	5	2	7	2	6	22
Actual number of Semitones. ...	5	...	7	...	...	12
Number of notes recognised and in ordinary use ...	5	2	7	2	...	16

41.

Chinnasami Mudaliar, M. A., P. 41.

the refined ear was found to be about twenty two as shown below; but as a good number of these rejected and some retained; while a few of the latter had to be treated as more or less identical ment, the names of the 22 Srutis are given merely for purposes of comparison; it will be seen that the 7 main notes, differs from the ordinarily accepted division into semitonic intervals, comprising

Varicties retained Govinda Dikshita's nomenclature.	Approximate European equivalents		Names of the 22 srutis more or less corresponding to these varieties.
	Syllabic.	Alphabetical.	
8	9	10	11
...	To	C. Flat ...	Sa { Tivra, Kumudvati, Manda, Chhandovati
Sa	Do	C. Natural ...	
...	Tê	C. Sharp ...	
...	... ...	... ...	Ri { Dayavati, Ranjani, Ratika
Ra	Ro	D. Flat ...	
Ri	Rê	D. Natural ...	
Ru	Ri	D. Sharp ...	
Ga	Mo	E. Double flat...	Ga { Raudri, Krodha
Gi	Mi	E. Flat ...	
Gu	Mê	E. Natural ...	
...	Fo	F. Flat ...	Ma { Vajrika, Prasarini, Priti, Marjani
Ma	Fa	F. Natural ...	
Mu	Fê	F. Sharp ...	
... ...	So	G. Flat ...	Pa { Kshiti, Rakta, Sandipini, Alapini
Pa	Sol	G. Natural ...	
...	Sê	G. Sharp ...	
Dha	Lo	A. Flat ...	Dha { Madanti, Rohini, Ramya
Dhi	La	A. Natural ...	
Dhu	Lê	A. Sharp ...	
Na ...	Jo ...	B. Double flat...	Ni { Ugra, Kshobhini
Ni	Si	B. Flat ...	
Nu	Jê	B. Natural ...	
16	21	21	22
...	12	12	...
16	12	12	...

Sixteenth.

The Enharmonic scale of the Western Musicians.

The Swarams used by the Western Scientists are in the order of 1, [illegible], [illegible], [illegible], [illegible], [illegible], [illegible], 9/10, [illegible] and [illegible]. (Vide Table 42).

The [illegible], the [illegible], the [illegible], the [illegible], the [illegible], the [illegible], the 9/10, and the [illegible] found in lines 19, 11, 8, 7, 6, 4, 3 and 2 are the measurements for the Swarams respectively. Here SA-PA is [illegible]. All writers (as seen from their tables) say that the majority of these Swarams are in use in their 22 Srutis. The difference in their measurements is given in cents in col. 7 of the Table. The difference of each of the Srutis in cents is given here. Here the Swarams are of five different measurements. This is nothing but the result of the wrong measurement of 3/4 and 2/3 for PA and MA, carried by Pythagoras from India. No music is possible with these measurements.

1. Though it resembles that of Parijatam in many respects, it does not entirely correspond with it.

2. It does not resemble either the view of Sangeetha Ratnakaram which advocates the SA-PA system.

3. Nor does it proceed on the principle of [illegible] from the beginning to the end of the Octave.

4. It does not correspond to the right system of Sarnga Dev.

5. The 22 Srutis of Sarnga Dev could never be reconciled with this.

6. Perhaps it may suit Hindustani music, but this we are not quite sure of.

TABLE 42.
Enharmonic Scale.

No. of Swaram or Sruti.	Name of Swaram or Sruti.		Location of Swarams in a wire 32 inches long.	Fraction for Swarams if Adhara SA be 1.	Cents.	Cents for the intervals between Srutis.	The Number of vibrations of each Swaram if SA-540.	The Number of vibrations of Swarams if SA-240.	The Number of vibrations of each Swaram if SA-256.
⊕ 1	⊕ 2	⊕ 3	⊕ 4	⊕ 5	⊕ 6	⊕ 7	⊕ 8	⊕ 9	⊕ 10
	C	S_1	32·00	1	0	71	540·00	240·00	256·00
1	C♯	S_2	30·72	24/25	71		562·50	250·00	266·67
2	D♭	R_1	30·00	15/16	112	41	576·00	256·00	273·00
3	D♭	R_1	28·80	* 9/10	182	70	600·00	266·67	284·44
4	D	R_2	28·44	8/9	204	22	607·50	270·00	288·00
5	D♯	R_3	27·31	64/75	275	71	632·81	281·25	300·00
6	E♭	G_1	26·67	5/6	316	41	648·00	288·00	307·20
7	E	G_2	25·60	4/5	386	70	675·00	300·00	320·00
8	F	M_1	24·00	3/4	498	112	720·00	320·00	341·33
9	F♯	M_2	22·76	32/45	590	92	759·38	337·50	360.00
10	G♭	P_1	22·22	25/36	631	41	777·60	345·60	368·64
11	G	P_2	21·33	2/3	702	71	810·00	360·00	384·00
12	G♯	P_3	20·48	16/25	773	71	843·75	375·00	400·00
13	A♭	D_1	20·00	5/8	814	41	864·00	384·00	409·60
14	A	D_2	19·20	3/5	884	70	900·00	400·00	426·67
15	A♯	D_3	18·20	128/225	977	93	949·22	421·88	450·00
16	B♭♭	N_1	18·00	* 9/16	996	19	960·00	426·67	455·11
17	B♭	N_1	17·78	5/9	1018	22	972·00	432·00	460·80
18	B	N_2	17·07	8/15	1088	70	1012·50	450·00	480·00
19	C	S	16·00	1/2	1200	112	1080·00	480·00	512·00

The Calculation in Columns marked ⊕ are our own.

Some exclude 9/10 and 9/16 and take the rest 17.

Table 43 gives the chief intervals for some of the Swarams accepted by Western musicians. These have been taken from the 332nd page of Ellis's "Sensations of Tone", and from the 50th page of "Text Book on Sound" by Barton. The Srutis and their fractions are given below :—

37th	[illegible]	10th	[illegible]	36th	16/15 × 1/2 = 8/15	27th	[illegible] × [illegible] = [illegible]	22nd	[illegible] × [illegible] = [illegible]	31st	[illegible] × [illegible] = [illegible]
26 ,,	[illegible]	8 ,,	9/10	35 ,,	[illegible] × 1/2 = [illegible]	23rd	[illegible] × [illegible] = [illegible]	20th	[illegible] × [illegible] = [illegible]	12th	[illegible] × [illegible] = [illegible]
17 ,,	[illegible]	6 ,,	[illegible]	29 ,,	[illegible] × 1/2 = [illegible]	11th	[illegible] × [illegible] = [illegible]	19th	[illegible] × [illegible] = [illegible]	16 ,,	[illegible] × [illegible] = [illegible]
15 ,,	[illegible]	3rd	[illegible]	28 ,,	[illegible] × 1/2 = [illegible]	30 ,,	[illegible] × 5/6 = [illegible]	21st	[illegible] × [illegible] = [illegible]	13 ,,	9/10 × [illegible] = [illegible]
14 ,,	[illegible]	1st	[illegible]	34 ,,	[illegible] × [illegible] = 9/16	24 ,,	3/4 × 9/10 = 27/40	33rd	[illegible] × [illegible] = [illegible]	5 ,,	[illegible] × [illegible] = [illegible]
										2nd	[illegible] × [illegible] × [illegible] = [illegible]

The first 15 Swarams are generally held as important. Many other Swarams may also be derived when we multiply the Srutis by different methods. But these will never suit the Karnatic Music.

When the Srutis proceed by multiplication, the Octave never comes to an end but has a few cents more or less. The interval that is thus over and above or less is called the *Comma*. We have already noted that when we proceed to determine the series of a scale by the measurements of 2/3 and 3/4 in a string we find Pa to be slightly flatter than 2/3, and Ma to be slightly sharper than 4/3. We need not repeat it here again.

Western scientists recognise,

The series, 1, 8/9, 4/5, 3/4, 2/3, 3/5, 8/15 and 1/2 as the Major Scale,

The series 1, 8/9, 5/6, 3/4, 2/3, 5/8, 5/9 and 1/2 as the Descending Minor Scale,

The series 1, 9/10, 4/5, 3/4, 2/3, 3/5, 9/16 and 1/2 as the Mode of the Fourth or Madhyama Gramam,

The series 1, 9/10, 4/5, 3/4, 2/3, 3/5 9/16 and 1/2 as the Mode of the Minor Seventh or Kaisika Nishada Gramam.

And the series, 1, 15/16, 5/6, 3/4, 2/3, 5/8, 9/16 and 1/2 as the mode of the Minor Sixth or Komala Dhaivata Gramam.

But all this does not suit the music of South India, it is clearly seen. We had to draw the attention of our readers to this Enharmonic scale because many have copied the fractions of this scale for their 22 Srutis and we wanted to prove that these Swarams will never suit the Karnatic music. We have shown by various Tables that the measurements 2/3 and 3/4 are but rough and approximate and that the Octave will never come to an end if we go by them. But, inasmuch as the concensus of opinion is that Sarnga Dev accounts for his 22 Srutis by the measurements 2/3 and 3/4 though some of them doubt it, and as we should necessarily find out the real view of Sarnga Dev and his measurement for Srutis, we now proceed to the view of Sarnga Dev as regards Srutis.

TABLE 43
CHIEF INTERVALS WITHIN AN OCTAVE.

Intervals.	No.	Diatonic Names.	Positions of the intervals in a 32" String. ●	Marks.	Equivalent Fractions.	Cents.	Vibrations if the Vibrations for Unison is 540. ●	Just Intonation, Meantone and other Names.
1	2	3	4	5	6	7	8	9
Unison ...		C	32·00			0	540·00	...
Minor Seconds ...	1		31·60	†	80/81	22	546·75	The Comma. J. I.
	2		31·25	†	125/128	42	552·96	G ♯ to A ♭. Mt. Great Diesis.
	3	C ♯	30·72	†	24/25	70	562·50	D to D ♯. J. I.
	4		30·63	†	67/70	76	564·18	C to C ♯ or Small Semitone. Mt.
	5		30·34	†	128/135	92	569·53	C to C ♯. J. I. Larger Limma
	6	D ♭	30·00	‡	15/16	112	576·00	Diatonic Semitone. J. I.
	7		29·91	†	100/107	117	577·80	Diatonic Semitone. Mt.
Major Seconds ...	8	D	28·80	‡	9/10	182	600·00	Small whole Tone. J. I. or Minor Tone.
	9		28·62	†	161/180	193	603·73	Every whole Tone. Mt.
	10	D	28·44	‡	8/9	204	607·50	Large whole Tone. J. I. or Major Tone.
	11	E ♭♭	28·13	*	225/256	224	614·40	Diminished minor Third.
Minor Thirds ...	12	D ♯	27·31	*	64/75	275	632·81	Augmented Tone.
	13	E ♭	27·00	*	27/32	294	640·00	Pythagorean minor Third.
	14	E ♭	26·67	‡	5/6	316	648·00	Minor Third. J. I.
Major Thirds ...	15	E	25·60	‡	4/5	386	675·00	Major Third. J. I.
	16	F ♭	25·00	*	25/32	427	691·20	Diminished Fourth.
Fourths ...	17	F	24·00	‡	3/4	498	720·00	Fourth. J. I.
	18		23·93	†	80/107	503	722·25	Fourth. Mt.
	19	F	23·70	*	20/27	520	729·00	Acute Fourth.
Sharp Fourths or Flat Fifths.	20	F ♯	23·04	*	18/25	569	750·00	Superfluous Fourth.
	21	F ♯	22·76	*	32/45	590	759⅜	Tritone.
	22	G ♭	22·50	*	45/64	610	768·00	Diminished Fifth.
	23	G ♭	22·22	*	25/36	631	777⅗	Acute diminished Fifth.
Fifths ...	24	G	21·60	*	27/40	680	800·00	Grave Fifth.
	25		21·40	†	109/163	697	807·52	Fifth. Mt.
	26	G	21·33	‡	2/3	702	810·00	Fifth. J. I. also Pythagorean.
Minor Sixths ...	27	G ♯	20·48	*	16/25	773	843¾	Grave superfluous Fifth.
	28	A ♭	20·00	‡	5/8	814	864·00	Minor Sixth. J. I.
Major Sixths	29	A	19·20	‡	3/5	884	900·00	Major Sixth. J. I.
	30	A	18·96	*	16/27	906	911¼	Pythagorean major Sixth.
	31	B ♭♭	18·75	*	75/128	926	922·00	Just diminished Seventh.
	32		18·29	†	4/7	969	945·00	Trumpet Seventh. J. I.
	33	A ♯	18·20	*	128/225	977	949⅗	Extreme sharp Sixth.
Minor Sevenths...	34	B ♭	18·00	‡	9/16	996	960·00	Minor Seventh. J. I.
	35	B ♭	17·78	‡	5/9	1018	972·00	Acute minor Seventh. J. I.
Major 7th.	36	B	17·07	‡	8/15	1088	1012·50	Major Seventh. J. I.
Octave ...	37	C	16·00	‡	1/2	1200	1080·00	Octave. J. I. and Mt.

*‡ Common to Messrs. Ellis and Barton. † Mentioned by Mr. Barton. * Mentioned by Mr. Ellis.*
J. I. Stands for Just Intonation and Mt. for Meantone.
The Calculations in Columns marked ● are our own.

Seventeenth.

IV.—The Sruti System of Sarnga Dev.

The Dwavimsati Srutis of South Indian music according to Sangeeta Ratnakaram.

Though many are of opinion that it is quite possible to determine the 22 Srutis in Indian music and to bring them to practical use, yet it seems to be a hopeless task owing to the conflicting opinions of the writers on the subject. Some of them have studied the Srutis of Hindustani music, and have given their opinion, while others pick out a line here and a line there from ancient authors and try to palm them off as their own. However, we will do well to point out the contradiction in their theories first and then speak about the Srutis in use in South Indian music. For, it is manifest from the writings of the above authors that they merely adopted the term Dwavimsati Srutis of Sarnga Dev and marked the Swarasthanams without trying to understand his real meaning in the determination of Srutis. Some gave Tables of Srutis which applied only to Hindustani music, which resembled more or less the modes of the Western musicians. Others copied the same Western modes, altering only a few Swarams here and there, and called them the Srutis of South Indian music. But it makes one smile to think that all these conflicting theories are palmed off as the Dwavimsati Srutis of poor Sarnga Dev!

The above writers merely made the term Dwavimsati Srutis the burden of their song, without understanding the real meaning and dignity of Sangeeta Ratnakaram, and distributed the Srutis in the octave in any way they liked. It is clear that they have not grasped even an iota of the meaning of Sarnga Dev. It is impossible to reconcile an ancient and impracticable theory with a modern one. The ancient works should be examined in the light of modern criticism, and all that is impracticable should be given up, and all that is good should be accepted. An ancient work may continue to be good even at the modern day, but it may also be superseded by a modern work owing to exigencies of time. It is the duty of wise men to discriminate between the two and hold fast that which is good. It is not advisable either to give up an ancient work which is good on the plea of its being impracticable now; on the other hand, an ancient work which conflicts with the modern practicability must certainly be discouraged. We shall understand presently that the system of Sarnga Dev is alien to South Indian music just as it does not suit the music of the North. We have to examine here the system of Sarnga Dev because Sangeeta Ratnakaram is held in high esteem as the standard work on Indian music. So we shall determine the Srutis according to his system and compare them with those of other writers who also swear by him, and then draw our own conclusions and not blindly grope about in the dark like the above writers.

The very fact that the octaves as they proceed should have the vibration of their Srutis in Geometrical progression shows that music of the ancient days was highly efficient. Just as the octaves proceed in the ratio of 1, 2, 4, 8 etc., so also the Swarams should do, he says. This should be carefully noted. Many have erred because they did not note this. We might clear all our doubts if we examine the 22 Srutis mentioned in his book, how they stand when the Gramams are changed and how far they agree. The different opinions given by the various writers on the 22 Srutis, namely, Sahasrabuddhi, Raja Surendra Mohan Tagore. Deval, Clements, Nagoji Row, Barve, Dr. Bhandarkar, Manickya Mudaliar who wrote Sangeeta Chandrika, Chinnasami Mudaliar, M.A., Subramania Sastrial, Panchapakesa Bhagavatar, Pratapa Ramasami Bhagavatar and others, made us conclude that the opinion of Sarnga Dev must be something different. The following Tables will show that the above writers who determined the Srutis, having his book as their authority, have gone clean out of his track as regards the Srutis. So we shall do well to find out the Srutis first according to his system, prove their correctness by seeing whether they stand the test of change of Gramam, and then compare them with the calculations of those who have interpreted him. Then we shall come to the conclusion either that these are not Dwavimsati Srutis or that the author of Ratnakaram gives a completely different view.

The main idéa of Sarnga Dev as regards Srutis given in his Chapter on Swarams is as follows:—

"An idea in the mind generates Agni, which in its turn generates Vayu. This Vayu proceeds upwards from the Brahmakranthi or Mooladharam through the stomach, the heart, the trunk, the head and the mouth in the shape of Nadam. In these five places, Nadam obtains the five corresponding names of Ati Sookshmam, Sookshmam, Pushtam, Apushtam and Krithrimum. The Nadam increases in intensity in the ratio of 1, 2 and 4 being Mandaram in the heart, Madhyamam in the trunk and Taram in the head. The sound which is thus produced has 22 varieties. The sound which could be distinctly heard is called Sruti. There are two breathing apparatuses going upwards from the heart which are called Idaikalai and Pinkalai. There are 22 (Nadis) arterial passages across these 22. When the air passes through them these passages dilate and the sound comes out. In the same manner there are 22 Sthanams in the trunk and the head. This may be proved with the help of two Veenas.

Have two Veenas with 22 strings each. In the first Veena, tune one of the strings so as to produce the lowest possible sound. Tune the second string so that it might sound the next possible note. No sound should be possible between the two. Arrange and tune all the wires on the same principle. Now the wires are arranged and tuned in a progressive series. Of these Sa has 4 Srutis. Fix the 4th of these Srutis as the Sa. Ri will have 3 Srutis, or in other words the 5th, the 6th and the 7th strings will be the varieties of Ri. The two Srutis of Ga will stand on the 8th and 9th wires. The four Srutis of Ma will be on the 10th. 11th, 12th and the 13th wires. The 14th, 15th, 16th and the 17th wires will sound the 4 Srutis of Pa, while the 3 Srutis of Dha will occur on the next three strings. The last two strings of the Veena will be responsible for the two Srutis of Ni. One of these Veenas is Dhruva Veena and the other Chala Veena. Alter the strings of the latter as directed below. If you arrange the Seven Swarams commencing them from the 3rd Sruti of Sa instead of the 4th, you will have one Sruti less. If you commence the series from the Second Sruti of Sa, Ga and Ni will obtain one of the Srutis of Ri and Dha. If three Srutis are left out, Ri and Dha will have the 4 Srutis of Sa and Pa. But when you commence the series leaving all the 4 Srutis of Sa on the left, Ri, Ga, and Ma of Dhruva Veena will correspond with the Sa, Ma and Pa of Chala Veena. In other words, Sa commences on the 22nd, Ma on the 9th and Pa on the 13th. By this means, the calculations of Srutis may be obtained. From these Srutis proceed the seven fundamental Swarams Sa, Ri, Ga, Ma, Pa, Dha and Ni.

SA is of two varieties—Suddha SA and Atchyuta SA. When you reduce the 4 Srutis of SA into 3, RI obtains 4 Srutis. In the same way when MA is reduced by one of its Srutis, it becomes Suddha MA. When two of the Srutis of SA are absorbed into Kakali Ni, it is called Achyuta SA. This is a Vikriti Swaram.

In the same way when MA gives two of its Srutis to Anthara GA and has only two Srutis, it is called Achyuta MA. This is also a Vikriti Sruti. When SA, with one Sruti less, commences the 22nd Sthanam, the 23rd Sthanam is Kaisika and the 24th Kakali. Both these Swarams are Vikriti. The SA which comes in the 3rd place after Kakali is Suddha SA. This is also a Vikriti Swaram. MA is likewise Vikriti. In the same manner when MA has only two Srutis it is called Achyuta MA, which is also Vikriti. When MA gets merged into Suddha GA, the first is Sadharana GA and the second, Anthara GA, which is also Vikriti. The MA which has three Srutis less is Suddha MA. When PA has only three Srutis, it is called Trisruti PA, which is also Vikriti. When PA obtains the fourth Sruti of SA, it is called Kaisika PA in spite of its four Srutis. This is also a Vikriti Swaram. When PA has four Srutis less, Dha gets one of the Srutis of PA and thus has four Srutis, which is also a Vikriti. So also when SA has one Srutis less, RI gets 4 Srutis, which additional one is a Vikriti Swaram. To sum up, then, the 12 Vikriti Swarams are:—

Sa—Suddham and Achyutam—2
Ni—Kaisikam and Kakali—2
Dha—while obtaining one of the Srutis of Pa—1
Ri—when obtaining one of Sa—1
Pa—Trisruti Pa and Kaisika Pa—2
Ma—Suddham and Achyutam—2
Ga—Kaisikam and Kakali—2

The Suddha Swarams are 7. The three Swarams are, Ri in SA, MA in GA, and DHA in PA.

The method adopted by Sarnga Dev for determining Swarams could be clearly understood by those who know the working and harmony of nature. There could be nothing there which they cannot understand. This is a place where the high-water mark of South Indian music is clearly seen. Just as it is clearly stated that the Sthayis should proceed at the ratio of 1, 2, 4 &c., so also the Swarams of a Sthayi should proceed with a uniform interval. We shall see how Sarnga Dev proceeds. He says, first take a Veena with 22 strings. Tune the first string so that it may produce the lowest possible sound. The next string must be tuned to sound the next possible note. There must be no possible sound between the two strings. So when the 22 strings are tuned on the above principle, the Srutis ascend in a regular serial order till the octave is reached. This is a natural series, and this has been stated in the easiest language possible. In addition to this he gives the measurement of each Sruti also in the clearest language.. But there is also something occult attached to it. He did not dilate upon it, because he knew that men of learning will easily read between the lines.

When a stone is thrown in the middle of placid water, waves are formed round the central point which gradually increase in diameter and decrease in intensity at a regular uniform interval. The vibrations of a Swaram are of the same nature. The Swarams in a wire proceed upwards at regular uniform intervals, whereas the Sthanams in the wire go on in an inverse ratio. This is what Sarnga Dev meant when he said that the Sthayis should proceed upward at the uniform ratio of 1, 2, 4, 8 &c. If the Swarams proceed at the ratio of 1 to 2 in the first octave, it is 2 to 4 in the second, and 4 to 8 in the third. But the length of wire for each octave is exactly the reverse. If the first octave finishes in the first half of the length of the string, the second octave finishes in the quarter of the length, the third in $\frac{1}{8}$ of the length and the fourth octave in $\frac{1}{16}$ of the length, and so on. The vibrations and length of wire vary in inverse ratio. Just as the first wave in the pond has a large intensity and small diameter, and just as the diameter increases the intensity diminishes, so is the case with sound waves also. Again, when a ray of light from the eye proceeds in a triangular form and falls upon an object, at the apex of the triangle the sight is distinct while it gets obscure at the base. But at the apex the area seen is small, but at the base the area seen is extensive so as to include even two hills. So is the case with sound waves also. Scholars will acknowledge that this rule is true of all objects of nature. The growth of leaves, flowers, petals of flowers, and seeds of grass, herbs and plants, the inner growth of trees, the growth of animals, the growth of pearls, corals, and oysters, and the inner growth of the layers of the earth — all these show a regular uniformity in their upward and onward progress just like sound waves. In the same way, heaven and earth and all creation obey the law of regular growth, support each other in their harmonious working and thus declare the omnipotence of the Creator. We all believe in what the Holy Bible says, "In the beginning was the Word." The whole world was created by the Word and the self same Word was the Life. The same Word was the cause of the variety of Nadam, which manifested itself as the Sapta Swarams, as the different Srutis and later on as Geetams. If Nadam did not obey the law of uniformity there could be no harmony or sweetness.

Sweetness is caused by uniformity. Whether it be colours, or sounds, or tastes, or qualities, or smells, or sensations of touch or knowledge, unless they be proportionately made up, they will be abhorred by every one. If in an article which is compounded of five different ingredients, there is one more or less, it will not taste well. This is our every day experience. The same with taste. In the same manner, if sound, its harmony and the calculations of it in a wire vary, how could it be sweet? It will be just the reverse. The series of sounds which have no uniform ratio between them will only form an abhorrent discord. Will musicians of repute accept such strange sounds and measurements? Every one must agree that any system, which has no uniformity in length of wire and its corresponding sounds, must be wrong. The very fact that it is said that the octaves must proceed upwards in the ratio of one to two, and that the series must proceed gradually with a uniform interval between them without admitting other possible sounds between, shows that the ancients had clearly understood the uniformity of the law of nature. People are quite at liberty to form their own theories with their own measurements and put them into practical use also. But what we object to is, that they should call it the system of Sarnga Dev!

In spite of the clear statement that the series must be uniformly progressive without admitting other Swarams between, one writer says that the octave should be divided into 22 equal parts.

Another locates Ma in the exact middle of the whole string and distributes 9 Srutis equally in the half length, namely 3 Ris, 2 Gas and 4 Mas. The other half he equally divides into 13 parts, 4 for Pas, 3 for Dhas, 2 for Nis and 4 for Sas.

Yet another mentions 4 Ris as well as 4 Dhas. This class of writers at least made equal divisions of the strings. But knowing that the length of wire will not exactly correspond with the sounds produced, they left off saying anything about the other half of the string.

Yet others, though they say the sounds must be of equal intervals, they forget the fact altogether, give measurements which do not agree either in sounds or the length of the string, and try to multiply them with fractions for equalising them, which has landed them in difficulties. These irregularities have been dealt with altogether. Their chief errors will also be pointed out hereafter from time to time.

How strange it is that the opinions of the ancient musicians of this Bharata-khandam noted for its excellence, and which was the birth place of so many eminent sages should be thus set aside and disregarded! How strange it is that their Sootrams should be changed and mutilated and mis-interpreted and added to in this reckless manner!! The ancients who were strong on account of the excellence of their penance and who were clever in Yogam, Gnanam, Vatham, medicine, astrology, Oviam, Geetam, use of weapons, Mantram, Vasyam and occultism have reserved the keynote of each science for the purpose of teaching it in person to those best fitted to receive it, and so have not stated them explicitly. This fact is mentioned in the books. Some have become perplexed owing to the voluminous pages of the books. Many have discredited them as pure lies. There were only very few who understood those mystic keynotes by learning them in person from those eminent men who knew them. They have said in their works,

"They are so hard-hearted that they will not tell them to every one they see."

"They will not tell the truth to anyone. Those who tell others are ignorant and wicked."

"Try to understand the mystery which is buried without your knowledge and prosper."

"Those who were willing to help wrote works, but hid the mystic truth from others."

"The science that is not learn't with the help of the Guru cannot be acquired even by the sweat of the body."

"It (the mystery) will seem to be plain to the eye of every one, but without the favour of the Guru, it can never be acquired."

The mystery of each science is taught at their last moments to a worthy disciple of theirs whom they could trust. In the chakram with forty triangles which is established in all the temples by Sankaracharíar, the Jagat Guru, all is plain with the exception of one little secret which is the key of the whole chakram, and which is not visible to the ordinary individual. Without knowing the secret key the chakram could never be understood. The key is so arranged that while you say thirteen it really means fourteen, that by an easy sign or writing on the ground you must indicate one should be added. In the same way there are such hidden mysteries in other sciences which cannot be understood unless told by the Guru. The same applies to the science of music. This secret has been revealed from time to time only to a select few and put into practice either by the special favour of God or as a result of unremitting labour. Such secrets pertaining to the science of music and the system of their interpretation will be mentioned later on.

The Calculation of a Sthayi.

What we have to notice specially now is to determine the measurements of Swarams from the fact that the Madhya Sthayi finishes in the first half of the string, and the vibrations of the Swarams from the fact that the Sthayis proceed in Geometrical Progression. Let us assume for this purpose that the length of wire is 32 inches, and the vibrations of Sa 540. The reason for the above assumption will be mentioned under the heading "The Srutis of South Indian music." The measurements of all writers have been reduced to this uniform standard so that they may be easily compared. Lovers of Indian music! We have determined to write at length and bring this affair to a satisfactory conclusion so that others may not laugh at us for quarrelling without understanding each other. But it is not an easy matter to reduce the various measurements to this particular standard. However, we have brought everything to a uniform standard and have given it in the form of Tables which might be easily understood by all.

We know very well that the ancients skilled for ages in the Science of Astronomy have devised mnemonics (Dhruva Vakkiams) for remembering the minute calculations. The primary numbers are called Moola Dhruvams, and the resultant integers are called Varundhruvams (products). Thus they have made this science easy as is seen from their writings here and there. From all this it is clearly seen that our ancestors must have had an easy key for even the most difficult of calculations. As we have no such keys in vogue at the present day we have made use of the Table of Logarithms of an eminent English Mathematician noted for his learning and researches.

The calculations of the Dwavimsati Srutis.

We shall first see how the 22 Srutis are a gradually ascending series beginning from Adhara Sa and ending with Tara Sa which is its double, according to the theory of Sarnga Dev.

The Logarithm of 1 is 0 and that of 2 is ·3010300. Now let us see how the 22 Srutis proceed gradually from 0 to ·3010300 without admitting any interval between. We can obtain the Logarithms for the Sthanams from 1 to 22 if we divide the Logarithm

TABLE 44.

Showing the 22 Srutis of South Indian music according to Sarnga Dev, the author of Sangeeta Ratnakaram.

No. of the Swaram or the Sruti.	Name of the Swaram or Sruti.	Logarithm.	No. of the Logarithm.	No. of vibrations if of Swarams if SA=540.	Decimal fractions showing the places of Swarams if the Adhara SA=1.	The location of Swarams in a wire 32 inches long.	The interval between Srutis.	Cents.	Cents for the interval between Swarams.
1	2	3	4	5	6	7	8	9	10
0	S_1	0	1·000000	540	1·0000000	32·000000	·9925	0	54·54½
1	S_2	·01368318	1·032008	557·28432	0·9689844	31·007501	·9617	54·55	54·54½
2	S_3	·02736636	1·065041	575·12268	0·9389310	30·045792	·9319	109·09	54·54½
3	S_4	·04104955	1·099131	593·53128	0·9098095	29·113904	·9030	163·64	54·54½
4	R_1	·05473273	1·134313	612·52848	0·8815912	28·210918	·8750	218·18	54·54½
5	R_2	·06841591	1·17062	632·1348	0·8542482	27·335942	·8478	272·73	54·54½
6	R_3	·08209909	1·208086	652·3686	0·8277522	26·488102	·8215	327·27	54·54½
7	G_1	·09578227	1·246758	673·2493	0·8020800	25·666560	·7916	381·82	54·54½
8	G_2	·10946545	1·286663	694·8000	0·7772029	24·870493	·7714	436·36	54·54½
9	M_1	·12314864	1·327849	717·0379	0·7530978	24·099130	·7474	490·91	54·54½
10	M_2	·13683182	1·370351	739·989	0·7297400	23·351680	·7243	545·45	54·54½
11	M_3	·15051500	1·414214	763·67556	0·7071068	22·627418	·7018	600	54·54½
12	M_4	·16419818	1·45948	788·1192	0·6851755	21·925616	·6800	654·55	54·54½
13	P_1	·17788136	1·506196	813·34584	0·6639245	21·245584	·6589	709·09	54·54½
14	P_2	·19156455	1·554406	839·37924	0·6433325	20·586640	·6385	763·64	54·54½
15	P_3	·20524773	1·604160	866·2464	0·6233790	19·948128	·6187	818·18	54·54½
16	P_4	·21893091	1·655507	893·9732	0·6040447	19·329430	·5995	872·73	54·54½
17	D_1	·23261409	1·708457	922.5878	0·5853100	18·729920	·5809	927·27	54·54½
18	D_2	·24629727	1·763182	952·1183	0·5671563	18·149000	·5629	981·82	54·54½
19	D_3	·25998045	1·819619	982·5948	0·5495656	17·586099	·5454	1036·36	54·54½
20	N_1	·27366364	1·877862	1014·04548	0·5325206	17·040659	·5285	1090·91	54·54½
21	N_2	·28734682	1·937968	1046·50272	0·5160040	16·512128	·5121	1145·45	54·54½
22	S	·30103000	2·000000	1080·00000	0·5000000	16·000000		1200	

of 2 by 22 and multiply the quotient by the numbers of the Srutisthanams one after another by 1, 2, 3, 4 &c. Now, if we divide the Logarithm of 2 or ·3010300 by 22 we get ·01368318 or the Logarithm of the first Sthanam. This is the Logarithm of the second of the four Srutis of Adhara SA. Multiplying this by 2 we get ·02736636. This is the Logarithm of the third of the Srutis of Adhara SA. Again, if we multiply the Logarithm of the first Sruti by 3 we obtain ·04104955, which is the Logarithm of the fourth SA. Likewise we may arrive at the Logarithms of the 22 Sthanams. They stand in the ratio of $2^{\frac{1}{22}}, 2^{\frac{2}{22}}, 2^{\frac{3}{22}}$ and so on and nothing more. The Logarithms for the 22 Sthanams may be found in column 3 of Table 44. If we determine the numbers for the Logarithms between 1 and 22, we may notice how they gradually rise in an equal ratio between Adhara SA=1 and Tara SA=2. We have stated before that the Logarithm of 1 is 0. Therefore for Logarithm 0 the number is 1. This is Adhara SA. So the Logarithm of the Adhara SA is 0. For Logarithm of the first Sruti or ·01368318 the number is 1·032008. The Logarithm of the second Sruti or ·02736636 obtains the number 1·065041. The same process will give the numbers for the series which may be found in column 4 of the Table. Here we may see clearly how the series proceed gradually with equal intervals. To test the correctness of these figures we have given their decimal fractions also correct to six, seven and even eight places. If we take the decimals only to two or three places they will be found still more easy to demonstrate. However, we shall do well to compare at least four places of decimals so that the calculations may not in course of time get out of reckoning gradually as was the case with the Srutis. Just as we found that the Logarithm of 2 was ·3010300, so we shall see clearly that the Logarithm ·3010300 gets 2 as its number.

The calculation of vibrations for the 22 Srutis.

We know that the theory of Sarnga Dev is—that if the first Sthayi is 1, its Octave must be 2. If Adhara SA is 1, its Octave must be 2. We noticed beforehand the 22 intervals between 1 and 2. In the same way we must observe how the number of vibrations beginning from Adhara SA=540, proceed upwards in equal ratio for the 22 Sthanams. Adhara SA has 540 vibrations per second. This has been noted in column 5 of the Table as 1 × 540=540 or the first number. In the same way, if we multiply the number 1·032008 equal to (the Logarithm of the first Sruti found in col. 4) by 540 we get 557·28432. Likewise, the number 1.065041 equal to the Logarithm of the second Sruti when multiplied by 540 gives 575·12268. So also, the numbers of the Logarithms for the 22 Srutis when multiplied by 540 respectively will give us the number of vibrations found in column 5 of the Table. The 22nd Sruti Sthanam will end with 2 × 540 or 1080 vibrations.

Till now we have noticed at what lengths the 22 Srutis occur in the wire and the number of vibrations of each Sruti. It is better to keep the calculations of the Srutisthanams in decimals and ensure their correctness up to two, three or four places. But if we take the calculations by vulgar fractions, the process of multiplying will cause much difference.

The calculation showing where the 22 Srutis occur in a wire 32 inches long.

We must next proceed to locate the 22 Sruti Sthanams in a wire 32 inches long. The Adhara SA occurs at the commencement and the Tara SA in the exact middle of the whole length of a wire. Therefore we must find out how the 22 Srutis gradually decrease in the length of the wire within half the total length. The Adhara SA has 540 vibrations. It sounds at the Meru which is 1. We have shown in the fifth column of Table 44 how the first Sruti has 557·28432 vibrations. If we divide 540 by 557·28432 we get ·9689844. In the same manner if 540 be divided by 575·12268, which is the number of vibrations of the second Sruti, we get ·9389310. In the same manner, if we proceed to divide 540 by the number of vibrations of the third, the fourth and the fifth etc., Srutis, we will obtain the lengths of the wire given in column 6.

We get ½ or ·5 for the 1080 vibrations opposite the 22nd Sruti. This shows how the 22 Srutis gradually decrease in the length of the wire from Adhara SA which is 1, to Tara SA which is ½ without admitting any other possible Sruti in the interval.

We shall next proceed to note where the Srutis occur in the wire which is 32 inches long. We all know that the Adhara SA sounds in the Meru, and the Tara SA sounds at the 16th inch or one half. These 22 Srutis must occur within these 16 inches, and they must rise step by step from the Adhara SA. Not only they should rise step by step but must not admit of any other Sruti in the interval and the Sthayi must come to an end exactly at half the length of the wire. In the fifth column of the above Table may be found the different lengths of the wire for the 22 Srutis in half the total length. We shall now proceed to locate them.

If we take the Meru to be 1, the 32 inches end there. So it becomes 1 × 32 or 32. This is the first measurement in column 7 of the Table. The first Sruti, or the second of the four Srutis of SA, is ·9689844 of the total length (see the second number in col. 6). If we multiply this by 32 we get 31·007501 which is the second measurement in col. 7. Likewise, if the 2nd, 3rd, 4th, 5th and the 6th Srutisthanams in col. 6 be multiplied by 32 we will be able to get the particular length in which each Swaram should sound. ·5 of the 22nd Sthanam when multiplied by 32 gives us 16. All these measurements are found in col. 7. We may notice a particular uniformity and harmony between the Swarams if we look into these calculations.

The harmony between the Srutis.

Just as the numbers in col. 1 are of a uniform order, just as they increase by a common uniform ratio, in the same way the figures in the other columns also have a certain uniformity in them. Any Sthanam may be taken as the standard and the measurements proceeded with, there will be no difference in the ratio. 1 will be to 4 as 4 is to 7; 7 will be to 10 as 4 is to 7; 5 will be to 9 as 1 is to 5 or 9 is to 13 or 13 is to 17 or 17 to 21. 9 will be to 17 and 13 to 21 just as 1 is to 9. 13 will be to the 3rd number of Tara Sthayi or 25 just as 1 is to 13 or 9 to 21. All measurements in the other columns will have the same uniformity.

We might also go a little deeper and see a little more clearly how these Sruti Sthanams stand in equal proportion to one another without any difference. The number obtained for the Logarithm of the first Sruti in col. 4 when multiplied by itself gives us the figure for the second Srutisthanam. In the same way, if the second be multiplied by the number of the first we obtain that of the third.
For example,

1·032008 × 1·032008 = 1·065041. If this be again multiplied by 1·032008 it gives us 1·099131, the figure for the third Sruti. If this again be multiplied by 1·032008 we get 1·134313, the figure for the fourth Sruti. In the same manner every figure when multiplied by that of the first Srutisthanam gives that of the next Srutisthanam. Again, the figure for the first Sruti in col. 6 namely ·9689844 when multiplied by itself gives the figure for the second Sruti and which if multiplied by that of the first Sruti gives the figure for the third, Etc.
For example,

.9689844 × ·9689844 = ·9389310; and .9389310 × ·9689844 = ·9098095. In the same manner the figure for each Sruti when multiplied with that of the first, will give us the figure for the next. Likewise, if the figure for the fourth Sruti found in cols. 4 and 6 be multiplied by itself we get the figure for the 8th Sthanam which is its *vargam*, and if the same figure be multiplied by itself thrice, we get the figure for the 12th Sthanam which is its *ghanam*, and the same when multiplied four times by itself gives the figure for the 16th Sthanam which is its *varga vargam*. In the same manner, any figure taken, when dealt with according to the above rule, will give us proportionate results.

We might also notice another uniformity. The figure for the first Sruti in col. 4 if multiplied by the figure for the same in col. 6 will give us 1. (1·082008 × ·9689844 = 1). The same holds good if the figures for the second Sruti be so multiplied (1·065041 × ·9389310 = 1). The figures for the 22nd Sruti when multiplied together give us the same result. (2 × ·5 = 1). Men of knowledge will clearly understand these truths.

Again, if we look at the cents calculation in cols. 9 and 10, we may find that they proceed by a common ratio, 54.54 or nearly 54½.

Besides this, the decimal fractions in col. 6 when multiplied in a particular order will always give us the product ½. For example, multiply the figures for Adhara and Tara Sa, or those for the first and the 21st Srutis, or those for the second and the 20th Srutis, or those for the 3rd and the 19th; the result will always be ½. In the same way, if the figures for Adhara and Tara Sa in col. 4 and for the 1st and the 21st, 2nd and the 20th, 3rd and the 19th be multiplied together the product will always be 2. The middle or the 11th Sruti must be multiplied by itself to obtain the same result.

These calculations might be multiplied and explained in many different ways. But what we have said is quite enough to determine the exact position of the Srutisthanams.

This is the method given by Saranga Dev for determining Srutis. We firmly assert that no other method could give the proper measurements, if, according to Saranga

Dev, the two Sthayis must be in the proportion of 1 to 2, and the 22 wires should produce a gradually ascending series of 22 Srutis in the octave without admitting any other sound in the middle. Men of understanding must certainly admit this. Unless the rungs of a ladder are equidistant, it will be impossible to go up and down the ladder. This is our everyday experience. If there is no such uniformity in the ladder of sounds it will be a stumbling block. It is strange that they have not understood this. They are not to blame. They stumbled because they tried to multiply the fractions head downwards. The Srutis also shared the same fate and became a discordant series. Each one believed that he was following the method of Sarnga Dev and it would be inexplicable to others, with the result they all completely strayed away from the method of Sarnga Dev. These writers who said they had all followed the one method, differed very much from each other. And they tried to perpetuate their different methods and tried to reconcile them with those of modern music by obtaining supporters for their respective theories ; yea, they went a step further and invented instruments to support the fraud. They only excite our pity. We fear that South Indian music will share the fate of the ship that is caught in the middle of the ocean during a terrific storm and darkness caused by the eclipse of the Sun in the sign of Thulam (துலாம்.)

Applying the principle of changing the Gramam to their new Swarams which stray away altogether from the principle of Sarnga Dev and finding they are not at all in agreement with his calculations, some of them say that a few Srutis are newly formed in the process. One of them says that three new Srutis generate from the Shadja Gramam, Madhyama Gramam and Gandhara Gramams respectively, while another foreseeing danger in such a process and knowing the Srutis will not agree, quietly omits them. Yet another, hoping that if there were 53 Srutis in the octave the trouble might be got rid of, establishes 53 Sthanams by the Sa-Pa series and says he has picked out 22 out of them. Are not the theories which try to establish 23, 24, 25 and even 53 Srutis in the octave quite contrary to Sarnga Dev and his 22 Srutis? We should particularly note that the 22 Srutis, when subject to change of Gramam, should not vary in their respective calculations or sounds and that they should satisfy the principle of harmony of Vadi and Samvadi. If the 22 Srutis are of a uniform order in calculations as well as sounds, they would certainly stand the test of Vadi and Samvadi in any Gramam, beginning from any Sruti whatever. If two ladders whose rungs are equidistant and of the same size were tied together exactly one over the other or tied in such a way that a rung of one is on any of the rungs of the other either in the three quarters or half or quarter part, they will certainly serve the purpose of going up and down conveniently. But if the two have different kinds of rungs which are not equidistant, the use of them separately will certainly be difficult. But if we attempt to tie $\frac{3}{4}$ of one with the $\frac{1}{2}$ of the other or $\frac{1}{4}$ of one with the $\frac{3}{4}$ of the other the result will be the production of a number of rungs at irregular intervals. The difficulties and objections raised against the system of 22 Srutis are to be traced to their irregular measurements. It will be more to the point if the advocates of the system will reduce to notation the Geetams which they sing and bring it into practical use. On the other hand, they adopt a system which is unnecessary and impracticable, and of which they are ignorant, and carry on a war of words which will certainly not be accepted by men with knowledge. Again, the more they attempt at change of Grahaswaram, the more the absurdities accumulate and land them in difficulties just like the accumulations of dust of the iron pestle of the Yadavakulam. Even these absurdities will have to be noted here. This will help people to understand whether the Srutis according to Saranga Dev or the Srutis according to these authors are correct.

The principle of changing Graham according to Sarnga Dev.

We noticed till now, the system of Sarnga Dev where the 22 Srutis are derived in the octave with the aid of the first Veena with 22 strings where they are arranged in a gradually ascending series without admitting any other sound in the middle. Let us now notice his principle of changing Graham. He says that the seven Swarams occurring in the 4th, 7th, 9th, 13th, 17th, 20th and the 22nd Sthanams of the first Veena should be made to sound in the 3rd, 6th, 8th, 12th, 16th, 19th and the 21st strings of the second Veena. This is exactly the same as beginning the fourth Sruti of Sa from the third Sruti of Sa and proceeding upwards so that the seven original Swarams occur at the Sthanam one Sruti less. In the same manner, if the fourth Sa starts from the second Sa then each Sruti will occur in places 2 Srutis less. So Ga and Ni will occur on Ri and Dha. Thirdly, if the fourth Sa commences on the first Sa, Ri and Dha lose three places and occur on the 2nd, 3rd and the 4th Srutis of Sa and Pa. Fourthly, when the fourth Sa commences on the 22nd Sthanam, Sa occurs on Ni, Ma on Ga, and Pa on Ma.

Beloved Readers! we understand from the work of Sarnga Dev that the names given by our ancestors to the Srutis were causing confusion even during his time. After him many writers have used many Srutis and Sruti names which are entirely conflicting with one another. To make matters worse, some modern writers have invented 53 Srutis and such fancy names as Vadiga and Chodika. So we have only numbered the Srutisthanams so that you may not get confused with the different names and that one right conclusion might be arrived at as regards Srutis. We do not make a display by giving a number of names of which we are not sure. We give only as many names as are necessary for a clear elucidation.

What we have to clearly note is the fact that just as the numbers 1, 2, 3, 4 have a certain uniform ratio between them, just like the regular rungs of a ladder, so these Sthanams are also in regular uniformity with the same ratio in whatever direction they may be taken. If they do not have such a ratio, it is a matter well known to men of understanding, that they will never agree with the first Swaram, when shifted here and there. If the 4 Sas, 3 Ris, and 2 Srutis of Ga were not of equal intervals how could the third Sruti of Ri agree with or coincide with the third Sruti of Sa, and the first Ga with the fourth Sa, when Sa commences on the 22nd Srutisthanam? Sarnga Dev made mention of a superior method where the Swarams also agree in the same manner. It is clear that he never advocated Srutis with unequal intervals.

Those who have doubts might easily clear them if they look at the Table in the next page.

TABLE 45.

The following Tables show clearly some of the remarks made about changing Grahams.

• Shadja Gramam.

According to Sangeetha Ratnakaram.

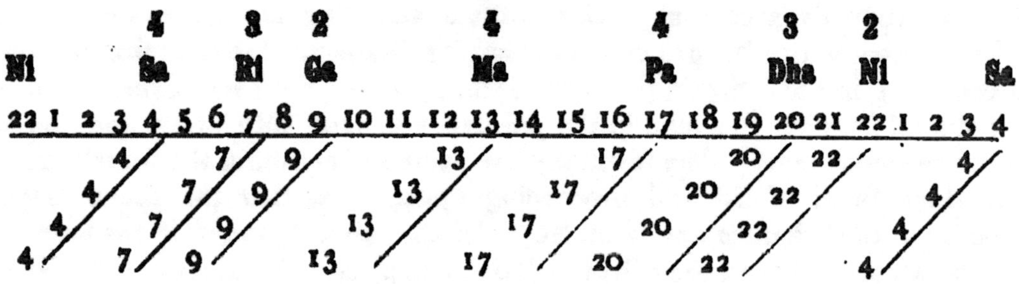

• Madhyma Gramam.

According to Sangeetha Ratnakaram.

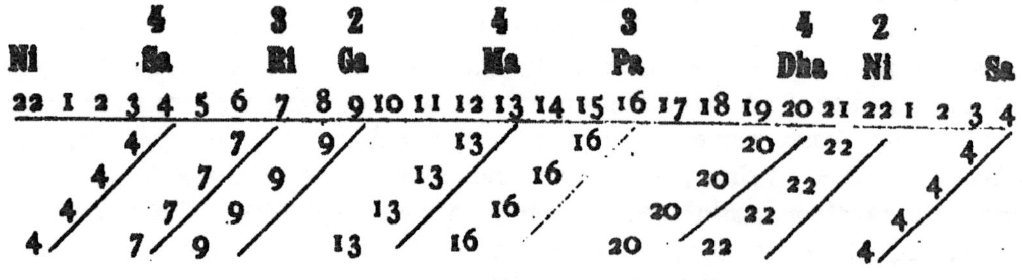

• Gandhara Gramam

According to Sangeetha Ratnakaram.

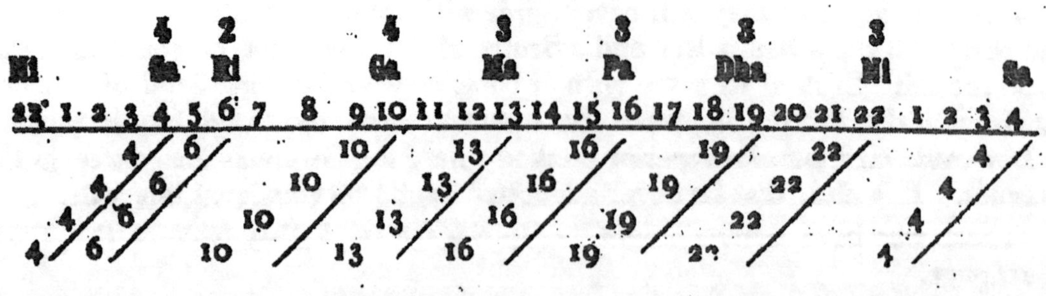

He says that when we take a Sruti less in each case beginning from Sa 4 we get the Moorchanas of the Sapta Swarams. This he calls Shadja Gramam. What we have to note here is, that if Sa should commence from the 22nd Sruti of Ni it is absolutely necessary that there should be a Sthayi below. For the first Sruti should be the lowest possible one, and so any Sthanam below the first Sa cannot possibly exist, for it cannot sound. So we should understand that the change of Graham is possible only from the Madhya Sthayi. We clearly see that for purposes of singing Graha Swaram and fixing the measurements there should be a Sthayi before Madhya Sthayi and one after.

Shadja Gramam.

Now we commence the Shadja Gramam. This has 22 Srutis with 4 Sas, 3 Ris, 2 Gas, 4 Mas, 4 Pas, 3 Dhas, and 2 Nis. Wherever we might commence the 1 Sruti, the Sapta Swarams should be similar in the measurement of the Sruti.

Madhyma Gramam.

In the same manner, this Gramam has 22 Srutis with 4 Sas, 3 Ris, 2 Gas, 4 Mas, 3 Pas, 4 Das and 2 Nis, while the Sapta Swarams should be used in the order of their Srutis in the various Ganams. We also note that Pa has one Sruti less or in other words, the third Sruti of Pa is used as its Pa and the fourth Pa goes along with Dha. While all the other Srutis sound in their own Sthanam, Pa alone sounds in its 3rd Sruti instead of the fourth. All the other Swarams remain Suddha Swarams.

Gandhara Gramam.

Next comes Gandhara Gramam the one that became celestial. He says that this Gramam should also have 22 Srutis with 4 Sas (1, 2, 3, & 4), 2 Ris (5 and 6), 4 Gas (7, 8, 9 and 10), 3 Mas (11, 12 and 13), 3 Pas (14, 15 and 16), 3 Dhas (17, 18 and 19) and 3 Nis (20, 21 and 22). When they change the Graham they must occur with the same regular intervals. Here, all the other Swarams with the exception of Sa, Ma and Ni lose the character of Suddha Swarams. For, the Ri instead of being the 7th Sruti becomes the 6th, the Ga becomes the 10th instead of the 9th Sruti, Pa becomes the 16th instead of the 17th Sruti, and Dha becomes the 19th Sruti instead of the 20th. Here Ri, Pa and Dha have each one Sthanam less, while Ga has one Sthanam more. So four Swarams get shifted from their usual Sthanam thus making Ganam difficult and involved. Perhaps on account of this difficulty all the great vidwans had it banished to the celestial regions. We do not know what other things will share the same fate. We pray that God may save at least the remnants of South Indian music from sharing the same fate.

As Sarnga Dev mentions that it was so banished even before his time, it is clear that it went out of use ages ago. We are afraid that the same might be the fate of the Shadjama and Madhyma gramams belonging to this Ga.

In the Table, the opinion of Sarnga Dev who said that they should have the same harmony while they changed the Graham, is indicated by numbers. For the measurements given by Sarnga Dev for the 22 Srutis have the uniform intervals as in the numbers 1, 2, 3, 4 &c., and those measurements and sounds exactly correspond with these. We have clearly proved there that they would not admit of any other measurement. We need not therefore repeat it here. The measurements found in the Table, when compared with the numbers found in the Table of Gramams, will be found to be exactly the same. They do not differ even in the slightest degree, they do not admit of any unequal intervals in the middle. While matters stand thus, one author boasts that he has discovered 2 more Srutis over 22, (22+2=24), another 3 more Srutis (22+3=25) while yet another claims to have discovered 31 more (or 31+22=53). Men of understanding will never accept these.

The application of Sa-Pa and Sa-Ma measurements to the theory of 22 Srutis of Sarnga Dev.

We know that Sarnga Dev has freely used the Sa-Pa and Sa-Ma systems which stand in the relation of Vadi and Samvadi. He says that where 8 Srutis occur between two Swarams they stand in the relation of Sa-Ma, and where 12 Swarams occur between two they stand in the relation of Sa-Pa. In other words, the 9 Srutis omitting the 1 will form Sa-Ma series, and 13 Srutis omitting the 1, the Sa-Pa series. All Swarams must conform to this system. This implies that if the Srutis were of unequal intervals and measurements they will never agree.

It is to be noted that everyone who advocates any system of Srutis says that he has proceeded by the Sa-Pa and Sa-Ma series. But their Swarasthanams are not of a uniform interval. Though this is contrary to the system of Sarnga Dev they will swear it is his. We have proved clearly by the Tables 15 and 16 on pages (306-307) that the 22 Srutis obtain perfection in Tara Sa, the Sa-Pa series in the 13th Sthayi and the Sa-Ma series in the 9th. The same is repeated in the 9th column of Table 44 which gives the system of Srutis of Sarnga Dev on page (406). When we proceed by nines we get the Sa-Ma series. If we multiply the cents against number 9 by 2 (*i.e.*,) if 490·91 be multiplied by two, we get the cents for the 18th place which is the next one, and then the cents for the fifth Sthanam. So when the cents of the Srutisthanams are multiplied by the numbers 4, 5 and 6 in order, we get those for the 22 Srutis.

In the same manner, if the cents against the 13th Sruti 709·09 be multiplied by 2, 3, 4 and 5 we get the cents for the 22 Srutis of the octave. These intervals are completely perfect without even the slightest difference of a fraction. In this Table if Ma and Pa are reckoned from the fourth Sa they will appear as the 12th and the 16th Sthanams respectively.

We shall presently see that if we do not admit of more than 22 Srutis in the octave according to Sarnga Dev and others, there will be a slight trouble when the change of Graham is made. In order to understand this clearly, let us compare the conflicting opinions of all the advocates of the Dwavimsati Srutis.

Eighteenth.

A comparison of the different opinions of writers as regards the Srutis in use in Indian Music.

We see clearly that among the writers about Sruti, Sarnga Dev is the primary author and that he has followed the method of Bharata who lived long before him. Writers in India and in the Western countries profess to follow the system of Sarnga Dev but in reality they make use of the measurements $\frac{2}{3}$ and $\frac{3}{4}$. But this is not at all the system of Sarnga Dev. They are ready to raise objections when we say that their method is contrary to that of Sarnga Dev. So it is absolutely necessary we should compare his with those of others in measurement, fractions and cents.

TABLE 46.

Here, in this Table, we have marked the measurements of Srutis of different writers in a Veena String which is exactly 16 inches long; which is the first half of a Veena wire 32 inches in length. Their measurements are accurately marked in the Madhya Sthayi 16 inches long. Those who want to test the accuracy of their measurements by sounding them in the Veena might easily mark their Swarasthanams by fixing a long strip of paper 16 inches long against the column opposite their names. They may then fix the frets in their Veenas from the Meru up to 16 inches and verify the Swarasthanams on the Veenas. The bridge of the frets should not be broad but very thin so that they may indicate exact measurements. They must be so made as to be fixed and removed with the greatest ease The Merusthanam should not be high, for then the strings will have to be held tight which might dislocate the Swarasthanams. The difference in frets between the Meru and the other Swarasthanams should be the thickness of a piece of paper and no more. But it must be understood that this is not for the purpose of producing music on the Veena but only for testing the Swarasthanams.

TABLE 47.

This Table marks the Swarasthanams in a wire 32 inches long. This is for the purpose of testing the accuracy of the measurements given before.

TABLE 48.

This Table shows the fractions corresponding to the measurements of Swarasthanams in the wire.

TABLE 49.

This Table gives the cents calculations of the different Sthanams bringing out the difference in the fractions. This will be useful for comparing the different views.

We shall only notice one or two important points here. The measurements of Sarnga Dev found in the first column closely follow his book. Those measurements and their uniformity should be clearly appreciated. The intervals, beginning from Adhara Sa, proceed upwards on a uniform ratio. In the same manner, the sound also increases gradually and finishes with 22 Srutis. We see that his superior system throws that of others completely into the shade. Those who professed to follow his regular method followed really the method of $\frac{2}{3}$ and $\frac{3}{4}$. So the systems of other writers never tally with his. There is a difference of 7 cents between the MA of Sarnga Dev (491 cents) and that of others (498) necessarily. There is also the difference of 7 cents between the PA of Sarnga Dev (709 cents) and that of others (702 cents). If the standard Swarams MA and PA are thus different, what can we expect about others? Measurements by two roads which are different will cause difference and trouble. The Table clearly shows this. Again, to bring out the discrepancy in measurements still more glaringly, if a red line be drawn from RI, in column 1 of Table 46, to all the RI Sthanams of the different writers, the line would never be a straight one. The same will be found as regards GA, DHA and NI and other Swarams. They are not of uniform intervals, nor do they follow Sarnga Dev, nor will they in any way suit Karnatic music.

Some of the Tables of other writers and their opinions have not been added here as they reached us after this Table was prepared.

TABLE 50.

From the above Table we see the different measurements of the Srutisthanam of the various writers. The fractions given by them are converted into the corresponding cents. Their Srutisthanams have also been indicated. Here Ma or $\frac{3}{4}$ with 498 cents occurs at the 24th inch of the wire and has 720 vibrations. Sahasrabuddhi makes it the 11th Sruti, Raja Surendra Mohan Tagore the 9th Sruti, Clements the 10th Sruti, Bhandarkar the 5th Swaram, while it occurs as the 7th Sruti in the Diatonic scale. But the author of Sangeetha Ratnakaram gives out that the Sruti with 491 cents and 717 vibrations occurring at the 24·10th inch of the wire is the 9th Sruti. So we find that $\frac{3}{4}$ is represented by various Srutisthanams as 7, 9, 10 and 11.

In the same manner if we notice Pa or $\frac{2}{3}$ with 702 cents, one gives it as the 10th Sruti, while another 12th, yet another 13th, 14th and the 15th. But according to Sarnga Dev the fraction $\frac{81}{122}$ with 709 cents should be the 13th Sruti. Thus each one gives a different Srutisthanam with many different irregular measurements. Just as the Bhootam appeared when the proverbial well was being dug, those who made efforts to establish the 22 Srutis have been responsible for many more which perplex them altogether! Sarnga Dev, the advocate of 22 Srutis, says in the same breath that there are but really 19 while the other three are the results of different names of the ones already existing. Some give 16 as the number of the Srutis, another gives 17, while another 18, and 20, and 21, and 24, and 25, and 27, and 29 while yet another gives 53 as the number. One of these while trying to establish the 22 Srutis, just as the man who fashioned a Pillayar found that it turned into a monkey, landed in 53 Srutis and finally had to satisfy himself only with 12! He has been responsible for 78 new Srutis in his search after the number of Srutis. They are found in Table 20, page 326-329 Taking into consideration the Srutisthanam mentioned by the others, we find we have a cropful of 158 different Sthanams in all. All these, apart from proving the 22 Srutis of Sarnga Dev, seem to support his statement "that the Srutis are many."

The above Table will clearly show that not one of the 158 Sthanams will agree with those in use in Karnatic music. This will be clearer when we go into the measurements of the Srutis in use in Karnatic music.

TABLE 50.

Table for comparing the different opinions of writers on Srutis and Swarams.

This shows in the first one of half the 32 inches of a wire the Srutis of Mạdhya Sthayi in (1) cents, (2) fractions, (3) measurements. (4) vibrations.

1	2	3	4	5	6	7	8	9	10	11	12	13	14	15	16	17	18	19	20	21	22	23	24	25	26
															Subramania Shastrial.						Parijatam				
Number.	Cents.	Fractions.	Location of Swarams in a wire 32 inches long.	Number of vibrations.	Sangeeta Ratnakaram.	Sahasrabuddhi.	R.S.M. Tagore.	Chinnasami Mudaliar.	Srutis of Western Music.	The diatonic scale.	E. Clements (Gramam).	E. Clements (own.)	K. B. Deval.	C. Nagoji Rau.	Srutis as given in the 3rd Conference.	The 53 Srutis by the Sa-Ma series.	Srutis as given in the 2nd Conference.	Srutis by the Sa-Pa series.	The Sa-Pa and the Sa-Ma series.	The view of Sangeeta Chandrika (Sa-Ma).	Bhandarkar's own.	P. R. Bhandarkar.	G. G. Barve.	Pratapa Ramasami Bhagavatar.	Fox Strangways.
		1	32·00	540	...	...	...	...	...	...	...	...	...	...	...	...	...	...	...	...	...	...	...	...	...
1.	22	80/81	31·60	546·75	...	...	...	...	1	...	...	...	...	...	...	...	1	...	...	...	...	...	...	...	1
2.	23	·9865	31·57	547·4	...	...	...	...	...	...	...	...	...	...	...	...	...	1	...	...	...	...	...	...	...
3.	40	43/44	31·27	552·6	...	1	...	...	...	...	...	...	...	...	...	...	...	...	...	...	...	...	...	...	...
A	42	123/128	31·25	552·96	...	...	...	...	2	...	...	...	...	...	...	...	...	...	...	...	...	...	...	...	...
4.	49	35/36	31·11	555·4	...	...	1	...	...	...	...	...	...	...	...	...	...	...	...	...	...	...	...	...	...
5.	55	125/129	31·01	557·3	1	...	...	...	...	...	...	...	...	...	...	...	...	...	...	...	...	...	...	...	...
6.	67	·9622	30·79	561·2	...	...	...	...	...	...	...	...	...	...	...	1	...	...	...	...	...	...	...	...	...
7.	70	24/25	30·72	562·50	...	...	...	1	3	1	1	...	...	1	1	...	...	...	...	...	...	...	...	...	...
B	76	67/70	30·63	564·18	...	...	...	...	4	...	...	...	...	...	...	...	...	...	...	...	...	...	...	...	...
8.	81	21/22	30·55	565·7	...	2	...	...	...	...	...	...	...	...	...	...	...	...	...	...	...	...	...	...	...
9.	84	20/21	30·48	567·	...	...	...	...	...	...	...	1	1	...	...	...	...	...	...	...	...	...	...	...	2

1	2	3	4	5	6	7	8	9	10	11	12	13	14	15	16	17	18	19	20	21	22	23	24	25	26
10.	90	243/256	30·38	568·9	...	...	...	...	...	...	...	...	...	...	...	1a	...	...	1	1	...	...	...	1	...
11.	92	128/135	30·34	569·5	...	...	...	...	5	...	...	...	...	...	1a	...	...	...	...	...	...	...	...	...	...
12.	99	17/18	30·22	571·8	...	...	2	...	...	...	...	...	...	...	...	...	...	...	...	...	...	...	1	...	...
13.	109	·9389=[illegible]	30·05	575·1	2	...	...	...	...	...	...	...	...	...	...	...	...	...	...	...	...	...	...	...	...
14.	110	·9384	30.03	575·4	...	...	...	...	...	...	...	...	...	...	...	2	...	...	...	...	...	...	...	...	...
15.	112	15/16	30·00	576·	...	...	...	...	6	2	2	2	2	2	2	...	2	...	...	...	1	...	...	2	3
16.	114	·9364	29.97	576·6	...	...	...	...	...	...	...	...	...	...	...	...	...	2	2	...	...	...	...	...	...
C	118	100/107	29·91	577·8	...	...	...	...	7	...	...	...	...	...	...	...	...	...	...	...	...	...	...	...	...
17.	122	41/44	29·82	579·5	...	3	...	...	...	...	...	...	...	...	...	...	...	...	...	...	...	...	...	...	...
18.	133	25/27	29·63	583·2	...	...	...	2	...	...	...	...	...	...	...	...	3	...	...	...	...	1	...	...	...
19.	137	·9238	29·56	584·6	...	...	...	...	...	...	...	...	...	...	...	...	...	3	...	...	...	...	...	...	...
20.	151	11/12	29·33	589·1	...	...	3	...	...	...	...	...	...	...	...	...	...	...	...	...	...	...	2	...	...
21.	164	·9098=[illegible]	29·11	593·5	3	...	...	...	...	...	...	...	...	...	...	...	...	...	...	...	...	...	...	...	...
22.	165	10/11	29·09	594·	...	4	...	...	...	...	...	...	...	...	...	...	...	...	...	...	...	...	...	...	...
23.	180	·9010=[illegible]	28·83	599·3	...	...	...	...	...	...	...	...	...	...	...	3	...	...	3	2	...	...	...	...	...
24.	182	9/10	28·80	600·	...	...	...	...	8	3	3	3	3	3	3	...	...	...	...	...	2	...	...	3	4
D	193	161/180	28·62	603·7	...	...	...	...	9	...	...	...	...	...	...	...	...	...	...	...	...	...	...	...	...
25.	200	·8906	28·5	606·3	...	...	...	...	...	...	...	...	...	...	...	4	...	...	...	...	...	...	...	...	...
26.	204	8/9	28·44	607·5	...	...	4	3	10	4	4	4	4	4	4	...	4	4	4	...	...	2	...	4	5
27.	209	39/44	28·36	609·2	...	5	...	...	...	...	...	...	...	...	...	...	...	...	...	...	...	...	...	...	...
28.	218	·8816=[illegible]	28·21	612·5	4	...	...	...	...	...	...	...	...	...	...	...	...	...	...	...	...	...	...	...	...
E	224	225/256	28·13	614·4	...	...	...	...	11	...	...	...	...	...	...	...	...	...	...	...	...	...	...	...	...
29.	225	640/729	28·09	615·1	...	...	...	...	...	...	...	...	...	...	...	...	5	...	...	...	...	...	...	...	...
30.	227	·8769	28·06	615·8	...	...	...	...	...	...	...	...	...	...	...	...	...	5	...	...	...	...	...	...	...
31.	254	19/22	27·64	625·3	...	6	...	...	...	...	...	...	...	...	...	...	...	...	...	...	...	...	...	...	...
32.	259	31/36	27·56	627·1	...	...	5	...	...	...	...	...	...	...	...	...	...	...	...	...	...	...	...	...	...
33.	267	6/7	27·43	630·	...	...	...	...	...	...	...	...	...	...	...	...	...	...	...	...	...	...	...	...	...
34.	273	·8542=[illegible]	27·34	632·1	5	...	...	...	...	...	...	...	...	...	...	...	...	...	...	...	...	...	...	...	...
35.	275	64/75	27·31	632·8	...	...	...	4	12	5	...	...	...	...	...	...	...	...	...	...	...	...	...	...	...
36.	294	27/32	27.00	640·	...	...	...	...	13	...	5	5	5	5	5	5	...	...	5	3	...	...	...	5	6
37.	300	37/44	26·91	642·2	...	7	...	...	...	...	...	...	...	...	...	...	...	...	...	...	...	...	...	...	...

1	2	3	4	5	6	7	8	9	10	11	12	13	14	15	16	17	18	19	20	21	22	23	24	25	26
38.	314	·8341	26·69	647·4												6									
39.	316	5/6	26·67	648·			6	5	14	6	6	6	6	6	6		6				3	3	3	6	7
40.	318	·8324	26·64	648·7														6	6						
41.	327	.8278 = $\frac{24}{29}$	26·49	652·4	6																				
42.	341	·8212	26·28	657·5														7							
43.	347	9/11	26·18	660·		8																			
44.	365	81/100	25·92	666·7							7														
45.	374	29/36	25·78	670·3			7																		
46.	382	·8021 = $\frac{77}{96}$	25·67	673·2	7																				
47.	384	·8009 = $\frac{6561}{8192}$	25·63	674·24												7			7	4					
48.	386	4/5	25·60	675				6	15	7	8	7	7	7	7						4			7	8
49.	396	35/44	25·45	678·9		9																			
50.	404	·7917	25·34	682·												8a									
50.	404	19/24	25·33	682·1																		4	4		
51.	406	405/512	25·31	682·7											8a										
52.	408	·7901 = $\frac{64}{81}$	25·28	683·4								8	8				7	8	8					8	9
53.	427	25/32	25·00	691·2				7	16					8	8										
54.	428	·7811	24·99	691·3												8									
55.	429	32/41	24·98	691·9													8								
56.	431	·7795	24·94	692·8														9							
57.	435	7/9	24·89	694·3			8																		
58.	436	·7772 = $\frac{171}{220}$	24·87	694·8	8																				
59.	446	17/22	24·73	698·3		10																			
60.	457	96/125	24·58	703⅛				8																	
61.	471	16/21	24·38	708·8								9	9												
62.	477	243/320	24·30	711·1							9														
63.	491	·7531 = $\frac{61}{81}$	24·10	717·	9																				
64.	498	3/4	24·00	720·		11	9	9	17	8	10	10	10	9	9	9	9	10	9	5	5	5	5	9	10
F.	503	80/107	23·93	722·3					18																
65.	520	20/27	23·70	729·					19			11		10			10								11
66.	522	·7399	23·68	729·8														11							

Table for comparing the different opinions of writers on Srutis and Swarams.

1	2	3	4	5	6	7	8	9	10	11	12	13	14	15	16	17	18	19	20	21	22	23	24	25	26
67.	543	19/26	23·41	738·9	...	...	10	...	...	...	...	...	...	...	...	...	...	...	...	...	...	...	...	...	...
68.	545	·7299	23·35	739·8	...	...	...	...	...	...	...	...	...	...	...	...	...	12	...	...	...	...	...	...	...
69.	545	$·7297 = \frac{27}{37}$	23·35	740·	10	...	...	...	...	...	...	...	...	...	...	...	...	...	...	...	...	...	...	...	...
70.	551	8/11	23·27	742·5	...	12	...	...	...	...	...	...	...	...	...	...	...	...	...	...	...	...	...	...	...
71.	565	·7216	23·09	748·4	...	...	...	...	...	...	...	...	...	...	...	10	...	...	...	...	...	...	...	...	...
72.	569	18/25	23·04	750·	...	...	...	10	20	...	11	...	...	...	10	...	...	...	...	...	...	...	...	...	...
73.	588	729/1024	22·78	758·5	...	...	...	...	...	...	...	...	...	...	...	10_a	...	...	10	6	...	...	...	10	...
74.	589	37/52	22·77	758·9	...	...	11	...	...	...	...	...	...	...	...	...	...	...	...	...	...	...	...	...	...
75.	590	32/45	22·76	759·4	...	...	...	...	21	9	12	12	11	11	$\overline{10}_a$	...	...	...	...	...	...	...	...	...	12
76.	600	$·7071 = \frac{70}{99}$	22·63	763·7	11	...	...	...	...	...	...	...	...	...	...	...	...	...	...	...	...	...	...	...	...
77.	606	31/44	22·55	766·5	...	13	...	...	...	...	...	...	...	...	...	...	...	...	...	...	...	...	...	...	...
78.	608	·7038	22·52	767·3	...	...	...	...	...	...	...	...	...	...	...	11	...	...	...	...	...	...	...	...	...
79.	610	45/64	22·50	768·	...	...	...	...	22	...	...	13	12	...	11	...	11	...	...	...	6	...	...	11	13
80.	612	$·7023 = \frac{312}{729}$	22·48	768·9	...	...	...	...	...	...	...	...	...	...	...	...	...	13	11	...	...	...	...	...	...
81.	631	25/36	22·22	777·6	...	...	...	12	23	10	13	...	...	12	...	...	12	...	...	...	...	6	6	...	...
82.	635	·6929	22·17	779·3	...	...	...	...	...	...	...	...	...	...	...	...	...	14	...	...	...	...	...	...	...
83.	637	9/13	22·15	780	...	...	12	...	...	...	...	...	...	...	...	...	...	...	...	...	...	...	...	...	...
84.	655	$·6852 = \frac{37}{54}$	21·93	788·1	12	...	...	...	...	...	...	...	...	...	...	...	...	...	...	...	...	...	...	...	...
85.	663	15/22	21·82	792	...	14	...	...	...	...	...	...	...	...	...	...	...	...	...	...	...	...	...	...	...
86.	678	·6758 = [illegible]	21·62	799·1	...	...	...	...	...	...	...	...	...	...	...	12	...	...	12	7	...	...	...	...	...
87.	680	27/40	21·60	800·	...	...	...	...	24	...	14	...	...	...	12	...	...	...	...	...	...	...	...	12	14
88.	685	35/52	21·54	802·3	...	...	13	...	...	...	...	...	...	...	...	...	...	...	...	...	...	...	...	...	...
G	697	109/163	21·40	807·5	...	...	...	...	25	...	...	...	...	...	...	...	...	...	...	...	...	...	...	...	...
89.	698	·6681	21·38	808·3	...	...	...	...	...	...	...	...	...	...	...	13	...	...	...	...	...	...	...	...	...
90.	702	2/3	21·33	810·	...	...	...	12	26	11	15	14	13	13	13	...	13	15	13	...	7	7	7	13	15
91.																									
	709	$·6639 = \frac{81}{122}$	21·25	813·3	13	...	...	...	...	...	...	...	...	...	...	...	...	...	...	...	...	...	...	...	...
92.	722	29/44	21·09	819·3	...	15	...	...	...	...	...	...	...	...	...	...	...	...	...	...	...	...	...	...	...
93.	723	160/243	21·07	820·1	...	...	...	...	...	...	...	...	...	...	...	...	14	...	...	...	...	...	...	...	...
94.	725	·6577	21·05	821·	...	...	...	...	...	...	...	...	...	...	...	...	...	16	...	...	...	...	...	...	...
95.	736	17/26	20·92	825·9	...	...	14	...	...	...	...	...	...	...	...	...	...	...	...	...	...	...	...	...	...
96.	764	$·6433 = \frac{9}{14}$	20·59	839·4	14	...	...	...	...	...	...	...	...	...	...	...	...	...	...	...	...	...	...	...	...

1	2	3	4	5	6	7	8	9	10	11	12	13	14	15	16	17	18	19	20	21	22	23	24	25	26
97.	769	·6415	20·53	841·7	...	...	...	...	...	...	...	...	...	...	...	14	...	...	...	...	...	...	...	...	...
98.	773	16/25	20·48	843·8	...	...	...	13	27	12	16	...	...	14	14	...	...	...	...	...	...	...	...	...	...
99.	783	7/11	20·36	848·6	...	16	...	...	...	...	...	...	...	...	...	...	...	...	...	...	...	...	...	...	16
100.	786	40/63	20·32	850·5	...	...	...	...	...	...	...	15	14	...	...	...	...	...	...	...	...	...	...	...	...
101.	787	33/52	20·31	850·9	...	...	15	...	...	...	...	...	...	...	...	...	...	...	...	...	...	...	...	...	...
102.	792	81/128	20·25	853·3	...	...	...	...	...	...	...	...	...	...	...	14a	...	...	14	8	...	...	...	14	17
103.	794	256/405	20·23	854·3	...	...	...	...	...	...	...	...	...	...	14a	...	...	...	...	...	...	...	...	...	...
104.	812	·6256	20·02	863·1	...	...	...	...	...	...	...	...	...	...	...	15	...	...	...	...	...	...	...	...	...
105.	814	5/8	20·00	864	...	...	...	14	28	13	17	16	15	15	15	...	15	...	...	...	8	...	...	15	18
106.	816	·6243 = 4096/6561	19·98	865	...	...	...	...	...	...	...	...	...	...	...	...	...	17	15	...	...	...	...	...	...
107.	818	·6234 = 5/8	19·95	866·2	15	...	...	...	...	...	...	...	...	...	...	...	...	...	...	...	...	...	...	...	...
108.	835	50/81	19·75	874·8	...	...	...	...	...	...	...	...	...	...	...	...	16	...	...	...	...	...	...	...	...
109.	839	·6159	19·71	876·8	...	...	...	...	...	...	...	...	...	...	...	...	...	18	...	...	...	...	...	...	...
110.	841	8/13	19·69	877·5	...	...	16	...	...	...	...	...	...	...	...	...	...	...	...	...	...	...	...	...	...
111.	845	27/44	19.64	880·	...	17	...	...	...	...	...	...	...	...	...	...	...	...	...	...	...	...	...	...	...
112.	853	11/18	19·56	883·6	...	...	...	...	...	...	...	...	...	...	...	...	...	...	...	...	...	8	8	...	...
113.	873	·6040	19·33	894	16	...	...	...	...	...	...	...	...	...	...	16	...	...	16	9	...	...	...	...	...
114.	882	·6007 = 19683/32768	19·22	899·	...	...	...	...	...	...	...	...	...	...	...	...	...	...	...	...	9	...	...	16	19
115.	884	3/5	19·20	900·	...	...	...	15	29	14	18	17	16	16	16	...	...	...	...	...	...	...	...	...	...
116.	895	31/52	19·08	905·8	...	...	17	...	...	...	...	...	...	...	...	...	...	...	...	...	...	...	...	...	...
117.	902	·5938	19·00	909·5	...	...	...	...	...	...	...	...	...	...	...	17	...	...	...	...	...	...	...	...	...
118.	906	·5926 = 16/27	18·96	911¼	...	...	...	...	30	...	19	18	17	17	17	...	17	19	17	...	...	...	...	17	20
119.	911	13/22	18·91	913·8	...	18	...	...	...	...	...	...	...	...	...	...	...	...	...	...	...	...	...	...	...
H.	926	75/128	18·75	921·6	...	...	...	...	31	...	...	...	...	...	...	...	...	...	...	...	...	...	...	...	...
120.	927	·5853	18·73	922·59	17	...	...	...	...	...	...	...	...	...	...	...	...	...	...	...	...	...	...	...	...
121.	927	1280/2187	18·73	922·6	...	...	...	...	...	...	...	...	...	...	...	...	18	...	...	...	...	...	...	...	...
122.	929	·5846	18·71	923·7	...	...	...	...	...	...	...	...	...	...	...	...	...	20	...	...	...	...	...	...	...
123.	933	7/12	18·67	925·7	...	...	...	...	...	...	...	...	...	...	...	...	...	...	...	...	...	9	9	...	...
124.	952	15/26	18·46	936	...	...	18	...	...	...	...	...	...	...	...	...	...	...	...	...	...	...	...	...	...
125.	955	72/125	18·43	937·50	...	...	...	16	...	...	...	...	...	...	...	...	...	...	...	...	...	...	...	...	...
126.	969	4/7	18·29	945·	...	...	...	...	32	...	...	19	...	...	...	...	...	...	...	...	...	...	...	...	...

·1	2	3	4	5	6	7	8	9	10	11	12	13	14	15	16	17	18	19	20	21	22	23	24	25	26
127.	977	128/225	18·20	949·2	...	...	...	...	33	15	...	...	...	...	...	...	...	...	...	...	...	...	...	...	...
128.	979	25/44	18·18	950·4	...	19	...	...	...	...	...	...	...	...	...	...	...	...	...	...	...	...	...	...	...
129.	982	·5672	18·15	952·1	18	...	...	...	...	...	...	...	...	...	...	...	...	...	...	...	...	...	...	...	...
130.	996	·5625 = 9/16	18·00	960·	...	...	...	...	34	16	20	20	18	18	18	18	...	...	18	10	...	...	...	18	21
131.	1011	29/52	17·85	968·3	...	...	19	...	...	...	...	...	...	...	...	...	...	...	...	...	...	...	...	...	...
132.	1016	·5561	17·79	971·	...	...	...	...	...	...	...	...	...	...	...	19	...	...	...	...	...	...	...	...	...
133.	1018	5/9	17·78	972·	...	...	...	17	35	17	21	21	19	19	19	...	19	...	...	...	10	10	10	19	22
134.	1020	·5549	17·76	973·1	...	...	...	...	...	...	...	...	...	...	...	...	...	21	19	...	...	...	...	...	...
135.	1036	·5496	17·59	982·6	19	...	...	...	...	...	...	...	...	...	...	...	...	...	...	...	...	...	...	...	...
136.	1043	·5475	17·52	987	...	...	...	...	...	...	...	...	...	...	...	...	...	22	...	...	...	...	...	...	...
137.	1049	6/11	17·45	990·	...	20	...	...	...	...	...	...	...	...	...	...	...	...	...	...	...	...	...	...	...
138.	1067	27/50	17·28	1000·	...	...	...	...	...	...	22	...	...	...	...	...	...	...	...	...	...	...	...	...	...
139.	1072	7/13	17·23	1002·9	...	...	20	...	...	...	...	...	...	...	...	...	...	...	...	...	...	...	...	...	...
140.	1086	·5239 = [illegible]	17·09	1011·4	...	...	...	...	...	...	...	...	...	...	...	20	...	...	20	11	...	...	...	...	...
141.	1088	8/15	17·07	1012·5	...	...	...	18	36	18	23	22	20	20	20	...	...	...	...	...	11	...	...	20	23
142.	1091	·5325	17·04	1014·0	20	...	...	...	...	...	...	...	...	...	...	...	...	...	...	...	...	...	...	...	...
143.	1106	19/36	16·89	1023·2	...	...	...	...	...	...	...	...	...	...	...	...	...	...	...	...	...	11	11	...	...
144.	1106	·5278	16·89	1023	...	...	...	...	...	...	...	...	...	...	...	$\bar{2}1$s	...	...	...	...	...	...	...	...	...
145.	1108	135/256	16·88	1024·	...	...	...	...	...	...	...	23	...	...	$2\bar{1}$a	...	...	...	...	...	...	...	...	...	24
146.	1110	128/243	16·86	1025·2	...	...	...	...	...	...	...	...	21	...	...	...	20	23	21	...	...	...	...	21	25
147.	1123	23/44	16·73	1033	...	21	...	...	...	...	...	...	...	...	...	...	...	...	...	...	...	...	...	...	...
148.	1129	·5208 = [illegible]	16·67	1036·8	...	...	...	...	...	...	...	...	...	21	21	...	...	...	...	...	...	...	...	...	...
149.	1130	·5207	16·66	1037·	...	...	...	...	...	...	...	...	...	...	...	21	...	...	...	...	...	...	...	...	...
150.	1131	64/123	16·66	1037·8	...	...	...	...	...	...	...	...	...	...	...	...	21	...	...	...	...	...	...	...	...
151.	1133	·5197	16·63	1039·3	...	...	...	...	...	...	...	...	...	...	...	...	...	24	...	...	...	...	...	...	...
152.	1135	27/52	16·62	1040·	...	...	21	...	...	...	...	...	...	...	...	...	...	...	...	...	...	...	...	...	...
153.	1146	·5160	16·51	1046·5	21	...	...	...	...	...	...	...	...	...	...	...	...	...	...	...	...	...	...	...	...
154.	1158	64/125	16·38	1054·7	...	...	...	19	...	...	...	...	...	...	...	...	...	...	...	...	...	...	...	...	...
155.	1173	32/63	16·25	1063·1	...	...	...	...	...	...	...	...	...	...	...	...	...	...	...	...	...	...	...	...	...
156.	1178	81/160	16.20	1066·7	...	...	...	...	...	...	24	...	...	...	...	...	...	...	...	...	...	...	...	...	...
157.	1196	·5010	16·03	1077·8	...	...	...	...	...	...	...	...	...	...	...	22	...	...	...	...	...	...	...	...	...
158.	1200	1/2	16·00	1080·	22	22	22	20	37	19	26	24	22	22	22	...	22	25	22	12	12	12	12	22	26

An abstract comparison of the different opinions of writers on Dwavimsati Srutis.

1. **Sahasrabuddhi** accepts the 22 Srutis and makes the Madhya Sthayi 22 inches long giving an inch for each Sruti. According to him Ma occurs exactly in the middle in the 11th inch. So it contradicts Sarnga Dev who says that Ma has 9 Srutis. In the same manner, Pa occurs at the 15th inch which has 13 Srutis according to Sarnga Dev. So his view does not agree with that of Sarnga Dev.

2. **Raja Surendra Mohan Tagore** accepts the theory of Saranga Dev and divides a Sthayi into 22 equal parts, 9 for the portion below Ma and 13 for the portion above it. Sangeetha Ratnaharam does not mention any such equal division. Again we see from Table I page 247 that according to Sahasrabuddhi the cents for Ri and Ga are 254 and 347 respectively, whereas according to Tagore they are 316 and 435. There is this kind of difference as regards other Srutis also.

3. **K. B. Deval** is also an advocate of 22 Srutis, and he accounts for them by Ma, or $\frac{3}{4}$ of the whole length, to be the exact middle of the Madhya Sthayi, and Pa to be $\frac{2}{3}$ of the whole. Though Sarnga Dev mentions that Srutis occur in the Sa-Pa and Sa Ma series satisfying the principle of Vadi and Sam Vadi, yet he never mentions that there will be 22 Srutis in the octave, nor does he mention that Sa-Ma is equivalent to $\frac{4}{3}$ and Sa-Pa to $\frac{3}{2}$. Again, though the method of proceeding by $\frac{3}{2}$ and $\frac{4}{3}$ is adopted by Pythagoras and the author of Parijatam, Deval does not adopt it fully but goes only three steps, from Sa to Pa, Pa to Ri, and Ri to Dha and while going from Dha to Ga he substitutes 300 vibrations in place of $303\frac{3}{4}$, and in the fifth step (from Ga to Ni) he gives 450 vibrations instead of $455\frac{5}{8}$. His real object is to fix Ga at $\frac{4}{5}$ and Ni at $\frac{8}{15}$. This will never suit Karnatic music nor is it the system of Sarnga Dev.

4. **Clements** adopts the theory of 22 Srutis of Deval but adds an eleventh and a nineteenth Sthanam thus making the Srutis out to be 24 (Vide Table 4 page 262). So we may be sure that his theory contradicts that of Sarnga Dev.

5. He (**Clements**) says that 3 new Swarams are obtained when the change of Gramams is made for (1) Sa (2) Pa and (3) Ga. (Vide Table 5, places 10, 16, 1). We have clearly shown in page (266) that while change of Graham is made with the 22 Srutis as made out by Sarnga Dev, such new Srutis will not result.

6. **Rao Bahadur C. Nagoji Rao** accepts the theory of 22 Srutis as given out by Deval with $\frac{3}{2}$ for Sa-Pa and $\frac{4}{3}$ for Sa-Ma. This does not agree with the system of Sarnga Dev. The Karnatic music will conflict with Srutis obtained by $\frac{3}{2}$ and $\frac{4}{3}$.

7. (*a*) **Subramania Sastrigal** accepts the theory of 22 Srutis of Sarnga Dev. He accounts for the Srutis by adopting the principle of Pythagoras and the author of Parijatam namely $\frac{3}{2}$ for Sa-Pa and $\frac{4}{3}$ for Sa-Ma. He accepts the theory of Pythagoras and Watson but alters some of the Slokas of Parijatam to account for the number 22. (Vide Table 7 page 285). This is neither the view of Sarnga Dev nor Parijatam, nor does it fully resemble that of Pythagoras and Watson, and it is totally unsuitable to Karnatic music.

(*b*) While he proceeds by the Sa-Pa series he purposely miscalculates, in order to obtain Ga_1, after Dha_1 in the fifth step, and Ga_2 after Dha_2 at the seventeenth step (Vide Table 8 page 286).

(*c*) He says that 22 Srutis are obtained by the Sa-Pa and the Sa-Ma series (Vide Table 9, page 288). But the Sthayi does not come to an end in these processes. We might see that many Swarams have irregular measurements and not gradual ones and that some Sthanams are omitted altogether if we proceed by $\frac{3}{4}$, (Vide Table 10, page 290).

(*d*) He says that he has found out a novel method by which 53 Srutis are obtained by the Sa-Ma series, (Vide Table 11 page 294, 295). Here in the second part we might see the names given by him to the Srutis. But no names are given to the Srutis from 17 to 35. He seems to have derived the first 12 Srutis by the ascending Sa-Pa series and the descending Sa-Ma series. It is clearly seen from the cents calculations that the same Srutis obtained by the two series are of different measurements.

(*e*) The 22 Srutis which he newly obtained by the Sa-Ma series are given in Table 12 page 299. It will be seen that with the exception of the 3 Srutis for Ma the rest are those of Nagoji Rao. But there is a world of difference between these 22 Srutis and the 22 Srutis he picks out from the 53 obtained by the Sa-Ma series.

(*f*) There is a vast difference between the 22 Srutis picked out from the 53 obtained by the Sa-Ma series (Vide col. 7 of Table 13 page 301) and his fractional calculations given in the 10th column of the Table. These differences are specially noted in col. 9 of the same Table.

(*g*) The 22 Srutis picked out from the 53 obtained by the Sa-Pa and the Sa-Ma series are found in col. 4 of Table 14, page 303. Knowing that the two series will never come to perfection at the 22nd Sthanam, he takes half of the one and half of the other. Even granting this process to be correct, there is a vast difference between Ma_8 below the 12th Sthanam and the Ma_5 above the 10th Sthanam. There is a difference of 157 cents. So this method is incorrect. Unless the series come back to the original starting place the octave can never be perfect. A series which does not come to perfection must certainly be wrong. We have shown in Table 15 (page 306) and 16 (page 307) how according to Sarnga Dev the octave comes to perfection while proceeding 13 steps by the Sa-Pa series and 9 steps by the Sa-Ma series, and how the Sa-Pa series could never end in 31 Sthayis and the Sa-Ma in 22 Sthayis.

(*h*) While proceeding with the series by 702 cents or Sa-Pa ($\frac{3}{2}$) and by 498 cents or Sa-Mà ($\frac{4}{3}$), at the fifth step of the former he lessens 2 cents and adds 2 cents at the fourth step of the latter series. He is not justified in adding and subtracting as he likes. He has done this to show that Aryan music resembles the Just Intonation of the Europeans. This method may be seen in Table 18 page 316.

(*i*) He says that the 2nd Swaram nearest Ma while proceeding by the Sa-Pa series from Ma (see page 311) and the 12th Swaram nearest Sa obtained as the 12th from the descending series of Sa-Pa commencing from Suddha Ma have not been approved by our ancestors. He does not support this ancestral disapproval by any facts. We have indicated the Swarams rejected by him (10 and 23) in Table 18 page 316. These two Swarams have small intervals and hence he says that our ancestors rejected them. But this is entirely wrong for intervals with 20 and 22 cents are approved, while one with 24 is rejected.

(*j*) He speaks of the three Sampradayas, Vydeeka, Swaya and Loukeeka on page 318. The cents for Srutis obtained by Vydeeka and Sama Veda Sampradayas may be seen on page 318. We find that Sama Vada Sampradayam and Vydeeka Sampradayam have different Srutis. So there must be four Sampradayas. The Vydeeka Sampradayam which proceeds by the SA-MA system, and the Sama Veda Sampradayam which gives 27 Swarams in the octave after the Just Intonation system of the Europeans, are very different from each other. Does the Sama Veda Sampradayam belong to Vydeeka or Lowkeeka class? We find from col. 10 of Table 13, page 301 that he says that the cents calculations in lines 2, 4, 6, 8, 11, 13, 16, 18, 20, 22, 24 and 27 belong to Sama Vedam, and the Srutis for which cents are given in col. 7 of the same Table in lines 2, 4, 6, 8, 11, 13, 16, 18, 20, 22, 24 and 27 are those of Vydeeka Sampradayam. Srutis are not divided by Sarnga Dev thus in his Dwavimsati system, nor does he (Sarnga Dev) pick out 12 Swarams out of 53 obtained by the SA-MA series. The fractions obtained by Mr. Shastrigal by the process of $\frac{81}{80}$ and $\frac{5}{4}$ added on to the fraction of Pythagoras produce Sama Vedam. We do not know what other novelty he will ascribe to Sama Vedam. If he says that the 12 Swarams obtained by the SA-MA series are those of Sama Vedam he will be nearer the mark. The chief Srutis in use in Sama Vedam, namely Chathur Sruti, RI, and DHA, do not have the correct measurements. Other Swarams have also the same defect. While advocating the cause of the theory of 22 Srutis, he has taken only 12 Swarams in Vydeeka and Sama Veda Sampradayas omitting others. He does not give any reason for this. We are at a loss to understand why he has done so.

(*k*) Table 20 in pages 326-329 clearly shows that deriving the same 53 Srutis by the SA-PA and the SA-MA series is distinctly wrong. In the same Table it is proved that the system dividing the octave into 53 equal divisions does not agree with his theory at all. The 78 different Srutis he obtains at different times, which we have only collected from his essays, are also shown there.

8. (*a*) **Panchapakesa Bhagavatar** of Tanjore also accepts the 22 Srutis of Sarnga Dev and says they ought to be the same that are in use in Karnatic music. He derives 53 Srutis in the octave, 31 by the SA-PA series, 22 by the SA-MA series and 17 by the SA-GA series, picks out 22 out of them and says these should be used in Karnatic music. But unfortunately, we find here that Devathatthan who proceeds by the right and Danavathatthan who proceeds by the left, after taking 11 steps each, find themselves landed in the nether regions! We have shown the absurdity of this system as well as the fact that Subramonia Shastrigal has omitted the right places obtained while proceeding by 12 steps at a time, in Tables 17 and 18 on pages 314 and 316.

(*b*) We have shown in Table 23, page 351 that it is wrong to say that we obtain 53 Srutis by the SA-GA system or $\frac{5}{4}$ with $386\frac{1}{3}$ cents. We have also proved (Vide Table 24, page 352) that this is contrary to the SA-PA and SA-MA system of Sarnga Dev and to the system of Karnatic music.

9. **Pratapa Ramasami Bhagavatar** of Poovanur is also an advocate of 22 Srutis according to Sarnga Dev. But instead of following the method of Sarnga Dev he flies off at a tangent and upholds that of the author of Parijatam by proceeding by 3/2, 4/3, 5/4 and 6/5. There is not the slightest connection, therefore, between his system and those of Sarnga Dev and Karnatic music. Moreover, it is seen from his Tables 25, 26, 27, 28, 29, 30 and 31 that there may be 16, 17, 18, 19, 22 and even 29 Srutis in the octave, and as Sarnga Dev mentions 1, 2, 3, 4, 9, 22, 66 and even multitudes of Srutis in the octave, it follows that any one can say anything as regards the number of Srutis. It seems impossible to come to the conclusion that there can be only 22 Srutis in the octave.

10. **Manicka Moodaliar** gives two different methods, one for those with a good musical ear and the other for the ignorant ones. Of these, the latter resembles that of Pythagoras and the author of Parijatam or, in other words, the Sa-Ma system or 4/3. So it is clear that Srutis arrived at by the rough method of 3/4 are not correct.

11. Though the author of Parijatam accepts the Dwavimsati Srutis of Sarnga Dev he follows the method of Narada with the measurements 3/2, 4/3, and 5/4. So this resembles more or less the method proposed by Manicka Mudaliar, the author of Sangeeta Chandrika, for the benefit of those who have no ear for music.

12. When we notice tables 34 and 35 where Bandharkar gives his own opinions and those of Parijatam respectively, we see they differ from each other in some respects, yet they are based upon the method of 3/2, 4/3, 5/4 and 6/5. But they take only 12 Swarams in the octave. Bhandarkar distinctly says they are intended for Hindustani music. He says further that the terms Theeviram and Komalam are copied from the same Hindustani music. Therefore it is neither suitable to Karnatic music nor is it the system of Sarnga Dev.

13. **G. G. Barve** accounts for 12 Swarams in the octave by proceeding by 3/2, 4/3 and 5/4 after the method of Parijatam. He gives two new Sthanams in Ri, with 151 and 99 cents respectively by giving a different interpretation to the Slokam in Parijatam. We think that, of these, the Komala Ri with 99 cents is correct. If we add to this the Chathursruti Ri (204 cents) which is obtained by another interpretation, the system of the author of Parijatam will be more or less correct. However, it is clear that the Srutis of Karnatic Music are not these. Though he does not definitely say that these Srutis occur in Hindustani Music, others are sure they are used only as such. So they do not suit Karnatic music.

14. **Fox Strongways** gives 22 Srutis in the octave after the system of Sarnga Dev, but he gives them for Hindustani music. Therefore, they will not suit South Indian music nor is it the system of Sarnga Dev.

15. **Chinnasami Mudaliar** gives the Swarams used by the Westerners, their names as well as measurements. They are based on the system of 3/2, 4/3 &c., recommended for those who have no ear for music.

Further, as the result of many researches on Srutis, he finds a good deal of confusion between ancient works and their practical use at present and concludes that it is safe not to interfere in the matter. However, he says that the matter can be easily decided by making reference to the Veena in use in South India. But he does not give any correct measurements for the same.

16. The enharmonic scale of the Westerners will not suit South Indian music as that is also based upon the principle of $\frac{81}{80}$, $\frac{25}{24}$, $\frac{4}{3}$ and $\frac{3}{2}$.

17. Sarnga Dev, the author of Sangeeta Ratnakaram, gives the right method of deriving 22 Srutis in the octave. Even while change of Gramam is made, his Srutis stand the test. He has also indicated the key, namely, the system of Sa-Pa and Sa-Ma. He gives 13 Vadi Swarams by the Sa-Pa series, and 9 Sam Vadi Swarams by the Sa-Ma series. But the intervals Sa-Pa and Sa-Ma in use in modern music do not satisfy his rule. Nor are they obtained by the process of $\frac{81}{80}$, $\frac{25}{24}$, $\frac{4}{3}$ and $\frac{3}{2}$ used by some of the Indian writers and a few of the Western Musicians like Pythagoras. They are not mentioned at all in Sarnga Dev's book. We do not think it right to refute it by an argument not mentioned in his book.

18. When we study the comparative Table which gives the different opinions of the advocates of the Dwavimsati Srutis, we do not see any uniformity eirher in their measurements or cents calculations. So we see clearly that they are not after Sarnga Dev. It also shows clearly that the Karnatic system of Srutis is one which is entirely different from them.

The opinions of some writers who say that the Dwavimsati Srutis will not suit modern Ganam.

We may conclude from the previous chapters that Dwavimsati Srutis will not suit modern Ganam. This is further supported by the following writers.

Introduction to the study of Indian Music, by E. Clements. P. 82.

"The author showed more perspicacity than the Karnatic writers, appropriating the Shuddh notes of the Ratnakar to the Kafi scale, and designating the Madras "Shuddh" notes "purva" but no scientific terminology could be expected of any writer who adhered to Sarangadevar's system. Nowadays, among the practical musicians of Western India, the Sangit Ratnakar is looked upon as belonging to a bygone age, although no one is able to say what it is which makes its theories inapplicable to modern practice. Professional musicians have constructed their own system; needless to say, they differ widely one from another."

The above extract shows that professional musicians have invented different systems of their own in accordance with their own traditions, and so they differ widely from one another. This is the truth. Those who make new compositions after practising ancient Geetams certainly do add a few beautiful Swarams which have been traditionally used. This becomes Desikam, violating the rules of Margam. Others who hear it, can not but object to them. But the succeeding generations are not cognisant of the reason for the new introduction. They only justify it by tradition. Only those who learn it by rote, without enquiring into the why of it, belong to this class. Only these people are petted and patronized to a large extent. On the other hand, these really good musicians who try to find out the cause of the new Swarams are sorely perplexed and stranded like the proverbial logician. who wanted to find out whether the ghee. supported the vessel made of plantain leaf or the vessel supported the ghee. and the man who lost the bran in his mouth as well as the fire he wanted to light by blowing it! All this results from want of a clear knowledge of the Dwavimsati Srutis. If others point it out to them they will pooh-pooh them by saying "all this is found in our old basket!" Musicians of Western India have distinctly stated that Dwavimsati Srutis would not suit modern music. But they do not state their reasons. But if a musician of South India would realise the incongruity between modern practice and the Dwavimsati system to the same extent as they have done. he would be able to pitch upon the real reason. When the question is asked of the Southern musicians. they merely harp upon the minuteness and subtlety of their Srutis, give a few wrong measurements and practically demonstrate their folly by singing something! This is no answer for the question. One reason for this perplexity is the fact that not one among the writers, who have adopted the system of Ratnakaram, says anything clearly about Srutis. Instead of studying and interpreting each separate work independently, they try to bring about an uniformity among different writers. That this has been the cause of such variety of opinions may be seen from the following extract.

Dr. P. R. Bhandarkar, B.A., L.M.S.

"It is a great relief, however, to find at least one sceptic in Captain Day" who says: –

"The translation must. of course. be more or less hypothetical; and as it is so entirely different in character and style to all modern Indian music, and airs heard now in India which are said to be very ancient, its correctness appears to be doubtful."

Here we find that he puts down the want of uniformity between modern music and the Srutis mentioned in ancient works to the translation. and says that the correctness of the Srutis seems to be doubtful because the writings declare that the Ragams now heard are very ancient. This is no doubt true. We have noted already that the system of Srutis found in ancient works did not suit modern requirements. It is sure that they cannot suit if there is no uniformity in the Swarams except Athara Sa and Tara Sa. We see here that practice contradicts what is found in books. The following extracts show that Sa is the foundation of all Swarams. and that the series of Swarams in harmony with Sa can never be obtained from the Dwavimsati series.

Introduction to the study of Indian Music, by E. Clements. P. 5.

"Now the modern system of tuning throughout India has Shadj as the principal drone accompanied by Pancham or Madhyam. Not only this but Shadj and Pancham are regarded as fixed notes which may never become "Vikrit," or in other words, sharpened or flattened, and Shadj has acquired the privilege of being regarded as the basis of all scales. All Jatis, therefore, start from Shadj, and all the scales of all the Ragas.

It is clear therefore. first that the modern Srutis and the ancient Srutis must differ in many cases, and secondly that there are no longer strings of Shuddh notes from which to construct Jatis and scales of Ragas."

We all know how an instrument is tuned. Having the ground note Athara Sa we get the Pa from it and then Tara Sa and from Tara Sa we arrive at Ma. Then we proceed by Sa-Pa and Sa-Ma and obtain all the chief Swarams. All Ragas start from Athara Sa. He says that Aroganam and Avarohanam of these Ragas and Swarajatis are quite contrary to the ancient Dwavimsati Srutis. This point should be noted. We have pointed out before in the previous Table that with the exception of the Sa used in modern Ganam no other Swarams agree with the Dwavimsati Srutis. When Pa itself is in discord we need not speak about the other Swarams derived by the Sa-Pa system. The minutest difference, when it gathers force, becomes as large as the hill Maha Meru. The Ma also is in discord. If Ma and Pa are not in concord with Athara and Tara Sa the result will be excruciating. We know the difference in taste between milk with which a plantain fruit is mixed and milk with salt in it. Ma and Pa which are not concords will make Sa unbearable just like the devil which spoils the life. If the Sapta Swarams are discordant, we need not describe their painful effect upon the ear. How could a series of sounds wanting in regular measurements produce harmony?

Introduction to the study of Indian Music, by E. Clements. P. XIV.

"When asked whether he (the head of one institution who finds the tempered harmonium an excellent means of teaching beginners 'the scale',) follows the teaching of Sarangadev, the author of the Sangit Ratnakar, he replies: "He (Sarangadev) is not really an old authority; we go back to the Sama Veda; we are of opinion that Sarangadev is wrong in many respects, and we reckon our Srutis downwards instead of upwards." To go back to the Sama Veda is a happy inspiration, as that work, so far as it touches the question of scales, deals in pure generalities."

We see here that the author is of opinion that Saranga Dev is not really an old authority, that he commits errors in many places, and that therefore we must adopt the Srutis of Sama Veda. He further says that even the Srutis of Sama Veda are not minute as it deals in pure generalities. We have noted before (page 99) that Sama Vedam was organised into a system by Ravana, that his Ganam was after the system that was in use in Southern India, and that it took the name of Sama Vedam only after particular Swarams were added to it by Ravana. We have also noted in page 105, the opinion of Kunte that through the systems of the North and South India and Hindustani music varied widely, yet the music of the Dravida country or the South was most useful for reciting Vedas.

The following extract shows that the enharmonic scale of the Westerners and that of the Karnatic music differ from each other.

The Music of Hindustan by Fox Strangways P. 121.

"The enharmonic seems to be opposed in principle to the Carnatic system".

So we find that the two systems are different from what Fox Strangways says. The Srutis of Northern India, those of Hindustani music and those used by Western musicians are different from those of Karnatic music and from one another.

Two important points which might help us in arriving at the Srutis of Karnatic Music.

Noble readers ! Many eminent musicians'have written about, and given their criticism on Srutis, that have been in use for the last 2400 years from the age of Pythagoras. We have seen that even today opinions vary as regards this subject. We have placed before you a few of those theories and pointed out how they contradict one another and how they are different from the systems of Sarnga Dev. Pythagoras and Ahobilar. Table 50 gives one the full idea of the subject.

From all this it appears that if a new system, based upon all that has gone before, could be evolved which has equal and uniform measurements, then that system will certainly help us in determining the Srutis in use in South Indian music. While trying to unify the many systems that were different and arrive at the truth, I came across a few ideas which were contained in an ancient Tamil literary work. This work is considered one of the best and most ancient of Tamil works on music and one that could throw considerable light upon the controversy as regards Srutis. Moreover it has the sanction of Shastras and gives a system of Srutis which might help in reciting the Sama Vedam. With the grace of learned sages I came across those ideas which I give below.

1. I hold that the system of Srutis of Saranga Dev is the right one for determining the Srutis in use in Indian Music, and that no one could improve on this system.

In other words the series should proceed upwards from Athara Sa gradually with equal intervals admitting of no other Swarams in the middle.

2. Secondly, because Western Musicians as well as writers on Indian Music unanimously declare that Sa-Pa is $\frac{3}{2}$ and Sa-Ma is $\frac{4}{3}$, these two series must be approximately taken to be $\frac{3}{2}$ and $\frac{4}{3}$ respectively.

According to modern writers while proceeding by $\frac{3}{2}$ or Sa-Pa system, we finish the series a little over the octave, and while proceeding by $\frac{4}{3}$ or Sa-Ma, we finish a little below the octave. This must never be. The measurements must be so accurate that the series must end exactly with the octave, neither more nor less. Then we shall arrive at the Srutis in use in South Indian music. and all doubts about Srutis will entirely vanish.

If we have the above facts in mind, we shall be able to find out how many Srutis there are in the Sthayi, with their respective measurements

Unless we adopt the system of Sarnga Dev, the Srutis cannot be changed for the purpose of Grahaswaram nor will they suit Karnatic music.

If we do not proceed by the approximate measurements of SA-PA and SA-MA the Srutis will not suit Karnatic music. Therefore we should adopt the system of Sarnga Dev along with the mysterious key for tuning instruments given by him, and the system of $\frac{2}{3}$ and $\frac{3}{4}$. By the latter we do not mean the one recommended for those who have no ear for music, but the minute and correct SA-PA and SA-MA series.

Before we arrive at the right method of determining Srutis by the above two methods, we shall do well to see what works on Isai-Tamil say, which were in use among the Tamilians, the most ancient of the inhabitants of India and the most renowned in South Indian Music.

END OF PART 2.

KARUNAMIRTHA SAGARAM.

FIRST BOOK.

THIRD PART.

ON SRUTIS.

KARUNAMIRTHA SAGARAM

FIRST BOOK.

THIRD PART.

The Srutis of South Indian Music according to Isai Tamil.

INTRODUCTION.

WE have noted before that the music of ancient renowned India was in the highest state of efficiency at one time, and that when it began to deteriorate, the scientific works of the period also were despised on the score of impracticability when compared with modern requirements.

We have also noted in the *Second Part* that though many writers have taken the greatest pains to interpret ancient musical works correctly and restore them to their original eminence, yet they have not determined the Srutis after the system of Sarnga Dev but according to their own fancy.

We were, therefore, naturally led to enquire whether South Indian Music which was held to be highly efficient and scientific could have any literary support from ancient Tamil works. Though we may not fully succeed in our expectations in this respect, we are sure, at least, of certain points which are found very useful for South Indian Music.

To add to this, we must understand that some of the standard Sanskrit works on music only contain those points found in South Indian music. We shall see clearly later on how the "Chathurdandiprakasika" of Venkatamahi, the musical works of Singarachariar and the "Ragamalika" of Maha Vydianatha Iyer treat of South Indian music only. All works treating on South Indian Ragas and the 72 Melakartas contradict the ideas contained in the "Sangeeta Ratnakaram" of Sarnga Dev. We should not be led away by the fact that these works are in Sanskrit, Telugu and other languages. Just as we do not find any resemblance between the Ganam of Northern India and the "Ratnakaram" of Sarnga Dev, so also there is no resemblance between the musical works of South India written in Sanskrit, Telugu and Tamil and "Sangeeta Ratnakaram." But men of understanding will know that there is unanimity between some of the Sanskrit works of South India and the music thereof. It is but the law of nature that a child which is just able to creep should attempt to walk, that a man who is able to walk should attempt to fly and that a man should love his wife more than the mother who gave birth to him and brought him up. Just as a man loves to describe the virtues of his mother in a foreign language though he is imperfect in it, the mysteries of South Indian music were written in a foreign language.

Those who looked upon music as a great acquisition and a lucrative one, kept it as a sealed book and stood guard over it like so many *bhutams* for fear it should be known to others. Moreover, those who wrote works on music pretended to help others but in reality they kept the key to the mysteries hidden in such a way that others might be in endless doubt.

Many thousand Keertanams of Theagaraja Iyer who flourished at Trivadi (Tanjore) about 60 or 70 years ago, have been destroyed by fire because those who learnt them up were unwilling to teach it to others and at the same were indifferent about reducing them to Swara notation. When they are advised to reduce at least the remnants to notation they decline because they are afraid to commit themselves. From this, there is reason to conclude that many ancient works gradually became defunct because they kept them as sealed book without imparting the knowledge in them to others.

We have noted before that the First Sangam which patronised the three Angams of Tamil (Iyal, Isai and Natakam) for 4000 years at the time of the first Ooli (i.e., about 8000 years from now) along with its kings, scholars and musical works were destroyed by the sea. After their destruction even the small remnants of deteriorated musical works were brought to nought by the Buddhists and the Jains. Even those works, which remained after this, came to an end because they could not be put into practical use as there was no one to interpret the mysteries contained therein and they disappeared like the host of Rávana before the bombs of Rama having been eaten away by the little insect Ramabhanam. Only a few points noted down by practical musicians here and there survive so as to render traditional music possible and practicable.

It is a matter for deep regret that we are not in a position to understand Indian music as it was from the earliest times. However some of the *hamsams* of it come to light through a few lines of "Silappadikaram" written by Ilankovadigal, the brother of Senguttuvan who ruled over the Tamil Chera country in ancient times i.e. about 1800 years ago, by the commentary on them by Adyarkunallar and by the work of Jayankondan, the Kavi Chakravarti, who wrote an annotation on the same. We read a few lines there about the singing, dancing and skill in Yal of Mathavi, and the musical genius (in playing the Yal) of the hero Kovala.

If we compare all these facts, we are led to believe that music was in a high state of efficiency at that age and must have been in a far eminent state many thousand years before that time. It goes without saying that the three Angams of the language, namely, Iyal, Isai and Natakam, flourished when the Sangam existed at South Madura, that many of those are not in use at present and that the cause of it was their destruction by the sea. However, we are able to lay our hands on some of them, namely, the names of the works, the instruments and their description and the number of Ragas in use through the words of the author, its commentator as well as the annotator mentioned above.

The very fact that the scholars of the first Ooli and the sovereigns considered their language the first part, music the second part, and Natakam the third, naming them Iyal Tamil, Isai Tamil and Nataka Tamil respectively and improved them by devising rules of grammar for the same, proves that Music was held to be very high at that time. If we notice the prosody, which, is one of the sub-divisions of Iyal Tamil, we find that all the parts thereof viz. Letters, Syllables, Seer, Thalai, Adi, Thodai, Koon, Ethugai and Monai are so arranged as to satisfy the rules of music. The Ragam and Thalam are so arranged that sweet Swarams may not sound out of their Sthanam, and that Thalam as well as the coherence of the subject may not be lost. The result of this has been the production of the different kinds of *Pah* such as Venpah, Asiriappah, Kalippah and Vanjippah and its varieties Thalisai, Thurai and Viruttham.

We may clearly understand that such productions based upon prosody and music are easily capable of being learnt by heart, are easily explainable to others and they are easily protected from the admixture of foreign element. The *pahs* which are the chief parts of Iyal Tamil become *Puns* when sung to Music or Isai Tamil. Though the term *pun* is a common name for Ragam and Swaram, it means *Pahs* sung to music. The *Puns* and the *Vachanams*, when used with their respective Abinayam (gestures), became Nataka Tamil. We know that attempt at poetry can be made only when we are proficient in reading and writing.

It was only after *Pahs* were made, that Isai Tamil or Music, which helped in reciting them, came into existence. After the advent of *Vachanams*, *Pahs* and *Puns*, *Abinayam* or gestures which brought out their meaning, came. Abinayam, because of its dancing and gestures, became *Natakam*. These three *hamsams* of the language are as necessary for a man as his Sthoola, Sookshma and Karana Sareerams. Having this in view, our ancestors made the three *hamsams* of the language into one and called it *Muttamil.* They have devised rules of grammar also unifying the three into one. Ahatyam is considered to be its Muthal Nool. There are also others who dealt with each of them separately and wrote grammars for them whose works appear to be very comprehensive and striking. But after their destruction by the sea, smaller works, which gave their purport in a condensed form, came into existence. We do not find in any language any grammar that deals with the language. *Pahs, puns* and *Natakam* in such an exhaustive manner. From this we conclude that a literary work which dealt with Isai Tamil or Sangeetam, and with Nataka Tamil or Bharatam, could never have been written for the first time in any other language. These two literary productions had attained high efficiency in the Tamil language from ancient times; hence the traditional name *Muttamil* for the three *hamsams.* This name was not given to it yesterday or the day before. It seems to have been in use during the time of Ahastya, the author of 'Ahathyam' and even before his time. Nor do we find the combination of these three words in any other language.

From these ancient works it is clear that although our ancestors were wanting in the requirements of modern civilisation such as steam engines, telegraphs, aeroplanes improved manners and customs, foods, drinks, I-O.U's, documents, registration offices, courts of law, rules of procedure, time bar, and the recognition of pauperism, yet they were scholars in the Tamil language, worshipping God by their *puns* and singing and dancing before Him, and their sovereigns were noted for their mercy, justice, truthfulness, patience, humility, love and other virtues.

They showed themselves the very embodiment of truthfulness, being bound by their words, in the midst of many trials and troubles. A promissory note written in four lines on a palmyra leaf four inches long bound them much surer than any registered document of the present day, for a period of seven succeeding generations. They made large transactions with no more living witness than fire which is easily put out after the fuel is burnt. Documents for gifts and sales were made only with the sprinkling of a handful of water which is easily sucked by the dry ground!

These three Angams of Tamil which were so helpful to one who aimed at attaining Mukti were also sources of abuse. When music which was helpful for the salvation of the soul was used for inferior purposes, it was but natural that it should degenerate into means of livelihood. Those who used it for such mean purposes would never care for its higher uses. When it lost prestige to such an extent, it naturally followed that it was seldom made use of and gradually stifled altogether. We know how the gold lace of the turban rests on the head and how the same in the shoe rests on the foot. Such has been the state of music patronised by crowned heads in ancient times and by the poor at the modern day.

We see the eminence of music as one of the finest of arts when we enquire into it. That the civilisation of a country and its inhabitants is proportionate to their attainments in music is accepted by learned men. When we apply this test to the Tamilians we find that they were very highly civilised at a very early stage of their existence. It is said that the ancient inhabitants of South Madura were using 12,000

Ragas with 14, 49, 84 and even 103 Moorchanas in place of seven Moorchanas of the seven Swarams, and were using Veenas with 17, 27, 100 and even 1000 strings. Their science of music was also proportionately of a high order.

There are some verses in Silappadikaram regarding music, which, though a small part of a long story, describe to perfection an important *hamsam* of music. This is a matter for gratification. Not only are those verses difficult to understand, but some of the words used there are not found in any modern work. Many precious words have gone out of use altogether. It is also difficult to understand the measurements of Ragas which were then in use. Moreover the commentators have made use of certain arguments well known in those days thinking that people who came 1000 years after them would understand them equally well. So they merely give the headings which only puzzle us. If they had been a little more explicit all the chief *hamsams* of music would have been brought to light. In spite of all this, even the little that we obtain from there are far superior to the opinions about Srutis expressed at the present day.

The grand expression "22 Srutis" is also found there. But when we go into the system of the change of Alagus of the 22 Srutis and the innumerable Moorchanas obtained while they change their Graham, the author of Sangeeta Ratnakaram is thrown into the shade. We have given below only those extracts from Silappadikaram of whose interpretation we were quite sure. The others have been omitted. However, we have examined thoroughly the system of determining the Srutis and the change of Graham. We have not made any original statements but only have made the road easy for all so that the meaning can be clearly understood. We know we have omitted many important extracts. If scholars could see the importance of such omissions and point them out to us we are sure to include them in the second edition.

There is a slight difference between the opinions of Adyarkunallar, the commentator, and Kavichakravarti Jayankondan, the annotator, as regards a few points. The latter seems to have flourished about a hundred years before Adyarkunallur, and he deals with principles of ancient music more minutely It is plain that Adyarkunallar based his opinions on those of Jayankondan. We have first dealt with only such matters which appear clear to us with the help of the commentaries and annotations of these two authors. Later on we have elucidated the mystic portion of their writings so that they may be clearly understood by all. One might ask why we give two interpretations, one according to what is written and one after elucidating the mysteries. We have done it, so that we may not mystify our readers still more.

It will be a matter for gratification when we realise that the principles given in this work written 1800 years ago are the principles that have been in use in our Karnatic music. The same system seems to have been in vogue at the time of the author of Tholkaupiam and in the previous age. The 12 Swarams of the Sthayi and its more minute quarter tones appear to have been carried to the countries to the east of India, namely, Malaya, Siam, Anam, China and Japan, and to the countries to the west, such as Persia, Arabia, Egypt, Asiatic Turkey and Greece. Though these countries copied it from India, so long as they were ignorant of the mystery of the Vattapalai and the right system of proceeding by the SA-PA and SA-MA series, it was no wonder that they all erred. As years rolled on, though the system of Karnatic music was lost, yet it has been preserved to a certain extent, no doubt mixed with Desikam, by means of music that has been traditionally handed down.

We may arrive at the truth by comparing music which is pure without the admixture of strange sounds and music which is so mixed. The beauty of Karnatic music is, that when its Ragas are sung without mixture according to the strict rules of Aroganam and Avaroganam they appear to be so varied and different. We have to dwell at length upon this ancient system as it will help us in eliminating the admixture of alien element and making Karnatic music pure.

The contents of Book II will be

(i) Rules to enable all people with musical ear to sing the Karnatic Ragas pure and free from admixture.

(ii) Rules by which errors in the existing Ragas may be easily rectified

(iii) Rules for making a Ragam with a given Aroganam and Avaroganam and for composing Gheetams, Varnams and Keertanams in the said Ragam.

We request our Tamil readers to try their best to bring to light those ancient gems of literature which are lying hidden and neglected. The Tamils owe a deep debt of gratitude to Mahamahopadhyaya V. Saminatha Iyer who has published this ancient literary work Silappadikaram which throws such considerable light upon many an ancient principle.

This part contains the following :—

I. The ancient musical system which gives the Swarams and Srutis in use in Isai Tamil.

1. The measurement of the Swarams as found in Isai Tamil practised by the ancient Tamilians.
2. The opinion of ancient Tamil works as regards the Srutis used in South Indian music.
3. How 14 Palais generate from the Ayapalai.
4. How Sempalai and other allied Palais (seven in all) generate.
5. The seven Palais derived from Kodipalai.
6. The three Sthayis, Mandaram, Madhyam and Tharam.
7. The Vattapalai used in Isai Tamil.
8. The 12 Palais which generate from Vattapalai while Graham is changed and their cycles. (Proceeding clock-wise to the right.)
9. The twelve cycles of Vattapalai, proceeding counter-clock-wise or to the left.
10. Regarding the four Yals, (Palai, Marutham, Kurinchi and Neythal) in use in ancient times in South India.

10. (a) How four different kinds of *Pans* generate from the four great *pans*.

II.—The description of some of the Kalais in use in Isai Tamil which the ancient Tamils were proficient in.

1. Kinds of Yal.
2. Some important points which the Tamils observed in the act of playing the Yal.
3. A summary of the Abinayams (gestures) in use in South India.
4. Instruments of percussion in South India.
5. A summary of the Thalam in use in South India.
6. The system of Alati or Raga Alapanam.

III.—The number of the Ragas in use in the ancient Tamil Country.

1. The Ragas used in the ancient Tamil Country.
2. The 103 *puns* mentioned by the Sage Pinkala.
3. The *Puns* used in Thevaram.
4. The Raganga Ragas and *puns* of the Tamil country given in the chapter on Ragaviveka in Sangeeta Ratnakaram.
5. Some Ragas and their description given in the work of Bharata.
6. The *Puns* found in the dictionary published by Mr. Ramanathan.
7. The names of the Tamil *Puns* found in Soodamoni Nikandu.
8. The names of the Tamil *Puns* found in the Bharata Shastram of Arabatta Navalar.
9. The Ragas found in Abithana Chintamoni.
10. The Ragas found in Paripadal.
11. Some points regarding the system of calculating Alagu which was in use in South Indian Music.
12. The minute mathematical system of the Tamils.
13. The distinguished Tamil scholars.
14. How the doubt about Srutis rose owing to certain mysteries in Isai Tamil.

IV.—The mystery in the works on Srutis of South Indian music and the key to it.

1. The system of determining the main Swarams.
2. The description of Inai Swaram.
3. How Kilai Swarams generate.
4. What is called Pahai Swaram.
5. All about Natpu Swaram.
6. About Pahai String.
7. The clearing of these mysteries.
8. The 12 Swarams obtained by the Sa-Pa series after clearing the doubt.
9. The 12 Swarams obtained by the Sa-Ma series after clearing the doubt.
10. How the Swarams of the Sa-Ga series harmonise.
11. How the Swarams of the Sa-Ri series harmonise.

12. About the Alagus of the Swarams.

13. How the 22 Alagus will never complete a Rasi Cycle.

14. To say that there are Dwavimsati Srutis in the Sthayi is wrong.

15. If there be 22 Srutis in the octave according to Vattapalai, they will never satisfy the principle of Vadi and Samvadi.

16. The system of Dwavimsati Srutis mentioned by the author of Sangeeta Ratnakaram will not satisfy the principle of Vadi and Sam Vadi nor will it have correct measurements.

17. The right system of Alagus which satisfies the principle of Vadi and Sam Vadi.

18. How the 22 Srutis were used in the octave.

19. If the 22 Srutis occur succesively in a Rasi Mandalam, the Sapta Swarams cannot be accounted for by the Vattapalai according to the rule that Oolai must proceed from Tharam, Kural from Oolai and so on.

20. The system followed by the Tamils in singing Grahaswaram.

21. The astronomical consistency of the Swarams used in Isai-Tamil.

22. The consistency of the Swarams found in the 'Paripadal' of Nallanduvanar who flourished in the period of the last Sangam before the age of Ilankovadigal.

23. Quotations in support of the statement that there were some mysteries in the Isai-Tamil used by the ancient Tamilians.

24. How the music was confined to 22 Srutis.

25. The system of Ayapalai.

26. The Yals and their parts used in ancient times.

27. The Swaram that generates from the four kinds of Yal.

28. How four Jatis generated from each Yal when once the doubt was cleared.

29. The cycle showing the generation of the four Jatis from the four kinds of Yal.

30. The six mother Ragas used by the Tamils.

31. How the ancient Tamils had six Alagus or Srutis for Kaikilai Tharam.

32. Some arguments in support of the fact that modern Ganam with 22 Srutis closely follows the custom of the ancient Tamils where they left out 2 Srutis out of the 24 of the Dha-Ga Series of the Vattapalai.

33. General remarks on Swarams and Srutis.

34. Establishment of the theory of 24 Srutis in the Sthayi.

I. THE ANCIENT SYSTEM OF SWARAMS AND SRUTIS USED IN ISAI-TAMIL.

1. The measurement of the Swarams of Isai-Tamil practised by the ancient Tamils.

Some of the statements found in Silappadikaram prove that the Tamil literature of the ancient times was very extensive, where the author describes the singing of Mathavi and her skill in playing the Yal. We find only very little said about music. But the commentators on the work have suited their work to the music which was then in use. But as the ancient system is now found nowhere, it is difficult even to understand them. Yet the folowing extract shows one of the ancient *hamsams* of music.

Annotation on Silapadikaram Page 31.

" மன்று மளிகள் மலர்தேடி மதுவை யுண்டு வரைதோறும்
பன்று சார லனைவெங்கும் பற்றி யார்க்கும் வகையேபோன்
முன்ன மோசை பலவாகி முழுதும் வேறாய் மிடற்றென்றாய்த்
தேன்ன வென்று மிசைவளர்த்துப் பண்ணு மாம தேன்போல் "

He says in this stanza that " bees which gather honey from different kinds of flowers on the hill side make each a different kind of sweet sound. In the same way when many Swarams with different sounds are tried and when Sancharam is made with such of them as are harmonious only, then we get what is called the *pun* which is sweet corresponding to the collected honey of the bees."

Annotation on Silapadikaram Page 7.

" மிடறுவென்பது மூலாதாரத் தொடக்கிய முந்தைக் காலாற் கிளப்பிக் கருத்தாவியக்கி நல்லோசைத் தாக்கி இரண்டொடைப் பகுத்துப் பன்னீரிலைவிளைப் பிறப்பிக்கப் பட்ட பாடலுடன் கலந்த மிடற்றுப் பாடு லென்றவாறு "

Here he says that " the breath which ranges as far as the *Moolatharam* is brought upwards by an effort and a sound is produced according to ones own will. This sound when doubled generates sweet Ragams." Here by *Moolatharam* he means the *heart* which is in the middle of the Arukonachakram or central *Moolam*. Of the three *Moolams* at the bottom, the centre and the top, as breath works between the top and the central *moolam*, we must hold that sound generates from here. The sounds of the Mandara Sthayi are produced in the space between the top of the lungs and the bottom of the throat, those of the Madhya Sthayi between the throat and the bottom of the tongue and those of the Tara Sthayi between the uvula and the nose. It is clear that the sounds of the different Sthayis are in the ratio of one, two and four for the Mandaram, Madhya and Tara respectively. The Tara Sthayi comprises those sounds above Ni, while according to ancient ideas, is the completion of the Sapta Swarams.

Silappadikaram, Achiarkuraval Page 409.

" இவ்வேழு நரம்பிற்கும் இசை பிறக்குமாறு: ச ரி க ம ப த நி என்னும் எழுத்திற்கும் பிறக்கும், என்னை?

" ச ரி க ம ப த நி யென் றேழெழுத்தாற் றானம்
வரிபரந்த கண்ணினாய் வைத்துத்-தெரிவரிய
வேழிசையுந் தோற்றி யிவற்றுள்ளே பண்பிறக்குஞ்
சூழ்முதலாஞ் சுத்தத் துளை "

Silappadikaram, Oorkankathai Page 341.

"ச ரி க ம ப த நி யென்று மெழுவகைப் பட்ட எழுத்தடியாகப் பிறக்கும் குரன் முதலாயே ழும்."

In the above lines he points out how the seven Swarams generate from the Kural. The seven Swarams proceed from the seven letters. These seven Swarams are the basis of all music. In the Isai Nool of Ahatya written in ancient times they were known as Ah, Ri, Ga, Ma, Pa, Dha and Ni, Ah. Next he proceeds to give the system by which the seven Swarms are sung as well as their calculations.

Silappadikaram, Arangetukathai Page 90.

[illegible]

"ஏற்றிய குரலிளி யென்றிரு நரம்பி
னொப்பக் கேட்டு முணர்வின னாகிப்
பண்ணமை முழவின் கண்ணெறி யறிந்து
தண்ணுமை முதல்வன் றன்னொடும் பொருந்தி
வண்ணப் பட்டடை யாழ்மேல் வைத்தாங்கு"

Silappadikaram, Arangetukathai Page 91.

[illegible]

"ஏற்றிய குரலிளி யென்றிரு நரம்பி
னொப்பக் கேட்டு முணர்வின னாகி"

யென்பது பதினாற் கோவையினிடத்துக் குரனரம்பு இரட்டிக்க வரும் பாலையையும், இளிநரம்பு இரட்டிக்கவரும் மேற்செம்பாலையையும் இவைபோல அல்லாதபாலைகளையும் இசைநூல் வழக்காலே இளி நரம்பு தொடுத்துப் பாடும் அறிவினை யுடையளுமென்க."

உரை.

"வண்ணப்பட்டடை யாழ்மேல் வைத்தாங் கென்பது"

பட்டடை—நரம்புகளின் இளிக்குப் பெயர்; என்னை? எல்லாப் பண்ணிற்கும் அடிமணையாதலின். வண்ணம்-நிறம் இதனையாழ் மேல்வைத் தென்க.

ஆங்கு-அசை. இளிக் கிரமத்தாலே பண்களை யாழ்மேல் வைத்தெனக் கூட்டினு மவையும்.

"குரல்வா யிளிவாய்க் கேட்டனள்"

குரல்முதலாக எடுத்து இளிகுரலாக வாசித்தாளென்க.

He says in these lines that each of these Swarams must be arranged so that it might harmonise with Pa or Kural with Ili. We know from experience that Ili or Pa perfectly harmonises with Kural or Sa. The sweetnees of the concord will be in proportion to the harmony of this Pa with Sa. He does not say here that this Pa sounds at ⅔ the length of the wire. We have no reason to suppose that the ancients were unware of this measurement. Our ancestors who were cognisant of even the minuteat things in relation to music had the ability to name the order of the Sthayi and sing also on harmonious strings. So they say that one must have such a cultivated ear so as to appreciate the complete concord of the Swarams Kural and Ili or Sa and Pa.

It is not easy to indicate a sweet sound which could be minutely appreciated by the ear by means of wire and calculations by the levelling rod. The internal ear as well as the nerve which differentiates auditory impressions are very subtle. The appreciation of sounds must be in proportion to the subtlety of the auditory organ. The first sound should be so appreciated and the Pa to it should be determined. Then if this Pa were made the Sa and if we proceed by the same process of fifths we obtain the 12 Swarams. These 12 Swarams are a gradually ascending series and are as concordant with one another as Sa is to Pa. They stand in the same relation with one another as that of the husband and wife of a family with perfect concord. The Panchamam is the Mathursthanam for all Swarams just as the Mathursthanam, the primal cause of man, is the genitive cause of all human beings with a body. Though the male is the originative cause of all living being it is but a comprehensive *Sookshma hamsam.* Though the first Swaram Sa comprehends in itself the Sapta Swarams, yet they obtain their shape only with the help of the Ili or the Panchamam. The relationship of Puthiran, Mithran and Chatru came by the concordant relation of Sa with Pa, and not by the individual existence of Sa like the Brahma. Therefore the seven Swarams must arrange themselves in the relation of Sa to Pa.

We must observe why our ancestors who were such expert mathematicians who dealt with integers up to 32 places and decimals down to many places, should have omitted to mention any measurement for determining these Swarams. They knew very well that even if there was the minutest difference in the Sa-Pa relation other Swarams could never be derived. They put the seal of Sa-Pa and Sa-Ma on the Sapta Swarams just as weights and measures are so sealed, that there might not be even the difference of a grain.

Even this seal is not measured or weighed but should be appreciated by the ear. It follows, therefore, that one must possess a highly advanced musical ear so that when one has once understood the harmony of Sa-Pa might apply the same test to all other Swarams.

We shall see that this standard has been used in different places at different times. We shall see in many places that Swarams in a Yal were arranged on the same principle, and the same recommended; that Yals were tuned on the same principle. The Swarams from Kural, the primary Swaram, to Ili formed the Mandhara Sthayi, then they proceeded upwards from Ili as Kural. Here we find that Kural is the first Swaram of the Mandhara Sthayi, and the Ili (which was fixed as the Kural) the first Swaram of the Madhya Sthayi. Here we shall find that the concord Sa to Ma is derived from the harmonious Sa to Pa. In the same way we shall find that they made their Ganam with no difference between the ascending series Sa, Ri, Ga, Ma and Pa, Dha, Ni, Sa, Ri, and in descending between Ri, Sa, Ni, Dha, Pa and Sa, Ni, Dha, Pa, Ma, for all Swarams were based on the principle of Sa-Pa. This may be seen from the following extracts and the cycles which will help in the elucidation thereof.

2. The opinion from ancient Tamil literature as regards the Srutis in use in South Indian Music.

Ilankovadigal mentions the first requisites of a musician who is a skilful player on the Yal as well as a teacher. The extract (an Ahaval) noted below, though very short, gives in detail the method of determining the Swarams used by the Tamilians in the ancient Isai Tamil. Though the ancient poems as well as prose literature are rather hard to understand, we have quoted the extracts below as they contain very rare ideas.

Silappadikaram, Arangetukathai Page 92, 93.

"ஈரேழ் தொடுத்த செம்முறைக் கேள்வியி
ஞேரேழ் பாலை நிறுத்தல் வேண்டி
வன்மையிற் கிடந்த தார பாகமு
மென்மையிற் கிடந்த குரலின் பாகமு
மெய்க்கிளை நரம்பிற் கைக்கிளை கொள்ளக்
கைக்கிளை யொழித்த பாகமும் பொற்புடைத்
தளராத் தாரம் விளரிக் கீத்துக்
கிளைவழிப் பட்டனை ளாங்கே கிளையுந்
தன்கிளை யழிவுகண் டவள்வயிற் சேர
வேனை மகளிருங் கிளைவழிச் சேர
மேல துழையிளி கீழது கைக்கிளை
வம்பு மரபிற் செம் பாலையாய
திறத்தி யாதி யாக வாங்கவை
பெயர்முறை வந்த பெற்றியி னீங்காது
படுமலை செவ்வழி யரும்பாலை யெனக்
குரல்குர லாகத் தற்கிழமை திரிந்தபின்
முன்னதன் வகையே முறைமையிற் றிரிந்தாங்
கிளிமுத லாகிய வேதிர்படு கிழமையுங்
கோடி விளரி மேற்செம் பாலையென
நீடிக் கிடந்த கேள்விக் கிடக்கையி
னிணைநரம் புடையன வணைவுறக் கொண்டாங்
கியாழ்மேற் பாலை யிடமுறை மெலியக்
குழன்மேற் கோடி வலமுறை மெலிய
வலிவு மெலிவுஞ் சமனு மெல்லாம்
பொலியக் கோத்த புலமை யோனுடன்."

The above extract gives the fourteen Kovais of Ayapalai, how they are derived, their names, the Swarams that are obtained on the right and the left from Yal and Kural respectively. The following is the commentary of Adyarkunallar on the same.

3. How the 14 Palais are derived from Ayapalai.

"ஈரேழ் தொடுத்த செம்முறைக் கேள்வியி
ஞேரேழ் பாலை நிறுத்தல் வேண்டி."

என்பது, ஆயப்பாலையாய் நின்ற பதினாற்கோவை, கேள்வியிது செய்ய முடைத்தாய்ப் பெயர்பெற்றுநின்ற நரை முடைய பாடலியல்பொருத்தமைந்த சிறப்புடைத்தாகலான், இதிலே செம்பாலை, படுமலைப்பாலை, செவ்வழிப்பாலை அரும்பாலை, கோடிப்பாலை, விளரிப்பாலை, மேற்செம்பாலை யெனப்பட்ட ~முறையாலிரண்டு இணைநரம்பு தொடுத்து நிரல் நிறுத்திக்கட்டல் ஏழாமிசை வேண்டி.

He says here that Ayapalai is the first of the chief four Palais (1) Ayapalai (2) Thirikonapalai, (3) Sathurapalai and (4) Vattapalai.

There are two kinds, the first commences with Tharam as Kural (SA) and the other with Oolai (or MA) as Kural. Each of these is capable of seven Palais, thus accounting for the 14 Palais in all.[1] The Swarams of these two series have the same concord with one another as SA has to PA. Their detail might be seen in the following Table. For these 14 *Moorchanas*, the first seven have seven names commencing with Sempalai, and the second seven, the names beginning with Arumpalai. The Swarams of the two series are in the relation of SA to PA.

Therefore, the Kural (SA) derived from Oolai (MA) gives us the seven Palais from Sempalai.

The Oolai (MA) derived from Tharam (Ni) gives us another seven Palais from Kodipalai.

Silappadikaram, Venirkathai Page 202.

"பிழையா மரபி னீரேழ் கோவையை
யுழைமுதற் கைக்கிளை யிறுவாய்க் கட்டி."

(இ-ள்) பையள மரபினையுடைய இப் பதினாற்கோவையாகிய சகோடயாழை உழை குரலாகக் கைக்கிளை தார மாகக் கட்டியென்க.

The 14 Swarams are from NI of the Mandhara Sthayi to DHA of the Tara Sthayi.

"தாரத்துட் டோன்று முழையுழை யுட்டோன்று
மோருங் குரல்குரலி னுட்டோன்றிச்—சேருமினி
யுட்டோன்றுந் துத்தத்துட் டோன்றும் விளரியுட்
கைக்கிளை தோன்றும் பிறப்பு."

என்பதனுள் தாரத்தில் முதற் பிறப்பதாகிய உழை குரலாய்க் கைக்கிளை தாரமாகிய கோடிப்பாலைமுதற் பிறக்கக் கட்டி யென்க.

When Oolai becomes kural (MA becomes SA) in the Saketayal and if GA (Kaikilai) is made NI (Tharam) the series MA, PA, DHA, NI, SA, RI, GA will result.

Again, when Oolai or MA is made into Kural or SA the series will be SA, RI, GA, MA, PA, DHA, Ni.

When MA (Oolai) commences on Ni (Tharam) the series will be Ni, SA, Ri, GA, MA, PA, DHA.

The different series, then, are:—

NI	SA	RI	GA	MA	PA	DHA
MA	PA	DHA	NI	SA	RI	GA
SA	RI	GA	MA	PA	DHA	NI.

These series will clearly demonstrate the meaning of the stanza commencing with the words "*தாரத்துட்டோன்றும் உழை* &c".

So by the Sa-Pa principle.

Oolai ...	(Ma)	will be derived	from	Tharam	(Ni)
Kural ...	(Sa)	"	"	Oolai	(Ma)
Ili ...	(Pa)	"	"	Kural	(Sa)
Thuttham ...	(Ri)	"	"	Ili	(Pa)
Vilari ...	(Dha)	"	"	Thuttham	(Ri)
Kaikilai ...	(Ga)	"	"	Vilari	(Dha)
Tharam ...	(Ni)	"	"	Kaikilai	(Ga)

This is the meaning of the expression that Kural became Ili. The above series are all on the principle of Sa-Pa. When Oolai (or Ma) is made into Kural (or Sa), Kaikilai (or Ga) which is before Oolai (or Ma) becomes Tharam (or Ni). This he calls Kodipalai.

4. The Seven Palais beginning from Sempalai and how they are derived.

Number.	Ma Kural Sa	Pa Thuttham Ri	Dha Kaikilai Ga	Ni Oolai Ma	Sa Ili Pa	Ri Vilari Dha	Ga Tharam Ni	Ma Kural Sa	Pa Thuttham Ri	Dha Kaikilai Ga	Ni Oolai Ma	Sa Ili Pa	Ri Vilari Dha	Ga Tharam Ni
1	Sa	Ri	Ga	Ma	Pa	Dha	Ni	Sa						
2		Sa	Ri	Ga	Ma	Pa	Dha	Ni	Sa					
3			Sa	Ri	Ga	Ma	Pa	Dha	Ni	Sa				
4				Sa	Ri	Ga	Ma	Pa	Dha	Ni	Sa			
5					Sa	Ri	Ga	Ma	Pa	Dha	Ni	Sa		
6						Sa	Ri	Ga	Ma	Pa	Dha	Ni	Sa	
7							Sa	Ri	Ga	Ma	Pa	Dha	Ni	Sa

1	Sa	Sa	When Kural is taken as Kural ... Sempalai.
2	Ri	Sa	When Thuttham is taken as Kural ... Padumalaipalai.
3	Ga	Sa	When Kaikilai is taken as Kural ... Sevalipalai
4	Ma	Sa	When Oolai is taken as Kural ... Arumpalai
5	Pa	Sa	When Ili is taken as Kural ... ... Kodipalai.
6	Dha	Sa	When Vilari is taken as Kural ... Vilaripalai.
7	Ni	Sa	When Tharam is taken as Kural ... Miraempalai.

In this Chakaram we have shown how the seven Palais are derived from the series MA PA DHA NI SA RI GA and SA RI GA MA PA DHA NI which are obtained by the SA-PA system taking Oolai (or MA) as the Kural (SA). When we deal later on with Vattapalai we may see how these Swarams are concordant by the SA-PA system. We must remember that when Oolai is taken as Kural, and Tharam as Oolai which in its turn is taken as Kural, they are all after the SA-PA system. When Tharam becomes Oolai and when this Oolai is taken as Kural, he calls it Kodipalai.

In the above Table, each of the seven Palais commencing from Sempalai (where Kural stands for SA) proceeds from Kural towards the right side and becomes a Moorchana. Each of these Moorchanas receives a separate name according to the Swaram from which it commences. For example,

The SA	which	commences	from	SA is Sempalai.
The SA	,,	,,	,,	RI is Padumalaipalai.
The SA	,,	,,	,,	GA is Sevvalipalai.
The SA	,,	,,	,,	MA is Arumpalai.
The SA	,,	,,	,,	PA is Kodipalai.
The SA	,,	,,	,,	Dha is Vilaripalai.
The SA	,,	,,	,,	NI is Merchempalai.

These names become different in the second Chakaram. They are purposely given different names there, inasmuch as they occur on doubled Swarams from SA-PA. Moreover, we shall see from the Tables of Palais to be given later on that these have different names when they proceed by the SA-PA system towards the right, and by the SA-MA system towards the left. These different names depend upon the place where SA commences in the various strings of Swarams such as SA-PA, MA-SA, PA-SA, NI-MA in the four kinds of Yal. This fact may be clearly seen from the Tables below.

"இதழி யாதி யாக வாங்கலை
பெருமுறை வந்த பெற்றியி னீங்காது."

என்பது, தார முதலாகப் பெருமுறையாய் வந்தபடியே நீங்காமல் என்றவாறு.

This means, "without changing the general way beginning from Tharam."

"படுமலை செவ்வழி யரும்பா லையெனக்
குரல்குர லாகத் தற்கிழமை திரிந்தபின்."

என்பது, கைக்கிளை குரலாகப் படுமலைப் பாலையும், துத்தம் குரலாகச் செவ்வழிப் பாலையும், குரல் குரலாக அரும் பாலையும் தற்கிழமை திரிந்தபின்னென்க.

அரும்பாலைக்கு நரம்பு இரட்டித்த பெற்றியென்க.

"When Kaikilai becomes Kural we get Padumalaipalai, when Thuttham becomes Kural Sevvalipalai, and when Kural is Kural we get Arumpalai when these changes are made."

"For Arumpalai the wire becomes doubled."

"முன்னைதன் வகையே முறைமையிற் றிரிந்தாங்
கிளிமுத லாகிய வெதிர்படு கிழமையுங்
கோடி விளரி மேற்செம் பாலையென
நீடிக் கிடந்த கேள்விக் கிடக்கையின்"

என்பது, முன்பிற்படியே தாரம் குரலாகக் கோடிப்பாலையும், விளரிகுரலாக விளரிப்பாலையும், இளி குரலாக மேற் செம்பாலையுமாய், மேற்செம்பாலை, இளி நரம்பிரட்டித்த நிலைமையினையுடைத்தாய், இப்படிச் சமைந்த பதினாற்கோவைப் பாலை நிலையிலென்றவாறு.

" As before, Kodipalai results when Tharam becomes Kural, Vilaripalai, when Vilari becomes Kural and Merchampalai when Ili becomes Kural. Merchampalai has double the pitch of Ili. Thus the 14 Kovaipalais result.

" இணைநரம் புடையன வணைவுறக் கோண்டாங்கு."

என்பது, இப்பதினாற் கோவைப் பாலை நிலையினும், பண்ணின்ற நிலையினுமிரட்டித்த குரல்குரலாகிய அரும்பாலையும், இளிகுரலாகிய மேற்செம்பாலையும் போல், அல்லாதன ஐந்து பாலையும், உழை குரலாகச்செம்பாலைக்கு உழை பெய்தும், கைக்கிளை குரலாகப் படுமலைக்குக் கைக்கிளை பெய்தும், துத்தங் குரலாகச் செவ்வழிக்குத் துத்தம் பெய்தும், தாரங் குரலாகக் கோடிப்பாலைக்குத் தாரம் பெய்தும், விளரிகுரலாக விளரிப்பாலைக்கு விளரி பெய்தும் பாடப்படுமென்றவாறு.

" Just like Arumpalai where Kural is Kural which resulted from these fourteen Kovaipalais and the doubling of sounds, and Merchempalai (where Ili is Kural) the other five Palais also are sounded. Sempalai is sounded when Oolai becomes Kural (thus Oolai comes to the aid), Padumalaipalai is sounded when Kaikilai becomes Kural (here Kaikilai comes to the aid), Sevvalipalai is sounded when Thuttham becomes Kural (here Thuttham comes to the help), Kodipalai is sounded when Tharam becomes Kural (here Tharam comes to the help), and Vilaripalai sounds when Vilari becomes Kural. (Here Vilari comes to the help.)

From the above extracts we see, that although each Palai has seven strings, the eighth Swaram which is the octave of the commencing Swaram must also be included in the ascending series like SA, RI, GA, MA, PA, DHA, NI and SA.

5. The Seven Palais derived from Kodipalai.

Number.	Sa Kural Ma	Ri Thuttham Pa	Ga Kaikilai Dha	Ma Oolai Ni	Pa Ili Sa	Dha Vilari Ri	Ni Tharam Ga	Sa Kural Ma	Ri Thuttham Pa	Ga Kaikilai Dha	Ma Oolai Ni	Pa Ili Sa	Dha Vilari Ri	Ni Tharam Ga	Sa Kural Ma	Ri Thuttham Pa
	Sa	Ri	Ga	Ma	Pa	Dha	Ni	Sa	Ri	Ga						
1				Sa	Ri	Ga	Ma	Pa	Dha	Ni						
2					Sa	Ri	Ga	Ma	Pa	Dha	Ni					
3						Sa	Ri	Ga	Ma	Pa	Dha	Ni				
4							Sa	Ri	Ga	Ma	Pa	Dha	Ni			
5								Sa	Ri	Ga	Ma	Pa	Dha	Ni		
6									Sa	Ri	Ga	Ma	Pa	Dha	Ni	
7										Sa	Ri	Ga	Ma	Pa	Dha	Ni

1	Ma	Sa	When Oolai is taken as Kural ...	Sempalai.
2	Pa	Sa	When Ili is taken as Kural	Mirsempalai.
3	Dha	Sa	When Vilari is taken as Kural ...	Vilaripalai.
4	Ni	Sa	When Tharam is taken as Kural ...	Kodipalai.
5	Sa	Sa	When Kural is taken as Kural ...	Arumpalai
6	Ri	Sa	When Thuttham is taken as Kural ...	Sevalipalai
7	Ga	Sa	When Kaikilai is taken as Kural ...	Padumalaipalai.

6. The Mandhara, Madhya and Tara Sthayis.

Silappadikaram, Aranketukathai P. 93.

" ஏனை மகளிருங் கிளைவழிச் சேர "

என்பது, இதனைப் பெண்டிருக்குரிய தானமாகிய பதினாற்கோவையிலே பொருந்தக்கட்ட வேண்டுமென்றவாறு. கட்டும்படி:

He says that " this should be added to the 14 Kovais which include the place for women."

" மேல துழையிளி கீழது கைக்கிளை
வம்புறு மரபிற் செம்பாலை யாயது."

என்பது, உழை முதற் கைக்கிளை இறுதியாக மெலிவு நான்கும், சமம் ஏழும், வலிவு மூன்றுமாய் உழை முதலாகச் செய்யப்படுவ தென்க.

He says here, there are four soft sounds from Oolai up to Kaikilai, middling sounds seven and hard sounds three.

From this we are able to conclude that when Oolai commences as the Kural we have four Swarams up to Oolai which takes the place of Tharam (Sa Ri Ga Ma) for the Mandara Sthayi (soft sounds), the seven Swarams from Oolai which takes the place of Tharam up to Kaikilai for the Madhya Sthayi (Middling sounds) and the three Swarams Pa, Dha, Ni above Oolai which commences in Tharam up to Tharam which commences in Kaikilai for the Thara Sthayi (hard sounds).

" வலிவு மெலிவுஞ் சமனு மெல்லாம்
பொலியக் கோத்த புலமை யோனுடன்."

என்பது, இப்படியால், வலிவும் மெலிவும் சமனுமெனப்பட்ட தானங்களிலேயுடைய இசைக்குற்றங்களெல்லாம் நரப்படைவு கெடாமலும், பண்ணீர்மை முதலாயின குன்றாமலும் புணர்க்கவல்லனும், அப்புணர்ப்பிற் கமைந்த எழுத்துக்களால் இசை செய்ய வல்ல யாழாசிரியனுமென்றவாறு. கிறுத்தல் வேண்டிப் பொலியக் கோத்த புலமையோனென்க.

Here he says that an expert in the playing of the Yal should be one who must be able to discriminate and adjust the different bard, soft and middling sounds so that the sweet harmony of the strings and the sounds may not be impaired and who could compose music by arranging these harmonious sounds.

Soft. Mandharam.	Middling. Madhyam	Hard. Taram
Ni, Sa, Ri, Ga	Ma, Pa, Dha, Ni, Sa, Ri, Ga	Ma, Pa, Dha
Ma, Pa, Dha, Ni	Sa, Ri, Ga, Ma, Pa, Dha, Ni	Sa, Ri, Ga

Here, we find that the four Swarams Ni Sa Ri and Ga of the top line belong to the lower Sthayi, the seven Swarams Ma Pa Dha Ni Sa Ri and Ga to the Middle Sthayi and the three Swarams Ma Pa and Dha to the upper Sthayi. In the bottom line the four Swarams Ma Pa Dha and Ni, as are in use at present, belong to the Mandhara Sthayi, the seven Swarams Sa Ri Ga Ma Pa Dha and Ni to the Middle Sthayi and the three Swarams Sa Ri and Ga to the Tara Sthayi. These are the hard, soft and middling sounds.

7. The Vattapalai which was in use in Isai-Tamil.

From the calculations of the Vattapalai we understand that there were four Palais, Ayapalai, Sathurapalai, Thirikonapalai and Vattapalai, and that the calculation of the Srutis of each of them was also given. Looking at the calculations of the Ayapalai, we find they resemble those of the Vattapalai. But we also find that Madavi played her Sakotayal tuning it on the principle of Sa-Pa and that this was the favourite music of women in those days. We have already noted the Sruti system of the Sakota-Yal. Apart from this he mentions how Vattapalai is arrived at, the order of its Swarams, the Srutis for each of the Swarams and the minuter Swarams derived from them. Particulars about Thirikonapalai and Sathurapalai will be given later on. But we are sure that the order of the Swarams of Ayapalai and the particulars about Vatta-palai are enough to determine the state of ancient South Indian music. This Vattapalai is illustrated in the form of a Rasimandalam. To those who have a knowledge of Astrology the Saptasthanams which are arrived at by computing the Sthanams seven by seven omitting the Rasi in which the Swaram occurs, the Kendrasthanams, the Sthanams for Mathru, Putthira, Kalathira and Pithur and the use of the Swarams for the respective Sthanams will be clearly known. These have been clearly set forth in the form of Tables. If one of the Chakarams could be studied and understood, the others will be quite easy. But as the matter contained in them are not in use at the present time, we have thought it well to give them separately.

Silappadikaram, Aychiarkuravai p. 405.

"குடமுத லிடமுறை யாக்குர லுழைத்தும்
கைக்கிளை யுழையிளி விளரி தாரமென
விரிந்த பூங்குழல் வேண்டிய பெயரே."

பாலை நான்கு வகைப்படும்; ஆயப்பாலை, சதுரப்பாலை, திரிகோணப்பாலை, வட்டப்பாலையென. என்னை?

"ஆயஞ் சதுரந் திரிகோணம் வட்டமெனப்
பாய நான்கும் பாலை யாகும்."

There are four kinds of Palai :—Ayapalai, Sathurapalai, Thirikonapalai and Vattapalai.

அவற்றுள் வட்டப்பாலை வருமாறு :

"வட்ட மென்பது வகுக்குங் காலை
போரேழ் நோக்கிய மண்டல மாகும்."

"ஈரணைவு கொண்ட தொகுவட்டத் தன்மேல்
பேணி யிருவகை பெருந்திசைக்—கோணத்
திருவகைய மேலோட்டு மென்பனவு முன்னம்
வகுமுறைய மண்டலத்தை வை."

என்பது [illegible], வட்டப்பாலை மண்டலம் வகுத்துத் [illegible] ஒரு வட்டத்தின் [illegible] மண்டலத்தின் [illegible] [illegible].

This says that a circle must be drawn whose diameter is one span (about 10 inches) and it should be divided into four great sections according to the cardinal points of the compass and the four sections should be divided into 12 equal compartments.

" எதிரும் ராசி வலமிட மாக
வெதிரா விடமீன மாக-முதிராத
வீராறி ராசிகளை யிட்டடைவே நோக்கவே
யோரார்த்த மண்டலமேன் றேண்"

என்பது சூத்திரம் என்னுதலிற்றோவெனின். இட்ட பன்னிரண்டு கோணத்தில் பன்னிரண்டிராசிகளை நிறுத்தினால் இவற்றுள் நரம்புடனியல்வன ஏழென்பதுணர்த்து நுதலிற்று.

If the 12 Rasis be distributed to the 12 compartments, seven of them would indicate the seven sounds.

" எத்து மிடப மலவனுடன் சீயங்
கோற்றனுக் கும்பமோடு மீனமிவை-பார்த்து
தான்முதற் குர மிவைவாய்க் கிடந்த
நிரலேழுஞ் செம்பாலை நேர் "

இவ்வேழும் இடபம், கற்கடகம், சிங்கம், துலாம், தனுசு, கும்பம், மீனமென இவற்றனிற்கும்.

These seven sounds would occur on the following seven signs of the Zodiac :—Idapam, Karkatakam, Simham, Thulam, Thanusu. Kumbam and Meenam.

" துலைநிலைக் குரலுந் தனுநிலைத் துத்தமு
நிலைபெற கும்பத்து நேர்கைக் கிளையு
மீனத் துழையும் விடைநிலைத் தினியு
மானக் கடகத்து மன்னிய விளரியு
மரியிடைத் தாரமு மமைவுறக் கோளலே "

This also illustrates the above. The Mathirais of these seven strings or sounds are indicated by what is quoted below.

இனி நரம்புகளின் மாத்திரைகள் வருமாறு :—

" குரைத்த நான்கு கிளைமுன் றிரண்டாங்
துழையா வுழையிளி நான்கு-விளையா
விளரியெனின் மூன்றிரண்டு தாரமெனச் சொன்னார்
களிசேர் கவின்னூற் றவர் "

எனக்கொள்க. இவற்றுள், தாரத்து உழைபிறக்கும்; உழையிற் குரல் பிறக்கும்; குரலுள் இளிபிறக்கும்; இளியுள் துத்தம்பிறக்கும்; துத்தத்துள் விளரிபிறக்கும்; விளரியுள் கைக்கிளை பிறக்குமெனக்கொள்க. இவற்றுள் முதலிற்றோன்றிய நரம்பு தாரம்; இவை விரிப்பிற்பெருகும்; வந்தவழிக் கண்டுகொள்க."

In the above he says that " Oolai generates from Tharam, Kural from Oolai, Ili from Kural, Thuttham from Ili, Vilari from Thuttham and Kaikilai from Vilari. Of these the first string is Tharam. We need not dilate on this, the others might be easily understood."

In accordance with the above Sootrams and their annotation, we may make the following Chakaram and divide it into 12 compartments for the 12 signs of the Zodiac commencing with Mesham and ending with Meenam. Within these 12 compartments, we should arrange the sapta swarams thus:—

(See next page)

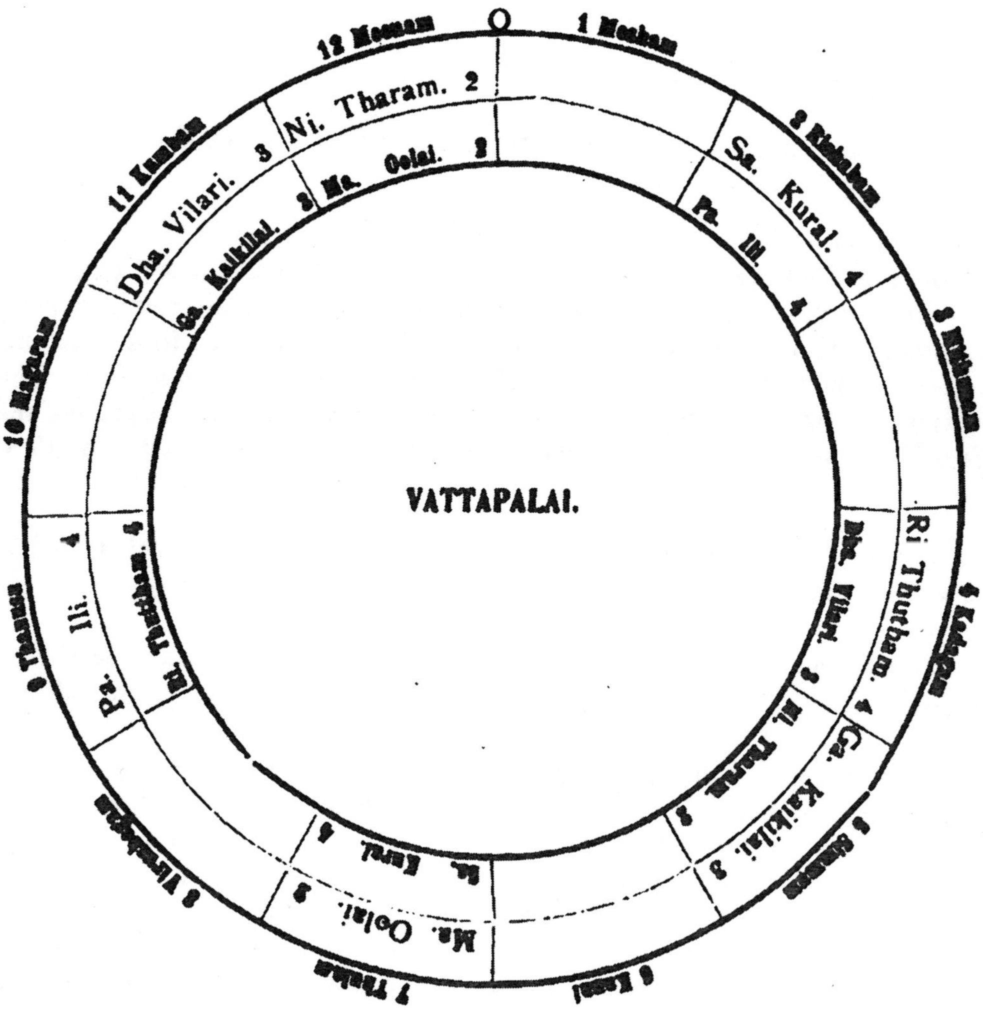

Kural	(Sa)	and Ili	(Pa)	in Rishabam	or the	2nd	compartment.
Thuttham	(Ri)	and Vilari	(Dha)	in Katakam	„	4th	„
Kaikilai	(Ga)	and Tharam	(Ni)	in Simham	„	5th	„
Oolai	(Ma)	and Kural	(Sa)	in Thulam	„	7th	„
Ili	(Pa)	and Thuttham	(Ri)	in Thanusu	„	9th	„
Vilari	(Dha)	and Kaikilai	(Ga)	in Kumbam	„	11th	„
Tharam	(Ni)	and Oolai	(Ma)	in Meenam	„	12th	„

Of these Kural has 4 Alagus, Thuttham 4, Kaikilai 3, Oolai 2, Ili 4, Vilari 3 and Tharam 2 or in all there are 22 Alagus.

Here the author says that Oolai will be derived from Tharam, in the 12th compartment or if we take the seventh place from there, this Oolai will be derived from Thulam, that Kural will be derived from Rishabam (2nd compartment) which is the seventh place from Thulam that Thuttham from Ili will be derived from Thanusu (9th compartment) which is the seventh place from Rishabam, that Vilari from Thuttham will be derived from Katakam which is the seventh place from Thanusu, and that Kaikilai from Vilari will be derived from Kumbam which is the seventh place from Katakam.

In the 12th compartment at the sign of Meenam, Oolai generates from Tharam and Kural from Oolai. This is the first born among sounds.

The Chakaram for Vattapalai also gives clearly the Swarams and their respective Alagus.

When we notice the Chakaram we find that Swarams occur in places which proceed by sevens. These proceed also by the Sa-Pa system. The first Swaram and its derived Swaram in the seventh place will stand in the relation of Kalathiram to each other. If the first Swaram be 1, the Kalathira Swaram will be 1½. If a Sthayi comes to an end on the first Swaram after a cycle, the end Swaram will be double the original Swaram, whereas a concordant Swaram will stand in the relation of 1 to 1½. The Swarams with the latter ratio will be as harmonious as the harmony between Sakti and Sivam, husband and wife. In Astrology, the seventh from the original Sthanam, is considered the Kalathira Sthanam, but here as Athara Shadjam is taken to be 0, if we proceed by sevens omitting the original Sthanam we shall obtain, as in Astrology, all the Swarams of a Ragam, their relation as Chathru and Mithru, Kalathira and Puthira, Mathur and Pithir and their respective uses. It will enable us to discord all the Chathru Swarams and include the Mithru Swarams. Of these more ater on.

8. The 12 Palais derived from Vattapalai while changing Grahams and their Chakarams.

Silappadikaram, Arangetukathai Page 93

வன்மையிற் கிடந்த தார பாகமு
மென்மையிற் கிடந்த குரலின் பாகமு
மெய்க்கிளை நரம்பிற் கைக்கிளை கொள்ளக்
கைக்கிளை யொழிந்த பாகமும் பொற்புடைத்
தளராத் தாரம் விளரிக் கீத்துக்
கிளைவழிப் பட்டன ளாங்கே கிளையுந்
தன்கிளை யழிவுகண் டவள்வயிற் சேர

என்பது

" தார பாகமுங் குரலின் பாகமு
நேர்கடு வண்கிளை கொள்ள நிற்ப
முன்னர்ப்பாகமும் பின்னர்ப் பாகமும்
விளரிகுர லாகு மென்மனார் புலவர் "

என்னுஞ் சூத்திரத்தின் விருத்தி, வட்டப்பாலையின் முடிவுதானமாய், வலித்த நிலைமையினையுடைய தாரம் பெற்ற இரண்டலகில் ஓரலகையும், இப்பாலையின் முதல் தானமாய் மெலிவினிற்கும் குரல் நரம்பு பெற்ற நாலலகில் இரண்டலகையும், தார நரம்பில் அந்தரக்கோலிலே கைக்கிளையாக நிறுத்தத், தாரந்தான் கைக்கிளையாயிற்று. அந்த நரம்பில், ஒழிந்த ஓரலகையும் பண்டை விளரியிலே கூட்ட, அவ்விளரி துத்தநரம்பாயிற்று. இப்படிப் பன்னிருகாற்றிரிக்கப், பன்னிரு பாலையும் பிறக்கும். பன்னிரு பாலையினுந், தொண்ணூற்றொன்றும் பன்னிரண்டுமாய்ப், பண்கள் நூற்றுமூன்றாதற்குக் காரணமாமெனக்கொள்க. இவ்விடத்துத் தார நரம்பின் அந்தரக் கோலைத் தாரமென்றார்.

According to the above Sootrams, one of the two Alagus of Tharam which belongs to the hard Sthayi, from the last Sthanam of Vattapalai, added on to the two out of the four Alagus of Kural (in the soft Sthayi) from the first Sthanam of this same Palai—when these Alagus are converted into Kaikilai in the Thara string, the Tharam becomes Kaikilai. When the single Alagu left out in the same string when added on to the old Vilari, the same Vilari becomes the string for Thuttham. In the same manner the twelve palais are dealt with. From these twelve palais are derived the 91 and 12 *Puns* or 103 *Puns* in all. Here the Andarakole of the Thara string is taken as Tharam.

This is also confirmed by the Sootram

" தன்னுமுந் தாரமுந் தன்வழிப் படூஉ ".

From the above words we conclude that when we place Ma with 2 Alagus on the fourth Alagu of Sa, the Sa becomes Ma.

Ga should be placed in the second Alagu of Sa. The first and second Alagus of Sa along with the twenty second Alagu of Ni become the three Alagus of Ga.

After this, the first or the twenty first Alagu of Ni when added on to the three Alagus of Dha, becomes four. Ri should be placed on the first Alagu of Ni or the twenty first place.

After the four Alagus of Ri, in other words, under Pa the 17th place, Sa should be located.

In the same manner the Pa with four Srutis from Ma located after the fourth Alagu of Sa, should be placed on the Ri which occurs as the 8th Sruti.

Above that, the Dha with 3 Srutis should come after Ga in the 11th place or the third from Ri.

The Ni with 2 Srutis should come under Ma the 13th which is two Srutis above Ga.

Now we find that the seven Swarams Sa, Ri, Ga, Ma, Pa, Dha and Ni or Ma, Pa, Dha, Ni, Sa, Ri and Ga commence from the Swarams with the following Alagus—Sa$_4$, Ri$_4$, Ga$_3$, Ma, Pa$_4$, Dha$_3$ and Ni$_2$. In the same manner the seven Swarams Ma, Ga, Ri, Sa, Ni, Dha and Pa commence from the fourth Sruti of Sa. These seven are called the Seven Primary Palais. Their names will be mentioned hereafter.

Moreover, the Ri which occurs on the first Alagu of Sa, the Sa on the second Alagu, the Ni on the second Alagu the Pa on the first Alagu, and the Ma on the second Alagu—these five are called the secondary Palais.

Thus he accounts for the 12 palais—seven primary and five secondary. These twelve palais are obtained while proceeding towards the right. The 12 palais obtained while proceeding towards the left, their Alagus, their names, and the seven palais derived from each of the seven primary palais will be mentioned in the chakarams that follow.

The 12 Palais of the Vattapalai.

The Chakaram showing the Vattapalai proceeding towards the right.

	M				P			D		N				S				R			G		M
	13	14	15	16	17	18	19	20	21	22	1	2	3	4	5	6	7	8	9	10	11	12	13
1	N				S				R			G		M				P			D		N
2	D		N				S				R			G		M				P			D
3		D		N				S				R			G		M				P		
4	P			D		N				S				R			G		M				P
5			P			D		N				S				R			G		M		
6	M				P			D		N				S				R			G		M
7	G		M				P			D		N				S				R			G
8			G		M				P			D		N				S				R	
9		R			G		M				P			D		N				S			
10			R			G		M				P			D		N				S		
11	S				R			G		M				P			D		N				S
12			S				R			G		M				P			D		N		

1. When Kural is taken as Kural it is Sempalai.
2. When Thuttham is taken as Kural it is Padumalaipalai.
3. When Kaikilai is taken as Kural it is Sevvalipalai.
4. When Oolai is taken as Kural it is Arumpalai.
5. When Ii is taken as Kural it is Kodipalai.
6. When Vilari is taken as Kural it is Vilaripalai.
7. When Tharam is taken as Kural it is Mirsempalai.

I

When Kural is taken as Kural it is Sempalai. (proceeding towards the right)

	N				S				R			G		M				P			D		N
	22	1	2	3	4	5	6	7	8	9	10	11	12	13	14	15	16	17	18	19	20	21	22
1	N				S				R			G		M				P			D		N
2			D		N				S				R			G		M				P	
3		P			D		N				S				R			G		M			
4	M				P			D		N				S				R			G		M
5			G		M				P			D		N				S				R	
6		R			G		M				P			D		N				S			
7	S				R			G		M				P			D		N				S

II

When Thuttham is taken as Kural it is Padumalaipalai. (proceeding towards the right)

	D		N				S				R			G		M				P			D
	20	21	22	1	2	3	4	5	6	7	8	9	10	11	12	13	14	15	16	17	18	19	20
1			S				R			G		M				P			D		N		
2	D		N				S				R			G		M				P			D
3		P			D		N				S				R			G		M			
4				P			D		N				S				R			G		M	
5	G		M				P			D		N				S				R			G
6		R			G		M				P			D		N				S			
7				R			G		M				P			D		N				S	

III

When Kaikilai is taken as Kural it is Sevvalipalai. (proceeding towards the right)

	P			D		N				S				R			G		M				P
	17	18	19	20	21	22	1	2	3	4	5	6	7	8	9	10	11	12	13	14	15	16	17
1			S				R			G		M				P			D		N		
2		N				S				R			G		M				P			D	
3	P			D		N				S				R			G		M				P
4	M				P			D		N				S				R			G		M
5	G		M				P			D		N				S				R			G
6	R			G		M				P			D		N				S				R
7	S				R			G		M				P			D		N				S

IV

When Oolai is taken as Kural it is Arumpalai. (proceeding towards the right)

	M				P			D		N				S				R			G		M
	13	14	15	16	17	18	19	20	21	22	1	2	3	4	5	6	7	8	9	10	11	12	13
1	N				S				R			G		M				P			D		N
2	D		N				S				R			G		M				P			D
3	P			D		N				S				R			G		M				P
4	M				P			D		N				S				R			G		M
5			G		M				P			D		N				S				R	
6		R			G		M				P			D		N				S			
7	S				R			G		M				P			D		N				S

V

When Ili is taken as Kural it is Kodippalai. (proceeding towards the rihgt)

	G		M				P			D		N				S				R			G
	11	12	13	14	15	16	17	18	19	20	21	22	1	2	3	4	5	6	7	8	9	10	11
1			S				R			G		M				P			D		N		
2	D		N				S				R			G		M				P			D
3			D		N				S				R			G		M				P	
4			P			D		N				S				R			G		M		
5	G		M				P			D		N				S				R			G
6		R			G		M				P			D		N				S			
7				R			G		M				P			D		N				S	

VI

When Vilari is taken as Kural it is Vilaripalai. (proceeding towards the right)

	R			G		M				P			D		N				S				
	8	9	10	11	12	13	14	15	16	17	18	19	20	21	22	1	2	3	4	5	6	7	8
1			S				R			G		M				P			D		N		
2		N				S				R			G		M				P			D	
3	P			D		N				S				R			G		M				P
4			P			D		N				S				R			G		M		
5		M				P			D		N				S				R			G	
6	R			G		M				P			D		N				S				R
7	S				R			G		M				P			D		N				S

VII

When Tharam is taken as Kural it is Mersempalai. (proceeding towards the right)

	S				R			G		M				P			D		N				S
	4	5	6	7	8	9	10	11	12	13	14	15	16	17	18	19	20	21	22	1	2	3	4
1	N				S				R			G		M				P			D		N
2	D		N				S				R			G		M				P			D
3	P			D		N				S				R			G		M				P
4	M				P			D		N				S				R			G		M
5	G		M				P			D		N				S				R			G
6	R			G		M				P			D		N				S				R
7	S				R			G		M				P			D		N				S

The above tables show the twelve palais obtained while proceeding towards the right, and the seven palais derived from each of the seven primary palais. Here we see that each Swaram occurs according to its regular Alagu system on the right side. We find that while they proceed on the right each row has 22 Alagus. The seven primary palais are named here. He says that these are used in Kulal. On the whole they show us how Grahams are changed and how different Ragas generate in the process.

9. The 12 Palais derived from Vattapalai proceeding to the left.

Silappadikaram, Venirkathai p. 202.

" குரல்வா யிளிவாய்க் கேட்டனள்."

(இ-ள்) குரல்முதலாக எடுத்து இளிகுரலாக வாசித்தாளென்க.

This means " She commenced from Kural, and then proceeded with Ili as Kural."

இனி வட்டப்பாலை இடமுறை திரிபு கூறுகின்றார்.

Next he goes to show how Vattapalai proceeds towards the left.

" குன்றுக் குரற்பாதி தாரத்தி லொன்று
கவே ளிளைகிளை யாக்கிக்—கோடியிடையாம்
தாரத்தி லொன்று விளரிமே லேறடவக்
கேரத் தருகுரலா மின்று "

என்-எனின், உழைகுரலாகிய கோடிப்பாலை நீக்க இடமுறை திரிபுமிடத்துக் குரல் குரலாயது செம்பாலை இதனிலே, குரலிற்பாதியும் தாரத்திலொன்றும் இரண்டின் அந்தரத்திலே கிளையாக்கித், தாரத்திலேநின்ற ஓரலகை விளரியின் மேலேறட, விளரி குரலாய்ப் படுமலைப்பாலையாம். இம்முறையே, துத்தம் குரலாயது செவ்வழிப்பாலையாம். இளி குரலாயது அரும்பாலையாம். கைக்கிளை குரலாயது மேற்செம்பாலையாம். தாரம் குரலாயது விளரிப்பாலையாம். என அந்தரமைந்து நீக்கி உறழ்ந்து கண்டுகொள்க. இவ்விடத்தில் தாரநரம்பின் அந்தரக்கோலைத் தாரமென்றது.

" தன்னமுந் தாரமுந் தன்வழிப் படர "

என்னுஞ் சூத்திர விதியாலென்க. இவ்வேழு பெரும்பாலையினையும் முதலாகத்து நூற்றுமூன்று பண்ணும் பிறக்கும். அவற்றுள் செம்பாலையுட் பிறக்கும் பண்கள் பாலையாழ், நகராகம், ஆகரி, தோடி, கௌடி, காந்தாரம், செந்துருத்தி, உதயகிரி யெனவிவை. பிறவும் விரிப்பின் உரை பெருகுமாதலின் அவற்றை வந்த வழிக்கண்டு கொள்க.

He says " omitting Kodipalai where Oolai is Kural, when we proceed towards the left, we get Sempalai where Kural is taken as Kural. Of these, when half of Kural and one of Tharam become the branch Swarams at the end of the Second, and when one of the Alagus of Tharam is added on to Vilari, Vilari becomes Kural and produces Padumalaipalai. In the same manner when Thuttham becomes Kural, it is Sevvalipalai. When Ili becomes Kural, it is Arumpalai ; when Kaikilai becomes Kural, it is Merchempalai. When Tharam becomes Kural, it is Vilaripalai. Thus you see that the five Antharams are omitted and the others taken. The authority for taking the Antharam of the Thara string as Tharam is the Sootram, " *தன்னமுந் தாரமுந் தன்வழிப்படர.*" The 103 *puns* generate from these Seven primary palais. Of these the *puns* derived from Sempalai are as follows :—Palaiyal, Nagaragam, Agari, Thodi, Goudi, Gandharam, Chenthurithi, Oothayagiri and others. Others may be found it in the same way. We omit them for the sake of being brief."

Here he gives the result of Vattapalai proceeding by the left. We noticed before the Vattapalai proceeding by the right and their chakrams. Both are based on the same principle. We should note here (1) the Kural appearing in Oolai in the Rasi Meenam (2) the Kural from Rishabam (3) the Kural from Thulam and (4) the Kural appearing in Thanusu. When we draw the attention to their importance we mean that they obtain a large number of concordant Swarams. They proceed by left and right. When they proceed from the 12th rasi as Sa, Ri, Ga and Ma in the order of Meenam, Mesham, Rishabam, Mithunam and Kadagam they go towards the right, when the Kural in Rishabam proceeds in the order of Mesham, Meenam, Kumbam and Maharam it goes towards the left. We noted the Swarams by the Sa-Pa system towards the right. Now proceeding left by the Sa-Ma system, we obtain (1) Sempalai in Rishabham when Kural appears in Kural (2) Vilaripalai in Meenam when Kural appears in Tharam (3) Padumalaipalai when Kural appears in Kumbam or Vilari, (4) Arumpalai when Kural appears in Ili which is in Thanusu (5) Kodipalai when Kural appears in Oolai in Thulam (6) Mirsempalai when Kural appears in Kaikilai which is

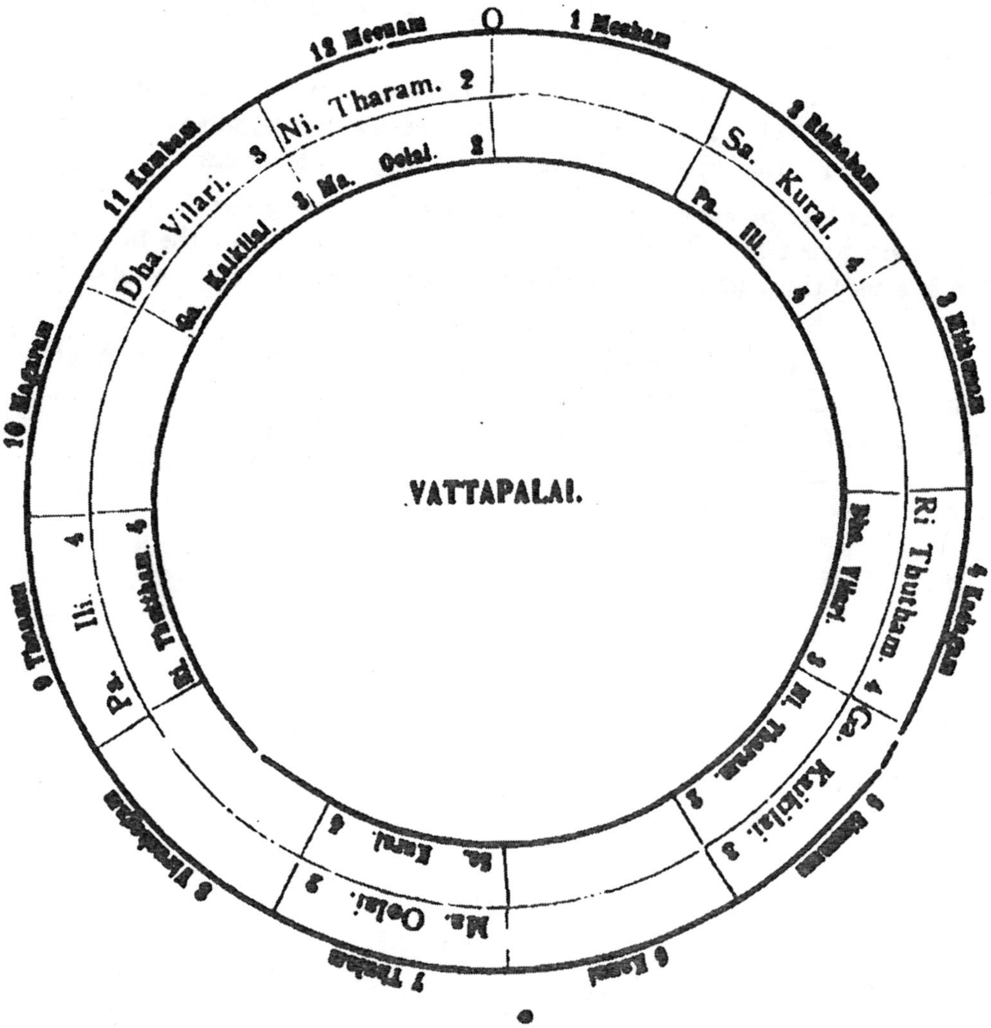

in Simham, (7) Sevvalipalai when Kural appears in Thuttham which is in Kadagam and (8) Sempalai when Kural is taken as Kural. In the same manner the Swarams of Arumpalai when Ili becomes Kural among the palais which change their places may be seen in the following chakaram.

It is said there "குரலாய் இளியாய்ப் பெட்டவள்". It means that she first played in Kural as the commencing Swaram and then made Ili the first. In other words she commenced from Kural in Rishabam and then made Ili into Kural. The four Swarams Sa, Ri, Ga and Dha commencing from Rishabam become Pa, Dha, Ni and Sa when they are taken in the Mandara Sthayi. The seven Swarams Sa, Ri, Ga. Ma, Pa, Dha and Ni from Thanusu to Thanusu become the Madhyasthayi. The three Swarams Pa, Dha and Ni become Sa, Ri and Ga and belong to Thara Sthayi. When Ili becomes Kural it appears to be Panchama Sruti, and when Oolai in Thulam becomes Kural, it appears to be Madhya Sruti. In other words, the Saranai string should be tuned to Pa of the Anusaranai string and Ma.

He says that the abovementioned Vattapalai proceeding towards the left is made use of in the Yal. This seems to have been used in Sakotayal, a very favourite Ganam of women. Its important hamsam will be given later on.

The twelve palais are thus generated while proceeding towards the left. The seven primary palais Ma, Pa, Dha, Ni, Sa, Ri, Ga derived from the fourth Sruti of Sa and the five secondary palais derived from its other Srutis will be given in a table later on.

When we proceed left we go by five Rasis at each step which stand in the relation of Sa-Ma. For example, Thanusu from Rishabam is the fifth rasi or Ili in Kural; Thulam from Meenam is the fifth or Kural in Oolai; Rishabam is fifth from Thulam; Kadagam from Thanusu is fifth; Kumbam from Kadagam is fifth. So this process towards the left forms the descending scale or Avaroganam or Sa-Ma series.

The 12 Palais of the Vattapalai.

The Chakaram showing the Vattapalai proceeding towards the left.

	M				P			D		N				S				R			G		M
	13	14	15	16	17	18	19	20	21	22	1	2	3	4	5	6	7	8	9	10	11	12	13
1	N				S				R			G		M				P			D		N
2			S				R			G		M				P			D		N		
3	S				R			G		M				P			D		N				S
4			R			G		M				P			D		N				S		
5		R			G		M				P			D		N				S			
6			G		M				P			D		N				S				R	
7	G		M				P			D		N				S				R			G
8	M				P			D		N				S				R			G		M
9			P			D		N				S				R			G		M		
10	P			D		N				S				R			G		M				P
11		D		N				S				R			G		M				P		
12	D		N				S				R			G		M				P			D

1. When Kural is taken as Kural it is Sempalai.
2. When Thutthain is taken as Kural it is Sevvalipalai.
3. When Kaikilai is taken as Kural it is Mirsempalai.
4. When Oolai is taken as Kural it is Kodipalai.
5. When Ili is taken as Kural it is Arumpalai.
6. When Vilari is taken as Kural it is Padumalaipalai.
7. When Tharam is taken as Kural it is Vilaripalai.

I

When [illegible] taken as Kural it is Sempalai. (proceeding towards the left)

	N				S				R			G		M				P			D		N
	22	1	2	3	4	5	6	7	8	9	10	11	12	13	14	15	16	17	18	19	20	21	22
1	N				S				R			G		M				P			D		N
2	S				R			G		M				P			D		N				S
3		R			G		M				P			D		N				S			
4			G		M				P			D		N				S				R	
5	M				P			D		N				S				R			G		M
6		P			D		N				S				R			G		M			
7			D		N				S				R			G		M				P	

II

When Thuttham is taken as Kural it is Sevvalipalai. (proceeding towards the left)

	D		N				S				R			G		M				P			D
	20	21	22	1	2	3	4	5	6	7	8	9	10	11	12	13	14	15	16	17	18	19	20
1			S				R			G		M				P			D		N		
2				R			G		M				P			D		N				S	
3		R			G		M				P			D		N				S			
4	G		M				P			D		N				S				R			G
5				P			D		N				S				R			G		M	
6		P			D		N				S				R			G		M			
7	D		N				S				R			G		M				P			D

III

When Kaikilai is taken as Kural it is Mirsempalai. (proceeding towards the left)

	P			D		N				S				R			G		M				P
	17	18	19	20	21	22	1	2	3	4	5	6	7	8	9	10	11	12	13	14	15	16	17
1			S				R			G		M				P			D		N		
2	S				R			G		M				P			D		N				S
3	R			G		M				P			D		N				S				R
4	G		M				P			D		N				S				R			G
5	M				P			D		N				S				R			G		M
6	P			D		N				S				R			G		M				P
7		N				S				R			G		M				P			D	

IV

When Oolai is taken as Kural it is Kodipalai. (proceeding towards the left)

	M				P			D		N				S				R			G		M
	13	14	15	16	17	18	19	20	21	22	1	2	3	4	5	6	7	8	9	10	11	12	13
1	N				S				R			G		M				P			D		N
2	S				R			G		M				P			D		N				S
3		R			G		M				P			D		N				S			
4			G		M				P			D		N				S				R	
5	M				P			D		N				S				R			G		M
6	P			D		N				S				R			G		M				P
7	D		N				S				R			G		M				P			D

V

When Ili is taken as Kural it is Arumpalai. (proceeding towards the left)

	G		M				P			D		N				S				R			G
	11	12	13	14	15	16	17	18	19	20	21	22	1	2	3	4	5	6	7	8	9	10	11
1			S				R			G		M				P			D		N		
2				R			G		M				P			D		N				S	
3		R			G		M				P			D		N				S			
4	G		M				P			D		N				S				R			G
5			P			D		N				S				R			G		M		
6			D		N				S				R			G		M				P	
7	D		N				S				R			G		M				P			D

VI

When Vilari is taken as Kural it is Padumalaipalai. (proceeding towards the left)

	R			G		M				P			D		N				S				R
	8	9	10	11	12	13	14	15	16	17	18	19	20	21	22	1	2	3	4	5	6	7	8
1			S				R			G		M				P			D		N		
2	S				R			G		M				P			D		N				S
3	R			G		M				P			D		N				S				R
4		M				P			D		N				S				R			G	
5			P			D		N				S				R			G		M		
6	P			D		N				S				R			G		M				P
7		N				S				R			G		M				P			D	

VII

When Tharam is taken as Kural it is Vilaripalai. (proceeding towards the left)

	S				R			G		M				P			D		N				S
	4	5	6	7	8	9	10	11	12	13	14	15	16	17	18	19	20	21	22	1	2	3	4
1	N				S				R			G		M				P			D		N
2	S				R			G		M				P			D		N				S
3	R			G		M				P			D		N				S				R
4	G		M				P			D		N				S				R			G
5	M				P			D		N				S				R			G		M
6	P			D		N				S				R			G		M				P
7	D		N				S				R			G		M				P			D

When we notice the above 12 palais proceeding towards the left, the seven primary palais derived from them, and the seven other palais derived from each of them we find that MA that takes the place of SA is a descending series though it resembles the Vattapalai that proceeds towards the right. In same way we find that each Swaram proceeds to the left commencing from MA the 13th Sruti in the top right hand side of the chakaram. For example, we find SA in MA, the 13th Sruti, SA in the 10th Sruti of the second GA, SA in the 8th Sruti of RI and so on. But in Vattapalai proceeding to the right, we find that SA commences from the 13th Sruti of MA in the top left hand side of the chakaram, and finishes at the 13th Sruti of MA at the bottom right hand side of the chakaram. He says, that though both of them appear like an ascending and descending series, their use is different. He says that the progression towards the left is for the use of Yal, and the progression towards the left is for that of Kulal (flute). We shall see later on the four primary palais derived from the Vattapalai proceeding towards the left which was used for the Yal and the chakarams giving the particulars about them.

10. The four kinds of Yal—Palai, Marutham, Kurinji and Neythal—in use in South India in ancient times.

Silappadikaram, Venirkathai Page 202.

" நாற்பெரும்பண்ணும் சாதி நான்கும்
பாற்படுத்திறனும் பண்ணெனப்படுமே "

We have noted before that there were four kinds of Palai—namely (1) Ayapalai (2) Vattapalai, (3) Thirikonapalai (4) Chathurapalai—in ancient times. No particulars are given about either Thirikonapalai or Chathurapalai. It will be out of place to give measurements for something about which no particulars have been given. Of these, he ascribe 14 Palais for Ayapalai, the first 7 palais from Kodipalai where Tharam becomes Kural and 7 palais from Sempalai where Kural is taken as Kural. They have been given in the previous table. He ascribes 12 palais for the fourth, namely, Vattapalai—7 primary palais from Kural and 5 Secondary palais. From these seven primary palais obtained by proceeding left, he derives the four Yals which are obtained as follows ;—

When Tharam becomes Kural it is Palai Yal, when Kural becomes Ili it is Marutha Yal, when Oolai becomes Kural it is Kurinji Yal and when Ili becomes Thuttham it is Neythal Yal. There is reason to believe that these are the primary *puns*.

To explain these Palais further,

(i) In the following Chakram, Palai Yal is derived when Oolai appears in Tharam proceeding towards the left. In other words, proceeding towards the left from Simham to the fifth rasi Meenam we get Palai Yal where Tharam becomes Kural.

(ii) Kural appears in Oolai. In other words, Kural occurs in Thulam, the fifth rasi from Meenam proceeding on the left side. This he calls Kurinji Yal where Oolai becomes Kural.

(iii) Marutha Yal is obtained when Kural becomes Ili in the fifth Rasi (Rishapam) from Thulam (proceeding on the left) where Oolai takes the place of Kural.

(iv) Neythal Yal is obtained when Ili takes the place of Thuttham in Thanusu, the fifth rasi to the left from Marutha Yal (Rishabam) where Kural takes the place of Ili.

Specially noting the above observations, we have reason to suppose that when Oolai appearing in Thulam becomes Kural towards the right side he intends it to be Kodipalai. It proceeds from Thulam up to Simham towards the right as Sa, Ri, Ga, Ma, Pa, Dha and Ni.

Now when we proceed from Simham towards the left by fifths we get the Swarams in Meenam, Thulam, Rishabam and Thanusu and ganam is made taking these Swarams as Kural. In other words when Kural commences in these Rasis the Alagus are not odd but even in Meenam (2, 2) in Thulam (2, 4), in Rishabam (4, 4) and in Thanusu (4, 4). But in other rasis they are odd as (4, 3), (3, 2) and (3, 3). So we see that he omits the Rasis with odd Alagus and takes only those with even ones. These he calls the four Primary *Puns*.

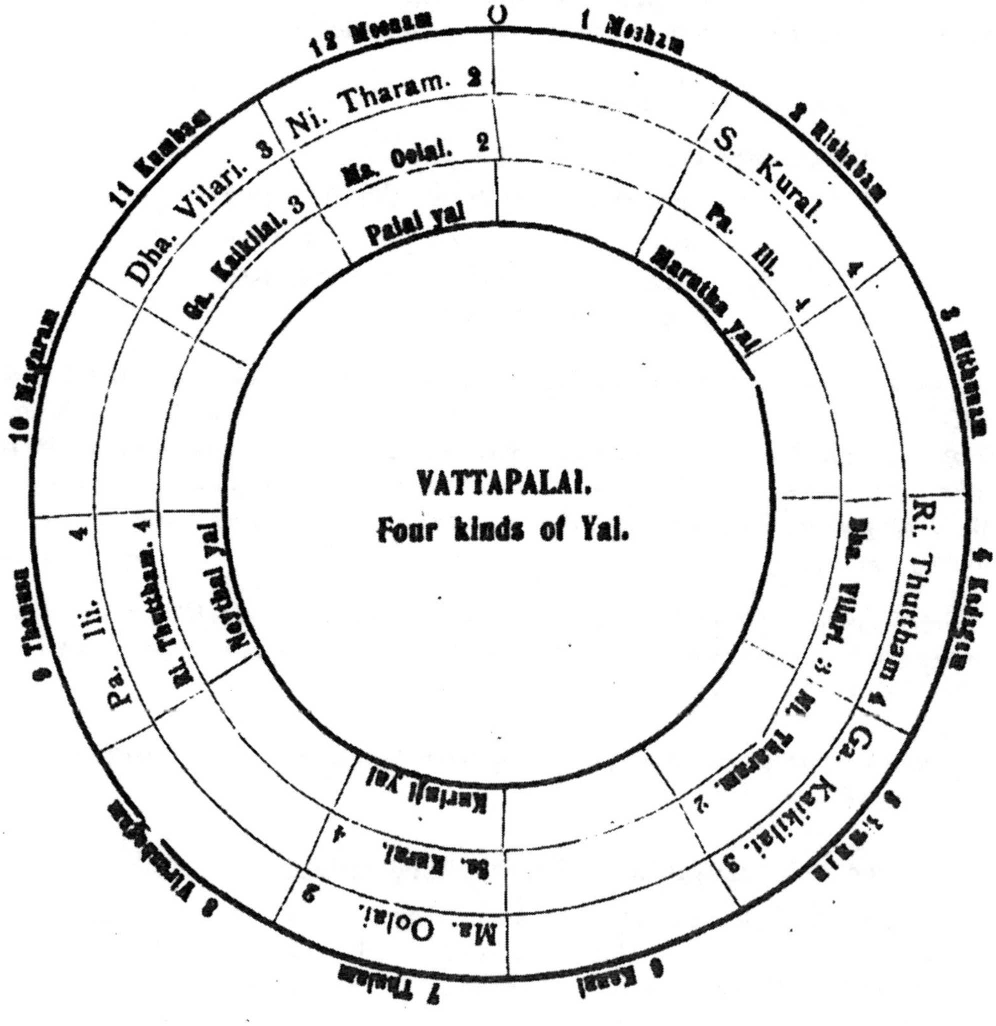

(i) These four are the most important among the seven primary palais. When Oolai appears in Tharam it is Palai Yal. In this Palai Yal, Tharam becomes Kural.

(ii) Kurinji Yal is obtained when Kural appears in Oolai.

(iii) Marutha Yal is obtained when Ili appears in Kural.

(iv) Neythal Yal results when Kural appears in Ili.

These are the four primary *Puns*. Each of these is capable of producing seven other *puns*. These are as follows :—

In the four Rasis Rishabam, Thulam, Thanusu and Meenam the four primary puns generate. As for the others the following quotation will explain.

Silappadikaram, Achiarkuravai Page 405 406.

"இப்பாலை யாழுள்ளே எழு பாலை யிசை பிறக்கும்.

"குரலிளியிற் பாகத்தை வாங்கியோ ரொன்று
வரையாது தாரத் துழைக்கும்—விரைவின்றி
யெத்தும் விளரி கிளைக்கீக்க வேந்திழையாய்
துத்தங் குரலாகுஞ் சோல்."

இந் நரம்பிற் பாலை பிறக்குமிடத்துக் குரலும் துத்தமும் இளியும் நான்கு மாத்திரை பெறும்; கைக்கிளையும் விளரியும் மூன்று மாத்திரை பெறும்; உழையும் தாரமும் இரண்டு மாத்திரை பெறும்; இவற்றுட் குரல் குரலாய் ஒத்து நின்றது செம்பாலை; இதனிலே குரலிற் பாகத்தையும் இளியிற் பாகத்தையும் வாங்கிக் கைக்கிளை உழை விளரி தாரத்திற்கு ஒரோ வொன்றைக்கொண்டு சேர்க்கத் துத்தங்குரலாய்ப் படுமலைப்பாலையாம். இவ்வாறே திரிக்க இவ்வேழு பெரும் பாலைகளும் பிறக்கும். பிறக்குங்கால் திரிந்த குரலேழும் முதலாகப் பிறக்கும். அவை பிறக்குமாறு :—

குரல் குரலாயது செம்பாலை; துத்தம் குரலாயது படுமலைப்பாலை; கைக்கிளை குரலாயது செவ்வழிப் பாலை; உழைகுரலாயது அரும்பாலை; இளிகுரலாயது கோடிப்பாலை; விளரிகுரலாயது விளரிப்பாலை; தாரம் குரலாயது மேற்செம்பாலை யென வரன்முறையே எழுபாலையுங் கண்டு கொள்க.

இதனை வரன்முறை யென்றும்; மேற்கே முகமாக விருந்து திரிதலான். கிழக்கே நோக்கியிருக்கில் இடமுறையாமெனக்கொள்க."

" From this Palaiyal Seven Palais will be derived.

Where the Palai is formed in this string, Kural, Thuttham and Ili have 4 Mathirais each ; Kaikilai and Vilari 3 Mathirais each ; Oolai and Tharam two each. Of these when Kural takes the place of Kural it is Sempalai ; of these when parts of Kural and Ili are added on to Kaikilai, Vilari and Tharam, Padumalaipalai is obtained, Thuttham becoming Kural. In this manner the seven Primary Palais are obtained. In the process of their formation the seven changed Kurals (as opposed to standard Kurals) will occur first. This is how they are obtained :—

When Kural stands for Kural we obtain Sempalai ; when Thuttham becomes Kural it is Padumalaipalai ; Sevvalipalai is obtained when Kaikilai becomes Kural ; when Oolai becomes Kural it is Arumpalai ; when Ili becomes Kural we get Kodipalai, Vilaripalai is obtained when Vilari becomes Kural and when Tharam becomes Kural it is Mersempalai. He says these Seven palais are obtained by *Varan Murai* or from the right side because they proceed westwards or towards the right. When it proceeds eastwards it is towards the left.

How the Seven Palais are derived. The Chakaram showing how they generate towards right and left.

		S	R	G	M	P	D	N			
I Towards the left. (East)	R 7	4	3	2	4	3	2	4	N	M	When Tharam takes the part of Oolai etc.
	G 6	3	2	4	3	2	4	4	D	G	When Vilari takes the part of Kaikilai etc.
	* M 5	2	4	3	2	4	4	3	P	R	When Ili takes the part of Thuttham etc.
	* P 4	4	3	2	4	4	3	2	M	S	When Ooli takes the part of Kural etc.
	D 3	3	2	4	4	3	2	4	G	N	When Kaikilai takes the part of Tharam etc:
	* N 2	2	4	4	3	2	4	3	R	D	When Thuttham takes the part of Vilari etc.
	* S 1	4	4	3	2	4	3	2	S	P	When Kural takes the part of Ili
II Towards the right. (West)	R 2	2	4	4	3	2	4	3	R	D	When Thuttham takes the part of Vilari etc.
	G 3	3	2	4	4	3	2	4	G	N	When Kaikilai takes the part of Tharam etc.
	M 4	4	3	2	4	4	3	2	M	S	When Ooli takes the part of Kural etc.
	P 5	2	4	3	2	4	4	3	P	R	When Ili takes the part of Thuttham etc.
	D 6	3	2	4	3	2	4	4	D	G	When Vilari takes the part Kaikilai etc.
	N 7	4	3	2	4	3	2	4	N	M	When Tharam takes the part of Ooli etc.

In the above Chakaram we may see the Alagus proceeding towards the left marked 7, 6, 5, 4, 3, 2 and 1 as well as the Alagus proceeding towards the right marked 1, 2, 3, 4, 5, 6 and 7. Here the change of graham of the Sapta Swarams according to the rules of Vattapalai may be clearly seen where they should occur as 4, 4, 3, 2, 4, 3, 2 or 22.

In each of the second lines we may see that when two out of the four of the Alagus of Kural and two of Ili are added on to the 3, 2, and 3, 2 of the Swarams Ga, Ma, Dha, and Ni, these four Swarams obtain 4, 3 and 4, 3 Alagus respectively and Kural and Ili lose two of their Alagus and have only 2 and 2 left. In the same way if two out of the four Alagus of the Swarams which stand in the relation of Kural to Ili be tacked on to Swarams with less Alagus the third line of Swarams will result. The system of change of Alagus is clearly shown here.

This is how the four different kinds of Yal obtain a different order of Alagus in each case.

This is as follows :—

In Marutha Yal where Kural becomes Ili the alagus are 4, 4, 3, 2, 4, 3, 2.
In Kurinji Yal where Oolai becomes Kural the Alagus are 2, 4, 3, 2, 4, 4, 3.
In Neythal Yal where Ili becomes Kural, the Alagus are 4, 3, 2, 4, 4, 3, 2.
In Palai Yal where Tharam becomes Kural, the Alagus are 2, 4, 4, 3, 2, 4, 3.

He says that from each of these yals seven palais are obtained. They may be clearly seen from the following chakarams.

The Alagu system of Marutha Yal where Kural becomes Ili.

	4	4	3	2	4	3	2
	P	D	N	S	R	G	M
S	4	4	3	2	4	3	2
R	2	4	4	3	2	4	3
G	3	2	4	4	3	2	4
M	4	3	2	4	4	3	2
P	2	4	3	2	4	4	3
D	3	2	4	3	2	4	4
N	4	3	2	4	3	2	4

I

Marutha Yal where Kural becomes Ili.

				P_4				D_4			N_3		S_2				R_4			G_3		M_2
	1	2	3	4	5	6	7	8	9	10	11	12	13	14	15	16	17	18	19	20	21	22
1				S				R			G		M				P			D		N
2		S				R				G			M		P				D			N
3			S		R				G				M			P		D				N
4				S			R		G				M				P			D		N
5		S				R			G		M				P				D			N
6			S		R				G			M		P				D				N
7				S			R		G				M			P		D				N

The Alagu system of Kurinji Yal where Oolai becomes Kural.

	2	4	3	2	4	4	3
	M	P	D	N	S	R	G
S	2	4	3	2	4	4	3
R	3	2	4	3	2	4	4
G	4	3	2	4	3	2	4
M	4	4	3	2	4	3	2
P	2	4	4	3	2	4	3
D	3	2	4	4	3	2	4
N	4	3	2	4	4	3	2

II

Kurinji Yal where Oolai becomes Kural.

		M_2				P_4			D_3		N_2				S_4				R_4			G_3
	12	13	14	15	16	17	18	19	20	21	22	1	2	3	4	5	6	7	8	9	10	11
1		S				R			G		M				P				D			N
2			S		R				G			M		P				D				N
3				S			R		G				M			P		D				N
4				S				R			G		M				P			D		N
5		S				R				G			M		P				D			N
6			S		R				G				M			P		D				N
7				S			R		G				M				P			D		N

The Alagu system of Neythal Yal where Ili becomes Kural.

	4	3	2	4	4	3	2
.	P	D	N	S	R	G	M
S	4	3	2	4	4	3	2
R	2	4	3	2	4	4	3
G	3	2	4	3	2	4	4
M	4	3	2	4	3	2	4
P	4	4	3	2	4	3	2
D	2	4	4	3	2	4	3
N	3	2	4	4	3	2	4

III

Neythal Yal where Ili becomes Kural.

				P_4			D_3		N_2				S_4				R_4			G_3		M_2
	14	15	16	17	18	19	20	21	22	1	2	3	4	5	6	7	8	9	10	11	12	13
1				S			R		G				M				P			D		N
2		S				R			G		M				P				D			N
3			S		R				G			M		P				D				N
4				S			R		G				M			P		D				N
5				S				R			G		M				P			D		N
6		S				R				G			M		P				D			N
7			S		R				G				M			P		D				N

The Alagu system of Palai Yal where Tharam becomes Kural.

	2	4	4	3	2	4	3
	N	S	R	G	M	P	D
N	2	4	4	3	2	4	3
S	3	2	4	4	3	2	4
R	4	3	2	4	4	3	2
G	2	4	3	2	4	4	3
M	3	2	4	3	2	4	4
P	4	3	2	4	3	2	4
D	4	4	3	2	4	3	2

IV

Palai Yal where Tharam becomes Kural.

		N_2				S_4				R_1			G_3		M_2				P_4			D_3
	21	22	1	2	3	4	5	6	7	8	9	10	11	12	13	14	15	16	17	18	19	20
1		S				R				G			M		P				D			N
2			S		R				G				M			P		D				N
3				S			R		G				M				P			D		N
4		S				R			G		M				P				D			N
5			S		R				G			M		P				D				N
6				S			R		G				M			P		D				N
7				S				R			G		M				P			D		N

The above chakarams give the Alagus for each of the Saptaswarams SA, RI, GA, MA, PA, DHA and NI and their Alagus while they change their graham. We find they commence from the seven Swarams in the order of 4. 4. 3, 2, 4, 3, 2. He gives direction by which two of the Alagus of two Swarams which have four Alagus by the SA-PA series are to be added on one each to the four Swarams which have only three and two Alagus each. In this process all the Swarams will have more or less Alagus by the SA-PA and the SA-MA series. We shall see later on how Swarams with three Alagus each were used in Karnatic music. On the whole we see that whichever of the seven Swarams of an octave be taken as the standard they must go in the order of 4, 4, 3, 2, 4, 3, 2. Of these, two of the Swarams obtained by the SA-PA and the SA-MA series should be sung with three Srutis each.

The two chakarams proceeding by the right and left resemble each other. As no names of the Ragas sung in them have been given we can definitely name the Ragams. But we shall understand from the calculations of Alagus to be given later on that the *Puns* which were derived from these Palais are now used as Ragas with different names.

To these same SA-PA and the SA-MA series, Sarnga Dev, the author of Sangeeta Ratnakaram, attributes 13 and 9 Srutis respectively. In his work on music he says that between the commencing or the Vadi Swaram, and the end or the Samvadi Swaram, there must be 12 Srutis by the SA-PA series and 8 Srutis by the SA-MA series. The 13 Srutis by the SA-PA series and the 9 Srutis by the SA-MA series make 22 in all. He says there distinctly that a Sthayi ends with 22 Srutis and they are so arranged that they might form a gradually ascending series without admitting any other possible Swaram between. It should be observed the same is said of the Swarams of the Palai system.

10 (a) How the four different kinds of Puns are derived from each of the four Primary Puns.

We have noted before how the four kinds of Yal are derived from Vattapalai, how each of them is capable of giving birth to seven palais and how their Alagus system is arranged. It is clear that they are the four primary *Puns*. The meaning of the Seotram

"நாற்பெரும்பண்ணும் சாதிநான்கும்
பாற்படுதிறனும் பண்ணெனப்படுமே"

that each of these *puns* are capable of producing four jathis seems to be thus clear. He names these four jathis Ahanilai, Puranilai, Arugial and Perugial and also mentions the standard or Kural Swarams for the commencement of each and the succeeding Swarams. From the line "பாற்படுதிறனும் பண்ணெனப்படுமே" we conclude that the Thiran or the Ragas with six swarams that generate from these are to be called *puns*. The extensiveness of the Isai Tamil used in those days and the Duruva Vakayams that are a key to the brief understanding of them are also mentioned there. Though it is hard to make them out fully yet we might gather some idea about them from the quotations that follow.

Silappadikaram, Venirkathai Page 203.

கஎ-அக. "உழைமுத லாகவு முழையீ றாகவுங்
குரன்முத லாகவுங் குரலீ றாகவு
மகநிலை மருதமும் புறநிலை மருதமு
மருகியன் மருதமும் பெருகியன் மருதமு
நால்வகைச் சாதியு நலம்பெற நோக்கி"

இனி உழை குரன்முதல் குரலீறாயுள்ள நான்கிற்கும் அகநிலை மருதமுதற் பெருகியன் மருதம் ஈறாயுள்ள நான்கும் நிரனிறை.

இ-ள். முன்னவளித்த முறையே, உழைகுரலாய கோடிப்பாலை அகநிலை மருதமாகவும், உழைகுரலாய்க் கைக்கிளை குரலாய மேற்செம்பாலை புறநிலை மருதமாகவும், குரல் குரலாய செம்பாலை அருகியன் மருதமாகவும், குரல் தாரமாய்த் தாரங்குரலாய விளரிப்பாலை பெருகியன் மருதமாகவும் இச்சொல்லப்பட்ட சாதிப்பெரும் பண்களையும் ஓசையினிமை பெற நோக்கி யென்றவாறு."

He says that the four Maruthams, namely Aganilai Marutham, Puranilai Marutham, Arugial Marutham and Perugial Marutham stand in the relation of Niranirai to the four Swarams Oolai to Oolai and Kural to Kural.

"Of these, as we have stated before, when Oolai is taken as Kural it is Kodipalai or Aganilai Marutham, when Kaikilai becomes Kural it is Mersempalai or Puranilai Marutham, when Kural is taken as Kural it is Sempalai or Arugial Marutham, when Kural becomes Tharam and in its turn Tharam becomes Kural it is Vilaripalai or Perugial Marutham. All these four primary puns are of complete concord."

In the Chakaram for Vattapalai given below the four kinds of Kurinji Yal are mentioned. It commences in Thulam and ends in the Rasis Kumbam Rishabam and Simham.

(1) In other words when Oolai is Kural it is Kodipalai. This is Aganilai Marutham.

(2) When Kural appears in Kaikilai in Kumbam which is the fourth Rasi from the previous one we get Mersempalai. This is Puranilai Marutham.

(3) When Kural is taken as Kural, it is Sempalai or Arugial Marutham.

(4) When Kural is Tharam and after that Tharam is Kural it is Vilaripalai or Perugial Marutham.

So we see that for the four kinds of Yal there were four kinds of jathis in use. It seems that he recommends that the Swarams Sa, Ga, Pa and Ni should be sounded after the standard grahaswaram and go on to different Ragas.

If the above Swarams be taken as Grahaswarams and the ganam made according to them they will never be in discord with the mother Swarams but begin and end very smoothly and in perfect concord.

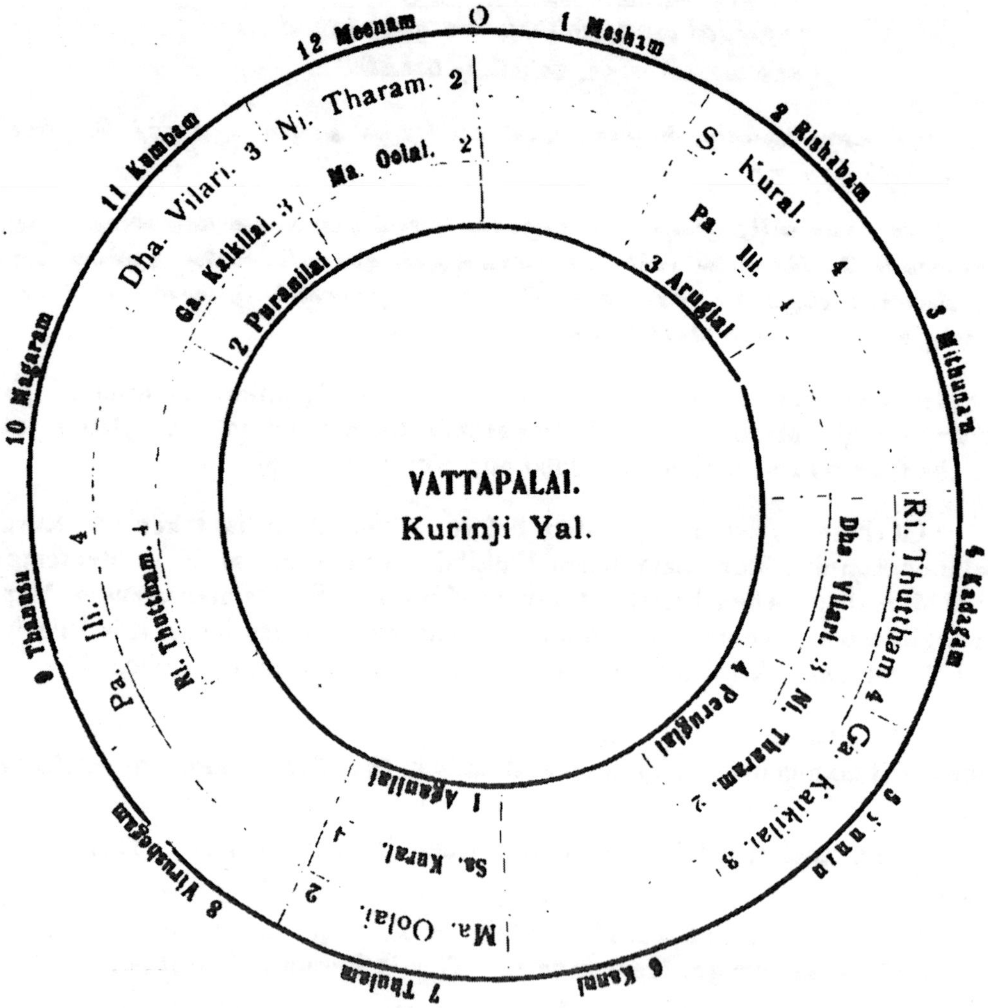

As these four are possible in every kind of Yal he says there are four jathis. In these MA and DHA are of the same concordant relation as between SA and GA. When two Swarams stand in the relation of SA and GA, if the first Swaram commences as SA, he calls it Puranilai Marutham. Again GA PA has the same relation as DHA and SA. The concord between GA and PA is rather doubtful here. If these have one Alagu less and if Kaikilai in Magaram has two Alagus then alone these will coincide with the Alagus in the rasis Magaram and Rishabam. If one Alagu is added we get the relation of SA-GA. Of these more anon.

When Kural commences as Kural he calls it Arugial Marutham. In this Marutbam Pa Ni stand in the relation of Sa-Ga. Here also there is an Alagu less in Tharam. When Vilaripalai which appears in Simham is Kural we get Perugial Marutham. In the same manner the other Yals also occur in fours.

To the four Swarams beginning from Oolai and Kural and ending with Kural the four Maruthams from Aganilai to Perugial stand in the relation of Niranirai. When Kural in Thulam becomes Aganilai Marutham, the Ili in Rishabam which is the seventh Rasi from it becomes Arugial Marutham. When the Tharam in Simham becomes Perugial Marutham, Kaikilai becomes Puranilai Marutham.

In the same way to the Aganilai Marutham which appears in Kural, the Swarams which occur in Rasis 1, 5, 8 and 11 become the four jathis. In the same manner, in the four kinds of Yal, the four jathis will commence in the Rasis 1, 5, 8 and 11.

Silappadikaram, Venirkathai, Arumpathavoorai.

Aganilai Marutham.

"ஒத்த கிழமை யுயர்குரன் மருதந்
துத்தமும் விளரியுங் குறைவுபெற னிறையே."

இதன் பாட்டு
ஊர்க திண்டே குருதற் கின்னே
நேர்க பாக நீயா வண்ணம்." The string has 16 mathiras.

Puranilai Marutham.

"புறநிலை மருதந் தாரவுழை கிழமை
துத்தங் கைக்கிளை குரலா மேனைத்
தாரம் விளரி யிளிநிறை வாகும்."

இதன் பாட்டு
"அங்கட் பொய்கை யூரன் கேண்மை
திங்க ளோர்நா ளாகுந் தோழி." Strings 16.

Arugial Marutham.

"அருகியன் மருதங் குரல்கிழமை கைக்கிளை
விளரி யிளிகுர னிறையா மேனைத்
துத்தந் தார மிளியிவை நிறையே."

இதன் பாட்டு
"வந்தானூரன் மென்றோள் வளைய
கன்றாய் போது காணாய் தோழி." Strings 16.

Perugial Marutham.

"பெருகியன் மருதம் பேணுங் காலை
யகநிலைக் குரிய நரம்பினை நிரட்டி
நிறை குறை கிழமை பெயமென மொழிப

இதன் பாட்டு
"மல்லூர்......கோவ வெம்முன்
சொல்லற் பாணா சொல்லுங் காலை
யெல்லி வந்த நங்கைக் கெல்லாஞ்
சொல்லுங் காலைச் சொல்லு நீயே." Strings 32.

Silappadikaram Venirkathai. Arumpathavoorai Page 31.

" அகநிலை மருதத்துக்கு நரம்பணியும்படி உழை, இளி, விளரி உ, கை, கு, உ, கு, தா, இ, தா, து, இ, உ இவை உரைப்பிற்பெருகும். தாரத்துட்டோன்றும் உழை ; உழையிற் குரல் பிறக்கும் ; குரலுள் இளி பிறக்கும் ; இளியுள் துத்தம் பிறக்கும் ; துத்தத்துள் விளரி பிறக்கும் ; விளரியுட் கைக்கிளை பிறக்கும். அகநிலை மருதமும் ... ... கொள்கவென்பது "

The strings for Aganilai Marutham are Oolai, Ili, Vilari, Oolai, Kaikilai, Kural, Oolai, Kural, Tharam, Ili, Tharam, Thuttham, Ili, Oolai &c., &c. We need not dilate on this. Oolai will appear in Tharam, Kural in Oolai, Ili in Kural, Thuttham in Ili, Vilari in Thuttham and Kaikilai in Vilari.

He gives the Swarams for the four jathis, just as he mentioned that seven Palais are derived from each of the four primary *puns*.

Aganilai is Kural which appears in Thulam. When it becomes Kural, Kaikilai becomes its Puranilai. When Kural is taken as Kural, it is Arugial. Vilaripalai, where Tharam becomes Kural, is Perugial. When we go into this deeper, we see it is only the system of singing Grahaswaram where Oolai becomes Kural, Kaikilai becomes Kural, and Kural and Tharam in their turn are taken as Kural. The commentators speek of Oolai appearing in Tharam, Kural appearing in Oolai, Ili appearing in Kural, Thuttham in Ili, Vilari in Thuttham, and Kaikilai appearing in Vilari. They represent them by the Tamil letters உ-கை-கு-உ-கு-தா-இ-தா-து-இ-உ. But their proper order should be தா-உ-கு-இ-து-வி-கை.

1. According to this system for Aganilai Marutham, Oolai will appear in Tharam, Kural in Oolai, Ili in Kural, Thuttham in Ili, Vilari in Thuttham, and Kaikilai in Vilari.

2. For Puranilai Marutham, Tharam will appear in Kaikilai, Oolai in Tharam Thuttham in Oolai, Vilari in Thuttham, Kaikilai in Vilari and Tharam in Kaikilai.

3. For Arugial Marutham, Kural will appear in Kural, Ili in Kural, Thuttham in Ili, Vilari in Thuttham, Kaikilai in Vilari and Tharam in Kaikilai.

4. For Perugial Marutham, Tharam appears in Simham. Oolai in Tharam, Kural in Oolai, Ili in Kural, Thuttham in Ili, Vilari in Thuttham and Kaikilai in Vilari.

Moreover it is distinctly seen that many ragas generate from each of the palais. The *puns* which generate from Sempalai are, Palayal, Nagaragam, Agari, Thodi, Goudi, Gandharam, Chenthurithi and Uthayagiri. He further adds that this is only an indication and the ragas may be multiplied but for brevity's sake they are omitted. This enables us to conclude that there are ragas, Swarams and their Alagu system for the other primary *puns* also.

Silappadikaram Oorkaukathai. Page 343.

" பண்களாவன : பாலை, குறிஞ்சி, மருதம், செவ்வழியென்பன. அவற்றின் திறங்களாவன:—பாலைக் குப்புறம்-தேனவி ; அருகு-சிகோதம் ; பெருகு-சீகாமரம். குறிஞ்சிக்குப்புறம்-செந்துரு ; அருகு-மருதவம் ; பெருகு-அரி மருதத்திற்குப்புறம்-நுதளி ; அருகு-சாயவேளர்கொல்லி ; பெருகு-ஸ்ரீராகம். செவ்வழிக்குப் புறம்-வேளாவளி ; அருகு-சீதம் ; பெருகு-பஞ்சுரம். பிறவும் வந்தவழிக்கண்டுகொள்க.

There are four *puns*:—Palai, Kurinji, Marutham and Sevvali. The ragas pertaining to these are:—*Devali* for Palai; *Seerkodigam* for Arugu; *Nagaragam* for Perugu; *Chenthu* for Kurinji; *Mandilam* for Arugu; *Ari* for Perugu; *Agari* for Marutham; *Sayavelarkolli* for Arugu; *Kinnaram* for Perugu; *Velavali* for Sevvali; *Sriragam* for Arugu; *Sandhi* for Perugu. The Ragas for the other *puns* may be imagined in the same way.

The four Jathis derived from the four kinds of Yal.

Aganilai.		*Puranilai.*		*Arugial.*		*Perugial.*
Paiai	...	Devali	...	Seerkodigam	...	Nagaragam.
Marutham	...	Agari	...	Sayavelarkolli	...	Kinnaram.
Kurinji	...	Chenthu	...	Mandilam	...	Ari.
Neythal	...	Velavali	...	Sriragam	...	Sandhi

Of these he mentions 16 strings for Aganilai, Puranilai and Arugial, but 32 for Perugial. These appear to have been arranged for the three Sthayis, hard, middling and soft. He also mentions, moreover, how from each of the Yals the four Jathis, Aganilai Marutham, Puranilai Marutham, Arugial Marutham and Perugial Marutham are derived.

I. The jathis and puns derived from Marutha Yal where Kural is Ili.

	4	4	3	2	4	3	2		
	P	D	N	S	R	G	M	Jathi.	Pun.
S	4	4	3	2	4	3	2	Aganilai.	Marutham.
R	2	4	4	3	2	4	3	...	...
G	3	2	4	4	3	2	4	Puranilai.	Agari.
M	4	3	2	4	4	3	2	...	...
P	2	4	3	2	4	4	3	Arugial.	Sayavelarkolli.
D	3	2	4	3	2	4	4	...	...
N	4	3	2	4	3	2	4	Perugial.	Kinnaram.

MARUTHA YAL.

Rishabam—Aganilai.

Ili in Kural	...	Thuttham in Ili	...	Vilari in Thuttham	...	Kaikilai in Vilari.
Tharam in Kaikilai	...	Oolai in Tharam	...	Kural in Oolai.		

K, I: I, T: T, V: V, K. K, T: T, O: O, K:
Sa, Pa: Pa Ri: Ri, Dha: Dha, Ga: Ga, Ni: Ni, Ma: Ma, Sa:

K, I, T, V, K, T, O.
Sa, Pa, Ri, Dha, Ga, Ni, Ma.

Kanni—Puranilai.

Tharam in Kaikilai ... Oolai in Tharam ... Kural in Oolai ... Ili in Kural.
Thuttham in Ili ... Vilari in Thuttham... Kaikilai in Vilari...

K, T: T, O: O, K: K, I: I, T: T, V: V, K:
GA, NI: NI, MA: MA, SA: SA, PA: PA, RI: RI, DHA: DHA, GA:

K, T, O, K, I, T, V.
Ga, Ni, Ma, Sa, Pa, Ri, Dha.

Thanusu—Arugial.

Thuttham in Ili ... Vilari in Thuttham ... Kaikilai in Vilari ... Tharam in Kaikilai.
Oolai in Tharam ... Kural in Oolai ... Ili in Kural ...

I, T: T, V: V, K: K, T: T, O: O, K: K, I:
PA, RI: RI, DHA: DHA, GA: GA, NI: NI, MA: MA, SA: SA, PA:

I, T, V, K, T, O, K.
Pa, Ri, Dha, Ga, Ni, Ma, Sa.

Meenam—Perugial.

Oolai in Tharam ... Kural in Oolai ... Ili in Kural ... Thuttham in Ili.
Vilari in Thuttham ... Kaikilai in Vilari ... Tharam in Kaikilai.

T, O: O, K: K, I: I, T: T, V: V, K: K, T:
NI, MA: MA, SA: SA, PA: PA, RI: RI, DHA: DHA, GA: GA, NI:

T, O, K, I, T, V, K.
Ni, Ma, Sa, Pa, Ri, Dha, Ga.

II. The Jathis and puns derived from Kurinji Yal where Oolai is Kural.

	2	4	3	2	4	4	3		
	M	P	D	N	S	R	G	Jathi.	Pun.
S	2	4	3	2	4	4	3	Aganilai.	Kurinji.
R	3	2	4	3	2	4	4	...	...
G	4	3	2	4	3	2	4	Puranilai.	Senthu·
M	4	4	3	2	4	3	2	...	...
P	2	4	4	3	2	4	3	Arugial.	Mandilam.
D	3	2	4	4	3	2	4	...	...
N	4	3	2	4	4	3	2	Perugial.	Ari.

KURINJI YAL.

Thalam—Aganilai.

Kural in Oolai ... Ili in Kural ... Thuttham in Ili ... Vilari in Thutham
Kaikilai in Vilari ... Tharam in Kaikilai ... ... Oolai in Tharam.

O, K: K, I: I, T: T, V: V, K: K, T: T, O:
Ma, Sa: Sa, Pa: Pa, Ri: Ri, Dha: Dha, Ga: Ga, Ni: Ni, Ma:

O, K, I, T, V, K, T.
Ma, Sa, Pa, Ri, Dha, Ga, Ni,

Kumbam—Puranilai.

Tharam in Kaikilai ... Oolai in Tharam ... Kural in Oolai ... Ili in Kural
Thuttham in Ili ... Vilari in Thuttham ... Kaikilai in Vilari.

K, T: T, O: O, K: K, I: I, T: T, V: V, K:
Ga, Ni: Ni, Ma: Ma, Sa: Sa, Pa: Pa, Ri: Ri, Dha: Dha Ga:

K, T, O, K, I, T, V.
Ga, Ni, Ma, Sa, Pa, Ri, Dha.

Rishabam—Arugial.

Ili in Kural ... Thuttham in Ili ... Vilari in Thuttham ... Kaikilai in Vilari.
Tharam in Kaikilai ... Oolai in Tharam ... Kural in Oolai.

K, I: I, T: T, V: V, K: K, T: T, O: O, K:
Sa, Pa: Pa, Ri: Ri, Dha: Dha, Ga: Ga, Ni: Ni, Ma: Ma, Sa:

K, I, T, V, K, T, O.
Sa, Pa, Ri, Dha, Ga, Ni, Ma.

Simham—Perugial.

Oolai in Tharam ... Kural in Oolai ... Ili in Kural ... Thuttham in Ili.
Vilari in Thuttham ... Kaikilai in Vilari ... Tharam in Kaikilai.

T, O: O, K: K, I: I, T: T, V: V, K: K, T:
Ni, Ma: Ma, Sa: Sa, Pa: Pa, Ri: Ri, Dha: Dha, Ga: Ga, Ni:

T, O, K, I, T, V, K.
Ni, Ma, Sa, Pa, Ri, Dha, Ga.

III. The Jathis and the puns derived from Neythal Yal where Ili is Kural.

	4	3	2	4	4	3	2		
	P	D	N	S	R	G	M	Jathi.	Pun.
S	4	3	2	4	4	3	2	Aganilai.	Neythal.
R	2	4	3	2	4	4	3	...	...
G	3	2	4	3	2	4	4	Puranilai.	Valavali.
M	4	3	2	4	3	2	4	...	...
P	4	4	3	2	4	3	2	Arugial.	Seeragam.
D	2	4	4	3	2	4	3	...	...
N	3	2	4	4	3	2	4	Perugial.	Santhi.

NEYTHAL YAL.

Thanusu—Aganilai.

Thuttham in Ili ... Vilari in Thuttham ... Kaikilai in Vilari ... Tharam in Kaikilai.
Oolai in Tharam ... Kural in Oolai ... Ili in Kural.

I, T: T, V: V, K: K, T: T, O: O, K: K, I:
Pa, Ri: Ri, Dha: Dha, Ga: Ga, Ni: Ni, Ma: Ma, Sa: Sa, Pa:

I, T, V, K, T, O, K.
Pa, Ri, Dha, Ga, Ni, Ma, Sa.

Mecham—Puranilai.

Oolai in Tharam ... Kural in Oolai ... Ili in Kural ... Thuttham in Ili.
Vilari in Thuttham ... Kaikilai in Vilari ... Tharam in Kaikilai.

T, O: O, K: K, I: I, T: T, V: V, K: K, T:
Ni, Ma: Ma, Sa: Sa, Pa: Pa, Ri: Ri, Dha: Dha, Ga: Ga, Ni:

T, O, K, I, T, V, K.
Ni, Ma, Sa, Pa, Ri, Dha, Ga.

Kadagam—Arugial.

Vilari in Thuttham ... Kaikilai in Vilari ... Tharam in Kaikilai ... Oolai in Tharam.
Kural in Oolai ... Ili in Kural ... Thuttham in Ili.

T, V: V, K: K, T: T, O: O, K: K, I: I, T:
Ri, Dha: Dha, Ga: Ga, Ni. Ni, Ma: Ma, Sa: Sa, Pa: Pa, Ri:

T, V, K, T, O, K. I.
Ri, Dha, Ga, Ni, Ma, Sa, Pa.

Thulam—Perugial.

Kural in Oolai ... Ili in Kural ... Thuttham in Ili ... Vilari in Thuttham
Kaikilai in Vilari ... Tharam in Kaikilai ... Oolai in Tharam.

O, K: K, I: I, T: T, V: V, K: K, T: T, O:
Ma, Sa: Sa, Pa: Pa, Ri: Ri, Dha: Dha, Ga: Ga, Ni: Ni, Ma:

O, K, I, T, V, K, T.
Ma, Sa, Pa, Ri, Dha, Ga, Ni.

IV. Jathis and Puns derived from Palai Yal where Tharam is Kural.

	2	4	4	3	2	4	3		
	N	S	R	G	M	P	D	Jathi.	Pun.
S	2	4	4	-3	2	4	3	Aganilai.	Palai.
R	3	2	4	4	3	2	4	...	...
G	4	3	2	4	4	3	2	Puranilai.	Davali.
M	2	4	3	2	4	4	3	...	...
P	3	2	4	3	2	4	4	Arugial.	Kodigam.
D	4	3	2	4	3	2	4	...	...
N	4	4	3	2	4	3	2	Perugial.	Nagaragam.

PALAI YAL.

Mesham—Aganilai.

Oolai in Tharam ... Kural in Oolai ... Ili in Kural ... Thuttham in Ili.
Vilalari in Thutham ... Kaikilai in Vilari ... Tharam in Kaikilai ...

T, O: O, K: K, I: I, T: T, V: V, K: K, T:
Ni, Ma: Ma, Sa: Sa, Pa: Pa, Ri: Ri, Dha: Dha, Ga: Ga, Ni:

T, O, K, I, T, V, K.
Ni, Ma, Sa, Pa, Ri, Dha, Ga.

Kadagam—Puranilai.

Vilari in Thuttham ... Kaikilai in Vilari ... Tharam in Kaikilai. ... Oolai in Tharam.
Kural in Oolai ... Ili in Kural ... Thuttham in Ili.

T, V: V, K: K, T: T, O: O, K: K, I: I, T:
Ri, Dha: Dha, Ga: Ga, Ni: Ni, Ma: Ma, Sa: Sa, Pa: Pa, Ri:

T, V, K, T, O, K, I.
Ri, Dha, Ga, Ni, Ma, Sa, Pa.

Thulam—Arugial.

Kural in Oolai ... Ili in Kural ... Thuttham in Ili ... Vilari in Thuttham.
Kaikilai in Vilari ... Tharam in Kaikilai ... Oolai in Tharam.

O, K: K, I: I, T: T, V: V, K: K, T: T, O:
Ma, Sa: Sa, Pa: Pa, Ri: Ri, Dha: Dha Ga: Ga, Ni: Ni, Ma:

O, K, I, T, V, K, T.
Ma, Sa, Pa, Ri, Dha, Ga, Ni.

Makaram—Perugial.

Kaikilai in Vilari ... Tharam in Kaikilai ... Oolai in Tharam ... Kural in Oolai.
Ili in Kural ... Thuttham in Ili ... Vilari in Thuttham.

V, K: K, T: T, O: O, K: K, I: I, T: T, V:
Dha, Ga: Ga, Ni: Ni, Ma: Ma, Sa: Sa, Pa: Pa, Ri: Ri, Dha:

V, K, T, O, K, I, T.
Dha, Ga, Ni, Ma, Sa, Pa, Ri.

When we notice the Alagú system of the four kinds of Puns derived from the above said four kinds of Yal, we find that they differ from each other in their Alagus and become different Ragams. The order of their occurrence and other particulars about them are given clearly in the following Table.

The commencing Swarams, the Alagu system and the names of the 16 Puns derived from the four kinds of Yal.

Four kinds of Yal.	Swaram.	Four kinds of Jathi.	Beginning Swaram.	S	R	G	M	P	D	N	Ragam.
Maruthayal...	S	Aganilai ...	S	4	4	3	2	4	3	2	Marutham.
,,		Puranilai ...	G	3	2	4	4	3	2	4	Agari.
,,		Arugial ...	P	2	4	3	2	4	4	3	Sayavelarkollai.
,,		Perugial ...	N	4	3	2	4	3	2	4	Kinnaram.
Kurinjiyal ...	M	Aganilai ...	M	2	4	3	2	4	4	3	Kurinji.
,,		Puranilai ...	D	4	3	2	4	3	2	4	Chenthu.
,,		Arugial ...	S	2	4	4	3	2	4	3	Mandilam
,,		Perugial ...	G	4	3	2	4	4	3	2	Hari.
Neythalyal...	P	Aganilai ...	P	4	3	2	4	4	3	2	Neythal
,,		Puranilai ...	N	3	2	4	3	2	4	4	Valavali.
,,		Arugial ...	R	4	4	3	2	4	3	2	Sriragam.
,,		Perugial ...	S	3	2	4	4	3	2	4	Sandhi.
Palaiyal ...	N	Aganilai ...	N	2	4	4	3	2	4	3	Palai.
,,		Puranilai ...	R	4	3	2	4	4	3	2	Devali.
,,		Arugial ...	M	3	2	4	3	2	4	4	Seerkotigam.
,,		Perugial ...	D	4	4	3	2	4	3	2	Nagaragam.

The above Table gives the four kinds of Yal, the commencing Swarams for each of them, the commencing Swarams for the four Jathis derived from them and their names corresponding to the commencing Swarams. If these 16 different *puns* be taken to be Mother-Ragams, we will find that seven different Ragams are derived from each of them. So there will be 16×7 or 112 Ragams. But the Alagu system for them should be changing in accordance with the Sootram.

“[illegible] etc.”

Sarnga Dev mentions that the Gramams should have the following Alagus :—

Shadja Gramam 4, 3, 2, 4, 4, 3, 2.
Madhyma Gramam 4, 3, 2, 4, 3, 4, 2.
Gandhara Gramam 3, 2, 4, 3, 3, 3, 4.

Of these the Alagus for Shadja Gramam resemble those of Neythal Yal (4, 3, 2, 4, 4, 3, 2) commencing from Pa in Vattapalai in accordance with the stanza " குரல் குரலாக வாசித்து இளி குரலாக வாசித்தாள் " (she played with Kural as Kural first and then with Ili as Kural.) In the same way the Madhyma Gramam may stand for Kurinji Yal with 4, 3, 2, 4, 3, 4, 2 Alagus, and the Gandhara Gramam for Palai Yal with Alagus arranged 4, 4, 3, 2, 4, 3, 2. But in Madhyma Gramam Pa has 3 Alagus and Dha 4. This is contrary to the order of 4, 3, 2. Moreover this will not occcur in the 112 Ragams derived from the above 16 puns. In the same manner the Gandhara Gramam with 3, 2, 4, 3, 3, 3, 4 Alagus is also wrong and will not agree with the system above. Again, the Gandhara Gramam of Sarnga Dev is contrary to the common rule where Sa-Pa should be 13 Srutis and Sa-Ma 9. The Alagus for the first four Srutis are 3+2+4+3 or 12 and 3+3+4=10.

We shall see from the succeeding table that the Alagu system of the three Gramams of Sarnga Dev cannot possibly be derived from the Alagus of the 16 Jathis given above. There seems to have been a doubt about these 2 Gramams even during the life-time of Sarnga Dev and the third, he says, was banished to the celestial regions.!

From this we are forced to think that he had his doubts about the system of Alagus of the four kinds of Yal—Marutham, Kurinji, Neythal and Palai—in use in ancient Tamil literature.

He has said before that seven out of the 12 Palais are primary and that from each of these seven Palais are derived. It is clear from the Sootram " நாற்பெரும் பண்ணும் சாதி நான்கும் " that four are primary puns from each of which four Jathis are derived and from the Sootram " பாற்படு திறனும் பண்ணொன்பதுமே " it is possible that seven Puns are derived from each of the 16 puns or there are 112 Puns in all. How these Puns are derived is shown in the following Table along with Alagus for each of them.

The 112 puns derived from the 16 different Puns.

1 Maruthayal-Aganilai — Where Kural is Kural.

S	4	4	3	2	4	3	2
R	2	4	4	3	2	4	3
G	3	2	4	4	3	2	4
M	4	3	2	4	4	3	2
P	2	4	3	2	4	4	3
D	3	2	4	3	2	4	4
N	4	3	2	4	3	2	4

1 Kurinjiyal-Aganilai — Where Olai is Kural.

M	S	2	4	3	2	4	4	3
P	R	3	2	4	3	2	4	4
D	G	4	3	2	4	3	2	4
N	M	4	4	3	2	4	3	2
S	P	2	4	4	3	2	4	3
R	D	3	2	4	4	3	2	4
G	N	4	3	2	4	4	3	2

2 Maruthayal-Puranilai — Where Kaikilai is Kural.

G	S	3	2	4	4	3	2	4
M	R	4	3	2	4	4	3	2
P	G	2	4	3	2	4	4	3
D	M	3	2	4	3	2	4	4
N	P	4	3	2	4	3	2	4
S	D	4	4	3	2	4	3	2
R	N	2	4	4	3	2	4	3

2 Kurinjiyal-Puranilai — Where Vilari is Kural.

D	S	4	3	2	4	3	2	4
N	R	4	4	3	2	4	3	2
S	G	2	4	4	3	2	4	3
R	M	3	2	4	4	3	2	4
G	P	4	3	2	4	4	3	2
M	D	2	4	3	2	4	4	3
P	N	3	2	4	3	2	4	4

3 Maruthayal-Arugiyal — Where Ili is Kural.

P	S	2	4	3	2	4	4	3
D	R	3	2	4	3	2	4	4
N	G	4	3	2	4	3	2	4
S	M	4	4	3	2	4	3	2
R	P	2	4	4	3	2	4	3
G	D	3	2	4	4	3	2	4
M	N	4	3	2	4	4	3	2

3 Kurinjiyal-Arugiyal — Where Kural is Kural.

S	2	4	4	3	2	4	3
R	3	2	4	4	3	2	4
G	4	3	2	4	4	3	2
M	2	4	3	2	4	4	3
P	3	2	4	3	2	4	4
D	4	3	2	4	3	2	4
N	4	4	3	2	4	3	2

4 Maruthayal-Perugiyal — Where Tharam is Kural.

N	S	4	3	2	4	3	2	4
S	R	4	4	3	2	4	3	2
R	G	2	4	4	3	2	4	3
G	M	3	2	4	4	3	2	4
M	P	4	3	2	4	4	3	2
P	D	2	4	3	2	4	4	3
D	N	3	2	4	3	2	4	4

4 Kurinjiyal-Perugiyal — Where Kaikilai is Kural.

G	S	4	3	2	4	4	3	2
M	R	2	4	3	2	4	4	3
P	G	3	2	4	3	2	4	4
D	M	4	3	2	4	3	2	4
N	P	4	4	3	2	4	3	2
S	D	2	4	4	3	2	4	3
R	N	3	2	4	4	3	2	4

1 Neythaiyal-Aganilai — Where Ili is Kural.

P	S	4	3	2	4	4	3	2
D	R	2	4	3	2	4	4	3
N	G	3	2	4	3	2	4	4
S	M	4	3	2	4	3	2	4
R	P	4	4	3	2	4	3	2
G	D	2	4	4	3	2	4	3
M	N	3	2	4	4	3	2	4

1 Palaiyal-Aganilai — Where Tharam is Kural.

N	S	2	4	4	3	2	4	3
S	R	3	2	4	4	3	2	4
R	G	4	3	2	4	4	3	2
G	M	2	4	3	2	4	4	3
M	P	3	2	4	3	2	4	4
P	D	4	3	2	4	3	2	4
D	N	4	4	3	2	4	3	2

2 Neythaiyal-Puranilai — Where Tharam is Kural.

N	S	3	2	4	3	2	4	4
S	R	4	3	2	4	3	2	4
R	G	4	4	3	2	4	3	2
G	M	2	4	4	3	2	4	3
M	P	3	2	4	4	3	2	4
P	D	4	3	2	4	4	3	2
D	N	2	4	3	2	4	4	3

2 Palaiyal-Puranilai — Where Thuttham is Kural.

R	S	4	3	2	4	4	3	2
G	R	2	4	3	2	4	4	3
M	G	3	2	4	3	2	4	4
P	M	4	3	2	4	3	2	4
D	P	4	4	3	2	4	3	2
N	D	2	4	4	3	2	4	3
S	N	3	2	4	4	3	2	4

3 Neythaiyal-Arugiyal — Where Thuttham is Kural

R	S	4	4	3	2	4	3	2
G	R	2	4	4	3	2	4	3
M	G	3	2	4	4	3	2	4
P	M	4	3	2	4	4	3	2
D	P	2	4	3	2	4	4	3
N	D	3	2	4	3	2	4	4
S	N	4	3	2	4	3	2	4

3 Palaiyal-Arugiyal — Where Golai is Kural

M	S	3	2	4	3	2	4	4
P	R	4	3	2	4	3	2	4
D	G	4	4	3	2	4	3	2
N	M	2	4	4	3	2	4	3
S	P	3	2	4	4	3	2	4
R	D	4	3	2	4	4	3	2
G	N	2	4	3	2	4	4	3

4 Neythaiyal-Perugiyal — Where Kural is Kural

S	3	2	4	4	3	2	4
R	4	3	2	4	4	3	2
G	2	4	3	2	4	4	3
M	3	2	4	3	2	4	4
P	4	3	2	4	3	2	4
D	4	4	3	2	4	3	2
N	2	4	4	3	2	4	3

4 Palaiyal-Perugiyal — Where Vilari is Kural.

D	S	4	4	3	2	4	3	2
N	R	2	4	4	3	2	4	3
S	G	3	2	4	4	3	2	4
R	M	4	3	2	4	4	3	2
G	P	2	4	3	2	4	4	3
M	D	3	2	4	3	2	4	4
P	N	4	3	2	4	3	2	4

In the above pages we see only a portion of the Isai Tamil practised by the ancient Tamilians. We see there that the three Sthayis, Mandhara, Madhya and Thara (soft Middling and hard) proceed upwards in the ratio of 1 to 2; that an expert musician is expected to discriminate the concordant relation between the Kural and the Ili strings, and that the Swarams of the Yal should be determined by the SA-PA system. We further see that out of the 14 Swarams thus obtained, the 7 between MA to GA were made the Madhya Sthayi, the four between SA to MA the Mandhara Sthayi and the three Swarams RI GA and MA, the Thara Sthayi and that Grahaswarams were sung in these and other ragams derived from them also. This is known as Ayapalai. This seems to have been sung in half Swarams and to have been the favourite ganam of women.

He then proceeds to speak of Vattapalai with 22 Alagus. He describes how these occur in the 12 different Rasis commencing from Mesham with different Alagus and as concordant Swarams. He shows how these Swarams occur in every seventh rasi proceeding by the right in the SA-PA series, and in every fifth place proceeding by the left in the SA-MA series. In addition to this how the Alagus change while proceeding towards right and left according to the change of Grahaswaram is shown.

The seven primary palais and the five secondary ones derived from the 12 main palais are also mentioned there. From these seven primary palais, the four Yals —Marutham, Kurinji, Neythal and Palai—are derived from the Swarams SA, MA, PA and Ni. From each of these Yals the four Jathis—Aganilai, Puranilai, Arugial and Perugial—are derived from the Swarams SA, GA, PA and Ni. The sytem of Alagus for each of them, their order of occurrence and their names are mentioned. The seven Puns that could be derived from each of these 16 Jathis are also given.

All these, namely, the chief hamsams of Srutis, their change of graham and the system of deriving ragams from them, distinctly indicate the eminence of the music of the Tamilians. We see there that a ragam was sung with 22 Alagus.

When we made enquiries about the names of such ragas and their scales we fortunately came across the Swarams and Alagu system for the 16 Puns derived from the four kinds of Yal. Thus we obtain the order of Swarams for the 112 Puns. But we are unable to ascribe to each separate order of Swarams its respective name. However we have to congratulate ourselves that we have been incidentally able to gather so much about music from a work which treats about Kovalan. We may come across differences of opinion of commentators. These differences only go to prove the excellence of the music of the age. We have quoted below only those ideas that could be derived from their annotations. Some of the hidden ideas in them will be dealt with later on.

Our beloved readers will be naturally curious to know whether the ancient Tamilians were really so highly proficient in music, whether four kinds of Yal really existed and the mode of playing on them. Their rules for producing sweet music from the Yal were quite commensurate with the knowledge they had attained as regards swarams and their concordant relationship. These will be noted in their due course.

Beloved readers ! though it is highly difficult to know the kinds of Yal and Ragas used by the ancient Tamilians, yet we shall quote below a few Sootrams from Silappadikaram that may be of help to us in determining them. Silappadikaram contains many minute hamsams of Isai Tamil. Some of the Tamil works which sprang up after Silappadikaram contain some points on the main principles of Isai Tamil. We have not thought it worth while to quote them here as they do not treat on the fundamental principles of music, namely. Srutis, formation of Ragas, change of grahams and the systems of Alagu. Ilankovadigal, the author of Silappadikaram, mentions in his work the important hamsams of music. Annotators of their period have tried their best to elucidate their ideas with the help of many quotations from various rare literary works of the period on Isai Tamil. However they have only indicated many points by mentioning the opening lines of particular Sootrams without explaining them. But for this imperfection we could have known much more about the music of the first Ooli.

There was a Tamil literary Sangam which was carried on for 4,400 years in destroyed Lemuria or South Madura at the close of the first Ooli. At the time of Nilandaruthiruvil Pandya, one of its rulers, Tholkaupiam, the illustrious work on grammar, was placed before the Sangam for the review of Athankotasan, a disciple of Ahastya. In this great work he makes mention of four kinds of Yal in connection with the products of four different kinds of soil. Ilankovadigal, on the other hand, mentions how these four kinds of Yal generate from Vattapalai, how four Jathis are derived from each of these Yals and other important relative hamsams. Again, Jayankondan, the prince of poets, as well as Adyarkunallar, who lived long after Ilankovadigal, have, in their commentaries, spoken about many rare points on Isai Tamil. We find that modern Karnatic music satisfies all the principles laid down by them, but owing to the interference of people with no ear for music many a mixture or desikam has been introduced in Karnatic music. We find here that Isai Tamil or Music has been in an exalted state for nearly 12,000 years. We think it highly important that we should understand the many hidden mysteries indicated therein as well as the Kalais in use in the Isai Tamil of those days. However as these points are of but secondary importance when compared with our subject of Srutis, we have not made much of them but only quoted a few Sootrams from Silappadikaram and the annotations thereon. Those who want to know more about them in detail are referred to Silappadikaram.

II.—THE DESCRIPTION OF A FEW KALAIS (ARTS & SCIENCE) IN USE IN ISAI TAMIL IN WHICH THE ANCIENT TAMILS WERE EXPERTS.

We have hitherto spoken about the system of Srutis in use in ancient Isai-Tamil practised by the Tamilians, the Palais to the right and left that are the results of the change of Grahaswaram, the Puns that generate from each of these, the four kinds of Yal — Marutham, Kurinji, Neythal and Palai — the four Jathis that generate from each of the above — Aganilai, Puranilai, Arugial and Perugial and their system of Alagus.

We find that, in keeping with the extensiveness of Isai Tamil, they had Yals where the 49 different graces were produced, that they sang them in different Thalams to suit, that they had an extensive system of Thalam which suited their vocal music to perfection, that they were proficient in dancing which suited their singing, that they were masters of Abinayam or gestures which were a perfect exposition of the ideas contained therein and that each of these has been exhaustively dealt with. Though our chief duty is to speak about Srutis, yet we want to prove clearly that the knowledge in Srutis of the Ancient Tamilians was only commensurate with their proficiency, from ancient times, in other Kalais of Isai Tamil, that they did not borrow anything from others and that, on the other hand, others borrowed from them.

I.—The kinds of Yal.

Here he speaks of the Yals in use at the first Ooli and the number of strings each of them had.

Silappadikaram Ooraipayiram P. 5.

உதயணன்கதை வந்தவகைகண்டம் யாழ் பெற்றது.

" தலைமுத லூழியிற் றனைவர் தருக்கறப்
புலமை யாளர் புரிநரப் பாயிரம்
வலிபெறத் தொடுத்த வாக்கமை பேரியாழ்ச்
செலவுமுறை யெல்லாஞ் செவ்வையிற் றெரிந்து
மற்றை யாழுங் கற்றுமுறை பிழையான்
பண்ணுந் திறனுந் திண்ணிதிற் சிவணி
வகையமைக் காணத்தந் தகைகய கவின
நாரத கீதக் கேள்வி யறிந்துப்
பரந்தவக் கற்கும் விருத்தியை வன்மீத்
தன்கோ ளம்பி தன்மைய ராதலிற் .
கல்பொற் காதலக் காவிய வழிகோள்
மன்னவன் முறைக்கீ வீரனைக் கொழுந்
யாழிசைப் பெரிதுந் திசையுடையாப் பயன்றுனு
தசை கேள்விக் கலைநிலை கேழ்
மக்க வேந்து வெந்திறை யுதிமீன
கொக்கினன் "

Silappadikaram Aranketukathai. P. 81.

" யாழ் நால்வகைப்படும் ; அவை பேரியாழ், மகரயாழ், சகோடயாழ், செங்கோட்டியாழென்பன. இவை நாலும் பெரும் பான்மை ; சிறுபான்மையான் வருவனவுமுள ; என்னை ?

" பேரியாழ் பின்னு மகரஞ் சகோடமுடன்
சீர்பொழியுஞ் செங்கோடு செப்பினர்-தார்பொலிந்து
மன்னுந் திருமார்ப வண்கூடற் கோமானே
பின்னு முளவே பிற "

என்று ராகலின். இந்நால்வகை யாழிற்கும் நரம்பு கொள்ளுமிடத்துப் பேரியாழிற்கு இருபத்தொன்றும், மகர யாழிற்குப் பதினேழும், சகோடயாழிற்குப் பதினாறும், செங்கோட்டி யாழிற்கு ஏழுங்கொள்ளப்படும்."

In the above lines he says that the four Yals such as Periyal etc., had 21, 17, 16 and 7 strings respectively. It appears that these were huge Yals like Perungalam or Periyal with 1000 strings in ancient times. The Yal with 21 strings seems to have been known as Periyal first, like the Yal with 1000 strings. Many ancient works confirm the existence of different kinds of Yal.

Of these Senkotyal seems to have been made of reddish wood and fitted with seven strings, four main strings and three side ones. This exactly resembles the modern Veena. As the top of the Meru was in appearance like the Yali, an ancient animal now extinct, the name Yal seems to have been given to it. In modern times it is made of jack wood. In Sanskrit it is known as Veena. In Thirukural written by Thiruvalluva Nayanar who lived 2000 years ago, it is said " குழல் இனிது யாழ் இனிது என்பர் தம்மக்கள் மழலைச் சொற்கேளாதவர் " (Only those who cannot appreciate the sweetness of the talk of their little children will go in raptures over the music produced by the flute and the Yal.) This distinctly proves that the Sanskrit word Veena could never have been in use then, and that Sanskrit words in music were of a later introduction.

On pages 518 and 519 of the book written by Kalladar, some seven or eight hundred years ago, he makes mention of four Yals named Periyal, Thoomburu Yal, Keechaka Yal and Marutthuva Yal. He commences his ahaval with the words " வடமொழி விதித்த இசை நூல் வழக்குடன்" (according to the rules prescribed for Isai Tamil by Sanskrit works). This distinctly shows that many of the instruments used in ancient Isai Tamil had become obsolete owing to want of patronage and the remnants were bolstered up by the works in Sanskrit of great men like Bharata and Sarnga Dev. The names of the Yal as given by Kalladar clearly prove their Tamil origin. The stanza " தலைமுதலூழியிற் றானவர் தருக்கறப் புலமகளாளர் புரிநரப் பாயிரம் வலிபெறத் தொடுத்த வாக்கமை பேரி யாழ்" shows that the Periyal with 1000 strings was one of those instruments used by the ancient Tamilians in Lemuria or South Madura. As it has become obsolete, only the name remains now. But no reference is made to it either in the writings of Bharata (5 century A. D.) or those of Sarnga Dev (13 century A. D.) based upon those of Bharata. But similar Yals seem to have been used in the Tamil country even in later times. We find these instruments used at the modern day under different names but not in the north. The Senkoti Yal used in thousands in the Chera and Chola country and Mysore at the present day is known as the Veena. These are very rare in the north.

We have been constrained to give here the description of the Yals given in Kalladam so as to compare it with the description of the four kinds of Yal in use among the ancient Tamilians.

Kalladam 13th Ahaval p. 90

" குடக்கோச் சேரன் கிடைத்திது காண்கென
மதிமலி புரிசைத் திருமுகங் கூறி
யன்புருத் தரித்த வின்பிசைப் பாணன்
பெறநிதி கொடுக்கென வுறவிடுத் தருளிய
மாதவர் வழுத்துங் கூடற் கிறைவன் "

This stanza refers to where the God Somasundra sent a message to Cheraman Perumal on behalf of Panapatthirar. This Cheraman Perumal was the friend of Sundaramoorti, one of the three leaders of Saivaitism. The age of Sundaramoorti is 9th cent. A.D. Therefore, the author of Kalladam who makes mention of Cheraman must have lived after him and could not possibly belong to the age of the Sangams.

Kalladam. Moolam and Oorai P. 518, 519.

" வடமொழி விதித்த விசைநூல் வழக்குட
னடுத்தன வெண்ணூன் கந்தலி யகத்தினு
நாற்பதிற் றிரட்டி நாலங் குலியினுங்
குறுமையு நெடுமையுங் கோடல் பெற்றதா
யாயிரந் தந்திரி நிறைபோது விசித்துக்
கோடி மூன்றிற் குறித்துமணி குயிற்றி
யிருநிலங் கிடத்தி மணங்கரங் கதுவ
வாயிரத் தெட்டி லமைந்தன பிறப்புப்
பிறவிப் பேதத் துறைபது போல
வாரியப் பதங்கோ ளுரைதப் பேரியாழ்
நன்னர்கோ ளன்பா னனிமுகம் புலம்ப."

Narada Yal.

This was 32 finger breadths broad, 84 finger-breadths long; it was triangular in form and had 1000 strings and bells. This was placed on the ground and played by the hands so as to produce 1008 different nadams. The three sides of the triangle must imply the three Sthayis—Mandara, Madhya and Thara—where the Swarams gradually proceed upwards while the length of the strings proportionately decreases, as we have noticed before. The strings of the Mandara Sthayi will be long and thick. As the length of the wire increases the sound will decrease. But as the length and thickness decrease the sounds will be of an increased pitch. The 1000 strings as well as their shape mentioned here remind us of the Kinnair of the Italians. This seems to have been the instrument at the first Ooli, but seems to have become obsolete in the second.

Kalladam P. 519.

" மூக்கான் கங்குலி முழுவுடற் சுற்ற
மைம்பதிற் றிரட்டி யாமுடன் கழித்த
வங்குலி நேமையு மமைத்துட் சேர்ந்தே
யொன்பது தந்திரி யுறுத்திரில நீக்கி
யறுவாய்க் காயிரண் டணைத்துவரைக் கட்டித்
தோள்கால் வதிந்து தொழிற்படத் தோன்றுந்
தும்புருக் கருவியுந் துன்னிநின் றிசைப்ப."

Thoombutu Yal.

Its dimensions were 12 finger-breadths in circumference, 94 finger-breadths in length with 9 strings. It was played resting on the shoulder and feet.

Kalladam p. 519.

" எழுவேண வுடம்புபெற் றெண்பதங் குலியின்
றந்திரி நூறு தழங்கிய முகத்த
கீசகப் பேரியாழ் கிளையுடன் முரல."

Keechaka Yal.

Its length was 80 finger-breadths. Its body was very heavy. It had 100 strings. This seems to have had the shape and characteristics of Narada Yal.

Kalladam p. 519.

" நிறைமதி வட்டத்து முயலுரி விசித்து
காப்ப ணொற்றை நரம்பு கடிப்பமைத்
தந்நரம் பிருபத் தாறங் குலிபெற
விடக்கரந் துவக்கி யிடக்கீ ழமைத்துப்
புறவிரன் மூன்றி னுனிவிர லகத்து
மறுபத் திரண்டிசை யனைத்துயிர் வணங்கு
மருத்துவப் பெயர்பெறும் வானக் கருவி
தூங்கலுந் துள்ளலுந் துவக்கிநின் றிசைப்ப
நான்முகன் முதலா மூவரும் போற்ற
முனிவரஞ் சலியுடன் முகம னியம்பத்
தேவர்க ளனைவருந் திசைதிசை யிறைஞ்ச."

Marutthuva Yal.

Its shape was circular like the moon. It was covered with hare's skin on the top surface. Its length was 26 finger-breadths. It had only a single string and was played by the ends of the fingers of the left hand so as to produce 62 Isais. This is also called Deva Yal.

When we notice the shape and formation of the four kinds of Yal, the Narada Yal with 1000 strings and the Keechaka Yal with 100 strings do not in any way resemble the modern Yal. But it is natural to conclude that the modern Thoomburu Yal, Marutthuva Yal, Sakota Yal, Magadi Yal, Katchabi Yal and other like instruments must have developed from the Narada Yal. Any how it should be noted that the modern Senkoti Yal has also a place there. Those who have had years of practice on stringed instruments are of opinion that Swarams played on one and the same string with different frets sound far sweeter than the same Swarams played on a number of distinct strings. One who has really understood and realised the sweetness and dignity of the Yal is on the threshold of understanding Nada Brahmam. Our ancestors who had realised this have been in the habit of constructing costly as well as cheap instruments to suit their own needs and tastes and called them by different names. This may be seen from the Table given below.

Gangamuttu Pillai of Tinnevelly, a distinguished scholar of Alavai Kshetram or Ootaramadura, has published a book called "Natanadi Vadhya Ranjanam" in 1898. He says it has been based on the Bharata Sastras in Sanskrit, Dravidian and Andra languages. He gives there 32 different kinds of stringed instruments and those who respectively used them. Though the words used there appear to be mixtures, yet many ancient Yals are mentioned there. Those who intended to keep music as a sealed book had them written and sung in Telugu so that others might not have the chance of knowing them. Are there not among us musicians even now who purposely pronounce the aksharams (letters) of their Pallavis a little indistinctly so that others might not understand them? Music which was kept as a hidden mystery is at this day published in different ways, in Sanskrit and other foreign languages, undergoing a daily change.

We must understand that the names of the Ragas, Thalams and Abinayam (gestures) used by the ancient Tamilians as well as the names of instruments on which they played, have been mutilated and changed and used in foreign languages with different names. Moreover, many who have Tamil as their mother-tongue prefer writing the beautiful language with mixture from strange languages to writing it pure. This is one of the causes for the deterioration of the beautiful Tamil language, which is purity itself. These people not only have murdered the language but the process is going on every day. We know that many Kalais flourished in ancient South Madura of which Isai-Tamil was one. The result of these mutilations has been to claim that all ancient Kalais were written in their own tongue, and to add many words to the old Tamil language so much so that people have doubts at the present day as to the priority of languages. So it is very difficult to know now what is what seeing that the language is neither this nor that. The foreign language that borrows a word from Tamil, removes the head and legs of the same and tacks on a tail to it and calls it its own and boasts that that is the prior language! Owing to these degenerate days, the names of the instruments used by the ancient Tamilians, the names of their Ragas and other vocabulary of Isai-Tamil have not only been changed, but the changes made permanent by being written down in books and sown broad-cast by means of Purana Kathas! Works on Isai-Tamil written at such a period are difficult to be recognised owing to mixtures. The names of the instruments given below appear to have been used in the 49 provinces of ancient Lemuria as they are connected with great men of yore.

Natanadi Vadhya Ranjanam Page 111.

The 32 different kinds of Veena and other stringed instruments along with the names of those who used them.

No.	Name		Instrument
1.	Brahma	...	Andam.
2.	Vishnu	...	Pindam.
3.	Rudhira	...	Sarasaram.
4.	Gowri	...	Rudrika.
5.	Kali	...	Gandhari.
6.	Lakshmi	...	Sarangi.
7.	Sarasvati	...	Katchabi (*Kalavati.*)
8.	Indra	...	Chithram.
9.	Kuperan	...	Athichithram.
10.	Varuna	...	Kinnari.
11.	Vayu	...	Thikuchikayal.
12.	Agni	...	Kolavali.
13.	Nama	...	Asthakoormam.
14.	Nirudi	...	Varaliyal.
15.	Athisheda	...	Vipanchakam.
16.	Chandra	...	Sara-Veena.
17.	Soorya	...	Naveetham.
18.	Viyalan	...	Vallabi Yal.
19.	Sukiran	...	Vathini.
20.	Narada	...	Magadi Yal (*Birukathi*)
21.	Thoomburu	...	Kalavati (*Magadi*)
22.	Visvavasu	...	Praharati.
23.	Puthan	...	Vidhyavadi.
24.	Arambai	...	Ekaveena.
25.	Thilotthama	...	Narayani.
26.	Menakai	...	Vani.
27.	Jayandan	...	Sathusoom.
28.	Agavooku	...	Nirmati.
29.	Chitrasena	...	Dharmavati (*Katchala*)
30.	Hanumar	...	Hanumatham.
31.	Ravana	...	Ravanesvaram
32.	Oorvasi	...	Laguvatchi.

The above list shows that those who used the particular instruments were kings and their ranis, some sages and dancing girls. The names Indra, Kupera, Varuna, Vayu, Agni, Nama, Niruthi, Athishedan, Chandra and Soorya appear to be those of some of the rulers of different provinces in South India. It will be absurd to say that the sun and the moon and the wind and the fire played on instruments! It will be going against nature to imagine anything long after the 49 provinces and the Kalais in them have been destroyed. This is the cleverness of those who write Puranas! These writers of Puranas, seeing that the rulers of Kishkinda in Mysore, namely, Vali, Sugrevan, Maruthi and others, had banners with the emblem of a monkey, made the rulers themselves monkeys by tacking on a tail to them! So here also they do not expressly say that they were rulers of these provinces, but give them names with something cut off! It is but the work of these writers to cut off a portion of a name or tack on a syllable to the already existing name for purposes of mutilation! Descriptions such as Vayu, the Prince of North-West, Varuna, the prince of West, Niruthi, the prince of South West, Yama, the prince of the South, Indra, the prince of the East, Chandra, the prince of North-East, Kupera, the prince of the North, and Agni, the prince of South East in ancient writings and expressions like Vayuputhiran, Varunakulam, Sooryakulam, Indrakulam, Chandravamsam and Agnikulam compel us to believe that these were human beings who had descendants. There is reason to believe that they ruled over the 49 provinces of Lemuria, each according to his share, and ruled over South India after the destruction of their original kingdom. There are many facts to show that these Kings were Tamilians. When South Madura was submerged, it is said that the seven sages escaped in a boat along with Satyavarada, the

Dravidian King, and settled in the Northern country. This makes us believe that the sages were also Tamilians. The number seven seems to be peculiarly that of the Tamil Country, for we hear of seven Kings, Sages, Maruthus, Women, Siranjeevis, Islands, Isais, and Thalams.

It is said that Brahma, Vishnu and Siva carry on the work of creation, preservation and destruction in all created world. This work corresponds to the Moorchanas of the Seven Swarams, the 12 palais derived from them, the 12 primary and the 5 secondary palais derived from the 12 main palais and the four kinds of Yal. So there is reason to think that all created world serve as their Yal. But in reality we believe they represent the shape of the Yals used by them respectively. To correspond to this, we find that Sarasvati, the incarnation of Sakti, used the Yal called Katchabi, Lakshmi, the Yal called Sarangi, and Gowri, the Yal named Rudrika. These three Yals used by them and the puns sung to them will be found later on to have been developments one upon another.

Sarnga Dev, who lived in the 13th century, says that he based his work upon those of Baharata, Madangar, Keerthitharar, Kambalar, Asvadavar, Anjaneyar, Abinavaguptar and Somesvarar who lived before him. Of these the date of Bharata the first of them is 5th century. The work of Bharata was taken to France and published in the French tongue in 1888. Mathangar and others seem to have lived after Bharata. From this we may conclude that these should have written their works at the time when the music of South India was in a retrograde state. Sarnga Dev who based his work on the above gives a list of instruments commencing from the 520th page of Sangeeta Ratnakaram. Here he gives the names of instruments with different numbers of strings, and the names of their particular owners. They are as follows :—

Sangeeta Ratnakaram p. 520.

Visvavasu	...	Brahadi Veena.	Naradha	...	Magadi.
Thoomburu	...	Kalavati.	Sarasvati	...	Katchabi.

Instrument with 1 string.	... Eka Thanthri.	Seven strings.
„ 2 strings.	... Nakula.	Nine strings.
„ 3 strings.	... Anvarthum or Juntra.	21 strings ... Mattha Kokilam
Kinnari, Alapini }	Lakuhi, Pragadi.	Pinahi, Nisanga Veena } partly made of bamboo.

Very little information is given here as regards particulars about instruments, the number of strings used therein and those who used them.

This work of Sarnga Dev was evidently written at a time when the music of India had degenerated. This is further supported by the fact that Doulabad, the place of Sarnga Dev, was one which very rarely came into contact with Karnatic music, and the time was as recent as 700 years ago. So those who came after Sarnga Dev fell into the same error as he did and they fulfilled the truth of the verse of the Bible, " if a blind man leads the blind, both will fall into the ditch." From the calculations of those who interpreted Sarnga Dev we came to the conclusion before that the 22 Srutis of Sarnga Dev became a " stumbling block and a rock of offence" to those who followed him without practically helping them in any way. Of this, more anon.

We read in Thiruvilayadal Puranam that Paramasivam overcame Emanatha, the expert in Veena from the north, by putting on the garb of a wood cutter and by singing the Ragam *Sathari*, and that the ruling Sovereign at the time was Varaguna Pandya. It is further said that Sivan is eternally listening to the music on the Veena of Kambalar and Asvadarar, the great experts, and keeps them with him always. From this we are able to conclude that Sivan was a great musical expert who conducted the Tamil Sangam as its first president and who was the patron of *Muttamil.* It is said when he sang the Sathari Ragam, all his hearers became petrified by losing their consciousness and that even dead trees began to shoot tender leaves and buds. In accordance with the rules followed by Paramasivam in playing and singing that Ragam, there are many hamsams and rules for perfect playing and singing laid down in ancient works on Isai Tamil. The rules are as perfect as the different kinds of Yal used by the Tamilians. Many words which are found there are no doubt extinct now. However there were many rules laid down for the Yal. But now even the name Yal has disappeared and the word *Veena* has taken its place. To add to this, all the rules laid down for playing the Yal are now printed in Sanskrit and the Tamils are taught those rules! However some of the rules for playing the Yal as used by the ancient Tamilians are given below for information.

2. Some important rules observed by the Tamilians in playing the Yal.

We have noticed till now the different kinds of Yal used by the ancient Tamilians in South Madura and the system of Alagu for the Swarams used in their ganam. We shall now enquire into the rules for holding the instrument, for tuning it and for playing the gamakams. Seeing that the Yal was of great help in concentrating their mind on devotion to God, they made much of it and called it "தெய்வஞ் சான்ற தீஞ்சுவை நல்யாழ்" (the beautiful and sweet Yal leading towards the deity), beautified it with garlands of sweet flowers, in accordance with the words "செழுங் கோட்டில் மலர் புனைந்து" and looked upon it as a God. Even at the present day we say that the Yal is a living instrument while others are dumb instruments. The Yal is the only instrument which could be played so as to bring out the distinct sounds of the long and short letters as pronounced by man. The extracts given below, though inadequate as regards giving full information, yet they show the proficiency of the ancient Tamilians in Yal playing.

Silappadikaram, Venirkathai p. 201.

The rule for playing the Yal is given below.

யாழ் வாசிக்கு முறைமை.

" நல்லிசை மடந்தை நல்லெழில் காட்டி
யல்லியம் பங்கயத் தயனினிது படைத்த
தெய்வஞ் சான்ற தீஞ்சுவை நல்யாழ்
மெய்பெற வணங்கி மேலொடு கீழ்புணர்த்
திருகையின் வாங்கி யிடவயி னிரீஇ,
மருவிய விசய மாட்டேல் கடனே "

என்பதனுணர்க. விநயம்-தேவபாணி.
விநயம் implies devotion.

“ வலக்கைப் பதாகை கோட்டொடு சேர்த்தி
யிடக்கை நான்விரன் மாடகந் தழீஇ ”

இ-ள், வலக்கையைப் பதாகையாகக் கோட்டின்மிசையே வைத்து இடக்கை நால் விரலான் மாடகத்தைத்தழுவி யென்க. பதாகைக்கையாவது பெருவிரல் குஞ்சித்து ஒழிந்த விரலெல்லா நிமிர்த்தல்; என்னை ?

The four fingers of the right hand (omitting the third finger) should be placed on the lines while the Matagam should be played by the four fingers of the left.

“ எல்லா விரலு நிமிர்த்திடை யின்றிப்
பெருவிரல் குஞ்சித்தல் பதாகை யாகும் ”

என்றாராகலின். மாடகம்-வீக்குங்கருவி. அது முன்னர் ஆணியென்பதனுட் கூறினும்.

Here he explains what பதாகை means, that is the four fingers to the exclusion of the third finger. By மாடகம் he means the plectrum.

“ செம்பகை யார்ப்பே யதிர்வே கூடம்
வெம்பகை நீக்கும் விரதுளி யறிந்து ”

செம்பகை ஆர்ப்பு அதிர்வு கூடமென்னு நான்கினும் செம்பகை தாழ்ந்த விசை = இன்பமின்றி இசைத்தல், ஆர்ப்பு மாத்திரை மிறந்த சுருதி = ஓங்கவிசைத்தல். அதிர்வு நரம்பைச் சிதறவுந்தல். கூடம் இசை நிறவாதது = தன் பகையாகிய ஆறாநரம்பினிசையிற் குன்றித் தன்னோசை மழுங்கலெனக்கொள்க.

Of these செம்பகை means playing in low tones without producing any charm, ஆர்ப்பு means playing too loud, அதிர்வு means making the strings vibrate loud, கூடம் means being submerged while sounding along with its sixth or பகை நரம்பு.

This is further supported by the stanza quoted from Panchabaratheeam,

இதனை,

“ இன்னிசை வழிய தன்றி யிசைத்தல்செம் பகைய தாகுஞ்
சொன்னமாத் திரையி னோங்க விசைத்திடுஞ் சுருதி யார்ப்பே
மன்னிய விசைவ ரர்து மழுங்குதல் கூட மாகு
நன்னுதலாய் சிதற வுந்த லதிர்வென காட்டி னாரே.”

என்பதனுற்கொள்க. இது பஞ்ச பாரதீயம்.

It is said that Narada published the work on Isai Tamil called Panchabaratheeam. This makes us believe that Narada was music master to the Tamilians of South Madura. The above stanza shows that Swarams which do not occur in the Sa-Pa or the Sa-Ma series will spoil the music, that Swarams with either more or less Mathiras than the standard and Swarams which sound out of the line have the same effect. We shall see later on that each of the points is of great importance and contains some of the mysterious ideas of Isai-Tamil.

Silappadikaram, Venirkathai p. 201.

“ செம்பகை யென்பது பண்ணோ டோரா
வின்பமி லோசை யென்மனார் புலவர்.”
“ ஆர்ப்பெனப் படுவ தளவிறந் திசைக்கும்.”
“ அதிர்வெனப் படுவ திழுமென லின்றிச்
சிதறி யுரைக்குந் குற்றிப் பிசையே.”

" கூட மென்பது குறியுற விளம்பின்
வாய்வதின் வராது மழுங்கியிசைப் பதுவே."

எனக்கூறினரு முளர். இவை நான்கும் மரக்குற்றத்தாற் பிறக்கும்; என்னை ?

These four are caused by mistake in the wood.

" நீரிலே நிற்ற லழுகுதல் வேத னிலமயக்குப்
பாரிலே நிற்ற லிடிவிழ்த ஞெய்மரப் பாற்படல்கோ
ணேரிலே செம்பகை யார்ப்போடு கூட மதிர்வுநிற்றல்
சேரினேர் பண்க ணிற்மயக் குப்பஞே சிற்றிடையே." என்றார்.

இ—ன். இச்சொல்லப்பட்ட பகை நரம்பு நான்கும் புகாமல் நீக்கும் விரகைக்கடைப் பிடித்தறிந்தெனக.

In order to avoid these four discordant strings the wood must be of proper choice

Silappadikaram, Kanalvari p. 177 -178.

" சித்திரப் படத்துட் புக்குச் செழுங்கோட்டின் மலர்புனைந்து
மைத்தடங்கண் மணமகளிர் கோலம்போல் வனப்பெய்திப்
பத்தருங் கோடு மாணியு நரம்புமென்
றித்திறத்துக் குற்றநீங்கிய யாழ்கையிற் றொழுது வாங்கி"

சித்திரப்படம்—உறை. கோட்டில் மலர்புனைந்து - கோட்டுறுப்பில் மலர்மாலையை அணிந்து ;

The Yal was decorated with a garland on the Kodu, before being played.

" விழ்மணி வண்டு பாய்ந்து மிதித்திடக் கிழிந்த மாலை
சூழ்மணிக் கோட்டு வீணை."

என்றார் சிந்தாமணியிலும் ; [காக்-உகூ] மணமகளிர்—கலியாண மகளிர். பத்தர் கோடு ஆணி நரம்பு என்பன யாழுறுப்புக்கள் ;

This is quoted from Chintamoni. மணமகளிர் implies that the Yal was decorated like a bride. பத்தர், கோடு, ஆணி and நரம்பு are the parts of the Yal.

" கோடே பத்த ராணி நரம்பே
மாடக மெனவரும் வகையின தாகும்."

என்பதனாலறிக. தொழுது—யாழ், மாதங்கியென்னும் தெய்வமிருத்தற் கிடமென்று நூல்கள் கூறுமாதலின்,

அதனைத் தொழுது. வாங்கி—வயந்தமாலை கையினின்றும் வாங்கி.

தொழுது shows that Yal was worshipped as it was the resting place of the goddess மாதங்கி. வாங்கி implies that it was received from the hand of Vayanthamalai.

Silappadikaram, Ooraipaiyiram p. 4.

இவற்றுட் பெருங்கலமாவது பேரியாழ் ; அது கோட்டினளவு பன்னிருசாணும் வணரளவு சாணும் பத்தரளவு பன்னிரு சாணும் இப்பெற்றிக்கேற்ற ஆணிகளும், திவவும் உந்தியும் பெற்று ஆயிரங்கோல் தொடுத் தியல்வது ; என்னை ?

Of these Perunkalam is Periyal. The measurement of its Kodu is 12 spans of its *Vanar* one span and of its *patthar* 12 spans. It has nails, belly &c., in proportion. It has 1000 koles.

" ஆயிர நரம்பிற் றுதியா ழாகு
மேனை யுறுப்பு மொப்பன கொளலே
பத்தர தளவுங் கோட்டின தளவு
மொத்த வெண்ப விருமுன் றிரட்டி,
வணர்சா ணெழித்தென வைத்தனர் புலவர்."

The following stanza describes how the Tamilians sang the Keertanams in praise of the deity avoiding all discordant Swarams, giving due importance to the Jeevaswarams, and with due Thalams, so that they might be blessed with everything good and delivered from all that is evil. It also describes how the Kulal (flute) and the Yal blended harmoniously with their vocal music and how the Mridangam which was known as Thannumai kept time with them all. It is difficult to come across a combination of these three instruments at the present day.

Silappadikaram, Aranketukathai p. 100.

" சீரியல் பொலிய நீரல நீங்க
வாரமி ரண்டும் வரிசையிற் பாடப்
பாடிய வாரத் தீற்றினின் றிசைக்குங்
கூடிய குயிலுவக் கருவிக ளெல்லாங்
குழல்வழி நின்றது யாழே யாழ்வழித்
தண்ணுமை நின்றது தகவே தண்ணுமைப்
பின்வழி நின்றது முழவே முழவொடு
கூடிநின் றிசைத்த தாமந் திரிகை "

சீரியல் பொலிய நீரல நீங்க, வாரமிரண்டும் வரிசையிற் பாடவென்பது நன்மையுண்டாகவும் தீமை நீங்கவும் வேண்டித் தெய்வப்பாடல் இரண்டினையும் பாடவென்றவாறு.

இனிச் சீரியல்பொலிய நீரலநீங்க வென்பதற்குத் தாளவியல்பு பொலிவுபெற அவதான நீங்கவென்றுமாம். வாரமிரண்டாவன ஓரொற்று வாரம் ஈரொற்று வாரமென்னுஞ் செய்யுள். அவை தாளத்து ஒரு மாத்திரையும் இரண்டு மாத்திரையும் பெற்று வரும்.

பாடிய வாரத்தீற்றினின் றிசைக்குங் கூடிய குயிலுவக் கருவிகளெல்லா மென்பது தெய்வப் பாடலின் இறுதியிலே நின்று கூடி இசையா நிற்கும் கருவிகளெல்லாமென்றவாறு.

இக்கருவிகள் எவ்வண்ணங் கூடி இசைத்தனவோ வெனின்.

'குழல்வழி நின்றது யாழே' என்பது வங்கியத்தின் வழியே நின்றது யாழ்ப்பாடலென்றவாறு.

எனவே, மிடற்றுவழியது யாழாகலான் மிடற்றுவழிப் பாடலும் யாழ்வழித்தெனக் கொள்க.

'யாழ்வழித், தண்ணுமை நின்றது தகவே' யென்பது யாழ்ப்பாடலின் வழியே தண்ணுமையாகிய மத்தள நின்றதென்க.

'தண்ணுமைப், பின்வழி நின்றது முழவே' யென்பது மத்தளக் கருவியின் பின்வழியே குடமுழா நின்றதென்க.

'முழவொடு, கூடிநின் றிசைத்த தாமந் திரிகை' யென்பது முழவொடு கூடிநின்று வாச்சியக் கூறுகளை அமைத்தது ஆமந்திரிகை யென்னுங் கருவி யென்றவாறு.

"*சீரியல் பொலிய* and *நீரல நீங்க வாரமிரண்டும் வரிசையிற் பாட*" means the two songs in praise of God were sung so that all good may result and all evil disappear.

These two lines imply that they were sung fulfilling all the strict rules of *Thalam*. *Varam* is of two kinds, one with a single Mathira and the other with two Mathiras. The next two lines mean the instruments which sound harmoniously together at the end of the song in praise of the deity. When asked how they sounded, he says that the Kulal and the Yal blended faultlessly together. This means the voice and the instruments were in perfect concord. The next lines mean that the Thannumai or Mridangam was in concord with the Yal, the Kudamula with the Thannumai, and the Amandrikai with the Kudamula.

Silappadikara Aroompathavoorai p. 32.

மதுரகீதம் பாடினள் மயங்கி-தாரங்குரலான மேற்செம்பாலை யென்னும் பண்ணைக் கண்டத்தாற் பாடி மயங்கி அப்பண்ணையே யாழினும்பாடிச் செய்வெனென்றவாறு. அதனுற் போந்த பொருள் :—நிலம் கலம் கண்ட மென்னும் நெறிமூன்றினும்,

மதுரகீதம் பாடினள் மயங்கி means she sang the *pun* Merchampalai (where Tharam is Kural) vocally and was so charmed she repeated the same playing it on the Yal. The importance of the harmonious combination of Nilam (Swarams) Kalam (the instrument) and Gantam (the human voice) is also seen from the following Sootram from Chollagathyam,

"கண்ட மல்லது நிரம்பக் காட்டக்
கருவிக் கின்பங் கோடப்ப துமது
பொருவரு நிலத்தைப் புணர்ப்ப ததுவே,"

என்னுஞ் சொல்லகத்தியச் சூத்திரத்தானும் முற்படக் கண்டத்தாலே பாடியெனவும் செம்பாலைப் பண்ணையா ழினும்பாடினளெனவுங் கொள்க.

This distinctly shows that the ancients were in the habit of singing the Puns first vocally and then perform the same on the Yal. We have seen how the sellers of cheap toy Kinnaries in the streets sing Anna, Anna and Renga, Renga and then exactly reproduce them on their toy instrument. This shows that all Isai and words that could be produced by the human voice can be faithfully reproduced in the Yal, that it would be very sweet and that other instrumental music are imperfect and unattractive. *Nilam* means the seven Swarams of the Yal, *Kalam* the particular Yal and *Gantam* the human voice. He emphasises the fact that the beauty of Isai-Tamil consists in singing the Swarams at their exact Sthanams. We are very glad to hear that this is a Sootram of Ahatyar. We hear there are a few more here and there.

His Muthal Nool on the subject of Iyal, Isai and Natakam, it is clear, speaks of very minute things.

Silappadikaram, Aroompathavoorai Page 25.

There are eight kinds of Isai. Of these the first is Pannal.

1. "வலக்கைப் பெருவிரல் குரல்கொளச் சிறுவிரல்
விலக்கின் நிளிவழி கேட்டு மிணைவழி
யாராய்ந் திணைகொள முடிப்பது
விளைப்படு மரபிற் பண்ணல் லாகும்.

The second is Parivattanai·

2. " பரிவட் டணையி னிலக்கணந் தானே
மூவகை நடையின் முடிவிற் ருகி
வலக்கை யிருவிரல் வணப்புறத் தழீஇ
யிடக்கை விரலி னியைவ தாகத்
தொடையொடு தோன்றியுந் தோன்ரு தாகியு
நடையொடு தோன்று நயத்த தாகும் "

The third is Araythal.

3. " ஆராய்த லென்ப தமைவரக் கிளப்பிற்
குரன்முத லாக விணைவழி கேட்டு
மிணையி லாவழிப் பயனொடு கேட்டுந்
தாரமு முழையுந் தம்மிற் கேட்டுங்
குரலு மிளியுந் தம்மிற் கேட்டுந்
துத்தமும் விளரியுந் துன்னறக் கேட்டும்
விளரி கைக்கிளை விதியுளிக் கேட்டுந்
தளரா தாகிய தன்மைத்தா தும் "

The fourth is Thaivaral.

4. " தைவர லென்பது சாற்றுங் காலை
மையறு சிறப்பின் மனமகிழ் வெய்தித்
தொடையொடு பட்டும் படாஅ தாகியு
நடையொடு தோன்றி யாப்பு நடை யின்றி
யோவாச் செய்தியின் வட்டணை யொழுகிச்
சீரேற் றியன்று மியலா தாகியும்
நீர வாகு நிறைய தென்ப "

The fifth is Chelavu.

5. " செலவெனப் படுவதன் செய்கை தானே
பாலை பண்ணே திறமே கூடமென
நால்வகை யிடத்து நயத்ததாகி
யியக்கமு நடையு மெய்திய வகைத்தாய்ப்
பதினே ராடலும் பாணியு மியல்பும்
விதிநான்கு தொடர்ந்து விளங்கிச்செல் வதுவே "

The Sixth is Vilayattu.

6. " விளையாட் டென்பது விசிக்குங் காலைக்
கிளவிய வகையி னெழுவகை யெழாலு
மளவிய தகைய தாகுமென்ப "

The Seventh is Kaiyool.

7. " கையூ ழென்பது கருதுங் காலை
யெவ்விடத் தானு மின்பமுஞ் சுவையுஞ்
செவ்விதிற் றேன்றிச் சிலைத்து வரலின்றி

நடைநிலை திரியாது நண்ணித் தோன்றி
நாற்பத் தோன்பது வனப்பும் வண்ணமும்
பாற்படத் தோன்றும் பகுதித்தாகும்."

The eighth is Kuroompokku.

8. " துள்ளற் கண்ணும் குடக்குத் துள்ளுந்
தள்ளாதாகிய வுடனிலைப் புணர்ச்சி
கோள்வன வெல்லாங் குறும்போக் காகும் "

இவையெல்லாம் ஈண்டு விரித்துரைப்பிற் பெருகும்.

We omit further detail for the sake of brevity.

Here the quotation from the third Araiythal " தாரமும் உழையும் தம்மிற் கேட்டும் etc " implies that the Swarams should be obtained by the SA-PA system, and the concordant Swarams should be determined from Kural.

Silappadikaram, Aroompathavoorai P. 25.

1. வார்தல் (Varthal) is the work of the second finger.

2. வடித்தல் (Vadithal) is the examination of the string both inside and outside by the second and the third finger.

3. உந்தல் (Onthal) is making the strings vibrate and find out whether the sound belongs to the soft or hard or middling sound.

4. உறழ்தல் (Oralthal) means examining the stings alternately and with two strings between.

5. உருட்டல் (Oruttal) is twisting the strings by the second finger or by the second finger and the third fiinger or by the two third fingers.

6. " தெருட்ட லென்பது செப்புங் காலை
யுருட்டி வருவ தொன்றே மற்ற
வொன்றன் பாட்டுமடை யொன்ற நோக்கின்
வல்லோ ராய்ந்த நூலே யாயினும்
வல்லோர் பயிற்றுங் கட்டுரை யாயினும்
பாட்டொழிந் துலகினி னொழிந்த செய்கையும்
வேட்டது கொண்டு விதியுற நாடி. "

எனவரும். இவை இசைத்தமிழ்ப் பதினறு படலத்துட் காரணவோத்துட் காண்க.

The above is a quotation from Isai-Tamil Sixteenth Padalam, Karanavote.

The different sounds made by the Yal are given in Sootram 1441 in Pingala Nigandu Page 176, 177.

" கலித்தல் சும்மை கம்பலை யழுங்கல்
சிலைத்த லுலைத்தல் சிலம்ப லிரங்க
லிமிழ்தல் விம்ம லிரட்ட லேங்கல்
கனைத்த முழங்கல் கறங்க லரற்ற
லிசைத்த லென்றிவை யாழ்நரம் போசை "

(இ-ள்.) யாழ்நரம்போசையின் பெயர்—கலித்தல், சும்மை, கம்பலை, அழுங்கல், சிலைத்தல், துவைத்தல், சிலம்பல், இரங்கல், இமிழ்தல், விம்மல், இரட்டல், ஏங்கல், கனைத்தல், தழங்கல், கறங்கல், அரற்றல், இசைத்தல்.

The names of the sounds of the Yal are:—Kalithal, Summai, Kampalai, Alungal, Silaithal, Thuvaithal, Silambal, Irangal, Imilthal, Vimmal, Irattal, Yankal, Kanaithal, Thalangal, Karangal, Yarattal, Isaitthal.

These seem to represent the various Gamakams of the Yal and other minute details.

In addition to this he gives the defects of the wood selected for Yal and the four kinds of playing that disturb the concord of sweet sounds.

Again, when we compare the Yal system of the time of Ilankovadigal and those which come after him we find there is a gradual deterioration.

For example, the rules for playing the Yal which existed during his time are for superior to those that were in use in later times. The same as regards Gamakams. Those of the days of the sage Pingala are far more varied. There were no Sanskrit words relating to music found in Isai-Tamil. These seem to have been a later introduction. The Tamilians of the past four or five hundred years are using Sanskrit words mainly in South Indian music.

Silappadikaram, Aroompathavoorai P. 33.

"இனி 'வலக்கைப் பதாகை கோட்டொடு சேர்த்தி' என்பது முதலாக 'புறந்தோந் றாணியிற் பூங்கொடி மயங்கி' என்பதீறாக முன்னர்ப்பாடிய ஒன்பான் கோவையின் மேற்செம்பாலைப் பண்ணெழீஇ பதினாற் கோவையாகிய சகோடயாழை வாங்கி வலக்கையைப் பதாகையாக்கி அக்கையாற் கோடு அசையாதபடி பிடித்து இடக்கை நாலு விரலும் மாடகத்தையுறப் பிடித்துச்செம்பகையும் ஆர்ப்பும் அதிர்வும் கூடமுமாகிய பகை நீங்க முறையிற் பிழையாத நரம்பினோர் பதினாலு நரம்பினையும் உழைமுதல் கைக்கிளை யிறுவாயாக "மெலிவிற்கெல்லை மந்தந் தாலே" என்பதனான் உழைகுரலான மந்தமும், "வலிவிற்கெல்லை வன்மைக் கிளையே" என்பதனாற் கைக்கிளையிறுவாயான வலிவும் இளி, கிளை, பகை, நட்பின் வழிகளிலே பொருந்தப் பார்த்துக் குரல் நரம்பினையும் யாழிற்கு அகப்பட்ட நரம்பாகிய இளி நரம்பையும் முற்பட ஆராய்ந்து இசை யோர்த்து அதன் முறையேயொக்காத நரம்புகளையும் ஆராய்ந்து இசையோர்த்துத் தீதின்மையறிந்து உழைமுதலாகவும் உழையிறுவாகவுமென மந்த முதலாகவும் மந்த விறுவாகவும் குரல் நரம்பு மந்தமானபோது குரல் நரம்பே முதலு முடிவுமாகவும் அகநிலைமருதமும் புறநிலைமருதமும் அருகியன்மருதமும் பெருகியன்மருதமுமென நால்வகைச் சாதிப்பெரும்பண்கள் விளங்கும்பெற வலிவு மெலிவு சமமென்னும் மூவகை இயக்கும் முறைமையிலே ஆராய்ந்து பாடிப் பின்னர் மாத்திரை குறைந்ததிற் பண்ணைப்பாடுமேல் வைக்கண் அப்பண்ணை இனிதாகப்பாடி நெகிழ்வுற்ற மனத்தினளாய் அடர்ந்தாளெனவுமாம்."

The above extract gives (1) how the Yal ought to be held while playing, (2) the four different discordant sounds that may spoil music, (3) the method of testing whether the Swarams satisfy the rules of the SA-PA system and (4) how to find out the four Jathis for the standard Swaram and determine what Swarams in the three Sthayis-hard, soft and middling-will be concordant with it.

Here இசையோர்த்து means tuning and மூவகை இயக்கம் the three Sthayis.

In ancient times the Yal and the Kulal seem to have been considered to be fitting accompaniments to vocal music. He gives the different kinds of wood with which the Kulal may be constructed, the age of the particular wood, the defects generally found in wood, the measurements of the Kulal and of the holes thereon.

Silappadikaram Arangetukathai P. 82, 83.

" குழலுமென்பது வங்கியப் பாடலு மென்றவாறு.

குழல் வங்கியம் ; அதற்கு மூங்கில், சந்தனம், வெண்கலம், செங்காலி கருங்காலியென ஐந்துமாம் என்னை ?

Kulal is an instrument. It is generally made of the bamboo, sandalwood, brass, rosewood or blackwood.

" ஓங்கிய மூங்கி லுயர்சந்து வெண்கலமே
பாங்குறுசெங் காலி கருங்காலி-பூங்குழலாய்
கண்ண னுவந்த கழைக்கிவைக ளாமென்றார்
பண்ணமைந்த நூல்வல்லோர் பார்த்து "

என்றாராகலின். இவற்றுள் மூங்கிலிற் செய்வது உத்தமம். வெண்கலம் மத்திமம். ஏனைய அதமமாம். மூங்கில் பொழுது செய்யும், வெண்கலம் வலிது, மரம் எப்பொழுதும் ஒத்து நிற்கும். இக்காலத்துக் கருங்காலி செங்காலி சந்தனம் இவற்றாற் கொள்ளப்படும்; கருங்காலி வேண்டுமென்பது பெரு வழக்கு. கழை-குழல். இவை கொள்ளுங்கால் உயர்ந்து ஒத்த நிலத்திற் பெருக வளர்ந்து நாலு காற்று மயங்கின் நாதமில்லையா மாதலான் மயங்கா நிலத்தின் கண் இளமையும் நெடும் பிராயமுமின்றி ஒரு புருடாயுப்புக்க பெரிய மரத்தை வெட்டி ஒரு புருடாகாரமாகச் செய்து அதனை நிழலிலேயாற இட்டுவைத்துத் திருகுதல் பிளத்தல் போழ்ந்துபடுதல் செய்கையறிந்து ஓர்யாண்டு சென்றபின் இலக்கணவகையான் வங்கியஞ் செய்ப்படும் ; என்னை ?

To make the Kulal of the bamboo is best. To make it of brass is middling, and of the rest, so so. The bamboo lasts long. Brass is strong and wood is invariably good. This is why they choose the Sandalwood, or Rose or Blackwood at the modern day. Kalai means Kulal. When the choice of wood is made it should not be a big tree on a raised mound exposed to the four winds of heaven as the Natham will not be good in such wood. But it should be of a tree grown in a protected place neither young not very old, grown quite straight and stout, dried in the shade, split and sawn and then constructed at the end of a year according to prescribed rules.

This is indicated in the stanza.

" உயர்ந்த சமதலத் தோங்கிக்கா லுன்கின்
மயங்காமை நின்ற மரத்தின்-மயங்காமே
முற்றி யமர்மரந் தன்னை முதறடிந்து
குற்றமிலோ ராண்டிற் கோளல் "

என்றாராகலின். இதன் பிண்டியிலக்கணம்: நீளம் இருபது விரல்; சுற்றளவு நாலரை விரல். இது துளையிடுமிடத்து நெல்லரிசியில் ஓர் பாதி மரனிறத்திக் கடைந்து வெண்கலத்தாலே அணைசு பண்ணி இடமுகத்தை யடைத்து வலமுகம் வெளியாக விடப்படும். என்னை ?

Next he proceeds to give the measurements of the Kulal.

The length should be 20 finger-breadths, the circumference $4\frac{1}{2}$ finger breadths. When the holes are made they should be of the dimension of the half of a grain of rice; the Kulal should have a band made of brass. The left end should be closed and the right end left open.

" சொல்லு மிதற்களவு நாலேந்தாஞ் சுற்றளவு
நல்லவிர லைரையா நன்னுதலாய்-மெல்லத்
துளையளவு நெல்லரிசி தூம்பிட மாய
வளைவலமேல் வங்கியமென் "

என்றாராகலின். இனித்துளையளவிலக்கணம்: அளவு இருபதுவிரல். இதிலே தாபமுகத்தின் இரண்டு நீக்கிமுதல்வாய்விட்டு இம்முதல் வாய்க்கு ஏழங்குலம்விட்டு வளைவாயினு மிரண்டு நீக்கி நடுவினின்ற ஒன்பது விரலினும் எட்டுத்துளையிடப்படும். இவற்றுள் ஒன்று முத்திரை யென்று கழித்து நீக்கிநின்ற ஏழினும் ஏழுவிரல்வைத்து ஊதப்படும். துளைகளின் இடைப்பரப்பு ஒரு விரலகலம் கொள்ளப்படும்.

Then he gives the measurement of the holes. The total length of the reed is 20 finger breadths. The holes should commence after two finger breadths. From this seven inches length should be marked. After two more finger breadths are marked, we shall have nine finger breadths. Eight holes must come in the nine finger breadths. Omitting the first hole, music should be played in the seven holes by seven fingers. The distance between holes should be one finger breadth.

" இருவிரல்க ணீக்கி முதல்வாயேழ் நீக்கி
மருவு துளையெட்டே மன்னும்-பெருவிரல்க
ளலஞ்சு கோள்க பரப்பென்ப நன்னுதலாய்
கோலஞ்செய் வங்கியத்தின் கூறு"

என்றாராகலின் இவ்வங்கியம் ஊதுமிடத்து வளைவாய் சேர்ந்த துளையை முத்திரையென்று நீக்கி முன்னின்ற ஏழினையும் ஏழுவிரல்பற்றி வாசிக்க. ஏழு விரலாவன: இடக்கையிற் பெருவிரலும் சிறு விரலு நீக்கி மற்றை மூன்று விரலும் வலக்கையிற் பெருவிரலொழிந்த நான்குவிரலும் ஆக ஏழு விரலுமென்க. என்னை ?

The seven fingers are : three in the left omitting the first finger and the last finger, four in the right omitting the first finger only.

" வளைவா யருகொன்று முத்திரையாய் நீக்கித்
துளையேழி னின்ற விரல்கள்-விளையாட்
டிடமூன்று நான்குவல மென்றார்கா ணேகா
வடமாரு மென்முலையாய் வைத்து

என்றாராகலின். இவ்வங்கியத்து ஏழுதுளைகளில் இசைபிறக்குமாறு: அஃது எழுத்தாற் பிறக்கும். எழுத்து ச, ரி, க, ம, ப, த, நி, என்பன. இவ்வேழெழுத்தினையும் மாத்திரைப்படுத்தித் தொழில் செய்ய இவற்றுள்ளே ஏழிசையும் பிறக்கும். ஏழிசையாவன: சட்சம், இடபம், காந்தாரம், மத்திமம், பஞ்சமம், தைவதம், நிடாத மென்பன. இவைபிறந்து இவற்றுளேபண்கள் பிறக்கும். என்னை ?

How sound is produced in these seven holes is given. They generate by the names of letters : the letters are Sa, Ri, Ga, Ma, Pa, Dha and Ni. When these seven letters are arranged and played according to Matthiras the seven Isais will generate, and these are Shadjam, Itapam, Gandharam, Madhymam, Panchamam, Dhaivatam and Nishadam. From these *puns* are derived.

" ச ரி க ம ப த நி யென் றேழெழுத்தாற் றானம்
வரிபரந்த கண்ணினாய் வைத்துத்—தெரிவரிய
வேழிசைப் தோன்று மிவற்றுள்ளே பண்பிறக்குஞ்
சூழ்முதலாஞ் சுத்தத் துளை"

என்றாராகலின்.

The Names of the Seven Isais, Shadjam, Itapam etc., are given in the commentary on the above stanza. But they are not found in the stanza itself. So we find that during the age of Adyarkunallar, and even four or five hundred years before his time, works on music were written in Sanskrit and Sanskrit words largely used in Isai Tamil. But there was no Sanskrit literature in the time of Ilankovadigal.

3. A few remarks on the Abinaya Shastram of South India.

Abinayam has three subdivisions :—(1) to dance according to the strict rules of Thalam in accordance with the singing of the master (2) to sing in conjunction with the master (3) and to show gestures by the head, hands and eyes to suit the ideas contained in the *pun*. Of these, the gestures of the head are of nineteen varieties, of the eyes 36, of the joint hands 15 and the combination of joint and disjoint hands 33. To add to these there are the varieties of gestures by the body—*Angam, Oopangam* and *Prathiyangam*. With the aid of these the nine *Rasams* as well as the actions, words, possessions and times of all the world can be easily expounded and explained. We find that our ancestors were in the habit of dancing in front of God and were in raptures by singing sweet songs, by dancing exquisitely and by making gestures which appealed to the innermost heart. At the same time we must not forget that those who devotedly worshipped God with the help of *Bhavam, Thalam* and *Ragam* were great Emperors of the world, sovereign rulers and Rishis. Those great men of the world who realise the degeneration of music, which is now solely in the hands of inferior people, are despising it just as they despise the artificial pith turban.

Though much is said in Silappadikaram as regards Abinayam, we have quoted here only what is most important. Those who want to know about it in detail are referred to the book itself. We deal here with the different kinds of dancing, and their rules, the rules for the fourteen kinds of gestures which should be avoided, the nine kinds of taste and the 24 kinds of gestures commonly known in dancing.

Silappadikaram, Aranketukathai P. 63.

The qualifications of the Dancing Master.

" இருவகைக் கூத்தி னிலக்கண மறிந்து
பல்வகைக் கூத்தும் விலக்கினிற் புணர்த்துப்
பதினோ ராடலும் பாட்டுங் கொட்டும்
விதிமாண் கொள்கையின் விளங்க வறிந்தாங்
காடலும் பாடலும் பாணியுந் தூக்குங்
கூடிய நெறியின கொளுத்துங் காலைப்
பிண்டியும் பிணையலு மெழிற்கையுந் தொழிற்கையுங்
கொண்ட வகையறிந்து கூத்துவரு காலைக்
கூடை செய்தகை வாரத்துக் களைதலும்
வாரஞ் செய்தகை கூடையிற் களைதலும்
பிண்டி செய்தகை யாடலிற் களைதலு
மாடல் செய்தகை பிண்டியிற் களைதலுங்
குரவையும் வரியும் விரவல செலுத்தி
யாடற் கமைந்த வாசான் றன்னொடும்"

இ-ள். இருவகைத்தாகிய அகக்கூத்தின் இலக்கணங்களையறிந்து பலவகைப்பட்ட புறங்களையும் விலக்குறுப்புக்களைச் சேரப்புணர்க்கவும் வல்லனாகி அல்லிய முதற் கொடுகொட்டியீறாகக் கிடந்த பதினொரு கூத்துக்களும் அக் கூத்துக்களுக்குரிய பாட்டுக்களும் அவற்றுக்கடைத்த வாச்சியங்களின் கூறுகளும் நூல்களின் விதித்தவழியே தெரிந்து கூத்தும் பாட்டும் தாளங்களும் தாளங்களின் வழிவந்த தூக்குக்களும் தம்மிற்கூடின நெறியையுடைய அகக்கூத்தும் புறக்கூத்து முதலாயின நிகழ்த்துமிடத்துப் பிண்டி பிணையல் எழிற்கை தொழிற்கையென்று சொல்லப்பட்ட நான்கினையும் நூலினகத்துக்கொண்ட கூறுபாட்டையறிந்து அகக்கூத்து நிகழுமிடத்துக் கூடைக்கதியாகச் செய்தகை வாரக்கதியுட் புகாமலும் வாரக்கதியாகச் செய்தகை கூடைக்கதியுட் புகாமலும் புறக்கூத்து நிகழுமிடத்து, ஆடனிகழுமிடத்து அவிநய நிகழாமலும் அவிநய நிகழுமிடத்து ஆடனிகழாமலும் குரவைக்கூத்தும் வரிக்கூத்தும் தம்மில் விரவாதபடியுஞ் செலுத்தி அமைந்த ஆடலாசிரியனுமென்க.

இது பொழிப்புரை.

௩௨. இருவகைக் கூத்தாவன:—வசைக்கூத்து, புகழ்க்கூத்து; வேத்தியல், பொதுவியல்; வரிக்கூத்து, வரிச்சாந்திக்கூத்து; சாந்திக்கூத்து, விநோதக்கூத்து; ஆரியம், தமிழ்; இயல்புக்கூத்து, தேசிகக்கூத்தெனப் பலவகைய. இவை விரிந்த நூல்களிற் காண்க.

The master must know the rules of the two kinds of dancing; he must know the particular gestures to be avoided in the different kinds; he must know the songs pertaining to the eleven kinds of dancing beginning from Allyam up to Kodukoti. He must conduct these dances in such a way that the dancing, singing and Thalam might satisfy the rules of Pindi. Pinayal, Elirkai and Tholirkai; he must see that rules of each of these do not run into one another; he must see that dancing is not sacrificed to the gestures, nor gestures sacrificed to the dancing.

The opposite kinds of dances are the following:—Vasaikoothu, Pugalkoothu; Vathial, Poduvial; Varikoothu, Varichandikoothu; Sandikoothu, Vinodakoothu: Aryam, Tamil; Iyalpukoothu and Desikam. These may be found in books that deal with them extensively.

The pairs of *Sandikoothu* and *Vinodakoothu* are

௩௨. என்று இருவகைக் கூத்தாவன:—சாந்தியும், விநோதமும் என்னை?

"அவைதாம், சாந்திக் கூத்தும் விநோதக் கூத்துமென்
றாராய்ந்துற வகுத்தன னகத்தியன் றனே" என்றாராகலின்.
"சாந்திக் கூத்தே தலைவ னவிநய
மேந்திநின் றாடிய வீரிரு நடமவை
சொக்க மெய்யே யவிநய நாடக
மென்றிப் பாற்படூஉ மென்மனார் புலவர்"

என்பதனால் நாயகன் சாந்தமாக ஆடியகூத்துச் சாந்திக் கூத்தெனப்படும். இவற்றுள்,—

சொக்கமென்பது சுத்த நிருத்தம். அது நூற்றெட்டுக் கரணமுடைத்து. மெய்க்கூத்தாவது தேசி, வடுகு, சிங்களமென மூவகைப்படும். இவை மெய்த்தொழிற் கூத்தாகலின், மெய்க்கூத்தாயின. இவை அகச்சுவைபற்றி வருதலின், அகமார்க்கமென நிகழ்த்தப்படும். அகச்சுவையாவன, இராசதம், தாமதம், சாத்துவிக மென்பன.

Sandikoothu is the dancing by the husband in a meek and mild manner.

Chokam means Pure dancing. It is of 108 different kinds. *Meykoothu* is of 3 kinds; *Desi, Vadugu, Singalam.* These are called *Meykoothu* because they are

Meytholirkoothu. As they are connected with *Agachuvai* they are called *Agamargam*. There are three different kinds of Agachuvai—*Rasatham*, *Thamatham*, and *Sadveegam*.

Kunanooludayar says

"குணத்தின் வழியதகக் கூத்தெனப் படுமே"

Sayanthanooludayar says

"அகத்தெழு சுவையா னகமெனப் படுமே"

அவிநயக்கூத்தாவது நிருத்தக்கை தழுவாது பாட்டினது பொருளுக்குக் கைகாட்டி வல்லபஞ் செய்யும் பலவகைக்கூத்து.

நாடகம்-கதை தழுவிவருங்கூத்து.

விநோதக்கூத்தாவது குரவை, கலிநடம், குடக்கூத்து, கரணம், நோக்கு, தோற்பாவை என்பர். இவற்றுள் :

குரவை என்பது காமமும் வென்றியும் பொருளாகக் குரவைச்செய்யுள் பாட்டாக எழுவரேனும் எண்மரேனும் ஒன்பதின்மரேனும் கைபிணைந்தாடுவது.

Abinayakoothu are the diffeient kinds of *koothu* where the gestures are made by the hands in accordance with the ideas contained in the song.

Natakakoothu is in connection with the story of the play.

Vinodakoothu is of six kinds :—*Kuravai*, *Kalinadam*, *Kudakootu*, *Karanam*, *Noku* and *Thorpavai*.

Kuravai is a combined dancing by seven, eight or nine persons with love or victory as subjects and with Kuravai *Cheyul* for song.

"குரவை யென்பது கூறுங் காலைச்
செய்தோர் செய்த காமமும் விறலு
மெய்தக் கூறு மியல்பிற் றென்ப" என்றாராகலின், குரவை, வரிக்கூத்தின் ஒருறுப்பு ; அவை வந்தவழிக்கண்டு கொள்க.

கலிநட மென்பது கழாய்க்கூத்து. குடக்கூத்தென்பது மேற் பதினொராடலுட் காட்டப்படும். கரணமாவது படிந்தவாடல் நோக்கென்பது பாரமும் நுண்மையும் மாயமுமுதலானவற்றை உடையது. தோற்பாவை யென்பது தோலாற் பாவை செய்து ஆட்டுவிப்பது.

இன்னும் நகைத்திறச்சுவை யென்பதனோடு எழென்பாருமுளர். அஃதாவது விதூடகக்கூத்து. இதனை வசைக்கூத்தென்பாருமுளர். வசை-வேத்தியல், பொதுவியலென இரண்டு வகைப்படும். அவை முந்து நூல்களிற் கண்டுகொள்க. வெறியாட்டு முதலாகத் தெய்வமேறியாடுமென்ற அத்திறக்கூத்துக்களுங்கூட்டி எழென்பாருமுளர். என்னை ?

This shows that *Kuravai* was one of the *angams* of *Varikoothu* ; how it was might be easily understood.

Kalinatam means *Kalaikoothu* ; *Kudakoothu* is one of the fourteen abovementioned ; *Noku* is a kind of *koothu* full of minuteness and full of tricks. *Thorpavai* is doll made of skin.

Others make out there are seven kinds of *koothu* along with *Naguithirachuvai*. In other words it is called *Vithudakoothu* or *Vasaikoothu*. *Vasai* is of two kinds, *Vathiyal* and *Pothuviyal*. They are found in previous works. Others give out seven *koothus* including the dance when one is under the influence of any God.

" எழுவகைக் கூத்து மிழிகுலத் தோரை
யாட வகுத்தன னகத்தியன் றானே " என்றாராகலின்.

12. The rules for these are.

13. இவற்றினிலக்கணங்களாவன.

" அறுவகை நிலையும் ஐவகைப் பாதமும்
ஈரேண் வகைய வங்கக் கிரியையும்
வருத்தனை நான்கு நிருத்தக்கை முப்பது
மத்தகு தொழில வாகு வென்ப."

13. பல்வகைக் கூத்தாவன :—வென்றிக் கூத்தும், வசைக் கூத்தும், விநோதக்கூத்து முதலியன. என்னை ?

The different kinds of koothu are :—Ventikoothu. Vasaikoothu and Vinodhakoothu.

" பல்வகை யென்பது பகருங் காலை
வென்றி வசையே விநோத மாகும்," என்றாராகலின்.
" அவற்றுள், மாற்றா னொடுக்கமு மன்ன னுயர்ச்சியு
மேற்படக் கூறும் வென்றிக் கூத்தே."
" பல்வகை யுருவமும் பழித்துக் காட்ட
வல்ல னுதல் வசையெனப் படுமே."
" எனவிவை தாளத்தி னியல்பின வாகும்."
" விநோதக் கூத்து வேடிபா னைடைத்து
வென்றி விநோதக் கூத்தென விளம்புவர்."

இதன் கருத்து : கொடித்தேர் வேந்தரும் குறுநிலமன்னரு முதலாக உடையோர் பகைவென்றிருந்த விடத்து விநோதங்காணுங்கூத்தென்பதாம்.

13. விலக்கினிற் புணர்த்து—விலக்குறுப்பிேனாடு பொருந்தவித்து : இன்—சாரியை ; மூன்றனுருபு ஐந்தனொடு மயக்கித்து ; வென்றிக்கூத்து முதலாகிய பலவகைப்பட்ட புறநடக்களையும் வேந்துவிலக்குப் படை விலக்கு ஊர்விலக்கென்று சொல்லப்பட்ட விலக்குகளாகிய பாட்டுக்களுக்கு உறுப்பாய் வருவனவற்றுடனே பொருந்தப்புணர்த்தி. பொருந்தப்புணர்த்தல்—கண்டுப்பாட்டெனுக்கு வரவு வகுத்தல்.

விலக்குறுப்பாவன :—பதினான்கு வகைப்படும் ; அவை பொருள், யோனி, விருத்தி, சந்தி, சுவை, சாதி, குறிப்பு, சத்துவம், அவிநயம், சொல், சொல்வகை, வண்ணம், வரி, சேதமென விவை ; என்னை ?

This kind of Koothu is performed when sovereigns with banners and cars and rulers of the Kurunilam enjoy themselves after their victories over their enemies.

These koothus should observe the rules of Vilaku *i.e.*, songs to be sung in respect of the King, in respect of the array and in respect of the town. The angams of these various vilakus must blend together.

The parts of Vilaku are 14 :—Porul, Yoni, Virudhi, Sandi, Suvai, Jathi, Kurippu, Sathuvam, Abinayam, Sol, Solvagai. Vannam, Vari and Setham.

" விலக்குறுப் பென்பது விரிக்குங் காலைப்
பொருளும் யோனியும் விருத்தியுஞ் சந்தியுஞ்
சுவையுஞ் சாதியுங் குறிப்புஞ் சத்துவமு
மவிநயஞ் சொல்லே சொல்வகை வண்ணமும்

வரியுஞ் சேதமு முளப்படத் தொகைஇ
யிசைய வெண்ணி னீரே முறைப்பே.'' என்றாகலின்.

அவற்றுள் :—பொருளாவது நான்கு வகைப்படும் ; என்னை ?

Of these Porul is of four kinds.

" அறம்பொரு ளின்பம் வீடென நான்குந்
திறம்படு பொருளெனச் செப்பினர் புலவர். என்றாகலின்.

இவை நாடகத்திற் பிரிந்துங் கூடியும் வருங்காற் பெயர் வேறுபடும். அவை நாடகம், பிரகரணப் பிரகரணம், பிரகரணம், அங்கமெனப் பெயராம் ; என்னை ?

When these four occur separately or together in a Natakam they have different names. They are Natakam, Praharanaprahafanam, Praharanam and Angam. Mathivanar says.

" அவைதாம், நாடகம் பிரகர ணப்பிர கரண
மாடிய பிரகரண மங்க மென்றே
யோதுப நன்னூ லுணர்ந்திசி னோரே.'' என்றார் மதிவாணனாரும்.

Cheyityanar says.

" அறமுத னன்கு மோன்பான் சுவையு
முறைமுன் னடக முன்னே னகும்'' எனவும்,
" அறம்பொரு ளின்ப மரசர் சாதி'' எனவும்,
" அறம்பொருள் வாணிகர் சாதியென் றறைப'' எனவும்,
" அறமேற் சூத்திர ரங்க மாகும்'' எனவும் சொன்னார் செயிற்றியனார் இவை நான்கும் நாடகமென் றறிக.

யோனி நான்கு வகைப்படும். உள்ளோன் தலைவனாக உள்ளதோர் பொருண்மேற்செய்தலும், இல்லோன் தலைவனாக உள்ளதோர் பொருண்மேற் செய்தலும், உள்ளோன் தலைவனாக இல்லதோர் பொருண்மேற் செய்தலு மெனவிவை ; என்னை ?

These four are Natakams.

Yoni is of four kinds :—

Making the story rest upon something that really exists with a rich man as hero ; making the story rest upon something that really exists with a poor man as hero; making the story rest upon something that does not exist with a poor man for a hero.

" உள்ளோற் குள்ளது மில்லோற் கில்லது
முள்ளோற் கில்லது மில்லோற் கில்லது
மென்னா துரைத்தல் யோனி யாகும்.'' என்றாகலின்.

விருத்தி நான்குவகைப்படும். அவை சாத்துவதி, ஆரபடி, கைசிகி, பாரதியென விவை. இவற்றுள் சாத்துவதியாவது அறம்பொருளாகத் தெய்வ மானிடர் தலைவராக வருவது. ஆரபடியாவது பொருள் பொருளாக வீரராகிய மானிடர் தலைவராக வருவது. கைசிகியாவது காமம் பொருளாகக் காமுகராகிய மக்கள் தலைவராக வருவது. பாரதியாவது கூத்தன் தலைவனாக நட்டன் நடிப் பொருளாகக் காட்டியும் உரைத்தும் வருவது. இச்சொல்லப்பட்ட நால்வகை விருத்தியுள்ளும் பாரதி விருத்தி, அந்த மூன்றுவிருத்தியும் போலப் பிறிதின் றலைவர் பிறிது பொருள் பற்றி விருத்தி கூறுமெனக் கொள்க.

சந்தி ஐந்துவகைப்படும். அவை முகம், பிரதிமுகம், கருப்பம், விளைவு, துய்த்தலெனவிவை. இவற்றுள் முகமாவது எழுவகைப்பட்ட உழவினுற் சமைக்கப்பட்ட பூமியுளிட்ட வித்துப் பருவஞ்செய்து முளைத்து முடிவது போல்வது. கருப்பமாவது அங்காற்று முதலாய்க் கருவிருந்து பெருகித் தன்னுட் பொருள் பொதிந்து கருப்பமுற்றி நிற்பது போல்வது. விளைவாவது கருப்பமுதலாய் விரிந்து கதிர் திரண்டிட்டுக் காய் தாழ்ந்து முற்றி விளைந்து முடிவது போல்வது. துய்த்தலென்பது விளையப்பட்ட பொருளை அறுத்துப் போரிட்டுக் கடாவிட்டுத் தூற்றிப் பொலிசெய்து கொண்டு போய் உண்டு மகிழ்வதுபோல்வது. இவை ஐந்து சந்தியும் நாட்டியக்கட்டுரை."

Virudhi is of four kinds. They are Sathuvathi, Arapadi, Kaisiki and Barathi. Of these Sathuvathi represents Aram as Porul with godlike men for heroes. *Arapadi* represents Porul as Porul with mighty men for heroes. *Kaisiki* makes Kamam into Porul and has lustful men for heroes. *Barata* makes the dancing master the hero and represents the dancing man and woman as Porul.

Of these the last one or Baratti Virutti has no alien subject or alien Porul for hero like the other three Viruthis but makes Porul the subject.

Sandi is of five kinds :—Mugham, Prathimugham, Karuppam, Vilaivu and Thooythal. Of these, *Mugham* represents the seed sprouting up from ground that had been ploughed by the seven kinds of Yoke. *Karuppam* represents the ear of corn nearly ripe containing the corn in itself. *Vilaivu* represents the fully ripened corn. *Thooythal* represents the harvest of the ripened corn, threshing and winnowing it and then taking it home for consumption. These five are some of the angams of Natyam.

Silappadikaram, Arangetukathal P. 66—67.

Suvai or taste is of 9 kinds. They are :—

1. Veera Chuvai Abinayam.
2. Baya Chuvai „
3. Ilipu Chuvai „
4. Arputha Chuvai „
5. Inba Chuvai Abinayam.
6. Avala Chuvai „
7. Nahei Chuvai „
8. Naduvu Nilai Chuvai „
9. Rudhira Chuvai Abinayam.

1. Veera Chuvai Abinayam.

“ வீரச்சுவை யபிநயம் விளம்புங்காலை
முரிந்த புருவமுஞ் சிவந்த கண்ணும்
பிடித்த வாளுங் கடித்த வெயிறு
மடித்த வுதடுஞ் சுருட்டிய நுதலுந்
திண்ணென வுற்ற சொல்லும் பகைவரை
யெண்ணல் செல்லா விகழ்ச்சியும் பிறவு
நண்ணு மென்ப நன்குணர்ந் தோரே.”

2. Baya Chuvai Abinayam.

“ அச்ச வவிநய மாயுங் காலை
யொடுங்கிய வுடம்பு நடுங்கிய நிலையு
மலங்கிய கண்ணுங் கலங்கிய வுள்ளமுங்
கரந்துவர லுடைமையுங் கையெதிர் மறுத்தலும்
பரந்த நோக்கமு மிசைபண் பினவே.”

3. Ilipu Chuvai Abinayam.

"இழிப்பி னவிநய மியம்புங் காலை
யிடுங்கிய கண்ணு மெயிறுபுறம் போதலு
மொடுங்கிய முகமு முனுற்ருக் காலுஞ்
சோர்ந்த யாக்கையுஞ் சொன்னிரம் பாமையு
நேர்ந்தன வென்ப நெறியறிந் தோரே."

4. Arputha Chuvai Abinayam

"அற்புத வவிநய மறிவரக் கிளப்பிற்
சொற்சோர் வுடையது சோர்ந்த கையது
மெய்ம்மயிர் குளிர்ப்பது வியர்த்தக வுடைய
தெய்திய திமைத்தலும் விழித்தலு மிகவாதென்
மையமில் புலவ ரறைந்தன ரென்ப."

5. Inba Chuvai Abinayam.

"காம வவிநயங் கருதுங் காலைத்
தாவுள் ளுவந்த வடிவுந் தொழிலுங்
காரிகை கலந்த கடைக்கணுங் கவின்பெறு
மூரன் முறுவல் சிறுநிலா வரும்பலு
மலர்ந்த முகனு மிரந்தமன் கிளவியுங்
கலந்தன பிறவுங் கடைப்பிடித் தனரே."

6. Avala Chuvai Abinayam.

"அவலத் தவிநய மறிவரக் கிளப்பிற்
கவலையொடு புணர்ந்த கண்ணீர் மாரியும்
வாடிய நீர்மையும் வருந்திய செலவும்
பீடழி யிடும்பையும் பிதற்றிய சொல்லு
நிறைகை யழிதலு நீர்மையில் கிளவியும்
பொறையின் றுகலும் புணர்த்தினர் புலவர்."

7. Nahei Chuvai Abinayam.

"நகையி னவிநய நாட்டுங் காலை
மிகைபடு நகையது பிறர்நகை யுடையது
கோட்டிய முகத்தது........................
விட்டெறி புருவமொடு விலாவுறப் புடையது
செய்வது பிறிதாய் வேறுசே திப்பதென்
மையமில் புலவ ராய்ந்தன ரென்ப."

8. Naduvanilai Chuvai Abinayam.

"நாட்டுங் காலை நடுவுநிலை யவிநயங்
கோட்பா டறியாக் கொள்கையு மாட்சியு
மறந்தரு நெஞ்சமு மாறிய விழியும்
பிறழ்ந்த காட்சி நீங்கிய நிலையும்

குறிப்பின் முகவுங் குணுக்கமில்லாத்
தகைமிக வுடைமையுந் தன்னேனை வுடைமையு
மளத்தற் கருமையு மன்போடு புணர்தலுங்
கலக்கமொடு புணர்ந்த நோக்குங் கதிர்ப்பும்
விலக்கா ரென்ப வேண்டுமொழிப் புலவர்."

9. Rudhira Chuvai Abinayam.

The Sootram for this Abinayam is not found in any copy. But the characteristics of the same may be understood from the following stanza :—

உருத்திரச் சுவையவிநயச் சூத்திரம் ஒரு பிரதியிலும் இல்லை. அச்சுவை மெய்ப்பாடென்ன,

"கைபிசையா வாய்மடியாக் கண்சிவவா வெய்துயிரா
மெய்குலையா வேரா வெகுண்டெழுந்தாள்" என்பதனுணர்க.

Silappadikaram, Arangetukathal p. 68.

Abinayam means gestures :—They are of 24 different kinds. They are as follows :—

1. The gestures of a man in a temper (வெகுண்டோன்)
2. The gestures of a man in doubt or suspicion (ஐயமுற்றோன்).
3. The gestures of a lazy man (சோம்பினோன்).
4. The gestures of one in raptures (களித்தோன்).
5. The gestures of one who is pleased (உவந்தோன்).
6. The gestures of a Jealous man (அழுக்கா றுடையோன்).
7. The gestures of a man who is joyful (இன்பமுற்றோன்).
8. The gestures of one possessed with God (தெய்வமுற்றோன்).
9. The gestures of one who is cheated (ஞஞ்ஞையுற்றோன்).
10. The gestures of one who is subject to another (உடன்பட்டோன்).
11. The gestures of one in sleep (உறங்கினோன்).
12. The gestures of one out of sleep (துயிலுணர்ந்தோன்).
13. The gestures of a dead man (செத்தோன்).
14. The gestures of one soaked in rain (மழை பெய்யப்பட்டோன்).
15. The gestures of one soaked in dew (பனித்தலைப்பட்டோன்).
16. The gestures of one exposed to the sun (வெயிற்றலைப்பட்டோன்).
17. The gestures of one ashamed of himself (நாணமுற்றோன்).
18. The gestures of one in grief (வருத்தமுற்றோன்).
19. The gestures of one with an eyesore (கண்ணோவுற்றோன்)
20. The gestures of one with a headache (தலைநோவுற்றோன்).
21. The gestures of one in a fit (அழற்றிறம்பட்டோன்).
22. The gestures of a phlegmatic man (சீதமுற்றோன்).
23. The gestures of a man with extreme heat (வெப்பமுற்றோன்).
24. The gestures of a poisoned man (நஞ்சுண்டோன்).

1. The gestures of a man in a temper.

" வெகுண்டோ னவிநயம் விளம்புங் காலை
மடித்த வாயு மலர்ந்த மார்புந்
துடித்த புருவமுஞ் சுட்டிய விரலுங்
கன்றின வுள்ளமொடு கைபுடைத் திதேலு
மன்ன நோக்கமோ டாய்ந்தனர் கொளலே "

2. The gestures of a man in doubt or suspicion.

" பொய்யில் காட்சிப் புலவோ ராய்ந்த
ஐய முற்றோ னவிநய முரைப்பின்
வாடிய வுறுப்பு மயங்கிய நோக்கமும்
பீடழி புலனும் பேசா திருத்தலும்
பிறழ்ந்த செய்கையும் வான்றிசை நோக்கலு
மறைந்தனர் பிறவு மறிந்திசி னோரே."

3. The gestures of a lazy man.

" மடியி னவிநயம் வகுக்குங் காலை
நொடியொடு பலகொட் டாவிமிக வுடைமையு
மூரி நிமிர்த்தலு முனிவொடு புணர்தலுங்
காரண மின்றி யாழ்ந்துமடிந் திருத்தலும்
பிணியு மின்றிச் சோர்ந்த செலவோ
டணிதரு புலவ ராய்ந்தன ரென்ப."

4. The gestures of one in raptures.

" களித்தோ னவிநயங் கழறுங் காலை
யொளித்தவை யொளியா துரைத்த லின்மையுங்
கவிழ்ந்துஞ் சோர்ந்துந் தாழ்ந்துந் தளர்ந்தும்
வீழ்ந்த சொல்லொடு மிழற்றிச் சாய்தலுங்
களிகைக் கவர்ந்த கடைக்கண் ணோக் குடைமையும்
பேரிசை யாளர் பேணினர் கொளலே."

5. The gestures of one who is pleased.

" உவந்தோ னவிநய முரைக்குங் காலை
நிவந்தினி தாகிய கண்மல ருடைமையு
மினிதி னியன்ற வுள்ள முடைமையு
முனிவி னகன்ற முகவனகை யுடைமையு
மிருக்கையுஞ் செறலுங் காணமும் பிறவு
மொருங்குட னமைந்த குறிப்பிற் றன்றே."

6. The gestures of a jealous man.

" அழுக்கா றுடையோ னவிநய முரைப்பி
னிழுக்கொடு புணர்ந்த விசைபொரு ளுடைமையுங்
கம்பிய வாயுங் கோடிய வுரையு

மோம்பாது விதிர்க்குங் கைவகை யுடைமையு
மாரணங் காகிய வெகுளி யுடைமையுங்
காரண மின்றி மெலிந்தமுக முடைமையு
மெலிவொடு புணர்ந்த விம்மலையு மேலாப்
போலியு மென்ப பொருந்துமொழிப் புலவர்."

7. The gestures of a man who is joyful.

" இன்பமொடு புணர்ந்தோ னவிநய மியம்பிற்
றன்ப நீங்கித் துவர்த்த யாக்கையுந்
தயங்கித் தாழ்ந்த பெருமகிழ் வுடைமையு
மயங்கி வந்த செலவுநனி யுடைமையு
மழகுள் ளுறுத்த சொற்பொலி வுடைமையு
மெழிலொடு புணர்ந்த நறுமல ருடைமையுங்
கலங்கள் சேர்ந் தகன்ற தோண்மார் புடைமையு
நலங்கெழு புலவர் நாடின ரென்ப."

8. The gestures of one possessed with God.

" தெய்வ முற்றோ னவிநயஞ் செப்பிற்
கைவிட் டெறிந்த கலக்க முடைமையு
மடித்தெயிறு கௌவிய வாய்த்தொழி லுடைமையுந்
துடித்த புருவமுந் துளங்கிய நிலையுஞ்
செய்ய முகமுஞ் சேர்ந்த செருக்கு
மெய்து மென்ப வியல்புணர்ந் தோரே."

9. The gestures of one who is cheated.

" ஞஞ்ஞை யுற்றோ னவிநய நாடிற்
பன்மென் றிறகிய நாவழி வுடைமையு
நுரைசோர்ந்து கூம்பும் வாயு நோக்கினர்க்
குரைப்பான் போல வுணர்விலாமையும்
விழிப்போன் போல விழியா திருத்தலும்
விழுத்தக வுடைமையு மொழுக்கி லாமையும்
வயங்கிய திருமுக மழுங்கலும் பிறவு
மேவிய தென்ப விளங்குமொழிப் புலவர்." இஃது எழுதுமாக்கணவிநயம்.

10. The gestures of one who is subject to another.

" சிந்தையுடம் பட்டோ னவிநயந் தெரியின்
முந்தை யாயினு முணரா நிலைமையும்
பிடித்த கைமே லடைத்த கவிழு
முடித்த வருத கரும நிலைமையுஞ்
சொல்வது யாது முணரா நிலைமையும்
புல்லு மென்ப பொருந்துமொழிப் புலவர்."

11. The gestures of one in sleep.

" துஞ்சா நின்றோ னவிநயந் துணியி
னெஞ்சுத லின்றி யிருபுடை மருங்கு
மலர்ந்துங் கவிழ்ந்தும் வருபடை யியற்றிய
மலர்ந்துயிர்ப் புடைய வாற்றலு மாகும்."

12. The gestures of one out of sleep.

" இன்புயி லுணர்ந்தோ னவிநய மியம்பி
லொன்றிய குறங்கோட் டாவியு முயிர்ப்புந்
தூங்கிய முகமுந் துளங்கிய வுடம்பு
மோங்கிய திரிபு மொழிந்தவுங் கொளலே."

13. The gestures of a dead man.

" செத்தோ னவிநயஞ் செப்புங் காலை
யத்தக வச்சமு மழிப்பு மாக்கலுங்
கடித்த நிரைப்பலின் வெடித்துப் பொடித்துப்
போந்துணி வுடைமையும் வலித்த வுயப்பு
மெலிந்த வகமே மேன்மைமிக வுடைமையும்
வெண்மணி தோன்றக் கருமணி கரத்தலு
முண்மையிற் புலவ ருணர்ந்த வாறே"

14. The gestures of one soaked in rain.

" மழைபெய்யப் பட்டோ [illegible]விநயம் வகுக்கி
லிழிதக வுடைய வி[illegible]ள் யுடைமையு
மெய்கூர் நடுக்கமு[illegible]லும் படாத்தை
மெய்பூண் டொடுக்கிய [illegible]தோடு புணர்தலு
மொளிப்படு மனை[illegible] கண்ணும்
விளியிலுக்[illegible]தசெவி யுடைமையுங்
கோடேவிட் [illegible] குளிர்மிக வுடைமையும்
நடுங்கு பல்லொலி [illegible]டைமையு முடியக்
கனவுகண் டாற்ற [illegible]முதலு முண்டே."

15. The gestures of one soaked in dew.

" பனித்தலைப் பட்டோ னவிநயம் பகரி
னடுக்கமு முடைமையு நகைப்படு நிலைமையுஞ்
சொற்றளர்ந் திசைத்தலு மற்றமி லவதியும்
போர்வை விழைதலும் புத்தியோ வுடைமையும்
நீரும் விழியுஞ் சேவ முனிதலு
மின்னவை பிறவு மிசைத்தனர் கொளலே."

16. The gestures of one exposed to the sun.

" உச்சிப் பொழுதின் வந்தோ னவிநய
மெச்ச மின்றி யியம்புங் காலைச்

சோரியா நின்ற பெருந்துய ருழந்து
தெரியா நின்ற வுடம்பெரி யென்னச்
சிவந்த கண்ணு மயர்ந்த நோக்கமும்
பயந்த தென்ப பண்புணர்ந் தோரே."

17. The gestures of one ashamed of himself.

" நாண முற்றோ னவிநய நாடி
னிறைஞ்சிய தலையு மறைந்த செய்கையும்
வாடிய முகமுங் கோடிய வுடம்புங்
கெட்ட வொளியுங் கீழ்க்க ணோக்கமு
மொட்டின ரென்ப வுணர்ந்திசி னோரே."

18. The gestures of one in grief.

" வருத்த முற்றோ னவிநயம் வகுப்பிற்
பொருத்த மில்லாப் புன்க ணுடைமையுஞ்
சோர்ந்த யாக்கையுஞ் சோர்ந்த முடியுங்
கூர்ந்த வியர்வுங் குறும்பல் லுயாவும்
வற்றிய வாயும் வணங்கிய வுறுப்பு
முற்ற தென்ப வுணர்ந்திசி னோரே."

19. The gestures of one with an eye sore.

" கண்ணோ வுற்றோ னவிநயங் காட்டி
னண்ணிய கண்ணீர்த் துளிவிரற் றெறித்தலும்
வளைந்த புருவத் தோடு வாடிய முகமும்
வெள்ளிடை நோக்கின் விழிதரு மச்சமுந்
தெள்ளிதிற் புலவர் தெரிந்தனர் கொளலே."

20. The gestures of one with a head-ache.

" தலைநோ வுற்றோ னவிநயஞ் சாற்றி
னிலைமை யின்றித் தலையாட் டுடைமையுங்
கோடிய விருக்கையுந் தளர்ந்த வேரோடு
பெருவிர லிடுக்கிய நுதலும் வருந்தி
யொடுங்கிய கண்ணொடு பிறவுந்
திருந்து மென்ப செந்நெறிப் புலவர்."

21. The gestures of one in a fit.

" அழற்றிறம் பட்டோ னவிநய முரைப்பி
னிழற்றிறம் வேண்டு நெறிமையின் விருப்பு
மழலும் வெயிலுஞ் சுடு மஞ்சலு
நிழலு நீருஞ் சேல முவத்தலும்
பனிநீ குவட்டும் பாதிரித் தொடையலும்
நனிவிர லீர மருநேர் யாக்கலும்
புக்க தன்போடு புலர்ந்த யாக்கையுந்
தொக்க தென்ப துணிவுறிந் தோரே."

22. The gestures of a phlegmatic man.

" சீத முற்றோ னவிநயஞ் செப்பி
னோதிய பருவர வுள்ளமோ டேத்தவ
மீர மாகிய போர்வை யுவந்தவ
மார வெயிலுந் தழலும் வேண்டலு
முரசியு முரன்ற முயிர்த்த முரைத்தலுந்
தக்கன பிறவுஞ் சாற்றினர் புலவர்"

23. The gestures of a man with extreme heat.

" வெப்பி னவிநயம் விரிக்குங் காலைத்
தப்பில் கடைப்பிடித் தன்மையுந் தாகமு
மேரிபி னன்ன வெம்மையோ டியைவும்
வெருவரு மியக்கமும் வெம்பிய விழியும்
நீருண் வேட்கையு நிரம்பா வலியு
மொருங்காலை யுணர்ந்தனர் கொளலே."

24. The gestures of a poisoned man.

" கோஞ்சிய மொழியிற் கூடுமெயிய மடித்தலும்
பஞ்சியின் வாயிற் பனிநுரை கூம்பலுந்
தஞ்ச மாந்தர் தம்முக நோக்கியோ
ரின்சோ லியம்புவான் போலியம் பாமையும்
நஞ்சுண் டோன்ற னவிநய மென்ப."

" சொல்லியு வன்றியும் வருவன வுளவெனிற
புல்வுவழிச் சேர்த்திப் பொருந்துவழிப் புணர்ப்ப " எனவரும்.

Silappadikaram, Aroompathavoorai P. 8.

" ஆடல்பாட..............முதல்வனுமென்பது—எல்லாக் கூத்துக்களும் எல்லாப் பாட்டுக்களும் எல்லா விசைகளும் வடவெழுத் தொரீஇ வந்த எழுத்தாலே கட்டப்பட்ட இசைக்கட்டளைக் கூறுபாடுகளும் எல்லாப்பண்களும், இருவகைத் தாளங்களும் எழுவகைத் தூக்குகளும், இவையிற்றின் முடக்குகளும் இயற்சொல், திரிசொல், திசைச்சொல், வடசொல்லென்னுஞ் சொற்களுமென்று சொல்லப்பட்டவற்றை யுணர்ந்து ஒருகுரவை இரட்டிக்கிரட்டி சேர்த்தவிடத்து நெகிழாதபடி நிரப்ப நிறுத்தவும் அவ்விடத்துப் பெருமிரட்டியை ஒப்பாக உருவான யதி நிற்குமாறு நிறுத்திக் கழியுமாறுங் கழிக்கவும் வல்லனாய் இப்படி நிகழ்ந்த உருக்களில் யாழ்ப்பாடலும் குழலின் பாடலும் கண்டப்பாடலும் இயைந்து ஈட்டிறபடி கேட்போர் செவிக்கொள அமைந்த வணத்தாற் குறியறிந்து சேர வாசித்தலும் மற்றைக் கருவிகளிற் குறை நிரப்புதலும் அக்கருவிகளின் மிகுதி யடக்குதலும் ஆக்குமிடத்தும் அடக்குமிடத்தும் இம்சயினிரக்திரக் தோன்றுதபடி செய்தலும் செய்யுமிடத்து கைத்தொழில் அழகுபெறச் செய்து காட்டலும் வல்லனாய் அழகு தக்க தன்னுமைக் கருவியினையும் அரிய தொழிலினையுமுடைய ஆசிரியனுமென்றவாறு."

The words " ஆடல்பாட..............முதல்வனும் " sum up the characteristics of a Dancing Master. He must be able to dance the different kinds of Koothus, sing all songs, all Isaias, he must know all the rules of sounds indicated by Tamil letters to the exclusion of Sanskrit letters, all puns, the two kinds of Thalams, the seven kinds of Thookus, and their varieties ; he must know the varieties of sol—Iyalsol, Thirisol, Thisaichol and Vadasol, he must know the doubling of the sounds of letters ; he must be able to combine the Yal, the Kulal and the human voice so as to please the audience; he must be able to manage a combination of instruments so that they may blend together harmoniously, one instrument not drowning another. He must be able to manage the Mridangam and other percussion instruments and must be a cunning hand at playing.

Silappadikaram, Aroompathavoorai P. 5.

" இருவகைக்கூத்தின் ....ஆடற்கமைந்த வாசான்றன்னொடு மென்றது—தேசியும் மார்க்கமுமென்று சொல்லப்படா நின்ற இரண்டு வகைப்பட்ட அகக் கூத்தினது இலக்கணங்களையறிந்து பலவகைப்பட்ட புறநடங்களையும் விலக்குறுப்புக்களைச் சேரப்புணர்க்கவும் வல்லனாகி அல்லிய முதலாகக் கொடுகொட்டியீறாக நின்ற பதினொரு கூத்தும் அகக்கூத்துகளுக்குரிய பாட்டுகளும் அவற்றுக்கடுத்த வாச்சியக் கூறும் நூல்களின் வழியே தெரிய வறிந்து அக்கூத்தும் பாட்டும் தாளங்களும் தாளங்களின் வழியே வந்த தூக்குகளும் தம்மிற்கூடி நிகழுமிடத்துப் பிண்டி பிணையல் எழிற்கை தொழிற்கையென்னும் அந்த நான்கினையும் நால்வகைத்துக் கொண்ட கூறுபாட்டை யறிந்து அகக் கூத்தினிடத்துக் கூடைக்கதியாகச் செய்தலை வாரக்கதியிற் புகுதாமலும் வாரக்கதியாகச் செய்தலை கூடைக்கதியிற் புகுதாமலும் புறக்கூத்தில் ஆடனிகழுமிடத்து அவிநய நிகழாமலும் அவிநய நிகழுமிடத்து ஆடல் நிகழாமலும் குரவைக் கூத்தும் வரிக் கூத்தும் தம்மில் விரவாதபடியும் செலுத்தவல்ல ஆடலாசிரியனுமென்றவாறு "

The words "இருவகைக் கூத்தின்..............ஆடற்கமைந்தவாசான்" also give the characteristics that should be found in an efficient master of dancing. He must know the rules of the two kinds of Ahakootu, namely Desikam and Margam; he must be able to combine the rules of Purakootu as well as Vilakuruppu; he must know the songs relating to the eleven kinds of Koothus from Allyam to Kodukoti; he must have studied from the literature the Achyakooru relating to these Koothus; he must be able to adjust the Thalams and the Thookus; he must be able to discriminate between the rules of Ahakoothu and Purakoothu and see that they do not get mixed; he must be able to direct the dancing so that it may not be sacrificed to the gestures and vice versa, and he must see that Kuravaikootu and Varikootu do not overlap each other.

The above extracts show the extensiveness of ancient Isai Tamil and the high proficiency of the Tamilians in them. We see that they cultivated the harmonious combination of the Kulal, the Yal and the human voice so that they might not overlap one another and sound as one so as to please the hearers. We find that the percussion instruments, as well as the dancing which was performed in correct Thalam blended harmoniously with the instruments and the voices. Further details about Abinayam may be found in Silappadikaram.

It is said that when Kali Devi, the expert dancer, was going round challenging any one to beat her in the art, Nataraja met her at Chidambaram and put her to shame by dancing the Oortavathandavam. The 93 varieties of that particular dancing are inscribed in the Eastern wall of the temple. Details of this may be seen from page 82 of the Archaeological Department G. O. No. 920 of 1913-14 dated 4th August 1914.

We have reason to believe that in many of the amsams of instruments, in the number of the Ragas, and in the system of their generation much curtailing has been done the names changed and the truth subverted. The fact that the extensive Adi Thivakaram, the work of the sage Thivakara, was curtailed by his son the sage Pingala, and called Pingalandai Negundu, and that Tholkaupiam was the outcome of the curtailing of Perahatyams of the sage Ahastya show that curtailing of ancient literature was very common. The extensiveness of the literature of the first Ooli may be better imagined than described!

Beloved Readers! We read often that the ancient people of South India were very rich, endowed with long life, of excellent and rare qualities, very devotional and were also great experts in Muttamil—Iyal, Isai and Natakam. We shall now proceed to enquire how far they were efficient in the use of percussion instruments and in Thalam.

4. The percussion instruments in use in South India.

The following Sootrams prove that the ancient Tamilians were equally efficient in making percussion instruments to suit different occasions and the dances just as they were experts in dancing.

Silapadikaram Arangetukathai P. 86.

" தாழ்குரற்றண்ணுமை யென்பது தாழ்ந்த குரலினையுடைய தண்ணுமைக் கருவி முதலாயின வாசித்தலுமென்க. அவையாவன :—பேரிகை படகம், இடக்கை, உடுக்கை, மத்தளம், சல்லிகை, கரடிகை, திமிலை, குடமுழா, தக்கை, கணப்பறை, தமருகம், தண்ணுமை, தடாரி, அந்தரி, முழவு, சந்திரவளையம், மொந்தை, முரசு, கண்விடுதூம்பு, நிசாளம், சிறுபறை, துடுமை, அடக்கம், தகுணிச்சம், விரலேறு, பாகம், உபாங்கம், நாழி கைப்பறை, துடி, பெரும்பறை யெனத்தோலார் செய்யப்பட்ட கருவிகள், என்னை ?

" தாழ் குற்றண்ணுமை" means that they used soft percussion instruments. A list of them is given.

" பேரிகை படக மிடக்கை யுடுக்கை
சீர்மிகு மத்தளஞ் சல்லிகை கரடிகை
திமிலை குடமுழாத் தக்கை கணப்பறை
தமருகந் தண்ணுமை தாவி றடாரி
யந்தரி முழவொடு சந்திர வளைய
மொந்தை முரசே கண்விடு தூம்பு
நிசாளந் துடுமை சிறுபறை யடக்க
மாசி றகுணிச்சம் விரலேறு பாகந்
தொக்க வுபாங்கந் துடிபெரும் பறையென
மிக்க நூலோர் விரித்துரைத் தனரே "

என்றாராகலின். இவை அகமுழவு, அகப்புறமுழவு, புறமுழவு, புறப்புறமுழவு, பண்ணமை முழவு, நாண் முழவு, காலைமுழ வென எழுவகைப்படும். அவற்றுள்

அகமுழவாவன :—மூன் சொன்ன உத்தமமான மத்தளம் சல்லிகை இடக்கை கரடிகை பேரிகை படகம் குடமுழா வெனவிவை.

அகப்புறக்கருவியாவன :—முன்சொன்ன மத்திமமான தண்ணுமை தக்கை தகுணிச்ச முதலாயின.

புறமுழவாவன :—முன் சொன்ன அதமக் கருவியான கணப்பறை முதலியன.

புறக்கருவியாவன :—முற்கூறப்படாத கொத்தப்பறை முதலாயின

பண்ணமை முழவாவன :—முன் சொன்ன வீரமுழவு நான்கும். அவையாவன முரசு நிசாளம் துடுமை திமிலையெனவிவை.

நாண்முழவாவன :—நாட்பறை ; அவது நாழிகைப்பறை.

காலைமுழவாவன :—முன் துடி யென்றது.

இனி இவற்றுள் மத்தளம் மத்து ஓசைப் பெயர் ; இசையிடனுமிய கருவிகட்கெல்லாம் தளமாத லான் மத்தளமென்று பெயராயிற்று. இக்கருவி பல கூத்திற்கும் உரித்தாகலானும் பாடல் எழுத்தான் உள்ளே பிறத்தலானும் முழவுகளெல்லாம் இதனுள்ளே பிறத்தலானும் இதனை நான்முகனுமென்றவாறு.

சல்லிகை என்பது சல்லென்ற ஓசையையுடைத்தாதலாற் பெற்ற பெயர்.

ஆவஞ்சியெனினும் குடுக்கையெனினும் இடக்கை யெனினு மொக்கும் ; அதற்கு ஆவினுடைய வஞ்சித்தோலைப் போர்த்தலால் ஆவஞ்சியென்று பெயராயிற்று ; குடுக்கையாக வடைத்தலாற் குடுக்கையென்று பெயராயிற்று ; வினைக்கிரியைகள் இடக்கையாற் செய்தலின் இடக்கை யென்று பெயராயிற்று.

கரடி கத்தினுற் போலும் ஓசையையுடைத்தாதலாற் கரடிகை யென்று பெயராயிற்று."

Mulavu is of seven kinds :—Ahamulavu, Ahapuramulavu, Puramulavu, Purappuramulavu, Pannamai Mulavu, Non-Mulavu and Kalai Mulavu. Of these,

Ahamulavu comprises the best instruments such as Madhalam, Sallika, Idakai, Karadikai, Perikai, Padagam and Kudamula.

Ahapurakaruvi :—The middling class of instruments such as Thannum., Thakkai and Thakunicham.

Puramulavu:—The inferior kinds of Kanaparai.

Purakaruvi :—Instruments like Neythalparai not mentioned before.

Pannamai Mulavu :—The four kinds of Veera Mulavu mentioned before namely, Murasu, Nisalam, Thudumai and Thimilai.

Non Mulavu :—This is Nal Parai indicating the Naligais of the day.

Kalai Mulavu :—The same as the Thudi referred to in the Sootram

Madhalam is derived from *Madhu*, the sound made by the instrument and *Thalam* which means *base*—the basis of all instruments. As it is used in all dances and as all songs and Mulavus are derived from this it is also called *Nanmugham*, the four faced.

Salligai is so called from the sound it makes. The words *Avanji*, *Kudukai* and *Idakai* mean the same. It is called *Avanji* because it is covered with the skin of the *Ah* or the *Cow*. As its shape is like that of a gourd it is called *kudukai* ; as it is chiefly worked on the left side by the left hand it is called *Idakai* (left hand).

Karadigai is so called because it makes the noise of the *bear* or *karadi*.

The above lines show there were seven kinds of Mulavu or percussion instruments. These are (1) Ahamulavu (2) Ahapuramulavu (3) Puramulavu (4) Purappuramulavu (5) Punnamai Mulavu (6) Non Mulavu and (7) Kalaimulavu. We must understood these were constructed and used so as to suit the four kinds of soil—Palai, Marutham, Kurinji and Neythal—the three divisions of the day Morning, Night and Noon, the different kinds of Rasams indicating victory, courage, pleasure and pain, and the different kinds of dancing.

5. The Thalam in use in South India.

Silappadikaram, Aranketukathai p. 73.

The word *Pani* implies Thalam.

" கொட்டு மசையுந் தூக்கு மளவு
மொட்டப் புணர்ப்பது பாணி யாகும்."

என்றாராகலின்.

இவை மாத்திரைப் பெயர்கள்; கொட்டு அரை மாத்திரை; அதற்கு வடிவு, க; அசை ஒரு மாத்திரை; அதற்கு வடிவு, எ; தூக்கு இரண்டு மாத்திரை; அதற்குவடிவு, உ; அளவு மூன்று மாத்திரை; அதற்கு வடிவு, ∴ எனக்கொள்க.

These are the names of the Matthiras. Kotu is half Matthira and its sign க. *Asai* means a full Matthira and its symbol எ. *Thooku* means two Matthiras and its symbol உ. *Alavu* is three Matthiras, its symbol being ∴

The function of each of these is given in the following stanza :—

" ககரங் கொட்டே யெகர மசையே
யுகரந் தூக்கே யளவே யாய்தம் "

என்றாராகலின். இவற்றின் தொழில் வருமாறு:

கொட்டாவது அமுக்குதல்; அசையாவது தாக்கி எழுதல்; தூக்காவது தாக்கித் தூக்குதல்; அளவாவது தாக்கின ஓசை நேரே மூன்று மாத்திரை பெறுமள.ம் வருதலெனக்கொள்க.

அரை மாத்திரையுடைய ஏகதாளமுதலாகப் பதினாறு மாத்திரையுடைய பார்வதிலோசன மீறாகச் சொன்ன நாற்பத்தொரு தாளமும் புறக்கூத்திற்குரிய; ஆறன் மட்டமென்பனவும் எட்டன் மட்டமென்பனவும் தாளவொரியலென்பனவும், தனிநிலை யொரியலென்பனவும், ஒன்றன் பாணிமுதலாக எண் கூத்துப் பாணி யீறாகக்கிடந்த பதினொரு பாணிவிகற்பங்களும் முதனடை வார முதலாயினவும் அகக்கூத்திற்குரிய வென்க.

தூக்குமென்பது இத்தாளங்களின் வழிவரும் செந்தூக்கு, மதலைத்தூக்கு, துணிபுத்தூக்கு, கோயிற் றூக்கு, நிவப்புத்தூக்கு, கழாற்றூக்கு, நெடுந்தூக்கெனப்பட்ட எழு தூக்குகளுமென்க;

Kottu means pressing the sound, *Asai* means making it rise. *Thooku* means lifting it up and *Alavu* means holding it on for the time of three Matthiras.

The forty-one kinds of Thalams commencing from Ekathalam with half a Matthira up to Parvatilochanam with 16 Matthiras belong to Purakootu. Aran Mattam Ettan mattam, Thalavorial, Thaninilai vorial, the eleven kinds of Pani beginning from the first to the Eighth Kootu Pani, Muthal Nadai and Varam belong to Aha Kootu.

Thooku implies the seven kinds :—Senthooku, Mathalithooku, Thunibut-thooku, Kovilthooku, Nivaputthooku, Kalaltooku and Nedunthooku.

" ஒருசீர் செந்தூக் கிருசீர் மதலை
முச்சீர் துணிபு நாற்சீர் கோயி
லைஞ்சீர் நிவப்பே யறுசீர் கழாலே
யெழுசீர் நெடுந்தூக் கென்மனார் புலவர் "

என்றாராகலின்.

கூடிய நெறியின வென்பது முற் சொல்லப்பட்ட கூத்தும் பாட்டும் தாளமும் தூக்கும் தம்மிற் கூடின நெறியை யுடைய அகக்கூத்தும் புறக்கூத்துமுதலாயினவு மென்க."

"கூடிய நெறியின்" implies a combination of Koothu, Song, Thalam, Thooku, Ahakoottu and Purakoothu.

Silappadikaram, Aroompathavoorai P. 9.

"வாங்கிய..............சேர்த்தியென்பது அப்படி நிகழ்ந்த உருக்களில் யாழ்ப்பாடலும், குழலிசையும் கண்டப்பாடலும் இயைந்து நடக்கின்றபடி கேட்போர்க்குச் செவி கொள்ளாநிற்கத் தண்ணுமைக் கருவியமைந்த கரணத்தாற் குறியறிந்து சேரவாசிக்க வல்லனுயென்றவாறு."

வாங்கிய...........சேர்த்தி implies that the master should be an expert in reproducing in the Yal the recognised songs, to the harmonious combination of the kulal and the human voice, so as to charm the audience with his music and he must also be able to use the percussion instruments to suit the whole combination.

We see from the above extracts that in ancient times the forty one different Thalams from Ekathalam with half the Matthira up to Parvatilochanam with 16 Matthiras were in use so as to suit Keethangam, Nirutthangam and Upangam and that the 108 kinds of Thalams taught by sage Ahatya to Raja Sekara Pandya were used in Gheetams and Dancing. To those accustomed only to Ekathalam these will appear like the capers of a mad man! The angams of Thalams, their Prastharas and their Chollukattus prove the pre-eminent state of South Indian music. The best of South Indian music can only be seen in Pallavis and dancing and not in mere verbal explanation or singing. The art of Abinayam was advanced proportionately to this superior art of Thalam.

6. The system of Alati or Raga Alapanam.

We are all acquainted with what is called Alati or Alapanam. The following extracts show some of the divisions of it as well as the letters which are generally emphasised in an Alapanam.

Silappadikaram, Arangetukathai p. 85.

The following shows how Alati is made.

இனி ஆளத்தியாமா றுணர்த்துகின்றது.

"மகரத்தி னொற்றுங் கருதி விரவும்
பகருங் குறினெடில் பாரித்து—நிகரிலாத்
தென்னு தெனுவென்று பாவேரே லாளத்தி
மன்னுவிச் சொல்லின் வகை"

முதற்பாடு மிடத்து மகரத்தி னொற்றாலே நாதத்தை யுச்சரிக்க மாபுபரிற் பாரித்து மூக்கூடிய நாதத்தினாற் றொழில் செய்யுமிடத்துக் குற்றெழுத்தாலும் நெட்டெழுத்தாலுஞ் செய்யப்படும். அவை அச்சு பாரணையென்று பெயர் பெறும். அச்சுக்கு எழுவாய் குற்றெழுத்து, பாரணைக்கு எழுவாய் நெட்டெழுத்து. அச்சு தாளத்துடனிகழும், பாரணை கூத்துடனிகழும். ஆளத்தி செய்யுமிடத்துத் தென்னவென்றும் தெனவென்றும் இரண்டசையுங்கூட்டித் தென்னதெனவென்றும் பாடப்படும். இவைதாம் காட்டாளத்தி, நிறவாளத்தி, பண்ணாளத்தி யென மூன்று வகைப்படும். இவற்றுட் காட்டாளத்தி அச்சுடனிகழும். நிறவாளத்தி திறக்குமோயாமற் பாரணையுடனிகழும். பண்ணாளத்தி பண்ணியையேகுறி வைக்கப்படும்.

When the singing commences the sound of ம் (M) should be commenced. Then as the singer proceeds he may use the long sound of it as Ma. The Alapanam is either Atchu or Paranai. When it is made with the short M (ம்) it is Atchu and when it is made with the long M (ன) it is Paranai. Atchu generally goes with Thalam and Paranai with dancing. Alati proceeds Thenna, Thena and then both together, Thenna Thena. These are of three kinds, Kattalati, Niravalati and Punnalati. Of these, Kattalati goes with Atchu, and Niravalati with Paranai. Punnalati will go in accordance with the Pun.

The words "மகரத்தினொற்றுஞ் சுருதி விரவும்" imply that the singer must commence the Nadam with the short sound ம் (M) and then proceed to the long sounds.

It is the custom to commence the Jeevaswaram or Athara Sa with the sound M as gamakam and then proceed as Tha-a-a-am or Na-a-a-am or Thanam. It is to be noted that the sound M is taken as the first sound which proceeds from the genitive place of all sound and which is given prominence in Pranava and other Mantrams and which is found in Karnatic music even at present. If we again note the rules of the letters that are used in Alati after the commencing sound M, no literature could have given such minute details as the rules of Isai Tamil have given.

> " குன்றாக் குறிலைந்துங் கோடா நெடிலைந்து
> நின்றார்ந்த மந்நாந் தவ்வோடே—நன்றாக
> நீளத்தா லேழு நிதானத்தா னின்றியங்க
> வாளத்தி யாமென் றறி."

என்பது ஆளத்திக்கு இன்னும் பலவேறெழுத்திலக்கண முணர்த்துகின்றது. குன்றாக்குறிலைந்துங்கோடா நெடிலைந்து மென்பது குற்றெழுத்தைந்தும்நெட்டெழுத்தைந்தும் ஆளத்தி செய்யப்படும். எ-று. குற்றெழுத்தைந்தாவன: அ, இ, உ, எ, ஒ. நெட்டெழுத்தைந்தாவன: ஆ, ஈ, ஊ, ஏ, ஓ எனவிவை. நின்றார்ந்தவென்பது மெய்யெழுத்தாகிய பதினெட் டெழுத்தினுள்ளும் மவ்வும், நவ்வும், தவ்வுமென மூன்றெழுத்தினுமல்லா மற்றையெழுத்துக்கள் ஆளத்திக்கு வரப்பெறா. எ-று. இம் மூவகை மெய்யினுள்ளும் மவ்வினம் சுத்தத்திற் குரித்து; நவ்வினம் சாதாரணத்திற் குரித்து; தவ்வினம் தமிழ்க்குரித்து. விரவவும் பெறும். இவ்வண்ணம் மூலாதாரந் தொடங்கி எழுந்திருந்தம் ஆளத்தியாய்ப் பின்னிசை யென்றும் பண்ணென்றும் பெயராம்.

Here he gives another rule as regards Alati. Five short sounds, அ, இ, உ, எ and ஒ (a, i, u, e and o) and give long sounds ஆ, ஈ, ஊ, ஏ and ஓ (Ah ee, oo, eh and oh) are to be used in Alati. Among the 18 consonants only three, namely Ma, Na and Tha (ம, ந, த) are allowed here. Of these three consonants Ma belong to Suttham, Na to Saralakam and Tha to Tamil. Variations may also occur. So Nadam which commences from the genitive organ becomes Alati and then is called Isai and Pun.

The above extracts show that only 13 sounds are allowed in Alati, namely long short and five vowels (அ, இ, உ, எ and ஒ) and three consonants (ம, ந and த). Others are forbidden. We know that at the present day that the end sounds of words which are sung are always either the long or the short vowels given above and that the indication of the Ragam is made by the sounds only, that Sarali Varisai is generally practised with these sounds and that in Raga Alapanams we use the pathams தம், நம் and இம். When Thanam is played in Madhymakalam we use the sounds Thanam, Tha-a-a-na-a-a-m-m-m. The fact that only 3 consonants are allowed in Alati as well as the sootram "நின்றார்ந்த மந்நாந் தவ்வோடே நன்றாக" prove without doubt that the rules of ancient Isai Tamil used many thousands of years ago are still being used in Karnatic music.

"பாவோ டணைத லிசையென்றார் பண்ணென்றார்
மேவார் பெருந்தான மெட்டானும்--பாவா
யெடுத்தன் முதலா விருநான்கும் பண்ணிப்
படுத்தமையாற் பண்ணென்றாம் பார்"

பல இயற்பாக்களுடனே நிரத்தை இசைத்தலால் இசையென்று பெயராம். பெருந்தான மெட்டினும் கிரியைகளெட்டானும் பண்ணிப்படுத்தலாற் பண்ணென்று பெயராயிற்று. பெருந்தான மெட்டாவன: நெஞ்சம் மிடறும் நாக்கும் மூக்கும் அண்ணாக்கும் உதடும் பல்லும் தலையு மெனவிவை. கிரியைகளெட்டாவன: எடுத்தல், படுத்தல், நலிதல், கம்பிதம், குடிலம், ஒலி, உருட்டு, தாக்கு எனவிவை."

Isai is so called because it has to be harmoniously joined with many *pahs*. *Pun* is so called (பண் = make) because it is the combined result of the eight organs of voice production as well as of the eight-different kinds of adjustment of these chords. The eight organs of voice production are, the chest, the throat, the tongue, the nostrils, the top portion of the mouth, the lips, the teeth and the head. The eight functions formed by the adjustment of the above are, Eaduthal, Paduthal, Nalythal, Kumbitham, Kudilam, Oli, Ooruttu, Thakku.

Silappadikara Aroompathavoorai p 8.

இசையோன் வக்கிரித்திட்டதை யுணர்ந்தாங் கசையா மரபினது பட வைத்தென்பது இசைப்புலவன் ஆளத்திவைத்த பண்ணீர்மையை முதலும், முறைமையும் முடிவும் நிறைவும் குறைவும் கிழமையும் வலியும் மெலியும் சமனும் வரையறையும் நீர்மையுமென்னும் பதினொரு பாகு பாட்டினுமறிந்து அவன் அவைதான் நிலையில் எய்த வைத்த திறம் தன் கவிவினிடத்தே தோன்றவைக்க வல்லனு மென்றவாறு.

The music master must be able to understand the hidden meaning of the author and must be able to determine the principle of Alati of the poet by the eleven kinds of songs and must be able to reproduce the beauty of the Thalam, Alati etc. of the poet by his own clever exposition.

The above rules of Alati show that there were two kinds of it, one with the short sound and the other with the long one, respectively called Atchu and Paranai. Atchu is Alati with the short sound அ with Thalam, whereas Paranai is Alati with long sound and goes with dancing. The former of these is called Kuttalathi and the latter Niravalathi. He says both the long and the short sounds may be combined and sung Thenna and Thenu. Pannalati is closely associated with the *Pun* and sung sweetly so as to bring out the idea in it and the exposition thereof is made very clear with the help of the eight Perunthanams and the eight Kiriyais given above.

Some important points as regards singing to the accompaniment of the Yal are also given here just as rules for Alapanam are laid down. The chief points to be remembered in connection with Alapanam are, the Ragam should be selected so as to suit the Seer, Adi, and the substance of the *pahs* chosen from Venpah, Asiriappah, Kalippah or Vanchipah; the Swarams in Aroganam and Avaroganam for the said ragam should then be determined; of these the perfect and the imperfect Swarams and their relation should be made out; the distribution of these Swarams in the three Sthayis—hard, soft and middling—should then be decided and then the special charm of the different Swarams. The words முதல், முறைமை and முடிவு seem to imply the commencing Swarams, the order of Swarams and the end Swarams of the four kinds of Puns derived from the four kinds of Yal. The words நிறைவு and குறைவு seem to imply Swarams with even number of Alagus as four or odd number of Alagus like three.

Silappadikaram, Kanalvari Aroompathavoorai p. 29.

"விளரிப்பண் பண்ணினோர் பாணர்."

Silappadikaram, Kanalvari, Aroompathavoorai p. 191.

"நுளையர் விளரி நொடிதருந் தீம்பாலை."

Jayankondan, the Prince of Poets, says that the Vilaripun referred to was sung by those who were in a merciful mood. This shows that the different kinds of puns derived from the Yals were sung to suit the different *rasams*. When Swarams change the ideas also change. The ancient Tamilians strictly adhered to Thalam in singing Ragas, but it is now very rare. But the custom is found at the present day only among those who play the Nagasuram.

Again one who composes *Pahs* must be able, he says, to insert the particular sound out of the seven sounds (Sa Ri Ga Ma Pa Dha & Ni) on which the Thalam falls into a composition of his own or existing pahs. We find at the modern day that many Annavis, dancing masters and Nattuvans have followed this principle in their Varanams, Thanams and Chitta Swarams. Others have copied them.

The above Sootrams distinctly show that the ancient Tamilians were experts in Alati or Raga Alapanam and that they had very minute rules on the same. This shows the extensiveness of the ancient system of Alati and the existence of 12000 Ragas to suit the different ideas of the singer. We find that even as 200 years ago musical experts were able to give the exposition of a ragam for ten consecutive days and even more. On the face of this some socalled Vidwans who are able to sing a few Keertanams only (and that with a good deal of desikam) and who are completely ignorant of the system of Alapanam deny completely the existence of Alapanam in ancient days and say that the system was in practice only 40 or 50 years ago. This only shows their crass ignorance of composing ragas out of given Swarams and their Prastharam.

III. THE NUMBER OF RAGAS USED IN THE ANCIENT TAMIL COUNTRY.

We have now dealt with the Sruti system of the ancient Tamil country, the four kinds of Yal, the four jathis derived from these yals, the 112 puns derived from the 16 puns the Yals (instruments) used in singing them, the minute gamakams of these instruments, Abinayam or gestures, Thalam and Alati or Raga Alapanam. It is clear that the Tamilians who were well acquainted with all Sciences connected with music used a very large number of Ragas. As we have been unable to obtain the full work treating on Isai Tamil we have just gathered together a few important points scattered here and there.

1. The Ragas used in the Tamil Country in Ancient days.

The following extracts prove the existence of 11991 Isais in ancient times.

Sillappadikaram, Arangetukathai P. 89.

" இசையென்பது நரப்படை வாலுரைக்கப்பட்ட பதினோராயிரத்துத்தொள்ளாயிரத்துத்தொண்ணூற்றொன்றாகிய ஆதியிசைகளும்."

The number of Isais in ancient times seems to be 11991.

" உயிருயிர் மெய்யள வுரைத்தவைம் பாலினு
முடறமி ழியலிசை யேழுடன் பகுத்து
மூவேழ் பெய்தந் ... ...
தொண்டு மீண்ட பன்னீ ராயிரங்
கொண்டன ரியற்றல் கோளைவல்லோர் கடனே."

என்னுஞ் சூத்திரத்தானுமுணர்ந்து கண்டு கொள்க.

The above lines seem to indicate the existence of 11,991 ancient Isais. Further calculations show that there were 12000 in all. As some of the lines relating to the calculations are missing in the stanza we cannot be definite about it. As the 12000 are said to be Isais the 103 puns should be the mother Ragas. But if the mother Ragas are fixed to be 103 the Jannya Ragas should certainly be more then 12000. We should not imagine that this number is an exaggeration. Just as we have Aroganams and Avaroganams for 1000 Ragas at the present day books, we can certainly imagine the existence of 12000 in ancient times. Just as musicians of the modern day are acquainted with, say, a 100 Ragas out of the 1000, and with only 10 specially out of the 100, so it is not beyond the limits of probability to suppose that there existed 12000 Ragas at first, afterwards it became 6000 and then reduced to a 1000. The ages of men in the ancient days and the amsams of musical instruments have gradually declined. So it is not surprising that this also should follow the general decline. It is traditionally said that there was a work called " Gouri katagam" treating about the 12000 Ragas derived according to the system of seven Palais from the twelve, and another called " Hanumath Katagam" dealing with 6000 Ragas derived in the same way, and another known as " Vyasakatagam" dealing with only 1000 of those Ragas. Just as 12000 became 6000 and afterwards 1000, many of the important amsams of music have gradually declined and disappeared altogether. From what is given in Silappadikaram we can be sure that they disappeared altogether.

As the superior and extensive systems of the first Ooli gradually declined in the later period there is now a contradiction between the science of music and what is actually practised. However, later writers only copied what had gone before, and still later writers committed to writing what they actually knew only. Thus in course of time the once eminent music deteriorated just as "the wooden pestle by constant use dwindled into a handle for the chisel." It was only at this stage the "Bharatam" of Bharata and the "Sangeeta Ratnakaram" of Sarnga Dev appeared on the scene. Many later works seem to have been written with "Ratnakaram" as the basis. This truth is clearly seen from Silappadikaram. Different writers have given different views without knowing this ancient truth and the mystery of modern practice. Many of the rules of Karnatic Music are still a mystery.

We shall see later on that the Raga Alapanam and Prastharam was quite in proportion to the eminence they had attained in Srutis and Swarams.

All these facts presuppose the existence of an infinite number of Puns. We have noted a few important points already about the generation of the four Yals from Vattapalai, their Swarams, the four Jathis derived from each of the Yals and the Swarams pertaining to them.

Where he makes mention of the number of the puns he says that there were 103 puns in all (91 + 12) derived from the twelve palais. But he does not give particulars. However we have a Sootram of the sage Pingala who was nearly a contemporary of his. This Sootram from Pingalandai Nigandu, No. 280, which says "ஈரிரு பண்ணு ஏழு மூன்று திறனும்" enables us to conclude that many Ragas generate from each of the Yals. Its meaning is from each of the four Yals seven palais are derived as well as the 21 Ragas used in ancient times, with imperfect number of Swarams, such as six (pun Iyal), five (Thiram) and four (Thirathiram). The names of the 103 puns derived from the four kinds of Yal of his time—Palai, Kurinji, Marutham and Sevvali—are as below.

2. The Names of the 103 Puns.

Pingala Nigandu P. 170, 171.

1375. நால்வகைப் பண்ணின் பெயர்.

பாலை குறிஞ்சி மருதஞ்செவ் வழியென
நால்வகை யாழா நாற்பெரும் பண்ணே.

(இ-ள்.) நால்வகைப் பண்ணின் பெயர்--பாலை, குறிஞ்சி, மருதம், செவ்வழி.

The names of the four kinds of Puns are:—Palai, Kurinji, Marutham and Sevvali.

1376. பாலையாழ்த் திறத்தின் பெயர்.

அராக நேர்திற முறைப்புக் குறுங்கலி
யாசா ரைந்தும் பாலையாழ்த் திறனே.

(இ-ள்.) பாலையாழ்த் திறத்தின் பெயர்—அராகம், நேர்திறம், உறுப்பு, குறுங்கலி, ஆசான்.

The names of the Thirams of the Palai Yal are :—Aragam, Nerthiram, Oorupu, Kurungali, Asan.

1377. குறிஞ்சியாழ்த்திறத்தின் பெயர்.

நைவளங் காந்தாரம் படுமலை மருளொடு
வயிர்ப்புப் பஞ்சர மரற்றைச் செந்திற
மிவ்வகை யெட்டே குறிஞ்சியாழ்த் திறனே.

(இ-ள்) குறிஞ்சியாழ்த்திறத்தின் பெயர்—நைவளம், காந்தாரம், படுமலை, மருள், அயிர்ப்பு, பஞ்சுரம், அரற்று செந்திறம்.

The names of the Thirams of the Kurinji Yal are :—Naivalam, Ghandaram, Padumalai, Marul, Ayirpu, Panjuram, Aratu, Chenthiram.

1378. மருதயாழ்த்திறத்தின் பெயர்.

நவிர்வடுகு வஞ்சி செய்திற நான்கு
மருத யாழ்க்கு வருந்திற னாகும்.

(இ-ள்.) மருதயாழ்த்திறத்தின் பெயர்—நவிர், வடுகு, வஞ்சி, செய்திறம்.

The names of the Thirams of the Marutha Yal are :— Navir, Vadugu, Vanchi, Seythiram.

1379. செவ்வழியாழ்த்திறத்தின் பெயர்.

நேர்திறம் பெயர்திறஞ் சாதரி முல்லையென
நாலுஞ் செவ்வழி யாழ்த் திறனே.

(இ-ள்) செவ்வழியாழ்த்திறத்தின் பெயர்—நேர்திறம், பெயர்திறம், சாதாரி, முல்லை.

The names of the Thirams of the Sevvali Yal are :—Nerthiram, Peyarthiram, Sathari, Mullai.

1380. பெரும்பண்ணின் வகை.

ஈரிரு பண்ணு மெழுமூன்று திறனு
மாகின் றனவிவை யிவற்றுட் பாலையாழ்
செந்துமண் டலியாழ் பவுரி மருதயாழ்
தேவ தாளி நிருபதுங் கராகம்
நாக ராக மிவற்றுட் குறிஞ்சியாழ்
ஆசாரி சாய வேளர் கொல்லி
கின்னராகஞ் செவ்வழி மௌசாளி சிராகஞ்
சந்தி யிவைபதி னாறும் பெரும்பண்

(இ-ள்.) பெரும்பண்ணின் வகை—பாலையாழ், செந்து, மண்டலியாழ், பௌரி, மருதயாழ், தேவதாளி, நிருபதுங்கராகம், நாகராகம், குறிஞ்சியாழ், ஆசாரி, சாயவேளர்கொல்லி, கின்னராகம், செவ்வழி, மௌசாளி, சிராகம், சந்தி. ஆக 16.

The different kinds of the Perum Pun are :—

Palai Yal, Chenthu, Mandaliyal, Bowri, Marutha Yal, Devathali, Nirupathunga Ragam, Nagaragam, Kurinji Yal, Asari, Sayavelarkolli, Kinnaragam, Sevvali, Mousali, Sriragam and Sandhi, 16 in all.

1381. பாலையாழ்த்திறன் வகையின் பெயர்.

தக்க ராக மந்தாளி பாடை
அந்தி மன்றல் நேர்திறம் வராடி
பெரிய வராடி சாயரி பஞ்சமம்
திராடம் அழுங்கு தனுசி சோமராகம்
மேக ராகந் துக்க ராகங்
கோல்லி வராடி காந்தாரம் சிகண்டி
தேசாக் கிரிசுருதி காந்தார ரம்மிவை
யிருபதும் பாலை யாழ்த்திற மென்ப.

(இ-ள்.) பாலையாழ்த்திறத்தின வகையின் பெயர்—நட்டபாடை, அந்தாளிபாடை, அந்தி, மன்றல், நேர்திறம், வராடி, பெரியவராடி, சாயரி, பஞ்சமம், திராடம், அழுங்கு, தனுசி, சோமராகம், மேகராகம், துக்கராகம், கொல்லிவராடி, காந்தாரம், சிகண்டி, தேசாக்கிரி, சுருதிகாந்தாரம். ஆக 20.

The names of the Thirams of the Palaiyal are :—Nattapadai. Andalipadai, Andi, Mandal, Nerthiram, Varadi, Periyavaradi, Sayari. Panchamam. Thiradam, Alungu, Thanasi, Somaragam, Meharagam, Thekkaragam, Kollivaradi, Gandharam, Sikandi, Desakiri, Sruti Gandharam, 20 in all.

1382. குறிஞ்சியாழ்த்திறன் வகையின் பெயர்.

நட்ட பாடையந் தாளி மலகரி
விபஞ்சி காந்தாரஞ் செருந்தி கௌடி
உதய கிரிபஞ் சுரம்பழம் பஞ்சுரம்
மேக ராகக் குறிஞ்சி கேதாளி
குறிஞ்சி கௌவாணம் பாடை சூர்துங்கராக
நாக மருள்பழந் தக்க ராகம்
திவ்விய வராடி முதிர்ந்த விந்தள
மநுத்திர பஞ்சமந் தமிழ்க்குச்சரி யருட்
புரிநா ராயணி நட்ட ராக
மிராமக்கிரி வியாழக் குறிஞ்சி பஞ்சமம்
தக்க ணாதி சாவகக் குறிஞ்சி
யாநந்தை யெனவிவை முப்பத் திரண்டுங்
குறிஞ்சி யாழ்த்திற மாகக் கூறுவர்.

(இ-ள்.) குறிஞ்சியாழ்த்திறன் வகையின் பெயர்—நட்டபாடை, அந்தாளி, மலகரி, விபஞ்சி, காந்தாரம், செருந்தி, கௌடி, உதயகிரி, பஞ்சுரம், பழம் பஞ்சுரம், மேகராகக் குறிஞ்சி, கேதாளி, குறிஞ்சி, கௌவாணம், பாடை, சூர்துங்கராகம், நாகம், மருள், பழந்தக்கராகம், திவ்வியவராடி, முதிர்ந்த விந்தளம், அநுத்திர பஞ்சமம், தமிழ்க்குச்சரி, அருட்புரி, நாராயணி, நட்டராகம், ராமக்கிரி, வியாழக்குறிஞ்சி, பஞ்சமம், தக்கணாதி, சாவகக்குறிஞ்சி, ஆநந்தை. ஆக 32.

The names of the Thirams of the Kurinji Yal are :—Nattapadai, Andali, Malahari, Vipanji, Gandharam, Cherundi, Koudi, Oodayakiri, Panchuram, Palam, Panchuram, Meha Raga Kurinji, Kedali, Kurinji, Gouvanam, Padai, Soorthunga Ragam, Nagam, Marul, Palandakaragam, Thivvyavaradi, Muthirntha Vindalam, Anudra Panchamam, Thamilkuchari, Arutpuri, Narayani, Natta Ragam, Ramakiri, Vyalakurinji, Panchamam, Thakannadi, Savaga Kurinji, Anandai—32 in all.

1383. மருதயாழ்த்திறன் வகையின் பெயர்.

தக்கேசி கோல்லி யாரிய குச்சரி
நாகதோனி சாதாளி யிந்தளந் தமிழ்வேளர்கோல்லி
காந்தாரங் கூர்ந்த பஞ்சமம் பாக்கழி
தத்தள பஞ்சம மாதுங்க ராகம்
கௌசிகஞ் சீகாமரஞ் சாரல் சாங்கிமம்
எனவிவை பதினாறு மருதயாழ்த் திறனே.

(இ-ள்.) மருதயாழ்த்திறன் வகையின் பெயர்— தக்கேசி, கொல்லி, ஆரியகுச்சரி, நாகதொனி, சாதாளி, இந்தளம், தமிழ்வேளர்கொல்லி, காந்தாரம், கூர்ந்த பஞ்சமம், பாக்கழி, தத்தள பஞ்சமம், மாதுங்க ராகம், கௌசிகம், சீகாமரம், சாரல், சாங்கிமம். ஆக 16.

The names of the Thiram of Marutha Yal are.—

Thakesi, Kolli, Aryakuchari, Nagadoni, Sathali, Indalam, Tamil Velarkolli, Gandharam, Keorntha Panchamam, Pakali, Thatthala Panchamam, Mathunga Ragam, Kousikam, Seekamaram, Saral, Sangimam—16 in all.

1384. செவ்வழியாழ்த்திறன்வகையின் பெயர்.—

குறண்டி யாரிய வேளர் கோல்லி
தனுக்காஞ்சி யியந்தை யாழ்பதங் காளி
கோண்டைக்கிரி சீவனி யாமை சாளர்
பாணி நாட்டந் தானு முல்லை
சாதாரி பைரவம் காஞ்சி யெனவிவை
பதினாறுஞ் செவ்வழி யாழ்த்திற மென்ப.

(இ-ள்.) செவ்வழியாழ்த்திறன் வகையின் பெயர்—குறண்டி, ஆரியவேளர் கொல்லி, தனுக்காஞ்சி, இயந்தை, யாழ்பதங்காளி, கொண்டைக்கிரி, சீவனி, யாமை, சாளர், பாணி, நாட்டம், தானு, முல்லை, சாதாரி, பைரவம், காஞ்சி, ஆக 16.

The names of the Thiran of the Sevvali Yal are:—Kurandi, Aryavelarkolli, Thanukanji, Iyanthai, Yalpathangali, Kondaikiri, Seevani, Yamai, Salar, Pani, Nattam, Thanu, Mullai, Sathari, Bhairavam, Kanji—16 in all.

1385. மற்றைத்திறத்தின் பெயர்.—

தாரப் பண்டிறம் பையுள் காஞ்சி
படுமலை யிவைமூன்று மற்றைத் திறத்தன.

(இ-ள்.) மற்றைத்திறத்தின் பெயர்—தாரப்பண்டிறம், பையுள்காஞ்சி, படுமலை இம்மூன்றும் நூற்றுமூன்று வகைப்படும்.

The names of the other Thirams are:—

Tharapandiram, Payulkanji, and Padumalai. These three are of 103 kinds.

The list of the 103 puns used in Pingalandai.

Of these 16 belong to PERUMPUN. These are :—

(1) Palai Yal.
(2) Chendu.
(3) Mandali Yal.
(4) Pouri.
(5) Marutha Yal.
(6) Devathali.
(7) Nirupathunga Ragam.
(8) Nagaragam.
(9) Kurinji Yal.
(10) Asari.
(11) Sayavelar Kolli.
(12) Kinna Ragam.
(13) Sevvali.
(14) Mousali.
(15) Seeragam.
(16) Sandi.

20 Belong to Palai Yal Thiran.

(1) Thakaragam.
(2) Anthalipadai.
(3) Andi.
(4) Mandal.
(5) Nerthiram.
(6) Varadi.
(7) Periya Varadi.
(8) Sayari.
(9) Panchamam.
(10) Thiradam.
(11) Alungu.
(12) Thanasi.
(13) Somaragam.
(14) Megaragam
(15) Thukaragam.
(16) Kollivaradi.
(17) Gandharam.
(18) Sikandi.
(19) Thesakiri.
(20) Srutigandharam.

16 Belong to Marutha Yal Thiran.

(1) Thakesi.
(2) Kolli.
(3) Aryakutcheri.
(4) Nagadoni.
(5) Sathali.
(6) Indalam.
(7) Tamil Velarkolli.
(8) Gandharam.
(9) Koorntha Panchamam.
(10) Pakali.
(11) Thatthala Panchamam.
(12) Mathungaragam.
(13) Kousikam.
(14) Seekamaram.
(15) Saral.
(16) Sangimam.

32 Belong to Kurinji Yal Thiran.

(1) Nattapadai.
(2) Andali.
(3) Malahari.
(4) Vipanji.
(5) Gandharam.
(6) Cherunthi.
(7) Koudi.
(8) Oodayagiri.
(9) Panchuram
(10) Palam Panchuram.
(11) Meba Raga Kurinji.
(12) Kethali.
(13) Kurinji.
(14) Kouvanam.
(15) Padai.
(16) Soorthungaragam.
(17) Nagam.
(18) Marul.
(19) Palamthakaragam.
(20) Thivya Varadi.
(21) Muthirntha Vindalam.
(22) Anudra Panchamam.
(23) Tamil-Kutchari.
(24) Arul Puri.
(25) Narayani.
(26) Nataragam.
(27) Ramakiri.
(28) Viyalakurinji.
(29) Panchamam.
(30) Thakanathi.
(31) Savaka Kurinji.
(32) Anandei.

16 Belong to Sevvali Yal Thiran.

(1) Kurandi.
(2) Arya Velarkolli.
(3) Thanukanji.
(4) Iyandaf.
(5) Yal Pathangali.
(6) Kondaikiri.
(7) Seevani.
(8) Yamai.
(9) Salar.
(10) Pani.
(11) Nattam.
(12) Thanu.
(13) Mullai.
(14) Sathari.
(15) Bhairavam.
(16) Kanji.

3 Belong to other Thirans.

(1) Tharapandiram. | (2) Payulkanji. | (3) Padumalai.

3. The Puns used in Thevaram.

1. Pun Gandharam.
2. „ Kolli.
3. „ Pyanthai Gandharam.
4. „ Sathari.
5. „ Palamthaka Ragam.
6. „ Pal·mpanchuram.
7. „ Indalam.
8. „ Seekamaram.
9. Pun Kurinji.
10. „ Natapadai.
11. „ Thakesi.
12. „ Vyala Kurinji.
13. „ Thiruviragam.
14. „ Meharaga Kurinji.
15. „ Yal Muri.
16. „ Senthuruthi.
17. Pun Nata Ragam.
18. „ Sèvvali.
19. „ Gandhara Panchamam.
20. „ Kousikam.
21. „ Panchamam.
22. „ Puraneermai.
23. „ Kolli Kouvanam.
24. „ Andali Kurinji.

The Puns mentioned in Thirumuraikanda Puranam.

Thirumuraikanda Puranam p. 5.

சொன்னட்ட பாடைக்குத் தொகையேட்டுக் கட்டளையா
மின்னிசையாற் றக்கராகத்தேழ் கட்டளையாம்
பன்னுபழந் தக்கரா கப்பண்ணின் மூன்றனதா
முன்னரிய தக்கேசிக் கோரிரண்டு வகுத்தார். —[illegible]

மேவுகுறிஞ் சிக்கஞ்சு வியாழகுறிஞ் சிக்காம
பாவுபுகழ் மேகரா கக்குறிஞ்சி பாலிரண்டு
தேவுவந்த விந்தளத்தின் செய்திக்கு நான்கினிய
நாவின்புகழ்க் காமரத்தின் றன்மைதனக் கிரண்டமைத்தார். —[illegible]

காந்தார மாகிய பியந்தையாங் கட்டளைக்கு
வாய்த்தவகை மூன்றுக்கி வன்னட்ட ராகத்திற்
கேய்ந்தவகை யிரண்டாக்கிச் செவ்வழியொன் றுக்கிசைக்
காந்தார பஞ்சமத்தின் கட்டளைமூன் றாக்கினார். —[illegible]

கொல்லிக்கு நாலாக்கிக் கவுசிகத்துக் கூறும்வகை
சொல்லிரண் டாக்கியிரு நான்கிசைசேர் பஞ்சமத்திற்
கொல்லையினி லொன்றாக்கிச் சாதாரிக் கொன்பதாப்
புல்லுமிசைப் புறநீர்மைக் கொன்றாகப் போற்றினார். —[illegible]

அந்தாளிக் கொன்றாக்கி வாகீச ரருந்தமிழின்
முந்தாய பலதமிழுங் கொன்றேனும் மொழிவித்து
சந்தாத கேள்வியாங் கொல்லிக்கு காட்டினிரண்
டெந்தாயுங் குறுந்தொகைக்கோர் கட்டளையா விசித்துரைத்தார். —[illegible]

[illegible] பாவுக்கோர் கட்டளையாத் தாமீந்துங்
காண்டகையார் [illegible]
[illegible] கிரண்டாக [illegible]
[illegible] ராகத்துக் கிரண்டாக [illegible] —[illegible]

கூறிய கட்டரா கத்திரண்டு கொல்லிக்கு
வேறுவகை மூன்ருக மிகுந்தபழம் பஞ்சரத்துக்
கேறும்வகை யிரண்டாக்கி யின்னிசைதேர் தக்கேசிப்
பேரிசையா ருக்கியதிற் காந்தாரம் பிரித்திரண்டாம். —௩௪

ஒன்ருகுங் காந்தார பஞ்சமத்துக் கோரிரண்டா
நன்ருன சீர்நட்ட பாடைக்கு நவின்மரைக்கிற்
குன்ருத புறநீர்மைக் கிரண்டாகுங் கூறமிசை
யொன்ருகக் காமரத்துக் கொன்ருகப் போற்றினர். —௩௫

உற்றவிசைக் குறிஞ்சிக்கோ ரிரண்டாக வகுத்தமைத்துப்
பற்றிய செந்துருத்திக் கொன்ருக்கிக் கவுசிகப்பாற்
றற்றவிசை யிரண்டாக்கித் தூயவிசைப் பஞ்சமத்துக்
கற்றவிசை யொன்ருக்கி யரனருளால் விரித்தமைத்தார். —௩௬

Thevara Puns of Thiragnana Sambanthar.

1. Natta Padai ... ... 8 Katalai.
2. Thaka Ragam ... ... 7 Katalai.
3. Palamthakuragam ... 3 Katalai.
4. Thakesi ... ... 2 Katalai.
5. Kurinji ... ... 5 Katalai.
6. Vyala Kurinji ... ... 6 Katalai.
7. Meharaga Kurinji ... 2 Katalai.
8. Indalam ... ... 4 Katalai.
9. Seekamaram ... ... 2 Katalai.
10. Pyandai Gandharam ... 3 Katalai.
11. Nataragam ... ... 2 Katalai.
12. Sevvali ... ... 1 Katalai.
13. Gandhara Panchamam ... 3 Katalai.
14. Kolli ... ... 4 Katalai.
15. Kousikam... ... ... 2 Katalai.
16. Panchamam ... ... 1 Katalai.
17. Sathari ... . 9 Katalai.
18. Puraneermai ... ... 1 Katalai.
19. Andali ... ... 1 Katalai.

Thevara Puns of Thirunavukarasu.

20. Nerisai 2 Katalai.
21. Kurunthugai 1 Katalai.
22. Thantagam 1 Katalai

Thevara Puns of Sundaramoorti.

23. Indalam ... ... 2 Katalai.
24. Thakaragam ... ... 2 Katalai.
25. Nataragam ... ... 2 Katalai.
26. Kolli ... ... 3 Katalai.
27. Palampanchuram ... 2 Katalai.
28. Thakesi ... ... 6 Katalai.
29. Gandharam ... ... 2 Katalai.
30. Gandhara Panchamam ... 1 Katalai.
31. Natapadai ... ... 2 Katalai.
32. Puraneermai ... ... 2 Katalai.
33. Seekamaram ... ... 1 Katalai.
34. Kurinji ... ... 2 Katalai.
35. Chenthuruthi ... ... 1 Katalai.
36. Kousikam ... ... 2 Katalai.
37. Panchamam ... ... 1 Katalai.

The names of the Ragas given above indicate that they have undergone a process of change in course of time according to circumstances. We find a difference in names and numbers of the Ragas given by the sage Pingala and those used in Thevaram. We also find that a great number of Ragas mentioned in Sangeeta Ratnakaram of a later date are an adaptation of the Puns of the Tamil country. For example, out of the 31 "Raganga Ragas" mentioned by him, 21 are either Ragas of the ancient Tamil country or their sub-divisions and even the "Upanga Bashanga Ragas" are Tamil ones. The following list will clearly show it.

4. The Raganga Ragas mentioned in the chapter on Raga Viveka in Sangeeta Ratnakaram.

(1) Suddha Sathari.
(2) Shadjagramam.
(3) Suddha Kaisikam.
(4) Pinna Kaisika Madhymam.
(5) Pinna thanam.
(6) Pinna Kaisikam.
(7) Kouda Kaisika Madhymam.
(8) Kouda Panchamam.
(9) Kouda Kaisikam.
(10) Vesara Shadavam.
(11) Pota.
(12) Malava Panchamam.
(13) Rupa Sathari.
(14) Pammana Panchamam.
(15) Nartha Ragam Nata
(16) Shadja Kaisikam.
(17) Madhyma gramam.
(18) Malava Kaisikam.
(19) Suddha Shadavam.
(20) Pinna Shadjam.
(21) Pinna Panchamam.
(22) Panchama Shadavam.
(23) Daka.
(24) Indolam.
(25) Suddha Kaisika Madhymam.
(26) Rebaguptam.
(27) Gandhara Panchamam.
(28) Kakupa.
(29) Savveeram.
(30) Suddha Panchamam.
(31) Daka Kaisikam.

The Bhashangas in the Jannya Ragas.

(1) Velavali.
(2) Pinjari.
(3) Natta.

The Upangas.

(1) Koundali.
(2) Thiravidi.
(3) Dakshana Kutchari.
(4) Dravida Kutchari.
(5) Mega Ragam.
(6) Soma Ragam.
(7) Daka Kaisika Dravida Bhasha.
(8) Sathari.
(9) Gandhari.
(10) Daka Kaishika Vipasha Dravida.
(11) Indala Basha.
(12) Nirupapatharagam.
(13) Natta.
(14) Pallavi.

The names of the Tamil Puns found in Ratnakaram.

(1) Daka Vibasha Devara Varthani. (2) Malava Kaisika Devara Varthani. (3) Pinna Shadja Vibasha Devara Varthani.

1. Karnada Bangalam.
2. Dravidi.
3. Dakshana Kutchari.
4. Dravida Kutchari.
5. Suddha Panchamam. (Dakshana Bhashangam).
6. Daka Kaisikam.
7. Dravidi Basha.
8. Mega Ragam.
9. Soma Ragam. (Dakshanathia Bhasha)

24. Indalam.
23. Daka.
1. Suddha Sathari.
13. Rupa Sathari.
15. Nata Ragam.
8. Kouda Panchamam.
12. Malava Panchamam.
14. Pammana Panchamam.
21. Pinna Panchamam.
22. Panchama Shadasam.
27. Gandara Panchamam.
30. Suddha Panchamam.

3. Suddha Kousikam.
4. Pinna Kousika Madhymam.
6. Pinna Kousikam.
7. Kouda Kousika. Madhymam.
9. Kouda Kousikam.
16. Shadja Kousikam.
18. Malava Kousikam.
25. Suddha Kousika Madhymam.
31. Daka Kousikam.

The above list of Ragas indicates that the 103 Puns are really Ragas according to the Sootram by which the 103 puns are made up of 91 and 12 derived from the 12 Palais. Some of these are Mother Ragas and others Jannya Ragas. Again, the terms "Karnataka Bhashanga Ragam", "Dravida Bhashanga Ragam" and "Dakshana

Bhashanga Ragam" are only the names of the Puns of the Tamil country. The same is the case with the names " Karnatakam" " Dravidi" " Dakshinakutchari" " Dravidakutchari" " Karnataka Bangalam". Again the names " Dakavibasha Theevara Varthini", " Malava Kaishika Devara Varthini" " Pinna Shadja Vibasha Thevara Varthini" are but the names of Tamil Ragas used in Thevara Puns.

We know that the Thevara Puns of the Tamil country are the production of Manikavasagar of the 4th century, Appar and Sambandar of the 7th century and Sundara Moorti of the 9th century. But the author of Sangeeta Ratnakaram lived in the 13th century and his work was written about 1247 A. D. So it is clear that he has copied some ragas of the Tamil country and a few of the Bhashanga and Desanga Ragas. The name " Daka" is a corruption of the Tamil name 'Thaka'. The term Deka Vibhasha Devara Varthani" implies the Thaka ragam used in singing Thevaram. We find many another corruption like ' Daka' for 'Thaka', 'Natai' for ' Nata' (the first letter elongated), 'Rupa Sathari' and 'Suddha Sathari' for ' Sathari' (with an additional word at the beginning,) ' Bhairavi' ' Indolam', ' Kuranji' for 'Vairavam' 'Indolam' and 'Kurinji' 'Danyausi' for ' Thanasi' (with additional letters) and 'Nirupatharagam' for 'Nirupathunga Ragam' (change of letter in the middle).

On the whole, it is clear that Sarnga Dev lived in the 13th century posterior to Ilankovidagal (1st century), Bharata (5th century), the authors of Thevaram (9th to the 11th century) Jayankondan, the prince of poets (11th century) and Adyarkunallar (12th century). The expression " Daka Vibhasha Thevara Varthani" clearly shows that he wrote his work after the appearance of Thevarams, putting together a number of amsams of Karnatic music. It is clear, then, that works on Isai Tamil existed many thousand years before the time of Bharata and Sarnga Dev, that many of them had been destroyed during their time and that subsequent works on music had been written without the writters really grasping the ideas about Srutis contained in them.

The following is a quotation from a work named " Vethagama Oonmai" (pages 22 and 23) ascribed to Maraithiruvan Swami Virudai Sivagnana Yogi.

" அவ்விசைகளில் முதலிசை (சுத்தசுரம்) வீற்றிசை (விகிர்தி சுரம்) என்பவற்றின் மாறலால் தோன்றிய ஏழுபாலை (மேளகர்த்தா-ராகாங்க ராகம்) களும் ஏழுபாலையினின்று தோன்றிய பண்கள் (ராகம்) 103உம் உள. அவை பண் 17, பண்ணியல் 70, பண்டிறம் 12, பண்டிறத்திறம் 4, என இசையின் எண்வகையால் நால்வகைப்படும். இவற்றை வடமொழியார் முறையே சம்பூரணம், ஷாடவம், ஔடவம், சதுர்த்தம் (சுராந்தரம்) என்றபெயரால் வழங்குகின்றனர். இவ்வேழுபாலைகளும் இசைப்புலவன் அறிவின் பெருமைக்குத் தக்கபடி பல்லாயிரம் பண்களாகிய அலைகளைத் தோற்றுவிக்கத்தக்க கடல்கள் போன்றன.

இப்பொழுது வடமொழியில் சங்கீதத்துக்கு முதல் நூலாய் விளங்கும் சங்கீதரத்னாகரத்தில் பண் தக்கராகத்தில்-1. இந்தளத்தில்-1. தட்டராகத்தில்-1. சாதாரியில்-2. பஞ்சமத்தில்-7. கௌசிகத்தில்-9. வகைகளும் வேறுவகைகளும் 10உம் ஆக 31 ராகாங்கராகங்களாக வகுத்து அவற்றை ராகாங்க பாஷாங்க கிரியாங்க உபாங்க ராகங்களாகப்பகுத்து அவற்றில் நாற்றுக்கணக்கான ஜன்யராகங்களும் (இனப்பண்) விரித்துக்கூறப்பட்டிருக்கின்றன. அஜ்ஜன்யராகங்களுள் மற்ற பண்களும் கூறப்பட்டுள்ளன. அன்றியும் தக்கராகம் கௌசிகம் என்ற ராகாங்கராகங்களில் ஜன்னியராகங்களுக்குத் தக்கவிபாஷா தேவாரவர்த்தநீ, மாளவ கைசிக தேவாரவர்த்தநீ என்று பெயரிட்டு அவை தேவாரத்தில் வழங்கும் பண்கள் என்பது குறிக்கப்பட்டிருக்கின்றது. அதற்கு வழி நூல் செய்வதாய்க் கூறிப்புகுந்த ராமாமாத்தியர் சுரமேளகலாநிதியில் 20 மேளங்களும் 45 ஜன்ய ராகங்களும் கூறினர்.

பின்னர்த் தமிழ் ஏழுபாலைகளில் செம்பாலைமுதல் 6 பாலைகளையும் உழையை (சுத்தமத்திமத்தை) வைத்து 6 வட்டங்கள் (சக்கரங்கள்) ஆகவும் மேற்செம்பாலையிலுள்ள வேற்றுழையை (பிரதிமத்திமத்தை) வைத்து 6 வட்டங்களாகவும் அமைத்து அவற்றால் பூர்வமேளம் 36, உத்தரமேளம் 36 ஆக 72 மேளங்களைக் கற்பித்து அதில் நூற்றுக்கணக்கான ஜன்யராகங்களும் வடமொழியில் விரிக்கப்பட்டுள்ளன. கி. பி. 1620ல் இருந்த வேங்கடமகி கூறிய மேளங்களும் இத்தன்மையனவே."

" There are seven Palais (Melakarta—Raganga Ragam) obtained by the change of Muthal Isai (Suddha Swaram) and Veetisai (Vikruti Swaram) and there are 103 Puns (Ragas) derived from the Seven Palais. These Puns are of four kinds, Puns 17, Pun Iyal 70, Pun Thiram 12, and Pun Thirathiram 4. These four kinds are known among the Scholars of Sanskrit as Sampooranam, Shadavam, Oudavam and Chathurtham (Surandaram) respectively. These seven Palais are like so many oceans capable of producing thousands of waves of Puns according to the dignity of the musical genius.

In Sangeeta Ratnakaram, held to be the pioneer work on Music, the author has indicated 31 Raganga Ragas (1 in Pun Thaka Ragam, 1 in Indalam, 1 in Nataragam, 2 in Sathari, 7 in Panchamam, 9 in Kousikam and 10 other different kinds) which have been sub-divided into Raganga, Bhashanga, Kiriyanga and Oopanga ragas and hundreds of Jannya Ragas (Kilai Puns) have also been extensively dealt with by him. Other Puns have also been mentioned as derived from the Jannya Ragas. Moreover the Jannya Ragas derived from the Raganga Ragas, Thakaragam and Kousikam have been named Thaka Vibsha Thevara Varthani and Malava Kousika Thevara Varthani—thus showing they were puns in Thevarams. Rama Matya, who wrote an interpretation for this work, speaks about 20 Melams and 45 Jannya Ragas in his " Swara Mela Kala Nithi".

Next, he proceeded to derive 6 chakarams from the 7 palais with Oolai (Suddha Ma) as commencing Swaram, and 6 chakarams with Vetuoolai in Merchempalai (Prathi Ma) as commencing Swaram. He thus accounted for the 72 Melams, (Poorva Melam 36 and Ootara Melam 36) and the hundreds of Jannya Ragas derived from them. All this has been extensively dealt with in his Sanskrit work. The Melams mentioned by Venkata Mahi (1620 A. D.) are of a like nature."

5. Some Ragas and their particulars mentioned in the work of Bharata.

As the author of Sangeeta Ratnakaram based his work on that of Bharata, we might like to hear what the latter says on the subject.

We shall do well, in this connection, to note what is said in pages 141, 142 and 143 of " Mathirga Vilasam " written by the Pandit Mandala Kandithar where he gives the substance of the Bharata Shastra.

" அதாவது சாமவேதத்திலிருந்து சுரங்கள் உற்பத்தியாயின. சுரங்களிலிருந்து கிராமம் உற்பத்தியாயிற்று. கிராமங்களிலிருந்து ஜாதிகள் உற்பத்தியாயின. ஜாதிகளிலிருந்து இராகம் உற்பத்தியாயிற்று. இராகங்கள் அந்தந்த தேசங்களுக்குத் தக்கபடி வெவ்வேறு பெயர்களால் வழங்கி வருகின்றன.

கிராம இராகங்களிலிருந்து பாஷாங்க இராகங்களும் பாஷாங்க இராகங்களிலிருந்து விபாஷா இராகங்களும் விபாஷா இராகங்களிலிருந்து அந்தரபாஷா இராகங்களுமுண்டாயின.

சப்தசுரங்களிலும் மூன்று கிராமங்களிலும் 21 மூர்ச்சனைகளிலும் 22 சுருதிகளிலுமிருந்து இராகம் தோன்றுகிறது.

ஷட்ஜாதியாக சுரம் ஏழு. ஷட்ஜ மத்திம கிராமங்கள் இரண்டு. சிலர் காந்தாரத்தைக் கூட கிராமமாகச் சொல்லுகிறார்கள். ஆனால் அது பூதலத்தில் இல்லை.

சுருதிகள் பதினாலும், மூர்ச்சனைகள் பதினாலும், பூமியில் மனுஷரால் பாடப்படுகின்றன. மற்றவை சொர்க்கத்தில் பாடப்படுகின்றன.

நிஷாத காந்தாரங்கள் உச்சத்திலும், ரிஷப தைவதங்கள் நீசத்திலும், ஷட்ஜம மத்திம பஞ்சமங்கள் சுவரிதத்திலுமிருக்கின்றன.

1. பஞ்சமம் மத்திமம் என்னும் இருசுரங்கள் ஆஸ்யம் சிங்காரம் என்னும் ரசங்களைக்கொடுக்கும்.

2. ஷட்ஜம ரிஷபங்கள் வீரரசத்தையும் ரௌத்ர ரசத்தையும் அற்புத ரசத்தையும் காட்டும்.

3. காந்தார நிஷாதங்கள் கருணாரசத்தில் வழங்கும். தைவதம் பீபத்சம் பயாநகம் என்னும் ரசங்களில் பாடப்படும்.

4 ஷட்ஜாதியான சப்த சுரங்களுக்கும் 4, 3, 2, 4, 4. 3, 2 என்ற சுருதிகள் வரும்.

" Swarams generated from Sama Vedam. Gramams were derived from the Swarams. Jathis were derived from Gramams and Ragas from Jathis. The Ragas are named in different ways to suit different countries.

The Bhashanga Ragas were derived from Grama Ragas. the Vibhasha Ragas from Bhashanga Ragas and Antharabhasha Ragas from Vibhasha Ragas.

Ragam is the result of the Sapta Swarams, the three gramams, the 21 Moorchanas and the 22 Srutis.

There are Seven Swarams commencing from SA. There are 2 gramas—Shadjama and Madhyma. Others speak of a Gandhara gramam also. But it does not exist in this world.

The 14 Srutis and the 14 Moorchanas are sung by mortals in this world. Others belong to celestial music.

NI and GA belong to the high Sthayi, RI and DHA to the Neecha Sthayi and SA, MA and PA to Swaritham.

1. The two Swarams PA and MA are responsible for Asya Rasam and Singara Rasam.

2. The Swarams SA and RI for Veera Rasam, Roudra Rasam and Arputha Rasam.

3. GA and NI for Karuna Rasam. DHA for Peepathsam and Payanaka Rasams.

4. The Sapta Swarams from SA have Srutis in the order of 4, 3, 2, 4. 4, 3, 2.

I shall next proceed to give the origin of the 36 Ragas.

1. Bhairavam.	3. Natam.	5. Koudamalavam.
2. Panchamam.	4. Mallaram.	6. Deshasam.

These Six Ragas are known all over the world. I shall give the Ragas derived from each of them.

I. From Bhairavam.	III. From Natam.	V. From Koudamalavam.
1. Vangapalam	1. Natanarayanam	1. Indolam
2. Kunahari	2. Poorvagandharam	2. Thiruguna
3. Mathyamathi Vasanthakam	3. Salagam	3. Thali
4. Thanniyasi	4. Karnatakam	4. Koudi
5. Seeragam	5. Ketharam	5. Kolakalam

II. From Panchamam.	IV. From Mallaram.	VI. From Deshasam.
1. Lalita	1. Mega Mallarikai	1. Poopali
2. Kutchari	2. Malavam	2. Arapalam
3. Thasi	3. Kousigam	3. Kamothi
4. Viradi	4. Prathimanjari	4. Thorinam
5. Ramakiriyai	5. Asaveri	5. Velavali

I shall now mention the Ragas found in very ancient works.

1. Bhairavam	3. Indolam	5. Mega Natham
2. Malava Kousikam	4. Theepakam	6. Sree Ragam

Each of the above has five Sthree Ragas.

1. Bhairavam.	2. Malavakousikam.	3. Indolam.
1. Bhairavi	1. Vichitrai	1. Vyravali
2. Nata Bhairavi	2. Pavini	2. Parathodi
3. Mala Sri	3. Maravani	3. Desakiyai
4. Padamanjari	4. Ramakiri	4. Chanavarigai
5. Lalitai	5. Koorshari	5. Mathavi

4. Theepakam.	5. Mega Natham.	6. Sree Ragam
1. Thanasari	1. Kaladigai	1. Vangali
2. Vasantha	2. Kouri	2. Megasali
3. Karnadi	3. Kakupa	3. Mothaga
4. Vyradi	4. Vipavari	4. Sama
5. Mathugari	5. Koudi	5. Asaveri

The different Ragas to be sung in the six different seasons are also noted.

1. *Theepakam*. in the months of Masi and Panguni.
2. *Meganatham*. in the months of Chithirai and Vaigasi.
3. *Sreeragam*, in the months of Ani and Adi.
4. *Malavakousikam*, in Avani and Puratasi.
5. *Bhairavam* in Aypasi and Karthikai.
6. *Indolam*, in Margali and Thai.

We see from the above that Sarnga Dev has closely followed Bharata in some parts. Further he says that these are the summary of what is found in Bharata Shastra. The following important points are to be noted here :

1. He says that Swarams originated from Sama Vedam. From this it does not follow that Rig Vedam has no Swarams. The two Vedams were chanted alike. Devotees of Rig Veda were in the habit of chanting in the five Swarams DHA, NI, SA, RI and GA. But Ravana added the two Swarams PA and MA above GA and below DHA, according to Karnatic music and completed the Octave by the seven Swarams PA, DHA, NI, SA, RI, GA and MA. He further developed the half Swarams proceeding from the Sapta Swarams as well as many another concordant Swaram derived from them and sang many different Sagais in many charming Ragas. Others have been following his example. Ravana was the first to use the Sapta Swarams and the Vikruti Swarams derived from them in the Sama Veda. But the Swarams used by him were in existence in the Karnatic music long before his time.

We read in ancient Tamil literature that Ahatya conquered Ravana, who aimed at conquering the Tamil country by his Gandarvam or Music, and prevented him from setting foot there. Ancient kings were in the habit of deciding a battle by a single combat between the best of the heroes on either side so that lives may not be needlessly lost and that the country may not become cursed. In the same manner there seems to have been a contest in music between Ahatya and Ravana in which the former was victorious. The following lines show that for this reason Ravana left the Tamil country.

Mathurakanji, the Sixth of the Pattupattu Edited by Maruthanar of Mangudi P. 183.

" தென்னவற் பெயரிய துன்னருந் துப்பிற்
றொன்முது கடவுட் பின்னர் மேயபொருந "

(இ-ள்) "இராவணனைத் தமிழ்நாட்டை யாளாதபடி போக்கின விட்டுதற்கரிய வலியினையுடைய பழமை முதிர்ந்த அகத்தியன் பின்னே எண்ணப்பட்டுச் சான்றோராயிருத்தற்கு மேவின ஒப்பற்றவனே.

'இதனால் அகத்தியனுடன் தலைச்சங்கத்துப் பாண்டியனிருந்து தமிழாராய்ந்த சிறப்புக் கூறினார்.' என்னும் நச்சினார்க்கினியர் உரையாலும்"

"O! thou peerless one who is considered only second to Ahastya, the ancient, the unapproachable and strong who drove Ravana from the Tamil country"

"This shows how Pandya of the first Sangam worked along with Ahastya in making researches into the Tamil literature." This is quoted from the annotation of Natchinarkinyar.

Tholkaupiam, Chirapupayiram, Annotation by Natchinarkinyar.

" பொதியிலின்கணிருந்து இராவணனைக் கந்தருவத்தாற் பிணித்து இராக்கதரை ஆண்டியங்காமை விலக்கி " என்னும் உரையாலும் அறியப்படுகின்றது.

" He beat Ravana by music from Pothiyil and routed the Rakshasas that they might not approach."

From this, the following facts are established. When the Pandyas were ruling over the Tamil country, Ravana who invaded the Tamil country with his Asurahs, challenged any one there to compete with him in Music, the incomparable art. Then

Ahastya, the well-known expert in Muttamil in the Sabha of Pandya, defeated him in the art. It is also proved that that the Tamil country was noted for its Isai-Tamil even before the age of Ravana.

"தென்னு தெந்தின, தென்னு தெந்தின
தினத்தெந்தின தினனு—"

The above words which have been in use from very ancient times show that they were sung either by a Thennavan or Pandyan or for the purpose of commemorating a Pandya King. In the rules for Alati it is said that it is sung to the same words Thenna, Thena etc. We have noticed that Sama Vedam became separate from Rig Vedam only from the time of Ravana. The fact that Swarams originated from Sama-Veda is mentioned only to prove that they originated from Vedas. We must understand that the art of Music, a portion of Isai Tamil used by the ancient Tamilians, was in a very advanced state even before the age of Sama Vedam.

2. It is said that gramams were derived from Swarams. He accepts the Shadja and the Madhyma Gramams and says that the Gandhara Gramam does not belong to this earth. But in Vattapalai four kinds of Gramam are mentioned--Shadja, Madhyma, Panchama and Thara Gramams. There is no doubt that Thara Gramam is the same as Gandhara Gramam. Four kinds of Yal are also mentioned there The order of Swarams mentioned in page (473) for the four Yals corresponds to the Gramams. As he gives the Alagu system of Srutis to be 4, 3, 2. 4, 4, 3, 2 it is the Alagu system for the Neythal Yal generally commenced from Panchamam. When Sa commences from Pa, we may have doubts about calling it Shadja Gramam. But the words "குரல் குரலாக எடுத்து இளிகுரலாக வாசித்தாள்" (she first began Kural as Kural and then Ili as Kural) indicate that they made ganam with the four Swarams Sa, Ri, Ga, Ma from Kural as Mandara Sthayi, and the Sapta Swarams Pa, Dha, Ni, Sa, Ri, Ga, Ma or Sa, Ri, Ga, Ma, Pa, Dha, Ni as the Madhya Sthayi. We call this the Panchama Sruti at the present day.

We know from experience that a singer first takes his lowest possible note as Sa, then tries his pitch for two Octaves, and then he sings from Pa of the first sthayi and takes it to be Sa. This he calls Shadja Gramam. In the same Madhyma Gramam should be said in Kurinji Yal. These are clearly seen in Vattapalai. Perhaps he said that Gandhara Gramam was not in use in this earth but only in the celestial regions as there were some doubts in the process! We fear that this statement was made because there was some difficulty in understanding these Alagu systems mentioned in ancient Isai Tamil and their order. Even now we have the custom of disposing of the stamping which a man had received in his body for a monetary consideration and giving him a passport to heaven so that he might be received with open arms by people who are there. This also seems to be suspicious like the above. Such doubts have arisen because the superior system of ganam by grahaswaram of the Tamils had become obsolete in later days.

3. It is said that Jathis are derived from gramams. We have already given the exposition of the line " நாற்பெரும் பண்ணும் சாதி நான்கும் " on page (491) When he says gramams are derived from swarams and Jathis from gramam, the two ideas are the same.

4. He says Ragams are derived from Jathis. This very much corresponds to the rule of the Tamilians by which the 112 puns are derived from the 16 puns from the four Jathis of the four kinds of Yal according to the Sootram.

" நாற்பெரும் பண்ணும் சாதி நான்கும்
பாற்படு திறனும் பண்ணெனப்படுமே."

5. He says further that Bhasha Ragas are derived from the Grama Ragas. Vibhasha Ragas from the Bhasha Ragas and Anthara Bhasha Ragas from the Vibhasha Ragas. This leads us to conclude (1) that Grama Ragas stand for the four kinds of Yal (2) that Bhasha Ragas are the puns of the four Jathis derived from the four great puns (3) that Vibhasha Ragas are the 112 puns derived from the 16 kinds of puns and that (4) the Anthara Bhasha Ragas are the Jannya Ragas from the 112 Puns. We are glad that these are based upon the system of the music of the ancient Tamilians. But as there is no definite system of calculations for the Gandhara Gramam he says it is found only in the celestial regions! In the same way the Alagu system of the Madhyma Gramam is also imperfect.

6. Though he makes mention of Sapta Swarams, three gramams, 21 Moorchanas. 22 Srutis and the fact that Ragams are generated from them, he does not appear to give the particulars how the 22 Srutis are derived. But he says that 14 Srutis and 14 Moorchanas are in use on this earth, and the rest in the celestial regions. We may think that the 14 Srutis are of the 22. But it is not so. By the 14 he means the 14 Swarasthanams of the two octaves which form the compass of the human voice. For, though three Sthayis—Mandara, Madhya and Thara or soft, middling and hard—are mentioned in works on Isai Tamil, yet only the Swarams of two Sthayis or 14 Kovais were generally possible for the human voice. It is difficult to make a sancharam in all the three Sthayis, in other words it is impossible to make a sancharam from SA, the first Swaram of the soft Sthayi, up to Taram, the limit of the hard Sthayi.

7. He next goes on to give the respective Swarams for the different kinds of *rasam* or taste. He says that DHA is used for representing fear and grief. The words " விளரிப் (ந) பண்ணிற் பாலைக் " are interpreted by Jayan-Kondan, the Kavi Chakravarti, to mean the pun sung by those in grief. The word 'இரக்கல்' means " to weep ", " to be melted to tears " or " to be in grief ". Again he gives the Swarams GA and NI for Karuna rasam, (or grace). We have already seen that GA and NI are concordant Swarams, that Tharam appears in Kaikilai and that in Thara or Gandhara gramam both Tharam and Gandharam are harmonious Swarams. Puns which commence with these Swarams are very sweet and have a tendency to melt even a stone. These two Swarams generally occur as Vadi and Samvadi. We have noted before that Thara Gramam was Palai Yal. The excellence of this Palai Yal is seen from the following Sootram found in page 41 of பொருநராற்றுப்படை written by Mudathamakanniar, one of the scholars of the last Sangam.

"ஆறலை கள்வர் படைவிட வருளின்
மாறுதலை பெயர்க்கு மருவின் பாலை"

(இ-ள்) வழியலை யலைக்கின்ற கள்வர் தங்கையிற் படைக்கலங்களைக் கைவிடும்படி அருளினது மாறுபாய மறத்தினை யவர்களிடத்து நின்று பெயர்க்கும் மருவுதலினிய பாலையாழை." என்று சொல்லியிருக்கிறார்.

"The charm of the Palai Yal is such that even the boldest of highway robbers when they listen to it are induced to give up their murderous intentions and throw away their arms."

The Same idea is contained in page 68 of Sirupanatupadai, the third out of the Pattupattus composed by Nattattanar of Idaikalinattu Nallur.

"நைவளம் பழுநிய நயந்தெரி பாலை"

(இ-ள்) நட்டபாடை யென்னும் பண் முற்றுப் பெற்ற இனிமை தெரிகின்ற பாலை" என்கிறார்.

He says here that the Pun called Natta Padai is a Palai which is a perfection of sweetness.

The above authors, we know, are among the scholars of the last Sangam which lasted for 2000 years before Christ. It is said that even at that early age the Palai Yal (where Tharam is taken as Kural) was in use, that Tharam was sung as Graha-swaram and that it had the tendency to melt even the heart of an enemy. In the same manner, we find that each Swaram and each Pun had its different taste and that they were used at seasonable times by the Tamilians. The age of these must be long anterior to the time of Bharata of the 5th century, at least a thousand or two thousand years before him.

8. If we notice the six mother Ragas and their Jannya Ragas we find that Bhairavam, Panchamam, Nadam, or Nattai, Thanyasi (Thanasi), Seeragam (Sriragam), Nata Narayanam (Narayanam), Kutchari, Poorvagandharam, Karnatam, Mega Mallari-kai (Maga Ragam), Kousikam, Intholam, Viradi (Varadi) Koudi and Velavali were Ragas of the period of the sage Pingala. We see distinctly that he wrote his work after the period of proficiency in music of the Tamilians inasmuch as many of the Puns used by them are found here.

9. Bharata first makes mention of the six Mother Ragas and their Jannya Ragas before speaking about his 36 Ragas. He says that those are also 36 in number. Of those the five Mother Ragas, namely, (1) Bhairavam, (2) Malavakousikam, (3) Indo-lam, (4) Mega Natham, (Mega Ragam) and (5) Sriragam (Seeragam) are ancient Ragas found in Tamil works. The other Mother Ragas, such as Bhairavi, Kurshari, Danasari, Karnati and Koudi are also Ragas used by the ancient Tamilians. It is to be particularly noted that the five out of these Six Mother Ragas,—Meganatham, Seeragam, Kousikam, Vairavam and Indolam—mentioned in ancient works long before the age of Bharata, are Ragas mentioned in Isai Tamil and used by the ancient Tamilians. These are the same which are mentioned by Bharata as found in ancient shastras. If Bharata, the pioneer among musical writers, makes such a statement, others who came after him cannot but endorse him.

10. It is also to be noted that the six ancient Mother Ragas mentioned by Bharata are set apart to be sung during the six seasons of the year. This clearly proves that, because there were Tamil Ragas of antiquity, the Tamilians of yore divided the year into six seasons and had the system of singing Ragas and Jannya Ragas to suit each of the seasons of the year.

In short when we note the chief amsams of music as given by Bharata, we come to the conclusion that they had been used in Isai Tamil and that the Puns were used in the same, but finding some difference in the gramams of Isai Tamil and their alagus he was landed in the region of doubt. We shall find more of this later on. Because Sarnga Dev mentions 'Thevara Varthini' it is clear that he lived after the age of Thevarams, and, inasmuch Bharata does not make mention of Thevarams, he lived before that period. It is generally said that Manickavasakar, the author of Thiruvachakam, lived about the 4th century A. D. But 5th century A.D. is the age of Bharata.

6. Names of the Puns found in the Dictionary edited by Mr. Ramanathan.

The Thirams of the Palai Pun are 5. (P. 483)

1. Thakaragam
2. Ner Thiram
3. Gandhara Panchamam
4. Somaragam
5. Gandharam

Venba.

" தக்கராக நேர்திறங் காந்தார பஞ்சமமே
துக்கழி சோமவி ராகமே-மிக்கதிறம்
காந்தார மென்றைந்தும் பாலைத் திறமென்றார்
பூந்தா ரகத்தியனார் போந்து."

The Thirams of the Palai Yal are 5. (P. 483).

1. Aragam
2. Asan
3. Oorupu
4. Kurungali
5. Nerthiram.

The Thirams of the Palai Yal are 21 (P. 483).

1. Andali.
2. Thakaragam.
3. Padai.
4. Andhi.
5. Mantral.
6. Nerthiram.
7. Varadi.
8. Periya Varadi.
9. Sayari.
10. Panchamam
11. Thiradam.
12. Alungu.
13. Thanasi.
14. Somaragam
15. Megaragam.
16. Thukaragam.
17. Kollivaradi.
18. Gandharam.
19. Sikandi.
20. Thesakari.
21. Sruti Gandharam.

The Thirams of the Marutha Yal are 16. (P. 495).

1. Thakesi.
2. Kolli.
3. Aryakutchari.
4. Nagadoni.
5. Sarathali.
6. Indalam.
7. Tamil Velaler Kolli.
8. Gandharam.
9. Koorntha Panchamam
10. Pakkali.
11. Thatthala Panchamam.
12. Mathunga Ragam.
13. Kousikam.
14. Seekamaram.
15. Saral.
16. Sangimam.

The Thirams of the Kurinji Yal are 32. (P. 457).

1. Andali.
2. Natta Padai.
3. Malahari.
4. Vipanji.
5. Gandharam.
6. Serunthi.
7. Koudi.
8. Oothayagiri.
9. Panchuram.
10. Old Panchuram.
11. Mega Raga Kurinji.
12. Kethali.
13. Kurinji.
14. Kouvanam.
15. Padai.
16. Soorthunga Ragam.
17. Nagam.
18. Marul.
19. Old Thaka Ragam.
20. Thivya Varadi.
21. Muthirntha Vindalam.
22. Aundra Panchamam
23. Tamil Kutchari.
24. Arulpuri.
25. Narayani.
26. Natta Ragam.
27. Ramakiriya.
28. Vyala Kurinji.
29. Panchamam.
30. Thakanathi.
31. Savagakurinji.
32. Anandei.

7. Names of the Tamil Puns found in Soodamani Nigandu.

The Thirams of the Palai Yal are 5.

1. Aragam. 2. Nerthiram. 3. Oorupu. 4. Kurungali. 5. Asan.

The Thirams of the Kurinji Yal are 8.

1. Naivalam.
2. Gandharam.
3. Padumalai.
4. Marul.
5. Ayirpu.
6. Panchuram.
7. Mey.
8. Atuchenthiram.

The Thirams of the Marutha Yal are 4.

1. Navir. 2. Padu. 3. Kurinji 4. Pyandie.

The Thirams of the Mullai Yal are 4.

1. Nerthiram. 2. Peyarthiram. 3. Yamei 4. Sathari.

The Thirams of the Neythal Yal are 2.

1. Thiravil Yal. 2. Vilari.

8. Names of the Tamil Puns mentioned in Bharata Shastra of Arabattha Navalar.

It appears that the ancient works on Music in Tamil contained rare things and were written exhaustively. If we see a difference in music between the period of Jayankondan, the Kavi Chakravarti, and that of Adyarkunallar—an interval of not more than 100 years—need we ask about the differences existing now? The names of Ragas used by the ancients are found in Thevaram and Thiruvachagam and it is very likely they are some of the ancient Ragas. Yet the names of the Ragas of the age of Pingala are not found there to any large extent. The names of many of the later Ragas do not correspond to the names of the ancient ones.

Though we hear that the names of the Puns used in Thevaram and Thiruvachakam and the Swarams and rules regarding them are in existence, it is very difficult to lay our hands on them. Perhaps they are destroyed.

In the small book 'Bharatam' written by Arabattha Navalar who lived 200 years ago the names of some of the Ragas and their Swarams are given. Though he says that his work is an abbreviation from the Bharatam of Ahatya we find that many other opinions also are mixed in it. However there is a correspondence between the names of modern Ragas and those given by him. The following is a list of them.

Bharata Shastram Ragavial Pages 99, 100, 101, 102, 103, 104.

பைரவி வசந்த பைரவி நாட்டை
பைரவி சந்திரகா பைரவி சாளக
பைரவி யாநந்த பைரவி யாகிரி
நாட்டை சாரங்க நாட்டை கேதார
நாட்டை நற்சல நாட்டை பூபாளம்
மஞ்சரி படமஞ் சரிச் ராகம்
ரஞ்சனி மனோரஞ் சனிஸ்ரீ ரஞ்சனி
சுருதி ரஞ்சனி சூலினி பியாகடம்
சுரசிந்து பிலஹரி சோம சுந்தரம்.
வசந்தங் கோபிகா வசந்தம் ஸ்ரீநாக
வசந்தஞ் சுத்த வசந்தம் வீர
வசந்தம் பங்காளம் வனஸ்பதி யமுனு
கௌளங் கேதார கௌள நாராயண
கௌளம் பூர்வ கௌளம் மாளவ
கௌளங் கன்னட கௌளஞ் சாயா
கௌள ரீதி கௌள மாயா
மாளவ கௌள மங்கள கௌசிகை
மாளவம் மாளவ ஸ்ரீ ராகந் தேசி
கல்யாணி யமுனு கல்யாணி பூரி
கல்யாணி பூர்வ கல்யாணி மோகன
கல்யாணி சாம கல்யாணி யமீரு
கல்யாணி தேசி கல்யாணி கம்பீர
கல்யாணி சாம கண்டஞ் சிந்தாமணி
காம்போதி யதுகுல காம்போதி கும்ப
காம்போதி நீல காம்போ தியரி
காம்போதி பல்லதி கமாஜு கைசிகம்
காந்தாரி தேவ காந்தாரி சூரிய
காந்தாரி சந்திர காந்தாரி யுதய
காந்தாரி பாண்டி களாநிதி களிங்கம்
சாவேரி சுத்த சாவேரி சோக
சாவேரி யோட சாவேரி சஹாணு
மனோஹரி தேவ மனோஹரி கமல
மனோஹரி மாதவ மனோஹரி மீச
மனோஹரி வாணி மனோஹரி யோகி

தன்னியாசி சுத்த தன்னியாசி மாருவ
தன்னியாசி தாயா தரங்கிணி முகாரி
குறிஞ்சி மேகார குறிஞ்சி நாட்டைக்
குறிஞ்சி கூர்ச்சரி குந்தல வராளி
வராளி புன்னாக வராளி நற்பந்து
வராளி நாகஸ்வர வராளியே நாக
வராளி சுபபந்து வராளி ராமனி
மோகன மோசேகன் மோகன மட்டாணு
நந்த பால கவரோஜு ஹோஷினி
இந்தோளம் லலிதை யிலலித பஞ்சமி
சுருட்டி மலாரந் தோடிரா மக்கலி
ஆந்தோளி யாரவி அபேரிணி மலாரம்
சேனு பதிதே சாக்ஷி சாதுளி
ஆனு வுதய பானுநா ராயணி
மங்கள பௌள மலகரி பாடி
பொங்கிய வேக வாகினி பூரண
சூத்திரிகா சயிந்தவி நூதன சந்திரிகை
சீர்த்த சஞ்சோளி சித்ரவே ளாவளி
வேளா வளியே வியன்மத்திய மாபதி
கீர ணாவளி கௌரிகன் டாரவம்
சாரங்கம் பிர்ந்தா ரவசா ரங்கம்
சாரு கர்ணட சாரங்கம் பிபாக
உதய சந்திரிகை யுயர்தேவ கிரியை
நாத நாமக் கிரியை நாராயணக்
கிரியை நாத ராமக் கிரியை
அரிய குண்டக் கிரியையுஞ் சிந்து
இராமக் கிரியை நாக நாதம்
உசேனி சாமந்த மோனிர்நீ லாம்பரி
சுஜாவந் திதுஜா வந்தி பௌளி
மேச பௌளி மேக விரஞ்சி
காபி கன்னடங் கன்னடங் காபி
வருணப் பிரியை கரஹரப் பிரியை
சண்முகப் பிரியை சௌராஷ் டிரமே
வண்மையாஞ் சிம்ம ஹேரக்தர் பாஜ
அம்சத் தோனியோ டாகுஞ் சரஸ்வதி
சங்கரா பரணந் தன்னோடே தீர
சங்கரா பரணஞ் சாணு வளியே
மணிரங்கு மாஞ்சி மகிழ்கர் ணாடகம்
சுருட்டிசேஞ் சுருட்டி ரதுப்தி கௌளி
பரக மாக்தாளி யாம்பல வுளவே.

The names of the Ragas given in the above stanzas are ;—

Bhairavi.	Svara Sindu.	Mangala Kousikai.	Mega Viranji.
Vasanta Bhairavi.	Bilahari	Malavam.	Pallathi.
Nattai Bhairavi.	Somasundaram.	Malava Sriragam.	Kamaju.
ChandrakaBhairavi.	Vasantam.	Desi Kalyani.	Kaisikam.
Chalaka Bhairavi.	Gopika Vasantam.	Yamuna Kalyani.	Gandhari.
Ananda Bhairavi.	Sri Naga Vasantam.	Poori Kalyani.	Devagandhari.
Agiri Nattai.	Suddha Vasantam.	Poorva Kalyani.	Soorya Kandari.
Sarnga Nattai.	Veera Vasantan.	Mohana Kalyani.	Chandra Kandari.
Kathara Nattai.	Bangalam.	Sama Kalyani.	Oothaya Kandari.
Chala Nattai.	Vanaspati.	Ameeru Kalyani.	Pandi.
Bhupalam.	Yamuna.	Desi Kalyani.	Kalanithi.
Manjari.	Koulam.	Gambeera Kalyani.	Kalingam.
Padamanjari.	Kethara Koulam.	Sama Kandam.	Saveri.
Sri Ragam.	Narayana Koulam.	Chintamoni.	Suddha Saveri.
Ranjani.	Poorva Koulam	Kambodi.	Soka Saveri.
Manoranjani.	Malava Koulam.	Neela Kambodi.	Asaveri.
Sri Ranjani.	Kannada Koulam.	Hari Kambodi.	Sahana.
Sruti Ranjani.	Saya Koulam.	Yathukula Kambodi	Manohari.
Soolini.	Nanda Palam.	Kumba Kambodi.	Kapi.
Deva Manohari.	Navaroju.	Sanjoli.	Kapi Kannadam.
Kamala Manohari.	Johini.	Chitra Velavali.	Kannadam.
Mathava Manohari.	Indolam.	Velavali.	Varuna Piriya.
Eesa Manohari.	Ilalitai.	Madhyamapati.	Karakara Piriya.
Sarasvati Manohari.	Ilalita Panchami.	Keeranavali.	Shanmuga Piriya.
Thannyasi.	Suruti Malavam.	Kouri.	Sourashtiram.
Suddha Thannyasi.	Thodi.	Kandaravam.	Simha Haram.
Maruva Thannyasi.	Ramakali.	Sarangam.	Durbaru.
Saya Tharangini.	Andoli.	Pirntharava Sarangam	Hamsa Doni.
Muhari.	Aravi.	Saru Karnada ,,	Sarasvati.
Kurinji.	Perani.	Pipasu.	Shankaraparanam.
Mahara Kurinji.	Malaram.	Oothaya Chandirkai	Deerashankaraparanam.
Nattai Kurinji.	Senapathi.	Devakiriya.	Suranavali.
Koorchari.	Desatchi.	Natha Namakiriya.	Moni Rangu
Kunthala Varali.	Sakuli.	Narayanakiriya.	Manji.
Varali.	Oothayabanu.	Natha Ramakiriya.	Karnatakam.
Punnaga Varali.	Narayani.	Guntakiriya.	Churuti.
Pandu Varali.	Mangala Boulam.	Sindu Ramakiriya.	Chenchuruti.
Nagasura Varali.	Malahari.	Naga Nadam.	
Naga Varali.	Padi.	Oosani.	
Suba Panthu Varali.	Vehavahini.	Samantham.	
Ramali.	Poorana Sootri.	Neelambari	

Mohanam.	Sayntavi.	Sujavandhi	Ragupti.
Jagan Mohanam.	Noothanachandrika.	Thujavauthy	Kouli.
Atana.	Reethi Koulam.	Pouli.	Parasu
Biakadam.	Mayamalava Koulam.	Mesa Pouli.	Mandali.

The Chief Ragas.

மேக விரஞ்சி குறிஞ்சி பூபாளம்
வாகுசேர் கைசிகம் வராளி மலகரி
பல்லதி யிந்தோளம் படமஞ் சரியே
நல்ல நாராயணை நாட்டை வசந்தம்
பௌளி சீராகம் பங்காளங் கூர்ச்சரி
கௌளி காந்தாரி காம்போதி லலிதை
தேவக் கிரியை தேசாக்ஷரி மாளவி
சாவேரி தேதி சாரங்கந் தோடி
இராமக் கிரியைவே ளாவளி பைரவி
குண்டக் கிரியை கூறுதன் னியாசியோ
டொன்றிய நாலெட் டாக வரைத்தவை
நிலைபெறு தலைமை நெறிப்படு மிசையே.

The following is a list of the chief Ragas he mention above :—

Mega Viranji.	Patamanjari.	Kouli.	Desi.
Kurinji.	Narayani.	Gandhari.	Sarangam.
Bhupalam.	Nattai.	Kambodi.	Thodi.
Kaisikam.	Vasantham.	Halitai.	Ramakiriya.
Varali.	Pouli.	Devakirya.	Velavali.
Malahari.	Seeragam.	Deshachari.	Bhairavi.
Pallathi.	Bangalam.	Malavi.	Gundakiriya.
Indolam.	Koortchari.	Saveri.	Thannyasi.

He says that he based his work on that of Bharata and that it was a summary of the same. We may see some kind of resemblance between the Ragas used during the time of this writer. who lived about 200 years ago. and those used during the time of Sarnga Dev. But there is a vast difference in the names of the Tamil Ragas of the period of the Sage Pingala who lived before him. So it is clear that these names came into use after the period when foreign names were habitually given to Tamil Ragas. Among his list of chief Ragas the following are Ragas used by the ancient Tamilians :—Megaviranji, Kurinji. Kaisikam, Varali, Indolam, Narayani, Nattai, Seeragam, Bangalam. Koorchari. Gandhari. Kouli. Velavali. Bhairavi and Thanniyasi. Because the ancient works treating about the 12,000 ancient Isais used by the Tamilians in the first Ooli. the order of their Swarams and the system of singing them have been lost, he mixes a number of foreign names used by writers of foreign languages and says that it is a summary of the work of Ahastya. From this we must not suppose that the Ragas he mentions were in existence at the time of Ahastya. Though it is out of place to give a list of his Ragas here, yet we give it in order to convince readers that the Tamilians who learnt foreign tongues gave foreign names to the Ragas they were singing and wrote musical works in foreign languages. This was the reason why all Isai Tamil came to be written in foreign tongues in course of time.

If we note carefully (1) the names of ancient Ragas used in the time of the sage Pingala who lived immediately after the period of the third Sangam, (2) the name of those mentioned by Bharata as belonging to ancient times, (3) the names of those of the period of Bharata, (4) the names of those mentioned in Sangeetha Ratnakaram based on the work of Bharata, (5) the names of those in use at the time of Arabattha Navalar, and (6) the names of those at the present day we shall be able to conclude that South Indian Music. and works relating to it even as early as the first Ooli. were very extensive, that during the time of the Second Sangam they were comparatively less extensive, that at the period of the third they became much more small like the middle portion of the Oodukai, that after the period of the third Sangam and during the time of Bharata (5th century A. D.) foreign words were introduced and works written which had doubts about Srutis, that more extensive works were written during the time of Sarnga Dev (13th century) and that the ancient Isai Tamil and its lakshanams are being written in a foreign language and used at the present time. We find that as no definite knowledge of Srutis existed after the third Sangam these gradually disappeared.

9. Ragas found in Abithana Chintamani.

The Chief Ragas Page 639-640.

1. Mega Viranchi.	9. Padamanjari.	17. Kouli.	25. Desi.
2. Kurinji.	10. Narayani.	18. Gandhari.	26. Sarangam.
3. Bhupalam.	11. Nattai.	19. Kambodi.	27. Thodi.
4. Kaisikam.	12. Vasantam.	20. Ilalitai.	28. Ramakiriya.
5. Varali.	13. Pouli.	21. Devakiriya.	29. Velavali.
6. Malahari.	14. Seeragam.	22. Desakshari.	30. Bhairavi.
7. Pallathi	15. Bangalam.	23. Malavi.	31. Guntakiriya.
8. Indolam.	16. Koorchari.	24. Saveri.	32. Thannyasi.

These are also found in the list of Arabattha Navalar.

The Male and Female Ragas.

Male Ragas	Female Ragas.	Male Ragas.	Female Ragas.
Bhairavi	Devakiriyai. Mega Viranji Kurinji.	Vasantam	Ramakiriya. Varali. Kaisikam.
Bhupalam	Velavali. Malahari. Pouli.	Malavi	Guntakiriya. Narayani. Koorchari.
Seeragam	Indolam. Pallathi. Saveri.	Bangalam	Thannyasi. Kambodi. Kouli.
Padamanjari	Desi. Ilalitai. Thodi.	Nattai	Deshakshari. Gandharam. Sarangam.

Thukka Ragas.	1. Agiri. 2. Kantaravam.	3. Neelambari. 4. Biyakatai.	5. Punnaga Varali. 6. Varali.
Joyful Ragas.	1. Kambodi.	2. Thannyasi.	3. Saveri.
War Ragam.	1. Nattai.		
Ragas of the Spring Season.	1. Kambodi.	2. Asaveri.	3. Thannyasi.
Ragas of the evening	1. Kalyani. 2. Kapi.	3. Kannadam. 4. Kambodi.	
Yama Ragam.	1. Agiri.		
Morning Ragas.	1. Indolam. 2. Ramakali.	3. Deshakshari. 4. Nattai.	5. Bhupalam.
Noonday Ragas.	1. Sarangam.	2. Deshakshari.	

With the exception of Agiri, Indolam. Ramakali, Sarangam and Bhupalam others may be sung at all times.

Ragas pertaining to different Pahs.

For Venba—Shankaraparanam,
,, *Ahaval*—Thodi
,, *Kalipah*—Panthuvarali.
,, *Kaliturai*—Bhairavi.
,, *Thalisai*—Thodi.

For Viruttham—Kalyani, Kambodi, Madhyamavati,
,, *Oola*—Sourashtiram,
,, *Devaram*—Bhupalam,
,, *Pillai Kavi*—Kethara Koulam,
,, *Parani*—Kandarvam.

The names of the above Ragas clearly show that they have been either changed in a foreign language or given an entirely new name in a foreign language and then brought into use. In the modern time we speak of 72 Mother Ragas and their Jannya Ragas, and 1008 such are in use along with their Swarams in Aroganam and Avaroganam. Besides these we find from a Telugu work that there are three Melams—Brahma Vishnu and Rudra—or Mother Ragas, with 4624. 200 and 72 Ragas in them respectively. But the author seems to be from a family of vidwans in Isai Tamil in Tinnevelly. According to him, Brahma Melam has 4624 Mother Ragas. There is a work in Telugu in the Tanjore Palace library Sarasvati Mahal—which gives the rules for Lakshanam as well as names for a 1000 of the above-mentioned Mother Ragas. It appears the author was a native of the Tamil country belonging to the Vellala community. But his work is in Telugu. The details about these will be given in the Part which treats about Ragas.

All the above facts enable us to conclude that the Tamilians were experts in Isai Tamil or Music from very early times, and that they were in the habit of singing different puns to the accompaniment of different instruments to suit the various seasons, occasions, circumstances and the soil, so as to bring out the nine different tastes in their religious devotions, in the Sabhas of the Kings and in their dances on different occasions. The fact that the different kinds of superior *Pahs* satisfy the chief rules of seer, adi, Ethugai, Monai and Matthirai shows that they have been sung with different

Thalams and with different puns from time immemorial. The Ahavals given below show that even the common Ahaval Pahs were sung along with the Puns. These Aahavals are taken from the 70 Paripadals of the last Sangam long before the age of Ilankovadigal. From the preface to Irayanar Ahaporul written by Nakeeranar we see that numerous Paripadals existed in South Madura also the seat of the First Sangam. So we should conclude that similar padals were in existence from the time of the First Sangam long before the first Ooli and that they were sung in different Ragas.

10. Ragas found in Paripadal.

Paripadal, the fifth of the Eight Thogais.

ஐந்திரு ளறநீக்கி நான்கினுட் டுடைத்துத்தம்
மொன்றாற்றுப் படுத்தநின் னார்வலர் தொழுதேத்தி
நின்புகழ் விரிந்தன கிளக்குங்கா லவைநினக்
கிறும்பூ தன்மைநற் கறிந்தோ மாயினு
நகுதலுந் தகுதியீங் கூங்குநிற் கிளப்பத்
திருமணி திரைபா டவிந்த முந்நீர்
வருமழை யிருஞ்சூன் மூன்றும் புரையு
மாஅ மெய்யொடு முரணிய வுடுக்கையை
நோனா வுயிரொடு முரணிய நேமியை
செய்தீர் செங்கட் செல்வநின் புகழ
புகைந்த நெஞ்சிற் புலர்ந்த சாந்தி
பிருங்கலா தன்பிணி பலப்பட வலந்துழ்
மலர்ந்த நோய்கூர் கூம்பிய நடுக்கத்
தலர்ந்த புகழோன் றாதை யாகலி
னிகழ்வோ னிகழா நெஞ்சின னாகி
யிகழாநன்று நட்டவன் மார்பு முயங்கி
யொன்றா நட்டவ னுறுவரை மார்பிற்
பிடிமதஞ் சாம்ப வோதுங்கி
யின்ன லின்னரோ டிடிமுர சியம்ப
வெடிபட வோடிதூண் டடியொடு நடிதடி
பலபட வகிர வாய்த்த வுகிரினை
பூருவத் துக்கரு வலகந் தாத்தாற்
றுங்கியிவ் வுலகந் தந்தடிப் படுத்தனை
நடுவ ணோங்கிய பலர்புகழ் குன்றினோ டொக்கு
நின் வெம்மையும் விளக்கமு ஞாயிற்றுள
நின் றண்மையுஞ் சாயலுந் திங்களுள
நின் சுரத்தலும் வண்மையு மாரியுள
நின் புரத்தலு நோன்மையு ஞாலத்துள
நின் னாற்றமும் வண்ணமும் பூவையுள
நின் னோற்றமு மகலமு நீரினுள

நின் னுருவமு மொலியுமா காயத்துள
நின் வருதலு மொடுக்கமு மருத்தினுள
அதனால், இவ்வு முவ்வு மவ்வும் பிறவு
மேம மார்ந்தநிற் பிரிந்துமேவல் சான்றன
வெல்லாஞ் சேவலோங் குயர்கொடி யோயே
சேவலோங் குயர்கொடி நின்னோன் றுயர்கொடிபனை
நின்னோன் றுயர்கொடி நாஞ்சில்
நின்னோன் றுயர்கொடி யானை
நின்னோன் றுயர்கொடி யொன்றின்று
விடமுடை யரவினுட லுயிருண் டுவணம்
அவன்மடி மேல வலந்தது பாம்பு
பாம்புதொடி பாம்பு முடிமேலன பாம்பு
பூண்பாம்பு தலைமேலது பாம்பு சிறைதலையன
பாம்பு படிமதஞ் சாய்த்தோய் பசும்பூணவை
கொடிமே லிருந்தவன் றாக்கிரையது பாம்பு
கடுநவை யணங்குங் கடுப்பு நல்கலுங்
கொடுமையுஞ் செம்மையும் வெம்மையுந் தண்மையு
முளவழி யுடைமையு மில்வழி யிலையே
போற்றா ருயிரினும் போற்றுந ருயிரினு
மாற்றே மாற்ற லிலையே நினக்கு
மாற்றா ருமிலர் கேளிரு மிலரேனும்
வேற்றுமை யின்றது போற்றுநர்ப் பெறினே
மனக்கோ ணினக்கென வடிவுவே றிலையே
கோளிரு ளிருக்கை யாய்மணி மேனியை
நக்கலர் துழாஅய் நாறிணர்க் கண்ணியை
பொன்னிற் றோன்றிய புனைபூண் மார்ப
நின்னிற் றோன்றிய நிரையிதழ்த் தாமரை
யன்ன நாட்டத் தளப்பரி யாயவை
நின்னிற் சிறந்த நிறைகட ளவை
அன்னோ ரன்ன வேறு முளவவை
நின்னோ ரன்னோ ருணரு மருமறை
அழல்புரை தழைநிழற் பகரும் பலசினை
யாலமுங் கடம்புநல் யாற்று நடுவேங்
கால்வழக் கறுநிலைக் குன்றமும் பிறவு
மவ்வவை மெய்வேறு வேறு பெயரோ
டெவ்வயி னோயு நீயேநின் னார்வலர்
தொழுதகை யமைதியி னமர்ந்தோயு நீயே
யவரவ ரேவ லாளனு நீயே
யவரவர் செய்பொருட் காரணமு நீயே.

கடவுள் வாழ்த்து. கடுவன் இளவெயினனார் பாட்டு
பெட்டனாகனார் இசை. பண் பாலையாழ்.

கார்மலி கதழ பெயறலை யேற்ற
நீர்மலி நிறைசுனை பூமலர்த் தனவே
தண்ணறுங் கடம்பின் கமழ்தா தூதும்
வண்ணவண் டிமிர்குரல் பண்ணையோன் றனவே
யடியுறை மகளி ராடுந் தோளே
நெடுவரை யடுக்கத்து வேய்போன் றனவே
வாகை யொண்பூப் புரையு முச்சிய
தோகை யார்குரன் மணந்து தணந்தோரை
நீடன்மின் வாரமென் பவர்சொற்போன் றனவே
நாண்மலர்க் கொன்றையும் பொலந்தார் போன்றன
மெல்லிணர் வேங்கை வியலறைத் தாயின
வழுகை மகளி ருழுவை செப்ப
நீரயற் கலித்த நேரிமுகைக் காந்தள்
வார்குலை யவிழ்ந்த வள்ளிதழ் நிறைதொறும்
விடுகொடிப் பிறந்த மென்கைத் தோன்றி
பவழத் தன்ன செம்பூத் தாஅய்க்
கார்மலிந் தன்மகின் றன்று போர்மலிந்து
சூர்மருங் கறுத்த சுடர்ப்படை யோயே
கறையில் கார்மழை பொங்கி யன்ன
நறையி னறும்புகை நனியமர்ந் தோயே
கெழீஇக் கேளிர் சுற்ற நின்னை
யெழீஇப் பாடே பாட்டமர்ந் தோயே
பிறந்த ஞான்றே நின்னை யுட்கிச்
சிறந்தோ ரஞ்சிய சீருடை யோயே
யிருபிறப் பிருபெ ரீர நெஞ்சத்
தொருபெய ரந்தண ரறனமர்ந் தோயே
யன்னை யாதலி னமர்ந்தியா நின்னைத்
துன்னித் துன்னி வழிபடு வதன்பய
மின்னு மின்னுமவை யாகுக
கொன்முதிர் மரபினின் புகழினும் பலவே.

எ-து—பருவங்கண்டழிந்த தலைமகள் கேட்ப முருகவேளைப் பரவுவாளா யிப்பருவத்தே தலைமகன் வருமென்பதுபடத் தோழி வற்புறுத்தியது.

கேசவனார் பாட்டு. இசையுமவர். பண்நோ திறம்.

Here the servant maid assures the lady of the time of the coming of the chieftain.

Kesavanar Pattu. The Isai by the same author. The Pun is Nar Thiram.

These padals were gathered from very old palmyra leaf writings relating on Medicine by M.R.Ry. Oolaganatha Pillai Avl., son of Mr. Lakshmana Pillai, Palace physician of Tanjore and Tamil Pandit, Kalyanasundram High School.

It appears that there were many *pahs* just like the Paripadals above quoted where the composer was one and he who set it to a *Pun* was another. The name of the Ragam is given. In some cases the composer of the stanza has set it to music himself. This means that all ancient poetry was capable of being sung to Ragas. This poetry reflects in a remarkable degree an excellence, pregnancy of meaning and devotion not found anywhere else. There are many reasons to suppose that this sweet and excellent Tamil and the different arts and Sciences written in it have degenerated owing to the mistake of the Tamilians themselves. We see at the present day the parents of children, who have become ungrateful when they grew up, being supported by strangers. In the same way after the destruction of the ancient Tamil province and the three Sangams, the literature has been saved to a certain extent and patronised and commentaries written on it by Aryans and other strangers who had appreciated its excellence. Even here only those works on grammar, and those written in prose have been preserved while other ancient works have all disappeared altogether. Yet we see here and there the traditional Tamil Music of the period of the commentators. If they had only collected together the different *amsams* of Tamil music in use at the time there will be no doubt that the Science of Tamil Music will be far superior to that of any other Music in the world.

II. Some remarks as regards the Calculation of Alagus which are said to have been used in the music of South India.

Though it is thousands of years since the works on Isai Tamil have been destroyed yet Karnatic music is held in eminence by all, because it is the most scientific as well as most practical. If we notice the four kinds of Yal mentioned in Silappadikaram the four Jathis of puns and their system of alagu we find that it beats all modern musical systems so far as its science is concerned. When we compare the Sootrams of this excellent Isai Tamil we find some contradictory statements here and there, chiefly in the system of Alagus.

Where he derives the Swarams by the Sa-Pa series (proceeding by fifths) on the right and the Sa-Ma series (proceeding by fourths) on the left, he makes mention also of the Swarams with a less number of Alagus Where Sa-Pa (by fifths) is 13 and Sa-Ma (by fourths) is 9, some swarams have only 12, and some 11 instead of 13. This doubt occurs in many places. It is this that led many people to say that there were 22 Srutis in the octave. Those who did not understand its real meaning wrote their theories in different ways. We are one of those who declare that the theory of 22 srutis in the octave will never suit the modern ganam and we can assure the advocates of the Dwavimsati Srutis that such a thing never existed.

Let us take the system of Alagus of Sarnga Dev who is considered a very ancient authority on music. His system is 4. 3. 2. 4. 4. 3. 2. Here if we notice the swarams with the 13 Srutis by the Sa-Pa series (by fifths) we find that Sa to Pa = 3. 2. 4. 4=13. Ri to Dha=2. 4. 4. 3=13. Ga to Ni=4. 4. 3. 2=13. Ma to Sa=4. 3. 2. 4= 13, while Pa to Ri =3. 2. 4. 3=12. Dha to Ga=2. 4. 3. 2=11 and Ni to Ma=4. 3. 2. 4= 13. This is the Alagu system of Neythal Yal. The same difficulty occurs in the Sa-Ma series (by fourths). Instead of SA-MA=9, we get different numbers. e. g. SA to MA =3. 2. 4=9, RI to PA=2, 4, 4=10, GA to DHA=4. 4. 3=11 and MA to NI=4, 3, 2=9. We have noted already in pages 491 to 495 that while change of graham is made the Alagus will also change in conformity with it. There the account of the Alagus is also different. Where the Swarams ought to be 13 by the SA-PA series (fifths) it is wrong to get 12 and 11. In the same manner the Swarams of the SA-MA series (fourths) which should proceed by 9's go by 10s and 11s. Calculations should aim at greater preciseness.

"ஏற்றிய குரல் இளி என்றிரு நரம்பின்
ஒப்பக் கேட்கும் உணர்வின னாகி"

This stanza says that the music master should have such a trained ear as to understand the perfect combination of the Swarams SA and PA. The ancient Tamilians who fixed such a rule can never admit SA PA to be 13 at one time and 12 and 11 at other times. If any body uses them who will admit that they are just? Is it right to have 10 and 11 in place of 9? Who will not declare that these are wrong? Can they not see that such an Alagu system is wrong?

12. The minute Arithmetical Calculations of the ancient Tamilians.

We see indications in different places that the ancient Tamilians had a very minute system of Arithmetical calculations. We have the expression "ஒரு இம்மி கூட விடமாட்டேன்"—"I shall not yield even an Immi (1/2150400)". The Tamilians are even at the present day in the habit of asking a man who wants to be very precise in his dealings, "What? Are you calculating down to the very Immi?"

If one is asked to divide 1 equally among three persons, this is how one proceeds.—

Three kals (quarters) make three quarters, remainder one kal or quarter.

Three Mahanis ($\frac{3}{16}$) make Mundani, remainder Mahani, or $\frac{1}{16}$.

Three Kanis ($\frac{3}{80}$) make Makani, remainder Half Ma ($\frac{1}{40}$).

Three Half kanis make kani Araikani, remainder Araikani (2 Munthiris) and so on.

Two Munthiris are the கீழ் இரண்டு. Again, when asked to divide two equally among three he proceeds thus :—

Three halves are equal to $1\frac{1}{2}$, remainder $\frac{1}{2}$.

Three eighths form $\frac{3}{8}$ and the remainder is $\frac{1}{8}$ ($2\frac{1}{2}$ Ma).

Three Makanis form two Makanis, remainder a kani.

Three Munthiris form Araikani Munthiri, remainder Munthiri (one keel Munthiri equals 21 Immis.)

Twenty one divided among three gives 7 each.

So we see that the Tamilians are in the habit of doing sums even now mentally without jotting down the items either on palmyra leaf or paper as Kalay

Magani, Kani, Araikani. Keel Arayarikal, Mukani, Munthiri, Immi or seven. We see that they had Tables to divide numbers like 3, 5, 7, 11, 13 and 17 and their products.

1/2,3238245,3022720,0000000	Therthugal	6¼	make	1	Nunmanal.
1/3575114,6618880,0000000	Nunmanal	100	,,	,,	Vellam.
1/35751,1466188,8000000	Vellam	60	,,	,,	Kuralvalaipidi.
1/595,8524436,4800000	Kuralvalaipidi	40	,,	,,	Kathirmunai.
1/14,8963110,9120000	Kathirmunai	20	,,	,,	Sindhai.
1/7448155,5456000	Sindhai	14	,,	,,	Nagavindam.
1/532011,1104000	Nagavindam	17	,,	,,	Vindam.
1/31294,7712000	Vindam	7	,,	,,	Baham.
1/4470,6816000	Baham	6	,,	,,	Bandham.
1/745,1136000	Bandham	5	,,	,,	Gunam.
1/149,0227200	Gunam	9	,,	,,	Anu.
1/16,5580800	Anu	7	,,	,,	Mummi.
1/2,3654400	Mummi	11	,,	,,	Immi.
1/2150400	Immi	21	,,	,,	Keel Munthiri
1/102400	Keelmunthiri	320	,,	,,	Mel Munthiri.
1/320	Melmunthiri	320	,,	,,	One.

We may say with certainty that such minute calculations were used in the dealing of precious stones, measurement of ground and in astronomy. Although such an elaborate system is not in use at present yet we cannot say that they are not altogether in use. Many a villager whom we treat with contempt as belonging to the Karnatic times is an expert in this ancient arithmetical system. We may think that such a minute and elaborate system is unnecessary at the present day when such things as monthly payments, daily wages, cubic contents of timber, square measurement of ground, weights, auspicious and other days with reference to the stars, the combination of grahams etc., are obtained from convenient pocket diaries! But for the diary we shall be completely nonplussed. But a boy who knows the Tamil system of Arithmetic can deal with them mentally. We may put down one of the three equal divisions of three as ⅓, and two of such divisions into ⅔, why, in fact ⅔ is the place where Pa is located in a Veena. But we are rest assured that the exact measurement of ⅔ can only be obtained by the Tamil system and not by any other.

They were acute enough to divide 1 into 2150400 Immis and to say that 716800 Immis were a third of it. When any calculation is asked of them they would go on working it out as Kalai Magani Kani Araikani Keel Ariya Araikal Mukani Munthiri Immi, seven and so on. Just as we use coins as Rupees, Annas and Pies and weights as Param, Maunds, Viss, Seer, Pallam, Virahanidai, and Panavidai the ancients were in the habit of using names for the minutest fractions. We find that the ancient Immi=1/2150400. In the same way they had different names for fractions down to Therthugal. In astronomy they had the following Table,

a Vitharparai	=	60 Tharparai.
a Tharparai	=	60 Vigalai.
a Vigalai	=	60 Kalai.
a Kalai	=	60 Pagai.
a Pagai	=	30 Rasi.
a Rasi	=	12 Mandalam.

This shows the minuteness of their astronomical calculations. It goes without saying that the ancients were experts not only from today or yesterday but from very early times in Isai Tamil, arithmetic and allied sciences.

13. The great experts in different Kalais of Tamil.

We have noted before that, after the first Ooli, i.e., after the advent of the Aryans into South India, they divided the people into four castes and also fixed the ceremonies for each of them. Of these the Sudras or Vellalas have held very high positions under the ancient Pandya and Chola Rajas as prime ministers, Sampratis, (Sampirithi Pillai) Ambassadors, (Thanathi Pillai) Monyagars, (Maniyakara Pillai) Accountants, (Kanakka Pillai) Karbars (Karwari Pillai) and Priests in the temple besides being Acharys, Thambirans, Matathipathis, Pandara Sannidhis, Samaya Gurus, Desikars, Kavirayars, Pulavars, Teachers and Annavis. In other words they have held first positions in Loukeeka as well as Vydeeka functions. The Tamil country was thus eminent for a very long time. But at the time of the last Sangam, the Aryans usurped the places occupied by the Vellalas in the Pandya kingdom which was the cause of its gradual downfall. Avayar who foresaid this said "மறையவனேலோ கோல் சாயும். தந்தமரேல் வெஞ்சமராம், கோமட்டியேலோ வாங்கே குடிசாயும், காராளன் மந்திரியுமானான் வழிக்குத்துணையாவான், அந்த அரசே அரசு" "If the Brahmins are made prime ministers they will influence him to do what they wish. If one's own relation are placed in such a position there will be strife. If a Vysya is made prime minister he will ill-treat the subjects. If the men of the fourth caste or Vellalas be made ministers they will do the work satisfactorily, yea, they will even give their life when rendering help." Here she seems to have given her advice to the Sovereigns as to how they should rule their kingdom. But the rulers never paid attention to her advice. They became degenerate. The Sangams became disorganised, and the kings gradually lost the prestige of their position. When the Pandya kings lost the help of the Vellalas, who defended them as their own lives, they (the kings) became poor and in course of time were despised by their own people. This is but the nature of the times. Like the proverb which says that "குளம் வற்றினாலும் குத்துக் கல்லுக்கு மயக்கமில்லை" "though the tank gets dry the stone with which the tank is built need not fear", though the Pandya kingdom is lost, the Vellalas who held chief positions in it are distinguished even to day in many arts and Sciences.

All the Tamils know M.R.Ry Meenakhisundaram Pillai Avergal who lived about 30 years ago. He had many distinguished scholars as his students, such as M. R. Ry. Theagaraja Chettiar Avl, M. R. Ry Shodasavathanam Subbaraya Chettiar Avl, M. R. Ry. Swaminatha Kavirayar Avl, M. R. Ry. Munsif Vedanayagam Pillai Avl, M. R. Ry. Varahaneri Savarimuthu Pillai Avl. Trichinopoly, M. R. Ry. Kandasami Pillai Avl. M. R. Ry. Ilakyam Perianna Pillai Avl. Trivadi, M. R. Ry.

Kandasami Pillai Avl, M. R. Ry. Subramania Desikar Avl, M. R. Ry. Mahamahopadhyaya V. Saminatna Iyer Avl, and others. He had during his time many another expert in Tamil literature. such as, M. R. Ry. Karunguli Ramalingam Pillai Avl, M. R. Ry. Arumuga Navalar Avl, M. R. Ry. Saravana Perumal Iyer Avl, and M. R. Ry. Visahaperumal Iyer Avl. We often hear about the distinguished scholarship of M. R. Ry. Nellayappa Kavirayar Avl, M. R. Ry. Thirikooda Rajappa Kavirayar Avl, M. R. Ry. Arunachalla Kavirayar Avl, M. R. Ry. Kandasami Kavirayar Avl, M. R. Ry. Arasan Shanmugam Pillai Avl. of Sholavandan, M. R. Ry. Ragavayengar Avl, M. R. Ry. Pandarasannadhi Ambalavana Desikar Avl, and M. R. Ry. Arumuga Thambiran Avl, and others. The names of the great Tamil Scholars of ancient times, such as, Avvai, Kapilar, Thiruvalluvar, Varaguna Pandyan. Athi Veera Rama Pandyan. Kulasekara Pandyan. Pillai Pandyan. Pugalendi. Kambar. Ambigapati. Perunthevanar, Thayumana Swamigal. Katchiappa Sivachariar, Nammalwar, Gnanasambanda Swamigal, Sundaramoorti Swamigal. Appar. Manickavasagar, Kulasekara Alwar, Seraman Perumal Nayanar, Pattinatthu Pillayar. Arunagiri Nathar, Sekilar, Kumaragurupara Swamigal, Swaminatha Desikar. Sivagnana Munivar. Katchiappa Munivar. Sivaprakasa Swamigal, and Veerama Munivar are well known to every one. From the list it is evident that the Vellalas were the majority among those Scholars who made researches into Tamil langaage and caused its growth from the earliest times, in the three Sangams and even at the modern day.

In the commentary on the 75th Sootram of Porul Athigaram of Natchinarkiniyar, the commentator on Tholkaupiam it is said that

"Logic and arithmetic are the subjects for the Vellalas"

and in other places of the same work that Isai Tamil and Nataka Tamil are their heritage.

In the commentary on the 19th stanza of Poral Padalam of Perundevanar, the Commentator on Veerasholyam of Putthamitranar it is said that the six functions of the Vellalas are :—giving gifts, ploughing, rearing of cows, carrying on of trade, learning stringed instruments, and walking in the path of goodness as pointed out by priests. From all these, as well as from the fact that many of the Vellalas of the present day are scholars in Tamil Grammar and Prose literature, in Astrology, Vedantam and Music, we can unhesitatingly say that the Tamilians were proficient in Iyal, Isai and Natakam—the Muttamil—from very ancient times, *i.e.*, from the age of the First Sangam in South Madura or Lemuria up to the present time. We can quite believe that the Tamilians were never in the habit of borrowing from others, nor calling other peoples' properties their own.

It is to be mentioned with deep regret that the Tamilians who had been scholars from the earliest times gradually lost the subtlety and extensiveness of their sciences and became degenerate. Ancient works not only had some hidden mystery in them but also gradually dwindled down so much so that they are not within the understanding of many. This applies also to the science of Music. Or else there will not be so much difference in the calculation of Alagus. Perhaps they did this so as to save it from the contumely of people, first like the egg which Columbus made to stand!

14. How the doubt as regards Srutis rose from the mystery common in Isai Tamil

Noble readers! What shall we say about the excellence of the music of South India as gathered from the Ayapalai and its fourteen kovais used by the ancients in South India, the Vattapalai and its 12 puns. the seven palais derived from each of the puns, the four Yals and their Jathis, the 103 puns and 12,000 Ragas derived from them, the innumerable Yals, the modes of singing. the extensiveness of the Thalams, the minuteness of the Abinayams, and the use of the different kinds of percussion instruments? Who is competent enough to describe the dignity and antiquity of of Iyal, Isai and Natakam, the Muttamil? When those who dwelt to the north of South India say that Music came from the east, do they not refer to the Tamil country? When they repeatedly declare that Karnatic Music is very scientific and is worthy of all praise, do they not refer to the music of South India? When they refer to the Swarams which are used in chanting the Vedas and in rendering the separate Ragas beautifully, are they not the Swarams of Ayapalai and Vattapalai? Are not the Swarams used by foreigners now the same as the Swarams obtained by the SA-PA and SA-MA principle, (Fifths and fourths) such as, Oolai from Tharam, Kural from Oolai, Ili from Kural, Thuttham from Ili, Vilari from Thuttham and Kaikilai from Vilari? Are these not the Swarams used in instruments like the Veena and in the vocal music of South India? Are these the Swarams that are now open to doubt and their very numbers in the octave doubted whether they are 22 or more? What injustice! We regret that this has been the fate of the music that flourished in South Madura after the destruction of that celebrated city of India! It is also a matter for pity that those who attempted to reestablish the music made matters worse! Those who knew it were not kind enough to instruct the ignorant. It is to be deeply deplored that though South Indian Music was borrowed from by everyone, the very shape of it has become unrecognisable.

Gentlemen! We have noticed before that on account of the preeminence of this science of music, the deity himself was pleased with it, that devotees made use of it in the praise of the deity, and that it was extensively used by kings, queens, princes and princesses, nobles and sages. If we enquire if such a custom exists now, we understand that every one who praises the deity makes use of the Thevara Puns which have a tendency to melt the heart. We see in our daily experience that a labourer who returns home alone after nightfall, a beggar with his cocoanut shell, a mendicant with his annakavadi, and a Thathan who begs his handful of rice from door to door are in the habit of singing these devotional puns. We are not strangers to the fact that the westerners sing their hymns in praise of God unanimously in one voice from the king down to a sweeper. It is a matter for regret that our ancestors who wrote about such excellent music left a few of its mysterious points hidden so that it might be known only to the few who might have the patience to learn the mystery of it from a guru. Just as sages themselves declare that there are hidden keys to the sciences of Alchemy, Medicine, Yogam and Gnanam, there is a hidden key to this science also. We shall do well to take note of a few amsams of it here as they would be of great use in removing the doubts about the Srutis of South Indian music. They say

"பனியை நம்பி உழுதுக் கரைதவைப்போலப்
பாடுநர் மறை பொருளாய்ப் பாடுநரே"

"Just as the man who attempted to plough the field trusting that the dew was enough for the sod to be turned was disappointed, the secret would be known only to those men of knowledge who took the greatest pains in understanding it and not to men like the silly farmer who mistook the dew for the rain". This is also supported by the stanza,

"மெய்ப்பாடு பட்டவர்க்கே எய்தும் எய்தும் மற்றவர் இங்கேவர் பாடுபட்டு உழல்வரே."

Thus they left their chief amsams a sealed book so that people might not easily obtain the key to them. This was possible only because of their great advance in the language and the knowledge thereof. Their object was to reveal the mystery of it only to the favoured man who would be capable of preserving it, and who would not abuse the excellent trust. Though the act was commendable in itself, it is to be regretted that even the favoured disciple was not informed of the key, and so practically the knowledge was not known to any. They were determined that the key should be studied only from a guru and hence the stanza

"எல்லார்கள் முன்னிற்கும் எடுத்துரைக்கும் குரு அருளில்லாமற் போனால் சொல்லா ஒம் வாராது"

"It will appear to be easily understandable even to ordinary eyes, but without the favour of the interpreting guru, nothing can possibly be known." It is also said "*சொன்னால் பெரு மோட்சம் சொல்லார் பெரியோர்*". "If explained, it will be a great mystery, but men of understanding will never reveal it". We shall do well to consider here the hidden mystery contained in the verses in Silappadikaram as regards the music of South India.

IV. The hidden mystery contained in ancient literature which treat about the number of Srutis in South Indian Music, and the system after the mystery is removed.

We have seen on different occasions from the Chakaram for Vattapalai, that the Srutis used in Isai Tamil were 22, and we have noted the different Alagus for the Sapta Swarams.

We have also distinctly noted the theory of 22 srutis of the Sanskrit writers on music like Bharata, Mathangar, Keertitharar, Kambalar, Aswatharar, Anjaneyar, Abinavaguptar and Saranga Dev.

We have repeatedly mentioned the fact that the ancient Tamilians had determined the Swarams thousands of years ago by the system of Kural—Ili by the right, and Oolai-Kural by the left and had put them into actual practice. In their Gandharva music 22 Alagus are mentioned.

We have also mentioned the fact that Karikal Cholan who ruled the Chola country during the latter part of the period of Third Sangam with Kaveripoompatnam as his capital, Ilankovadigal the brother of Sengutuvan who wrote about Madavi, (the great expert in Yal), Kovalan, the chastity of Kannagi and about many important things regarding the Pandya Kingdom, his contemporary Nakeerar, Nedunchelian, the Pandya and Kayavagu, the ruler of Lanka—all these were more less people who flourished during the first century A. D. We have noted the fact that even during their time Isai Tamil was very extensive and that the Tamils had attained great proficiency in the science.

Paripadal, which was written prior to the first century during the period of the third Sangam, Tholkaupiam, which was approved in the assembly of Nilantharu-theruvil Pandya, in the presence of Athankote Asan, about the first Ooli or the latter part of the age of the first Sangam, a few Sootrams on Isai Tamil written by Ahastya during the age of the first Sangam the Sootrams of Narada—all these definitely prove that, for 12000 years and more, Isai Tamil was in a highly efficient state in South Madura, in Lemuria, later on in Kapatapuram, and then in North Madura or Koodal Alaway.

The Alagus or Srutis which were in use at that age were only 22. The same number of Srutis are found in Bharatam written in the V century A. D. Sarnga Dev, who based his treatise on that of Bharata also mentions 22 Srutis. We might think, therefore, that it would be unjust to contradict what was first said by the ancient Tamils as well as by later Sanskrit writers.

But we may see clearly that it is impossible to make ganam in the 22 Srutis of octave if they are derived by the SA-MA series as 9 and the SA-PA series as 13, and that it will not suit any gheetam in use at the modern day. We have already noticed the opinions of those who have declared that ganam is impossible with the Dwavimsati Srutis.

On the other hand, it is clear that in the music of the ancient Tamil country, they have divided the octave into 12 compartments corresponding to the 12 Rasis of the Zodiac, have selected 22 Alagus out of them and have derived separate Ragas from them by the process of change of graham. It is said that they have made ganam in the 22 Alagus, but it is not said that there were only 22 Alagus in the octave. They have divided a cycle of Rasis into 12 compartments and not 11.

Thus, we find that a great system has been in use for ages, as mentioned in ancient Tamil works, but with the key to it hidden.

Bharata and Sarnga Dev and others, who had no knowledge of this mystery, declared that there were only 22 Srutis in the octave, wrote works in support of it, changed the grahams to suit their theory and banished a few of the gramams to the celestial world! Others who have read their works, considered the theory of 22 Srutis to be the correct one, and have come forward to teach and establish the theory. Some of the vidwans of Karnatic music are hanging perplexed between the two theories, unable either to learn the Aryan music with the 22 srutis or give up the Karnatic music they have learnt.

It is very necessary that we should enquire how there are no 22 Srutis in the octave, how the ancient Tamils made ganam in the 22 Srutis of the Octave and how minuter Srutis occur in the Karnatic music. We shall do well, therefore, to note in the first instance the hidden secret contained in the works on Isai Tamil, and the system of ganam in the 22 Srutis, and then proceed to the enquiry of the minute Srutis. After examining closely the modern Karnatic music and the system of the 22 Srutis, the utter impossibility of ganam in the 22 Srûtis struck us forcibly as well as the idea that there must be some hidden mystery in it. So, on our going through Silappadikaram we came across some points which were a clue, as it were, to the hidden mystery. They are as follows.—

1. The system of determining harmonious Swarams.

We have till now noted the elaborateness of the music of South India, and the system of making ganam with the help of the Swarams determined by the Sa-Pa and the Sa-Ma series. The system clearly states what Swarams will harmonize and what Swarams will be discordant. The dignity of Indian music consists in the harmony of different Swarams and, at the same time, their separate individual existence up to the present day.

The rules for the individual Ragas of the Karnatic music are the cause of their peculiar charm and suitability to different seasons. In other words, the incomparable charm of these melodies is to be attributed to the rules laid down by our ancestors who were experts in Isai-Tamil. We do not know how far they are mentioned in the rules on Isai Tamil. There are only a few lines in Silappadikaram on the subject. Even here we find that there are some contradictory opinions owing to the difference of interpretation of commentators. However, what we find there is quite enough for our purposes. We could understand a good many things from what little we see there.

The ideas of Ilankovidigal, the author of Silappadikaram, and those of Adyarkunallar, the commentator, who lived a 1000 years after him and the views of Kavi

Chakravarti Jayankondan who wrote the Aroompathavoorai may not be one in some points. Yet, the ideas of the author can be easily made out if due attention is paid to the stanzas. We shall note below the stanzas and their commentaries.

Silappadikaram, Venirkathai p. 202.

> " இணைகிளை பகைநட் பென்றிந் நான்கின்
> இசைபுணர் குறிநிலை யெய்த நோக்கி "

இணை கிளை பகை நட்பென்று சொல்லப்பட்ட நான்கினும் இணை-இரண்டு நரம்பு; என்னை ?

Of the four strings Inai, Kilai, Pagai and Natpu, Inai has two strings. What are they ?

> " இணையெனப் படுவ கீழு மேலு
> மணையத் தோன்று மளவின வென்ப"

கிளை-ஐந்து நரம்பு; என்னை ?

Kilai has five strings. What are they ?

> " கிளையெனப் படுவ கிளக்குங் காலைக்
> குரலே யிளியே துத்தம் விளரி
> கைக்கிளை யெனவைந் தாகு மென்ப "

Silappadikaram, Aroompathavoorai p. 31.

"வரன் முறையாவது முன் கூறின வகையே ஐந்தாக நரம்பாக முறைநிறையின், இளிகுரலாக ஏழு நரம்பும் வாசித்தாளென்க. குரல் குரலாகவும் குரல் தாரமாகவும் வாசித்தாளென்றவாறு."

The Varan Murai is, as stated above, played by fifths in the seven strings which stand in the relation of Ili to Kural. First she played Kural as Kural and then Tharam as Kural.

பகை ஆறும் மூன்றும்;

The Pagai strings are the sixth and the third.

> " நின்ற நரம்பிற் காறு மூன்றுஞ்
> சென்றுபெற நிற்பது கூடமாகும் "

கூடமென்றும் பகையென்றும் ஒக்கும். நட்பு நாலாம் நரம்பு.

' Koodam' and 'Pagai' are identical. The Natpu string is the fourth string. Kilai is the fifth string and Pagai the sixth. This is another version.

☛ This is the interpretation of Mahamahopadhyaya V. Saminatha Iyer.

Silappadikaram, Aroompathavoorai p. 29.

"இளிகிளையிற் கேடல்—நின்ற நரம்பிற்கு ஆறாநரம்பு பகை; அது கூடமென்றும் குற்றம்; இளி முதலாகக் கைக்கிளை யாறுவதாம். இளிக்குக் கைக்கிளை பகையென்றது. நல்ல மயக்கத்தாலே பகைநரம்பிலே கைசென்று தடவ."

The relation between Ili and Kilai (Kaikilai) is Pagai, in other words, the relation between the standard string and its sixth is Pagai. it is called *Koodam*. From Ili to Kaikilai the interval is sixth. Ili and Kaikilai do not form a concord. When they are perplexed they misplace their fingers on the discordant string.

Silappadikaram, Venirkathai p. 201.

"கூட மென்பது குரிபுற விளம்பின்
வாய்வதின் வராது மழுங்கிபிசைப் பதுவே"
"மன்னிய விசைவ ராது மழுங்குதல் கூட மாகும்"

From the above extracts we understand that in ancient Karnatic music where Ragas which suited different seasons, times, and ideas were sweetly sung, the difference between four different relations of Swarams, as Inai Swaram, Kilai Swaram, Pagai Swarams and Natpu Swaram, was clearly noted.

2. What Inai or Concordant Swaram is.

Inai means two strings or two concordant strings. This term is applied to Swarams obtained by the Sa-Pa relation. Those that are concordant like Sa and Pa are Inai Swarams.

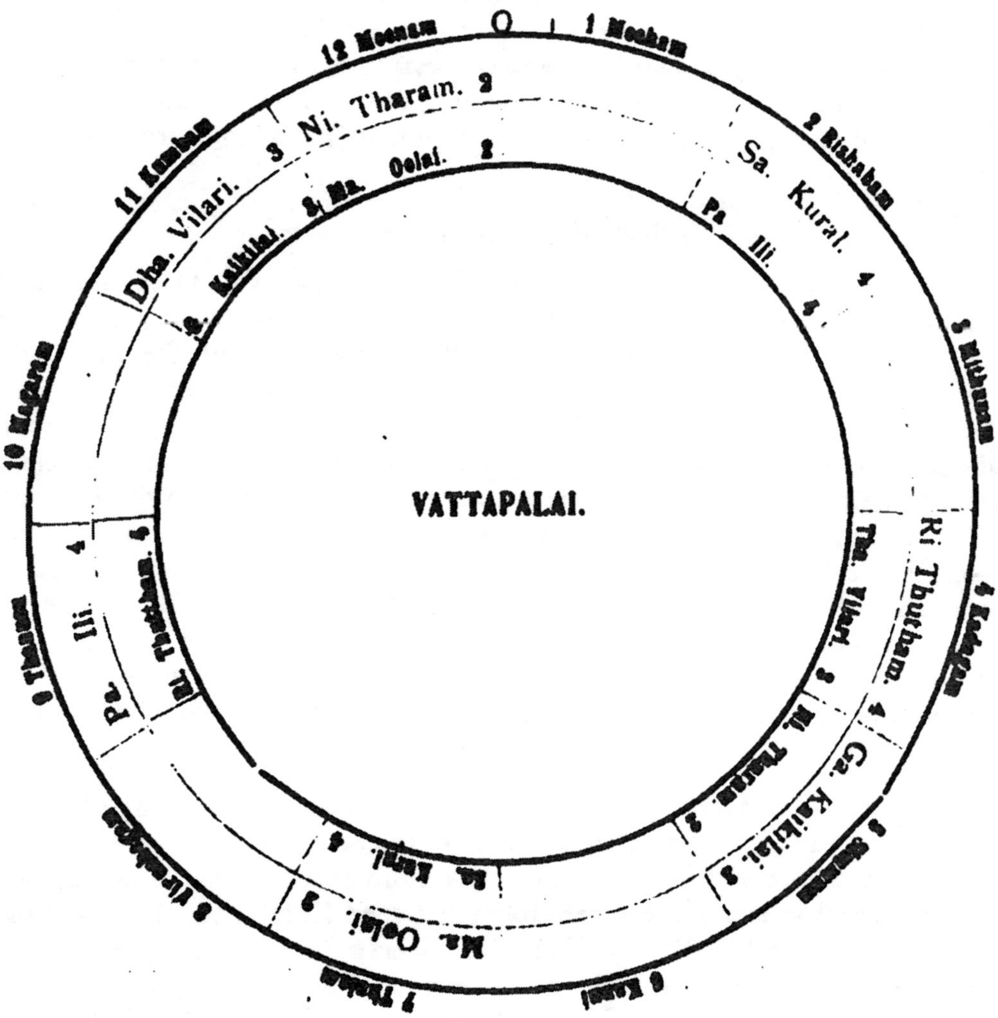

The Oolai that occurs in the seventh Rasi from Tharam (Ni-Ma),
The Kural that occurs in the seventh Rasi from Oolai (Ma-Sa),
The Ili that occurs in the seventh Rasi from Kural (Sa-Pa),
The Thuttham that occurs in the seventh Rasi from Ili (Pa-Ri),
The Vilari that occurs in the seventh Rasi from Thuttham (Ri-Dha),

and such like swarams that occur in the seventh Rasis are Inai Swarams. For example, Kural (Itapam) and Ili (Thanusu, seventh Rasi from Itapam) are Inai Swarams. This is in the ascending order.

Again Ili (Thanusu) and Kural (Itapam, or seventh Rasi backwards from Thanusu) are Inai Swarams in the descending order. This illustrates the meaning of the words "இணையெனப் படுவ கீழும் மேலும், கிளையத் தோன்றும் அவையே".

The Swarams that occur in the seventh Rasis either upwards or downwards are Inai swarams. These are the ascending Sa-Pa series and the descending Sa-Ma series. These are the Swarams indicated by the words, "இணை நரம்புடையன" "இணை நரம்பு தொடர்ந்து" "குரல் நரம்பு இரட்டிக்க வரும் அரும்பாலையும், இளி நரம்பு இரட்டிக்க வரும் செம்பாலையும் இசைநூல் வழக்காலே இணை நரம்பு தொடர்ந்துப் பாடும் அறிவினையுடையனாகி" (the music master must be one who could understand the Arumpalai, the doubling of the Kural string, Sempalai, the doubling of the Ili string and the concordant relation of Inai strings according to rules of Isai Tamil).

3. What Kilai Swarams are.

We have noted that the seven swarams of the octave should be arrived at by the Sa-Pa series. In the same way he says that the Swarams from Sa to Pa must occur in a particular order. He gives rules for the concordance of Swarams between the Inai strings Sa and Pa. Just as he said that the relation between the first and the second Sthayis should be as one is to two, he also says how the Swarams within the octave should be obtained by the Sa-Pa principle and how a concordant relation should exist between them. The calculations he says are those pertaining to the Inai strings Sa and Pa. When an article is measured it is first calculated by a foot rule and that which remains is calculated in inches. So also this is done. He mentions the seven Rasis obtained by sevenths in the 12 compartments of the Zodiac by the Sa-Pa principle and also mentions such of them that are concordant with the Kural and Ili. The meaning of this is clear, that the Swarams of particular Rasis in the six Rasis between Sa and Pa will be concordant while ascending and descending. We shall note these concordant Rasis as well as the Swarams in them later on.

The word Kilai means, relation, branch, off-shoot or surrounding object. That swaram is considered Kilai which stands almost in the same relation as that between Kural, the standard note and Ili, but slightly less concordant. That Swaram, he says, is Kilai which occurs in any of the seven Rasis between Kural and Ili and which is concordant with the standard Kural. The Kilai Swarams will always occur within the seven Rasis belonging to the Inai strings. It seems that a Kilai Swarams occurs in the fifth Rasis from any given Swaram. This is the relation of Oolai to Kural or Sa to Ma.

This can be exemplified from the previous Chakaram.

The Thulam which is the fifth Rasi from Itapam is its Kilai or SA-MA.

So the fifth from Thulam is its Kilai or SA-MA.

Itapam which is the fifth Rasi from Thanusu is its Kilai, i.e., PA to SA or SA-MA. In the same manner the Swarams in the fifth Rasis stand in the relation of Kilai to the Swarams of the given Rasi.

We may view these in another way also. If we commence from Thulam and proceed by seven compartments on the right side we get a series of Swarams with the relation of SA PA, and if we proceed by five compartments to the left we get the same series with the relation of SA-MA.

For example, we find from the above Chakaram that Itapam is fifth (proceeding left wards) from Thulam, Thanusu is fifth from Itapam, Katakam is fifth from Thanusu, and Kumbam is fifth from Katakam.

This means;

Kural in Itapam and Oolai in Thulam (MA-SA).

Ili in Thanusu and Kural in Itapam (SA-PA).

Thuttham in Katakam and Ili in Thanusu (PA-RI).

Vilari in Kumbam and Thuttham in Katakam (RI-DHA) are Kilai Swarams.

In the same manner, proceeding on the right.

Kural in Thulam is Kilai to Ili in Itapam (PA-SA).

Ili in Thanusu is Kilai to Thuttham in Katakam (RI-PA)

Kural in Itapam is Kilai to Ili in Thanusu (PA-SA).

Oolai in Thulam is Kilai to Kural in Itapam (SA-MA).

Tharam in Meenam is Kilai to Oolai in Thulam (MA-NI.)

Kaikilai in Simham is Kilai to Tharam in Meenam (NI-GA.)

These concordant Swarams MA-SA, SA-PA, PA-RI and RI to Dha are Kilai Swarams proceeding leftwards in SA-PA relation, and the Swarams PA-SA, RI-PA, PA-SA, SA-MA, MA-NI and NI to GA are Kilai Swarams proceeding rightwards in SA-MA relation.

He says Kilai is five strings. It is to be observed that instead of calculating by fifths from the given string he mentions only five Swarams obtained by fifths. For a fifth from the fifth string and another fifth over it is possible. We accept without hesitation the other version which says that Kilai is the fifth string. We accept the five strings obtained by fifths and there is a possibility for more. It is said in the Text that she played on the seven strings by the SA-MA principle proceeding by fifths taking Ili as Kural. So there must be seven Swarams by the SA-MA principle.

So it is clear that the Swarams occurring in the fifth Rasis with Kural as Oolai are the Kilai Swarams which stand only next in concordance to the Inai Swarams obtained by the SA-PA principle with Kural as Ili. We decidedly conclude, then, that the Swarams obtained by fifths with Kural as Oolai or the SA-MA principle are the Kilai Swarams. Again, when we say fifth string we are apt to think that PA of the series SA RI GA MA PA is the fifth. This is wrong because he also says "இணைகிளை பகைநட்பென்றிந் நான்கின்" (Of the four strings Inai Kilai Pagai and Natpu). He speaks of four separate strings and it is wrong to suppose Inai and Kilai to be the same. We have noted clearly how Inai is in the seventh Rasi and Kilai in the fifth. So it is certain that Inai is seventh string and Kilai fifth string.

4. What Pagai Swaram is.

We know that *Pagai* means *Enmity, Enemy* and *hatred.* This he calls 'Koodam'. 'Koodam' means 'harm'. By the words "[illegible]" he means that the third and the sixth from the given Swaram will sound discordant or destroy harmony. The third and the sixth from the standard string will be abominable. So it is clear that out of the seven Rasis of the SA-PA series the third and the sixth should be studiously avoided. It is incorrect to say that by the sixth and the third he means the Vilari and the Kaikilai respectively in other words DHA and GA. We will note later on how this interpretation will not hold.

5. What Natpu Swaram is.

Natpu means 'friendship'. The Swarams obtained by fourths from a given Swaram are Natpu Swarams. These mostly adjoin the chief Kilai strings. Viruchikam between Thulam and Thanusu is the sixth from Itapam. This is a Pagai string. He calls the Kanni Rasi a Natpu Swaram. Simham or the third Rasis is Pagai. From all these it is distinct that the Swarams of the third and the sixth Rasis are Pagai Swarams, the fourth Swaram is Natpu, the fifth, a Kilai Swaram and the seventh, an Inai Swaram. PA in the concord SA-PA obtains the top RI as its Inai Swaram. Just as Kural and Ili are SA and PA, so also are Ili and Thuttham. PA which is a concord with SA, obtains RI as its Inai Swaram. As this stands in the second Rasi above Kural, if we take it to be an Inai Swaram, the Swaram in the Second Rasi above SA is also an Inai Swaram. In the same manner. Thanusu in relation to Thulam, Kumbam in relation to Thanusu, and Itapam in relation to Meenam stand in the relation of Inai Swarams. So we conclude that the Swarams in the second Rasi, the fourth Rasi, the fifth Rasi and the seventh Rasi to any given Rasis are concordant swarams.

6. What Pagai String is.

The third and the sixth to a given string are Pagai strings. The sixth from the given Rasi is Pagai e. g. Viruchikam is Pagai to Kural which occurs in Itapam. Simham is Pagai to Kumbam.

Kaikilai is Pagai to Ili because it is the sixth string from it. This seems to be above SA-PA measurement. When we say sixth string we mean that DHA is sixth in the series SA, RI, GA, MA, PA, DHA and NI.

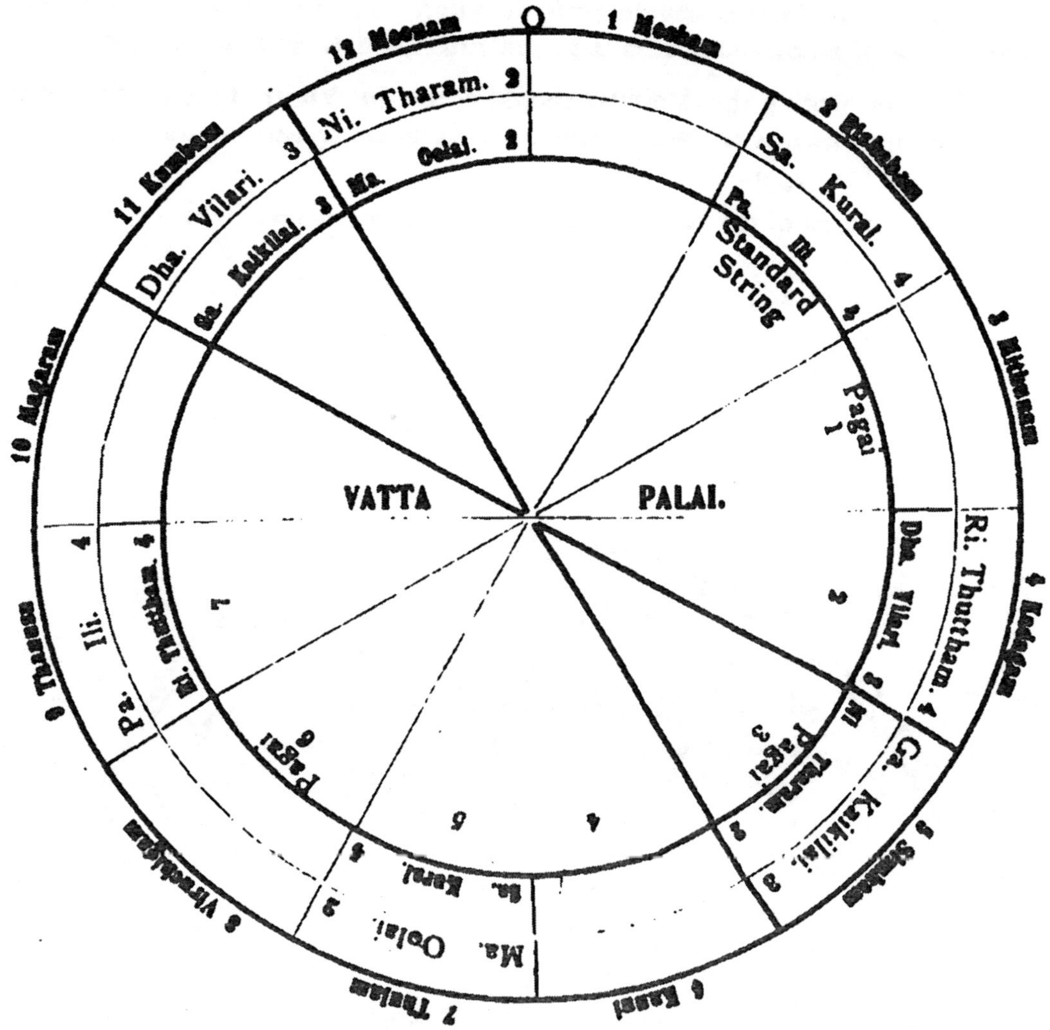

GA is the Sixth in PA, DHA, NI, SA, RI, GA and MA. We have noted before that the relation of Pagai, Kilai and Natpu does not apply to Swarams above SA-PA, but the relations appear when we preceed by the SA-PA series.

When we say that the Pagai string is the sixth, it refers to the sixth Rasi and not the sixth Swaram. Kaikilai is Pagai because it is the sixth from Ili.

7. How the mystery is cleared.

We have to note something here. This is the place which appears to be involved in mystery in the Vattapalai Chakaram. He called Kaikilai to be Pagai which was in Simham which is the sixth from the given Swaram. But if we enquire how Kaikilai occurred in Simham we shall find that it has not occurred in the usual order.

He has first said that Kaikilai should occur in Vilari, but says later on that Kaikilai and Tharam should be placed in Simham, and Vilari and Kaikilai in Kumbam.

After first stating that Kaikilai should occur in Vilari, to say that Kaikilai occurs in Simham which is the sixth place from Kumbam creates a doubt. The sixth place is the place for Pagai.

Yet the words of the commentator " the fourteen Kovais which are beyond all doubt" and the words of Ilankovadigal, the author, " the fourteen Kovais of the fault-less marabu " imply clearly that the system is fault-less. We must note these words carefully.

Chakaram where the mystery is cleared.

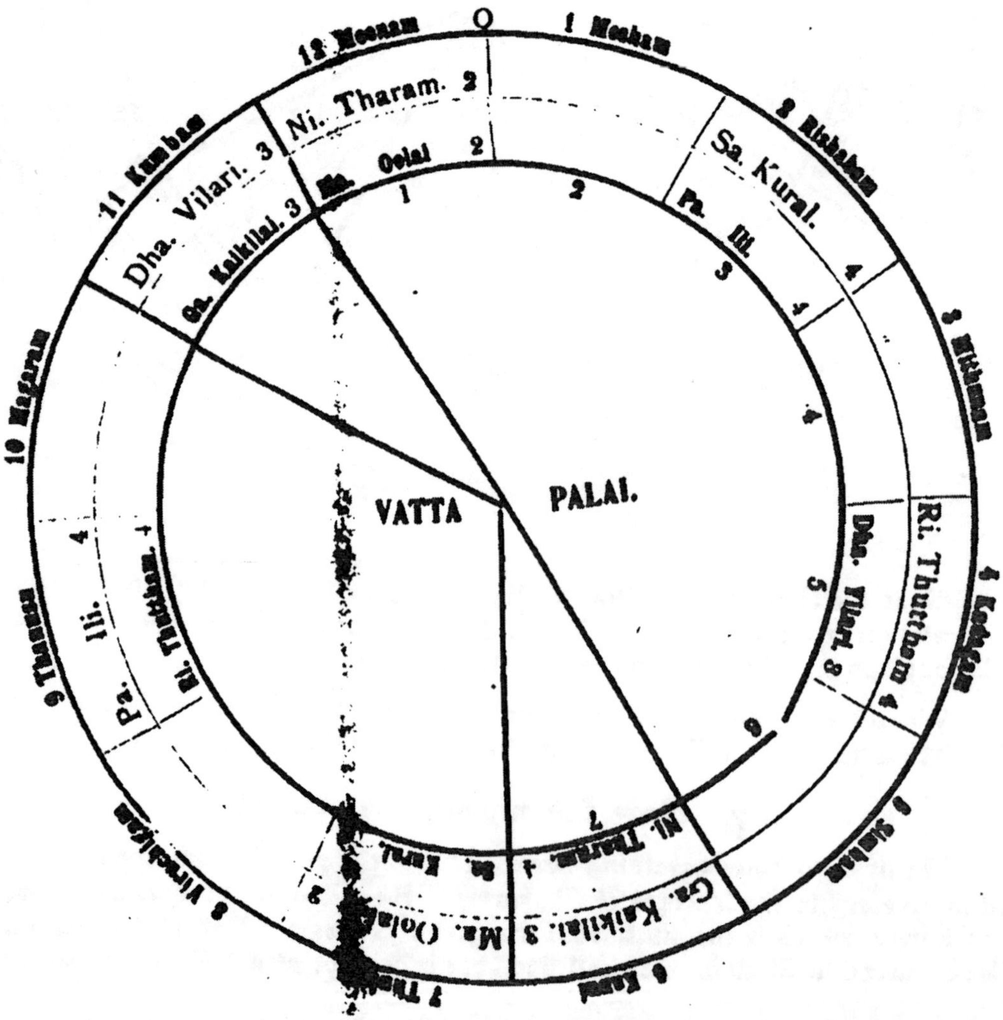

Besides this, Kavichakravarti Jayankondan, who wrote the Aroompathaveorai, says " Kaikilai is the sixth if Ili is the first. Ili and Kaikilai are Pagai strings. In their perplexity they pass their fingers over the Pagai String". In their ignorance they placed Kaikilai, which is in SA-PA relationship with Vilari, in the Simha Rasi and computed it as the sixth Swaram and so it turned out to be a Pagai Swaram. The Swaram that occurs in the seventh Rasi from any given Rasi will be in the relation of SA-PA. The following may be verified from the Vattapalai Chakaram given above :—

Oolai appears in Tharam. This is Thulam or the seventh Rasi from Meenam.
Kural appears in Oolai. This is Rishabam or the seventh Rasi from Thulam.
Ili appears in Kural. This is Thanusu or the seventh Rasi from Rishabam.
Thuttham appears in Ili. This is Kadagam or the seventh Rasi from Thanusu.
Vilari appears in Thuttham. This is Kumbam or the seventh Rasi from Kadagam.
Kaikilai appears in Vilari. This is Simha or the *sixth* Rasi from Kumbam.

It will no doubt perplex any one because he places the last one in the Simham or the sixth Rasi instead of in Kanni which is the seventh. You must first clear this doubt, and then everything will run smooth. If you clear the apparent errors you will understand the mystery hidden in Vattapalai.

We see from the above Chakaram where the mystery is cleared that all the Swarams are obtained by the Kural—Ili series. Of these Oolai appears in Tharam, or in other words Oolai appears in Thulam which is the seventh place from Meenam (which is the 12th). This occurs in the seventh compartment above Meenam.

Thus we see that the Swarams occur in the series of seventh houses from the given house. The Rasi Chakaram will clear all difficulties, and give all details.

In the same Chakaram the Alagus after the Vattapalai system are also made mention of. We may see there that the Swaram in the seventh Rasi from any given Rasi is a concordant Swaram. It is marked in the inner first compartment of the Cycle. We may see that they are after the SA-PA and the SA-MA series.

Kural commences in the Thulam. The Swarams that are found in the inner second compartment in each Rasi form a series of ascending scale SA RI GA MA PA DHA NI to the Kural in Thulam.

When Kural commences in Rishabam Rasi which is Panchamam to the Kural in Thulam it becomes the second line. From the Kural, commencing from the second line of Rishabam, the Rasis Kadagam, Kanni, Thulam etc., become the ascending series SA RI GA MA PA DHA NI.

So it is clear that the Swarams in the second and the third line in each of the Rasis are obtained by the SA-PA series.

In the same way the Swarams in the third and the second lines stand in the relation of MA-SA.

MA-SA in Thulam will become SA-PA in Rishabam by the Panchamam principle. We can see distinctly that it occurs as SA-MA in the fifth place in Thulam. In the same manner PA RI in Thanusu becomes SA-PA and RI-PA becomes SA-MA.

To conclude, then, the fifth Swaram from any given Rasi is SA-PA.

The expression " Kural which appears in Thulam " implies that it is taken as the standard Swaram. This is the seventh Rasi from Meenam proceeding rightwards. Proceeding five Rasis leftwards from Meenam we get Thulam. MA or Oolai is in this Meenam. This is the fifth place from Kural in Thulam, and the place for MA. We also know that Kural occurs in Thulam, the Seventh place from Meenam.

In the same manner we find that Rishabam is the seventh place rightwards from Thulam and that Ili or PA occurs there.

Kural occurs in Thulam, the fifth place rightwards from Rishabam. The series SA-MA, MA-SA and SA-PA, PA-SA are in the relation of 5 to 7 and 7 to 5.

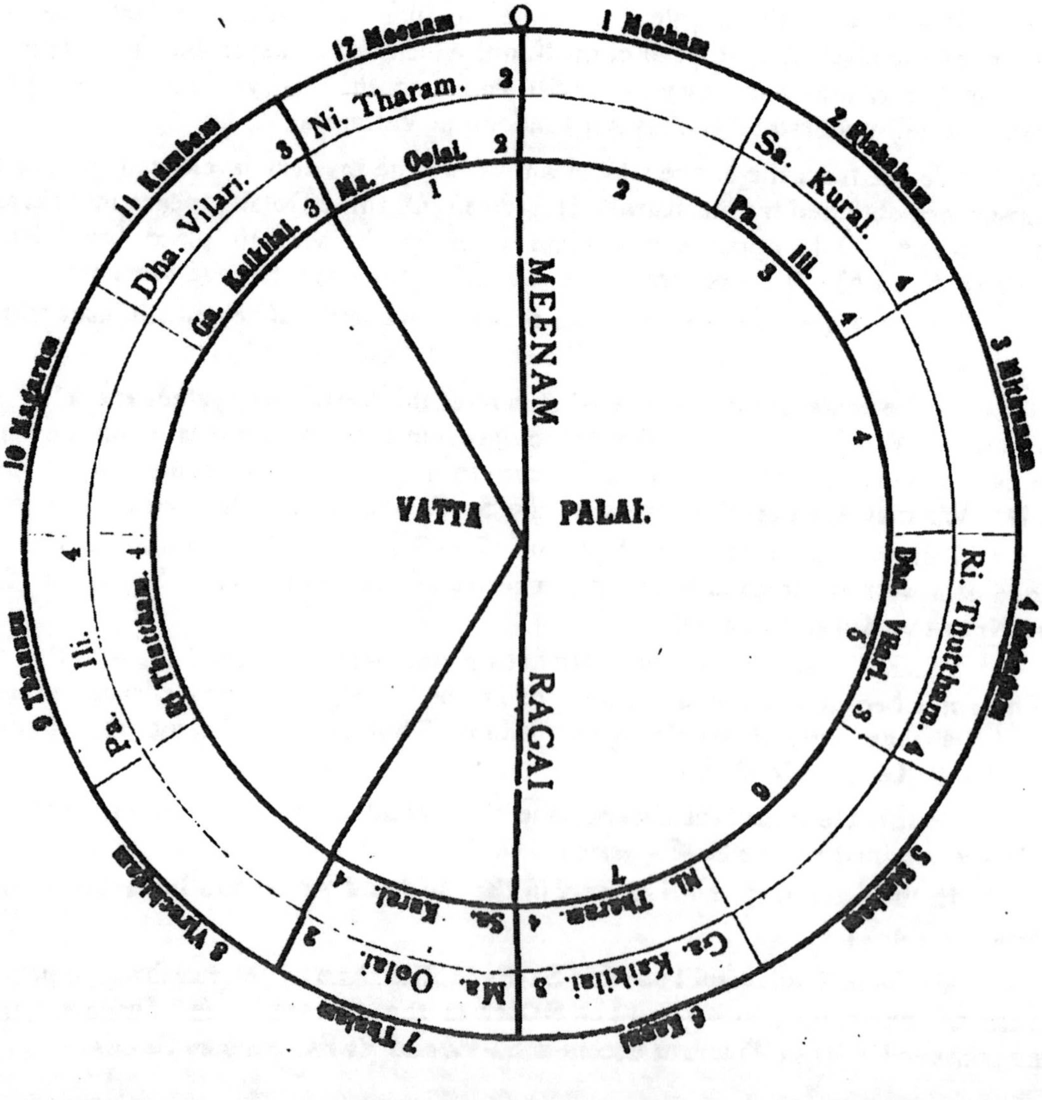

We must note there are four Rasis between SA and MA and six between SA and PA. The fifths from a given Rasi stand in the relation of SA-MA. There will be four Rasis between SA and MA.

In the same manner the seventh from a given Rasi will be concordant as SA-PA. There will be six Rasis between them. All the other Swarams should be derived in the same manner.

Again, the line that passes between Meenam and Mesham passes though Kanni and Thulam and divides the Chakaram into two equal parts. We find that it has six Rasis on either side. To the right side of this line or to the right of Meenam there are six Rasis.

Now, Kural commences in Thulam at the bottom to the left of the Meena Ragai. We see Oolai in Meenam at the top. The Tharam occurs at the sixth Rasi from Oolai which is the concordant Rasi in Meena Ragai from Kural. There are four Rasis in the middle.

In the same way there are eight compartments to the right side of Oolai in Meenam up to Thulam. Besides the two Rasis for Kural and Oolai there are six Rasis in the middle.

In the same manner, Ili which appears in Kural, and Kural which appears in Oolai are in the first half to the right of Mesha Ragai. This is the fifth Rasi to the right of the Rasi for Kural and seventh to the left of it.

Likewise, we find that Thanu Ragai to the right of Thanusu occurs between Mithunam and Kadagam.

Vilari in Kadagam becomes the seventh Rasi to the Thuttham which commences in Thanusu which is at the bottom of this Ragai. Thanusu becomes the fith Rasi on the right side from Kadagam. The former has the SA-PA relation and the latter SA-MA.

Again, when PA occurring in Rishabam becomes SA to the Kural in Thulam, the Kural that occurs in Thulam becomes Oolai, or SA-MA. Thuttham in Thanusu becomes Ili or PA. When PA in Thanusu becomes Kural, the Thuttham in Kadagam becomes PA. When Kural commences in Kadagam it becomes PA. When Kural commences in Kadagam Vilari in Kumbam which is seventh to it becomes PA. This system can be easily understood from the Chakaram.

We find, then, that the ganam of the ancient Tamilians was by the SA-PA and the SA-MA principles without even the remotest error. Though we had dealt with them in the Vattapalai Chakaram and the details thereon we had to refer to it again here in order to emphasise the importance of SA-PA or Kural to Ili.

8. The Swarams obtained when once the mystery is cleared.

In this system, if Kaikilai appears in Kanni it has the relation of Natpu. This is the relation of SA-GA. The GA in Simham will never agree with SA, but with PA in Thanusu. It will have the relation of GA-PA.

In the same way, Ni in Kanni or Ga will be concordant with the Pa in Rishabam. But the Ga or Ni in Simham will not be so. Making mention of such a discordant interval in the middle is the cause of the perplexity. He asks us to clear this doubt.

Now Kaikilai in Vilari is Kanni. This is seventh Rasi as before. The following Chakaram will help in clearing this.

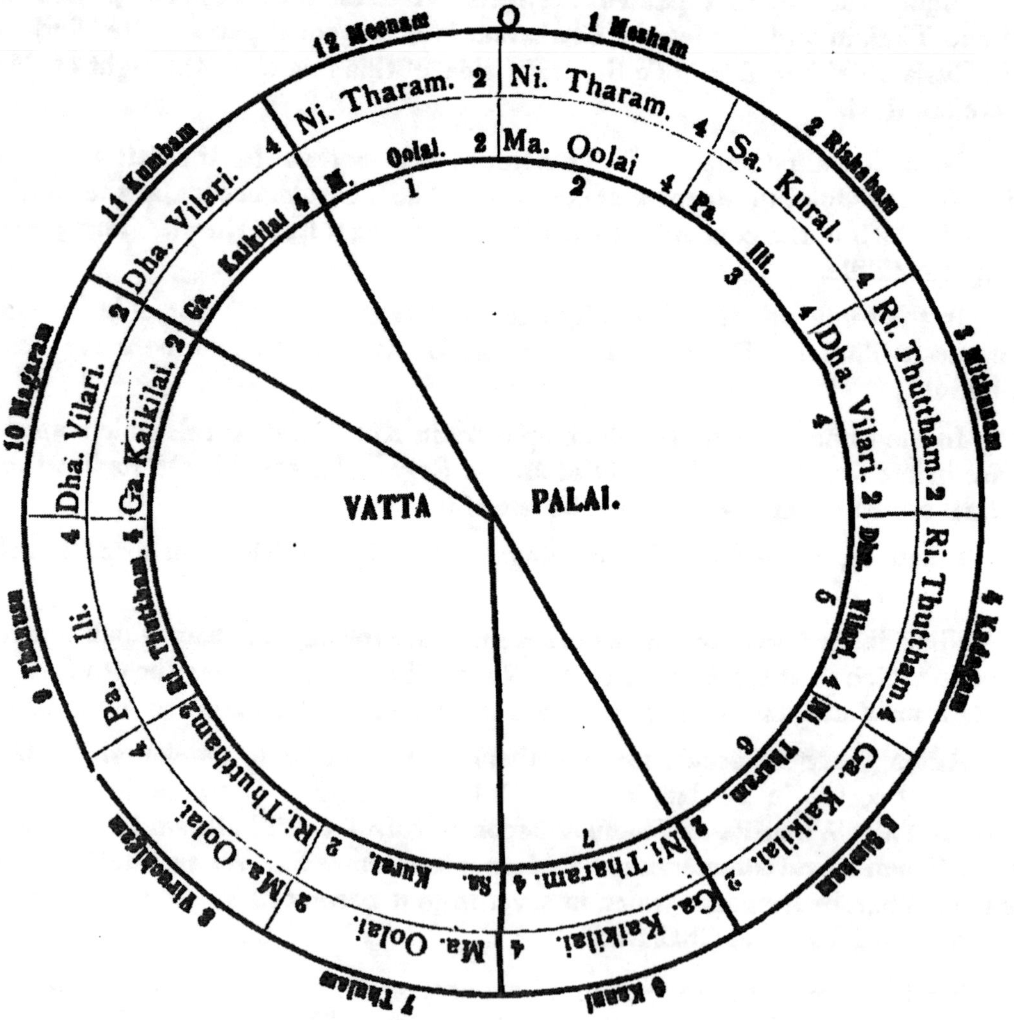

Kaikilai in Vilari, Dha_1—Ga_1. This is the seventh from Kumbam to Kanni.
Tharam in Kaikilai. Ga_1—Ni_1. This is the seventh from Kanni to Mesham.
Oolai from Tharam, Ni_1—Ma_1. This is the seventh from Mesham to Viruchigam.
Thuttham from Oolai, Ma_1—Ri_1. This is the seventh from Viruchigam to Mithunam.
Vilari from Thuttham, Ri_1—Dha_2. This is the seventh from Mithunam to Magaram.
Kaikilai from Vilari Dha_2—Ga_2. This is the seventh from Magaram to Simham.

By the above method, the five Rasis that had no Swarams in them have Swarams now. According to the rule "Tharam occurs in Kaikilai" Swarams were obtained by sevenths from Kanni to Mesham. Now if we proceed from Simham where Kaikilai was obtained from Vilari we will have

Tharam in Kaikilai GA_2—NI_2. This is the seventh from Simham to Meenam.
Oolai in Tharam. NI_2—MA_2. This is the seventh from Meenam to Thulam.
Kural in Oolai MA_3—SA_4. This is the seventh from Thulam to Rishabam.
Ili in Kural SA_4—PA_4. This is the seventh from Rishabam to Thanusu.
Thuttham, in Ili PA_4—RI_1. This is the seventh from Thanusu to Kadagam.
Vilari in Thuttham. RI_1—DHA_4. This is the seventh from Kadagam to Kumbam.
Kaikilai in Vilari DHA_4—GA_4. This is the seventh from Kumbam to Kanni.
Tharam in Kaikilai GA_4—NI_4. This is the seventh from Kanni to Mesham.

Now we find that there are 12 Swarams in the 12 Rasis, and that these Swarams have been used by the Tamilians.

We also find that the five Rasis Mesham, Mithunam, Kanni, Viruchigam and Magaram mentioned in Vattapalai without any Swarams attached to them have Swarams given to them as seen from the system of the change of Alagus for the four kinds of Yal.

Moreover, when one of the two Alagus of Tharam, and two of the four Alagus of Kural are held as Kaikilai at the Antharakole of the Thara string Tharam becomes Kaikilai. When the Alagu left out in the string is added on to the old Vilari, that becomes the Thuttham string. So in accordance with the stanza "[illegible]" noticed above it is clear that ganam was made in the 12 Swarams in the 12 Rasis.

In as much it is said that six and three are in the relation of Pagai to the standard Swaram the Kural, it is clear that the Swaram in the sixth Rasi and that in the third Rasi are in such relation.

On the other hand, if the sixth Rasi is dealt with according to the principle that Kaikilai appears in Vilari, Meenam from Simham and Thulam from Meenam will result as usual in repetition. According to the proverb "Just as the green ([illegible]) bends even when cut down, so each one wil! have the result of one's intelligence", be appended a mystery to the Simha Rasi. When this is once understood all doubts will vanish.

9. The 12 Swarams obtained by the Sa-Ma principle when the mystery is cleared.

Just as the 12 Swarams result by the Sa-Pa principle proceeding by sevens in the same way the 12 Swarams are derived from the Sa-Ma principle proceeding by fifths.

The following method will clearly show it.

1. $Sa_4 - Ma_2$ ... Here Thulam is the fifth from Rishabam.
2. $Ma_2 - Ni_2$ ... " Meenam " Thulam.
3. $Ni^2 - Ga_2$ ... " Simham " Meenam.
4. $Ga_2 - Dha_2$ ... " Magaram " Simham.
5. $Dha_2 - Ri_2$ ... " Mithunam " Magaram.
6. $Ri_2 - Ma_4$ ... " Viruchigam " Mithunam.
7. $Ma_4 - Ni_4$ ... " Mesham " Viruchigam.
8. $Ni_4 - Ga_4$ ... " Kanni " Mesham.
9. $Ga_4 - Dha_4$ ... " Kumbam " Kanni.
10. $Dha_4 - Ri_4$ ... " Kadagam " Kumbam.
11. Ri_4 to Pa_4 ... " Thanusu " Kadagam.
12. $Pa_4 - Sa_4$ ... " Rishabam " Thanusu.

If we do not proceed this way, the progression from Simham will land us in difficulties. The Kaikilai in this Simham is in the relation of a Pagai Swaram to Sa. In the same way Tharam is in the same relation to Ili in Rishabam. The Kaikilai in Kanni is only Tharam (Ga-Ni). The Kural in Rishabam is in the relation of Natpu to Ili (Sa-Pa). As it is said that the fourth string is Natpu and as Sa-Ga is very harmonious it is clear that the fourth Rasi from the given Rasi is in the relation of Natpu. The third from the given Rasi is Pagai. Though it is said that Kaikilai results from Vilari the sixth Rasi with the relation of Pagai, it appears that a warning is given that we should not get perplexed.

10.—How the Swarams agree when they are considered after the relation of Sa-Ga.

Kaikilai in the fourth Rasi above is Natpu to Kural in Rishabam.
Pa in the fourth Rasi above is Natpu to Kaikilai in Simham.
Vilari in Kumbam in the fourth Rasi above is Natpu to Oolai in Thulam.
Tharam in Mesham in the fourth Rasi above is Natpu to Ili in Thanusu.
Thus these Swarams stand in the relation of Sa-Ga.

Here Pa Ga Sa are exactly in the same relation of Sa Ga Pa. The Sa Ga Pa in Rishabam, Kanni and Thanusu are the ascending series, while Pa Ga Sa in Thanusu, Simham and Rishabam form the descending series. So we find that the third Rasi from the given Swaram is Pagai and that the fourth Rasi is Natpu. It does not follow from this that a Swaram has a particular relation in the ascending series and a different one in the descending series.

11.—How the Swarams agree while they stand in the relation of Sa-Ri.

It is clearly seen that the Swarams have been harmoniously arranged in sevens, fives, fours and twos or with the intervals that occur in Sa-Pa, Sa-Ma, Sa-Ga, and Sa-Ri. If we accede that the above Swarams are in concordant relationship, it goes without saying that Sa-Dha (sixth) and Sa to Ni (seventh) are also harmonious.

For Sa-Ri has the same relation as Pa-Dha. Ma-Pa is just the same. Oolai appearing in Meenam has the same relation to Sa in Oolai as Sa-Ma. Vilari in Kumbam has the same relation to Thuttham in Kadagam. Dha in Kumbam becomes the Swaram in the second house to Pa which is concordant with Kural in Rishabam. If the intervals for Sa and Pa be rightly arranged first, we may find that the Swarams above them are in the same concordant relation.

The Chakaram showing the order of Swarams commencing from Kural.

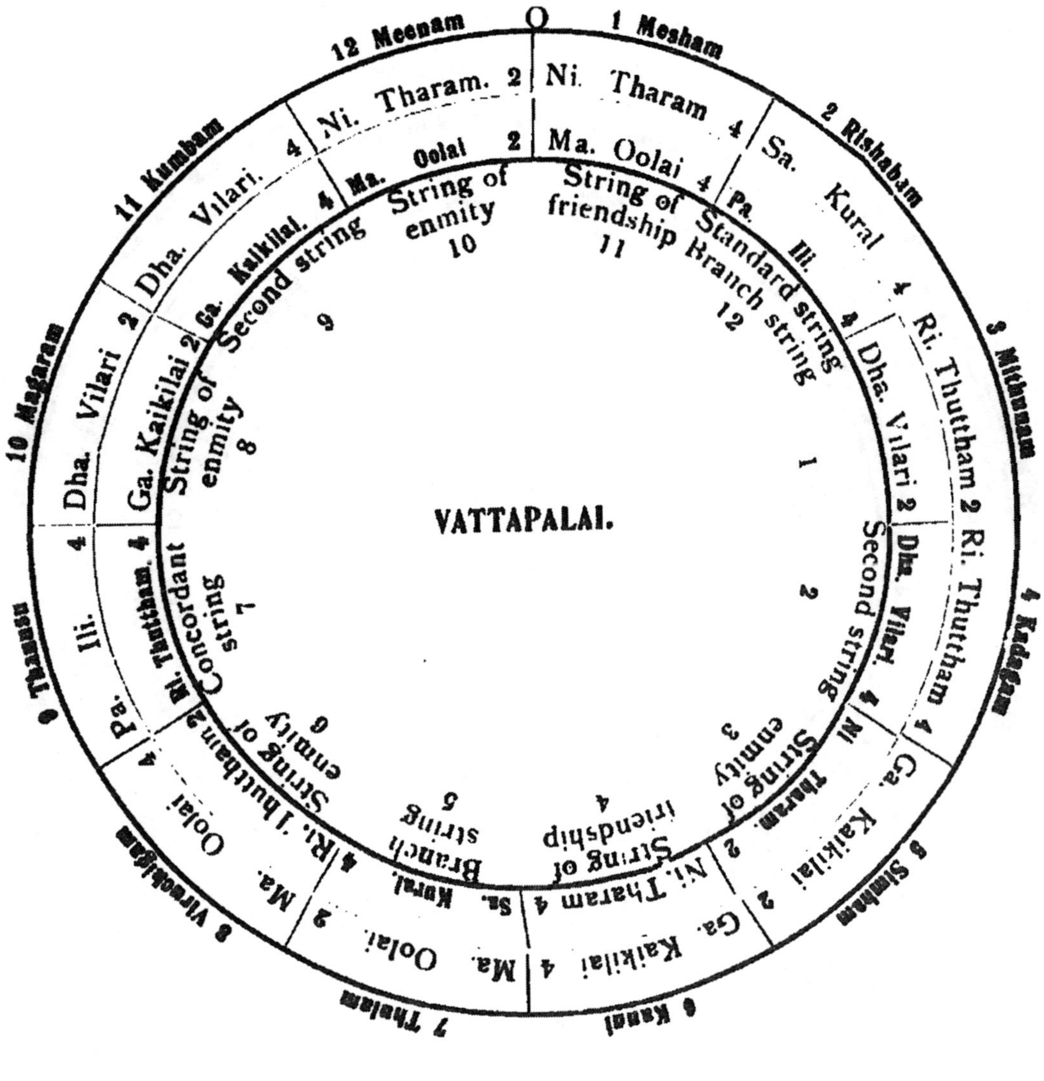

In the above Chakaram we find that there are two strings, Kural and Ili, in Rishabam. According to the principle that when Kural is taken as Kural it is Sempalai, we may find out from the Chakaram, which of the Swarams of the 12 Rasis form the seven Swarams along with the Kural commencing from Kural itself.

The string that stands in the Meru is the Kural string. **The seven Swarams** above this formed of the Swarams in the Rasis two, four, five, seven, nine, eleven, and twelve are the seven Swarams which are concordant with the standard string Kural. The strings in one, three, six, eight and ten are in the relation of Pagai (enmity) to the standard Kural.

The Chakaram showing the order of Swarams of the Sthayi commencing from Ili.

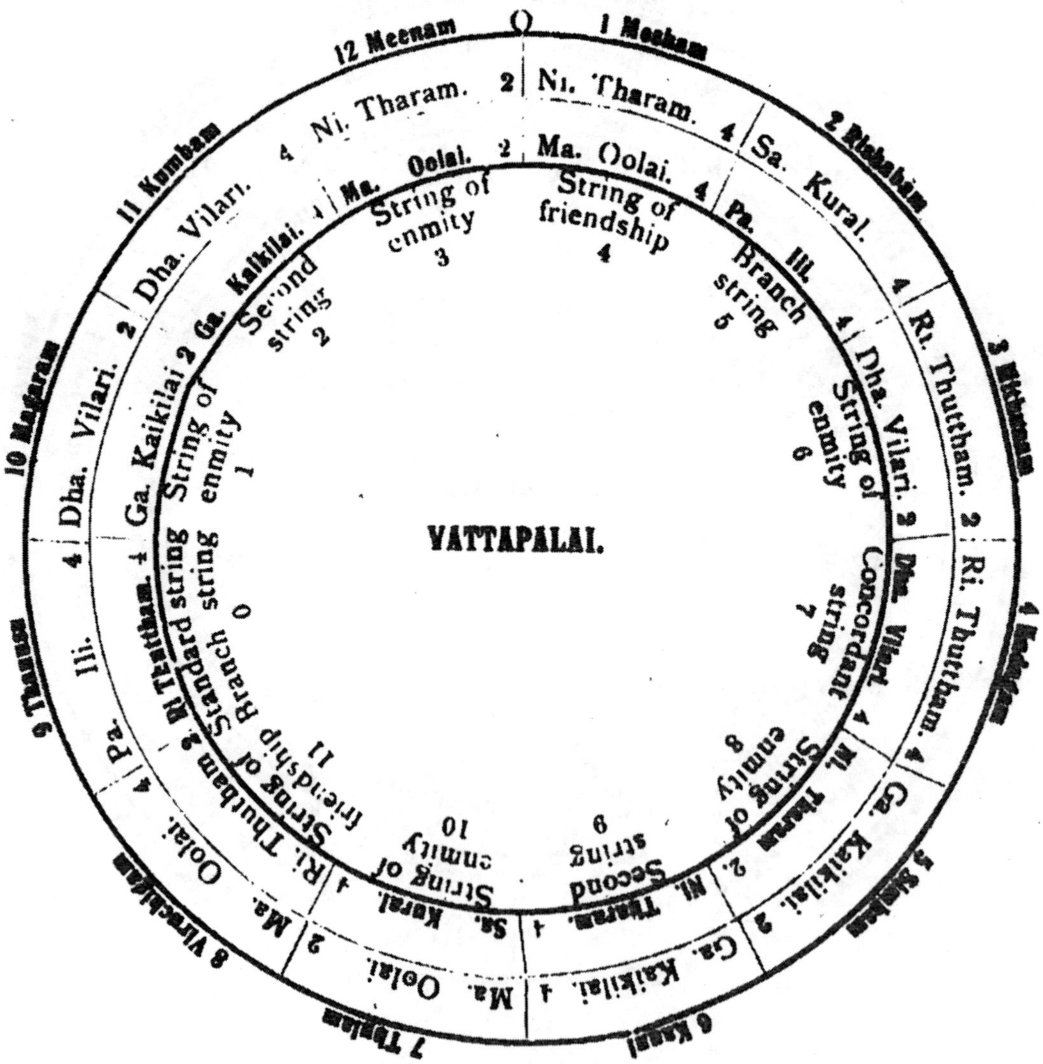

We may see the order of Swarams of a Sthayi when Kural commences from Ili from this Chakaram. When Ili is taken as the standard we find that only seven Swarams are concordant with it. This is known as Areempalai.

The stanza " She first played Kural as Kural and then made Ili as Kural" shows that the seven Swarams commencing from PA formed the Madhya Sthayi or Swarams of the SA-MA series and that Ganam on that principle was made by the ancient Tamils.

It is also seen that the ancient Tamils made Alati in the fourteen Kovais having the four Swarams SA RI GA MA below Ili as PA DHA NI SA, and the Swarams DHA NI SA above Ili SA RI GA (hard) of the Thara Sthayi.

The Chakaram Showing the order of Swarams commencing from Oolai.

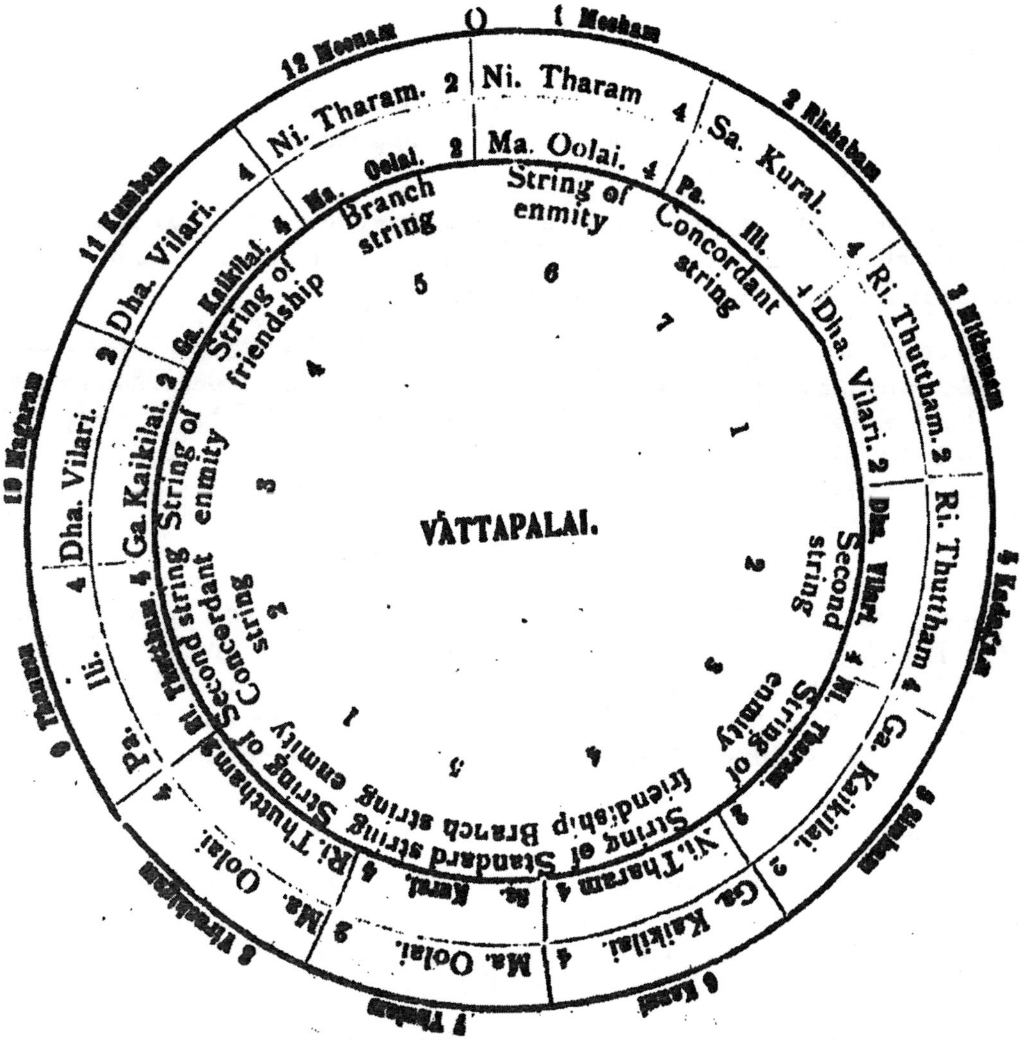

This Chakaram shows the seven Swarams of Kodipalai when Oolai is taken as Kural. That is, when Kural commences in Oolai in Thulam from Sempalai (where

Kural is taken as Kural in Rishabam), we may find which of the 12 Swarams above the Kural agree with it thus producing the seven Swarams of the octave.

According to the previous system, here also the five strings namely the first, third, sixth, eighth and the tenth stand in the relation of Pagai to Kural.

We may notice that the seventh string from the standard or commencing Swaram from the Meru is in the relation of Inai, and when that is made the commencing Swaram and other concordant Swarams calculated from it the Kural or the original standard string will come again as a Kilai string.

The seventh string from Kural in Meru towards the right is in the relation of Inai. On the other hand, proceeding leftwards to the standard Kural, the Inai string becomes a Kilai string.

It appears, then, that these SA-PA and SA-MA principles which make strings stand in the relation of Inai and Kilai have been applied as the measurement for determining the 12 Swarams of a Sthayi.

When we notice the fact that the standard string becomes Kilai and Inai, we come to the conclusion that each of the 12 Swarams of the octave must be in the relation of either Inai or Kilai to every other Swaram.

To conclude, then, from the words "இடமுறைமெலிய பண்ணிடுதற் கிளைப் பண்ணிடு பாலையுள்ளடம்" what has been already said is clear that the seven Palais obtained by the principle that Oolai appears in Tharam and Kural in Oolai are the Primary Palais, and the five Palais obtained by the principle that Tharam appears in Kaikilai in Kanni and Oolai in Tharam in Mesham, are the secondary Palais.

12. About the Alakus of the Swarams.

Silappadikaram gives 22 Alakus for the seven Swarams of Vattapalai thus :— SA^4 RI^4 GA^3 MA^2 PA^4 DHA^3 NI^2. The author of Sangita Ratnakar gives SA^4 RI^3 GA^2 MA^4 PA^4 DHA^3 NI^2 or 22 Alakus. The latter 4-3-2-4-4-3-2 resembles the Alaku system of Neythal Yal where PA is taken as Kural and nothing more. He does not mention any particulars about these either. The Gandhara Gramam he mentions has been banished to the celestial regions even during his time! while the Madhyma and Shadja Gramams in modern use do not agree with his system.

Again, if we note his words carefully, we find that some of the *amsams* mentioned in Silappadikaram were a sealed book even to him. For though he gives the measurements of Swarams as SA-PA and SA-MA, yet he implies that there should be 12 Srutis between SA and PA and 8 between SA and MA.

We have already noticed in the calculations as regards Dwavimsati Srutis that if we divided the Sthayi into 22 parts and examine the SA-MA and SA-PA as 8 and 12 Srutis respectively, we would find that none of the Swarams in modern use correspond to that series. In other words it was pointed out that SA-MA or the 9th Sruti from the given Swaram and SA-PA or the 13th Sruti from the given Swaram will never correspond to the modern Pa and Ma. We have noted in the same breath that when we proceed by ⅔ or 9 Srutis and ¾ or 13 Srutis at each step, the Sthayi never comes to an end.

On the other hand we see the Swarams proceed regularly in the Sa-Ga or Sa Ma or Sa-Pa series and finish the octave perfectly with their respective measurements.

If we had known that such a sound and ancient system had existed already we need not have wasted our words. We would have been spared the irregularity of using scales having one Swaram in Aroganam and a different one in the Avaroganam. We would have been saved from conflicting theories, such as 22 Srutis, 53 Srutis and 25 Srutis in the octave. The musical world would not have been in such grave doubts.

Many of the authentic works which elucidated the mysteries of the ancient music of South India seem to have disappeared after the age of Silappadikaram. For the commentators make remarks which contradict practical music.

For example, they make remarks which amount to saying that the Inai string and the Kilai string are identical. Instead of saying the fifth string, they give five series of Swarams which agree with one another as Sa with Ma. Though the idea is not incorrect, they say that Kilai is the fifth string and the series are the result of the application of the principle Sa-Ma. These are the five series of Swarams obtained by proceeding leftwards by the Sa-Ma principle in Vattapalai and none else. The five series end with Simham. If we proceed onwards we shall only repeat the Seven Swarams but never arrive at the 12.

The other version says that Kilai is the fifth string. This enables us to think that Pa, the fifth string, is Kilai. But we have repeatedly said that the other strings are deriv l from Panchamam or the Inai string. So to call this Kilai string also will be contradictory.

In the same manner he says the sixth string is Pagai string. Dha, which is sixth from Sa occurs in the seventh Rasi from Rishabam. Dha is to Pa as Thuttham is to Kural. Just as Pa is in the relation of Inai string to Sa, so Dah is Inai string to Ri. This is the sixth Swaram. It will be contradictory to say that this is Pagai string. The sixth Rasi should be in the relation of Pagai.

In the same manner, the Ga which is the sixth Swaram from Pa is called Pagai. We noticed before that the Ga in Simham is not arrived at rightly by the Principle of Sa-Pa. It will be just to say that it is Pagai to Vilari. But it is true that the Ga and Ni which appear in Simham, the third Rasi, stand in the relation of Pagai to Sa and Pa which occur in Rishabam. Those experts who have a thorough knowledge of Karnatic music only can know its truth and not others. There are also musicians who hold that this Pagai Swaram in the third Rasi is really a Natpu Swaram. This is the result of ignorance. If this ignorance is found in the residents of South India who practise Karnatic music, we need not be surprised that Sarnga Dev who lived very far north had erred. Just as we said that concordant Swarams according to the

Alakus given by him are not in practice at the modern time we also clearly see that the Alakus given by the author of Silappadikaram also do not correspond to the Swarams in modern use.

For example, GA, the third Swaram, and DHA, the sixth, are in the relation of Pagai. In other words, as they do not agree with SA, they are Pagai Swarams. If these two fundamental Swarams are to be omitted in an important primary scale, the Ragam will be classified not as Sampoorana but as one of the Oudava.

So it is clear that the Swarams in Vattapalai which stand in a particular relation according to the Rasis are the most ancient ones. We could also accept these as correct as they correspond exactly to the Swarams in use at the present day. Though it is said here that the number of Alakus is 22, when observed closely we shall find that it is incorrect and that a different interpretation should be put upon the words.

13. How the 22 Alakus can never completely finish an octave.

As we see from the Vattapalai Chakaram, attached we get 22 Alakus from Thulam to Simham. Kanni is left out. But inasmuch as Simham is sixth house from Kumbam we called it Pagai. The relation between Kumbam and Kanni is Inai. So it must have the Swaram of the Kanni Rasi. A Swaram with four Alakus in Kaikilai should be located there.

Below it there must be a Swaram with 4 Alakus in Tharam. If so, Vilari and Kaikilai which are in the relation of Kilai strings should also have four Alakus each.

Then, Vilari in Kadagam which is in the relation of Kilai string to Kumbam will also have four Alakus. Thus each Rasi will have two Alakus.

In the cycle of 12 Rasis, if two intervals are left out then we might say there are only 22 intervals. But they are continued and complete in the calculation.

Again, Tharam and Oolai in Meenam have two Alakus each.

Kural and Ili in Rishabam have four Alakus each. The two Alakus in Mesham and the two in Rishabam make up the four for SA. In the same way the two Alakus for PA in Mesham receive two more from Rishabam and go to make up the four for PA. Again, Thuttham obtains its four Alakus from Mithunam and Kadagam with two Alakus each.

Tharam stands with two Alakus in Simham. Kaikilai which stands with two Alakus in Kanni above it obtains two Alakus in Simham and four in Kanni.

Oolai ends in Thulam with two Alakus and Kural with four in its second Rasi.

PA and Thuttham in Thanusu end with four Alakus in the second rasi.

In the same manner Vilari and Kaikilai in Magaram should fiinish with two Alakus each.

Then Vilari and Kaikilai in Kumbam will finish with four Alakus each.

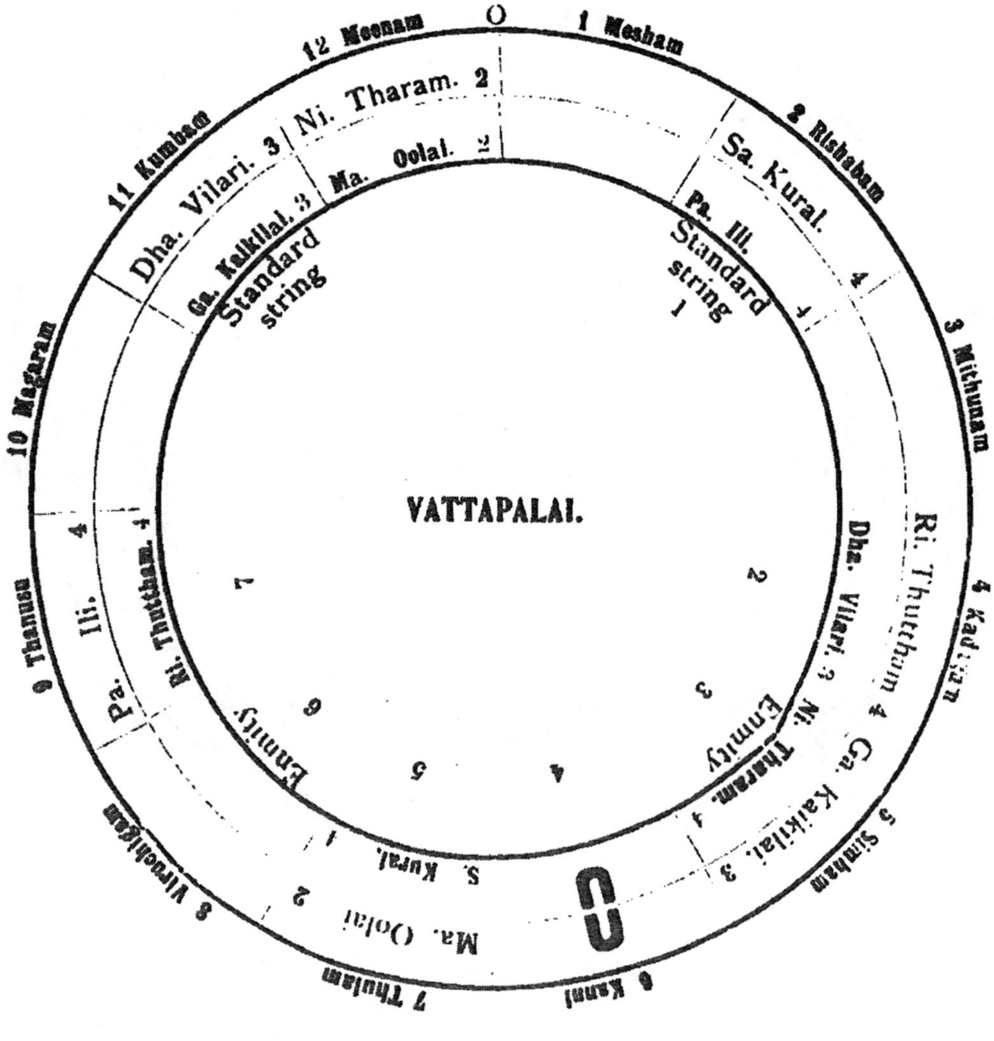
O
1 Mesham
2 Rishabam
3 Mithunam
4 Kadagam
5 Simham
6 Kanni
7 Thulam
8 Virochigam
9 Thanusu
10 Magaram
11 Kumbam
12 Meenam
Ni. Tharam. 2
Ma. Oolai. 2
Dha. Vilari. 3
Ga. Kaikilai. 3
Standard string
Sa. Kural.
Pa. Ili.
4
Standard string 1
Ri. Thuttham 4
Dha. Vilari. 3
Ni. Tharam. 4
Ga. Kaikilai. 3
Enmity
VATTAPALAI.
S. Kural.
Ma. Oolai 2
Pa. Ili.
Ri. Thuttham. 4
Enmity
1
2
3
4
5
6
7

14. Showing the error of the opinion that there are Dwavimsati Srutis in the Sthayi.

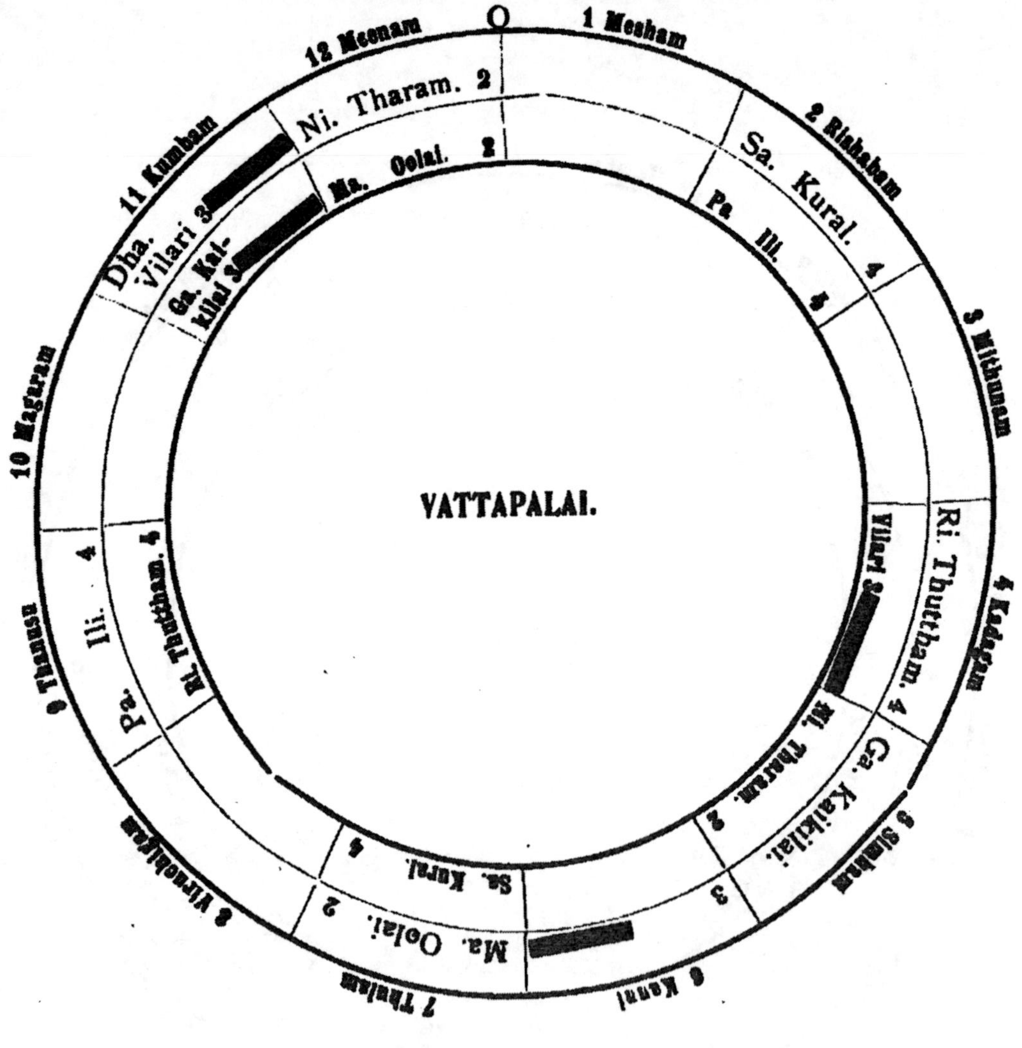

Vilari has one Alaku less in the second row in Kadagam which is the fourth Rasi commencing from Mesham. On the same principle, the Tharam with two Alakus in the second row of Simham, the fifth Rasi, will not agree with Kaikilai which has three Alakus. One of the Alakus should be given to Kanni. Then Kaikilai gets one Alaku less in Kanni. Vilari and Kaikilai end with three Alakus each in the eleventh Rasi or Kumbam. Therefore Kumbam should have one Alaku less in the latter part. When we notice, then, that there are two Alakus less in the second and the first rows, we find that Alakus are arranged in the Rasi mandalam with intervals between. If they are continuous, the two Alakus which are wanting now must go along with the 22.

If we take four Alakus each for Vilari and Kaikilai, we will see that all the calculations for the Swarams of the Vattapalai are in the relation of SA-PA, SA-MA and SA-GA. The Swarams will also be continuous and all doubts removed.

When we notice the Swarams which are computed to be 24 according to Vattapalai and their mode of changing Graham, we find that they had fixed the Srutis to be 24, and have made Ganam with one Sruti less in Swarams obtained by the SA-PA principle, such as RI DHA, DHA GA, GA NI, NI MA, and PA RI. In the same way, looking at the Alakus we find the very same principle has been adopted for SA-MA and SA-PA. On the other hand, if they had fixed only 22 Srutis, they would never get the concordant series by the SA-PA and SA-MA principles but quite a different discordant series.

If the author had not given the system by which the Swarams are arranged in the relation of SA-PA and SA-MA with 12 RASIS of Vattapalai then we might believe the statement that there are 22 Alakus in the octave. But he has distinctly stated it. Those who try to learn the 22 Srutis will get only perplexed and will never be able to practically realise it. Even if it is practicable, who is here to listen to it? None even in the three mandalams. What shall we say about the Ganam where even the fundamental Swarams SA RI GA MA and PA are not concordant? We might, perhaps, appear to be in the wrong, for Sarnga Dev speaks about 22 Srutis, the ancient Tamil works give 22 and many other works have copied the same.

The Mandara Sthayi proceeds from the heart, the Madhya Sthayi, from the Kantam and the Tara Sthayi, from the head. 22 Nadis proceed from each of these places. 22 Nadis go across them. And the 22 Srutis proceed from them. These are the statements made by the advocates of 22 Srutis, and they may mislead many.

Sound is produced by the current of air passing through the breathing apparatus. Just as sounds of a high pitch are produced through the small holes, and those of a lower pitch through the bigger holes of a Nagasuram, so sounds of different pitches are produced from the human throat through the lip, the teeth, the tongue, the nostrils, the lower part of the throat, the mouth and the palate with the help of air passing through them. But to say that there are 22 Nadis here and 22 across them and that sound is produced through them is perplexing. Those who never tested the truth of this, blindly repeated this and confounded others also.

Even now, there are some in India who, without understanding the truth, have created some wrong theories, fathered them on sages who knew the truth and thus are perplexing many. Such perplexities abound in works on Medicine and in Puranas. Their presumption is that if their wrong opinions and fables could be called 'Ahastya's Katakam' and "Vyasa's Katakam", every one would believe them.

Knowing that the human embryo is in the womb which is surrounded on all sides by water, could Ahastya have made the astounding statement that the child absorbs part of the mother's food through an opening on the top of the skull? He knows there is no opening between the top of the skull and the stomach. He compares the body to the Karunelli tree and the pipe attached to the navel to the side roots. The tree is generally fed from the roots and not from the top. Can the sperm which is swallowed reach the stomach and be converted into the embryo?!! Is not this against all laws of nature? Such unnatural inferences abound in some of their works.

It appears that the cycle of years, as far as the Andam was concerned, was calculated by the solar month, and that for the Pindam, by the lunar month. It is said that by the lunar month calculation the time that the human embryo takes for full development is ten months. The lunar month has but 28 days. They calculated then about 28 days for the whole period—280 for the 10 lunar months and the number of days between menstruation and conception. On the other hand they speak of the period as 300 days calculating 30 days for each solar month and father it upon sages! What ignorance! They blow their big trumpets on the strength of the venerable names of these sages!

It seems that Ilankovadigal wrote the Silappadikaram at a time when the glory of the music of South India of the first Ooli had nearly departed. There are some points of difference between the commentary of Kavichakravarti Jayankondan, who lived 10 centuries after Ilankovidigal and that of Adyarkunallar who lived 100 years later.

Where he speaks about the four different kinds of Yal, Jayankondan makes mention of Ahanilai Marutham, Puranilai Marutham, Arugial Marutham and Perugial Marutham and their rules. This shows that the author had somewhat realised the extensiveness of the music which then existed. Adyarkunallar has written his commentary on the musical portion of it closely following his ideas and having his words for a basis. Now, Saranga Dev, who lived still 100 years later, takes only the 22 Alakus of Vattapalai and generates Ragas on the principle of change of Graham by shifting the four Srutis of Sa to the left one after the other. He supports his number 22 by analogy to what is found inside the human anatomy. The perplexity caused by Vattapalai led him into this error. If he had paid attention to the words 'இணையா மரபின்' of Ilankovadigal and noted the position of Simham which is the sixth house from Kumbam, he would have had his position clear. If there is doubt about Srutis what will be the fate of music which rests on them? We request our noble readers not to think that we are belittling the opinions of our ancient sages. The following calculations will make our position clear.

15. Showing how the Swarams will not stand in the relation of Vadi and Samvadi and in the right places if 22 Srutis occurred in the Vattapalai as follows :—

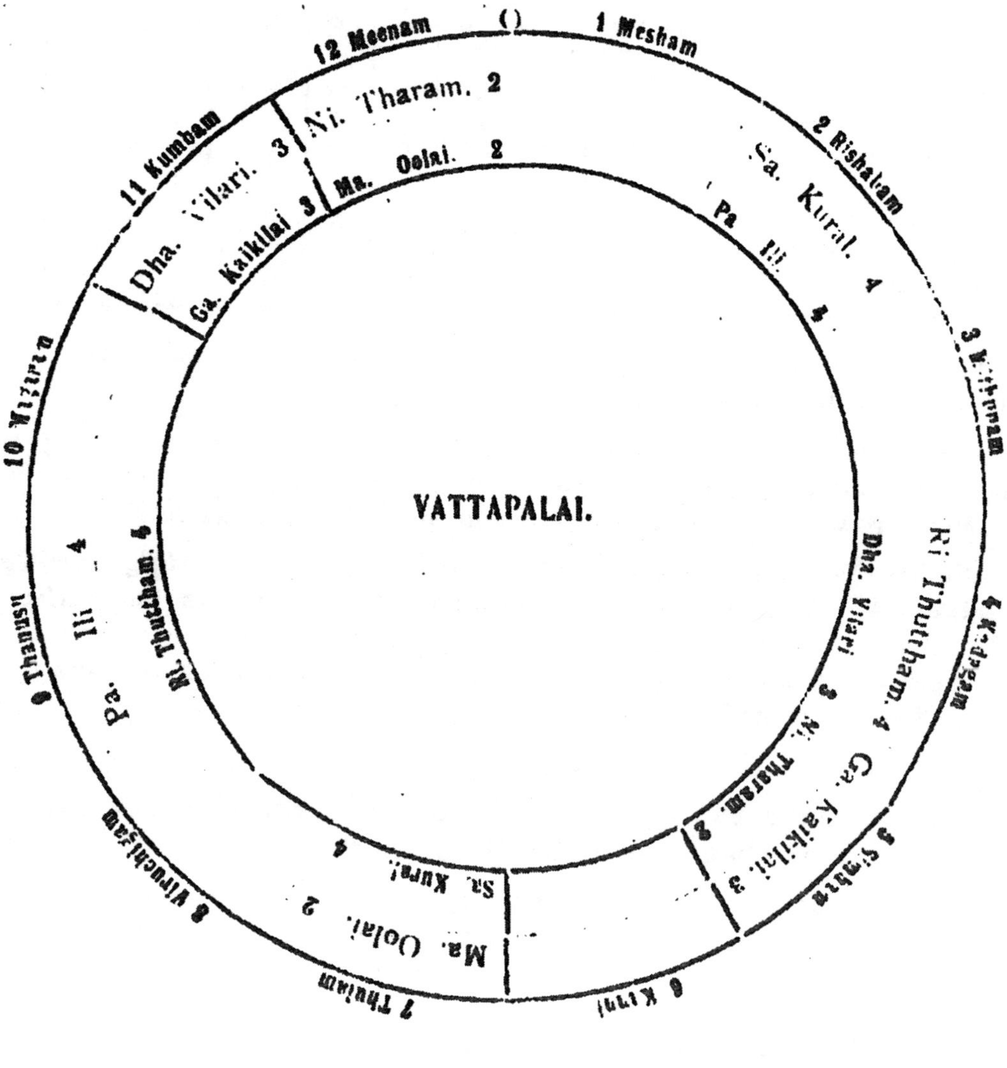

How the Alakus occur for the Sapta Swarams.

He gives the numbers of Alakus or the numbers for Srutis as SA^1, RI^1, GA^2, MA^2, PA^1, DHA^1 and NI^1. According to the above calculation Kural appears in Oolai (MA^2 SA^1) or MA PA DHA NI SA. In the same way if we put down the series SA^1-PA^1, PA^1-RI^1, RI^1-DHA^1, DHA^1-GA^1 and GA^2-NI^1 and add up their Alakus we shall see the truth of what we say. The following Table will show that NI SA RI GA MA has 13 Alakus.

I

1	Oolai	appears in	Tharam	2 2 N-M	N	4 S	4 R	3 G	2 M	13
2	Kural	„	Oolai	2 4 M-S	M	4 P	3 D	2 N	4 S	13
3	Ili	„	Kural	4 4 S-P	S	4 R	3 G	2 M	4 P	13
4	Thuttham	„	Ili	4 4 P-R	P	3 D	2 N	4 S	4 R	13
5	Vilari	„	Thuttham	4 3 R-D	R	3 G	2 M	4 P	3 D	12
6	Kaikilai	„	Vilari	3 3 D-G	D	2 N	4 S	4 R	3 G	13
7	Tharam	„	Kaikilai	3 2 G-N	G	2 M	4 P	3 D	2 N	11

The first four rows and the sixth row end with 13 Srutis each, but the fifth ends with 12 and the seventh with 11 only.

This is the calculation for 22 Srutis in the octave. Here there are 13 Srutis in the five rows from the given Swarams on the principle of SA-PA. But in the fifth and the seventh rows, there is one sruti and two Srutis less respectively.

We have already noted the words, 'ஏற்றிய குரல் இளி யென்றிரு நரம்பினொப்பக் கேட்கு முணர்வினனாகி' (he must possess the knowledge to discriminate the perfect concord of Kural and Ili Strings). Will such an expert give up one Sruti in one, and two Srutis in another, and have Ri-DHA 11 in one, GA-NI, 12 in another and SA-PA thirteen in a third? He will never have it.

16. The Swarams will not stand in the relation of Vadi and Samvadi and will not have the right calculations according to the system of Dwavimsati Srutis of Sarnga Dev.

Just as we proved that the Alaku system was wrong in Vattapalai, we find the same here also. The system 4, 3, 2, 4, 4, 3, 2 resembles the system of Neythal Yal which is obtained when Ili is made Kural in Thanusu Rasi in Vattapalai. We have stated this before. This stands as Ili to the Kural in Rishabam. We have also noted before that they had the Mandara Sthayi from Kural up to Ili, the Madhaya Sthayi from Ili in Thanusu up to Oolai in Thulam, the Thara Sthayi from Ili to Meenam above, and sang the 14 Kovais. This appears to be the Panchama Sruti. We find it in use even now. Saranga Dev calls this Shadja gramam and proceeds to give the Alaku system. He calls the Swarams that occur in Neythal Yal in Vattapalai, namely, PA^4 DHA^3 NI^2 SA^4 RI^4 GA^3 MA^2 and their Alakus, by the name of Shadja Gramam. We must be thankful that Sarnga Dev agrees with us at least in this point, namely the Alaku system of one of the Yals in Vattapalai. We are led to believe that the Alaku system of Vattapalai and its Yals were getting out of use during his time. The following table gives his Alaku system.

II

1	Thuttham	appears in	Ili	4 3 P-R	P	3 D	2 N	4 S	3 R	12
2	Vilari	„	Thuttham	3 3 R-D	R	2 G	4 M	4 P	3 D	13
3	Kaikilai	„	Vilari	3 2 D-G	D	2 N	4 S	3 [illegible]	2 G	11
4	Tharam	„	Kaikilai	2 2 G-N	G	4 M	4 P	3 D	2 N	13
5	Oolai	„	Tharam	2 2 N-M	N	4 S	3 R	2 G	4 M	13
6	Kural	„	Oolai	2 4 M-S	M	4 P	3 D	2 N	4 S	13
7	Ili	„	Kural	4 4 S-P	S	3 R	2 G	4 M	4 P	13

Just as we get Thuttham in Ili, and Vilari in Thuttham by the Vattapalai, the series Pa Ri, Ri Dha, Dha Ga, Ga Ni, Ni Ma, Ma Sa and Sa Pa are derived as Vadi and Samvadi Swarams. Each of these should have 13 Srutis. On the other hand the first series Pa Ri gets 12 Srutis while the third, Dha Ga gets only 11. How can this be justified? If Saranga Dev was quite sure about his position, will he not have given some explanation for the discrepancy? He had said that if 12 and 8 Alakus occurred between two Swarams which were the beginning and the end they stood in the relation of Vadi and Samvadi. But when the series obtain 10 and 11 Srutis, excluding the commencing and the ending Swarams, how could they be concordant? We find by the Alaku system given above that such a discordant Thuttham and Kaikilai occur in the ascending as well as the descending series. It is clearly seen that this has been written without understanding the mystery contained in the Vattapalai system of the ancient Tamils.

It is seen that the ancient Tamils had Swarams in the 12 Rasis, in the 12 Palais and in the 7 Swarams taking for granted that the seventh string was Inai, the sixth Pagai, the fifth Kilai and the fourth Natpu. They have declared the Srutis to be 22 knowing the mystery of it, whereas Sarnga Dev has blindly stated that the Srutis are 22.

17. The Alaku system for Srutis when they are concordant as Vadi and Samvadi.

Let us now see how they should be. As we saw in the previous Vattapalai Chakaram, if the Alakus of the two strings Kaikilai and Vilari be taken as 4 each instead of 3, the regularity and uniformity of the series is secured. It can be seen from the following Table :—

III

1	Oolai	appears in	Tharam	$\overset{2\ 2}{\text{N-M}}$	N^{2}	N	S^{4}	R^{4}	G^{4}	M^{2}	14
2	Kural	,,	Oolai	$\overset{2\ 4}{\text{M-S}}$	M^{2}	M	P^{4}	D^{4}	N^{4}	S^{2}	14
3	Ili	,,	Kural	$\overset{4\ 4}{\text{S-P}}$	S^{4}	S	R^{4}	G^{4}	M^{2}	P^{4}	14
4	Thuttham	,,	Ili	$\overset{4\ 4}{\text{P-R}}$	P^{4}	P	D^{4}	N^{4}	S^{2}	R^{4}	14
5	Vilari	,,	Thuttham	$\overset{4\ 4}{\text{R-D}}$	R^{4}	R	G^{4}	M^{2}	P^{4}	D^{4}	14
6	Kaikilai	,,	Vilari	$\overset{4\ 4}{\text{D-G}}$	D^{4}	D	N^{4}	S^{2}	R^{4}	G^{4}	14
7	Tharam	,,	Kaikilai	$\overset{4\ 4}{\text{G-N}}$	G^{4}	G	M^{2}	P^{4}	D^{4}	N^{4}	14

Here we see that each series obtains 14 Alakus. This is the sum total of the Rasis which stand in the relation of Sa Pa. We noted before that each Rasi should have 2 Alakus or 24 Alakus in all. This is just the same. Perhaps Sarnga Dev did not understand this clearly and said there ought to be 12 Srutis between the commencing and the ending Swarams? The six Rasis between get the 12 Alakus.

Again he gave 8 Alakus between Sa and Ma. This also means 8 Alakus for 4 Rasis between the commencing and the ending Rasis. But it is clear that one Alaku in a Rasi has not been added. If added, we will get 24 Alakus in all with 14 for Sa-Pa and 10 for Sa-Ma. We shall find that all the Swarams are perfectly concordant with one another by this system. We noted before that Kaikilai in Simham of the Vattapalai series of the ancient Tamils should be properly placed in Kanni and it has the relation of Sa-Pa and Sa-Ma. When that doubt is cleared and when the Swarams are obtained by the Sa-Pa principle we shall see that series (Sa-Ma) ends in the Meenam Rasi which was also the commencement.

18. How 22 Srutis were in use in the Sthayi.

Then, we shall find that the two Swarams, Kural and Ili, have two Alakus each and the other five Swarams, four Alakus each. This is how matters stand when the mystery in Vattapalai is explained. It is clear, that in ancient times the 24 Alakus were sung as the 24 Srutis. It is also clear that they lessened a quarter in each of those Swarams or one Alaku, but in a single Aroganam and Avaroganam as a whole they had lessened two Alakus. So it is incorrect to lay stress upon the fact that 22 Alakus are mentioned in ancient works ignoring altogether the calculations for Vattapalai and the 24 Alakus of a Sthayi. The division of the octave into 22 had confounded many people. We noticed before how deeply this idea had taken root.

From the Vattapalai Chakaram we learn the Sapta Swarams, the two half Swarams of each of Ri, Ga, Ma, Dha and Ni, the seven and the 12 Swarams on the whole, the calculation by which each of the 12 Swarams have 2 Alakus, and how the 24 Alakus are distributed among the Srutis. We also understand that Ganam was made in the 24 Srutis with one Alaku less in the seventh and the fifth Rasis which occur by the Sa-Pa and the Sa-Ma systems.

It was a custom to make Ganam with one Alaku less in a Swaram occurring at the Poorvabagam in a scale, and with one Alaku less in a Swaram occurring in Ootarabagam. It is this that led them to say that there are 22 Srutis in the octave, but they have not said that there are only 22 in the octave. Further details may be seen from the Chakaram attached.

According to the statement that Kaikilai should appear in Vilari there must be a Kaikilai with four Alakus in Kanni, which is the seventh Rasi from Kumbam. In Simham there must be a Kaikilai with two Alakus seeing that the Kaikilai in Simham which is the sixth Rasi from Kumbam is Pagai to Panchamam. The Kaikilai in Kanni gives five more Swarams by the Sa-Pa system and the 12 Swarams of the Sthayi. These are the 12 Swarams which we sing and hear at the present day. These are the very Swarams used by Madhavi with great pleasure. These were the seven Swarams arranged in the Sakota Yal after the Sa-Pa and the Sa-Ma principles. The fourteen Kovais or fourteen Swarams which are divided from these 12 Swarams in the Mandara, Madhya and Tara Sthayi is belong to Ayapalai.

To play music in the 24 Alakus is the Ganam for men. To lessen two Alakus out of the 24 appears to be the Vattapalai. It does not mean that all the 22 Srutis occur in one and the same Ragam. The one Alaku, obtained when the Sthayi is divided into 24, is lessened for the two out of the seven Swarams which stand in the relation of Vadi and Samvadi, while the other five are sung according to the Rasi. It is clear that they had the 12 Swarams as the basis, and lessened one Alaku in the Poorvabagam or Sa Pa, and another in the Ootarabagam or Pa Sa. The Vattapalai and its rules were given to make clear which of the Swarams of the Scale had lesser Alakus when they mentioned the number 22, they emphasised the fact that a Sthayi should not be divided into 22 parts. So they also gave the Rasi Mandalam with 12 compartments and at the same time the Sa Pa and the Sa Ma principles.

We have repeatedly pointed out so that every one may clearly see that in the Rasi Mandalam 7, 5, 4 and 2 Rasis stand concordant on the principle of Sa Pa, Sa Ma, Sa Ga and Sa Ri respectively. Those who understand this will never say there are 22 Srutis or 25 or 53 Srutis in the Sthayi. We may see in the second book that in the Sa Pa and Sa Ma series occurring in the Poorvabagam and Ootarabagam there shall be an Alaku less and how excellent that system is. We have omitted them here as they have to be spoken in detail.

If we reject the system of 24 Alakus according to Vattapalai and accept the theory of 22 Alakus, we shall never get even a single Swaram on the principles of Sa Pa or Sa Ma.

The following Chakaram shows the series of 22 Alakus commencing from Mesham.

Here, the series commencing from Sa is given in the second inner circle, and that which commences from Pa in the third. We find here that Mesham and Rishabam have 4 Alakus each and stand in the relation of Kural-Ili or Sa Pa.

In Kadagam we see Thuttham having 4 Alakus whereas Vilari has only 3. The second Alaku of Tharam ends in the first half of Simham and Kaikilai ends with the third Alaku in the first half of Kanni. Oolai with 2 Alakus and Kural with 4, end in the first half of Thulam. Ili and Thutham with 4 Alakus each end in the first half of Thanusu. We might also see that in Magaram, Vilari and Kaikilai end with 3 Alakus each, and Tharam and Oolai with 2 Alakus each in Kumbam.

The two Alakus of Meenam are not found in either of the circles. We see that no two Swarams in the relation of Sa Pa can exist in this compartment.

For, unless Kural and Ili in Rishabam end in the second Alaku of Thanusu they will never have the relation of Sa Pa and Pa Ri. But as they end in the first Alaku of Thanusu, Sa Pa has one Alaku less.

In the same manner, If the secondary relation of Sa Ma and Pa Sa should result from Rishabam there should be 5 Rasis complete above Rishabam. On the other hand, the Oolai and Kural which should occur in the second Alaku of Thulam occur in the first. In this way eight Alakus occur between Sa and Ma and 12 between Sa and Pa.

Though we find this agreeing with the theory of Sarnga Dev that there should be 8 and 12 Srutis between two Swarams, yet we have seen in detail that they do not stand in the relation of Sa Pa or Sa Ma. We also noted that this will be quite contrary to the rules of South Indian Music.

19. If we arrange the series of 22 Srutis in a Rasimandalam, the Sapta Swarams derived will never satisfy the principle that Oolai must appear in Tharam, and Kural in Oolai according to the system of Vattapalai.

The following Chakaram shows the calculation of the 22 Alakus commencing from Mesham.

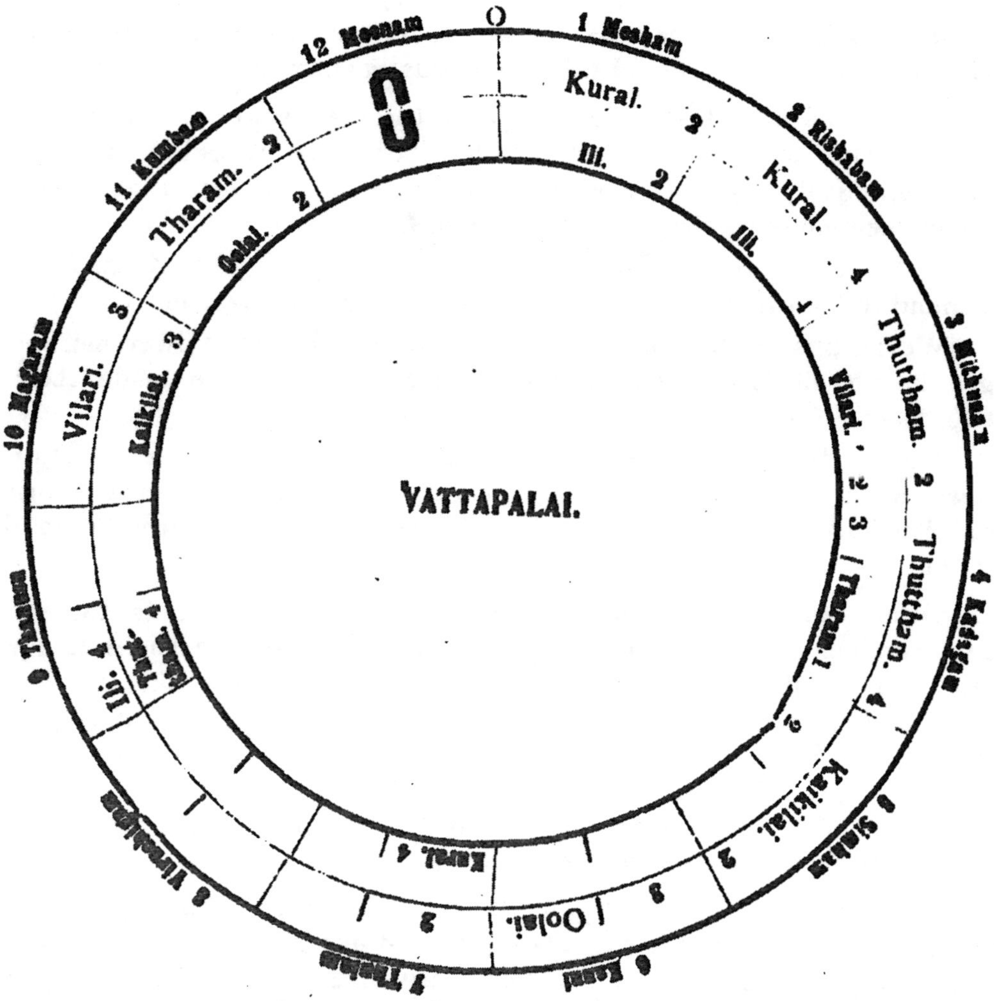

The ancient Tamil works distinctly state that concordant Swarams should satisfy the theory that Oolai should appear in Tharam. But such concordance will never be found here. For, Tharam, which should end in Meenam, ends in Kumbam. Kanni is the seventh place for Kumbam by the principle of SA PA. Instead of the Oolai commencing from here it ends in the first Alaku of Thulam. This has one Alaku more than what it ought to have.

Again contrary to the principle that Oolai should appear in Kural, the Oolai ends in Kumbam instead of Meenam. The Oolai which should end in the second Alaku of Thulam inasmuch as it commenced in the first Alaku, does not do so, so we should say that here also there is an Alaku less. Just as Oolai does not agree with the Kural which commences from Rishabam (SA-MA), the Oolai which stands in Thulam will also be discordant. If there is no agreement even in the fundamental principles of SA-PA and SA-MA, how could other concords exist among the Swarams?

We noticed in the first table on page 596 that there could be no concord between RI GA MA PA DHA, GA MA PA DHA NI and MA PA DHA NI SA as they have 12, 11 and 13 Srutis respectively. We see from Vattapalai that such a discordant system was never made mention of by the ancients in South India.

Just as the system of Sarnga Dev will never agree with Karnatic music, it will be found that it can never agree with any other existing system.

We see plainly that the Tamils had 24 Alakus for the 12 Swarams, and having arranged them by the SA-PA and the SA-MA principles they have made their ganam with two Alakus less.

Because Sarnga Dev failed to understand the location of the 22 Srutis when ganam was made with 2 Alakus less, and was mystified with the ancient work which declared that Kaikilai should appear in Vilari, he gave his own interpretation of it and brought out his work.

Others, thinking that the beauty of their music was due to the 22 Srutis, began to examine it. Even though they knew there was not the slightest agreement between the music of South India based on concordant Swarams like SA GA, SA-MA and SA-PA and other music, they wanted to support the theory of Sarnga Dev by introducing small Srutis between the intervals as they pleased. If even those who are traditional experts in Karnatic music are taken in by this fancy theory need we say about others? We know from our experience that the concordant Swarams of Vattapalai were the ones used by our ancestors.

What can we say about people who deny the truth? They try to hide the big pumpkin inside their plate of rice! They are blind like the brother-in-law who caught hold of the supposed man inside the drum! (Two villagers who had never seen the drum thought there was a man inside making the noise. So put their hands in and caught hold of each other's hands and each cried out he had caught the man inside the drum!) We can only laugh at such people!

We shall notice later that minuter Srutis than these are also used in the ganam of South India.

20. How the Tamils sang Grahaswaram.

We have noted till now how the ancient Tamils were efficient in Isai Tamil, how they made ganam in Swarams which had the relation of SA-PA, SA-MA, SA-GA and SA-RI, how they divided a Sthayi into 12 corresponding to the 12 compartments of the Zodiac, how they had made ganam in the 7 Swarams out of the 12 and how in two of those Swarams which stand in the relation of SA-PA and SA-MA they made ganam with an Alaku less.

We have also noted that, consequently, only 7 Swarams were used in the ganam, that they were divided into 12 which stood in the relation of Inai, Kilai, Natpu and Pagai and that these 12 had two Alaku each or 24 in all. We have also noted that if there were 22 Srutis in the octave their calculations would never satisfy the rules of Vadi and Samvadi, how the series would never come to a finish in the Zodiac, how the system is entirely wrong and how the advocates of 22 Srutis had erred because they failed to understand the meaning of the Tamil works. We have also seen how Sarnga Dev makes mention of Neythal Yal only out of the 4 Yals as Shadjagramam whose Alakus are 4, 3, 2, 4, 4, 3, 2 and even there the Swarams do not satisfy the principle of Vadi and Samvadi as in some cases there are 11 and 12 Srutis instead of 13. We have seen how his theory will never suit Karnatic music and how not a single Swaram on the principle of SA-PA and SA-MA could be found in it.

We found on page 418 of the Second Part how they gave many calculations contradicting one another and many measurements which were never uniform. The Tamils have divided the Sthayi into 24 parts and made ganam in them for many thousand years, with two Alakus less. We also noted that the Tamils, after the destruction of the major portion of their habitation, and after the destruction of South Madura and Kapatapuram declined in their status. Many of the Kalais used by them became obsolete owing to absence of patronage. Even the few that remained owing to want of practice were given up as beyond comprehension. When such was the condition of affairs Bharata in the 5th Century and Sarnga Dev in the 13th became the chief writers on music.

Ever since the advent of their works the theory of 22 Srutis lifted up its head. However, people of understanding, who found the theory to contradict science and practice, raised objections and began to argue against it. Many works were written. They were all conflicting in their opinions. They found that their opinions could never be uniform unless the Ghandara Gramam which was sent up to the celestial regions was brought down once more! They were further discouraged by the saying of Sarnga Dev that the Srutis may be 1, 2, 3, 4, 9, 22, 66 and Srutis may be innumerable. Thus the strife came to an end.

Though we have repeatedly said that the theory of 22 Srutis was the result of not having clearly understood the mystery contained in ancient Isai Tamil, we have also said that the series was not practicable for singing Grahaswaram. The ancient Tamils used the 12 Palais or 12 Swarams in their ganam. In the process of singing Grahaswaram they shifted the Swarams with 2 Alakus each and not the single Alaku.

of the series 24. We may see from the following extract that Grahaswaram was used only for the 12 Swarams. We know that a ganam which does not admit of Grahaswaram is imperfect. So, in examining Srutis, if we could find out in what relationship the Swarams stood while Grahaswaram was sung, we shall get clear of the doubt about Dwavimsati Srutis.

One or two points about Grahaswaram are mentioned below :—

Silappadikaram, Aroompathavoorai Page 55.

" குடமுதல்-குடமுதல்-மேற்றிசை முதலாக. வட்டப்பாலை வருமாறு.

" ஆழியு மாரும்போற் கீறிச் சிறதிசைக்க
ணூழி ஞெரோவோன் மடன்கீறிச்-சூழ
வெருதாதி கீழ்த்திசைக்கொண் டீராறு மெண்ணிக்
கருதி நிலக்கயிற்றைக் காண் "

(இ-ள்) ஆழி ஒன்றுபோல வட்டம் ஒன்று கீறி வட்டத்தினுள்ளே ஆழியின் பாறகள் 2 குறுக்கும் நெடுக்குமாக ஒன்றன்மேலொன்று வைத்திருந்தாற்போலக் கிழக்கிலிருந்து மேற்களவும் ஊடுருவலாக இரேகைகள் 2-ம் வடக்கிலிருந்து தெற்களவும் ஊடுருவலாக இரேகைகள் 2-ம் ஆக இரேகைகள் நான்கு கீறி தென்கிழக்கு தென்மேற்கு வடமேற்கு வடகிழக்கு ஆகிய மூலைகள் 4-லும் நான்கு இரேகைகள் ஊடுருவாது அங்கங்கே தனி டித்து நிற்றலாகத் தனித்தனி ஒவ்வொன்று கீறி இராசிகளினெதிர்க்கயிறு அவ்வவற்றின் எதிரிலே தானே யிருக்கும் என்பது கருதி ரிஷபத்தை நேர்கிழக்காக கொண்டு ரிஷபம் முதல் மேஷம் இறுதியாக இராசிகள் டை-உம் வலமுறையே எண்ணிக் காணப்படும் எ-று.

Describe a circle, draw two radii across it from east to west and two others from north to south intersecting the first two. Draw four radii in the four corners south east, south west, north west and north east. These should stand in the corners without intercepting the main radii. Let Rishabam be placed in the east and so the 12 compartments from Rishabam up to Mesham proceeding towards the right can be obtained.

" இளியிடபங் கற்கடக மாம்விளரி சிங்கத்
தளராத தார மதுவாந்-தளராக்
குரல்கோற் றனுத்துத்தங் கும்பங் கிளையாம்
வரலா வுழைமீன மாம் "

(இ-ள்) இடபத்தில் இளியும், கற்கடகத்தில் விளரியும், சிங்கத்தில் தாரமும், துலாத்தில் குரலும் தனுவில் துத்தமும், கும்பத்தில் கைக்கிளையும் மீனத்தில் உழையும் நிற்கும் எ-று.

Ili will stand in Rishabam, Vilari in Karkadagam, Tharam in Simham, Kural in Thulam, Thuttham in Thanusu, Kaikilai in Kumbam and Coiai in Meenam.

" குரலிலை விற் றுத்தங் கைக்கிளையே கும்பம்
பரிய வுழைமீனம் பாவா-யரிதாரஞ்
சொல்லே யிளிவிளரி கற்கடகங் கோட்பமைந்த
தொல்லே ழிசைநரம்பிற் காம்."

(இ-ள்) குரல் துலாத்திலும், துத்தம் தனுவிலும், கைக்கிளை கும்பத்திலும், உழை மீனத்திலும், தாரம் சிங்கத்திலும், இளி இடபத்திலும், விளரி கடகத்திலும் வரிசையாக நின்றன.

இப்படி ஏழு நரம்புகளையு நிறுத்தி 'எழுவ ரிளங் கோதையர்' என்ற ஏழு பெண்களையும் ஏழு நரம் பாக்கி அவர்களை நரம்பு நிற்கு நிலைகளிலே நிறுத்தி * * *

Kural stands in Thulam, Thuttham in Thanusu, Kaikilai in Kumbam, Oolai in Meenam, Tharam in Simham, Ili in Rishabam and Vilari in Kadagam in a serial order.

Thus the seven strings were arranged, the seven damsels in 'எழுவ ரிளங் கோதையர்' were made seven strings and they were placed where the strings were * * *

Silappadikaram, Aiychiarkuravai Page 398.

> " குடமுத லிடமுறை யாக்குர மத்தங்
> கைக்கிளை யுழையிளி விளரிதா ரமேன
> விரிதரு பூங்குழல் வேண்டிய பெயரே "

(இ-ள்) குட திசையிற் குரல் நரம்பு முதலாகக் குரல், துத்தம், கைக்கிளை, உழை, இளி, விளரி தாரமெனை இவர்க்கு நிரலே யிட்ட பெயரே மாதரி விரும்பும் பெயரென்க.

On the east, the Kural string was made the first string followed by Thuttham, Kaikilai, Oolai, Ili, Vilari and Tharam. These are the seven names given and these are the names appreciated by damsels.

> " மாயவ னென்றாள் குரலை விறல்வெள்ளை
> யாயவ னென்றா ளிளிதன்னை-யாய்மகள்
> பின்னையா மென்றாளோர் துத்தத்தை மற்றையார்
> முன்னையா மென்றாண் முறை "

அவருள்

" மாயவனென்றாள் " — மாயவனென்றாள் குரலை; மற்றை வெள்ளையாயவனென்றாள் இளி நரம்பை; ஆய்மகள் பிஞ்ஞையாமென்றாள் துத்தத்தை; மற்றைப் பெண்களைக் கைக்கிளை உழை விளரி தார மென்றாள்.

She called Kural by the name of Mayavan, the Ili string was called Vellai Ayavan; Thuttham she (the shepherdess) called Pingai and the rest of the damsels were called Kaikilai, Oolai, Vilari and Tharam.

> " மாயவன் சீருளார் பிஞ்ஞையுந் தாரமும்
> வால்வெள்ளை சேரா குழையும் விளரியுங்
> கைக்கிளை பிஞ்ஞை யிடத்தாள் வலத்துளாண்
> முந்தைக்கு நல்விளரி தான் "

" மாயவன்சீர் " — மாயவனென்ற குரனரம்பைப் பின்னையான துத்தமும் தாரமுஞ் சேர நின்றன; பலதேவராகிய இளி நரம்பை உழையும் விளரியுஞ் சேர நின்றன; கைக்கிளை யென்கின்ற நரம்பு பின்னைக்கு இடப்பக்கமே நின்றது; முந்தையாகிய தாரத்துக்கு வலப்பக்கமே நின்றாள் விளரி."

Thuttham and Tharam stood along with Kural or Mathavan; Oolai and Vilari stood along with Ili or Paladevar; the string Kaikilai stood to the left of Pingai, while Vilari stood to the right of Tharam or Munthei.

First, how the Grahaswaram was sung in a Sthayi by Kilai Swarams only.

The Chakeram Showing how the Swarams occur leftwards from Thulam.

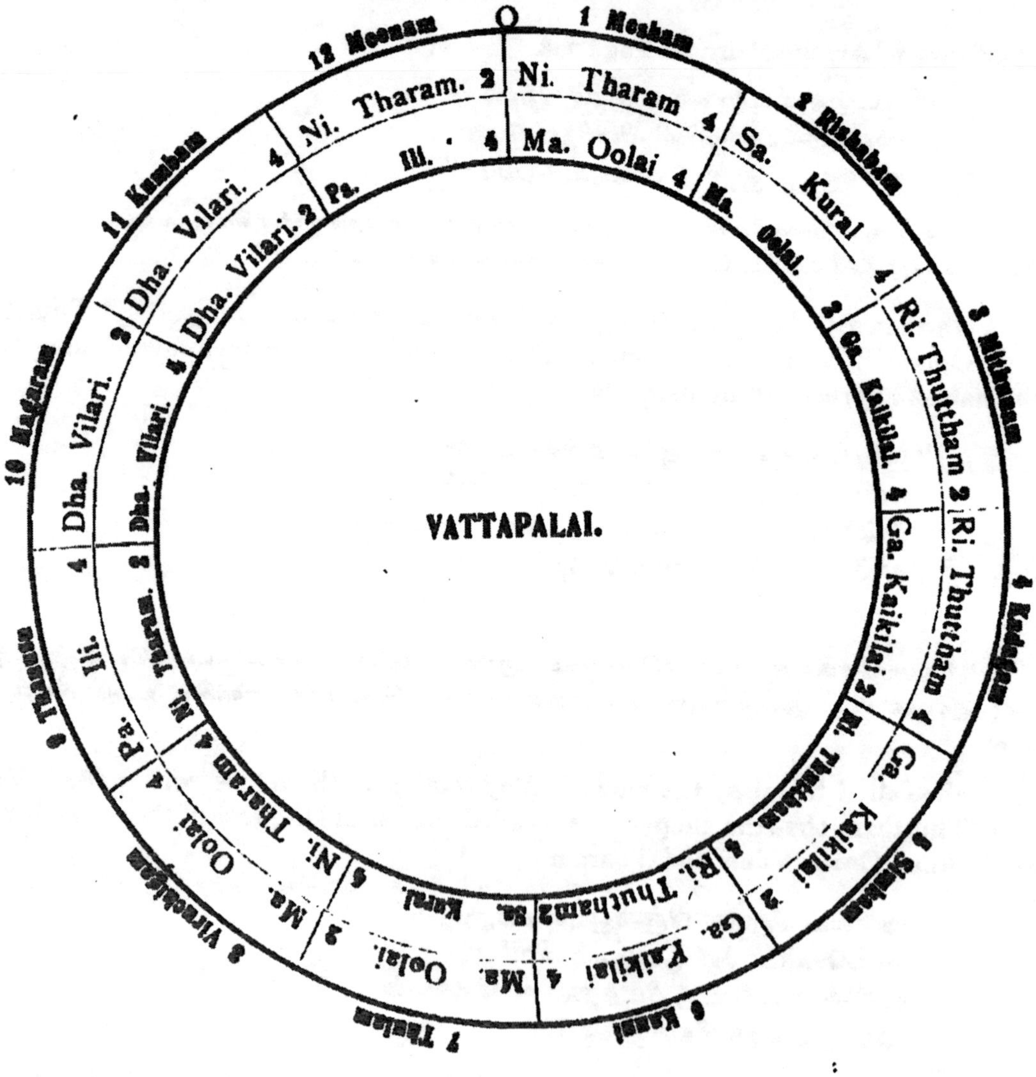

Silappadikaram, Aychiarkuravai Page 406.

(இ-ள்) மாயவனென்று பெயர் கூறப்பட்ட குரனரம்பைச்சேரப் பின்னை யென்னும் துத்தமும் தாரமும் நின்றன ; வெள்ளையாயவனென்று பெயர் கூறப்பட்ட இளியென்னு நரம்பைச்சேர உழையும் விளரியு நின்றன ; கைக்கிளை யென்னு நரம்பு பின்னைக்கு இடப்பக்கத்தே நின்றது ; மூத்தை யென்னும் தார நரம்பிற்கு வலப்பக்கத்தே விளரி நின்றதென்க.

Name of Swaram.	Swaram.	Name of seven Puns.	The order in which the seven stood.
Kural	SA	Mayavan	Thuttham and Tharam stand on either side of the Kural string called Mayava as NI SA RI
Thuttham	RI	Pingai	
Kaikilai	GA	Kaikilai	Kaikilai stood to the left of Pinnai as NI SA RI GA
Oolai	MA	Oolai	
Ili	PA	Paladevar	Oolai and Vilari stood by the side of Paladeva or Vellayavan or Ili string as MA PA DHA
Vilari	DHA	Vilari	Vilari stood to the right of Munthei or Tharam as MA PA DHA NI
Tharam	NI	Tharam	

Thuttham or Pingai and Tharam stood on either side of the string Kural which is called Mayavan; Oolai and Vilari stood on either side of Ili or Vellai-Ayavan; the string Kaikilai stood to the left of the string called Pingai; Vilari stood to the right of the Thara string called Munthei.

When we note the above Sootrams and their exposition, we find that the sons of the soil Mullai styled Kural Mayavan and Ili Vellai to suit their own soil, made the seven puns into seven strings, arranged them on the strings on the principle of Vadi and Samvadi, made ganam thereon and danced linking their hands.

The term Aychiar distinctly points to the sons of the Mullai soil whose occupation is to tend cattle.

He also gives the system by which the Swarams arrange themselves into Inai and Kilai to the given string when the Kural commences in the Kudam (east) and proceeds leftwards.

Silappadikaram, Arangetukathai Page 64.

குரவை என்பது காமமும் வென்றியும் பொருளாகக் குரவைச் செய்யுள் பாட்டாக எழுவரேனும் எண்மரேனும் ஒன்பதின்மரேனும் கைபிணைந்தாடுவது ;

" குரவை என்பது கூறுங் காலைச்
செய்தோர் செய்த காமமும் விறலும்
மெய்தக் கூறும் இயல்பிற் றென்ப "

The term 'Kuravei' means the dancing of seven, eight or nine persons with their hands linked singing a song whose subject is either love or victory.

From the above we see that they styled SA, Mayavan; RI, Pingai; GA, Kaikilai; MA, Oolai; PA, Vellai; DHA Villari and NI, Tharam. "Thuttham and Tharam stood by the side of Kural or Mayavan" means NI and RI stood on either side of SA or Mayavan as NI SA RI. "Oolai and Vilari stood by the side of Paladeva" means that

Ma and Dha stood on either side of Ili or Ma Pa Dha. Kaikilai stood to the left of Thuttham or Ni Sa Ri became Ni Sa Ri Ga. Vilari stood to the right of Tharam or Munthei. This is Ma Pa Dha Ni. This shows that he means the two series Ni Sa Ri Ga and Ma Pa Dha Ni should be identical. Ni Ma should be identical with Sa Pa, Ri Dha and Ga Ni. The intervals between the series Ni Sa Ri Ga should be equal and identical with those between Ma Pa Dha Ni. Thus we see that they satisfy the principle of Kural Oolai.

For the two series Ni Sa Ri Ga and Ma Pa Dha Ni form the ascending series Ni Sa Ri Ga Ma Pa Dha Ni. Here, according to the principle that Oolai must appear in Tharam, Ma is derived from the Ni of the first series. According to the principle that Kural appears in Oolai, Ma, the first Swaram of the second series is derived from Ni of the first series. In the same manner, Ili should be derived from Kural, Thuttham from Ili, Vilari from Thuttham, Kaikilai from Vilari and Tharam from Kaikilai. In other words, the couples Ni-Ma, Ma-Sa, Sa-Pa Pa-Ri, Ri-Dha, Dha-Ga and Ga-Ni should stand concordant in the relation of Shadjam and Madhymam. Proceeding leftwards these same became Kilai strings. We see that only Swarams so derived occur as Sa Ri Ga Ma Pa Dha Ni in a Sthayi. In other words Swarams which do not satisfy the Sa-Ma principle are never concordant.

Just as Kaikilai was mentioned to stand to the left of the series Ni Sa Ri, from the fact that Vilari is mentioned to stand to the right of Tharam or Munthei in the series Ma Pa Dha, we see that Tharam added to Ma Pa Dha becomes Ma Pa Dha Ni. Thus the Aroganam Ni Sa Ri Ga Ma Pa Dha Ni and the Avaroganam Ni Dha Pa Ma Ga Ri Sa Ni are complete. We are reminded here of the song of little girls when they have their Kanni saying "Eight persons for a Vattam, but if there is one less we shall have *nattam* (or loss)" Just as little girls stand in a circle and join their hands two by two and dance, the series Ni Sa Ri Ga Ma Pa Dha Ni not only suited repetition one after another but was also suitable for singing them to the exclusion of one or more Swarams. We do not mean that these two series were repeatedly sung by the two sides. But if one side sang Ma Pa Dha Ni the other side echoed by singing Ni Sa Ri Ga, and if one side repeated Ma Pa Dha, the other side said Ni Sa Ri and Sa Ri Ga was answered by Pa Dha Ni and so on in different ways. Though the habit of varying Swarams is extant at present, experts who sing Pallavi now never sing the Inai Kilai (Vadi Samvadi) Swarams within the Sthayi. But they sing the higher notes in the lower octave. This seems to have been very common among the sons of the Mullai soil in the ancient Tamil country.

The words "குடமுதல் இடமுறையாக் குரல் துத்தம்" indicate that if you proceed from the west it is towards the right and if you proceed from the east it is towards the left. In other words, if we proceed from Rishabam to Mithunam and Kadagam etc., it is rightwards, and it is leftwards if we begin from Thulam and go towards Kanni, Simham, Kadagam etc. Astrology says that the Rasis Mesham, Rishabam and Mithunam are those of the east and that Thulam, Viruchigam and Thanusu belong to the west.

From the above Chakram we see that according to this system the Swarams commence from Rishaba Rasi (Taurus) and go towards the right as Sa Ri Ga Ma in Aroganam, while they proceed leftwards beginning from Thulam (Libra) in the same order Sa Ri Ga Ma. Here the order of Swarams is given when Kural commences in the Oolai of Thulam (Libra) and proceeds leftwards. Here we see that this series Ni Sa Ri stand on either side of the Kural which appears in Thulam (Libra) and Kaikilai to its left. After this we find Ili in Meenam (Pisces) and the Swarams Dha Ma on either side, thus forming the series Ma Pa Dha. From the words ' Vilari stood to the right of Tharam ' the series Ma Pa Dha became Ma Pa Dha Ni. In the series Ni Sa Ri Ga, Tharam is the first Swaram. If the same series are repeated in Aroganam then a Sthayi is complete. So he says that Vilari stood to the right of Tharam because he wanted the Ni which was the first Swaram of the first series to become the last Swaram of the second series. According to this system when the series Sa Ri Ga Ma Pa Dha Ni proceeds leftwards it is Aroganam while Ni Dha Pa Ma Ga Ri Sa when it proceeds rightwards it is Avaroganam. He also says it in another form by mentioning that the Swarams proceeding leftwards are of a higher pitch, while they are of a lower pitch proceeding rightwards.

Silappadikaram Arangatukathai, Page 94.

" யாழ்மேற் பாலை யிடமுறை மெலியக்
குழன்மேற் கோடி வலமுறை மெலிய என்பது.

யாழினிடத்து அரும்பாலை முதலாயின இடமுறை மெலியவும் குழலினிடத்துக் கோடிப்பாலை முதலாயின வலமுறை மெலியவும் பாடப்படுமென்றவாறு" என்று கூறப்பட்டுள்ளது.

In the Yal Aroompalai and other Palais proceeding leftwards produce notes of a lower pitch while in the Kulal (or Flute) Kodipalai and others proceeding leftwards produce tones of a lower pitch.

Here we see that from Kodipalai where Oolai is Kural the series Sa Ni Dha Pa Ma Ga Ri Sa results towards the right. Here he says that towards the right the sounds decrease in pitch. This is so far as the Kulal is concerned. The same, proceeding leftwards, becomes the Aroganam. He calls the Aroganam going leftwards as decreasing in pitch. This shows that the ancient Tamils put the Yal on the ground with its belly downwards and played on it. Thus the Swarams decreased in pitch as one proceeded upwards towards the left in the Yal, while on the Kulal the Swarams decrease towards the right and increase in pitch towards the left.

We know from experience that in the Kulal the ascending scale proceeds towards the left whereas in the Yal it is towards the right. The Yal which in ancient times was known as, '*தெய்வஞ் சான்ற தீந்தொடை நல் யாழ்*" (the celebrated Yal where God lived and which possesed a mellifluous tone) and held in the highest esteem by the Tamils has lost its very name and has now become the Veena. The erect position in which the Yal was held when played made the actions, உந்தல், உறுத்தல், and உருட்டல் possible, but the modern way of making it lie down makes such actions very difficult. The ancient Tamils were capable of many excellent devices in playing without even looking at the instrument. This was very common among them and even at the present day we see such glimpses of them in the playing of M.R.Ry. Sri Venkataramana Doss

Avergal of Vijianagaram. But what we see most at the present day is that though the Swarasthanams are clearly marked and though they have the instrument on their own lap, only false Swarams are heard most!

How Grahaswaram was sung in the three Sthayis with Inai Swarams.

Silappadikaram Aychiarkuravai, Page 407.

" குரன்மந்த மாக விளிசம ஞக
வரன்முறையே துத்தம் வலியா-வுரனிலா
மந்தம் விளரி பிடிப்பா ளவணைட்பின்
பின்றையைப் பாட்டேடுப் பாள் "

அடியார்க்கு நல்லார் :

(இ-ள்) பாட்டெடுக்கின்றவள் குரலென்னும் நரம்பு மந்தரமாக இளியென்னு நரம்பு சமநரமாக வந்த முறையே துத்தமென்னு நரம்பு வலிசரமாக விளரியையும் வலிமையில்லாத மந்தரமாகப் பிடிக்கின்றவள் தன்னட்பு நரம்பாகிய துத்த நரம்பாயவட்குப் பற்றுப்பாடுமென்றான்."

He gives the compass for the three Sthayis Mandham, Oocham and Samam (soft, hard and middling).

Comment:—The damsel who commences the singing takes the Kural string as the beginning of Mandara string, the Ili string as the Madhya string and the Thuttham string as the hard string and the Vilari. The damsel who commences next with the Mandara string commences from the Natpu string or Thuttham and keeps in concordance with the first.

From the above sootram and its comment we see that instructions are given how the series of Swarams should be sung in Mandara, Oocha and Sama Sthayis. The words "குரல் மந்தமாக இளிசமமாக" imply that from Kural in Rishabam to Ili in Dhanus it is Mandara Sthayi, the Kural commencing from Ili in Dhanus up to the next Dhanus it is the Madhya Sthayi and from that up to Meenam it is Tara Sthayi. This he calls வலன்முறை or proceeding rightwards.

Modern Name	Mandara Sthayi.	Madhya Sthayi.	Tara Sthayi.
Ancient Tamil Name.	Mandam. Lower pitch.	Samam. Middling.	High Pitch. Ootcham.
	Sa, Ri, Ga, Ma. Ma, Pa, Dha, Ni.	Pa Dha Ni Sa Ri Ga Ma. Sa Ri Ga Ma Pa Dha Ni.	Pa Dha Ni. Sa Ri Ga.

Here, the first series Sa Ri Ga Ma are the notes of the Mandara Sthayi where Kural is of a low pitch. The series Pa Dha Ni Sa Ri Ga Ma are the Madhya Sthayi where Ili is of a middling pitch. Pa Dha Ni are notes of the Tara Sthayi or very high pitch. These series occur in Vattapalai in two cycles beginning from Rishabam. The same has been called the 14 Kovais in many places. It is clear that the complete *Sancharam* of a ragam was possible in these 14 Swarams in the three Sthayis—Mandara,

Madhya and Tara—, that the Tamils adopted this system and that even Graha Swaram was sung within these 14 Swarams. When these 14 Kovais occurring in the three Sthayis are transferred to Shadjam, the second series given above beginning Ma Pa Dha Ni is the result. This is what we are singing at the present time. This is also called Panchama Sruti now because Shadjam is commenced from the place where Panchamam stands in Vattapalai. Instead of the series Pa Dha Ni Sa Ri Ga Ma we use the series Sa Ri Ga Ma Pa Dha Ni. Each of these notes satisfies the relation of Inai and Kilai of the series Sa-Pa, Pa-Ri, Ri-Dha, Dha-Ga, Ga-Ni, Ni-Ma and Ma-Sa. So it is quite appropriate that it should be called Panchama Sruti.

The Sempalai Series (where Kural is taken as Kural) should form the series for Shadja Gramam. In the same manner he giyes seven Palais for the seven Swarams. Of these, Arumpalai which appears in Panchamam is called Shadja gramam by Saranga Dev. Apart from this, it is clear that when one party sang Ri Ga Ma Pa or Ri Ga Ma Pa Dha, commencing from Rishabam in the Tara Sthayi, the opposite party responded by singing the series Dha Ni Sa Ri or Dha Ni Sa Ri Ga commencing with the Dha or Vilari which is the Inai Swaram for Rishabam from the Mandara Sthayi up to Madhya Sthayi. The words " துத்தம் வலியாய்" imply that Thutthham was sung in Tara Sthayi or Oocham, and the words" உரனிலாமந்தம் விளரி பிடிப்பாள்" indicate that she sang Vilari which occurs in Mandara Sthayi as Grahaswaram while its Inai Swaram or Itapam was commenced as Graha Swaram. The Ga and Ni were exactly in the same way as Rishabam and Da. They sang Sa Ri Ga Ma and Sa Ri Ga Ma Pa in the higher or Oocha Sthayi and Pa Dha Ni Sa and Pa Dha Ni Sa Ri in the Mandara Sthayi. Thus they sang each Swaram in all the Mandara, Madhya and Tara Sthayis. This was the method of ganam of the ancients. But if we enquire whether such a system exists even among the best exponents of Indian Music who sing Pallavis we find that the majority of them are ignorant of it. For in the modern times it is the practice to repeat the same notes in the different Sthayis—Sa Ri Ga Ma in the Tara Sthayi is followed by Sa Ri Ga Ma in the Madhya Sthayi. If they sing variations in Sa Ri Ga Ma in the Tara Sthayi the same variations will occur in the Mandara Sthayi also. The same notes will be repeated in different octaves but they will never be Inai or concordant Swarams. The sounds Ni Sa Ri Ga in the Tara Sthayi should have Ma Pa Dha Ni of the Mandara Sthayi as grahaswarams and not the Ni Sa Ri Ga of the Mandara Sthayi which is quite against the rules of Isai Tamil. So when one set sings the Swarams of one Sthayi with its variations the other set begins with the Inai Swaram of the series in the other Sthayi and goes on introducing variations. For example if one commences with Thuttham as Graha Swaram in the higher Sthayi and finishes after many variations the other starts with Dha of the Mandara Sthayi as Grahaswaram and goes through the identical variations where the Swarams of the two different octaves stand in the relation of Inai Swarams.

As the ganam of the ancient Tamils is not much in use now, we find it necessary to give below a few series so that it may be clearly understood. It should be noted that the swarams with a dot on the top belong to the higher octaves and those with a dot under, to the lower octaves.

Sankarabaranam.

1

மபதநி
mpdn
மபத பதநி
mpd pdn
மப பத தநி
mp pd dn
மபத பதநி தபம
mpd pdn dpm
மதபத பநிதநி தபம
mdpd pndn dpm
மபபத பததநி தபம
mppd pddn dpm
மப பத தநிநித தப பம
mp pd dnnd dp pm
மபபம பததப தநிநித தபபம
mppm pddp dnnd dppm
மமபப மத பநி நிப தம பபமம
mmpp md pn np dm ppmm

நிஸரிக
nsrg
நிஸரி ஸரிக
nsr srg
நிஸ ஸரி ரிக
ns sr rg
நிஸரி ஸரிக ரிஸநி
n sr srg rsn
நிரிஸரி ஸகரிக ரிஸநி
nrsr sgrg rsn
நிஸஸரி ஸரிரிக ரிஸநி
nssr srrg rsn
நிஸ ஸரி ரிக கரி ரிஸ ஸநி
ns sr rg gr rs sn
நிஸஸநி ஸரிரிஸ ரிககரி நிஸஸநி
nssn srrs rggr nssn
நிநிஸஸ நிரி ஸக கஸ ரிநி ஸஸநிநி
nnss nr sg gs rn ssnn

2

ரிக்ம்ப்த்
rgmpd
ரிரிக் க்க்ம் ம்ம்ப் ப்ப்த்
rrg ggm mmp ppd
ரிக்ரி க்ம்க் ம்ப்ம் த்ப்ம் ப்ம்க் ம்க்ரி
rgr gmg mpm dpm pmg mgr
ரிக்ரிக் க்ம்க்ம் ம்ப்ம்ப் த்ப்ம்க்ரி
rgrg gmgm mpmp dpmgr
ரிக்க்ம்ம்ம்ப்த் த்ப்த்ப்ப்ம்ப்ம்க்ரி
rgagmammapd dpdppmpmgr
ரிம் க்ப் ம்த் த்ம் ப்க் ம்ரி
rm gp md dm pg mr
ரிம்க்க்ப்ம் ம்த்ப் த்ப்ம்ப்ம்க் ம்க்ரி
rmggpm mdp dpmpmg mgr
ரிக்க்ம்க்ம்ம்ப்ம்ப்ப்த் த்ப்ப்ம்ப்ம்ம்க்ரி
rggmgmmpmppd dppmpmmgr
ரிம்க்ரி ரிக் ப்ம்க்க்ம் த்ப்ம்ம்ப்ம்க்ரி
rmgr rg pmggm dpmmpmgr

தநிஸரிக
dnsrg
த தநி நிநிஸ ஸஸரி ரிரிக
d dn nns ssr rrg
தநித நிஸநி ஸரிஸ கரிஸ ரிஸநி ஸநித
dnd nsn srs grs rsn snd
தநிதநி நிஸநிஸ ஸரிஸரி கரிஸநித
dndn nsns srsr grsnd
தநிநிஸஸரி ரிக கரிகரிரிஸரிஸநித
dnnssr rg grgrrsrsnd
தஸநிரி ஸக கஸ ரிநி ஸத
dsnr sg gs rn sd
தஸநி நிரிஸ ஸகரி கரிஸ ரிஸநி ஸநித
dsn nrs sgr grs rsn snd
தநிநிஸநிஸஸரிஸரிரிககரிரிஸரிஸஸநித
dnnsnssrsrrggrrsrssnd
தஸநிதத நிரிஸநிநி ஸகரிஸஸ ரிஸநித
dsndd nrsnn sgrss rsnd

3

ச ரி க ம ப	ப த நி ச ரி
s r g m p	p d n s r
ச ரி க ம ரி க ம ப	ப த நி ச த நி ச ரி
s r g m r g m p	p d n s d n s r
சச ரிரி கக கக ம பா	பப தத நிநி சரி
ss rr gg gg m p	pp dd nn sr
ச ரி க ரி ரி க ம க க ம பா	ப த நி த த நி ச நி நி ச ரி
s r g r r g m g g m p	p d n d d n s n n s r
ச க ரி ச ரி ம க ரி க ப ம க ரி ச	ப நி த ப த ச நி த நி ரி ச நி த ப
s g r s r m g r g p m g r s	p n d p d s n d n r s n d p
ச க ரி ம ரி ம க ப ப ம க ரி ச	ப நி த ச த ச நி ரி ரி ச நி த ப
s g r m r m g p p m g r s	p n d s d s n r r s n d p
ச ச க ரி ரி ரி ம க க க ப ம க ரி ச	ப ப நி த த த ச நி நி நி ரி ச நி த ப
s s g r r r m g g g p m g r s	p p n d d d s n n n r s n d p
ச க ரி க ரி ரி ம க ம க க ப ம ப ம க ரி ச	ப நி த நி த த ச நி ச நி நி ரி ச ரி ச நி த ப
s g r g r r m g m g g p m p m g r s	p n d n d d s n s n n r s r s n d p
ச ரி ச க ரி ரி ரி க ரி ம க க க ம க ப ம ம க ரி ச	ப த ப நி த த த நி த ச நி நி நி ச நி ரி ச ச நி த ப
s r s g r r r g r m g g g m g p m m g r s	p d p n d d d n d s n n n s n r s s n d p

Here we see that one party repeated the series of Vadi Swarams and its variations while it was echoed by the opposite party which sang the Samvadi Swarams and its variations. Moreover Pahs were composed in those Swarams which satisfied the above principle and were sung antiphonally. We shall note below one or two examples of their antiphonal singing :—

Silappadikaram Aychiarkuravai, Page 408.

க   "கன்று குணிலாக் கனியுதிர்த்த மாயவ
னின்றுநம் மானுள் வருமே லவன்வாயிற்
கொன்றையந் தீங்குழல் கேளாமோ தோழீ"

(இ-ள்) தோழீ, நிரை மேய்க்கின் றழி விளவின் கனியையுதிர்க்கவேண்டி அவ்விடத்தில் மேய்கின்ற பசுவின் கன்றைக் குறுந்தடியாகக்கொண்டு உதிர்த்த மாயவன் நம் வழிபாட்டால் இங்குள்ள பசு நிரையிடத்து வருவன்; அங்ஙனம் வந்தால் அவனூதும் கொன்றையங் குழலோசையைக் கேட்போமென்றுளென்க.

Comment. "Oh damsel ! Mayava who brought down the Vilam fruit (wood apple) growing in the fields by using a calf as a stick may be attracted by our song and come into the field where the cows are grazing : if he does come we may have a chance of hearing him play his sweet flute made of the Kondrai tree."

உ   "பாம்பு கயிறாக் கடல்கடைந்த மாயவ
னீங்குநம் மானுள் வருமே லவன்வாயி
லாம்பலந் தீங்குழல் கேளாமோ தோழீ"

(இ-ள்) தோழீ, கடலைக் கடைகின்ற காலத்து மேருவரை மத்தாகிற் சுற்றுக் கயிறு வாசுகி யென்னும் பாம்பாகச் சுற்றிக் கடைந்த மாயவன் நம் வழிபாட்டால் ஈங்கு நம் மானிடத்து வருவான்; அங்ஙனம் வந்தால் அவனூதும் இனிய ஆம்பலங் குழலோசையைக் கேட்போமென்றுளென்க.

Comment. "Oh! damsel! Mayava who used the Meru as the Matthu (revolving dasher) and the serpent (Vasuki) as the cord to churn the Sea of Milk might be attracted by our song and come near the field here. If he comes, we may have a chance of hearing him play his sweet flute made of the Ambal.

ஈ " கொல்லையஞ் சாரற் குருந்தொசித்த மாயவ
னெல்லைநம் மானுள் வருமே லவன்வாயின்
முல்லையந் தீங்குழல் கேளாமோ தோழீ"

(இ-ள்) தோழீ, நம் புனக்கொல்லையைச் சார்ந்த விடத்து வஞ்சனையால் வந்து நின்ற குருந்தை முறித்த மாயவன் நம்வழிபாட்டாற் பகலே இங்குள்ள நம் ஆனிரையுள் வருவன்; அவன் அங்ஙனம் வந்தால் அவனூதும் இனிய முல்லையங் குழலோசையைக் கேட்போமென்றுரைக்க

Comment. Odamsel ! Mayava, who destroyed Kuranda who came with deceitful intentions into our field, may be attracted by our song and come into the field during the day. If he does come, we may hear him play his sweet flute made of the Mullai.

On pages 409 to 415 of Silappadikaram we find the same kinds of Pahs repeated. They invariably express a wish that their people and their cattle should live long without any disease. They also express a wish that their ruler Thennavan should triumph over his enemies and that his victorious drum should ever be heard. They said these antiphonally and danced their Kuravai.

We have noticed the following game of children in the streets. One party asks in the same tone " what will you do when the people of the two kingdoms come against you?" The other party answers in a slightly higher pitch. " We shall all escape with one accord." The singing of Aychiar Kuravai was something like this. But the ganam of the ancient Tamils seems to have been highly efficient in the system of Gheetams and in the excellent ideas contained therein.

This is exactly the way to sing Grahaswaram. By this means, Ragas do not change, exposition is not spoiled and the relationship of Inai Swarams is also kept up. Though it is out of use at present, it can be easily brought into practice.

Saranga Dev in his Raga Viveka Adhyaya makes mention here and there of Dhaivata Gramam, Madhyma Gramam, Gandhara Gramam and such like. They could be sung only according to the system of Karnatic music but never according to the principle of 22 Srutis.

If Srutis are different in Aroganam and Avaroganam, that which binds the different *amsams* of a Ragam will be undone. Even supposing that a Sruti is same while ascending and descending, if proceeded with by thirteens, the same Sruti will not result in Avaroganam. Even when ganam is made by shifting the four Srutis of Shadja Gramam, the Srutis will not be the same in Aroganam and Avaroganam nor will we obtain the beautiful and charming Ragas which are in practical use at the present day.

After such a clear exposition, we need not accept any theory however it may differ from this wholesale. Those who bring forward such wrong theories and those who accept them should be considered as people without any music in them. Those who after hearing the Sa Pa series sounded to them still continue in doubt will never understand what is written in books and shall ever continue in a state of uncertainty. Could any body be still in doubt when it is proved that Swarams are derived by the Sa-Pa and the Sa-Ma principles and stand as sevenths and fifths to the standard Swaram in the Rasi-mandalam (Zodiac)? We understand that Pa-Sa which is like

Sakti-Sivam and SA-MA which is like Sivam-Sakti stand as the Alpha and the Omega of the Sapta Swarams, as the underlying principle for the 12 Swarams of the Sthayi, as the Moorchana with seven Swarams and as the sound which occurs as a regular and uniform series.

21. How the Swarams of Isai Tamil agree with the principles of Astrology.

The Tamils have clearly mentioned how the 24 Srutis used in the music of South India can be distributed in the Rasi Mandalam, (zodiac), how the 12 Swarams occurring in the 12 Rasis (Signs) form the 12 palais, how they stand in the relation of Inai, Kilai, Pagai and Natpu, how a particular series will be concordant with another series and which of these concordant Swarams will go to make up the number 7. Just as seven planets move through the cycle of Rasis and just as the Sun goes round the 12 Rasis passing through a Sign each month, so also in music the Kural or SA keeps changing in each of the 12 Swarams and the location of the seven Swarams concordant with the above is made possible.

We have noted before this that the efficiency of the Tamils in astrology was quite in proportion to the efficiency they had attained in the science and art of music. Many of the minute principles of astrology were used by them in music also. Though we are unable to come across any work on astrology now yet the fact that the Tamils were proficient in that science from very early times is accepted. We give below a Sootram by Nallanduvanar, one of the writers of the last Sangam which flourished nearly 1900 years to 2000 years ago. It is a Paripadal pointing out the time when the rain commenced in the Sayya hill, and the commentary said to have been written on it by Parimelalagar.

In the Paripadal composed by Nallanduvanar and set to music by Naganar, it is said,

ஆசிரியர் நல்லந்துவனார் பாடியதும் நாகனார் இசையமைத்ததுமாகிய அடியிற்கண்ட பரிபாடலில்,

'விரிகதிர் மதியொடு வியல்விசும்பு புணர்ப்ப
வெரிசடை யெழில்வேழத் தலையெனக் கீழிருந்து
தெருவிடைப் படுத்தமூன் றொன்பதிற் றிருக்கையு
ளுருகெழு வெள்ளிவந் தேறியல்சேர வருடைப்
படிமகன் வாய்ப்பப் பொருடகுபுந்தி மிதுனம்
பொருந்தப் புலர்விடிய லங்கியுயர்நிற்ப வந்தணன்
பங்குவி னில்லத்துணைக்குப் பாலெய்த விறையமன்
வில்லிற் கடைமகர மேவப்பாம் பொல்லை
பொதியின் முனிவன் புரைவரைக் கீறி
மிதுன மடைய விரிகதிர் வேனில்
திரவரவு மாரி யியைகென விவற்றுற்
புரைகெழு சையம் பொழிமழை தாழ
நெரிதரூஉம் வையைப் புனல்'

(இ-ள்) விசும்பு மதியத்தொடு புணர்ப்பனவாகிய வெரியுஞ் சடையும் வேழமு முதலாக வவற்றின் மேழிருந்த வீதியால் வேறுபடுக்கப்பட்ட வோரோன் றொன்பது நாளாகிய மூவகை இராசிகளுள் மேலவாய நாண்மீன்களைத் தொழுதாகிய மதிபுணர்தலாவ தவ்வோர்நிற்றன் மாத்திரமாகலின் அவற்றை விசும்பு புணர்ப்பன வென்றார்.

எரி—அங்கியைத் தெய்வமாகவுடைய கார்த்திகை; அதனுலதன் முதலாதலையுடைய விடப முணர்த்தப்பட்டது.

சடை—சடையையுடைய வீசனைத் தெய்வமாகவுடைய திருவாதிரை; அதனுலதனையுடைய மிதுன முணர்த்தப்பட்டது.

வேழம்—வேழத்திற்கு யோனியாகிய பரணி அதனுலதனையுடைய மேழ முணர்த்தப்பட்டது.

இவை முதலாக விவற்றின் மேழிருத்தலாவ திவற்றது பெயரான் இடபவீதி மிதுனவீதி மேடவீதி யென வகுக்கப்பட்ட இம்மூவகை வீதியுள்ளுமடங்குதல்.

அவற்றுள், இடபவீதி கன்னி துலா மீன மேடமென்பன ; மேடவீதி, இடபம் மிதுனங் கற்கடகஞ் சிங்கமென்பன.

ஓரிராசியாவது இரண்டேகா லாளகலின் நாலான்கிராசியாகிய விவை யோரோன் றொன்பது நாளாயின. கோட்களுக் கெடனுகலானிவை பன்னிரண்டு மிருக்கையெனப்பட்டன.

சிறத்தையுடைய வெள்ளி இடபத்தைச் சேரச், செவ்வாய் மேடத்தைச் சேரப், புதன் மிதுனத் தைச் சேரக், கார்த்திகை யுச்சமாக விடிதலுண்டாக வியாழஞ் சனியினில்ல மிரண்டாகிய மகரங்கும்பங் கட் குப்பாலையாகிய மீனத்தைச் சேர, யமனைத் தமயனுகவுடைய சனி வில்லுக்குப் பின்னுகிய மகரத்தைச் சேர, விராகு மதிமறையும்படி வருநாளின்கண் ஆதித்தன் மேத்தையடையவென்பார் 'புலர் விடியலங்கியுயர் நிற்ப'என்றார்.

பாம்பு மதியமறையவொல்லை வருநாளென்றது அவ் வாவணிமாதத்து மதிநிறை நாளாகிய வவிட்டத்தை எனவே, மதியுமிராகுவு மகரத்து நிற்க வென்பதூஉம், கேது வதற் கேழாமிடமாகிய கற்கடகத்து நிற்க வென்பதூஉம் பெறப்பட்டன.

இதனுற் சொல்லிய தாவணித்திங்க ளவிட்ட நாளி னிக்கோட்க டமக்குரிய நிலமாகிய விவ்விராசி களி னிற்பச் சோமனை யரவு தீண்ட வென்பதாயிற்று.

அகத்திய னென்னுமீன் உயர்ந்த தன்னிடத்தைக் கடந்து மிதுனத்தைப் பொருந்த அப்பொதியிலே யிட்டெனவுந் தோன்ற நின்றது.

முதுமினை வெயிலையுடைய முதுவேனிற்குப் பின்வருங் கார்காலத்து மழைபெய்கவென்ற விவ்வீதி வழியாதுயர்ந்த சையமலைக்கண் மழைபெய்ய.

Eri :—Asterism Krithika (Y. Tauri, Alcyone) whose deity is fire ; it denotes sign Taurus.

Sadai :—Asterism Ardhra (a Crionis) whose deity is Iswara ; it denotes sign Gemini.

Vêzham :—Asterism Bharani (35 Arieties and Musca) to which is ascribed the organ of reproduction in the elephant ; it denotes sign Aries.

These and the other signs constitute what are known as Idapa (Taurus) Veedhi (Range), Mithuna (Gemini) Veedhi and Mesha (Aries) Veedhi. Idapa Veedhi comprises Virgo, Libra, Pisces and Aries ; Mesha Veedhi comprises Taurus, Gemini, Cancer and Leo. Each Veedhi of four signs has nine days, each sign representing two days and a quarter. The twelve Rasis (Signs) are the houses of the Planets.

It seems that Parimelalagar flourished at the time of Natchinarkiniyar where as Nallanduvanar belongs to the last Sangam. He may be said to have lived about 1000 years ago. He was the author of Kalithogai. The Rasi Chakaram given below will explain the ideas contained in Paripadal quoted above.

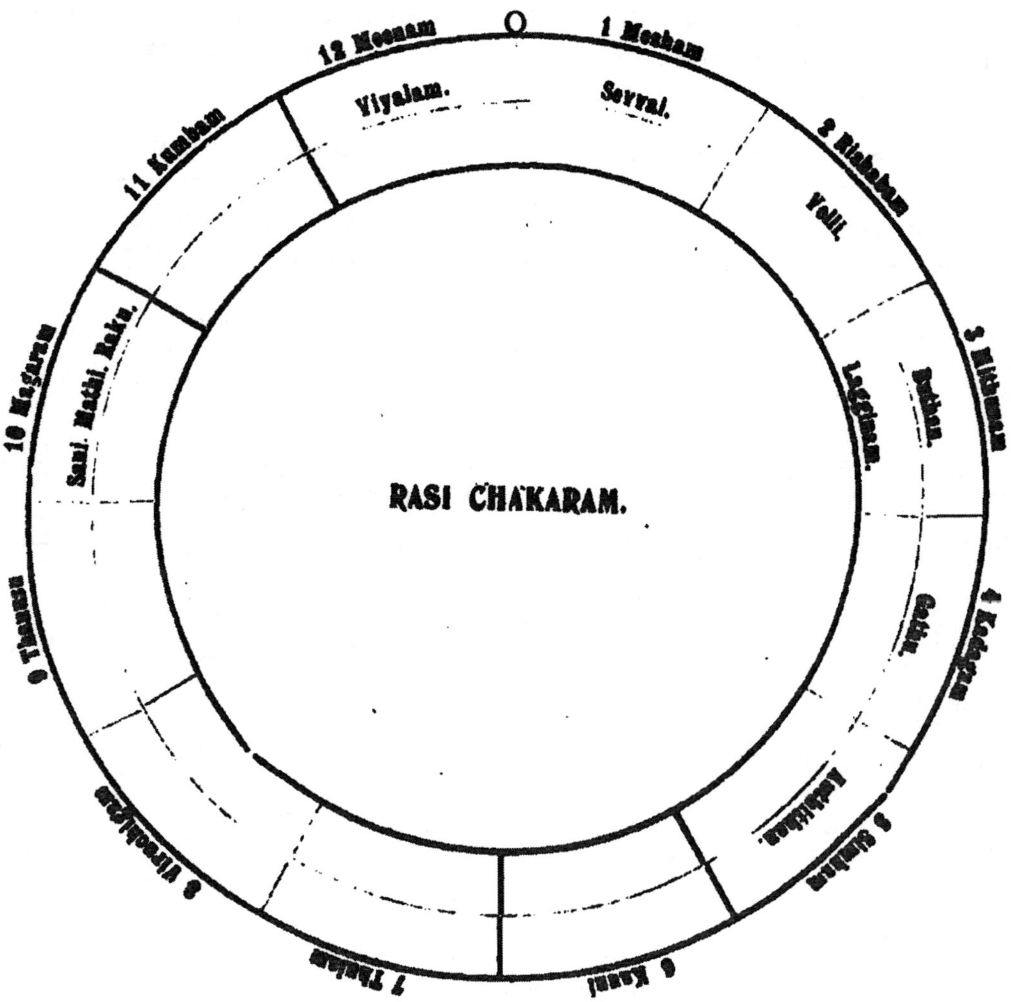

Though there are many things in connection with Astrology that might be noted here we have only selected a few ideas necessary to establish the fact that the ancient Tamils were efficient in the science.

When we look into the Vattapalai and its construction given by the ancient inhabitants of South India, we not only see that they had made researches and were efficient in music but they had adopted into music many of the Amsams of Astrology in which they were equally efficient. The 12 Swarams were arranged in the 12 Rasis, commencing from Mesham; they were classified into Inai, Kilai, Pagai and Natpu and their relationship defined. As the commencing Swaram or SA is near the Meru, if we suppose it to be the closing twelfth place to the Sthayi below it, then the commencing Swaram for the sthayi above it will be Itapam. The twelfth Swaram for this rightwards will be Rishabam if we commence from Mithunam. The 12th Sthanam has been styled the Moksha Sthanam.

For the 12 Sthanams from the Lakinam to the Moksham they have given the particular results for the particular Sthanams. The following extracts as given from works on Astrology will illustrate it. Although the results for each Sthanam are given in detail we have copied only such brief results as are recognised in the modern day.

1	2	3	4	5	6
Lakinam	Wealth	Brothers and Sisters	Mother	Intelligence	Enemies
Life	Family	Prowess	Acquisition of knowledge	Sons	Diseases
Physique	Eyes	Servants	Carriages	Good deeds of previous birth	Calamity
Period of life	Words		Earth	Uncles	Enmity
Appearance			God		

7	8	9	10	11	12
Kalathiram	Length of life	Pithur	Occupation	Ayam	Moksham
Health	Death	Happiness	Deeds	Profit	Extravagance
Pleasure	Loss	Charity	Profession	Elder brother	House
Marriage	Enmity	Guru	Travelling		Sleep
Ornaments		Father	Sacred duties		
		Knowledge			

The twelfth place is called Moksha Sthanam. The seventh is called Kalathrasthanam. In the same way the Sthanams 1, 2, 3 generally called by the name on the first line, may also be called by the names given under. This system should be compared with the quotations given below :—

In addition to this some Sthanams are productive of good results and some portend calamity. This is given in Astrology as quoted below. These very nearly correspond to what is given in music also.

Kendiram	1, 4, 7, 10
Thirikonam	1, 5, 9,
Maraivu	3, 6, 8, 12
Panaparam	2, 11
Parvai	5, 7, 9
Full Parvai	7,

Three quarters Parvai 5, 9
Complete lucky Sthanams 1, 2, 4, 5, 7, 9
Unlucky Sthanams 3, 6, 8, 10 and 12.

The powerful Sthanams for all Grahams are Ootcham, Atchi, Kendiram, Moolathirikonam. All planets give pleasant results in 5 and 9 while 3, 6, 8 and 12 invariably give bad results. If the Grahams to the given Lakinam are in Kendiram, Thirikonam, Atchi and Ootcham they invariably give good results.

The sun from the first to the sixth Rasi is called life and after six it is called body.

We noted before that the Swaram in the fifth Rasi to the given Swaram and the Swaram to the fifth of it and the Swaram to the fifth of it and so on, are in the principle of Sa-Ma. In the same way we noted that the Swarams in the seventh Rasi to the given string were in the relation of Sa-Pa. This very same principle has been followed by Astrologers as Kendiram and Thirikonam. But there is one difference. Musicians have always omitted the commencing Rasi whereas Astrologers have included that also in counting by sevens. In music, the seventh Rasi is calculated omitting the commencing Rasi whereas in Astrology the commencing Rasi is included in calculating by sevens. The truth of this may be known from the following stanza and its comment.

Sinendiramalai, Kandapolipu p. 17.

" ஐந்துமதற் கைந்து மதற்கைந்து மென்னுமிவை
யைந்தோன்ப தோடுதய மாகுமே-முந்திய
கோண முதயமைந்தேன் கோணமிரண் டொன்பஃதேன்
கோணமூன் றாகக் குறி "

(இ-ள்) கோணங்களாவது ஐந்தாமிராசியும் ஐந்தாமிராசிக்கு ஐந்தாமிராசியும், ஐந்தாமிராசி ஐந்தாமிராசிக்கு ஐந்தாமிராசியுமாம். இவைமுறையே ஐந்தாமிராசி ஒன்பதாமிராசி உதயவிராசி என்றின்றனவாம். இவற்றில் உதயவிராசியை முதற்கோணமென்றும் ஐந்தா மிராசியை இரண்டாங்கோணமென்றும் ஒன்பதாம் இராசியை மூன்றாங்கோணமென்றுஞ்சொல்லப்படும்.

Comment.—The Konams stand by fifths. There are the fifth Rasi, the ninth Rasi and the Oothaya Rasi. Here Oothaya Rasi is the first Konam, the fifth Rasi the second Konam and the ninth Rasi, the third Konam.

" எழுவதற்கு நான்காகு நீர்க்கீ ழிதற்குப்
பழுதின்றிப் பாநோன் காகும்-வழுவின்றி
யுச்சியத னன்கா மதற்குதய நான்கேன்ப
விச்சைகோணற் கண்டத் தியல் "

(இ-ள்) கண்டங்களாவது நான்காமிராசியும் நான்காமிராசிக்கு நான்காமிராசியும் நான்காமிராசி நான்காமிராசிக்கு நான்காமிராசியும் நான்காமிராசி நான்காமிராசிக்கு நான்காமிராசியுமாம். இவை முறையே நான்காமிராசி ஏழாமிராசி பத்தாமிராசி உதய விராசி என்றின்றனவாம். இவற்றில் உதயவிராசியை உதயகண்டமென்றும், நான்காமிராசியை நீர்க்கீழ்க்கண்டமென்றும், ஏழாமிராசியைப்பாட்டுக்கண்டமென்றும் பத்தாமிராசியை உச்சிக்கண்டமென்றும் சொல்லப்படும்".

Comment :—The Kandams proceed by fourths. There are the fourth, the seventh, the tenth and the Oothaya Rasis. Of these the Oothaya Rasi is called Oothayakandam, the fourth is called the Neerkeelkandam, the seventh Pattukandam and the tenth Ootchikandam.

In the above stanzas he makes mention of the Kendira Sthanams, namely, 4, 7, 10 and 1 obtained while proceeding by fourths and the Thirikona Sthanams, 5, 9, and 1 obtained while proceeding by fifths. We have noted before that the fourth Rasi is the Natpu string and that the Swarams arrange themselves therein as SA-GA ; that the fifths are the Kilai strings and that proceeding by the SA-MA principle we might obtain therein the 12 Swarams of the Sthayi.

In the same way, proceeding by sevens is the SA-PA principle. This is also an excellent system for obtaining the 12 Swarams of the Sthayi. Ilankovadigal calls the seventh place Vannapatadai. The word 'Vannam' means 'colour' or 'letter'. Here he gives the particular name 'Varnam' to the seven Swarams. Again, a difficulty may be presented on account of the fact that in Astrology the Rasis proceed by fourths or fifths or sevenths including the commencing Rasi where as in music the commencing Rasi is left out in the calculation. In music the commencing Swaram is the standard from which all the other Swarams are derived. The sound in the Meru is the Shadjam. This may be made of a higher or a lower pitch to suit the compass of the human voice. So if the SA is first determined the other Swarams might stand in different concordant relations, the finishing SA of the Madhya Sthayi can be arranged to have double the intensity of the first SA ; the finishing SA of the Mandara Sthayi is rightly called the Standard Swaram.

Even at the present day Srutis are calculated from Itapam. Besides this, in astrology, when the results of the seventh house are declared it is done in view of those of the eighth house. Again when the results of the Lakina Sthanam which is the seventh from the seventh house are given out, they are declared in proportion to the strength of the next house. The result of the Kalathira Sthanam or the seventh is determined in conjunction with that of the eighth or the Kudumba Sthanam, and the result of the Kalathira Sthanam to the Kalathira Sthanam or Purusha Sthanam is declared in conjunction with the next or its Kudumba Sthanam. So we are able to determine how the wife will behave, how she will look after the household, how a bride will agree with the bridegroom, how she will manage the household and so on. In the same way points 1, 2, 3 and 4 can be clearly decided in conjunction with the respective Kudumba Sthanam. The result of the second house or Kudumba Sthanam can be determined in conjunction with the third house which is its Kudumba Sthanam. It is of general use that the result of the fourth or the Vidya Sthanam is decided in conjunction with its fourth or the seventh house, that of the ninth with the ninth from it, and that of the tenth with the tenth from it. In the same way the 12 Swarams which are a regular series of fifths are arranged as a gradually ascending series. In the same way the 12 Inai Swarams which are a series of the SA-PA relationship are the results of proceeding by sevenths.

Again, just as results are different in the different points 1, 2, 3, 4 for the given Lakinam in a Rasi vattam and when the Lakinam changes to the different Rasis the results are proportionately different so also when Kural changes the graham it derives the different Swarams from that Rasi which stand in the relation of Inai, Kilai. Pagai and Natpu.

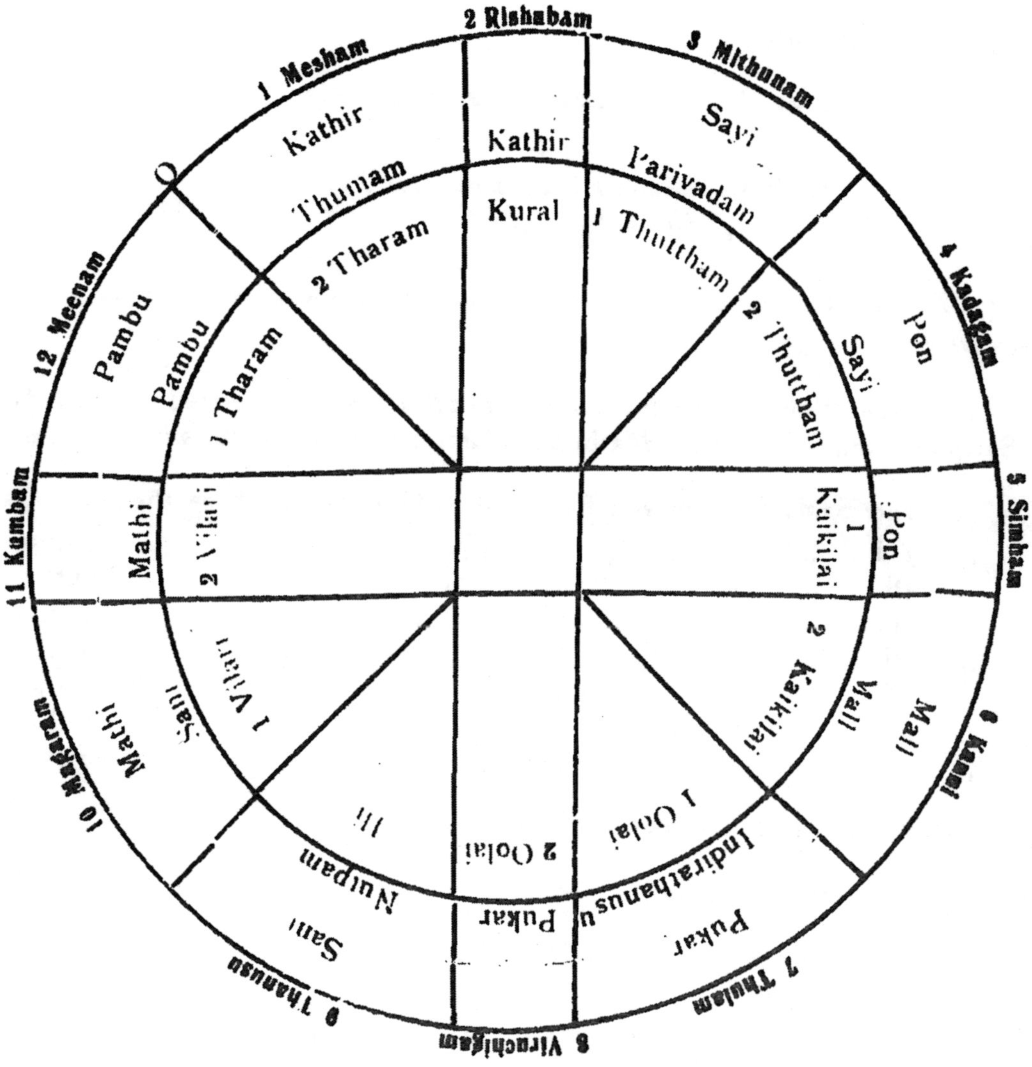

We noted on Page 604 the stanza " ஆறிலு மாகும் போர்க் கீர்த் தெறிநிலைக் கண் " and its meaning. In the same way all the Vattapalai Chakarams have been divided into 12 Rasis and explained. However, the above Chakaram should also be studied in the light of Astrology. Here we notice that we commence from Mesham and end with Meenam and that the compartments Kadir. SA, PA, Maul, Pugar, Sani, Mathi and Pambu are to the right.

In the same manner, commencing from Itapam and up to Mithunam the following stand to the left, namely. Kadir, Thoomam, Pambu, Mathi, Sani, Nutpam, Pugar, Indira Thanusu, Mal, Pon, Sai, and Parivedam in the third enclosure. These are known as *சார்துறைக் கோட்கள்.*

The following stanza explains the above.

Sinendramalai Kandapolipu p. 40.

" கதிர்சேய்பொன் மாலோன் புகர்சனியுங் கற்றை
மதிபாம் பறதியாய் வைத்து-மதியார்
கதிராதி காலங்கோண் டேழுரையா லோட்ட
லதிராத வெண்கோட்கு மாம்."

(இ-ள்.) *கதிர் சேய் பொன் மால் புகர் சனி மதி பாம்பு ஆகிய ஆருடக்கோட்கள் எட்டையும் நிறுத்த முறையே உதித்தொரு சாமத்திற்கு*

Comment.—When the right arooda compartments are arranged in the order of Kadir, Sai, Pon, Mal, Pugar, Sani, Mathi and Pambu. a samam results in each case

The	2nd	Samam	is	derived	from	the 8 directions	such as the	East
,,	3rd	,,	,,	,,	,,	,,		South-east
,,	4th	,,	,,	,,	,,	,,		South
,,	5th	,,	,,	,,	,,	,,		South-west
,,	6th	,,	,,	,,	,,	,,		West
,,	7th	,,	,,	,,	,,	,,		North-west
,,	8th	,,	,,	,,	,,	,,		North
,,		,,	,,	,,				North-east

All these proceed towards the right.

Sinendramalai Kandapolipu p. 42.

" இரவி யெழுதூமம் வாளரவ மிந்து
பரவுசனி நுட்பம்பார்க் கோனும்-விரவிய
வில்லோடே மால்பொன்சேய் வேடமிவை யீராறு
நல்கடிகை யவ்வைந்தாய் நாட்டே "

இ-ள். *கதிர் தூமம் பாம்பு மதி சனி நுட்பம் புகர் இந்திரதனுசு மால் பொன் சேய் பரிவேடம் ஆகிய ஆருடக்கோட்கள்-கூ யும்-நிறுத்த முறையே உதித்து.*

Comment.—The 12 arooda compartments such as Kadir, Thoomam, Pambu, Mathi, Sani, Nutpam, Pugar, Indra Thanusu, Mal, Pon, Sai, and Parivedam when arranged in order.

The	1st	Vattam falls in the 12 Rasis beginning with	Rishabam
,,	2nd	,, ,, ,, ,, ,, ,, ,,	Mesham
,,	3rd	,, ,, ,, ,, ,, ,, ,,	Meenam
,,	4th	,, ,, ,, ,, ,, ,, ,,	Kumbam
,,	5th	,, ,, ,, ,, ,, ,, ,,	Magaram
,,	6th	,, ,, ,, ,, ,, ,, ,,	Thanusu
,,	7th	,, ,, ,, ,, ,, ,, ,,	Viruchikam
,,	8th	,, ,, ,, ,, ,, ,, ,,	Thulam
,,	9th	,, ,, ,, ,, ,, ,, ,,	Kanni
,,	10th	,, ,, ,, ,, ,, ,, ,,	Simham
,,	11th	,, ,, ,, ,, ,, ,, ,,	Kadagam
,,	12th	,, ,, ,, ,, ,, ,, ,,	Mithunam

These are arranged on the left.

These are called *கரந்துறைக்கோட்கள்* commencing from Thoomam.

> " கதிர்முதற்பாம் பீறகக் காட்டியவெண் கோட்க
> தேதருநீ கானமுதற் றேன்றி-விதியே
> யிடம்வரும் வாராதி யெல்லாரும் பின்ன
> ரடையவரு மூன்றேமுக் கால் "

இ-ள். கதிர், சேய் பொன் மால் புகர் சனி மதி பாம்பு ஆகிய ஆருடக் கோட்கள் எட்டும் நிறுத் முறையே அவற்றை வாராதிபன் முதலாக உதித்து

Comment.—The eight arooda compartments such as Kathir, Sai, Pon, Mal, Pugar, Sani, Mathi and Pambu commencing from Varathibam (Meenam) are arranged thus :—

The	1st	Muhoortham occurs in the eight directions beginning from	North-east
,,	2nd	,, ,, ,, ,,	North
,,	3rd	,, ,, ,, ,,	North-west
,,	4th	,, ,, ,, ,,	West
,,	5th	,, ,, ,, ,,	South-west
,,	6th	,, ,, ,, ,,	South
,,	7th	,, ,, ,, ,,	South-east
,,	8th	,, ,, ,, ,,	East

The other 8 Muhoorthams are arranged in the eight directions leftwards. When we say that Varathiban stands to the North East when the Muhoortham commences means that Meenam or Varathiban has four quarters in the first part and two quarters in the next part of the Rasi. The same rule obtains for the others also. These Arooda compartments are called *வாரக்கோட்கள்* as they commence from Varathiban. A Muhoortham is $3\frac{3}{4}$ Naligais.

Here he mentions how the Varakoals such as Kathir, Sai, Pon &c., are arranged to the right, and how the Karanthurai Koals such as Kathir, Thoomam, Pambu &c., are arranged towards the left in the 12 Rasis such as Itapam &c. The day is divided into 8 Samams and the Varakoals commencing from Kathir are made to occur one after the other rightwards. Again, the Naligais of a day are divided into 12 and how the 12 Karanthurai koals commencing from Thoomam are arranged leftwards in the Rasis commencing from Mesham is also shown. The facts that the Varakoals change the Graham every week and the Karanthurai koals keep changing leftwards are spoken at length there. In accordance with the same system we have seen how the Sapta Swarams Sa Ri Ga Ma Pa Dha Ni stand concordant by the relation of Sa-Pa towards the right and by the relation of Sa-Ma towards the left. The fact that the Sa-Pa series proceeding rightwards is towards the Kulal, and the Sa-Ma series proceeding leftwards is towards the Yal implies that much more is meant than what is expressly said. In the same manner, when he mentions the opposite Kayir of a Rasi, the Rasi that stands opposite to the given one becomes the sixth Rasi. The sixth string from the Swaram of the commencing Rasi is said to be the Pagai string in music and is to be avoided. On the same principle Kaikilai is the opposing Rasi to Vilari. This we called a Pagai Rasi. In Astrology this is called the opposite Kayir. So we are at a loss to understand the many things in common between Music and Astrology. However we shall notice presently some amsams common to both the sciences.

The Swarams that commence as first and second in a Sthayi complete the octave in Meru Sthanam or the twelfth. On the same principle the 12th Sthanam to any given Rasi is the Moksha Sthanam.

We noted before that the Inai Swaram stands in the seventh place to a given Swaram in the Moksha Sthanam. This is the Kalathira Sthanam. This is the Sthanam that produces happiness to the given Swaram. The Kalathira Sthanams proceed by sevens.

The sixth place from Shadjam is Chathuru Sthanam. He calls this by that name because the fourth Alaku of the Oolai that stands in it and the second Alaku of the Thuttham, do not stand in the relation of Kural Ili, but are discordant. The Chathuru Sthanam is the one that gives the detail about a man's enemies, such as disease, war, loss and calamity. On the same principle the Swarams that stand in the position of Pagai to the given Shadjam or stand sixth will never produce concord but discord.

The Swarams that stand fifth from the Kural in Meru are Swarams of the Putthirasthanam. The fifth Swaram is called the Kilai Swaram just as the fifth place is called Putthira Sthanam. The terms "Kilai Swaram" and "Putthira Swaram" are very apt, because the fifth place from the Shadjam produces and other Shadjam just as branches spring from the tree.

He says the Natpu Swaram stands the fourth above the Meru. The Natpu Swaram or the fourth place is the Sthanam indicating mother, knowledge, carriages, house, land, God etc. This is generally known as the Mathir Sthanam, Vidya Sthanam, or Vagana Sthanam in astrology. On this principle Kaikilai stands as the Mathir-Sthanam for the Shadjam in Meru

The third Sthanam below the Shadjam is known as the Veeria Sthanam and Sahothara Sthanam. So in music, the Kaikilai that occurs in the third place from Shadjam is in the relation of Pagai.

In Astrology, the second place is called the Kudumba Nethira Sthanam. So also in music the second Swaram from Shadjam should be in close concordance with it. The Second is like the 'eye' to the Shadjam The Sthanam next to the twelfth appears to be of secondary impoitance.

The eighth Sthanam above the seventh is Death Sthanam Just as this Sthanam denotes disease, trouble, loss, enmity etc., the Vilari which is the eighth from the Meru Shadjam will never be in concord with it.

The ninth Sthanam indicates ancestors, guru, grace, knowledge, character, penance, good conduct, riches etc. So also the Vilari with 4 Alakus, which is the ninth from any given Swaram, stands to it in the relation of Pithur Sthanam.

The tenth Sthanam gives a clue to karmam, fame, rule, houses, cities, temples, tanks, devotion, wisdom, occupation etc. So the Ni with 2 Alakus in the tenth Sthanam above Shadjam stands in the same relation.

The eleventh Sthanam is the Aya Sthanam like the first. It is also called Lapa Sthanam. We must note here, that, in astrology, the Kendira Sthanams one, four and seven, the Thirikona Sthanams one, five and nine, and the Panapara Sthanams two and eleven are considered 'lucky' Sthanams. So also in music, we see that the Sapta Swarams of an Aroganam namely, the Rishabam with 4 Alakus which is the second from Shadjam, the Gandharam with 4 Alakus in the fourth place, the Ma with 2 Alakus which is in the fifth place, the Pa which is the Inai Swaram in the seventh place, the Dha with 4 Alakus in the ninth place and the Ni with 4 Alakus in the eleventh place, stand as a perfectly concordant series.

Again, Simham the third Rasi, Viruchikam the sixth, Magaram the eighth and Meenam the tenth Rasi are known as Pagai Sthanams in astrology. Note that in music the 3rd, the 6th and the 8th Swarams are completely disagreeable.

Lucky Rasis are the Kendira Sthanams 4 and 7 and the Thirikona Sthanams 5 and 9, so also the 4th 5th 7th and 9th Swarams are concordant.

All Grahams if they can control the fifth and the ninth will invariably give lucky results whether they be bad or good. In the same way the Swaram which is the fifth from Kural is Putthira Sthanam and the Natpu string which is the fourth from it (or ninth from the Kural) is the Puthira Sthanam for Sa.

The Grahams which control the 3rd the 6th and the 8th places will invariably give unlucky results. Note that in music also the 3rd, the 6th and the 8th strings are discordant.

All Grahams have their faces turned towards the seventh place, just as all Swarams face their sevenths or are in concordance with them.

The third, the sixth, the eighth and the twelfth places are hidden Sthanams, just as the Swarams which stand in the 3rd, the 6th, and the 8th Rasis should never show their faces to the Shadjam as they cannot agree in consonance.

Just as each Graham has Atchi, Oocham, Kenthiram and Thirikonam as lucky Sthanams each Swaram has four concordant relations.

The seventh and the fouth places are Kenthirams, the seventh from the Neecha Rasi is Oocham, the fifth is Thirikonam, the Meru is Atchi and the second Kudoomba-Sthanam.

The first six Rasis of the Sun are said to be its life and the next six, its body. So also the Swarams from Sa to Pa are the life and the remaining Swarams from Pa to Sa are the body.

We may also note that the fourth place or the Mathuru Sthanam and the ninth place or the Pithur Sthanam are concordant as Sa-Ga and Sa-Ma ; the fifth or the Puthira Sthanam and the ninth or the Pithur Sthanam are in the relation of Sa-Ga ; the seventh or the Kalathira Sthanam stands in the relation of Sa-Ma to the twelfth or the Moksha Sthanam ; the seventh or the Kalathira Sthanam stands in the relation of Sa-Ma to the second or the Kudoomba Sthanam ; and the Lapa Sthanam or the eleventh place stands as Natpu to the Kalathira Sthanam just as in the case of a woman who desires to make money.

Just as the fifth place is Puthira Sthanam to the given Kural, the given Kural becomes Puthira Sthanam to the Kalathira Sthanam or the seventh place. We find also that Sa-Ma and Pa-Sa are Kilai strings.

Just as a man's life is harmonious with that of his family in the 2nd Sthanam, with his mother in the 4th Sthanam, with his children in the 5th Sthanam, with his wife in the 7th Sthanam, with his father in the 9th Sthanam, with his riches in the 11th Sthanam and with his Moksham or house in the 12th Sthanam. so also the commencing Swaram is in perfect harmony with the six succeeding Swarams Ri Ga Ma Pa Dha and Ni.

For, the Sa in the 12th place stands in harmony with Itapam with 4 Alakus in the second place. with Ga with 4 Alakus in the fourth place, with Ma with 2 Alakus in the fifth place, with Pa in the 7th place, with Dha with 4 Alakus in the ninth place and with Ni with 4 Alakus in the eleventh place.

Our ancestors have given the Vattapalai Chakaram with a complete knowledge of the above facts. Just as they base the results of a graham on the strength of its Sthanam by examining the Ashta Varka Bindhu. so also they have indicated the way by which a Ragam can be composed and its correctness examined. We shall see them in the second Book relating to Ragas. When we find that these precious truths are gathered from a few Stanzas of Silappadikaram where music is casually mentioned, can we not imagine how many precious things would have been said in the works of the first Sangam on music itself such as Ahatyam, Perunarai, Perunkurugu, Panchaparatheeam ? We regret we have not been fortunate enough to see them. However a few important secrets which are the very life of music, as it were, will be mentioned in the Second Book.

22. The concordance of Swarams as found in the Paripadal of Nallanduvanar, a writer of the third Sangam before the time of Ilankovidigal.

(This Paripadal is dated about 3000 years ago).

Noble readers! We noted till now how the Swarams and Srutis of the ancient Tamils were concordant with one another, the peculiar consonance of the Inai Kilai and Natpu Swarams and the dissonance of the Pagai strings and how some of the chief Amsams of music were in accordance with the principles of astrology. We quoted only a few Sootrams found in Silappadikaram written by Ilankovadigal and their commentary in support of the above facts but never sought the help of any later works. For the later writers, like Bharata and Sarnga Dev, have been confounded by the theory of Dwavimsati Srutis.

In Tholkaupiam which was written long before the time of Ilankovadigal, first century A. D., and which was placed before the first Sangam at the time of Nilandaru-thiruvil Pandya at the close of the first Ooli which was still anterior to the 1st century the four Yals, Palai Kurinji, Marutham and Neythal are mentioned. So there is reason to suppose that from the very ancient times the Yal, the rules of the Yal, Alathi and the rules of Alathi, the 12000 ancient Isais and the order of Swarams have been mentioned in an extensive manner. But we are not able to substantiate this by means of literary works. However the quotations from Silappadikaram have been closely studied by us and without any doubt they will be found quite practicable. We did not get these ideas at the beginning. After we had proceeded thus far in our work we came across these Sootrams in Paripadal written by Nallanduvanar, who flourished about a 1000 years before Adyarkunallar, and the commentary on them by Parimelalakar. We quote them below.

In the Paripadal that begins "விரிகதிர்மதியொடு" it is said.

"விரிகதிர் மதியொடு" என்னும் பரிபாடலில்,

'நீனெய்தாழ கோதை மகள்விலக்க நில்லாது
பூவூது வண்டினம் யாழ்கொண்ட கொளைகேண்மின்
கொளைப்பொரு டெரிதரக் கொளுத்தாமற் குரல்கொண்ட
வின்னிசைத் தாங்கொளைச் சீர்க்குங் கிளைச்சுற்ற
வுழைச்சுரும்பின் கேழ்கெழு பாலை யிசையோர்மின்
பண்கண்டு திறனெய்தாப் பண்டாளம் பெறப்பாடிக்
கொண்ட வின்னிசைத் தாளங் கொளைச்சீர்க்கும்
விரித்தாடுந் தண்டும்பி யினங்காண்மின்'

(இ-ள்) நீலநிறத்தையுடை தேனெய்தங்கிய கோதையையுடைய மகளிர் விலக்க நில்லா தங் கோதையிற்பூவை யூதும்வண்டினம் யாழோசைக் கொத்ததற்குக் காரணமாகிய பாட்டைக் கேண்மின்; குரல்கொண்ட கிளையாகிய விளிக்குக்கிளையாப் பொருந்தின.

உழை குரலான்வரும் பாலையிற்றோன்றிய மருதப்பண்ணாகிய விசையெனக் கூட்டுக. இட முறையாற் குரற்கு ஐந்தாவதாகையால் உழை இளிக்குக் கிளையாயிற்று.

பண்கண்டு திறனெய்தாப்பண் விளரிப்பாலையிற் றோன்றும் யாமயாழ். அதனைத் தாளத்தோடு பொருந்தப்பாடி யவ்விசைத் தாளத்திற்கேற்ப மாறுபாடு பொருந்தின'

Comment.—The noise of the beetles that were singing from inside the flowers worn in their hair by damsels, in spite of their efforts to drive them off, resembled the Yal. This was in the relation of Kural to Ili which is Kilai Swaram.

This was the Pun Marutham which appeared in the Palai where Oolai is Kural. Oolai is Kilai to Ili as it is fifth to the Kural leftwards. The words "பண் கண்டு திறனெய்தாப்பன்" imply that it is the Yama Yal appearing in Vilari Palai. The beetles sang them harmoniously according to the Thalam.

We see the idea of Nallanduvanar from the words "கொண்டைப்பொருநர் இசைபோன்றன." The Swarams stand in the relation of Kilai as Kural is to Ili. The words "as used in the Yal leftwards" imply the rule that Oolai appears in Tharam, and Kural in Oolai, and on this principle the ancients seem to have understood that Sempalai is where Kural becomes Kural whereas it is Marutha Pun when Kural itself commences as Kural. Again when we consider the Sootram "she first commenced Kural as Kural and then played with Ili as Kural," we find that the Kural which appears in Oolai Stands in Itapam. The Swaram that appears in Thanusu becomes its Panchamam. Kural which appears in Oolai becomes Panchamam in Itapam proceeding rightwards. Pa or Ili in Itapam is in the same relation to Kural in Thulam on the right side and Kural stands in the same relation to it on the left side. These facts have been repeatedly noted by us. Where he mentions the relation of strings as Inai, Kilai and Pagai, the fifth string is called the Kilai string. On this principle, Oolai is Kilai to Kural on the right, and Kural and Ili are Kilai to Oolai on the left. Kural in Thulam becomes Kilai to Ili in Itapam on the right.

So he is plain in saying that Oolai is Kilai Swaram to Ili which in turn is Kilai Swaram to Kural on the left side. We have mentioned this principle before so many times. So we find clearly that the Tamils were excellent musicians for many thousands of years, before the time of Adyarkunallar in the 11th Century (prior to Sarnga Dev in the 12th Century), before the time of Jayankondan Kavichakravarti in the 10th Century, before the period of Bharata in the 5th Century, before the time of Ilankovadigal in the 1st Century, before the age of Nallanduvanar one of the Savants of the last Sangam which flourished 1000 years ago, before the age of Tholkaupiam which is 8000 years ago, yea, before the age of the first Sangam established 12000 years ago and which continued for 4400 years!

As the rare music of the Tamils gradually deteriorated, others who did not understand the mystery of the Srutis used started the theory of 22 Srutis in the Octave. All writers on 22 Srutis appear to have been thoroughly ignorant of the Srutis used in Isai Tamil. They also appear to have been written after the disappearance of works on Isai Tamil.

The Srutis used in Isai Tamil were 24, at the rate of 2 for each of the 12 Rasis which are a continued series satisfying all principles of consonance. We noticed before that seven Swarams were sung out of the 12, and that two Swarams had an Alaku less in each case. This truth seems to have been a kind of mystery. Hence the necessity of a system with the mysteries removed with the help of a few Sootrams whose meaning was hidden.

We thought there might be also a mystery hidden in the 22 Srutis system of Sarnga Dev. But inasmuch as he gives the measurements for the Saptaswarams as 4, 3, 2, 4, 4, 3, 2 and says that SA-MA has 9 and SA-PA 13 Srutis there does not seem to be any mystery in it.

When we were making researches into the Srutis of Isai Tamil we concluded there might be a mystery there also. Tracing the mystery, we found that the arrangement of strings into Inai, Kilai, Pagai and Natpu implied the division of the Sthayi into 24 Alakus and that ganam was made with 2 Alakus less. It was also stated that in Sakota Yal with 12 Swarams in the Sthayi or 12 Palais, Mathavi sang 14 Swarams in the two Sthayis. It was clearly seen that men made ganam with 2 Alakus less and that Mathavi also adopted the system. So we understand the truth which is corroborated in different ways yet we were at a loss to give convincing reasons to say there was a hidden mystery. At this juncture we were glad we came across a few quotations which would satisfy any critic.

23. A few quotations to prove that there were hidden mysteries in the Isai Tamil used by the ancient Tamils.

There is an explanation found in the work on grammar known as Thandi Alankaram written by Thandi who lived about seven or eight hundred years ago. This Thandi is held to be the son of Ambikapati, the son of Kavichakravarti Kamba Nadan. In his Thandi Alankaram, at the close of Sollani Iyal, he gives seven Malayyus and their rules—namely, those relating to place, time, Kalai, world, justice and books—மலைவு means enmity as given there. It might also mean doubt or contrariness. Of these the rule for Kalai Malayvu is as follows :—

Thandi Alankaram, Sollani Iyal P. 169.

அ. கலைமலைவு.

கஉஅ கலையெனப் படுவ காண்டக விரிப்பிற்
காமமும் பொருளு மேமுறத் தழுவி
மறுவறக் கிளந்த வறுபத்து நான்கே "

(இ-ள்) கலை யென்று சொல்லப்படுவன காமத்தினையும் பொருளினையுந் தழுவிச் சொல்லப்பட்ட அறுபத்து நான்குமாம். எ-று.

கலை சாஸ்திரம்; அவை கீதம், வாத்தியம், கணிதம் முதலியன. இவற்றிற்கு விரோதமாக வருவது கலை மலைவாகும்.

Comment :—The Kalais are 64 relating to lust and property. The science of Kalai implies music, musical instruments, arithmetic etc. Those which contradict this are Kalai Malayvu.

உதாரணம்.

" ஐந்தாம் நரம்பாம் பகைவிரவா தாருக
வந்த கிளைகொள்ள நான்காய-முந்தை
இணைகொண்ட யாழியற்ற மேற்றிசைதன் னாவித்
துணைவன் புகழே தொடுத்து."

இங்கே நின்ற நரம்பிற்கு ஐந்தாவதாகிய கிளையைப் பகையென்றும், ஆறாவதாகிய பகையைக் கிளை என்றும் நான்காவதாகியநட்பினை எட்டாவதாகிய இணை என்றுஞ் சொன்னமையினாற் சங்கீத நூற்கு விரோதமாயிற்று.

Here he calls the Kilai String which is the fifth to the given string as Pagai, the Pagai or the sixth string is called Kilai and the Natpu or the fourth string is given as the eighth or Inai. This is all contrary to the established rules of music.

Here Kalai Malayvu appears to mean that the central idea of any of the Kalais practised by the ancient Tamils is hidden (just like the leaf hides the fruit) and has to be interpreted with the help of the next. It means that, though each Kalai is dealt with in an extensive manner, some central idea is hidden so that it might be known only to the initiated and not to common people. Compare the case of a painter who paints a beautiful human figure but hides the eye which at one touch of the brush with an ordinary colour can be made to come to life. A house full of precious things will certainly be kept under lock and key. Such a system of hiding the central idea is known in Tamil works on grammar as உய்த்துணர வைத்தல் which is one of the many cunning devices. Whatever sages mention in order that we might attain charity, riches, happiness and Moksham are embodied in a literary work. Each work should speak about the seven different opinions, should eschew the seven kinds of errors, should have the ten kinds of merit or beauty and should have the thirty two kinds of cunning devices. These have been clearly mentioned by the ancient Tamils. The 32 literary devices are the following :—

Nannul Pothupayiram P. 11.

நுதலிப் புகுதல் ஒத்துமுறை வைப்பே
தொகுத்துச் சுட்டல் வகுத்துக் காட்டல்
முடித்துக் காட்டல் முடிவிடங் கூறல்
தானெடுத்து மொழிதல் பிறன்கோட் கூறல்
சொற்பொருள் விரித்தல் தொடர்ச்சொற் புணர்த்தல்
இரட்டுற மொழிதல் ஏதுவின் முடித்தல்
ஒப்பின் முடித்தல் மாட்டெறிந் தொழுகல்
இறந்தது விலக்கல் எதிரது போற்றல்
முன்மொழிந்து கோடல் பின்னது நிறுத்தல்
விகற்பத்தின் முடித்தல் முடிந்தது முடித்தல்
உரைத்து மென்றல் உரைத்தா மென்றல்
ஒருதலை துணிதல் எடுத்துக் காட்டல்
எடுத்த மொழியி னெய்த வைத்தல்
இன்ன தல்ல திதுவென மொழிதல்
எஞ்சிய சொல்லி னெய்தக் கூறல்
பிறநூன் முடிந்தது தானுடன் படுதல்
தன்குறி வழக்க மிகவெடுத் துரைத்தல்
சொல்லின் முடிவி னப்பொருண் முடித்தல்
ஒன்றின முடித்த றன்னின முடித்தல்
உய்த்துணர வைப்பென உத்தியெண் ணான்கே.

Comment :—நுதலி புகுதல் :—to state the subject before hand.

ஓத்துமுறை வைப்பு :—to bring the Iyals under some principle of classification.

தொகுத்துச் சுட்டல் :—to mention ideas in a comprehensive manner.

வகுத்துக் காட்டல் :—to give the particulars of a comprehensive principle.

முடித்துக் காட்டல் :—to finish in imitation of great men.

முடிவிடம் கூறல் :—to give instances for the particular rules one quote.

தான் எடுத்து மொழிதல் :—to quote old sootrams at the proper places.

பிறன்கோள் கூறல் :—to incorporate other people's opinions in one's book.

சொல்பொருள் விரித்தல் :—to explain clearly the ideas so that they might be understood.

தொடர்சொல் புணர்த்தல் :—to group allied words together.

இரண்டு உற மொழிதல் :—to give a double meaning to a sentence.

ஏதுவின் முடித்தல் :—to explain an idea which was first left unexplained and convince the reader.

ஒப்பின் முடித்தல் :—to convince by means of analogy even an apparent contradiction.

மாட்டெறிந்தொழுகல் :—to extend a particular rule to an allied subject and connect it with it.

இறந்தது விலக்கல் :—To expunge obsolete words and ideas.

எதிரது போற்றல் :—To adopt a rule which has been recently introduced and which did not exist before.

முன் மொழிந்து கோடல் :—to adopt wherever necessary a rule which has been once quoted.

பின் அது நிறுத்தல் :—to place behind what should invariably be placed before.

விகற்பத்தின் முடித்தல் :—to establish a rule by bringing together the beauty of many apparently contradictory rules.

முடிந்தது முடித்தல் :—to establish a rule by connecting such contradictory rules with a common rule.

உரைத்தும் என்றல் :—to say that an idea will be explained later on but really to say it out then and there briefly.

உரைத்தாம் என்றல் :—to abstain from repeating an idea just to imply that it has been previously stated.

ஒரு தலை துணிதல் :—to argue for a particular side boldly where two sides exist.

எடுத்துக் காட்டல் :—to plainly state the particulars from which a generalisation has been made.

எடுத்த மொழியின் எய்த வைத்தல் :—to fit the particular into the rule established by one.

இன்னது அல்லது இது என மொழிதல் :—to state boldly the idea whenever there is room for doubt.

எஞ்சிய சொல்லின் எய்த கூறல் :—to bring under the formula even a particular which has been omitted.

பிறநூல் முடிந்தது தான் உடன்படுதல் :—to accept the conclusions of another work.

தன்குறி வழக்கம் மிக எடுத்துரைத்தல் :—to make much of an idea newly introduced by one in many different places.

சொல்லின் முடிவின் அப்பொருள் முடித்தல் :—to end the idea where the word ends.

ஒன்றின முடித்தல் தன்னினம் முடித்தல் :—to bring together cognate ideas which could be comprehended under a rule ; to bring together analogous ideas.

உய்த்துணர வைப்பு :—to leave an idea to be comprehended by established sootrams.

உத்தி :—literary devices, which are 32 in number.

We understand from the above Stanza and its commentary that the ancient Tamils were efficient in literary compositions and that they were guided therein by excellent rules. It is also clear they have some Sootrams which could be easily understood by those who study those rules. The same system is found in the Sootrams of Silappadikaram. We have called this the mystery of a work. In the same manner [illegible] means the indication of the hidden meaning by a subject analogous to it. We noted before that the term "[illegible]" comes under the same category.

It appears that the 64 Kalais in use among the ancient Tamils were excellent ones which called forth the admiration of every one. As they were so rare, they were considered to be the manifestations of the Virisadai Kadavul who was considered to be the very origin of the Tamil language.

Sculpture, Astrology, Medicine, Drama, Dancing, Yal, Kulal, Mulavu and Thalam are among the 64 Kalais. They may be studied in detail from books treating on those special subjects.

Of these, the singing by the Yal and the flute and vocal music were, owing to their charm, considered to be very rare accomplishments. We see that the Tamils had special Ragas to influence cobras and uncontrollable elephants knowing that cobras spread their hoods and dance to particular music and that elephants which could not be controlled by the goad are influenced by singing on the Yal. Of the 12,000 ancient Ragas Nagaragam is one. What the snake charmers play at the present day for influencing cobras is the Nagaragam. This is otherwise known as Punnagavarali now. The ancient Tamils associated the different Swarams with different female deities and made ganam to please them by describing their favourite food, dress, ornaments etc. The fact that the cobra which hides itself from the gaze of man-kind comes out at the playing of the particular ragam and spreads out its hood and becomes so meek and tame as to be handled by the player is a proof for it. We know it is a well known fact that Thennava, one of the distinguished rulers of the ancient Tamil country, kept large herds of elephants for war purposes. It is also seen that when male elephants burst their chains and could not be controlled even by the sharp goad of the mahout they were influenced by the music of the Yal. The following stanzas show that this custom was in existence, even about 3000 years ago.

Kalithogai - First Palai, first page—8.

" தாழ்வரை நில்லாக் கடுங்களிற் றொருத்தல்
யாழ்வரைத் தங்கி யாங்கு "

(இ-ள்.) பரிக்கோலாற் குத்தவுந் தன்னெறியில் நில்லாத செலவு கடகளிற் றொருத்தல் மெல்லிய யாழோசையின் எல்லையிலே தங்கினாற் போல "

Comment :—" Just as obstreperous elephants which treated the mahout's goad with contempt were controlled by the mellow music of the Yal."

Perungathai - Narumathai Churukam.

" அணியிழை மகளிரும் யானையும் வணக்கு
மணியொலி வீணை "

Merumanthara Puranam.

" மகரயாழ் வல்லமைந்த தொருவனைக் கண்டு மதத்தப்
புகர்முகக் களிற்றின் "

The above stanzas show that the science of the Yal and the science of music among the ancient Tamils were of a very high order. The doubt as regards Dwavimsati Srutis and the destruction of the purity of Karnatic music owing to the introduction of Desikam is due to the facts that the ancient works on Isai Tamil have been destroyed and consequently people have been unable to understand the ideas underlying them. We know that the Karnatic Ragas are sung and instruments like the Yal and the flute are played even at the present day by the servants in temples where the Tamils worshipped for ages and even before that time during the period of the first Sangam. Yet this truth is not known because some important *amsams* of music are found hidden in works relating to music and because the practice of ancient Tamil has declined. How could common people understand the truth when it is said that the fifth string is the sixth, the sixth string is fifth, and the fourth or the Natpu string is the eighth string which is really Inai string? He calls the eighth string Inai!

But we have noted before that the seventh is the Inai string. This is an example of a hidden mystery, we presume. While writing a commentary on Kalai Malayvu, he himself introduces a mystery therein! We have often seen in the Vattapalai Chakaram that Kaikilai appears in Vilari. But inasmuch as the Kaikilai is sixth from Vilari it stands in the relation of Koodam or Pagai. But in reality Kaikilai is that which appears as the seventh Rasi in Kanni. We have noted before that placing Kaikilai in Simham is another mystery. We have also said that they made ganam in 22 Alakus, lessening an Alaku each in Kaikilai in Kanni and Vilari in Kumbam. We have also stated that there are 24 Srutis and not 22 in the Octave. Though it is a mistake to have placed the Kaikilai in the sixth Rasi from Vilari instead of the seventh he gives a justification for it. This is what is called Kalai Malayvu Amaithi. We have stated before that when we lessen one of the two Alakus in a Rasi and play it as a gamakam from the next Swaram it will be very charming. We have also repeatedly stated that they had 12 frets according to the Rasi Chakaram in the Sakota

Yal and played seven Swarams in them and that they made ganam in two other Swarams with an Alaku less in each. So the author placed Kaikilai in Vilari so that Kaikilai may be sounded from Simham and Vilari from Kumbam just to point out where the sweet Swarams should sound from when the Alaku is lessened. In other words the Swaram in the seventh Rasi should be played from the sixth Rasi. The point is made clear by the following Chakaram as well as the stanza.

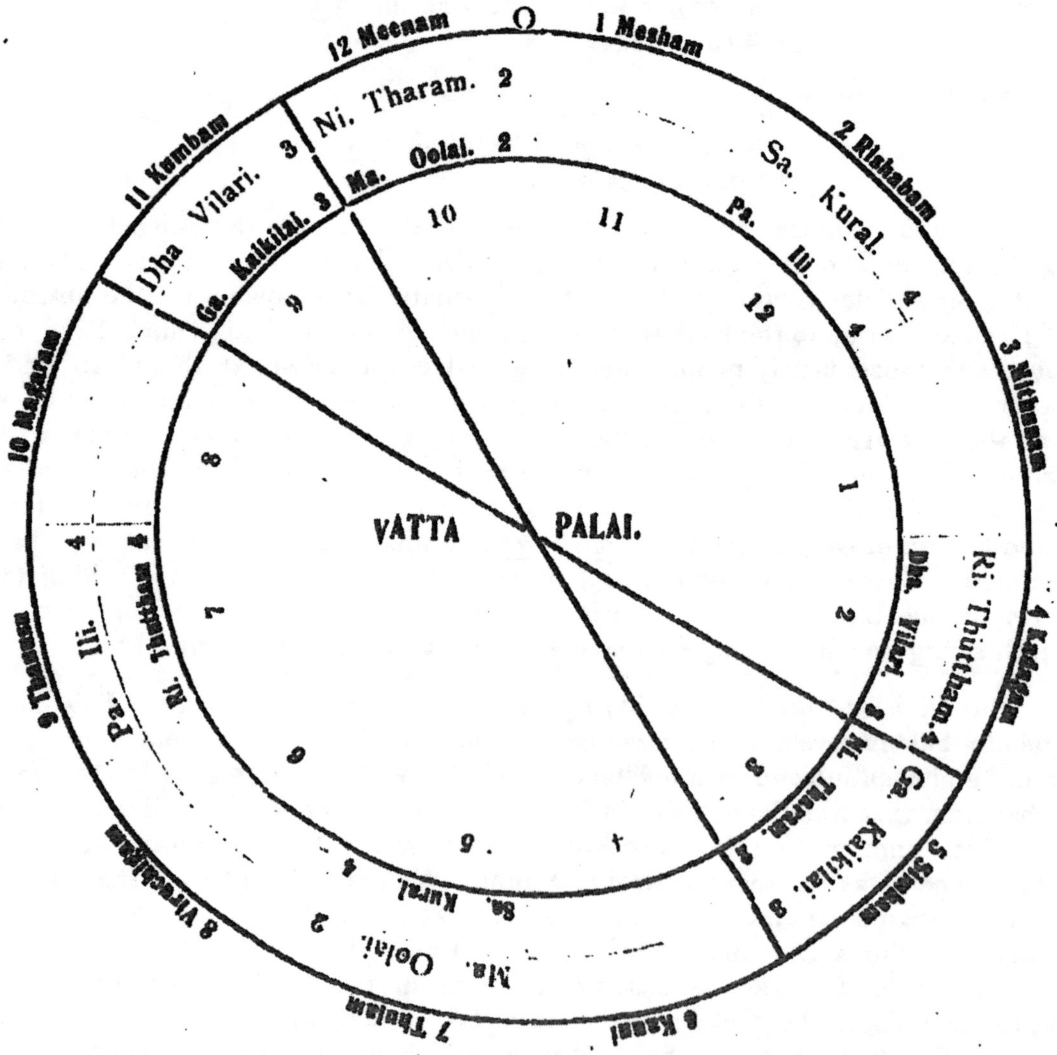

3. Kalaymalaivamaythi.

Thandi Alankaram, Sollani Iyal, 173.

> " கூடம் விரலிக் குறைநிலத்தா னத்தியன்ற
> பாட லமுதம் பருகினன்-ஆகேன்ற
> னசலயற் றேன்றி யொளியிழைக்கு நாணளித்த
> ஆசில் வடிவே லவன்."

இங்கே ஆறும் நரம்பாகிய பகையோடு கூடிக் குறைநிலத்தா னியன்றதனைப் பாடலமுதம் என்றது கிளைமலைவாயினும் புணர்த்துரை யாதலிற் பொருந்துவதாயிற்று.

Comment:—Here he calls the lessening of an Alaku and sounding it along with the sixth string by the expression "பாடலமுதம்" or the most charming place in music. This is plain from the context though it is an example of Kalaimalaivu (கிளைமலைவு.)

When he mentions here that Kaikilai appears in Vilari as regards the sixth string it is an example of கிளைமலைவு. The Vilari and Kaikilai in Kumbam and Kanni respectively should have three Alakus each, or an Alaku less as in the case of Kumbam and Simham. The reason why he suggests Kaikilai in Vilari is because when those two Swarams are sung a little flatter it is delicious. The words "ஆறும் நரம்பாகிய பகையோடு கூடி குறை நிலத்தானியன்றதனை" mean that an Alaku should be lessened in the seventh string and made flatter and should be played from the sixth. குறைநிலம் means a flatter Swaram. To sound it from the sixth instead of from the seventh will be very sweet. This he calls பாடலமுதம் or the most charming place in a Ragam. Such Swarams are generally sung sharper at the modern day.

From the above Chakaram we see that the Kaikilai in the sixth string has 3 Alakus. The extra Alaku after deducting the two belonging to the Rasi should occur in Kanni. The GA with 4 Alakus which should occur in Kanni has been placed in Simham because it should have one Alaku less and should be played from Simham which is a Pagai Rasi. It appears, then, that the ancients made ganam with 2 Srutis less in the 12 Palais, in the 4 different kinds of Yal and in the Palais of the 4 jatis and made complete ganam with 12 Swarams of the Rasis. There was a Malayvu or doubt because concordance was given with a Pagai string. Inasmuchas it was sweet to have one Alaku less in the seventh string he tacked it on to the sixth string. This is an example of Kalai Malayvuamaythi. The words புணர்த்துரையாதலிற் பொருந்துவதாயிற்று imply that though a Pagai string is given as concordant, as taking them together is sweet, we may accept it. We do accept it as concordant.

We would like to enquire whether such ganam was really made in ancient times and whether it is supported by modern practice. We shall go into the question now.

24. How ganam was made in the 22 Srutis.

The ancient Tamils were very efficient in playing the Yal and the Kulal. We have repeatedly said that just as they made ganam in the seven Swarams of the Rasi Mandalam they also made sweet music in the 24 Alakus or Srutis of the seven

Swarams. There is reason to believe that under the same system 12000 ancient Isais derived from the 24 Srutis were also in use. However, from the following quotation we understand that Srutis minuter than the 12 Swarams were also in use among them.

Silappadikaram, Aroompathavoorai p. 33.

"இனி வலக்கைப் பதாகை கோட்டொடு சேர்த்தி' என்பது முதலாக' புறத்தொகு பாணியிற் பூங் கோடி மயங்கி' என்பதிறுக முன்னர்ப்பாடிய ஒன்பான் கோவையின் மேற்செம்பாலைப் பண்ணெழுந்த பதினாற் கோவையாகிய சகோடயாழை வாங்கி வலக்கையைப் பதாகையாக்கி அக்கையால் கோடு அசையாதபடி பிடித்து இடக்கை நாலு விரலும் மாடகத்தையுறப் பிடித்துச்செம்பகையும் ஆர்ப்பும் அதிர்வும் கூடமுமாகிய பகை நீங்க முறையிற் பிழையாத நரம்பினாற் பதினாலு நரம்பினையும் உழை முதல் கைக்கிளை யிறுவாயாக "மெலிவிற் கேள்வி மந்தக்குரலே" என்பதனான் உழைகுரலான மந்தமும், "வலிவிற் கேள்வி வன்கைக் கிளையே என்பதனாற் கைக்கிளை யிறுவாயான வலிவும் இணை, கிளை, பகை, நட்பின் வழிகளிலே பொருந்தப்பார்த்துக் குரல் நரம்பினையும் யாழிற்கு அகப்பட்ட நரம்பாகிய இளி நரம்பையும் முற்பட ஆராய்ந்து இசையோர்த்து அதன் முறையேயல்லாத நரம்புகளையும் ஆராய்ந்து இசையோர்த்துத் திண்மையறிந்து உழைமுதலாகவும் உழையீறாகவுமென மந்த முதலாகவும் மந்த மீறாகவும் குரல் நரம்பு மந்தமானபோது குரல் நரம்பே முதலு முடிவுமாகவும் அகநிலைமருதமும் புறநிலைமருதமும் அருகியன்மருதமும் பெருகியன்மருதமுமென நால் வகைச் சாதிப்பெரும்பண்கள் விளைநிலம்பெற வலிவு மெலிவு சமமென்னும் மூவகை இயக்கும் முறைமையிலே ஆராய்ந்து பாடிப் பின்னர் மாத்திரைகுறைந்ததிற் பண்ணைப்பாடுமேல் வைக்கண் அப்பண்ணை இனிதாகப்பாடி நெகிழ்வுற்ற மனத்தினளாய் அயர்ந்தாளெனவுமாம்."

The above quotation gives the chief rules to be observed in playing the Yal. We understand that the player understood the Swarams for the four kinds of Primary puns, and the concordance of Swarams for the three Sthayis—Mandhara. Madhya and Tara—and played them on her Sakota Yal with 12 frets for the Octave. She afterwards sang the same pun very sweetly with less *mathiras*, and was so charmed with it that she sank unconsciously into sleep. We understand from this that she first sang a Ragam where seven Swarams of the 12 of Ayapalai occurred and then sang another with 2 Alakus less according to the system of Vattapalai. It is clear from this that a Ragam in Vattapalai with 2 Srutis less is sweeter and better able to melt the heart than one in the 12 Swarams. The Vattapalai was given just to indicate the places in the four kinds of Yals and its different puns where the Alakus should be lessened while change of graham is made while 2 Srutis are lessened out of the 24. Before we look into the Ragas derived from Vattapalai we think it necessary to look into the system of changing Graham in Ayapalai and Vattapalai.

25. The System of Ayapalai.

We spoke till now about the Sruti systems as found in Silappadikaram. The statement that Kaikilai must appear in Vilari contradicts the SA-PA principle and the idea that the sixth string is Pagai. Kaikilai has been placed in Simham because that implies that an Alaku in the seventh string should be played as gamakam from the sixth. The seventh is the concordant string, and when one Alaku is lessened in it, it sounds very sweet and it should be played from the sixth. We have said that this is an example of Kalai Malayvu. The fact that a flattened Swaram is sweet is Kalai Malayvu Amaytai or the hidden mystery.

Now, we shall do well to note how Swarams are arranged in Ayapalai and Vattapalai. In other words, we must note the 12 Swarams of the Sthayi that are obtained by the SA-PA and the SA-MA principles rightwards and leftwards, the Ragas that generate from them when the change of graham is made, the four primary puns and the four Jatis derived from the 24 Alakus of Vattapalai with 12 Swarams and how the 22 Srutis are used out of them. For when once the mystery is cleared, after a slight change, i.e., the substitution of the seventh for the sixth string, they follow the general rule by which Swarams are classified under the relation of Inai, Kilai, Pagai and Natpu. We had to rewrite the original Tables and Chakarams with slight modification so that every one might clearly understand them and have their doubts removed.

We have noted already how the Suddha Swarams of Ayapalai change their Grahams. They are the 7 Moorchanas out of the 12 Swarams of the Sthayi arranged by the SA-PA and the SA-MA principles. But we must now observe whether they satisfy the relations of Inai, Kilai, Pagai and Natpu, in what particular Ragas they were used in ancient times while changing graham and whether there is any connection between them and those in use at the present day.

We have noted time and often that the Isai Tamil now in use among the Tamils is the same as the one used by them for thousands of years for 12000 years from now, and that it is sung as pure Karnatic music traditionally by the temple servants such as gandharvas. At the same time we have noted that others who came to the south country about the time of the third Sangam learnt the three kinds of Tamil, became members of the Sangam owing to their profound erudition, made excellent researches in the field of Tamil literature, and wrote many works and commentaries also on some of them. Some of them who took a fancy to Isai Tamil during the course of their researches forgot even the Veda Ganam in Sanskrit, eschewed even the devotional element in the music of the Tamils, took a delight only in Gandharva music and have been making some progress in it. We have to congratulate ourselves that, at least, through their perseverance and intelligence South Indian music has been brought to a stage in which all can enjoy it.

We know that the professional musicians who were held in such high esteem in ancient times gradually declined and lost their character so much so that one abhors hearing any music from them at the present time. So it is just that we should feel gratified that we are in a position to hear such music from others. It is also a matter for pride that times have come that we are enabled to hear Harikathas from the lips of some excellent women. It is said in the Upanishads that those who make secular ganams to the exclusion of Veda Ganams are not allowed to partake in a feast along with others. But it is a fact that patronage was extended to musicians and they were held in esteem only after the time of Brahamasri Theagaraja Iyer of Tiruvadi, Brahmasri Maha Vydianatha Iyer of Vyacheri and other equally eminent musicians who not only composed many Keertanams noted for their excellent devotional element but also sang them in a manner which could melt people's hearts.

We feel glad that they are also practising playing the percussion instruments such as Gengira, Gatam and Mridangam. Though Karnatic music is preserved by these expert musicians, yet we must not forget that the music deteriorates owing to the mixture of desikam.

When those who could not appreciate other Thalams but Eka Thalam, sing Avartha Swarams four times in an Eka Thalam belonging to a particular jathi, it is found that there is an admixture of five Ragas in it. To add to this, if the 22 Srutis system which compels one to sing different Swarams in Aroganam and Avaroganam gets mixed with Karnatic music we may imagine the consequences! Why? Karnatic Ragas are being now sung in Hindustani style! We need not point out that many Ragas would get mixed with one another and become one. It is said that the ancient Tamils were using 12000 old Isais, each independent of the other, with ineffable sweetness, each having a separate idea and a particular charm. And those who try to make them all into one now are considered expert musicians! What is the cause of this? The destruction of works on Isai Tamil and the existence of mysteries in the remnants that were saved. Karnatic music did not make any progress owing to the absence of a definite system of Srutis and the method for composing Ragas in them. Yet some of its excellent *amsams* have been preserved by being traditionally handed down. Then, without understanding the number of Srutis of ancient Karnatic music, they began to ascribe 22 Srutis to the Octave, to describe ancient ganam in the light of those 22 Srutis and to divide the Sthayi into 22 Swarams and Srutis. This confusion is not of yesterday or to day but has been confounding Karnatic music for nearly 1400 years from the time of Bharata in the 5th Century A. D.

To add to this, the controversy about SA-PA $\frac{2}{3}$ and SA-MA $\frac{3}{4}$ system of Pythagoras has been raging for the past 2500 years. One may think that we are criticising this system in order to establish the system of Swarams by Ayapalai and Vattapalai mentioned in the Isai Tamil used by the ancient Tamils. But a careful observer will readily see that the very Ragas used by the ancient Tamils are now used with altered names. One may clearly see by examining Vattapalai that 12 kinds of Swara Varisais or Moorchanas result from the change of graham of the Swarams of Ayapalai.

The ganam in 7 Swarams picked out of the 12 half Swarams is Ayapalai. There are 7 primary Palais mentioned here. The other 5 there are called secondary Palais. The manner in which these 12 Palais generate may be seen from the Chakarams below. We may see there that in changing graham the Shadjam gets two Alakus for every change and the Swarams satisfy the principle of Inai, Kilai, Pagai and Natpu. The names for the seven primary and five secondary Palais are also given there according to the names of the 72 Meḷa Kartas now in use.

The first Table gives the 24 Srutis into which a Sthayi is divided and the 12 Swarams with 2 Alakus each. The names of the Swarams and the Alakus for each are given. We find that 12 Moorchanas are obtained when we shift the SA rightwards to the extent of 2 Alakus at each step. If the other Swarams are also shifted on the same principle, the 12 Ragas will appear as one. We noticed them before in the 12 puns obtained by proceeding rightwards and leftwards in Vattapalai (Vide pages 459—479). They are arranged according to the system of 22 Srutis in the Octave where GA and DHA have 3 Srutis each. We have also noted how they divided the Octave into 24 Alakus or Srutis, how they arranged the Swarams on the principle of Inai and Kilai (SA-PA 14 and SA-MA 10) and made ganam in the 12 Swarams, and how they lessened an Alaku each in GA and DHA and played them as gamakams from the adjacent Swaram on the Sakota Yal. We have also proved by many instances, Alaku calculations and the system of Vattapalai from ancient works that the books which advocated Dwavimsati Srutis were written in ignorance of the secret in Karnatic music and that the devil of doubt, namely the 22 Srutis, would never lift its head again. We have also removed the doubt in the minds of those advocates by going into their own calculations in the second part. We have also shown by many Tables that the system of calculation by $\frac{3}{2}$ for SA-PA and $\frac{4}{3}$ for SA-MA might also produce very nearly 24 Srutis in the Octave. To remove the doubt about the 22 Srutis for ever we have demonstrated with the help of Vattapalai of the ancient Tamils how Swarams arrange themselves on the SA-PA and SA-MA principles and how there are 24 Alakus in the Octave at the rate of two for each of the 12 Swarams. The ancients emphasise the fact that Swarams should arrange themselves on the principle of Inai, Kilai, Pagai and Natpu. Those Ragas which do not stand this test are surely incorrect.

So all Ragas should be sung on the principle of Inai, Kilai, Pagai and Natpu. The Swarams should change their graham after the Vattapalai system. The Shadjam should shift 2 Alakus to the right at each step, and the other six Swarams should occur in their order as indicated at the top of the Table. Some of these may not agree with the Swarams in Aroganam. Such will not be included under the Mother Ragas. For example, Ragas 2, 4, 7, 9 and 11 are of such nature. The same holds good for Suddha Thodi without Panchamam in the twelfth row. These are called secondary Palais. We also see that this Suddha Thodi is included among the 7 primary Palais. But Mother Ragas should invariably consist of 7 Swarams.

Contrary to this principle, we must note (Vide second Table) that Suddha Thodi commencing with NI is included among the seven Mother Ragas. Sarnga Dev and Bharata before him and ancient works before the time of Bharata mention 6 Mother Ragas with 5 branch Ragas from each and that their total is 36. We have quoted many instances to prove that the ancient Mother Ragas were 6 and that they have been called by different names at different periods. In the same manner, though all the six Mother Ragas mentioned here do not have their ancient Tamil names, some of them do have their Tamil names. They may be seen in the system of Yal given below.

The Moorchana in the first row seen in the Table is after the ancient Vattapalai system. The Moorchana or Ragam commencing from Kural in Itapam is called Marutha Pun in Vattapalai. The series of Swarams of this pun satisfies the concord of Swarams. He gives also the principle by which the Swarams of each Ragam should

The 12 Swarams of Ayapalai and the Ragas resulting from change of Graham.

Parumpalai	Standard String 0		Second String 2		String of friendship 4	Branch String 5		Concordant String 7		Second String 9		String of friendship 11	Branch String 12	According to the modern system. Names of Ragas.	Swarams for Ragas.	
	S	2R	4R	2G	4G	2M	4M	P	2D	4D	2N	4N				
	23 24	1 2	3 4	5 6	7 8	9 10	11 12	13 14	15 16	17 18	19 20	21 22	23 24			
1	1 S		4R		4G	2M		P		4D		4N		Dheerasankaraparanam	S 4R 4G 2M P 4D 4N S	29
	2	S	2R		*2G	4G M		4M P		2D		2N		Kusumboki	S 2R 4G 4M 2D 2N S	50
2	3 2N		S		4R	2G		2M		P		4D		Karakarapiriya	S 4R 2G 2M P 4D 2N S	22
	4 4D N			S	2R	4R *G		2G M		4M P		2D		Dharmani	S 2R 4G 4M 2D 1N S	49
3	5 2D		2N		S	2R		4G		2M		P		Hanumat Thodi	S 2R 2G 2M P 2D 2N S	8
4	6 P		4D		4N	S		4R		4G		4M		Mecha Kalyani	S 4R 4G 4M P 4D 4N S	65
	7 4M P		2D		2N		S	2R		2G		*2M		Bavani	2R 2G 4M 2D 2N S	44
5	8 2M		P		4D	2N		S		4R		4G		Harikambodi	S 4R 4G 2M P 4D 2N S	28
	9 4G M		4M *P		2D	4D N			S	2R		2G		Mecha Kambodi	S 2R 2G 4M 2D 1N Ṡ	43
6	10 2G		2M		P	2D		2N		S		4R		Nata Pairavi	S 4R 2G 2M P 2D 2N S	20
	11 4R G		4G M*		4M P	P D		4D N			S	2R		Santhrajothi	S 2R 1G 4M P 4D S	41
7	12 2R		2G		2M	4M *P		2D		2N		S		Suddha Thodi	S 2R 2G 2M 2D 2N S	8

TABLE II.

The 7 primary Palais derived from the 12 Palais.

	Standard string 0			Second string 2				String of friendship 4		Branch string 5				Concordant string 7				Second string 9				String of friendship 11		Branch string 12	Modern system.		
	24	1	2	3	4	5	6	7	8	9	10	11	12	13	14	15	16	17	18	19	20	21	22	23	24	Modern Ragas.	The Swaram for Ragas.	
	S		R^2		R^4		G^2		G^4		M^2		M^4		P		D^2		D^4		N^2		N^4		S			
1	S				R^4				G^4		M^2				P				D^4				N^4			Sankraparanam	S 4R 4G 2M P 4D 4N S	29
2	N^2				S				R^4		G^2				M^2				P				D^4			Karakarapiriya	S 4R 2G 2M P 4D 2N S	22
3	D^2				N^2				S		R^2				G^2				M^2				P			HanumatThodi	S 2R 2G 2M P 2D 2N S	8
4	P				D^4				N^4		S				R^4				G^4				M^4			Mesha Kalyani.	S 4R 4G 4M P 4D 4N S	65
5	M^2				P				D^4		N^2				S				R^4				G^4			Harikambothi.	S 4R 4G 2M P 4D 2N S	28
6	G^2				M^2				P		D^2				N^2				S				R^4			Nata Bairavi...	S 4R 2G 2M P 2D 2N S	23
7	R^2				G^2				M^2		M^4 P^4				D^2				N^2				S			Suddha Thodi.	S 2R 2G 2M 2D 2N S	8

be concordant with one another. This Marutha Pun is known as Shankaraparanam in modern music. So when change of graham is made for the 12 Palais, Shadjam should have 2 Alakus at each step while other Swarams should stand on the principle of Inai, Kilai, Pagai and Natpu as given on the top of the Table.

We know that the Sun has its sancharam in the 12 Rasis for the 12 months of the year, at the rate of one each month. So also the Sahdjam has its move in the 12 Rasis or Swarams. But just as the seven Grahams have their sancharam in their respective signs, the Sapta Swarams also keep changing on the principle of Inai, Kilai, Pagai and Natpu. The six mother Ragas and other innumerable Ragas derived from them while change of Graham is made will be given in detail with their chakarams in the second Book.

We have already noted the Yals derived after the 12 palais. But as they have been calculated on the principle 'Kaikilai will appear in Vilari' after the system of 22 Srutis, and inasmuchas the Swaram is a Pagai Swaram we had to repeat it here just to show that it is entirely wrong.

26. The Yals and other allied instruments used by the ancient Tamils.

We know that the ancient Tamils made much use of the excellent Yal and the Flute called Vangiam which could faithfully produce even the minutest of Swarams, in proportion to their advancement in music. These instruments are held in high esteem even now, and are respectively known as the Veena and Flute. He gives the system of Vattapalai to show how the Swarams are arranged in these instruments. We have referred to this very often. We might be led to think that the Swarams of the Vattapalai are for the Yal and the Flute only. But the Ayapalai is derived from the Vattapalai as mentioned before. We shall do well to understand the relation between them. It may be seen from the following Chakaram.

The Alaku system for the 12 Swarams in Ayapalai and Vattapalai.

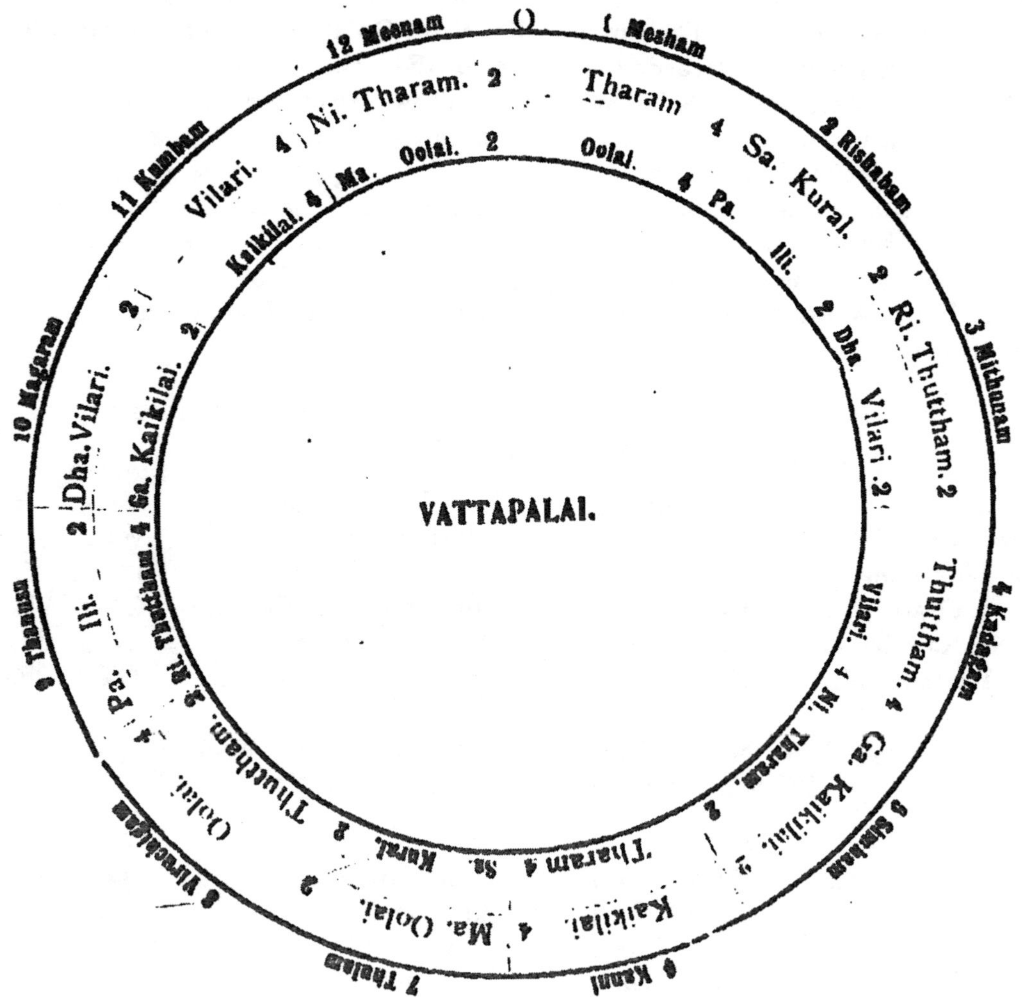

In the above Chakaram if we insert a line between Itapam and Mesham and straighten it out by making Itapam the beginning and Mesham the end, in the outer circle we have the series Sa Ri Ga Ma Pa Dha Ni, and in the inner one, the series Pa Dha Ni Sa Ri Ga Ma. This is at present known as the Panchama Sruti series. In the same way if we divide the chakaram, commencing from Thulam and ending with Kanni, we get the two series Ma Pa Dha Ni Sa Ri Ga and Sa Ri Ga Ma Pa Dha Ni. We call this the Madhyama Sruti series. This is the Sruti for women's voices. Here the two series commencing from Itapam are the concordant series obtained when we proceed rightwards by the Sa Pa principle. For the Pa in the inner circle is an

Inai Swaram (or Kural Ili) to the Sa in the outer circle. In the same way the Ri in the outer circle is an Inai Swaram to PA in the inner circle. In the same manner the series SA-PA, PA-RI, RI-DHA, DHA-GA, GA-NI, NI-MA and MA-SA are obtained. These are the same as the Ili in Kural, Thutham in Ili, Vilari in Thutham, Kaikilai in Vilari. Tharam in Kaikilai, Oolai in Tharam and Kural in Oolai spoken of in ancient Tamil works. When we proceed leftwards the series MA-SA, SA-PA, PA-RI, RI-DHA, DHA-GA, GA-NI and NI-MA stand as Kilai Swarams. These are the series known in ancient works as Kural in Oolai, Ili in Kural, Thutham in Ili, Vilari in Thutham, Kaikilai in Vilari, Tharam in Kaikilai and Oolai in Tharam. These appear to be all correct. But these are the result of the system that Kaikilai appears in Vilari. On this principle if we take the Inai Swaram in Kanni the 12 Swarams in the 12 Rasis occur as Inai Swarams. We mentioned this fact on pages 580 to 583. On the same principle we see that Inai Swarams are Inai and Kilai Swarams are Kilai as seen from the following Tables.

The 12 Swarams obtained in Vattapalai proceeding rightwards on the Sa-Pa principle.

Ili in Kural ...	SA 2	PA 2		Thuttham in Oolai ...	MA 4	RI 2
Thuttham in Ili ...	PA 2	RI 4		Vilari in Thuttham ...	RI 2	DHA 2
Vilari in Thuttham ...	RI 4	DHA 4		Kaikilai in Vilari ...	DHA 2	GA 2
Kaikilai in Vilari ...	DHA 4	GA 4		Tharam in Kaikilai ...	GA 2	NI 2
Tharam in Kaikilai ...	GA 4	NI 4		Oolai in Tharam ...	NI 2	MA 2
Oolai in Tharam ...	NI 4	MA 4		Kural in Oolai ...	MA 2	SA 2

The 12 Swarams obtained in Vattapalai proceeding leftwards on the Sa-Ma principle.

Kural in Oolai ...	MA 2	SA 2		Oolai in Tharam ...	NI 4	MA 4
Ili in Kural ...	SA 2	PA 2		Thuttham in Oolai ...	MA 4	RI 2
Thuttham in Ili ...	PA 2	RI 4		Vilari in Thuttham ...	RI 2	DHA 2
Vilari in Thuttham ...	RI 4	DHA 4		Kaikilai in Vilari ...	DAH 2	GA 2
Kaikilai in Vilari ...	DHA 4	GA 4		Tharam in Kaikilai ...	GA 2	NI 2
Tharam in Kaikilai ...	GA 4	NI 4		Oolai in Tharam ...	NI 2	MA 2

It appears they have made ganam in the seven swarams chosen out of the 12 strings which satisfy the relation of Inai, Kilai, Pagai and Natpu. This is Ayapalai. The Sakota Yal was played on this principle with 12 frets for the Sthayi. From the fact that she played 14 Kovais on it, it is clear that the Yal had 24 frets, 12 each for the first and second Sthayis, and that it had a second string (Panchama string) under the first or Sarana string. So it is clear that the ancient Senkoti Yal is the same as the modern Veena where we have 24 frets for the 24 swarams of the Madhya and the Tara sthayis, 4 main strings known as Saranai. Panchamam, Anusaranai and Thakupanchamam with 3 side strings for the purposes of Thalam known as Anusaranai. Panchamam and Mel Shadjam (seven strings in all), and made of seasoned jack wood. There is reason to believe that the ancient Senkoti Yal was of the same structure as the Sakota Yal. From the series of Swarams used we find the ganam of the two yals is identical. We find that, even at the present day expert players on the Yal tune their instrument and adjust the frets on the principle of Inai Swarams SA-PA, PA-RI etc. This is Ayapalai. We see clearly the concordant series of the Ayapalai from the Vattapalai Chakaram. The swarams of the Ayapalai have been always clean Suddha notes without any sharpening or flattening.

On the same principle Alakus for swarams in Vattapalai are given. There is no difference any where except where he gives the Kaikilai only 3 Alakus, which should have four Alakus in Kanni and places it in Simham, and where he gives the Vilari 3 Alakus which should really have 4 Alakus in Kumbam. Of the series SA RI GA MA PA DHA and NI the two Swarams GA and DHA are given three Alakus instead of four. The Vattapalai system is mainly given so that we may understand in which two Swarams there should be a lessening of Alakus when we change Graham and what different ragas result from the process.

Four kinds of Yal are mentioned in Vattapalai. And these are the four series commencing respectively from Itapam, Thulam, Thanusu and Mesham. These are respectively known as Marutham, Kurunji, Palai and Neythal. Each of these has four Jathis known as Aganilai, Puranilai, Arugial and Perugial. We shall do well to notice these carefully as we have insufficient data to understand the music of the ancients. So we shall note below the order of Swarams of each Yal and of the 4 Jathis that are derived from each of them with the help of the Vattapalai Chakaram.

27. The Swarams for the four kinds of Yal.

"தாரத் துழைதோன்ற பாலையாழ் தண்குர
லோருழைத் தோன்ற குறிஞ்சியாழ்-நேரே
இளிகுரலிற் றோன்ற மருதயாழ் துத்த
மிளியிற் பிறக்கநெய்தல் யாழ்."

Here he says that Palai Yal is obtained when Oolai appears in Tharam, Kurinji Yal is obtained when Oolai appears in Kural, Marutha Yal is obtained when Ili appears in Kural and Neythal Yal is obtained when Thuttham appears in Ili. When we observe this system more minutely, we find that Palai Yal generates from the Thara string which stands in the relation of string of friendship to the standard string, when we obtain 24 Srutis in the octave after once the mystery has been cleared, although we have mentioned in the Vattapalai system given before, that Palai Yal is obtained when Oolai appears in Tharam (NI 2 MA 2). The tenth to the standard string is the string of enmity. We see by various means that Palai Yal never occurs in the string of enmity but in the string of friendship. In the system of Vattapalai given below, MA which is the branch string to the string taken as the standard commencing from Idapam, PA which is the relative string to the standard string and NI which is the string of friendship to PA should be taken for the four kinds of Yal. We mentioned before that Palaiyal will generate from Tharam which is the string of enmity to PA. This is the hidden mystery which is now solved.

The system with the mystery removed in connection with the four kinds of Yal.

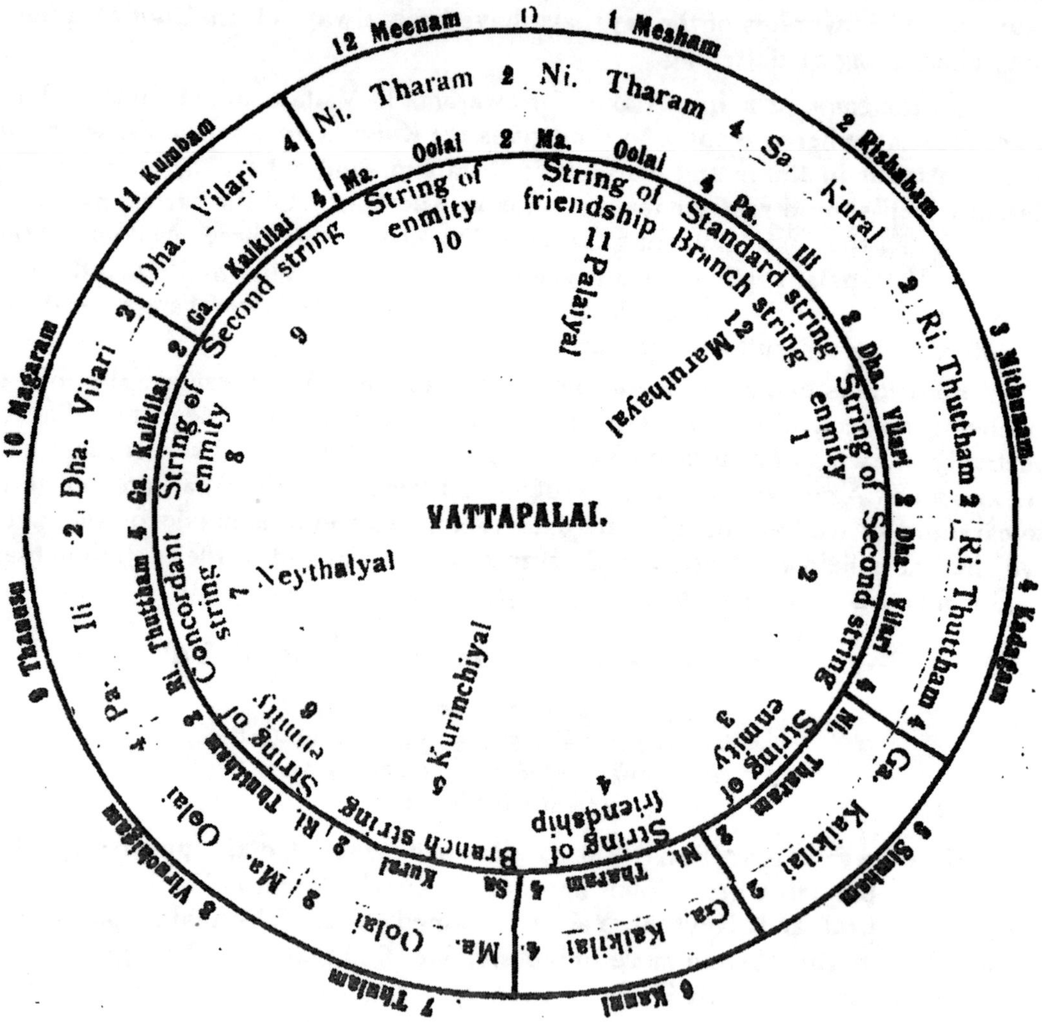

28. How the four Jathis generate from each Yal when once the mystery has been cleared.

It has become a necessity to consider once more the four Jathis Ahanilai Puranilai, Arugial and Perugial derived from the four kinds of Yal mentioned in the previous Chakaram.

Silappadikaram Venirkathi P. 203.

"உழைமுத லாகவு முழையீ றாகவுங்
குரன்முத லாகவுங் குரலீ றாகவு
மகநிலை மருதமும் புறநிலை மருதமு
மருகியன் மருதமும் பெருகியன் மருதமு
நால்வகைச் சாதியு நலம்பெற நோக்கி"

இனி உழை குரன் முதல் குரலீறாயுள்ள நான்கிற்கும் அகநிலைமருத முதற் பெருகியன் மருதம் ஈறாயுள்ள நான்கும் நிரனிறை ;

Commentary—The four strings commencing from Oolai and Kural and ending with Kural will be Ahanilai Marutham. In the same manner the Kodipalai where Oolai becomes Kural is Ahanilai Marutham ; the Merchempalai with Oolai as Kural and Kaikilai as Kural is Puranilai Marutham ; the Sempalai with Kural taken as Kural is Arugial Marutham ; and Vilaripalai with Kural as Tharam and Tharam as Kural is Perugial Marutham. All these Jathis have harmonious Swarams.

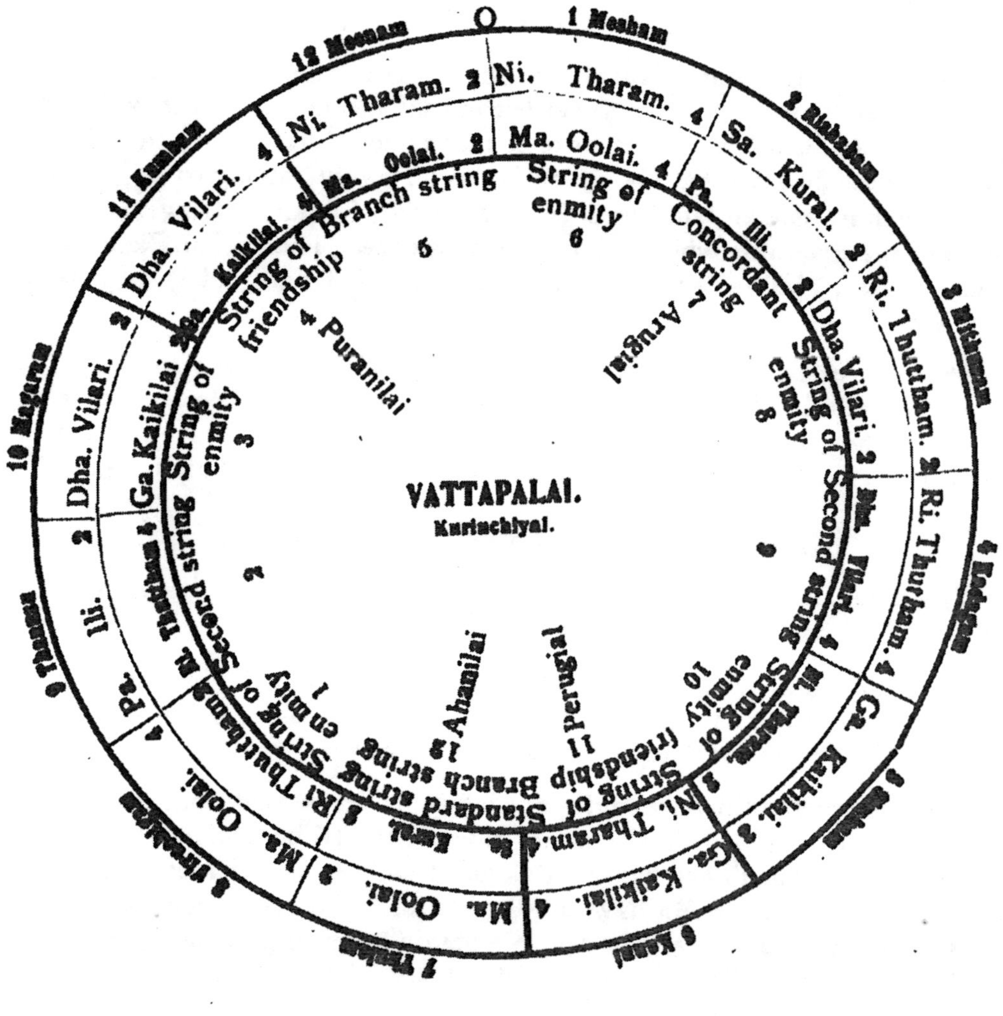

He first makes mention of the four kinds of Yal obtained in the following manner :—

When Oolai is first and last, or in other words to have the Kural that appears in Thulam as the first and last, is one; to have the Kural that appears in Itapam as first and last is another ; to have the Thuttham that appears in Thanusu as first (Kural) and last is a third, and to have the Oolai as first (Kural) and last that appears in Mesham is the fourth Yal. Then he proceeds to mention the four Jathis which are the sub-sections of the four kinds of Yal. He gives the name of Kodipalai to the Kural that appears in Thulam. The seven concordant Swarams derived from Kodipalai are the Ahanilai Marutham.

If we commence Kural from Kaikilai, which is the fourth string from the Kural that appears in Thulam, we obtain Puranilai Marutham. These are friendly Swarams of the SA-GA type.

When Kural which appears in Oolai is taken as Kural we get Arugial Marutham. These are concordant Swarams of the SA-PA type.

Going onwards, when Kural becoms Tharam and *vice versa* it is Perugial Marutham. When he says " while Kural becomes Tharam " it means while Kural is Kural or the first and last Swaram and the commencing Kural is NI ; this is Perugial. Proceeding further, he says that GA which is the 'friendly' string to Sa (the standard string), PA which is 'concordant' with SA and NI the 'friendly' string to the 'concordant' string are the Swarams where all Jathis commence. The ancient Tamilians seem to have used these 16 Jathis derived from the four kinds of Yal. They may be clearly seen in the Chakaram.

There is reason to think that Ganam under this system and the Ragas derived from them were held in high esteem by the ancient Tamilians. We are at a loss to know what further subtle methods they had. However, I think we shall do well to see the use of the four different kinds of Yal—Palai, Kurinji, Marutham and Neythal.

The Marutha yal and its four Jathis.

The Sempalai derived when Kural is taken as Kural is the Aganilai of the Maruthayal. This may be seen from the chakaram given below.

Here the Kural which appears in Itapam is the Aganilai Marutham. To which the Swarams in 4, 7 and 11 form Puranilai Arugial and Perugial. Here he leaves out the Pagai strings 1, 3, 6, 8 and 10 and chooses 7 strings.

Here Kural should have only 2 Alakus as it is said that the Tharam in Mesham is the forth Alaku. On the same principle the Ili in Thanusu should have 2 Alakus as Oolai in Viruchikam has 4 Alakus. Shadjam and Panchamam should be given 4 Alakus when Ni and MA have only 2 Alakus. Otherwise we shall have either 2 Alakus less or 2 Alakus more than 24. We obtain according to this system the series SA 2, RI 4, GA 4, MA 2, PA 4, DHA 4 and NI 4. These are the Swarams for the modern Dheerashankaraparanam. This is otherwise known as Maruthayal pun. But the same series with an Alaku less or 3 Alakus each for Kaikilai in Kanni and Vilari. Kumbam was called by the ancient Tamils Aganilai Marutha Pun or Marutha Pun. We must understand distinctly that with the exception of Vilari and Kaikilai the other five strings are perfect.

In the Chakaram given for Marutha Yal Aganilai, the Swarams of the outer circle must be taken to be the permanent ones and those in the inner circle to be the ones derived while change of Graham is made. When we commence Kural as Kural the top Swarams result. This is known as Chempalai Pun in Ayapalai and Aganilai Marutham in Vattapalai in the system of the ancient Tamils. The Alaku system for the same may be found from the Chakaram. We call the old Sempalai Pun by the modern name of Dheerasankaraparanam.

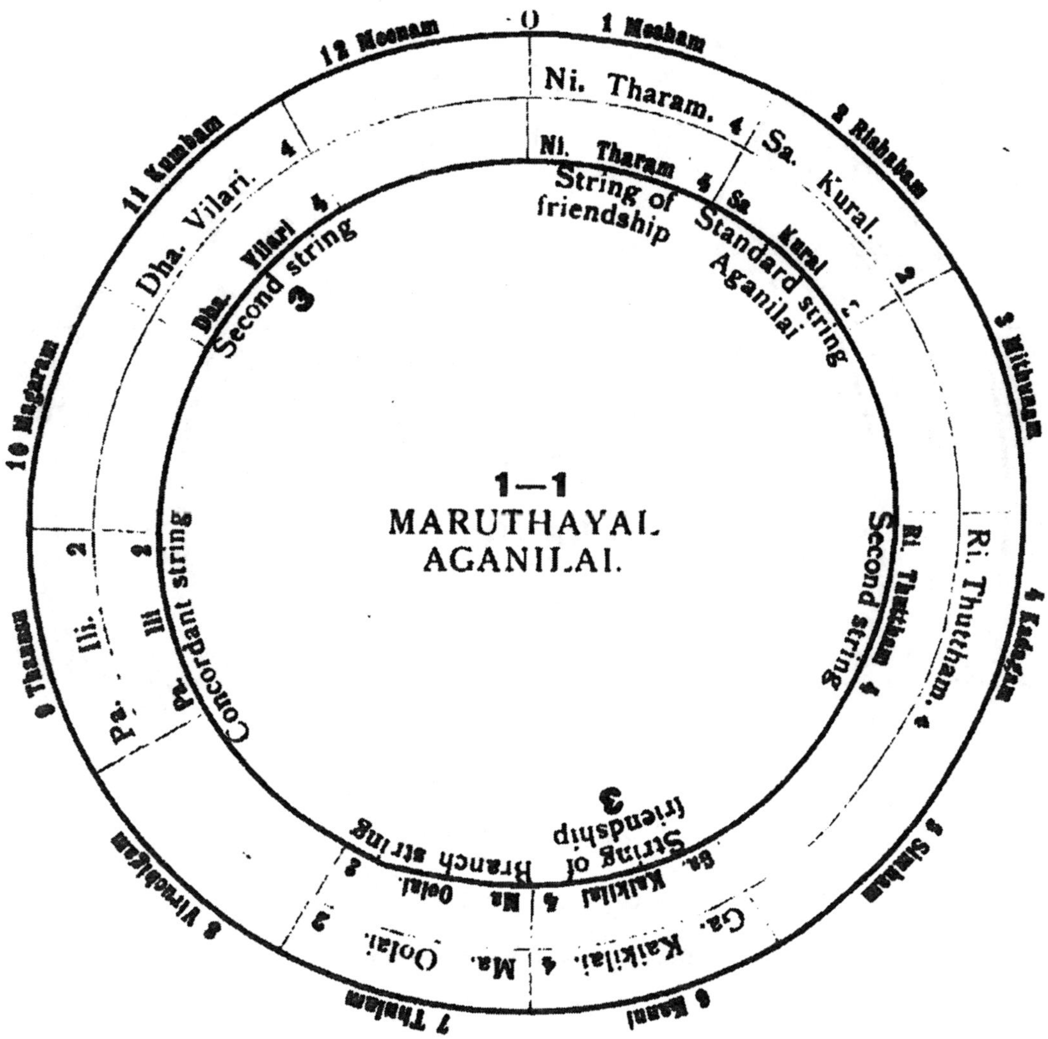

Chempalai Pun in Ayapalai has the series Sa, Ri 4, Ga 4, Ma 2, Pa, Dha 4 and Ni 4—Dheerashankaraparanam.

Aganilai Marutham in Vattapalai has the series Sa, Ri 4, Ga 3, Ma 4, Pa, Dha 3 and Ni-4—Marutham.

In the next Chakaram given below we shall note the series derived when Kaikilai in Kanni in the inner circle is taken as Kural. This he calls Sevvali Palai in Ayapalai and Puranilai Marutham in the Vattapalai system. It may be understood from the resultant series given below. He calls this Ragam by the name of Agari. It is used in the modern day as Hanumathodi and Agari its Jannya ragam. Here we find that the Kural is played from the 23rd Alaku above Kakali Nɪ. In the same manner Oolai is played from the 9th Alaku above Anthara Gᴀ. In other words it has an odd Alaku.

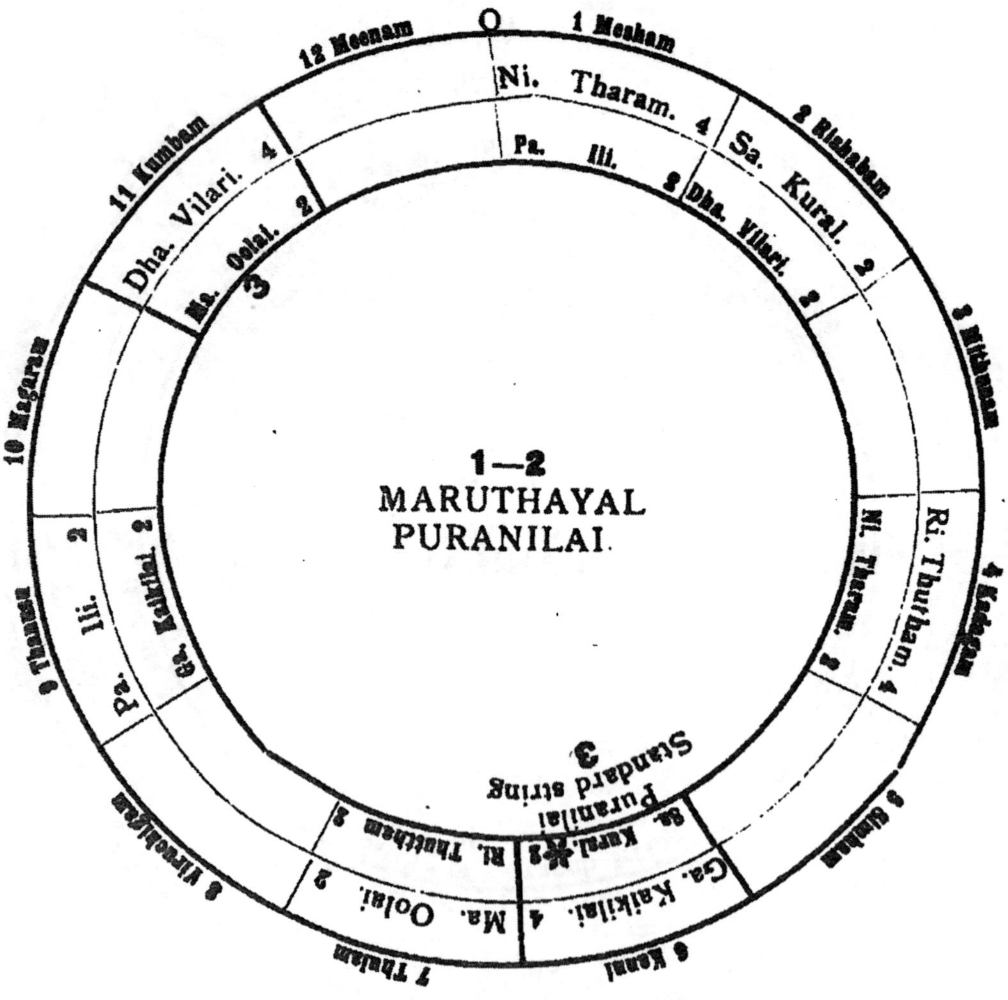

Sevvalipalai in Ayapalai has the series Sᴀ, Rɪ 2. Gᴀ 2, Mᴀ 2. Pᴀ. Dʜᴀ 2 and Nɪ 2—Hanumathodi.

Puranilai Marutham in Vattapalai has the series Sᴀ 3, Rɪ 2, Gᴀ 2, Mᴀ 3, Pᴀ, Dʜᴀ 2 and Nɪ 2—Agari.

When Kural commences from Ili in Thanusu he calls it Kodipalai Pun in Ayapalai, and Arugial Marutham in the Vattapalai system. The series may be seen below. Thutham and Vilari have only 3 Alakus each. But when they appear without lessening the Alakus, the series is Harikambodi and according to the 24 Alakus system it is Sayavelarkolli.

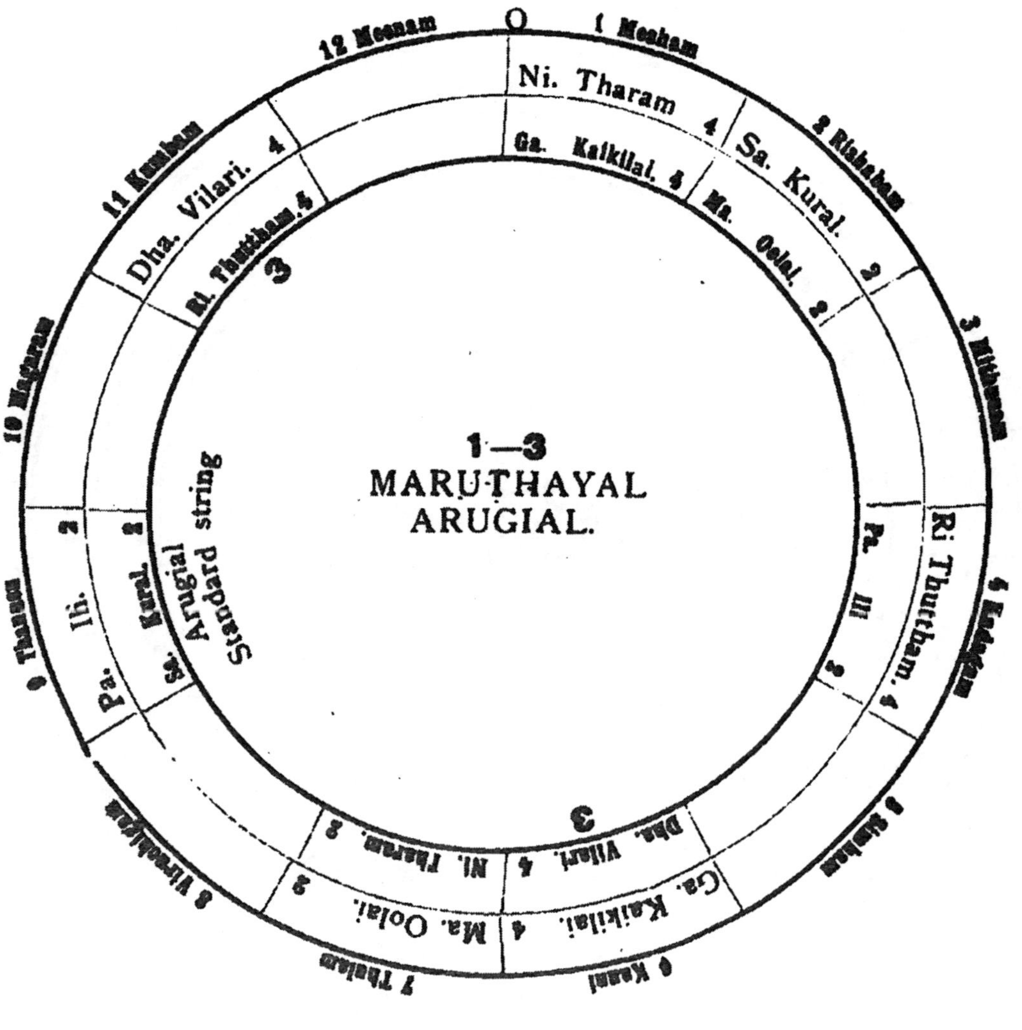

The Kodipalai Pun in Ayapalai has the series Sa, Ri 4, Ga 4, Ma 2, Pa, Dha 4 and Ni 2—Harikambodi.

Arugial Marutham in Vattapalai has the series Sa, Ri 3, Ga 4, Ma 2, Pa, Dha 3, and Ni 2—Sayavelarkolli.

It is Merchempalai Pun in Ayapalai when Kural commences from Tharam in Mesham. It is now called Suddha Thodi. As there are two Madhymams here it becomes a source for Desika Ragas. Of the two Alakus for Ma in Kanni and for Tharam in Kumbam one Alaku should be lessened. The idea is that Alakus in Rasis with the number 3 should be odd.

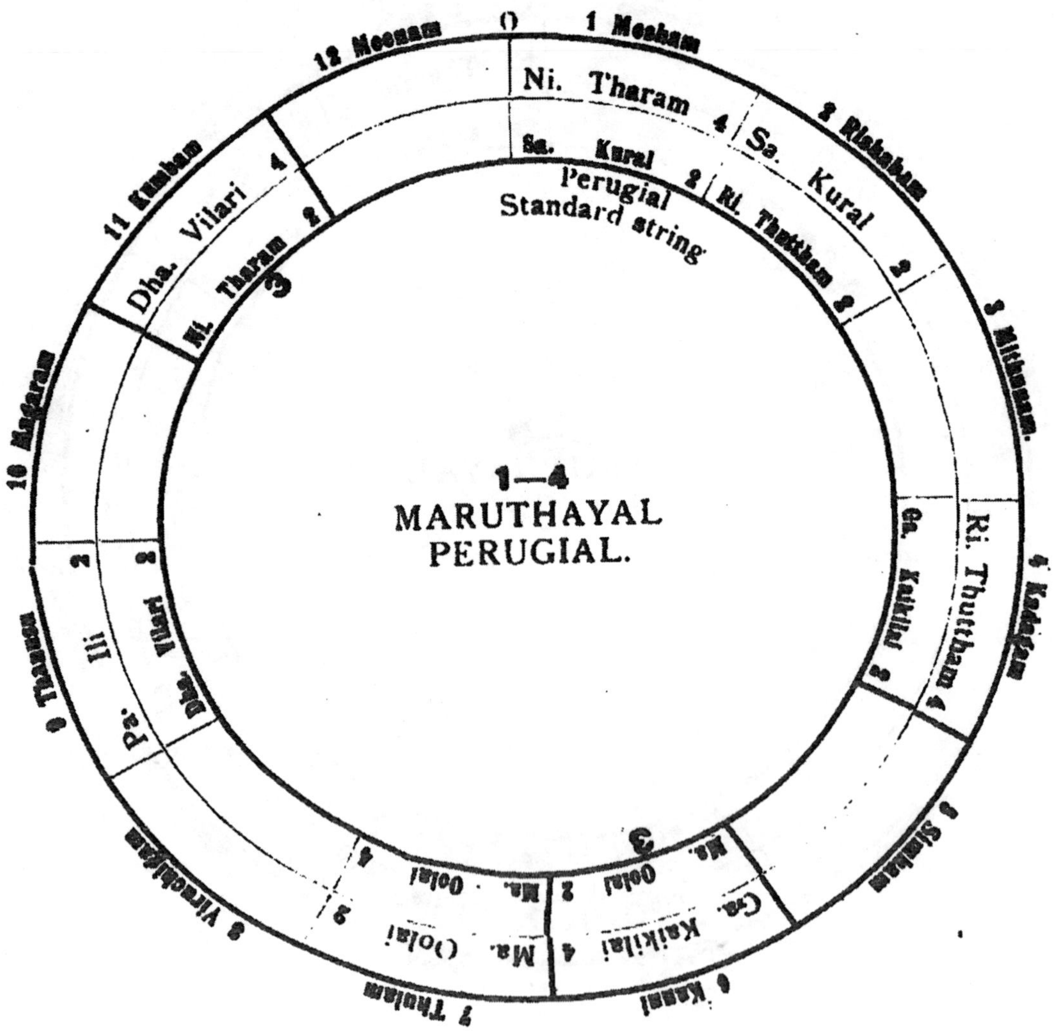

The Merchempalai Puń in Ayapalai has the series Sa, Ri 2, Ga 2, Ma 2, Ma 4, Dha 2, and Ni 2—Suddha Thodi.

The Perugial Marutham in Vattapalai has the series Sa, Ri 2, Ga 2, Ma 3, Ma 4, Dha 2 and Ni 2—Kinnaram.

The Kural in Thulam is Aganilai Marutham to the Kurinji Yal where Oolai commences as Kural. This is called Arumpalai Pun in Ayapalai, and Aganilai Kurinji in Vattapalai. The Ragam in Ayapalai is now called Mechakalyani.

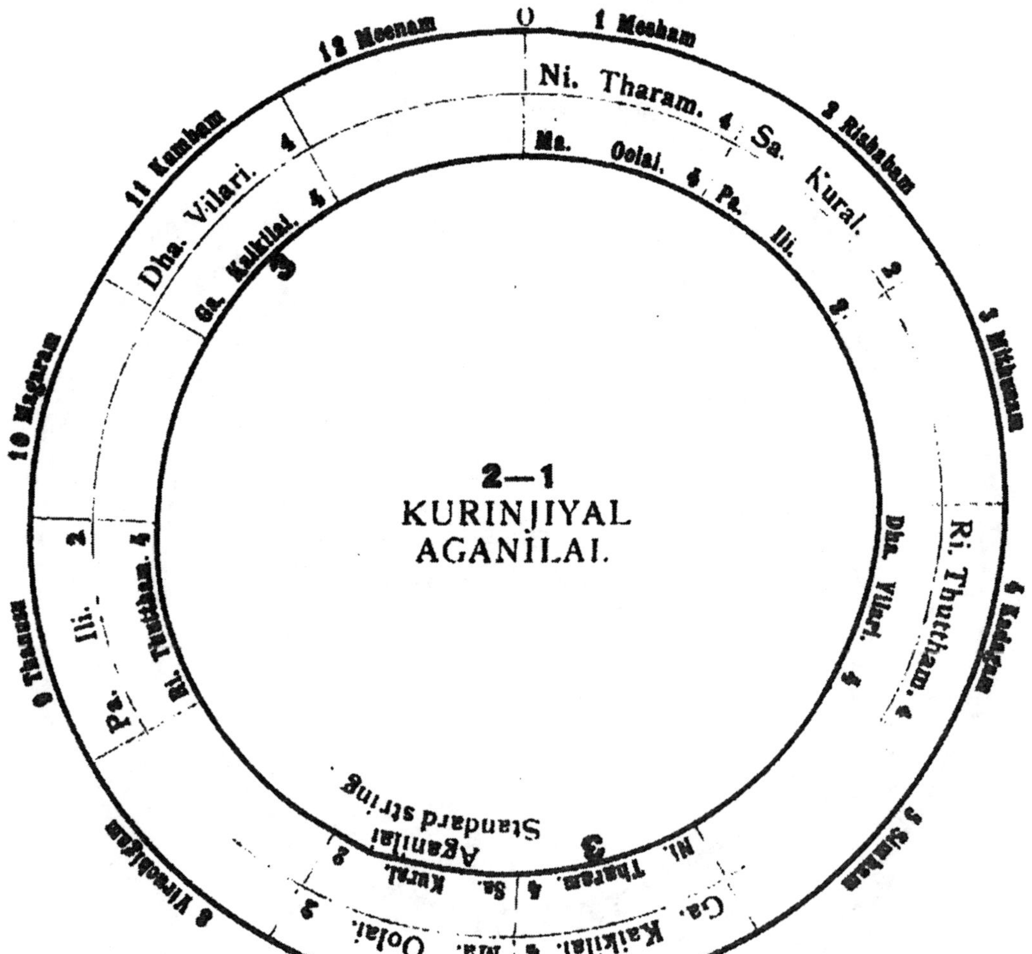

The Arumpalai Pun in Ayapalai has the series Sa, Ri 4, Ga 4, Ma 4, Pa, Dha 4, and Ni 4—Mechakalyani

The Aganilai Kurinji in Vattapalai has the series Sa, Ri 4, Ga 3, Ma 4, Pa, Dha 4 and Ni 3—Kurinji.

When Kural Commences in Kumbam which is Puranilai to Kurinji Yal we get Vilaripun in Ayapalai and Puranilai Kurinji in Vattapalai. Vilari Pun is now known as Natabairavi. We must not forget that in the following Chakaram if there are 4 Alakus in a Rasi printed in bold letters it should be sung with one Alaku less and where there are 2 Alakus it should be sung as 1. Here Kural and Ili obtain their *Karvai* (Gamakam) in the 23rd and 13th Alakus respectively. The following series will show this. In other words, they are the 3rd Alakus of Ni and Ma.

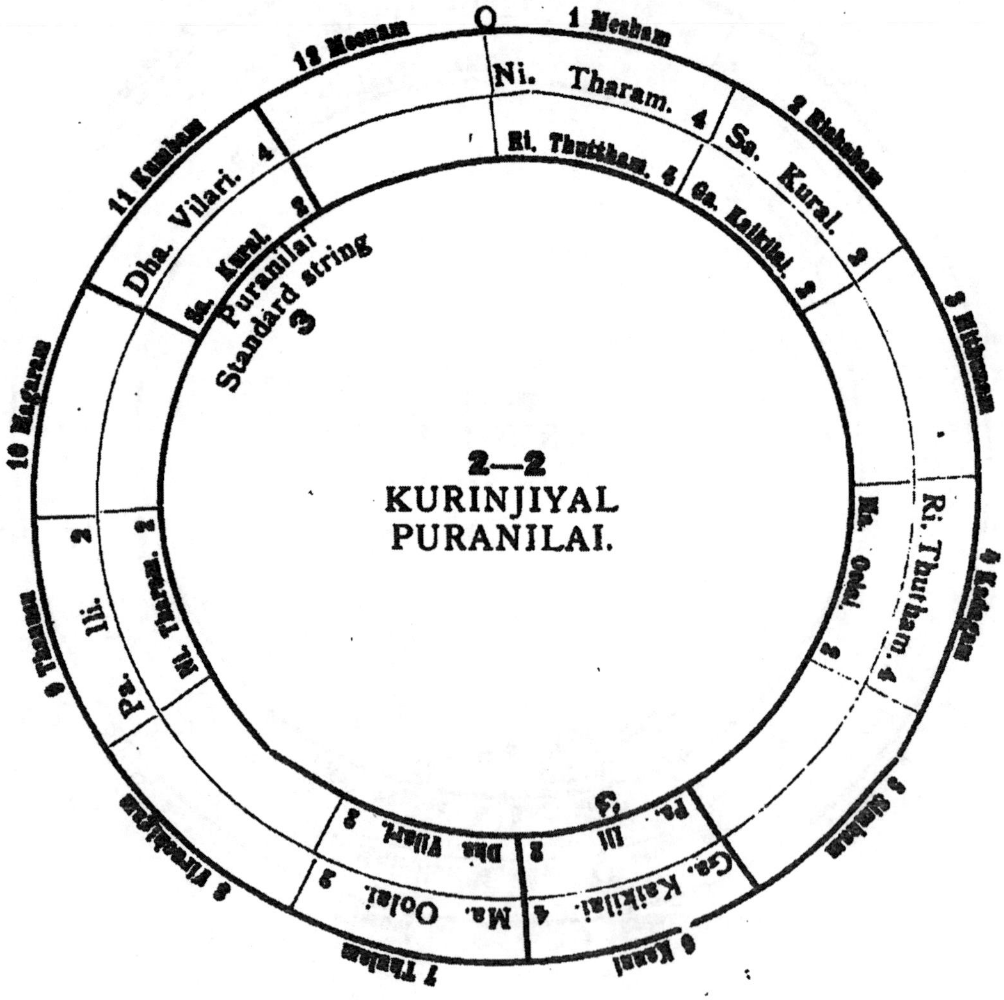

Vilari Pun in Ayapalai has the series Sa, Ri 4, Ga 2, Ma 2, Pa, Dha 2, Ni 2—Natabairavi.

Puranilai Kurinji in Vattapalai has the series Sa 3, Ri 4, Ga 2, Ma 2, Pa 3, Dha 2, Ni 2—Senthu.

When Kural commences as Kural it is Kurinji Yal Arugial Marutham. This is Sempalai Pun in Ayapalai and Arugial Kurinji in Vattapalai. And also it is called Mandilam in Vattapalai. Though it was seen in the first Chakaram as Aganilai Marutham, as Kurinji Yal Arugial is called Mandilam there is a difference between the two. The difference in names shows they are not one.

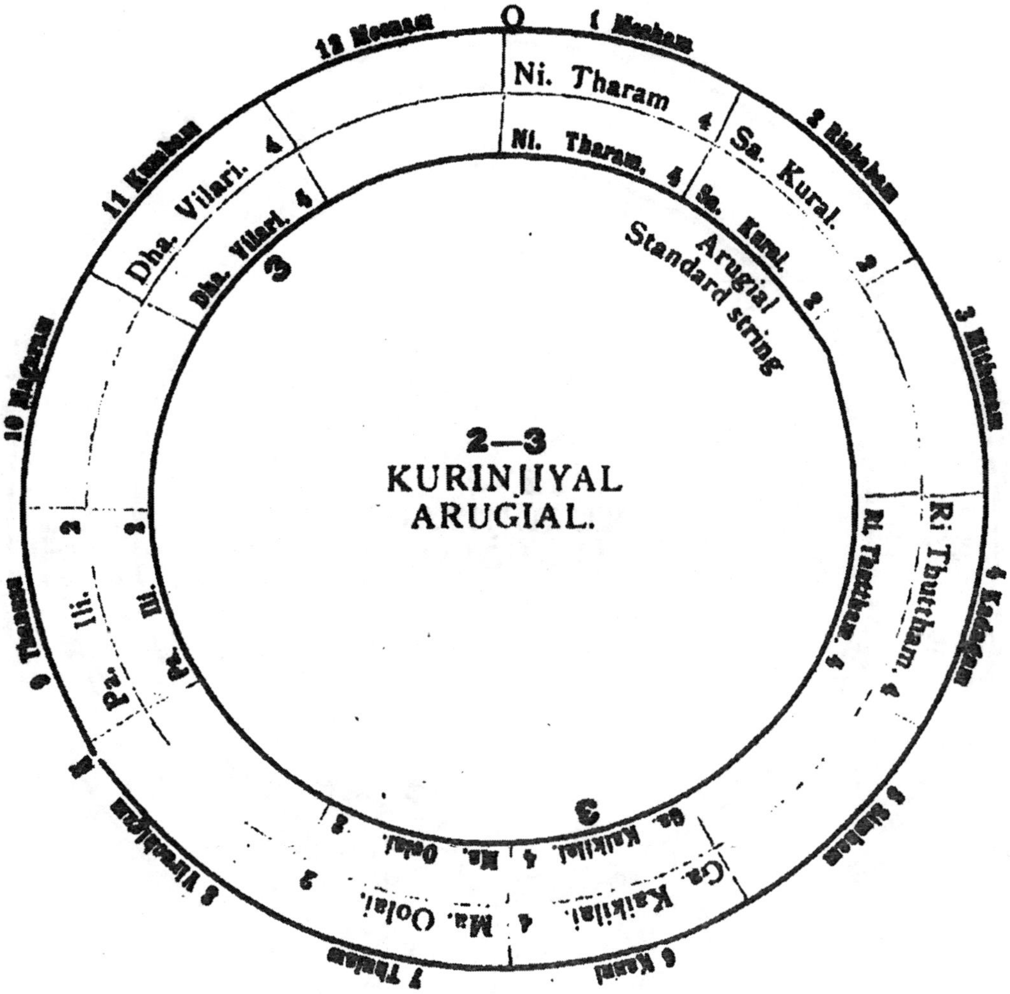

Sempalai Pun in Ayapalai has the series Sa, Ri 4, Ga 4, Ma 2, Pa, Dha 4, Ni 4—Dheerashankaraparanam.

Arugial Kurinji in Vattapalai has the series Sa, Ri 4, Ga 3, Ma 2, Pa, Dha 3, Ni 4—Mandilam.

To the Kurinji Yal Perugial, the Kaikilai in Kanni commences as Kural. This is called Sevvali Palai Pun in Ayapalai and Perugial Kurinji according to Vattapalai. It is also known as Hanumathodi in Ayapalai and Hari in Vattapalai. Though this looks like Marutha Yal Puranilai Marutham. the Ragam must be an entirely different one as it is called Agari there and Hari here.

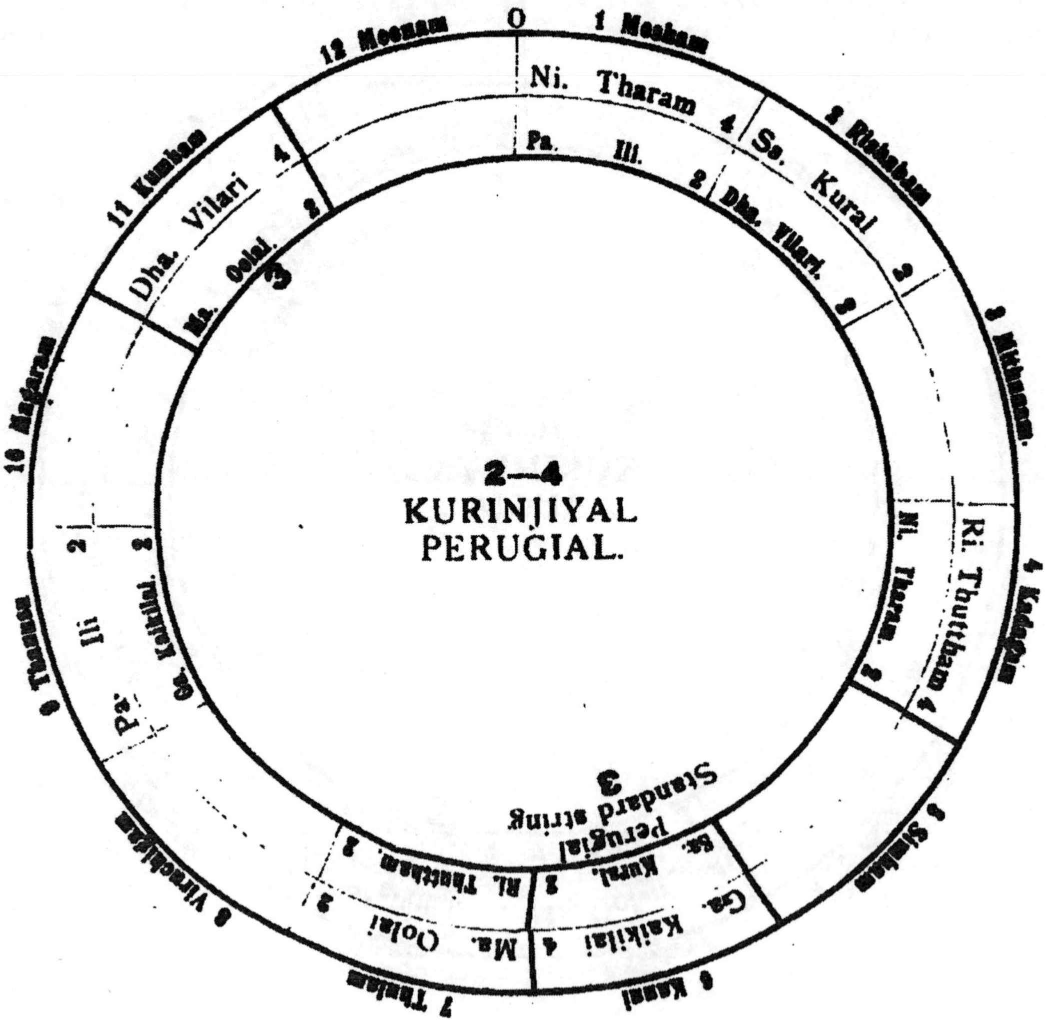

Sevvalipalai Pun in Ayapalai has the series SA, RI 2. GA 2, MA 2, PA, DHA 2, NI 2—Hanumathodi.

Perugial Kurinji in Vattapalai has the series SA 3, Ri 2. GA 2, MA 3, PA, DHA 2, NI 2,—Hari.

It is Neythal Yal when Ili becomes Kural. It is known as Kodipalai Pun in Ayapalai and Neythal Pun in Vattapalai. This is known as Harikambodi at the modern day in the system of 12 Swarams. There is no difference except in the fact that the Ri and DHA have 3 Alakus when the division as to Jatis is made it is known as Aganilai Neythal Pun.

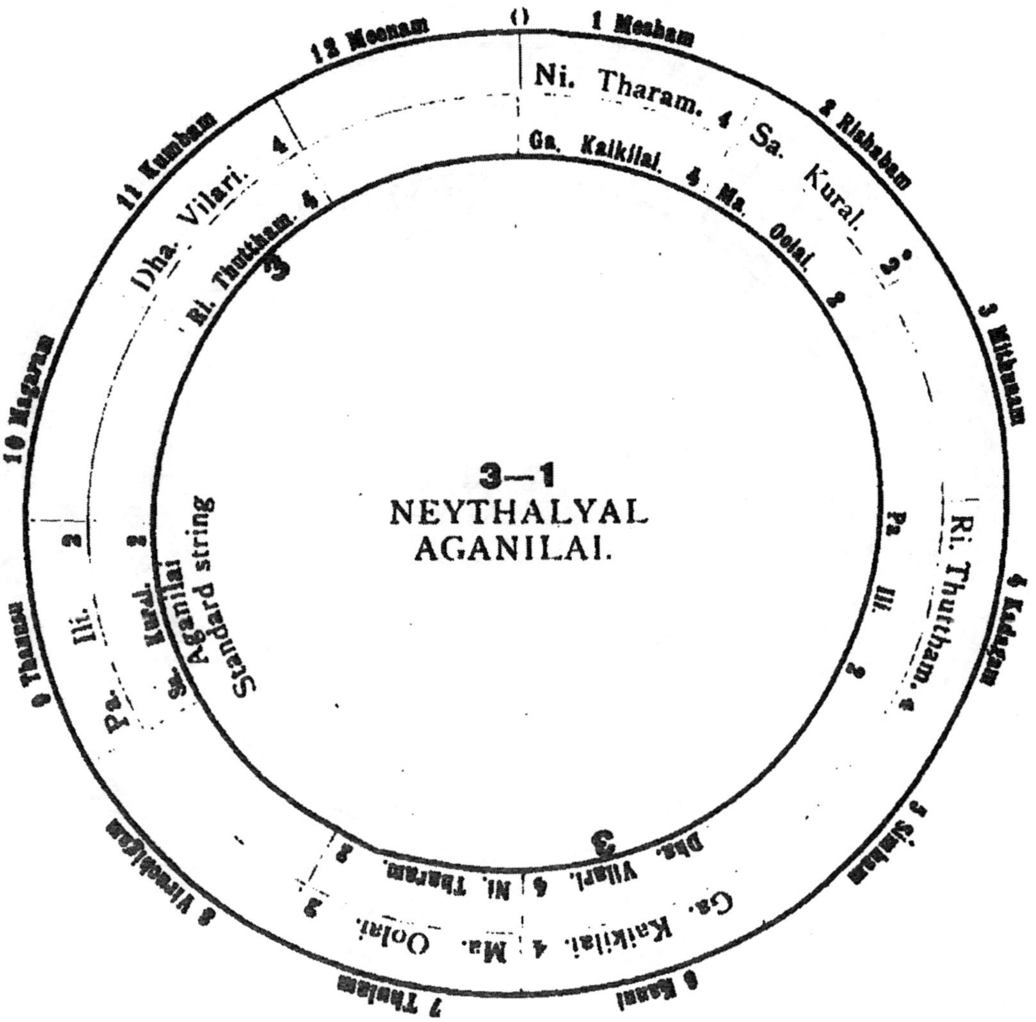

Kodipalai in the system of Ayapalai has the series SA, RI 4, GA 4, MA 2, PA, DHA 4, NI 2—Harikambodi.

Neythal Yal in Vattapalai has the series SA, RI 3, GA 4, MA 2, PA, DHA 3, NI 2—Aganilai Neythal Pun.

When Ili which appears in Thanusu becomes Kural its fourth string or Taram becomes Puranilai. The Ragam which commences from it as the first string or Kural is called Neythal Yal Puranilai. It is called Merchempalai and Suddha Thodi in Ayapalai and Neythal Yal Puranilai and Velavali in Vattapalai.

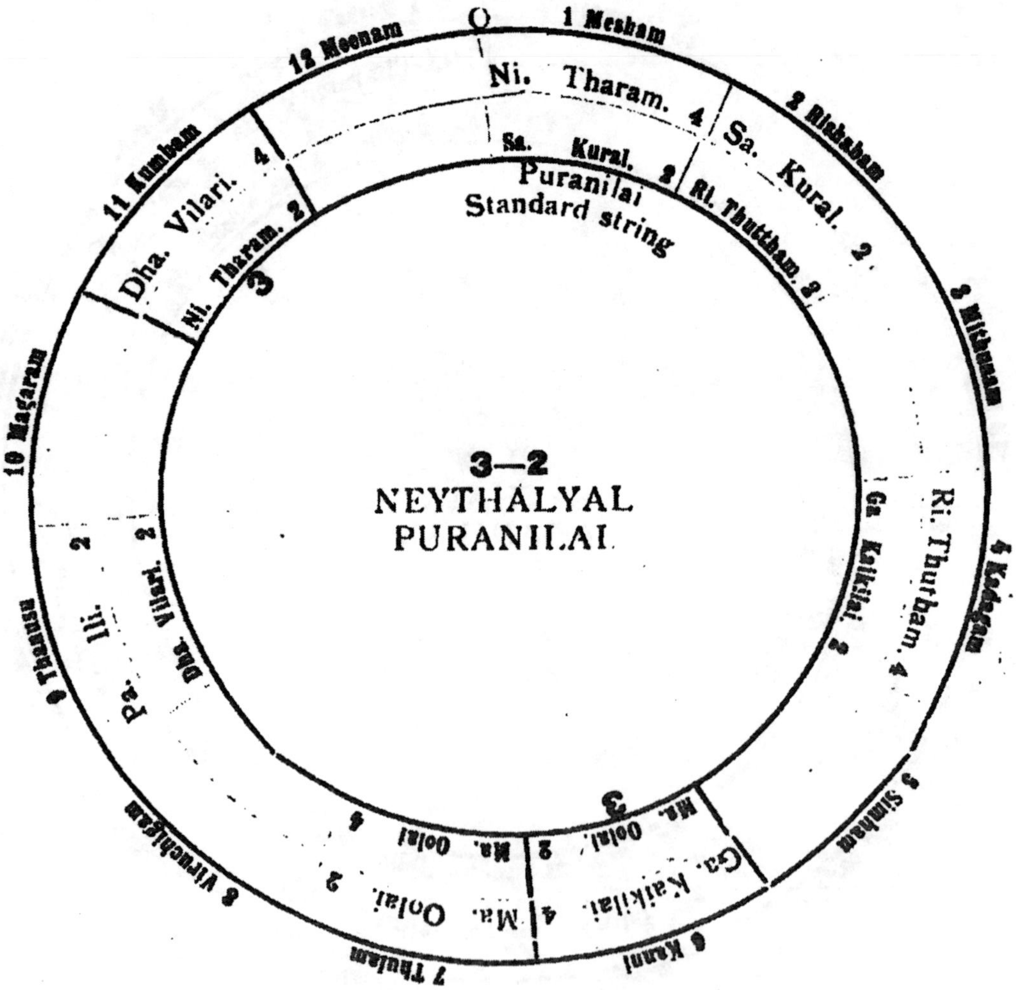

Merchempalai in Ayapalai has the series Sa, Ri 2, Ga 2, Ma 2, Ma 4, Dha 2, Ni 2—Suddha Thodi.

Neythal Puranilai in Vattapalai has the series Sa, Ri 2, Ga 2, Ma 3, Ma 4, Dha 2, Ni 3—Velavali.

To the Neythal Yal which is obtained when Kural commences in Ili in Thanusu, the Swaram which stands in the Rasi which is seventh to it becomes Arugial. When Kural commences in Kadagam it is known as Padumalai Palai in Ayapalai and Neythal Yal Arugial in the Vattapalai system. It is also known as Karaharapirya in Ayapalai and Seeragam in Vattapalai.

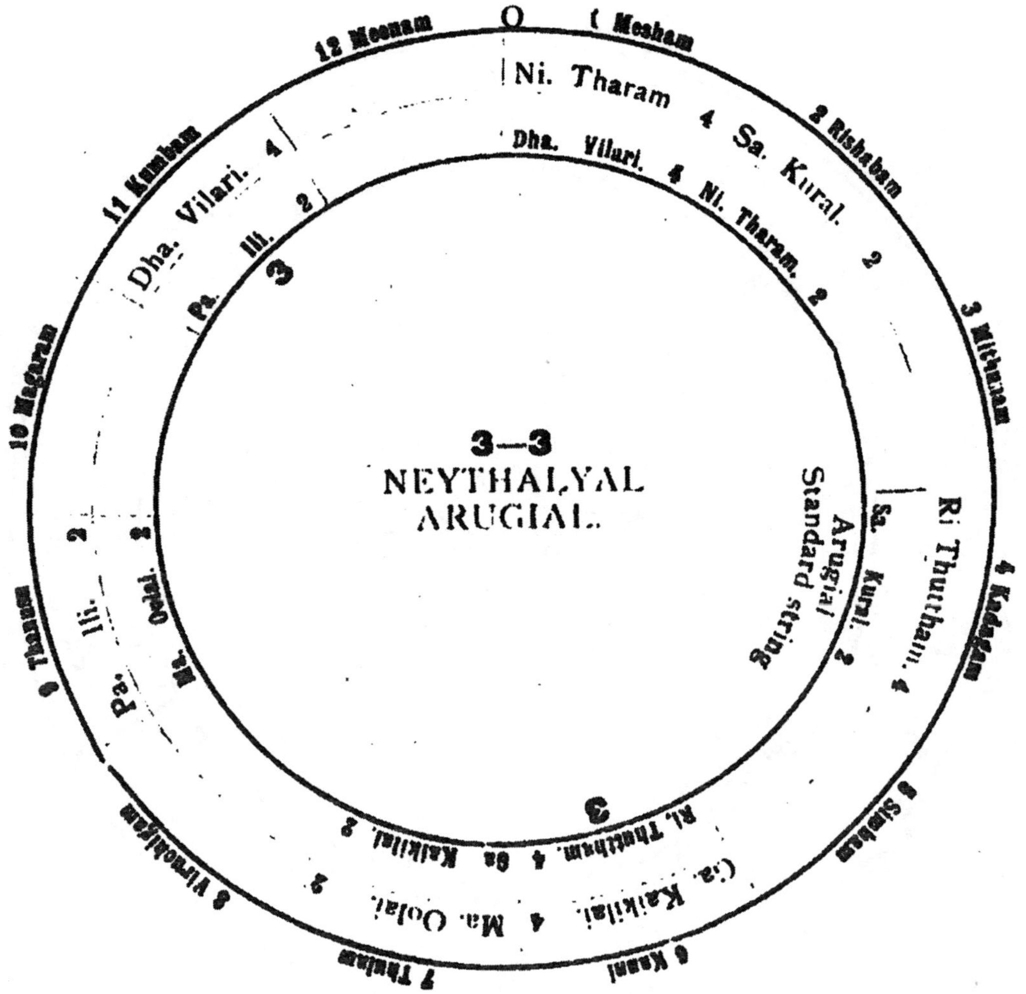

Padumalai Palai in Ayapalai has the series SA. RI 4, GA 2, MA 2, PA, DHA 4, NI 2—Karaharapiriya.

Neythal Yal Arugial in Vattapalai has the series SA, RI 3, GA 2. MA 2, PA 3. DHA 4, NI 2—Seeragam.

To the Neythal Yal which is formed when Kural commences in Ili in Thanusu, the 12th. Rasi will be Viruchigam. And when Kural commences in this Viruchigam it is Perugial. The Ragam which results when Kural commences in Oolai with 4 Alakus or Prathi Mathimam is known at present as Bavani in Ayapalai. It is one of the five secondary Palais according to the ancient system. It has been known as Neythal Yal Perugial and Sandi according to Vattapalai.

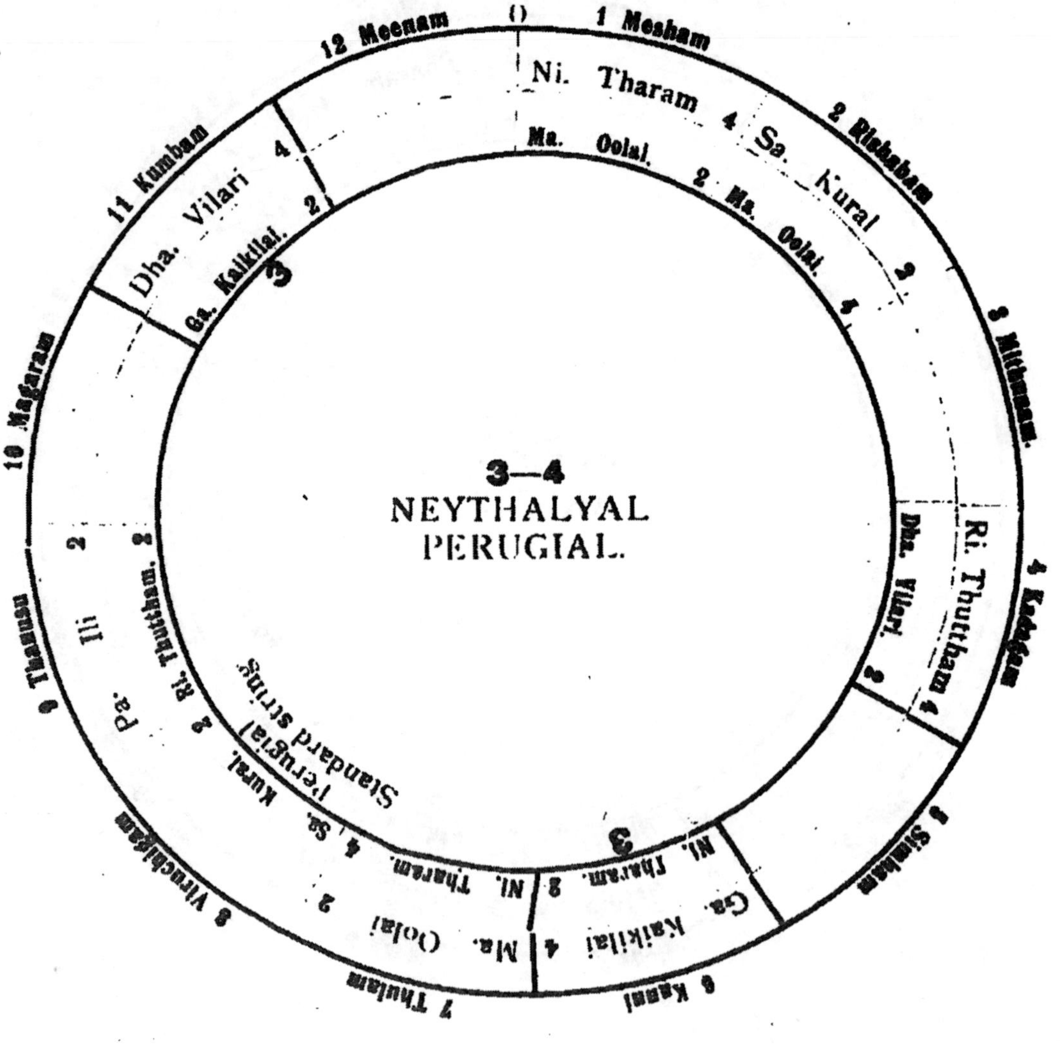

One of the 5 secondary Palais in Ayapalai has the series SA, RI 2, GA 2, MA* 2, MA 4, DHA 2, NI 2, NI* 4—Bavani.

Neythal Yal Perugial in Vattapalai has the series SA, RI 2, GA 3, MA 2, MA 4, DHA 2, NI 3, NI 4—Sandi.

When Kural commences in Thulam in Mesham it is Palai Yal or Aganilai. It is called Merchampalai in Ayapalai and Palai Yal Aganilai in Vattapalai. It is also known as Suddha Thodi in Ayapalai and Palai according to the Vattapalai system. Though there seems to be a repetition of the Ragas in Ayapalai yet they are different in Vattapalai having Swarams with less Alakus.

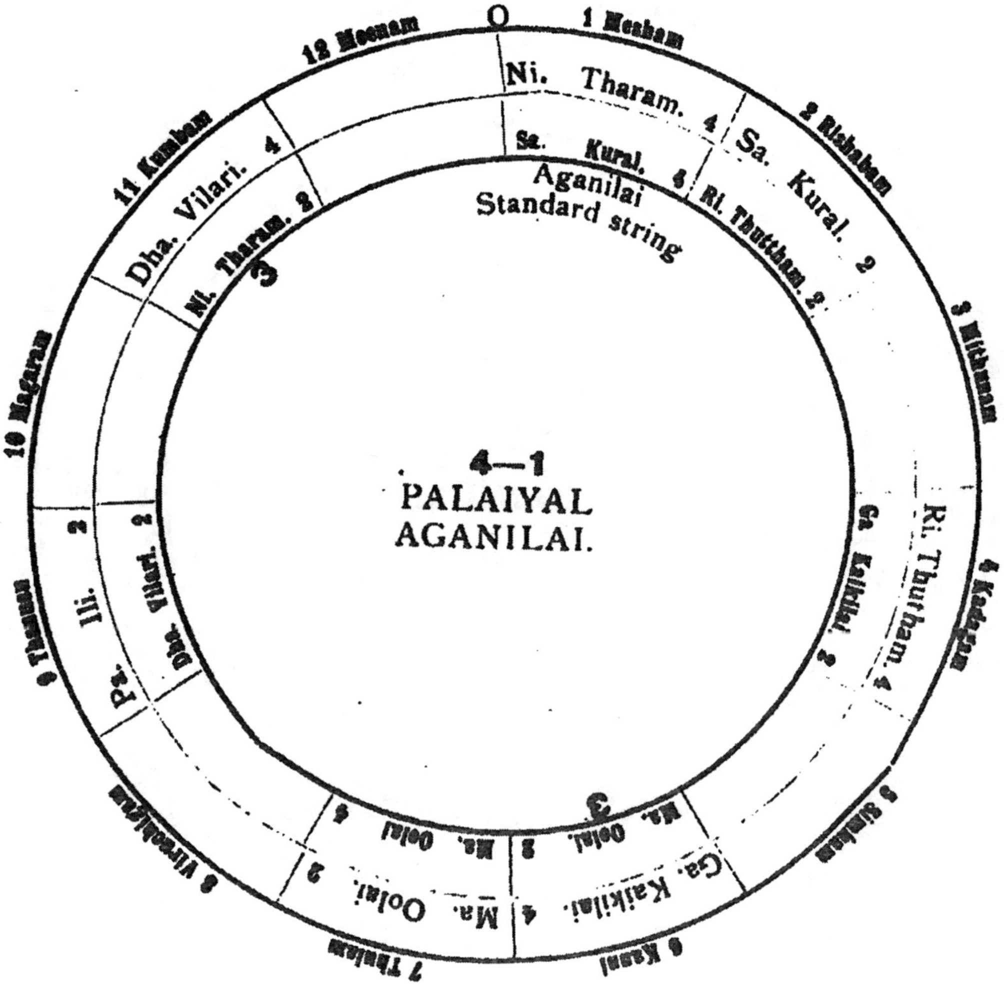

Merchempalai in Ayapalai has the series Sa, Ri 2, Ga 2, Ma 2, Ma 4, Dha 2, Ni 2—Suddha Thodi.

Palai Yal Aganilai in Vattapalai has the series Sa, Ri 2, Ga 2, Ma 3. Ma 4. Dha 2, Ni 3—Palai.

When Kural commences in the fourth string from Tharam in Mesham it is Puranilai. This is known as Sevvali Chiru Palai in Ayapalai and Palai Yal Puranilai in Vattapalai. It is known at present as Dharmani and Devali in Vattapalai.

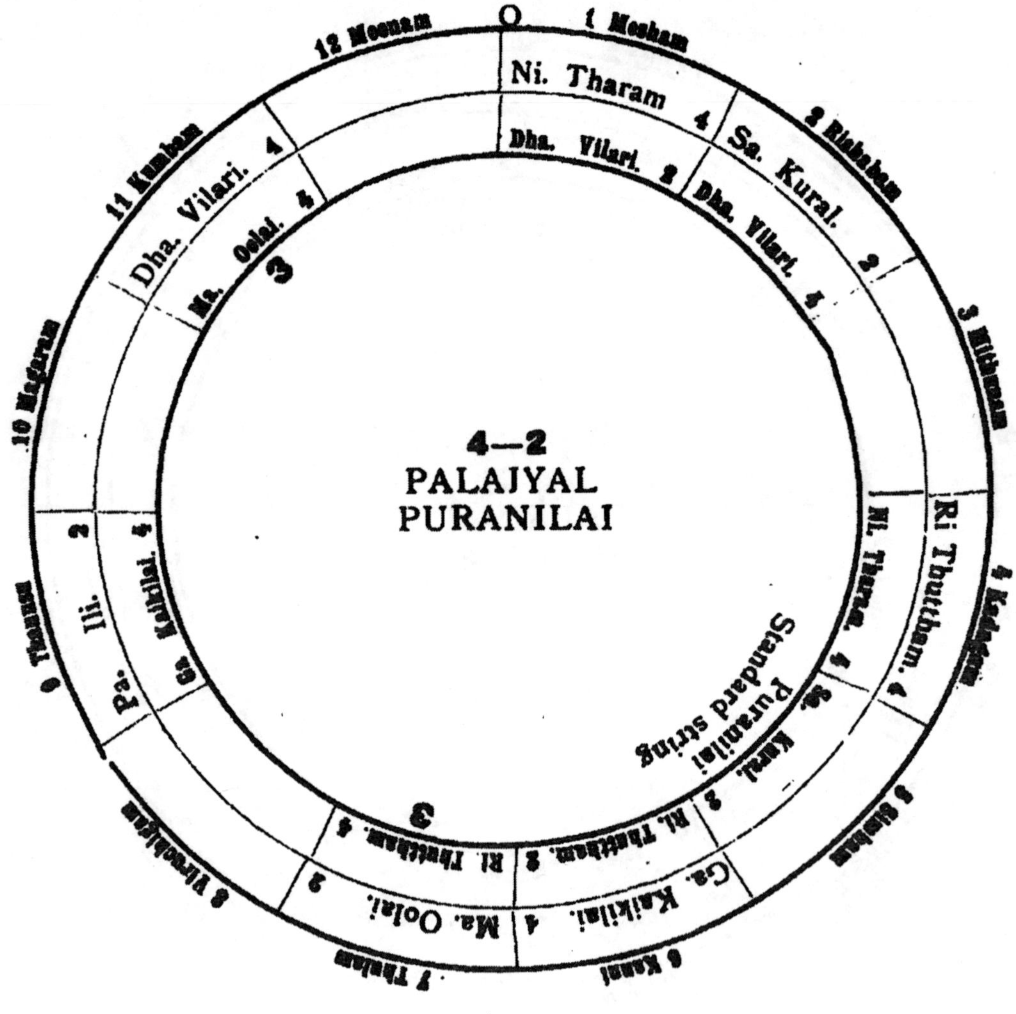

Sevvali Chiru Palai in Ayapalai has the series Sa, Ri 2, Ri 4, Ga 4, Ma* 4, Dha 2, Dha 4, Ni* 4—Dharmani.

Palai Yal Puranilai in Vattapalai has the series Sa, Ri 2, Ri 3, Ga 4, Ma 4, Dha 2, Dha 3, Ni 4—Devali.

The Swaram in Virichigam becomes Inai Swaram to the Kural in Mesham. When that swaram itself is taken as Kural it is Palai Yal Arugial. It is known as the Chiru Palai in Aroompalai in Ayapalai and Palai Yal Arugial in Vattapalai. It is used as Bavani by the system of 12 Swarams and Seerkodigam according to the system of 24 Srutis.

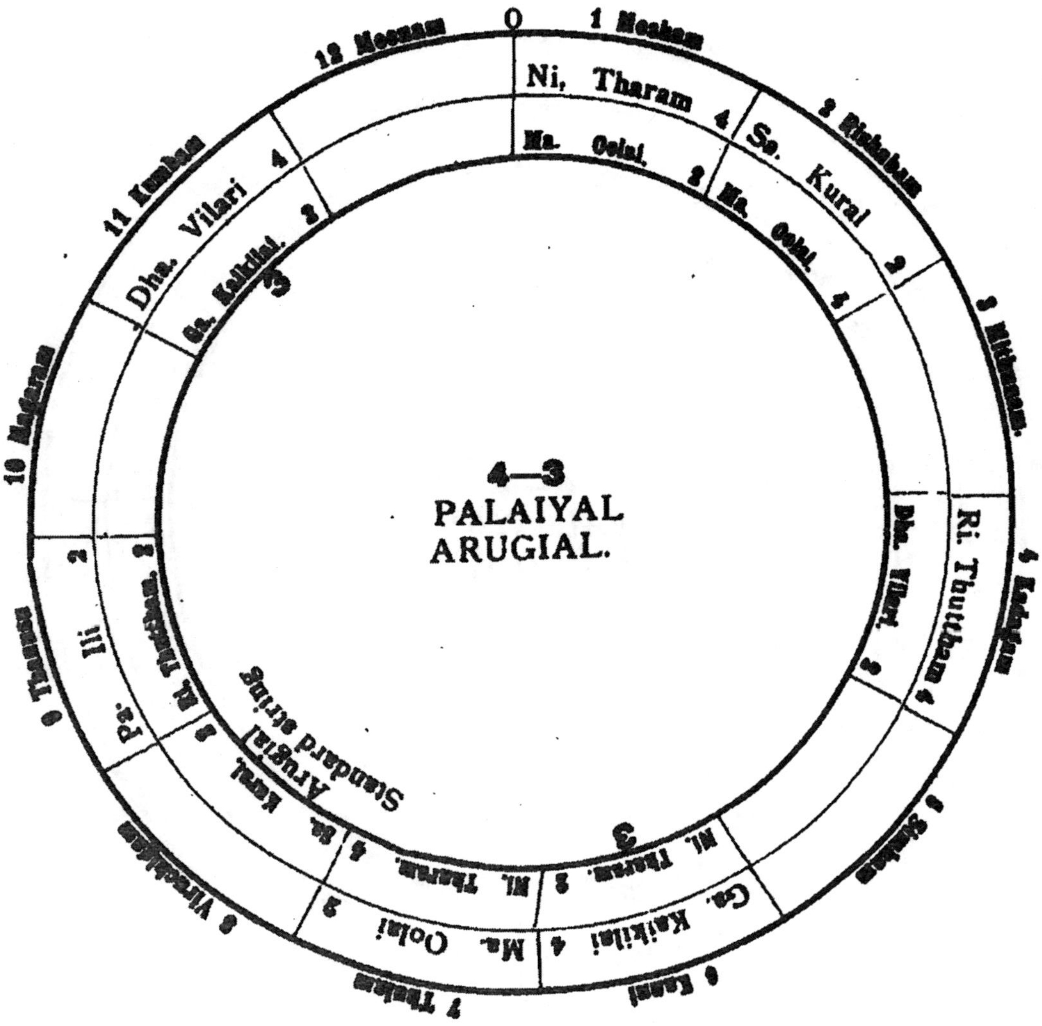

Chiru Palai in Aroompalai according to Ayapalai has the series Sa 2, Ri 2, Ga 2, Ma 2, Ma 4, Dha 2, Ni 2, Ni 4—Bavani.

Palai Yal Arugial in Vattapalai has the series Sa 2, Ri 2, Ga 3, Ma 2, Ma 4, Dha 2, Ni 3, Ni 4—Seerkodigam.

The swaram in Meenam stands in the relation of Perugial to the Kural commencing from Mesham. When Kural commences in Meenam it is called Chiru Palai in Merchempalai according to 'Ayapalai, and Chandrajothi in the modern day. It has been known as Palai Yal Perugial in Vattapalai and Naga Ragam in ancient times.

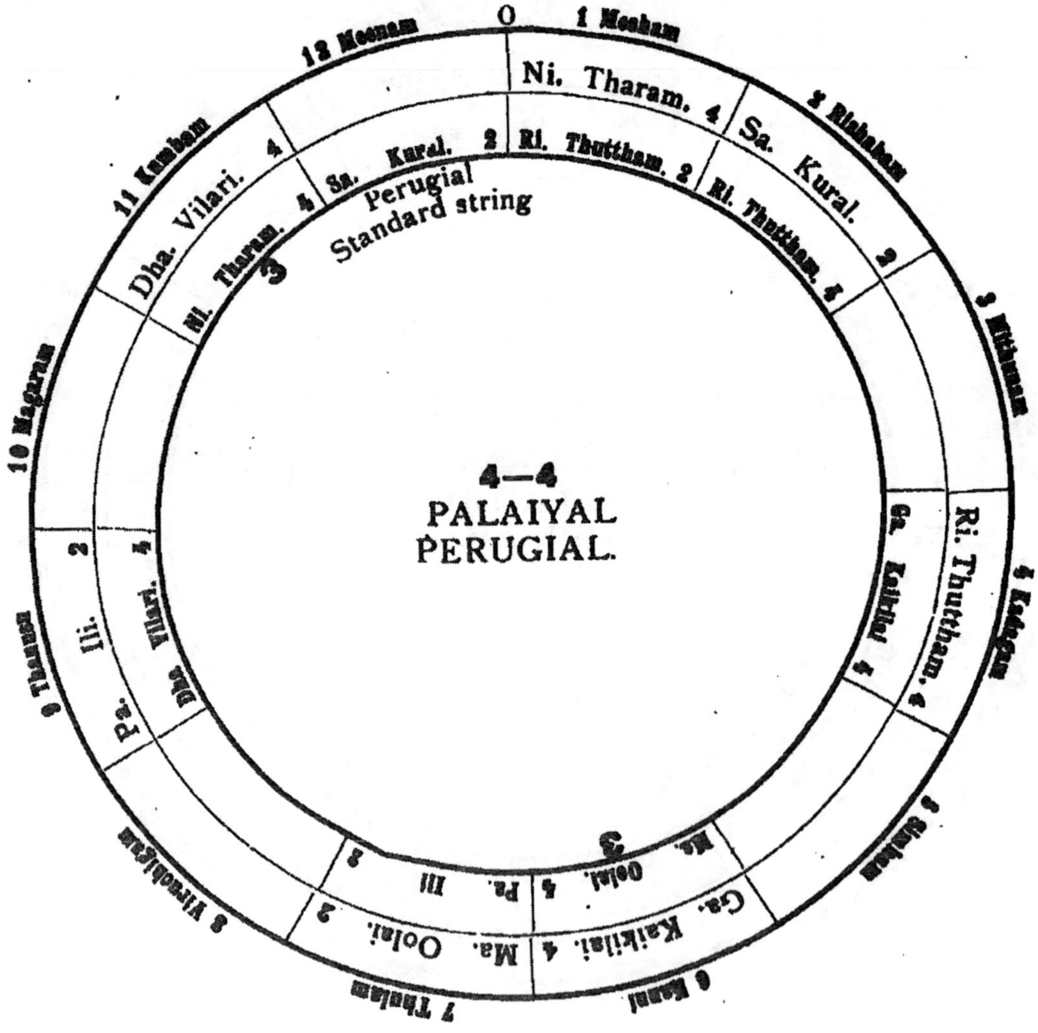

Chiru Palai in Merchempalai in Vattapalai has the series Sa, Ri* 2, Ri* 4, Ga 4, Ma 4, Pa, Dha 4, Ni 4—Chandrajothi.

Palai Yal Perugial in Vattapalai has the series Sa, Ri 2, Ri 4, Ga 4, Ma 3, Pa, Dha 4, Ni 3—Nagaragam.

We see, then, from the above Chakarams the order of the four kinds of Yal, the four Jathis derived from each of them and their names. We also see that the ancient Tamils had their general ganam with 12 primary Swarams whereas the experts among them made ganam with an Alaku less in Swarams that were concordant as Vadi and Samvadi or SA-PA and SA-MA or Vilari-Kaikilai. Their ganam consisted of 22 Srutis whereas the Sthayi was made up of 24 Srutis. The 24 Srutis were determined by the 12 Swarams which stood in the 12 Rasis. Each Rasi had 2 Alakus, and SA-PA had 7 Rasis and 14 Srutis and SA-MA had 5 Rasis and 10 Srutis. The rule was laid down that the Swarams of the seventh Rasis with 14 Alakus were Inai Swarams, and the Swarams that occurred in the fifth Rasis with 10 Alakus were Kilai Swarams. On the same principle the Swaram that occurred in the fourth Rasi with 8 Alakus was Natpu Swaram and that in the second Rasi with 4 Alakus was also a concordant one. We see distinctly that the ancient Tamils had used these Swarams with great effect even 12,000 years ago.

We noted in Part I that many of the great works which spoke about the music that was in use at the time of the three Sangams were destroyed. Ilankovadigal mentions only their essence and a few important points in his Silappadikaram. The Tamil works which speak about music in detail at the present day are rare. Yet, the systems of Yal have been given with the help of a few remarks found in Silappadikaram and its commentaries. More points will be given when we obtain works that speak more in detail about music. Yet there are data enough to prove that the ancient Tamils divided the Sthayi into 24 Srutis, but made ganam in them with 22 Srutis (two Alakus less) and in 7 Swarams.

Among the 16 kinds of Puns shown above we find that one or two Ragas are repeated. Yet, as they have different names, there must have been some rules to avoid their repetition. Again, the names of the 14 Primary Puns are mentioned in Pingala Nigandu, and these names are different in the different Yals. The Table showing the 16 kinds of Puns is given below.

The names of the 16 Puns derived from the four Yal, their commencing Swarams and their Alaku system.

4 Yals.	Swaram.	4 Jathis.	Beginning Swaram.	Sa	Ri	Ga	Ma	Pa	Dha	Ni	Ragam.
Marutha Yal.	Sa	Aganilai ...	Sa	2	4	3	2	4	3	4	Marutham.
,,		Puranilai ...	Ga	3	2	2	1	4	2	2	Agari.
,,		Arugial ...	Pa	4	3	4	2	4	3	2	Sayavelarkolli.
,,		Perugial ...	Ni	4	2	2	1*	0	2	1	Kinnaram.
Kurinji Yal ...	Ma	Aganilai ...	Ma	2	4	3	4	2	4	3	Kurinji.
		Puranilai ...	Dha	3	4	2	2	3	2	2	Senthu.
		Arugial ...	Sa	2	4	3	2	4	3	4	Mandilam.
		Perugial ...	Ga	3	2	2	1	4	2	2	Ari.
Neythal Yal ...	Pa	Aganilai ...	Pa	4	3	4	2	4	3	2	Neythal.
		Puranilai ...	Ni	4	2	2	1*	0	2	1	Valavali.
		Arugial ...	Ri	4	3	2	2	3	4	2	Siragam.
		Perugial ...	Ma	2	2	1	2*	0	2	1*	Santhi.
Palai Yal ...	Ni	Aganilai ...	Ni	4	2	2	1*	0	2	1	Palai.
		Puranilai ...	Ga	2	1*	4	3	0	2*	4	Davali.
		Arugial ...	Ma	2	2	1	2*	0	2	1*	Seerkodigam.
		Perugial ...	Ni	2	2*	4	3	2	4	3	Nagaragam.

If the number of Alakus for the Rasis left out be added, the Total will be 22.

* It must be understood that the Swaram of the next Rasi is implied where the Star mark appears, and that the Swaram in such Rasis is left out.

29. The explanation of the Chakaram where the four Jathis generate from the four kinds of Yal.

We are very familiar with the outer Rasi Chakaram of the following Chakaram. It shows how the Sapta Swarams stand complete in the 12 Rasis with their Alakus. The inner circle shows how the Swarams stand concordant on the principle of Inai, Kilai, Pagai and Natpu, the principle that guided the ancient Tamils. According to the Sootram "கிளை நரம்பிற்கு மூன்றும் ஆறும் பெற நிற்பது பகையாகும்", the Swarams in the 3rd and 6th compartments to that in the 12th will be in the relation of Pagai, and when the Inai Swaram in the seventh is taken as the standard the Swarams in the 10th and the 1st (3rd and 6th) will be in the relation of Pagai.

According to this system, the Rasis which occur as 2, 4, 5, 7, 9, 11 to the standard Rasi and the Swarams in them are the seven Swarams of the Aroganam. It also shows that the two Swarams Dha and Ga which are Vadi and Samvadi Swarams rightward and leftward should have only 3 Alakus instead of 4 according to the system that Kaikilai appears in Vilari. It also shows the Swarams from which the four kinds of Yal generate. We noted before that when Kural in Itapam commences as Kural it is Marutha Yal. We also noted the seven Swarams concordant with it. If you want to see the same in this Chakaram you should do this. The Rasi with number 12 in the inner circle should be placed right opposite to Itapam in the outer circle. Then the Swarams of the two circles are concordant. The series will be Sa 2, Ri 4, Ga 3, Ma 2, Pa 4, Dha 3 and Ni 4 with 22 Alakus. This is Sempalai Pun or Shankaraparanam when it comes in the 12 Rasis as half-swarams without lessening two Alakus. But when two Alakus are lessened it is Marutha Pun.

In the same way if the 5th Rasi of the inner circle be placed against Itapam and Oolai is made the standard string, the following series will result, namely, the Swarams in 5, 7, 9, 11, 12, 2, 4, of the outer circle. The series will be Sa 2, Ri 4, Ga 3, Ma 4, Pa 2, Dha 4, Ni 3 with 22 Alakus. This is Kurinji Pun. When it is sung in Ayapalai without lessening the 2 Alakus it is called Arumpalai Pun or Mecha Kalyani. So also the four kinds of Yal and the Aganilai, Puranilai, Arugial and Perugial from them which occur at 12, 4, 7 and 11 respectively might be seen clearly there.

The recurrence of the 3 Alakus for Vilari and Kaikilai will be in different Swarams when seen in the inner circle as stated above. We have noted already that the 12 Palais will be formed when the 12 Rasis in Ayapalai become the commencing strings. But there should be no lessening of Alakus for the 12 Palais when change of Graham is effected. Dha and Ga should invariably have 4 Alakus each. In that case we obtain the Ragas given in the Table on Pages 640 and 641. This he calls Ayapalai. There is not much difference between the methods used for deriving Ragas from Ayapalai and Vattapalai. The only difference is that the Ragas derived from Vattapalai should be sung in 22 Srutis only with an Alaku less in Dha-Ga. The other Swarams of Vattapalai are identical with those of Ayapalai. On the other hand, there is much difference in charm between singing the 7 out of the 12 Swarams of Ayapalai

The double Chakaram showing how the four Jatis spring from the four kinds of Yal.

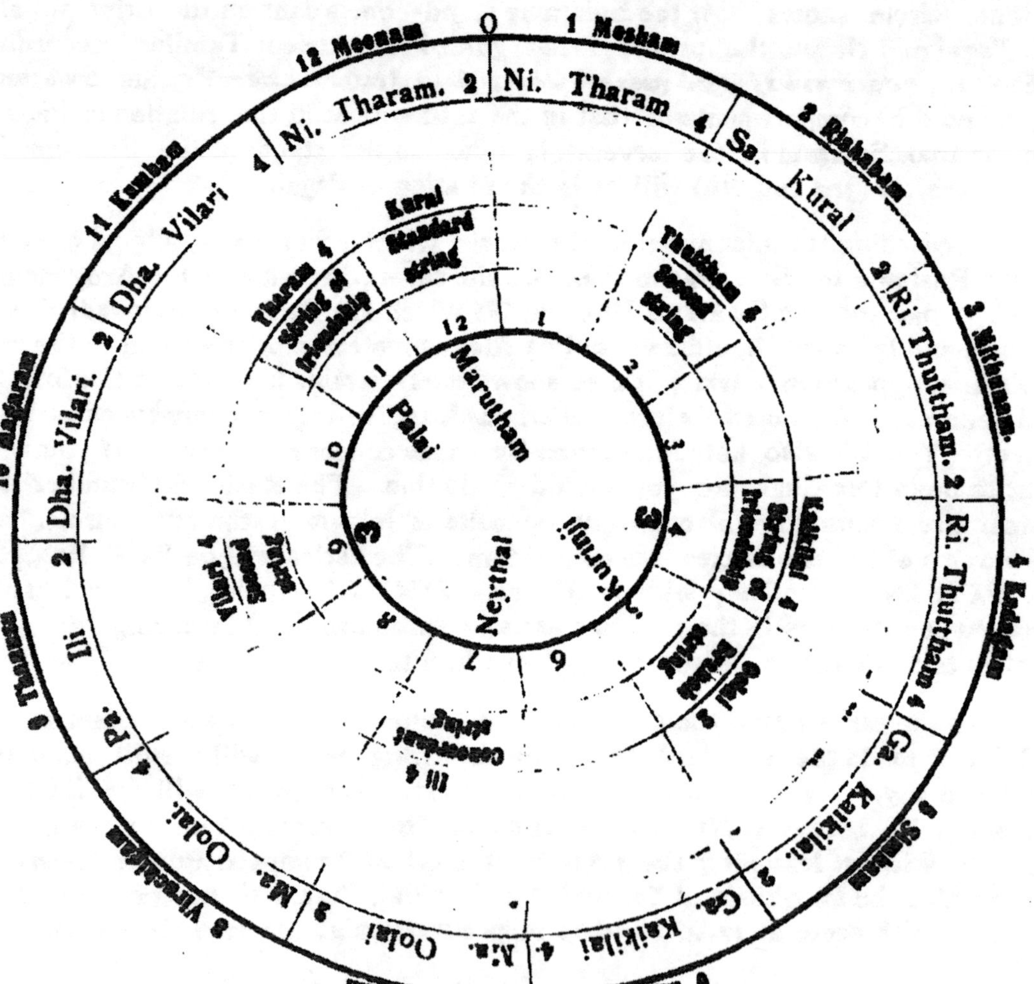

and the 7 Swarams of Vattapalai with 2 Alakus less. But in the Swara system and the system of Ragas the identity between the two is complete. We have said before, that they first sang according to the system of Ayapalai and then according to Vattapalai with 2 Alakus less. So we understand that the Karnatic Music we use at present has been sung extensively without any doubt, most clearly and with great charm.

30. The six mother Ragas of the Tamil country.

If we notice the Ragam on the first line of Table 2 on page 641. We may find that it has harmonious Swarams and also contains in itself the common rule from which Ragas are generally derived with the help of such harmonious Swarams. This is the Mother of all Ragas. Its ancient name Sempalai Pun has disappeared and it is now known as Shankaraparanam. This Mother-ragam has been considered one of the best of Ragas by Vidwans and others up to the present day. Its jannya ragas are held in the same estimation. Are there Tamilians who are not familiar with Ragas such as Amsadoni, Atana, Arabi, Kanada. Ketharam, Byagu, Bilahari, Suddha Saveri, Garudathoni, Devagandari, Durbar, Biagatai and Neelambari? Is there a baby which is not lulled to sleep by hearing the Neelamburi Ragam? It is said in Thiruvilayadal Puranam that Paramasivam in the garb of a woodcutter sang the Ragam Neelambari, the ancient Sathari, before Yemanatha, on behalf of Panapathiran. The Ragam is considered by all to be so charming as to make even a dead tree shoot forth young tendrils.

The fact that we find the Sathari or Neelambari Ragam so commonly sung as lullaby by mothers and girls is proof enough for its extensive use in the Tamil country. Just as Shankaraparanam or Chempalai Pun is the mother of all Ragas, Neelambari or Sathari is the first of all Ragas which is sung by mothers in lulling their babies to sleep and is of a melting nature.

From this we are enabled to say that Virisadai Kadavul, the originator of Muttamil, even at the commencement of the first Sangam (i.e. 12000 years ago) was a patron of Isai Tamil among Muttamil, that he instituted the Chempalai Pun or Shankaraparanam which contains in itself the principle of order of Swarams, and that he derived many Ragas from it by the change of Swarams in Aroganam and Avaroganam.

When we come to the chapter on modern names of Ragas for the ancient Ragas used in Thevaram and Thiruvachakam we shall understand why we give the name Sathari to the ancient Neelambari.

Referring to Table 2 on page 641 we find that Chempalai Pun which is the mother of all the mother Ragas is called Shankaraparanam at present. When we change the graham for the seven Swarams of Chempalai Pun we get six mother Ragas.

When Kural commences in Thuttham with 4 Alakus we get Padumalaipalai Pun. This is the modern Karaharapiriya.

When Kural commenced in Kaikilai with 4 Alakus it was called Chevvalipalai by the ancients. It is called Hanumathodi at present.

The modern Mechakalyani is the Areompalai Pun of the ancients where Kural commenced in Oolai with 2 Alakus.

Harikambodi of the modern day is the Kodipalai Pun of ancient times where Kural commenced in Ili.

The modern Natabairavi is not different from the Vilaripalai Pun or Vilaripalai when the Vilari with 4 Alakus is commenced as Kural according to Isai Tamil.

Suddha Thodi is the same as the Merchempalai Pun of the ancient Tamils where the Tharam with 4 Alakus commences as Kural.

We find that the seventh of these Ragas, Suddha Thodi, occurs without the Panchamam. But as the Sampoorna Ragam Hanumathodi results when GA is the first Swaram, this Suddha Thodi has been omitted from the list of mother Ragas and only six mother Ragas are made mention of. Hence we think that the first is called Chempalai Pun while the seventh is Merchempalai, the identity between them being clear.

The Tamilians are quite familiar even at the present day with the 6 mother Ragas—Shankarabaranam, Karaharapiriya, Hanumathodi, Mechakalyani, Harikambodi, and Natabhairavi and the more than 300 Jannya Ragas derived from them.

31. How the ancient Tamils used 6 Alakus or Srutis for Kaikilai and Tharam.

We find 5 secondary Palais, leaving aside the 7 primary Palais noted before in the Chakaram on page 640 which explains the formation of the 12 Palais. There is a special point to be noted in connection with this. We see from the table the Swarams for the six mother Ragas. They are the 12 half Swarams of Ayapalai. They appear to be irregular without mixing with their respective Alakus. In other words, each Swaram occurs in its second and fourth Alakus. But the Swarams of the secondary Palais appear to mix with the adjacent Swarams. In other words NI occurs in DHA and GA in RI.

NI appears in the boundary of DHA with four Alakus in the Ragam Dharmani which is found in the fourth Palai of the Table of the 12 Palais. Instead of standing with its four Alakus under SA, it stands in the second house of DHA. Likewise, NI occurs in the forth Alaku of DHA in Mecha-Kambodi which is the ninth Palai. There is a recurrence of this in the eleventh Palai also. In the same manner, GA occurs under RI with 4 Alakus in the fourth as well as the eleventh. We conclude, therefore, that GA and NI occur with six Alakus of the three Rasis. The six Alakus are obtained by adding two Alakus of the second of the Rasis of RI and DHA. In the same manner RI and DHA may obtain 2 Alakus from each of the boundaries of GA and NI. From the above points, we are enabled to conclude that the ancient Tamils understood by means of the secondary Palais the GA and NI occurring under RI and DHA and *Vise Versa* and that they used the many Ragas obtained through the secondary Palais. We shall find later on that the above four Swarams had 5 Srutis each and that they were so used. We call at the modern day the Swarams with two Srutis by the name of Suddha Swaram, the Swaram with four Alakus by the name of Chathursruti, Satharanam or Kaisikam while the Swarams with 6 Srutis are called Shatsruti, Antharam and Kakali.

We find here, then the chief Amsams of the 72 Melakartas of the present day. We have noted often the 24 Alakus at the rate of 2 for each of the Rasis and the Swarams of the 12 Rasis occurring as 24 Alakus. There is no reason for any doubt in this matter. It follows as a matter of course, then, that when RI, DHA, GA and NI mix together and occur in the 3 Rasis they get six Alakus or Srutis. So the 72 Karta Ragas and the Ragas derived from them form about a 1000 which are included under the 12000 ancient Isais of the Tamils. Even this 1000 is never wholly sung but only two or three hundred of them. Even among these, the four primary Puns of Vattapalai, the 16 different kinds of Jatis derived from them and their Jannya Ragas are found mixed with less Alakus. They will be dealt with later on. When the Ragas for Ayaplai and Vattapalai are so clearly stated, without being able to discriminate between the 12 Palais or half Swarams and their Jannya ragas and the quarter Swarams of Vattapalai and their Jannya ragas, many writers divided the Sthayi into 22 Srutis, gave them different names, confounded the Ragas of Ayapalai and Vattpalai and wrote different works which led to the confusion of many. The confusion became worse confounded when they could not reconcile their theory with their practice. This doubt affected every one that was enquiring about the question of Srutis.

On the other hand, we have made quite clear that the ancient Tamils were quite sure about arriving at the 12 Swarams of a Sthayi on the SA-PA principle, that they made ganam in them lessening an Alaku in two of those Swarams and that they reckoned the number of Srutis to be 24 in a Sthayi.

We have given a table showing how the 12 Swarams of an octave are approximately derived on the principle of SA-PA $\frac{3}{2}$ and SA-MA $\frac{4}{3}$. Their minute calculations will be given in Part IV.

We shall do well now to quote a few practical illustrations to show that many of the modern Ragas are sung in the 24 Srutis.

32. Some evidence to show that our modern ganam resembles that of the ancient Tamils who cut out 2 Srutis in Dha-Ga according to the system of Vattapalai or the 24 Srutis of the Octave.

Noble readers ! After the destruction of the works on music and rules on Isai Tamil of the first Ooli, even the remnants of those perserved at the period of the last Sangam are brought to light by references in Silappadikaram of Ilenkovadigal and its commentary. Even the ideas of this excellent system have been confounded by differences of opinion. As the later works on music were all in sanskrit, musicians have been unable to understand them completely, and they have been floundering since in the mire with their theory of 22 Srutis.

We see clearly from history that those who entered India two and three thousand years ago either for purposes of trade or mere pleasure of travel have taken the Srutis of the precious South Indian Music to their own country. We also find that as South India lost its prestige in course of time its music also gradually lost its lustre. However, the musicians of the present day only see that their traditional music is not wholly forgotten and that it is deteriorating day by day by the admixture of Desikam. They do not care to study those works which give the reason for their deterioration and which show them the way of improving their music but break their heads over other works.

Many of the Tamil works are obsolete. As many of the Tamils have become Sanskrit scholars they only interpret such works as are written in that language. They knock their heads against the 22 Srutis mentioned there and try to establish something which they really do not know. Bharata and Sarnga Dev are the cause of this confusion. Their followers neither follow their method nor examine what they are practising themselves, but just like a man who applies to himself the scandalising words of his neighbour some of them pass off the Srutis of foreigners for those of Sarnga Dev, some, especially in the north, ascribe the same Srutis to Hindustani music while some of the musicians of South India ascribe the same to Karnatic music. This is a matter for surprise.

We have to regret that South Indian music is like a field from which the corn has been removed and like the snail whose pearl has been extracted. Perhaps it may be a matter for surprise that the efficient music of the Ayapalai system is in use up to the present day with 2 Alakus less which stand in the relation of Inai. But if we note it a little carefully we shall find very clearly that the ancients have been using a number of Ragas, the concordance of whose Swarams was according to the system of Vattapalai. We have noted before that the 12 Swarams, which even women could easily understand, were arranged in the 12 Rasis, that the 7 Moorchanas and the order of Swarams of the 14 Kovais in the three Sthayis Mandara, Madhya and Tara were all in common use.

We may find that these 12 Swarams are the ones used in South Indian music and these are the series used by those interested in music and by those who are gifted with keen musical ear.

These are the 12 Swarams of Hindustani music also, and the chromatic scale of the Westerners. We must note the words of Ilankovadigal that this is the system for women and that this was the system which Mathavi was fond of. For the system for men was the Alaku systsm of Vattapalai. He says that the ganam for men should be in the 22 Srutis or Alakus. For, Kaikilai and Vilari should have 3 Srutis each. In short, there must be 24 Alakus at the rate of two for each of the 12 Rasis, but that ganam should be made in them lessening two of the Alakus. Here the 4 Alakus of the 2 Rasis for Kaikilai and Vilari become 3 in each case. In the same manner, Aganilai, Puranilai, Arugial and Perugial are given where an alaku is lessened in the Poorvabagam and Ootarabagam of two concordant Swarams.

Now, singing with an Alaku less is only a recognised convention among musicians. The third Alakus of Kaikilai and Vilari should be sounded as gamakams from the second Alaku by pulling the string inwards. This kind of playing will equal the human voice in sweetness. He considers this kind of playing to be the system for males alone as the women have very delicate fingers which could not pull a string as to produce a gamakam. If we notice the tips of fingers of celebrated Veena players we see that they are full of grooves like those of a Star-Gooseberry (அரிநெல்லிக் காய்). Perhaps this kind of playing was not recommended for women as it might spoil their fingers which are as delicate as the petals of the Kendal (காந்தள்) flower. But we may notice that even females who understand the delicacy of sweet music practise the Veena in spite of this.

We understand, then, that there were two systems—one in which the Swarams of Karnatic music were played purely as Suddha Swarams and the other in which the Alakus were lessened. In my researches on the Srutis of Karnatic music, I examined the Swarams of some of the Ragas with the help of experts four or five years ago even at a time when I was ignorant of the Vattapalai system mentioned in Silappadikaram. I found that 24 Srutis were used there and that the same 24 Alakus of Vattapalai are in use even at present. It was clear, therefore, that the ancient system of Vattapalai was correct and that that was the system copied by others from South India. Did any good result from this? None. It became lifeless like the precious gem which had lost its lustre. It existed in mere theory and not put into practice. But all the same South Indian music on the 24 Srutis as a basis is considered scientific and each separate ragam thereof is considered to have its own peculiar beauty. On the other hand, those who admire this music in others are ignorant of the Srutis which they use in their own music. We will notice the Srutis of South Indian Ragas later on.

We may find that some of the Swarams of Karnatic Ragas have different Swarams in Aroganam and Avaroganam and the position of some of the Swarams have been entirely changed. This is due to different masters and the natural differences caused by oral transmission. We have written only those in modern use though there are slight differences when compared to the ancient Vattapalai system. Again when we note places where Srutis occur in addition to the 12 Swarams we find they are of a very minute character. Of these more anon.

In the following three Tables, series of the nature of RI-DHA and GA-NI are slightly sharper or slightly flatter than the Srutis of the ancient system. This will be found to be more glaring in some of the Ragas of the present day. We have picked out only a few out of them which people are very familiar with.

We shall find later on that the Ragas mentioned in the Tables have far minuter Srutis. These Ragas were examined on the Veena as well as vocally in the presence of great professional experts such as M. R. Ry Muthia Baghavatar Avl. of Harikesavanallur, and M. R. Ry. Vencatachallam Iyer Avl. son of M. R. Ry. Athiappa Iyer Avl., musician of Tanjore.

TABLE I.

No.	Name of Kartha Ragas.	Melam.	Name of Ragas.	SA	RI			GA			MA		PA	DHA			NI		
					2	4	6	2	4	6	2	4		2	4	6	2	4	6
1	Mayamalavam.	15	Goulibandu ...	SA	1	...	...	...	...	6	3	...	PA	1	...	...	...	...	7
2	„ ...	15	Arutharadesi ...	SA	1	...	...	...	...	6	2	...	PA	1	...	...	...	...	6
3	„ ...	15	Poorvi ...	SA	1	...	...	...	...	7	...	...	PA	1	...	...	...	...	5-6
4	„ ..	15	Kummakambodi ...	SA	1	...	...	...	...	6	3	...	PA	1	...	...	...	...	5
5	Hanumaththodi...	8	Asavari	SA	1	...	...	...	3	...	2	...	PA	1	...	...	...	5	...
6	Karakarapriya	22	Nayaki *	SA	...	4	...	...	3	...	2	...	PA	...	4	...	..	3	...
7	„ ...	22	Sri Ragam ...	SA	...	4	...	...	3	...	2	...	PA	...	4	...	...	3	...
8	Hanumaththodi...	8	Thodi	SA	2	...	...	...	3	...	2	...	...	2	...	...	...	3	...
9	Mayamalavam.	15	Suddha Kiriya ...	SA	3	...	...	...	...	...	2	...	PA	3	...	...	...	...	...
10	Hanumaththodi...	8	Bhoopalam... ...	SA	3	...	...	...	5	...	...	...	PA	3	...	...	...	...	...

From the above Table we notice that RI and DHA occur in their first Alakus in the Ragas Goulibandu, Arutharadesi, Poorvi, Kummakambodi and Asaveri. This is the same as lessening the second Alaku in Thutham (RI) and Vilari (DHA)

We find that Kaikilai (GA) and Tharam (NI) have only 3 Alakus where they should have four in the Ragas Nayaki, Sriragam and Thodi.

On the other hand Thuttham and Vilari (RI and DHA) have 3 Alakus where they should have only 2, in the Ragas Suddha-Kiriya and Bhoopalam.

In Table II we may find that RI, DHA and GA, NI have an Alaku less out of the 2, but RI and DHA have one in addition to their 4 Alakus in the Yathukula-kambodi, Kurinchi, Navarooj and Shankaraparanam.

According to the system of modern 72 Melakartas they will hold that this is a flattened Gandharam, but a sharpened Sruti when its position is considered.

TABLE II.

No.	Name of Kartha Ragas.	Melam.	Name of Ragas.	SA	RI			GA			MA		PA	DHA			NI		
					2	4	6	2	4	6	2	4		2	4	6	2	4	6
1	Mayamalavam	15	Savari	SA	2	...	...	...	...	5	3	...	PA	2	...	...	...	...	5
2	Hanumaththodi..	8	Danyasi	SA	2	...	...	...	5	...	2	...	PA	2	...	...	...	5	...
3	,, ...	8	Agari	SA	2	...	...	...	5	...	2	...	PA	2	...	...	...	5	...
4	Nadabairavi...	20	Annanda Bhairavi.	SA	...	4	...	...	5	...	2	...	PA	3	...	...	...	5	...
5	,, ...	20	Poorana Shadjam.	SA	...	4	...	...	5	...	2	...	PA	...	...	...	...	5	...
6	,, ...	20	Indolavasantam ...	SA	...	...	...	...	5	...	2	...	PA	2	...	...	...	5	...
7	Karakarapriya.	22	Jayanarayani ...	SA	...	4	...	...	5	...	2	...	PA	...	4	...	...	5	...
8	,, ...	22	Oosani	SA	...	4	...	...	5	...	2	...	PA	...	4	...	...	5	...
9	,, ...	22	Kapi	SA	...	4	...	...	5	...	2	...	PA	...	5	...	...	5	...
10	Dheerasankaraparanam.	29	Durbar * ...	SA	...	4	...	...	...	5	2	...	PA	...	4	...	...	...	5
11	,, ...	29	Neelambari * ...	SA	...	4	...	...	...	5	3	...	PA	...	4	...	...	...	5
12	Harikambodhi	28	Yathukulakambodi	SA	...	5	...	...	...	6	2	...	PA	...	5	...	...	5	...
13	Dheerasankaraparanam.	29	Kurinchi	SA	...	5	...	...	...	6	2	...	PA	...	5	...	...	...	7
14	,,	29	Navarooj	SA	...	5	...	...	...	6	1	...	PA	...	5	...	...	...	6
15	,,	29	Atana	SA	...	4	...	...	...	5	2	...	PA	...	5	...	...	...	5,6
16		29	Shankaraparanam.	SA	...	5	...	...	...	6	2	...	PA	...	5	...	...	...	6,7

Again, the Kaikilai and Vilari (GA and NI) occur in Danyasi, Agari Annanda-Bhairavi, Poornashadjam, Indola Vasantam. Jayanarayani, Oosani, Kapi, Durbar and Neelambari occur as Inai Swarams according to the system of 72 Melakartas in their third Sruti which is really their fifth.

In the same manner, the GA and NI in Saveri and Neelambari have only five Srutis instead of 6.

TABLE III.

No.	Name of Kartha Ragas.	Melam.	Name of Ragas.	SA	RI 2	RI 4	RI 6	GA 2	GA 4	GA 6	MA 2	MA 4	PA	DHA 2	DHA 4	DHA 6	NI 2	NI 4	NI 6
1	Mayamalavam	15	Maruva	SA	2	...	...	...	...	7	2	...	PA	2	...	...	...	...	7
2	„ ...	15	Barasu	SA	2	...	...	...	...	7	2	...	PA	1	...	...	...	...	7
3	„ ...	15	Goulibandu ...	SA	1	...	...	...	...	7	3	...	PA	1	...	...	...	...	7
4	Salanattai ...	36	Nattai	SA	...	...	7	...	...	6	2	...	PA	...	...	7	...	...	6

In Table III we find that the GA and NI occurring in Maruva, Barasu and Gouli Bandu appear in the first Sruti of Oolai (MA) and in the first Sruti of Kural (SA) respectively.

Natai Ragam has RI and DHA with 7 Alakus. In other words, they occur in the fifth Alakus of Kaikilai and Tharam. Thus we see that ganam was made with an Alaku less in Inai and Kilai Swarams in the SA-PA and SA-MA systems.

It appears, likewise, they had made ganam with an Alaku less either in the Poorvabagam or Ootharabagam and that even two, three or four Alakus were added or lessened in their ganam.

When Alakus are less in a Swaram it will be very difficult to sing but delicious when sung. We may see instances of it in the modern Ragas, such as, Anandabhairavi, Saveri, Punnagavarali, Poorvi, Barasu, Mathyamavati, Kapi, Sahana, Palamsa, Kedaragoula, Ketharam and Ameerkalyani. So we see that Ragas with less number of Alakus in many Swarams will be particularly charming. Just as we sing 22 Alakus or less number in the system of Vattapalai, it is presumed that such must be the case with the Ragas of Thirikonapalai and Chathurapalai. On the other hand, though such of the 14 Kovais obtained from Ayapalai have 24 Alakus, they are made up of the Swarams of the 12 Rasis with 2 Alakus each and never made up of any flattened Swarams. According to the system of the 72 Melakartas of the modern day only half Swarams were used in Ayapalai.

So, Ayapalai is ganam with 7 Swarams out of the 12 half Swarams occurring in a Rasi cycle.

Vattapalai is where the 7 Swarams are sung in the 22 out of the 24 Alakus of the 12 Swarams of a Rasi cycle, lessening an Alaku in each of two Swarams.

Thirikonapalai has its music with less Alakus in 3 Swarams which stand to one another in the relation of Inai, Kilai and Natpu.

There is reason to believe that the music of Chathurapalai was with 4 Alakus less in the 4 Swarams which stood in the relation of Inai, Kilai, Natpu and Second string to one another. We say now that Swarams with less Alakus should be produced as gamakams If they are not played so, Ragas will lose their charm.

The Ragas which satisfy their Alaku system and the rules common to them will be dealt with in the second book.

We see in the Ragas we commonly use at the present day the 72 Karta Ragas according to Ayapalai, other Ragas where two Alakus are lessened according to Vattapalai and yet a few others where three and four Srutis are lessened.

33. A few general remarks as regards Swarams and Srutis.

It seems that the author of Sangeeta Ratnakar has put together a few points from hearsay after the destruction of Tamil works on Isai-Tamil. His saying that Shadja, Madhyma and Gandhara gramas have 22 Srutis instead of clearly saying that 22 Alakus out of 24 in a Sthayi are sung, and his theory that Sa-Pa should have 12 Srutis and Sa-Ma 8 Srutis in the middle led to all this confusion. If this doubt is cleared, we may say that his other theories are somewhat useful. As his work was written long after the disappearance of the truth of Vattapalai system which was the basis of all ancient music of South India it is hard to say whether his theory was meant as a mystery or whether he was himself floundering in doubt. If he had expressed himself clearly there is hardly any doubt that the Sruti systems of India would have been held in high esteem by all. As there was some doubt they stopped short with the 12 half Swarams, and expert musicians of South India had their doubts even about the standing 12 Srutis. Others bother themselves with 53 Srutis. The reason for all this is the 22 Srutis theory of Sarnga Dev.

During the time of the first Sangam all the four Palais seem to have been used, but in later times only the first two seem to have survived and in still later days Vattapalai seems to have disappeared and only Ayapalai held its head. Then came Sarnga Dev with his work treating on 22 Srutis. The author of Parijatam as well as Venkatamahi seem to have dealt only with the system of Ayapalai with its 12 Swarams. Though their works speak of the 12 swarams of Ayapalai, they made ganam in the 24 Alakus of Vattapalai which had been handed down to them for generations.

One chief cause for doubt at the present day is the fact that the theory in their books is quite contrary to their practice.

Our doubts will be cleared if we study chiefly the system of Vattapalai used by our ancestors in the ganam of South India. The 24 Alakus there are the 24 Srutis.

The ancient system was to make ganam in the 24 Srutis, but with an Alaku less in any two Inai Swarams.

To lesson a Sruti means to sound the higher Swaram from the lower one as gamakam.

Even in gamakams there are minute calculations, which will be explained later on. Though it is a little hard to understand the extensiveness of South Indian Music, as a number of pieces taught by our ancestors who used the most minute Srutis have been preserved, it is possible to understand them.

We must accept the correctness of these Swarams which occur as Inai, Kilai, Natpu and second string. It is also true that in other works is contained the warning that this system should be determined clearly, emphatically and minutely. We understand from ancient works that experts of South Indian Music were very efficient in this system. It is also seen that tuning by the principle of Sa-Pa and making ganam in many Ragas were very common in ancient times.

When we note the Kurinchi Yal where Oolai is commenced as Kural in the Sa-Pa system, the Neythal Yal where Thuttham is Kural, the Palai Yal where Tharam commences as Kural, the Marutha Yal where Ili is Kural and the Sootram of the author of Tholkaupiam where he speaks about the productions of the four different kinds of soil, we understand clearly that this system of Vattapalai as well as the calculations of Srutis according to the Sa-Pa system were in existence even at the period of the author of Tholkaupiam *i.e.* even 8000 years ago. Though the age of Ilankovadigal and that of Adyarkunallar are slightly later, yet the age of Tholkaupiam seems to be very ancient and it is also clear that these systems were also equally ancient.

Though works like Ahatyam and Isai-Noonukam are extinct, yet as the four kinds of Yal and the system of deriving puns from them are mentioned in Tholkaupiam which separates Iyal Tamil from Ahatyam, it can be established without the slightest doubt that South Madura to the South of South India was the cradle of all music in the world.

It appears that after the destruction of South Madura even the remnants of Musical works gradually deteriorated owing to want of patronage. But even these remnants with the help of the little practical knowledge that had been kept up in South India were enough to indicate in a way the ancient scientific system.

Some of the truths of South Indian Music were carried to foreign countries by means of traders and travellers. For example, the Buddhist monks of India carried this music to China, Japan, Burma, Siam, Tibet, Persia and other countries. But through the Arabs who came into India long before this period for selling horses and buying spices in return, this was carried to Arabia and Egypt and used extensively there.

We read in the 22nd verse of the 10th Chapter of the First Book of Kings that monkeys and peacocks, the products of the tropical South India, hill products such as pepper, cardamum, cloves and sandalwood, ivory (tusks of elephants) and the precious gold of Ophir were taken to Tarsish *via* the Red Sea and were given to King Solomon by Hiram, the King of Tarsish. This seems to be about 2930 years ago. The city of Tarsish is an important city in the East Mediterranean Coast in Asiatic Turkey. We know that reaching this city through the land route is much nearer than its approach through the Red Sea. Those who carried spices, monkeys and ivory from South India as precious products 2930 years ago carried also the precious gold from Ophir in South India.

These traders cannot but have carried its music also which is considered far more precious than gold. Because the people of Tarsish as well as the Phoenician traders were acquainted with commerce long before this period, it can be presumed that music of South India must have been disseminated by them in different countries long anterior to the period mentioned above.

Many of the foreigners who had heard accounts of the fertility and the civilisation of India have travelled into India. Of these travellers, Pythagoras, who is held to be the founder of Western music, was one. It is said that he travelled through India for many years and learnt a few precious ideas from its people. He lived about 2400 years ago. We noted before the age of Tholkaupiam (i.e. 8000 years ago) and the efficiency of the music of that age. When it is said that Pythagoras came to India nearly 5000 years later and learnt a few ideas about regeneration and Yogam, he should be held as a great sage.

The Sa-Pa and the Sa-Ma system used in South India seem to have been to a certain extent common through out the whole of India. There is reason to think that Pythagoras who transferred to the strings this Sa-Pa and Sa-Ma and reckoned them roughly as $\frac{2}{3}$ and $\frac{3}{4}$, carried this measurement with him. He seems to have apprreciated the beauty of the Puns sung in South India and to have taken this measurement of $\frac{2}{3}$ and $\frac{3}{4}$ to determine the Sapta Swarams.

This measurement of $\frac{2}{3}$ for Sa to Pa was never in use in India. Further, they had no instruments like the Tuning Fork to indicate the pitch of Sa-Pa or other Swarams.

We must understand that in the case of adjusting frets for a new Yal and other instruments and for tuning instruments, the musical ear which has been cultivated for generations is made use of and not any standard pitch. They had no such standard instrument of any kind for the above purpose. Before commencing the tuning of the Veena, they adjust the three small strings by the side of it to the concordance of Sa-Pa and Sa. As these Swarams satisfy the Sa-Pa and the Sa-Ma principles, as the top Sa is exactly double that of the commencing Sa and as the sounds stand in the relation of 1. $1\frac{1}{2}$ and 2. the concordance will be very striking. The Pa which is $1\frac{1}{2}$ when tuned with Sa, which is 1, and Sa which is 2, the harmony will be complete.

Then the Pa in the Sarana string of the Yal will be tuned in accordance with that. Then this Pa will be made Sa in its turn and the next Pa determined. Thus in determining the Sapta Swarams the Sa-Pa in the main strings and the side strings will often be compared and proceeded with. We have never heard nor seen that a measurement rod was ever used, nor is such a thing mentioned in ancient works on music.

Again. when we notice the Karta Ragas obtained by change of graham of the Swarams derived by the Sa-Pa system. we find no reason to believe that the Swarams have been changed. In whichever Rasi of Vattapalai we commence the fifth and the seventh places are invariably on the principle of Sa-Ma and Sa-Pa. Though this ancient system was largely used in South India, as some doubtful points had been introduced in works on music, one was not able to emphasise certain points and the result was doubt in many points. Many who saw the state of affairs took certain instruments such as the Yal and the flute and their measurements with them to their own country and made researches in them. They made their ganam in the Swarams which they were sure of as the result of their enquiry. They are making corrections also in them most carefully. But it is plain they have never yet come across a system which is in any way superior to the tuning of instruments by the SA-PA principle.

We have to regret that men of other countries have not yet understood the minuteness of the music of South India based on the SA-PA principle and the extensiveness of its Ragas. Even though some of the *Amsams* of South Indian music, such as the Sapta Swarams, the 12 half-Swarams derived out of them and the 24 quarter Swarams are made mention of by others it is highly doubtful whether they could have put them into practice.

It is certain that all foreigners who came to India must have carried with them some of the mysteries of Indian music. When it was thus carried to Tarshish, Egypt and Greece it is but natural that the people of those countries who had any knowledge of the Science should declare it to have been indigenous. It is a custom for those who have borrowed ideas from others to take pride in saying that they were their original ideas. People at the present day copy things from books but palm them off as their own saying that they were discovered accidentally by them. To add to this when such things are forgotten after a lapse of years what they emphasise passes for truth. Though our statement that Pythagoras copied his music from India may be open to doubt, yet what about the writers of the west who declare that Europe learnt its music from the east and that the musical system of India is wholly scientific?

The Swarams used in the chanting of the Roman Catholic priests in Rome are identical with the chanting of the Rig Veda at the modern day. What is the conclusion? Did this chanting go from India to the west or was borrowed from the west by us? However different opinions may be on this point, the excellence and the antiquity of South Indian music can never be doubted and we can boldly say that it will take years before people are able to understand this system thoroughly.

34. Some final remarks to be noted.

Till now we enquired into the Sapta Swarams, the 12 half Swarams and the 24 Srutis of Isai Tamil, one of the three divisions of Muttamil or South Indian music. Of these ganam was made in seven Swarams which stand in the relation of Inai, Kilai and Natpu out of the 12 Swarams of Ayapalai. Again, ganam was made in the 22 Srutis of Vattapalai lessening 2 Alakus in 2 Swarams which are in the relation of Inai and Kilai out of the seven. We noticed also the system of 4 Kinds of Yal and 4 Jathis derived out of them. We also observed how they used 12000 ancient Isais by understanding the different Gamakams used in the Yal for singing a ragam, the letters for Alathi, the different kinds of thalams, the minute rules of the act of dancing, the nine kinds of taste and many other minute points in connection with music. We also observed how they had 103 puns in use, how their names were gradually changed and how after the period of the third sangam owing to the influence of Buddhists and others music completely deteriorated.

We see clearly that after the destruction by deluge of the works on Isai Tamil of the first and second Sangams, even the remnants deteriorated as there were none to take care of them and owing to constant wars. However, some of the rules of Isai Tamil and some Ragas have been preserved to a certain extent till this day mainly by oral transmission for generations. Some of the very important *amsams* of Isai Tamil have been preserved to us by the casual mention of them in Silappadikaram and its commentaries. These *amsams* are quite in accordance with rules of modern practice and appear to have a minuteness which requires still further elucidation.

It also appears that Isai-Tamil was in an excellent condition at the time of Ilankovidigal 2000 years ago and even many thousand years before that period, that after the disappearance of the extensive treatises dealing on music it was kept up by mere practice, and that these practical musicians in later times wrote works on them in different languages of their own.

The work of Bharata in the 5th cent. A. D. is considered prior to the Sangeeta Ratnakar written in the 13th Century a little more extensively. This latter is held in high esteem as it is considered to be full of important ideas. Though this work treats to a certain extent on Srutis which are the life of all music, yet it has erred in saying the number of Srutis to be 22 without understanding the two Srutis hidden in the principle of DHA-GA in Vattapalai. We have given our own reasons for this mystery as regards the lessening of two Alakus in DHA-GA.

The Vattapalai Chakaram is the repository which holds within itself many of the precious ideas of music. The lock to this store house is the pointing to Simham as the sixth Rasi under the rule Kaikilai appears in Vilari. The key to it is the dictum that Kaikilai appears from Vilari in Kanni. The principles of Inai, Kilai and Natpu are the lights which disclose the property in the house. We find that people have been floundering in the theory of 22 Srutis and writing books on it without caring to understand this system and clearing their doubt.

When once this theory was published in books others adopted it and wrote works upholding it. From this it is clear that all works advocating 22 Srutis are posterior to those of Bharata and Sarnga Dev. Or if at all they were prior the ideas contained in Sarnga Dev must have been interpolated into them. We have seen that this custom has been very much adopted.

There are only 12 Swarams in a Sthayi which are obtained on the principles of Inai and Kilai or SA-PA and SA-MA. Those who have no belief in this are men of doubt. If one notes the minute amsams of South Indian Music one can unhesitatingly say that among all countries and nations of the world no country or nation can excel South India and the Tamil language which contains within itself the Muttamil—Iyal, Isai and Natakam.

When we observe the important *amsams* of South Indian Music we find that it was in a very progressive state for many thousands of years 12000 years ago, that it degenerated gradually and had to confine itself to the 12 Swarams of Ayapalai. It appears that, after the deterioration of the 12000 ancient Isais, even the works relating to them disappeared at the period of the last Sangam, that after the period of the last Sangam when rules of practice had disappeared some Sruti systems and systems of generating Ragas were in a doubtful state, that at a later period the works of Bharata and Sarnga Dev and later sanskrit works had taken the 22 Srutis into their head and were tottering, that the Gandhara Gramam held to be very sweet in ancient times had been banished to the celestial regions and that 14 alone out of the 22 Srutis had their existence in this earth.

We find that after the 13th century many disputes and dissensions arose as it was found there was no unanimity between the 22 Srutis and what they were really practising. As a result of this contradiction only the 12 Swarams of the Sthayi were reconciled with the ganam of the ancient Tamils, and musicians like Purandra Vittal Das, Ahobilar, Somanathan, Ramamatyar and Venkatamahi wrote works in Sanskrit and Telugu based on these 12 Swarams alone. The system of change of Graham found here and the Swarams used as 2, 4 and 6 Srutis are identical with the Ayapalai of the ancient Tamils. We are using only a small part of the system of the ancient Tamils with the names changed while we are ignorant of the most extensive portions of it.

Again, though we find the Alaku system of Vattapalai and that of Sarnga Dev to resemble in some respects, yet by means of calculations for Alakus it has been clearly established that there were not 22 but 24 Alakus in the Sthayi but that we have our ganam in 22 of them lessening 2 Alakus in Swarams related as Inai and Kilai and have also demonstrated the fact by means of a few modern Ragas.

We have also indicated the connection between Music and Astrology by the cycle of 12 Rasis, drawn out their relation and have established beyond doubt that the Srutis should be 24 in number. By the singing of Aychiarkuravai we have indicated the system of singing Grahaswarams in the Isai Tamil of the ancient Tamils and have established by that means the 12 and the 24 Srutis of the Octave.

We have shown that Shankaraparanam was the Mother Ragam which had been in use among the Tamils of South Madura, that this is the first of the Ragas of Ayapalai and that other Ragas should be obtained by the order of Swarams indicated here. In that mother Ragam, when ganam is made in 22 Alakus *i. e.* in two Alakus less which stand in the relation of DHA-GA or Vilari-Kaikilai, it is called Marutha Pun. There are but 24 Srutis according to this system.

Calculations by which SA-PA is taken as $\frac{2}{3}$ in a wire and SA-MA as $\frac{3}{4}$ are not mentioned in Isai-Tamil. Nor are they found in the works of Bharata and Sarnga Dev who modelled their works after the ideas found in Isai-Tamil.

The idea of Sarnga Dev that SA-PA is 13 Srutis and SA-MA is 9 Srutis is nowhere found in Isai Tamil. There SA-PA or Inai Swaram occurs in 7 Rasis with 14

Alakus, while SA-MA or Kilai Swaram occurs in 5 with 10 Alakus. If PA and MA were to get an Alaku less they will never be concordant. The existence of Swarams which are not concordant as SA-PA, SA-MA, SA-GA or SA-RI and ganam in such Swarams are both impossible.

The measurements [illegible] and [illegible] are found in the West and not in musical works in India. The 12 Swarams which the Tamils were able to obtain by their musical ear after the SA-PA and SA-MA systems could only be obtained by the others by measurements and calculations. Can a minute sound be obtained by calculations and instruments? No. We find that a stone cast into the mud sticks there without producing any movement while the one cast into muddy water produces a few waves. But if it is cast into clear and pure water it produces a good number of waves and even these waves sometimes have wavelets. And yet again when a stone is cast into a tank of petrol which is $\frac{1}{4}$ lighter than water will it not produce twice and thrice the number of waves and counter-waves? In air which is 773 times lighter than water, we hear sound producing echoes and reechoes on the hills. In the same manner, when we place our hands behind our ears we hear distant sounds; when we put the narrow end of a long tube with a wide mouth to our ears we hear distinctly speeches and sounds coming from a long distance, but if we take our stand on a high place we hear sounds from a still greater distance and more clearly also.

Of the organs of the five senses, the ear is given a high position and among the five senses sound or Natham is held to be supreme. When we closely observe this sound and its sense organ, its high place in man, its big size among animals which could be controlled by man, its very small size in animals not necessary for man, and the presence in such animals of eyes which are unable to absorb sun light or artificial light, we are at a loss to understand the wonderful wisdom of the Creator.

He who tries to approach Natham approaches God who is in the shape of Natham. Who can understand the omnipotence of the Natham who created the world, the vegetable and the animal kingdoms by a word? How many new things are being introduced into the world by the words we utter, by the prayers we offer and the songs we sing!

Even the power of God is reflected in the words of man though we have not witnessed the dissolution of the granite stone yet the melting of a hard heart is within our ken. Though granite stone may not be powdered by our command we see people giving up their pride and hard heart and becoming humble. Though we do not see vegetable kingdom springing up at our word of command, yet we see the growth of the tree of life which yields fruits of the spirit. Christ, the Paramanma, says "For every idle word that men shall speak, they shall give account thereof in the day of judgment." (St. Matt. XII. 36)

Can the walls of a fortress be destroyed by the noise made by breaking of pots? Can a speech procure water out of the stony rock? Can wild beasts, serpents, evil spirits and diseases be tamed or got rid of by swearing on a person? Can an evil spirit forget its evil by hearing the sweet sounds of the harp? Yet all this is possible by sound. In the same manner, the facts that the three functions of creation, preservation and destruction should be accomplished by Natham only speaks for its greatness.

The sciences which treat of this Natham are very precious. Their minuteness cannot be gauged by calculations and the footrule. All writers on Srutis measure Sa-Pa and Sa-Ma by instruments, multiply their product by another number, add a few digits here and cut off a few there and show a multiplicity of calculations. If they agree with one another we may take them to be correct. If two blind men tumble into the same ditch at least they may be of help to each other. But they fall into different ditches!!

The ancient Tamils of South Madura never gave such calculations. In nature when the five elements are sub-divided by fives, the parts will get gradually smaller. But will all the elements be alike in measurement weight and quality? Will the weight of land and that of air be alike? These are very extensive and subtle points.

Our attempting to give the calculation of sound which should be completely accurate even in the minutest amsam is like weighing the body and the spirit in separate balances and saying that the former weighs one Param and the latter one Maund! Though personally we were disinclined to enter into the calculations of Srutis, yet to satisfy those great mathematicians who will not accept anything unless it is mathematically shown to be accurate, we made bold to give approximately the measurements and calculation for the Srutis of South Indian music.

As sound is very minute, when fractions such as $\frac{3}{4}$, $\frac{3}{4}$, $\frac{1}{2}$, $\frac{1}{4}$, $\frac{1}{8}$ and $\frac{1}{8}$ are multiplied together the result will never give the exact measurement of a Sruti. Hence the necessity for being very minute.

At least the experts in Karnatic music will understand that the ancients had used minuter Srutis than the 12 Swarams of Ayapalai and the 24 Srutis of Vattapalai. As it is very necessary to understand those very minute Srutis, illustration by means of minute calculations is absolutely necessary to clear our doubts as we are knocking our heads over the 22 Srutis. We give them in Part IV under the heading "calculations for Srutis used in Isai Tamil or Karnatic music" with the assurance that it will make us understand the excellence of our ancestors and the minuteness of Isai Tamil.

END OF PART 3.

KARUNAMIRTHA SAGARAM.

FIRST BOOK.

FOURTH PART.

The Calculations for Srutis used in Isai-Tamil, which is another name for Karnatic Music.

KARUNAMIRTHA SAGARAM.

FIRST BOOK.

FOURTH PART.

The Calculations for Srutis used in Isai-Tamil, which is another name for Karnatic Music.

Preface.

MEN of intelligence will accept the fact that the science of Music which is an excellent means for understanding the limit of Karunamirtha Sagaram is an exalted science which, when sung according to rules, is capable of making people concentrate their attention on God and obtaining for them the Moksham.

We should realise that the words and sounds said in praise of the deity from the innermost hearts of devoted Saints of God are the seeds of the science of music, they are the Vedas and they are the basis for all rules relating to music.

These first songs in praise of the deity were prior to many Shastras which were derived from them. Just as oil is extracted from the sesamum and jaggery from sugar-cane all Shastras, we may say, had their origin from the songs of praise uttered by devoted sages. They were delighted when they realised that the shape of the Omnipresent God was the embryo of nature and that this tallied with their personal experience also.

As often as they felt that all created beings with their Sthoolam were realised as one and indivisible in their Sookshama Sareera and that they had the same sensations and rendered mutual help, they knew that they had seen in themselves the sacred form of the deity, they realised that God lived in them, they praised him as the incarnation of love and kindness and themselves as beings full of love.

The First Being who is inseparable from creation as brightness from a precious gem, as fragrance from a flower, as sweetness from honey and as life from the body became Natham and disseminated this sweetness everywhere. Just as Natham was the cause of the seven kinds of appearances, the Sapta Swarams and Srutis originated from the sound of the living beings which were part of the seven appearances.

Just as life in animate objects is seen in 12 places, six above and six below representing different functions, the Sapta Swarams also appear as distinct sounds, six above and six below the Madhymam.

The truth that the First Being who was in the form of Natham is seen through the seven kinds of appearances and lives in 12 places in the Sthoola and Sookshama Sareeras of animate beings is proved by the fact that Shadjam, the first of the Sapta Swarams becomes gradually the seven Swarams in the regular order of 1, 2, 3, 4, 5 and 6 and distributes itself into six Swarams above and six Swarams below Madhymam.

The devoted saints of God who realised the structure of the Sthoola Sareeram, the seat of life and its different functions, constructed the excellent Yal, which resembles the human body in all respects and used it as an adjunct of their ganam in praise of the deity.

Being assured that the structure of the Yal and its sweet music reflect completely and openly some of the mysteries of the human body, that it is the most delicate of all musical instruments and that it is the only instrument which could faithfully produce short and long sounds with their respective duration, they laid down that God should be praised with the help of the Yal and that a service without the Yal was utterly useless.

The outward appearance of the Yal completely resembles the Sthoolam of the human body and its sound, the life of living beings. There are many reasons to suppose that this mysterious fact was made the basis of all musical science by our ancestors who were noted for their devotion to God.

Just as the created objects of the world are the result of a regular evolution for ages, so also the Sapta Swarams appear to have been brought into music by different devotees and to have attained perfection many thousand years ago. We see clearly that the 4400 Tamil experts who lived at the period of the first Sangam in the first Ooli about 8000 years ago were efficient in the Muttamil—Iyal, Isai and Natakam—for the past 4,400 years. When we reflect on the fact that music was considered a part of their literature and that every one,—even crowned kings and nobles,—was efficient in it there is reason to believe that South Madura in the South of India was the cradle of all music.

Again, when we compare the four kinds of Yal mentioned in Tholkaupiam dated 8000 years ago with the four kinds of Yal spoken of in Silappadikaram written by Ilankovadigal about 1800 years ago, we may conclude with pride that the Southern part of India excelled other countries in music, that Chera and Chola Kings largely patronised music after the destruction of the Pandya Kingdom and that the Dravidian musical experts who spoke the Tamil, Telugu, Malayalam and Canarese dialects have composed a large collection of Padams, Varnams, Keertanams, Ragamalikas and Pallavis. We may boldly say that no country or language can boast of such large collection of pieces of music as those of Purandara Vittal Das, Kshetringar, Theagaraja Iyer, Arunachala Kavi, Gopala Bharati and other Karnatic experts. We must not forget that the music of others can only boast of easy pieces like Thurubath, Thillana, Kyal, Tappa, Dumoori, Pathyas, Thindi, Jaki etc.

Again, some of the experts of the Dravidian country such as Venkatamahi of Tanjore, Muttusami Dikshitar of Tiruvarur, and Mahavaidyanatha Iyer of Vyachari wrote some pieces in Sanskrit and Telugu also, though they were born in the Tamil country and were experts in that language. It is also clearly seen that though the music of South India deteriorated in the later Ooli after the destruction of South Madura and the first sangam which had lasted for 4400 years, yet it was fostered to a certain extent by the rulers of the Chera, Chola and the Pandyan Kingdoms and with the help of lands attached to temples Though, after the dis-appearance in the later Ooli of the Muttamil-Iyal, Isai and Natakam owing to absence of patronage and music was preserved by a few professionals, yet we must note with regret that all ancient literature on music which formed the very foundation of all music has been completely destroyed.

Many of the precious works of expert musicians of the Karnatic country which had been preserved mainly by oral transmission disappeared because they failed to teach them to every one but confined them to one or two of their favourite disciples. Their disciples in their turn kept them all to themselves. Thus many precious pieces of Karnatic music gradually disappeared and people at the present day are satisfied with Parsi and Hindustani music and music played on the Harmonium or heard through the Gramoph ne! We do not like to be misunderstood. There is no denying the fact that every one is interested in music. But it is a matter for regret that people are satisfied with cheap substitutes instead of hearing Ragas with minute Srutis just as at the present day people are content if they get the pearl of Surat in place of the real pearl, the imitation ruby in place of the real gem, and the cheap pith turban in place of the silk turban!!

After the first Ooli, Music which was to a certain extent disliked by the Jains and the Buddhists, was looked upon as a means of livelihood. It is but true that a country which has advanced in music should also be highly civilised. In addition to it, it must be ruled by Kings who consider it their duty to maintain truth, who look upon the welfare of their subjects as their own and who prevent wars and ensure peace in their borders. We know that music can make advance only in the time of peace and plenty, when there is no famine in the country owing to want of rain and when people are free to divert their attention to the reading, writing and preaching of books on justice and truth. Could a man sing with an empty stomach? Could he listen to another man's music when he is in such a famished condition? Could you imagine music parties during the reign of terror of Hyder? Morever, it is certain that people praise God, do service to him and celebrate festivals only when they are free from trouble. Where can music be when kings out of hatred fight against one another and destroy the subjects of the enemies, when people fly for refuge to other countries to beg there, burying all their treasures and precious books in the hurry of their flight? At such times we must understand that all industries and sciences which reflect civilisation must come to nought. We have a good deal of experience of the terrors of the modern war with Germany. It is but certain that when South Madura lost its rulers, the science of music as well as many precious works on the subject gradually declined owing to the internecine wars of the Cholas, and completely disappeared during the Muhammadan ascendency.

Many who have observed the collection of literary works in the Sarasvati Mahal of Tanjore, once the seat of the Cholas, will know that a number of precious works have been filched from there even before a catalogue was made. Many works dealing on astrology, music, medicine and other sciences have disappeared. We may see even to day a note by those who made out the catalogue that of the remnants, such works as Chathurthandi prakasika and Sukkira Nadi relating to Music and Astrology respectively are missing. This fact enables us to affirm that in every Presidential city there must have been libraries which must have perished along with the kingdom. So it will not be wrong if we affirm that the first Sangam which had existed for 4000 years should have had a large Tamil library. Though there might not have been printed books there must have been a large collection of palmyra leaf records.

When we hear that when Burma was captured the Sepoys made a bonfire of the precious records on palm leaves left by the Buddhist monks called Pongis, it reminds us of the fact that Omar, the Ottman general, used the books in the library of Alexandria as fuel for six months! We know that in the present great war the Germans destroyed by fire not only many libraries in Belgium, but also an ancient and magnificent church in France, besides other churches noted for their beautiful sculptural work and beautiful pictures. The library of the first Sangam was destroyed by sea. Some of the books saved from this destruction were carried away by the sea at Kapatapuram. We have reason to believe that the library at Madura or Koodalalaway, where the Third Sangam was, was destroyed owing to various disturbances while the remnants surely went out of existence during the Mahammadan rule.

Men of intelligence will accept the fact that the present time is a period of decay of the Tamil Language or Iyal Tamil because of the disappearance of its beautiful style, its rules of prosody, and many rare words and the introduction of foreign element into it, while the two other parts of Muttamil—Isai and Natakam—had disappeared long ago. After the disappearance of these three angams of Muttamil, the ideas contained in them appear to have been written in other languages.

It seems that Ilankovadigal wrote his Silappadikaram when the extensive literature on music of the first Ooli and the regular use of the 12000 Ragas had been forgotten to a certain extent. The commentators on Silappadikaram wrote them only about 800 years ago when the musical system of Ilankovadigal had declined to a certain extent. And we who are 800 years after the time of the commentators are unable to understand their meaning. The names of the Ragas of those days, certain technical terms and instruments have completely disappeared and foreign words either from Telugu or Sanskrit are at present in use. We are sure that Sarnga Dev, the author of Sangeeta Ratnakaram, lived about 700 years ago. This Sangeeta Ratnakaram written in Sanskrit is considered to be the pioneer work on Music.

We see clearly that the author of Sangeeta Ratnakaram lived a century or two after Adyarkunallar and Kavichakravarti Jayankondan, the commentators on Silappadikaram, and a thousand years after Ilankovadigal.

The fact that Dwavimsati Srutis are mentioned in the work of Saranga Dev and in Bharata Sastram which is its basis indicate the idea that there are 22 Srutis in the octave. There are 13 Srutis between Sa and Pa and 9 between Sa and Ma. Sarnga Dev says that Sa-Pa and Sa-Ma should be 12 and 8 Srutis excluding the commencing and the finishing Swarams. By this rule Sa and Pa will never be concordant. We must understand that concordant Swarams alone are sweet, while discordant Swarams are disagreeable.

The Sa and Pa should completely blend in concordance. We have noted in part III that if this is not satisfied no concordance will result and that this concordance of Sa-Pa is the basis of the ganam of South India by the minute discrimination of which the 12 Swarams and the 24 Srutis of the Sthayi are derived. We have indicated by means of Tables how by the lessening of certain Srutis 22 are found in the Sthayi and have also pointed out such Swarams occurring in the modern Ragas. These are quite enough, we are confident, for intelligent men who strive to understand the Srutis found in the music of South India. We have also made bold to establish the Srutis by means of calculations just with a view to make out the different calculations given by different writers. On the other hand the knowledge of the Srutis should be established purely by a musical ear.

Again, when we were making enquiries into the question of Srutis used in South Indian Music we came to the conclusion that 24 Srutis could be obtained in a Sthayi. When we went deeper into the question there appeared the possibility of still minuter Srutis being found there. There is a necessity not only to give mathematical calculations for these Srutis but to indicate the places where they occur in modern Ragas. Some vidwans who are unable to understand even the 12 Swarams and the 72 Melakartas derived by their combination will also howl at this demonstration of ours. So we are constrained to give the calculations for the very minute Srutis also for the benefit of our intelligent readers.

The life which could not be understood by any means except by the functions of the body has been divided into the ten kinds of Vayu—Piranan, Apanan, Samanan, Oothanan, Vyanan, Nagan, Koorman, Kirukaran, Devathatthan and Thananjayan;

their places and functions in the body have been determined; the diseases which result either from the excess or want of these Vayus have been given; oxygen has been subdivided into five elements, the time each of them runs through each nostril and the corresponding results have been given. All this is mentioned in the Shara Shastram. Further, the science of embryology speaks about the process of determining length of life from the change of this breath at different seasons, and the process of determining shortness of life, defect of organs, ill-health and untimely death from the strengh of the breath in the nostrils and the diminution of oxygen even when a hundredth part of it is lessened at the time of conception. On the other hand, the Yoga Shastrám treats about prolonging of life by practising exhaling of less quantity of oxygen by one hundredth or even two hundredth part every day. We earnestly request those sages who have a knowledge of the above Shastras to forgive us for being so bold as to give calculations for Natham which is derived from oxygen itself.

When desire originated from Brahmam who is the first cause or seed of all creation, Natham resulted from this desire, and all creations of the vegetable and animal kingdoms from this Natham. In the same manner, the first cause appears in each created being in the form of desire in the Karana Sareeram, of Natham in the Sookshma Sareeram and of action in the Sthoola Sareeram. The world thought differently of Him at different times according as He appeared small or gigantic in form.

Though different waves with different dimensions result from a central force, yet the central force is one. So the sages of old understood that the central figure of the seven different kinds of forms is God. They have also declared that all things were created by Him, for Him, nothing was made without Him and that He is the life of all creations.

They said that the action of all creation is His play and His Chitthu Vilasam. They knew that everything received its action from Him. God who became the word in the Sookshma Sareeram dances with delight in the form of Natham just as the Sapta Swarams obtain 16 Kalais with 12 Sthanams, and the seven kinds of action and become Mother Ragas as well as innumerable jannya Ragas having the differences in Swarams such as Pun, Punniam, Thiram, Thirathiram, or Sampoornam, Shadavam, Oudavam and Swarantham in Aroganam and Avaroganam with extensive Prastharam.

The ancients, understanding the extensive Natha Soroopa of the deity by the extensive Ragas derived out of the Saptaswarams made ganam in the different Ragas with the Amsa Swarams corresponding to his actions as the Jivaswarams.

Our ancestors, who realised the importance of such a ganam, first determined the Srutis and then constructed rules relating to them.

Our ancestors who attached a good deal of importance to the well-being of the soul laid great stress on knowing God and living up to His standard. We clearly understand from their works that as their knowledge became perfect they realised first the twenty-five Pancheekarana Tatvas of this andam and its chief or the twentyfifth Tatvam which is annam, the twenty-five Tatvas of Annamayakosam derived from Annam, the lust which is the chief and at the same time its twenty-fifth Tatvam, the twenty-five Tatvas of the Sookshma Sareeram bound by lust, the Anthakarna which is the twenty-fifth Tatvam and the same time its chief and the knowledge and ignorance contained therein; their works make us understand that the end and aim of their existence was to realise the 25 Tatvas of the Karana Sareeram through knowledge, the chief Tatvam of the Sookshma Sareeram, and through this to realise the Brahmam, the end of all knowledge which is the chief and the 25th Tatvam of the Karana Sareeram.

That which is obtained by the five actions of the Andam is annam. It was derived from Prithvi, the first Tatvam of Andam. Moham or lust is the 25th Tatvam of Sthoola Sareeram derived from Annam. The 25 Tatvas of the Sookshma Sareeram are derived from lust; of these, the genital organ, which is an amsam of the Prithvi of the Sookshma Sareeram is the first Tatvam.

Anthakarnam is the 25th Tatvam. Brahma is the first Tatvam of the Karanasareeram derived from Anthakaranam as the basis. This is the amsam of Prithvi. Parabrahmam is the 25th Tatvam among those derived from Panchakaranam which is a mixture of the Panchakartas and the Panchasaktis. This is known among sages as the knowledge of all knowledge, the Mounam or Silence, the Soonyam or nothingness, the extensive perfection, and Satthu, Chittu and Anandam.

Thus in the presence of the Brahmam, the 25th Tatvam of the Karanasareeram, the three gunams Satva, Rajas aud Thamas generated. These three gunams mixed according to the rules of the Panchabootas and the Panchakaranam, and the result was the creation which enables man to enjoy the functions of this body and its organs and also enables him to have wordly experience. Of this creation the human form is very superior.

This supreme human being behaves either according to knowledge or ignorance which is derived from Anthakaranam, the head of the Sookshmasareeram. If he chooses ignorance or, in other words, if he conducts himself to suit the gross body the result is ignorance, interest from ignorance, lust of me and mine from interest, evil deed from lust, taking on this gross body as the result of evil, the bondage of family life owing to the gross body and ultimate hell owing to this bondage of family life. On the other hand if he chooses knowledge he obtains discretion by knowledge, disinterestedness by discretion, destruction of Karma by this absence of desire, exemption from Sthoola Sareeram by this destruction of Karma, exemption from bondage owing to exemption from Sthoola Sareeram or the Ego and finally obtains Moksham by this exemption from bondage.

The lust which is the cause of life and death is the prime cause for the two Andams above and the two Andams below. The being which is influenced by lust owing to the preponderance of ignorance loses the effect of the prestige and good actions of the Sookshma Sareeram and is destined for hell thus fulfilling the word of God "dust thou art and to dust thou shalt return."

On the other hand, the being who directs his conduct by knowledge, the 25th Tatvam of the Sookshma Sareeram, thus destroying lust which is the 25th Tatvam of the Sthoola Sareeram, understands the superiority of the Sookshma Sareeram, subdues it, understands one by one the godly qualities and Saktis of the Karana Sareeram by Pancheekaranam, brings it into practice and finally realises in himself the Brahmam or the Satthu, Chittu and Anandam.

The sages of old, knowing that the realisation in themselves of the one true God and his viceroy, the Paramatma, was life eternal, they enquired by day and night in order to obtain this life everlasting. They wrote in the form of works their experiences out of generosity so that others might also obtain the benefits of the Saktis of the Karana Sareeram which they themselves had realised in proportion to the severity of their respective penance. Speaking about the nine different kinds of the Sthoola, Sookshma and the Karana Sareerams and the nine gunams that are reflected out of them, they gave the Panchabhootas and the actions of Panchee Karanams for Andam, and Pindam and the Sookshma and the Karana Sareerams.

They pointed out that Sthoolam, Sookshmam and Karanam were Sareerams, that mind, word and body were their respective places, that Anavam, Kamam and Maya were Malams, that Sathmeegam, Rajasam and Thamatham were Gunams, that Swargham, Madhyam and Pathalam were lokas, that the Sun and the Moon were Agnimandalams, that Mandaram, Madhya and Taram were Sthayis, that Ah, Oo and Ma were Aksharams, and that creation, preservation and destruction were actions and taught also kindred ideas to enable them to understand the above. They wrote about animal creation commencing from beings with a single sense up to beings with seven senses such as human beings with the amsam of God. Each vargam was divided into seven different kinds and the key to understand them was laid down. They gave the thirteen different kinds of evil which spoil the animal kingdom and the way to avoid them. They gave similes as well as the Pancha Bhootas and their modifications most clearly to prove that what holds good for the Andam (the whole) also holds good for the Pindam (the part). They sought the help of God who shines as the seed of the Karana Sareeram in order to have a perfect conception of all these.

The life breath or the oxygen which is diffused in the Kalais of the Sun and the Moon was controlled by them and confined to the Soorya Kalai alone. They saw the glorious presence of the Nandi as of myriads of suns in the place where the three roads met at the top of the Ongara pillar which is the result of the mixture of the functions of the two ears, the two eyes and oxygen, and obtained in that presence all that they wanted to know or to hear or to see. The saints who attained this exalted stage reflected the glory of God in them and looked like angels. Such men never recognised the difference of caste, creed or culture, and taught to the world the excellent principle of looking upon the life of every created being as their own by their example and experience. There is reason for us to be proud that such sages who gave up the world and loved God were found primarily and in great numbers in the south Tamil country. We know that Satyavaratha, king of the south Tamil country, and the seven sages who came with him were saved from the deluge by a boat, that they took refuge in the north country, that people multiplied through that sage and that he was known later as Vyvasutha Manu. We may also boldly say that all sciences and arts originated from the Kumari Nadu, the abode of these sages, and spread to other places.

In all their sciences, they state that the chief amsams of the Pindam (the part) were found in the Andam (the whole). We shall find later on that this truth is the basis of the science of music. They found that the chief Tatvas of the Andam were the basis of music also. They found from their experience that the prime calculation of the Sthoola Sareeram was the right one for the Nadam of the Sookshma Sareeram which is the very life of the Sthoola Sareeram. Those who experienced this divided the Natham according to that calculation and praised him by sweet music derived from the changes of Natham and declared his good works. Their chief business was to commune with God; the incarnation of the six Atharams, to praise him, to write during leisure hours works that may be useful to their children and to be kind to all living Beings.

They found that Karana Sareeram was based on the six fundamental Sthanams of the Sookshma Sareeram just as life stands on the six fundamental Sthanams of the Sthoola Sareeram. Just as Om, the primary sound, became seven Swarams through the six intermediate gradual steps, Brahmam, the prime Being, obtained gradually the seven appearances with seven different kinds of knowledge. This Brahmam with the seven different appearances passed through the six Sthanams of the Sthoola Sareeram—namely, Moolatharam, Swathishtanam, Monipooragam, Anagatham, Visuthi and Akinai —and the six Sthanams of the Sookshama Sareeram, namely, Sakiram, Swarpanam, Suluthi, Thuryam, Thuryatheetham and Atheetham, rose step by step became the 12 Sthanams and obtained the layam in the Karana Sareeram. In the same way, the first Shadjam or Om develops into the six Swarams up to Suddha Ma, and the six Swarams from the Pratti Ma or the 12 fundamental Swarams in all and comes back to the Shadjam again.

When we observe the fact of the seven appearances, it seems that the eighth one is the basis of all appearance. In other words, the eighth place is the one where the seven appearances loose their Sthoola, Sookshama and Nama appearances and get merged into the Prime Being. On the same principle the seven Swarams commencing from the Shadjam end in the eighth Swaram or the upper Sa. The Prime Being appearing with seven different forms and coming back to his original form is an example of the play ot the deity.

He who danced for joy with the seven kinds of appearances and the seven paruvas loses the form and the paruvam and reaches the stage of Mukti. The case is analogous to that of the Sa which gradually rises upwards through the seven Sthanams and obtains perfection at the eighth step or the octave.

Natham or sound by its sancharam in the 12 Sthanams produces sweetness just as life is contained in the 12 Sthanams and the Sun lives in the 12 Rasis.

Just as the Sapta grahams by their sancharam in the 12 Rasis preduce numerous seasons and Jathaka Chakarams and just as the Sapta Swarams in the 12

Sthanams by change of graham produce innumerable Ragas, so also the living beings in the seven kinds of appearances obtain numerous differences in the Sthoola and Sookshma Sareerams.

We may find that some of the other Amsams of the Sthoola and Sookshma Sareeras satisfy this uniformity. Just as the measurement of the Sthoola Sareeram is 8 spans and each span is 12 inches according to the principle that "even the length of the ant is 8 spans measured by its own span", the seven appearances must also have a uniform measurement.

In the same manner, the sages have made mention of the fact that life in the breath of 12 inches lives as 16 Kalais, and stands normal in a breath of 8 inches. These sages who knew the nature of the Sthoola, Sookshama and Karana Sareeras were eternally praising the deity. When we note that all the saints were eternally praising God before Him, we may understand clearly that some of the important Amsams of music have been so constructed as to suit the structure of the Sthoola, Sookshma and the Karana Sareeras.

It is but fit that the Being who first appeared as Natham, after the seven appearances should practise the music with the seven Swarams and return back to his original stage as Natha Brahmam. Besides music there is no other easy means by which living beings can concentrate their mind on God or realise him. Those devoted saints who sing the puns or songs in praise of the deity so as to melt the hearts will understand the truth of our statement.

Just as the bottom Sa is in complete harmony with the upper Sa, so also through music the saints practised perfect harmony with the deity. Just as they found from experience that the concord with Sa was the most charming place in music, they realised that their happiness was in being in perfect harmony of oneness with God and so spent their lives in being kind to all living beings. Just as fragrance is the special excellence of a blossomed flower, and sweetness that of a ripe fruit their lives were one round of fragrance and sweetness to the rest of mankind. They fully believed that Puns in praise of the Deity were the vessels which would take them safely out of the ocean of this painful family life and lead them to God.

Some important musical mysteries which were naturally held in enimence during the first Ooli in South Madura when the practice of the Music of the Tamilians was very extensive, lost their importance in the later Ooli. Some parts of the work on Music written by Ilankovadigal at such a period were also held to be doubtful.

At this period of doubt other writers put together in the form of works many ideas which they came across during their researches in their own language. Of these Sarnga Dev alone wrote very extensively. We do not say that he did not understand the theory of Ilankovadigal who lived 1200 years before him, or that of Tholkaupiam dated about 8000 years before that period nor the opinion of the savants of the first sangam which lasted for nearly 4000 years. It is but natural that in course of years some ideas should gain preeminence while others gradually go out of use altogether. We have to be glad that he preserved in his writings at least some of the amsams of Music. But he would have done better if he had not given 13 and 9 Srutis for Sa-Pa and Sa-Ma to establish the stumbling block of the 22 Srutis.

The measurement which he has given has led to the discordance of Srutis used in the ganam and has made all the enquirers on Srutis break their heads over his system.

The author of Parijatam, Somanatha and others who lived about 300 years after him have, to a certain extent, adopted the views of Sarnga Dev as regards Srutis and the Swarams of the Yal. It is clear they give contradictory opinions as regards names, swarasthanams and their system of exposition. They were unwilling to contradict the theory of Sarnga Dev who was their predecessor and who was held to have very clear views on Music nor were they willing to give up the Swarams of Karnatic Music which were within their practical experience. The result was they were in the midst of the region of doubt. So it is clear that even at that period the Dwavimsati Srutis were impracticable and open to doubt and many musicians wrote their works to clear this doubt and establish the truth of the Karnatic Music.

Instead of insisting on tuning by the Musical ear according to the Sa-Pa system they gave a rough measurement for the benefit of the carpenter who constructed the Yal. It is but natural that those who have no Musical ear should make much of such a rough measurement. On the same principle Pythagoras, the Greek philosopher, evidently carried this rough measurement of $\frac{2}{3}$ and $\frac{3}{4}$ in the determination of the Srutis of the Yal to the Western countries. The Swarams that are determined according to this measurement are altered in a very slight degree by those gifted with Musical ear to suit their Ganam. When altered, though the Ragas played by them appear to be correct owing to constant practice, yet there will be a slight difference when their calculations are examined. This difference added on to the rough measnrement intended for carpenters, the minute and subtle Srutis used in Ragas and the confusion of the 22 Srutis, landed everyone in the region of doubt.

To clear ourselves of this doubt we must first establish the facts that the shape of the Yal resembles that of the Sthoola Sareeram, the sound of the Yal that of the Sookshma Sareeram and that the vibrations of the Swarams of the Yal resemble those of the human breath.

Secondly, we must note the calculations of the 12 Swarams of Ayapalai, the 24 Srutis of Vattapalai, and the calculations of the minuter Srutis and examine the Ragas where such minute Srutis occur.

Thirdly, we should examine the opinions of those who wrote about the Swarams and Srutis in use in the Music of South India.

If the correct calculation for the 12 Swarams in use in Karnatic Music could first be established, it will be easy to understand the Srutis and minuter Srutis used there.

No other instrument could help in determining this but the Yal, the queen of instruments. The shape, the structure and the vibrations of this excellent instrument resemble those of the human body. Some of the important structures of the human body are seen here.

Therefore, if we note, in the first place, some of the amsams of the Yal which are said, by our ancestors, to be found in the human body, it will be of use to us who want to know something about the calculations of Swarams and Srutis used in Music. We have purposely stated very briefly many points which ought to have been dealt with extensively for the sake of avoiding voluminousness.

I. The Human being and the Yal.

1. The excellence of the Yal used by the ancient Tamils.

We have noted before that during the preeminent period of the First Ooli, for thousands of years the Tamil language which had been divided into Iyal, Isai and Natakam was in a highly efficient condition. Many kinds of Yal seem to have been mentioned there, as well as many ragas which generate from the change of Graham of its Swarams, the system of Alakus as well as extensive and minute rules of practice. Though the different Yals used at that period slightly vary in structure from one another, we find that, on the whole, they resemble the human body and its measurements. Instruments which did not resemble the human body and shape never attained any eminence in ancient times.

We have noted the kinds of Yal used by the ancient Tamils and their names, how they had 1, 2, 3, 4, 7, 9, 16, 17, 21, 100 and even 1000 strings to suit the shape and measurement desired by the player. The one most used by the Tamils from that date up till now seems to have been the Senkoti Yal having 7 strings, being made of red wood like the jack wood and known as Veena in the modern time. However, sweet insruments with 1, 2 and 3 strings known in those days as Maruthuvayal, Sundari and Kinnari are found even now in the South Country, though of lesser importance.

We know that even now the practice of the Veena is held in high esteem by the Tamils of South India. The Tamils who worship Paramasiva who has a partiality for the Music of the Veena think it best to praise him by Music on that instrument. The use of the Yal is fast disappearing and cheap foreign instruments which could be got for a Rupee or a Rupee and a half such as the Fiddle, Mouth harmonicon, Harmonium, Piano which is played on pieces of steel or on wires and northern instruments such as Saranda, Surabath, Mayil Veena and Zithar are being gradually introduced in South India. We may see even to day that those who have not the patience and perseverance to learn the Veena and become experts in it after 12 years of constant practice with the Yal master have learnt easily to play some mutilated tunes on a foreign instrument. It is a fact that expert players on the Yal look down upon other instruments. We know Paramasivam who bears Asuvatharar and Kumbalar, the Yal experts, as his ear ornaments and who played the Yal for the sake of his devotee Panapathiran in the guise of a wood-cutter. We do not see that he brought any other instrument but the Yal. It would have been easier for him to have brought a light instrument like the fiddle seeing that he had to carry a heavy load of undried fuel fixing a prohibitive price on it and himself toiling with the heavy burden. Such instruments seem to have been unknown in those days. We see clearly that the Yal so much admired for its shape, measurement. sound and sweetness seems to have been the only instrument practised by the ancient Tamils. No other instrument can so faithfully produce Suddha Swarams snd minute Srutis. This alone could serve as an accompaniment to the human voice in the singing of Puns. The short and long sounds, Otu and Gamakam produced by the human voice can faithfully be reproduced only by this instrument As the other musical instruments are not so clear in reproducing the human voice, the Yal alone is known as the living instrument and the instrument of Gods, while the others are known as dumb instruments. We understand by the expressions 'living instrument' and ' instrument for Gods' that a devotee who praises God by his sweet music resembles the Yal, that the structure of the Yal made of wood resembles his own and that the sweetness of the Yal combined with his own pleases the Deity. The man was called Kathira Veena and the Veena on which he plays, Tharu Veena. The following slokam from Sama Vedam supports it.

" தாருவீ காத்ர வீணைச த்வே வீணே கான ஜாதிஷு "
ஸாமிகோ காத்ர வீணைது தஸ்யா ச்ருணுத லட்சணம்

The Kathira Veena or the Sareeram, and the Tharu Veena made of wood are instruments for ganam. We shall now give the characteristic of the Kathira Veena which alone could perform the Sama Veda Ganam.

2. How the Yal resembles the human body.

We noticed just now that a man should praise the Deity with his Sareeram or the Veena which the Deity likes, to the accompaniment of the Veena made of wood. We give below a number of quotations which emphasise the fact that the Yal completely resembles the human body.

Pages 24 and 25 of the Essay read by M. R. Ry. Veena Venkataramanadoss of Vizianagaram, at the third Conference of the Tanjore Sangeetha Vidya Mahajana Sangam :—

"தவிரவும் விஷ்ணுவின் ஸ்தானத்திற்குக் காரணமாயிருக்கும் பிரம்மாண்டத்துக்கு வீணையொத்திருப்பதால் ஐத்ரேய ஆரண்யகத்தில் சொல்லியபடி மனுஷ்ய வீணையும் தைவ வீணைக்குச் சரியாகும். ஆகையால் வீணையைக் கொண்டாடப்பியசிக்கவேண்டும்.

பாகவதம், 3வது ஸ்கந்தம், 12-ம் அத்தியாயத்தில் சொல்லியபடி ககாராதிமகாரம் முடிய 25 அக்ஷரங்களான ஸ்பர்சங்கள் சப்த பிரம்மத்தின் ஜீவன். அகாரம்முதல் 16 அக்ஷரங்களாகிய ஸ்வரங்கள் தேகம். ச, ஷ, ஸ, ஹ, என்கிற 4 அக்ஷரங்களாகிற ஊஷ்மா இந்திரியங்களாகச் சொல்லப்பட்டிருக்கிறது. ஸ்பர்ச ஸ்வர ஊஷ்மா ரூபமான சப்தபிரமம் விக்ருதி அவஸ்தை அடைந்து விஷ்ணு என்றபெயர் அடையுங்காலத்தில் அதன் அம்சம் பிருத்வியில் இருப்பதால் பிருத்வி விஷ்ணுரூபமாகவும் அவ்விதமாகவே அந்தரிக்ஷம் ஸ்வர்க்கங்களும் விஷ்ணுரூபமாகவும் இருக்கிறது. பிருத்வி, அந்தரிக்ஷம், ஸ்வர்க்கம் ஆக 3 லோகங்களும் ஸ்பர்சாதிகளால் பிரதி பாதிக்கப்பட்டு 3 லோகத்திற்கும் அதிஷ்டானமாகிறது. 3 லோகத்தின் ஸாரமான அக்கினி, வாயு ஆதித்தியன் என்னும் தேவர்களுக்கு அதிஷ்டானமாகிறது. 3 தேவதைகளுக்கும் ஸாரமான ருக் யஜுர் ஸாமமென்கிற 3 வேதத்திற்கும் அதிஷ்டானமாகிறது. அத்யாத்மமான சக்ஷுச்ச்ரோத்திரம், மனது இவைகளுக்கும், பிராணன், அபானன், வியானன் இவைகளுக்கும் அதிஷ்டானமாகிறது. ஆகையால் ஸ்பர்சாதிகளால் பிரதி பாதிக்கப்பட்ட பிரம்மாண்டத்துக்கே தைவீ வீணை என்று பெயர் அடைகிறது. விஷ்ணுவின்

கானத்துக்கு நேரானதாக இருப்பதால் தேவனுமாகிற விஷ்ணுவின் வீணை என்று பெயர். அப்படியிருக்கையில் மரத்தினால் செய்யப்பட்ட மனுஷிய வீணைக்கும் வீணை என்று பெயர் சொல்லலாமா? பிரம்மாதி தேகத்தின் ஸாதிருசியம் மனுஷிய வீணையிலும் இருப்பதால் அதற்கும் வீணை என்று பெயர் சொல்லலாம். இதைப்பற்றி ஐத்ரேய 3-ம் ஆரண்யகம் 2-ம் அத்தியாயம் 5-ம் அநுவாகத்தில் சொல்லியிருக்கிறது.

Comment :—Again, as the Veena resembles the body of the Brahma which is the cause of the ganam of Vishnu, the human Veena resembles Deva Veena as mentioned in Itraya Aranyakam. So one must practise with the Veena.

As mentioned in the 12th chapter, 3rd Skandam of Baghavatam, the 25 Aksharams ending with Kakarathi Makaram or sparisas form the life of the Sapta Brahmam. The 16 Aksharas or Swarams beginning with Agaram form the body. The 4 Aksharas Cha, Sha, Sa and Ha or Ooshma form the Indiriyas. So when the Saptabrahmam in the forms of Sparisa, Swara and Ooshma undergo Vikriti or change and obtain the name of Vishnu, as their amsam is in Prithvi (worlds-middle, air and heaven), both the Prithvi and Antharikshasvargas are in the shape of Vishnu. Prithvi, Anthariksham and Swargam or the three worlds are each explained by Sparisa and form the basis of the three worlds. It also forms the residence of the three Gods, Agni, Vayu and Athityon which are the basis of the three worlds. It also becomes the residence of the three Vedas, Rig, Yajur and Sama, the basis of the three goddesses. It also becomes the residence of Chakshush, Srotram and Manas which are very imporant factors as well as Pranan. Apanan and Vyanan. So Brahma and other bodies explained by Sparisa obtain the name of Daiva Veena. As it is useful for Vishnu ganam it is called Daiva Veena or the Veena of Vishnu. When such is the case, can the human instrument made of wood be also called Veena? Yes, because the amsams of Brahmam and other bodies are also found in the human Veena. The following quotation in the 3rd Aranyakam, 2nd Chapter and 5th Anuvagam of Itraya is in support of the above :—

Prithivya rupam sparsah ; antarikshasyosh manah ; divah svarah. Agne rupam sparsah ; vayorushmanah ; adityasya svarah. Rigvedasya rupam sparsah ; yajurvedasyoshmanah ; samavedasya svarah. Chakshusho rupam sparsah ; srotrasyoshmanah ; manasoh svarah. Pranasya rupam sparsah ; apanasyoshmanah ; Vyanasya svarah. Atha khalviyam daivi vina bhavati. Tadanukritirasau manushi vina bhavati. Yathasyah sira evamamushyah sirah; yathasyah udarame; vamamushyah ambhanam ; yathasya jihvai vamamushya vadanam ; yathasyas tantrya evamamushyangulayah ; yathasyah svara evamamushyah svarah ; yathasyah sparsa evamumushyah sparsaha yatha hyeveyam sabdavati tardmavati ; evamasau sabdavati tardmavati, yatha hyeveyam lomasena charmana pihita lomascna ha sma charmana pura vina apidadhati. Sa yo haitam vinam veda srutavadano bhavati.

Comment:—The forms of the Prithvi are Sparisas (or touch,) that of Antariksham Ooshmas (or heat) and that of Swarga logams. Swarams. In the same manner the Rupas of Agni, Vayu and Athityan, are the Swarams of Sparisa and Ooshma ; the Rupas of Rig, Yajur and Sama Vedas, the Rupas of Chakshus, (the eye) Srotram (the ear) and Manas (Mind) and those of Pranan, Apanan and Vyanan are the Swarams of Sparisa and Ooshma. This is called Daivi Veena. That which is constructed of wood according to the same shape is called the human Veena. The organs found in Brahmam and other bodies are also found in the human Veena. The

Veena has also a head like that of the human body, a belly or middle part like that of man, a plectrum like the tongue, wires and sounds of high pitch like the fingers of man, Swarams like SA (C) like letters commencing from அ; just as the Daiva Veena produces a tone and a sound of higher or lower pitch in the wires through the fingers like the letters SA-PA and SA-MA or Sparisas, the human Veena also is capable of producing sounds. Just as the Daiva Veena is covered with skin and hair, so also the Veena in the Kirta Yogam is covered with skin and hair. Whoever thinks devotedly of Brahma and other bodies as Vishnu Veena to him is given the gift of music. So we must understand first the character of Veena and then practise music on it. We have heard that Narada who practises Nada Brahmam does his ganam with the Veena."

In the above lines we notice a number of points in which the Veena resembles the human body. As they are clearly stated we need no further dwell on the subject. The picture on the next page will clearly illustrate this.

The Spinal column in the above picture which is known as Veenathandam has 24 separate bones. In the same way there are 24 frets in the Thandu of the Veena. The same space which is found between the 24th fret and the base of the strings is also found between the spinal column and the head.

We know that the human body is 8 spans in length, according to the measurement of each one's span. Of these, there will be 4 spans from the genital organ to the head and 4 spans from the same to the foot. In the same manner, we must know that the measurement of the Veena from the Meru to the Mettu must be 4 spans. Just as the Thandu of the Veena is 3 spans, the spinal colum of man will also be 3 spans. The circumference of man's head is also 3 spans. The circumference of the belly of the Veena must also be of the same measurement.

Just as we infer that if the head which is the seat of the five senses of touch, taste, smell, hearing and sight be big, the man's knowledge is proportionately wide, we find that if the belly of a Veena has a larger circumierence than 3 spans the volume of its sound is also proportionately greater. But any Veena with a belly more than 4 spans in circumference will be not only disproportionate but also against fixed rules.

Just as a man's body reaches perfection by receiving the Seven Thathus, skin, bone, flesh, braim, sperm, blood and marrow, so also the Veena attains perfection by means of the seven strings. Just as a man with the seven thathus obtains life and knowledge and becomes capable of sweet deeds and sweet sounds, the Veena with seven strings should have Reku (ரேக—a little brass plate placed under the wires in the Mettu of the Veena so as to produce sweet sound) in the Mettu. If it is not so the sound of the Veena will be lifeless and wooden. It must be placed very minutely in the Reku plates that are placed on the Mettu. If we do not do so we will be compelled to have silk strings as in the case of the Tambura. The sound generates from the middle of the place where the Reku is placed. So when we measure the strings to know the calculations of sounds, the Mettu should exactly be placed where the wire sounds and we should locate the SA of Madhya Sthayi in the exact centre of the wire. Or else the measurements of Swarasthanams will slightly differ.

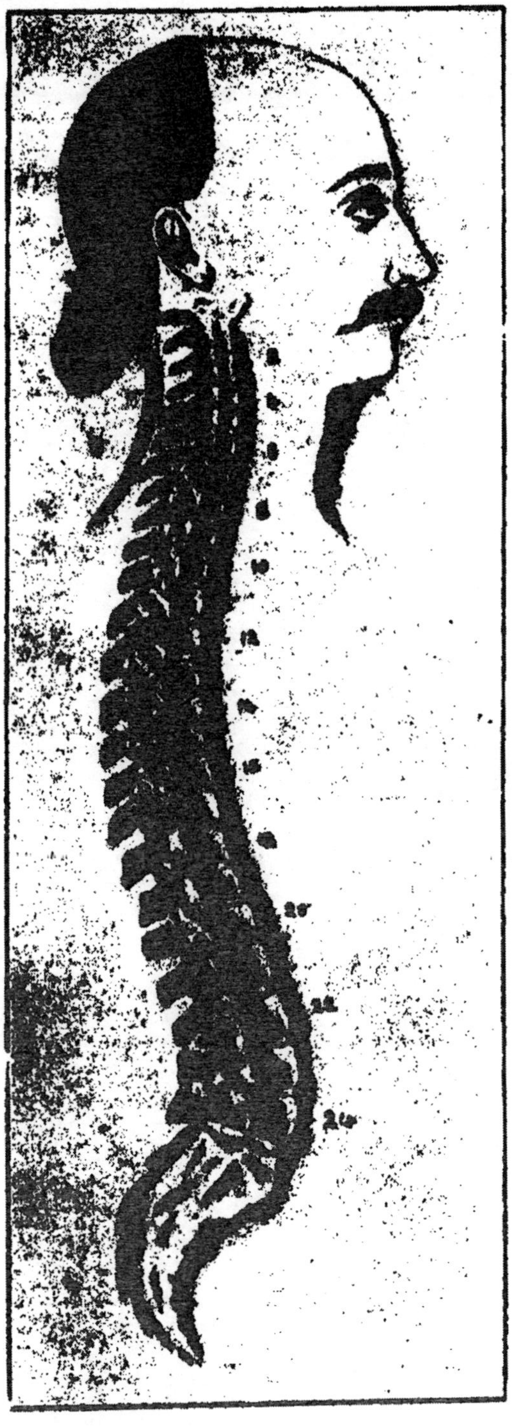

We know that a span is made of 12 digits of our fingers. So the length of the Veena from the Meru to the Mettu will be 48 inches. In the same manner it will be 48 inches from the middle of the brow of a man to his genital organ.

We also see clearly that the Swarasthanams of a Veena gradually become less and are in Geometrical Progression from the Meru to the Mettu just as the bones of the spinal column gradually get smaller and smaller commencing from the genital organ and proceeding upwards. Moreover, just as the intervals from the Meru to the Mettu gradually get less and less so also we know that sound gradually rises in pitch without admitting any other possible sound between. The following quotations will show that sound rises from the middle of the Reku in the Merusthanam which is of the breadth of a digit.

In the same way the Oxygen which keeps moving in the Sthoolam can be measured and said at what exact inch from the genital organ it moves and how sweet music springs from that region. The following stanzas prove this :—

Silappadikaram, Arangetukathai p. 83.

"பூதமுதற் சாதனத்தாம் புற்கலத்தின் மத்திமத்து
நாதமுத லாமெழுந்து நாலாகி—வீதி
வருவரத்தாற் றுனத்தால் வந்து வெளிப்பட்
டிருவரத்தாற் றேற்ற மிசைக்கு."

என்பதனுணர்க. புற்கலம்—உடம்பு. அப்புற்கலத்துக்கு முதலாயுள்ள பூதமாவன :—மண் நீர் தீ வளி வானெனவிவை. என்னை ?

Comment :—Here he says that Natham generates from the middle of the Purkalam or body.

"மண்ணுட னீர்தெருப்புக் கால்வான மென்றிவைதா
மெண்ணரிய பூதங்க ளென்றறிந்து—நண்ணரிய
மண்ணாக்கு மண்கோடுத்து மாற்றாக்கு விண்கோடுத்த
தெண்ணரவர்கோ மாமே தெளி."

என்றாராகலின். இப்பூதங்களிக்குள்ளும் புற்கலமாமென்ற ஆசானை மாணுக்கன் பணிந்து பூதங்கடாம் ஒன்றோடொன்று கூடமாட்டா ; மண் செறிதலைக் குணமாக வுடைத்து ; நீர் நெகிழ்தலைக் குணமாகவுடைத்து; தீ தெறுதலைக் குணமாக வுடைத்து ; காற்று நிலைபெறாது திரிதலைக் குணமாகவுடைத்து ; ஆகாயமென்பது உருவுடையதன்று ; அன்றியும்,

Comment :—The disciple made his obeisance to the guru who declared that the body is made up of these five elements. Then the disciple said that the nature of the elements was such that they could never mix. To which the guru replied, the earth has cohesion for its character ; water, relaxation ; fire, burning ; air, blowing and not being fixed to any particular sphere while as regards atmosphere we cannot say whether it has a form or not. Besides this,

" செப்பிய பூதங்கள் சேர்க்தோர் குறியன்றே
யப்பரிச மண்ணைந்து நீர்நாலா—மொப்பரிய
தீயாகின் மூன்றிரண்டே காற்றம் பரமோன்று
வேயாயக் தோளி விளம்பு."

என்பதனுல் மண் ஐந்து பயனுடைத்து ; நீர் நான்கு பயனுடைத்து ; தீ மூன்று பயனுடைத்து ; காற்று இரண்டு பயனுடைத்து ; வான் ஒரு பயனுடைத்து ; ஆதலால் இவை ஒன்றோடொன்று கூடுவனவல்ல வாகவும் இவற்றின் கூட்ட முடம்பென்றீராதலால் இவ்வைந்தின் கூட்டம் உடம்பாவது எவ்வாறெனின், இதற்கு விடை :—

Comment :—Earth has five uses, water four, fire three, air two and atmosphere one. So these can never mix together. But a combination of the five is the body. How this is so is seen from the following stanza:—

" மெய்வாய்கண் மூக்குச் செவியெனப் பேர்பெற்ற
வைவாயு மாயவற்றின் மீதேத்து—துய்ய
சுவையொளியூ றோசை நாற்றமேன் றைந்தா
லவைமுதற் புற்கல மாம்."

என்பது பூதங்கள் பரிணமித்து உடம்பாமாறு கூறுகின்றது. பூதங்களைந்தும் தத்தம் தன்மை நீங்கி மண் உடம்பாயும், நீர் வாயாயும், தீக்கண்ணாயும், காற்று மூக்காயும், ஆகாயம் செவியாயுநின்று உடம்பாம். பொறிகடோறும் வினியோகப்பட்ட புலன் சுவைமுதல் ஐந்துவகைப்படும். இவ்வைந்தும் பொறியைத்திறுமேறி, மண்ணால் உடம்பு ஊறுயும், நீரால் வாய் சுவையாயும், தியாற் கண் ஒளியாயும், காற்றால் மூக்கு நாற்றமாயும் வானாற் செவி ஓசையாயும் வந்து உடம்பாம். அன்றியும் மண்ணின் பகுதி நரம்பு இறைச்சி என்பு மயிர் தோலெனவைந்து, நீரின், பகுதி நீர் மூளை சுக்கிலம் நிணம் உதிரமெனவைந்து.

Comment :—The five Bhutas by the process of change become the body. The earth becomes the human trunk, water the mouth, fire the eye, air the nostrils and atmosphere becomes the sound. There are five distinct senses corresponding to the respective sense organs. By earth the body becomes the organ of touch, by water the mouth becomes the organ of taste, by fire the eye becomes the organ of sight, by the air, the nose becomes the organ of smell, by the atmosphere the ear becomes the organ of sound. Again the earth is responsible for the five, namely nerve, the flesh, the bone, the hair and the skin of the human body while water is responsible for the five, namely the urine, the brain, the sperm the fat and the blood of the human body.

" பசிசோம்பு மைதுனங் காட்சிநீர் வேட்கை
தேசின்ற தீக்குணமோ ரைந்து—மோசின்ற
போக்கு வரவுநோய் கும்பித்தன் மெய்ப்பரிசம்
வாக்குடைய காற்றின் வகை."

என்பது தீயின் குணமும் காலின் குணமுமுணர்த்துகின்றது ; அவை; பசி சோம்பு மைதுனம் காட்சி நீர்வேட்கை யென வைந்து தீக்குணம். போக்கு வரவு நோய் கும்பித்தல் பரிசமெனவைந்து காற்றின் குணம்.

Comment :—The resultant characteristics of fire and air are here given :— Those of fire are, hunger, laziness, sexual intercourse, sight and thirst. Those of air are, going, coming, disease, regulation of breath and touch.

" ஓங்கும் வெகுளி மதமான மாங்கார
நீங்கா வுலோபமுட னிவ்வைந்தும்—பாங்காய
வன்னை முகிலமடவாய் வானகத்தின் கூறென்று
ரென்னவிக நூலவர்க்கோ ரேன்."

இது ஆகாயத்தின் குணமுணர்த்துகின்றது. வெகுளி மதம் மானம் ஆங்காரம் உலோபமெனவிவை இப்பூதகுணம் இருபத்தைந்துங்கொண்டு உடம்பாம்.

Comment :—This gives the characteristics of the atmosphere. These five are: anger, lust, self-respect, selfishness and greediness. That which contains the 25 characteristics of the elements is the Body.

" ஒப்பார் பிராண னபான னுதானனுடன்
றப்பா வியானன் சமானனே—யிப்பாலு
நாகன் றனஞ்சயன் கூர்மன் கிருகரன்
நீதிலாத் தேவதத்த னே."

என்பது தச வாயுக்களையுமுணர்த்துகின்றது. அவை : பிராணன் அபானன் உதானன் வியானன் சமானன் நாகன் கூர்மன் கிருகரன் தேவதத்தன் தனஞ்சயனெனவிவை.

Comment :—This shows the ten Kinds of Vayus. They are, Pranan, Apanan, Oothanan, Viyanan. Samanan, Nagan, Koorman, Kirukaran, Devathathan and Thananjayan.

" இடைபிங் கலைசுழுனை காந்தாரி யத்தி
புடைநின்ற சிங்குவை சங்கினி பூடாவோ
டங்குகு கன்னி யலம்பு வெனவுரைத்தார்
தங்குதச நாடிக டாம்."

தசநாடிகளாவன : இடை, பிங்கலை, சுழுமுனை, காந்தாரி, அத்தி, சிங்குவை, சங்கினி, பூடா, குகு, அலம்பு எனவிவை ;

Comment :—The ten Nadis are :—Idai, Pingalai, Shulumunai, Kanthari, Atthi, Singuvai. Sangini, Pooda, Kuku and Alambu.

" பூத வகைகளோ ரைந்தாய்ப் பொறியைந்தாய்
வாதனையோ ரையைந்தாய் மாருதமு—மேதகுசீர்ப்
பத்தாகு நாடிகளும் பப்பத்தாம் பாரிடத்தே
முத்திக்கு வித்தா முடம்பு."

என்பது பூத பரிணாம முணர்த்துகின்றது. பூதங்களைந்தாவன : மண் முதலாயின ; பொறியைந் தாவன : செவி முதலாயின ; புலனைந்தாவன : சத்த முதலாயின ; வாதனையையைந்தாவன : வாம்பு முதலிய ஐந்தும், நீர் முதலிய ஐந்தும், பரி முதலிய ஐந்தும், போக்கு முதலிய ஐந்தும், வெருளி முதலிய ஐந்தும். தச வாயுக்களாவன, பிராணன் முதலிய பத்தும். தச நாடிகளாவன ; இடை பிங்கலை முதலிய பத்தும். மூலாதாரத்து எழுபத்தீராயிர நாடிகளும் பிக்கங்கட்டின் மூன்று கன்றுபோல இடைபிங்கலை சுழுமுனை யென்னும் மூன்று நாடிகளுமாய் நடுவு நின்ற சுழுமுனையொழிய இரண்டாலும் வேறுவேறே இரண்டு மூக்காலும் ஓரோர் பரிசத்து ஐந்து நாழிகையாகச்செல்லும் ஒரு மாத்திரையில் நாற்றிருப்பத்தெட்டு கலைதயாய் ஒரு கலாநத்திலே பன்னிரண்டங்குலி வாயு புறப்பட்டு நாலங்குலி தேய்ந்து எண் விரலடக்குகின்றது பிராண வாயுவென்க. மாத்திரையாவது : இரண்டரை நாழிகையை எட்டிக்கூட்டிட்ட ஒரு கடிகையென்றறிக. அபான

வாயு மலமூத்திரங்களைப்பெய்விக்கும். உதானன் கண்ட தானத்தில் நிற்கும். வியான வாயு போக்கு வரவு செய்து இயங்கப்பண்ணும். சமான வாயு அறுவகைச் சுவையையும் அன்னத்தையும் பிரித்து எழுவகைத் தாதுவின் கண்ணுங்கலப்பிக்கும். கூர்மன் இமைப்பும் விழிப்பும் உறக்கமும் உணர்ச்சியும் பண்ணும். நாகன் விக்கலிடுவிக்கும். கிருகரன் கோபத்தைப் பண்ணுவிக்கும். தேவதத்தன் உடம்பெரிப்பைப் பண்ணுவிக்கும். தனஞ்சயன் பிராணன்போன பின்னும் உடம்பை விடாதே நின்று மூன்று நாளுநிப்பித்து உச்சந்தலையிற் பிற் கூற்றிலே மூன்று நெற்றிடை வெடித்துப்போமென்றறிக. நாடிகள் எழுபத்திராயிரத்திலும் தச நாடிகளும் தச வாயுக்களும் பிரதான மெனக்கொள்க என்னை ?

Comment :—This shows the process of change of the Elements. The Bhutas are five, such as fire &c; the sense organs are five, such as the ear &c; the senses are five, such as hearing &c; The Vathanai or the bodily troubles are 25, such as the five commencing with nerves, the five commencing with urine, the five commencing with hunger, the five commencing with excretion and the five commencing with anger. In all 25. The vayus are 10 commencing with Pranan. The Nadis are 10 such as Idakalai, Pingalai &c. The 72,000 Nadis of the Moolatharam, distribute themselves into the three main Nadis Idaikalai, Pingalai and Shulumunai which are like the three partitions of a dried Peerkam fruit. Of these, with the exception of the Shulumunai in the centre, the other two Nadis go up by the two nostrils. On each side they stay for five Naligais and they become 125 breathings in a mathira. From each of these breaths a 12 inch vayu is generated, and of these 4 inches get wasted and 8 inches of vayu or 8 digits alone are made use of by the body. This is the rule for the breathing of Oxygen by the nostrils. A mathira is one-eighth of 2½ Naligais. Apana Vayu is responsible for the excretions. Oothanan works in the trunk itself or Kantam. Viyana Vayu is responsible for the easy breathing in and breathing out. The Samana Vayu divides the six kinds of taste and the food and mixes them with the seven Thathus. The Koorman is responsible for the movement of the eyelashes, sleep and wakefulness and feeling. The Vayu Nagan causes hiccough. Kirukaran creates anger. Devathathan causes the burning sensation in the body. Thananjayan stays in the body even after its demise and reaches the top of the head on the third day and then dissolves itself, separating the soul from the body. Of the 72,000 Nadis, the Dasa Nadis and the Dasa Vayus are important.

The following are quotations in support of the above from Sikandiar, the author of Isai Nunukam. They are.

" இடைபிங் கலையிரண்டு மேயம் பிராணன்
புடைநின் றபானன்மலம் போக்குந்—தடையின்றி
யுண்டனகீ ழாக்கு முதானன் சமானனெங்குங்
கொண்டேறியு மாறிரதக் கூறு."

எனவும்,

" கூர்மா னிமைப்புவிழி கோணுகன் விக்கலாம்
பேர்வில் வியானன் பெரிதியக்கும்—போர்மலியுங்
கோபங் கிருகரனுங் கோப்பி னுடம்பெரிப்புத்
தேவதத்த னுதமென்ற தேர்.

எனவும்,

" ஒழிந்த தனஞ்சயன்பே ரோதி யுயிர்போய்க்
கழிந்தாலும் பின்னுடலைக் கட்டி — யழிந்தழியா
மூக்கா ளுதிப்பித்து முன்னியவான் மாவின்றிப்
பின்று வெடித்துவிடும் போந்து.

எனவும், இசை நுணுக்கமுடையசிகண்டியாரும் கூறினாராகலின்.

Silappadikaram, Arangetukathai P. 85.

Thus by the process of change of the Bhutas, the sense organs, the Vayus and the Nadis life is generated with Sukilam and Sironitham as body having within itself (life) the control of the two kinds of actions.

" துய்யவுடம் பாவன தோண்ணூற்று றங்குலியா
மெய்யெழுத்து நின்றியங்கு மெல்லத்தான் — வையத்
திருபாலு நாற்பத் தெழுபாதி நீக்கிக்
கருவாகு மாதாரங் காண்."

Comments:—This stanza gives the place of generation of all sound. The measurement of a man's body is 96 inches by his own hand. Of these 47½ inches form the top and 47½ inches from the bottom the Moolatharam or the genital organ occupies one inch. Four finger breadths above this is the seat of the generation of sound. The following stanzas illustrate the above.

" ஆதாரம் பற்றி யசைவ முதலெழுத்து
மூதார்ந்த மெய்யெழுத்து முன்கொண்டு — போதாரு
முந்தி யிடைவளியா யோங்குமிடை பிங்கலையால்
வந்துமே லோசையாம் வைப்பு."

" ஐவகைப் பூதமு மாய சரீரத்து
மெய்பெற நின்றியங்கு மெய்யெழுத்தாற் — ஐய
வொருநாடி நின்றியங்கி யுந்தமே லோங்கி
வருமா லெழுத்துடம்பின் வந்து."

The stanza *பூதமுதற்............தோற்றமிசைக்கு* and the succeeding ones give the five elements, the five sense organs, the five senses, the actions of the 25 bhutas in them, the ten Vayus and their actions. He also says that the height of each man is 8 spans by his own fingers. Each span is sub-divided into 12 digits, so that the total height is 96 digits. Of these from the centre or the Moolatharam we have 47½ digits above and 47½ digits below. He further says that this Moolatharam is the seat of the production of sound.

Varahopanishad P. 405.

சகல ஜந்துக்களுடைய தேகமானது தொண்ணூற்றாறு அங்குல முள்ளதாக விருக்கிறது. அதின் மத்தியில் அபான ஸ்தானத்திற்கு இரண்டங்குலத் திற்குமேலும் மேட்டிரத்திற்கு இரண்டங்குலத் திற்குக் கீழும் மத்தியப்பிரதேசமென்று சொல்லப்படுகிறது.

Comment :—The height or length of all animals is 96 inches In the centre of the body, two inches above the anus and two inches below the navel, is the Madhyapradesam.

This enables us to understand that the Yal should be constructed according to the measurement of each man's body and that the length of the string from the Meru to the Mettu is the place for the Natham. If we note the structure of the Yal and that of the sound which is its life we may find that the Yal resembles the human body and its life in the Sthoolam by its shape and in the Sookshmam by the shape of its sound.

Again, we find Slokas even at the commencement of Sama Veda, which say, that the sages worship God with the help of the Yal which resembles the human body and obtain Mukti knowing the facts that the human body is so constructed as to enable it to praise God with the help of sweet Puns and that it is just that we should ever be praising him.

3. The Sookshma Tatvas of man and the Structure of the Yal.

We noted before some points of resemblance outwardly as Sthoolam between the Yal and the human body. Now we shall note the resemblance between them in the Sookshma plane. Just as we noted life in the human body and the various actions of oxygen we shall note the sound of the Yal and its different divisions.

Just as life makes its Sancharam in the 12 sthanams of the Sthoola Sareera, six above and six below, and reflects the actions of all living beings, so also Natham makes its Sancharam in the 12 sthanams of the Yal, six below the Madhymam and six above, and causes numerous Raga moorchanas.

Just as the three Moolasthanams of the body represent the three lokas Swargam, Madhyam and Pathalam, so also the Yal has Swarams in the three Sthayis Mandaram, Madhyam and Tharam.

We observed before that just as the Sthoola Sareeram has 25 Pancheekarana Tatvas the Sookshma Sareeram has a like number of Pancheekarana Tatvas. We shall find that in like manner, the Yal has 24 Mettus in the shape of the Sthoolam while it has 24 sounds in the Sookshmam. Just as the Pancheekarana Tatvas of the three Sareeras are 25 in number, so also the three Sthayis Mandara, Madhya and Thara have 25 Srutis. For we know when the Sthayi commences with the Sa and ends with the top Sa, the Srutis are 25. But when the Scale commences with the Ri, omitting the Meru Swaram, and ends with the top Sa, the nnmber is 24. In the same manner, we may say that the Tatvas are really 24 in number, because the 25th tatvam of the Sthoola Sareeram becomes the basis for the Sookshma Sareeram, the 25th tatvam of the Sookshma Sareeram becomes the basis for the Karana Sareeram while the 25th tatvam of the Karana Sareeram becomes the seed for all creation. Arguing from analogy, though the ending Swaram of the three Sthayis is considered the 25th Swaram, yet the ending Swaram of each of the three Sthayis becomes the commencing

Swaram of the next Sthayi, and therefore we conclude the Srutis are really 24. We observed before that there were 7 Swarams in a Sthayi which were divided into 12. We arranged these 12 Swarams in the Rasi Cycle, gave their Alaku system, stated what the concordant Swarams were, picked out clearly the Swarams which should have a lesser number of Alakus and demonstrated how ganam was made in them.

We also noted that just as the Sthoola Sareeram is perfected by the Seven Thathus, the Veena is also made perfect by seven strings. In the same way, in the Sookshma Sareeram life obtains the seven kinds of knowledge and becomes active. Similarly, the seven concordant Swarams in the 12 Sthanams obtain their Moorchana and become what is commonly known as a Ragam. The following quotations show that the numbers 7, 12, and 24 found in the Isai-Tamil of the ancient Tamils are commonly found in Vedantam, Medicine, Astrology, the Holy Bible and the Upanishads.

We know to a certain extent, the ideas and meanings of the following quotations. So they are very briefly stated. Here after, while dealing with the mathematical calculations of Srutis we shall refer to these and the like wherever necessary.

Mythrayanni Upanishad P. 97.

சுருதி சொல்லுகிறதென்னவெனில், சப்த பிரம்மம் பரபிரம்ம இரண்டையும் அறியவேண்டியது. சப்த பிரம்மத்தில் செவ்வையாய்த் தேர்ந்தவன் (பிரணவமாகிற ஓங்காரத்தைப் பிரம்ம சுவரூபமாய்த் தியானித்து அதில் நிலையுற்றவன்) பிரம்மத்தை யடைகிறான்.

Comment :—" What the book says is, both the Sapta Brahmam and the Parabrahmam should be realised. One who becomes an expert in the Sapta Brahmam, or one who fixes his attention in Brahmam by taking Ongaram or Pranavam to be the shape of Brahmam, realises the Brahmam in himself."

Here we should take Saptabrahmam to mean the Vedam which was recited with sweet geetam.

Mythrayanni Upanishad P. 61.

சூரிய சம்பந்தமான, ருக்காகிய காயத்திரியினாலேயும் உபாசிக்கவேண்டியது. பிரம்மத்திற்கு மூர்த்தம் அமூர்த்தம் என இரண்டு ரூபங்களுண்டு. எது மூர்த்தமோ (உருவமோ) அது அசத்தியமானது. அமூர்த்தம் எதுவோ அது சத்தியமானது. இதுதான் பிரம்மம். அதே தேஜஸ். எது தேஜஸோ அது சூரியன். இந்த சூரியன்தான் ஓம் என்கிற ஆத்மாவாகிறான். அவன் (அந்த சூரியன் பிரணவமாகிய) தன்னை மூன்று விதமாய்ச் செய்தான். ஓம் என்பது மூன்று மாத்திரைகள். (அவையாவன அ. உ. ம் இவைகள்தான். இந்த மூன்று மாத்திரைகள்தான் அவயவங்கள்.) "இவைகளினாலே இந்த (பிரபஞ்சம்) சகலமும் குறுக்கும் நெடுக்குமாய் (குறுக்கும் நெடுக்குமாய் நெய்யப்பட்டிருக்கிற துணி போல) கோர்க்கப்பட்டிருக்கிறது. இதுவென்று (சூரியன்) சொன்னான்."

Comment :—" The deity should be approached by Gayatri or Rig which is related to the Sun. Brahmam has two forms—Moortham and Amoortham. That which is Moortham (shape) is untrue and that which is Amoortham (absence of shape) is true. This is Brahmam

This is Brightness. That which is bright is the Sun. This Sun became the Atma or the Om This Sun made himself into three different kinds. Om is three mathiras. (They are, Ah, Oo, and M. These three mathiras are the organs.) By means of these the whole creation is woven, just as the cloth is the result of the crossing of the warp and the woof. The Sun said it was himself,"

Threads crossing one another as warp and woof result in a cloth, just as two opposite forces produce motion or just as a top spins by means of the rotation of a rope worked with one hand against the pulling force of the other. This simile is given here as we see it daily in common use. We have seen how the letter அ goes leftwards while உ goes rightwards from the centre in writing them. Similarly sages say that all the activities of this world are the result of two saktis pulling at opposite directions. Just as brightness is inseparable from the gem, fragrance from the flower, sweetness from honey, the female from the male, life from the body so we should understand that the inseparable combination of two saktis—one seen and the other unseen—are the Sakti and the Sivam and all actions result from this combination. These three (Sakti, Sivam and the effect) are known as the அ, உ and the ம or Satthu, Chittu and Anandam. We know that when we make prastharam above and below the Jivaswaram in a Moorchana formed by the Aroganam and Avaroganam of a scale, the result will be very sweet. Likewise every object obtains its action and appears as Anandam. This was called by sages the play of the deity or the Om.

All Mantras, Prayers, Penance and Vedas were declared on this principle only. We know that of these, Astronomy, Grammar, Vedantam, Physiology, Music and Midwifery are of paramount importance and are closely related to one another each being excellent in itself. If we understand the underlying idea of any one of the above the rest is easy.

The fire or Agni in the centre of the earth—just like the pupil in the centre of the eye, the centre right in the exact middle of the wheel and the central peg in the middle of a grind stone—the agni of the stomach (hunger) in the centre of the human body, the fire in the centre of the eye which is the middle of the Sookshma Sareeram, and the fire of wisdom, the centre of the Karanasareeram form the 13th tatvam each among the 25 tatvas. Similarly the Sun which supports this Andam and millions of other Andams revolves round its own axis. Every one is aware of this. He mentions here how all creation, animate and inanimate, derive their heat, brightness, life, action, fragrance and character from the Sun and how the living beings get their life and mortality from the same source. Similarly things that move and things which are motionless are either preserved or destroyed by the same Sun. This Sakti he mentions as Brahmam or Atma or Satya or Pranava (அ, உ and ம்) or Soorya, that this Mantram should be said by all and that he who mentions this mantra obtains Mukti. We have to note that from this fundamental letter came the seven letters (ஸ, ரி, க, ம, ப, த, நி, the six Shastras, the twelve Sthanams, the Rasis, the seven kinds of appearances, the seven Swarams and their multitudinous permutations and combinations.

Mythrayanni Upanishad P. 65.

மற்றொரு விடத்திலும் (வேறு சுருதியிலும்) சொல்லப்பட்டிருக்கிறது. (அதாவது) "ஓங்காரமானது இதற்கு (பிராண ஆதித்திய ஆத்மாவுக்கு) சப்த சரீரம் (உதாத்த அனுதாத்த சுவரிதமாகிற சப்தம்தான் சரீரம்) அவனுக்கு ஆண்பால் பெண்பால் அஃறிணைப்பால் இவைகள் லிங்கசரீரம். அவனுக்கு அக்கினி, வாயு, ஆதித்தன் பிரகாச சுவரூபமான சரீரம்.

Comment:—"This is mentioned in another Book also. What is Om has Sapta Sareeram—Oothatha, Anuthatha and Swaritham (high, low and middling). The masculine, feminine and Neuter genders form its Linga Sareeram, while Agni, Vayu and Sun form its bright and usual Sareeram.

Mythrayanni Upanishad P. 147–149.

மூலாதாரத்திற்கு மேலிருக்கிற அக்கினி மண்டலமானது அதிலிருக்கிற அக்கினியினாலும் உஷ்ணத்தை யடைந்து அதானது சுவாசமாகிற காற்றினால் ஊதப்பட்டு பிரம்ம தேஜசாகிற நாத மாத்திரமான ஓங்காரமானது விபாகமில்லாத ஓமென்கிற அக்ஷரமாக பிரகாசப்படுகிறது. அக்ஷர உற்பத்தி ஸ்தானங்களாகிய கழுத்து நாக்கு முதலான விடங்களில் சம்பந்தப்படும்போது பல அக்ஷர சுவரூபமாகி வேதத்தினுடைய பல சாகைகளாகிறது.

Caimment:—"The Agni Mandalam above the Moolatharam receives its heat from the Moolatharam. It becomes inflated by the air or breath, receives the brightness of the Brahmam, becomes Natham or the bright letter Om. When it comes in contact with the places where letters take their rise, say the neck and the throat, it takes the shape of numberless letters and becomes different branches of the Vedas."

Mythrayannia Upanishad P. 149–151.

மனமானது தேகத்திலிருக்கிற அக்கினியை எழுப்புகிறது. அந்த அக்கினியானது வாயுவை எழுப்புகிறது. வாயுவானது மார்பில் சஞ்சரித்து மந்தரத்துவனியை உண்டாக்கிறது. அக்கினியுள்ள கடைகிற கட்டையானது இருதயத்தில் அசைவையுண்டாக்கிறது. அதானது (அந்த துவனியானது) அணுவாயிருக்கிறது. பிறகு (கண்டத்தினிடத்தில்) இரட்டிக்கிறது. நாக்கு நுனியில் மும்மடங்காகிறது. அது (வார்த்தையாக) புறப்படுகையில் (சப்தங்களுக்கு) உற்பத்தி ஸ்தானமாக சொல்லுகிறார்கள்.

Comment:—"The Manas or the Mind rouses the Agni in the body. This rouses Vayu in its turn. This Vayu lives in the chest and produces the very lowest sound. The Central rod which churns this heat produces a movement of sound in the heart. This sound is infinitesimal at first, then it doubles itself in the trunk, it trebles itself at the tip of the tongue. When it comes out as word or Saptam, the heart becomes the seat of all sound."

From the above we understand that sound generates from the Sthanam of the heart, that it is infinitesimal at the beginning, that it becomes double at the throat and treble at the tip of the tongue. All this agrees with the science of Music. We have noted before that if we take Athara SA, the sound of the Meru, to be one, Taca SA sounds in half the length of the whole string, Athithara SA in quarter of the length and that the top Sthayi SA sounds in one-eighth the length of the whole string. According to the same principle Sarnga Dev also says that if Athara Shadjam is 1, Tara SA is 2, and Athithara SA 4. This is what is found in ancient Tamil works also. We know that each Octave commences in the whole, half. quarter and one-eighth of the whole string. But sound increases in the inverse ratio as 1, 2, 4, 8 & etc. Everyone accepts this fact.

Nirusimhathapani Upanishad, fifth Upanishad P. 418, 419 & 420.

1. பிறகு தேவர்கள் பிரஜாபதியை அடியில் வருமாறு கேட்டார்கள்.

"எல்லாக்காமங்களையும் கொடுக்கின்றதாயும் மோக்ஷத்திற்கு துவாரமாயும், எதை யோகிகள் சொல்லுகின்றார்களோ அந்த மகா சக்கிரமென்று பெயருள்ள சக்கிரத்தை எங்களுக்குச் சொல்லும்."

அதற்கு பிரஜாபதி சொல்லுகிறதாவது ; இந்த மகா சக்கரம் ஆறு அரங்களுள்ளது ; 'ஸுதர்சனம்' என்று பெயர் கொண்டது ; ஆறு ருத்துக்களும் ஆறு பத்திரங்களாக விருக்கின்றன. மத்தியில் நாபியிருக்கின்றது ; அந்த நாபியில் இந்த அரங்கள் கோர்க்கப்பட்டிருக்கின்றன. மாயையினால் இது எல்லாம் சூழப்பட்டிருக்கின்றது. மாயை ஆத்மாவை தொடுகிறதில்லை. ஆதலால் இந்த ஆகத் மாயையால் வெளியில் சூழப்பட்டிருக்கின்றது.

அந்த சக்கரம் எட்டு அரங்களுள்ளதாகவும், எட்டு பத்திரமுள்ளதாகவும் இருக்கின்றது. காயத்ரி எட்டு அக்ஷரமுள்ளது ; அதுடன் சேர்ந்திருக்கின்றது. ஆகையால் வெளியில் மாயையால் எல்லாம் சூழப்பட்டிருக்கின்றது. இந்த மாயை எல்லா இடங்களையும் அடைகின்றது.

இந்த சக்கரம் பன்னிரண்டு அரங்களுள்ளதாகவும் பத்திரங்களுள்ளதாகவும் இருக்கின்றது. புருஷன் பதினாறு கலைகளுடையவன். இதெல்லாம் புருஷன் ; புருஷனுடன் சேர்ந்திருக்கின்றது. வெளியில் மாயையால் சூழப்பட்டதாக விருக்கின்றது.

இந்த சக்கரம் முப்பத்திரண்டு அரங்களும் பத்திரங்களுமுள்ளது. அனுஷ்டுப் மந்திரம் முப்பத்திரண்டு அக்ஷரங்களுள்ளது அதுடன் சேர்ந்திருக்கிறது. வெளியில் மாயையால் சூழப்பட்டிருக்கின்றது.

இந்த ஸுதர்சன சக்கரம் அரங்களால் ஸ்திதியுள்ளது. தேவர்கள் தான் அரங்கள் ; இந்த சக்கரம் பத்திரங்களால் சேர்ந்திருக்கின்றது. பத்திரங்கள் சந்தஸ்கள்.

2. இந்த சக்கரமே ஸுதர்சனமென்று பெயருள்ள மகா சக்கரம். அதின் மத்தியத்தில் நாபியில் தாரகம் (பிரணவம்) இருக்கின்றது. நரசிம்மமாகின்ற ஏகாக்ஷர மெதுவுண்டோ அதாகவே இருக்கின்றது, அந்த சக்கரத்தின் ஆறு பத்திரங்களில் ஆறு அக்ஷரமுள்ள ஸுதர்சன மந்திர மிருக்கிறது. எட்டு பத்திரங்களில் எட்டு அக்ஷரங்களுமுள்ள நாராயணமந்திரம் இருக்கின்றது. பன்னிரண்டு பத்திரங்களில் பன்னிரண்டு அக்ஷரங்களுள்ள வாசுதேவ மந்திரமிருக்கின்றது. பதினாறு பத்திரங்களில் விந்துக்களுடன் கூடிய பதினாறு மாத்ருகா அக்ஷரங்களான பதினாறு கலைகளிருக்கின்றன. முப்பத்திரண்டு பத்திரங்களில் முப்பத்திரண்டு அக்ஷரங்களுள்ள மந்திர ராஜ நரசிம்ஹ அனுஷ்டுப் மந்திரம் இருக்கின்றது.

இதுதான் சர்வ காமங்களையும் கொடுப்பதாகவும், மோக்ஷ துவாரமாகவும், ருக், யஜுஸ், ஸாம, அதர்வணவேதமயமாகவுமிருக்கின்ற மகா சக்கரம். இதற்கு முன் பக்கத்தில் வஸுக்களும் பின் பக்கத்தில் ஆதித்யர்களும், இடது பக்கத்தில் விச்வேதேவர்களும், நடுப்பக்கதில் பிரமன், விஷ்ணு, மகேசுவரர்களும் இருக்கின்றார்கள். சூரிய சந்திரர்கள் பக்கத்திலும் இருக்கின்றார்கள்.

இதற்கு ரிக்கு, முன் 5-வது உபநிஷத்தின் இரண்டாவது கண்டத்தில் சொல்லப்பட்டிருக்கின்றது.

இந்த மகா சக்கரத்தை அறிகின்ற பாலனாகட்டும், யுவனாகட்டும் அவன் மகானும், குருவாயும், எல்லாமந்திரங்களையும் உபதேசிக்கக் கூடியவனுமாகின்றான். இந்த அனுஷ்டுப் மந்திரத்தால் ஹோமம் செய்யவேண்டும். இது ராக்ஷஸர்களை நாசம் செய்கின்றது. மிருத்யுவைத்தாண்டச் சக்தியைக்கொடுக்கின்றது குருவினிடமிருந்து கிடைத்த இந்த சக்கரத்தைக் கழுத்திலாவது கையிலாவது சிகையிலாவது கட்டிக்கொள்ள வேண்டும். இதற்கு ஏழு தீவுகளுள்ள பூமியே தக்ஷிணையாக ஏற்படும். ஆனால் இதற்காக ச்ரத்தையுடன் எதைக்கொடுப்பினும் அது தக்ஷிணையாகும்.

Comment:—1. Afterwards the Gods asked Prajapati as follows :—

" Please tell us about the great Chakaram (wheel) which is believed by sages to be capable of satisfying all that one desires and which is the gateway of heaven."

To which Prajapati answered :—This great wheel has six spokes or bars. It is called Sudarsanam. The six double months or Rutthus are six Pathiras. There is the navel in the centre. The spokes are attached to the central nave. All this is surrounded by Maya. But Maya does not touch the soul. This world is surrounded by Maya on the outside.

This wheel has eight spokes or Pathiras. Gayatri is of 8 letters. It is connected with it. So everything is covered by Maya on the outside. This Maya has access to all places.

This wheel has 12 spokes or Pathiras Man has 16 Kalais. All this is of man, surrounded by Maya on the outside.

This wheel has 32 spokes and Pathiras. Anushtup Mantram has also 32 letters. It is related to it and surrounded by Maya on the outside.

The Sudarsana Chakaram is made strong by spokes. Gods are the spokes. This chakaram is kept together by Pathiras or Chanduses.

2. This Chakaram is the great wheel known as Sudarsanam. In the centre of it, in the nave, is the Tharaka or (Pranavam). It is the single letter which becomes the Narasimham. In the six spokes of the wheel is the Sudarsana Mantram with six letters. It has also the Narayana Mantram with 8 letters in the eight Pathiras. It has also the Vasudeva Mantram with 12 letters in the 12 Pathiras. In the 16 Pathiras there are the 16 Kalais which are the 16 Mathiruga letters along with the Bindu (sperm.) In the 32 Pathiras is the Mantra Raja Narasimha Anushtup Mantra with 32 letters.

This is the great Chakaram which gives all desires, which is the door of Moksham and which has the appearance of the Rig, Yajus, Sama and the Atharvana Vedas. In front of it are the Eight Vasus (Ashta Gods) to the back of it the Athityas, to the left side of it the Visava Devas and in the centre of it, Brahma, Vishnu and the Mahesvaras. The Sun and the Moon are by the side of it also.

The support for this from the Rig Veda is given in the second Kandam of the 5th Upanishad.

One who understands this great Chakaram, whether he be a baby or a youth, he becomes a sage and a guru qualified to teach all Mantras. Homam should be performed only with the help of this Anushtup Mantram. This destroys Rakshasas. It gives power to overcome death. This wheel obtained from the guru should be worn round the neck or tied to the hands or the hair. The reward or Thatchina for this Mantram is the land of the seven isles. Whatever may be given for this with great trouble will be considered a Thatchina.

Prushnopanishad, Six Prushnam P. 438—439

1. ஸுகேசர் என்கிற பாரத்வாஜர் கேட்டதாவது தேவ! பகவானே! கோசல தேசியாகிய ஹிரண்யநாபன் என்ற (ஒரு) ராஜபுத்திரன் என்னிடத்தில் வந்து பதினாறு கலைகளுள்ள புருஷனை அறிவீரா வென்ற இந்தக்கேள்வியைக்கேட்டான்.

இப்பொழுது அந்தக்கேள்வியை உம்மைக் கேட்கிறேன். அந்த புருஷன் எங்கு இருக்கிறார்.

2. இவர் பதில் சொன்னதாவது எந்த புருஷனிடத்தில் இந்த (அடியில் கண்ட) பதினாறு கலைகள் உண்டாயினவோ, அந்த புருஷன் இவ்விடத்திலேயே சரீரத்திற்குள்ளேயே இருக்கிறார்.

4. அவர் (ஹிரண்யகர்ப்பர் என்று பெயருள்ள) ப்ராணன், சிரத்தை, ஆகாசம், வாயு, அக்னி, ஜலம் பிருதிவி, இந்திரியம் (தசேந்திரியங்கள்) மனஸ், அன்னம், பலம், தபஸ், வேதங்கள், கர்மம், (அதன் பலனாகிய ஸ்வர்க்காதி லோகங்கள் நாமம் இவைகளை (இந்தப்பதினாறு கலைகளை) சிருஷ்டித்தார்.

5. எப்படி சமுத்திரத்திலிருந்து உற்பத்தியான இந்த நதிகள் பெருகா நின்றுகொண்டு மறுபடியும் சமுத்திரத்தையடைந்து பெயர், ரூபம் இவைகளை இல்லாமல் செய்து, (அப்படி கலந்த பிறகு) சமுத்திரமென்றே சொல்லப்படுகிறதோ அப்படி புருஷனிடத்திலே நின்றும் உண்டான இந்தப் பதினாறு கலைகளும் மறுபடியும் புருஷனை யடைந்து அதனின் நாம ரூபங்களைப் போக்கடித்து, பிறகு புருஷன் என்றே சொல்லப்படுகின்றன. அந்த இந்த புருஷன் அகலனும், அமிருதனும் இருக்கிறான். அதற்கு இந்த ச்லோகம் இருக்கிறது.

6. ரத சக்கரத்திலுள்ள ஆரங்கள் போல இந்தக் கலைகள் எந்த புருஷனிடத்தில் வைக்கப்பட்டிருக்கின்றனவோ, வேத்யனுயிருக்கிற அந்த புருஷனை அடையுங்கள். உங்களை மிருத்யு பீடிக்காமல் இருக்கட்டும்.

1. Sukesar or Bardwajar, addressing God, said "Oh! God! A Rajput by name Hiranyanapan from the Kosala country came to me and asked me if I knew a man who knew the 16 Kalais.

I ask you the same question. Where is such a man?"

2. He answered and said the man who knew the 16 Kalais given below is here within this body.

4. He created the following 16 Kalais such as pranan (life), Sraddha (trouble), Ahasa (the atmosphere), Vayu (wind), Agni (fire), Jalam (water), Prithvi (the earth), Indiriam (the sperm), Manas (the mind), Annam (food), Palam (strength), Thapas (penance) Vedas, Karmam (actions) Swargam and the other logas and Namam (Name).

5. Just as the rivers which take their rise from the sea, expand themselves, and finally reach the sea again causing their name and shape to be changed and called sea once more, so also these 16 Kalais which generate from the Purusha reach the purusha once more changing their name and shape and are called Purusha ever after. Thus this Purusha is faultless and immortal. This slokam proves it.

6. Whosoever possesses these Kalais just as the wheel of a car has its spokes, him alone should you all try to obtain. Let not death overtake you.

Prushnopanishad P. 425.

ஐந்து பாதங்களுள்ளவரும் (ஆறு ருதுக்களில் ஹேமந்த சிசிருதுக்களில் ஒன்றாய் வைத்து, பாக்கி ஐந்து ருதுக்களாகிற பாதங்கள்); பன்னிரண்டு விதமான ஆகிருதியை உடையவரும் (12 மாதங்கள் ஆகிருதிகள்); பிதாவாயும் (எல்லோரையும் ஜனிப்பிக்கிறவர்) உதகமுள்ளவராயும் இருக்கிறவரை (காலாத்மாவையே) தேவலோகத்திற்கு மேலே (எல்லாவற்றிற்கும் உயர) இருப்பதாக (இருக்கிற பரமாத்மாவென்று) காலத்தை யறிந்த சிலர் சொல்லுகிறார்கள்; மற்ற சிலர் ஸர்வஞ்ஞராயிருக்கின்றவரை ஆறு ஆரங்களையுடைய (6 ருதுக்கள் ஆரங்கள்), ஏழு குதிரைகள் கட்டின சக்கரத்தில் (ரதத்தில்) வைக்கப்பட்டிருக்கும் வஸ்துவாக ஆதித்யனாகிற காலாத்மாவாக) சொல்லுகிறார்கள்.

Some who understand the mystery of time say that the Paramanma who possesses five Pathams (the five remaining Rhuthus with the exception of Hemanda Sisrithu out of the six), the 12 kinds of Akrithis (the 12 months are the 12 Akrithis), who is the father of all (as creating all) and who has the Oothagam lives above the abode of Gods, above all. Some others declare the omnipresent one as the object placed in the car having six spokes in its wheel and drawn by seven horses.

Mundagopanishad Second Mundagam P. 447.

8. அவரிடத்திலிருந்து ஏழு பிராணன்கள் (இந்திரியங்கள், காது 2, கண் 2, மூக்கு 2, வாய் 1, ஆக 7); அவைகளின் ஏழு அர்ச்சிஸ்கள் (பிரகாசங்கள்); ஏழு ஸமித்துக்கள் (விஷயங்கள்); ஏழு ஹோமங்கள் (மேற்படி விஷய ஞானங்கள்); ஏழு லோகங்கள் (இடங்கள்) உண்டாயின. அவைகள் ஹ்ருதயத்தில் ஏழேழாக வைக்கப்பட்டன.

10. புருஷனே (பரமாத்மாவே) இந்த ஜகத், கர்மம், தபஸ், பிரம்மம், என்றது பரமாமிருதம் என்றது; எல்லாம் அதுவே; அப்படிப்பட்ட ஆத்மா (தம்முடைய) ஹ்ருதயத்தில் இருப்பதாக யார் அறிகிறானோ அவன், இவ்விடத்திலேயே, அவித்யா முடிச்சை அவிழ்த்து விடுகிறான்.

8. From him there generated seven sense-organs (2 ears, 2 eyes, 2 nostrils and 1 mouth), their seven Archises (prakasas), seven smits (Vishayas), seven homams and seven lokas. They were arranged in sevens in the heart.

10. This Purusha (Paramatma) is this Jagath (world), Karmam, Thapas and Brahamam or Paramamirtham. He is everything. Whoever realises that such Atma is in his heart undoes the avidya knot (ignorance) even in this life.

Varahopanishad P. 409.

மூலாதாரம் முதலான ஆறு சக்கரங்கள் சக்தி ஸ்தானமென்று சொல்லப்படுகின்றன. கழுத்து முதல் தலையுச்சி வரையில் சம்புவினுடைய ஸ்தானமென்று சொல்லப்படுகிறது.

The six Chakrams such as the Moolatharam etc., are the birth place of all Sakti. From the neck to the top of the head is called the Sthanam of the Sambu.

Varahopanishad P. 405.

இந்த ஆரங்களிலே பிரதக்ஷிணக்கிரமமாய் நாடிகள் பன்னிரண்டு வாயுக்களைச் சுமந்துகொண்டிருக்கின்றன. நாடிகள் வஸ்திரங்கள்போலிருக்கின்றன. அவைகள் பல வர்ணங்களுடையனவாகச் சொல்லப்பட்டிருக்கின்றன. வஸ்திரத்தின் மத்திய பாகம் நாபீசக்கரமெனப்படுகிறது.

In these spokes, the Nadis carry the 12 Vayus beginning from left proceeding to right, (clockwise). The Nadis are like clothes. They are said to be of different colours. The centre of the cloth is called the Nabi Chakaram.

Narada parivirajagopanishad P. 299.

பதினாறு மாத்திரா ஸ்வரூப மெப்படி யென்றால், அகாரம் முதலாவது. உகார மிரண்டாவது. மகாரம் மூன்றாவது. அர்த்த மாத்திரை நான்காவது, நாத மைந்தாவது. பிந்து ஆறாவது. களா ஏழாவது. களாதீதம் எட்டாவது. சாந்தி ஒன்பதாவது. சாந்தியதீதம் பத்தாவது. உன்மனி பதினொன்றாவது, மனோன்மனி பன்னிரண்டாவது. புரீததி பதின்மூன்றாவது. தனுமத்தியமா பதினான்காவது. பதி பதினைந்தாவது. பரா பதினாறாவது.

The shapes of the 16 Mathiras are as follows :—Aharam, first ; Oogaram, second ; Magaram, third ; Arthamathira, fourth ; Natham. fifth ; Bindu, sixth ; Kala, seventh ; Kalatheetham, eighth ; Sandi, ninth ; Sandyatheetham, tenth ; Oonmani, eleventh ; Manonmani, twelfth ; Pureethathi, thirteenth ; Thanumatyama, fourteenth ; Pathee, fifteenth and Para, sixteenth.

Kalisaantaranopanishad P. 417.

(இச்சப்பதினாறு நாமங்கள்) பதினாறு கலைகளால் சூழப்பட்டிருக்கிற ஜீவனுடைய ஆவரணத்தை (ஞானத்திற்கு மறைவாயிருக்கிற அவித்தையை) நாசம் செய்கிறது. அதற்குப் பிறகு, மேகம் போன பிறகு சூரிய மண்டலம் பிரகாசமாவதுபோல பரப் பிரம்மம் பிரகாசிக்கிறது.

These sixteen names destroy the ignorance of life surrounded by the sixteen Kalais. When once the ignorance is removed, the Parabrahmam shines like the Sun after the clouds are removed.

Sareeragopanishad P. 357.

மனது, புத்தி, அகங்காரம், ஆகாசம், வாயு, அக்கினி, ஜலம், பூமி இந்த எட்டும் பிரகிருதிகள். காது தொக்கு, கண், நாக்கு ஐந்தாவதாகிய மூக்கு, பாயு, உபஸ்தம், கைகள், கால்கள், பத்தாவதாகிய வாக்கு சப்த ஸ்பரிச ரூபரஸ கந்தம் இவைகள் பதினைந்து ஆக இந்தத்தத்துவங்கள் இருபத்துமூன்று. இருபத்து நான்காவது அவ்வியக்தமாகிய பிரதானம். அதற்கு அந்நியன் அல்லது சிரேஷ்டன் புருஷன்.

Mind, wisdom, ego, Akasa, Vayu, Agni, Jalam and Bhumi—these eight are Prakritis. The tatvas are 23 such as the five sense-organs, Payu. Oopastham, hands, legs, words, and the five senses touch, taste, smell, hearing and sight. The 24th tatvam is the imperishable man. The important tatvam is the Purusha.

As it is said that an enquiry into the tatvas is very necessary. I give the tatvas below :—The five tatvas of the Gnana Indiriams, the five tatvas for the Karma Indiriams, the five tatvas of Pranan etc., the five Satthus and the four Anthakaranas—Total 24 tatvas.

Vasudavamananam of Vivahasaram, Twentysixth Nirupagam, Page 168.

சுருதியாதிகளில் தத்துவவிசாரம் பண்ணவேண்டுமென்று சொல்லுகிறபடியால் தத்துவங்களை தேடெனின் உ-ம்-ஞானேந்திரிய பஞ்சகமும் கன்மேந்திரிய பஞ்சகமும் பிராணாதி பஞ்சகமும் சத்தாதி பஞ்சகமும் அந்தக்கரண சதுஷ்டயமுங்கூடி (24) தத்துவங்களாம்.

Varahopanishad P. 359.

சில வாதிகள் தத்துவம் இருபத்து நான்கென்றும் சிலர் முப்பத்தாறென்றும் பின்னும் சிலர் தொண்ணூற்றாறென்றும் கிளக்கிறார்கள். அவைகளின் கிரமத்தைச் சொல்லுகிறேன் கவனமான மனதுடன் கேளும்.

காது தொக்கு கண் முதலிய ஞானேந்திரியங்கள் ஐந்து ; வாக்கு கை கால் முதலிய கன்மேந்திரியங்கள் ஐந்து ; பிராணாதிகள் ஐந்து ; சப்தாதிகள் ஐந்து மனோபுத்தி அகங்காரம் சித்தம் நான்கு ; இப்படி இருபத்து நான்கு தத்துவங்களென பிரம வித்துக்களறிகிறார்கள்.

இவைகளுடன் பஞ்சீகிருத பூதங்களான பூமி ஜலம் அக்கினி வாயு, ஆகாசம் ஐந்து என்றும், ஸ்தூல சூக்ஷ்ம காரணங்களென மூன்று தேகங்களென்றும், ஜாக்கிர ஸ்வப்ன சுஷுப்திகளென மூன்று அவஸ்தைகளென்றும் ஞானிகளறிகிறார்கள். ஆக தத்துவங் கட்டங்கள் முப்பத்தாறென்று முனிவரறிகிறார்கள்.

Some say there are 24 tatvas, others give 36 while yet others say there are 96. Listen to me carefully.

Gnana Indirias or the sense Organs of superior type are five; The Karma Indirias or those of the lower type like hands and legs are five; the pranas etc. are five; Saptam etc., are five; Manas, Buddhi, Ahankaram and Chittam are four. These 24 tatvas are recognised by those who have the seed of Brahma in them.

Besides these, wise men recognise the five Pancheekrita elements, fire, air earth, water and Akasa, the three bodies such as Sthoola, Sookshma and Karana, the three troubles such as Jakira, Swapna and Sushupti. So the tatvas recognised by the wise are 36.

Varahopanishad P. 361.

இந்த தத்துவங்களுடன் இருத்தல், உண்டாதல், வளருதல், திரிதல், குறைதல், நசித்தல் இவ்வாறும் ஷட்பாவ விகாரங்கள். பசி, தாகம், சோகம், மோகம், ஜரை (கிழத்தனம்) மரணம் இவ்வாறும் ஷடூர்மிகள் என்று சொல்லுகிறார்கள். தோல், ரத்தம், மாம்ஸம், கொழுப்பு, மஜ்ஜை, எலும்பு இவ்வாறும் ஷட்கோசங்களென்று சொல்லப்படுகின்றன. காமக் குரோத லோப மோக மத மாச்சரியம் இவ்வாறு அரிஷட்வர்க்கங்களும், விச்வன் தைஜஸன் பிராக்ஞன் என்ற மூன்று ஜீவன்களும், சத்துவ ரஜஸ் தமஸ் என்ற குணங்கள் மூன்றும், பிராரப்தம் ஆகாமியம் ஸஞ்சிதமென்ற கருமங்கள் மூன்றும், பேசுதல் எடுத்தல், நடத்தல், மலஜலம் விடுதல் ஆனந்தம் இவைகளாகிய கருமேந்திரிய வியாபாரங்களைந்தும். சங்கற்பம் பிரயத்தினம், அபிமானம் நிச்சயம் இவைகளும், சந்தோஷம் தயவு மோகம் அசட்டை இந்நான்கும், திக்குகள், வாயு, சூரியன், வருணன், அசுவினிதேவதைகள், அக்கினி, இந்திரன், உபேந்திரன், மிருத்யு, அப்படியே சந்திரன் சதுர்முக பிரம்மா, ருத்திரன். க்ஷேத்திரக்ஞன், ஈசுவரன் ஆக தத்துவங்கள் தொண்ணூற்றாறென்று சொல்லப்பட்டன.

Many more are added to these tatvas.

The six changes such as existence, formation, growth, change, lessening and decay are recognised. Six other changes such as hunger, thirst, ennui, lust, old age and death are also recognised. The six gosas recognised are, skin, blood, flesh, fat, marrow and bone. Six emotions are recognised such as love, hatred, greed, lust, and selfconceit jealousy; the three jivas—Visvan, Thyjasan and Pragnan, the three gunas—Satva, Rajas and Thamas, the three Karmas—Praraptam, Ahamyam and Sanjitam, the five actions of the Karma-Indiriams or lower organs—talking, taking, walking, passing excreta and enjoying are also recognised. Other actions such as fixing conventions, endeavour enthusiasim, and arriving at definiteness, gladness, favour, friendship and disregard are also recognised. The eight directions, Vayu, Soorya Varuna, the twenty seven goddesses such as Asvani etc. goddesses, Agni, Indra, Upendra and Yama, Moon, Sathurmuka Brahma, Rudhira, Kshetringan and Isvara—all these put together make up the 96 Tatvas.

Varahopanishad P. 405.

சகல ஜந்துக்களுடைய தேகமானது தொண்ணூற்றாறு அங்குல முள்ளதாக விருக்கிறது. அதின் மத்தியில் அபான ஸ்தானத்திற்கு இரண்டங்குலத்திற்குமேலும் மேட்டிரத்திற்கு இரண்டங்குலத்திற்குக் கீழும் மத்தியப்பிரதேசமென்று சொல்லப்படுகிறது.

The bodies of all creation are 96 inches in length. In the centre of it is the Madhyapradesa two inches above and two inches below the Apanasthanam.

To understand the 96 tatvas the following quotations from Gurunool are given.

குருநூல் உ௱௭.

தொண்ணூற்றாறு தத்துவம் காணுதிகளறியவும்

“ வட்டமென்ற வுள்பட்ட முடியு மாகி
மம்முடியி லாதார மாய மாகி
அட்டகசங் துவாரபா லர்க ளாகி
யவ்வட்டம் பஞ்சகர்த்தாக்கள் மூர்த்தமாகி
நட்டமென்ற கண்ணேட்டஞ் சுழுனை யிலாகி
நவசரா சரங்களெல்லா மதற்குள் ளாகி
கட்டவொண்ணுக் கருவிகர ணாதி யாகிக்
கருவியென்ற தொண்ணூற்றாய தத்துவமா மென்றே. ”

குருநூல் ௪௱௬௪.

“ தும்பித்துச் சுழுமுனையில் வாசி யோட்டிக்
குமுறவே பிராணையத் தங்கி நாட்டி
வம்பித்து யிடைகலையால் தம்பித் தாக்கல்
வருஷிக்கு மதியமூர்த மூன்றுக்காலே
வெம்பித்து மதியமூர்த ருசியை கண்டு
விளங்கவே யவ்வமூர்த முண்டா லையா
கம்பித்த நசல்களெல்லா மோடிப் போச்சு
கழன்றிடுங்காண் தொண்ணூற்றாய சட்டை போச்சே, ”

குருநூல் ௬௱௫௭.

“ ஆமென்ற குன்றிமணிப் பிரமாணங் கொண்டா
லதீதமென்ற போதையாவோர் சட்டை கழலும்
ஞாமென்ற குன்றிமணி தொண்ணூற்று மண்டால்
தோற்கருவி தொண்ணூற்றாய முரியும் பாரு
நூமென்ற குன்றிமணி நூறுமணி யுண்டால்
நன்மையது வாசிலும் நூறுகோடி வயதாம்
பாமென்ற பத்துநூறு குன்றிமணி யுண்டால்
பாடினேம் லோகாதி கர்த்த ரீயாமே. ”

திருமந்திரம் யாக்கை நிலையாமை பாட்டு ௧௨.

“ முப்பது முப்பது முப்பத் தறுவருஞ்
செப்ப மதிளுடைக் கோவிலுள் வாழ்பவர்
செப்ப மதிளுடைக் கோவிற் சிதைந்தபின்
ஒப்ப வரிவரு மோட்டெடுத் தாரே ”

திருமந்திரம் மத்திய சாக்கிராவத்தை பாட்டு ௫

" வைச்சவ னவச்ச வகையிரு பத்தஞ்ச
முச்ச முடன்மரின வாறெரு வன்னுளன்
பிச்சன் பெரியன் பிறப்பிலி யென்றென்று
நச்சி யவனரு ளுணுய்ந்த வாறே "

திருமந்திரம் மத்திய சாக்கிராவத்தை பாட்டு ௯.

" நாலா றுடன்புருட னற்றத் துவமுடன்
வேறான வையைந்து மெய்ப்புரு டன்பரங்
கூறுவி யோமம் பரமெனக் கொண்டனன்
வேறான நாலேழு வேதாந்த தத்வமே "

திருமந்திரம் மத்திய சாக்கிராவத்தை பாட்டு ௧௧.

" நாலொரு கோடியே நாற்பத்தெண் ணாயிர
மேலுமோ ரைந்நூறு வேறா யடங்கிடும்
பாலவை தொண்ணூறோ டாறுட் பமேவை
கோலிய வையைந்து ளாகுங் குறிக்கிலே "

The following quotations in support of the above are from the Holy Bible.

The seven branched candlesticks. Exod 25 : 31, 32.

" பசும்பொன்னினால் ஒரு குத்துவிளக்கையும் உண்டாக்குவாயாக. அது பொன்னினால் அடிப்பு வேலையாய்ச் செய்யப்படவேண்டும். அதின் தண்டும் கிளைகளும், மொக்குகளும் பழங்களும் பூக்களும் பொன்னினால் செய்யப்படவேண்டும்

ஆறு கிளைகள் அதன் பக்கங்களில் விடவேண்டும். குத்துவிளக்கின் மூன்று கிளைகள் அதன் ஒரு பக்கத்திலும் குத்துவிளக்கின் மூன்று கிளைகள் அதன் மறுபக்கத்திலும் விடவேண்டும். etc

" And thou shalt make a candlestick of pure gold ; of beaten work shall the candlestick be made ; his shaft and his branches, his bowls, his knops, and his flowers, shall be of the same.

And Six branches shall come out of the sides of it ; three branches of the candlestick out of the one side, and three branches of the candlestick out of the other side."

The seven churches, the seven stars and the seven Angels. Rev. I. 12, 13. 14, 15, 16 & 20.

அப்பொழுது என்னுடனே பேசின சத்தத்தைப் பார்க்கத் திரும்பினேன். திரும்பினபோது ஏழு பொன் குத்துவிளக்குகளையும், அந்த ஏழு குத்துவிளக்குகளின் மத்தியிலே நிலையங்கி தரித்து மார்பருகே பொற்கச்சைகட்டியிருந்த மனுஷகுமாரனுக்கொப்பானவரையும் கண்டேன். அவருடைய சிரசும் மயிரும் வெண் பஞ்சைப்போலவும் உறைந்த மழையைப்போலவும் வெண்மையாயிருந்தது. அவருடைய கண்கள் அக்கினி ஜுவாலையைப்போலிருந்தது.

அவருடைய பாதங்கள் உலைக்களத்தில் எரிக்கிற பிரகாசமான வெண்கலம் போலிருந்தது. அவருடைய சத்தம் பெருவெள்ளத்து இரைச்சலைப்போலிருந்தது. தமது வலது கரத்திலே ஏழு நட்சத்திரங்களை ஏந்திக்கொண்டிருந்தார். அவர் வாயிலிருந்து இருபுறமும் கருக்குள்ளபட்டயம் புறப்பட்டது. அவருடைய முகம் வல்லமையாய்ப் பிரகாசிக்கிற சூரியனைப்போலிருந்தது. etc etc

என் வலது கரத்தில் நீ கண்ட ஏழு நட்சத்திரங்களின் இரகசியத்தையும் ஏழு பொன் குத்துவிளக்குகளின் இரகசியத்தையும் எழுது ; அந்த ஏழு நட்சத்திரங்களும் ஏழு சபைகளின் தூதர்களாம் ; நீ கண்ட ஏழு குத்துவிளக்குகளும் ஏழு சபைகளாம்."

" And I turned to see the voice that spoke with me. And being turned, I saw seven golden candlesticks ; and in the midst of the seven golden candlesticks one like into the Son of Man, clothed with a garment down to the foot, and girt about the paps with a golden girdle. His head and his hairs were white like wool, as white as snow ; and his eyes were as a flame of fire ;

And his feet like unto fine brass, as if they burned in a furnace ; and his voice as the sound of many waters. And he had in his right hand seven stars : and out of his mouth went a sharp two edged sword ; and his countenance was as the sun shineth in his strength. etc., etc.

Write the mystery of the seven stars which thou sawest in my right hand, and the seven golden candlesticks. The seven stars are the angels of the seven churches ; and the seven candlesticks which thou sawest are the seven churches."

Similarly, in many places of the Bible we read about seven golden vessels, seven trumpets, seven kine, the seven last plagues. seven spirits, seven seventies, seven seals, seven eyes, seven horns, seven heads, seven times seven years etc.

The number 12 is also frequently used. We see them in the 21st and the 22nd chapters of the Book of Revelation which admits of a philosophic interpretation.

Rev. XXI. 11-22.

" *அதின் பிரகாசம் மிகவும் விலையுயர்ந்த இரத்தினக்கல்லைப்போலவும் பளிங்கொளியுள்ள வச்சிரக் கல்லைப்போலவும் இருந்தது.*

அதற்குப் பெரிதும் உயரமுமான மதிலும் கிழக்கே மூன்று வாசல்கள், வடக்கே மூன்று வாசல்கள் தெற்கே மூன்று வாசல்கள், மேற்கே மூன்று வாசல்கள் ஆகப் பன்னிரண்டு வாசல்களும் இருந்தன.

வாசல்களின் அருகே 12 தூதர்களிருந்தார்கள் ; அந்த வாசல்களின் மேல் இஸ்ரவேல் சந்ததியாராகிய பன்னிரண்டு கோத்திரத்தாருடைய நாமங்களும் எழுதப்பட்டிருந்தன.

நகரத்தின் மதிலுக்கு பன்னிரண்டு அஸ்திபாரக்கற்களிருந்தன. அவைகள் மேல் ஆட்டுக்குட்டியானவருடைய பன்னிரண்டு அப்போஸ்தலரின் பன்னிரண்டு நாமங்களும் பதிந்திருந்தன.

என்னுடனே பேசினவன், நகரத்தையும் அதின் வாசல்களையும். அதின் மதிலையும் அளக்கிறதற்கு ஒரு பொற்கோலைப் பிடித்திருந்தான்.

அந்நகரம் சதுரமாயிருந்தது. அதின் அகலமும் நீளமும் சமமாயிருந்தது. அவன் அந்தக்கோலினால் நகரத்தை அளந்தான். அது பன்னீராயிரம் ஸ்தாதி அளவாயிருந்தது.

அவன் அதின் மதிலை அளந்தபோது, அது தூதனுடைய அளவாகிய மனுஷ அளவின்படியே நூற்று நாற்பத்து நான்கு முழமாயிருந்தது.

அதின் மதில் வச்சிரக்கல்லால் கட்டப்பட்டிருந்தது ; நகரம் தெளிந்த பளிங்குக்கு ஒப்பான சுத்தப் பொன்னாயிருந்தது.

நகரத்து மதில்களின் அஸ்திபாரங்கள் சகலவித இரத்தினங்களினாலும் அலங்கரிக்கப்பட்டிருந்தன. முதலாம் அஸ்திபாரம் வச்சிரக்கல், இரண்டாவது இந்திரநீலம், மூன்றாவது சந்திரகாந்தம், நான்காவது மரகதம், ஐந்தாவது கோமேதகம், ஆறாவது பதுமராகம், ஏழாவது சுவர்ணரத்தினம், எட்டாவது படிகப்பச்சை, ஒன்பதாவது புஷ்பராகம், பத்தாவது வைடூரியம், பதினோராவது சுநீரம், பன்னிரண்டாவது சுகந்தி இவைகளே.

பன்னிரண்டு வாசல்களும் பன்னிரண்டு முத்துக்களாயிருந்தன ; ஒவ்வொரு வாசலும் ஒவ்வொரு முத்தாயிருந்தது. நகரத்தின் வீதி தெளிவுள்ள பளிங்குபோலச் சுத்தப் பொன்னாயிருந்தது."

Rev. XXI. 11-21.

"And her light was like unto a stone most precious, even like a jasper stone, clear as crystal;

And had a wall great and high, and had twelve gates, and at the gates twelve angels and names written thereon, which are the names of the twelve tribes of the children of Israel;

On the east three gates; on the north three gates; on the south three gates; and on the west three gates.

And the wall of the city had twelve foundations, and in them the names of the twelve apostles of the Lamb.

And he that talked with me had a golden reed to measure the city, and the gates thereof and the wall thereof.

And the city lieth foursquare, and the length is as large as the breadth; and he measured the city with the reed, twelve thousand furlongs. The length and the breadth and the height of it are equal.

And he measured the wall thereof, an hundred and forty and four cubits, according to the measure of a man, that is, of the angel.

And the building of the wall of it was of jasper; and the city was pure gold, like into clear glass.

And the foundations of the wall of the city were garnished with all manner of precious stones. The first foundation was jasper; the second, sapphire; the third, a chalcedony; the fourth, an emerald; the fifth, sardonyx; the sixth, Sardius; the seventh chrysolyte; the eighth, beryl; the ninth, a topaz; the tenth, a chrysoprasus; the eleventh, a jacinth; the twelfth, an amethyst.

And the twelve gates were twelve pearls; every several gate was of one pearl and the street of the city was pure gold, as it were transparent glass."

Rev. XXII. 2.

"நகரத்து வீதியின் மத்தியிலும் நதியின் இருகரையிலும் பன்னிரண்டு விதமான கனிகளைத் தரும் ஜீவவிருட்சம் இருந்தது; அது மாதந்தோறும் தன் தன் கனியைக் கொடுக்கும்; அந்த விருட்சத்தின் இலைகள் ஜனங்கள் ஆரோக்கியமடைகிறதற்கு ஏதுவானவைகள்."

"In the midst of the street of it, and on either side of the river, was there the tree of life, which bare twelve manner of fruits, and yielded her fruit every month: and the leaves of the tree were for the healing of the nations."

The use of the number 12 is given here in 12 gates, 12 angels, 12 tribes, 12 foundation stones, 12 apostles, 12 thousand furlongs, the twelve times twelve cubits, 12 precious stones, 12 pearls, the tree of life yielding 12 manner of fruits and the 12 months.

Besides these, we read of the 12 loaves of shewbread, 12 disciples, 12 patriarchs, 12 baskets, 12 hours for the day, the crown with 12 stars etc,, in many places of the Bible.

Again the number of the redeemed is said to be 1,44,000 at the rate of 12 thousand for each of the 12 tribes, as given in scripture.

The following verse shows that the number 24 also was of common use.

Rev. IV. 4.

அந்தச்சிங்காசனத்தைச் சூழ இருபத்து நான்கு சிங்காசனங்களிருந்தன ; இருபத்துநான்கு மூப்பர்கள் வெண் வஸ்திரந்தரித்து தங்கள் சிரசுகளில் பொன்முடி சூடி அந்த சிங்காசனங்களின் மேல் உட்கார்ந்திருக்கக் கண்டேன்.

"And round about the throne there were four and twenty seats: and upon the seats I saw four and twenty elders sitting. clothed in white raiment; and they had on their heads crowns of gold."

The following verse shows that 24 sacrifices were offered at the rate of two for each of the 12 tribes.

Ezra VIII. 35

"சிறைப்பட்டுமீண்டவர்கள் இஸ்ரவேலின் தேவனுக்குச் சர்வாங்க தகனபலிகளாக இஸ்ரவேல் அனைத்தினிமித்தம் பன்னிரண்டு காளைகளையும் தொண்ணூற்றாறு ஆட்டுக்கடாக்களையும், எழுபத்தேழு ஆட்டுக்குட்டிகளையும், பாவநிவாரணத் தக்காசப் பன்னிரண்டு வெள்ளாட்டுக் கடாக்களையும் பலியிட்டு அவை யெல்லாம் கர்த்தருக்குச் சர்வாங்கதகன பலியாகச் செலுத்தினார்கள்"

"Also the children of those that had been carried away, which were come out of the captivity, offered burnt offerings unto the God of Israel, twelve bullocks for all Israel, ninety and six rams, seventy and seven lambs, twelve he goats for a sin offering; all this was a burnt offering unto the Lord."

Again it is said in the 23rd verse of the 52nd chapter of the Book of Jeremiah that 96 pomegranates were placed at the rate of 24 for each of the four corners in the brazen sea or reservoir borne by the 12 brass oxen.

"The 96 pomegranates were against the four corners."

The numbers and calculations found in the above quotations are those referring to the tatvas of the Sthoola, Sookshma and Karana Sareeras from very ancient times. In short, they all refer to one and the same subject. All the divisions of this Pindam are applicable to the Andam, and those found in the Andam apply to those in Astrology, Music and Medicine.

So these numbers have been used in Physiology, Vedantam, Astrology, Music, Yoga Sastram and other important Sciences.

We know that the human voice and the sounds of the Yal resemble each other. We noted how they are the same in measurements and calculations. We shall now do well to note the relation between the vibrations of a sound and the breath of man.

4. How the vibrations of the sound of the Yal resemble human breath.

We noted some points as regards the resemblance between the Sthoola shape of the Yal and that of the human body. Next, we proceeded to establish the resemblance between the tatvas of the Sookshma Sareera of man and those of the Sookshma Sareera of the Yal or different sounds. Similarly, we must now compare the motion of oxygen which is the cause or the karanam for the human body with the vibrations of sounds in the Yal which resemble the movement of oxygen. As it is slightly metaphysical we note here only a few points which could be understood by intelligent people.

We know that change of sounds is caused by the movement of oxyzen. We all believe that this whole creation is the result of the words or Nathams which proceeded out of the sacred mouth of God or the first being.

We have observed little children blowing soap bubbles by means of a stalk dipped in soap water or the milk of the wild amanakku. When they blow gently through the stalk small and large globes are formed and disappear in the air. When they blow fast only small bubbles are formed, but big bubbles are formed when they blow with the proper force. As the bubbles last only for a minute we see little boys constantly repeating this process and enjoying it just as learned people observe the innumerable stars and planets in the sky and feel happy over it. We may see that the play of the Divine being exactly resembles this. Our ancestors have declared that His great delight was to produce numerous created beings with different shapes, different measurements and different character. The Holy Bible says that when God breathed His spirit into the nostrils of the first man made of earth, he obtained life. We also know that every living being blessed with His spirit naturally propagates its own species. But it is not easy to understand Natham and its minute vibrations. Though all mankind possess the same kind of sense organs—body, mouth, eye, nostrils and ears, and the same five senses of touch, taste, smell hearing and sight, yet men are different in colour, form and character.

Do we not wonder at the Gramophone which faithfully records in a wax cylinder at the back the words spoken through its wide mouth and which faithfully reproduces the whole thing? Do they not reproduce by means of the apparatus of wireless telegraphy placed on an elevated ground words spoken hundreds of miles away? The very minute vibrations of sounds passing through air have their counterpart in letters and *vice versa*. The letters representing these sounds are not different like the different letters of different languages we speak, but are common to all sounds of nature. The shape of these letters is found in the structure of every animate being, and every member of the vegetable and mineral kingdoms. The action, character and size of every object is in proportion to this Prime letter. Wise men are striving night and day to understand this Prime letter. Though we are unable just now to give any definite conclusions regarding it, we shall do well just to note a few external points.

A man breathes 21,600 times in a day of 60 Naligais night and day Similarly, our ancestors have said that the Sun comes round Mahameru 21,600 times in a day. The following quotations will throw light on the point.

Mythrayanni Upanishad P. 59.

[illegible] (21,000)

அல்லது சரியாய்ச் சொல்வதானால் (21,600) சுவாசமாக தேகத்திற்குள் சுற்றி வருகிறது. சூரியனுடைய கால அளவைக்கொண்டு இவ்வளவு சுவாசமாகுமென்றும் சுவாசத்தினுடைய அளவைக்கொண்டு சூரியனுடைய (நாழிகை விநாடி முதலிய) அளவைக் கணக்கிடலாமென்றும் தாத்பரியம். இதன் பேரில்தான் மனிதனுக்கு நூறுவயது கணக்கிடப்பட்டிருக்கிறது.

Comment:—He says that the progression of the external Atma is decided by that of the Antaratma. For in a day of 24 hours the Sun comes round the Mahameru from left to right (Prathakshana). In one day oxygen circulates through the body as 21,000 or, to be more accurate, 21,500 breaths. The idea is that the number of breaths can be decided by the position of the Sun and *vice versa*. On this principle man's age is reckoned to be 100 years."

Varahopanishad P. 401.

இந்தத் தேகத்திலே வாயுமண்டலத்தினுடைய மோதுதலினாலே இருபத்து ஓராயிரத்து அறுநூறு (21,600) சுவாசம் உண்டாகிறது. பிருதிவிமண்டலம் குறைந்தால் தேகத்தை யுடையவர்களுடைய தேகத்தில் மடிப்புகளுண்டாகின்றன. ஜலபாகம் குறைந்தால் கிரமமாய் நரையுண்டாகிறது. தேஜஸ் குறைந்தால் பசியும் காந்தியும் குறைகின்றது. வாயுபாகம் குறைந்தால் எப்போதும் நடுக்கமுண்டாகிறது. ஆகாசபாகம் குறைந்தால் ஜீவித்திருக்கிறதேயில்லை.

Comment:—In this body by the motion of air there result 21,600 breaths. If the Prithvi Mandalam declines folds are found in the human body. If watery portion declines grey hair results. If the Thejas (brightness) declines hunger and glossy appearance also declines. When the Vayu declines continual tremor is caused, but when Akasa declines death results.

Silappadikaram, Arangetukathai P. 84.

" தசநாடிகளாவன; இடை பிங்கலை முதலிய பத்தும் மூலாதாரத்து எழுபத்தீராயிரநாடிகளும் பீர்க்கங்காயின் மூன்று கண்ணும் போல இடை பிங்கலை சுழுமுனையென்னும் மூன்று நாடிகளுமாய் நிலைநின்ற சுழுமுனையொழிய இரண்டாலும் மேனோக்கியோடி இரண்டு மூக்காலும் ஓரோர்பாரிசத்து ஐந்து நாழிகையாகக் கொண்டு ஒரு மாத்திரையில் நூற்றிருபத்தைந்து சுவாசமாய் ஒரு சுவாசத்திலே பன்னிரண்டங்குலி வாய்வுபுறப்பட்டு நாலங்குலி தேய்ந்து எண்விரலடங்குகின்றது பிராணவாயு வெனக்கொள்க. மாத்திரையாவது: இரண்டரை நாழிகையை எட்டுக்கூறிட்டு ஒரு கூறென்றறிக."

Comment:—The Dasa Nadis are Idakalai, Pingalai &c. The 72,000 Nadis of the Moolatharam, distribute themselves into the three main nadis, Idakalai, Pingalai and Shulumunai which are like the three partitions of a dried Peerkam fruit. Of these, with the exception of the Shulumunai in the centre, the breath of the two Nadis goes up by the two nostrils. On each side they stay for five Naligais and they become 125 breaths in a Mathira. From each of these breaths a 12 inch Vayu is generated, and of these 4 inches get wasted and 8 inches of Vayu or 8 digits alone are made use of by the body. This is the rule for the breathing of oxygen by the nostrils. A Mathira is one-eighth of 2½ Naligais.

Here we have 24,000 breaths for 60 Naligais at the rate of 400 per each. But the common view is 21,600 breaths. There is reason to think that 21,600 is the least number of breaths of a man in a day and 24,000 is the most. We think that those who intend practising yogam must begin with 21,600 only.

Veemesura Oollamudaian P. 19.

> " கூறவேன் விமகாதர்நாள் சென்னிமேற்
> கோண்கேவாச மிருபத்தோராயிரத்
> தாறனுமகிரேதாயுகமென்பதி
> ஞற்பெருக்கத்தி ரேதமஙபதா
> லேறுநாற்பத்தி லேற்றத்துவாபர
> மிருபதாலே பெருக்கக்கலியுக
> மீழிச்சென்றது மூவாயிரத்தோரு
> நூறமேழ்பத்து மோன்பதாப் மேவுமே."

(இ-ள்) விமேசுரர்திருவடியை சென்னிமேல் வைத்துக்கொண்டு சுத்தகணிதாங்கம் பிறக்கும்படி அண்டநாயகனுக்குச் சரம் இரவி முதலான கிரகங்கள் இராசிநட்சத்திரங்கள். ஒரு சுவாசம் விடுகிறதுபகல்-௩௰ நாழிகையாம் உள்ளே வாங்குகிற சுவாசம் இராத்திரி ௩௰ நாழிகையாம். இதை ௬௰ நாழிகையாம் அண்ட நாயகனுக்கு ஒரு சுவாசமென்றறிக. இந்த ஒரு சுவாசம் பூலோக நாயகனுக்கு ஒரு தினமென்றறிக. இப்படி அண்ட நாயகனுக்கு-௨௧௲௬௱-சுவாசமும் ஒருதின மென்றறிக. இந்த அண்ட நாயகனின் சுவாசமே தேவர்களும் கிரகங்களும் ரிஷிமுனீசுரரும் மற்றுமுள்ளவை களெல்லாம் இப்படி நடக்கிறதென்றறிக. இந்த அண்டநாயகனின் சுவாசம் ஒன்று பூலோகநாயகனுக்கு-௨௧௲௬௱ சுவாசமாய் நடக்கும். ௨௧௲௬௱-யும்-௮௰-ல் பெருக்க-௧௭-லட்சத்து-௨௮௲ வருஷம் கிரேதாயுகமென்றறிக. இனி திரேதாயுகம்-௬௰ல் பெருக்க ௧௨-லட்சத்து-௯௬௲ வருஷமென்றறிக. இனி துவாபரயுகம்-௪௰-ல்-பெருக்க ௮ லட்சத்து ௬௪௲-வருடமென்றறிக. இனிக்கலியுகம் ௨௰-ல் பெருக்க ௪-லட்சத்து ௩௨௲-வருஷமென்றறிக. இப்போது கலியுகத்தில் சாலிவாகனன் அண்டதற்குமுன் சென்றது-௩௲௱௭௰௯ வருஷமாம். எ-று.

Comment:—I shall give the method of calculating the true measurement for time, placing the sacred feet of God against my cheeks. The Rasi stars for the ruler of the world are the planets Saram and Iravi (Sun). The exhaling breath during the day is 30 Naligais and the inhaling breath during the night forms 30 Naligais. This 60 Naligais is one breath to the Andanayakan (God). This simple breath to the man is one day. In the same manner 21,600 breaths are one day to the Andanayakan. The calculation about the breath of the Andanayakan applies also to Gods, planets, Rishis and Munis also. One of the breaths of this Andanayaka will be equal to 21,600 of those of the Bhulokanayaka (Man). If we multiply this 21600 by 80 we get 17,28000 years or Kretayugam. Threthayugam is obtained by multiplying it by 60 i.e. 12,96000 years. Dvaparayugam is 8,64,000 years obtained by multiplying it by 40. Kaliyugam is 4,32000 years obtained by multiplying it by 20. The present year is 3179 years before Salivahana in the Kaliyugam."

The time that the Sun takes to go rouud Maha Meru 21600 times is reckoned as one day. In other words, a day in the life of man is reckoned as one revolution for the earth and one breath for the Sun, So the 21600 Rechaka Pooraka days become one Pariviruthi for man or 60 years. Two of this Pariviruthis form a Kalachakaram. This is reckoned to be the full life of man. This is equal to two days for the Sun. In astrology the years for the direction of the Nine Grahams is said to be 120 years. One breath or one revolution of the Sun is a day of 24 hours for man. Man breathes 21600 times a day. So 21600 human days are one day for the Sun. We understand that according to the old rule, what applies for the Andam holds good for the Pindam also, there is a connection between human breath and the revolution of the Sun. On the same principle, if we reckon a day to be 60 Naligais, a Naligai to be 60 Tharparais, and a Tharparai to be 60 Vitharparais, a day is equal to 2,16,000 Vitharparais. So man breathes 21,600 times at the rate of one breath for 10 Vitharparais. Likewise a day has 24 hours, each hour has 60 minutes and each minute 60 seconds or 86,400 seconds for the whole day. Here man breathes 21,600 times a day at the rate of one breath for 4 seconds or 15 breaths for a minute.

Because there is a certain amount of resemblance between the Sthoola and the Sookshma Sareera of man and shape of the Yal and the Swarams and Srutis of it we preseume that there must be some resemblance between human breath and the number of vibrations of a sound in the Yal. We know that if we want to twirl a small vessel filled with water without spilling any of the water we must do the twirling very rapidly. So also if we twirl a rupee placing it in the open palm of the hand we must twirl it with a force more rapid than is necessary to bring it to the ground. On the same principle the revolutionary force of the Sun, that of the Earth or the Andam, which rotates by the force and gravitation of the Sun, this Pindam which exists by the rotatory force and gravity of the earth and that of the Yal which resembles it must be in a proportionately declining ratio.

It takes 216000 Tharparais for the earth to revolve round its own axis. This is one day. A man breathes 21600 times during the day. This is a tenth of 2,16,000 Vitharparais for the day. If 21600 be the breathings of a man in a day, the number of vibrations of the Yal must be 21600 or a tenth of it. In other words the Thara Sthai Shadjam, the highest of the three Sthayis—Mandaram. Madhya and Thara—should have 2160 vibrations per second. As pitch increases at the rate of 1, 2 and 4 for the three Sthayis so the number of vibrations of the 3 Shadjams should be as follows: 2160 for Thara Sa, 1080 for Madhya Sa and 540 for the Mandara Sa. The finishing Sa of the Mandara Sthayi should be reckoned as Athara Sa. The finishing Sa of the Madhya Sthayi should be the Madhya Sa, and the finishing Sa of the Tara Sthayi the Thara Sa.

We know that a man who earns 60 Rs. a month and spends 30 Rs. saves Rs. 30 but that the same man spending Rs 70 a month is a debtor to the extent of Rs 10. Similarly, our ancestors have declared that a man who has been blessed with 120 years of life at the normal rate of 21,600 breaths per day will shorten his life if he breathes more than 21,600 times a day, but will lengthen it in proportion to the number of breaths he saves in a day. They have also struck a note of warning and said. "If the Kalai is lessened life is shortened." Note also their words "forget not to turn the breath through the right nostril." They say this because they clearly understood that we spend twelve and save four inches of breath out of 16 inches breathed through Soorya Kalai while we waste four inches of breath by receiving 12 inches and letting out 16 by the Chandra Kalai. The following quotations clearly explain this :—

Romarishi Sootram. 100 padal 81.

" வாரான மதியமிர்தம் பீரிட்டோடி வருகுதேன்ற சிறிஜனம் மாண்டார் ஐயா
நீரேது நீர்குடிக்க ஆறங்கேது நினைவுகேட்ட தோசிகளே நிறுத்திப்பார்க்க
கூரான சந்திரனில் வாலேமிச்சம் குடிக்கிறதும் பிடிக்கிறதும் அதுதான் ஐயா
சீரான மேல்வாசல் தமதுக்குள்ளே சிங்குவைவா லங்குலமுஞ் செலுத்திடாயே "

Romarishi Sootram 100 padal 72.

வாங்கியத்த பன்னிரண்டி லுள்ளே ரேசி
வன்னி நின்ற விடமல்லோ ரவியின் வாழ்க்கை
யோங்கியித்த ரெண்டிடமு மறிந்தோன் யோகி
உற்பர மடிதானே பதினு றுகுர்
தாங்கி நின்ற காலடிதான் பன்னிரண்டே
சார்வான பதினுறில் மெள்ள வாங்கி
யேங்கினதைப் பன்னிரண்டில் நிறுத்தி பூத
எழுந்தபுரி யட்ட மடங் கித்துப் பாரே.

Here the lines " உற்பர மடிதானே பதினாறும் தாங்கி நின்ற காலடிதான் பன்னிரண்டே " explain the allusion to the fact that when Kali who was so very conscious of her superiority in dancing challenged the whole world in that art Natesa, in order to teach her a lesson, danced with his left foot up and thus conquered her. Here he teaches mankind always to practise the excellent system of breathing in the Soorya Kalai (16 breaths) without breathing in the Chandra Kalai which is the amsam of Sati. The following lines also indicate this idea :—

காட்டிய நாதம் நல்வழி செலுத்தியே
நீட்டிடக் குறைக்கிட நினைத்தவாறு செய்தி
அட்சரத் தாலே அளந்திடும் உபாயம்
காட்டியே நாதம் லயித்த பதவி
தக்தோம் என்றடித் தாளம் உரைத்தானே.

They have indicated secrets like these in various places by many analogies and illustrations. They have also written extensively about the Yoga Shastra which treats about the control of breath and obtaining eternal life and the rules relating to its practice. Again, knowing that the deep sighing in times of trouble and sorrow and the short breathing during sleep, anger and actions of lust lead to an increase of the number of breaths and lessening of the number of days they, like a bird caught in a flood eschewed such actions and concentrated their attention in the art of breathing. We know that as a result of their penance they lived longer than ordinary men. If the letter Om be taken as one Mathira, they recommended that one should inhale 2 Mathiras of breath, suspend the respiration for 4 Mathiras and exhale 1 Mathira. They laid down rules for improving this kind of respiration gradually and also had mathiras to be repeated during the process. They gave out easy suggestions for the practice of the same in accordance with the words, " நடக்கையிலும் இருக்கையிலும் வாசி பாரு." We know how we commonly inhale and exale. But the process of suspending breath is not commonly known. So we must first practise the process of inhaling according to the Mathira of the letter Om and exhaling proportionately and suspend the breath in the middle. The Mathiras should be increased gradually for every separate function. As a first step they appointed that the Gayatri with three divisions should be practised in the three processes of Rechakam, Pooragam and Kumbagam. Instead of understanding the secret of this, what shall we say of those people who catch hold of their nostrils and repeat the Mathiras with their mouths open? How will they obtain the benefit of it? If the secret is first known many may successfully practise it.

It is said that he who repeats 108 Gayatris per day is held in esteem by his dead ancestors and the goddesses. When we think over this we find if a man reduces his 21600 breaths per day 200 times, he should breathe 108 times a day. In other words he saves 200 days in 1 day or he makes one year of his life into 200 years. The following is what sage Patanjali says about it.

" நாழிலேறு போதிலாறு கேணியாகும் விந்தடா
நூறு நூறு சேருமாகின் மாரிபெய்யு மாறடா
வேறுமீச னேதுஞான வீதியேறு போதிலே
வேதனுரு மாயனுரு மீசனுரும் வாசமாய்
கூறுநாவ தேதடாசொன் மூல நாடி யூதவே
கோணமாமூ வாச லேறப் பாழின் மீதி லேறடா
சாறடா கணேசர்பாத கேசாதி வீதியிற்
சாருசேரு தாரக சதாசிவாய பிரம்மமே "

The great sages who practised this excellent Yogam, though they appear to have given up everything connected with this world, they never gave up the Yal and its sweet ganam. When their body got heated owing to their difficult practice of respiration they played on the Yal and returned to their normal condition by the help of its sweet music. We know that when we sing the seven Swarams in Aroganam and Avaroganam and say many Ravai Jati Varisais we have to do the three practices of Rechakam, Pooragam and Kumbagam in excess contrary to nature. We also know from experience that suspending the breath abnormally leads to the swelling and bursting of some parts of the body. Therefore when we say that in singing our breath must not exceed one tenth of the total number of normal breathings, and that for the sake of distinctness when we gradually increase the speed in singing the number of vibrations of the sounds we use should be one-tenth of the whole 21,600 breaths, we state a fact that is agreed.

We are able to make ganam in 3 Sthayis only—two above the Athara SA and one below, that is Mandara Sthayi. In these three Sthayis, ganam is made in 14 Swarams only, 4 in the Mandara Sthayi, 7 in the Madhya Sthayi and 3 in Thara Sthayi as for as Kaikilai. This is in accordance with the practice of the ancient Tamils who made their Ganam in the 14 Kovais. These are the very 14 Sruṭis mentioned by Bharata (V century A. D.) as having been practised in this earth. Only very few rarely practise the 21 Swarams of the three Sthayis. Though sounds may be possible in the wires above the Thara Sthayi and below the Mandara Sthayi, yet the compass of the human voice being restricted to the three Sthayis only we may reckon the number of vibrations for sounds within that compass alone. For the sounds above and below we may double the number of vibrations and halve them respectively. Though our calculations are approximate here yet we made bold to say this knowing the truth of the old adage that what is true of the universe is true of the body and what is true of the body is true of the Yal.

We have given before 540 vibrations for the Athara SA, 1080 for the finishing SA of the Madhya Sthayi and 2160 for the finishing SA of the Thara Sthayi. In like manner, the length of the Yal from the Meru to the Mettu as well as the trunk of men measures 4 spans by each man's hand. Assuming that a span is 8 inches, we have reckoned the four spans as 32 inches or 48 digits and the length of the string of the Yal as 32 inches. The half of the 32 inches is 16. We have given measurements and calculations for the Swarams, Srutis and minuter Srutis up to Madhya SA, taking Athara SA to be at the 16th inch. From this it is clear that the Yal should be constructed according to the measurements of the player's hand and the Swarasthanams should be proportinately marked to suit his hand while any other measurement will be inconvenient. Swarasthanams of a Yal which is either over or under 4 spans of the player will not suit him as they may be too long or too short for his fingers. Swarasthanams will not also sound accurate if the measurement is less than 4 spans. Sweetness and accuracy of sound will result only if the measurement is correct.

5. How the Tamils were advanced in all sciences.

We may doubt whether the ancient Tamils were so efficient in Isai Tamil and other sciences. Many Tamilians know that sages like Ahastya, Thirumoolar, Chattamuni and Matchamuni have spoken about very minute points in the four sciences of Medicine, Vatham, Yogam and Gnanam. The most important of all these, namely Vatham and Yogam are called by the same name owing to their close resemblance. In the 500 Paripadals of Ahastya where he makes mention of the names of Brahma salts we may find the numbers 1. 2, 3. 5. 7. 10. 25 and 96 which also suit the Sthoola Tatvas.

We find from many sources that similar precious numbers are mentioned in Astrology also. This reminds us of the big Siva temples, the images found in them and many buildings made of granite stone in the Tamil Country built on principles of the science of Architecture and Sculpture practised by the ancient Tamils. If we observe the dimensions of the temples and their surrounding courts we may see their resemblance to the measurements of our Sthoola Sareeram. Just like a tailor who makes a coat with only the measurement of the neck given, our ancestors were capable of writing the picture of a man with only the circumference of the small finger as a clue. With the help of a lock of hair picked up from the flowing river and its length they were able to reproduce the original of the damsel. Measurements like these and sciences dealing with them seem to have been abundant in the Tamil language.

They seem to have had some conventional terms for the silent letter Om, and for each of the five letters Na, Ma, Si, Va and Ya. For example, the letter Om has been known as Yakaram, Vyttham, Thaltham, Mathu-Kalanjam, Navalatham, Oopanigaltham and Pathilkaram; the letter Na has been otherwise called Brahmala, Chathuram, Nicharalam, Tharalathakam, Vindulam, Vilachalasam and Kalavitham; the letter Si has been known by the several names of Rudrangam, Sivarangam, Naduvanaipati, Vilaichapasarikam, Thayadakam, Noanpuram, Nadapatham and Niruvi; similarly we see from their literature that different names had been given for similar letters, Tatvas, Astrological names, Green leaves, Metals, the 120 compounds of metals, the nine poisons, the 64 drugs of China, living beings which walk, fly or creep and grass and herbs and other species of the Vegetable Kingdom.

When we closely observe the names given to the five elements—fire, air, earth, water and atmosphere. the names of the five sensory organs—body, mouth, eye, nostrils and ear and the names of the five senses of touch, taste, smell, hearing and sight, the brevity of the names, the beauty of the words and the sweetness of their sound strike us prominently and indicate the excellence of the Tamil language. Many other more precious words, words relating to tatvas and other conventional terms have gradually disappeared and foreign words have usurped their places. We are aware that commentators of ancient Tamil works, later writers of fiction and translators introduced a number of foreign words and hybrid words, changing the names of Tamil works into foreign ones and mutilating them in many different ways.

Similarly there are people who claim many Tamil words as belonging to their own language. For example 'Kattam' has become 'Kadam'; 'Thattam', 'Thadam'; 'Vattam', 'Vadam'; 'Kannam', 'Kanam'; 'Atthai', 'Athai'; 'Putthu', 'Puthu'; 'Thattha', 'Thatha'; 'Thakkai', 'Thahai'; 'Mutthu', 'Muthu', and so on. These are examples of hard consonants losing their reduplication. There are examples of hard consonants mixed with vowels and other consonants becoming soft in other languages. We have noted on pages 336 & 337 how the hard consonants க, ச, ட, த, ப and ற becom soft when placed before and after the soft consonants ங, ஞ, ண, ந, ம and ன. There are many Sanskrit writers of Dictionaries who without understanding the pronunciation of Tamil words converted them wholesale into Sanskrit words.

The ancient Tamils had separate Dictionaries to explain the words in the separate sciences they had. Though Iyal Tamil had a separate dictionary they had also separate ones for Medicine, Astrology, Music, Physiology and other sciences. Of these the dictionaries referring to the words used in Iyal Tamil, Isai Tamil and Nataka Tamil and other sciences were destroyed by the sea. In spite of this wholesale destruction, some words and Sootrams which remained in the memory of those Tamils saved from the general deluge came into use. Even those words were found to be difficult for use in course of time and forgotten and the result was the large importation of foreign words into the language.

We noted before how many of the rare ideas of Isai Tamil used in South Madura 12000 years ago and names of Ragas were changed into the foreign language so much so it is doubted now whether such ideas ever existed in the Tamil literature at all. In spite of the fact that the work of Saranga Dev in Sanskrit advocating 22 Srutis in the octave and giving different names for Ragas, recognising 9 and 13 Srutis respectively for SA-MA and SA-PA on the principle of Vadi and Samvadi was written in complete ignorance of measurements of Swarams, the system of Alakus of Srutis and the 12000 ancient Isais, confusing the true ideas of the Karnatic Music, yet the first Ragam Chempalai Pun or Shankaraparanam used by the ancient Tamils from time immemorial, Padumalai Palai Pun or Karaharapiriya, Chevvali Pun or Thodi, Aroompalai Pun or Kalyani, Kodipalai Pun or Harikambodi, Vilari Pun or Nata-Bhairavi, Thara Pun or Thodi without Panchamam and a few other Ragas—all these are preserved in use even at the present day.

We are aware also that there is some kind of relation between some facts of astrology, and some ideas of the Sthoola, Sookshma and Karana Tatvas of the human body with the calculations for the Swarams, small Swarams. Srutis and minuter Srutis of Karnatic Music.

Though the traditional Musicians of South India have been unable to understand the works containing the minute amsams of Music, yet, many of the ancient puns have been preserved by them alone. In spite of this, the disappearance of principles of the science which enables one to compose new ragas and correct the errors in the old caused the confusion about the 22 Srutis advocated by foreign writers.

Those who realised that more Srutis than the 12 half Swarams were used in the Ganam of the Tamils put down the number of Srutis as 22. They gave calculations to show they were derived by the SA-PA and the SA-MA principles and by the principles of $\frac{3}{2}$ and $\frac{4}{3}$. We pointed out in the second part how these calculations could never agree with Karnatic Music:

We also examined the calculations of Srutis according to the eminent system of Sarnga Dev. He says clearly that Swarams should stand in their most natural order and should have their calculations according to Geometrical Progression. He has said that the three Sthayis—Mandara, Madhya and Thara—should stand in the proportion of 1: 2: 4.

But without understanding the secret of the Vattapalai system which divides the Sthayi into 12 Rasis and 24 Alakus and makes ganam in them with 2 Alakus less in Vilari and Kaikilai, nor the ganam of the Tamils nor the four kinds of Yal, he gives 22 Srutis for the octave, says they change the graham and become Shadja, Madhyma and Gandhara gramams, declares that the Gandara gramam has gone up to the celestial regions and confuses the Neythal Yal Alaku system of 4, 3, 2, 4, 4, 3, 2 with Shadja Gramam. If he had said there were 24 Srutis instead of 22, that the Inai Swaram SA-PA from any given Rasi has 7 Rasis or 14 Srutis, that SA-MA has five Rasis or 10 Srutis and that two Srutis should be lessened in Vilari and Kaikilai there could never have been any doubt about the number of Srutis in an octave. The

Lakshanams and arrangements for Ragas and the names given to them having 22 Srutis as the basis quite contradict the Karnatic Ragas handed down by oral transmission and sung at the present day.

We were compelled to give our own opinion as regards Srutis and their calculations seeing the mischief caused by the measurement of $\frac{2}{3}$ for Pa and $\frac{1}{2}$ for Sa carried to the west 2500 years ago and the doubt and confusion caused by the writings of Bharata and Sarnga Dev and the other advocates of 22 Srutis who came after them. Our object is for the purpose of removing these doubts. We are aware that oxygen in the air in course of time eats up even an iron pillar though the old world saying is "can the iron pillar be eaten up by white ants?" A piece of iron eaten up by air is as brittle as a mud pot. So, for fear that the truth of the Karnatic Music practised by the ancient Tamils and the minuteness of Isai Tamil may altogether disappear we are constrained to make mention of the 12 Swarams of Ayapalai, the 24 Srutis of Vattapalai and the minute Srutis made mention of in their ganam.

Though our making mention of a thing that had been in use for 12000 years and over may appear novel, we had to refer to the ancient glory of Isai Tamil—one of the divisions of Muttamil—and assert our rights at a time when antiquity is discarded and things belonging to others are claimed as their own. Not to do so will be derogatory to the position of a Tamilian.

Moreover, when we were making researches day and night for many years as regards the system of composing a Ragam from a given Moorchana we heard the discouraging remarks of many expert musicians who said, "this man is music-mad; let him not trouble himself on the subject any longer; one may measure the seven seas and fix their limits but it is impossible to fix rules for a ragam which is generated from the seven Swarams; it is a waste of labour; this is possible with God alone and not with man; I have wasted 20 years of labour on this impossible subject." Such remarks were made by different persons. When Mr. Louis Dickinson of the Cambridge university and Mr. R. C. Travelian paid a visit to our place in the middle of January 1913 for the purpose of gathering some ideas as regards Indian Music, after a number of enquiries they asked if we had any system of composing a Ragam from a given Aroganam and Avaroganam. We placed before them our manuscript describing the principle of making a Ragam out of a Moorchana and writing a Geetam for the same giving the Jivaswaram, Grahaswaram, Vivadi Swaram, the system of singing it and the various combinations of Swarams. They were surprised and said "We have travelled through the whole of India. When we made enquiries from Vidwans in many places if they had any definite system for composing ragas, they invariably answered that such a thing was possible in the case of only a favoured few who might be considered incarnations of the Deity and who did it from their own experience and that there was no such written system." They further requested us to send them a copy of this book as soon as it was ready.

It is necessary that the calculations for Srutis should be given prior to the system of composing Ragas. It is but just that the doubts as regards the Srutis that exist in India and other places must be first cleared before establishing the true system. So there arose the necessity of examining the theories of different writers and giving our opinions on the same.

Though our efforts in the direction of the system of composing Ragas extended for 15 years, they did not obtain fruition, till the year 1909 aud that also providentially. The definite system of making Ragas will soon be published as the Second and the Third books. We found out later on that that system was the one in use in ancient Isai Tamil. After we tried the truth of this system by practical demonstrations we had to declare to the world that a comparison of the 12 Swarams of Ayapalai in use in ancient Isai Tamil, the 24 Alakus of Vattapalai and the ganam with 2 Alakus less, the Ragas of the ancient Tamils and those in use at the modern day with our own practical experience enabled us to say that the modern Srutis were the very Srutis of Isai Tamil that were practised by the Tamils in South Madura and those of the Three Sangams and that the calculation for their minute Srutis were exactly the same as for the minute Srutis we used now.

II. The calculations for the Swarams, Srutis and minute Srutis and the Puns in which they are used.

1. General remarks on the Seven Swarams of the twelve Rasis.

We know that Tamil was the spoken language in South Madura, spoken of by all for its excellence as 'Thiruvidam'. in the Seven islands belonging to it and in the 49 provinces of these seven islands (at the rate of 7 for each), and that the three angams of Tamil--Iyal, Isai and Natakam—and other sciences were practised by the ancients. We noted in Part 1 that these 49 provinces formed Lemuria, that it was now submerged in the Indian Ocean, that the ancient inhabitants of Lemuria were now scattered in different countries and that many of the Tamil words spoken by the Tamils of the country known as Lemuria were now found mixed in other languages.

There is reason for us to surmise that to the exclusion of the many rare ideas of Isai Tamil which were the result of the patient labours of the ancient Tamils, some of the most common of the amsams such as the twelve Swarams of Ayapalai spread in other parts of the world when the Tamil country was destroyed by sea.

When we understand that Western Musicians have heard even the apes which escaped from Lemuria and reached the near shores singing the 12 Swarams (the chromatic scale) in order, our remark that the remnants of those saved from Lemuria made their ganam in the 12 Swarams of Ayapalai is not very surprising.

The following extracts show that monkeys reproduce the 12 Swarams of Ayapalai and that other living beings are also fond of Music.

Art of teaching as applied to Music : Page 97, 98.

" Insects and some few spiders are the lowest animals which voluntarily produce any sound, and this is generally effected by the aid of beautifully constructed stridulating organs. The sounds thus produced consist, I believe, in all cases, of the same note repeated rhythmically.

The auditory hairs with which Crustaceans are provided have been seen to vibrate in response to musical sounds ; as also have the antennæ of gnats. As we ascend the scale of mammalian development, so is the capacity for appreciating differences in musical sounds increased, until we reach the Hylobates agilis, an ape having many characteristics in common with man. According to Mr. Waterhouse ("general introduction to natural History of Mammalian Animals," by W. C. L. Martin), this gibbon possesing an extremely loud but musical voice, appeared to him to ascend and descend the musical scale in exact half-tones, and he was sure that the highest note was the exact octave to the lowest ; and he continues : "I do not doubt that a good violinist would be able to give a correct idea of the gibbon's composition, excepting as regards its loudness.' Professor Owen who was a musician, confirms this view and says that this gibbon alone of brute mammals, may be said to sing."

Were it not beyond the scope of this work, it would be easy, and in some respects profitable, to trace the evolutionary process by which the gibbon, in arriving at his chromatic scale, proves the general truth of the assumption that in proportion to the complexity and age historically of the organism is the discrimination of degrees of pitch in musical sound developed. We have however, referred to the fact (sec. 74) that in the more advanced mammals the several stages of mental progress are all passed through (though more rapidly in the life of the individual itself than in the lower forms), and it is this fact that enables even young children not only to imitate accurately sounds heard but to label mentally their relations one to another."

From this extract we understand the apes of Lemuria as well as men were singing easily the 12 Swarams of Ayapalai or those used in the modern 72 Melakartas. The following stanza from the Aychiarkuravai of Silappadikaram shows that the daughters of herdsmen sang Grahaswaram on the Sa-Pa principle antiphonally, which is a proof for the efficient state of music at that time.

"குரன் மந்தமாக விளிசம னாக
வரன்முறையே துத்தம் வலியா—வுரனிலா
மந்தம் விளரி பிடிப்பா ளவனட்பின்
பின்றையைப் பாட்டெடுப் பாள்."

The music of those days appears to have been very eminent judged from the systems of Vattapalai, Thirikonapalai and Chathurapalai. In addition to these palais they have given the number of Srutis, their concordance and the Swarams that are discordant with one another. They have demonstrated from their practical experience that if the discordant Swarams are retained the Ragams become lifeless and useless. They were able to control even elephants by singing Puns in strict accordance to rules. They were able to make cobras come out of their holes and dance with their hoods extended and let them off. They were able to melt even the hardest of hearts with their music. They praised Goddesses with their music and obtained what they desired. Just to show that they should avoid in their music all Vivadi Swarams if they wanted to obtain what they desired they have laid down the rules "[illegible]" and "[illegible]."

These who have not realised the excellence of these rules have got into the habit of adding Vivadi Swarams in their ganam thus spoiling the beauty of ancient ragas. To those who use such mixed Swarams these rules may appear hard. To those who strictly adhere to the Margham these infringements are Desikam. But to those who habitually infringe the rules and practise Desikam, these become Desikam of Desikam. The ganam of the ancient Tamils is Margam. We have clearly said in Part III how this is the best system containing rules for composing innumerable Ragas and for correcting the errors that had crept into the old ragas.

We have dealt before about the different kinds of Yal used by the ancient Tamils, the 12000 Isais sung by them, the 12 Palais that are obtained by the change of Grahaswaram, the seven Primary Palais and the fact that these are the modern ragas. We have also given tables dealing with the Ragas for the 7 Swarams, the 12 half swarams and the 24 Srutis.

We have also noted how these calculations are also found in the sciences of astrology, medicine and physiology. It now behoves us to give the mathematical calculations for the 12 Swarams of Ayapalai, the 24 Srutis of Vattapalai and the minuter Srutis occurring in the various Puns.

We have proved before that the Swarasthanams obtained by assuming Sa-Pa to be $\frac{2}{3}$ of a wire and Sa-Ma $\frac{3}{4}$ and multiplying them ad. lib. necessitate an addition here and a subtraction there and therefore they are false. Now it becomes our duty to give the right calculations for the right Swarasthanams.

So we shall do well first to speak about the seven Swarams of Isai Tamil, next about the 12 Swarams of Ayapalai and the 24 Srutis of Vattapalai, next about more minute Srutis and lastly to point out where such Srutis are used in modern Ragas with foreign names.

We have spoken about two points which should be primarily considered in determining Srutis, (see P. 431 Part II). These two points should be first considered here also. They are :--

(1) The system of Sarnga Dev for determining Swarams and Srutis, and

(2) The system of $\frac{2}{3}$ for Sa-Pa $\frac{3}{4}$ for Sa-Ma adopted by Western Musicians as well as a few Indian Musicians.

We may perhaps think that the calculations given by writers on Srutis are correct according to these two systems.

We see that Sarnga Dev has adopted the principle of Geometrical Progression both in determining the Srutis and in the relation of the three Sthayis and bases his system of changing the graham also on the same principle.

But he gives the number of Srutis to be 22 in a Sthayi and gives names of Ragas and Ragalakshanam accordingly without saying that the Tamils made ganam in the 22 Alakus lessening 2 Alakus in Vilari and Kaikilai. From the calculations we see that when we divide the octave into 22 even Ma and Pa do not obtain the proper measurements.

Other writers without adopting the excellent system enunciated by Sarnga Dev and at the same time being unwilling to give up the number 22, determine the 22 Srutis by multiplying the Pa and Ma or $\frac{2}{3}$ and $\frac{3}{4}$ of the Veena. Not two of them agree in their calculations.

This necessitated the enquiry whether a system which all could adopt really does exist and the demonstration of it.

If we could only fix our attention on some of the stanzas found in Isai Tamil in order to understand the music of South India we shall find there clearly stated that the Swarams in Ragas should stand in the relation of Inai, Kilai or Natpu, that Swarams should be arranged on the principle of Kural—Ili and that the number of Srutis according to Vattapalai is 24. The Alakus of Vattapalai proceeding upwards as 1, 2, 3, 4 &c satisfy the principle laid down by Sarnga Dev that the Srutis of a sthayi should rise gradually without admitting any possible sound between and end with the octave.

The rule of the ancient Tamils says that the sound which appears at the throat first begins with the breath at the genital organ by the legs in the proportion of 1 which afterwards becomes doubled and in this proportion of 1: 2 all the Puns are derived. It is this very rule that Sarnga Dev upholds when he says that the Mandira, Madhya and Tara Sthayis should be in the proportion of 1: 2: 4. The words "ஒன்றெனத் தாக்கி இரண்டெனப் பகுத்துப் பண்ணீர்மைகளைப் பிறப்பிக்க" clearly establish the above proportion between the Sthayis.

The Srutis should also be determined according to the uniform principle adopted by westerners as well as Indian Musicians that Sa-Pa and Sa-Ma occur in the $\frac{2}{3}$ of the whole length of wire and $\frac{3}{4}$ of the whole length respectively and that the Swarams of a Sthayi should be decided on this system. If we note carefully the ancient Tamil works and those of Bharata and Sarnga Dev, we shall find that the measurements $\frac{2}{3}$ and $\frac{3}{4}$ are not mentioned in any of these works. But it is clearly mentioned in the ancient works on Isai Tamil and in Sangeeta Ratnakar that the Swarams should be of the Sa-Pa and the Sa-Ma series. The following stanzas from Silappadikaram distinctly indicate the fact that the ancient Tamils made their ganam in the Yal clearly understanding the concordance between Swarams on the principle of Sa-Pa owing to their high efficiency in music, and deriving other Swarams according to the same rule :—

"ஏற்றிய குரல் இளி என்றிரு நரம்பின்
ஒப்பக் கேட்கும் உணர் வினைஞர்"

and

"வண்ணப் பட்டடை யாழ்மேல் வைத்தாங்கு"

"குரல்வாய் இளிவாய்க் கேட்டனள்."

We noticed in the third para how the 12 Swarams of Ayapalai were derived from Vattapalai as seventh Rasi from the given rasi rightwards on the principle of Inai or SA-PA, and how the same series are derived as fifths leftwards on the principle of Kilai. We find, therefore, that the method of arriving at Swarams by the ancient Tamils is far superior to the principle of $\frac{3}{2}$ and $\frac{4}{3}$. Such is the music of the ancient Tamils satisfying the above two principles.

Therefore we propose to enquire into the question of (1) Swarams, (2) Swarams of Ayapalai, (3) Srutis of Vattapalai and (4) minuter Srutis by their calculations and examine later on whether such Srutis occur in the Ragas of the modern day.

2. The Seven Swarams of a Sthayi.

It is said that the Seven Swarams of Isai Tamil sprang from the seven islands known in ancient times as the Tamil Country. They are Noval (Jambo), Irali (Itthi), Kuchai (Darpa), Krounja (Andil), Putkara (Elephant), Thengu (Cocoanut) and Kamugu (Areca nut). These seven Isands seem to have been discovered by the seven sages. So we say that the seven Swarams originated in the Tamil Coutnry made up of the seven isles. Sarnga Dev also derives them from seven isles. They are, Jambu, Saga, Kuchai, Krounja, Salmali, Swatha, and Pushkara isles. Just as the Puns of the Tamil country are known as, Thakka Vibbasha Devara Varthani, Malava Kaisika Devara Varthani, Pinna Shadja Vibasha Devara Varthani, Dakshanakutcheri, Thiravidi, Thiravida Kutcheri, Thiravidi Bhasha Soma ragam, Dakshinathya Bhasha, Suddha Panchamam, Dakshana Bhashangam, he says that the seven Swarams originated from the Seven Isles of the Tamil Country. India in which we live is one of the Seven Isles. It is called Noval isle. We know that a great part of South India or South Madura was destroyed by sea, that the Tamil Country extended far north as far as the Himalayas and that Kumarikode the Southern limit of the South Tamil province as well as the River Patruli dug by Vadimbalamba Nindra Pandya were also destroyed

We see that these islands obtained their names from the product that was abundant in them. For instance, the island filled with Jambo trees was called Noval; Irali isle, on account of its Itthi trees; Kuchai on account of its long grass; Krounja on account of its Andil (a kind of water bird); Pushkara was called after the numerous herd of elephants found there; Thengu on account of its many Cocoanut trees and Kamugu on account of its groves of Areca-nut palm. We may note that these seven products are very common even to day on the shores of the countries bordering the Indian Ocean. They are also found in large quantities all through India.

So it is clear that the province of South Madura to the South of India was very extensive, that it was a prominent country ruled by eminent Pandya Rajas and that Tamil was the language spoken in all these Seven Isles.

We find that the most prominent rulers of these islands became Raja Rishis on account of their penance, Sages and Manus. On pages 16 & 17 of this book it is stated how it is mentioned in Bhagavatam that Satyavarada, the King of South Madura (the Dravida Country) became Vyvasutta Manu. There is reason to believe that the Seven Swarams were discovered by them from time to time and completed,

Just as it is mentioned in the Holy Bible that through the sage Noah who was saved from the Deluge, mankind increased in numbers, it is commonly stated that the people of India had their origin from Satyavarada, the King of the Tamil Country who went north after being saved from the deluge, that according to his calculation 23 Chathuryugas have already passed, that Kaliyugam occurred in the present 24th Chathur Yugam and that 5015 years of that Yugam have already passed. Though we cannot definitely subscribe to this statement we may safely say that the Pandya Sovereign who ruled over Lemuria or the South Tamil Country or South Madura and his descendants were the renowned ancient inhabitants of India

Just as seven Swarams are apportioned to seven isles, seven Srutis for each of the Srutis are given for each of the seven Nadams which are the sub-divisions of the seven islands. The details for these will be given in Book II. The word 'ஏழு' possesses a letter which is peculiarly the heritage of the Tamil language. Similarly, things represented by the number seven belong preeminently to the Tamil Country and they were primarily found or used there alone.

In all the sciences of the Tamils, we see that this number has been largely used. The expressions 7 Isais, 7 strings of the Yal, 7 grahams, 7 days of the week, 7 puns, 7 vangiams, 7 kinds of appearances, 7 isles, 7 provinces, 7 Thalams, 7 Thathus the 7 steeds of the Sun, 7 seas, 7 worlds, 7 seasons, 7 Palais, 7 continents, 7 damsels, 7 Mulavus, 7 sages, 7 clouds, 7 rulers etc. show that these were commonly used in connection with sciences such as Music, Astrology, Grammar, Vedantam etc.

Of these the expressions 7 Swarams, 7 Thalams, 7 palais, 7 Mulavus, 7 Vangiams, 7 Puns and 7 strings of the Yal are solely used in Music and form the calculations of the science. We have noted before that the Tamil country was made up of seven large islands. The mathematical calculations also are seven and its multiples. There are many other calculations occurring in the same figure. We should now see in what measurements the Swarams with number 7 occur.

Just as the celestial expanse was divided into 12 Rasis and the sancharams of the 7 grahams in it were mentioned, the ancient Tamils divided the Octave also into 12 Swarams and mentioned the sancharam of 7 Swarams in it. We must then understand that there are 12 Swarasthanams in the Sthayi and that 7 of them form different Ragas with their separate calculations. Similarly, there are 12 vowels in Tamil and 7 of them are long; there are 12 months in the year and 7 days for the week; there are 12 Mettus for the yal and 7 Swarams; there are 12 Atharas (6 above and 6 below) in living beings and 7 appearances, and there are 12 Suns with their 7 horses.

Of the 12 Swarams of the Sthayi, the two Swarams Sa and Pa are primary Swarams, like Sati and Sivam; so these are always stationary and permanent in all Ragas. These two stand by themselves in the Rasis, Itapam and Thanusu. The other 5 Swarams, Thuttham, Kaikilai, Oolai, Vilari and Tharam or Ri, Ga, Ma, Dha and Ni appear each in 2 Rasis and get two places. In other words, the Swarams are arranged in the 12 Rasis as follows :—Sa 1, Ri 2, Ga 2, Ma 2, Pa 1, Dha 2 and Ni 2. The ancient Tamils have used these 7 Swarams in the Sthanams 1, 2, 2, 1, 2, 2, 2. We may see on pages 640 & 641 that when these 7 Swarams change their graham according to this calculation we get the mother Ragas or the 7 primary puns and when change of graham is made in the 12 Swarams we get the 12 palais.

Of these, they say 7 palais are primary and 5 secondary. The Chempalai Pun among the 7 primary palais is now known by the foreign name of Shankaraparanam, Padumalai Palai Pun as Karaharapiriya, Chevvali Pun as Hanumathodi, Aroompalai Pun as Mechakalyani, Kodipalai Pun as Harikambodi, Vilaripun as Natabhairavi and Merchempalai Pun as Suddha Thodi. We may note that in the accompanying table these Ragas appear in the order 1, 2, 2, 1, 2, 2, 2.

In the next Table, in the first row, seven numbers are given for the seven Swarams. Of these leaving aside the number for the first Swaram or Sa, if we commence the second series from number 2 of Ri and the third series from number 2 of Ga and proceed leftwards, the number for the seven series will be arrived at. If we note the 7th row, we get Ma with 4 Alakus in place of Pa in the 5th. Because Pa is a fixed Swaram, and Ma with 2 Alakus and Ma with 4 Alakus cannot occur in the same ragam and if it does it would contradict established rules, the Pa occurring in the place of the Ma with 4 Alakus has been given up altogether and the Ragam named Suddha Thodi. This is why it seems to have been called Tharapun-thiram. We call it Suddha Thodi. There is reason to believe that the seventh row was abolished, the mother Ragas taken to be only 6 and the 7th has been called Merchampalai Pun. However this is a stumbling block and leads to the formation of many Desika Ragas. The calculations of these Alakus may be clearly seen in the Table of the seven Primary Palais given below.

The Table showing the position of the Seven Primary Puns derived from Sempalai in the 12 Rasis, with their respective intervals

Six Mother Ragas.	Change of Graham of Swarams.	Beginning Swaram.	Standard string. 12 ச Sa	Second string. 2 ரி Ri	String of friendship. 4 க Ga	Branch string. 5 ம Ma	Concordant string. 7 ப Pa	Second string. 9 த Dha	Branch string. 11 நி Ni	Ancient Tamil names.	Modern names.
1	When Kural is taken as Kural.	ச Sa	1	2	2	1	2	2	2	Chempalai Pun.	Dhira Sankaraparanam.
2	When Thuttham is taken as Kural.	ரி Ri	2	2	1	2	2	2	1	Padumalaipalai Pun.	Karakarapriya.
3	When Kaikilai is taken as Kural.	க Ga	2	1	2	2	2	1	2	Chevvali Pun.	Hanumat Thodi.
4	When Oolai is taken as Kural	ம Ma	1	2	2	2	1	2	2	Arumpalai Pun.	Kalyani.
5	When Ili is taken as Kural ...	ப Pa	2	2	2	1	2	2	1	Kodipalai Pun.	Harikambothi.
6	When Vilari is taken as Kural.	த Dha	2	2	1	2	2	1	2	Vilari Pun.	Nata Bayravi.
	When Tharam is taken as Kural.	நி Ni	2	1	2	2	0	2	2	Merchampalai Pun.	Suddha Thodi.

The Table showing the intervals of the Swarams belonging to the Six mother Ragas which result from the change of Graham of Chempalai Pun or Shankaraparanam.

Standard string. 0		Second string. 2				String of friendship. 4		Branch string. 5				Concordant string. 7				Second string. 9				String of friendship. 11		Branch string. 12		Modern system.		
24	1	2	3	4	5	6	7	8	9	10	11	12	13	14	15	16	17	18	19	20	21	22	23	24	Modern Ragas.	The Swaram for Ragas.	
S		R^2		R^4		G^3		G_4		M^2		M^4		P		D^2		D^4		N^2		N^4		S			
1 S				R^4				G^4		M^2				P				D^4				N^4			Sankraparanam	S 4R 4G 2M P 4D 4N S	29
2 N^2				S				R^4		G^2				M^2				P				D^4			Karakarapiriya	S 4R 2G 2M P 4D 2N S	22
3 D^2				N^2				S		R^2				G^2				M^2				P			Hanumat Thodi	S 2R 2G 2M P 2D 2N S	8
4 P				D^4				N^4		S				R^4				G^4				M^4			Mesha Kalyani.	S 4R 4G 4M P 4D 4N S	65
5 M^2				P				D^4		N^2				S				R^4				G^4			Harikambothi.	S 4R 4G 2M P 4D 2N S	28
6 G^2				M^2				P		D_2				N^2				S				R^4			Nata Bairavi...	S 4R 2G 2M P 2D 2N S	20
7 R^2				G^2				M^2		M^4 P^2				D^2				N_2				S			Suddha Thodi.	S 2R 2G 2M 2D 2N S	8

It is clearly seen from the above Table that the primary Ragam is Chempalai-pun, that it was sung in Swarasthanams 1, 2, 2, 1, 2, 2, 2, that it is known as Shankaraparanam in modern music and that the calculation of intervals for the Swarams of Ragams should be in accordance with what is given for this. Just as the seven Swarams of the standard string, second string, friendly string, branch string, concordant string and then again of the second string, friendly string and branch string occur in the 12th, the 2nd, the 4th, the 5th, the 7th, the 9th and 11th Rasi for the Chempalai Pun, it must occur for the others also. S› Chempalai Pun primarily sets forth the common rule for all. Because the other six mother Ragas are formed after this system, this might be called the mother of all mother Ragas. The details of these are given in the 3rd part where we treat about the system of Yal with all mysteries cleared.

However, from the Chakaram given below we may see that the 12 Swarams of Ayapalai are obtained as Inai Swarams or the SA-PA series (Kural Ili) proceeding rightwards by sevens commencing from kural in Itapam, the second Rasi. Here, 2 Alakus are taken for each of the Rasis. We had to do this for comparing the calculations of modern Swarams. But we must understand that Kural and Ili occur in single Rasis and the other five Swarams in two Rasis each.

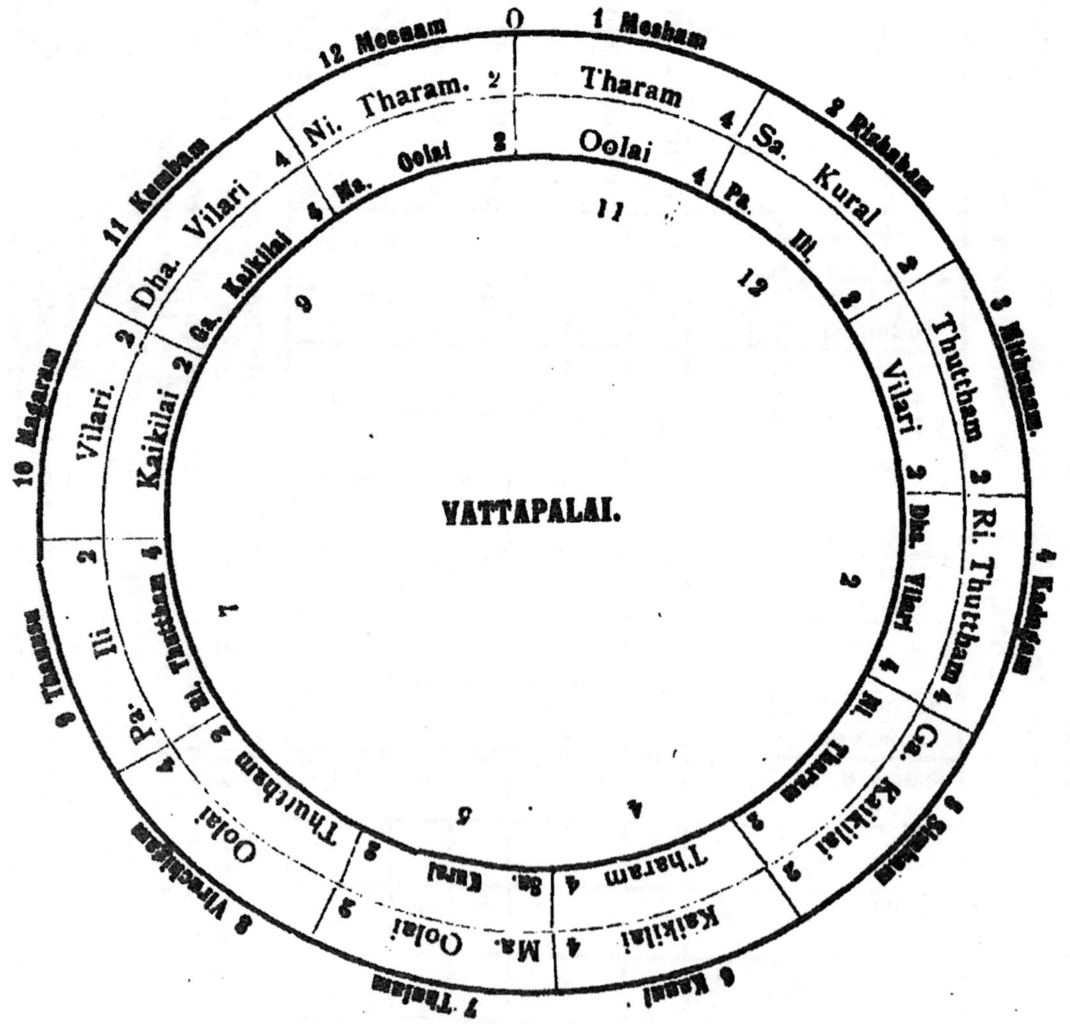

The 12 Swarams in Vattapalai obtained by the Sa-Pa principle proceeding rightwards.

Ili in Kural	SA2 PA2	Thutham in Oolai	MA4 R12
Thutham in Ili...	PA2 R14	Vilari in Thutham	R12 DA2
Vilari in Thutham	R14 DA4	Kaikilai in Vilari	DA2 GA2
Kaikilai in Vilari	DA4 GA4	Tharam in Kaikilai	GA2 N12
Tharam in Kaikilai	GA4 N14	Oolai in Tharam	N12 MA2
Oolai in Tharam	N14 MA4	Kural in Oolai	MA2 SA2

The 12 Swarams in Vattapalai obtained by the Sa-Ma principle proceeding leftwards.

Kural in Oolai	MA2 SA2	Oolai in Tharam	N14 MA4
Ili in Kural	SA2 PA2	Thutham in Oolai	MA4 R12
Thutham in Ili	PA2 R14	Vilari in Thutham	R12 DA2
Vilari in Thutham	R14 DA4	Kaikilai in Vilari	DA2 GA2
Kaikilai in Vilari	DA4 GA4	Tharam in Kaikilai	GA2 N12
Tharam in Kaikilai	GA4 N14	Oolai in Tharam	N12 MA2

These are the seven out of the 12 Swarams of Ayapalai used by the Tamils in the ancient Tamil country. The ganam that is contrary to the rules laid down by ancient Tamils can never be a Margam. When irregular Swarams like the creation of Visvamitra are introduced even though it may sound sweet it will only be considered Desikam and the music of the ignorant. The mathematical calculation for the Chempalai Pun is margam. When puns are sung according to rules. then alone we shall obtain their desired effect.

If in the Ragam Punnagavarali if the Kumba Vilari or Vilari with 4 Alakus be used in place of the Magara Vilari, the cobras lose their entranced state, are roused to anger and they will sting. This is within our experience.

When a man, in an entranced state, dances to the Ragam Anandabairavi, if the Vilari in Kumbam instead of that in Magaram be used, he loses the particular state and comes back to his normal condition.

The Various names given by others for Isai-Tamil.

Others who heard the ganam of the Tamils in which each Ragam had its own peculiar charm and which had strict rules for its Isai-Tamil gave different names to the music of the Tamils. Those living in the North of India called it by the name of South Indian Music. Sanskrit writers who called South India or Thiruvidam by the names of Thiravidam and later on 'Thiravidam' called the Tamil music by the name of Thiravida Sangeetam and said that it was eminently satisfactory. The merchants from the west who occupied the Karnatic kingdom which extended from Tanjore to Nellore on the East-Coast and their descendants called it by the name of Karnatic music. Others speaking broadly call it Indian Music. The ancient Tamils of South Madura called it Isai-Tamil. So we clearly see that the Isai-Tamil which has such excellent rules has been called 'the ganam of South India', 'Thiravida music' and "Karnatic music'.

Again, there are some who say that music was first in the Sanskrit language as the sound of some of the letters SA, RI, GA, MA, PA, DHA, and NI, resembles that of Sanskrit letters. But here the sounds of SA, GA, PA and DHA are open to dispute. We have pointed out before that the letter ச when sounded with a soft consonant resembles the third SA of Sanskrit, but when it comes after an cttu it sounds like the second SA. Again, when hard consonants occur as first letters of words with vowel consonants they become soft in character. The ச that occurs in words like சது, சக்கொண்டை, சரி, சரிகை, சரிபாதி, சருகு, சலசலப்பு, சட்டெப்பு, சலவை வெள்ளை has only the first sound of the SA series. The first ச of the series ச, ஜ, ஸ, ஷ, seems to have been used according to the usage in Tamil words. This seems to have been used as அ by the ancients.

Again, it is common in Tamil that the hard consonants which are sounded either before or after the soft ம, become themselves soft. The same is true of ஞ and ச with ந. These sounds are common in the Tamil language and nothing peculiar.

The following tables will show the isles where the seven Swarams criginated, the place of origin, the names of the discoverers, Athidevatas, the names of those who use them, flowers, vahanam, jewels, arms etc. mentioned in works in Tamil, Sanskrit and Telugu.

If we note the Table given below we shall see that in the Isai-Tamil of the Tamils the cast, the soil, the colour, the day, the Rasi and the graham which are mentioned in connection with the rules of prosody should be satisfied in the case of the four kinds of Pahs. Again, when the poet sings about the chief man or the chief woman, he takes care to see whether the commencing word satisfies the ten kinds of பொருத்தம் (harmony) such as harmony in mangalam, conventional usage words, letters, thanam, gender, caste or colour, food, day, jati and ganam.

Some common points as regards the seven Swarams given in Isai-Tamil and other works.

Number.	Swarams.	Names of Swarams.	The birth place of Swarams.	Comparison of Srutis.	Comparison of Tastes.	Comparison of Smells.	Letters.	Matthiras.	Palai.	How they generate.	The author.
1	2	3	4	5	6	7	8	9	10	11	12
1	SA.	Kural ...	Throat...	Peacock.	Milk ...	Mavval ...	அ. ஆ.	4	Chempalai ...	Kural in Oolai.	Visvamitra.
2	RI.	Tuttham	Tongue.	Ox ...	Honey ...	Mullai ...	இ. ஈ.	4	Padumalaip-palai.	Thuttham in Ili.	Samathkini.
3	GA.	Kaikilai.	Palate...	Goat ..	Curd ...	Kadambu ...	உ. ஊ.	3	Chevvalippalai	Kaikilai in Vilari	Chandran.
4	MA.	Oolai ...	Head ...	Stork ...	Ghee ...	Vanchi ...	எ. ஏ.	2	Arumpalai ...	Oolai in Tharam.	Soorya.
5	PA.	Ili ...	Forehead	Cuckoo.	Cardamum.	Neythal ...	ஐ. இ.	4	Kodippalai ...	Ili in Kural ...	Gouthama.
6	DHA.	Vilari ...	Chest ...	Horse ...	Plantain ...	Ponnavirai ...	ஒ. ஓ.	3	Vilarippalai...	Vilari in Thuttham	Kasipa.
7	NI.	Tharam.	Nostrils.	Elephant.	Pomegranate	Punnai ...	ஔ. உ.	2	Merchempalai	Tharam in Kai-kilai.	Isan.

Some common points as regards the seven Swarams given in Isai-Tamil and other works.

Number.	Swarams.	Wife.	Athi Devatas.	Food.	Clothing.	Vahanam.	Precious stones.	Arms.	Isles of Origin	Trees.	Age.	Stars.	Days of the Week.
1	2	3	4	5	6	7	8	9	10	11		12	13
1	SA.	Gandarvas.	Sevvai...	Curd ...	White ...	Swan ...	Pearl ...	Knife ...	Sampu ...	Mango...	10	Chathayam.	Monday.
2	RI.	Kinnaras	Brahma.	Milk ...	Gold ...	Lion ...	Sapphire ...	Spear ...	Saga ...	Date ...	20	Chitra ...	Wednesday.
3	GA.	Yatchas.	Sarasvati	Flour Cakes.	Red ...	Kandaperundam	Diamond...	Gata ...	Kusa ...	Plantain.	30	Avittam ...	Thursday.
4	MA.	Kimburudas.	Isan ...	Chitrannam.	Blue ...	Deer ...	Chrysoprasus.	Wheel ...	Krounja ...	Lemon...	40	Magam ...	Tuesday.
5	PA.	Nagadevas.	Vishnu.	Flour ...	Yellow...	Chakaravagam.	Emerald ...	Pindipalam.	Salmali ...	Pomegranate.	50	Oothiram.	Friday.
6	DHA.	Rakshasas	Pillayar.	Good Food.	Parti-Colour.	Parrot ...	Sardonyx...	Narasam ...	Sweta ...	Vine ...	60	Pooradam.	Sunday.
7	NI.	Females.	Soorya...	Rice ...	Samalam	Minah ...	Topaz ...	Goad ...	Pushkara...	Punnai.	70	Anusham...	Saturday.

Here, we see that we can infer many things from the pah, the colour, the soil the star, the rasi and the graham from the special pah sung for the headman. Some points are mentioned for the seven Swarams on this principle.

It appears from the above table that the ancient experts in Isai-Tamil first made out by calculation the Jiva Swaram of a particular Ragam and then determined the athidevatas, the food, the clothing, the vahanam, the precious stones, the arms, and the trees etc. of that Jivaswaram. Along with these the table gives the place of origin of the seven Swarams, the particular sounds and the isles from which they generate. Many of these have fallen into disuse and have disappeared. Works relating to them are not now in existence. We shall know more about them when such books can be obtained.

3. The Calculation of the 12 Swarams that occur in Ayapalai which is found in works on Isai-Tamil.

We have hitherto noted clearly the seven Swarams which were in use in Isai-Tamil, and the 12 Swarams of Ayapalai which are derived in the 12 Rasis by arranging them in the concordant string, branch string, inimical string, friendly string and the second string. We have also noted how the 12 Swarams of the octave are obtained by the Sa-Pa system (concordant series) in the Vattapalai Chakaram proceeding by the right, and how the same are obtained (branch series) by the Sa-Ma system proceeding by the left.

We have also stated before, (in pages 740-741) the intervals of the six mother Ragas and their modern names and we have given the 12 Swarams obtained by proceeding on the right by the order of Kural, Ili &c., and their respective Alakus. In the same manner, the 12 Swarams obtained while proceeding on the left by the order of Oolai, Kural &c., and their respective Alakus are also given in page 743.

I think that all men with knowledge of music will accept that these are the 12 Swarams that are in use in Karnatic music at the present day. These 12 Swarams are not an innovation but what have been in use under the Ayapalai and Vattapalai systems among the Tamilians for many thousand years, even before the age of the first Sangam.

There is reason to think that the 12 Swarams of the Ayapalai used in ancient times in the South Tamil country were carried to many places and adopted with slight modifications. This we have to emphasise in spite of the fact, that when Lemuria was submerged, the remnants of the Tamilians went and settled in the lands opposite to them, and that though they appeared to be different races with different colours and languages owing to peculiarities of the climate and the natural surroundings of their new homes, yet from the Tamil words found mixed in their new languages and the 12 Swarams which they had been using in music, it is established without doubt that they came from a common stock.

It appears that the knowledge of the 12 Swarams which was kept up for many thousand years mainly by the strength of a well-developed ear for music, must have varied here and there slightly. Then came the new measurement of Pythagoras 2500 years ago, when he fixed $\frac{2}{3}$ of a string for Sa-Pa and $\frac{3}{4}$ of it for Sa-Ma. Though these Swarams may be approximately correct when taken by themselves, yet when fixed as the standard, and multiplied many times over, their result does not tally with the measurements of many well-known resultant Swarams.

To add to this, the theory of Sarnga Dev, advocating 22 Srutis in the octave, gave room to many doubts. As it is very necessary to clear these doubts, we have treated about them in Part II.

It is necessary to understand the calculations of the 12 Swarams of Ayapalai before entering into the Swarams and minuter Srutis of Indian Music.

We have noted already that the measurement of the Sthayis given in ancient Isai-Tamil—if Athara Sa be 1, Madhya Sa should be 2 and the end Sa of the Tara Sthayi should be 4—concurs with Sarnga Dev's measurement for the Sthayis. We must examine how the Sthayis proceed upwards in the ratio of 1, 2 and 4 producing a gradually ascending series of 12 Swarams without admitting any other possible sound in the middle.

When we take Kural to be the end Swaram or standard Swaram in the three Sthayis, low, middling and high, the seven Swarams which follow, namely, Thuttham, Kaikilai, Oolai, Ili, Vilari, Tharam and Kural, become 12 Swarams in the 12 Rasis. We have noted this already. Here the commencing Swaram should be calculated from Itapam and the last Swaram should be Kural. When we follow this calculation, if the Sa below the Mandara Sthayi be $\frac{1}{2}$, the finishing Sa of the same will be 1, if the ending Sa of Mandhara Sthayi be 1, the ending Sa of the Madhya Sthayi will be 2. If the ending Sa of Madhya Sthayi be 2, the ending Sa of the Tara Sthayi will be 4.

In all the three Sthayis the progression of the series of Swarams should be uniform. For, commencing from Athara Sa or 1, the 12 Swarams should ascend gradually with equal intervals without admitting any other possible Swaram in the middle. The end Swaram which is 2 will be the Madhya Sa. How we proceed from 1, the Adhara Sa, to 2, the Madhya Sa, is shown in the table in the next page

The calculations to show that the Swarams used by the ancient Tamilians in Ayapalai are the ones used at present in Karnatic music.

Number.	Rasi.	Names of Srutis And Alakus.	How the 12 Swarams proceed gradually upwards from 1 to 2. by powers of $\sqrt[12]{2}$	The logarithm of the powers of $\sqrt[12]{2}$	The Anti—logarithms for the numbers in col. 4.	Vibrations of each Swaram if Sa=540	Vibrations of each Swaram if Sa=240	The location of the 12 Swarams in the first half of the whole string.	The position of the Swarams in a wire 32 inches long.	Measurement by inches of the Swara Sthanams while proceeding upwards from Athara Sa.	The intervals (in length) between Swarams.	The cents of Ellis for the 12 Swarams
1	2		3	4	5	6	7	8	9	10	11	12
0	Idabam	S	$(\sqrt[12]{2})^0$	·000000000	1·000000	540·00	240·00	1·0000000	32·0000	0		0
1	Midunam	R_2	$(\sqrt[12]{2})^1$	·025085833	1·059463	572·11	254·28	0·9438743	30·2040	1·7960	1·7960	100
2	Kadagam	R_1	$(\sqrt[12]{2})^2$	·050171667	1·122462	606·13	269·40	0·8908986	28·5088	3·4912	1·6952	200
3	Simmum	G_2	$(\sqrt[12]{2})^3$	·075257500	1·189207	642·17	285·41	0·8408963	26·9087	5·0913	1·6001	300
4	Kanni	G_1	$(\sqrt[12]{2})^4$	·100343333	1·259921	680·36	302·38	0·7937005	25·3984	6·6016	1·5103	400
5	Thulam	M_2	$(\sqrt[12]{2})^5$	·125429167	1·334840	720·81	320·36	0·7491535	23·9729	8·0271	1·4255	500
6	Viruchigam	M_1	$(\sqrt[12]{2})^6$	·150515000	1·414214	763·68	339·41	0·7071069	22·6274	9·3726	1·3455	600
7	Thanusu	P_2	$(\sqrt[12]{2})^7$	·175600833	1·498307	809·09	359·50	0·6674199	21·3574	10·6426	1·2700	700
8	Magaram	D_2	$(\sqrt[12]{2})^8$	·200686667	1·587401	857·20	380·98	0·6299601	20·1587	11·8413	1·1987	800
9	Kumbam	D_1	$(\sqrt[12]{2})^9$	·225772500	1·681793	908·17	403·63	0·5946036	19·0273	12·9727	1·1314	900
10	Meenam	N_2	$(\sqrt[12]{2})^{10}$	·250858333	1·781797	962·17	427·63	0·5612309	17·9594	14·0406	1·0679	1000
11	Medam	N_1	$(\sqrt[12]{2})^{11}$	·275944167	1·887749	1019·38	453·05	0·5297315	16·9514	15·0486	1·0080	1100
12	Idabam	S_1	$(\sqrt[12]{2})^{12}$	·301030000	2·000000	1080·00	480·00	0·5000000	16·0000	16·0000	0·9514	1200

The logarithm of 1 is 0. The logarithm of 2 is ·301030000. These may be seen in Chamber's Mathematical Tables in the first and second lines in page 2. If this ·301030000 be divided by 12 we get ·025085833 which is the logarithm of the first of the 12 Swarams (which have 2 for their number). If this be multiplied by 2, we get the logarithm for the second Swaram, and if multiplied by 3 we get the logarithm for the third Swaram and so on. The logarithms of all the 12 Swarams are obtained in this manner. These are found in Col. 4 of the above table.

The logarithm of 2 has been divided by 12 and multiplied in order by the numbers 1 to 12. This is given in col. 3. The second column gives the Alakus for the 12 Swarams in the 12 Sthanams with their respective Rasis.

If we notice the numbers of the logarithms for the 12 Swarams we find ·0000000000 to be 1. The 12th logarithm ·301030000 gets 2. The fourth column gives the root numbers of the 12 Swarasthanams of the Sthayi progressing from 1 to 2. In the same way the numbers of the 12 Swarasthanams from 1 to 2 should be noted.

1. We may see in the 10th line on page 7 of Chamber's Mathematical Tables that the number 1.059463 is the anti-logarithm for the logarithm of ·025085833 as seen in column 4 against number 1.

2. The same book tells us (P. 8 line 23) that the number 1·122462 is the anti-logarithm for the logarithm of ·050171667 (See col. 4 against number 2).

3. The number 1·189207 is found in page 9 and line 40. (See col. 5 against 3).
4. The number in col. 5 is found in p. 11 line 10.
5. The fifth number in col. 5 is found in p. 12 line 35.
6. The number in the sixth line of col. 5 is found in p. 14 line 15.
7. The seventh number in p. 15 line 49.
8. The eighth number in p. 17 line 38.
9. The ninth in p. 19 line 32.
10. The tenth in p. 21 line 32.
11. The eleventh in p. 23 line 39.
12. The twelfth in p. 26 line 1.

These 12 antilogarithms of the fifth column are given in decimals.

The 5th column indicates the measurements of the 12 Swarams in the octave if Athara Sa be 1 and the end Sa of the Madhya Sthayi be 2. These proceed in geometrical progression. The fixed number is 2. The twelve logarithms of 2 are mentioned in Col. 4. The antilogarithms for the logarithms in Col. 4 are given in Col. 5.

We find, then, that this is the opinion of the ancient Tamilians, that this is the system of Vattapalai and the one advocated by Sarnga Dev. This is the measurement of the natural series. Having this as the basis, we may determine the vibrations and the position of the Swarams in the wire. The measurements have been calculated down to several places of decimals so that they may be minute and at the same time accurate without causing any doubt. To examine only two or three places of decimals may be easy, but there is a chance of the calculations causing doubt if we stop there. So we request those who are earnest about it, to examine the calculations down to four places at least.

The calculation of vibrations of the 12 Swarams of Ayapalai.

We noticed how the series of 12 Swarams in the octave proceeded gradually upwards from 1 to 2 according to the established rule if Athara Sa be 1, Madhya Sthayi Sa is 2. Now we should note how we obtain the vibrations for the 12 Swarams found in Col. 5. We have stated in Part IV, pages 722-729 that if we suppose Athara Sa to have 540 vibrations per second, then Madhya Sa will have double or 1080 vibrations and Tara Sa will have 2160 vibrations or double that of Madhya Sa and that this is in conformity with the breath of man and the sound of the Yal. We see in column 6 of the table how the upward progression of 540 vibrations to 1080 is a gradually ascending series of 12 steps from Athara Sa to Madhya Sa and from Madhya Sa to Thara Sa.

We see from col. 5 that the logarithm of 0 is 1·000000. When we multiply this by 540 we get 540. This is the number of vibrations for Athara Sa If we multiply 1·059463, the anti-logarithm (of 1) in Col. 5 by 540, we get 572·11, and if 1·122462 the anti-logarithm (of 2) in col. 5 by 540, we obtain 606·13. In the same way if the anti-logarithms given in col. 5 in all the 12 lines be multiplied by 540, we get the vibrations of all the 12 Swarams. These are given in col. 6.

We have given the vibrations for the 12 Swarams in col. 7 supposing Athara Sa to be 240, as this measurement is advocated by some writers. We should proceed to find out the position of the 12 Swarams in a wire 32 inches long.

The location of the 12 Swarams in the exact half of a wire 32 inches long where the Madhya Sthayi ends.

The number 1 seen at the top of col. 8 of the above table is the length of the wire. The Madhya Sa occurs exactly in the middle of this length, and Tara Sa is located in exactly a quarter of this length. The number 1 which is found in col. 5 is the number for the logarithm 0 in col. 4. The product of the numbers found in cols. 5 and 8 is always 1. The numbers in col. 5 found opposite the Swarams of the 12 places when made to divide 1, give us the measurements of the 12 Swarasthanams found in col. 8.

The ·5 which is obtained for the 12th place or Sa of the Madhya Sthayi is half of the Athara Sa. The Sthanams for the 12 Swarams are found in col. 8. We should next see the places where they occur in a wire 32 inches long with the same measurements.

The measurements of the Swarams up to Madhya Sa in a wire 32 inches long.

We noted in col. 8 that if the whole length of the wire be 1, the Madhya sthayi Sa occurs exactly at the middle of the whole length. We have also mentioned in pages 700 to 708 in Part IV, how the Yal resembled the human body.

This distance from the centre of the brow to the *Moolatharam* is 48 (or 47½) inches. This should be divided into 4 equal parts of a *chan* (or nearly a foot) each. Of these the distance of 3 *chans* is the place for Swarams and the remaining space is left vacant. We have there pointed out the relation between the measurement of the Sthoola Sareeram according to the measurement of the human hand and the distance of Swarams in the Yal. According to this measurement the Athara SA will sound at the 16th inch or half the length of the wire which is 32 inches long from the Meru to the Mettu. The Madhya Sthayi SA sounds at the 16th inch from Meru. We must see how these 12 Swarams ascend gradually from the Meru up to the 16th inch.

If each of the measurements of the 12 Swarams (given in col. 8) which proceed from 1 to ½ be multiplied by 32 we get the measurements for the 12 Swarams given in col. 9. We see that the 12th Swaram or Madhya Sthayi SA is located exactly at the 16th inch in a wire 32 inches long.

The 10th column gives the intervals of each of the 12 Swarams beginning from the Meru and ending at the 16th inch. These measurements of the Swarasthanams are obtained by subtracting the measurements given in col. 9 from the wire 32 inches long.

The table also shows how the 12 Swarams gradually increase in pitch up to the Madhya Sthayi SA (found in line 12) and come to an end at the 16th inch of the wire whose total length is 32 inches.

Col. 11 gives the length of wire of the intervals between Swarasthanams. The difference of the intervals is shown here. We see, then, that the 12 Mettus of the Yal gradually decrease in intervals but increase in pitch in conformity with the natural growth of the human spine.

The cents calculations for the 12 Swarams.

The 12th column gives the cents measurements. Here the Sthayi is divided into 1200 cents. There is a regular and uniform progression in the number of cents also. This shows that the Sruti system of Sarnga Dev which speaks of the 12 Swarams as a gradually ascending series without admitting any other Swaram in the middle and the system of Ayapalai of the ancient Tamilians by the SA-PA and the SA-MA principles are quite correct. The 12th col. gives the cents which anybody could easily understand.

In all the 12 columns of the above table, we have given the calculations, the number of vibrations, the length of wire and the cents corresponding to the 12 Swarams of the octave.

We think that this system is the one where the minuteness of the difference in sounds is clearly seen. All other systems which do not agree with this are surely at fault. This is the measurement of the series of sounds which correspond with nature.

We have stated before that to take SA-PA as $\frac{3}{2}$ and SA-MA as $\frac{4}{3}$ is only a rough way of calculating. Although this calculation is approximately correct when we proceed by the system we shall be never able to obtain the other Swarams namely $\frac{1}{2}$, $\frac{1}{3}$, $\frac{1}{4}$, $\frac{1}{5}$, and $\frac{1}{6}$.

Again, we have seen in one of the previous tables that when we proceed by SA-PA as $\frac{3}{2}$ the Sthayi does not end exactly but has 24 cents over, and 24 cents less when proceeding by SA-MA as $\frac{4}{3}$. Therefore it is quite clear that this system will never agree with that mentioned in ancient Isai-Tamil where the calculations are made by the trained ear of the musician. We consider that the calculation by geometrical progression is the one best suited to understand the system of the ancient Isai-Tamil.

We think that this system of the calculation of Srutis alone will satisfy the author of Tholkaupiam who speaks of the four different kinds of Yal — Marutham, Kurinji, Neythal and Palai,—Ilankavodigal, who mentions the four Jathis,—Abanilai, Puranilai, Arugial and Perugial when change of Graham is made for each of the Yals, and Sarnga Dev who advocates change of Graham of Srutis. Any other system will not be so very minute as this.

We might have heard the gramaphone which records the sweet sounds of man and reproduces them. We also know that the reproduced voice does not altogether resemble the particular human voice. When we ask the why of it, we find that it is due to the fact that the recorder which receives the human sound is made of mica and thin plates of zinc, and that there is a vast difference between this and the recorder inside the human ear. In the same way the recording of sounds by the siren and that by the human ear will only be approximately the same and not completely so.

In the systems of Ayapalai and Vattapalai in use among the ancient Tamils, it is distinctly stated that the Sthayi comes to an end in the 12 Rasis by the SA-PA or the concordant series and SA-MA or branch series. It is this calculation for the 12 Swarams of the Sthayi that corresponds with that system. We have noted in page 740 how the seven Swarams out of the 12 occur in the six mother Ragas with particular intervals. We have also stated in p. 741, the different Alakus for the six mother Ragas in the 12 Swarams. The Alakus for the 12 Swarams obtained by the SA-PA and the SA-MA series are given in pages 742 and 743.

These are the 12 Swarams used in Ayapalai pertaining to the 14 Kovais found in Senkotiyal. These are the Swarams used even by the apes which lived on the shores of Lemuria noted for its Isai-Tamil.

There was a good deal of controversy and doubt as regards these 12 Swarams and these came to an end only about 120 years ago in Europe. These were first used by Haydn (1732-1809) and Mozart (1756-1826). As the 12 Swarams of the octave were equally divided and pianos constructed, modulation in all the keys became possible. This modulation was brought to perfection by the celebrated Beethoven (1770-1827) about 120 years ago. So Equal Temperament was introduced as recently as 120 years ago. These are the 12 Swarams divided into equal semitones in Equal Temperament.

Captain Day mentions that before Equal Temperament was introduced into Europe, Indian musicians have used it in the music of the Yal. These are the 12 Swarams used by Mathavi 2000 years ago in the Sakota Yal with 2 Sthayis and 14 Kovais.

These are the 12 Swarams of the Vattapalai (where Oolai occurs as Kural) mentioned in the *Paripadal* of the poet Nallanduvanar who flourished at the close of the third Sangam about 3000 years ago. The Stanza is as follows :—

"பூஊது வண்டினம் யாழ் கொண்ட கொளை கேண்மின்
கொளைப்பொரு டெரிதரக் கொளுத்தாமற் குரல்கொண்ட
இன்னிசைத் தாங்கொளைச் சீர்க்குங்கிளைச்சுற்ற
வுழைச்சுரும்பின் கேழ்கெழு பாலையிசை யோர்மின்"

The four kinds of Yal, Marutham, Kurinji, Neythal, Palai, mentioned by the author of Tholkaupium who flourished at the close of the first Sangam about 8000 years ago, and the four kinds of Yal in Vattapalai derived from Sa-Ma and Pa-Ni are all derived from these 12 Swarams.

So we conclude from the above that even as early as 8000 years ago, and even at an earlier age from the commencement of the first Sangam i.e., 12000 years ago, the ancient Tamilians have had their Ganam with these 12 Swarams as the basis.

Some more beautiful points of coincidence which are found in the above calculations will be noticed in the calculation of Srutis that follows.

The 12 Swarams of the Ayapalai of the ancient Tamilians and the mathematical calculation of the Swarams compared with the calculations of other writers.

We have noticed till now what the measurements of the 12 Swarams of the Ayapalai were. The mathematical calculations of Srutis and Swarams by various writers were mentioned in Part II We think it necessary to compare in this place their fractional lengths of wires and cents calculctions with ours, especially in places where they most agree.

For, the measurement $\frac{2}{3}$ for Pa and $\frac{3}{4}$ for Ma has been used by many musicians of repute for many thousand years. We now take it upon ourselves to controvert their time-honoured theory by giving a new one which is in accordance with the systems of Ayapalai and Vattapalai in use among the Tamilians of South Madura for ages. Hence the necessity for the comparison.

The following table is divided into two sections. The first section shows how the Swarams proceed gradually upwards from Athara Sa or 1 to Madhya Sa or 2 in the order of 1, 2, 3, 4 &c. These are the Swarams that satisfy the rule of the ancient Tamilians and of musicians like Sarnga Dev and Bharata that Swarams should be a gradually ascending series which do not admit of any other possible Swaram in the middle. We do not think that there is any other correct method. Musicians of repute must acknowledge this.

If the logarithms found in Col. 4 be each of them multiplied by 1200 and divided by the logarithm of 2, we get the cents found in col. 5. These also are an ascending series like 1, 2, 3 with equal intervals. This is the opinion of the ancient Tamilians as well as that of Sarnga Dev. The mathematical calculations for the Sruti system of Saranga Dev are seen in the Table in page 406.

The 12 Swarams of the Ayapalai of the ancient Tamilians and the mathematical calculation of the Swarams compared with the calculations of other writers.

The calculation of the 12 Swarams which are in Geometrical Progression with equal measurements.						The calculation of others who take SA-PA to be $\frac{2}{3}$ and SA-MA to be $\frac{3}{4}$.		
Number.	Rasi.	Names of Srutis and Alakus.	How the 12 Swarams proceed gradually upwards from 1 to 2, by powers of $\sqrt[12]{2}$	The logarithm of the powers of $\sqrt[12]{2}$	The cents of Ellis for the 12 Swarams	The fractional length of wire.	The cents corresponding to the fractions.	The intervals for the 12 Swarams.
1	2		3	4	5	6	7	8
0	Idapam	S	$(\sqrt[12]{2})^0$	·000000000	0			
1	Midunam	R_2	$(\sqrt[12]{2})^1$	·025085833	100	$\frac{15}{16}$	112	112
2	Kadagam	R_1	$(\sqrt[12]{2})^2$	·050171667	200	$\frac{8}{9}$	204	92
3	Simham	G_2	$(\sqrt[12]{2})^3$	·075257500	300	$\frac{5}{6}$	316	111
4	Kanni	G_1	$(\sqrt[12]{2})^4$	·100343333	400	$\frac{4}{5}$	386	71
5	Thulam	M_2	$(\sqrt[12]{2})^5$	·125429167	500	$\frac{3}{4}$	498	112
6	Viruchigam	M_1	$(\sqrt[12]{2})^6$	·150515000	600	$\frac{32}{45}$	590	92
7	Thanusu	P_2	$(\sqrt[12]{2})^7$	·175600833	700	$\frac{2}{3}$	702	112
8	Magaram	D_2	$(\sqrt[12]{2})^8$	·200686667	800	$\frac{5}{8}$	814	112
9	Kumbam	D_1	$(\sqrt[12]{2})^9$	·225772500	900	$\frac{3}{5}$	884	70
10	Meenam	N_2	$(\sqrt[12]{2})^{10}$	·250858333	1000	$\frac{9}{16}$	996	112
11	Mesham	N_1	$(\sqrt[12]{2})^{11}$	·275944167	1100	$\frac{8}{15}$	1088	92
12	Idapam	S_2	$(\sqrt[12]{2})^{12}$	·301030000	1200	$\frac{1}{2}$	1200	112

Because of the difference owing to the necessity of accounting for the 22 Srutis in the octave there is an addition of 9 cents for each of the Swarams. Otherwise they will be correct. This will be seen in col. 10 of the Table in page 406.

In the second part the Swarasthanams which are in dispute at the present day, the fractions showing their respective lengths in the wire, their corresponding cents and their differences are given. They say that these measurements are those of the natural series and resemble the measurements which are determined by the siren. But we see the discrepencies in them in col. 8.

As these proceed with the presumption that SA-PA=$\frac{2}{3}$ and SA-MA=$\frac{3}{4}$ they have been driven to the necessity of selecting some from the SA-PA series, some from the SA-MA series and a lew cthers from SA-GA series. As these have different measurements we see without any doubt that they cannot be used for singing Grahaswaram nor can they account for the six mother Ragas derived by the change of Grahaswaram. We have noted above how the 12 Swarams are obtained as a gradually ascending series in Vattapalai either as SA-PA or concordant Swarams or as SA-MA or branch Swarams without any other possible Swaram in the middle.

To sum up, then, we distinctly see that the Swarams and their measurements as given in Ayapalai by the ancients are the correct ones. The System of $\frac{2}{3}$ and $\frac{3}{4}$ of Pythagoras, and the theory of 22 Srutis of Sarnga Dev and Bharata are completely wrong and they are altogether unfit for the purposes of Grahaswaram.

4. The mathematical calculations to prove that the 24 Srutis of the Vattapalai of the ancient Tamilians are the Srutis of the modern Karnatic music.

We have established now beyond doubt that the 12 Swarams obtained by the ancient Tamilians by the SA-PA and SA-MA systems are the Ayapalai, that these 12 are the very Swarams in use in modern Karnatic music, and that by rising gradually in geometrical progression they satisfy the principle that the series should be a gradually ascending one without admitting any other possible sound in the middle. Their number of vibrations has also been recorded. We should next proceed to find out how many of these Srutis occur between Athara SA and Madhya SA and give their mathematical calculation also.

In Part III we have divided a Sthayi into 12 Rasis, stating the concordant and discordant Swarams in each. We have also stated that two Swarams in particular Rasis should each of them be sung with one Alaku less and the Srutis then will be 24 in number when these 2 Alakus are added on.

Out of the 7 Swarams of an ascending and descending scale, the ancient Tamilians had made Ganam with 2 Alakus less either in two of the concordant or 2 of the branch Swarams.

From this it is clear that the ancients divided a Sthayi into 12 parts, and made 24 Srutis with 2 Alakus for each of the 12, and made their Ganam with 2 Alakus less in some cases, and not that they divided the octave itself into 22 Alakus. This theory of 22 Srutis seems to have been given out by mistake by Sarnga Dev, about 700 years ago when those who knew the rules and secrets of ancient music had become extinct.

The mathematical calculations to show that the 24 Srutis of Vattapalai of the ancient Tamilians are the identical Srutis in use in modern Karnatic music.

Number.	Rasi.	Name of Sruti and Alaku.	How the 24 Srutis proceed upwards gradually from 1 to 2 by the powers of $\sqrt[24]{2}$	The logarithm of $\sqrt[24]{2}$	Anti-logarithms for logs. given in col. 4.	Number of vibrations of each Swaram if SA 540.	Number of vibrations of each Swaram if SA=240.	Location of the 24 Swarams in the first half of the total length of wire	Location of the 24 Swarams in a wire 32 inches long.	Measurement by inches of each Swaram while proceeding from Allai in SA.	The intervals between Swarams.	Cents for the 24 Swarams.
1		2	3	4	5	6	7	8	9	10	11	12
		S.	$\sqrt[24]{2}$	·000000000	1·0000	540·0000	240·00	1·0000000	32·00000			0
1	Midhunam	R.	„ t[1]	·012542917	1·0293	555·8232	247·03	0·9715320	31·08902	·9110	·9110	50
2		R.	„ t[2]	·025085833	1·0595	572·1103	254·28	0·9438743	30·20398	1·7960	·8850	100
3	Kadagam	R.	„ t[3]	·037628750	1·0905	588·8743	261·72	0·9170042	29·34413	2·6559	·8599	150
4		R.	„ t[4]	·050171667	1·1225	606·1295	269·40	0·8908986	28·50876	3·4913	·8354	200
5	Simmam	G.	„ t[5]	·062714583	1·1554	623·8905	277·30	0·8655366	27·69717	4·3028	·8115	250
6		G.	„ t[6]	·075257500	1·1892	642·1719	285·41	0·8408964	26·90868	5·0913	·7885	300
7	Kanni	G.	„ t[7]	·087800417	1·2241	660·9890	293·78	0·8169577	26·14265	5·8574	·7661	350
8		G.	„ t[8]	·100343333	1·2599	680·3574	302·38	0·7937005	25·39842	6·6016	·7442	400
9	Thulam	M.	„ t[9]	·112886250	1·2968	700·2934	311·23	0·7711055	24·67538	7·3246	·7230	450
10		M.	„ t[10]	·125429167	1·3348	720·8136	320·36	0·7491535	23·97291	8·0271	·7025	500
11	Viruchigam	M.	„ t[11]	·137972083	1·3740	741·9350	329·76	0·7278265	23·29045	8·7096	·6825	550
12		M.	„ t[12]	·150515000	1·4142	763·6754	339·41	0·7071069	22·62742	9·3726	·6630	600
											·6441	

The mathematical calculations to show that the 24 Srutis of Vattapalai of the ancient Tamilians are the identical Srutis in use in modern Karnatic music.

Number.	Rasi.	Name of Sruti and Alaku.	How the 24 Srutis proceed upwards gradually from 1 to 2 by the powers of $\sqrt[24]{2}$	Logarithms of $\sqrt[24]{2}$	Anti-logarithms for logs. given in col. 4.	Number of vibrations of each Swaram if Sa=540.	Number of vibrations of each Swaram if Sa=240.	Location of the 24 Swarams in the first half of the total length of wire	Location of the 24 Swarams in a wire 32 inches long.	Measurement by inches of each Swaram while proceeding from Athira Sa.	The intervals between Swarams.	Cents for the 24 Swarams.
1		2	3	4	5	6	7	8	9	10	11	12
13	Thanusu	P_1	$\sqrt[24]{2}^{t13}$	.163057917	1·4557	786·0528	349·37	0·6869768	21·98326	10·0167		650
14		P_2	,, t^{14}	.175600833	1·4983	809·0858	359·50	0·6674199	21·35744	10·6426	·6259	700
15	Magaram	D_1	,, t^{15}	·188143750	1·5422	832·7939	370·13	0·6484198	20·74944	11·2506	·6080	750
16		D_2	,, t^{16}	·200686667	1·5874	857·1966	380·98	0·6299601	20·15872	11·8413	·5907	800
17	Kumbam	D_3	,, t^{17}	.213229583	1·6340	882·3145	392·16	0·6120268	19·58486	12·4151	·5738	850
18		D_4	,, t^{18}	·225772500	1·6818	908·1681	403·63	0·5946036	19·02732	12·9727	·5576	900
19	Meenam	N_1	,, t^{19}	·238315417	1·7311	934·7794	415·46	0·5776764	18·48564	13·5144	·5317	950
20		N_2	,, t^{20}	·250858333	1·7818	962·1707	427·63	0·5612310	17·95939	14·0406	·5262	1000
21	Medam	N_3	,, t^{21}	·263401250	1·8440	990·3644	440·16	0·5452539	17·44812	14·5519	.5113	1050
22		N_4	,, t^{22}	·275944167	1·8877	1019·3844	453·05	0·5297315	16·95141	15·0489	·4967	1100
23	Idabam	S_1	,, t^{23}	·288487083	1·9431	1049·2546	466·34	0.51465110	16·46883	15·5312	·4826	1150
24		S_2	,, t^{24}	·301030000	2·0000	1080·0000	480.00	0.5000000	16·00000	16·0000	·4688	1200

We have mentioned here and there in many places that there can be but 24 Srutis in the octave and that any system which advocates either more or less can never satisfy the rules of Karnatic music which had always used 24 Srutis in its Ganams.

We have given a few Ragas as examples where even modern Karnatic music uses only 22 Srutis out of the 24 omitting two concordant and branch Srutis. The author of Sangeeta Ratnakaram speaks of the number of Srutis as 1, 2, 3, 4, 9, 22, 66 and even says there are numberless Srutis but finally settles it as 22. These 22 Srutis are nothing but the 22 out of the 24 Alakus of Isai-Tamil used by the Tamilians. Two Alakus have been reduced in Vilari and Kaikilai.

We emphatically say that Sarnga Dev is wrong when he says that there are 22 Srutis in the octave and that if the octave be so divided the resultant Swarams and Srutis will never satisfy Karnatic music.

We, again, emphatically assert that the ancient Tamilians about 12000 years ago used the 7 Swarams of the Sthayi, the 12 half Swarams of a Rasi Vattam, and the 24 Alakus of Srutis which have 2 Alakus in each of the 12 Rasis, as Ayapalai and Vattapalai of Isai-Tamil. Their system of Vattapalai clearly indicates that the Srutis of Karnatic music are 24 and that they never mentioned 22 Srutis in the octave.

Just as we gave before the mathematical calculations and measurements of the 12 Swarams, we must now determine the measurements of the 24 Srutis in the octave.

Granting that, according to the theory of the ancients, if Athara SA be 1 Madhya SA is 2, the 24 Alakus or Swarams should be produced here just as the 12 Swarams generated from Ayapalai as a gradually ascending series with no other possible Swarams between.

For, the logarithm of the fixed number 2 is ·301030000. When divided by 24 this gives us ·012542917 which is the logarithm of the first Sruti. If we multiply this by 1 up to 24 in succession we get the logarithms given in column 4 of the Table. The anti-logarithms for each of these is given in column 5. The logarithms for the 12 Swarams which occur by twos are given in page 749.

The logarithms for the 12 Srutis occurring in odd Alakus are given in the following pages and lines of Chamber's Mathematical tables :—

(1)	RI¹	·012542917	6th page	line 30.
(3)	RI³	·037628750	7th ,,	,, 41.
(5)	GA¹	·062714583	9th ,,	,, 6.
(7)	GA³	·087800417	10th ,,	,, 25.
(9)	MA¹	·112886250	11th ,,	,, 47.
(11)	MA³	·137972083	13th ,,	,, 25.
(13)	PA¹	·163057917	15th ,,	,, 6.
(15)	DHA¹	·188143750	16th ,,	,, 43.
(17)	DHA³	·213229583	18th ,,	,, 35.
(19)	NI¹	·238315417	20th ,,	,, 32.
(21)	NI³	·263401250	22nd ,,	,, 45.
(23)	SA¹	·288487083	24th ,,	,, 44.

It is shown in column 4 how the 24 Alakus proceed upwards from 1 to 24. Here the figure 1·0293 found in column 5 against Ri is the anti-logarithm for ·012542917 which is a 24th of ·301030000, the logarithm of the integer 2. If this number is multiplied by 1, 2, 3, 4......24 in succession, at the 24th step it will give the product 2. The sixth column gives the number of vibrations for the 24 Srutis assuming that Athara Sa has 540 vibrations. These are obtained by multiplying each of the figures in column 5 by 540.

In column 7 we have given the resultant figures obtained by multiplying each of the figures in column 5 by 240, as some suppose that Athara Sa has 240 vibrations.

The Sa of the upper Sthayi sounds in exactly half the length of the wire from Meru to Mettu. So the 8th column gives the measurements for the Srutis commencing from Athara Sa as 1 and proceeding upwards to the Madhya Sa which is the exact half of the whole string. Here, if the number 1 at the top of column 8 be divided by the numbers 1, 2.........24 found in column 5 in succession, the length of the wire where the Srutis speak will be indicated.

The exact half of a wire 32 inches long from Meru to Mettu is 16 inches. Column 9 gives the measurement for the 24 Alakus as they occur in the wire up to 16 inches. They show the Swarasthanams for the 24 Alakus in the 16 inches, which are obtained by multiplying the lengths of wire in column 8 by 32.

The 10th column gives the measurements for the 24 Srutis in the 16 inches wire from Athara Sa to Madhya Sa. This is obtained by subtracting 32 inches given at the top from each of the measurements given for the 24 Srutis in column 9.

The 11th column gives the length of wire between each of the Srutis. This shows the difference in measurements of the 24 Srutis as given in column 10.

The cents calculations are given in column 12. We noted before at the end of column 4 that the logarithm for the fixed number 2 was ·301030000. The 24 Srutis of the Sthayi finish with the number 2. If we divide the Sthayi into 1200 cents, we may obtain the respective cents for the 24 Srutis by multiplying the numbers 1, 2, 3......24 given in column 4 by 1200 and dividing each of them by the logarithm of 2. Here each Sruti progresses by 50 cents. In other words, we get 24 Srutis in the Sthayi where each Sruti progresses upwards by 50 cents without admitting any possible sound between, having a total of 1200 cents for the Sthayi.

We may like to know what the meaning of 'cents' is. The western expert Mr. Ellis gives this measurement for the minute Srutis of a Sthayi. He seems to have travelled through Asia, Europe and America to study the musical system of these countries. Finding that each country had a different Sruti System, he gave this cents system with a view to mark the minute Srutis and unify them all. He divides the Sthayi into 12 Swarams, and each of the Swarams into 100, thus getting 1200 parts for the whole. It is easy to determine Swarasthanams by means of cents. Minute differences in measurements may easily be reckoned by this method. We had to speak about this method as it is useful in determining the calculations for the minute Srutis of Karnatic music.

The concord among Srutis.

We noted the measurements for the 24 Srutis just now, so we shall do well to note the concordant relation among them.

We have observed before that the ancient Tamils knew well the calculations of Srutis standing in the relation of Inai, Kilai, Natpu and Second string. They made their ganam on the above principle avoiding the discordant Pagai strings, third and sixth. The Srutis proceed by fourteens in the relation of Inai. Thus Ri^4 in line 4 and Dha^4 in line 18 are derived. We may find that the 12 Swarams of the Sthayi are obtained on the principle of Inai occurring in the seventh Rasis and as fourteenth Srutis.

In the same manner the Sa-Ma series are obtained on the principle of Kilai or the fifth Rasi or the 10th Swarams. For example, Ni^2 occurs on the 20th line, Ga^2 in the 6th line above it Dha^2 in the 16th line above and Ma^1 in the 12th line above and so on. Thus the 12 Swarams proceed by tens.

In the same manner the Natpu string in the fourth Rasi has eight Srutis. In other words this is the Sa-Ga series. The Ga^1 in line 8, Dha in line 16, and Sa in line 8 above it stand concordant in the relation of Natpu.

Likewise, among the odd Rasis the Ri in line 1 is in concordance with Dha in line 14, and Ri^3 in line 3 with Dha^3 in the 14th line from it on the principle of Sa, Pa. The same rule applies to others also.

Just as Sa-Ma is the 10th Sruti, so also is Ma^3 to Ri^1, Pa^1 to Ri^3, Dha^1 to Ga^1, Ni^1 to Ma^1 and so on. Again, just as 1 is to 4, 4 is to 7, 7 to 10, 10 to 13 and so on. Again as 1 is to 6, so is 6 to 13, 11 to 16 and so on. No matter what interval is taken the Swarams that are concordant with it will stand in the same harmonious relation.

We see clearly, then, that according to this system 24 Srutis are obtained in the Sthayi as a progressive series without admitting any other possible sound between, that these were the Srutis used by the ancient Tamils in their ganam, that these are the present ones in use and also the Srutis of the future.

Again, if the logarithm of Ri^1 given in column 4 be multiplied by 2 we get the logarithm of Ri^2, and if it be multiplied by 3 we get the logarithm of Ri^3, if we multiply it by 4 we get the logarithm of Ri^4 and so on for the rest of the Srutisthanams.

Again, if 1·0293 the antilogarithm of the logarithm of Ri^1 given in column 5, be multiplied by itself we get the figure for Ri^2, if the antilogarithm of Ri^2 be multiplied by that of Ri^1 we get the figure for Ri^3, and if the antilogarithm for Ri^3 be multiplied by that for Ri^1 we get the figure for Ri^4 and so on for all the Sruti Sthanams.

Again in column 5 we may see that the fractions for Srutis gradually increase and finish with two, while the length of wire in column 8 gradually decreases ending in ½. If the figure in column 5 against Ri^1 be multiplied by the figure in column 8, the product will be 1. Likewise, the figure against Ri^2 in column 5 and column 8 be multiplied, the product will be 1. The same product will result if the figures in column 5 and column 8 were multiplied. The figures in column 5, and column 8 for the 24th Sruti, namely 2 and ·5, when multiplied give the product 1.

Besides this, the first figure of column 8 when multiplied with that for the 23rd line will give the product ½. Likewise the figure in column 8 against 2 when multiplied with that against 22, the product will be ½. Similarly the multiplication of the 3rd with the 21st, the 4th with the 20th, the 5th with the 19th. the 6th with the 18th. the 7th with the 17th, the 8th with the 16th, the 9th with the 15th, the 10th with the 14th. the 11th with the 13th, in column 8 will give the product ½. If the figure in the 12th be squared, the product will also be ½. Unless such a relation exists between Swarams and Srutis, change of graham and singing of grahaswaram will be absolutely impossible. If this system is not adopted some of the beautiful lakshanams of music will be lost, Srutis will differ, different kinds of measurements will result and innumerable tables full of doubt will have to be formed like the ones given above.

All these doubts resulted from the fact that Sarnga Dev mentioned 22 Srutis in the octave though he adopted the excellent system of the ancient Tamils as regards arriving at Srutis. If Sarnga Dev had mentioned these 22 Srutis as an example of Kalaimalayvu given in the rules of ancient Isai Tamil we would have made much of his theory. It would have been better if he had not said that Sa-Pa has 12 Srutis and Sa-Ma 8. Including the commencing and the ending Swarams Sa-Pa has 14 and Sa Ma 10 Srutis. We may doubt here whether the numbers 14 and 10 agree with the 14 Inai Srutis and 10 Kilai Srutis and whether this was the system of the Tamils. If we observe a little deeply we may see that if we exclude the commencing Sruti Sa-Pa has 14 and Sa-Ma. 10 Srutis. But when the commencing Swaram is included Sa-Pa should be 15 and Sa-Ma 11. But Sarnga Dev, omitting the commencing Swaram, gives 13 for Sa-Pa and 9 for Sa-Ma or 22 Srutis in all. Isai Tamil distinctly says there are 12 Rasis, (7 in the relation of Inai, and 5 in the relation of Kilai,) 12 Swarams in the Rasis and 24 Makus or Srutis in the Sthayi (14 in Sa-Pa and 10 in Sa-Ma).

Isai Tamil gives excellent rules for the 7 Swarams, 12 half Swarams and 24 Srutis as represented in the Rasis with excellent measurements. These could never change though the sun and the moon may change their course. We regret that many people did not understand these precious rules and gave different theories. Other points to be noted in connection with the determination of Srutis are mentioned at the end of Part II pages 400-414.

5. The calculations for the minute Srutis employed in South Indian or Karnatic Music.

We have showed before how according to the system of Vattapalai (where the Srutis are obtained by the principles of Inai and Kilai) as used by the ancient Tamils in South Madura.

(1) There are 12 Swarams.

(2) That the Seven Isais or Swarams are in the Rasi order of 1, 2, 2, 1, 2, 2. 2.

(3) That the six Northen Ragas are generated by the change of graham of the Swarams of the 12 Rasis.

(4) That an Alaku was lessened in Vilari and Kaikilai or 2 Alakus were lessened out of the 24 and Ganam was made in the 22.

(5) That we are at present using in the Karnatic Music the seven Isais used by them.

(6) That the 12 Swarams of Ayapalai are within our practical experience.

(7) That there is doubt about the 22 out of the 24 Alakus of Vattapalai.

We have given mathematical calculations also for the 24 Srutis so that there may be no longer any doubt about the question of Srutis.

To those scholars who are anxious to know the antiquity and minuteness of South Indian music we are sure what we have stated hitherto is quite enough to convince them. It is a matter for great wonder that such rare things have been mentioned many thousands of years ago, and that they throw into shade the advanced opinions of the modern day. However we must not stop here but consider another thing of very great importance. The sweet Ragas we are in the habit of singing are not confined to the seven Swarams or the 12 half Swarams or even the 24 Swarams. Unless we have a definite knowledge of this, our doubts will be often recurring.

If we notice the Swarams used in the 10000 ancient Isais found in works on Isai-Tamil in use in the ancient Tamil country or the Swarams used in the *Puns* like Thirugnanam, Thevaram and Thiruvachakam according to the ancient system, we shall be surprised to find that more Srutis than 24, and minuter ones, are found in them. The *Puns* and Ragas of ancient times have had their names changed and sung at the modern day as Parsi, Hindustani and English notes to suit modern tastes. Very seldom we come across the beautiful chanting of the ancient Thevara *Puns* and the rare excellence which they had in convincing the minds of the hearers. Next to them in beauty come the Kshetrya *Pathams*. Even these, we find, have become rare.

The beauty of old Ragas should be attributed to the minute Srutis in which they were sung. As it was difficult to determine what those Srutis were, even the seven primary Swarams were doubted. When one of these minute Swarams occurred along with the seven Swarams, it was found to be a little higher or lower in pitch. So this made them say "there is a difference between your Swarams and ours, your Swarams are incorrect." They not only argued this way but tried to produce different measurements in support of their statement. But this only increased the confusion still more, and no definiteness was arrived at.

So long as we do not understand these minute Srutis, the minuteness of ancient Isai-Tamil will be a sealed book to us, nor could we understand the subtlety of modern Ragas which are sung according to ancient rules. We could not write out the Swarams and Srutis for the modern Ragas either. The result will be that the minuteness of the musical system will gradually disappear and we shall have to rest content with 12 Swarams only. Others might also accuse us of singing Karnatic Ragas incorrectly, without knowing the Srutis. Just as the Karnatic Ragas have lost their ancient Tamil names and are called by foreign names, so they might, in course of time, lose their minute Swarams also and be reduced to music with 12 Swarams only. So we see the necessity of studying these minute Srutis deeply.

We have noted before from pages 687-729 that the calculations given in Physiology, Vedantam, Astrology, Music and Sarasastra have close relation to each other. The minute Srutis must also conform to those calculations.

Our ancestors have said that just as the measurement of the Sthoola Sareeram is 96 inches, so also the man who has the Sthoola, Sookshma and Karana Sareeras possesses the 96 Tatvas. There is reason to believe that the minute Srutis of a Sthayi way also be 96 in number.

When once we establish the existence of 96 Srutis in the octave, all doubts as regards the Srutis will be made clear. But we may ask why not argue this way. The five Swarams Ri, Ga, Ma, Dha and Ni and each of them divided into two halves and with the addition of Sa and Pa form the 12 half Swarams of Ayapalai, which when further halved become the 24 Swarams of Vattapalai. Extending this division still further we arrive at 48 Srutis. Why not stop here? But it is very clear that unless we proceed a step further we cannot account for some of the very minute Srutis which occur in a very large number of Ragas.

We can assure our readers that we must acknowledge 96 Srutis in order to understand the truth of the Tamil Ragas that have been sung for many thousands of of years and to impart them to others.

Many may doubt the truth of the existence of 96 Srutis and may think that they do not occur in ancient Ragas. They may ask whether each of these very minute Srutis do really occur in our ganam. We must understand that one or two of these very minute Srutis may occur along with the seven primary Swarams in a Ragam and not all together in the same. These minute Srutis will never occur by themselves. So there will be no difficulty in understanding them. We are singing these minute Srutis in many a Ragam but we are ignorant we are singing them. It is not necessary to divide the Sthayi into 96 equal parts and place 96 frets over them. It is enough if we divide the 12 half Swarams of Ayapalai into two, halve each division once more, get at the 24 Srutis and subdivide each of these into four by means of frets and arrive at 96.

According to the system of Vattapalai, only the 2nd, 4th, 7th, 9th and the 11th strings to the standard string and the 12th or the octave—these seven Swarams alone will be concordant. Here according to the system of lessening an Alaku in Vilari and Kaikilai, these minute Srutis will occur only in the 4th and the 9th strings from the given string and in the Kilai and Inai strings and not in all the Swarams. So it is very easy to understand this.

These minute Srutis may be marked in the Yal as follows :—There are already the 12 frets in the Yal placed at intervals. Make the wax level between the existing frets. New frets either of ivory or bamboo splits should be made according to the height between the wax and the string. These new frets should be about $\frac{1}{16}$ of an inch bread on one side and tapering to a point on the other. Each of these new frets should be 2½ inches long. These may be placed between the intervals and the Swarasthanams marked. For example Suddha Ri, or Ri with 2 Alakus, may be divided into halves and the Ri with one Alaku marked. Then this interval for Ri,, may be divided into four equal parts marking ¼, ½ and ¾, thus arriving at 72+24 or 96 Srutis. This may be done easily and the Srutis occurring in the various Ragas marked without difficulty. But those who are accustomed to sing these minute Srutis sometimes flat and sometimes sharp will find this a nuisance. Unless we determine the Srutis accurately there will be no end of doubts and discussions.

1. We have noted before that the 12 Swarams obtained by the Sa-Pa and Sa-Ma principle, or the concordant and branch Swarams of Vattapalai in the 12 Rasis, are the 12 Swarams of Ayapalai. Of these seven Swarams, each of the Swarams Ri, Ga, Ma, Dha and Ni with the exception of Kural and Ili (Sa and Pa) is divided into two and thus (10+2) the 12 Swarams are obtained.

2. The 12 half Swarams of Vattapalai have 2 Alakus each, thus accounting for the 24 Srutis or Alakus of Vattapalai.

3. We see from experience that the 24 Alakus of Vattapalai had each of them 2 Sub-Alakus and were used in South Indian music.

4. Further, these 48 Sruti Sthanams are still subdivided into halves and the resultant 96 Srutis are profusely used in our Karnatic music.

To sum up, then, we have reason to think that Ayapalai is the division of the seven Swarams into the twelve.

The 12 Swarams of Ayapalai when divided into 24 Srutis become Vattapalai.

The 24 Srutis of Vattapalai when sub-divided into 48 Srutis or Alakus become Thirikonapalai.

And the 48 Srutis of Alakus of Thirikonapalai when halved into 96 quarter Srutis become Chathurapalai.

For, mention is made of four Palais, Ayapalai, Vattapalai, Thirikonapali, and Chathurapalai. We see from their calculations that just as they used half Swarams in Ayapalai they have used quarter Swarams in Vattapalai. So the third and fourth sub-divisions naturally formed the Thirikonapalai and Chathurapalai. There is evidence, then, to conclude that

the 12 half-Swarams are Ayapalai
the 24 quarter Swarams are Vattapalai
the 48 one eight Swarams are Thirikonapalai
the 96 one-sixteenth Swarams are Chathurapalai

(1) They have said that there are 12 Palais, 7 primary and 5 secondary, in the system of Ayapalai, and have derived the six mother Ragas –Chempalai, Padumalaipalai, Chevvalipali, Arumpalai Kodipalai and Vilaripalai corresponding to the modern Sankaraparanam, Karaharapiria, Hanumathodi, Kalyani, Harikambodi and Natabhairavi, from them and also the four branch Ragas or Janiya Ragas, viz Pun, Punniam, Thiram, Thiratthiram corresponding to Sampooranam, Shadavam, Oudavam and Suvarantham.

(2) They have also stated clearly the four primary Puns derived from Vattapalai, namely, Marutham, Kurinji, Neythal and Palai, the four Jathis derived from each of them, namely Ahanilai, Puranilai, Arugial, and Perugial, as well as the system of making ganam with one Alaku less in Vilari and Kaikilai. There is reason to think that Ilankovadigal might have omitted the details of Thirikonapalai and Chathurapalai as he had explicitly stated the first two very minutely.

We can never clear our doubts if we take the standard of $\frac{3}{2}$ and $\frac{4}{3}$ which never completely finishes an octave. We can never make ganam with only 22 Srutis in the octave. If we admit the 22 Srutis for the octave some of the Srutis used in South Indian music will never be found there. It will be more to the point if the Sthayi were divided into 12 parts, and if one or more of $\frac{1}{8}$ Srutis be added along with the seven main Swarams. Therefore it is necessary to give those mathematical calculations and practically demonstrate the fact by means of the Ragas in which those very minute Swarams occur.

We need not dilate upon these mathematical calculations as they are the same given before for the 12 Swarams and the 24 Srutis.

" மூலாதாரந் தொடங்கிய மூச்சைக் காலாற்கிளப்பிக் கருத்தாலியக்கி ஒன்றேனைத்தாக்கி இரண்டேனைப் பகுத்துப் பண்ணீர்மைகளைப் பிறப்பிக்கப்பட்ட மிடற்றுப்பாடலும் "

According to the above ancient Sootram which means that the breath which generates from the *Moolatharam*, proceeds upwards, is held in the mind, becomes a musical sound which increases in pitch from 1 to 2 ; Puns are derived from this music which proceeds from the throat. We must see how between 1 or Athara Sa and 2 or Madhya Sa there are 96 equal divisions and 96 minute Srutis which form a gradually ascending series without admitting of any other possible Sruti between. As we have noticed before, if we divide the logarithm of 2 by 96 and multiply the result by the series 1, 2, 3, 4 up to 96 we get the figures in col. 4. The decimal fractions for the logarithms are found in col. 5 ; the vibrations, in col. 6 and 7 ; the parts of the length of the wire, in col. 8 ; the measurement of the wire in col. 9 ; the measurements of the respective Srutis, in col. 10 ; and the cents for each of the Srutis in cols. 11 and 12. All the above are clearly stated in the Table in the page 768.

The four minute Srutis for each of the major Srutis are separately shown in the Table.

Each Rasi is divided into 2 Alakus and each Alaku into 4 Srutis.

When any of the above Srutis is to be sounded, the modern method is to sound it as a Gamakam by pulling the string towards the player from one of the twelve frets. We must first determine exactly the resemblance between the Sruti played as a Gamakam and that sounded by the human voice and try to reproduce it in the Veena by the help of small frets. We may thus arrive at the minute Srutis $\frac{1}{4}$, $\frac{1}{2}$ and $\frac{3}{4}$. Again, the 12 Sthanams of the Table, namely like 8, 16, 24, 32, 40 &c. are the 12 half Swarams of the Ayapalai. And the Sthanams like 4, 8, 12, 16, 20, 24 &c. are the 24 quarter Swarams of the Vattapalai. The others are more minute Srutis which are the $\frac{1}{4}$, $\frac{1}{2}$ or the $\frac{3}{4}$ of any particular Sruti.

These indicate the Srutis of the Vattapalai known to the ancient Tamilians in the 12 Rasis. These are shown separately and distinctly, so that the 24 Srutis obtained by dividing each Rasi into 2 Alakus, and the more minute Srutis obtained by sub-dividing each Alaku into 4, might be clearly understood.

Each of the Swarams here will stand to the other either in the relation of concordant or branch Swaram. In the same way among these concordant and branch Swarams, any Alaku which comes as Gamakam and its four minute Srutis will be in the same harmonious relation

For example, the Ri 4 Alakus ending in Kadakam (line 16) will have the Sa-Pa or concordant relation with Dha which ends in Kumbam. In the same way when this Ri is used as Gamakam by adding the 2 Srutis in the 18th Sthanam, the Dha also in Kumbam will be used as Gamakam by taking in the 2 Srutis in line 74. These are the Ri and the Dha used in Sankaraparanam. They must be stated as Ri and Dha with $4\frac{1}{2}$ Alakus each.

Again, the Ri with $4\frac{1}{2}$ Alakus occurring in Arabi derived from Deera Shankaraparanam (line 17) and the Dha with $4\frac{1}{2}$ Alakus (in line 73) are concordant Srutis. Examples of the same kind of minute Srutis may be seen in the Tables that follow.

When these concordant and branch Swarams are mentioned in the 12 Rasis, they become Gamakams either as $\frac{1}{4}$, $\frac{1}{2}$, $\frac{3}{4}$, 1, $1\frac{1}{4}$, $1\frac{1}{2}$ or $1\frac{3}{4}$ Srutis obtaining the names of the Swarams which stand in the respective Rasis. For instance the Ri which ends with four Alakus in Kadagam obtains $4\frac{1}{4}$, $4\frac{1}{2}$, $4\frac{3}{4}$, 5, $5\frac{1}{4}$, $5\frac{1}{2}$, $5\frac{3}{4}$ Alakus in the 17th, 18th, 19th, 20th, 21st and 23 places (with the exception of the 24th place) while occurring in Simham, and is used as Gamakam.

Again, the Ri with 2 Alakus which finishes at the 8th place in Mithunam occurs in thr 16th Sthanam in Kadagam with $2\frac{1}{4}$, $2\frac{1}{2}$, $2\frac{3}{4}$, 3, $3\frac{1}{4}$, $3\frac{1}{2}$ and $3\frac{3}{4}$ Alakus (omitting Ri with 4 Alakus) corresponding to the places 9, 10, 11, 12, 13, 14 and 15. These may be clearly seen in the Tables that follow.

We presume our readers do now clearly understand the mathematical calculations for the 12 half Swarams of Ayapalai, the 24 quarter Srutis of Vattapalai, the 48 one eight Srutis of Thirikonapalai and the 96 one sixteenth Srutis of Chathurapalai. Though we come across many varied names for the Swarams, the Srutis of South Indian music have been made clear by works on Isai-Tamil and Telugu literature. Therefore, it is clear that the modern names do correspond with these given in ancient Tamil works, and the Sanskrit names derived from the ancient Tamil names may also be used.

The mathematical calculations for the 12 Swarams of the Ayapalai known among the ancient Tamilians, the 24 Srutis of the Vattapalai and the 96 minute Srutis.

Number.	Rasi. Swaram.	How the 96 Srutis are a gradually ascending series from 1 to 2 shown by the powers of $\sqrt[96]{2}$	Sruti.	The logarithms of the powers $\sqrt[96]{2}$	Anti-logarithms for the figures given in col. 4.	Number of vibrations of each Swaram if SA=540.	Number of vibrations of each Swaram if SA=240.	Location of the 96 Swarams in the first half of the total length of wire	Location of the 96 Swarams in the first half of a wire 32 inches long.	Measurement by inches of each Swaram while proceeding from Athara SA.	Cents for the 96 Swarams.	The intervals between the Swarams.
1		2	3	4	5	6	7	8	9	10	11	12
		$\sqrt[96]{2}$		.000000000	1·0000	540·00	240·00	1·000000	32·000000	·0000	·0	
1	1 Midunam Ri	,, t^1		·003135729	1·0072	543·89	241·73	0·992805	31·769760	·2302	12·5	12·5
2		,, t^2		·006271458	1·0145	547·83	243·48	0·985663	31·541216	·4588	25·0	12·5
3		,, t^3		·009407187	1·0219	551·83	245·26	0·978572	31·314304	·6857	37·5	12·5
4		,, t^4	1	·012542917	1·0293	555·84	247·08	0.971532	31·089024	·9110	50·0	12·5
5		,, t^5		·015678646	1·0368	559·87	248·83	0·964542	30·865360	1·1346	62·5	12.5
6		,, t^6		·018814375	1·0443	563·92	250·63	0·957603	30·643296	1·3567	75·0	12·5
7		,, t^7		.021950104	1·0518	567·97	252·43	0·950714	30·422848	1·5772	87·5	12·5
8		,, t^8	2	·025085833	1·0595	572·13	254·28	0·943874	30·203968	1·7960	100·0	12·5
9	2 Kadagam Ri	,, t^9		·028221563	1·0671	576·30	256·10	0·937084	29·986688	2·0133	112·5	12·5
10		,, t^{10}		·031357292	1·0749	580·48	257·98	0·930342	29·770944	2·2291	125.0	12·5
11		,, t^{11}		·034493021	1·0827	584·67	259·85	0·923649	29·556768	2·4432	137.5	12·5
12		,, t^{12}	3	.037628750	1·0905	588·87	261·72	0·917004	29·344128	2·6559	150.0	12·5
13		,, t^{13}		.040764479	1·0984	593·14	263·62	0·910407	29·133024	2·8670	162·5	12·5
14		,, t^{14}		.043900208	1·1064	597·46	275·54	0·903857	28·923424	3·0766	175·0	12·5
15		,, t^{15}		·047035938	1·1144	601·78	267·46	0·897355	28.715360	3·2846	187·5	12.5
16		,, t^{16}	4	·050171667	1·1225	606·15	269·40	0·890899	28·508755	3·4913	200·0	12 5

1		2	3	4	5	6	7	8	9	10	11	12
17	3 Simmum GA Swaram.	$\sqrt[96]{2}^{17}$	Sruti.	·053307396	1·1306	610·52	271·34	0·884490	28·303664	3·6963	212·5	12·5
18		,, t^{18}		·056443125	1·1388	614·95	273·31	0·878126	28·100032	3·9000	225·0	12·5
19		,, t^{19}		·059578854	1·1470	619·38	275·28	0·871809	27·897872	4·1021	237·5	12·5
20		,, t^{20}	5	·062714583	1·1554	623·91	277·30	0·865537	27·697170	4·3028	250·0	12·5
21		,, t^{21}		·065850313	1·1638	628·45	279·31	0·859310	27.497910	4·5021	262·5	12·5
22		,, t^{22}		·068986042	1·1722	632·99	281·33	0·853118	27·299760	4·7002	275·0	12.5
23		,, t^{23}		·072121771	1·1807	637·58	283·37	0·846990	27·103688	4·8963	287·5	12·5
24		,, t^{24}	6	·075257500	1·1892	642·17	285·41	0·840896	26·908650	5·0913	300·0	12·5
25	4 Kanni GA	,, t^{25}		·078393229	1·1978	646·82	287·47	0·834847	26·715104	5·2849	312·5	12·5
26		,, t^{26}		·081528758	1·2065	651·51	289·56	0.828841	26·522912	5·4771	325·0	12·5
27		,, t^{27}		·084664688	1·2152	656·21	291·65	0·822878	26·332096	5·6679	337·5	12·5
28		,, t^{28}	7	·087800417	1·2241	660·97	293·78	0·816958	26·142646	5·8574	350·0	12·5
29		,, t^{29}		·090936146	1·2329	665·77	295·90	0·811080	25·954560	6·0455	362·5	12·5
30		,, t^{30}		·094071875	1·2419	670·63	298·06	0·805245	25·767840	6·2322	375·0	12·5
31		,, t^{31}		·097207604	1·2509	675·49	300·22	0·799452	25·582464	6·4175	387·5	12·5
32		,, t^{32}	8	·100343333	1·2599	680·35	302·38	0·793701	25·398416	6·6016	400·0	12·5
33	5 Thulam MA	,, t^{33}		·103479063	1·2691	685·31	304·58	0·787990	25·215680	6·7843	412·5	12·5
34		,, t^{34}		·106614792	1·2783	690·28	306·79	0·782322	25·034288	6·9657	425·0	12·5
35		,, t^{35}		·109750521	1·2875	695·25	309·00	0·776693	24·854176	7·1458	437·5	12·5
36		,, t^{36}	9	·112886250	1·2968	700·27	311·23	0·771106	24·675376	7·3246	450·0	12·5
37		,, t^{37}		·116021979	1·3062	705·35	313·49	0·765558	24·497843	7·5022	462·5	12·5
38		,, t^{38}		·119157708	1·3157	710·45	315·77	0·760050	24·321600	7·6784	475·0	12·5
39		,, t^{39}		·122293438	1·3252	715·60	318·05	0·754582	24·146624	7·8534	487·5	12·5
40		,, t^{40}	10	.125429167	1·3348	720·80	320·36	0·749154	23·972912	8·0271	500·0	12·5
41	6 Virchigam MA	,, t^{41}		·128564896	1·3445	726·04	322·68	0·743764	23·800448	8·1996	512·5	12·5
42		,, t^{42}		.131700625	1·3543	731·32	325·03	0·738413	23·629216	8·3708	525·0	12.5
43		,, t^{43}		·134836354	1·3641	736·61	327·38	0·733100	23·459200	8·5408	537·5	12.5
44		,, t^{44}	11	·137972083	1·3740	741·96	329·76	0·727827	23·290448	8·7096	550·0	12.5
45		,, t^{45}		·141107813	1·3839	747·31	332·14	0·722591	23·122896	8·8871	562·5	12·5
46		,, t^{46}		·144243542	1·3939	752·71	334·54	0·717392	22·956544	9·0435	575·0	12·5
47		,, t^{47}		·147379271	1·4040	758·16	336·96	0·712231	22·791392	9·2086	587·5	12·5
48		,, t^{48}	12	·150515000	1·4142	763·67	339·41	0·707107	22·627421	9·3726	600·0	12·5

The mathematical calculations for the 12 Swarams of the Ayapalai known among the ancient Tamilians, the 24 Srutis of the Vattapalai and the 96 minute Srutis.

Number.	Rasi.	How the 96 Srutis are a gradually ascending series from 1 to 2 shown by the powers of $\sqrt[96]{2}$		The Logarithms of the powers $\sqrt[96]{2}$	Anti-logarithms for the figures given in col. 4.	Number of vibrations of each Swaram if SA=540.	Number of vibrations of each Swaram if SA=240.	Location of the 96 Swarams in the first half of the total length of wire	Location of the 96 Swarams in the first half of a wire 32 inches long.	Measurement by inches of each Swaram while proceeding from Athara SA.	Cents for the 96 Swarams.	The intervals between the Swarams.
1		2	3	4	5	6	7	8	9	10	11	12
49	7 Thanusu PA Swaram.	$\sqrt[96]{2}^{49}$	Sruti.	·153650729	1·4245	769·23	341·88	0·702020	22·464644	9·5354	612·5	12·5
50		,, ^{50}		·156786458	1·4348	774·79	344·35	0·696969	22·303008	9·6970	625·0	12·5
51		,, ^{51}		·159922188	1·4452	780·41	346·85	0·691955	22·142560	9·8574	637·5	12·5
52		,, ^{52}	13	·163057917	1·4557	786·08	349·37	0·686977	21·983258	10·0167	650·0	12·5
53		,, ^{53}		·166193646	1·4662	791·75	351·89	0·682035	21·825104	10·1749	662·5	12·5
54		,, ^{54}		·169329375	1·4768	797·47	354·43	0·677132	21·668234	10·3318	675·0	12·5
55		,, ^{55}		·172465104	1·4875	803·25	357·00	0·672256	21·512205	10·4878	687·5	12·5
56		,, ^{56}	14	·175600833	1·4983	809·08	359·50	0·667420	21·357440	10·6426	700·0	12·5
57	8 Magaram DHA	,, ^{57}		·178736563	1·5092	814·96	362·21	0·662618	21·203776	10·7962	712·5	12·5
58		,, ^{58}		·181872292	1·5201	820·85	364·82	0·657851	21·051232	10·9488	725·0	12·5
59		,, ^{59}		·185008021	1·5311	826·79	367·47	0·653119	20·899792	11·1002	737·5	12·5
60		,, ^{60}	15	·188143750	1·5422	832·79	370·13	0·648420	20·749440	11·2506	750·0	12·5
61		,, ^{61}		·191279479	1·5534	838·83	372·82	0·643755	20·600160	11·3998	762·5	12·5
62		,, ^{62}		·194415208	1·5646	844·88	375·50	0·639124	20·451952	11·5480	775·0	12·5
63		,, ^{63}		·197550938	1·5760	851·04	378·24	0·634526	20·304816	11·6952	787·5	12·5
64		,, ^{64}	16	·200686667	1·5874	857·20	380·98	0·629960	20·158723	11·8413	800·0	12·5

1		2	3 Sruti.	4	5	6	7	8	9	10	11	12
65	Dha Swaram.	√2^{65}		·203822396	1·5989	863·41	383·74	0·625429	20·013715	11·9863	812·5	12·5
66		,, ^{66}		·206958125	1·6105	869·67	386·52	0·620929	19·869728	12·1303	825·0	12·5
67		,, ^{67}		·210093854	1·6222	875·99	389·33	0·616462	19·726984	12·2730	837·5	12·5
68		,, ^{68}	17	·213229583	1·6340	882·56	392·16	0·612027	19·584858	12·4151	850·0	12·5
69	9 Kundam	,, ^{69}		·216365313	1·6458	888·73	394·99	0·607624	19·443952	12·5560	862·5	12·5
70		,, ^{70}		·219501042	1·6577	895·16	397·85	0·603252	19·304974	12·6959	875·0	12·5
71		,, ^{71}		·222636771	1·6697	901·64	400·73	0·598912	19·165184	12·8348	887·5	12·5
72		,, ^{72}	18	·225772500	1·6818	908·17	403·63	0·594604	19·027315	12·9727	900·0	12·5
73	10 Mosanam Ni.	,, ^{73}		·228908229	1·6940	914·76	406·56	0·590326	18·890432	13·1096	912·5	12·5
74		,, ^{74}		·232043958	1·7062	921·35	409·49	0·586[illegible]79	18·754528	13·2455	925·0	12·5
75		,, ^{75}		·235179688	1·7136	928·04	412·46	0·581863	18·619600	13·3804	937·5	12·5
76		,, ^{76}	19	·238315417	1·7311	93[illegible]·79	415·46	0·577676	18·485645	13·5144	950·0	12·5
77		,, ^{77}		·241451146	1·7436	941·54	418·46	0·573520	18·352640	13·6474	962·5	12·5
78		,, ^{78}		·244586875	1·7563	948·40	421·51	0·569394	18·220608	13·7794	975·0	12·5
79		,, ^{79}		·247722604	1·7690	955·26	424·56	0·565298	18·089536	13·9105	987·5	12·5
80		,, ^{80}	20	·250858333	1·7819	962·17	427·63	0·561231	17·959392	14·0406	1000·0	12·5
81	11 Medam Ni	,, ^{81}		·253994063	1·7947	969·14	430·73	0·557193	17·830189	14·1698	1012·5	12·5
82		,, ^{82}		·257129792	1·8077	976·16	433·85	0·553185	17·701304	14·2981	1025·0	12·5
83		,, ^{83}		·260265521	1·8208	983·23	436·99	0·549205	17·574560	14·4254	1037·5	12·5
84		,, ^{84}	21	·263401250	1·8440	990·36	440·16	0·545254	17·448125	14·5519	1050·0	12·5
85		,, ^{85}		·266536979	1·8473	997·54	443·35	0·541331	17·322592	14·6774	1062·5	12·5
86		,, ^{86}		·269672708	1·8607	1004·74	446·57	0·537457	17·197968	14·8020	1075·0	12·5
87		,, ^{87}		·272808438	1·8742	1012·07	449·81	0.533570	17·074240	14·9258	1087·5	12·5
88		,, ^{88}	22	·275944167	1·8877	1019·36	453·05	0·529732	16·951468	15·0486	1100·0	12·5
89	12 Idadam Ni.	,, ^{89}		279079896	1·9014	1026·76	456·34	0·525920	16·829440	15·1706	1112·5	12·5
90		,, ^{90}		·282215625	1·9152	1034·21	459·65	0·522137	16·708384	15·2916	1125·0	12·5
91		,, ^{91}		·285351354	1·9291	1041·71	462·98	0·518380	16·588160	15·4118	1137·5	12·5
92		,, ^{92}	23	·288487083	1·9431	1049·27	466·34	0·514651	16·468835	15·5312	1150·0	12·5
93		,, ^{93}		·291622813	1·9571	1056·83	469·76	0·510949	16·350352	15·6496	1162·5	12·5
94		,, ^{94}		·294758542	1·9713	1064·50	473·11	0·507273	16·232726	15·7673	1175·0	12·5
95		,, ^{95}		·297894271	1·9856	1072·22	476·54	0·503623	16·115936	15·8841	1187·5	12·5
96		,, ^{96}	24	·301030000	2·0000	1080·00	480·00	0·500000	16·000000	16·0000	1200·0	12·5

6. Names of Swarams and Srutis.

What we now call Suddha Ri and Chathursruti Ri, and Suddha Dha and Chathursruti Dha are only the Swarams of Ayapalai with 2 Alakus and 4 Alakus. What the ancient Tamilians called Alakus, modern writers name Srutis. The Swarams Ri, Ga, Ma, Dha and Ni with two Srutis each are now called by us Suddha Ri, Suddha Ga, Suddha Ma, Suddha Dha, and Suddha Ni. In the same manner the Swarms Ri, Ga, Ma, Dha, and Ni with 4 Alakus each are known at the present day as Chathursruti Ri, Chathursruti Dha, Sadarana Ga, Prathi Ma and Kaisika Ni.

The Swarams in the Table that follows appear to have names in correspondence with the Alakus in the 12 Rasis.

The ancient and modern names for the 12 Swarams of Ayapalai.

No.	Ancient Names.			Modern Names.	
1	Sa	Kural	Idapam	Sa	Shadjam.
2	Ri^{2}	Thuttham with 2 Alakus.	Midunam	Ri^{2}	Suddha Rishapam.
3	Ri^{4}	„ 4 „	Kadagam	Ri^{4}	Chathursruti Rishapam.
4	Ga^{2}	Kaikilai with 2 „	Simmum	Ga^{2}	Suddha Gandharam.
5	Ga^{4}	„ 4 „	Kanni	Ga^{4}	Sadarana Gandharam.
6	Ma^{2}	Oolai with 2 „	Thulam	Ma^{2}	Suddha Madhyamam.
7	Ma^{4}	„ „ 4 „	Viruchigam	Ma^{4}	Prathi Madhyamam.
8	Pa	Ili	Thanusu	Pa	Panchamam.
9	Dha^{2}	Vilari with 2 Alakus.	Magaram	Dha^{2}	Suddha Daivatam.
10	Dha^{4}	„ „ 4 „	Kumbam	Dha^{4}	Chathursruti Daivatam.
11	Ni^{2}	Tharam „ 2 „	Meenam	Ni^{2}	Suddha Nishatham.
12	Ni^{4}	„ „ 4 „	Mesham	Ni^{4}	Kaisika Nishatham.
13	Sa	Kural	Idapam	Sa	Shadjam.

But it is within our experience that we see Ga in the house belonging to Ri, and *vice versa*, and Dha in that of Ni and *vice versa*. This is also seen in the 12 Palais obtained by the 12 Swarams of the Rasis by taking each of the Rasis as the compartment of Sa in order. It may be seen in line 4 of the Table of change of Graham on page 640 that in the fourth secondary Palai Ga occurs in the compartment of Ri with 4 Alakus, and Ni in the compartment of Dha with 4 Alakus. In the same way in line 9 Ni occurs in the compartment of Dha$_2$, and in line 11, Ga in that of Ri$_4$ and Ni in that of Dha$_4$. In other words Ni gives up its two compartments and comes as far as one of the compartments of Ri. So we find here that Ga and Ni occur in three Rasis with six Alakus. In the same way when Ri gives up its second compartment and takes the third which belongs to GA, it obtains six Alakus in all the three Rasis. These RI and DHA with six Alakus we call Shat Sruti. To bring out the same meaning the GA with six Srutis is called by us Anthara Gandharam or end Gandharam and the second NI as Kakali or sweet NI. All these details may be seen in the Table that follows.

These are used for the purpose of generating Ragas by using the 12 Swarams only without other intervals. The two alterations in RI and GA, and two others in DHA and NI (four different names in all) only indicate 16 names but not 16 different Swarams. The Swarams of a Sthayi are but 12. We see clearly from the traditional Ragas and puns that our modern ganam is with the help of the 12 Swarams as given in the Table below and that this is also the system in use at the modern day. Ancient works on music, without specifying the minute Srutis that occur with these 12 merely said that some of them should be sung as gamakams and they should be acquired with the help of a guru. On account of this the Srutis that were to be played as gamakams by pulling the strings of a Yal disappeared in course of time so much so that doubts arose even about the 12 Srutis.

The Table showing how the 12 Swarams of Ayapalai are used as 16 Swarams.

Modern Swarams and the names of the Vikruti Swarams.				Ancient Names.
Shadjam	SA	SA	Shadjam	
Suddha Rishapam ...	RI^{2}			RI with 2 Alakus
Chathursruti Rishapam ...	RI^{4}	GA^{2}	Suddha Gandharam ...	RI with 4 Alakus or GA with 2 Alakus
Shatsruti Rishapam ...	RI^{6}	GA^{4}	Satharana Gandharam.	RI with 6 Alakus or GA with 4 Alakus
		GA^{6}	Anthara Gandharam ...	GA with 6 Alakus
Suddha Madhymam ...	MA^{2}			MA with 2 Alakus
Prathi Madhymam ...	MA^{4}			MA with 4 Alakus
	PA	PA	Panchamam	PA or Ili
Suddha Daivatam ...	DHA^{2}			DHA with 2 Alakus
Chathursruti Daivatam ...	DHA^{4}	NI^{2}	Suddha Nishatham ...	DHA with 4 Alakus or NI with 2 Alakus
Sat Sruti Daivatam ...	DHA^{6}	NI^{4}	Kaisika Nishatham ...	DHA with 6 Alakus or NI with 4 Alakus
		NI	Kakali Nishatham ...	NI with 6 Alakus
	SA	SA		SA or Kural

The names of 24 Alakus of Vattapalai with the modern names of Srutis and their position.

Number.	The names used at present and the names that ought to be used.						The names of Srutis according to the system of Vattapalai.
1	...			S		Nathasadjam or Achutha-sadjam ...	Sa or ... ... Kural
2	Ega Sruti Rishabam ...	1	R				1 Alaku Ri Thuttham
3	Suddha Rishabam ...	2	R				2 Alaku Ri ... „
4	Tis Sruti Rishabam ...	3	R	G	1	Ega Sruti Gandharam ...	3 Alaku Ri or 1 Alaku Ga Kaikilai ... ...
5	Chatur Sruti Rishabam ...	4	R	G	2	Suddha Gandharam ...	4 Alaku Ri or 2 Alaku Ga Kaikilai ... ...
6	Pancha Sruti Rishabam ...	5	R	G	3	Tis Sruti Gandharam ...	5 Alaku Ri or 3 Alaku Ga Kaikilai ... ...
7	Shat Sruti Rishabam ...	6	R	G	4	Sadarana Gandharam ...	6 Alaku Ri or 4 Alaku Ga Kaikilai ... ...
8	Sutha Gandara Rishabam	7	R	G	5	Pancha Sruti Gandharam.	7 Alaku Ri or 5 Alaku Ga Kaikilai ... ...
9	...			G	6	Andhara Gandharam ...	6 Alaku Ga Kaikilai
10	Sutha Madhimum ...	1	M	G	7	Sutha Madhima Gandharam	7 Alaku Ga or 1 Alaku Ma Oolai ... ...
11	Suddha Madhimum ...	2	M				2 Alaku Ma ... Oolai
12	Tis Sruthi Madhimum ...	3	M				3 Alaku Ma ... „
13	Prathi Madhimum ...	4	M				4 Alaku Ma ... „
14	Sutha Panchama Madhimum	5	M	P		Sutha Panchamum ...	5 Alaku Ma or 1 Alaku Pa Oolai ... ...
15	...		P	P		Panchamum or Achutha-panchamum ...	Pa or ... Ili
16	Ega Sruti Dhaivatham ...	1	D				1 Alaku Dha
17	Suddha Dhaivatham ...	2	D				2 Alaku Dha ... Vilari
18	Tis Sruti Dhaivatham ...	3	D	N	1	Ega Sruti Nishadam ...	3 Alaku Dha or 1 Alaku Ni Tharam ... ...
19	Chatur Sruti Dhaivatham ...	4	D	N	2	Suddha Nishadam ...	4 Alaku Dha or 2 Alaku Ni Tharam ... ...
20	Pancha Sruti Dhaivatham	5	D	N	3	Tis Sruti Nishadam ...	5 Alaku Dha or 3 Alaku Ni Tharam ... ...
21	Shat Sruthi Dhaivatham ...	6	D	N	4	Kaisika Nishadam ...	6 Alaku Dha or 4 Alaku Ni Tharam ... ...
22	Sutha Nishada Dhaivatham	7	D	N	5	Pancha Sruti Nishadam ...	7 Alaku Dha or 5 Alaku Ni Tharam ... ...
23	...			N	6	Kakali Nishadam ...	6 Alaku Ni ...Tharam
24	Sutha Shadjam ...		S	N	7	Sutha Shadja Nishadam ...	7 Alaku Ni or 1 Alaku Sa
25	Shadjam ...		Ṡ			Natha or Achutha Shadjam	Sa

In addition to this, it is necessary that we should note the names of the 24 Alakus of the Vattapalai and those of the Vikruti Swarams derived from them.

In the above Table we see clearly the modern names of Swarams as well as their ancient names which were never open to doubt.

Of these, the names of the 12 Swarams with 2 Alakus each are the same as given in the previous Table. We know that it is quite possible to have a third Alaku between the second and the fourth and a fifth between the fourth and the sixth Alakus. On the same principle I have marked a Dwisruti Ri between Suddha Ri and Chathursruti Ri and a Pancha Sruti Ri between Chathursruti Ri and Shatsruti Ri. It is clearly seen that Sutha Sa and Sutha Pa have each a Sruti less than Sa and Pa, and that Achyuta Sa and Achyuta Pa are Niyata Srutis. Of these, Niyata (நியத) Sa and Pa, being the very fundamental Srutis of all music, can admit of no change. But the Ni below Sa and the Ma below Pa are called Sutha Shadja Ni and Sutha Pancha Ma respectively. From this it does not follow that we should make Ganam with the 2 Srutis of Sa and the 2 Srutis of Pa left out. On the other hand, the Ragas should be made after changing the Graham according to the system of Ayapalai, and Ganam should be made with a few Alakus less according to the system of Vattapalai. Perhaps we may hesitate a little and say that if we change the Graham in accordance with the four Srutis of Sa and Pa we should obtain innumerable sweet Ragas, and this is recommended by the author of Sangeeta Ratnakaram. But this was never the custom either with the ancients or with modern musicians. The ancient system was to make Ganam in the 12 concordant and branch Śwarams with 22 Alakus omitting one Alaku each for 2 of those Swarams. Without understanding this ancient Tamil method, they have advocated 22 Srutis in the octave, and the names given by them to the Srutis make confusion worse confounded. Literature on music clearly proves that there was doubt as regards numbers and names of Srutis.

Moreover, in the Telugu work called 'Melathikaram' the names of the 24 Srutis of the Brahma Melam are given. The table is given below.

In the Table below, odd Srutis have the name 'Prathi' and even Srutis are called Suddham, Chathur Sruti and Shat Sruti. The names which we use at present for half-Swarams are found here. So there is reason to believe that a similar system was in use in ancient times in the Tamil country, that the same was written in Telugu and that the works in Tamil became obsolete in course of time. But the author of this Telugu work is a Tamil Vellala from Tinnevelly.

The names of Swarams found in Brahma Veena called Brahma Melam.

No.	How the Vikruti Swarams are formed.				
			SA		Achyuta Shadjam.
1	Prathi Suddha Rishabam ...	... 1	RI		
2	Suddha Rishabam	... 2	RI		
3	Prathi Chathursruti Rishabam	... 3	RI	GA	1 Prathisuddha Gandharam.
4	Chathursruti Rishabam ...	... 4	RI	GA	2 Suddha Gandharam.
5	Prathishatsruti Rishabam ...	... 5	RI	GA	3 Prathi Sadarana Gandharam.
6	Shatsruti Rishabam ...	... 6	RI	GA	4 Sadarana Gandharam.
7	Sutha Gandara Rishabam ...	... 7	RI	GA	5 Prathi Andara Gandharam.
8				GA	6 Andara Gandharam.
9	Sutha Madhimum	... 1	MA	GA	7 Suthamadhima Gandharam.
10	Suddha Madhimum ...	... 2	MA		
11	Uppratlii Madhimum ...	... 3	MA		
12	Prathi Madhimum ...	... 4	MA		
13	Suthapancha Madhimum ...	... 5	MA	PA	1 Sutha Panchamum.
14				PA	2 Panchamum.
15	Prathisuddha Dhaivatham	... 1	DHA		
16	Suddha Dhaivatham ...	... 2	DHA		
17	Prathi Chathursruti Dhaivatham	... 3	DHA	NI	1 Prathisuddha Nishadam.
18	Chathursruti Dhaivatham ...	... 4	DHA	NI	2 Suddha Nishadam.
19	Prathishatsruti Dhaivatham	... 5	DHA	NI	3 Prathikaisika Nishadam.
20	Shatsruti Dhaivatham ...	... 6	DHA	NI	4, Kaisika Nishadam.
21	Suthanishatha Dhaivatham	... 7	DHA	NI	5 Prathikakali Nishadam.
22				NI	6 Kakali Nishadam.
23	Suthashadjam	...	SA	NI	7 Suthashadja Nishadam.
24	Nathashadjam	...	SA	SA	

We obtained this from M. R. Ry. Venkatasubbier Avergal, Manager of a Zemindari, Maniyachi, through M. R. Ry. Mutthaya Baghavatar Avergal of Harikesavanallur. There are two other palmyra leaf records similar to this in Tanjore. The work called "Melathikara lakshanam" which gives lakshanasootra for over 1000 Ragas out of the 4624 Ragas of Brahma Melam may be found even to day in the Sarasvati Mahl of the Tanjore Palace.

When we note this Brahma Melam shown above we see that the ancient Tamil names have been changed in foreign languages. But the names of the Swarams correspond to the number of Alakus of ancient times. The system of Vattapalai is to make ganam in conformity with the Swarams mentioned in Brahma Veena. This Vattapalai system seems to date from about a 1000 to 1500 years before the time of Ilankovadigal.

The following is a quotation from the 41st to the 46th stanzas in Paripadal and its commentary by Parimelalagar. These stanzas are in praise of the deity commencing with the words "*நிலவரையழுவத்தான வானுறை புகறந்து*" set to music in Pun Gandharam by Maruthanallachuthanar and composed by Nappannanar.

"தெய்வப் பிரமஞ் செய்குவோருங்
கைவைத் திமிர்குழல் காண்குவோரு
மிர்திகாம விளிகுரல் சமங்கொள்வோரும்
வேள்வியி னழகியல் விளம்பு வோருங்
கூர்நாண் குரல் கொம்மென வொலிப்ப
வூழுறு முரசி னொலிசெய் வோரும்"

(இ-ள்) *தெய்வத்தன்மையையுடைய பிரமவீணையை யெழுப்புவோரும், கைவைத்து இக் குழலினிசையை யெழுப்போரும், யாழின்க ணிளிவாய்ப் பாலையையும் குரல்வாய்ப் பாலையையும் வலியவு மெலியவுந் தாக் காது சமனுத்தாக்கி யதனின்பத்தைக் கொள்வோரும். வேள்வி-பூசை.*

யாழினது நாண்குரல் கொம்மென வொலித்த வளவிலே யத்தாளத்திற்கேற்ப முரசினொலியை யெழுப்புவாரும்.

Comment:—"Those who get music out of the divine Brahma Veena, those who create music with their fingers out of the kulal (flute), and those who enjoy the music of the Yal by producing the Palai from the Ili and the Kural, neither too loud nor too soft but in a middling degree, (வேள்வி=sacrifice).

Those who make the noise of the Murasu to be in complete combination with the thalam of the music of the Kural in the Yal."

When we note the expression the "divine Veena" and the fact that the Brahma Veena is called Rudra Veena in the work 'Melathikaralakshanam' we see that the modern Veena where we make ganam with 12 half Swarams is the Rudra Veena, and that making ganam in it by the 24 Alakus of Vattapalai, but with 2 Alakus less, is the Brahma Veena. We observed before that the Palai commencing from Ili in the Veena was Neythal Yal and that commencing from Kural is the Marutha Yal. According to the above principle, it is said that one after the other sang the Chempalai where Kural was taken as Kural and the Kodipalai where Ili was taken as the Kural and delighted in such music. We also see that the strings vibrated in harmony with the human voice and the percussion instrument Murasu kept strict time in conjunction. When we observe that those who sang having Kural as Kural and those who sang having the same Kural as Ili sang them with a middling voice and revelled in it, it seems that this was sung exactly like the Aychiar-Kuravai found in pages 610–613 of this book. When one party sings the variations in the Swarams Sa, Ṛi, Ga, Ma and Pa the other party responded by singing variations in the Swarams PA, DHA, NI, SA and RI. The idea is the other party began with PA while this party began with SA. This shows that the ancients were experts in the Kulal and the Thannumai (Thalam) and that they made ganam according to the Vattapalai system or Brahma Veena.

We have pointed out in page 209 that in the 'Chathurthandi Prakasika' of Venkatamahi he says that he has constructed the 72 Melakarthas. We find that the Suddha RI and Chathur Sruti RI mentioned there are the modern names respectively for the RI, GA, MA, DHA and NI with 2, 4 and 6 Alakus.

We have seen a copy of the book Vyasa Katakam (which appears to have been written prior to the above) in the hands of M. R. Ry. Sreenivasa Iyengar Avl., the Samasthana Vidwan of Ramnad. There also we find that Raga lakshanam with Grahanyasa Amsam has been given for the Swarams RI, GA, MA, DHA and NI with 2, 4 and 6 Alakus using the modern names of such Swarams. The names have been so distinctly given as Kanakangi, Ratnangi, Ganamurti etc., and with other particulars that we are easily able to distinguish the numbers of the Ragas.

But Venkatamahi has completely changed the 72 names and given them new names and claims that the 72 Melams were his handi-work.

The Table in the next page will show that the name of each of the Melakartas has been changed and a good many of the Jannya Ragas have been given the place of Mother Ragas.

The fact that the names of the 15th Kartha Ragam Mayamalavam, the 29th Kartha Ragam Dheerashankaraparanam and that of the 36th Kartha Ragam Jala Natai have not been changed presupposes the existence of a work with the 72 Melakartas long before his time. There is reason to believe that because these three Ragas have a world-wide reputation and because their Jannya Ragas have been so particularly used in the Tamil country, he was not bold enough to change their names.

We may think that the system of 72 Melakarthas with the names Kanakangi and Ratnangi were really written by Vyasa. But it is not true. For if Vyasa had been the author of "Vyasakatakam", Baratha in the 5th and Sarnga Dev in the 13th century would not have failed to make mention of it in their writings. Moreover if we notice their Ragas and their system the custom of giving names by the Kadapayathi Sangai method seems to have been unknown to them.

We conclude, therefore, that the names of the 72 Melakarthas must have been written by a Vyasa who lived after Sarnga Dev and before Venkatamahi, *i. e.* between the 13th and the 16th centuries. There is reason to suppose these changes of names were effected after the advent of foreigners into this country.

However, we note that some mother Ragas are found which have the Srutis of Vattapalai and more minute Srutis. This shows that foreigners who came into India changed the names of the Swarams and the Ragas completely after having learnt up the system of music of the Tamil country and wrote works to make it appear that they were original. They may be seen from the following Table.

The ancient names of Ragas and the New Names given to them by Venkatamahi.

No.	Ancient Names.	Names given by Venkatamahi.	No.	Ancient Names.	Names given by Venkatamahi.
1	Kanakangi	Kanahambari	37	Salagam	Sougandani
2	Ratnangi	Penathuthi	38	Jalarnavam	Jaganmoganam
3	Ganamurti	Gana Samavarali	39	Jalavarali	Thali Varali
4	Vanaspati	Panumati	40	Navaneetham	Nabomoni
5	Manavathi	Manoranchini	41	Bavani	Kumbini
6	Thanarubi	Thanukeerti	42	Ragapirya	Ravikirya
7	Senavathi	Senakirani	43	Kavambothi	Keervani
8	Anumathodi	Janathodi	44	Bavapirya	Bavani
9	Thenuka	Thoni pinna Shadjam	45	Subabanduvarali	Sivabanduvarali
10	Natakapiriya	Natаparanam	46	Shatvitamarkini	Sthavarajamu
11	Kokilapirya	Kokilarapam	47	Swarnangi	Souveeram
12	Rupavati	Rupavati	48	Thivyamoni	Jeevanthini
13	Kayakapiriya	Koyaketchatchi	49	Thavalambari	Thapalangam
14	Vakulaparanam	Vadi Vasanta bairavi	50	Nama narayani	Namadesi
15	Mayamalavagoula	Maya malava goula.	51	Kamavartani	Kasiramakirya
16	Chakravagam	Thoya Veha Vahini	52	Ramapirya	Ramamanokari
17	Sooryakantham	Sapavati	53	Kamanapirya	Kamagakirya
18	Atakambari	Jaya suddha malavi	54	Visvambari	Vamsavati
19	Jangarathvani	Jangara brahmari	55	Syamalangi	Samola
20	Natabairavi	Nari reethi goula	56	Shunmugapirya	Samara
21	Keeravani	Kranavali	57	Simyentra mathyamam	Sumatthuthi
22	Karaharapirya	Sriragam	58	Hemavati	Thesi simkaravam
23	Kourimanohari	Kouri Velavali	59	Tharmavati	Thamavati
24	Varunapirya	Veera Vasantam	60	Neethimathi	Nishatham
25	Mararanjani	Saravali	61	Kanthamoni	Kundalam
26	Sarukesi	Tharangini	62	Rishabapirya	Rethipirya
27	Sarasanghi	Sourasena	63	Lathangi	Geethapirya
28	Arikambodi	Harikathara goula	64	Vasaspati	Bousavati
29	Dheerasankaraparanam	Dheerasankaraparanam	65	Mechakalyani	Santha kalyani
30	Naganandi	Nagaparanam	66	Chithrambari	Chathurangani
31	Yagapiriya	Kalavati	67	Susarithra	Santhana manjari
32	Ragavarthani	Raga Soodamani	68	Jothisvaroopini	Jothiragam
33	Kangayabusani	Gangatharangini	69	Thathuvarthani	Thoutha panchamam
34	Vahatheesvari	Bokthasaya nada	70	Nasikabushani	Nasamoni
35	Soolini	Sylathesatchi	71	Kosalam	Kusumikaram
36	Salanada	Chala natta	72	Rasikapirya	Rasamanjari

Sarnga Dev who wrote about Srutis gave certain names for Swarams such as Kaisika Ni, Kakali Ni, Satharana Ga, Antara Ga, Sutha Sa, and Sutha Pa and fixed 22 Srutis in the Sthayi. The same names have been used in Karnatic music for the 12 Swarams of Ayapalai and the 24 Alakus acccrding to the system of Vattapalai.

In ancient times they seem to have been reckoned as having 2, 4 and 6 Alakus. This is quite in accordance with the Alaku Nilai of the Mathematical Table of the ancient Tamils known as எண்சுவடி.

So it appears that everybody can easily name the Swarams and Srutis according to the number of their Alakus according to the system of the ancient Tamils, for example, we may place the number of the Alakus after the Swaram and say Ri with 1 Alaku, Ri with 1¼ Alakus, Ri with 1½ Alakus, Ri with 1¾ Alakus, Ri with 2 Alakus and Ri with 4 Alakus or place the number of Alakus before the Swaram and say 4 Alakus Ri, 4¼ Alakus Ri, 4½ Alakus Ri, 4¾ Alakus Ri or 5 Alakus Ri and so on. This will enable us to understand the Swarasthanams without any doubt.

We are of opinion that it is important to find out the Ragas where the Swarams, Srutis and minuter Srutis of the ganam of South India occur.

7. Examples showing the particular Srutis used in modern Ragas which follow the system of the ancient Tamils.

We made a few remarks about the Swarams, Srutis and very minute Srutis used in Isai-Tamil, sweeter than nectar, in which the ancient Tamilians were so highly proficient. We find that their excellence was quite in keeping with the efficiency they had attained in other sciences such as Anatomy, Physiology, Astronomy, Medicine and Philosophy. Music has also been developed in proportion as the inner meaning and calculations of other sciences had advanced.

We see that the ancient Tamilians, the Pandya sovereigns who ruled in South Madura and the scholars of the Tamil Sangams were efficient in Isai-Tamil, that they completely understood even the very minute Srutis used in music, and that they sang the praises of God in Pahs proportionate to the subtlety of those Srutis. We knew that the several religious *puns* such as Thirugnanam, Thevaram and Thiruvachakam which are sung from the very ancient times and that several other religious *puns* anterior to that time are sung up to the present day in accordance with the rules of ancient Isai-Tamil.

It is a fact that we are singing only the ancient *puns* and Ragas according to the ancient methods and we are singing nothing new. But we have reached the stage where the names of these Puns and Ragas have been completely changed by strangers, nay, the Tamilians are accused of ignorance of music! Such is the times!

It is said that Narada gave the Suvadi treating about the minuteness of Ragas to Theagarajayar, who lived at Tiruvadi, as a great devotee of Rama, about 60 years ago. But ancient works on Isai-Tamil speak of Narada as Yal-asirian. Though we see in his Keertanams the Srutis of the four Palais of the ancient Tamilians, as modern musicians have no idea how the ancient Puns were chanted, we had to quote a few of his Keertanams here for demonstration. The result of our researches on Puns as well as on Ragas and Srutis will be published later on.

My opinions may appear very strange to many advocates of 22 Srutis who live in this age when there is a great doubt about Srutis. However, I have stated them hoping perhaps it might be of some use to unbiassed musicians who are close observers.

I have to state again and again that the ancients divided the octave into 12 half Swarams by the principle of concordant and branch Swarams (SA-PA and SA-MA systems), then divided them into 24 Alakus according to the system of Vattapalai and made their Ganam with 2 Alakus less.

We arrived at the conclusion that there were 24 and not 22 Srutis in the octave by various experiments. We examined a number of Ragas both vocally and on the Veena with the help of M. R. Ry. Muthaya Baghavatar Avl, of Harikesava Nallur and M. R. Ry. Vencatachallam Iyer, the Veena Vidwan of Tanjore Palace, noted down the minute Srutis used in them and roughly marked the 24 Srutis. But the former did not concur with my theory of 24 Srutis till he saw the "Brahma Melam" 2 years later. Even this work was doubted by the latter till he saw the "Melathikara lakshanam" constructed after the 24 Srutis system, found in the Sarasvati Mahal of the Tanjore Palace. However, the idea that there must be minuter Srutis than 24 was often worrying us. When we gave out the idea of 24 Srutis in the octave, many musicians raised their objections and made fun of the theory.

In addition to this they fought tooth and nail about this theory in the Tanjore Sangeeta Vidhya Mahajana Sangam and tried to establish 22 and 53 Srutis in the octave. So we were unable to expect any help from that quarter.

However, with the help of my talented daughter Srimati Maragathavalli Ammal who is no mean exponent of the Karnatic music and who has the distinction of having passed the Higher Local Examination of the Theory of Music of the Trinity College, London, we were able to examine the minuter Srutis of Karntic music for a considerable time.

The Tables have been shown separately according to the system in use among the ancient Tamilians. Table 5 gives some of the Desika Ragas and Hindustani Ragas which have different Swarams in Arohanam and Avarohanam. Tables 1, 2, 3 and 4 give some of the Marga Ragas which satisfy the rules of South Indian music.

We have already noticed that the Tamilians were highly proficient in Isai-Tamil, that they were competent to use and discriminate between the minutest Srutis, and that the Ragas of the present day date from very ancient times though their names have been mutilated in many ways.

We see that dealers in grains and miscellaneous articles and other merchants have been using uniform measures like one measure, ½ a measure, ¼ of a measure, ⅛ of a measure and $\frac{1}{16}$ of a measure and weights like 1 palam, ½ a palam, ¼ of a palam, ⅛ of a palam and $\frac{1}{16}$ of a palam, and many such devices so that there may be no difficulty in their dealings with others, and such devices exist even at present.

In the same manner in music also the different measurements such as Ayapalai, Vattapalai, Thirikonapalai and Chathurapalai have been used so that the Swarams which they use in any music might be easily classified.

The term '*Palai*' means "that which is divided" and "one of the sweet tastes of music". This shows they had four divisions to suit the different sounds of the *puns* sung.

Of these, Ayapalai admits of ganam in the 12 Swarams of a Sthayi derived by the SA-PA and the SA-MA systems.

Vattapalai consists of 24 Srutis with 2 Alakus for each of the 12 Swarams of the Sthayi, but the ganam is made with an Alaku less in each of the two concordant or branch Swarams like Vilari and Kaikilai. The other Swarams belong to Ayapalai.

Thirikonapalai admits of ganam with half the Alakus of the concordant and branch Swarams of Vattapalai. The other Swarams are those of Ayapalai.

Chathurapalai admits of ganam with quarter Alaku Swarams of the Vattapalai series, in other words, it has very minute Srutis like ¼, ¾, 1¼ and 1¾. The other Swarams are those of Ayapalai. By this, we do not mean that all Swarams should lose their original position in the octave and sound with the minutest Srutis. But only the two Swarams which are Jeevaswarams in Arohanam and Avarohanam should admit minute Srutis with 1 Alaku, ½ Alaku, ¼ Alaku and so on.

The Tables 1, 2, 3 and 4 give the Ragas with Srutis according to the 4 Palais given above. They are easily understood. Of these

the first Table gives the Ragas where the 12 half Swarams of Ayapalai are used,

the second Table gives those where the quarter Swarams of Vattapalai are also used,

the third gives those Ragas where the ⅛ Srutis of Thirikonapalai also occur along with other Swarams,

the fourth gives those Ragas where the $\frac{1}{16}$ Srutis of Chathurapalai are used along with other Swarams.

and the fifth contains the Ragas which contain Srutis mixed with Desikam in Karnatic music and Hindustani music.

Table I showing the Ragas of Ayapalai.

The Ragas of Ayapalai in the 12 half Srutis.

No.	Kartha.	Ragam.	SA	RI							GA						MA				PA	DHA							NI						SA
				1	2	3	4	5	6	7	2	3	4	5	6	7	2	3	4	5		1	2	3	4	5	6	7	2	3	4	5	6	7	
1	Dhirasankarabaranam.	... ...	2				4								6		2				2				4								6		
2	Harikambothi ...	... ...	2				4								6		2				2				4						4				
3	Kharakarappiriya ...	... ...	2				4						4				2				2				4						4				
4	Natapyravi ...	... ...	2				4						4				2				2		2								4				
5	Hanumaththodi ...	... ...	2		2								4				2				2		2								4				
6	Methakalyani ...	... ...	2				4								6				4		2				4								6		
7	Mayamalavam ...	... ...	2		2										6		2				2		2										6		
8	Chakravaham ...	... ...	2		2										6		2				2				4						4				
9	Dhirasankarabaranam	Pankala	2				4								6		2				2				0								6		
10	Kanakayabhooshani...	Kankayapooshani	2						6						6		2				2		2										6		
11	Valntheesvari ...	Sayanattai ...	2						6						6		2				2				4						4				
12	Vanaspathi	Vanaspathi ...	2		2						2						2				2				4						4				
13	Harikambothi ...	Kunthalavarali ...	2				0								0		2				2				4						4				
14	Natapyravi	Jayantha Sri ...	2				0						4				2				2		2								4				
15	Dhirasankarabaranam.	Karudathoni ...	2				4								6		2				2				4								6		
16	Karakarapiriya ...	Salakhapyravi ...	2				4						4				2				2				4						4				
17	Harikambothi ...	Kokilathoni ...	2				4								6		2				2				4						4				
18	Dhirasankarabaranam.	Kolakalam ...	2				4								6		2				2				4								6		
19	Harikambothi ...	Sinthukannada ...	2				4								6		2				2				4						4				
20	Dhirasankarabaranam.	Sinthumanthari...	2				4								6		2				2				4								6		

The Ragas given in Table I are the ones most commonly in use in Karnatic music. These are sung in half Swarams only in Ayapalai by the ancient Tamilians. These occur with 2, 4 or 6 Alakus in the 12 Rasis. They stand in the Relation of Vadi and Samvadi Swarams or concordant and branch Swarams to one another.

We may notice that as a rule, Ri with 2 Alakus is followed by Dha with 2 Alakus, Ri with 4 Alakus by Dha with 4, Ga with 4 Alakus by Ni with 4, and Ga with 6 Alakus is followed by Ni with 6.

The corresponding Arohana and Avarohana Swarams are found in the Table below. The Ragam should proceed strictly by the Swarams in Arohanam and Avarohanam and according to the Alakus given in the Table. This is Margam. We shall give in book II some of the rules relating to this.

Table I showing the Ragas of Ayapalai.

No.	Ragams.	Arohanam.	Avarohanam.
1	Dhirasankaraparanam.	s r g m p d n s	s n d p m g r s
2	Harikambothi	s r g m p d n s	s n d p m g r s
3	Karakarappiriya ...	s r g m p d n s	s n d p m g r s
4	Natapyravi	s r g m p d n s	s n d p m g r s
5	Hanumathodi	s r g m p d n s	s n d p m g r s
6	Mechakalyani	s r g m p d n s	s n d p m g r s
7	Mayamalavam ...	s r g m p d n s	s n d p m g r s
8	Sakravaham	s r g m p d n s	s n d p m g r s
9	Pankala	s r g m p n p s	s n p m r g r s
10	Kankayabhoosani ...	s r g m p d n s	s n d p m g r s
11	Sayanattai	s r g m p m p s	s n d n p m r s
12	Vanaspathi	s r g m p d n s	s n d p m g r s
13	Kunthalavarali ...	s m p d n d s	s n d p m s
14	Jayantha Sri	s g m d n s	s n d m p m g s
15	Karudathoni	s r g m p d n s	s d p g r s
16	Salakapyravi	s r m p d s	s n d p m g r s
17	Kokilathoni	s r g m d n d s	s n d n p m g r s
18	Kolakalam	s p m g m p d n s ...	s n d p m g r s
19	Sinthukannada ...	s m g m r g m p s ...	s n d p m g r s
20	Sinthumanthari ...	s r g m p s	s n d p g m d p m r s

Table II. Ragas of Vattapalai.

The Ragas of Vattapalai in the 24 quarter Srutis.

No.	Kartha.	Ragam.	SA	RI							GA						MA				PA	DHA							NI						SA
				1	2	3	4	5	6	7	2	3	4	5	6	7	2	3	4	5		1	2	3	4	5	6	7	2	3	4	5	6	7	
1	Dhirasankarabaranam	Piyakadai ...	2				4								6			3			2				4							5			
2	Mayamalavam ...	Saveri	2	1										5			2				2	1										5			
3	Neethimathi ...	... Kaikavesi ...	2				4						4							5	2						6							7	
4	Harikambothi	... Sahana	2				4									7	2				2				4							5			
5	Bavapriya ...	... Bavapriya ...	2	1								3½							4½		2	1								3½					
6	Dhirasankarabaranam.	Devagandhari ...	2				4½							5	*		2				2				4½							5	*		

Table II. Ragas of Vattapalai.

This is the system of Ganam by which the ancient Tamilians divided each of the Rasis into 2 Alakus according to the Vattapalai system thus obtaining 24 Srutis in the octave and made Ganam with one Alaku less in two of the Rasis which are related as concordant or branch.

We see here that some of the Swarams of Ayapalai with even number of Alakus such as 2, 4 and 6 occur as Swarams with odd numbers of Alakus. For example, Saveri and Bhavapriya have Ri_1 and Dha_1 instead of Ri and Dha with 2 Alakus. In the same manner Saveri has Ni_3 and Ga_3 in place of Ni_4 and Ga_4. But in Bhavapriya Ga_3 and Ni_3 are a little sharper. In Devagandhari Ga and Ni have 5 Alakus each but Ri and Dha have 4½ Alakus Sahana has Ga_5 and Ni_1. Kaikavasi has the 5th Alaku of Ma and the 7th Alaku of Ni. Biakatai has Ma_3 and Ni_5. We find that all the above have odd Srutis in the 24 Srutis of Vattapalai but have even Swarams according to those of Ayapalai.

Devagandari has Ga and Ni with 6 Alakus very rarely. They may be found to have different Srutis while being sung. The Arohanams and Avarohanams of Ragas are given below.

No.	Ragams.	Arohanam.	Avarohanam.
1	Byakadai	s g r g m p d p s ...	s n d p m g r s
2	Saveri...	s r m p d s...	s n d p m g r s
3	Kaikavesi	s r g m p d n s	s n p m g r s
4	Sahana	s r g m p m d n s ...	s n s d p m ga m r s
5	Bhavapriya	s r g m p d n s... ...	s n d p m g r s
6	Devagandhari ...	s r m p d s	s n d p m g r s

Table III. Ragas of Thirikonapalai.

The Ragas sung with 48 one-eighth Srutis according to the system of Thirikonapalai.

Number.	Kartha.	Ragam.	SA	RI							GA						MA				PA	DHA							NI						SA
				1	2	3	4	5	6	7	2	3	4	5	6	7	2	3	4	5		1	2	3	4	5	6	7	2	3	4	5	6	7	
1	Dhirasankaraparanam...	Sankarabaranam...	2				4½								6		2				2				4½								6		
2	Hanumaththodi ...	Thodi	2		2							3½					2				0		2							3½					
3	Do.	Thanniasi ...	2		2								4½				2				2		2								4½				
4	Bavappiriya ...	... Bavappiriya ...	2	1								3½							4½		2	1								3½					
5	Thanuka ...	... Thanuka... ...	2		2							3½					2				2		2										6		
6	Salanattai ...	... Nattai	2						6½						6		2				2						6						6½		
7	Mayamalavam	... Phouli	2		2										6½		0				2		2										6½		
8	Harikambothi	... Palahamsa ...	2				4½								6		2				2				4½						4				
9	Karakarapiriya	... Aboki	2				4						4½				2				0				4							0			
10	Shunmugappiriya	... Shunmugappiriya	2				4					3½							4½		2		2							3½					
11	Kamavarthani	... Kamavarthani ...	2		2										6				4½		2		2										6		
12	Harikambothi	... Nattaikurinji ...	2				4½								6		2				2				4						4½				
13	Karakarapiriya	... Sriranjini ...	2				4						4½				2				0				4						4½				
14	Dhirasankaraparanam	Hamsadhoni ...	2				4½								6½		0				2				0								6½		
15	Harikambothi	... Mohanam ...	2				4½								6½		0				2				4½						0				

Table III. Ragas of Thirikonapalai.

The Swarams in the above Table with an even number of Alakus such as 2, 4 and 6 are those of Ayapalai. But we see some of those Swarams either with half an Alaku more or half an Alaku less, such as $4+\frac{1}{2}=4\frac{1}{2}$ and $4-\frac{1}{2}=3\frac{1}{2}$. The Ri and Dha of Sankarabharanam have $4\frac{1}{2}$ Alakus each, while the other Swarams are Suddha. The Ga and Ni in Thodi have $3\frac{1}{2}$ Alakus each. The Ga and Ni of Thanyasi have $4\frac{1}{2}$. In the Natai Ragam (about whose Srutis there was such a discussion at the first meeting of the Tanjore Mahajana Sabha and at which no definite conclusion was arrived at) the Ri and Ni have $6\frac{1}{2}$ Alakus. In Hamsadoni the Ga and Ni have $6\frac{1}{2}$ Alakus. In the same way the Table will show that Ma has $4\frac{1}{2}$ and Ri, Ga, Dha and Ni $6\frac{1}{2}$ Alakus each. The other Swarams are those of Ayapalai.

This is used as Thirikonapalai by the ancient Tamilians. These Ragas have been in use from the ancient times as seen from the Puns and Keertanams found in ancient Isai-Tamil.

The Arohanams and Avarohanams of Ragas are given in the following Table.

No.	Ragams.	Arohanam.	Avarohanam.
1	Sankarabharanam ...	s r g m p d n s	s n d p m g r s
2	Thodi	s r g m d n s	s n d m g r s
3	Thannyasi	s g m p n s	s n d p m g r s
4	Dhenuka	s r g m p d n s	s n d p m g r s
5	Nattai	s r g m p d n s	s n p m r s
6	Bhouli	s r g p d s	s n d p g r s
7	Balahamsa	s r m p d s	s n d p m r m g s
8	Apohi	s r g m d s	s d m g r s
9	Shanmukhapriya ...	s r g m p d n s	s n d p m g r s
10	Kamavardhini ...	s r g m p d n s	s n d p m g r s
11	Nattaikurinji	s r g m n d n p d n s...	s n d m g s
12	Sriranjeni	s r g m d n s	s n d m g r s
13	Hamsadhoni ...	s r g p n s	s n p g r s
14	Mohanam	s r g p d s	s d p g r s

Table IV. Ragas of Chathurapalai.

The Ragas sung with 96 one-sixteenth Srutis according to the system of Chathurapalai.

Number	Kartha.	Ragam.	SA	RI							GA						MA				PA	DHA							NI						SA
				1	2	3	4	5	6	7	2	3	4	5	6	7	2	3	4	5		1	2	3	4	5	6	7	2	3	4	5	6	7	
1	Karakarapiriya.	Madhimavathi...	2				4¾						0				2				2				0						4¾				
2	,, ...	Nayaki ...	2				4					3¾					2				2				4					3¾					
3	Thiruchiharaharanam.	Dhevaganthari.	2				4¾							5	*		2				2				4¾							5	*		
4	,, ...	Arabi ...	2				4¼								6		2				2				4¼								6		
5	,, ...	Purnachandrigi	2				4½								6		2				2				4¼								6		
6	,, ...	Kakanakuthukalam.	2				4¼								6		2				2				¼								6		
7	Harikambothi...	Sanjuriti ...	2				4¼								6		2				2				4¼						¼				
8	,, ...	Navarasakannada	2				4								6		2				2				4					3¾					
9	,, ...	Nagaswarawali	2				0								6		2				2				4¼						0				
10	Hanumaththodi	Himanki ...	2		2							3¾					2				2		2							3¾					
11	Karakarapiriya.	Kanada ...	2				4						4¾				2				2				4						4¾				

Table IV. Ragas of Chathurapalai.

When we examine the above Ragas we find that with the exception of ¼ and ¾ Swarams the rest belong to Ayapalai. Ri and Dha have ¼ or ¾ Alaku added on to the 4 Alakus, and Ga and Ni have 3¾ and 4¾ Alakus. The other Swarams are the half Swarams of Ayapalai.

But in Devagandari the Ga and Ni have one Alaku less and so have only 5. This system of lessening an Alaku for Ga and Ni by the Vattapalai, and adding a ¼ or ¾ Alaku for the same by Chathurapalai adds a peculiar charm to the ganam. Lessening an Alaku for Ga, and Ni, (Vattapalai) and adding a ¼ or ¾ Alaku for Ri, and Dha, (Chathurapalai) according to the different systems is the cause of the sweetness of the Ragas.

If we notice Devagandari and Arabi which generate from Dheerasankarabaranam and which have the same Arohanam and Avarohanam (Sa Ri Ma Pa Dha Sa and Sa Ni Dha Pa Ma Ga Ri Sa), the Ri and Dha in Devagandari have 4¾ Alakus each while the same occur in Arabi with 4¼ Alakus. Again, Ga and Ni have one Alaku less or 5 according to Vattapalai in Devagandari but in Arabi Ga with 6 Alakus or Anthara Ga and Ni with 6 Alakus or Kakali Ni occur.

So this system with one Alaku less than that of Ayapalai (which is Vattapalai) and ¼ an Alaku less than that of Ayapalai (which is Thirikonapalai) and ¼ Alaku more than that of Ayapalai (which is Thirikonapalai) has been in use from very ancient times.

These sharp Swarams, we know, are played as Gamakams in the 12 frets of the Veena. The ancient Tamilians have called Gamakam by the name 'Padalamutham' or 'the nectar of music' or the most charming parts in a melody. There is reason to think that others applied the name Padalamutham to the Jeeva Swarams.

For, in the above Table, Ri and Dha are sharper by ¼ or ¾ Alaku. It is these sharp Swarams that are the very life of the particular Ragas. In the same manner the Ri Dha Ga Ni and Ma which are made sharp in each of the Ragas from the Jeevaswarams.

We find from the Table that Ri and Dha in Sankarabaranam and Ga and Ni in Thodi are mentioned as Jeevaswarams. There are reasons why these particular Swarams should be Jeevaswarams. There is also a method for determining the Jeevaswarams in each Ragam. They will be given in detail in Book II. The Arohanams and Avarohanams of Ragas are given in the Table below.

No.	Ragams.	Arohanam.	Avarohanam.
1	Madhimavathi ...	s r m p n s	s n p m r s
2	Nayaki	s r m p d n d p s	s n s d p m r g r s
3	Dhevaganthari ...	s r m p d s	s n d p m g r s
4	Arabi	s r m p d s	s n d p m g r s
5	Poornachandrigai ...	s r g m p d p s...	s n p d p m g m r s
6	Kakanakuthukalam ...	s r m d n g p s...	s n d p m g r s
7	Sanjuriti ...	d s r g m p d n	d p m g r s n d p
8	Navarasakannada ...	s g m p s	s n d m g r s
9	Nagaswarali	s g m p d s	s d p m g s
10	Himangi	s r g m p d n d s	s n p d m g r s
11	Kanada	s r g m p m d n s... ...	s n p m n d p m g m r s

Table V. Some Desika Ragas and Hindustani Ragas.

Number.	Kartha.	The opening words of songs.	SA	RI							GA						MA				PA	DHA							NI						SA
				1	2	3	4	5	6	7	2	3	4	5	6	7	2	3	4	5		1	2	3	4	5	6	7	2	3	4	5	6	7	
1	Saranga ...	... Nee vadala kana ...	2				4								6		2		4		2				4								6		
2	Pyak ...	... Mangalam Sleika ...	2				4								6		2		4		2				4						4		6		
3	Thesiga Kalyani ...	Singara vana kanitha...	2				4								6		2		4		2				4								6		
4	Gaupi ...	... Dheem na thera dheem	2				4						4				2				2		2		4						4				
5	Bhairavi ...	... Koluvai yunadha ...	2				4						4				2				2		2		4						4				
6	Anantha Bhairavi...	Atharamunai alhall ..	2				4						4				2				2		2		4						4				
7	Kaumbothi ...	... Eppadium pavikalai ...	2				4								6		2				2				4						4		6		
8	Adana ...	... Pala kanakamaya ...	2				4								6		2				2				4						4		6		
9	Muhari ...	... Ennaod kirupa kalkuno	2				4						4				2				2		2		4						4				
10	Pyahak ...	... Savalisurattha Paramgi	2				4								6		2		4		2				4						4		6		
11	Ameerakalyani	... Thurasa pola pola ...	2				4								6		2		4		2				4								6		
12	Kamas ...	... Nathiyakinari pasiyan.	2				4								6		2				2		2		4						4		6		
13	Maunt ...	... Mee abarathikaravidow	2				4								6		2				2				4						4		6		
14		Kona daya karathutha	2				4								6		2				2				4						4		6		
15	Hindustani Kanada	Soapara mesarasasani	2				4						4	5			2				2				4						4	5			

Table V. Some Desika Ragas and Hindustani Ragas.

We find from the above Table that Ragas have the 12 half Swarams of Ayapali but the fixed rule is that a Swaram which has a particular number of Alakus in Arohanam should have the same in Avarohanam also. This is Margam.

Sometimes a Swaram or two may be omitted or their order changed either, in Arohanam or Avarohanam. But the number of Alakus should never be changed.

For example, a Ri with 4 Alaku should never be changed either in Arohanam or Avarohanam into one with 2 or 6 Alakus. The same rule applies to Ga Ma Dha and Ni. If they so occur, they infringe one of the fixed rules of South Indian music or Margam. This infringement of rules is called Desikam. No doubt these Desika Ragas are very pleasant as the mixture of sweetmeats like Boondhi and Ladu with salted mango or salted lemon which add flavour to the sweetness. But this can never be compared to the Ganam made strictly in accordance with the rules of Karnatic Music, which independently by itself has the power of charming even elephants and inducing cobras to spread their hood and dance. So we have not dealt with Desikam to any extent. I think what I have already given about Desikam in the first part is enough. The following Table gives the Arohanam and Avarohanam of Desika Ragas.

We notice in Table IV that in the system of Chathurapalai, in the Ragam Kanada, Ga and Ni had 4¾ Alakus each. When the same Ragam is sung as Hindustani, the Ni and Ga have 5 Alakus sometimes and even 4 Alakus at other times, while the other Swarams resemble those of the Karnatic Kanada. I am not able to give more examples of Hindustani Ragas as I am not well acquainted with them.

Again, if we notice Hindustani Ragas, we find that each of the Swarams in particular Ragas occurs continuously with one or more Swarams, indicating the Swarams pertaining to that Ragam and thus makes the Sancharam in Arohanam and Avarohanam. It is the custom to indicate the top Swarams while making Sancharam in the lower Swarams in Arohanam and *vice versa*. These are mostly the 12 half Swarams of Ayapalai. A few of the 24 Srutis of Vattapalai also rarely occur as in Hindustani Kanada. Those who are well acquainted with Hindustani music should inquire into this and give us the result of their observations.

No.	Ragams.	Arohanam.	Avarohanam.
1	Sarnga	s r g m p d n s...	s n d p m r g m r s
2	Piyake	s g m p d n s	s n d p m g r s
3	Dhesikakalyani ...	s r g m p d n s...	s n d p m g r s
4	Kabi	s r g m p n s	s d n p m r g m r s
5	Bairavi	s r g m p d n s...	s n d p m g r s
6	Ananthabairavi ...	s g r g m p d p s,n s...	s n d p m g r s
7	Kambothi	s r g m p d s	s n d p m g r s
8	Adana	s r m p nee s	s n da p d n d p m g r s
9	Muhari	s r m p d s	s n d p m g r s

If the Ragas could be arranged, as shown in the above tables, under Ayapalai, Vattapalai, Thirikonapalai and Chathurapalai with their respective Swarams in Aroganam and Avaroganam, there could never arise any doubt in the future as regards Swarams and minute Srutis. It will also be of help to the students of music of the present day.

With the exception of the 12 half Swarams of Ayapalai, the other minute Srutis should be played according to their respective pitch as gamakams by pulling the strings of the Veena. When Swarams are played as gamakams they are as sweet as the re-production of the human voice. It will not be possible to play them as separate notes by means of frets.

We must understand, then, that permanent frets should be had on the Yal only for the half Swarams of Ayapalai while the rest of the Srutis should be played as gamakams.

8. Calculations to determine the position of Swarams in the Yal.

We see clearly that the Yal and the Kulal were the most important of the instruments long used by the ancient Tamils. We know from experience that these two instruments are capable of reproducing even the minutest Swarams.

Here, instead of saying what the minuter Srutis were, they seem to have employed the terms Vattapalai, Thirikonapalai and Chathurapalai. When this system fell into disuse, it became impossible to bring Ragas under their respective palais until recent times when they were classified under the 72 Melakartas.

Though Ragas have been classified under the 72 Melakartas they are not correct as there are minute differences like ¼, ½, ¾ and 1 Alakus, as may be seen from the Table. For example, we use Arabi with 4¼ Alakus in Deerasankaraparanam which should have R_1 with 4 Alakus, and we sing also Sankaraparanam and Amsadoni with 4½ Alakus and Devagandari with 4¾ Alakus. We have to be thankful that so much at least has been done where everything was dark.

We have observed before that the Yal has been so constructed as to satisfy the measurements of the human body, the tatvas of man and the calculations of the human breath. Just as the height of a man when seated is 4 spans, the Swarasthanams of a Yal from the Meru to the Mettu should also be 4 spans of the player. If not, the different beauties of the sound of the Yal could never be brought out. We think it, therefore, necessary to give, in a way, the measurements of the Swarams and the minute Srutis of the Yal.

As we have already made mention of ivory or bamboo frets for determining the sounds of the minute Srutis on page 764 it is enough if we give the measurements here for the Sthanams of the frets and calculations to test their accuracy in a Yal 32 inches long.

We also give here the measurements of the Dwavimsati Srutis of Sarnga Dev, the author of Sangeeta Ratnakaram, for comparison showing where the 22 Srutis of the Madhya Sthayi (16 inches long) occur, proving at the same time their incompatibility with the ganam of the ancient Tamils.

We observed before on pages 757-758 in the Table of calculations for the 24 Srutis of Vattapalai how the length of wire for each Sruti is obtained by multiplying the decimal fractions in column 8 by 32 inches.

These calculations are based on the following facts:—(1) that if 1 be the length of wire where Athara SA sounds, the Tara SA sounds in half the length, (2) if Athara SA be 1 in sound, Tara SA should be double that, (3) the length of the wire and the pitch of the respective sounds vary in an inverse ratio, (4) the principle of proceeding upwards by Geometrical Progression does not admit of any possible sound between notes and (5) wherever the sounds may be they are all of the same proportionate measurement that the series does not present any difficulty while change of graham is made.

We have to note something here. If 4 spans be equal to 31 inches only, then the decimal fractions in col. 8 should be multiplied by 31 and the measurements for Swarams calculated. On the other hand, if 4 spans are equal to 33, 34, 35 or 36 inches the fractions in col 8. should be multiplied by these figures so as to suit the different measurements. The centimetre should be used where each inch is divided into 100 equal parts.

What we mean when we say that the measurements in the Yal should be in proportion to the length of fingers is that growing youths should add $\frac{1}{2}$ or $\frac{1}{4}$ of an inch while grown up adults should reduce by such lengths as the case may arise. For example, if a player whose 4 spans are $32\frac{1}{2}$ inches be under 25 years of age, the $32\frac{1}{2}$ inches may be reckoned as 33, and if such a person be over 25 years, the $32\frac{1}{2}$ inches may be reckoned as 32, and the measurements marked accordingly on the Veena.

We all know that if the total length of the wire be 32 inches, the Madhya SA sounds in the 16 inches or half the length of the whole wire. So the 12 Swarasthanams are marked in this 16 inch wire. Over and above this, the 24 Srutis of the Sthayi and the $\frac{1}{48}$ and $\frac{1}{96}$ minuter Srutis are marked inside. Measurements and names are given for the 12 half Swarams and the 24 quarter Swarams. Details about the other minute Srutis may be found in the Table which commences on page 768.

If the Swarasthanams are to be marked in a Yal on this principle, the length of the wire in a Yal from the Meru to the Mettu should be 32 inches. Wherever the wire falls in the Meru and the Mettu the measurement should be very minutely taken or else it may sound $\frac{1}{8}$ or $\frac{1}{16}$ of a Swaram sharper.

To give an instance, it is within our experience that wooden articles expand in moisture and contract when dried. It is customary to have an interval of a quarter or three-eighths of an inch between the brass plate and the string to enable it to sound sweet when the top plank of the Yal expands in cold weather. At such times there is a diminution of an interval of $\frac{1}{16}$ or $\frac{1}{8}$ of an inch. So the total length of the wire diminishes and the Swarams are slightly sharper.

During the hot season, when the top plank of the Veena contracts, the intervals become enlarged and the Swarams become slightly flatter. This necessitates some adjustment during the different weathers. This truth is well known to all players on the Veena. This is why we have to be very particular and minute in the measurement of the wire.

Now, to proceed to fix the frets on the Yal, the Swarasthanams should first be made level by wax. Then the measurement given in the book should be marked in a long strip of paper 16 inches long, and this paper should be placed parallel quite close to the top part and the different Swarasthanams should be minutely marked in the Yal, where the wax is level and the frets placed on the Swarasthanam. The measurement in the paper as well as the measurement of the frets on the Yal should be constantly checked in order to ensure accuracy.

Though placing of frets is not a difficult task to those who possess a musical ear, it will take some time to arrive at the accurate Swarasthanams by comparing them with the Swarams that occur in various ragams. Even then, there may be a slight inaccuracy in the swarams. But if one proceeds by the method given above the whole process can be accurately finished within an hour's time. Not that we cry down the process of fixing the Swarasthanams by the ancient Sa Pa principle of the Tamilians indicated by the lines "குரல் இளி என்றிரு நரம்பின் ஒப்பக்கேட்கும் உணர்வினனாகி" which is possible to a man with an ear for music. But we are surely against doing this by the rough measurement of 3/2 for Sa-Pa and 4/3 for Sa-Ma with their respective number of vibrations. There are those, in the modern day, who advocate this principle. But we know that multiples of 3/2 never finish an octave.

Our method is chiefly given to show that there is a very minute and accurate process by which even the minutest Srutis can be accurately arrived at. Hence these calculations and these Tables.

Just as invertebrate animals are weak, sciences and arts without accurate measurements are also weak. If the rules of art arrived at by long experience are not jotted down according to the commfon rules and measurements they will not last. Just because the ancient Tamils who were experts in music failed to record the measurements expecting that their generations will also be equally clever, Pythagoras had to give roughly his theory of Sa-Pa 3/2 and Sa-Ma 4/3, 2500 years ago and the author of Parijatam his theory that Pa sounds in 2/3 and Ma in 3/4 of the total length of string about 250 years ago.

Perhaps they failed to give the measurements because they had stated clearly how the 12 Swarams of a Rasi arranged themselves on the principles of Inai or Sa-Pa in a Rasi chakaram as sevens, how the same Swarams arranged themselves as fifths by the Sa-Ma principle proceeding leftwards. When such was the case and when it was brought into practical use also in the Veena they thought perhaps the measurements would never be open to doubt.

Though detailed measurements are not stated in works on music yet the author of Sangeeta Ratnakar writes as if he perfectly understood the system of determining Swarams and of tuning instruments. His calculations for the Sthayi and for the Srutis and his principle of change of graham are in perfect accord with the system of the ancient Tamils. But the only difference is that the ancient Tamils divided the Sthayi into 24 Alakus and made ganam in them with an Alakus less in each of the Swarams which were in the relation of Inai and Kilai.

The Tamils have very clearly stated the four primary puns in Vattapalai, namely, Marutham. Kurinji, Neythal and Palai, the 16 puns derived from each of the four Jatis Ahanilai, Puranilai, Arugial and Perugial, how they are affected by the change of graham and the Swarams where the Alakus should be lessened. As 22 Alakus are mentioned there, Bharata and Sarnga Dev fell into the error of saying that there were 22 Srutis in the Octave.

When once this doubtful theory was placed before the world, musicians like the author of Parijatam and Venkatamahi wrote works to remove the doubt. Anyhow the theory of Sarnga Dev confounded every one. Later writers adopted the number 22, gave names and Ragalakshanam in accordance with the Alakus of Swarams and thus filled their writings with conflicting ideas.

We know from experience that not a single Ragam could be sung according to the Ragalakshanam given by him and according to the system of Dwavimsati Srutis.

We can assure our readers that all the Ragas sung at the modern day are the Puns used in Isai Tamil by the ancient Tamils and none else. Only later writers gave different names to these Puns as well as the Swarams and perpetuated them by writing books on them.

The minute Srutis in these puns are sung even at the present day. We see that the ancient puns with minute Srutis were sung in the services of temples owing to their devotional nature, and those who sung them were rewarded with gifts of lands, houses and regular salary. We must understand that the puns used in poems of praise like Thevaram, Thiruvachagam and Thirumarei were according to the ancient system.

The Ragam and Thalam for these puns are very cleverly arranged to suit the ideas expressed by them. If one sings them strictly according to the rules, one who hears them will certainly be entranced and shed tears of joy. As this ancient system is arranged according to Thalam and the letters of the Swarams, many gave it up owing to its difficulty. Just as a child which cannot walk when it attempts to stand and take a few steps forward has a fall because it could not balance itself, so also an attempt at ancient music made the moderners to stumble.

The best of experts to day held that the Puns and the Padams sung so as to bring out the structure of Ragas and in conformity with the Thalam are very charming. Some of such Puns and Padams are practised by them and sung so that the hearers are melted to tears. As these Puns are difficult to sing the system of singing Puns has now been changed and they are sung in quick time. Some of these Puns are sung to English and Parsi tunes and consequently their structure and ideas are completely changed.

9. The names of Tamil Puns found in Thevaram and Thiruvachakam and the names of the modern Ragas which stand for them.

Though the Puns contained in Thevaram, Thiruvachakam and Thirumarei were written by great sages who lived between the 4th and the 10th centuries and used up to the present time it appears that even prior to that period many devotional

Puns had been written by great men from the time of the first sangam in ancient South Madura and they have been called by the collective name of 'Thevarathiratu'.

It has been a custom from very ancient times for Tamil Vidwans to sing a few compositions when they appeared in the presence of Kings and God. The holy actions of the deity when represented as musical poems appeal more to the heart and give more pleasure than when merely recited in prose. Puns which melt the heart make the singer as well as the hearer to be in complete unison with God.

Those who are unable to appreciate the beautiful and the lofty ideas of ancient puns and bring them into practical use, sing them in easy varnamettus. This practice is of recent origin.

Many of our readers might have personally known M. R. Ry. Maha Vaidyanatha Iyer Avl., of musical fame, well known in South India for his life of devotion and his elder brother M. R. Ry. Ramasami Iyer Avl., the author of Keertanams from Periya Puranam. They might have also heard their music. These two brothers paid a visit to Sri Subrahmania Desikar, the Matathipathi of Kallidakurichi in Tinnevelly. The Matathipathi took a fancy to Maha Vydianatha Iyer, kept him with him for a long period and had the Thevaram and Thiruvachagam sung in the temple of Nellaiappar in the ancient Puns known to Sri Salivateesvara Othuvar, Sri Thandavaraya Thambiran, Sri Shunmugam Pillai, the Puraneekar and others. He then asked Maha Vydianatha Iyer to repeat them before him and enjoyed their divine music.

In the Peria Puranam which he possessed then, and which is now in the custody of his younger brother Appasami Iyer Avl., of Vyacheri, the modern names for the ancient Ragas and their thalam are given. We are giving the list below as it may be of use to us.

Though the ancient Puns exist even now without any change in the system of their singing, it is clearly seen that their old names have been changed and they appear with foreign names. Though the resemblance between the old and new names is seen in some cases, some of the Ragas have had their old names completely changed. We may also see that some of the names of the ancient Ragas are found in four or five of the modern ones.

As they have been in existence from very old times it is but natural that some of the good Ragas might have become obsolete while others have taken their places. The Puns in the period of Thevarams seem to have been fewer than those at the time of the sage Pingala. Can there be a comparison in numbers between the 12000 ancient Isais of the first sangam and 103 puns of the last sangam? In the same manner even the few Ragas used in Thevaram appear to have entirely disappeared now with their names changed.

In the Table of Ragas given below may be found the Pathigas of Thevarams, the places from which they originated, the ancient names of Puns, their modern names, their Thalam and their opening lines. We think this might be of use to the Tamils who sing Thevara Puns.

Page.	Sthalam.	Ancient Pun.	Modern Ragam.	Thalam.	Opening line.
78	Thiru Irumpoolai	Pun Inthalam ...	Anandabairavi.	Sangeerna Jamby.	சீரார்கழலே தொழுவீர்
78	Thiru Arathai Perumbali ...	Pun Kolli	Sudhasaveri ...	...	பைத்தபாம்போடரைக் கோவணம்
79	Thirucherai	Thiruviragam Pun Sathari.	Neelambari ...	Athithalam	முறியுறு நீர்மல்கு
79	Thirunalur Mayanam ...	Pun Seegamaram ...	Like 'Thiruch Shalal'	...	பாலூரும் மலைப்பாம்பும்
79	Thirukudavayil	Pun Inthalam ...	Saveri	...	திகழும் திருமாலொடு நான்முகனும்
79	Thirunarayur	Pun Piyanthai kantharam.	Nattai	Athithalam	கேசியனுரு மல்லொருபாதுமேனியரியான்
80	Thirupputhur	Pun Thakkaragam ...	Bairavi ...	Athithalam	வெங்கள் விம்மு வெறியார் பொழிற்சோலை
80	Thiruchivapuram	Pun Vyalakurinji ...	Kurinji ...	Athithalam	இன்குரலிசை கெழும்யாழ்முரல
81	Tirukudamooku	Pun Panchamam ...	Anandabairavi Like 'Keedaminia Kuila'	...	அரவிரி கோடனீடலணி காவிரி
81	Thirukudanthaiga Karonam...	Pun Thakkasi ...	Kapi	Athithalam	வாரார் கொங்கை மாதோர் பாகமாக
82	Thirunakecharam	Pun Inthalam ...	Saveri	Athithalam	பொன்னேர் தருமேனியனே
82	Thiruvidaimaruthu	Pun Vialakurinji ...	Sankaraparanam.	Misram ...	விரிதருபுலியுரிவிரவிய வரையினர்
83	Thirukurankaduthurai ...	Pun Inthalam ...	Kalyani ...	Thisram ...	பரவக்கெடும் வல்வினை
84	Thiru Avaduthurai	Pun Gandhara Panchamam.	Sankaraparanam.	...	இடரினும் தளரினுமெனதுறுநோய்
85	Thirukolambam	Pun Inthalam ...	Anandhabairavi.	Athithalam	நீற்றுலர்கீர் சடைமேல்
86	Thiruvykal Madakoil ...	Pun Gandhara Panchamam:	Saveri	Athithalam	துளமதியுடை மறிதோன் றுகையினர்

Page.	Sthalam.	Ancient Pun.	Modern Ragam.	Thalam.	Opening line.
86	Thirunallam ...	... Pun Kurinji ...	Like 'Pitthapirai-soodi'	...	கல்லால் நிழல்மேய
86	Thiruallunthoor ...	... Pun Inthalam ...	Sarangam ...	Athithalam	தொழுமாறு வல்லார் துயர்தீர
87	Thiruththurtthi ...	... Pun Nattaragam ...	Theerasankara-paranam Note	...	வரைத்தலைப் பசும்பொன்னோடு
87	Thirumayiladuthurai	... Pun Thakkaragam ...	Ananthabairavi	Athithalam	கரவின்றி நன்மாமலர்கொண்டு
88	Thiruchempon Palli...	... Pun Thakkaragam ...	Kaliyani ...	Jambai ...	மருவார்குழலி மாதோர்பாகமாய்.
88	Thiruvilamar ...	... Pun Sathari ..	Neelambari ...	Athithalam	மத்தகமணிபெற மலர்வதோர்
88	Thirupparíyaloor ...	... Pun Megaragakurinji	Yethukula Kambothi	Jambai ...	கருத்தன் கடவுள் கனலேந்தி
89	Thiruvettakkudi ...	... Pun Panchamam ...	Sourashtiram ...	Athithalam	வண்டிரைக்கு மலர்க்கொன்றை
89	Thirutharumapuram...	... Pun Viyalakurinji ..	Yethukula Kambothi	Thisram ...	மாதர்மடப்பிடியும் மடவன்னமும்
91	Thirumallaru ...	... Pun Palanthakka-ragam	Sourashtiram ...	Athithalam	போகமார்த்தபூண்முலையாள்தனோடும்
92	Thiruchathamangai	... Pun Panchamam ...	Neelambari ...	Athithalam	திருமலர்க் கொன்றைமாலை
92	Thirunagaikkaronam	... Pun Sevvali ...	Neelambari ...	Athithalam	கூனற்றிங்கள் குறுங்கண்ணி
93	Thirukkeevaloor ...	... Pun Nattaragam ...	Nattai ...	... Athithalam	மின்னுலாவிய சடையினர்
96	Thiruchenkattangudy	... Pun Nattapadai ...	Ananthabairavi	Thisram ...	அங்கமும் வேதமுமோதுநாவர்
96	Thiruppugaloor ...	... Pun Sevvali ...	Neelambari ...	...	வாழ்ந்தநாளும் இனிவாழும் நாளும்
97	Thiruppugaloor ...	... Pun Piyanthaik-kantharam	Arabi ...	... Thisram ...	ஈசனேமர் கடவுளின்னமுதெந்தை

Page.	Sthalam.	Ancient Pun.	Modern Ragam.	Thalam.	Opening line.
98	Thiruvirkudiveerattam ...	Pun Nattaragam ...	Nattai... ...	...	வடிகொள் மேனியர்
99	Thiruvaroor	Pun Kurinji ...	Sourashtram ...	Athithalam	சித்தத்தெளிவீர்காள்
100	Thiruvaroor	Pun Kovsikam ...	Saveri... ...	Athithalam	அந்தமாயு லகாதியுமாயினான்
101	Thiruvalivalam	Pun Viyalakurinji ...	Bairavi ...	...	பூவியல் புரிகுழல்
102	Thirukkolili	Pun Palanthakkaragam	Senchurutti ...	...	நாளாய போகாமே
102	Thiruvaroor	Pun Gandharam ...	Neelambari ...	...	பவளமாய்ச் சோடையாய்
103	Thiruppanayoor	Pun Thakkaragam ...	Piyaku ...	Athithalam	அரவச்சடைமேன் மதிமத்தம்
103	Thiruppugaloor	Pun Nattapadai ...	Nattaikurinji ...	...	குறிகலந்த இசைபாடலினான்
105	Thiruambarpperunthirukkoil ...	Pun Gandhara Panchamam	Saveri	Athithalam	வையகன் மலைமகள்
106	Thirukkadavoor	Pun Gandhara Panchamam	Nathanamakkiriyai	Athithalam	சடையுடையானும்
106	Thirukkadavoormayanam ...	Pun Gandharam ...	Madhyamavathi	Thisram ...	வரியமறையார் பிறையார்
107	Thiruakkoothanthonrimadam	Pun Seegamaram ...	Sourashtram ...	Athithalam	அக்கிருந்த வாரமும்
107	Thirumeeyachoor	Pun Gahdharam ...	Bairavi ...	Athithalam	காயச் செவ்விக்காமற்காய்ந்து
107	Thiruppampuram	Pun Thakkaragam ...	Bairavi ...	Athithalam	சீரணிதிகழ்திரு மார்பில் வெண்ணூலர்
109	Thiruveelimilalai	Pun Nattapadai ...	Nattaikkurinji	...	சடையார் புனலுடையான்
110	Sri Pugalithiruveelimilalai ...	Pun Nattapadai ...	Sagana ...	Thisram ...	மைம்மரு பூங்குழற் கற்றை

Page.	Sthalam.	Ancient Pun.	Modern Ragam.	Thalam.	Opening line.
113	Thiruvanchiyam ...	... Pun Inthalam ...	Kalyani	Kandalagu	வன்னி கொன்றை
113	Thirupperuvalloor ...	... Pun Panchamam ...	Like 'Kochagam'	——	[illegible]
113	Thirukkaraveeram ...	... Pun Palanthakkaragam	Piyagu ...	Athithalam	அரியும் நம்வினையுள்ளன
113	Thiruvilamar ...	... Pun Sathari ...	Neelambari ...	Athithalam	மத்தக மணிபெயரவருமலர்
114	Thirukkarayil ...	... Pun Inthalam ...	Thodi ...	... Thisram ...	நீரானே நீள் சடைமேல்
114	Thiruthevoor... ...	... Pun Gundharam ...	Kalyani	... Jambai ...	பண்ணிலாவிய மொழி உமைபங்கன்
115	Thirunellikka ...	... Pun Inthalam ...	Saveri ...	... Athithalam	அறத்தாலுயிர்க் காவலமர்ந்தருளி
115	Thirukkaichinam ...	... Pun Seegamaram ...	Like 'Kochagam'	Nathanamakkiriyai	தையலோர் கூறுடையான்
115	Thiruthengoor ...	... Pun Pyanthaik Gandharam	Sathari ...	Thisram ...	புரைசெய் வல்வினை தீர்க்கும் புண்ணியர்
115	Thirukollikadu ...	... Pun Gandhara Panchamam	Saveri ...	... Athithalam	நிணம்படு சுடலையின் நீறுபூசி
116	Thirukottoor... ...	... Pun Nattaragam ...	Nattai ...	... Thisram ...	நீலமார் தருகண்டனே
116	Thiruvendurai ...	... Pun Panchamam ...	Arabi ...	... Thisram ...	ஆதியன் ஆதிரையன் அனலாடி
116	Thiruthandalainelneri	... Pun Kousikam ...	Saveri ...	... Athithalam	விரும்புந் திங்களுங் கங்கையும்
117	Thirukalar	... Pun Seegamaram ...	Saveri ...	.... Thisram ...	நீருளார்கயல் வாவி சூழ்பொழில்
118	Thirumaraikadu ...	... Pun Inthalam ...	Kalyani	... Jambai ...	சதுரம் மறைதான் துதிசெய்து வணங்கும்
120	Thiruvaimoor ...	... Pun Nattaragam ...	Nattai ...	... Athithalam	தளிரிள வளரொளியுமைபாட
120	Thirumaraikadu ...	... Pun Pyanthaik Gandharam	Arabi ...	... Thisram ...	பொங்குவெண் மணற்கானல்

Page.	Sthalam.	Ancient Pun.	Modern Ragam.	Thalam.	Opening line.
123	Vayurutholi	Pun Piyanthai kantharam	Nattai	Athithalam	வேயுறுதோளிபங்கன்
124	Thiruaghathiyanpalli ...	Pun Gantharam ...	Ananthapairavi	...	வாடியவெண்டலைமாலை
124	Thirukadikulam	Pun Nattaragam ...	Nattai	Athithalam	பொடிகொண்மேனி
124	Thiruidumbavanam	Pun Nattapadai ...	Like 'Pitthapirai-soodi'	...	மனமார்தரு மடவாரொடு
125	Thiruusathanam	Pun Kolli	Thodi	Athithalam	நீரிடைத் துயின்றவன் தம்பி
126	Thirukodungkunram ..	Pun Nattapadai ...	Like 'Pitthapirai-soodi' Thira-sankaraparanam	...	வானிற்பொலி வெய்தும்
130	Thiruvalavai	Pun Kousigam ...	Saveri	Athithalam	காட்டுமாவதுரித்துரி போர்த்து
139	Thiruvalavai	Pun Palampanjuram	Poorvikaliyani	Sabu ...	வேதவேள்வியை
141	Thirubrahmapuram	Thiruchackramatru	Sankaraparanam	Athithalam	பிரமனூர் வேணுபுரம்
154	Thiruyadagam	Pun Kolli	Saveri	Athithalam	வன்னியுமத்தமும்
157	Thiruvalavai	Thiruviamagam ...	Nathanamakirya	...	ஆலநீழலுகந்த திருக்கையே
158	Thirukalumalam	Pun Kolli	Saveri	Athithalam	மண்ணினல்லவண்ணம்
159	Thiruparangkunram	Pun Kurinji ...	Kabi	Athithalam	நீடலர் சோதி வெண்பிறையொடு
159	Thiruappanoor	Pun Kurinji ...	Like 'Pitthapirai-soodi'	...	மற்றுஞ்சடைமுடிமேல்
160	Thiruputthoor	Pun Thackaragam ...	Saveri	Athithalam	வெங்கள் விம்மு வெறியார்பொழில்
160	Thirupoovanam	Pun Thackesi ...	Ananthapairavi	Athithalam	அறையார் புனலுமாமலரும்
160	Thirukanapare	Pun Kolli	Like 'Pitthapirai-soodi'	...	பிடியெலாம் பின் செல்ல
161	Thirukutralam	Pun Kurinji ...	Kalyani ...	Kandalagu	வம்பார்குன்றநீடுயர்சாரல்

Page.	Sthalam.	Ancient Pun.	Modern Ragam.	Thalam.	Opening line.
161	Thirukurumbala	Pun Gandharam ...	Sourashtram ...	Thiripudai	திருந்தமதி குடி
161	Tinnevelly	Pun Gandharapanjamam	Neelambari ...	Athi ...	மருந்தவை மந்திரம்
162	Thiruiramashvaram ...	Pun Gandharapanjamam	Ananthapairavi	Misra Athi	அலைவளர் தண்மதி
162	Thirukonamamalai	Pun Puraneermai ...	Kaliyani ...	Athi ...	நிரைகழலரவம்
163	Thirukatheechuram	Pun Nattaragam ...	Nattakurinji ...	Athi ...	விருதுகுன்ற மாமேரு
163	Thiruadanai	Pun Nattaragam ...	Saveri	Athi ...	மாதோர் கூறுகந்தேற
163	Thirupunavayil	Pun Gandharapanjamam	Neelambari ...	Athi ...	மின்னியல் செஞ்சடை
164	Thirupathaleechuram ...	Pun Kurinji ...	Kurinji ...	Thisram ...	மின்னியல் செஞ்சடைமேல்
165	Thirukollampoothoor ...	Pun Gandharapanjamam	Nathanamakirya	Sap ...	கொட்டமேகமழும்
166	Thirunallarumthiruvalavayum ...	Pun Nattapadai ...	Sankaraparanam	...	பாடகமெல்லடிப்பாவை
166	Thiruthelicheri	Pun Indalam ...	Sankaraparanam	Jambai ...	பூவலர்ந்தனகொண்டு
173	Thirukalumalam	Thiru Iyamagam ...	Sankaraparanam	Thisram ...	உற்றுமை சேர்வது
175	Thirumanikuli	Pun Sathari ...	Mathyamavathi	Jambai ...	பொன்னியல் பொருப்பரையன்
175	Thirupathiripuliyur	Pun Sevali	Kalyani ...	Jambai ...	முன்னநின்ற
175	Thiruvadukoor	Pun Kurinji ...	Like 'Pitthapirai-soodi'	Thisram ...	சுடுகூடெரிமாலை
176	Thiruvakarai...	Pun Panjamam ...	Arabi	Thisram ...	கறையணிமாமிடற்றான்

Page.	Sthalam.	Ancient Pun.	Modern Ragam.	Thalam.	Opening line.
176	Thiruirumbaimagalam ...	Pun Sevali	Ananthabairavi	Jambai ...	மண்டுகங்கைச்சடையில்
176	Thiruathikai Veerattanam ...	Pun Thackaragam ...	Like 'Pitthapirai-soodi'	...	குண்டைக்குறட்பூதம்
177	Thiruamatthoor	Pun Seeragam ...	Nathanamakirya	Sapu ...	குன்றவார்சிலை
177	Thirukovalveerattam ...	Pun Nattaragam ...	Note	Athi ...	படைகொள்கூற்றம்
178	Thiruaraiyaninalloor... ...	Pun Gandharam ...	Like 'Matrupa-trena'	Tisram ...	பீடிகுற்பெரியார்களும்
178	Thiruvannamalai	Pun Nattapadai ...	Like 'Pitthapirai-soodi'	Tisram ...	உண்ணாமுலையுமை
179	Thiruvannamalai	Pun Thackesi ...	Kabi	Tisram ...	பூவார் மலர்கொண்டடியார்
180	Thiruothoor	Pun Palanthcka ragam	Bairavi ...	Athi ...	பூத்தொத்தாயின கொண்டு
180	Thirunagaral	Pun Sathari ...	Madhyamavathi	Jambai ...	விங்குவிளைகழனி
181	Thirukuranganinmuttam ...	Pun Thackaragam ...	Kaliyani ...	Jambai ...	விழுநீர்மழுவாட்படை
182	Thiruyagambam	Pun Indalam ...	Ananthapairavi	Tisram ...	மறையானை மாசிலாப்புன்சடை
184	Thirunerikaraikadu	Pun Punjamam ...	Senchuriti ...	Tisram ...	வாரணவும் முலைமங்கை
185	Thirumarparu	Pun Palanthacka ragam	Poorvikalyani ...	Sapu ...	வடியார் தருகஞ்சினை
185	Thiruvallam	Pun Vialakurinji ...	Saveri	Athi ...	எரித்தவன் முப்புரம்
185	Thiruilampayangkottoor ...	Pun Kurinji ...	Like 'Thillaival-anthanar'	Roobagam	மலையினுர் பருப்பதம்
186	Thiruvirkolam	Pun Gandhara panjamam	Saveri	Athi ...	உருவினுருமையொடு

Page.	Sthalam.	Ancient Pun.	Modern Ragas.	Thalam.	Opening line.
186	Thiruooral	Pun Vialakurinji ...	Like 'Variyamaraiyar	...	மாறிலவுண ரரணம்
187	Palaiyanoorthirualangadu ...	Pun Thackaragam ...	Sourashtram ...	Athi ...	துஞ்சவருவாரும்
188	Thirupasoor	Pun Gandharam ...	Yathukulakambothi	Athi ...	சிந்தையிடையார்
189	Thirukalatthi	Pun Sathari ...	Kaliyani ...	Jambai ...	வாளவர் கடாசலர்கள்
190	Thirukailayam	Pun Thackesi ...	Ananthapairavi	Athi ...	பொடிகொளுருவர்
190	Thirukatharam	Pun Sevali	Saveri	Athi ...	தொண்ட ரஞ்சுகளிறு
191	Thirukogaranam	Pun Sathari ...	Kurinji ...	Jambai ...	என்று மரியானயலவர்க்கு
191	Thiruindraneelaparupatham	Pun Indalam ...	Saveri	Athi ...	குலவு பாரிடம்போற்ற
191	Thiruparupatham	Pun Vialakurinji ...	Like 'Pithapiraisoodi'	Tisram ...	சுடுமணியுமிழ் நாகம்
192	Thiruvanegathangapatham ...	Pun Indalam ...	Kaliyani ...	Thiripudai	நீடல்மேவு நிமிர்புன்சடை
192	Thirukalatthi	Pun Kolli	Suddhasaveri ...	...	சந்தமாரகிலொடு
193	Thiruverkadu...	Pun Palantharagam	Saveri... ...	Athi ...	ஒள்ளிதுள்ளக் கதிகாம்
193	Thiruvalithayam	Pun Nattapadai ...	Like 'Thodudaiya'	...	பத்தரோடு பலரும்பொலிய
193	Thiruvotriyoor	Pun Panjamam ...	Neelambari ...	Athi ...	விடையவன் விண்ணுமண்ணும்
205	Thiruvanmiyoor	Pun Indalam ...	Kaliyani ...	Thiripudai	கரையுலாங் கடலிற்பொலி
206	Thiruidaichuram	Pun Kurinji ...	Saveri	Sapu ...	வரிவளரவி ரொளியரவரை

Page.	Sthalam.	Ancient Pun.	Modern Ragas.	Thalam.	Opening line.
207	Thirukkalukkunram ...	Pun Kurinji ...	Sankarapharanam	Thisram ...	தோடுடையானொருகாதில்
207	Thiruchirupakam	Pun Kurinji ...	Note, ...	Kandachapu	பொன்றிரண்டன்னபுரிசடை
208	Thiruarisili	Pun Piyanthaik-Gandharam	Sourashtiram ...	Thiribudai	பாடல் வண்டறை
209	Thiruvenupuram	Pun Nattapadai ...	Like 'Pithapirai-soodi'	...	வண்டார் குழலரிவையொடு
210	Srikali	Pun Nattaragam ...	Note	Roobaham	நம்பொருணமக்கென்று
221	Nalloor Thirupperumanam ...	Pun Anthalikkurinji	Bairavi ...	Athi ...	கல்லூர்ப்பெருமணம் வேண்டாகழுமலம்

Here we find that a number of modern Ragas are attributed to a single Pun. In the same way a single Ragam is attributed to a number of Puns. This may be explained by what is stated on page 542 as found in Thirumuraikanda Puranam by such expressions as Nattapadai Eight Kattalais, Thaka Ragam, Seven Kattalais. Sathari Nine Kattalais, Vyalakurinji Six Kattalais, Thakesi Six Kattalais etc., where he gives the Kattalais for the 37 Puns. This seems to account for the difference in Ragas noticed. It may also be accounted for by the fact that musicians of the later days changed the names of the ancient Ragas and gave them beautiful new names and new mettus. We have a mind to publish separately the result of our researches into the system of the ancient Puns. However, we hope that this is enough to satisfy those who are experts in the chanting of Puns.

10. Some points of resemblance between the Swarams of South Indian Music and the notes of Equal Temperament of the westerners.

From the following figure one may understand clearly how the 12 Swarams of Ayapalai in a Sthayi are distributed in western instruments.

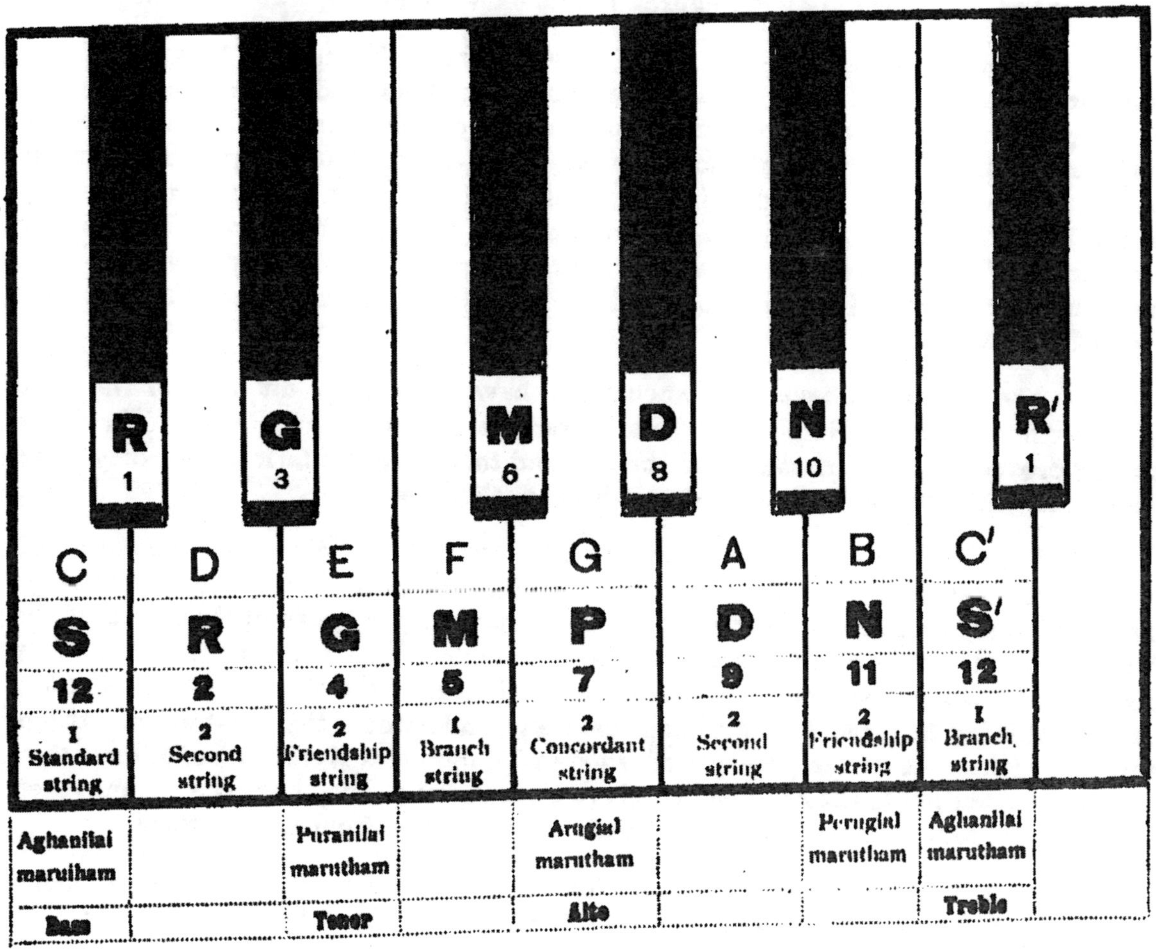

Here we see that six black keys appear at the top with the letters Ri, Ga, Ma, Dha, Ni, Ri and the figures 1, 3, 6, 8, 10, 1.

Below the black keys we see eight white keys indicated by the letters Sa, Ri, Ga, Ma, Pa, Dha, Ni, Sa and C D E F G A B C and with the figures 12, 2, 4, 5, 7, 9, 11 and 12 to shew the Swarasthanams. These white keys stand for the 7 Swarams of a Sthayi from Sa to Pa.

Here while we take SA to be the commencing string, the Sa where the Madhya Sthayi ends becomes the 12th Swaram from RI. The order of the 12 Swarams from RI_{11} to SA_{12} is the serial order 1, 2, 3, 4 etc. The Swarams of the bottom row are arranged according to the system of concordance.

The seven Swarams of this series when sounded in order we call Dheera-shankaraparanam. The ancient Tamils have been calling this by the name of Chempalai Pun. According to their system, the concordant series as well as the discordant series indicated by the figures 1, 3, 6, 8 and 10 are separately shown.

When the SA or the first white key becomes the ending Swaram of the Mandara Sthayi he calls it [illegible] நரம்பு or commencing string. Because the SA occurs as the commencing and the ending Swaram of a Sthayi, he calls the RI of the second Rasi (out of the 12 Swarams obtained by the Kural-Ili or SA-PA principle from the commencing string) the Second string, the Kaikilai of the fourth Rasi, the fourth string or the Natpu string, the Oolai or the MA of the fifth Rasi the fifth or the Kilai string and the Ili (PA) of the seventh Rasi the seventh or the Inai string. Of these the Swarams that occur in Rasis 1, 3, 6, 8 and 10 have been set aside as discordant or Pagai Swarams.

The sthanams above the Panchamam have also been divided on the same principle into Second, Natpu and Kilai Swarams and used in Ragas. These are clearly proved by the stanzas quoted below and their commentaries. As they have been dealt with already we have only slightly touched them here.

We see clearly how the ancient Tamils received the Yal with reverence and sat down to play on it, how they ran their fingers through the concordant strings avoiding all the discordant Swarams and how they were particular in the choice of the Yal knowing the defects of the various kinds of wood. We also see clearly that they understood exactly what the 14 Swarams of the Mandara Sthayi were when Madhya Sthayi extended from Oolai to Kaikilai, that they understood the relation of strings appearing leftwards on the principle of Oolai in Tharam and Kural in Oolai, that they paid great attention to the relation of strings as Inai, Kilai, Pagai or Natpu and then produced the four primary Puns and the four Jatis derived from each of them.

It appears that the Bass, Tenor, Alto and Treble of the westerners correspond to the Aganilai, Puranilai, Arugial and Mel Aganilai of the four Jatis respectively.

Besides this, the same Ragam may be sounded, say Sankaraparanam, commencing from any of the Key's so long as the order of the semitones of the scale is maintained. This is the arrangement of the Swarams with equal intervals or equal semitones. This is called the system of Equal Temperament.

The westerners held for a long time that the Swarams obtained by multiplying $\frac{3}{2}$ by $\frac{3}{2}$ and $\frac{4}{3}$ by $\frac{4}{3}$ were the result of the Just Temperment or the series of the Natural scale. But they found it was very inadequate for purposes of harmony and modulation.

Experts who realised this difficulty when they proceeded to arrange the series of 12 Swarams on the SA-PA principle, slightly flattened their fifths and thus arranged the series with equal intervals. So this system of Equal Temperament was derided by many who are ignorant of the excellence of this system and they are speaking against it even to day. If calculation for it had been given by Geometrical Progression no body would have objected to the system. If they could only realise that this system was in use among the ancient Tamils with excellent rules, they will at once understand that the modern Puns sung by the Tamils of South India and the Swarams and Srutis used in them are very minute, that they have the hall mark of advancement and that they are in use even now. More minute details about them may be found in the second book.

The Puns or the Ragas where the 12 Swarams of Ayapalai occur as shown in the above figure may be played without any doubt on the Piano or the Harmonium or any other similar western instrument. They are played on them even now. Ragas of Ayapalai will never lose their charm by being played on them. These very Ragas were played by Mathavi on the Sakota Yal in three Sthayis and in the 14 Swarams. This is nothing new, but what has been in use for many thousands of years in South Madura during the period of the first Sangam. We may do well to consider the following quotations from Silappadikaram written by Ilankovadigal.

Silappdikaram Venirkathei P. 200

23-26. அதிரா மரபின் யாழ்கை வாங்கி
மதுர கீதம் பாடினள் மயங்கி
யோன்பான் விருத்தியுட் டலைக்கண் விருத்தி
நன்பா லமைந்த விருக்கைய ளாகி

இ-ள். மாதவி, பணிமொழிகூற, அதற்கு விரும்பி [illegible] ஒன்பது வகைப்பட்ட இருப்பினுள் முதற் கண்ணதாகிய பதுமாசனமென்னும் ஆசனத்திருந்து கோவை கலங்கா மரபினையுடைய யாழைக் கையில் வாங்கிக் கண்டத்தால் முற்பட மதுரகீதமாகப்பாடி அது மயங்கிக் கலத்தாற்பாடத் தொடங்கினள யென்க.

இதனுள் விருத்தியென்பது இருப்பு. ஓவிய நூலுள் நிற்றல் இருத்தல் கிடத்தல் இயங்குதலென்னும் இவற்றின் விகற்பங்கள் பலவுள. அவற்றுள் இருத்தல் திரிதரவுடையனவும் திரிதரவில்லனவுமென இருவகைய. அவற்றுள் திரிதரவுடையன யானை தேர் புரவி பூனை முதலியன; திரிதரவில்லன ஒன்பது வகைப்படும். அவை, பதுமுகம், உற்கட்டிதம், ஒப்படியிருக்கை, சம்புடம், அயமுகம், சுவத்திகம், தனிப்புடம், மண்டிலம், சுபாதம் எனவிவை, என்னே !

Comment:—Mathavi, using courteous words, placed herself in the posture of Pathumasanam, (placing the feet transversely on the two thighs and turning the soles up that they may be seen) one of the nine kinds of posture, took the Yal in her hands in which the Kovais could be reproduced without any confusion, sang first in a delicious manner vocally, pleased every one, and then began her instrumental music.

Here விருத்தி means 'posture'. In the art of painting are many different postures such as standing, sitting, lying down, and moving. Of these the sitting posture may be with motion or without motion. Under the former heading come the postures of the elephant, the car, the horse and the cat. These without motion are of 9 kinds.

They are, பதுமுகம், உற்கட்டிதம், ஒப்படியிருக்கை, சம்புடம், அயமுகம், சுவத்திகம், தனிப்புடம், மண்டிலம், ஏகபாதம். If you ask what these are, their description is given in the following stanzas from Perungkathei.

"பதுமுக முற்கட் டிதமே யோப்படி
யிருக்கை சம்புட மயமுகஞ் சுவத்திகந்
தனிப்புட மண்டில மேக பாத
முளப்பட வொன்பது மாகுந்
திரிதர வில்லா விருக்கை யென்ப

என்றாகலானும்,

பண்ணுள் கழிந்த பின்னர் முன்னு
ளெண்மெய்ப் பாட்டினு ளிரக்க மெய்ந்நிறீஇ
யோண்வினை யோவியர் கண்ணிய விருத்தியுட்
டலையத னும்பர்த் தான்குறிக் கொண்ட
பாவை நோக்கத் தாரணங் கெய்தி

எனப்பெருங்கதையுட் கூறினமைபானுங்கொள்க. இனி நாடக நூலார் இவ்விருப்பை ஐம்பதென விரிவரையறைபாற் கூறித் தொகைவரையறை கூறுவார் அவற்றை ஒன்பதி னடக்கினாரெனவுணர்க: என்னை?

Comment:—The author of the Nataka has held these to be fifty, speaking widely, but brought them under 9 for the sake of brevity.

This is explained by the following stanza

ஆதிப்பா விருத்தி யைம்பதிற் புலவோ
ரோதிக் கொண்டன ரொன்பான் விருத்தி

என்றாகலின். அவற்றுள் தலைக்கண் விருத்தியாவது பதுமாசனம். இதனுற் சொல்லியது அதிராமர பிணையுடைய யாழைக் கையின் வாங்கிப் பதுமாசனமாக விருந்தவள் தனக்கு நாயகனின்மையால் தியாதகாய கனுமானதத் தாளுக்கு எதிர்முகமாகவிருந்து வாசித்தலைக் கருதினாளென்பது. என்னை?

முதற்க ணெதிர்முக நோக்கி நயத்தக
வொருவ னாகிய தோற்றமும்

என்றாகலின்.

Comment:—She got the Yal—unshakeable in its nature—in her hands and sat down in the posture of Pathumasanam. As she had no husband of her own, she imagined herself as if she was seated in front of one whom she worshipped in her heart and desired to play the Yal.

How she played the Yal is indicated in the following stanza

யாழ் வாசிக்கு முறைமை,

"நல்லிசை மடந்தை நல்லெழில் காட்டி
யல்லியம் பங்கயத் தயனினிது படைத்த
தெய்வஞ் சான்ற தீஞ்சுவை நல்யாழ்
மெய்பெற வணங்கி மேலொடு கீழ்புணர்த்
திருகையின் வாங்கி யிடவயி னிரீஇ
மருவிய விசய மாட்டேல் கடனே"

என்பதனுணர்க. விசயம்-devotion.

Silappadikaram Venirkathei P. 201.

27-28 " வலக்கைப் பதாகை கோட்டொடு சேர்த்தி
யிடக்கை நால்விரன் மாடகந் தழீஇ"

இ-ள். வலக்கையைப் பதாகையாகக் கோட்டின்மிசையே வைத்து இடக்கை நால் விரலான் மாடகத்தைத் தழுவியென்க. பதாகைக்கையாவது பெருவிரல் குஞ்சித்து ஒழிந்த விரலெல்லா நிமிர்த்தல்; என்னை ?

Comment :—She used the four fingers of the right hand excluding the thumb on the Yal and touched the screw pin of the Yal with the four fingers on the left.

The description of பதாகை is given in the following stanza.

" எல்லா விரலு நிமிர்த்திடை யின்றிப்
பெருவிரல் குஞ்சித்தல் பதாகை யாகும் "

என்றாராகலின். மாடகம்-வீக்குங்கருவி. அது முன்னர் ஆணியென்பதனுட் கூறினும்.

மாடகம் is the plectrum. It is implied in the word ஆணி given before.

Silappadikaram Venirkathei P. 201.

29-30 " செம்பகை யார்ப்பே யதிர்வே கூடம்
வெம்பகை நீக்கும் விரகுளி யறிந்து"

செம்பகை ஆர்ப்பு அதிர்வு கூடமென்று நான்கினும் செம்பகை தாழ்ந்த விசை = இன்பமின்றி இசைத்தல். ஆர்ப்பு மாத்திரை யிறந்த சுருதி = ஓங்கவிசைத்தல். அதிர்வு நரம்பைச் சிதறவுந்தல். கூடம் இசை சிறவாதது = தன் பகையாகிய ஆறாம்பினிசையிற் குன்றித் தன்னோசை மழுங்கலெனக்கொள்க.

Comment :—Of these four, செம்பகை means playing without taste ; ஆர்ப்பு is playing loud ; அதிர்வு is playing so as to make the string vibrate and கூடம் means merging of one's music by the music of the sixth string or string of discordance.

This is also corroborated by the following quotation from Panchabaratheeam.

இதனை,

" இன்னிசை வழிய தன்றி யிசைத்தல்செம் பகைய தாகுஞ்
சொன்னமாத் திரையி னோங்க விசைத்திடுஞ் சுருதி யார்ப்பே
மன்னிய விசைவ ராது மழுங்குதல் கூட மாகு
நன்னுதால் சிதற வுந்த லதிர்வென நாட்டினாரே."

என்பதனுற்கொள்க. இது பஞ்ச பாரதீயம்.

Besides this the following stanzas also explain the four kinds of defects in playing.

அன்றி,

" செம்பகை யென்பது பண்ணொ டொரா
வின்பமி லோசை யென்மனார் புலவர்."

" ஆர்ப்பெனப் படுவ தளவிறந் திசைக்கும்."

" அதிர்வெனப் படுவ திழுமென லின்றிச்
சிதறி யுரைக்குஞ் சுச்சரிப் பிசையே."

" கூட மென்பது குறியுற விளம்பின்
வாய்வதின் வராது மழுங்கியிசைப் பதுவே."

எனக்கூறினரு முளர். இவை நான்கும் மாசுக்குற்றத்தாற் பிறக்கும் ; என்னை?

The four kinds of defects may be due to choice of bad wood or material for the construction of the Yal.

The following stanza shows how the choice of wood should be made thus avoiding the defects in playing.

"நீரிலே நிற்ற லழுகுதல் வேத னிலமயக்குப்
பாரிலே நிற்ற லிடிவீழ்த லேய்மரப் பாற்படல்கோ
ணேரிலே செம்பகை யார்ப்போடு கூட மதிர்வுநிற்றல்
சேரினோர் பண்க ளிறமயக் குப்பகேஞ் சிற்றிடையே." என்றார்.

இ-ள். இச்சொல்லப்பட்ட பகை நரம்பு நான்கும் புகாமல் நீக்கும் விரகைக்கடைப் பிடித்ததின்றென்க.

Silappadikaram Venirkathei P. 202.

31-32 "பிழையா மரபி னீரேழ் கோவையை
உழைமுதற் கைக்கிளை யிறுவாய்க் கட்டி,

(இ-ள்) மயக்கா மரபினையுடைய இப் பதினாற்கோவையாகிய சகோடயாழை உழை குரலாகக் கைக்கிளை தாரமாகக் கட்டியென்க.

The Swarams of the Sakota Yal, with its 14 Kovais of doubtless existence, were arranged on the principle of Oolai-Kural and Kaikilai-Tharam.

இக் குரல் முதலேழினும் முற்றோன்றியது தாரம்

"தாரத்துட் டோன்று முழையுழை யுட்டோன்று
மோருங் குரல்குரலி னுட்டோன்றிச்-சேருமிளி
யுட்டோன்றுந் துத்தத்துட் டோன்றும் விளரியுட்
கைக்கிளை தோன்றும் பிறப்பு."

என்பதினால் தாரத்தில் முதற் பிறப்பதாகிய உழை குரலாய்க்கைக்கிளை தாரமாகிய கோடிப்பாலை முதற் பிறக்கக் கட்டியென்க.

Comment :—As he says that out of the Seven Swarams what is first obtained is Tharam, Oolai which just appears in Tharam becomes Kural, and when Kaikilai becomes Tharam Kodipalai is just formed.

Silappadikaram Venirkathei P. 202.

33-34 "இணைகிளை பகைநட் பென்றிந் நான்கி
னிசைபுணர் குறிநிலை யெய்த நோக்கி"

இணை கிளை பகை நட்பென்று சொல்லப்பட்ட நான்கினும் இணை-இரண்டு நரம்பு; என்னை?

Comment :—Of the four strings Inai, Kilai, Pagai and Natpu. Inai is the second string. Because it is said,

"இணையெனப் படுவ கீழு மேலு
மிணையத் தோன்று மளவின வென்ப"

கிளை-ஐந்து நரம்பு; என்னை?

The Kilai string is the fifth. For it is said,

"கிளையெனப் படுவ கிளக்குங் காலைக்
குரலே யிளியே துத்தம் விளரி
கைக்கிளை யெனவைந் தாகு மென்ப"

பகை ஆறும் மூன்றும்;

The Pagai strings are the third and the sixth. For he says,

"நின்ற நரம்பிற் கைம முன்னஞ்
சென்றபெற நிற்பது கூட மாகும்"

கூடமெனினும் பகையெனினு மொக்கும். நட்பு நாலா நரம்பு.

இ-ள். இந்நான்கனுள் இசைபுணருங் குறி நிலையைப் பொருந்த நோக்கியென்க.

The words கூடம் and பகை mean the same.

The Natpu string is the fourth. Of these four strings only the concordant ones should be taken.

Silappadikaram Venirkathei P. 202.

"குரல்வாய் இளிவாய்க் கேட்டனள்"

இ-ள். குரல்முதலாக எடுத்து இளிகுரலாக வாசித்தாளென்க.

Comment :—She played the Kural first and then continued with Ili as Kural.

Next he proceeds to give the results of the leftward progression in Vattapalai.

இனி வட்டப்பாலை இடமுறைத்திரிபு கூறுகின்றார்.

"குன்றாக் குரற்பாதி தாரத்தி லொன்று
கடவ ளிளைகிளை யாக்கிக்—கோடியிடையாய்
தாரத்தி லொன்று விளரிமே லேறுடவர்
நேரத் தகுகுரலா நின்று"

என்-எனின், உழைகுரலாகிய கோடிப்பாலை நிற்க இடமுறை திரியுமிடத்துக் குரல் குரலாயது செம்பாலை; இதனிலே, குரலிற்பாதியும் தாரத்திலொன்றும் இரண்டின் அந்தரத்திலே கிளையாக்கித், தாரத்திலேயின்ற ஓர லகை விளரியின் மேலேறுட விளரி குரலாய்ப் படுமலைப்பாலையாம். இம்முறையே, துத்தம் குரலாயது செவ் வழிப்பாலையாம். இளி குரலாயது அரும்பாலையாம். கைக்கிளை குரலாயது மேற்செம்பாலையாம் தாரம் குரலா யது விளரிப்பாலையாம். என அந்தரமைந்து நீக்கி உறழ்ந்து கண்டுகொள்க இவ்விடத்தில் தாரநரம்பின் அந் தரக்கோலைத் தாரமென்றது.

"தன்னமுந் தாரமு தன்வழிப் படுர"

என்னுஞ் சூத்திர விதியாலென்க. இவ்வேழு பெரும்பாலையினையும் முதலடுத்து நூற்றுமூன்று பண்ணும் பிறக்கும். அவற்றுள் செம்பாலையுட் பிறக்கும் பண்கள் பாலையாழ், நாகராகம், ஆகரி, தோடி, கௌடி, காந்தாரம், செந்துருத்தி, உதயகிரி யெனவிவை. பிறவும் விரிப்பின் உரை பெருகுமாதலின் அவற்றை வந்த வழிக்கண்டு கொள்க.

Comment :—Leaving aside Kodipalai where Oolai is Kural, when we proceed leftward we get Chempalai where Kural is taken as Kural. Here, an half Alaku in Kural and one Alaku in Tharam become Kilai at the end of the second, while one Alaku of Tharam is taken to Vilari. Then Padumalai Palai results, Vilari becoming Kural. On the same principle we get Chevvalipalai when Thuttham becomes Kural, Arumpalai when Ili becomes Kural, Merchempalai when Kaikilai is Kural and Vilaripalai when Tharam becomes Kural. The meaning should be found after eschewing the five Antarams. Here the Antharakole of the Tharam is taken as Tharam. This is also supported by the Sootram.

The 103 Puns are derived from these seven Primary Palais. Of these, Palai Yal, Nagaragam, Agari, Thodi, Gowdi, Gandaram, Chenthuruthi and Oothayagiri are derived from Chempalai.

For the sake of brevity we do not go into detail. Others may be derived in the same manner. Again he gives the definition of Pun in the stanza below.

"நாற்பெரும் பண்ணுஞ் சாதி நான்கும்
பாற்படு திறனும் பண்ணெனப் படுமே"

என்றார்

Silappadikaram Venirkathei Page 203.

36. அன்றியும்
வரன்முறை மருங்கி னைந்தினு மேழினு

(இ-ள்) அங்ஙனம் இளிகுரலாக வாசித்தலேயன்றி முற்கூறியவகையே ஐந்து நரம்பான முறைமையின் ஏழு நரம்பு வாசித்தாரென்றவாறு.

Comment:—Besides playing with Ili as Kural as stated before she played by fifths and sevenths.

Silappadikaram Venirkathei P 203.

37-41. உழைமுத லாகவு முழையீ றாகவுங்
குரன்முத லாகவுங் குரலீ றாகவு
மகனிலை மருதமும் புறநிலை மருதமு
மருகியன் மருதமு பெருகியன் மருதமு
நால்வகைச் சாதியு நலம்பெற நோக்கி

இனி உழை குரன்முதல் குரலீறுயுள்ள நான்கிற்கும் அகநிலை மருத முதற் பெருகியன் மருதம் ஈறுயுள்ள நான்கும் கிரனிரை.

(இ-ள்) முன்னனிர்த்த முறையே உழை குரலாய கோடிப்பாலை அகநிலை மருதமாகவும், உழை குரலாய்க் கைக்கிளை குரலாய மேற்செம்பாலை புறநிலை மருதமாகவும், குரல் குரலாய செம்பாலை அருகியன் மருதமாகவும், குரல் தாரமாய்த் தாரங்குரலாய விளரிப்பாலை பெருகியன் மருதமாகவும் இச்சொல்லப்பட்ட சாதிப் பெரும் பண்ணையும் இசையினிமை பெற நோக்கியென்றவாறு.

He gives the four Maruthams beginning with Aganilai and finishing with Perugial obtained by taking the Oolai as the the first and the last Swaram and the Kural as the first and the last Swaram.

Comment:—As said before, Kodipalai where Oolai becomes Kural is taken as Aganilai Marutham, Merchempalai obtained by Oolai becoming Kural and Kaikilai becoming Kural is taken as Puranilai Marutham, Chempalai obtained by taking Kural as Kural is taken as Arugial Marutham while Vilaripalai derived by taking Kural as Tharam and Tharam as Kural is taken as Perugial Marutham. These primary Puns mentioned here were played with an ear for complete concordance.

Silappadikaram Venirkathei P. 203.

42. மூவகை யியக்கி முறையுளிக் கழிப்பி

(இ-ள்) வலிவும் மெலிவும் சமனு மென்னும் மூவகைப்பட்ட சுருதியும் நிற்கு நிலைமையிலே நிறுத்தி முறைபாலை அந்தொழிலைக் கழித்தென்க.

Comment:—She played in such a way that the Srutis of the hard soft, and middling Sthayis were each played in their respective positions, leaving out discordant Swarams.

Silappadikaram Venirkathei P. 203.

43-44. திறத்து வழிப்படூஉந் தெள்ளிசைக் காணத்துப்
புறத்தொரு பாணியிற் பூங்கொடி மயங்கி

(இ-ள்) திறங்கட்குப் பிறப்பிடமாயுள்ள நாற்சாதிப் பெரும் பண்களுட் புறநிலை மருதப்பண்ணை வாசித்தவிடத்தே மயங்கியென்க.

Comment:—When she played Puranilai Marutha Pun out of the Puns from which generate all Thirams, she became enraptured.

We see that the province of South Madura was noted for its fertility, riches, sciences and arts and that the people were noted for their devotion to God. In preporation to this they were well advanced in Music, Astrology, Medicine, Yoga Sastram and other renowned sciences. Just as a modern expert on the Veena plays different Kinds of Gamakams, the ancient Tamils were noted for the production of the eight kinds of sounds from the Yal, such as *பண்ணல், பரிவட்டணை* and *ஆராய்தல்* and also very cleverly produced the eight Kinds of Isaikaranams such as *வார்தல், வடித்தல், உந்தல், உறழ்தல்* etc., (For explanations of these terms see. below). The following stanzas and their annotations will give an idea of the above devices in the playing of the Yal.

Silappadikaram, Kanalvari P. 177.

சித்திரப் படத்துட் புக்குச் செழுங்கோட்டின் மலர்புனைந்து
மைத்தடங்கண் மணமகளிர் கோலம்போல் வனப்பெய்திப்
பத்தருங் கோடு மாணியு நரம்புமென்
றித்திறத்துக் குற்றநீங்கிய யாழ்கையிற் றொழுதுவாங்கிப்
பண்ணல் பரிவட்டணை யாராய்த றைவரல்
கண்ணிய செலவு விளையாட்டுக் கையூழ்
நண்ணிய குறும்போக் கென்று நாட்டிய
வெண்வகையா லிசையெழீஇப்
பண்வகையாற் பரிவுதீர்ந்து
மரகதமணித் தாள்செறிந்த மணிக்காந்தண் மெல்விரல்கள்
பயிர்வண்டின் கிளைபோலப் பன்னரம்பின் மிசைப்படர
வார்தல் வடித்த லுந்த லுறழ்தல்
சீருட னுருட்ட றெருட்ட லள்ள
லேருடைப் பட்டடை யென விசையோர் வகுத்த
வெட்டு வகையி னிசைக்கர ணத்துப்
பட்டவகைதன் செவியினோர்த்
தேவலன்பின் பாணியாதெனக்
கோவலன் கையாழ் நீட்ட வவனுங்
காவிரியை நோக்கினவுங் கடற்கானல் வரிப்பாணியு
மாதவிதன் மனமகிழ வாசித்தற் றொடங்குமன்.

சித்திரப்படம்-உரை. *கோட்டில் மலர் புனைந்து-கோட்டுத் தலைப்பிற் மலர் மாலையை அணிந்து ;*

The Yal was decorated with flower garlands at the top. The following Seotram from Chintamani also supports the above.

வீழ்மணி வண்டு பாய்ந்து மிதித்திடக் கிழிந்த மாலை
சூழ்மணிக் கோட்டு வீணை

என்றார் சிந்தாமணியிலும் ; [கார்-உ.௬.௫] மணமகளிர்-கலியாண மகளிர். பத்தர் கோடு ஆணி நரம்பு என்பன யாழுறுப்புக்கள்.

மணமகளிர் means the bridegroom and the bride, பத்தர், கோடு, ஆணி and நரம்பு are the different parts of the Yal. This is given in the lines,

கோடே பத்த ராணி நரம்பே
மாடக மெனவரும் வகையின தாகும்

என்பதனுலறிக. தொழுது-யாழ், மாதங்கி யென்னும் தெய்வமிருத்தற்கிடமென்று நால்கள் கூறுமாதலின் அதனைத் தொழுது. வாங்கி-வயந்த மாலை கையினின்றும் வாங்கி, பண்ணல் முதலிய எட்டும் கலைத் தொழிலென்று சொல்லப்படும். அவற்றன்

The Yal was worshipped as it was believed that it was the dwelling place of the Godess Mathangi. வாங்கி implies that the vayanda garland was taken from the hand. The eight devices such as பண்ணல் etc., are considered arts.

பண்ணல் is arranging the Inai, Kilai, Pagai and Natpu strings in relation to the Pun to be sung in accordance with their nature and Mathira.

பரிவட்டணை is examining the particular string by the forefinger and the back finger ;

ஆராய்தல் is examining the correctness of the Isai by trying the Aroganam and the Avaroganam.

தைவரல் is tuning the concordant strings ;

செலவு is singing it fully by the process of Alati

விளையாட்டு is the variations of the player on the Pun to be sung.

கையூழ் is the rendering of the Puns to be sung in a very charming manner.

குறும்போக்கு is singing the Pun in very fast or in very slow time.

These interpretations may be seen in the annotations for the 165th stanza of Gandaruvathatthayarilambakam in Jeevakachintamani. The annotator deals with it more minutely. இசைஎழீஇ=produced the Swarams. பண் வகையால் பரிவு தீர்த்து=eschewing all kinds of defects in the Pun. உருபு மயக்கம் and பரிவு are the defects. மரகதமணித்தாள் is an emerald ring. In the Kadaladukathei also he makes mention of "மரகதத்தாள் செறி." பயிர் வண்டு means the beetle that sings. பயிர் means sound.

வார்தல் is working with the little finger.

வடித்தல் is examining the string inside and outside by the little finger and the thumb.

உந்தல் is pulling the strings out to find out the hard, soft and middling.

உறழ்தல் is breaking the strings at intervals of one and two.

உருட்டல் may be done by the little finger of the left hand or by the joint action of the little finger and the thumb, or of the two thumbs together. Others may be understood as they occur. பட்டவகைதன்செவியிதேர்ந்து.= Mathavi understood by her ear the nature of the Swarams. ஏவலன் = I do not press you to play this. பின்பனியமா

தென=indicating further instructions. கோவலன் கை யாழ் நீட்ட=She handed over the Yal to Kovalan thus giving him predominance and asking him to play first. காவிரியை நோக் கின=implies the river Cauvery; கானல்வரிப்பாணி is the Pun referring to kanal. தொடங்கும் means 'will commence.' The Stanzas running "புக்குப்புனைந்து எய்தி நீங்கிய யாழை தொழுது வாங்கி எழீஇ ஓர்த்து" and which mean that she handed over the Yal to Kovalan and then both of them sang many puns to their heart's delight have also a different reading where the words 'கோட்டுமலர்' 'இத்திறத்த' 'செவியோர்த்து' and 'பாணியாதென' occur.

Details about these may be found on a reference to the ahavals mentioned in pages 508-510 of this book.

Silappadikaram Aroompathavoorai P. 33.

இனி "வலக்கைப் பதாகை கோட்டொடு சேர்த்தி" என்பது முதலாக "புறத்தொரு பாணியிற் பூங்கொடி மயங்கி" என்பதீறாக முன்னர்ப் பாடிய ஒன்பான் கோவையின் மேற்செம்பாலைப் பண்ணொழிந்து பதினாற் கோவையாகிய சகோடயாழை வாங்கி வலக்கையை பதாகையாக்கி அக்கையால் கோடு அசையாதபடி பிடித்து இடக்கை நாலு விரலும் மாடகத்தையுறப் பிடித்துச் செம்பகையும் ஆர்ப்பும் அதிர்வும் கூடமுமாகிய பகை நீங்க முறையிற் பிழையாத நரம்பினாற் பதினாலு நரம்பினையும் உழைமுதல் கைக்கிளை யிறுவாயாக "மெலிவிற் செல்லா மந்தக் குரலே" என்பதனான் உழைகுரலான மந்தமும் "வலிவிற் செல்லா வன்கைக் கிளையே" என்பதனாற் கைக்கிளை யிறுவாயான வலிவும் இணை, கிளை, பகை நட்பின் வழிகளிற் பொருந்தப் பார்த்துக் குரல் நரம்பினையும் யாழிற்கு அகப்பட்ட நரம்பாகிய இளி நரம்பையும் முற்பட ஆராய்ந்து இசையோர்த்து அதன் முறையேயல்லாத நரம்புகளையும் ஆராய்ந்து இசையோர்த்துத் தீதின்மையறிந்து உழைமுதலாகவும் உழையீறாகவுமென மந்த முதலாகவும் மந்த ஈறாகவும் குரல் நரம்பு மந்தமானபோது குரல் நரம்பே முதலும் முடிவுமாகவும் அகநிலை மருதமும் பெருகியன் மருதமுமென நால்வகைச் சாதிப் பெரும் பண்கள் விளைநிலம் பெற வலிவு மெலிவு சமமென்னும் மூவகை இயக்கும் முறைமையிலே ஆராய்ந்து பாடிப் பின்னர் மாத்திரை குறைந்ததிற் பண்ணைப்பாடு மேல் வைக்கண் அப்பண்ணை இனிதாகப் பாடி நெகிழ்வுற்ற மனத்தினளாய் அயர்ந்தாளெனவுமாம்.

Comment:—The words "வலக்கைப்பதாகை கோட்டொடு சேர்த்தி" up to புறத்தொரு பாணியிற் பூங்கொடி மயங்கி" mean the following:—Leaving aside the Merchempalai pun sung before with 9 Kovais, she got hold of the Sakota Yal with 14 Kovais, made her right hand the Pathakai, held the Yal in the right line with that hand, took hold of the Matakam by the four fingers of the left hand, avoided carefully the four kinds of errors,—Chempagai, Arpu, Athirvu and Koodam— and ran her fingers through the 14 strings without a single fault. Then she played from Oolai to Kaikilai in the soft Sthayi where Oolai becomes Kural (மெலிவிற் செல்லா மந்தக் குரலே) as well as the hard Sthayi which ends with the Kaikilai (வலிவிற் செல்லா வன் கைக்கிளையே) paying strict attention to the rules of Inai, Kilai, Pagai and Natpu. On the light of the above she examined the Kural and the Ili strings and tuned the Yal avoiding carefully all discordant Swarams. When she was satisfied that the concordance was complete, she played the four primary puns such as Aganilai Marutham, Perugial Marutham etc., arranging the Kural and the Oolai strings according to rules in the three sthayis—hard, soft and middling. Later on she sang these with less mathiras and was so enraptured that she went to sleep."

The above stanzas and their commentaries show that the ancient Tamils were highly efficient in playing the Yal. They also seem to have had excellent rules and sang the puns in the most effective manner. Though the ancient works as well as the Sootrams quoted from them by annotators have become extinct, which places us in a very disadvantageous position about understanding all the details of the music of the Tamils, yet the few references made in Silappadikaram, full of pregnant ideas, appear to be quite enough to make us understand the minuteness of ancient music. A little drop of water is enough to test the taste of the water of a large ocean made up of many smaller seas. Do we want five different drops of water to test the water of the five different seas? Just as a small quantity of sour buttermilk is enough to make sour a big pot full of milk, the few hints of Ilankovadigal given in Silappadikaram are enough to make us understand the minuteness of ancient Tamil music.

We must understand that he only casually makes mention of Tamil music as much as it was necessary by indicating a few points, in his major attempt to describe the powers of dancing of Mathavi, her musical genius in playing the Yal and the chastity of Kannahi. Because the annotators found that the efficiency of the music of the period of Ilankovadigal had declined during their time, they only put down a few Sootrams which came to their memory and wrote their annotations basing them on the remnants of the musical works. Even their annotations are very meagre and they hardly help us in clearly understanding the great works. There are people who say that Adyarkunallar has only made mention of two lines referring to music in Silappadikaram, being in total ignorance of the Sootrams quoted above.

Here we read about Swarams and their concordance, the four primary puns and the four Jatis derived from them and the fact that ganam was made in less number of Alakus. We have noted already that the Puns of the ancient Tamils were divided into those of Ayapalai, Vattapalai, Thirikonapalai and Chathurapalai and that modern ganam was according to the very system.

With the exception of the Ragas of Ayapalai it is impossible to reproduce on western instruments the minutest Swarams of other Palais.

Many who could not discriminate between these minute Swarams played them on the Harmonium along with the Swarams of Ayapalai and lost their ear for these minute Swarams. Even to day, many Vidwans murder ancient Tamil Puns, the Pathams of Kshetringar and the Keertanams of Theagaraja Iyer by teaching their pupils to play them on the Harmonium and also sing them. It does not matter much if the number of these murderers is a few but they are a legion!

As this wrong practice had taken root for a number of years it was absolutely necessary to enquire into the Srutis of South Indian music. Nobody can be particularly blamed for this for it is due to the nature of the times. However we think it may be useful to give here a few general points and notation which may be of use to all people and which may be used by those playing on western instruments as well as the Yal which is largely used in South india.

11. How the Staff notation may be used for easily reproducing the music of South India.

It is a matter for regret that Indian Music, which has been held in high esteem from ancient times, has, for the last 2000 years or so, degenerated owing to want of patronage; times have so changed that, at present, researches are being made about Srutis which are the basis of all music! This is something like trying to find out the Alphabet of a language which was once noted for its high style and eminent literature! But we hope the time has come for the regeneration of Indian Music.

Given the particular Ri, the particular Ga, Ma, Dha or Ni which occur in a Ragam, professional musicians who have made it their life-work will easily understand the ramification of the Ragam and will be able to compose many Keertanams and Varnams in the same. When they commit them to writing, they group all the Swarams one after another, in the form of an ordinary language, without employing any musical measure or symbol.

Even clever musicians will not be able to make it out at times, so much so that its real meaning is completely lost to their successors. Sometimes they will merely mention the particular Thalam (time) of a piece of music without giving its parts which might cause endless doubts. So we see the necessity of clearing all these doubts by having a new method of Notation which might be useful to all. No doubt there are differences of opinion on this subject.

We are all agreed that a system of Notation easily understandable by all will be of great use to students of music. To indicate them merely by letters will not be enough, for the letters of a particular language may not be known to speakers of other languages. So it is best to mark them on the staff which is known to all people.

We should understand that the members of the Tamil Sangam which existed in South Madura eight thousand years ago and other musicians of that age used 12 half-Swarams of Ayapalai obtained by the Sa-Pa and the Sa-Ma principles in their ganam. The succession of the same 12 Swarams is now known among the renowned musicians of Europe as the chromatic scale under Equal Temperament. This is considered highly useful for purposes of harmony and modulation and modern western musical instruments like the Piano and the Harmonium are constructed on this principle. For over 2500 years, from the time of Pythagoras, controversy has been going on about the measurements of the 12 Swarams of an octave obtained while supposing Sa-Pa to be $\frac{3}{2}$ and Sa-Ma $\frac{4}{3}$. The celebrated western musicians Haydn, Mozart and Beethoven, about 120 years ago, found out the advantage of Equal Temperament and the result was the dawn of a new era in music and the perfection of symphony. Since then Europe has advanced by leaps and bounds in instrumental as well as vocal music, parts being written for wind as well as percussion instruments. Many an Indian has advanced in European music so much so that one is able to interpret the music of the west as well as make original compositions in the same. We have seen how a piece of

English Music composed by an Englishman at one end of the world when written in Staff notation is faithfully interpreted and reproduced by an Indian at the other end. We have seen the excellence of the English Staff notation. The signs which indicate (1) the duration and (2) the increasing or decreasing intensity of different notes, (3) the signs to denote speed. (4) expression, and (5) pauses, (6) the signs giving special directions to the performer as to where a piece of music ends or where it is repeated from, (7) time-signatures and (8) key-signatures, and (9) a variety of abbreviations and (10) embellishments are the distinguishing features of European music. So our humble opinion is that to reproduce those Indian Ragas where these 12 half Swarams only occur, the Staff notation of the west is quite enough. This notation is already known to many Indians constituting military bands, and other private bands, to Indian organists who play on the organ or the Harmonium in Christian churches, even to students of Indian music who play their Ragas on a Harmonium and to those students of the science of English Music. So it will be of advantage to put them down on the Staff. By so doing we should understand that those Ragas made up of the 12 half-Swarams of the Ayapalai only are capable of being thus transferred and played on the Harmonium or the Piano.

We should bear in mind two other points. In the first place, the bars should be so divided as to suit the different Thalams in use in India, and secondly, special signs should be given to indicate the minute Srutis over and above the 12 Swarams. Though these minute Srutis could not be reproduced on the piano or the Harmonium they might be of use to vocal musicians as well as players on instruments like the Yal or the Veena, the Violin and the Flute.

We may notice on pages 783—791 that concordant Swarams in an octave like Ri-Dha, Ga-Ni and Ma-Ni occur a little sharp sometimes. We have Ri not only with 2 Alakus but with $2\frac{1}{4}$, $2\frac{1}{2}$, $2\frac{3}{4}$, 3, $3\frac{1}{4}$, $3\frac{1}{2}$, and $3\frac{3}{4}$ Alakus also. So we may indicate the $\frac{1}{4}$, $\frac{1}{2}$, $\frac{3}{4}$, 1, $1\frac{1}{4}$, $1\frac{1}{2}$ and $1\frac{3}{4}$ by the numbers 1, 2, 3, 4, 5, 6, 7 respectively. These numerals tacked on to a Swaram will indicate what minuter Srutis they should add on. For example, Ri 4' and Dha 4' will mean that $4\frac{1}{4}$ Alagus are meant in each case. These occur in Sankaraparanam. But the Signs Ri 4' and Dha 4' will indicate $4\frac{1}{4}$ Alagus for the two Swarams. These occur in Ragas like Arabi, Poornachandrika and Chenchuruti. Ragas with minute Srutis such as these in Vattapalai, Thirikonapalai and Chathurapalai might be found in the Tables given. So, to conclude, then, we are of opinion that (1) the English Staff notation with certain modifications may be advantageously used for the Ragas composed of the 12 half Swarams of Ayapalai.

(2) Indicating the minuter Srutis by means of numerals from 1 to 7 will be of use to vocalists as well as players on instruments with the exception of the Harmonium and the Piano.

(3) Bars should be so divided as to suit the variety of Thalams in use in Indian music. The following Ragas will illustrate what we said.

1 AYAPALAI RAGAM.

Ragam: Garudadoni. Athithalam. 8-4-4

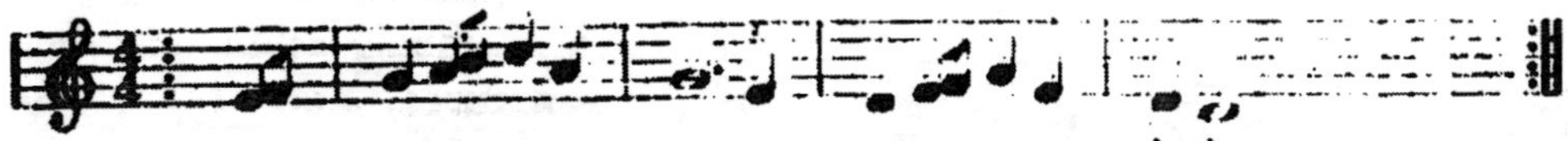

E - mi Ne - - ra mu nan - nu-pro - su da ku

gm p dn s d pa - g r gm p g r sa

E - mi Ne - - ra mu. - - - - - - - - - -

gm p dn s d pa- dp ga- pg r- gr sa-

2 VATTAPALAI RAGAM.

Ragam: Kaikavachi. Athithalam. 8-4-4

Ya - ral cholla - - mu di yum m - na dai

g g r gr r s ne s r re sr g r

A thi va nna tham ma - - - the - - - va se ya lai

s s pa m pa- dn sn n d n p m m p

Ya - ral chol la. - - - - -

m m ga r rs ne sa - - sa-

3 THIRIKONAPALAI RAGAM.

Ragam: Shunmugapiria. Athithalam. 8-4-4

Ma ru ve ra thi ge va rai ya ra - ma

p d pa m pa- p d ni n n d da

Mat ti mat ti ki - ni - - the lu - p va la - - - - -

m m ga g re r g r s s g r g m p d da n s ne n

Ma - - ri-ve ra - - -

n d da pa m pa - - pa- - pa -

4 CHATHURAPALAI RAGAM.

Ragam: Chenchuruti. Athithalam. 8-4-4

Van tha tha ri ver pa rn chontha main da no.

p d sa ri ga - m g re s - s n d

Van tha tha ri ver surar thu thi ka nam na rar va di va tha nil.

p d sa r ga - mg ri ga g r - s r s n d n d p

Of the four examples given above, the first is that of a Ragam in Ayapalai. What we have to note here is that the twelve half swarams of Ayapalai are the same as the 12 semitones of the westerners and so the Staff notation may be equally applied for both. To transfer such Ragas to the Staff notation and reproduce them will be very easy for all. To harmonise a few easy Keertanams and Swarajatis of the Ragas of Ayapalai and sing them in four parts will be very charming and the process easy.

Now let us take the Kaikavasi Ragam given as an example of a Ragam in Vattapalai. We may note that in the third bar the number 4 is placed over Ni (B), in the sixth bar the number 4 is over Ma (F sharp), while the same number is placed over the Ma (F sharp) in the 9th and the 10th bars and over the Ni (B) in the 11th bar. We have treated about these numbers already. Yet we go over the ground again for the sake of clearness.

Let us divide the half swaram of the Ayapalai or 2 Alakus into 8 parts, making each of the quarter Alakus into a separate division calling each division or Alaku by the numbers 1, 2, 3 up to 8.

In the following plan a half Swaram of Ayapalai is divided into 8 equal parts. The top numbers show how the Srutis should be marked while the bottom figures show the number of Alakus.

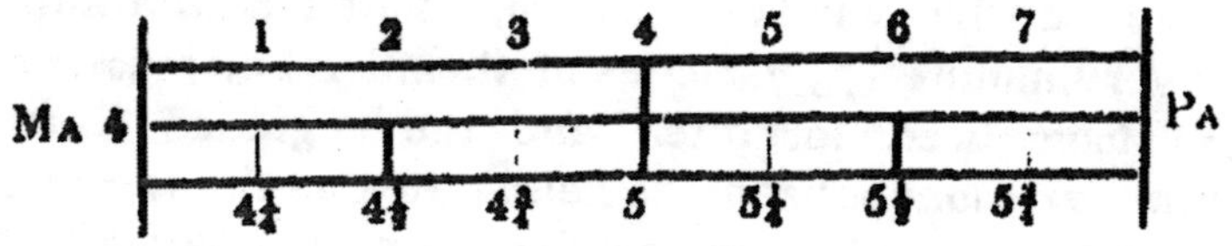

The Ma with four Alakus used here is called Prati Madhyamam at the present day. The interval between Ma 4 and Pa has been reckoned by the ancients as one Rasi with 2 Alakus. Between Prati Ma 4 and Pa comes Ma 5. This Ma 4 gathers momentum by quarter as 4¼, 4½, 4¾, 5, 5¼, 5½ and 5¾ and ends in Pa. Instead of marking these intervals as ¼, ½ and ¾ it is easier to mark them by integers as 1, 2, 3 etc.

The number 4 on a Swaram means, the addition of 4 quarter Alakus or 1 Alaku with the given Swaram. If the number 2 is placed it means that 2×¼ or ½ an Alaku is added. The number 3 implies an addition of ¾; the number 6 implies an addition of 1½, the number 1 implies an addition of 1×¼ or ¼, while the number 7 implies 7×¼ or 1¾ Srutis to the given Swaram.

We can understand the measurements of the Srutis in the four Palais if the interval between any two of the 12 Mettus used in the Yal could be divided into 8 parts according to the measurements given by us (*i. e.* according to Geometrical Progression) and the Swarasthanam of the particular Sruti marked in these divisions. This is possible only on the Yal. These measurements have been clearly given in the Tables in this book.

Now for the Srutis of Thirikonapalai the Ragam taken as example is Shunmukapiriya. We may see the number 2 on the Prati Ma (F sharp) and the number

6 on the Ri and Dha (D and A) with four Srutis each. It means that Ma (F sharp) should be played with an additional $\frac{1}{2}$ Alaku while the Ri and Dha (D and A) should be sharpened by $1\frac{1}{2}$ Alakus.

In the Chenchuruti Ragam given as an example of Thirikonapalai, we may notice number 1 placed over the Ri and Dha (D and A) with 4 Alakus each. This means they should be played with $4\frac{1}{4}$ Alakus.

So we see that Alakus like $\frac{1}{4}$, $\frac{1}{2}$, $\frac{3}{4}$, 1, $1\frac{1}{4}$, $1\frac{1}{2}$ and $1\frac{3}{4}$ are added on to the 12 Swarams. These minute Srutis are reproduced as gamakams by the human voice as well as on the Yal. They are not capable of being played on the western instruments: But modern players of Indian music on the harmonium play $\frac{1}{4}$, $\frac{1}{2}$, $\frac{3}{4}$ and 1 Alaku on the lower half Swaram and $1\frac{1}{4}$, $1\frac{1}{2}$ and $1\frac{3}{4}$ Alakus on the higher half Swaram.

Thus the charm of minute Srutis of the ancient Tamils has disappeared and people are satisfied with the ganam of the 12 half Swarams of Ayapalai, while ganam with 24 Srutis of Vattapalai, 48 Srutis of Thirikonapalai and 96 Srutis of Chathurapalai has been completely forgotten.

In the same manner, the seven different kinds of Thalams, the 35 different divisions derived from the five Kinds—Thisram, Chathusram, Kantam, Misram and Sankeeram, and the very minute 175 varieties of them by Thisrakalai and Chathurthakalai ($7 \times 5 \times 5 = 175$) have been forgotten and the degraded Ekathalam which is considered the easiest has monopolized the field. Just as the 12 Swarams have taken the field of all Srutis so also Sarvalegu which gives many ekathalams in the 12 Aksharas has come to stay on account of its ease.

So we see what immense difference there is between the ganam of the ancient Tamils and that of the people of other countries. The minuteness of the Srutis of the four Palais of the ancient Tamils has gradually dis-appeared so much so that one has to decide the 12 Swarams of Ayapalai and remove the doubt regarding them! To add to this doubt, the system of determining Srutis by the principle of $\frac{3}{2}$ and $\frac{4}{3}$ and the theory of 22 Srutis for the octave have come into the field. The truth of these theories will be manifest to all intelligent men. Only the ignorant will argue in an irrational manner. However, we understand that the ancient Tamils were using very minute Srutis in their ganam, that they had made proportionate progress in Thalam, that they used wind and percussion instruments such as the Flute, and the Yal and the Thunnumai and the Amandrigai and sang to the harmonious combination of all these instruments, playing them neither too loud or too soft so as to bring out the timbre of each instrument for satisfying their audience. As we think that the time is come for reviving this ancient music and placing it on an eminent position we had to speak about the method of making ganam wtth minute Srutis.

As the press letters were not enough to exemplify each Keertanam more fully by Staff notation we had to be satisfied with merely touching them.

III. Some inscriptions to show that the Pandya sovereigns of the Tamil country fostered Mut-tamil.

We have, till now, noted that the ancient Tamils who had much advanced in all sciences and arts were also efficient in Isai-Tamil, one of the divisions of the Tamil language, that they made their ganam with a complete knowledge of many of the minute amsams of Music, that their culture in these sciences is beyond comparison with that of any other nation, and that because of the gradual deterioration of many of the minute points of music many people wrote in different ways and doubted the very Srutis.

If appears that the efficiency of the ancient Tamils in Music should be attributed to the Sovereign rulers of the country. Judging from the Paiyiram of Irayanar Agaporul dated 2000 years ago, it is clear that the Pandya rulers of the period of the Sangam in South Madura, Korkai and Madura had a peculiar fascination for the Muttamil—Iyal, Isai and Natakam, and that they conducted the Sangams themselves besides possessing the literary preeminence for presiding over such Sangams. Though the period after the last sangam was a period of trouble for the Pandya sovereigns, the interest in Muttamil and the patronage on the part of the rulers never diminished. Even after the fall of the Pandyas, the minor rulers over the dismembered kingdoms continued to foster Music, and this is seen even at present. It is a well-known fact that experts in Iyal Tamil, in Music and in Drama are even to day patronised by the rulers of Samasthanams.

We think it will be satisfactory to examine by means of inscriptions how for the Pandya sovereigns showed their appreciation of the Tamil language and the music.

Besides it will open the eyes of those critics who declare that Sangeeta Ratnakar of Sarnga Dev is the primary work on Music and that the Tamils are completely ignorant of the science. It will also prove the fact that the Tamils were highly proficient in Music long before the time of Bharata of the 5th century and Sarnga Dev of the 13th century besides showing the excellent Tamil of these inscriptions which gradually deteriorated by admixture of foreign words.

While examining ancient inscriptions on this subject we obtained a few from M. R. Ry. Harihara Bharatiar Avl., Head Tamil Pandit of the High School at Amba-Samudram, Tinnevelly District, through M. R. Ry. Mutthaya Baghavatar Avl., of Harikesavanallur. These are given below.

The genealogical tree of the renowned Pandya rulers has never been made public till now, owing to absence of inscriptions. The following has been published as the result of a few inscriptions on copper plates.

பாண்டிய ராஜ வம்சாவளி
வேள்விக்குடிச் செப்பேடு
10-வது
|
பாண்டியாதி ராஜ பரமேஸ்வர பல் யாக சாலை முதுகுடுமிப் பெருவழுதி.

இவனே பல்யாக சாலை முதுகுடுமிப் பெருவழுதி என்பவன். இவனைப்பற்றிய வரலாறு வெகு சுருக்கமாகவே புறநானூற்றில் கூறப்பட்டிருக்கிறது.

|

ஞளபார்

இவனைப்பற்றி விசேஷமாய் ஒன்றும் தெரியவில்லை. இவனுக் கப்பாலுஞ் சில தலைமுறைகளுள. அவைகளும் இன்னும் வெளிப்படவில்லை.

|

பாண்டியாதி ராஜக்கடுங்கோன்

இவனைப்பற்றிய விசேஷங்களுந் தெரியவில்லை.

|

செழியன் சேந்தன்

|

மாறவர்மன் அரிகேசரி அசமசமன்.

இவன் வில்வேலி சைனியத்தை நெல்வேலி வென்றவன்.

|

கோச்சடையன் ரணதீரன்

இவன் மகா பராக்கிரமசாலி; மருதூரில் போர் புரிந்தவன். மங்களபுரத்து மஹாரதரை ஜெயித்தவன். கொங்கர் கோமான்.

|

அரிகேசரி பராங்குச-மாறவர்மன்

இவன் பெயரோடு தேர்மாறன், என்றோர் ஒட்டுப்பாடு முளது. இவன் குழுப்பூர், சங்கரமங்கை என்னுமிடங்களில் பல்லவர்களை ஜெயித்தான். இவனையே முதலாவது இராஜசிம்மனென்பர். பிற்காலத்தில் இவன் பல்லவ மல்லனை வென்றதோடு, கூடல், வஞ்சி, கோழி என்ற நகரங்களையும் சிறப்புறப் புதுப்பித்தான். மாளவ கன்னிகையை மணந்திருக்கொண்டு, மழகொங்களை கீழ்ப்படுத்தினான். கங்க அரசர்க்குக் கிட்டின உறவினன். மற்றொரு காலத்தில் இவன் நெடுவயல், குறுமடை, மன்னிக்குறிச்சி, பூவலூர், கொடும்பாளூர் என்னுமிடங்களிற் பெரும் போர் புரிந்து வெற்றி மாலை சூடியிருக்கின்றான். திருப்பாண்டிக் கொடுமுடியில் ஸ்ரீ பசுபதீஸ்வரரை ஆத்துமார்த்த தெய்வமாகக்கொண்டு வழிபட்டான். மேற்படி ஆலயத்தில் அநேக திருப்பணிகளும் இவனே செய்தானென்பர். முத்தமிழிலும் பேரபிமானம் படைத்தவன் எனத் தெரிய வருகின்றான்.

|

ஜடிலன் கலிப்பகை நெடுஞ்சடையன் பராந்தகன் காலம் கி. பி. 770.

இவன் பெண்ணாகடத்துக் காடவனையும், நாட்டுக் குறும்பு என்னுமிடத்து ஆய வேளையும் குறும்பரையும் வெற்றி பெற்றிருக்கின்றான். வைத்தியர் குலத்து வந்த மூவேந்த மங்கலப் பேரரையனாகிய மாறன்காரி என்பவர் இவனுடைய முக்கிய மந்திரி. இம்மந்திரிக்கு மதுரதரன் என்றும் பெயருளது. இவரது நகரம் கரவந்தபுரம். ஆனைமலைச் சாசனத்தால் இவ்வரசன் காலம் கி.பி. 770 என்று தெரிகிறது. மதுரதரன் என்னும் மந்திரியே பன்னிரண்டு ஆழ்வார்களில் ஒருவராகிய மதுரகவி ஆழ்வார் எனப்படுவரென்பர்.

|

இராஜ சிம்மன் 2-வது

இவனைப்பற்றி விசேஷமாய் ஒன்றுந் தெரியவில்லை.

|

வரகுண மஹாராஜா

இவன் மகா வீரன். இடைப்பட்டுச் சோர்வடைந்து போன பாண்டிய இராஜ்யத்தை மிகு கம்பீரத்துடன் விளங்கச் செய்தவன். இவன் பட்டத்துக்கு வந்த சில காலத்துள் தெற்கே குமரி, வடக்கே இமயமலை, மேற்கும் கிழக்கும் கடல்கள் ஆகிய எல்லைக்குட்பட்ட பூமியை யெல்லாம் தன் வசப்படுத்திக்கொண்டவன். இவனைப் பற்றிய சிலா சாசனங்கள் எல்லா நாட்டிலுமிருக்கின்றனவாம். பாண்டி நாட்டிலுள்ள அம்பாசமுத்திரம் ஸ்ரீ காசிபேஸ்வரர் ஆலயத்தில் இவனது சிலா சாசனமொன்றுளது. அது பின்வருவது :—

1-வது சாசனம்.

ஸ்வஸ்தி ஸ்ரீ படாரனுக்ககத்திலை முள்ளி நாட்டிளங்கோய்க்குடித் திருப்போத்துடையார் ஸ்ரீ கோயில் படாரர்க்கு முதல் கெடாமை பொலிகொண்டு நாந்த காலமுந்திருவமிது செலுத்துவதாக வரகுண மஹா ராஜர் தொண்டை நாட்டுப் பெண்ணைக்கரை அரைசூர்விற்றிருந்து இளங்கோக்குடிச்சபையார் கையிற் குடுத்த காசு இருநூற்றெண்பது இவற்றுற் காசின்வாயிருகலமாக ஆண்டு வரை சபையாரளக்கும் பொலி நெல் ஐந்நூற்றெண்பதின் கலம். இவைகொண்டு படாரர் பணி மக்களும் இளங்கோக்குச் சபை வாரியரும் உடனின்று வரகுண மகா ராஜர்க்கு ராஜவர்ஷம் நான்காவதுக்கு எதிர் பன்னிரண்டாயாண்டு துலா ஞாயிறு முதலாக நிசதியாக நாந்த காலமுந்திருவமிது செலுத்தும்படி ஒரு பொழுதைக்கு வேண்டுவன அரிசி செந்நற் றீட்டல் நாழி தும்மாயத்துக்கு பயற்றுப் பருப்பு நிவேதிக்க பசுவின் நெய்யாழாக்கு பசுவின்றேயிர் தயிருரி கருவாழைப் பழம் நான்கு சர்க்கரை ஒரு பலம் கறியமிது காய்க்கறி ஒன்று புளிங்கறி இரண்டு புழுக்குக்கறி ஒன்று பொறிக்கறி ஒன்று எற்றிக்கறி ஐஞ்சினுக்கும் கறி பதின் பலம் கறிதுமிக்கவும் பொறிக்கவும் பசுவினது நெய் ஆழாக்குக் கூட்டுக்குப் பசுவின் றேயிர் தயிருரி காயம் இருசெவிட்டு இலை அமிது வெள்ளிலை ஈரடுக்கு அடைக்காய் பத்து நூறு ஒரு செவிட்டு ஆக நிசதி நான்கு பொழுதைக்கு வேண்டுவன அரிசிசெந்நற்றீட்டல் பதி னறு நாழி ....நியதிப்படி முட்டாமல் நெடுங்காலமுஞ் செலுத்துவதாக வைத்தார் ஸ்ரீ வரகுண மகா ராஜர்.

இச்சாஸனம் பெரிதாதலால் பிற்பாகத்தைப் புள்ளிக்குறியிட்டு விடுத்துச் சுருக்கமாக வரைந்துளேன். இப்பொழுது இச் சிலை மெற்ருஸ் மியூஸியத்திலிருக்கிறது.

திருச்செந்தூர் ஸ்ரீ சுப்பிரமணிய சுவாமி கோவில் மேல உட்பிரகாரம் மாலைகட்டு மிடத்தில் நாட்டியிருக்கும் இரண்டு சிலையிலுள்ள சாஸனமும் மேற்படி வரகுண மஹாராஜரைப் பற்றியது. அதனையும் இங்கு சிறிது வரைந்துளேன்.

2-வது சாசனம்.

..................ஸ்ரீ வரகுண மஹாராயற்குயாண்டு..................னெதிர் பதின்மூன்று இவ்வாண்டு திரு [ச்செந்தூர்]ச்சுப்பிரமணிய படாரர் உபாஸலையார் திருமூலத்தானத்துப் படாரர்க்கு முதல் கெடாமைப் பொலிகொண்டு செலுத்துவதாக உடையாராடியாரா இன வரகுண மாராயர் பொற்றுர் இருட்டைக் குடி கிழவனும் சாத்தன் பெருமானும் அளந்து நாட்டுக்கொளும் ஐயா இசுத்தான்............கொண்டு வைத்த நிறை குறையாப் பழங்காசு ஆயிரத்து நானூறு இக்காசிற்............கொற்கை மாரார் கை இன் முதற் கெடாமைப் பொலி ஊட்டுக் கொண்டு செலுத்துவதாக வைத்த நிறை குறையாப் பழங்காசு தொள்ளாயிற்று பொன் வட்டு இக்காசால் ஒரு காசுக்கு ஆண்டு வரை பொலி நிறைமதி நாராயத்தால் இருகல நெல்லாக வந்த நெல்லு நாற்பத்தொன்பதாற்று முக்கலனேய் ஒன்பதின் குறுணி. இந்நெல்லால் நியதிப்படி இவர்கள் கொண்டு வந்து செலுத்தக் கடவன நாழி அரிசிக்கு முன்னுழி நெல்லாகத் திருவமுதினுக்கு அரிசி செந்நெற்றீட்டல் ஒரு போதைக்கு நானாழியாக நான்கு போதைக்கு அரிசி செந்நெற்றீட்டல் பதினறு நாழியாக மார்கழித் திருவாதிரை மாசி மகமும் வைய்யாசி விசாகமும் படி இரட்டி செலுத்துவது இப்பரிசு செலுத்தாது குற்றுக் காற்படில் இந்தேவர்க்கேய் இருபத்தைந்து காசு தண்டமுந் தூப்பது இந்நாட்டு..................

இச்சாஸனமும் மிகப் பெரிதாதலால் சுருக்கமாக எடுத்துக் காட்டப்பட்டது.

இங்குக் காட்டிய சாஸனங்களால் வரகுண மகா ராசர் சிறந்த வையத்தரென்று தெரிகின்றது. இவர் கோயில்களுக்குச் செய்து வந்த வழிபாடுகள், பண்டைக் காலந்தொட்டு முறை பிறழாது இப்பவும் நடந்தேறி வருகின்ற சேரன் காட்டரசர் தருமங்களை ஒத்திருக்கின்றன. திருச்செந்தூர் சாஸனத்தின் கடைசி பாகத்தில் இவ்வரசர் தேசப்பிரியராயிருந்தாரென்று வாசிக்கப்படுகிறது. அனால் அப்பாக மிகவும் மழுங்கிப் போய் விட்டது.

சிலர் இவ்வரகுண பாண்டியர் காலத்திருந்த சோழன் விஜயாலயன் என்றும் இவன் அவரால் தோல்வியுற்று சிற்றரசனும்த் தஞ்சாவூரை முதன் முதல் தனக்கு இராஜதானியாகக் கொண்டானென்றும் வேறுள்ள சிலாசாஸனங்களால் ஊகிக்கின்றனர். ஒருவாறு இவ்விஷயம் பொருந்தவுங்கூடும். இவர் கி-பி 862-ல் பிரிட்டர்தரித்தவர். இவர் மாதா ஓர் சோழன் மகள். இன்னும் இவ்வேந்தரைப் பற்றிய சரித்திரங்கள் பல விரிவஞ்சி விடுக்கப்பட்டன.

ஸ்ரீ மாறஸ்ரீ வல்லப ஏகவீரபர சக்ரகோலாகலன்.

இவன் சேரர் சிங்களர் பல்லவர் வில்லவர் முதலானவர்களை ஜெயித்தவன். "பல்லவ பஞ்சனன்" என்றோர் பட்டப் பெயருமிவனுக்குண்டு

வரகுணவர்மன்.

பராந்தகன்வீரநாராயணசடையன்.

இவன் கரகிரியிற் போர்புரிந்தவன், பெண்ணுகடமழித்தவன் இவன் மனைவியின்பெயர் வானவன் மாதேவி.

இராஜ சிம்மன் மூன்றவது

மந்தர கௌரவ அபிமானமேரு

இவன் விஜயாலயன் பேரன் பராந்தகன் காலத்திலுள்ள வனுமிருன்.

இதுவரை வேள்விக்குடிச் செப்பேட்டை ஆதாரமாய்க் கொண்டு விளக்கப்பட்டது. இனி வருவன பல இடங்களிலுமுள்ள சிலாசாஸனங்களின் சுருங்கிய ஆராய்ச்சி என்றறிக.

வீரபாண்டியன்

இவனைச் சோழன் தலைகொண்ட வீரபாண்டியன் என்று சாஸனங்கள் கூறும். இவன் இராஜசிம்மன் குமாரனெனக் கூறுவர். கி-பி. 925-ல் தன்னுடன் போருக்கெழுந்த ஆதித்திய கரிகால சோழன்தலை கொண்டவன். இவனைப்பற்றிய சாஸனங்கள் பாண்டி நாட்டிலும் வடநாடுகளிலும் மற்றுமுள்ள தமிழ் நாடுகளிலும் சிறிது அருமையாகவே காணப்படுகின்றன. அம்பாசமுத்திரம் ஸ்ரீ மூலநாதர் கோவிலில் ஒரு சாஸனமுளது. அது பின்வருவது —

3-வது சாசனம்.

ஸ்வஸ்தி ஸ்ரீ சோழன்றலை கொண்ட வீரபாண்டியர்க்கு யாண்டு நாலு இதனெதிர் நாலு இவ்வாண்டு முள்ளி நாட்டுப் பிரமதேயம் இளங்கோய்க் குடித்திருக்காலத்துறை நின்றருளின எம்பெருமானுக்கு ஸ்ரீ கரணத்திருச் சித்திரக்கூடத்திருந்து முப்பத்திரண்டு அச்சை உம் ஐந்சு வாரமோதிதானம் புக்கார் தன் [நேர] சோதி நான்மைக் காட்டேன்பதாக வெண்பு நாட்டு கூர்த்திரளைக்கனத்த சாத்தன் பிரவிறை கொண்டு சபையார் காட்ட............இச்சாஸனம் குறைவாகவேயிலங்கிறது.

இந்த வீரபாண்டியன், பராக்கிரம பாண்டியன் குமாரனென்றும், குலோத்துங்க சோழனுற் கொல்லப்பட்டானெனவும் கூறுவர்.

அப்பால் சில காலம் சோழ மன்னவர்களால் பாண்டி நாடு காக்கப்பட்டு வந்ததாகத் தெரிகிறது. சிதைந்துபோன பாண்டிய ராஜ வம்சத்தில் சோச்சடையன் குலசேகரன் என்னுமோர் பாண்டியன் கி. பி. 1190-ல் பிரசித்தி பெற்றான். திரண்ட சைன்யத்துடன் பல நாடுகளையும் தன் வசப்படுத்திக்கொண்டான். இவனுடைய பிரதாபமனைத்தையும் பின்வரும் மெய்க்கீர்த்திப் பாகரங்களாலறிந்து கொள்க.

4-வது சாசனம்.

ஸ்வஸ்தி ஸ்ரீ

பூவின் கிழத்தி மேவி வீற் றிருப்ப
மேதினி மாது நீதியிற் புணர
வயப்போர் மடந்தை ஜயப்புயத் திருப்ப
மாக்கலை மடந்தை வாக்கினில் விளங்க
திசையிரு நான்கும் இசைநிலா வெறிப்ப
மறைநெறி வளர மனுநெறி திகழ
அறநெறிச் சமயங்க ளாறுந் தழைப்ப
கான வேங்கையை வில்லுடன் துரந்து
† மீனுங் கனகா சலத்துவீற் றிருப்ப
எண்கிரி சூழ்ந்த எழுகட லெழுபொழில்
வெண்குடை நிழற்றிச் செங்கோல் நடப்ப
கோமேங்கலி நடேத்தி நேமியெலத் தெளிப்ப
வில்லவர் செம்பியர் விராடர் களுடவர்
பல்லவர் திறையுடன் முறைமுறை பணிய
இருநேமி யளவும் ஒருநேமி யோங்க
‡ இன்னமு தாகிய இயலிசை நாடகம்
* மன்னி வளர மணிமுடி சூடி
விளங்கிய வீரசிம்மாசனத்து

வீற்றிருந்தருளிய ஸ்ரீ கோச்சடைய பன்மரான திரிபுவன சக்கரவர்த்திகள் ஸ்ரீ குலசேகர தேவர்க்கு யாண்டு மூன்றாவது நாள் இராஜ்யாபிஷேகத்து பழ நூற்று ஐப்பத்தஞ்சு மதுரோதயவள நாட்டு மாடக்குளக் கீழ் மதுரைக் கோயில் பள்ளியறைக் கூடத்துப் பள்ளிப்பீடம் காலிங்கராயனில் எழுந்தருளியிருந்து கீழ் வேம்புநாட்டுத் திருநெல்வேலி . ...

இச்சாஸனம் திருநெல்வேலி நெல்லையப்பர் கோவில் சபைப் பிரகாரம் தென்புறத்திலுள்ளது.

5-வது சாசனம்.

ஸ்வஸ்தி ஸ்ரீ

பூதல வனிதை மேதக விளங்க
சுந்தர மார்பில் இந்திரை இருப்ப
புயல்வரை தழுவிய வயமகள் நனிப்ப
* மயலறு சிறப்பின் மாமுனி தேர்ந்த
‡ இயலிசை நாடகம் எழில்பெற வளர
அந்திவெண் கூரி மதக ளிடத்து
வெந்திற வேங்கை வில்லுட னேளிப்ப
திக்கடிப் படுத்திச் சக்கரஞ் செல்ல
எவ்வெவ் மாநிலப் பார்த்திவர் பொதுவற
† தெய்வ மேதவில் செல்வினை யாட
.....................இருவகைப் பிறப்பின்
முந்நூல் மார்பின் நான்மறை யாளர்
மாக விசும்பின் வானவர்க் கமைந்த
யாக வேள்வி விடத்தொறு மியல
அம்புவி அடக்கு மதுமைசா லறுவகை

செங்கோதுட் சம்யக் சிறுடன் துலவ
எழுபொழில் கவித்த முழுமதிக் கவிகை
திருநிலவு சொரிந்திங் கிருநில வரைப்பின்
வெங்கலி கடிந்து செங்கோல் நடப்ப
விண்பொத சிகர மாதிர வெண்கோட்
டெண்பெரு களிறு......................
ஒன்பது கண்டத்து உயர்குல வேந்தரும்
அன்புடன் வணங்கி அருந்திறை காட்டி
யணிதட முடிமே லடிமலர் சூடி
....
....
....
ஓடரி நெடுங்கண் ஒண்டொடி மகளிர்
திலத நுதல்மேற் சேவடி வைத்தும்
உலகு முழுதுடையாரோமே வீற்றிருந்தருளிய
ஸ்ரீ கோச்சடைய பன்மரான திரிபுவன
சக்ரவர்த்திகள் ஸ்ரீ குல சேகர தேவர்க்கு
யாண்டு மூன்றவது நாள் இராசு நாஞ்சி
நாட்டு.........................

இதுவும் திருநெல்வேலி நெல்லையப்பர் கோவில் சபைப் பிரகாரத்திலிருக்கிறது.

இங்குக்காட்டிய சாஸனங்களிரண்டும் சடையன் குலசேகரபாண்டியன் மூவகைத்தமிழையும் நல்ல வண்ணம் ஆதரித்து வந்தனன் என்பதைத் தெளிவாய் விளக்குகின்றன.

அப்பால் கி. பி. 1216ல் சுந்தரபாண்டியன் மாறவர்மன் அரசாக்ஷி செய்தான். இவன் மகா வீரன். தோல்வி என்பதே இவனுக்குத் தெரியாது. தமிழிடத்தும் எழுவகை இசையிடத்தும் பேரபிமான முள்ளவனுயிருந்தான். இவன், சோணாட்டை அக்காலத்தி லாண்டுகொண்டிருந்த மூன்றாவது இராஜாதி ராஜனைக் காட்டில் ஓட்டிக் கருணையால் மீண்டும் அவனுக்கு அரசளித்தான். அதனுல் இவனுக்கு (முதலாவது) சுந்தரபாண்டியன் எனவும், சோணாடு கொண்டு சோளபுரத்து வீராபிஷேகங் கொண்டருளிய சுந்தரபாண்டியன் எனவும், சோணாடு வழங்கிய சுந்தரபாண்டியன் எனவும் பெயர்கள் வழங்கலாயின.

6-வது சாசனம்.

ஸ்வஸ்தி ஸ்ரீ

பூமருவிய திருமடந்தையும் புவிமடந்தையும் புயத்திருப்ப
நாமருவிய கலைமடந்தையும் ஜெய மடந்தையும் நலஞ்சிறப்ப
கோளார்ந்த சினப்புலியும் கோதேஞ்சிலையும் நிலந்தோன்ற
† வானார்ந்த பொற்கிரிமேல் வரிக்கயல்கள் விளையாட
இருங்கடல் வலயத் திவிதறம் பெருக
கரிங்கலி கடிந்து செங்கோல் நடப்ப
ஒருகுடை நீழலி லிருநிலங் குளிர
* மூவகைத் தமிழு முறைமையின் விளங்க
நால்வகை வேதமும் நவின்றுடன் வளர
ஐவகை வேள்வியு மெய்வகை விளங்க
அறுவகைச் சமயமும் அழகுடன் திகழ
* எழுவகைப் பாடலு மிசையுடன் பரவ

எண்டிசை யனைவுஞ் சக்கரஞ் செல்ல
கொங்கணர் கலிங்கர் கோசலர் மாளவர்
சிங்களர் தெலுங்கர் சீனர் குச்சரர்
வில்லவர் மாகதர் விக்கலர் செம்பியர்
பல்லவர் முதலாப் பார்த்திவ ரெல்லாம்
உறைவிட மதுவென வொதுவர்முன் றொழுதவர்
முறைமுறை கீழ்வந் திறைஞ்ச விளங்கொளி
மணிமுடி யிந்திரன் பூட்டிய பொலங்கதிர்
ஆர மார்பினிற் பொலியப் பனிமலர்
திசைமுகன் படைத்த..............................
மறுநெறி தழைய மணிமுடி சூடி
பொன்னிசூழ் நாட்டிற் புலியாணை போயகல
* கன்னிசூழ் நாட்டிற் கயலாணை கைவளர
வெஞ்சின விவுளியும் வேழமும் பரப்பித்
தஞ்சையும் உறந்தையும் செந்தழல் கொளுத்திக்
காவியும் நீலமும் நின்றுகவி னழிப்ப
ஆவியு மாறு மணிநீர் நலனழித்துக்
கூடமா டங்களுங் கோபுரமு மாடரங்கும்
மாடமா ளிகையு மண்டபமும் பலவிடித்துத்
தொழுது வந்தடையா நிருபர்தந் தோகையர்
அழுத கண்ணீ ராறு பரப்பிக்
கழுதைகொண் டுழுதுக் கவடிவித்துச் செம்பியனைச்
சினம்பெரியப் பொருது சுரம்புக வோட்டி
வம்பொன்மணி முடிபறித்துப் பாணனுக்குக் கொடுத்தருளி
பாடருஞ் சிறப்பிற் பருதிவான் றோயும்
ஆடகப் புரிசை யாயிரத் தளியில்
சோழ வளவன் அபிஷேக மண்டபத்து
வீராபி ஷேகஞ் செய்துபுகழ் விரித்து
நாளும் பரராசர் நடுத்தலை விழுங்கி
மீளுந் தறுகண் யானைமேற் கொண்டு
நீராழி வையம் பொதுவற வொழித்துக்
கூராழியுஞ் செய்ய கோலுமே கொண்டுபோய்
ஐயப் படாத அருமறைதே ரந்தணர்வாழ்
தெய்வப் புலியூர்த் திருவெல்லை யிற்புக்குப்
பொன்னம் பலம்பொலிய நின்றவோர் பூவையு
மன்றுந் திருமேனி கண்டு மனங்களித்துத்
தாமமலர் மேலயனுந் துளிர்துழாய் மாலும்
அரிய மலர்ச்சேவடி வணங்கிச் சிறையன்னஞ்
துயிலொழிய வண்டெழுப்பும் பூங்கமல வாவிசூழ்
பொன்னம ராவதியி லணைந்துலகந் தாங்குமர்
மேதகைத் தொணர்ந்து வைத்தவன் சோணாட்டைப் பக்கந்தந்து
தோகை மயில்புனற் சோணாடு தானிழந்த
தாரவளை முடியுந் தவறுக வொன்றுமொழி
மான நிலைகுலைய வாணகிரிக் கப்புறத்துப்

சோனை வளைவ ஞரிமை பொருநிம்புகுந்து
பொய்ய புநல்வளைநிர் செருவேற்று முற்காட்டி
வெற்றி பரியனைக்கீழ் வீழ்ந்து தொழுதிறைஞ்சு
நாடோடி முற்றிகழ்ந்த வேம்பைமொல்லாங் கைகொள
தமிழ்நாடும் பண்ணிக் தமிழ்நாடர் முடியுடனே
…………புநலிடங்கொண்டு………இது பிடிபாடகவொர
பொருந்திலை நாலத்துப் பூமலர் தொழுவிளங்கு
செங்கையல் தோய்ந்தேர் திருமுகமும் பண்டிமுக
சோணாடு பொன்னு தமமுக தொல்லைநதி
மீனை வழங்கி விடைநொடிந்து விட்டதுளி
…………ஹோமத்திலை நாட்டிய
ஸ்ரீ கோமாறவர்மரான திரிபுவன சக்கரவர்த்திகள்

ஸ்ரீ சோணாடு கொண்டு முடிகொண்ட சோழபுரத்தில் வீராபிஷேகம் பண்ணி அருளிய ஸ்ரீ சுந்தர பாண்டியதேவருக்கு யாண்டு [illegible] நாள் [illegible]……………

இதுவும் திருநெல்வேலி நெல்லையப்பர் கோவிலிலுள்ளது.

அப்பால் கி.பி. 1234-ல் இரண்டாவது மாறவர்மன் சுந்தரபாண்டியனும் கி.பி. 1251-ல் எம்மண்டலமுங் கொண்டருளிய சுந்தரபாண்டியனும், கி.பி. 1268-ல் எம்மண்டலமுங் கொண்டருளிய மாறன்குலசேகர பாண்டியனும் வெகு கம்பீரத்துடன் அரசியற்றி வந்திருக்கின்றனர். இவர்களுக்குரிய மெய்க்கீர்த்திகளை எல்லாமெடுத்துக் காட்டல் சாத்தியமல்லவென விடுக்கப்பட்டன.

பிறகு கி. பி. 13-வது நூற்றாண்டில் இத்தமிழ் நாடுகளோடு வட நாடுகளையும் தன் வசப்படுத்திக் கொண்டாண்டவன் சடாவர்மன் சுந்தரபாண்டியன். இவனுடைய தண்டத்தலைவனே கப்பற்கோவைக்கு நாயகனுவான். இவ்வேந்தன் கருநாட்டரசனையும் வென்றனான். கப்பற்கோவையாலுரிதனை அறியலாகும்.

இந்த சடாவர்மன் சுந்தரபாண்டியன் பரிசுத்தமான சிவபக்தன் எனவும் பண்ணோடு தேவாரமோதத் தெரிந்தவனெனவும் தெரிகின்றன். பாண்டிய நாட்டிலுள்ள கோவில்களில் திருஞானபோதகம்—தேவாரமோதுதலை ஏற்படுத்தியிருக்கின்றான். இவ்விஷயத்தைக் கீழ்வரும் சாஸனத்தாலறியலாகும்.

7-வது சாசனம்.

திரிபுவனசக்க……………………திருவேம்புகொடு உடையார் திருநெல்வேலியுடைய நாயனார் கோவில் [illegible] தேவாரம் [illegible] ஸ்வாமிகளுக்கு [illegible]…திருமுறைப்பு திருஞான [illegible] தவசிகளில் விஷபாடதேவர் சந்தானத்து [illegible] தேவர் சிஷ்யரில் [illegible], [illegible] சந்தானத்து [illegible] தேவ சிஷ்யரில் [illegible], திருவாதூர் [illegible] சிவபாத இருதய சிஷ்யரில் திருஞான் [illegible] பெருமானுக்கும் பிக்ஷாமட சந்தானத்து [illegible] தேவ சிஷ்யரில் [illegible] திருவாதூர் மடத்து [illegible] அஸ்தா தேவ சிஷ்யரில் ஞான [illegible] தேவர்தன் தேவனுக்கும், பிக்ஷாமட சந்தானத்து திருநாகீஸ்வரத்து [illegible] சிஷ்யரில் திருஞானசம்பந்தருக்கும், [illegible] சந்தானத்து [illegible] தேவ சிஷ்யரில் [illegible] மதுரா [illegible] சந்தானத்து நீலகண்ட சிஷ்யரில் திருநெல்வேலி மாளிகை மடத்து அழகிய தேவர் சிஷ்யரில் திருநெல்வேலி யுடையானுக்கும், பிக்ஷாமட சந்தானத்து [illegible] தேவ சிஷ்யரில் [illegible] நாட்டிறைவனுக்கும், திருநெல்வேலி கோயிலில் மடத்து [illegible] சந்தானத்து [illegible] சிஷ்யரில் [illegible] பெருமாளுக்கும் [illegible] திருஞானம் [illegible] வைக்க………இதுவும் திருநெல்வேலிசாசனம்………………

அப்பால் மூன்றாவது மாறன் சுந்தரபாண்டியன் பட்டத்திற்கிருந்தல் வேண்டும். கீழ்வரும் மெய்க் கீர்த்தி அவனது பிரதாபத்தை விளக்காநிற்கும்.

8-வது சாசனம்.

ஸ்வஸ்தி ஸ்ரீ

பூமலர்த் திருவும் பொருஜெயமடந்தையும்
தாமரை......முலைஜாயர் புயத்திருப்ப
செந்நாவில் வெள்ளிதழ்த் தாமரை
அமல மாது [illegible]
பொற்றொடியை [illegible]
இருநில மடந்தை [illegible]
[illegible] நீரும் தருமழை [illegible]
முறைமையாள் விழாக்கோடி [illegible]
கருங்கலி [illegible]
அறுதொழில் வேள்வி [illegible]
[illegible] தமிழும் [illegible]
பொருநிய [illegible] பூதல [illegible]
ஒருகை [illegible] ......
[illegible]..................
........................[illegible]
[illegible]............[illegible]
[illegible]............[illegible]
கலிங்கமும் கடாரமும்............[illegible]
தெலிங்கத் சோலகத் [illegible]
விக்ரமை [illegible] குளிந்து
முழுநில [illegible]
[illegible]
............முடிசூடி [illegible]
[illegible] குளிர்த்து [illegible]
............[illegible] வீர
............[illegible] சிங்காசனத்து
[illegible] வீற்றிருந்தருளிய
[illegible] விளங்கிய
[illegible] ஸ்ரீ [illegible]

இவ்வரசன் அருதியின்மேலும் தமிழின்மேலும் வைத்துள்ள பேரபிமானத்தையே இங்கு காணலாகத் தக்கது திருவாலீஸ்வரத்து சாசனம்.

அப்பால் இரண்டாவது விக்ரமபாண்டியன். மேல்வருவது இவனது மெய்க்கீர்த்திச் செய்யுள்.

9-வது சாசனம்.

திருமகள் ஜெயமகள் திருப்புயத் திருப்ப
பெருநில [illegible]
[illegible]
[illegible]

நேமி வளைத்து நெடுநிலை முழுதுந்
த............வெண்குடை நிழலிற் பூர்ப்பச்
............செங்கோல் நடப்பக் கருங்கலிதுரந்து
வேதவிதியில் நீதி நிலவ
............நிறை கோணர்ந்திரந்த
வீரமும் புகழு மேதக விளங்க
நதிப்பெருஞ் சடைமுடி நாதன் சூடிய
மதிக்குலந் திகழ மணிமுடி சூடி
விளங்கிய வீரசிம் மாசனத்து
வீற்றிருந்தருளிய கோமாறபன்மரான திரிபுவனசக்ரவர்த்திகள் ஸ்ரீ விக்ரமபாண்டியதேவர்க்கு
....

இச்சாசனம் பத்தன் மடைப்பெருமாள் கோவிலிலுள்ளது.

அடுத்தவன் மூன்றாவது குலசேகரபாண்டியன் எனச்சிலர் கூறுவர். கீழ்வருவது இவனைப்பற்றிய மெய்க்கீர்த்திச் செய்யுள்.

10-வது சாசனம்.

தேர்போலும்............வார்பூணு மணிவடமுலை
திருப்பாவை திருமார்பிலும் வரைப்பாவை வரைத்தோளிலும்
கலைவனிதை மலர்மனத்திலும் துணிபிரியாதினி திருப்பச்
செங்கோல் நடப்ப வெண்குடை நிழற்றக்
கருங்கலி முருங்கப் பெரும்புகழ் பரப்பந்
நானத் தனல்வழி நடுமேபுலி சேர
† மீன் பொன்வரைமிசை யோங்க
* முத்தமிழ்ப் பனுவலும் நான்மறை முழுது
மெய்த்தவச் சைவசமயத்துடன் விளங்க
சிங்கள............எழும்............விங்கத்தே............எழும்
தனக்குதிர............எழும் துச்சரங்கி..............எழும்
நெடுமுடி............எழு...யாவனையும்............எழும்
வியந்செயி............எழும்............வின்ன
நிறைமுன் காட்டி மிதபுடை பொருந்தி
விசிகதிர்த் தவசி வீசற் றென்றலும்
வாடையு மின்ன வீசந் தவத
சிம்மாசனத்தைத் தைடேறவிருந்தி
பகையரசோட்டி.......................... ......
....வீற்றிருந்தருளிய

ஸ்ரீ கோமாறபன்மரான திரிபுவன சக்ரவர்த்திகள் ஸ்ரீ குலசேகர தேவர்க்கு ஆண்டு நாலாவது திருப்புடைமருதூர் சுவாமிநாதரும் பூநாதர் கோவில் சாசனம்.

11-வது சாசனம்.

கீழ்வரும் வம்சாவளி, தென்காசிக் கோவிலிலுள்ள சிலாசாசனங்களையும் செப்பேடுகளையும் ஆதாரமாகக் கொண்டு வரையப்பட்டது.

அபிராமபாண்டியன் சகம் 1474
- பராக்ரம பாண்டியன்
  - அபிராமபாண்டியன்
    - பராக்ரமன்
      - குணராம பாண்டியன்
      - வரதுங்கராம பாண்டியன்
    - சாலிவாடபதி
      - அழகன் பெருமாள் அதிவீரராம பாண்டியன்
  - ஆகவராமபாண்டியன்
    - ஸ்ரீ வல்லபன் மானுபரணன்
      - ஸ்ரீ வல்லபன்

இதில் தென்காசி ஸ்ரீ விசுவநாதஸ்வாமி கோவில் கட்டின பராக்ரமபாண்டியன் மெய்க்கீர்த்தி வருமாறு.

12-வது சாசனம்.

குடமலந்து.

பூமிசை வனிதை மார்பினிற் பொலிய
நாமிசை கலைமகள் நலம்பெற விளங்க
புயத்துணை மீது ஜயமகள் புணர
† நயவினை உலகங் கண்ணெனத் திகழச்
சந்திர குலத்து வந்தவ தரித்து
முந்தையோர் தவத்தின் முளையென வளர்ந்து
• தென்கலை வடகலை தெரிவுறத் தெளிந்து
ஐம்படை புரங்க யணிமுடி வனைந்து
சங்கர சரண பங்கயஞ் சூடி
செங்கோ லோச்சி வெண்குடை நிழற்றி
மறங்களை பறித்துநல் லறப்பயிர் விளைந்து
சிங்கையி லனுரையி லிராரையிற் செய்யில்
விந்தையில் அயந்தையில் முதலையில் விளையில்
வைப்பாற்றே......................
............னுரைவந் கண்டோட மாற்றி....................
பதினெண் பாஷைப் பார்த்திவ ரிசைவதும்
திறையுஞ் சின்னமு முறைமுறை கொணர்ந்து
துறை.........விர்ந்து துறைகழ விறைஞ்ச
அவரவர் வேண்டிய தரவிக்கருளி

அந்தமர் அ[illegible] சேந்தழ லோம்ப
[illegible]தழுத [illegible] ஐந்த[illegible] [illegible]
சிவநெறி போற்றித் சிவார்ச்சனை புரிந்து
மருதா ரார்ந்த [illegible] மணைந்து
மூவே[illegible]ருத்தார் மூங்கிலா[illegible] புக்கிருந்த
சி[illegible]ர் தம்மை [illegible] [illegible]
பொ[illegible] கழுது [illegible]வில் தருவிச்
[illegible] [illegible]ந்து [illegible] தமர்த்த
[illegible] [illegible]ந்து மணிமுடி சூடி
[illegible] மணி [illegible] விரைபுர [illegible]
[illegible] [illegible] மலர்ந்து [illegible]
[illegible] [illegible]யும் [illegible]
[illegible] [illegible] துறுபுரல்[illegible]
[illegible] [illegible] [illegible]
[illegible] புனசிய [illegible]புர [illegible]
[illegible]தால் [illegible] [illegible]
[illegible]சிபெருங் கோயில் [illegible]
நல்லா [illegible] [illegible]
எல்லாப் பூசையு [illegible]
பொருள்முத லனைத்தும் பு[illegible]
திருமலி செம்பொ[illegible]
[illegible] முழுது[illegible]
[illegible] கருணை [illegible] [illegible]
அம்மையு [illegible] [illegible] [illegible]
[illegible] [illegible] [illegible]
[illegible] நல்கி வீற்றிருந்தருளிய
ஸ்ரீ.......... [illegible] [illegible]து.................

கீழ்வரும் சாசனம், நைடதம் காசி காண்டம் கூர்ம புராணம் கருக்கொலகை முதலாய நூல்களியற்றினவனும் அதிவீரராம பாண்டியனது. இவ்வரசனுக்கு அழகன் பெருமாள், ஸ்ரீ வல்லபன் முதலிய சிறப்புப் பேர்களுமுள.

13-வது சாசனம்.

[illegible]து.

[illegible] [illegible] [illegible] [illegible] [illegible] [illegible] [illegible] [illegible] [illegible] [illegible] [illegible] [illegible] [illegible] ஸ்ரீ [illegible] அழகன் பெருமாள் அதிவீர[illegible] ஸ்ரீ [illegible]...........

மற்றுமுள்ள அரசர்க்கும் மெய்க்கீர்த்திகளுள. இங்கு விரிவஞ்சி விடுக்கப்பட்டன.

இங்குக் கடைசியாய்க் காட்டிய அதிவீரராம பாண்டியன் காலத்திற்கு சில நூற்றாண்டுகளுக்கு முன்னரே தமிழ் நாடுகளில், விஜயநகரத்தார் ஆட்சியும் நாயக்கர் முதற்களுடைய அதிகாரங்களும் வேறுவேறாகவும் ஒன்றிகலந்தும் மற்றும் பல பெயருடைய அதிகாரங்களும் நிகழ்ந்தனவாகத் தெரிகின்றன. அவையவையெல்லாமிங்கு வருஷமுறையாகத் துணிந்து கூறச் சரியான சாசனங்கள் இன்னும் கிட்டில.

ஊழிகாலந்தொட்டுத் தலைசொண்டு பரம்பரையால் நீண்ட வெகு சம்பிரதாயத்துடன் இராச்சியாதிகாரம் படைத்து வந்த பாண்டியராஜ பரம்பரை இக்காலத்திலில்லாமற் போகவில்லை. அப்பரம்பரையோர் இன்னுமிக் காலத்திலிருக்கவே செய்கிறார்கள். அவர்கள் உலகபரிபாலனஞ் செய்யும் பதவியைக் காலகெதியால் இழந்து விட்டாலும் பெயர் மாத்திரையால் சிற்சில அடையாளங்களுடைமையால் இன்னுமிவ் வுலகத்திலிருக்கவே செய்கிறார்கள். இவ்விஷயத்தை மற்றொரு காலத்தில் விரிவாய் வரையப்படும்.

வேள்விக்குடிச் செப்பேட்டில் சமஸ்கிருத பாகத்தில் கூறப்பட்டுள்ள பாண்டியராஜ பரம்பரை சந்திரகுலத்தின் பூர்வ வம்சத்தார்.

1 சந்திரன்
2 புதன். பாண்டியனுக்கு அவதரித்தான்
3 புரூரவன்
4 மாறவர்மன்
5 ரணதீரன்
6 மாறவர்மன் ராஜசிம்மன
7 ஜடிலன

The genealogy of the Pandya Sovereigns
The copper plate found in Velvikudi.
roth
|
Pandyathi Raja Paramesvara Pal salai Muthukudumi Peruvaluthi.

Particulars about this sovereign are given briefly in Purananooru

|
Kalaparar.

Nothing definitely is known about this ruler There are some generations of sovereigns after him They are not known at present

|
Pandyathi Rajakadunkoan

Particulars about this Sovereign are not known

|
Sheliyan Chenthan

|
Maravarman Harikesari Asamasaman

He conquered the army from Vilveli at Nelveli

|
Kochadayan Ranadeeran.

He was a great man of prowess. He fought at Maruthoor He conquered the Maharathars of Mangalapuram. He was sovereign over Konkars

|
Harikesari Parankusa Maravarman.

The appellation Thermaran is also added to his titles He won victories over the Pallavas in Kulupoor and Sankaramangai. He is the one known as the first

Rajasimhan. In the later part of his reign besides defeating the Pallava King Mallavan he renewed and beautified the cities of Koodal, Vanchi and Koli. By marrying a Malava damsel he subjugated Malakonker. He was a close relation to the rulers of the Kanga province. At one time he fought great battles at Neduvayal, Kurumatai, Vallikurichi, Poovalur and Kodumpalur and wore the garland of victory. At Thirupandi Kodumadi he worshipped Sri Pasupatheesvara as the God of his soul's devotion. It is also said that he performed many services in person in that temple. He appears to have showed the keenest interest in Muttamil.

Jadilan Kalipagai Nedunchadayan Parantakan Period 770 A. D.

He has defeated the Kadavas of Pennakatam, Aya Vel at Nattukurumbu, and the Kurumbas. His chief minister was Marankari, the Mooventha Mangala Perarayan of the Vydiar Kulam. This minister is also known as Mathuratharan. His capital is Karavandapuram. With the aid of the Anaimalai inscription his period is fixed as 770 A D. It is this minister Mathuratharan that is known as Mathurakavi Alvar, one of the twelve Alvars.

Rajasimhan II.

No particulars are known.

Varaguna Maharajah.

He was a great hero, who revived the nearly extinct Pandya Kingdom and brought it to a highly efficient state. Within a few years after his accession he conquered a large extent of territory which was bounded by Kumari on the South, the Himalayas on the north and the Seas on the eastern and western borders. Stone inscriptions about him are found in all provinces. There is a stone inscription about him in the temple of Sri Kasi Pesvararin Ambasamudram in the Pandya Kingdom.

The first Sasanam (see page 827) speaks about the instructions left by Varaguna Maharaja as to the daily supply that should be made to the temple Padarars or servants.

As this inscription is very long the latter portions have been omitted which are indicated by dots. This inscription is now found in the Museum at Madras.

Another inscription in two stones found in the place where they tie the garlands in the inner court of the Sri Subramania Swami Kovil at Tiruchendoor also refers to Varaguna Maharaja. It is the second Sasanam.

The second Sasanam (See page 827) also speaks about the instructions left by the sovereign as regards the various charities to the temple and temple servants.

This inscription has also been curtailed owing to its length.

These inscriptions show that Varaguna Maharajah was a devoted Sivite. His gifts and charities to temples are carried on regularly even to this day like the charities of the Kerala Kings. At the close of the Tiruchendoor inscription he is spoken of as one who was interested in Music. But the inscriptions are far from being distinct.

With the help of inscriptions some conclude that his contemporary Chola sovereign was Vijayalayan, that after the defeat of the latter by Varaguna he became a second-rate ruler and made Tanjore his capital. This may be true to a certain extent. Varaguna was crowned in 862 A. D. His mother was the daughter of a Chola sovereign. Many other particulars about him have been omitted for the sake of brevity.

|

Sri Mara Sri Vallapa Ekaveerapara Chakra Kolakalan.

He won victories over the Kerala, Singala, Pallava, Villava and other kings. He was known as "Pallava Panjana."

Varagunavarma

Parantaka Veeranarayana Shadayan

He fought at Karagiri. He destroyed Pennagatam. His wife was Vanavan Mathevi.

|

Rajasimhan III

Mandara Gourava Apimana Meru

He was the Grandson of Vijayalaya and the contemporary of Parantaka.

Hitherto we based our conclusions on the copper plate inscriptions found at Velvikudi. What follows has been gathered from various other inscriptions.

|

Veera Pandya

He is known in some inscriptions as "Veera Pandya who carried off the head of Chola." He is said to be the son of Rajasimhan. He cut off the head of Athitya Karikala Chola who came against him in 925 A. D. Inscriptions relating to him are very rarely found in the Pandya Kingdom, in the North country and the Tamil provinces. There is an inscription in the Temple of Sri Moola Nathar at Ambasamudram. It is as follows :—

The *Third Sasanam* (see page 828) speaks about the charities to the temple given by Veera Pandya. This inscription is defective.

It is said that this Veera Pandya was the son of Parakirama Pandya and that he was put to death by Kulotunga Chola.

For some time after, the Pandya Kingdom seems to have been under the protection of the Chola Sovereigns. But about 1190 A. D. a certain Pandya sovereign *Kochadayan Kulasekaran* distinguished himself by conquering many provincess with the help of a large army. His greatness may be gathered from the Stanzas speaking about his fame, given below.

The *Fourth Sasanam* (see page 829) speaks about the progress of the country in all arts and sciences, the victory over enemies. the justice of the administration and the progress of Iyal Isai and Natakam under Kochadayan Kulasekara Pandyan.

This inscription is found in the south inner court of the temple of Nellayappar in Tinnevelly.

The *Fifth Sasanam* (see page 829) also speaks about the excellence of the administration of Kochadayan Kulasekara Pandyan, the progress of Muttamil during his time, the tribute paid to him by the superior sovereigns of the nine provinces and the advancement of arts and sciences during his rule.

This inscription is also found in the same temple.

The two inscriptions quoted above prove distinctly that the three angams of Tamil were fostered by the Pandya sovereign Kulotunga.

After him ruled *Sundara Pandyan Mara Verma* in 1216 A. D. He was a great hero who did not know what defeat was. He took a lively interest in the Tamil language and the seven kinds of Isais. He drove Rajathi Raja III who was then ruling over the Chola Country into the forest but afterwards graciously restored him his kingdom. So he was known by the appellations of " Sundara Pandyan the First ", " Sundara Pandyan who conquered the Chola country and had himself victoriously crowned at Cholapuram " and " Sundara Pandyan who used the Chola Province as his own"

The *Sixth Sasanam* (see page 830) speaks of the fame of Sundara Pandian, the progress of Muttamil and the seven kinds of Isais, the perfect peace among his subjects, the tribute paid to him by different rulers, his even administration of justice, the fertility of the country, the enemies he had conquered and the column of victory he had built etc.

This inscription is also found in the temple to Nellayappar in Tinnevelly.

After this sovereign came *Maravarma Sundara Pandian II* in 1234 A. D ; and in 1251 A. D., *Sundara Pandian* who had conquered all Mandalams and after him ruled *Maran Kulasekara Pandian* in 1268. These were all very famous sovereigns. We have omitted the glorious acts of the sovereigns as it will be impossible to enumerate them.

After these in the 13th century ruled *Jatavarman Sundara Pandian* who conquered not only the whole of the Tamil Province but also the countries in the North. The head of his army was also the head of the navy. He conqured also the King of Karunadu. The fact that he possessed a navy proves this.

He appears to have led a pure life as a reputed devotee of Siva and is said to have been able to sing Thevarams along with the Pun. He has introduced the chanting of Thirugnanam and Thevaram in temples. The Sasanam given below proves all this.

The *Seventh Sasanam* (see page 832) gives a list of singers who were appointed to chant the above and speaks about the gifts for such singers in the temple..

This is also an inscription found in Tinnevelly.

This sovereign was probably succeeded by *Maran Sundara Pandian III.* The following stanzas describe his fame.

The *Eighth Sasanam* (see page 833) speaks about his fame as an administrator, his patronage of arts especially Music and Tamil language etc.

This sovereign's great interest in Sruti and Tamil should be noted here. This is an inscription found in Thiruvaleesvaram.

Then followed *Vikrama Pandian II.* The Stanzas given below speak of his fame.

The *Ninth Sasanam* (see page 833) speaks about the greatness of Vikrama Pandia and the success of his administration.

This inscription is found in the temple of Patthan Madai Perumal.

Some think that his successor was *Kulasekara Pandian III.* The following reflects his greatness.

The *Tenth Sasanam* (see page 834) speaks of the great success of the administration of Kulasekara Pandia, the progress of Vedas and Muttamil, his conquest of the various provinces, the golden throne on which he sat etc. This is an inscription found in the temple to Poonathar in Tirupudamarudur.

The *Eleventh Sasanam* (see page 835) is based on the stone and copper plate inscriptions found in the temple at Tenkasi which gives the following genealogy.

- Abirama Pandyan 1474
  - Parakirama Pandyan
    - Abirama Pandyan
      - Parakiraman
        - Gunarama Pandyan
        - Varathungarama Pandyan
      - Salivateepati
        - Alagan Perumal Athiveerarama Pandyan.
        - Sri Vallapan
    - Ahavarama Pandyan
      - Sri Vallaban Manabaranan

The greatness of *Parakirama Pandian* who built the Sri Visvanatha Swami temple at Tenkasi is set forth in the following inscription.

The *Twelfth Sasanam* (see page 835) speaks about the excellence of the administration of Parakirama Pandyan, the fostering of 18 different languages by him, the progress of the worship of Siva, the temples built for the God Sankara and Visvanatha at Tenkasi, the arrangements made by him for the poojas in the temples, the golden throne on which he sat etc., etc.

The Sasanam given below speaks of *Athiveerarama Pandya* the author of Naidatham, Kasikandam, Koorma Puranam, Narunthogai etc. This sovereign is otherwise known also as Alagan Perumal and Sri Vallapa.

The *Thirteenth Sasanam* (see page 836) speaks about the honorific titles of Athi Veera Raman. Other sovereigns also have stanzas on their greatness. But they have been omitted for the sake of brevity.

It seems that some centuries before the period of Athi Veera Rama Pandya the Tamil country was overrun by the Vijayanagaram Kings, the Naick Kings, Muhammadan rulers and others either jointly or severally. Inscriptions are not available to arrange them in a chronological order.

The descendants of this ancient and renowned Pandya sovereigns are not altogether extinct. Some of them do remain still in the Tamil country. Though they have lost their ruling prestige by the vicissitudes of the times, yet the names and some other signs show that they are still in the land of the living. We shall speak about this in detail some other time.

The genealogy of the Pandya rulers given in the sanskrit portion of the copper plate inscription found in Velvikudi.

The ancient families of the Chandra Kulam.

1. Chandran.
2. Puthan, who became incarnate as Pandya.
3. Pruravan.
4. Maravarma.
5. Ranadeeran.
6. Maravarman Rajasimhan.
7. Jateela.

The following quotations from the above Sasanams such as

" இன்னமு தாகிய இயல் இசை நாடகம்
மன்னி வளர மணி முடி சூடி " in the fourth,
" மயலறு சிறப்பின் மாமுனி தேர்ந்த
இயல் இசை நாடகம் எழில் பெறவளர " in the fifth,
" மூவகைத் தமிழும் முறைமையின் விளங்க
எழுவகைப் பாடலும் இசையுடன் பரவ " in the sixth,
" இவர்கள் வர்க்கத்தில் திருஞானமோதும் பேர்க்கும்
போஜன முள்ளிட்டு வேண்டு வளவுக்கு " in the seventh.
" சுருதியுந் தமிழும் தொழு வளங்குலவ " in the eighth,
" முத்தமிழ்ப் பனுவலும் நான்மறை முழுதும் " in the tenth,
" தென்கலை வடகலை தேற்றெனத் தெளிந்து " in the twelfth.
and " சங்கீத சாகித்திய சார்வ பௌம " in the thirteenth,

seem clearly to show that the Pandya sovereigns of the ancient Tamil country were great admirers of the Muttamil and patronised them. Though their period seems to be ten centuries after the third sangam, yet they appear to have fostered Muttamil according to the requirements of their respective period. We conclude from the writings of commentators that many precious works on Isai Tamil were destroyed to a certain extent during their period. Jata Varman Sundara Pandian, who flourished in the 13th century, appears to have been a devoted Sivite who introduced the chanting of Thevarams with Puns in the different temples of the Pandya Kingdom. We have already observed that the chanting of Thevaram was in vogue in the Tamil country before the time of Jatavarman Sundara Pandyan, that the Ragas used in Thevaram were known by Tamil names and they were found in Pingala Nigandu of the period of the last Sangam. We have noted on page 540 that many of those Ragas were extinct and that 24 of them were in use at the period of Thevarams. We have also stated on page 543 that many of these Ragas had been borrowed by the author of Sangeeta Ratnakar and made use of in his book.

The names of Ragas with many syllables, such as, Thaka Vibasha Thevara Varthani, Malava kaisika Thevara Varthani, Thakshana Bhashangam, Thiravida Bhasha, Thakshana Kutcheri and Thiravida Kutcheri indicate that he wrote his Sangeeta Ratnakar after the period when Thevarams were freely used in the Tamil country, that the names of many of these Tamil Puns were retained by him while others were mutilated by the addition or subtraction of a prefix or suffix, while yet others were given new names and all incorporated in his so called original work.

If only they had known of the existence of Isai Tamil capable of melting even the hardest heart with its Ragas and lofty ideas long before the time of Sangeeta Ratnakar, will a musician born and bred in the Tamil country dare to say " the Tamils are ignorant of Music. They learnt their music only after the appearance of the Sanskrit work Sangeeta Ratnakar ?"

The author of Sangeeta Ratnakar went wrong where he made mention of the Alaku system where they made ganam lessening an Alaku in Vilari and Kaikilai which stand in the relation of Inai and Kilai in the sixteen Puns derived from the four Jathis Aganilai, Puranilai, Arugial and Perugial which were in their turn derived from the four Yals of the Vattapalai system of the ancient Tamils namely Marutham, Kurinji, Neythal and Palai. He added these Alakus together, established 22 Srutis for the octave and gave names and Ragalakshanam for the 22. So the science of Music of Sarnga Dev went crooked to the end in accordance with the well known Tamil saying, " the starting was crooked and so the whole thing went crooked". When asked for a small specimen of a Keertanam or Ragam in accordance with the 22 Srutis of Sarnga Dev, will an advocate of the Dwavimsati Srutis take refuge for the occasion by saying " I shall practise the same in two months time and then sing it before you ? " There is reason to believe that with the exception of the principle of tuning given by Sarnga Dev, his 22 Srutis for the octave, the names he gives for them and the Ragas he derives from those names are all but castles in the air.

We have noted before that of the 36 Ragas mentioned by Bharata, six are spoken of by him as found in ancient works. Of these six mother Ragas—Bhairavam, Malava Kaisikam, Indolam, Theepakam, Mehanadam and Sriragam—with the exception of the fourth, namely, Theepaka, all the other five are the ones used by the ancient Tamils. We hope that by pointing this out the ignorant idea that the Tamils had no music of their own will, for ever, be dispelled.

It is generally known that the Pandya sovereigns of the Tamil country had profound knowledge in Muttamil, they were well known for their devotion to God and that some of them ruled over countries as far as the Himalayas

There is also data to establish the fact that some of the most celebrated of those rulers conquered the whole of India by defeating many of the sovereigns and ruled over them as emperors under their sole regime.

In addition to this, we see that they were hereditary sovereigns of the Chandrakulam except for a few breaks here and there.

We have stated before that there was a great deluge during the time of Satya Viratha, the devoted ruler over South Madura in ancient days, and that he and the seven sages were taken to the foot of the Himalayas and were saved from the deluge by means of a boat. We learn from the Puranas that this very same King Satya Viratha of the South became Vyvasutha Manu and that his descendants were known as the rulers of the Chandra line of Kings. It is the custom, when a traditional name is to be mentioned, to name the founder, and to add the names of some of the celebrated rulers of the line and the names of one's grandfather, father and one's own. So also when the ancient traditional name of the Pandyas is to be stated, it seems to have been the custom to give the names of Chandran, Puthan, Pruravan, Maravarman *Ranadeeran *Rajasimhan *Jateela and then add the names of the sovereigns of the time. Here the three names marked with an asterisk are those of later sovereigns, while the names given at the commencement are those of the very ancient founders.

As it is impossible to mention the names of all the successors of Vyvasutha Manu it is the custom to make mention of a few celebrated rulers and then add on their own names. According to this rule, we are enabled to state clearly that the descendants of a single Tamil ruler who was well-versed in Muttamil were the inhabitants of the whole of India, that they were the rulers of India, that they were well-known for their devotion to God and that they were the founders of all music.

We have stated before how the South Pandya Province where the Southerners had ruled became the seven Theebas, that seven Sages lived there who orginated the seven Swarams. This very same fact is indicated by Sarnga Dev when he says that the seven Swarams originated from the isles through the seven Sages. There is evidence for us to believe that these seven Sages belonged to the Southern Pandya country, that they fostered the seven Isais and the seven Puns derived from them, that these were the Sages that accompanied Satya Viratha to the foot of the Himalayas, that these were Tamils and that the Tamil languages and its arts and sciences were disseminated by them. Again, historians make mention of the facts that Tamil Kings ruled over Tibet to the North of the Himalayas, over Mesopotamia, in Asiatic Turkey, over the region from the Northern extremity of Russia to Australia and the neighbouring provinces and over the large islands of Sumatra and Java, that they were advanced in civilization which resembled that of the people of South India. These facts lead us to conclude that even at an early age when there was no language or nationality there was a ruler of the Tamil province, that Tamil was spoken and that there were Isai Tamil or Music and other arts and sciences in the Tamil country. These conclusions are enough for our purpose.

The stanza

"இன்னமுதாகிய இயல் இசை நாடகம்
மன்னி வளர மணிமுடி சூடி"

shows in what esteem Muttamil was held by the Tamils and the Tamil Sovereigns.

We have purposely omitted similar inscriptions about the Pandya Sovereigns and other historical remarks on the inscriptions as we thought them unnecessary.

We hear that the inscriptions here stated and other Pandyan inscriptions may be found in detail in the First Volume of the Travancore Archæological series written by Mr. Gopinatha Row M. A. As the book is not with us, we are unable to make mention of those inscriptions.

We have observed already that Raja Raja Chola who ruled over the Chola country from 985 to 1013 A.D. built the Bragatheesvara Temple at Tanjore. Two of the inscriptions in the temple walls to the North-West have been quoted on pages 127-147. It is stated in the first of those inscriptions that 48 Pidaras, one permanent player on the Oodookai and one player on the Koti Madhalam, 50 in all, were appointed to chant the Thirupathyam in front of the deity in turns. This Thirupathyam is now known as Thevara Thirupathigam or Thirupathigam. In the book Thevarathiratu which contains these Thirupathigams each pathigam appears to have been mentioned along with its ancient Tamil Pun. We have noted before that in chanting of these Puns and in their Thalam the ancient Tamils were highly efficient.

Further, E. Hultzsch in his South Indian Inscription Vol. II Part III page 252 says.

"This inscription records an order of King Rajarajadeva, by which he assigned a daily allowance of paddy to each of forty-eight persons, whom he had appointed before the 29th year of his reign, in order to recite the *Tiruppadiyam* in the temple and to two persons who had to accompany the other on drums. This statement is of considerable importance for the history of Tamil literature as an unmistakable proof of the existence of the Siva hymns which go by the name of *Padiyam* or padiyam, and which are collected in the Devaram in the time of Rajaraja. The names of the fifty incumbents serve to corroborate this identification of the Tirupadiyam with the *Devaram*, as part of them are derived from the names of the authors of the *Devaram*, viz., Tirugana-sammandan (Parragraph 7) or Sammandan (10, 22, 34, 38, 42), Tirunavukariyan (6, 12, 14, 19, 28, 43, 45,) and Nambi-Aruran (41, 44) or Aruran (19, 22)."

He gives here the substance of the inscription. As these are facts well-known to the Tamils what he says about Thirupathigams is enough. Even during the reign of Rajaraja Cholan he collected together the remnants of the Thevara Pathigams and made arrangements for their chanting in the temple. It is said in Thirumurai Kanda Puranam that owing to the absence in the Chola country of those who knew how to chant the Thevara Thirupathigams, they sent for a woman, who was a descendant of Thiruneelakanta Yalpana Nayanar, and heard her sing all the Puns. This enables us to conclude that even during the reign of Rajaraja Chola, *i. e.* 900 years ago, many of the Thirupathigams had disappeared and only a few remained. It is likely that the Ragas for these Puns must have disappeared at the same time. Names are given only for the remnants of the Ragas found in the remnants of the Thevarapathigams. Even these puns have been mutilated and given different names by foreigners so that one is unable to recognise their Tamilian origin.

From inscriptions we understand that the period of Rajaraja Chola is the 10th century A. D. But the age of Sangeeta Ratnakar is 1210—1247. So we have put it down to the 13th century. So we must say that the expression "*தக்க [illegible] தேவார வர்த்தினி*" used by Sarnga Dev must be posterior to the time of the appointment of the 50 men in the Big Temple at Tanjore for chanting Thevara Puns. It is clear that Sarnga Dev wrote his work after the time of the Puns in the Tamil country. When such is the case we advise those who say that Sangeetha Ratnakar is the pioneer work on music, that music came after the Sanskrit language and that Tamils are completely ignorant of music to refer to the stone inscription stated above.

2. Some proofs to show that Isai Tamil or Music was largely used in Tamil Country.

We have already noted how the Tamils, who were the most ancient of all the inhabitants of the world and who spoke the sweet Tamil language which is the oldest of languages since the origin of man, how advanced in all arts and sciences even 22000 yeas ago, that they fostered the Muttamil and other arts and sciences for 12000 years and up to the last 2000 years with the aid of the three Sangams and that they are encouraging the Tamil language even at the present day. We also noted how they praised God by means of the 12000 ancient Isais with very minute Swarams according to the system of Ayapalai with its 12 Swarams, and Ragas according to the system of Vattapalai with its 24 Srutis and Ganam in the 22 Srutis with two Alakus less in Swarams which stand in the relation of Inai or Kilai deriving 4 primary Puns and their 4 Jathis, according to the system of Vattapalai singing half the Alakus of Thirikonapalai and quarter Alakus of Chathurapalai.

We who live in an age of advanced culture will wonder when we hear of the Tamil language of 12000 years ago and its different Kalais, the three Sangams and the works written by the scholars of the period, their music or Isai Tamil, the minuter Swarams such as $\frac{1}{4}$, $\frac{1}{8}$ and $\frac{1}{16}$ used in it at the present time, the four Palais, the four primary Puns and the four different kinds of Puns derived from them. We shall be surprised at the advancement they had made in music and will consider it a novelty. We will be inclined to enquire whether modern practice of music in the Tamil Country presupposes such an advancement in the earliest ages. We think of giving a few remarks to such intelligent gentlemen who are anxious to know something on this subject.

We have already noted how the Tamil language is a combination of natural sounds found in different animals, and that the words of the language are found in various languages either in a mutilated form or as they were.

The Pandya sovereigns as well as the Tamils who divided the Tamil country with seven isles known as Lemuria into 49 provinces and ruled over them with South Madura as the capital, have divided the living beings and their voices or sounds into 7 different kinds and have prescribed rules for them. The Almighty who is the Creator of the universe delights in hearing the sweet sounds emanating from all living beings. The Tamils devised rules for the seven sounds out of these and for the minuter Srutis derived from them and praised God with the help of these Swarams. We must not forget that others advanced in music and are advancing only after the Tamils. Many being ignorant of the harmony of the 12 Swarams of Ayapalai in use for many thousands of years, floundered in them and came to the right conclusion only 120 years ago. Even to day many disputes are going on as there is a difference between the measurements according to the sound and measurements according to calculations. If in an age the bird sings and the idiot also then we may conclude that all men of that period are singers. But if there is a dispute about 12 Swarams and 22 Srutis even at the present day in conferences, who can speak with authority on the four Palais of the ancient Tamils and the minute Swarams used by them.

Only experts on the Yal or the Veena who are capable of playing the 12 Swarams of Ayapalai on the Yal on the principle of Inai and Kilai and who could play the minuter Srutis there as Gamakams could understand this. As the excellent Yal practised with such difficulty by the Ancient Tamils has disappeared and cheap and easy instruments like the fiddle and the harmonium have taken its place, the Swarams and Srutis have come to be doubted.

Again, if we notice the life, the profession and culture of the Tamils, we may see the important part played by music there. When we declare that the Tamils have used music in their every day transaction more copiously than other nations have done it may excite the wonder of our readers.

Astronomy and its calculations are set to music. Astrology and its results are given out in music. Arithmetic and its minute divisions are in music. Medicine, the nature of herbs and different mixtures are given in music. Physiology and the functions of organs are in music. Karpa Shastram, Yoga Shastram, Gnana Shastram, Manthram and Vedam are in music. The rules relating to all the above sciences are in music. The dictionary of the Tamil language is in music. Letters which one writes to another are in music; yea. Sasanams which are executed are in music.

It is impossible to find Poetry not set to music or any literary work without Poetry in the Tamil Country. As others say that it is impossible for the Tamils to write in an easy prose style and as all works of devotion, works of science and art of the Tamils are in poetry, one may imagine how easy poetry was to the Tamils. All poetry is so arranged with Thalam. Ethugai and Monai (Rhythmical flow) that they can be sung to the rules of Puns. The Tamilians who have read Thirupugal will understand how some of the rare Thala Prastharas are used in Tamil as Chandakulippu. In addition to these they have given rules for various Osais—such as Thoongal Osai, Thullal Osai, Ahaval Osai and Cheppal Osai—to be sung as Pahs, and for the various Chandams—such as, Thuttha Chandam, Thantha Chandam, Thanna Chandam and Thayya Chandam—to satisfy the rules of Chandakulippu. From these we may have an idea of the excellent style of the language and the harmonious combination of the Thalams with the Puns and of the fact that they are within our practical experience up to the present day.

We know, further, that music plays a very prominent part in the temple festivals, morning and evening services, in the dramas played during festivals and in royal palaces and that this is peculiar to the South Tamil country.

Music there must be when a child is rocked to sleep, and during festive and marriage occasions. Music there must be when he sows the seed for his daily food. when he transplants the seedlings, when he binds the sheaves of corn, when he separates the grain from the husk, when he measures the corn and when the paddy is ground.

Music there is when the cotton necessary for man's apparel is gathered, when it is beaten, when the thread is made, when the woof is prepared when the cotton ball is bound together and when it is woven into a cloth.

Many of us must have heard—yea, we hear them daily—how a beggar who begs a handful of rice, a pandaram who begs grain from door to door, the paradesi who carries the Annakavadi, the man of vow who bears the Kavadi, and the man of vow who rolls on the ground duriug hot sun sing devotional songs and heart-melting Puns such as Ekalakanni, Paraparakanni, Oodarkooru, Pambati Chittar Padal, Alukanni Chittar Padal, Kilikanni, Pallikathal, Nanjari Vilakam, Patnathu Pillayar Padal and Thayumana Swami Padal.

We have heard some professional beggars sing extracts from the story of Nalla Thangai, Pavalakodi Malai, Alli Arasani Malai and other songs giving practical advice to women and even Kurathis who live by tattooing and Oddars who level grinding stones singing songs during the process. We hear during festive occasions for Grama Devatas annually in villages Chiruthonda Natakam, Harichandra Natakam, Kuravanji Natakam, Rama Natakam, Markanda Natakam, Mukoodarpallu and other Natakams and songs while performing Villadi Pattu, Kuravai Koothu, Oyil Kummi, Kaliyaladi Pattu, Oonchal Pattu, Kappal Pattu and the like. We often hear the songs sung while the gardeners water the garden, while flour is being ground, while cows are milked and when chunam is pounded.

Is there any one who has not heard the lullaby for sending infants to sleep? Little boys playing in the streets speak to one another alternately in songs while playing games. When children learn to read the letters one party sings sweetly the words Anah, Anah, Anah (GA-RI, GA-RI, RI-GA.) while the opposite party answers Avannah, Avannah, Avannah (PA-MA, PA-MA, MA-PA). These series of Swarams stand in the relation of fourths or Natpu Swarams. PA stands in the relation of Natpu to GA with 2 Alakus. So also MA with 4 Alakus is in the relation of Natpu to RI with 4 Alakus. We shall be delighted when we find that these Swarams stand in the relation of Natpu to one another and that the four Swarams RI, GA, MA and PA are learnt by children when quite young.

So also Athichoodi with two words and Kondrai Vendan with four words are songs. Vakundam, Oolaganeethi, Vettiverkai, Velamugam, Moothurai, Nalvali, Nanneri, Naladiar, Kural, Thivagaram and Nigandu are Phas. So also are Enchuvadi, fractional figures, tables of multiplication and division. Kuliperukkam, Thanaperukkam, cube measure, square measure, tables of weights and measures in Pahs. It is not a matter for surprise that one accustomed to prosody should write them all out in poetry set to music. If one sings these various Swarams and takes a delight in them within five or six years he could master all the important rules of these various sciences. It is the custom for school children to sing the songs pertaining to the festivals of Mahara Nonbu, eighteenth day of Adi, dress themselves to suit the season and play Kolattam. By these means, Iyal, Isai and Natakam, the three Amsams of Tamil were easily taught to the Tamils.

The knowledge of the three kinds of Tamil thus inculcated at the earliest age stood them in good stead when they grew up, according to the proverbs "Learn when you are young" "The learning while young, lasts for ever like the inscription on stone" and it was easy for them to cultivate them according to their respective inclinations and become experts in those Amsams of Tamil. All Tamils know that it is very common to find poets composing new poems and teaching people to dance beautifully.

There is nothing in other countries to compare with the sweet folk lore songs of little cow boys, little girls who watch over corn fields and of bandy drivers.

When we note that the aliens who came and settled in the South Tamil country are superior to others in their good manners and customs and are well-known for their Tamil Music and Poetry, we may say without doubt that the South Tamil Country has been and is the cradle of all civilisation, manners, devotion to God and music.

We may have heard the people of Jaffna who are reputed to be speakers of pure Tamil and also those who speak Malayalam, the sister language. Their speech is full of all the Swarams of music. The ancient Tamils must have spoken something like it. As people speaking different languages mixed with the Tamils, the language has undergone many changes.

From the above facts we are able to say that the ancient South Tamil Country was the birth-place of all nations, that it was the soil where music flourished that the Tamils were the pioneers of Iyal, Isai and Natakam, that these people taught others some of its very important Amsams, and that the field of Tamil music is capable of teaching many new ideas to others.

We shall do well to make mention here the remarks of others on the points mentioned above by us.

IV. SOME IMPORTANT POINTS AS REGARDS INDIAN MUSIC AND INDIA MENTIONED BY OTHERS.

I. Some general remarks on Indian Music.

We noted above how in the Tamil country where the Tamil language Sweeter than nector was exclusively used Muttamil—Iyal, Isai and Natakam—attained great efficiency how works corresponding to it were written, how Sangams were established and carried on with vigour, how all Kalais in relation to the language and their rules were steadfastly improved, how they have been written with a view to satisfy the rules of prosody, Ragam and Thalam, how all such poetry had been written with a view to be sung as Puns, how they were used in the Tamil country and how they are being sung even at the present day.

As works relating to the rules for chanting the Puns sung with the minute Srutis, the excellent system for composing Ragas and the determination of Srutis have disappeared in the Tamil country where everything was tinged with the colour of Music, we are in a position where we are unable to say definitely the Swarams and Srutis used in ancient Puns. Vidwans of Karnatic music who have learnt up and used in their Kalekshepams the Puns (Ragas), the varunams, Thanams and Keertanams of the Tamil country either in Sanskrit or Telugu are unable to make further researches into them and are satisfied with spending their time in singing the old Ragas over and over again.

Some of these Sanskrit Vidwans who made attempts to enquire into the number of Srutis, only tried to establish the 22 Srutis and came to grief catching a Tartar as the man in the proverb who mistook the bear floating down the stream for a goat, embraced it and came to grief. Hence there was a necessity for conference enquiring into the Swarams and Srutis of Karnatic music and disputes on the subject. So it was seen that the system of Srutis of the ancient Tamils and its excellent rules were completely forgotten.

There was difference of opinion among enquirers after Srutis and among the writers on Srutis. The same was true of the Calculations for Srutis. Though they differed in many respects, yet they were ignorant that what they were all singing was one and the same. There was no difference there. We have referred to some of these points before. We shall do well to note here a few points which support the Swarams, Srutis and minute Srutis used in the four kinds of Palais in which the Tamils were experts.

Revival of Hindu Music.

"Patriotic Hindus have of late endeavoured to bring about a musical revival upon the old Sanskrit basis. No Englishman has yet brought an adequate acquaintance with the technique of Indian instrumentation to the study of Hindu music. The art still awaits investigation by some eminent western professor; and the contempt with which Europeans in India regard it, merely proves their ignorance of the system on which Hindu music is built up."

Here the author says that endeavours were made to revive Indian Music on the basis of the old Sanskrit works but in vain, and that the art still awaits with eagerness the advent of a European professor to set it up.

This reminds us of the art attempt made some time back at Poona to enquire into the system of Dwavinsati Srutis. In the assembly made up of many northern Vidwans there was such a sharp difference of opinion that they left things as they were "being satisfied with the old Soku" as the proverb says. We have referred to this on page 361. From that time forwards many different calculations as regards the 22 Srutis sprang up in the field and culminated in the great All India Music Conference held on the 20th of March 1916 organized by His Highness, the Gaekwar of Baroda. Here different essays on different subjects were read by Vidwans and many demonstrations and discussions made.

Here Mr. V. N. Bhatkande brought in a proposition that there should be an easy Staff Notation for the beginners of Hindustani Music which is largely used in the North. Then I gave my opinion that the 12 Swarams of Ayapalai of the ancient Tamils were the ones used in Karnatic Music now, they were the equal Temperament series of the Westerners, that these were the very Swarams of the Veena and the Piano, and that the Staff Notation will be of great use to Hindustani Music.

Mr. E. Clements I.C.S. District Judge, proposed that the Srutis should be 27 and not 22 and he tried to demonstrate his theory by means of a Harmonium specially constructed for that purpose, and this was seconded by Mr. K. B. Deval, Retired Deputy Collector. Then this special Harmonium was tested to see whether it satisfied the Swarams in Arohanam and Avarohanam for the Ragas Shankaraparanam, Karaharapirya (Belawal and Kafi) used in Karnatic as well as Hindustani Music. The Swarams of the Harmonium were really flatter when compared with the Swarams in practical use. This was demonstrated vocally by M. R Ry. Zakruddin Sahib, the Samasthanam Vidwan of Oodaipoor.

Before the conference assembled on Wednesday the 22nd of March, I criticised the various theories as regards the Srutis used in Indian Music and made a practical demonstration of the four Palais used by the ancient Tamils—Ayapalai, Vattapalai, Thirikonapalai and Chathura Palai and the Swarams, Srutis and minute Srutis used in them. This instrumental and vocal demonstration lasted for three hours and a half. This demonstration was accepted to be correct by the Hindustani and Karnatic vidwans assembled there without any demur and with great joy and applause. As the conference unanimously approved of this it was resolved the next morning that the 12 Swarams with the staff notation may be commonly accepted for Karnatic and Hindustani Music.

Men of intelligence will see how difficult it is to convince the truth of these 12 Swarams in use for thousands of years which have equal intervals. One says that he was confounded by the 12 Swarams obtained in the Octave by the principle of Sa-Pa. Another says that 22 Srutis are obtained in the octave where Sa-Pa gives 13 Srutis. A third says 22 Srutis are found in the octave by proceeding by $\frac{3}{4}$. Another that 27 Srutis are obtained by Sa-Pa, while yet another, that he obtains 53 Srutis on the same principle.

The saying of Sarnga Dev is broad enough to support all, for he says the Srutis are 1, they are 2, they are 3, they are 4, 9, 22, 66, yea, Srutis are innumerable. If Sarnga Dev who is held to be the pioneer of Indian Music makes such a confounded statement, need we ask about others?

The question of Srutis became very hard to chew like அவல் made of iron, as different writers made different statements and as very minute Srutis were used along with Swarams. When this was difficult to be understood by Indian musicians singing very minute Srutis, especially vidwans of Karnatic music, how can we blame others who had confined their ganam to the 12 Swarams of Ayapalai alone?

The author says that Indian music awaits the advent of a European to let it up because he knows that Indians are lacking in endeavour to make researches in such sciences and arts which may promote the good of the country. The following extract shows that many such attempts failed as they were unable to grasp the exact meaning of what they wanted to solve.

Introduction to the study of Indian Music by Mr. E. Clements Foreword by Dr. Kumaraswamy P. 6.

The neglect of centuries, as in so many analogous cases, has proved less disastrous than the renewed patronage of a few decades."

The above shows that Indian music suffered more from the patronage of recent years than from the neglect of centuries.

These words are spoken by Dr. Kumaraswami. I know that he was earnestly making enquiries on Sculpture and Music of India during his travels. Receiving no satisfactory answers as to the Alakus of Ri and Dha in Shankaraparanam he came to me for an answer. When he heard that these two Srutis should be slightly sharper he was much delighted. To Dr Kumaraswami making researches into ancient sciences and arts Mr. Clement's book which speaks of 27 Srutis in the octave will surely appear a stumbling block!

We have given the different opinions of writers on Srutis of Indian Music in the second part of this Book. We have discussed 20 different opinions there and given mathematical calculations for the same, we have pointed out how they contradict one another besides contradicting the views given in ancient books.

Neither Bharata nor Sarnga Dev Speak of Sa Pa as $\frac{3}{2}$. There is no connection between the series obtained by $\frac{3}{2}$ and the Swarams derived after the system of Sarnga Dev. There is no kind of resemblance between the series obtained by $\frac{3}{2}$ and the Swarams of Karnatic Music. There is not the slightest connection between the Swarams sung vocally and the Swarams or intervals put by them on paper. It is but natural that by a conglomeration of such varied and contradictory opinions truth should disappear and doubt be caused.

Is it not strange that a Vidwan of Karnatic Music who has learnt by heart the system of Srutis and who has advocated for many years the Dwavimsati Srutis according to Sarnga Dev when asked to sing a Keertanam where the 22 Srutis occurred should say in reply that he would be able to do so after two months' practice?

Is the music he lives by one thing. the music to which he gives the calculation by multiplying $\frac{2}{3}$ and $\frac{3}{4}$ another. and the music of the 22 Srutis which he said he would practise in 2 months' time a third. If the same thing is said in three different ways, can there be any good in it?

This will be only analogous to the case of the Brahmin and his sacrificial goat! Some rogues were determined to appropriate the goat which a Brahmin carried with him for the purpose of a Yagam. So one of them said it looked like a dog, another that it looked like a donkey while a third wondered whether it was a dead calf. The Brahmin thought on the other hand it must be a devil (as it changed its shape so often) and let it go!

The following extract shows that different writers gave different opinions owing to their ignorance of the truth of what the ancient Tamils had said about Isai Tamil.

Introduction to the Study of Indian music by E. Clements.

"Modern Text Books may appear learned to the uninitiated; the historian will, however frankly admit that, since the days of the Sankit Ratnakar, Indian musical systems have fallen into such confusion that no one has been able to reconcile the teaching of that authoritative treatise with later works on the subject, or with the practice or theory of modern musicians. The art is also in grave danger of being spoiled as other Indian arts have in the past been spoiled by cheap imitation. Contact with the west has resulted in a blend of Indian music with European intonation, a combination in the highest degree inartistic and likely to prove more harmful than the neglect of centuries."

The above remarks are those of Mr. E. Clements I. C. S. District Judge. These are found in the preface of his book. He says that after the advent of Sangeeta Ratnakar, Indian musical systems have fallen into confusion. that many works were written after it and that there is no kind of unanimity between the practice and the theory of modern musicians since his time.

The system of tuning according to Sarnga Dev is that there should be 22 Srutis in the octave which should be a gradually ascending series without admitting of any possible sound between.

Works written after him give calculations dividing the wire into $\frac{1}{2}$, $\frac{2}{3}$ and $\frac{3}{4}$. They recommend Swarams by dividing them into $\frac{3}{4}$ and $\frac{4}{5}$. There will be a slight difference between these Swarams and those in practice.

The division of Swarams according to the system of Sarnga Dev alone will enable one to sing grahaswaram. If, on the other hand, we divide the octave into 22 Srutis we shall not obtain even a single Swaram now in use.

If we follow the system of the author of Parijatam we shall find that small minute Swarams occur in conjunction with the Swarams now in use. As this minute difference was noticed even in the 12 Swarams of the octave even the standard 12 Swarams of the Ayapalai were doubted.

We showed in the Tables on pages 368 and 369 that different versions have been given for the names of Swarams, names of Srutis, names of Swarasthanams and their calculations. We have given also the opinions of modern writers in four tables from pages 416-417 so that all might clearly understand them. We have also shown clearly that none of these contradictory opinions can ever agree with the principles of Karnatic music.

The sixth and the seventh columns of these Tables give the Sruti system of Mr. Clements. The criticism of his theory given there was practically proved to be so at the All India music Conference as his Sruti Harmonium for 27 Srutis was found to be inaccurate. If he had known that his theory was wrong and his harmonium false he would not have made the statement "the art is in grave danger of being spoiled as other Indian arts have in the past been spoiled by cheap imitation."

If Mr. Clements had tried to find out truth as it is, he would not have added two Srutis more over those of Sarnga Dev, nor would he have derived three Srutis more while change of Graham is made and accounted for 27 Srutis in the octave. If he had made a study of at least the Srutis found in the common Ganam of the whole of India we might have accepted his conclusions with advantage. When it is not so he himself becomes guilty of the "cheap imitation" and becomes a stumbling block to the progress of Indian music.

That differences of opinion are found among writers is proved by the following extract.

Captain Day.

"Parijata differs from that of the Ratnakara, in that it admits of greater intervals than a tone or four Sruties and of less intervals than a semi tone or two Sruties being therefore capable of forming numerous enharmonic scales. All the notes except the first and fifth are occasionally shifted above or below and the fourth is never omitted. This work contains the key to the present Karnatic system."

Captain day who has written about South Indian Music recognising to a certain extent the existence of 24 Srutis on the octave points out that there is a difference between Sangeeta Ratnakar and Parijatam. We see his opinion in the above lines. He says there may be greater intervals than four Srutis and lesser intervals than two Srutis.

Here four Srutis are one full tone like Chathur Sruti Ri. Two Srutis are a semitone. We have showed on page 789 how in Chenchuruti, the seventh of the Chathurapalai Ragas, an $\frac{1}{16}$ Swaram or Sruti with $\frac{1}{4}$ of an Alaku comes along with a full Swaram. In the same manner we have observed that in Chathurapalai Ragas Swarams with 5—$\frac{1}{4}$ Alakus and 4—$\frac{3}{4}$ Alakus occur. When $\frac{1}{16}$ of a Swaram comes along with a full Swaram it is customary to call it a full Swaram owing to the difficulty of discriminating the minute Swaram. In the same manner Swarams which have a minute Alaku less are also considered to be full Swarams.

In Shankaraparanam belonging to Thirikonapalai, Ri and Dha have 4$\frac{1}{2}$ Alakus. In other words, $\frac{1}{2}$ of a Swaram is added on to a full one for Ri with 4 Srutis is a full tone. But in giving calculations we say that Shankaraparanam has four Srutis for its

RI and DHA. But we sing 1¼ Swaram or Swaram with 4½ Alakus. The RI of Chenchuruti with 4¼ Alakus and the RI of Shankaraparanam with 4½ Alakus are popularly known as Chathur Sruti RI, without observing this minute difference in sound they have practically been called Chathursruti RI.

It was the common practice of the ancient Tamils who played the Yal to play these additional Srutis as gamakams either from the full Swaram or half Swaram. Musicians who were not dexterous in வார்தல், வடித்தல் and உந்தல் etc.—the different devices of an expert—had their mettus at longer or shorter intervals to suit the minute Swarams. But this custom is found among the instrument players of the North and not among the players of the Yal or other instruments of the South country.

It is a matter for joy that those foreigners who are ignorant of the minute Swarams of the Isai Tamil of the South Tamil country have recognised the existence of minute Srutis and try to produce them by means of Mettus.

Again, he says that Parijatam is a key to Karnatic Music. We have shown on pages 374, 375, 378, 383 and 385 the Sruti system of Parijatam. There we may note that mention is made of $\frac{1}{16}$ Swaram and ¼ Swaram in place of sounds with very minute calculations made use of by the ancient Tamils. This shows the possibility of still minuter Swarams.

He divides the strings into ⅓, ¼ &c., But his system, we have said before, is more or less that of Karnatic Music and that he has determined the 12 Srutis of the octave.

There is no kind of connection between the 22 Srutisthanams of Sarnga Dev and the 12 Srutisthanams of the author of Parijatam. From this, we clearly see that Sarnga Dev wrote his work in ignorance of the Sruti system of the South Tamil country, that great disputes resulted from it and that Parijatam and other works were written in elucidation of the Swarams used in Karnatic Music

The author of Parijatam who began discussing the generation of Nadams and Srutis after Sarnga Dev, suddenly turns round and says he is adopting the system of Narada in tuning Srutis. So it is clear he gives up the tuning system of Sarnga Dev and adopts that of Narada. The system of Narada is the system of Karnatic Music. Narada was held in high esteem as a Yalasirian in the South Tamil country. It is a custom even now in Ramnad and other Samasthanams that a descendant of the line of Narada receives a gift called Narada Mariyadai during the Dussera festivitie and Navaratri golu. So it is plain that the author of Parijatam made mention of only the Swarams of Karnatic Music.

We may think that the music of Parijatam and that of Sangeeta Ratnakar are different. But all sweet music is made up of the seven Swarams which became 12 half Swarams. Sarnga Dev made mention of 22 Srutis in the octave without being able to understand the minute Srutis used along with the 12 half Swarams. This was the cause of the difference and the dispute. There was no music after the system of Sarnga Dev, there is no music according to that system nor will ever in future be music based on his system.

Of the evils that beset South Indian Music at a time when it was declining owing to want of definite works the system of Sarnga Dev and the system of Pythageras with the inevitable $\frac{3}{2}$ and $\frac{4}{3}$ were the two great ones. Others who call their system that of Sarnga Dev but who adopt the $\frac{3}{2}$ and $\frac{4}{3}$ of Pythagoras should also be classified with them.

Hindu Musical Scale and the 22 Srutis by K. B. Deval P. 6.

"Narad sat watching from time to time his large Veena (sonometre or monochord) which by the impulse of breeze, yielded notes that pierced succesively the regions of his ear, and proceeded by musical intervals."

We see that the large Veena of Narada produced music with regular intervals when the breeze passed over it as mentioned by Sir, W. Jones in the 6th page of his book. If we note this minutely, we may conclude that Narada must have laid down rules for the playing of the Yal where minute Swarams with equal intervals in the four Palais Ayapalai, Vattapalai, Thirikonapalai and Chathurapalai occurred.

We must also note here what Mr. K. B. Deval says in his second Book.

Hindu Musical Scale and the 22 Srutis by K. B. Deval.

"The Hindus must have followed a system similar to the equal 'temperament' system at present in vogue in Europe."

He says here that the Hindus must have followed a system of equal Temperament. If the Srutis between intervals were equally divided, the Swarams must also have been dealt with accordingly. We have spoken in detail how they had divided the Swarams and Srutis equally and also devised calculations to show how they were concordant. This system of equal divisions has been in the South Country from very early times. In Europe this system of dividing the intervals by equal Temperament was only introduced about 150 years ago. As they were unable to understand the minute Srutis used along with the 12 Swarams of Equal Temperament different opinions as regards Srutis came in.

Mr. Deval, in spite of the equal intervals advocated by Narada, gives irregular cents such as Sa, 'Ri-84, "Ri-27, "'Ri-71, ''''Ri-22, 'Ga-90, and "Ga-22 etc. How surprising! What uniformity is there between 90 and 22 and between 84 and 27?

While making the remark that ancient Hindus divided Srutis equally why is he not aware that he gives a calculation for irregular intervals? How can he discard a theory advocated by Narada which has been carefully calculated? Sarnga Dev never says that 4 Srutis each should be given for Ri, Ga, Ma, Dha and Ni. He does not fix his Srutis by the system of $\frac{3}{2}$ or $\frac{4}{3}$, nor does he add to some Srutis and subtract from some.

It is not a matter for surprise that music should suffer by those writers who think they help music by perpetuating a number of irregularities. Music there never was according to the system of 22 Srutis. This trouble has arisen through writers who try to read the 22 Srutis into their practical experience of Karnatic music. Through such men ancient systems are losing their minuteness and prestige. The following extract illustrates this.

A. J. Hipkins.

"Under Captain Day's guidance, we find that, in India, an ancient quarter-tone system has become in modern times a half tone one, substantially our Equal Temperament, but permitting an expressive or ornamental use of smaller intervals than the half-tone according to the players."

Mr. Hipkins quotes Captain Day and says that the ancient quarter-tone system in India has given place to the system of half-tone, which gives room to the use of minuter intervals than half tone as gamakams, and that this is not far different from Equal Temperament. This shows how he has clearly understood the mystery of South Indian Music.

The Swarams of the ancient Ayapalai are but 12. They are obtained by the principle of Inai or SA-PA in the seventh Rasis. They are also obtained by the system of SA-MA or Kilai as fifths. Why should we not call this series the series of Equal Temperament?

If Swarams, as Mr. Deval says, were not of equal intervals, but irregular with cents like 84, 27, 71, 22 and 90, how do we arrive at the 12 Swarams of the octave? As the excellent system of the ancient Tamils, which had been in use for thousands of years, was forgotten, the $\frac{2}{3}$ system of Pythagoras, which could never completely finish the octave, and the stumbling block of the 22 Srutis created endless doubts in the minds of experts.

The ancient Tamils had their ganam in the 12 half Swarams of Ayapalai, by change of graham and the formation of many Ragas. We have pointed out before that they added to these 12 Swarams the 24 Alakus or $\frac{1}{4}$ Swarams of Vattapalai, the $\frac{1}{8}$ Swarams of Thirikonapalai and the $\frac{1}{16}$ Swarams of Chathurapalai, which were all played as gamakams from the 12 main Swarams. We have to be thankful that he at-least noted the half and the quarter Swarams used in ancient South Indian Music.

He would have been much pleased if he had found out that $\frac{1}{8}$ and $\frac{1}{16}$ Swarams were more frequently used in South Indian Music than $\frac{1}{2}$ and $\frac{1}{4}$ Swarams. He would have also spoken about the minute Srutis in use, at present. It is a matter for congratulation that he advocated 24 Srutis in the octave, in the midst of the cry every where, for the 22 Srutis.

This will be a good place to note the remarks of Hermann Smith, a Western musician, who has written very clearly about the art of tuning the Pianoforte. This book is considered very useful by many and is held in high esteem. This is what he says :—

The art of tuning the Pianoforte by Hermann Smith P. 75, 76.

"Mr. W. H. B. Woolhouse remarks truly, "It is very misleading to suppose that the necessity of temperament applies only to instruments which have fixed tones. Singers and performers on perfect instruments must all temper their intervals, or they could not keep in tune with each other, or even with themselves; and an arriving at the same notes by different routes would be continually finding a want of agreement. The scale of Equal temperament obviates all such inconveniences, and continues to be universally accepted with unqualified satisfaction by the most eminent vocalists; and equally so by the most renowned and accomplished performers on stringed instruments, although these instruments are capable of an infinite variety of intonation. The high development of modern instrumental Music would not have been possible, and could not have been acquired without the manifold advantages of the tempered intonation by equal semitones, and it has, in consequence, long become the established basis of tuning."

He says here that the system of Equal Temperament is equally useful for purposes of harmony as well as solo singing, that it is useful for a combination of orchestral instruments as well as individual stringed instruments. He says this system is the basis of all musical progress. This system of tempered intervals dates from very recent times, as noticed before.

We pointed out on page 116 that Captain Day says that the Veena taken to Europe from Tanjore over 150 years ago was tuned according to Equal Temperament. But we understand that, for thousands of years anterior to the time of the Tanjore Veena in the British Museum at London, the ancient Tamils had their ganam with Swarams of Equal intervals in the four palais, where the minute Srutis were played as gamakams. We have to feel glad that the system of tuning, which had long been forgotten, has been placed before us at least now.

We presume that the Swarasthanams of the Veena placed in the British museum, taken from Tanjore, one of the capitals of the Chola kingdom, might have helped the Equal Temperament system of the Westerners.

The art of tuning the pianoforte by Hermann Smith, Page. 17.

"The two cardinal points of the system are :

1. All octaves shall be tuned perfect.
2. All the fifths shall be a little flatter than perfect."

The opening Sa, as well as its octave the 8th Swaram, should be in complete unison. Just as an adult is an improved edition of a youth and a youth in his turn a developed image of an infant, so are the Tara Sthayi Sa, Madhya Sthayi Sa and Authara Sa in their relation to one another. The three Sthayis Munda, Sama and Ootcha increase in the proportion of 1 : 2 : 4. Just as ¼ measure is included under ½ a measure and ½ a measure within the full measure, so also sound increases gradually with a uniform ratio leaving no remainder.

If there is no such uniformity, a Sthayi cannot be said to have been perfectly completed. If the wire of a Veena be equally divided, a Sa sounds on the bisected point. There is complete unison between the Sa that sounds on the whole string and that which sounds on the bisected half string. If these do not agree, the octave is wrong.

The eighth note completes one octave or the Sthayi. Now, we may obtain the 12 Swarams of the Sthayi by the Sa-Pa system or system of fifths (Sa Ri, Ga, Ma, Pa,) or according to the principle of Inai and Kilai, or the seventh and the fifth Rasis spoken of by the ancient Tamils. We have pointed out already that, if we proceed by multiplying $\frac{3}{2} \times \frac{3}{2}$ and so on, according to Pythagoras, or take $\frac{1}{3}$ of the string for Panchamam, according to Parijatam, at the 12th step we go over the Sthayi. So the division of the string into thirds and obtaining the 12 Swarams on that principle can never be. It will never end the octave.

So, Hermann Smith says all fifths should be tuned a little flatter than perfect so that the 12 Swarams may be perfectly obtained within the octave. So, we understand that the squaring of $\frac{3}{2}$ will never give Swarams satisfying the ear. In the same manner, the fourths should be tuned a little sharper, or else the Swarams will fall short of the octave for SA-MA, or $\frac{4}{3}$ is not a perfect 4th.

The following extract shows that, unless we tune the fifths a little flatter, the concordance will be abhorrent.

The art of tuning the pianoforte by Hermann Smith, Page. 54.

"These trials, as they are called, afford at each step a check, by which the correctness of the progress may be indicated, or, unfortunately, probably the incorrectness of your first estimates of "how much" and "how little."

The last is the severest test, as the two notes of which this fifth is formed have been obtained by different series of fifths, and any imperfection in the gradation of the beatings allotted to the previous fifths will mainfest itself here. Hence this fifth, from the frequent harshness and howlings of its beats, has been technically termed the wolf, and strict injunctions are "Look out for the wolf," "Reckon yourself fortunate if no wolf appears."

He does not say how much flatter the fifths should be. He says it is difficult to derive the 12 Swarams by SA-PA or fifths. It is quite true. This is possible only in the case of tuners with very efficient ear for music, as pointed out in ancient works on Isai Tamil, who say that the tuner must be

"ஏற்றிய குரலிளி என்றிரு நரம்பின்
ஒப்பக் கேட்கும் உணர்வினனாகி"

Again the ancient custom was to make the Veena the standard for Swarasthanams. The Veena is very expedient for marking the Swarams by fifths or SA-PA. As others had not practised this system to any large extent, many discordant Swarams crept in.

To add to this, the wolf namely $\frac{3}{2}$, $\frac{4}{3}$ and the Fox namely the 22 Srutis of the octave howl in union! He says, "beware of the wolf", and we add "beware of the Fox"! then you will be happy. We, living in India, may think lightly of the wolf, but people living in cold countries like our author will know that herds of wolves are more dangerous to man than even lions!

He has used the analogy of the wolf as sharp Swarams spoil concord. We know for a fact, when $\frac{1}{3}$ is divided, it will never come to an end even if the world ends, for it is a recurring fraction with a dot at its head, and when it is multiplied, the fraction becomes bigger and bigger and never comes to an end.

He calls this wolf. But a wolf may die in a few years, but this has lived for 2500 years! So we must really call it the devil! Many have adopted this devil of a system and have come to grief. We must say these are bad times for Music, resulting from ignorance of rules of the ancient Tamil ganam.

I have made a demonstration of the ancient system of the Tamils in use for thousands of years, with the help of a few Keertanams, now in use, distributed in the four Palais, before the All India Music Conference, held in Baroda, on the 22nd March 1916. This was done in the presence of distinguished Karnatic musical experts such as

M. R. Ry. Ramakrishna Iyer Avl., B.A., B.L., Retired Sub-Judge, Palghat.
,, Veenai Krishna Row Avl., B.A., Mysore.
,, Panchapakesa Baghavatar Avl., Tanjore.
,, Ramasamy Baghavatar Avl., B.A., B.L., Madura.
,, Sreenivasa Iyengar Baghavatar Avl., B.A., L.T., Madras
,, Chitti Babu Naidu Garu Avl., Madras.
,, Pratapa Ramasami Baghavatar Avl., Poovanur.
,, Hari Nagabooshanam Iyer B.A., B.L., Masulipatam.
,, Veenai Venkataramana Doss, Avl., Vizianagaram.
,, K. T. Sreenivasa Iyengar, Trichinopoly.

and Hindustani Musical experts such as

Mr. Thakur M. Nawab Ali of Akbarpur.
Prince Faluknaz Md. Bakar Ali Bahadur.
Mr. V. N. Bhatkande B.A., L.L. B.
,, S. N. Karnad.
,, Rao Sahib K. B. Deval.
,, E. Clements I.C.S.
,, N. V. Chatre.
,, D. K. Joshi.
,, N. B. Divatia.
,, K. B. Divatia,
,, Prem Valabh Joshi.
Mrs. Atiya Begum Fyzee Rahimin.
Mr. G. S. Khare.
,, Lakshmidas Aditram
,, Vishnu Digamber Pluskar.
,, Mangesh Rao R. Telang.
,, Abdul Halim Sharar.
,, Zakruddin Saheb of Oodaipur.
,, Samasthana Vidwan of Baroda.

and in the presence of a cultured and learned assembly.

When this demonstration was made, when the measurements of the Swarasthanams, the calculations for the sounds of Swarams, and their cents were clearly set forth by means of logarithm and geometrical progression, in accordance with the system recommended by Saranga Dev, and when the Swarams, Srutis and minute Srutis of Karnatic music were demonstrated vocally and on the Veena by my daughters Maragatavalli Ammal and Kanakavalli Ammal, the delight universally experienced by the learned assembly could not possibly be described.

Some remarked that a new era had dawned for music, others that they need no longer trouble about enquiry into Srutis, and yet others that the Sruti systems of such and such writers have been sent to the bottomless pit, and the applause of the whole assembly was deafening. The demonstration by Swarams and measurements was made so as to satisfy the doubts of the various people assembled there. It was shown that sounds should be of uniform measurement; that singing of Swarams with different cents such as 84, 27, 71, 22 and 90 would sound like the howling of the wolf; that it would not be music; that such measurements would spoil the beauty of music and cause doubts; that they could never be of help to music.

But we give them credit for the good intentions they possessed for advancing the cause of music.

The following extract proves that placing of frets on the Veena to produce equal Swarams is peculiar to Indians.

P. R. Bhandarkar B.A., L. M. & S.

"But the scale used on the Vina since the 16th century, at least by one school viz., the Karnatic, has been Temperament, except for any accidental defects in tuning. What circumstances led to the adoption of this scale will have to be discussed on a future occasion. But it may be remarked here that this temperate scale is a capital discovery and the Hindus deserve to be congratulated on it, unless indeed it was borrowed like many other things in music from the Persians and Arabs. If any Indian perceives the Vina music to be defective, now that he has been made aware that its scale is one of equal temperament, let him taboo the instrument altogether or introduce modifications, which will allow of the use of what he thinks to be a better scale."

He says here that even as early as the 16th century, Karnatic measurements had divided the Swarasthanams of the Veena on the principle of Equal Temperament. We have, on the other hand, declared that it had existed from very ancient times. He says that the Indians were indebted to the Arabs and the Persians for many amsams of Music. But we understand that the South Tamil Country, its administration and civilisation were very ancient and that the civilisation, &c., of the other nations was of recent origin. The ganam in very minute Swarams was the peculiar heritage of the Tamils. The fact that this has not been yet understood by many show that Arabia or Persia never influenced the music of South India.

Perhaps, this statement was due to the fact that the Mughals were ruling in Northern India and Hindustani music was largely used there. He says that it is praised (or) that Indians had divided the Swarams and Srutis on the principle of Equal Temperament. If one understands that the system adopted for fixing the frets by equal divisions of intervals on the Veena by the ancient Tamils and the system of Equal Temperament are one and the same, one will never say that the Swarams of the Veena are incorrect.

Knowing that the Swarams of the Veena were identical with the Swarams of Western instruments, a Veena was prepared for the benefit of Sevappa Naicker, one of the rulers of Tanjore, on the principle of Western instruments. I earnestly beseech the readers of this work, but who obstinately disbelieve my statement, to believe that this system of equal divisions and the 12 Swarams of Ayapalai derived by the SA-PA system were played on the Yal even 2000 years ago, yea, for many thousands of years before that, by the Tamils as indicated by the words "வண்ணப்பட்டடை யாழ்மேல் வைத்தாங்கு."

We have pointed out how the 12 Swarams derived by SA-PA principle with equal divisions were made the basis of all ganam, how minute Swarams were played as gamakams from them, how grahaswaram was sung in the very Swarams, how they derived different Ragas by the change of grahaswaram from the same Swarams, and how the same system was in practice even now.

The above remarks point to the conclusion how the Conference held sometime back for the purpose of reviving Indian Music with the aid of Sanskrit Srutis came to nought, how confusion between theory and practice was caused by enquirers after Srutis (the basis of all music) and writers on them, owing to their conflicting opinions, and that different writers wrote in different strain on the subject of Srutis, some having Ratnakar as the basis, and some Parijatam, which was just its opposite, while others had later writings for their support. The result was a cartload of conflicting theories!

On the other side, we have the support of Narada, who recognises equal intervals, and that of the Hindus of the Tamil country, who have for generations used Swarams with equal intervals. The latter have used 24 quarter Swarams in their ganam, which could be played as gamakams with the 12 Swarams as the basis.

To add to this testimony, we have that of the Western musicians, who recently came to the conclusion that Tempered intervals served best the purposes of harmony and modulation. Though they have adopted $\frac{3}{2}$ as an approximation, yet they advocate a slight flattening of the fifths in progression, which must be the result of musical experience and they say that all Swarams should be of equal intervals.

Again, the Swarams of the Veena are found to be in Equal Temperament and the Indians are praised for working this theory out themselves, without being indebted to Persians or Arabs for the same. The author says that the Swarams of the Veena can never be improved upon, owing to their perfection.

We conclude then, that the Swarams used by the ancient habitants of India were of equal intervals, that the same equal intervals are used in Karnatic music and on the Veena, that the Westerns adopted the same system about 120 years ago, that those who wrote on Indian music theorised that Indian music had equal intervals, yet by adopting the progression of $\frac{3}{2}$ and $\frac{4}{3}$ they had to give wrong calculations, adding in one place and subtracting in another. They have gone to the length of constructing instruments to suit their theory but have found them impracticable.

But the Isai Tamil system of the ancient Tamils is equal division, which has been in practice for the past 12000 years. These very intervals are found in the excellent Senkoti Yal practised by them. These are the very intervals divided into four palais and used in Karnatic music even now. The division of equal intervals is the only system that can aid the progress of the world in music.

We may note here what Mr. A. Ghose, who has made researches into the ancient history, culture and migrations of the ancient Tamils, wrote to the Madras Mail on 2nd December, 1915.

2. The Civilisation of Ancient Indians and their political administration.

Ancient Indians in Mesopotamia

History repeats itself in the strangest manner. This is not the first time that Indians (now forming the Expeditionary Force) are playing an important part in altering the history of the fertile valley, drained by the waters of the Tigris and Euphrates. Archaeological researches have tended towards the establishment of the most remarkable fact that colonists from ancient India in remote ages settled in Mesopotamia.

What leading part they played in that cradle of civilisation will be realised when it is stated that an eminent archaeologist of great experience, after patient studies, is inclined to come to the startling conclusion that the wonderful Mesopotamian culture displayed by the ancient Babylonians and Assyrians was derived from the Sumerians. These were no other than Dravidian settlers from India, who had migrated to the head of the Persian Gulf at the very dawn of civilisation.

Mr. H. R. Hall, of the British Museum, thus expresses the latest views on the origin of the Sumerians, who were the pioneers of the high degree of civilisations, to which the ancient nations of the Euphrates valley attained :—

> The Sumerian culture springs into our view ready-made, as it were, which is what we should expect, if it was, as seems on other grounds probable, brought into Mesopotamia from abroad. The earliest scenes of their culture development had, perhaps, not been played upon the Babylonia stage at all, but in a different country, away across the Persian mountains to the eastward.

> The ethnic type of the Sumerians, so strongly marked in their statues and reliefs, was as different from those of the races, which surrounded them, as was their language, from those of the Semites, Aryans or others. They were decidedly Indian in type. The face-type of the average Indian of to-day is, no doubt, much the same as that of his race ancestors thousands of years ago. And it is by no means improbable that the Sumerians were an Indian race which passed, certainly by land, perhaps, also by sea, through Persia to the valley of the Two Rivers. It was in the Indian home (perhaps the Indus valley) that we suppose for them that their culture developed.

> There, their writing may have been invented, and progressed from purely pictorial to a simplified, and abbreviated form, which afterwards in Babylonia took on its peculiar "cuneiform" appearance, owing to its being written with a square ended stylus on soft clay. There is little doubt that India must have been one of the earliest centres of human civilisation, and it seems natural to suppose that the strange un-Semitic, un-Aryan people, who came from the East to civilise the West, were of Indian origin, especially when we see with our eyes how very Indian the Sumerians were in type.

The origin of the Dravidian race, the most primitive of the Indian types, is lost in obscurity. No satisfactory theory has yet been forthcoming to point out their original home (if they had any other than India) from which they migrated. Huxley's theory as to their connection with the aborigines of Australia, although apparently supported by Slater's hypothesis of a vast continent now submerged under the Indian Ocean, which once embraced Africa, India and Australia, has been traversed by Sir William Turner's comparative studies of the Australian and Dravidian crania.

Sir W. W. Hunter's assumption, which assigned a trans-Himalayan origin to the Dravidians, has been discounted for various reasons. The failure of all theorists to assign a foreign home to the Dravidians appears to justify the conclusion that they were among the original inhabitants of India.

There is every reason to suppose that pre-Aryan Dravidian culture flourished in their great home, well-endowed as it was by bountiful nature. Whether the Dravidians from India who migrated to Mesopotamia were compelled to seek a new home forced by famine or by persecution, or whether they were traders or adventurers, we have no means of ascertaining. We are also in the dark as to whether they took the difficult land route across Baluchistan and Persia or they went by sea along the coast.

The presence of the Brahuis in Baluchistan, who have a dialect showing strong affinity with the Dravidian languages, appears to lend much support to the former theory, specially when we take into consideration the fact that their ancestral neighbours, who inhabited ancient Persia, most probably belonged to the Dravidian race.

These ancient non-Aryan inhabitants of Persia were called "Anarikoi" by the Greeks which is undoubtedly a corrupted form of "Anarya,' by which name the Dravidians were known to the first Aryan settlers in India.

Several years ago, Mr. Hewitt pointed out that the Euphrates valley was the home of the Hindu lunar astronomy, which was introduced into India before 4700 B. C. He also produced evidence pointing to the existence of trade relations between India and Mesopotamia in very ancient times.

The discovery of indigo and muslin in Egyptian tombs conclusively showed that Indian products found their way into Egypt, so long ago as at least 1700 B. C. There is also evidence that the Sumerians traded in teak and muslin, which were exclusive products of India. Mr. Hewitt was of opinion that these commercial transactions between Western India and Sumeria took place in 6000 B. C. He also endevaoured to trace the presence of Sumerians in ancient Gujarat. Later researches have not only confirmed some of the conclusions of Mr. Hewitt, but, as we find from the above quotation from a leading authority on archæology and ancient history, the identification of the Sumerians with the ancient Dravidians of India leaves little room for doubt.

The linguistic evidence as supplied by the Brahuis of the survival of a Dravidian language, in the remote central Highlands of Baluchistan, forms a strong link for establishing the identity of the Sumerians. If the opinion of Dr. Grierson to the effect that of all Dravidians the Brahuis alone retain the true ethnic type owing to their isolation, be accepted, then we are led to the conclusion that the Sumerians were imigrants from Southern India, as is evidenced from their strong resemblance to the Dravidian ethnic type as modified by admixture, with aboriginal nationalities.

If the Brahuis really represent the true Dravidian ethnic type, an alternative theory may be proposed, pointing to Baluchistan as the original home, from which a great Dravidian emigration to India took place in very ancient times.

The recent geological investigations of Mr. Vredenburg appears to favour such a hypothesis, as there is, now, good reason to surmise, on the basis of Mr. Vredenburg's explorations, that the desert tracts of Baluchistan were once covered by fertile lands, which were well populated. The exhaustion of the water resources and consequent production of famine conditions threatened the ancient inhabitants, rendering migration on a vast scale imperative.

That the Sumerians, who settled in Southern Babylonia (Sumer), were the founders of Babylonian culture is abundantly shown by the relics recovered by archæologists from the excavation conducted on the sites of the ancient cities. The early history of Babylonia is a record of Sumerian domination and progress.

The excavations of the city mounds at the lowest levels disclose Sumerian culture so advanced that the people were already using copper. The Sumerian copper implements, found at Tello in Babylonia, probably go so far back as 4000 B. C. A bronze statue of Gudea, perhaps the greatest of all the Sumerian Kings, dating back to 2500 B. C., is a landmark in the history of the antiquity of copper.

More than one eminent archæologist have advanced the opinion that India was the first home of the bronze industry. Even such a conservative historian as Mr. Vincent Smith admits that copper was used in India in very ancient times. Some of the prehistoric copper implements (probably dating back to about 2000 B. C.) of the most remarkable hoard, discovered in 1870 at Gungeria, in the Central Provinces, bear a close resemblance to those found in Babylonia.

Although very valuable work has been done in Southern India by Mr. Rhea, by his discoveries of prehistoric metal implements, a great deal has yet to be done in this direction, in the way of discovery and serious study to throw light on the ancient history of metallurgy in India and its possible connection with Mesopotamian culture.

The Sumerians were great builders of towns and irrigation works. They were the first town-planners known to history. They developed the City State to a marked extent. Each city had its temple with a city-god, who was the owner of all the city land. Every city was governed by a hereditary ruler, who was also the high priest of the local god with the title of "patesi" or vicegerent of the god. We do not know much about the Sumerian deities.

Nippur, which was the chief city of ancient Babylonia, had a great temple dedicated to Enail. The identity of this name with the Dravidian name for the moon god is significant. The corresponding Dravidian name, Bal, is most prominent in Babylonian mythology.

The temple at Nippur was a great repository for votive offerings of the Sumerian Kings which have yielded valuable material for ancient history, showing that the Sumerians who lived 6,000 years before us lived in great and populous cities under organised civil and religious government.

They had long ago emerged from the savage state, as they were already using metal and had their own system of writing. From their statues, we see them with shaven heads and wearing long garments. Their physiognomy and fashions of dress bear such close resemblance to the Dravidian that their common origin is not improbable, as such striking similarity cannot be merely accidental.

Dr. Buhler traced the derivation of the ancient Brahui script, the parent of most of the known alphabets of India, from Mesopotamia, fixing the date of its introduction into India at about 800 B. C.

It is acknowledged by some authorities that the Tamil alphabet, with its peculiar characters of a primitive type, was in existence long before the introduction of Brahui or Kharosthi. The supposition that the Tamil alphabet was derived from a Semitic source and is a variety of the Aramaic or Hymiaritic script, which originated in Mesopotamia, ought to undergo modification in the light of recent researches which appear to reverse the country of origin of the Tamil alphabet.

When another Champollion is found to unearth the deeply buried relics of the ancient Dravidian culture, in all probabilty, it will be discovered that lunar astronomy as well as the very first alphabet originated in India, just as it is now being recognised that the advanced civilisation of ancient Mesopotamia owed its inception to the Sumerians from India. How far the world is thus indebted to the ancient Dravidians, as appears to be disclosed by recent researches, is a subject which finds no place in the works of the modern historians of ancient India.

A. GHOSE.

We see here some remarks about the ancient Indians who migrated to Mesopotamia. Mesopotamia is the fertile land between the two rivers Euphrates and Tigris in Asia Minor. It is said that the Euphrates was one of the rivers that fertilised the garden of Eden, mentioned in Creation. History tells us that the land watered by these rivers was extremely fertile, capable of producing excellent fruits and different kinds of grain.

The Indians were called Sumerians. The Sumerians resembled the Dravidians of South India in their physiognomy and build. These Dravidians must have migrated to Mesopotamia from South India. As the Sumerians resemble the race of South India in their manners, customs and culture, they must have originally come from South India. They seem to have founded and ruled over the ancient Kingdoms of Babylon and Assyria and to have made great advancement in Sculpture and Astronomy and in weaving, dyeing, agriculture, and in making metallic statues, as also in trade.

It is said that there were commercial relations between the Sumerians and the Dravidians, 6000 years ago. We see that Astronomy was carried to Mesopotamia from India about 4700 years ago. As the language spoken in the highlands of Baluchistan and Persia was Dravidian, it is possible that their inhabitants originally came from India. Their language was called Brahuis.

It is said that the Dravidians settled in the lands adjoining Mesopotamia and that they spoke the Dravidian language. The Greeks called them 'Anarya'.

The copper and bronze tools made by the Sumerians were dug up in the ruins of Tello, a town in Babylon. These are dated over 4000 years.

The bronze statue of Gudea, one of the renowned Sumerian kings, dates as far back as 2500 B.C. This shows that the Indians were clever, from very ancient times, in copper and bronze work and in metallurgy. Again, the copper implements discovered in 1870 at Gungeria, in the Central Provinces, bear a close resemblance to those found in Babylonia. These seem to have been used as early as 2000 B.C.

The Sumerians were experts in building and irrigation works. They planned towns, built forts and temples and were the foremost in doing works in temples.

It seems that Nippen, the chief city of Babylonia, had a great temple dedicated to Ennil, which is identified with the Dravidian name for the moon, and that the corresponding Dravidian name 'Bal' is most prominently used in Babylonian mythology. In addition to this it is stated that they were noted for their devotion to religion and were very cultured in their manners and customs.

He says their language was known as Brahuis and the characters of the language are found in the bricks of the buildings in Babylon. It is further stated that the letters are purely Tamil and are not derived from the Aramaic tongue, one of the dialects of the Semitic language.

Many of the above remarks are based on the researches of historians. Some remarks, supported by the above, may be found in Part I. All this shows that, before the period of the Deluge, the ancient Tamils who belonged to the royal family of the Pandyas and others, who ruled at South Madura, must have migrated to Mesopotamia and established the kingdoms of Babylon and Assyria there.

As they belonged to Chandrakulam, it is probable that they gave the name of Ennil (Chandran) to the God at Babylon which they built.

It is not possible that subject races who find it difficult to eke out their own livelihood can possibly have built great cities and forts and established renowned kingdoms. The builders of cities and empires must have been the rulers, or, descendants of the royal house of Pandya. We have noted, at the commencement of this book that the city of Babylon was built on either side of the Euphrates, comprising 225 square miles in extent, with walls 75 feet by 32 feet, and possessing 120 huge bronze doors, that in the centre of the city were placed the royal palace, the temple and other wonderful structures.

The description of this beautiful city reminds one of the beauties of South Madura, about which the sage Vanmeeka spoke to the best of the Vanaras saying, "you will see the gates of the Pandya sovereigns, set with precious stones and glittering with gold, and connected with the main walls of the fort."

The civilisation of South Madura and its beauty must have been in proportion to the royal feast made by king Ahasuerus, mentioned in page 14, when it is said that he ruled over 127 provinces, from India to Ethiopia; his capital city of Shushan and the province of Persia must be identical with the new cities and provinces ruled over by the royal Pandyan family of South Madura, after their migration.

From inscriptions we see that South Pandya Kings' rule extended as far north as the Himalayas and that their flag, having the emblem of a fish, was planted on the top of those mountains.

We have read about Nimrod who built Erech, Accad and Calneh, the chief cities of Babylonia and its provinces, and Nineveh, Rehoboth, Calah and Resen, the chief cities of the Assyrian Kingdom. These cities and kingdoms are near Mesopotamia and its adjacent provinces, watered by the Euphrates and the Tigris, to the south of Asia Minor.

We have observed how the Sumerians ruled over Mesopotamia, how they were originally the inhabitants of South India, how they migrated to Baluchistan, and Persia through Baluchistan, that their language was Brahuis or Tamil, and how their letters were those of the Tamil Alphabet. These enable us to establish that the Tamils of the South Pandya Kingdom ruled, once upon a time, as far as the Himalayas and the countries of Baluchistan, Persia and Mesopotamia and beyond, by founding various Kingdoms there, and extended their administration over 127 provinces from India to Ethiopia.

This enables us to make further remarks and say that the language of these 127 provinces was Tamil, and that, at a later time, the language became changed, owing to mixture, and called by different names. The truth of this may be seen from the fact that the majority of the words of these different languages are Tamil.

It appears that others must have learnt the Sciences of Architecture, Astrology, Music and Medicine from those who spoke the Tamil language. When we note the minuteness of Astronomy and Music, we see that they must have been in a highly efficient state in South Madura, from ancient times, and deteriorated, in later days, owing to want of patronage.

If we read verses 2-5 of the 10th chapter of the book of Genesis in the Bible, we read there that Japheth had seven sons, and that the different tribes descended from them; their isles, their languages and provinces were also seven.

" The sons of Japheth : Gomer, and Magog, and Madai and Javan and Tubal and Meshech and Tiras.

And the sons of Gomer : Ashkenaz and Riphath and Togarmah.

And the sons of Javan : Elishah and Tarshish, Kittim and Dodanim.

By these were the isles of the Gentiles divided in their lands ; every one after his tongue, after their families, in their nations."

There is reason to think that the seven sons of Japheth became the founders of the seven nations, that they lived in the seven isles and that each of these isles was sub-divided into seven provinces. It is likely, therefore, that the remnants of the Lemurians, saved from the Deluge, kept up the number 7 and divided themselves on that principle which might remind them that their original land of Lemuria, or, South Madura has also comprised of 7 isles, and each of the 7 isles sub-divided into 7 provinces. So the original Tamil custom seems to have been kept up.

We may say, then, that the Tamils, when they escaped to different places during the Deluge, migrated to many regions, conquered different provinces and established their administration there.

This shows that the 127 provinces from India to Ethiopia, were under the Tamil sway and the Tamil language was spoken there. These 127 provinces seem to have been in the Arabian sea region, from the southernmost corner of India to the southernmost corner of Africa.

It is impossible to find parallels to the court at Shushan and to the build of the cities of Babylon and Nineveh. When it is proved that the magnificence of these kingdoms, their power and antiquity is to be attributed purely to the Tamil race, who can adequately express the antiquity of the South Tamil country, the glory of the Muttamil, practised there, and their supreme and minute knowledge of music?

Who will believe a Tamil when he says that the ancient South Tamil country was the most distinguished of provinces, that music was extensively practised there and in other provinces under the sway of the Tamils, that they had practised Tamil under the three amsams of Iyal, Isai and Natakam, and that music had attained such proficiency among them that they made their ganam in very minute Swarams like $\frac{1}{2}$, $\frac{1}{4}$, $\frac{1}{8}$ and $\frac{1}{16}$? Who will believe a man when he declares that the Tamil language, spoken by the Sumerians in Mesopotamia, was the one spoken in Persia and Baluchistan, that they were Tamils who had founded such magnificent kingdoms such as Babylonia and Assyria, and that they were experts in all arts?

It is likely that the Tamil language, spoken in Persia and Baluchistan by the Sumerians, was called Brahuis, that this language after undergoing many alterations in different countries, became the Prakrit language, which in turn was converted into the Sanskrit tongue.

We have observed before that the mother tongue Tamil was found in the south of India, its sister languages Telugu, Malayalam and Canarese in Central India, and that the Pali tongue, which is a mixture of the Dravidian languages, was found in the North.

It appears, therefore, that the Tamil language, which was the language of the emigrant Tamils of Mesopotamia, became corrupt while spoken in Persia, Baluchistan, Afghanistan, Sind, Guzerat and other western provinces of India, and was known as the Prakrit, and an admixture of these various dialects gave birth to the Sanskrit language.

The majority of words in the different dialects of the Prakrit language are Tamil. The presence of a very large number of Tamil words in the Pali language and Malayalam, Telugu, Canarese and Tulu languages, derived from Tamil, shows that Tamil must have been the original for all these languages.

Again, among the letters of the Tamil alphabet, the hard consonants க, ச, ட, த, ப and ற have a single sound in the language but have two and three and four sounds in later languages.

Scholars declare that a comparative study of Greek, Hebrew and Latin dictionaries discloses the fact that more than half the words of these languages are Tamil.

Works similar to those on Alchemy, Medicine, Yogam and Gnanam, written by the seven sages and eighteen siddhas who were among the ancient Tamils of India, are not found in any other language, either in the past or the present. But these works are being interpreted in other languages now.

The 64 drugs of China and the system of preparing them, the nine kinds of poison and the rules for preserving and refining them, the method for calcining, converting them into red preparations or reducing them to potash, their antidotes, the system of preparing various salts and acids, the system for reviving suspended animation, the methods of preparing stones. plants and pills, the method of preparing different mixtures of herbs, the 120 metallic preparations. the remedies by talisman and Mantrams for serpent bites, the system of surgery and incision for abscesses, the system of Yoga Sadhana, the system of inuring the body to hardship by medicine and practice, and the system of Gnanam are very extensively spoken of in Tamil works. These are very sparingly found in other languages.

The four kinds of Pahs of Isai Tamil or Music. their different divisions, the Chandakulippus, the arrangement of Thalam, the four Palais, the four varieties of Yal generating from the Palais, the four Jatis derived from each of the Palais, and the 12000 ancient Isais, sung sweetly, are not found in any other language.

We should not forget that others who heard the Thevaram, Thiruvachakam, Thiruvaimoli, Thiruppugal, Keertanams and Padams, sung in the sweet Tamil Chandam, knowing the absence of such charming pieces in their own languages, are trying to compose Keertanams in them, in their respective languages.

Some of us might have heard the new Padals in Sanskrit composed according to the Chanda system of the modern Tamils, by M. R. Ry., Narayana Sastrial, Senior Professor in the Sanskrit college at Trivadi, near Tanjore.

If such compositions, after the model of the Tamil Chandams, were even 40 or 50 years old, admirers of Sanskrit are sure to claim them to be Sanskrit originals !! The real truth may be forgotten. Many of the rare productions of the Tamilians have lost their antiquity by such means!

Mr. Ghose says that the Sumerians had commercial dealings with South Indians 6000 years ago B. C.—really means they had such dealings for nearly 8000 years. So it is seen that Indians migrated to Mesopotamia, 8000 years ago, and established kingdoms there.

An American merchant, who excavated the ruins of the city of Nineveh, says he found there many valuable relics of antiquity and, among them, four figures whose heads were of gold, and who had wings of silver and bodies like that of an animal. He also came across a large number of burnt square tiles of clay, ½ and ¾ inch in thickness, in which were inscriptions written by iron styles, tapering to a point like the spear. The letters in them belong to the Sumerian language. Documents relating to land, judgments and scientific truths were found written in them. There were also tiles, in which was written a description of Creation, as given in Genesis, written by Moses. We have noted before that this great city of Nineveh, and other great cities as also the kingdoms of Babylon and Assyria were founded by Nimrod.

To support our theory that the ancient Tamils were the Sumerians, who established the kingdoms of Assyria and Babylon, the inscriptions on these square tiles are also in Sumerian characters. Signs of civilisation and culture are found in abundance there. It is seen from the inscriptions that they had established great kingdoms even in the prehistoric period, that they were proficient in arts and sciences, and that they were Tamils.

The following extracts also support the contention that the relics, found in the ruins of Nineveh and Babylon, prove the ancient culture and civilisation of the Sumerians who were Tamils.

The Popular Encyclopedia Vol I Page 370.

"The advanced condition of the Assyrians in various other respects is sufficiently evidenced by the representations on the sculptures, and by the remains discovered among their ruined buildings. We now know that they understood and applied the arch; that they constructed tunnels, aqueducts and drains; that they used the lever and the roller; that they engraved gems in a highly artistic way; that they understood the arts of inlaying, enamelling and overlaying with metals; that they manufactured porcelain and transparent and coloured glass and were acquainted with the lens; that they possessed vases, jars, and other dishes, bronze and ivory ornaments, bells, gold earrings and bracelets of excellent design and workmanship.

Their household furniture also gives us a high idea of their skill, taste, minuteness, and accuracy.

The cities of Nineveh, Assur and Arbela had each their royal observatories, superintended by astronomers-royal, who had to send in their reports to the king, twice a month.

At an early date the stars were numbered and named, a calendar was formed in which the year was divided into twelve months (of thirty days each), called after the Zodiacal signs, but as this division was found to be inaccurate, an intercalary month was added, every six years. The week was divided into seven days, the seventh being a day of rest; the day was divided into twelve *casbu* of two hours each, each casbu being subdivided into sixty minutes, and these again, into sixty seconds.

Eclipses were recorded from a very remote epoch, and their recurrence roughly determined. The principal astronomical work, called the Illumination of Bel, was compiled for the library of Sargon of Agane; it was inscribed on seventy tablets, and went through numerous editions, one of the latest being in the British Museum.

It treats, among other things, on observations of comets, the polar star, the conjunction of the sun and moon and the motions of Venus and Mars. The study of mathematics was fairly advanced, and the people who were acquainted with the sun-dial, the clepsydra, the pulley, and the lever must have had considerable knowledge of mechanics."

We noticed in the previous pages that the Sumerians, who inhabited Mesopotamia, built the great cities of Babylon, Nineveh and Shushan, that they ruled over these great kingdoms, that they traded with India, that they originally came from South India, that they resembled the South Indians in features, and that their language resembled that of the Tamils. To support the above statements, we find from the extract, quoted, that one of the kingdoms ruled by them, namely, Assyria, was much advanced, as seen from its progress in many modern arts and sciences and, especially, in astronomy. As they are clearly stated, we need not dilate upon the subject.

Their civilisation resembles that of the ancient Tamils of South Madura. We shall note here some remarks upon the God worshipped by them.

Discoveries in the ruins of Nineveh and Babylon by Austen H. Layard, M. P. Page 343.

"On the north side of the chamber were two doorways leading into seperate apartments. Entrance was formed by two colossal bas-reliefs of Dagon, or, the fish god. Unfortunately the upper part of all these figures had been destroyed, but, as the lower remained, from above the waist we can have no difficulty in restoring the whole, especially as the same image is seen entire on a fine Assyrian cylinder of a gate in my possession. It combined the human shape with that of the fish. The head of the fish formed a mitre above that of the man, whilst its scaly back and fanlike tail fell as a cloak behind, leaving the two human limbs and feet exposed. The figure wore a fringed tunic, and bore the two sacred emblems, the basket and the cone.

We can scarcely hesitate to identify this mythic form with the Oannes, or, sacred man-fish, who, according to the traditions preserved by Berossus, issued from the Erythræan sea, instructed the Chaldaeans in all wisdom, in the sciences, and in fine arts, and was afterwards worshipped as a God in the temples of Babylonia. Its body, says the historian, was that of a fish, but under the head of a fish was that of a man and to its tail were joined women's feet. Five such monsters rose from the Persian gulf at fabulous intervals of time. It was conjectured that this myth denotes the conquest of Chaldaea at some remote and prehistoric period, by a comparatively civilised nation coming in ships to the mouth of the Euphrates.

I had already identified with the Babylonian idol, a figure in a bas-relief at Khorsabad having the human form to the waist, and the extremities of a fish. Such figures are also frequently found on antique cylinders and gems, but those at Kouyunjik agreed even more minutely with the description of Berossus, for the human head was actually beneath that of the fish, whilst the human feet were added to the spreading tail."

The above extracts say that the Chaldaeans worshipped a man-fish and that this denoted the conquest of Chaldaea at a remote prehistoric period by a more civilised nation coming in ships to the mouths of the Euphrates, the ships resembling the shape of a fish.

These fish-shaped figures are found in abundance in the large cities of ancient times, such as Nineveh and Babylon. Berossus calls this figure by the name of Oannes. On the strength of this, we may say that the ancient Tamils migrated to Chaldaea, and that the sovereigns of the South Pandya Kingdom also ruled over Chaldaea. For, we read that, when Satya Viratha. King of the ancient Dravidian country, was making his ablutions in the river Kritamala, when he took up a little water in his hand, a small fish was found there which grew under his care. When the fish became big, it advised him thus :—"This city is about to be destroyed by a flood. I shall bring you a boat within eight days. You and your relatives and the seven sages may save your lives by getting into it with all necessary provisions. I shall take you to a place of safety." The king believed the fish got into the boat, and, they all reached the foot of the Himalayas and were saved. This Satya Viratha became Vaivaswatha Manu afterwards and became the ancestor of the Indian race. He was the founder of the Chandra dynasty and of the Pandya line of kings. We have also stated before that the flag of the Pandyas had the figure of a fish in it, and that it was flying on the Himalayas. It is but natural that they should worship the God who saved them in the form of a fish, and have the figure as a precious emblem in their banners also. We may also notice that Meenambal is worshipped as a goddess in South India, and the name is very commonly given to the females there. The Pandya sovereigns, who made voyages in their ships, had also this emblem on the stem of their ships. All these clearly show that the Tamils of the South Pandya country migrated in ships to Babylon, Nineveh, Persia, Mesopotamia and other places. Even now we may see that the game of 'Pandi', called after the Pandya sovereigns, is played on a board which has the shape of a fish (in the districts of Tinnevelly and Madura), that it is given as a part of the dowry when a girl is given away in marriage, that the pan-supari box has also a similar shape, that fish are worshipped at Papanasam, where the Tambiraparani takes its rise, and that Pandya sovereigns are called by the title of "Meenavas". The Pandi board, the pansupari box, and the emblem on the flag have the shape of a "Sale Fish". This makes us bold to say that the ancient rulers from India to Ethiopia were the Tamils.

To add to this testimony, the Indian cow was also found there, as seen from the following extract :

Discoveries in the ruins of Nineveh and Babylon by Austen H. Layard, M. P. Page, 604.

"On others of the same age we find the gods represented under various forms : —the king and priests worshipping before them, altars and various signs peculiar to the period, and the usual mythic emblems. On a small cylinder in which porcelain or quartz is engraved a cow of the Indian breed suckling a calf, an Assyrian emblem, which occurs amongst the ivory carvings discovered at Nimroud."

We know that the monkey, the elephant, the cow and the peacock are animals generally found in nature in India. From the facts that the Indians regarded the cow as indispensable to their daily life and looked upon it as sacred and as a goddess, that they worshipped fish as sacred, that the ox was the vahanam of Paramasivam who is known to the Tamils as Perumal who knows Tamil, Perumal who could be melted by Isai and who is the founder of Muttamil, and that the Nandi (ox) is the favourite figure in the Sannadi of all Siva temples, we may conclude that the Tamils inhabited Mesopotamia, Babylon, Assyria, Persia and other provinces.

We shall do well to make a few remarks on the language spoken by the Sumerians or the Tamils in Mesopotamia. Discussing the question of language, we must note the shape and sound of letters and the grammatical rules and their relation to one another. We cannot deal with them in detail as the subject in our hand is only Srutis. But as the minute swarams of music are made mention of in Isai Tamil, one of the divisions of the ancient Muttamil, the Tamil language must have been the original one. To examine this the following extract is given :—

The Popular Encyclopedia Vol. XI Page 34.

"Lastly come the Inflectional Languages represented by the two groups of the Semetic and Indo-Germanic languages. It is from the speakers of languages of these two groups that almost everything, most beneficial to the development of the human race, has sprung. The Semetic languages are (*a*) Hebrew, closely akin to which were the other ancient dialects of Canaan, Mobite, Phoenician etc; (*b*) Arabic, widely spread as the result of Mohamadan Conquests; (*c*) Aramaic, the languages of Ancient Syria which in Palestine also had taken the place of Hebrew as a spoken language before the Christian era; and (*d*) Assyrian, which has been recovered from countless inscriptions upon clay tablets found on the sites of ancient cities like Nineveh and Babylon. The different Semetic languages do not differ more from one another than do Romance languages like French, Italian and Spanish. They are, however, generally divided into a northern and a southern group; the southern group being formed of the various dialects of Arabic; the northern groups of the other languages though Aramaic deviates considerably from the rest of the group. The most characteristic feature of the Semitic languages is that, with rare exceptions, all roots have three consonants or semi-consonants, which, in combination with vowels, form series of words. The verb system is much less perfectly developed than that of the Indo-Germanic system.

To the Indo-Germanic or Indo-European system belong a number of languages and dialects which fall easily into eight groups. These languages are widely spread, extending from India to Iceland in the Old World, and since the end of the fifteenth century having been disseminated over the whole of America, Australia, New Zealand, and the East India as the language of European conquerors or colonizers of those lands. The system has been called by other names as Aryan, which is however, more appropriately applied to the most easterly group of the languages. The name Indo-European is commonly used, but seems to imply that the languages are spoken only in India and Europe, which is inaccurate, as is also the notion that all Indian and European languages belong to this system. In Southern India the Dravidian languages, of which the chief representatives are Tamil and Telugu, are agglutinative languages and therefore of a different type; while in Europe, Turkish, Hungarian, Finnish, and Lapp belong to an agglutinative system, and Basque, as we have seen, is an incorporating language. The names Indo-Germanic and Celt-Indic are each an attempt to express the family by the extreme links of the chain. The languages belonging to the system are descended from an original language long since lost. Where this language was spoken it is difficult definitely to decide."

It is not easy to give clear opinions as regards languages. We may venture to make remarks on languages, reformed in recent times or were discovered in our own time; but to attempt generalisations about very ancient languages is an impossible task. Malayalam, which is spoken in Travancore, adjacent to the Tamil country, and the Telugu language have undergone great modifications recently by borrowing many words and letters from Sanskrit. We know that the Sourashtra language—the language of the silk weavers—became a written language with an alphabet only in very recent times. It is but the way of the world to try and progress after other models. We have stated before that Sanskrit became a language a few thousand years ago, by borrowing many words and rules from Brahuis, the language of the Sumerians, from the different Prakrit dialects, from Pali and Indo-Germanic tongues, and devising a few new rules of its own. Languages which have merely borrowed a few letters and words from Sanskrit may be said to be derived dialects of Sanskrit, a few years hence!

Just as the pure rain water that falls from the clouds flows into channels, the channel water into tanks, the tank water into fields, the field water into rivers, and the river water into the sea, and obtain, each in its field, a variety of taste, smell and colour, so also the words of a language obtain different spellings and pronunciations by contact with other languages. We have given examples of such on pages 43—45. The ancient language of the early emigrants changes its letters, words and shape, to suit the climate, dress, productions, vegetable and mineral, and manners of the various countries where it spreads, and appears like a different language altogether. When the changed language extends over vast territories, ruled by different sovereigns, the language appears to be the language of a different country altogether and has no resemblance with the original tongue at all!

In a grocer's shop where the different grains and articles get mixed it is difficult to separate them. So also is the work of a goldsmith who wants to get the alloy out of the mixed gold. He has to first separate the alloy by using the பாதரசம் (Mercury) which has the tendency of uniting itself with gold, silver, copper, lead and other metals, then put them in lime crucibles to separate the gold and silver alone, and then burn the gold and silver in the refining vessel to separate the pure gold from the silver. The case of analysing an old language is equally difficult. Only scholars, interested in studying histories of languages, with the help of ancient relics, will be interested in such philological analysis, and not others.

The above remarks appear to be correct in the light of what Mr. Ghose says which is found in page 865. He says there, "when another Chompollion is found to unearth the deeply buried relics of the ancient Dravidian culture, in all probability, it will be discovered that lunar astronomy as well as the very first alphabet originated in India just as it is now being recognised that the advanced civilisation of ancient Mesopotamia owed its inception to the Sumerians from India. How far the world is thus indebted to the ancient Dravidians, as appears to be disclosed by recent researches, is a subject which finds no place in the works of the modern historians of ancient India." So we make bold to make a few remarks on the subject.

It has been already said that the extensive land to the south of India was Tamil country, that it was ruled by Pandya sovereigns, that Muttamil made progress there, and that ganam with even $\frac{1}{16}$ of a Swaram was made there. Many examples were also given on page 46 that Tamil was proficient in many arts having actions found in nature and the natural sounds of all living beings.

He mentions here that all languages are derived from Indo-Germanic or the Semitic stock. Semitic group comprises the Hebrew, Arabic, Aramaic and the Assyrian languages. The Indo-Germanic group seems to imply the languages and the dialects spoken in the Old World, from India to Iceland in Northern Europe.

We find the same groups of languages spoken after the XV century in America, Australia, New Zealand, East India Islands and other countries. He says that the term Indo-European does not necessarily mean that the languages under the group were spoken in India and Europe, and that 'Indo' does not confine itself to Tamil and Telugu languages. Just as many countries lay between India and Iceland, so also languages, with the Indian language as the ancient mother tongue and

Germanic language as the modern tongue, are included in the term. Just as the first and the last links are indicated, while naming the whole chain, this group of languages is also named. The analogy of Hindu, Germanic, Celtic and Hindi languages may also be noted. He says that many languages of the group have disappeared; some have been so thoroughly influenced by other languages that it is impossible to trace their origin or determine the places where they were spoken, or, say anything about the original language from which they were derived.

We may say with certain degree of certainty that Tamil was prior to the Hebrew language (derived from the Semitic group), as many Tamil words are found in Hebrew and no Hebrew words are found in Tamil. The same must be true of the Semitic group also. As it is said that the Aramaic tongue was spoken in Palestine before the birth of Christ, and after the Hebrew language, the Hebrew language with a good admixture of Tamil words must also have influenced the Aramaic dialect.

The facts that the Assyrian language was spoken in Nineveh and Babylon; that clay tiles with inscriptions in that language were dug up from ruined cities; that the various letter-sounds of the language correspond to the letter sounds of Tamil; that the Sumerians built those cities and ruled over them; that the Sumerians were Dravidians; that they migrated there from the south of India; that a powerful nation ruled there before the period of the Chaldaeans; that they reached the place on ships through the Persian Gulf; that they worshipped a god in the shape of a fish; and that the figure of the fish was found in precious stones, such as diamonds and rubies—all these facts clearly prove that, at an age whose time cannot possibly be fixed, the Tamils migrated to Mesopotamia and the surrounding countries, such as Persia and Baluchistan, that they ruled over those countries, and that their own language was spoken in those countries with slight modifications. To add to these we have the proof of the existence of a number of Tamil words in the Indo-Germanic languages and their branches.

We have given, on page 44, 100 Tamil words which are found in the languages of Europe. These words appear to be the most common ones used by the people in their ordinary avocations. But no single word of any languages of the Germanic or European groups is found in the Indian or Tamil language. Thus the Tamil language seems to have had a peculiar excellence of its own with its own literature and grammar, with its own excellent sciences, with its own efficient system of music with minute divisions quite alien to other languages—these facts embolden us to say that the Tamil language which was once extensively used in India is the most ancient of all the languages.

The term 'Indo-Germanic' is like the two-end links of a chain. As there are other intermediate links in the chain many mixed languages must have been spoken which are derived from the Indo-Germanic group.

It is said that king Ahasuerus who ruled over 127 provinces, from India to Ethiopia, made a feast for six months to all his princes and nobles. The Tamils who migrated from the Tamil province, or, the Sumerians ruled over Babylon, Nineveh and other cities. The Brahuis dialect, spoken in Mesopotamia, Persia, and the hills of Baluchistan, implies that they were the Tamils. The Fish-God (Dagon) as well as the cow, worshipped by the inhabitans of these countries before the time of the Chaldaeans, clearly indicate their Tamil origin.

The following quotations from the Bible show that the Dagon mentioned there was the shape of a fish and that the Philistines worshipped it.

I. Samuel V ·2.

" When the Philistines took the ark of God, they brought it into the house of Dagon, and set it by Dagon."

Judges XVI 23.

" Then the lords of the Philistines gathered them together for to offer a great sacrifice unto Dagon their God and to rejoice : for they said, Our God hath delivered Samson our enemy into our hand."

Biblical Cyclopaedia Page 190.

" Dagon. (1 Sam. V. 2). This was the name of a celebrated idol of the Philistines; worshipped at Gaza, (Judg. XVI. 23) at Ashdod (1 Sam. V. 1. 3) at Beth-dagon, (" the house or temple of Dagon ") in the bounds of Judah, (Josh XV. 41) in a town of Asher, (Josh. XIX. 27) and elsewhere. There are various opinions as to the appearance of this idol, but it is usually represented with the head, hands, and face of a man, and the body like that of a fish. The name was probably derived from *dag* signifying a large fish. One of the incarnations of the Hindu god Vishnu was of the same form."

The above quotations prove that the Philistines and their neighbours worshipped the shape of the fish, or Maha Vishnu, who became incarnate to deliver his devotee Satya Viratha, ruler of the South Madura kingdom, from the deluge. So we may say that the Tamils of the South Pandya kingdom, who settled in Mesopotamia and ruled over many kingdoms, became divided into many nations, races and country-men, speaking different languages, and that, though the languages, spoken by the different nations, became independant tongues, yet there is an admixture of Tamil words in them all. Just as the fish-God was common to them all, so also the Tamil language must have been their common tongue.

Pure Tamil words found in Sanskrit, Tamil words common to sanskrit and Tamil, Tamil words found in European and Scythian languages are given in pages 43—45 of this book.

We do not find in Tamil works of 2000 years and upwards any admixture of Sanskrit, or European or Scythian words. This shows that Tamil was the most ancient of languages, that it was efficient in Muttamil—Iyal, Isai and Natakam and that Isai-Tamil or Music was well arranged, and that it had a system of Ragas which could reflect all possible human emotions.

Again the 12 Swarams or the chromatic scale sung in succession even by apes are taken as the 12 swarams of Ayapalai. This takes us back to the very time of the origin of Man from the Tamil country. A comparison of the origin of the Tamil language, the origin of Music, and the excellent ideas contained in the sciences of the Tamils renders it impossible for any one to gauge adequately the antiquity of Tamil and the minuteness and charm of their Isai-Tamil or Music.

The irregularity of the Swarams of the natural scale obtained as $\frac{9}{8}$, $\frac{5}{4}$, $\frac{4}{3}$, $\frac{3}{2}$, $\frac{5}{3}$ and $\frac{15}{8}$ and the regularity of the Sa-Pa and the Sa-Ma series, obtained as sevenths and fifths in the 12 rasis, or, the regularity of the Swarams of Ayapalai make one doubt whether other nations had reached the very first step in Music. Though other nations had determined the 12 Swarams of Ayapalai by slightly flattening the fifths, yet their system of Equal Temperament is divided, because of their inability to give correct calculations for the same.

Sanskrit writers on Music erred, even at the second step, by dividing the sthayi into 22 Srutis (being ignorant of the system of Vattapalai of the ancient Tamils), and singing Ragams on that false principle.

When they are doubtful about the first and second steps, what is the use of troubling them about the third and fourth steps? Those who practically realise the truth of the four Palais of the ancient Tamils, the minute Srutis used there, and the Puns derived from them, may understand the antiquity of Tamil and the excellence of its Isai Tamil.

Music, which could express the emotions of human beings, animals, birds, creeping things and trees, which could move the singer as well as the hearer, and which could charm even the deity, has been in existence in Isai Tamil with minute Srutis. It has been sung in the shape of 12000 ancient Isais, while other nations do not even possess the right calculation for the 12 Swarams, and they are bothering their heads about the progression of multiplying $\frac{3}{2}$ and $\frac{4}{3}$! All these show clearly that Tamil was the most ancient of languages and that Isai Tamil was the most ancient of all music.

3. The number of the Srutis occurring in Ayapalai, Vattapalai, Thirikonapalai, and Chathurapalai.

My beloved readers!

I have hitherto put down only such points as could be clearly derived from the stanzas in Silappadhikaram, which could be clearly interpreted from them and which could probably be guessed from them. None of these contradict the theory and practice of music of the modern day. Only such practical points as could be established with the help of ancient works have been mentioned. Though the ideas, mentioned in ancient works, are very minute, yet the extensive interpretation, put upon them, are quite capable of being derived from the originals. I can boldly say that the Sruti system of the ancient Tamils is highly proficient and minute, and, at the same time, clear.

This book, I may point out, was not written after I had completely grasped all the ideas contained therein. From time to time I have come across ideas, quite providentially, and they have been declared in the easiest possible manner. The new ideas that came to me, I am glad to say, have been quite in accordance with the ideas contained in the ancient Tamil works. Whenever I studied the ideas in ancient works, and, whenever I illustrated them, though no man was present with me to cheer me up, yet I was conscious of the presence of God and was much encouraged. I was assured of the correctness of what I had written by the data I obtained later, in support of what I had written. I may mention one particular instance of this in the stanza quoted "from Isaimarabu" before the Tanjore Sangeeta Vidya Mahajana Sangam by Swami Sivagnana Yogigal of Virudupatti which will be of use to my readers. This is the stanza :—

"ஆயத்துக் கீரா றுநான்கு வட்டத்துக்
கேயுங்கோ ணத்துக் கிரட்டிப்புத்—தாயவிசை
நண்ணுமைக் கதிலிரட்டி நோனலகு மோர்ரிலக்கிங்
கேண்மூன்ம கேள்விகோண் டேன்."

This stanza clearly says that Ayapalai had 12 swarams; Vattapalai, 24 Srutis; Thirikonapalai, 48 Srutis; and Chthurapalai, 96 Srutis.

The expression இசை நுண்மை clearly states that further minute divisions of Srutis is possible neither to sing nor to hear. This is quite clear, practicable and definite, unlike the blind words of Sarnga Dev. "Srutis are one ; they are two ; they are three, four, nine, twenty two, sixty six ; nay, they are a legion" and the impracticable theroies of those who say that Srutis are 25, 27, 53, 42 and 66.

When once it is stated that the Srutis are a legion in number, it gives room for any one to say anything and to take refuge under it. This was the cause of all doubt as ragards Srutis.

But here he definitely says that the minimum soundable and the minimum audible is $\frac{1}{96}$ of a Sthayi, and this implies that a more minute sound is impossible. This can be easily seen from the veena where no minuter sound than $\frac{1}{96}$ is possible.

We had to write at great length as we were not able to obtain many clear works on Isai Tamil. We hear that some of the parts of Isai Marabu, from which the above stanza is quoted, are found in the library of Thiruvavaduthurai Mutt. As the Sruti calculations of this book are based on the stanza, quoted above, I think it is enough for intelligent men to understand the whole system.

4. The names of the Saptaswarams Sa, Ri, Ga, Ma, Pa, Dha and Ni are of Tamil and not of Sanskrit origin.

Some who are ignorant of the object of this work imagined that I had changed or was going to change the system of modern music and that I had completely upset the theory of Sarnga Dev who wrote his work in Sanskrit. Imagining such things, they induced certain so-called Tamil Vidwans who are daily spoiling the Tamil language purposely, by mixing a number of Sanskrit words into it to dispute my position. I have given them proper answers from time to time.

One of those vidwans said that the series Sa, Ri Ga, Ma, Pa, Dha and Ni is named after the seven Sanskrit words Shadjam, Rishabam, Gandharam, Madhymam, Panchamam, Dhaivatam and Nishadam, that their pronunciation is entirely Sanskrit and that I would do well to give them new names altogether. As many are under the impression that the series are derived from Sanskrit, I had to write this to disabuse them, once for all, of that idea. I have slightly touched upon it already on page 744.

We have repeatedly stated that the names of the series have first been used in Tamil only and that the science of music was a part of Muttamil. The following stanza, by the sage Sikandi, proves that this series was in existence even at the age of the Middle Sangam. It is as follows :—

ச ரி க ம ப த நி யென்றேழெழுத்தாற் றானம்
வரி பரந்த கண்ணினாய் வைத்துத் தெரிவரிய
வேழிசையுந் தோன்றுமிவற்றுள்ளே பண் பிறக்குஞ்
குழ் முதலாஞ் சுத்தத்துளை.

We clearly understand that, during his time and the time of Ahatya (Agastya) in the first Sangam and long prior to that time also, Iyal, Isai and Natakam were in use. We cannot get at the works of that period. But the customs of the first Sangam was followed by the second. The same system was indicated by the sage Sikandi of the middle Sangam in the above stanza.

We know that this system of naming the series was long prior to the time of Bharata (V century), and Sarnga Dev (XIII century). The Aryans who brought a dead language with them to the ancient Tamil country tried hard to appropriate all the sciences of the Tamil world to themselves. Sarnga Dev is one of them. Though he has used many derivatives and told a number of stories to differentiate between the music of the Tamils and that of the Aryans, while basing his writing on Tamil works, yet we know that he has failed. For example, the following words are direct translations of Tamil into Sanskrit and nothing original :—Thiruvenkadu (Swetaranyam), Maraikadu (Vedaranyan), Thiruvayar (Panchanadakshetram), Kudamuku (Kumbakonam), Thiruvavaduthurai (Gomuthikshetram), Thiruvidamarudur (Madhyarjunam), Puliyoor (Vyagrapuram), Chittambalam (Chidambaram) and Thayumanavar (Mathurboothesvarar). In the same way he has altered the names of Ragas as mentioned in pages 543—547 of this book.

When we notice the names of places that have been changed we find that they have been considered sacred from ancient times, that they have been made the subject of verses by gifted sages of yore, and that they have been made much of by the ancient Tamils. The name of 'Thiruvayar' means the place watered by five sacred rivers. Though the name of it has now been changed into Panchanadakshetram, yet we know that the present Tamils call it by the same name, as was given to it by ancient Tamils, and that it is not derived from Sanskrit. We find the name 'Aiyarappan' to the deity presiding at Thiruvayar.

The history of the seven letters ச ரி க ம ப த நி must have been mentioned clearly in works on Isai-Tamil. As they are not now at hand, we have to think in different ways as to their origin. Sarnga Dev accounted for the Swarams, Shadjam, Rishabham and Gandharam in one way, for Madhyamam and Panchamam in a different way, and for Daivatam and Nishadham in a third.

He says Madhyamam was so called because it sounds in the middle of the string between Adhara Shadjam and its octave.

He says Panchamam was so called as it was the fifth in the order of seven Swarams. But it is the seventh in the half-swaram series. If he had followed the same principle for the first, fourth, sixth and seventh Swarams, he would have been consistent.

Again he says Rishabham is so called because it resembles the sound of a Rishabham (bull). Why not we extend the analogy and say that Nishadham should be called க because it resembles the sound of a கஜம் or elephant, and Daivatam should be called அ because its sound is that of an அசுவம் or horse, and Panchamam be called கோ because its sound is that of கோகிலம் or the cuckoo, and Madhyamam be called கி for its sound resembles that of the கிரவுஞ்ச bird and Shadjam be called ம because its sound is that of the மயில் or peacock? There are so many similar words whose first letters are one or other of the series.

Again, others who are ignorant of the fact that the hard consonants க, ச, ட, த, ப and ற combine with soft and middling consonants and with vowels and are being pronounced in different ways according as they come at the beginning, the middle or the end of a word, contend that, as the first letter of the series, ஸ is from Sanskrit other letters also are from the same language.

I have heard others again who say that Shadjam comprises *six* Swarams, that it is so called because the sound emanates from *six* places and that, therefore, names of all Swarams are derived from Sanskrit. A little close observation will show that this theory is wrong.

For the prefix *shad* means *six* as in the words 'Shadvargam', 'Shadoormi', 'Shadragam', and 'Shashti'. The suffix 'ஜம்' (Jam) means 'is born' 'generates' and 'causes to generate'. If the seven Swarams Ri, Ga, Ma, Pa, Dha, Ni and Sa generate from Shadjam then only the Sthayi becomes complete. If the first Adhara Shadjam is the mother, then her seven children Ri, Ga, Ma, Pa, Dha, Ni and Sa will generate from her. From the seven children will generate another seven from Sa, the daughter who resembles the mother. If there is no daughter resembling the mother there can be no Thara Sthayi and Madhya Sthayi.

Again, Shadjam, for the matter of that many letters are said by them to proceed from six places; this is not peculiar to the letter Sa alone. The throat, the palate and the tip of the tongue along with other organs are said to be the organs for the production of sound and not six places.

Again there is no connection between the first letter in the word Shadjam and the first of the series SA, RI, GA, MA. There is no rule by which Sha can become SA; but I have quoted many examples (see page 144 of the book) where the Tamil letter ச becomes the softened SA or ஸ. Here ஸ may be a substitute for the Tamil ச and the sound has no connection whatever with the Sanskrit letter.

There is no support for deriving the consonants ரி from the sanskrit word 'Rishabham'; nor is there any data for the transformation of கா in Gandharam into the letter க and the letter தை of Daivatam into the letter த. So we find that the writer who attempted to trace the origin of the letters SA, RI, GA, MA, PA, DHA and NI to Sanskrit sounds has failed in his attempt.

Again the fact that the letters GA, PA and DHA have the third Sanskrit sound misleads many to suppose that the names of these Swarams must have been originally in Sanskrit. This is not true, for I have already spoken in page 336 of this book that the hard sounds of certain letters become soft or middling according as they are preceded by soft or hard sounds and so resemble the sounds of Sanskrit letters.

If we note, again, that GA changes its sound owing to its being followed by a soft MA, PA changes its sound because it is preceded by a soft MA and that DHA changes its sound as it is followed by a soft ந and that this is a very ancient custom in many Tamil words, even the little doubt we may have on the subject will be cleared.

5. The opinion of M. R. Ry., Narayana Sastrial, Professor, Sanskrit College, Trivadi, as regards the sounds of the Saptaswarams.

Though I have given my own opinion as regards the sounds of Swarams, I requested M. R. Ry., Narayana Sastrial, Senior Professor of the Sanskrit College at Trivadi to study the subject with the help of the two volumes of Sangeeta Ratnakaram. The following letter is the result of his study :—

"I publish to the world the result of my careful study of Karunamirta Sagaram written by M. R. Ry., Rao Sahib M. Abraham Pandither Avergal and also the volumes of Sangeeta Ratnakaram of Sarnga Dev.

The saying of Sarnga Dev, that the seven sounds SA, RI, GA, MA, PA, DHA and NI are names given with a cause, contradicts what is said by the Sage Sikandi, who lived before the birth of Christ, that they are original names. To say that ச was derived from Shadja, ரி from Rishabha, க from Gandharam, ம from Madhya, ப from Panchama, த from Daivata, and நி from Nishadham is not possible, for there is no rule in Sanskrit grammars to change the Sanskrit SHA (ஷ) into SA (ஸ), to change the vowel ரு (Ru) into the consonant ரி (RI), to change the long கா (GA) into the short க (GA), and to convert தை into த with a vowel sound. Again, the fact that Sarnga Dev adopts one principle to explain Rishabham, Gandharam and Daivatam and quite another to explain Shadjam, Madhymam, Panchamam and Nishadham, and further states without reason that these are the commencing letters of the Sanskrit words Shanta, Rutham, Gathram, Mathuram, Pattalam and Dhairiam. My opinion is that he has done this with a view purposely to change the original names given to them by the Dravidians.

Though the sounds SA, GA, DHA do not pertain to the Tamil language, yet as the word 'Hoom' in Sanskrit in the old Sama Veda manuscripts is sounded as 'him', in Tamil also we have the sounds, SA, GA, DHA, JA, THA, BHA, DA and PA. This has been admirably pointed out by Rao Sahib Pandither Avl, in his Karunamirta Sagaram. Though the initial mistake is committed by great sages like Mathanga, yet as it does not stand to reason such thing can never be blindly accepted as correct in this advanced 20th century. I make bold to say that the Sanskrit works on music written by great sages like Narada have been made obscure by Sanskrit Pandits of later days who derived music and attacked what was true."

(Sd.) NARAYANA SASTRIAL.

6. Concluding remarks about the Srutis used in Karnatic Music.

We studied till now the Swarams, Srutis and minute Srutis which are as it were the limits of Karunamirta Sagaram. I consider this a very important factor in music.

The letters of the Tamil alphabet—vowels, consonants, vowel-consonants and Ayutham—are indispensable for the language. Integral as well as fractional numbers are absolutely necessary for Arithmetic. So also the 12 Swarams of Ayappalai, the 24 quarter Srutis of Vattappalai, the 48 one-eighth Srutis of Trikonapalai and the 96 one-sixteenth Srutis of Chathurappalai are necessary for understanding the sounds of music. These minute Srutis have been played as Gamakams on the Yal by the ancient Tamils and are being played now by Yal experts. After the disappearance of the works which clearly described this minute system, different kinds of calculations were given for these minute Srutis like the blind-men who described the elephant.

To add to this, Pythagoras, the Philosopher who visited India about 2500 years ago, took the measurement of the Veena $\frac{2}{3}$ for SA-PA and $\frac{3}{4}$ for SA-MA to Europe; and different theories resulted from it.

Bharata and Sarnga Dev, among the Sanskrit writers of India, spoke of 22 Srutis for the octave and gave calculations for the Swarams and wrote Ragalakshanam also to suit. The result was confusion and doubt as regards Swarams and Srutis of Karnatic and other music.

It is certain that it will be impossible to compose a raga or sing it with special charm unless one is sure of the Swarams and Srutis of Karnatic Music. When

I discovered a system which would be of help in composing new ragas and correcting the errors that have crept into the old, I founded the Sangeeta Vidya Mahajana Sangam at Tanjore for the purpose of placing this system before musical experts and advance the cause of music, on the 27th May, 1912.

In that Conference enquiry was made as to the Swarams that occurred in Ragam Nattai. Some were for arriving at them by the 72 Melakartas while others spoke for deriving them according to the Dwavimsati Srutis ; while the majority were for arriving at them as they were found in the Veena. As no definite conclusion was arrived at, the discussion was postponed for the next Conference. And so it was completely enquired into at six Conferences.

As the calculations and practical experience of many were different and conflicting. I had also to give my view on the subject. Hence there was the necessity for criticising the various contradictory opinions and to prove the impracticability of the 22 Srutis for Karnatic music. The importance of enquiring into the minuteness of the Isai Tamil used by the ancient Indians was also keenly felt.

I had to deal with the four Palais of the ancient Tamils, the mathematical calculations according to that system, the system of 12 Palais obtained while change of Grahams is made and 7 primary Palais derived from them. The number of vibrations and cents calculations according to modern ideas had also to be given for the 7 Swarams, the 12 half-Swarams and the 24 Srutis and minuter Srutis.

As the fractional measurements of $\frac{8}{9}$, $\frac{3}{4}$, $\frac{4}{5}$, $\frac{5}{6}$ &c., do not give the right sounds, calculations for Swarams and Srutis have been given based on the logarithm of 2 according to the idea found in ancient Tamil works and in conformity with the view of Sarnga Dev on the subject. The length of the wire for the Swarams and Srutis according to the logarithm of 2 and the respective sounds produced in the Swarams have been indicated in separate tables.

Just to show that the Swarams pointed out in the tables correspond to the Swarams used in Karnatic music now, 67 Karnatic Ragas under four tables, one for each of the Palais, are also given.

A system of staff notation for Karnatic music is given and the unanimity of the Swara system of Western music and Indian music is also shown. Some inscriptions have been quoted to show that later sovereigns fostered the ancient Isai Tamil.

Some historical data have been given to establish that the Tamils of South Madura migrated to Mesopotamia and built the towns of Nineveh and Babylon and ruled there, that they spoke Tamil and many languages sprung from that mother-tongue, that the sciences of music, astrology, medicine and other rare ones spread in other countries from the Tamil country, that Tamil must have been the original tongue as it is pure without any admixture while Tamil words are found in many other languages, and that the Tamils must have been the pioneers of music as the very minute Swarams used by them are not found among any other nation.

I had to write at length to refute the theory of Dwavimsati Srutis advocated by Bharata and Sarnga Dev who are considered to be very ancient authorities. I had also to write against those who contended that $\frac{2}{3}$ and $\frac{3}{4}$ are the measurements for the Natural Series, and that the Tamils had no music. What I have said about music, its history, Srutis and their calculations is very little. Though the quotations and illustration on the subjects are not many, yet I hope they are enough to make one understand them.

Some important rules of music which will enable one to compose new Ragas and rectify the old ones will be found in Book II.

7. The Srutis of South Indian Music and the All-India Music Conference held at Baroda under the patronage of His Highness the Maharajah the Gaekwar of Baroda.

When I requested the Dewan Sahib V. P. Madhava Row Avl., to preside over the deliberations of the fourth Conference of the Sangeeta Vidya Mahajana Sangam held at Tanjore on 9th August 1913, he readily consented and conducted the Conference with great tact and efficiency. The idea struck him then that if such a Conference were conducted by one of the Indian Rajas, the cause of music might be greatly advanced. He then requested me that if such a thing came to pass I should be present and render necessary help. Accordingly he arranged a Conference at Baroda for the December of the year 1915 and requested me to attend. But I told him it would be convenient to me if the Conference could be arranged for the end of February or the beginning of March of 1916, after the dewy season was over. So the great All-India Conference was fixed for the third week of March (20th to the 25th) during the Kaman feast which was considered a time of convenience for His Highness and his subjects.

About 23 members from among those who were making researches in the field of music from different parts of India, along with many professional experts in Karnatic and Hindustani music were invited to the Conference. There were also present a number of princes and obles interested in the cause of music. Excellent arrangements had been made for the convenience and comfort of the various guests. As the date of the conference conicided with the annual festival of the State, many music parties, the birthday celebrations of the Rajah, the music conference—all these united together in such a manner that it was one long festivity without distinction of day or night!

His Excellency the Dewan Saheb was in charge of all these arrangements besides that of conducting the conference. The music conference commenced at 8 A. M. on Monday, the 20th of March. Their Highnesses and the princes arrived at the conference punctual to the appointed time and the whole assembly did obeisance to them.

His Excellency the Dewan then told the Maharajah that all arrangements had been completed according to His Highness's desire and requested him to open the conference. The Maharajah then thanked the audience for responding to his invitation and expressed his delight at meeting them. Then he requested Mr. Thakur M. Nawab Ali Khan Saheb Avl., to take the Presidential Chair.

The President then spoke a few words of welcome to the members assembled. The opening speech of His Highness the Gaekwar, that of His Excellency, the Dewan Saheb, that of the President and that of the other members were published in the Bombay Chronicle, the Madras Mail and other dailies. The proceedings of the Conference are published in the Appendix attached to this book.